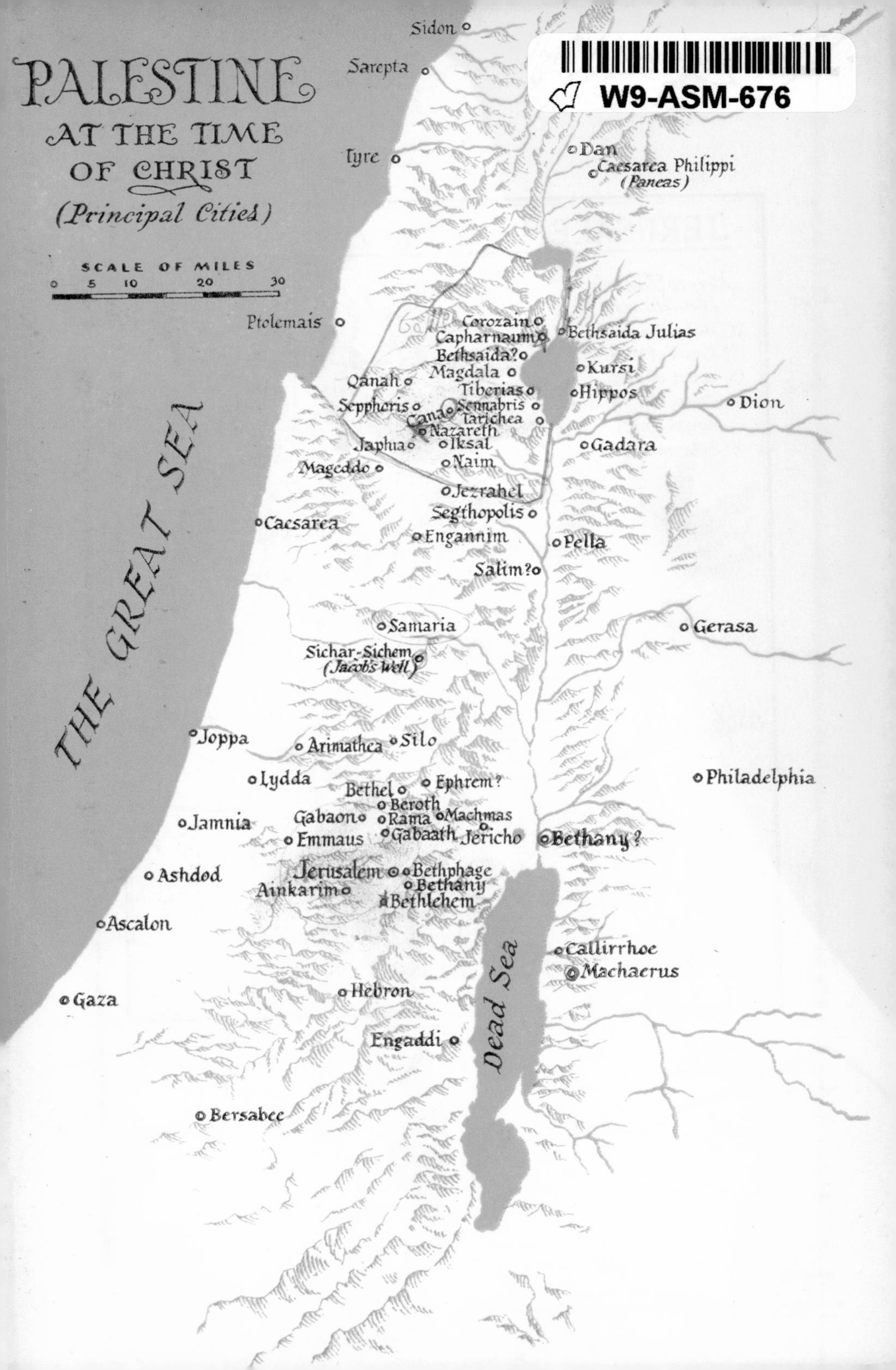

PALESTINE
AT THE TIME
OF CHRIST
(Principal Cities)
SCALE OF MILES
0 5 10 20 30
THE GREAT SEA
Dead Sea
Sidon
Sarepta
Tyre
Dan
Caesarea Philippi
(Paneas)
Ptolemais
Corozain
Capharnaum
Bethsaida Julias
Bethsaida?
Magdala
Kursi
Qanah
Tiberias
Hippos
Dion
Sepphoris
Sennabris
Cana
Tarichea
Nazareth
Japhia
Iksal
Gadara
Mageddo
Naim
Jezrahel
Scythopolis
Caesarea
Engannim
Pella
Salim?
Samaria
Gerasa
Sichar-Sichem
(Jacob's Well)
Joppa
Arimathea
Silo
Philadelphia
Lydda
Bethel
Ephrem?
Beroth
Jamnia
Gabaon
Rama
Machmas
Emmaus
Gabaath
Jericho
Bethany?
Jerusalem
Bethphage
Ashdod
Bethany
Ainkarim
Bethlehem
Ascalon
Callirrhoe
Machaerus
Gaza
Hebron
Engaddi
Bersabee

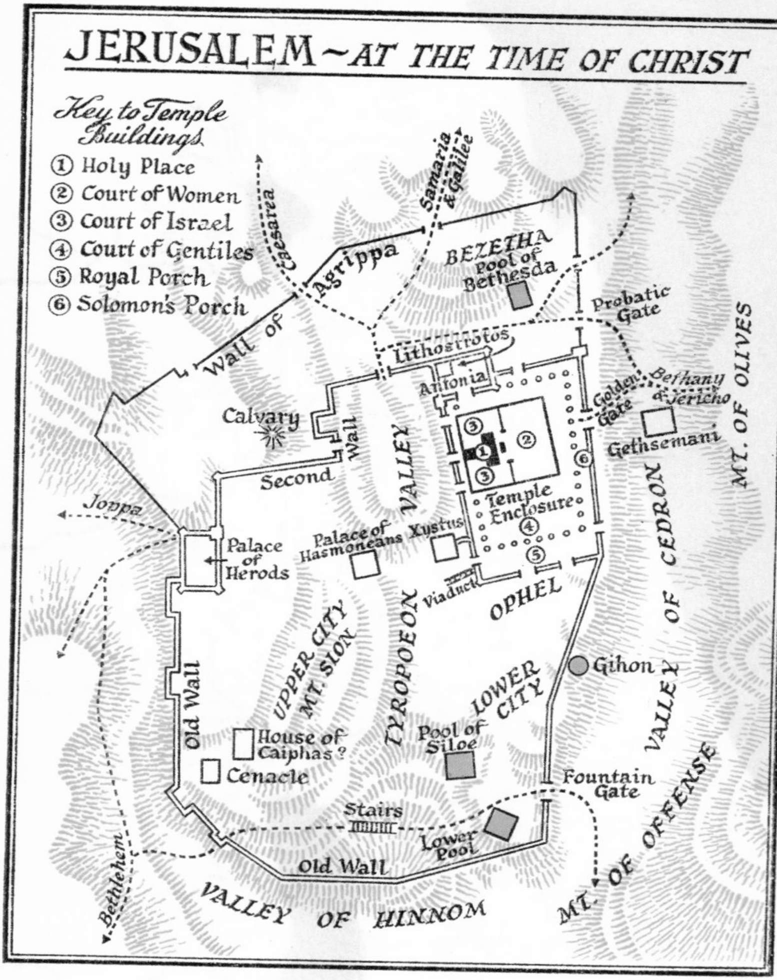

JERUSALEM ~ AT THE TIME OF CHRIST
Key to Temple Buildings
① Holy Place
② Court of Women
③ Court of Israel
④ Court of Gentiles
⑤ Royal Porch
⑥ Solomon's Porch
Caesarea
Samaria & Galilee
Wall of Agrippa
BEZETHA
Pool of Bethesda
Probatic Gate
Lithostrotos
Antonia
Golden Gate
Bethany & Jericho
MT. OF OLIVES
Calvary
Second Wall
VALLEY
Gethsemani
Temple Enclosure
Joppa
Palace of Herods
Palace of Hasmoneans
Xystus
Viaduct
OPHEL
VALLEY OF CEDRON
UPPER CITY MT. SION
TYROPOEON
Gihon
LOWER CITY
Old Wall
House of Caiphas ?
Cenacle
Pool of Siloe
Fountain Gate
Stairs
Lower Pool
Old Wall
Bethlehem
VALLEY OF HINNOM
MT. OF OFFENSE

JESUS CHRIST

JESUS CHRIST

HIS LIFE, HIS TEACHING, AND HIS WORK

VOLUMES I & II COMPLETE

by Ferdinand Prat, S.J.

TRANSLATED FROM THE SIXTEENTH FRENCH EDITION

JOHN J. HEENAN, S.J.

THE BRUCE PUBLISHING COMPANY
MILWAUKEE

Imprimi potest: David Nugent, S.J., Provincialis
Nihil obstat: John A. Schulien, S.T.D., Censor librorum
Imprimatur: ✠ Moyses E. Kiley, Archiepiscopus Milwaukiensis
28 iulii 1950

Library of Congress Catalog Card Number: 50–58219

MADE IN THE UNITED STATES OF AMERICA
(FIFTH PRINTING — I & II — 1963)

Note

THIS English translation is the work of the Rev. John J. Heenan, S.J., of Georgetown University. For a considerable part of Volume I the translator had the valuable assistance of a draft prepared by the Rev. Edward Gannon, S.J., but Father Gannon was prevented by circumstances from completing the work. The Scripture quotations throughout were rendered directly from Father Prat's own French version; in the matter of vocabulary and style, however, the approved English versions as well as the Vulgate and the Greek were constantly consulted. The numerous Scripture references were checked and, where necessary, corrected. Some few references to English translations of books mentioned in the course of the work have been inserted in the footnotes, and the Alphabetical Index has been substantially expanded. These emendations are aimed at increasing the usefulness of the book for English readers. The few bibliographical notes indicated by the initials *J.C.* are by Rev. Jean Calés, S.J., editor of the sixteenth French edition.

Abbreviations

Billerbeck, *Kommentar: Kommentar zum neuen Testament aus Talmud und Midrasch,* Strack-Billerbeck

J.T.S.: Journal of Theological Studies

MG: Migne, *Patrologiae Cursus Completus, Series Graeca*

ML: Migne, *Patrologiae Cursus Completus, Series Latina*

R.B.: Revue Biblique

Recherches: Recherches de Science Religieuse

T.U.: Texte und Untersuchungen

Schürer, *Geschichte: Geschichte des jüdischen Volkes*

Contents

VOLUME I

Book One

THE YEARS OF PREPARATION

III. *The Mystery of the Hidden Life*

IV. *Jesus and John*

V. *The Gradual Manifestation of Christ*

BOOK TWO

THE GOSPEL IN GALILEE

I. *The Choice of the Apostles*

II. *The Divine Mission of Christ*

APPENDIX: CONCORD OF THE GOSPELS

VOLUME II

BOOK THREE

THE GOSPEL IN PEREA AND JUDEA

JESUS CHRIST

Introduction

THE Gospel is a book for everyone; in it the simplest souls as well as the most cultivated intellects find nourishment. But to press from it the essence of its meaning and taste the flavor of its charm, some initiation is needed. This divine book, written by men and for men of another age, product of a distant era and another civilization, reflects manners, customs, institutions, and ways of thinking and speaking very different from our own. Before reaching us, divine revelation has passed through social contexts whose coloring it tended to assume; and to catch its spirit it is often necessary to relive the past and breathe its atmosphere. There is, of course, no substitute for direct contact with the Gospel itself, and to presume to supply for it by dissertations and commentaries would be like conducting a worshiper around the outside of a temple into which he was denied entrance. The faithful know this well. Consequently, among the Lives of Christ — all of them distinguished by some particular merit, be it their learning, their style, their piety, or their eloquence — those stay longest in favor with the public that aim at being simply an introduction to a reading of the Gospels, and that follow very closely the sacred text.

The Gospels are not biographies, properly speaking. They present to us various aspects of the figure of Jesus Christ in sufficient detail to command faith in him as the Son of God, the revealer of the Father, the light and salvation of men; but the material in them is fragmentary and full of gaps. Considerable periods of the Saviour's public life are, as it were, but blank pages; chronology and topography, those two eyes of history, are barely sketched. And yet, if we were to depend on pagan authors and

Rabbinical and apocryphal writings to fill in the gaps, we should be quite disappointed.

1. Sources Other Than the Gospels

Up to the middle of the second century, profane authors provide only brief bits of information and passing allusions; this is as we would expect. Tacitus, Suetonius, Pliny the Younger, and the Emperor Hadrian, never suspecting the miraculous nature of the expansion of Christianity, regarded it merely as a sect which happened to be gaining members rapidly in the Greco-Roman world of the time.[1]

Tacitus, with laconic contempt, notes as an item of news, the ferocious persecution of the Christians in A.D. 64, following the burning of Rome, and adds carelessly: "The name (Christian) comes from Christ, who was put to death by Pontius Pilate, the Procurator, in the reign of Tiberius. This detestable superstition was smothered for the time, but burst forth again, not only in Judea where the evil thing began, but even in Rome whither flows everything that is horrible and abominable in the world to find there a large following."

Suetonius mentions in passing the punishments inflicted on the Christians, "that race of men given over to a new and baneful superstition," as also the expulsion of the Jews, perpetual foment-

---

[1] Tacitus, *Annales,* xv, 44. On the sources of Tacitus cf. Corssen in *Z.N.T.W.,* 1914, Vol. XV., pp. 114–141, and Battifol, *Orpheus et l'Evangile,* 1910, pp. 46–49.

Suetonius, *Nero,* 16: "Afflicti suppliciis christiani genus hominum superstitionis novae et maleficae"; *Claudius,* 25: "Judaeos, impulsore Chresto assidue tumultuantes Roma expulit." It is now agreed that *Chrestus* is *Christus.* Cf. Preuschen, in *Z.N.T.W.,* 1914, Vol. XV, p. 96. The form *chrestiani* also appears often for *christiani.*

Pliny the Younger, *Epist.,* x, 96; the rescript of the Emperor Trajan, *ibid.,* x, 97. Cf. Allard, *Le christianisme et l'empire romain,* 6 ed., 1903, pp. 31–40 (*Le rescrit de Trajan*) and pp. 289–311 (*Choix de textes relatifs aux rapports des empereurs avec les chrétiens jusqu'au règne de Constantin*).

Hadrian to Fundanus, in Eusebius, *Hist. eccl.,* iv, 9. St. Justin alludes to it in his first *Apology,* lxxiv.

Cf. Kurt Linck, *De antiquissimis veterum quae ad Jesum Nazarenum spectant testimoniis,* Giessen, 1913. The pagans had scarcely more understanding of Judaism than they had of nascent Christianity. Cf. Th. Reinach, *Textes d'auteurs grecs et romains relatifs au judaïsme,* Paris, 1895. The historical account given by the sedate Tacitus of the origins of the people of Israel contains almost as many errors as it has lines (*Hist.,* v, 2–5).

ers of discord, "at the instigation of Chrestus" — a name that could hardly designate anyone but Christ.

The letter written in A.D. 112 to the Emperor Trajan by Pliny the Younger, Governor of Bithynia, and the one sent a few years later by the Emperor Hadrian to Fundanus, Proconsul of Asia, are both valuable for the history of the early Church, whose rapid growth they describe; but they are of slight interest to the historian of Jesus.

Although these documents afford little information about the life of Christ, they are quite adequate to silence the champions of the fantastic theory that Jesus was a myth. They prove that, from A.D. 64 onward, Christianity was a force which could arouse hate and fear; that, at the beginning of the second century, in certain provinces it counterbalanced the cult of idols; that the bloody persecution, started by Nero to stifle it in its cradle, continued, with greater or lesser intensity, without the need of any new edict; and, finally, that as far back even as that Christ was adored as God. This is not much, still it is something.

The much earlier text of Josephus would be of greater importance, were it authentic: "There appeared about this time a wise man named Jesus; if indeed he is to be called a man: for he was a doer of marvelous works, master of those who receive the truth with joy, and he drew to himself many Jews and many converts from Hellenism. He was the Christ. Those whom he had won from the beginning did not cease to love him, even after he had been denounced by the leaders of our nation, and condemned by Pilate to be crucified; for he appeared to them on the third day, as our divine prophets had foretold of him, together with countless other marvels. The sect of Christians, named after him, still exists."[2]

The tradition of the manuscripts favors the authenticity of the text, but it must be noted that we have only three manuscripts for this particular section of Josephus, and the earliest of them is from the eleventh century.[3] Is it not a little too much to

---

[2] Josephus, *Antiq.*, XVIII, iii, 3. On this text cf. L. De Grandmaison, *Jésus-Christ,* 1928, Vol. I, Note A (English transl., Vol. I, pp. 190–195. *Josephus and Primitive Christianity*), and Tricot, in *Revue apol.*, April–May, 1922. A bibliography may be found in the latter.

[3] Eusebius cites the text twice (*Hist. eccl.*, i, 11, and *Demonstr. evangel.*, iii, 3);

attribute the following phrases to a Jewish historian: " . . . if indeed he is to be called a man. . . . He was the Christ . . . he arose on the third day, as our prophets had foretold"? And if, with the majority of those who defend the text, we consider those phrases interpolated, there is nothing left of the famous testimony except a dry and colorless reference. Josephus who kept a systematic silence about would-be Messiases, from the moment Rome annexed Judea, would have held to the same line in the matter of Jesus. Justus of Tiberias, his rival and contemporary, followed the same policy.[4] And if Josephus does speak of the death of the Baptist and the martyrdom of James, the brother of the Saviour, it is because he had not the same reasons for silence, since neither had put forth any Messianic pretentions.[5]

Thus, in the century that followed the death of Jesus, neither pagan authors nor Jewish historians tell us anything about his person. An examination of the Koran and the Talmud yields no happier results.

Several *Suras* of the Koran contain lengthy passages on the Virgin and her Son, but the fact that Mohammed confused the mother of Jesus with Mary, the sister of Moses and Aaron, is sufficient commentary on their historical worth.[6] Whatever Mohammed knew of the Saviour, his virginal birth, his miracles, and his divine mission, he drew from the Apocrypha, from the Arabic Gospel of the Infancy or some similar work; or else from oral traditions circulating among the Christians of his time in Medina and Mecca. His insistent defense of Mary's perpetual virginity, and even, according to the words which some commentators attribute to him, of her Immaculate Conception, can be nothing else than an authentic echo of Christian beliefs

---

Origen, however, does not appear to have known it, since he says that Josephus did not believe that Jesus was the Christ (*In Matth. Series,* x, 17; cf. *Contra Cels.,* i, 47). At least he did not read it as we now have it.

[4] Photius, *Bibliotheca,* cod. 33.

[5] The authenticity of the texts of Josephus, *Antiq.,* XVIII, v. 2 (on John the Baptist) and *Antiq.,* XX, ix, 1 (on James) is scarcely disputed nowadays. Still, Schürer (*Geschichte,* 4 ed., Vol. I, p. 581) expresses some doubts about the second passage.

[6] The Koran, *Suras,* 2, 3, 4, 5, 19, 43, 57, 61, etc. Cf. Hughes, *Dictionary of Islam,* 2 ed., 1896, s.v. *Jesus Christ,* or Fleming, in Hennecke *Handbuch zu den neutest. Apokryphen,* 1904, pp. 165–171, especially the article on "Isa," etc.

at this remote period. Besides, the miracles which he attributes to the founder of Christianity are all rather puerile and fantastic. Jesus talks in his cradle to vindicate his mother; he molds clay birds and gives them life by breathing upon them; he calls down a food-laden table from heaven. This is the sort of thing the Koran has to offer.

In the enormous compilation known as the Talmud there is very little space devoted to our Saviour. The *Mishnah,* drawn up toward the end of the second century; the *Tosephta,* which in the following century completed this codification of Jewish law; and the first three *Midrashim,* which possibly go back to the same period, all barely mention Jesus.[7] It seems a conspiracy of silence. And yet we know from St. Justin and Origen that the Jews of the time carried on a skillful campaign of defamation against him. They did not contest his miracles, which were too well known to be denied; but they attributed them to magic, as their fathers had given the credit for them to the prince of devils. They did not deny the fact of the empty tomb; instead they claimed that the Apostles, or Judas, or the gardener had spirited away the corpse. To disqualify Jesus as Messias, they centered their attack chiefly upon his descent from the line of David. They said his mother was a beggar girl, repudiated by her husband after her conviction as an adulteress. In her distress she was forced to flee to Egypt with her illegitimate son; there he learned the art of prodigies, in which the Egyptians excelled; and on his return, in the pride of his power to work miracles, he sought to pass himself off as God. Things like this were being said everywhere in the Jewish world, but were put down in writing only in the Talmud of Jerusalem, composed toward the end of the fourth century, and in the Babylonian Talmud, which appeared two centuries later. It is better not to mention a scurrilous pamphlet, entitled *Toledoth Jeshu,* published after the time of Charlemagne. It is universally agreed today that this pamphlet is an "out-and-out lampoon; certain passages in it are disgusting."

---

[7] The only texts cited are one in the Mishnah, *Yebamoth,* iv, 13, and a Tosephta, *Hullin,* ii, 22–23.

Jews themselves have the honesty to scout the historical value of similar lucubrations. One of them writes: "Many of the legends have a theological origin. For polemical purposes, it was necessary for the Jews to insist on the illegitimacy of Jesus as against the Davidic descent claimed for him by the Christian Church. Magic was imputed to him to nullify the value of the miracles recorded in the Gospels; and the legends about his shameful lot, both before and after his death, are perhaps directed against the accounts of his Resurrection and Ascension."[8] The Babylonian Talmud actually says that Jesus, the son of a hairdresser and a soldier named Pandira, seduced the world by his marvels, was excommunicated for the crime of heresy and condemned to death at Lydda. Witnesses for the defense were sought for forty days, but when none appeared he was executed on the eve of the Passover and hung on a gibbet. Accounts like these furnish polemical material, but are worthless as history.

It is difficult to imagine a work more completely devoid of a critical sense than the heterogeneous ensemble called the Talmud. It is said that one can find pearls in this mire: this may possibly be true, but one would have to rake over much mud to discover them. Places, dates, and persons are outrageously confused and falsified. A pupil in elementary school capable of listing Charlemagne, Joan of Arc, and Napoleon as contemporaries could not commit more staggering anachronisms. There is no attempt at verisimilitude, no idea of distances or numbers. Here are a few examples among a thousand. Sepphoris, a city near Nazareth, is supposed to have had a hundred and eighty thousand public squares. At Bether (the modern Bettir), the last refuge of the insurrectionist Jews, the blood of those massacred by the Romans formed torrents which went rushing down to the sea, fifteen leagues away, and reddened the water as far as six kilometers from the coast. The trumpets in the Temple were heard in Jericho, and the incense burned on the Altar of Incense

---

[8] Samuel Krauss in the *Jewish Encyclopedia,* 1904, Vol. VII, p. 170. By the same author, *Das Leben Jesu nach jüdischen Quellen,* Berlin, 1904. Cf. also Laible, *Jesus Christus,* Berlin, 1891, with texts from the Talmud in the appendix, by Dalman; R. Travers Herford, *Christianity in Talmud and Midrash,* 1904, summarized in the *Dict. of Christ and the Gospels,* 1909, Vol. II, pp. 877–882; A. Mayer, *Jesus im Talmud,* in Hennecke, *Handbuch der neutest. Apokryphen,* 1904, pp. 47–71; Rabbi J. Klausner, *Jesus of Nazareth,* London, 1923, pp. 18–54.

in the interior of the sanctuary made the goats on the mountains of Moab sneeze. In Jerusalem it was forbidden to have furnaces, because of the smoke; gardens, for fear of offensive odors; domestic fowl, for fear they would scratch up human bones — a longer litany would be monotonous. Not all is in this style; but there is more than enough to justify the severe verdict of a very learned Jew: "The numerous juridical and theological discussions, mixed up with all sorts of digressions, leave scant room for historical information. There is no information about the Jews of the Diaspora, and a great deal of ignorance and fantasy in the information about Palestine. . . . In no case are the data certain."[9]

What one could expect from this literature is a more precise notion of the evangelical milieu and some light on the framework of the life of Christ. The better exegetes of the past did not neglect this source of information, and since direct contact with Rabbinical writings requires an initiation which not all can acquire, patient scholars — such as Lightfoot, Schoettgen, Meuschen, Wetstein, Wuensche, Edersheim, and others — have furnished ready-made material to the uninitiated. But their esteemed contributions are now out of date, and have been supplanted by the four-volume work of Strack and Billerbeck. With admirable care and indefatigable labor, using more recent and more correct editions, these authors have scrutinized the Talmud and the Midrashim for texts which might throw light, by comparison or contrast, on the books of the New Testament. Moreover, the principal source, the Mishnah, has always been accessible to Biblical students, and there is now a French translation of the Talmud of Jerusalem.[10]

[9] J. Juster, *Les Juifs dans l'empire romain,* 1914, Vol. I, p. 23. Neubauer's appraisal with respect to the geography is no less unfavorable. According to the Talmud, Palestine was 160,000 square *parsas,* about 1,852,800 square miles (more than eight times the area of France). Neubauer remarks (*Géographie du Talmud,* 1868, p. 4): "Such exaggerations are well known to students of the Talmud." Cf. Farrar, *Life of Christ,* Excursus xii, whose opinion is summarized in these words: "Anything more utterly unhistorical than the Talmud cannot be conceived."

[10] Strack and Billerbeck, *Kommentar zum neuen Testament aus Talmud und Midrasch,* Munich, 1922–1928. The fourth volume contains the Excursus. A critical edition of the *Mishnah* with a German translation and commentary is being published at Giessen. The French translation of the *Jerusalem Talmud* by Schwab (Paris, 1878–1889) is well known.

However, the importance of these sources must not be exaggerated. Rabbinical writings are consistently silent on many interesting points. The glorious epoch of the Hasmoneans, which was so important in the evolution of Judaism, is almost completely ignored. The exploits of Judas Machabeus and his brothers seem unknown; in connection with the Feast of the Dedication only their father, Mathathias, is mentioned. The reign of Herod apparently never happened. And we find in the Talmud next to nothing on the city of Jerusalem itself, or its walls and buildings, which were the wonder of the world. The Temple is described more according to Ezechiel than according to reality!

Since the memory of manners and customs is not as quick to change as the oral tradition of events, we may hope to find in the Talmud, the *corpus juris* of Judaism, a faithful picture of the social habits and religious institutions of the time of Christ. But here again we have to make reservations. The Talmud is exclusively the work of the Pharisaic party, and treats the rest of the people as almost nonexistent; it omits whole periods when the Pharisees were not in the ascendant. The whole of history is seen from the point of view of Pharisaism. The Sanhedrin as it existed at the end of the second century is used as a description of the Sanhedrin as it existed in ancient times; in consequence, the High Priest not only does not preside over it, but has no role whatever in it. It would be hard to conceive anything more daring than this distortion of one of the best attested facts of history. The Talmud is the tradition of a school — a very wooden school — which after the catastrophe of the year 70 emigrated successively to Jamnia, Sepphoris, and Tiberias, bearing its narrow and particularist spirit with it everywhere. The Tannaim and Amoraim of the second and third centuries codified an artificial legislation, partly theoretical and impractical, which they supposed to have been in force always. It is surprising to see otherwise estimable historians of Jesus placing blind faith in these lucubrations. If we had only the Talmud, it would be very difficult to reconstruct Palestinian society at the time of Christ.

Fortunately we have Josephus. The author of the *Jewish Antiquities* and the *Jewish War* has been criticized for his subservient attitude toward Rome, his desperate eagerness to exculpate the people he had deserted, his exaggerations and his bragging. It has been justly enough said that he was "a bad judge of distance," and it may be added that he had no very exact sense of figures. When he describes places from memory or gives a general estimate of crowds, he is often more or less unreliable; but when he gives measures or precise numbers, he can be followed. He has not been convicted of error in such cases, though he is quite capable of giving things a turn favorable to his thesis. At all events, we are not looking for such details in his works, but for the description of social and religious institutions, which his birth, offices, and sacerdotal rank qualified him to know better than anyone else. We want the picture of the environment in which he lived and the country which he traveled through in every direction. In these respects the reading of the *Jewish War* and the last book of the *Antiquities* is an indispensable preparation for a scientific study of the Gospels.

Several New Testament apocryphal books, the *Gospel According to the Hebrews,* the *Gospel of Peter,* the *Gospel of Thomas,* and the *Protoevangelium of James,* date from the middle of the second century and are earlier than the oldest Rabbinical writings; but as trustworthy history they are hardly of greater worth.[11]

The first two recount the life of the Saviour from his baptism to his Resurrection. A lucky discovery has given us some pages on the Passion of Christ from the *Gospel of Peter;* but they add nothing to what we already know, and are marked by the obvious leaning to Docetism that led Serapion, the bishop of Antioch, after careful examination, to proscribe the book.[12] The author

[11] The following are the principal works to consult on the Apocryphal Gospels: Tischendorf, *Evangelia Apocrypha,* 2 ed., Leipzig, 1876; Hennecke, *Handbuch der neutest. Apokryphen,* Tubingen, 1904 (German translation and notes); Variot, *Les Evangiles Apocryphes* (literary history, original form, transformations), Paris, 1878; James, *The Apocryphal New Testament* (excellent notes and English translation), Oxford, 1924; Frey, in the *Supplément* to *Dict. de la Bible,* Vol. I, 1926, coll. 475–483.

[12] The fragment found at Akhmin (Egypt) in 1884 is divided by Robinson into 14 sections; by Harnack, into 60 verses. This Gospel is quoted by Origen (*In Matthaeum,* lib. x, n. 17) and by Eusebius (*Hist. eccl.,* vi, 12) who takes the story from Serapion. For the text with a French translation and an account, cf. *R.B.,* 1894, pp. 522–560. The very complete study of Vaganay (*L'Evangile de Pierre,* 1930) supersedes all previous works.

sets out to exonerate Pilate by throwing all the odium for the condemnation of Jesus on the Jews and the Tetrarch Herod. The *Gospel According to the Hebrews* must have been orthodox, since St. Jerome, who translated it into Latin and Greek, was inclined to accept it as the original of St. Matthew. It was shorter than our canonical Gospel by about one fourth, according to the stichometry of Nicephorus. Judging from citations in the Fathers, it differed notably from St. Matthew. The fragments that have come down to us create no very favorable impression.[13]

The other apocryphal Gospels aim at supplementing the little we know about the early years of the Saviour and the days following the Resurrection. The *Protoevangelium of James* tells of the miraculous birth and the still more miraculous infancy of the Virgin Mary, up to the day when she gave birth to her only son. The author, who betrays a remarkable ignorance of Jewish customs and Mosaic legislation, tries to prove factually the virginity of Mary before, during, and after the birth of our Lord. This eminently orthodox thesis won him the favor of the Greek Fathers. The episode of the midwives brought in to verify the virginity of Mary, however offensive to our sensibilities, was less shocking to the ancients. There are some historical facts here and there, such as the names of the parents of the Virgin and the fact that she was born at Jerusalem; but the work adds little to our knowledge.[14] The *Gospel of Thomas* is a silly piece of writing in which Jesus is depicted as a capricious and temperamental child, and so vindictive that he strikes comrades of his own age dead if they have the misfortune to interrupt his games; he is insufferable to the neighbors and deserves the scoldings he gets from Joseph, and even Mary herself. It is unintelligible how anything so inane and blasphemous managed to last so many centuries, or why anyone bothered to transcribe it, even for the purpose of toning it down.

The Latin Church, with St. Augustine and St. Jerome, was always severe on the Apocrypha. Pope Innocent I ordered St.

---

13 Cf. Lagrange, *R.B.*, 1912, pp. 161–181 and 321–349; L. de Grandmaison, *Jésus-Christ*, 1928, Vol. I, Note D, pp. 210–215 (English transl., Vol. I, pp. 214–220).

14 Amann, *Le Protévangile de Jacques et ses remaniements latins* (text, translation, and commentary), Paris, 1910.

Exuperius, bishop of Toulouse, not only to reject but also to condemn books falsely carrying the names of Matthias, James the Less, Peter, John, Andrew, and Thomas. One would think that the decree of Gelasius would have finished them once and for all; but a clever forger gave them a new vogue by his fabrication of a supposed correspondence between St. Jerome and his friends, the bishops Heliodorus and Chromatius. They are made to say they heard that the solitary of Bethlehem possessed a history written in Matthew's own hand. Jerome replies that he actually has this volume, and had intended to keep it a secret; but, since the Manicheans had published a falsified version of it, he is sending a faithful translation of it to his correspondents. Thus was born the *Gospel of the Infancy,* or the Pseudo-Matthew, which had great influence on the plastic arts and pious literature of the Middle Ages. It is a combination of the *Protoevangelium of James* and the *Gospel of Thomas* (considerably polished) and a collection, of uncertain origin, of miracles occurring during the journey of the Holy Family to Egypt and during their sojourn there.[15]

An unknown author, who may well have been a monk of the time of Charlemagne, worked over the *Protoevangelium of James,* carefully expunging the more shocking incidents, such as the first marriage of St. Joseph and his advanced age when he was betrothed to Mary, the preposterous "bitter-water test" and the episode of the midwives. From this came the *Nativity of Mary,* a work of rather pure style, for the time, and animated with a tender devotion to the Queen of Heaven. It was incorporated almost entirely into the *Golden Legend.*[16]

A brief word must be said about the *Agrapha,* those sayings of Jesus not included in our canonical Gospels. St. Paul cites one of them in his discourse to the elders of Ephesus, and two or

---

[15] Michel, *Protévangile de Jasques, Pseudo-Matthieu, Evangile de Thomas* (with notes and translation), Paris, 1911; P. Peeters, *L'Evangile de l'enfance, rédactions syriaques, arabe et arméniennes traduites et annoteés,* Paris, 1914. Cf. also Charles, *The Apocryphal New Testament,* 1924, pp. 70–79.

[16] The book *De nativitate Mariae,* mistakenly attributed to St. Jerome, the earliest known manuscript of which is from the eleventh century, may go back two or three centuries farther. The opusculum is substantially the same as that in the *Golden Legend* for the eighth of September.

three others in his Epistles, giving at least their sense. Catalogues have been made of hundreds of these stray sayings, patiently collected from Biblical manuscripts, the writings of the Fathers, papyri exhumed from the sands of Egypt, and even from the Koran and the Talmud. Very few stand up under critical examination; at most a dozen seem worthy of Jesus. We would not dare quote with any confidence more than the following three: "Be good money-changers, rejecting what is to be rejected, and retaining what is good." "Ask for great things and the little things will be given besides." "Rejoice not except when you look on your brother with love."[17]

Obviously, then, outside of our canonical books there is very little material for the historian of Jesus; we must therefore turn to the four Gospels to know the life and teaching of the Saviour. But before making use of them, it is important to study the purpose, characteristics, and style of each.

2. The Quadriform Gospel

According to Eusebius, Papias had the following tradition from the ancients: "Matthew arranged in the Hebrew tongue the oracles (of the Lord) and each interpreted them as he could."[18] This short sentence, in spite of its brevity, is a good indication of the purpose, object, and character of the first Gospel. Since

---

[17] On the *Agrapha,* cf. Ropes, in Hastings, *Dict. of the Bible,* Vol. IV, 1904, pp. 343–352; Hennecke, in *Realencycl. f. prot. Theol.,* 3 ed., 1913, Vol. XXIII, pp. 16–25; Vaganay, in *Suppl.* of the *Dict. de la Bible,* Vol. I, 1926, coll. 159–198 (copious bibliography).

[18] Eusebius, *Hist. eccl.,* iii, 39 (MG, XX, 300): Ματθαῖος μὲν Ἑβραΐδι διαλέκτῳ τὰ λόγια συνετάξατο, ἡρμήνευσεν δ' αὐτὰ, ὡς ἦν δυνατός, ἕκαστος. Papias, the bishop of Hierapolis in Phrygia, composed about the year A.D. 125 a work in five books called *An Explanation of the Oracles of the Lord* (Λογίων κυριακῶν ἐξήγησις). He was more interested in the *oracles* (i.e., the sayings, the discourses) of Jesus than he was in the Gospel events, and these discourses he found chiefly in St. Matthew. This does not mean, as was once held, that St. Matthew had written a book called Λόγια, but that he had gathered together and *put in order* the λόγια (sayings) of the Saviour. This is what is meant by the word employed by Papias, according to the genuine reading ageed upon by the critics (συνετάξατο, Schwartz ed., Berlin, 1903, p. 292), instead of the old and faulty reading συνεγράψατο. The verb συντάσσεσθαι means *dispose, put in order, line up* (an army, or a fleet), *arrange, organize, compose artistically* (a discourse, a book), with an eye to the ordering and harmonious grouping of parts. And that is exactly one of the characteristic features of the first Gospel.

St. Matthew wrote in Hebrew (Aramaic), the language then in use among the Palestinian Jews, he was addressing especially them, and it is logical to expect his work to carry the imprint of the Semitic genius and echo the concerns of his readers.

For every Jew faced with the Gospel, the capital question was: Is or is not Jesus of Nazareth the Messias? It is universally agreed that the Evangelist intends to show forth the firm foundation of the affirmative answer by proving that Jesus is the Messias promised by the prophets, the son of David, the hope and salvation of Israel. This is why the testimonies from the prophets appear so often in his pages; he quotes no less than twenty-two passages. Not all, of course, have the same probative value. Some are taken in the literal sense, others in the typical, and still others in the accommodated sense. This last, though devoid of value as a proof, is not to be disregarded. "The ease with which the actions of God toward his chosen people and their prophets could be applied to the life of Christ showed, or at least suggested to the Jews, who were very responsive to this sort of parallel, that the same Spirit which formerly watched over Israel also guided Jesus during his earthly life."[19]

Let us go more into detail. According to St. Matthew, Jesus is not the Messias of the popular imagination heightened by apocalyptic visions, but the Messias as described by the prophets: an ineffable blending of lowliness and grandeur. The kingdom which he came to found is not that of the nationalist and the zealot; it is terrestrial by reason of its component elements, but

---

[19] J. Huby, in *Etudes,* Vol. CLVIII (1919), p. 13. He often (8 times) quotes the prophecy without any formula of citation. In other cases (14 times) the formulae of citation are of three kinds: (1) *for it is written* in the prophet; (2) *thus was fulfilled* the word of the prophet; (3) this happened *in order that* (ἵνα or ὅπως) the word of the prophet might be fulfilled. It must, however, be noted that in the New Testament ἵνα may very often be translated *in such a way that.*

On the various ways in which a prophecy is fulfilled, cf. Maldonatus on Matt. 2:15: "Dicitur prophetia, quantum observare potui, quatuor modis adimpleri: primum, cum ipsum fit de quo proprie et litterali sensu intelligebatur. . . . Secundo, cum fit non id, de quo proprie intelligebatur prophetia, sed id quod per illud significabatur. . . . Tertio, cum nec fit id, de quo proprie intelligitur prophetia, nec illud quod per illud significatur, sed quod illi simile est et omnino eiusmodi, ut prophetia non minus apte de eo, quam de quo dicta est, dici potuisse videatur. . . . Quarto, cum idipsum quod per prophetiam aut Scripturam dictum erat, quamvis iam factum fuerit, tamen magis ac magis fit."

spiritual in nature, tendency, and final destination. That Jesus was repudiated by his people proves nothing against his divine mission, because that was the result of willful blindness on the part of those who could not bring themselves to acknowledge him. St. Matthew's plan is, therefore, at once dogmatic, polemical, and apologetic.

The praise given to him by Papias for having put in order the oracles of the Saviour is well deserved. He was, indeed, careful to group together utterances on the same theme and to make of them five long discourses which define the various features of the kingdom of God and form, as it were, the skeleton of his Gospel:

1. The Sermon on the Mount, the program of the kingdom;
2. The discourse to the Twelve, the program of the Apostolate;
3. Dogmatic parables, the essence and nature of the kingdom;
4. The organization of the kingdom and relations between its members;
5. The consummation of the kingdom at the Parousia.

This structure is not the result of accident; it is the fruit of deliberation and reflection on the part of the author, for he puts a period to each discourse by a uniform formula. "When Jesus had brought these words to a close, the multitude was struck with admiration," or "when he had finished speaking, he departed thence for other places."[20] And so we have a natural explanation of the phenomenon of doublets, which is so frequent in St. Matthew. After including an idea of the Saviour's in a discourse on an analogous theme, he repeats it in the episode in which it was uttered and where it is impossible to omit it without doing violence to the sense of the passage.[21]

The Semitism of the First Gospel needs no demonstration; it is clear at first glance, though not so much in the syntax and vocabulary (the work of the translator, who was enough master of his language to write correctly and with a certain ease), but in the turn of thought and the manner of conceiving and expressing things. Almost every page has instances of Biblical parallelism

[20] Matt. 7:28; 11:1; 13:53; 19:1; 26:1.

[21] Hawkins, *Horae Synopticae,* Oxford, 1909, pp. 80–99, is the best study of the doublets in St. Matthew.

and other figures of speech familiar to the Hebrews. The author realizes that he is writing for readers conversant with Jewish customs and institutions, and finds it superfluous to explain them. A reading, with this in mind, of the Sermon on the Mount or of the indictment leveled against the Scribes and Pharisees, will make the point clear.

St. Mark, on the other hand, either simply leaves out or else explains matters like these that would be unintelligible to his readers. According to a well-established tradition, he wrote primarily for the Gentiles or the Hellenistic Jews. Here again we have Papias' testimony: "Mark, the interpreter of Peter, wrote down accurately but not in order the works and words of the Saviour which he remembered; for he had not been a companion or hearer of Jesus, but, as I have said, he attached himself later to Peter, who taught as the occasion demanded, and not with the intention of giving a coherent record of the words of the Lord in their entirety. Thus Mark is not at fault if he wrote certain things (or certain words) as he recalled them. He was concerned only with omitting nothing that he had heard and with telling it truthfully."[22]

If this testimony is reliable — and there is no doubt that it is, since it is confirmed by the unanimous tradition of antiquity — St. Mark's purpose in writing his Gospel must have been identical with St. Peter's, when he preached at Rome. To make Jesus acceptable to a largely polytheistic audience, he had to present him not as a superior human being nor as some superhuman being nor even simply as Son of God (for the pagans knew an infinity

---

[22] Eusebius, *Hist. eccles.*, III, 39 (MG, XX, 300; in the Schwartz edition, Leipzig, 1903, p. 290): Μάρκος *μὲν ἑρμηνευτὴς* Πέτρου *γενόμενος, ὅσα ἐμνημόνευσεν ἀκριβῶς ἔγραφεν, οὐ μέντοι τάξει, τὰ ὑπὸ τοῦ κυρίου ἢ λεχθέντα ἢ πραχθέντα· οὔτε γὰρ ἤκουσεν τοῦ κυρίου οὔτε παρηκολούθησεν αὐτῷ· ὕστερον δέ, ὡς ἔφην,* Πέτρῳ, *ὃς πρὸς τὰς χρείας ἐποιεῖτο τὰς διδασκαλίας, ἀλλ' οὐχ ὥσπερ σύνταξιν τῶν κυριακῶν ποιούμενος λογίων, ὥστε οὐδὲν ἥμαρτεν* Μάρκος *οὕτως ἔνια γράψας ὡς ἀπεμνημόνευσεν· ἑνὸς γὰρ ἐποιήσατο πρόνοιαν, τοῦ μηδὲν ὧν ἤκουσεν παραλιπεῖν ἢ ψεύσασθαί τι ἐν αὐτοῖς.*

Papias here refers to the testimony of a person whom he calls the *Elder* (*ὁ πρεσβύτερος*). Zahn, Schmiedel, Lagrange, and others think that Papias is again speaking for himself at the words *οὔτε γὰρ ἤκουσεν*, and, as a matter of fact, *ὡς ἔφην* would be very strange in the mouth of his informant. Besides, what follows seems to be Papias' own comment on the lack of order which the *Elder* attributed to St. Mark.

of divine generations), but as the sovereign God, exalted beyond comparison above pagan divinities. It is thus that St. Mark presents him. He does not call him God, but portrays him acting as God, as the supreme Ruler of the world and the absolute Lord of the spiritual forces to which the pagans gave divine honors. Although the Second Gospel is by far the shortest, it recounts almost as many miracles as the other Synoptics and has two which they do not mention, exclusive of those to which it refers repeatedly *in globo*.[23] It notes circumstances of time, place, and persons which throw into relief the almighty power of the Wonder-Worker and registers the astonishment, admiration, stupefaction, and fright which the miracles aroused in the souls of the spectators. On catching sight of Jesus, the crowd could not resist crying out: "He has done all things well. He has made both the deaf to hear and the dumb to speak. . . . Never have we seen the like."

St. Mark is not an abbreviator (*breviator*) of St. Matthew, nor his follower and footman (*pedisequus*), so to speak, as St. Augustine would have it. He has a way all his own. He can be called, as St. Jerome called him, the interpreter (*interpres*) of Peter, in the sense that he faithfully reproduces Peter's catechesis. Certain critics deny this, on the ground that Peter is less gently handled in the Second Gospel than in the others. Their objection is really proof of the point they are denying. Would they have St. Peter exploit his own teaching to put himself on a pedestal? He spoke of himself modestly, as he should, and deliberately passed over his greatest title to honor. This is precisely what the account of his interpreter does.

It is somewhat surprising, but quite intelligible, that Papias reproaches Mark for a lack of order. Chronological order, for Papias, as for most of his contemporaries, was a kind of disorder. He would have preferred a grouping of the *Oracles of the Lord* according to subject matter. He misses the beautiful and skillful arrangement of Matthew. He excuses Mark because "Peter taught as the occasion demanded and not with the intention of giving a coherent record of the words of the Lord in their

---

[23] The deaf-mute (Mark 7:32–37) and the blind man of Bethsaida (Mark 8:22–26). [Note of J. Calés.]

entirety." Mark needs no excuse, however, and what was to Papias a defect is to us an excellence.[24]

To the first recipient of his Gospel, St. Luke clearly expresses his aim and plan: "Inasmuch as many have attempted to draw up a narrative of the things that have been accomplished among us, according to the tradition of those who, from the first, were eyewitnesses and ministers of the word, it has seemed good to me also, after applying myself to learn all from the beginning, to make for thee an orderly account thereof, excellent Theophilus, that thou mayest realize the certainty of the teachings that thou hast received."[25] Though St. Luke addresses this directly to a

---

[24] In oratorical or literary work, the ancient rhetoricians distinguished three things: the *invention* (εὕρησις), the *order* or *arrangement* (τάξις), the *style* or *diction* (λέξις or φράσις). So understood, *order* was the harmonious arrangement of parts. *Invention,* by itself, gave only a formless body; it was *order* that gave to it beauty of form (Lucian, *De conscrib. histor.,* 48). Dionysius of Halicarnassus reproaches Thucydides for following the chronological order too strictly, because his division by winters and summers forced him to place the beginning of the siege of Plataea in the second book and the end of it in the next book. Papias finds that Mark's Gospel is not a *work of art* comparable to Matthew's because he merely repeats Peter's catechesis, without caring to put in order, to group together, the Saviour's discourses, which were of primary interest to Papias. The logical order, St. Matthew's great merit, at times leaves something to be desired in St. Mark. Cf. Colson, Τάξει in *Papias,* in *J.T.S.,* Oct., 1912, Vol. XIV, pp. 62–69, and Wright, *ibid.,* pp. 298–300.

[25] Luke 1:1–4: Ἐπειδήπερ πολλοὶ ἐπεχείρησαν ἀνατάξασθαι διήγησιν περὶ τῶν πεπληροφορημένων ἐν ἡμῖν πραγμάτων, καθὼς παρέδοσαν ἡμῖν οἱ ἀπ' ἀρχῆς αὐτόπται καὶ ὑπηρέται γενόμενοι τοῦ λόγου, ἔδοξε κἀμοὶ παρηκολουθηκότι ἄνωθεν πᾶσιν ἀκριβῶς, καθεξῆς σοι γράψαι, κράτιστε Θεόφιλε, ἵνα ἐπιγνῷς περὶ ὧν κατηχήθης λόγων τὴν ἀσφάλειαν.

a) ἐπιχειρεῖν has no unfavorable meaning and does not indicate an abortive effort. *Conari* implies too much; rather it is *aggredi,* "to undertake, take in hand." St. Luke is not finding fault with his predecessors, nor does he mean to imply any failure on their part. He proposes to imitate them: what they have done, he too can do (ἐπειδήπερ . . . κἀμοί).

b) ἀνατάσσεσθαι is a very rare word. It is scarcely to be found except in Irenaeus (*Haeres.,* III, xxi, 2) where it is translated into Latin by *rememorare,* and in Plutarch (*De solertia animalium,* 12) where the meaning appears to be "rehearse, repeat a lesson." In St. Luke the meaning would be "retrace" (*recolere*), or simply "compose"; but it is not "to put in order" (συντάσσεσθαι).

c) πληροφορεῖν is merely a more expressive synonym for πληροῦν which means "to fill up, to accomplish, to complete." The second meaning is the only one applicable here. If, with Zahn, Loisy, and others, we take the Prologue as a Preface common to the Gospel and the Acts, we would read: "the things that

catechumen, or more probably to a neophyte of noble birth or high position, he envisions beyond his first reader all the new Greek-speaking Christians, Gentiles like himself, and wants to confirm them in their faith. He forthrightly declares that he has not been an eyewitness of the things he is going to relate; but he has sedulously culled his information from firsthand witnesses and official heralds of the Gospel. He has diligently studied and attentively followed the course of events from the beginning. He possesses an exact and detailed knowledge of them. He thus fulfills the three requirements demanded of a trustworthy historian, and no one has the right to reject his testimony. Several others, strangers like himself to the events, have undertaken to write of them; he does not criticize or judge their attempts, but limits himself to stating the fact, as a precedent for his own venture.

---

have been accomplished among us (ἐν ἡμῖν) Christians"; otherwise ἐν ἡμῖν must be taken in a more general sense, "in our time" (as in Justin, *Dialog.*, 81).

d) St. Luke distinguishes two classes of men: those who *hand down* (παρέδοσαν) the word of the Gospel of which they have been the *eyewitnesses* (αὐτόπται) or *ministers* (ὑπηρέται), and those who receive it. He puts himself in the latter category (ἡμῖν).

e) He enumerates his qualifications as a historian: he has *followed all the events* (παρηκολουθηκότι πᾶσιν), not as a spectator, but as an observer who has questioned eyewitnesses and explored written documents; he has followed them *diligently* (ἀκριβῶς) and ἄνωθεν. This word can mean "for a long time" (Lagrange, Dibelius, Klostermann, etc.) or "from the beginning" (Schanz, Loisy, Plummer, etc.). In either case, the author is qualified to write the Gospel.

f) He will write καθεξῆς "in order," but not necessarily in chronological order. "It is above all a linking of cause and effect, a story which holds together, whose beginning looks forward to its ending, in which everything and all the characters are in their proper place" (Lagrange, *Saint Luc,* 1921, p. 6). The order of history is, to be sure, chronological, but "we must not exaggerate to the extent of thinking that Luke intends to write a chronicle or a diary" (Schanz). On the contrary, St. Luke betrays a certain indifference to questions of time, and his formulas of transition are of the vaguest. On this point we share the opinion of Maldonatus, to whose explanation of the words *ex ordine scribere* we refer the reader.

A comparison of the Prologue with the introduction of the treatise *De materia medica* by the physician Dioscorides is interesting, but it does not, in our opinion, prove the existence of any imitation or even of any direct reminiscence; cf. Lagrange, *Saint Luc,* p. 2; or Zahn, *Lucas,* 1920, pp. 40–41.

Cf. also Cadbury, "Commentary on the Preface of Luke," in *The Beginnings of Christianity,* first part, Vol. II, London, 1922, pp. 489–510. The author gives numerous examples and instructive parallels, but his theory is to be accepted with caution.

What they have done, he can do. Nothing could be less pretentious.

He does not say what he finds fault with in his predecessors, nor does he insinuate that their work leaves anything to be desired. All he does is to set forth what he himself proposes to do. Some of the previous efforts were doubtless very fragmentary. Others, like St. Mark's, began *ex abrupto* and threw the reader *in medias res*. St. Luke will go back to the beginning and write a coherent narrative of the life of Christ, from his birth to his glorious Resurrection. Not that the chronology is obtrusive; no other Evangelist seems so indifferent to matters of time and dates. He has not the intention, at times imputed to him, of correcting St. Mark, at least in the order of his narrative. It should rather be said that he follows Mark closely, and in the two cases where he departs from him, critics generally prefer the order of his predecessor. Besides, exact chronological sequence, though a necessity for a chronicler or an annalist, is a secondary quality in a historian.

An attempt has been made to present St. Luke as a painter. An author of the sixth century tells us that the Empress Eudoxia discovered at Jerusalem a picture of the Blessed Virgin painted by the author of the Third Gospel. The work was of much later date, as was easy to see. However, if St. Luke did not himself wield a brush, he has given rise to masterpieces on canvas and his pen has sketched pictures that have been the inspiration of the greatest artists: the Annunciation, the Visitation, the adoration of the shepherds, Jesus among the doctors, the repentant woman, the Prodigal Son, the Good Samaritan, Christ weeping over Jerusalem, the disciples at Emmaus, and many other unforgettable scenes.

Though treating the same subject, the Synoptics resemble one another very little. Their distinctive characteristics show up readily in any comparison of parallel passages. Let us take as an example the raising from the dead of Jairus' daughter, and the cure of the woman with an issue of blood, which is inseparable from it.

Matthew 9:18–26

18. While he was speaking these things,

behold, a certain ruler prostrated himself before him, saying: "My daughter has just now died, but come, lay thy hands upon her, and she shall live.

19. And Jesus arose and followed him, with his disciples.

20. And behold, a woman with an issue of blood for twelve years

21. came up behind him and touched the hem of his cloak;
for she said within herself: "If I do but touch his cloak, I shall be made safe."

22. But Jesus turning and seeing her, said: "Have confidence (my) daughter; thy faith has healed thee." And the woman was healed from that same moment.

Mark 5:21–43

21. And when Jesus had reached the other bank in a boat, a great multitude again gathered together about him, and he was on the seashore.

22. And a ruler of the synagogue named Jairus comes to him, and seeing him, falls at his feet,

23. and prays him earnestly, saying: "My daughter is at the point of death; come lay thy hand upon her that she may be safe and live.

24. And he went with him, and a great multitude was following him and pressing upon him.

25. And a woman afflicted with a loss of blood twelve years,

26. who had suffered much from many physicians and had spent all her goods without gaining any relief, but rather growing worse,

27. hearing about Jesus came behind him and touched his cloak,

28. for she said: "If I touch but his cloak, I shall be made safe."

29. And immediately the flow of blood was dried up, and she felt in her body that she was cured of her affliction.

30. And immediately Jesus, knowing that power had gone forth from him, turned toward the multitude and said: "Who touched my cloak?"

31. And his disciples said to him: "Thou seest the multitude pressing about thee, and dost thou ask: 'Who touched me?' "

32. And looking round about him he sought out her who had done this.

33. But the woman, frightened and trembling, knowing what had happened to her, came and prostrated herself before him and told him the whole truth.

Luke 8:40–56

40. Now it came to pass that on the return of Jesus the multitude welcomed him, for all were awaiting him.

41. And behold, a man named Jairus, who was the ruler of the synagogue, came and fell at the feet of Jesus and prayed him to enter his house,

42. for he had an only daughter about twelve years old who was dying. And as he went the multitudes pressed upon him.

43. And a woman afflicted with a loss of blood twelve years, who had spent all her substance on physicians, and could not be healed by any,

44. came up behind him and touched the hem of his cloak; and at once the flow of her blood ceased.

45. And Jesus said: "Who touched me?" Since all denied, Peter and those that were with him said to him: "Master, the multitude presses about thee and stifles thee."

46. But Jesus said: "Someone touched me, for I know that power has gone forth from me."

47. But the woman, seeing that she was discovered, came trembling and prostrated herself before him, and declared before the whole people why she

Matthew 9:18–26	Mark 5:21–43	Luke 8:40–56
		had touched him, and how she had been instantly cured.
	34. He said to her: "Daughter, thy faith has made thee safe. Go in peace, and be healed of thy affliction."	48. He said to her: "Daughter, thy faith has healed thee. Go in peace."
	35. While he was yet speaking, they come to say to the ruler of the synagogue: "Thy daughter is dead; why trouble the Master further?"	49. While he was yet speaking, they came to say to the ruler of the synagogue: "Thy daughter is dead; trouble the Master no further."
	36. But Jesus, hearing these words, says to the ruler of the synagogue: "Fear not, only believe."	50. But Jesus, having heard this, answered: "Fear not; believe only, and she shall be made safe."
	37. And he allowed no one to follow him but Peter, James, and John the brother of James.	51. When he had come to the house, he suffered no one to enter with him except Peter, John, and James, with the girl's father and mother.
23. And when Jesus had come to the ruler's house and saw the flute-players and the noisy crowd, he said:	38. And they come to the house of the ruler of the synagogue, and he sees the tumult, and the people wailing and lamenting greatly.	
24. "Retire, for the girl is not dead, but sleeps." And they laughed him to scorn.	39. And entering he says to them: "Why this uproar and this weeping? The child is not dead, but sleeps."	52. And all were weeping and mourning for her. He said: "Weep not, she is not dead, but sleeps."
25. And when the multitude was cast out,	40. And they laughed him to scorn. But casting them all out, he takes the father and mother of the child and those who were with him, and goes toward the place where the child was.	53. And they laughed him to scorn, knowing that she was dead.
he entered and took her hand,	41. And taking the child's hand, he says to her: *"Talitha cumi,"* which is to say, "Girl, I command thee, arise."	54. Taking her by the hand, he said to her: "Girl, arise."
and the girl arose.	42. And immediately the girl arose and walked. She was twelve years old. And immediately they were struck with amazement.	55. And her spirit came back into her, and she arose at once.
26. And the report of it spread throughout the country.	43. And he insistently charged that no one should know of it. And he bade them to give her to eat.	56. And he commanded that they should give her to eat.
		57. And her parents were beside themselves, but he charged them to say nothing to anyone of what had come to pass.

A single episode is a very slim basis for comparison; nevertheless an examination of it is instructive.

What stands out everywhere in the first Evangelist is the contrast between the fullness of the discourses and the brevity of the narratives. The episode we have just transcribed is twice as long in St. Luke and almost three times as long in St. Mark. St. Matthew achieves his condensation in two ways: he omits accessory details to get on quickly to the climax, and he has a group take the place of individuals. This can be called the synthetic procedure, as against the analytic method of St. Mark and St. John. Jairus, the father, approaches Jesus and says, "My daughter has just now died." Only later will Jairus actually know of her death, but this anticipatory mention of it eliminates a repetition of his request and cuts down the narrative accordingly.[26] St. Matthew mentions only very briefly the cure of the woman with the issue of blood, and does not think it necessary to say that Jesus was accompanied into the young girl's room by her mother and father and three disciples. The detail is interesting, but adds nothing to the miracle. Whether it be from lack of imagination or indifference to the externals of events, he goes straight to the point without a pause. Sometimes his account seems a trifle dull compared to the lively descriptions of St. Mark. It is schematic, in the ordinary sense of the word; it portrays only the essential traits — the skeleton, as it were — of the object. It is condensed to an extreme.

St. Mark is at the opposite pole to St. Matthew in his way of telling things. Yet his narrative, for all its weight of details, does not drag, but gives an impression of rapidity. There are three reasons for this: his very frequent use of the historical present, a lavish use of the adverb *immediately*, and small co-ordinated phrases joined together with the conjunction "and."[27] Picturesque

[26] Jansenius of Ghent remarks on this subject (Matt. 9:18): "Qui breviter aliquid narrare gaudet cogitur nonnumquam ob narrationis convenientiam aliquid aliter narrare quam quo modo gestum est, quod tamen facit sine falsitatis et mendacii nota, si modus ab ipso narratus in rei gestae ordine saltem comprehendatur."

[27] There are 151 historical presents in St. Mark (as against 78 in St. Matthew and only 4 or 6 in St. Luke); cf. Hawkins, *Horae Synopticae,* 2 ed., 1909, pp.

features abound. St. Mark has a visual memory. He excels in describing the gestures and expression of Jesus, and the attitude and feelings of his interlocutors. This is what gives such charm to his narrative; his is the most realistic of all.[28] His style, of course, is at times somewhat rough, and his expression, with its pleonasms and repetitions, is less literary; but these defects are greatly redeemed by his fresh pictures and his ingenuousness. Look at the vivacity and richness of the pages transcribed above! The woman with the issue of blood had consulted many doctors, who were not satisfied with tormenting her to no avail, and impoverishing her, but actually made her worse. After curing her, Jesus looks searchingly around and finally fixes his eyes on her. Thanks to St. Mark, we know the very words the Saviour spoke when he brought the dead girl back to life. On the other hand, there is some slight carelessness. The order to the crowd to stay back is repeated twice without necessity. The moment when her father interceded for her would have been a better place to state the young girl's age rather than after her resurrection; and though Jesus' instruction to her parents to give her something to eat is a moving touch, it would seem to belong before the injunction to say nothing about the miracle, rather than after it.

St. Luke's narrative is of a more highly literary quality. Historical presents yield to imperfects; the little co-ordinated phrases are rounded out into periods; pleonasms are avoided. It is not to be concluded, however, that St. Luke had St. Mark's text before him and was correcting it. He seems certainly to have

143–149. The historical present, which is frequent in Josephus, was also common in ordinary speech, if we may judge from the papyri.

The adverb *immediately* (εὐθύς) occurs 42 times in St. Mark and loses much of its force by its frequency. It appears only 18 times in St. Matthew, and 10 in St. Luke. Cf. J. Weiss, Εὐθύς *bei Markus, in Z.N.T.W.*, p. 124.

St. Mark is sparing in his use of the particle δέ (150 times as against 496 in Matthew and 508 in Luke). On the other hand, he is partial to the conjunction καί which the other two Synoptics replace by δέ in 26 parallel cases.

[28] On the characteristics of the second Gospel, cf. Hawkins, *Horae Synopticae,* 1909, pp. 114–153; Turner, *Marcan Usage* (a series of articles published in *J.T.S.* from October, 1924, to October, 1926); Swete, *The Gospel According to St. Mark,* 2 ed., 1908, *Introduction;* Lagrange, *Saint Marc,* 4 ed., 1929, pp. lxvii–cvii: *Le style et la langue de Marc* and *Le caractère sémitique de Marc.*

read it, but his own version is not a mere emendation of St. Mark. He draws from him freely, as from his other sources, but has his own way of telling the facts that had come to his knowledge in more than one way. Let us not make a purist out of him. He writes the language of the Hellenists, correctly and not without a certain elegance, but does not strive for Atticism, as Lucian of Samosata and Clement of Alexandria did later. He does not shrink from using common expressions and Semitic turns of phrase picked up in much reading of the Septuagint. Yet his two books are the most literary works of the New Testament, as is shown by his rather frequent use of the optative, which had dropped almost completely from the spoken idiom. His style is easily recognizable: practically all philologists, at least those of any importance, agree today that the Third Gospel and the Acts are from the same pen.[29] An attempt has been made to prove from the language alone that they are the work of a physician, but with hardly decisive success; all that is evident is that the author, a man of culture, had read medical works, that he was interested in medicine, and that he keeps in mind a certain number of technical terms.[30] St. Luke is an artist. The fact that he wrote his first two chapters in a Biblical style does not prove that he translated them from a Hebrew or Aramaic document, but is an indication that he was familiar enough with the Greek version of the Bible to imitate its language.

Passing from the Synoptics to the Fourth Gospel is like going into a new world. We shall speak here only of the quality of the narrative, not of the discourses. In his preface, Westcott, the best English commentator on St. John, shows that the author was a Jew, and a Jew of Palestine, as well as an eyewitness, one of the

---

29 Zahn, *Einleitung,* 3 ed., Vol. II, pp. 431–446; Hawkins, "The linguistic similarity between Luke and Acts," in *Horae Synopticae,* pp. 174–189; Harnack, *Lukas der Arzt, der Verfasser des dritten Evangeliums und der Apostelgeschichte,* Leipzig, 1906; Stanton, *The Gospels as Historical Documents,* Cambridge, Vol. II, 1909, pp. 240–260 and 276–322; also in *J.T.S.,* Vol. XXIV, 1923, pp. 361–382. The theory of unity of authorship is unhesitatingly admitted by Blass, Moulton, Deissmann, etc.

30 Hobart, *The Medical Language of St. Luke,* Dublin, 1882; Harnack, *Lukas der Arzt,* Leipzig, 1901; more briefly in Plummer, *The Gospel According to St. Luke,* 4 ed., Edinburgh, 1906, pp. lxiii–lxvii, and Lagrange, *Saint Luc,* 1921, pp. cxxv–cxxvii.

twelve Apostles, and the beloved disciple of Jesus. Read without prejudice and stubborn preconceptions, St. John gives the irresistible impression of being a man who is telling what he personally saw. In the other Evangelists, exactitude in matters of time and place is rather rare, but in St. John it is more frequent. Many concrete and precise details are casually scattered throughout the whole narrative, as the occasion for them occurs, and without appeal to other authority. Except to give their names, the Synoptics scarcely ever speak of any Apostles except Peter and the sons of Zebedee. St. John, on the other hand, keeps an obviously deliberate silence about his brother and himself, but furnishes enough characteristic traits of most of his colleagues — Peter, Andrew, Thomas, Philip, Jude, and Bartholomew-Nathanael — to bring them vividly to life.

There is the same care for accuracy in topography and chronology. He carefully distinguishes the two Bethanys, one beyond the Jordan and the other about two miles from Jerusalem; he expressly speaks of Cana of Galilee and Bethsaida of Galilee to prevent the reader from confusing them with the two better known towns, the Cana neighboring on Tyre and the Bethsaida of Philip. He notes that Ennon, where John last baptized, was near Salim, because Ennon, which means *Springs,* could be used to designate several places. On the question of Sichar, in which critics thought he was in error, present-day discoveries are proving him right. It is with the topography of Jerusalem, however, that the author of the Fourth Gospel shows himself most familiar. He is the only one to mention the pool of Siloe, Solomon's Porch where Jesus taught in the winter, the torrent of Cedron which had to be crossed to get to Gethsemani, the pool with five porticoes, the site and form of which have been recently established by excavations. He knows that the place where Jesus was judged was called Lithostrotos in Greek and Gabbatha in Aramaic.

There is the same precision in mentioning the times of day and measurements. The other Evangelists confine themselves to the common division of the day into four parts, similar to the four watches of the night. They seem to know only morning, noon, evening, and the third, sixth, and ninth hours. St. John makes further subdivisions. He recalls that he met Jesus for the first time at the tenth hour of the day (four o'clock in the afternoon), and that the son of the imperial official was cured of fever at the seventh hour (one o'clock in the afternoon). He points out that Golgotha was near the city, and the tomb of Joseph of Arimathea very near Golgotha. He tells us that the water jars of Cana each held two or three measures; that the Bethany of Lazarus was fifteen stadia from Jerusalem; that in their struggle against the storm the Apostles had advanced only twenty-five or thirty stadia; that the risen Jesus stood on the beach of the Sea of Tiberias, some two hundred cubits away from Peter's boat.

It may be objected that at the time of life when St. John wrote his Gospel he could not have remembered such details so accurately, and that they must be the invention of a forger who was conversant with Palestine. But this would be to forget that the adolescent memory is extraordinarily retentive of facts that have made a vivid impression on the imagination. Who of us does not find deep somewhere in his memory, even at the end of a long life, passages of authors he admired long ago but has not since had the opportunity to reread? The Fourth Gospel is composed of a small number of such unforgettable episodes: the first contact with the divine Master, the cure of the paralytic at Bethesda, the first multiplication of the loaves, the incidents at the Feast of Tabernacles, the raising of Lazarus, the anointing at Bethany, the history of the Passion, and the apparition on the shore of the Sea of Tiberias.

The reproduction of extended discourses after the passage of so many years creates a real difficulty, and we cannot deny it. Observe, however, that the Apostle had repeated them hundreds of times, probably in the same terms, and that they had become, as it were, stereotyped on his memory. Besides, we do not claim that he gives them word for word, just as he first heard them. He puts them in his own style, too personal to be missed, and perhaps in his own order. We know that St. Matthew reduced the teachings of the Saviour to five themes, without being too much concerned about their topographical or chronological setting. Why refuse to allow St. John the same privilege? As a matter of fact, when he touches on a subject, he does not leave it until he has exhausted it; and he does not come back to it again. For example, Jesus speaks only once to his Apostles: in the long discourse after the Supper. It is possible that the Evangelist here inserted instructions and advice given on previous occasions. Perhaps the same could be said about the group of discourses addressed to the hostile crowd during the Feast of Tabernacles, or at the unnamed feast of the fifth chapter. And what does it matter whether the discourses are composite or not, provided they give us the true thought of Jesus, not always as the Apostles understood it at the time (St. Luke says their souls were covered with a veil), but as they understood it after the Resurrection and the descent of the Holy Ghost?

Let us cease treating the Evangelists as men on trial whose every word is suspect. When one of them is alone in stating something, certain modern critics who pride themselves on their independence reject his testimony as isolated; when several say the same thing, it seems, we are told, that they must have copied from one another, and their testimony is equally worthless. Were such radical norms applied to profane writers, history could not be written.

3. Harmony of the Gospels

St. John chooses to put only his favorite memories in his work; St. Mark depends chiefly or perhaps exclusively on oral tradition; St. Luke draws sometimes on oral tradition and sometimes on previous writings. The result is that each Evangelist's presentation of the subject matter is very different from the others, and each follows his own path. How can we derive from their combined writings a coherent and harmonious history? St. Augustine, the first and only Father of the Church to treat the question *ex professo,* formulated two illuminating principles to serve as guides: one treats of divergent expositions of the same theme, the other has to do with the order of events.

1. THE DIFFERENCES IN EXPRESSION — The inspired authors have imprinted on their works the stamp of their own personalities, but have not mixed error with divine revelation. When Erasmus broached his theory about *lapsus memoriae* on the part of the Evangelists, Catholics opposed him mercilessly. Nor did Newman have any greater success with his suggestion on *obiter dicta.* But error is one thing, and imperfect expression of

the truth another. Our eye takes in at one glance only a limited horizon, and cannot take the full measure of the object. Human speech practically swarms with inadequate expressions which do not stand up under philosophical analysis and are excused only by usage, necessity, or a sort of tacit convention. God could certainly have transformed the intelligences of his interpreters and elevated them to the fullness of vision that is the prerogative of the Blessed. He could even have created expressly for them a more accurate language; but another miracle would have been necessary to make it intelligible, because though more exact, if you will, it would be an enigma to the rest of mankind. But God has not willed to do this, because the heralds of revelation were to speak to men in the speech of men.

Every artifice of expression, every literary form, every type of composition in use among profane writers appears in the sacred writers. Everything from the strictest history to fiction, including poetry, which is halfway between history and fiction, is used by those God chose as his mouthpieces. The lyrical form, the dialogue, the apologue, the allegory concealing under a more or less transparent veil some dogmatic or moral truth, can all serve as vehicles of religious teaching, and may be expected in the Bible. The Canticle of Canticles is all sublime allegory, from beginning to end.

Though language is the mirror of thought, it cannot be its perfect reflection. It is a recognizable image, but not a photograph. It outlines the important features, but is not a finished portrayal of the lines, coloring, movement, or vitality in the object. That is why great writers wrestle so desperately with language to force it to express what they have in their hearts. A perfect language, used by a perfect intelligence, would dispense with figures. They are legitimized only by usage, which gives the word its proper value and heightens or softens down the speech to the level of the idea. On this account, figurative language is not purely arbitrary; it is regulated by a sort of tacit convention, which is at the same time imperative and demanding. To indicate a large and indefinite number, the Greeks said *ten thousand,* the Latins *six hundred;* the French stop at *a hundred* or go to *a thousand* at will. All translate exactly the same idea with quite different figures. All speak correctly with that relative correctness men consider sufficient, and could be accused of falsehood or error only if they were to depart from the accepted usage of their time and country.[31]

Round numbers, meanings that do not fit etymology, figures of speech that touch only the surface — all these are part of the necessary and hence excusable imperfections of human speech. I may say eight days for a week, or fifteen for two, without scruple; usage in some other language may forbid it. I readily speak of the heresy of Luther and Calvin as the *Reform,* of the sophisms of the Encyclopedists as *Philosophy,* of the schism of Constantinople as the *Orthodox Church.* I am certainly using language that is inexact, that I inwardly condemn, but it is authorized by current usage, and, when necessary, carries with it the corrective of irony. Isolated words are crude ore; words joined in phrases are metal minted into coins by usage, which determines their circulation and is itself subject to fluctuations and change.[32]

It would be superfluous to bring up these elementary notions if some exegetes did not show themselves too inclined to forget them when they handle the Sacred Books. After all, some commentators have felt obliged to extol the maternal tenderness of the stork, because its Hebrew name means *kind,* or to justify the use of the word *firmament* (raq'a), which the author of Genesis uses to designate the vault of the heavens. At that rate, one would be reduced to silence. It would be impossible to name God,

---

[31] This is St. Augustine's answer to Faustus, who proposes to him as an objection the divergences of the Evangelists (*Contra Faustum,* xxxiii, 7; ML, XLII, 516): "Quid ergo? Cum legimus obliviscimur quemadmodum loqui soleamus? An Scriptura Dei aliter nobiscum fuerat quam nostro more locutura?" Let one of these quibblers try to tell the same thing twice in exactly the same way; he will not succeed. "Utrum non aliquid plus minusve diceret, aut praepostero ordine, non verborum tantum, sed etiam rerum; aut utrum non aliquid ex sua sententia diceret, tanquam alius dixerit, quod eum dixisse non audierit, sed voluisse atque sensisse plane cognoverit; aut utrum non alicujus breviter complecteretur sententiae veritatem, cujus rei autem quasi expressius articulos explicasset?" etc. (*ibid.,* xxxiii, 8).

[32] A theologian as reliable as Pesch does not hesitate to write (*De Inspiratione S. Scripturae,* p. 520, note): "Nihil obstat quominus hagiographus utatur notionibus geographicis tunc sparsis etsi forte minus correctis; at ea quae in notionibus falsa sunt non potest ipse ut vera affirmare." Certainly, but why limit the statement to "widespread notions of geography"?

heaven, the soul, the spirit, any immaterial things whose etymology is based on a false or less exact primitive conception. We could not say the sun rises or sets, or mounts or descends toward the horizon, or stands still at solstices and moves backward about the time of the equinox. In things like this, usage is a safe guide; and if I can be sure that, in the first century of our era, Greeks called those afflicted with epilepsy or some other nervous disorder demoniacs, I would no more rely on this word itself to show the reality of diabolical possession than I would admit the influence of the moon because of the etymology of the word *lunatic*.

St. Jerome warns us that when the Evangelists quoted from the Old Testament they concerned themselves more with meaning than words.[33] We should do the same in interpreting them. In discussing the quelling of the storm at sea, St. Augustine asks what words the Apostles used to wake Jesus. Were they, "Master, we perish," or "Lord, save us, we perish," or "Master, does it not concern thee that we perish?" And did Jesus answer, "Where is your faith?" or "Why are you afraid, O men of little faith?" or "Why fear? Have you not yet faith?" It does not matter, says St. Augustine, whether they said one or the other, or something equivalent given by no Evangelist, since the sense is the same. In another place, the holy Doctor formulates this general principle: "The use by the Evangelists of different but not contrary expressions to designate the same things furnishes us with a very useful and very necessary lesson. It is that we should consider the intention and not the words, and that it is not a lie to express the thought of another in different words than his. Otherwise we would be miserable syllable-pickers, tying truth down to the shapes of letters, when the meaning of the writer is to be gathered not only from his words but from all the other signs of his thought."[34]

---

[33] St. Jerome, *Epist. ad Pammachium* (ML, XXII, 576), "Ex quibus universis perspicuum est apostolos et evangelistas, in interpretatione Scripturarum sensum quaesivisse non verba, nec magnopere de ordine sermonibusque curasse, dum intellectui res pateret."

[34] St. Augustine, *De consensu Evang.*, ii, 28, n. 67 (ML, XXXIV, 1111): "Quae cum ita sint, per hujusmodi evangelistarum locutiones varias sed non contrarias, rem plane utilissimam discimus et prenecessariam, nihil in cujusque verbis nos debere inspicere nisi voluntatem, nec mentiri quemquam si aliis verbis dixerit

It is true that sometimes differences can be accounted for by supposing that actions or discourses that were basically identical, were repeated several times. But this explanation is not always possible. The words of the consecration were said only once. The Lord did not teach the "Our Father" twice; and the best commentators agree that the two versions of the Sermon on the Mount are really both the same discourse.

Everybody knows how liberally Greek and Roman historians put their own eloquence at the service of their heroes. The speeches with which they provided them were often no more than exercises in rhetoric. Whether they are to declare war or seal a peace, march out to battle or beat a retreat, snuff out a revolution or overthrow tyranny, great men are expected to declaim, and declaim they do, in an elegantly florid or sober and terse style — and always with such finish that their words stand as models for future generations. This peculiar practice has given us the *Conciones,* which are real masterpieces. Whether there was a record or any living memory of the speech, or whether it was ever actually given at all, was entirely incidental and does not seem to have been a matter of concern to classical historians. Thucydides alone, by way of praiseworthy exception, has the honesty to let us know that, in default of absolute truth, he has confined himself to probabilities. Lacking certitude, the historian often has to be content with probabilities; and if the reader is forewarned, he has nothing to complain about.

Far be it from us to claim for the sacred writers the license of profane authors. The tender memory of the words of the Master and the reverence and devotion which engraved them on their minds were sufficient guarantee against liberties and abuses, even apart from Inspiration. But it is thoroughly evident that faithful reproduction of them is a matter of sense, and not of the actual words. Now, a single sense lends itself to a great variety of expressions, especially in figurative style, in the speech of proverbs, and still more in apologues or parables. In speaking of the Saviour, did John the Baptist say, "I am not worthy to bear his sandals,"

---

quid ille voluerit cujus verba non dicit; ne miseri aucupes vocum apicibus quodammodo litterarum putent ligandam esse veritatem, cum utique non in verbis tantum sed etiam in ceteris omnibus signis animorum non sit nisi animus inquirendus."

as Matthew has it, or, "I am not worthy to loose the straps of his sandals," as St. Luke says, following St. Mark? St. Augustine calls this an idle question; both phrases come to the same thing; by two synonymous metaphors John declares his unworthiness to be the servant of Christ and to discharge the functions of his servant.

Compare the parable of the Talents in St. Matthew with the parable of the Minas in St. Luke. The resemblances are obvious: the journey of the master, the deposit confided to the servants to test their fidelity, the rendering of accounts on his return, the identity of replies given by the diligent servants and also by a negligent servant, and the identity of the moral. But the differences are not less notable. In St. Luke, the master entrusts a single mina to each of his ten servants; the first increases his tenfold, the second fivefold. On his return, the master makes the second the governor of five towns, and the first of ten, giving the latter also the mina of the idle servant. But in St. Matthew the master distributes talents instead of minas, ten to one, five to another, and one to a third. The first two are industrious and double their holdings and are rewarded equally. The third, for allowing his talent to lie idle, is deprived of it and is severely punished. Despite these differences, Maldonatus thinks the two parables are identical and says that most of his contemporaries are of the same opinion. They are right. What difference does the amount of the deposit make as far as the moral of the parable goes? In an allegory and a parable, minas and talents can very well designate the same thing. The number of servants, the gain they acquired, and the nature of the reward are all immaterial, and do not change the thought fundamentally: for the truth of real fact is not the same thing as the truth of fiction, whether it be allegory or parable.

Natural or conventional signs sometimes complete and point up the thought of an orator. They can be gestures, tone of voice, what has gone before, circumstances of time and place, the dispositions and prejudices of the audience. In such a case, the conscientious narrator has a choice between mentioning the things that modify the import of the words and giving the words a slight change to bring out their full meaning. In St. Mark there is a sentence omitted by the other Synoptics: "Every woman who repudiates her husband and takes another is guilty of adultery." A woman repudiating her husband would have been an anomaly to a Jewish audience. But did St. Mark, writing in a civilization where the law gave the woman the right to take the initiative in a divorce, add this explanatory sentence as an authentic commentary? Possibly, if it emerged from the circumstances or previous teachings that the duties and rights of spouses in marriage are equal and reciprocal. His sentence would then be virtually contained in the verse which is in all three Synoptics. To prevent misunderstanding on the part of his Roman readers, St. Mark would repeat the idea in two forms, displaying its full content, not adding anything of his own, but altering the manner of expression.[35]

2. DIFFERENCES IN THE ORDER OF EVENTS — A careful student of the Gospels knows that chronological order is not always observed. But lack of order in historical writing is quite compatible with a respect for truth. It is, if you wish, a carelessness, a defect in composition; but it is not a moral failing, still less a betrayal of the truth. Besides, there are different kinds of order. In addition to order of time, the most desirable in history, there is a logical and a psychological order, ruled by the association of ideas and the memory of the writer. The order of Tacitus and Thucydides, in which the periodic recurrence of years and seasons governs the progress of the narrative, is not that of Sallust and Polybius, where the chain of causes and effects, the portrayal of situations and characters, and general surveys all unfold regardless of time and place. Nor is it

---

[35] St. Augustine summarizes his teaching on this subject in a passage of more than twenty lines (*De cons. evang.*, ii, 12, n. 28; ML, XXXIV, 1090–1091). There is no falsehood (*mendacium*): (1) if several eyewitnesses and earwitnesses report the same thing in different ways, in different terms, and in different orders, provided that they safeguard the sense; (2) if they omit some things through forgetfulness or for the sake of brevity or because they consider them virtually contained in what they have already said; (3) if one who has the authority to do so makes additions, not to the sense, but to the words, in order to clarify or better explain the thought (sive ad illuminandam declarandamque sententiam, nihil quidem rerum verborum tamen aliquid addat, *cui auctoritas narrandi concessa est*); (4) if, though grasping the subject well, he does not succeed, despite his efforts, in fully reproducing from memory the words which he has heard (sive rem bene tenens non assequatur, quamvis id conetur, memoriter etiam verba quae audivit ad integrum enuntiare).

anything like the more popular method of Herodotus, Suetonius, and Plutarch, who simply collect anecdotes which are linked together only by the identity of the hero.

If profane historians may adopt at will one or the other of these three orders, why deny the sacred writers the same privilege? Inspiration does not restrict them to one determined literary form. In directing their pen and preserving them from error, God leaves their minds free to choose their own methods and to search for their own material. Inspiration is like grace: it does no violence to the mind and will, and often accomplishes God's design by what pagans call chance, but Christians correctly call supernatural Providence.

Maldonatus repeats the same idea more than twenty times in his commentary: "I have already said that we should not look too anxiously for consecutive thinking in the Evangelists, for they do not intend to report the words and actions of Christ in the order in which they took place. This is particularly true of the discourses. . . . The Evangelists are no more in the habit of following chronological order in their writings than the other sacred writers."[36] Perhaps the great exegete generalizes a little too much; but the Bishop of Hippo is on his side. St. Augustine keeps constantly returning to this principle, and thinks it of supreme importance in resolving contradictions. On the visit of Jesus to Nazareth, which he regards as obviously transposed in St. Luke, he has this to say: "And so we can infer — and it is of great consequence in handling the problem of agreement between the Evangelists — that sometimes they deliberately omit some facts, or, not knowing themselves the chronological order in which they occurred, follow the order of their memory of them."[37] And he offers a very interesting psychological reason for this. St. Matthew does not relate the cure of Peter's mother-in-law in the same set of circumstances as St. Luke. The difference is irrelevant, because "the mere fact that one event is put down after another does not necessarily mean that it actually happened after it." Thus, "whether an Evangelist places an event in its actual chronological setting, or, by anticipation or to fill in some-

[36] Maldonatus on Matt. 7:1. See the same author on Matt. 4:5; 18:21; Luke 1:56; 12:1; 14:1; 16:15; Mark 9:41–42, etc.

[37] *De consensu evang.*, ii, 42, n. 89–90 (ML, XXXIV, 1121).

thing he forgot, mentions it in some other place, is of little consequence, provided that he does not contradict himself or the others. For just as it is impossible for a person, no matter how conversant he is with his subject, to recall something at a given moment (for a succession of thoughts does not depend on our own wills, but on the way God chooses to give them to us), it is also probable that each Evangelist thought he should put things down the moment God recalled them to his memory, but only on those occasions when the order (whatever it was) would not impair the authority or the truth of the Gospel." His conclusion is this: "Hence, if the order is not evident there is nothing to worry about. If it is evident, and seems to involve a contradiction, the problem must be examined and a solution sought."[38]

The case comes up when the Evangelists say in so many words that something happened "before" or "after" something else, or "at the same time." But this does not occur very often. In general, they use vague phrases like "then," "afterwards," "at that time," "as he was speaking," and so forth — phrases which may be merely transitional. No general rule can be formulated, however, and each text has to be examined separately.

From the Synoptics alone it would be very difficult to reconstruct a coherent account of the public life of Christ. We could not say how long it lasted, or in what order events occurred; we would have almost nothing more than a series of anecdotes. The green grass which, according to St. Mark, carpeted the theater of the first multiplication of loaves suggests springtime. The ears of corn plucked by the Apostles to appease their hunger bring us to the beginning of summer. That is almost all there is in the Synoptics to indicate time, for the "second-first" Sabbath of St.

---

[38] *De consensu evang.,* ii, 21, n. 51–52 (ML, XXXIV, 1102). Similar texts abound (*ibid.,* ii, 39, n. 86; ML, XXXIV, 1119): "Quis non videat superflue quaeri quo illa ordine Dominus dixerit, cum et hoc discere debeamus per evangelistarum excellentissimam auctoritatem non esse mendacium si quisquam non hoc ordine cujusque sermonem digesserit quo ille a quo processit, cum ipsius ordinis nihil interest ad rem sive ita sive ita sit." — (*Quaestiones xvii in Matth.,* qu. 15; ML, XXXV, 1374): "Nonnumquam alius evangelista contexit quod diversis temporibus alius indicat. Non enim omnimodo secundum rerum gestarum ordinem, sed secundum quisque suae recordationis facultatem narrationem quam exorsus est ordinavit."

Luke is probably interpolated; and, if it is authentic, it defies all interpreters.

The case of St. John is different. From him we know that Jesus inaugurated his apostolate at Jerusalem during the Passover, about three months after his baptism, and that it was forty-six years after the reconstruction of the Temple. Synchronization with profane history enables us to determine this date. Toward the month of May of this same year the Saviour returns to Galilee, where St. John leaves him, to avoid encroaching on the territory of the Synoptics. The four Evangelists finally come together again in the description of the first multiplication of the loaves, which St. John expressly puts at Paschal time. Then comes the Feast of Tabernacles, six months before the Passion, and, thanks to the Fourth Gospel, we can follow Jesus' movements from that time on. We have therefore a very solid chronological framework; only details are uncertain.[39]

---

[39] We reserve our examination of the facts and a discussion of the dates to a special note on the "Chronology of the Life of Christ" and an Appendix on "The Concord of the Gospels."

VOLUME I

BOOK ONE

THE YEARS OF PREPARATION

CHAPTER I

The Mystery of Nazareth

1. Gabriel's Message
(LUKE 1:26–38)

THE little village of Nazareth, where heaven was mysteriously wedded to earth in the person of Jesus, was at the time only an unknown, straggling village, whose name appears for the first time under the pen of the Evangelists. The fact that it had no history was due even more to its isolation than to its unimportance. The great roads linking the capitals of the ancient world lay at its foot, alongside the mountain range in which it nestled, but they did not pass through it or come in sight of it. As it snuggles at the bottom of a valley enclosed on all sides by a circle of hills, Nazareth in the spring is like a lone flower blossoming in its green chalice.

In this sanctuary of recollection and prayer there lived, five or six years before the Christian era, a young orphan girl called Mary. We know today that in her, grace had forestalled the course of nature. No impure breath had ever touched her; by a miracle of preservative redemption, she alone of Adam's children had escaped the original contagion. God seemed to have exhausted the treasures of his infinite power to make her body and soul beautiful; and her perfect fidelity continually invited more and more advances from heaven, multiplied her merits beyond measure, and made her the loveliest, noblest, most sublime of the works of the hand of the Most High. But her fellow townsfolk had no suspicion of all this; and when she went in the evening to fill her pitcher at the village well, only her gentleness, her modesty, and a certain air of simple but compelling majesty distinguished her from her companions. She was a precious pearl overlooked by men, her pricelessness known only to the divine Artist who had chosen her out of all women.

A reputable tradition says that she was born to her pious parents, Ann and Joachim, when they were advanced in age. She seems to have lost them when she was quite young, for the Gospel does not mention them. They called her Mariam, once a very rare name. In the Old Testament it had belonged only to the sister of Moses, but toward the beginning of our era, it became very common; there were no less than five Marys in Herod's household.

God often gives to holy persons whom he wishes to make the instruments of his justice and mercy a symbolic name in keeping with their role or mission; and those devoted to Mary are reluctant to believe that he would have done less for the mother of his Son. Much has been written on the mysterious meaning of her name; but it must be admitted that the conclusions have not been very satisfying. After all, the name of the first Mary, as that of her brothers Moses and Aaron, could be of Egyptian origin. In that case, Mariam would mean "Beloved of Jehovah"; but this hypothesis is too doubtful to detain us.

In any case, the etymologies drawn from the Hebrew ("sea of bitterness," "myrrh of the sea," and others) are either meaningless or confronted by insurmountable philological difficulties. The title "Star of the Sea" so generally given to Mary seems to be the result of a misunderstanding. Perhaps we should not look for a strict etymology of the name. It is certain that at the time, when Aramaic was the popular tongue, the name Mary, pronounced Mariam, called up the idea of dominion and sovereignty. This popular derivation is scarcely in accord with strict philological rules, but would explain why St. Jerome says, "In Syriac, Mary means Lady." And it is precisely under the title of "Our Lady" that Christian piety loves to invoke her.[1]

---

[1] On the meaning and etymology of the name Mary, we refer the reader to Bardenhewer (*Der Name Maria,* Freibourg i. Br., 1895, in the collection *Biblische Studien,* I, 1). The author rejects as impossibilities words composed of two substantives (*mar-yam* — myrrh of the sea), or of an adjective and a substantive (*Mar-yam — amarum mare*), or of a substantive and a suffix (*mari-am* —

As a matter of fact, nowhere except in certain apocryphal writings of slight antiquity and even slighter authority is it said that God intervened to choose a name for the predestined Virgin. He did incomparably more for her than for any other creature, and to give her a very common name, which would not distinguish her from so many namesakes, would have added nothing to her glories.

Despite her youth, Mary was betrothed to a kinsman named Joseph, sprung like herself from the tribe of Juda and the house of David. With the Hebrews, betrothal was not a simple promise of marriage as it is with us. It had the effect of a marriage, with its mutual rights and duties and all its juridical consequences. "Betrothal," writes Philo, a contemporary of Jesus, "has the same force as marriage."[2] In Deuteronomy, as in the Gospel, the betrothed girl is called the *wife* of her fiancé, since that is what she actually was. If she is unfaithful, she is punished as an adulteress. If her fiancé dies she is considered a widow and benefits by the Law of Levirate, which obliges the brother of her deceased and childless husband to marry her. She can be repudiated only with the formalities required in the case of a legitimate wife. One difference, however, was that cohabitation

---

their revolt). He regards the ending *am* as a name formation and retains only the two roots *marah* (rebellious being) and *mara'* (fat being); the first would give quite correctly the adjective *miriam* (rebellious), and the second, though not quite as easily, *mir'iam* (fat, stout). He adds that in the East plumpness in a woman is considered an indication of wealth and an element of beauty, and that thus Miriam (from *mara'*) is a perfectly acceptable feminine name. This is the whole result of the learned monograph.

The hypothesis of Egyptian origin is that of P. Zorell, S.J. (*Lexicon Graecum N.T.*). In Egyptian, the participle *meri* (beloved) is common in so-called theophorous names: *Meri-Ra, Meri-Ptah,* etc.; on the other hand, *Iam* is found at the end of words as the divine name *Iahweh* or *Iahu* (abbreviated into *Iaw* and then into *Iam*). Thus *Abiyahu* is the same as *Abiyam*. There are several examples in Schrader, *Die Keilinschriften und das A.T.*, 3 ed., 1902, pp. 466–467. Fr. Zorell is less positive today.

St. Jerome twice proposes the etymology, *stella maris* (*De nomin. hebr.*, on Exod. 15:20 and Matt. 1:16); but many suspect that the correct reading is *stilla maris* instead of *stella*. As a matter of fact, no Hebrew word of the form *mor, mar, mir,* means "star" (*stella*), whereas *mar* does mean a "drop of water" (*stilla*). St. Jerome adds: "Maria sermone *Syro,* Domina nuncupatur." In the same way, the French say *Notre-Dame,* and the Italians say *Madonna* (*mia donna*).

[2] Philo, *De special. legibus* (Mangey, II, 811). The same was true among the Egyptians.

was generally postponed, sometimes for as long as a year or even longer. This was done to give the husband an opportunity to fulfill the onerous clauses in the contract, or to allow the virgin, who was ordinarily betrothed as a young girl, to come of age in her father's house. It was then that the wedding festivities took place, varying with the circumstances of those concerned, but always as solemn as the position and means of the bride and groom permitted.[3]

As we shall soon see, Mary had vowed her virginity to God, and the marriage of a virgin consecrated to God seems so strange that it would be well to offer some explanation. The only one that has been found so far (apart from the secret designs of Providence, which works in unexpected ways) is the obligation which the Old Law imposed on heiresses to espouse one of their relatives, in order to prevent their patrimony from passing into a strange family. Poor as we conceive Mary's parents to have been, they most probably owned a house and a plot of ground. This was the modest heritage Mary was bound to save for the tribe of Juda and the family of David. Hence it was proper that she be betrothed to her kinsman Joseph.[4]

According to the Apocrypha, which were anxious to fill in the silence of the Gospels, the scene of the betrothal was very dramatic. Mary had been brought up in the shadow of the Sanctuary, where she had been nourished by angels. When she reached her twelfth year, the High Priest Zachary, after consulting the Lord, decided to see to her betrothal. All widowers were summoned by the sound of a trumpet up and down the length and breadth of Palestine. They arrived in great numbers, carrying their staffs, as they had been bidden. When they were all gathered together, the staff of Joseph blossomed and out of the flower sprang a dove, which circled awhile in the air and finally alighted on his head. Then the High Priest said to him, "Thou art the one destined to take the virgin of God under thy care."

---

[3] In Billerbeck (*Kommentar,* Vol. II, pp. 303–398) may be found the Talmudic teachings on the obligations of marriage, the age and choice of partners, the celebration of marriage, etc. The doubtful point is whether the lucubrations of the Talmud are applicable to Gospel times — something which writers of Lives of Christ too readily suppose.

[4] Num. 36:6–12 (the daughters of Salphaad). Cf. Num. 27:1–6.

But the holy man excused himself, pleading, "I am old and I have children. If I took this young girl as a companion, I would be the laughing-stock of the world!" (According to these absurd legends Joseph was ninety years old, and James, his eldest son, was forty.) But when the High Priest threatened him with the divine wrath, he finally acquiesced and took her into his house, but on some pretext or other left her soon afterward, returning only six months after the Annunciation.[5]

This sketch of the apocryphal accounts is given not because any faith is to be placed in them, but to explain why some painters who are too much inclined to draw their inspiration from apocryphal stories often represent Joseph as an old man with white hair. Yet the guardian and protector of the Virgin, the foster father and defender of Jesus, who will accompany him to Egypt, bring him back to Nazareth, and support him with the fruit of his toil, could hardly have been a broken-down old man. There are proprieties to be observed, and it is not likely that God would have exposed the Holy Family to ridicule by permitting such an incongruous union. All the evidence suggests that Joseph was in the full vigor of life, young enough to fulfill his role and mature enough to inspire respect.

Betrothals were sometimes sealed in writing, but more often concluded by word of mouth. In the presence of two witnesses, the man offered his betrothed a small gift, such as a coin, and said to her, "By this token you are my betrothed." She answered by accepting the gift. The pact was usually ratified by a private meal at the home of the girl's father. Then the newly betrothed would put off living together to a more or less distant date.

It was in the interval between the espousals and the celebration of the marriage that the event described in such divinely simple terms by St. Luke took place: "The angel Gabriel was sent

---

[5] The *Protoevangelium of James, The History of Joseph the Carpenter,* the *Book of the Nativity of Mary,* the *Gospel of the Pseudo-Matthew.* According to the first of these writings, Joseph excuses himself on the score of old age (ix, 2, Tischendorf, p. 18); according to the second (xiv and xv, translation from the Coptic and the Arabic, by Peeters, S.J., Paris, 1911, pp. 208–209) he was ninety years old at the time, and lived for twenty-one years afterward. The third (viii, Tischendorf, p. 118) presents him as merely *grandaevus.* In the last (viii, Tischendorf, p. 69), Joseph pleads, as in the *Protoevangelium of James,* "Senex sum et filios habeo."

from God to a town of Galilee called Nazareth, to a virgin betrothed to a man named Joseph, of the house of David. The virgin's name was Mary. And when the angel had come to her, he said, 'Hail, full of grace, the Lord is with thee (blessed art thou among women).' But she was troubled at his words and wondered what could be the meaning of this salutation."

The choice of messenger gives us some inkling of the nature and importance of the message. Gabriel had been charged to explain to the prophet Daniel the secret of the seventy weeks of years which would end in the days of the Messias.[6] Now that the time has come, it is he who is commissioned to carry the news and take part in the execution of the plan of redemption. He is pictured sometimes as cleaving the air with his great pinions, like some winged giant. But he doubtless appeared as a young man, in no way frightening or monstrous, but with something heavenly and supernatural about him. Those artists who depict Mary at prayer, meditating on the prophecy of Isaias about the Virgin who is to bring forth a son, are nearer the truth. The Gospel leaves us in ignorance on the matter, but what other attitude are we to suppose in the Virgin Mother at a moment of such importance to her and to the world?[7]

"Hail, full of grace." The Greeks, on meeting, wished one another joy, the Latins health, and the Semites, then as now, peace, which we translate by the word "Hail!" Several illustrious men of the Old Testament — Abraham, Josue, David, Isaias, Jeremias, and others as well — had been assured of help from on high and of the particular protection of God; and it was always to entrust to them some glorious mission or to prepare them for great sacrifices. But no human creature ever heard himself called "full of grace." Mary becomes uneasy and wonders what such an unusual greeting can mean, especially now that she

---

[6] Dan. 8:16; 9:21. About the Archangel Gabriel in Jewish theology, cf. Billerbeck, Vol. II, pp. 89–98.

[7] The *Protoevangelium of James* (xi, 1–2) states that as Mary was on her way to draw water at the fountain, she heard a voice saying: "Hail, full of grace, the Lord is with thee." In fright, she hastened to return home. The angel rejoined her there, and said to her: "Fear not, Mary, etc." On the strength of this apocryphal writing, the Orthodox Greeks have built a church under the title of St. Gabriel at the place of the spring, a little beyond the present fountain. But this tradition formally contradicts the text of St. Luke, in which the angel "went into" Mary's house and said: "Hail, full of grace."

has probably discovered that her visitor is an angel. What mysterious meaning is she to find in these words? As she thinks of them, she becomes more and more disturbed and confused.

Some pious authors conjecture that it was because of her modesty that she was alarmed. St. Ambrose says that "we should expect a virgin to tremble at the approach or the sight of a man." But would God have allowed his messenger, quiet of mien and of gentle manners, to awaken distrust in Mary? Besides, the Gospel is quite clear: *Quae cum audisset, turbata est in sermone eius*. It is not what she sees, but what she hears, that troubles her. Only in her humility is she disturbed, not in her purity, which is in nowise threatened. What has she done to merit this praise? Whence this overwhelming honor? The more she turns it over in her mind, the less can she believe that it refers to her. And her doubt is understandable, since all her prerogatives — her divine maternity, her immaculate conception, her stainless purity — are radically contained in the phrase, "full of grace."[8]

Gabriel reassures her, this time calling her by name: "Fear not, Mary, for thou hast found grace before God. Behold, thou shalt conceive and shalt bring forth a son, and thou shalt call his name Jesus. He shall be great and shall be called the Son of the Most High. The Lord God shall give to him the throne of David his father, and he shall reign over the house of Jacob forever, and of his reign there shall be no end."[9]

Mary was too familiar with the Holy Books to misunderstand the meaning of these words; they repeated the prophecies of the birth and eternal kingship of the Messias. Isaias had sung of the Virgin who would bring forth Emmanuel, "God-with-us"; the Psalmist had announced that this child would sit on the throne of David his father; and Daniel had said that his reign would

[8] Luke 1:26–29. The words, "Blessed art thou among women," are missing here in the best Greek manuscripts. Most critics (even Vogels) think that they are borrowed from Verse 42, where they are addressed to Mary by Elizabeth. "Full of grace" (κεχαριτωμένη). Verbs in όω always indicate abundance and fullness. Origen (*Homil. viii in Lucam;* MG, XIII, 1816) says rightly: "Soli Mariae haec appellatio servatur." No one before her, whether man or woman, had ever heard such words.

Instead of *cum audisset,* several manuscripts of the Vulgate have *cum vidisset,* which does not correspond to the original text.

[9] Luke 1:30–32. The allusions to the Old Testament are numerous and easily recognized. Cf. Isa. 7:14; 9:6; Ps. 88 (89):4–5; Dan. 7:14, etc.

last forever. Now doubt is no longer possible. To the Virgin of Nazareth is reserved the honor of being the mother of the new David, the Messias, the Son of God, Emmanuel.

Mary puts full and unlimited faith in the divine messenger. She asks no sign as Zachary did, and draws no reproaches from the angel. She deserves the praise the divinely inspired Elizabeth will give her: "Blessed art thou for having believed." What she does not understand and has a right to know is how her coming maternity can be reconciled with her determination to remain a virgin — a determination she knows God has found acceptable. It is on this point that she respectfully asks an explanation. "How shall this be done, since I know not man?"[10] Sara had never dreamed of asking this question, nor had the wife of Manue, nor the mother of Samuel, nor any of the women to whom God had promised a son. If Mary had not been betrothed at the time of the Annunciation, her question could be taken as naïve simplicity, and interpreted thus: "I live alone and do not know anyone to whom I can join my destiny." But she was already united to Joseph by a bond which was a true marriage, and her words would be absolutely devoid of meaning if she were not expressing her determination to remain a virgin. Heterodox writers, who take umbrage at such words as vow and virginity, can see in Mary's words only an impetuous cry of surprise, wrung from a young girl so upset by the strangeness of the message that she hardly

---

[10] Some of Mary's devotees interpret her question somewhat differently. According to them, it should be admitted that she perfectly understood the prophecy of Isaias about the Virgin Mother; else she must be classed as inferior to the Jewish doctors; she also understood "clearly that the Angel was proposing to her that she should be this Virgin Mother"; but "all the other circumstances of the marvel were hidden from her eyes"; it is about these that she inquires. Cf. Médebielle, *Annonciation,* in *Dict. de la Bible, Supplément,* Vol. I, coll. 280–281.

The prophecy of Isaias was less clear before the event and before the labor of Catholic theology. Billerbeck (Vol. I, p. 75) and Edersheim (*Life and Times,* Vol. II, p. 274) cannot find *a single Jewish doctor* who understood the text in a Messianic sense. The Septuagint translated *almah* by *παρθένος*, but there is nothing to indicate that they understood "the virgin shall give birth" *in sensu composito.* If Mary was so well instructed in God's designs *before the explanation of the angel,* she had only to say her *fiat* immediately, without questioning the angel about the accompanying circumstances. All in all, we would still prefer St. Bernard's interpretation, according to which Mary would have been prepared to sacrifice her virginity if such were the will of God, though, to tell the truth, this interpretation does seem somewhat realistic. Cf. Knabenbauer, *In Lucam,* p. 69.

knows what she is saying. But common sense rebels against such a forced interpretation, which is so much to the discredit of the Mother of God. It is pointless and absurd to urge that she uses the present and not the future, because we all refer in this way to things we are determined to do or not to do; and since there is question here of a future event, "I know not man" cannot be limited to the present.

Protestants find this meaning shocking and scandalous, but it seemed quite natural to the Fathers of the Church. In the words of St. Augustine, "Mary would not speak thus if she had not vowed her virginity to God. It is because Jewish customs demanded it, that she was betrothed to a just man, who, far from ravishing her virginity, would be its guardian."[11] This is an idea which Bossuet developed with great brilliance later, in his panegyric on St. Joseph. And St. Gregory of Nyssa says the same: "Since it was necessary to keep the flesh consecrated to God intact and without stain, Mary seems to say (to the divine envoy): Even though you are an angel, and from heaven, even

[11] St. Augustine, *De virginitate,* iv; ML, XL, 898; St. Gregory of Nyssa, *In diem natalem Christi* (MG, XLVI, 1140). This discourse is given in Migne as doubtful, but it bears all the marks of authenticity. Cf. Bardenhewer, *Geschichte der altchristl. Liter.,* 1912, Vol. III, p. 208. The text of St. Bernard is well known. St. Thomas (*Summa Th.,* p. III, q. xxviii, a. 4) thinks that before her marriage Mary's vow was not absolute, but was conditioned on the divine will: "Postmodum vero, accepto sponso, secundum quod mores illius temporis exigebant, simul cum eo votum virginitatis emisit." Though there are examples of such conduct in the lives of the saints, we prefer to believe that Mary would not have accepted Joseph's hand without having been previously assured of his agreement. Discussion would remain open only on the meaning of "vow," "promise," "firm resolve."

Zahn presents a ridiculous objection, which we have just answered: "If she had made a vow of virginity, she would have broken it by espousing Joseph." As though virginity were incompatible with marriage! Protestants, Anglicans included, try their best to evade the difficulty. To Plummer, a vow seems "not very natural"; for Grotius, Mary's question is nothing but a cry of "wonder"; for Godet, it is "the astonished cry of a pure conscience." Machen (*The Virgin Birth of Christ,* 1930), who ably and with conviction defends Mary's virginity *ante partum,* thinks St. Luke would have expressed himself more clearly if he had wished to speak of a vow; he admits, however, that Mary's question, in that case, is not "very logical" (p. 148). Quite so! Bengel (*Gnomon,* Stuttgart, 1892, p. 220) is, perhaps, the Protestant author who most closely approximates the Catholic interpretation; he will not hear of any vow or promise, but he agrees that "I know not" looks to the future and is the same as "I will not know," and that Mary understood from the angel's answer that her virginity would be respected.

though you appear to be a superhuman being, I am not permitted to approach a man. And how, without a man, could I be a mother?"

Thus Mary's fixed resolution shines forth with full clarity. This vow was so dear to her that she would perhaps have hesitated, had it been necessary to pay the price of her virginity for the honor of being the mother of God. On reflection, one cannot help thinking that Joseph knew and approved of her resolution, and shared it. Would Mary have plighted her troth to him without telling him her secret and being certain of his agreement? Would she say, "I do not know man," if there could be any question of carnal intercourse between her and her spouse?

In Mary's question there was neither insulting distrust nor indiscreet curiosity. She was asking only what she must know in order to conform herself to the divine will. And far from reprehending her, the angel hastens to enlighten her: "The Holy Spirit shall come upon thee and the power of the Most High shall overshadow thee. Therefore the child to be born (of thee) shall be holy, and shall be called the Son of God." Mary's fears for her virginity are at rest. Already full of grace, she will receive a new infusion of grace the moment God overshadows her with his creative power. The presence of God in her womb will be more real than it was in the Ark of the Covenant, when the luminous cloud threw its shadow over the Tabernacle. He who will be born of her, without the concurrence of man and by the divine action of the Holy Ghost alone, will be truly the Son of God.

Gabriel has given his message, and waits only for Mary's consent. She cannot refuse this consent; but in the present order of Providence it is necessary that she give it. The human race, not to be saved despite itself, had to accept its Liberator, and it does accept him, in the person of the Virgin Mother. It was fitting too that a woman take part in our restoration, for a woman had contributed to our ruin. And it was proper that Mary's freedom be respected and she be allowed to gain merit by an act of obedience which would bring her new graces. "Behold the handmaid of the Lord; be it done to me according to thy word. *Fiat mihi secundum verbum tuum.*" How ineffably powerful this *fiat!*

Just as the priest, in the name of the eternal High Priest, calls down the Son of God upon the altar by five words of authority, so Mary, in the name of humanity which she represents, brings him into her womb by five words of obedience.

The promise God made to his people more than seven centuries before has just been fulfilled: "The virgin shall conceive and bear a son, and his name shall be called Emmanuel (which means God-with-us)."[12] The Jews had not understood this prophecy. Perhaps they were incapable of understanding it in the half-light of the revelation of old. At least they should have suspected in it a mystery which the future would clarify, for it was obvious that the Child celebrated in such magnificent terms could not be the son of Achaz, nor the son of Isaias: "A child is born to us, and a son is given to us. And he bears the sovereignty upon his shoulders. He is called Counselor, Admirable, God the Mighty, Father of Eternity, Prince of Peace."

The event has thrown full light on this mysterious text. The Son whom the Virgin will bring forth will be in reality God-with-us. What does it matter that the Hebrew *almah* can mean "young girl" or "young woman"? Its most natural meaning is "virgin," which the Septuagint gave it before our Vulgate. And all the Fathers from the beginning have seen in the mystery of the Incarnation the accomplishment of the prophecy of Isaias.

2. The Word Made Flesh[13]

(JOHN 1:1–14)

While St. Luke unrolls the august drama of Nazareth before our eyes, the Beloved Disciple opens heaven to us and allows us to contemplate the intimate life of the Son of God who is about to become the Son of Mary.

[12] Isa. 7:14. Cf. J. Calès, *Le Sens de Almah en Hébreu,* in *Recherches,* Vol. I, 1910, p. 161.

[13] It is known that three of the most illustrious of the Fathers — St. John Chrysostom, St. Augustine, and St. Cyril of Alexandria — wrote commentaries on the Fourth Gospel. Of the thirty-two books of Origen, only nine have come down to us, among them the first two. We have an admirable homily of St. Basil on the first chapter. The best patristic and theological commentary is probably that of Toletus, published in 1587 with the permission of Sixtus the Fifth. Naturally it needs to be filled in and occasionally corrected by more modern works.

In the beginning was the Word,
and the Word was with God
and the Word was God.
He was in the beginning with God.
All things were made through him,
and without him was made nothing that was made.[14]

In three singularly pregnant words St. John reveals the eternity, personal character, and divinity of the Word.

If we go farther and farther back, to the origin of the first creature from God's hands, we find before it the Word. He himself is not drawn from nothing; he does not receive his being as things that exist in time. He is without beginning, because he was in the beginning; and so he is eternal.

He was not only *in* God, as wisdom and goodness, which are identified with God's substance; He was *with* God, as the son with his father, turned *toward* God, as a living image equal to its archetype, yet distinct from the Father, for to speak of Son and Father is to name two distinct Persons.

"And the Word was God." He was not the Father; that would be an evident contradiction; but he possessed the nature of God and shared fully the divinity of the Father.

Since the nature is common to both, so of necessity will operation be common to both; the Son does nothing without the Father, and the Father nothing without the Son. Indeed, all that exists outside of God, all that can become, is the work of the Son acting with the Father and, with him, calling beings into existence by one and the same operation.

Raised to such inaccessible heights, is not the Word so beyond the reach of humanity that he is incapable of being Mediator between God and men? Is he not like some planet lost in space whose rays never come to our eyes? Philo was so anxious to have his *Logos* play the role of mediator that he made him a god of second rank, somewhere in between creator and creature, and

[14] These verses offer no difficulty except such as is inherent in the mystery itself. One will note the emphasis with which St. John places the Word *outside the category of created beings* and puts him *with* the Father, *beside* the Father (πρὸς τὸν Θεὸν, not ἐν Θεῷ), ὁ Θεός designating the Father, the principle of divinity.

by that token more fitted to act as messenger, interpreter, and representative of the sovereign God. The Word, in St. John, while fully God, equal to his Father, is also our Mediator, because he is the Life and the Light of the world, and brings us life and light from the bosom of the Father.

In him was (the) Life,
And the Life was the Light of the world;
and the light shines in the darkness,
and the darkness grasped it not.[15]

By his essence, the Word is the Life and Principle of all natural life; but that is not the meaning of the Evangelist when he says that in the Word is the Life. For St. John, the Light and the Life are always the light of faith and the life of grace which make us sharers in the very life of God. In the mysterious divine plans, the Word, who took upon himself the task of restoring mankind by becoming man, is the only source of that supernatural life for fallen humanity. All graces come from him, since they are given only because of his redemptive mediation. Hence also they are attributed to him by anticipation, before the time of his appearance on earth. If we understand St. John in this way, we see the advance and progress in his thought. We saw the Word in the bosom of the Father, in the mystery of his divine life; then in relation to the world to which he gives being. Now we see him in relation to men, to whom he carries the light that gives them life. Between light and darkness there is utter opposition, but we are not to fear that the darkness will conquer the light. The light will finally scatter the darkness.

On the appearance of that glorious youth, St. John the Baptist, his enthusiastic disciples were ready to believe that he was the sun destined to illumine the world. But he was not the sun; he was but the dawning. He had been lifted up by God to be the witness and precursor of the Light.

He existed, the true Light
That enlightens every man coming into the world.
He was in the world,
And the world was made through him,
and the world knew him not.

[15] John 1:4. Cf. Note C: *The Word as Life and Light.*

He came into his own domain
and his own received him not;
but to as many as received him
he gave the power of becoming children of God.[16]

---

[16] John 1:9–12: ἦν τὸ φῶς τὸ ἀληθινόν, ὃ φωτίζει πάντα ἄνθρωπον ἐρχόμενον εἰς τὸν κόσμον. The Fathers have observed that the first phrase of the second part is ambiguous. The participle ἐρχόμενον can be in the nominative neuter and agree with τὸ φῶς, or in the accusative masculine agreeing with τὸν ἄνθρωπον. The Vulgate has chosen the second alternative, which is also adopted by most of the commentators, Greek as well as Latin. In fact, it is more natural to refer the participle "coming into the world" to the nearer word, i.e., "every man." Though in itself complementary, the complement may lend emphasis: the light of the Word is destined for all; no man, absolutely none, is excluded except by his own fault; just as the only way to block out the sun, which of its nature illumines everything, is to close one's eyes. The other translation ("which illumines every man *when it comes* into the world") would permit the meaning that the Word illumines men only when he becomes man: but the phrase following contradicts this.

This objection would not touch those who refer all that follows to the illuminative action of the Word after the Incarnation. In their opinion, St. John is here making no progress in thought, but is simply presenting various aspects of the same phase of illumination. But it seems quite clear that the words "He was in the world" refer to a phase before his appearance in a mortal body, and thus it is that all the Fathers and ancient commentators have understood it. Maldonatus, who strives to sustain the probability of the opposite opinion, is forced to recognize that the Fathers are against him. But even an impartial examination of the text itself shows his interpretation to be mistaken. There is a clear gradation, a succession of phases, each of which has three divisions: the activity of the Word, the theater of his activity, and the result obtained. Thus:

First phase (v. 10): the *presence* of the Word in the *world,* ending in *failure.*

Second phase (v. 11): the *invisible coming* of the Word *among his own,* with *partial success.*

Third phase (v. 14): the *visible appearance* of the Word *in our midst, in all fullness* (v. 16).

For the condition of humanity during the first phase, before the Mosaic revelation or apart from it, it is necessary to compare St. Paul (Rom. 1:18–32) and the Book of Wisdom (13:1–9). St. John does not say that the pagans should have known the Word *as* the Word, but he makes it clear that they should have known and honored him as God, and desired him as Saviour. Moreover, men were not then left to themselves; they had behind them a primitive revelation, and they had supernatural and natural graces which they could have put to profit to lead them, indirectly but infallibly, to the justification of which the Incarnate Word is the author and meritorious cause.

In the second phase, the activity of the Word becomes more forceful. He lives in the midst of his own people, but his success is mediocre, and it is true as a general statement that "his own did not receive him." But in the mass of unbelievers, he always had a *faithful few,* and it is to this nucleus that he gives "the power to become the sons of God."

From the *fiat lux,* the Word was in the world and operative in it. His creative act continued in the conservation of creatures. He manifested himself to rational creatures by his works; and if, instead of losing themselves in vain thinking and squandering on creatures the glory due to God, men had availed themselves of the light of reason, the Word, always ready to save them, would not have refused them the true light of faith, which would have given them a pledge of eternal life. But of this first phase of human history it may well be said that the world knew him not, neither as the Word nor as God.

Yet the presence of the Word in the world was not altogether without effect. Noe, Henoch, Abraham, Isaac, Jacob, Adam himself, and all the just who lived before the revelation of Sinai were enlightened by the Light. To bring himself nearer to humanity, the Word came toward that people which he did not tire of calling in Scripture his own, his possession, his heritage, his domain. He drew them out of Egypt, guided them in the desert, established them in the Promised Land, gave them a lawgiver. But this people, taken as a whole, did not know him; the objurgations of the prophets are proof of it. Yet, even in the midst of this general apostasy, there was always a "remnant," a faithful few from whom salvation would spring. To these true children of Israel the Word gave power to become children of God.

And now the fullness of time has come. The day is at hand when the Word will no longer speak to the world by the voice of creation, or by the prophets, but with his own lips:

> And the Word was made flesh,
> and set up his tent among us,
> and we have seen his glory,
> glory such as an only-begotten son,
> full of grace and truth, receives of his father.[17]

---

[17] The Word undertook three times in some way to dissipate the darkness of ignorance and error. His presence in the pagan world had been a failure; his coming to the chosen people had been only a half-success; then "the Word was made flesh," he made his dwelling among us Christians (ἐσκήνωσεν, "he pitched his tent," because his stay was to be only transitory); he manifested to us his glory, the glory which befitted him as the only Son of God (δόξαν ὡς μονογενοῦς

His first two manifestations — through his creative activity and through supernatural revelation — have not had the desired effect. Now he goes a step further. He takes flesh like to ours, or rather, clothes himself with our flesh. In the present order of Providence, redemption is to be achieved in accordance with the principle of solidarity, humanity restoring itself and itself making reparation for its offenses against God, through its Head, its Representative and Epitome — just as Adam represented and epitomized the human race which sprang from his loins. This is why the body of the new Adam was not formed from nothing or fashioned from the dust of the earth as the first man's; for then he would not be our Brother, our Head, our High Priest. He would be a stranger, not of our race, and we would have no part in the satisfaction offered for us.

Instead of writing, "The Word was made flesh," the Evangelist could have written, "The Word was made man," because in Scripture the two are synonymous. But by saying, "The Word was made flesh," he contrasts two extremes: the Word, God of God and equal to the Father; and the flesh, symbol of all that in us is feeble, weak, frail, and perishable.

The greatest event in history has just taken place, and the world is so absorbed in its petty preoccupations that it has no

---

παρὰ πατρός), i.e., a glory such as an only son should receive from his father: thus the work of enlightenment is complete:

"And of his fullness we have all received,
and grace upon grace;
for the Law was given through Moses;
grace and truth have come (to us) through Jesus Christ."

The Incarnate Word possesses two plenitudes; one that is incommunicable, from the very fact of the Hypostatic Union; the other communicable, the plenitude of grace which the holy Humanity of Christ derives from the union with the Word and its own merits.

It does not matter whether we understand χάριν ἀντὶ χάριτος, "grace upon grace," as we have taken it (there are examples of this sense in Greek: Chrysostom, *De sacerdotio,* iv, 13; MG, XLVIII, 692; σὺ δέ με ἐκπέμπεις ἑτέραν ἀνθ' ἑτέρας φροντίδα ἐνθεὶς), or, with Toletus, "gratiam nos accepimus pro gratia Christi" (qua Christus plenus est). Moses has given only the Law (with prophetic figures of future grace). Christ alone *confers grace* and *gives truth* (i.e., realizes the prophetic types prefiguring grace). Cf. Bover, in *Biblica,* 1925, pp. 454–460. Joüon is inspired by this article to translate (*L'Evangile de N.-S. J.-C.,* 1930, p. 463): "It is from his fullness that we have all received, namely, a grace corresponding to his grace."

suspicion of it. A little while ago Augustus closed the temple of Janus for the third time, proclaiming by this gesture that all lands were enjoying a Roman peace and that Caesar's power was no longer challenged. He had vanquished the Dalmatians, the Pannonians, the Sicambrians, the Alpine mountaineers. Singers in poetry and prose vied with one another in praising him. Everywhere trophies were set up in his honor, and temples and triumphal arches, with extravagant inscriptions like this: "Caesar, lord of the sea and its continents, the new Jupiter, holding the title of liberator from Jupiter his father, a star risen over the world, shining with the brightness of Jupiter Salvator." Popular adulation had never gone so far nor fallen so low.

In Palestine, Herod was closing his monstrous thirty-three years of rule with an insane orgy of crime and debauchery. He had just murdered two of his sons, Alexander and Aristobulus, and was now begging the Emperor's permission to put to death a third, Antipater. His subjects trembled for their lives, and all attempts at revolt were swiftly drowned in blood. Neither Augustus in his house on the Palatine nor Herod in his palace at Jericho had the slightest notion that the King of heaven and earth had descended among us.

No spot on earth should be dearer than the place where the mystery of God made man was enacted. For many years the disciples of Christ were forbidden to venerate it or even to visit it. After the total destruction of their Temple and their nation, those Jews who escaped massacre were expelled from Jerusalem and its vicinity and took refuge in Galilee, carrying their wild fanaticism with them, furious at their defeat and misfortunes. They drove all strangers indiscriminately from the towns over which they managed to become master. St. Epiphanius tells us that no pagan, no Samaritan, no Christian was tolerated in four Galilean villages: Tiberias, Capharnaum, Sepphoris, and Nazareth. This last was made a sacerdotal city and served as a seat of one of the twenty-four sections of the Levitical priesthood.[18] With the triumph of Christianity everything changed. There were no reprisals against the Jews, but the Christians regained their freedom. In the year

---

[18] Dalman, *Orte und Wege Jesu,* 1924, p. 65 (English transl. by Levertoff, *Sacred Sites and Ways,* 1935, p. 60).

359, St. Epiphanius met a converted Jew at Scythopolis, Joseph, Count of Tiberias, commissioned by Constantine to build churches in the towns of Galilee, where the intolerance of his former coreligionists had raged with the greatest violence.[19] It is doubtless to this period that we should assign the first church of the Incarnation which was later rebuilt by the Crusaders. It was a large basilica of three naves, and recent excavations have revealed its general plan and the principal features of its architecture. The sons of St. Francis are working to rebuild this monument worthy of the thrice-hallowed spot where the Word became flesh.[20]

3. The Angel Gabriel and Zachary

(LUKE 1:5–25)

Six months before his visit to the Virgin of Nazareth, the Archangel Gabriel had been charged with another message, to a priest called Zachary, married to a woman named Elizabeth, both of the blood of Aaron. Although they were a couple of exemplary piety, God had withheld from them the blessing promised to faithful observers of the Law; they were childless and had lost all hope of having children, for Elizabeth was barren and both were advanced in age.

The Jewish priesthood, numbering about twenty thousand, was divided into twenty-four groups, each of which served in the Temple a week at a time. When it came the turn of the eighth group, that of Abia, to which Zachary belonged, he set out for Jerusalem to be at his post at the required time, a little before the start of the Sabbath. To avoid rivalry and intrigue, lots were drawn each day for the most honored roles, which were naturally

---

[19] St. Epiphanius, *Haeres.*, xxx, 11–12 (MG, XLI, 425–428).

[20] The ancient basilica measuring 246 by 98 feet was much larger than the present church (82 by 56 feet). It faced in the usual direction, whereas the seventeenth-century church, which is without style or character, is from south to north. Cf. Prosper Viaud, O.F.M., *Nazareth et ses deux églises de l'Annonciation et de Saint-Joseph d'après les fouilles récentes,* Paris, 1910. There are diagrams in *Rev. Biblique,* 1901, p. 490, and the *Dict. de la Bible,* Vol. IV, 1535.

About 100 or 150 yards from the basilica there was another church which is said to have marked the site of St. Joseph's house. The Franciscans have rebuilt it into a vast and elegant edifice (91.84 by 54.12 feet). The large convent of the Franciscans joins this church to the new basilica.

also the most coveted. And so this year the privilege of offering incense on the altar fell to Zachary. It was the first time he had fulfilled this function, and would be the last, for this particular honor was never repeated and those who received it were barred from taking part in the drawing of lots.

The offering of incense was made twice a day, before the morning and after the evening sacrifice, and was the high point of the daily liturgy. Thus it was with lively emotion that Zachary, holding in his hands a golden incense plate full of incense, walked into the Sanctuary and advanced toward the Altar of Incense, having on his left the great seven-branched candelabrum, and on his right the table of the loaves of proposition. He had just spread the incense on the burning coals, which had been prepared beforehand, and a cloud of fragrant smoke was filling the sanctuary, when lifting his eyes he saw the angel of the Lord standing over against the altar beside the golden candelabrum. Celestial apparitions always threw fright into the souls of the Hebrews, and Zachary stood paralyzed with terror at the sight of the angel. But the angel reassured him:

"Fear not, Zachary, for thy petition has been heard. Thy wife shall bear thee a son, whom thou shalt call John. He shall be a source of gladness to thee, and many shall rejoice at his birth, for he shall be great before the Lord. He shall drink no wine nor strong drink. He shall be filled with the Holy Spirit even from his mother's womb; and many of the children of Israel shall he convert to the Lord their God. He shall go before him in the spirit and power of Elias. He shall turn the hearts of fathers to their children, and shall lead back the rebellious to the wisdom of the just, to prepare for the Lord a well-disposed people."

What great honors are heaped upon the head of this miraculous child! Like Samuel, he will lead the penitential life of the Nazirites; like Jeremias, he will be marked for the apostolate from his mother's womb; like Elias, he will prepare the world for the coming of the Saviour. But, greater than all this, he will be filled with the Holy Spirit before his birth; and, by a privilege that is unique, if we except Mary, who must always be set apart when there is question of graces, the day of his birth will be joyfully celebrated by the Church.

There was a time when Zachary had ardently desired a son; but now it is probable that he was no longer thinking of one and that his prayers had another object. With all the people whom he represents, he keeps praying for the speedy advent of the Messias. God fulfills his dreams of yesterday and today at the same time, by promising him a son who will clear the way for the Liberator of Israel and the Saviour of the world.

The news was so unexpected and so extraordinary that Zachary, losing his self-possession and fearing himself the dupe of a dream, dared to ask for a sign that would guarantee its fulfillment. "How shall I know that this is to be, for I am an old man and my wife is advanced in years?" The question, though partly excusable by reason of anxiety and distraction, implied a doubt offensive to God. The angel's answer was stern: "I am Gabriel who stand before the face of God. I have been sent to bring to thee these glad tidings. And behold, thou shalt be dumb and unable to speak a word, because thou hast not believed my promise, which is to be fulfilled in its own time." In cases of the same kind, Abraham, Moses, Gedeon, and Ezechias had also asked for signs, and they had not been refused them: but we are now on the threshold of the Gospel, and God now asks men for a readier and fuller faith. Zachary receives his sign, but it is a punishment as well as a favor: a punishment for his imperfect faith, and a favor for others, for they will be unable to doubt the providential mission of John.

The exchange of words between the angel and the priest did not take longer than it takes to retell them, but the people outside were already restless. The offering of the incense was usually a brief matter, and they were impatient to intone the joyous strains of the hymn. When Zachary finally appeared, they knew from his manner and gestures that an extraordinary event with something mysterious about it had caused the delay.[21]

---

[21] We suppose, with the majority of authors, that the scene took place at the daily morning sacrifice, the more solemn of the two. At daybreak lots were drawn to determine who should offer incense in the Holy Place. Zachary was designated, and chose two relatives or friends to make ready the Altar of Incense. One of them cleared out the ashes from the day before, the other put the burning coals on the altar. When this was done they retired, and Zachary entered *alone,* but waited for a signal from outside before spreading the incense on the live coals. Meanwhile, the people all prayed in silence. When the rite was over, the priest

When this week was over, Zachary returned to his village and some time later Elizabeth realized that she was to be a mother. Joyfully and deeply thankful, she stayed five months in confinement in her home. "Behold what the Lord has done to me, when it pleased him to lift the reproach that pressed upon me before the eyes of men."

Several authors attribute the voluntary seclusion of Elizabeth to shame and fear of that kind of ridicule that is leveled by the worldly at a late fertility. But had she yielded to this foolish feeling, she would have withdrawn from the gaze of people, not at the beginning, but rather toward the end of her time. Did she not rather wish to keep precious and secret the divine gift of which Mary was to be the first to learn, and that by divine revelation? Zachary doubtless shared her isolation. His dumbness separated him from the company of men and he had no craving to satisfy importunate curiosity. The two spouses lived therefore in retirement until the day when the unexpected visit of the Blessed Virgin drew them from their solitude.[22]

4. Mary at the Home of Elizabeth

(LUKE 1:39–55)

One of the purest feelings and the most delicate pleasures of the human heart is joy in another's good fortune and the desire to become part of it, especially when the persons concerned are united by the bond of friendship or the ties of blood. With Mary, divine inspiration had anticipated natural inclination. When she learned of the favor her relative had received, her first thought was to go to congratulate her.[23] She was not moti-

went out *immediately* and the flame on the sacrificial altar consumed the previously slain holocaust to the accompaniment of chants and musical instruments. The ceremony is described in the *Mishnah,* in the treatise *Tamid*. Cf. also Billerbeck, Vol. II, pp. 71–79, or Edersheim, *Life and Times,* Vol. I, pp. 133–143.

[22] Luke 1:24–25. "After those days, Elizabeth his wife conceived and secluded herself for five months, saying, etc." It would certainly be an error to conclude that this voluntary seclusion ended after the fifth month; the time is mentioned only to prepare for the account of the Annunciation; a familiar practice of St. Luke in his Gospel and in the Acts.

[23] Luke 1:39. "In those days, Mary went in haste into the mountain country to a town of Juda." The Greek μετὰ σπουδῆς (with haste, without losing time)

vated by curiosity or any inclination to verify the celestial message, for she did not doubt it; she wanted only to fulfill a duty of charity and make herself useful. She could not make such a long journey alone, so she had to wait for one of her neighbors to consent to accompany her, or for a caravan of pilgrims on the way to Jerusalem. The traditional date of the Annunciation, toward the end of March, around Paschal time, bears out the second possibility.

What relationship existed between Elizabeth, daughter of Aaron and of the tribe of Levi, and Mary, of the line of David and the tribe of Juda? Their difference in age suggests that Elizabeth was Mary's maternal aunt. It may be, on the other hand, that their mothers were sisters. That is possible, too, because there was nothing against a woman of the house of Aaron marrying a member of the tribe of Juda. But whether Mary was the niece or the cousin of Elizabeth, they were certainly close relatives, which is all that St. Luke says and all that we need to know.[24]

Ten places claim the glory of having sheltered the crib of the Precursor, and the Gospel, which confines itself to mentioning a "village in the mountains of Judea," offers little help in making a choice. All of Judea, from Bethel to Hebron, is mountainous country.[25] The only place, however, whose claim is supported by any reputable tradition is the village of Aïn Karim, in the moun-

---

is not as strong as the Latin *cum festinatione,* and the accompanying circumstance "in those days" (ἐν ταῖς ἡμέραις ταύταις), after the account of the Annunciation, leaves some latitude.

The words "into the mountain country" (εἰς τὴν ὀρεινήν) can be taken in a general sense "into the mountain range of Judea" or in the special sense "into the district called *the Mountain*" of which Jerusalem was the capital.

The words "to a town of Juda" (εἰς πόλιν Ἰούδα) could mean strictly "to a town called Juda"; but, if St. Luke had wished to say that, he would have phrased it differently to avoid ambiguity. We should therefore understand him to mean "a town of Juda" which he does not name, either because of its unimportance, or because he did not know its name.

24 A writer of the seventh or eighth century, named Hippolytus of Thebes, says that Mary and Elizabeth were first cousins, born of two daughters of the priest Mathan. But of what value is so late a witness? The fact that he is quoted by Nicephorus Callistus, who mistakes him for Hippolytus of Porto, adds no new value to his testimony.

25 Buzy (*S. Jean-Baptiste,* 1922, p. 54) mentions Machaerus, Sebaste, Bethlehem, Jerusalem, Hebron, Yuttah, Juda of Nephthali, Beit-Skaria, Beit-Cha'an, Aïn Karim. None of these places except the last can produce any real claim.

tains of Judea, about five miles from Jerusalem. Even a tradition that was already ancient by the time of the Crusades would not be decisive if it were opposed by a rival tradition; but that is not the case, and Aïn Karim, fitting in well with the data of the sacred text, wins out over its unsupported competitors.[26]

The meeting between Mary and Elizabeth has often inspired the brush of Christian artists. There is a striking contrast between the matron with the wrinkled brow, respectfully bowing, and the radiant youth of the most pure Virgin. Painters usually people the scene with witnesses, and they are probably right, for Mary did not come alone; besides, the arrival of a stranger in an Oriental village generally attracts more than one visitor. At the sound of Mary's voice, Elizabeth felt the infant in her womb leap for joy. She herself was filled with the Holy Spirit, and her words show that the mystery of the Incarnation has been revealed to her. In a burst of prophetic enthusiasm she cries:

"Blessed art thou among women, and blessed is the fruit of thy womb. Whence comes to me this favor, that the mother of my Lord should deign to come to me? As soon as thy salutation

---

[26] Aïn Karim, a large village called by the Christians St. John-in-Montana, is about five miles from Jerusalem, in a pretty little valley at the foot of green hills. It owes its name to the beautiful spring (*Aïn*) and to the vineyards which surround it (*kerem* in Hebrew and *karm* in Arabic mean "vine").

The tradition favoring Aïn Karim is constant from the twelfth century on, but it goes back much farther. The pilgrim Theodosius (around 530) places Elizabeth's house five miles from Jerusalem, which is the same as the distance of Aïn Karim. The monk Epiphanius (ninth century) gives the distance and direction as "six miles west of Jerusalem." The Russian *hegumen* Daniel (around 1110) gives a description of it and mentions a church there.

According to St. Luke (1:39 and 1:65), Elizabeth lived in "the mountain country" (ἐν τῇ ὀρεινῇ). Now, in the division of Judea into ten toparchies (Pliny) or eleven (Josephus), the mountain country (ἡ ὀρεινή) indicated the environs of Jerusalem. "Orine in qua fuere Hierosolyma" (Pliny, *Hist. nat.*, v. 14; cf. Josephus, *Bellum*, IV, viii, 2): another confirmation of the claims of Aïn Karim. The Church of St. John, which was given to the Franciscans, thanks to the intervention of Louis XIV, and restored by them, antedates the Crusades in its more ancient sections.

After Reland (1714) many authors translate εἰς πόλιν Ἰούδα by "to a village called Juda," and think this refers to *Yuttah* (Josue 15:55 and 21:16, *Jota*), a priestly city which they identify with a village situated on a high hill some six miles south of Hebron. But Ἰούδα cannot be a transcription of *Yuttah* (note the emphatic *t* and its reduplication; the Septuagint gives Ἰεττά). The present pronunciation of the name of the town in question is *Yaththa*. Add to this the absence of tradition and *Yuttah* may be dismissed from consideration.

struck my ear, the child in my womb leaped for joy. Blessed is she who has believed that which the Lord announced to her."[27]

The stirring in her womb that the divinely inspired mother recognizes as a leap of gladness is indeed mysterious. Joy implies knowledge, which is why many Fathers held that the Precursor received a flood of prophetic illumination in the presence of him for whom he was one day to prepare the way. Some are even inclined to believe that the child's intelligence, awakened at the time of the visitation, thereafter suffered no eclipse. But neither Scripture nor tradition allows us to follow them that far, and it is perhaps better to reserve such an extraordinary privilege to the Blessed Virgin alone.[28]

What Scripture and tradition permit us to infer with confidence is that the Precursor was invested with sanctifying grace before he saw the light of day. St. Paul's predestination for the Apostolate and Jeremias' sanctification in his mother's womb were of an entirely different nature. Predestination to the Apostolate does not confer sanctifying grace, and sanctification in the Old Testament often means only a consecration to God's service. The fullness of the Holy Spirit, on the other hand, always renders the soul holy or supposes it to be already holy. Thus, though the Church has never defined the point, it is commonly believed that the Baptist was sanctified before his birth — and it would be rash to depart from this opinion.

In the presence of all these marvels, Mary's soul overflows with enthusiasm and she intones the *Magnificat*:

"My soul glorifies the Lord and my spirit exults in God my Saviour, because he has cast his eyes upon the lowliness of his

---

[27] Luke 1:42–45. The best manuscripts of the Vulgate, conformably to the Greek text, have "Beata quae *credidit* quoniam perficientur ea quae dicta sunt ei." Mary is the one referred to, though in a general maxim. She is blessed for having believed *because* it shall be accomplished etc.; or better, she is blessed for having believed *that* it shall be accomplished. ὅτι (*quoniam*) has both these meanings, but the second is preferable.

[28] Luke 1:15. "He shall be filled with the Holy Ghost while still in the womb of his mother" (ἔτι ἐκ κοιλίας). On the case of Jeremias, see Condamin, *Recherches,* 1912, pp. 466–467. On the opinions of the Fathers about these questions, see Buzy, *S. Jean-Baptiste,* 1922, pp. 64–96. St. Ambrose, Origen, and several good theologians are of the opinion that "reason, like grace, was given to him as a permanent gift" before his birth.

handmaid. Behold all generations shall call me blessed, for the Almighty has wrought great things in me, and holy is his name.

"His mercy is extended from generation to generation upon them that fear him. He has displayed the strength of his arm. He has scattered the proud. He has cast down the mighty from their thrones and has exalted the lowly. He has filled the hungry with good things, and the rich he has sent away empty-handed.

"He has come to the aid of Israel, his servant, mindful of his mercy, according to the promise made to our fathers, for Abraham and his race forever."[29]

Mary's hymn is neither an answer to Elizabeth nor, properly speaking, a prayer to God; it is a lifting of soul, an ecstasy. It is crowded with Biblical reminiscences, most of the ideas being borrowed from the prophets and the Psalms. Two or three expressions recall the cry of gratitude of Anna, the mother of Samuel, and the cry of joy of Lia, the adoptive mother of Aser. But the words of Anna and Lia take on new meaning in the mouth of the Immaculate Virgin.

Poetical improvisations were not rare among the ancient Hebrews, and it is as true of the Semitic world today as it was of remoter periods, that "Poetry is the language of strong impressions and lofty ideas, which among peoples of the East well forth in inspired words."[30] And it is at moments of national crisis or religious fervor that the soul is most eager to sing. Thus the heroines of Israel found lyric measures to celebrate help from on high, the salvation of their country, and their own exploits: Mary, Moses' sister, at the passage through the Red Sea; Debbora,

---

[29] Luke 1: 46–55. The theory of Harnack, Loisy, and others, which attributes the *Magnificat* to Elizabeth, is merely a curiosity of historical interest. Cf. Durand, in *R.B.*, 1898, pp. 74–77, or Lagrange, *Saint Luc*, pp. 44–45.

Plummer (in his *Commentary,* 1896, pp. 30–31) gives a synoptic table of the Magnificat together with the allusions to the Old Testament. There is not a verse without one or more reminiscences.

There is no agreement on the division into strophes, and with good reason. Many mark off four strophes (Schanz, Plummer, etc.); others find five (Grimm and Zorell, in their translations of the *Magnificat* into Hebrew). We prefer to divide the text according to the three sentiments expressed, without troubling about the too uncertain division into strophes.

[30] Didon, *Jésus-Christ,* 1891, p. 112 (English transl., Vol. I, pp. 38–39).

after the defeat of the Chanaanites, whose corpses were dragged along by the torrent of Cison; Judith, at the death of Holophernes, fallen by her dagger. When inspired, their chanting took on rhythm and cadence, without the trammels of metrical laws. Mary for her part sings of the power of the arm of the Most High and the liberation of her people, remembering herself only to proclaim her lowliness. She gives free play to the three feelings that fill her soul: humble gratitude for the great things God has wrought in her, admiration of the wisdom and mercy of Him who humbles the powerful and exalts the weak, and joyous confidence that God is making ready to fulfill his promises by sending a Liberator to his people.

5. The Birth and Circumcision of the Precursor

(LUKE 1:57–80)

Mary stayed at the home of Elizabeth about three months. This bit of summary information does not permit us to say that she waited for the birth and circumcision of the child. If we had to settle the question by marshaling authorities, we would come to no conclusion, for they are equally divided. But we cannot suppose that after such a long journey undertaken to assist her relative, and after a whole season with her, Mary left her abruptly just when her condition would require more care, on the eve of the day when the two families would be rejoicing in the birth of the Precursor of the Word Incarnate. We would not expect such conduct in the case of any other woman; should we, then, attribute to Mary less concern about family obligations and social propriety?[31]

When the child was born, relatives and friends gathered in numbers to congratulate the mother. The crowd was still larger on the eighth day, when the baby was to be circumcised and given his name. The assembled relatives proposed that he be called Zachary. It was not quite usual to give a child his father's

[31] Luke 1:56. "Mary remained with her about three months and returned to her own house." This brief note is put before the birth of John because St. Luke wishes to conclude everything relating to the Visitation. It does not follow that Mary left before the birth of the Precursor. Opinions on both sides are enumerated by Knabenbauer; the reasons for and against are discussed by Maldonatus.

name, but they doubtless thought that the aged and failing Zachary would not have long to live, and that the child would soon inherit an honored name. But Elizabeth insisted that he be called John. In vain did they point out that no one in the family had ever had that name; she persisted in her determination, either moved by divine inspiration, or because her spouse had made known to her the formal command of the archangel. The father was then questioned by signs, for he was, or they believed that he was, deaf as well as mute. He called for a stylus and a waxed tablet and traced the words, "John is his name." The guests were surprised and could not understand the agreement of the mother and father on a name which had never been in the family before; but their surprise changed to amazement when they heard Zachary sing in prophetic terms the praise of God:

"Blessed be the Lord God of Israel, because he has visited and redeemed his people, raising up for us a mighty Saviour in the house of David his servant. Such was the promise proclaimed of old through his holy prophets, to save us from our enemies, to rescue us from the hands of them that persecute us, to show mercy to our fathers, to be mindful of his holy covenant. For he had sworn to Abraham our father that, delivered from the hand of our enemies, we should be able to serve him without fear, in holiness and justness all the days of our life.

"And thou, my child, shalt be called the prophet of the Most High; thou shalt walk before the Lord to prepare his ways, to give to his people the knowledge of salvation through forgiveness of sins. Such is the merciful kindness of our God, who has made his light to shine on us from on high, to enlighten those that sat in darkness and the shadow of death, to guide our feet in the path of peace."[32]

---

[32] Luke 1:68–79. Plummer (*Commentary,* p. 39) places before us parallel passages from the Old Testament. He mentions *six* reminiscences from the Psalms and *seven* from the prophets. Only one verse has no parallel (the remission of sins).

The *Biblical* language of the passage presents some obscurities. The "fathers" are the Patriarchs; the "people seated in the shadow of death" are the pagans plunged in mortal ignorance; a "horn of salvation" (*cornu salutis*) means a powerful savior; the "oath that he swore to Abraham" is an allusion to Genesis 22:16, Exodus 2:24, etc.

The division into two parts is clear (68–75 and 76–79). Most authors count five strophes, but Grimm (*Die Oden Salomos,* p. 112) finds seven distychs. The best course to follow is to divide according to sense.

The *Benedictus* of Zachary, which, like the *Magnificat,* is as rhythmical as a hymn, is a tissue of passages borrowed from the Psalms and especially the prophets. Five strophes may be distinguished: the first three sing of the realization of the promises that God had made under oath, to deliver his people and give to them a Saviour, a descendant of David; the last two predict the glorious future of the child who has just been born. He will walk before the Lord to prepare his ways, by disposing men to receive him; he will be the dawn of the sun of justice and holiness, which is about to rise on the world, to shine on the human race, as the prophets had foretold.

Let us now leave the miraculous child to "grow and become strong in spirit" and return with Mary to Nazareth, where a cruel trial is awaiting her.

6. St. Joseph's Ordeal

(MATTHEW 1:18–25)

We said above that among the Hebrews betrothal was the same as marriage, and differed from it only as far as the cohabitation of the spouses was concerned. On the other hand, Mary's answer to the angel, "I know not man," evidently excludes all marital relations for the future as well as the past. And so we must suppose that there was an express or tacit understanding between the spouses before the contract, by which Joseph pledged himself to be the faithful guardian of Mary's virginity, so that she should have nothing to fear under his patronage.

Jewish ideas on marriage and continence had undergone an evolution in the course of centuries. The time was past when the daughter of Jephte would go grieving to the mountains to bewail her virginity, consecrated to God by her imprudent father. Elias, Eliseus, Jeremias, and other holy persons had lived in celibacy, and at the beginning of our era celibacy was generally observed by the Essenes, as well as the Therapeutae, if these latter are not a product of Philo's creative imagination. The continence of the Baptist had imitators, therefore, and widowhood, too, was universally held in honor. Thus the mutual agreement of Joseph and Mary has in itself nothing improbable. Besides, we are not to set ourselves up as norms when we judge saints blessed with extraordinary graces, nor to confine to our own narrow ideals those whom God has placed upon a lofty pedestal, to serve as models and ideals for the rest of men.

At the time of the Annunciation, the two spouses, though united by a true marriage, were not living under the same roof. Hence it is not probable that Joseph accompanied Mary when she visited Elizabeth. Had he been present at their meeting, he would have known the mystery of the Incarnation; and his anxiety shows that he was ignorant of it. The Blessed Virgin had decided that she was not to tell him the angel's message; either she kept it to herself out of instinctive reserve and virginal modesty, or, what is more likely, she felt that she was not free to divulge the divine secret entrusted to her alone, until heaven should dispose otherwise.

Shortly after Mary's return to Nazareth, the first signs of maternity became noticeable to Joseph and to others. The anguish of the holy patriarch was inexpressible. He knew Mary's holiness and her decision to remain always a virgin. Convinced of her innocence, he found himself faced by a torturing mystery, and did not know how to lift the veil. Could she have been the victim of violence during her double journey and prolonged stay with Elizabeth? If so, her determined silence would be explicable. It may be, too, that the idea of a miracle and virginal conception came to Joseph's mind. At all events, he asked himself if his place was still at Mary's side and if he had the right to act as the father of the child she was about to bear. But how was he to break the bond which united them without endangering her reputation?

His apparently insoluble problem was how to give Mary her freedom and still safeguard her honor. It was one of those moments in life when it is much easier to do one's duty, no matter how difficult, than to see clearly where it lies. "And Joseph, her spouse, being a just man and unwilling to expose her to reproach, was minded to put her away privately."[33] The difficulty was in

[33] Matt. 1:18–20. We should place before us the various aspects of this little drama, which is somewhat obscured by the extreme conciseness of the narrative:

a) *The condition of Mary* — She was the *fiancée*, or, if you wish, the *betrothed* of Joseph μνηστευθείσας τῷ Ἰωσήφ, but this is to be understood as a true marriage after the manner of the Jews. Hence Joseph is called her *husband* (ἀνὴρ αὐτῆς) and she is called the *wife* of Joseph (Μαρίαν τὴν γυναῖκά σου).

effecting this purpose. A public act, executed before witnesses, permitting the repudiated wife to contract a new union, was as necessary for the annulment of a betrothal as for the dissolution of a marriage. Perhaps a long absence, on some plausible pretext, would best serve the purpose. This would be a precarious measure, but it would gain time, and time has a way of clearing up many situations. Yet, wherever he turned, Joseph saw chiefly the disadvantages, and could not make up his mind. After all, nothing was yet settled; all was in suspense. Had he believed her guilty, it was his duty, or at least his right, to hand her a bill of divorce, regardless of the consequences. But knowing her to be innocent, he vainly sought some way to reconcile his desire to free her with his anxiety not to dishonor her.

In such perplexities, the wise man turns to prayer. This is what the just Joseph must have done; he lifted his eyes to heaven to implore help from on high. God at last had pity on

---

b) *The time of the crisis*—This was *before* the two spouses lived together (πρὶν ἢ συνελθεῖν αὐτούς). Many understand συνελθεῖν (*convenirent*) of conjugal relations; but this meaning is improbable, for the Evangelist immediately adds that Mary had conceived of the Holy Ghost; and the angel commands Joseph to "take unto him his wife" (παραλαβεῖν) which obviously means to take her to his home to begin their life together. St. Matthew uses a different word for conjugal relations (*non cognoscebat eam,* οὐκ ἐγίνωσκεν).

c) *The discovery of Mary's pregnancy*—This discovery happened after her return to Nazareth, about four months after the Annunciation, and from natural signs that Joseph would notice as would anyone else. *Inventa est in utero habens de Spiritu Sancto* (εὑρέθη ἐν γαστρὶ ἔχουσα): "She was found to be with child"; or better, "It was found that she was with child." Joseph is not specially mentioned, and few subscribe to the singular view of St. Jerome: "Non ab alio inventa est nisi a Joseph, qui paene licentia maritali futurae uxoris omnia noverat."

d) *Joseph's state of mind*—He was ignorant of the mystery of the Incarnation. The angel's words showed that he needed instruction. "Because he was a just man (δίκαιος ὤν), he did not wish (μὴ θέλων) to discredit her (δειγματίσαι); he purposed (ἐβουλήθη) to send her away secretly (ἀπολῦσαι λάθρᾳ)." The very rare word, δειγματίζειν, has the same meaning as παραδειγματίζειν, "to make an example of," "to disgrace." In an Egyptian papyrus δειγματισμός is coupled with λοιδορία. Cf. Moulton-Milligan, *Vocabulary,* pp. 137–138. For Mary, disgrace would be exposure to feminine raillery and gossip. This is what Joseph wishes to avoid (μὴ θέλων) at any price. He deliberates (ἐβουλήθη) what to do. Βούλεσθαι is not a synonym for θέλειν. It means "desire," "plan"; and Plato in the *Protagoras* gently chides a Sophist who finds a shade of difference between βούλεσθαι and ἐπιθυμεῖν. Besides, the meaning is explained further on: "While he was reflecting on these things (ταῦτα αὐτοῦ ἐπιθυμηθέντος)." He had not yet come to a definite decision.

him and released him from his distress. The angel of the Lord appeared to him in a dream and said to him: "Joseph, son of David, fear not to take to thyself Mary thy wife; what has been conceived in her is of the Holy Spirit. She shall bring forth a son, and thou shalt call him Jesus, for he is to save his people from their sins."[34]

The Fathers are very much divided in their interpretations of this distressing incident. According to some, the mystery of the Word Incarnate had been revealed to Joseph, and he understood the virginal conception at the first signs of Mary's maternity. He was not saddened and perplexed, but seized with an overpowering humility at the thought of playing in her regard a role of which he thought himself altogether unworthy. The opinion would be attractive, if it were less devoid of evidence and more in harmony with the Gospel text. Many other Fathers believe that Joseph really doubted Mary's innocence. But in this hypothesis his conduct is incomprehensible. A wise man would not base important resolutions on a simple suspicion, and his first duty would be to clear up his doubt. Yet, derogatory as this opinion might seem to be to Jesus, his mother, and Joseph himself, we would embrace it without hesitation if the Gospel invited us to do so. The Gospel, however, upon close examination suggests nothing of the kind. Perhaps the middle term proposed by St. Jerome will win favor: "How could Joseph be called *just* if he concealed the guilt of his spouse? What speaks in defense of Mary is precisely the fact that Joseph, knowing her chastity and marveling at what had happened, buried in silence a fact whose mystery he did not understand."[35] He kept his peace, because he

---

[34] Matt. 1:20–21. The angel appeared κατ' ὄναρ (*in somnis*), a favorite expression of the first Evangelist, who uses it five times (2:12, 13, 19, 22; 27:19). Dreams of their nature are deceptive, but κατ' ὄναρ does not mean "in a dream." It is opposed to ὕπαρ, as in Plato (*Theatetus,* 158b): ὄναρ τε καὶ ὕπαρ, a state of *sleep* and a state of *waking*. God can speak to someone during sleep and later give him assurance that he has spoken to him (Gen. 20:3–6; Num. 12:6; Deut. 13:1; Job 33:15–16, etc.).

[35] For the exegesis of this passage consult Patrizi (*De evangeliis,* Dissert. XV, Vol. II, pp. 122–135); for a presentation of the various opinions, consult Knabenbauer's commentary.

Most of the Fathers whose opinions we know (St. Justin, St. Hilary, St. Ambrose, St. John Chrysostom, St. Augustine, and others more recent) admit that Joseph had a *real suspicion,* and, if they are logical, even more than a suspicion.

was sure of only one thing, Mary's virtue. His only concern was to protect the honor of the Blessed Virgin, until heaven spoke to him. Then he hastened to obey the injunctions he received. He welcomed Mary into his house with traditional ceremony. Both gave themselves to the usual festivities and solemnized their union as far as their modest resources and their lowly status permitted. No outward detail was to distinguish them from any ordinary couple. Charged with giving the child a name, Joseph assumed his role as head of the family. Since the mystery of the virginal conception could not yet be revealed to a world ill-disposed to receive it, everything had to take place under the protection of marriage, and the presence of Joseph at Nazareth was indispensable for safeguarding the honor of the Virgin Mother and her divine Son.

There was also another reason. The prophets had predicted that the Saviour would be a descendant of David, and his successor on the throne of Israel. It is because of Joseph, his legal father, that Jesus will be recognized as the heir of David, for his mother was not qualified to pass on to him the right to the crown. This

---

They are followed, even in our own time, by many exegetes. Thus Fouard (*Vie de N.-S. J.-C.*, Vol. I, p. 44; English transl., Vol I, p. 39): "He could not hesitate as to his duty of repudiating this affianced maiden whom honor would not permit him to retain." Schanz and Fillion also, though not as crudely.

On the other hand, Salmeron believes that Joseph *knew the mystery of the Incarnation and wished, out of pure humility, to leave Mary*. In support of his opinion he cites Origen and St. Basil (the texts cited by him are not from these two authors) and some sixteenth-century theologians, not to mention St. Bridget.

The explanation we have chosen, following St. Jerome and the *Opus Imperfectum* mistakenly attributed to St. John Chrysostom, claims many adherents today. Maldonatus approves of it: "Sententia (haec) nec a veritate nec a pietate discedit." Fr. Durand apparently wishes to reconcile it with the first (*Saint Matthieu,* 1927, p. 8): "He did not feel that he had the right to treat Mary as a faithless spouse, so much did her virtue place her above all suspicion; on the other hand, he did not wish to expose himself to a violation of the law by becoming an accomplice to a fault." Le Camus (*Vie de N.-S. J.-C.*, 1921, Vol. I, p. 180) is franker, but he supposes that Mary was united to Joseph only by "a simple promise of marriage, a simple verbal tie," which could easily be broken without causing surprise. Fr. Lagrange's formula is, in our opinion, better: "In the midst of all his anxiety, it seemed to him the wisest thing he could do was to restore to Mary her freedom, but in such a way as to prevent the possibility of anyone thinking that she had been guilty of any crime" (*L'Evangile de J.-C.*, 1928, p. 27; English transl., Vol. I, p. 29). But it should be noted that he had not yet made up his mind.

is why the two Evangelists who give brief accounts of the infancy of Jesus end his genealogy with Joseph and not with Mary.[36]

7. The Heir of David

The Semites attached such importance to their lineage that among the Arabs every biography, be it of warrior, poet, or scholar, begins with a long list of ancestors. The Hebrews had a higher reason to keep alive the memory and proofs of their descent. We know that, at the return from captivity, many priests were excluded from the sacerdotal rank because they could not produce evidence that they were of the blood of Aaron; and some private individuals were deprived of citizenship because they could not show that they were Israelites. At the time of jubilee, moreover, all had to prove that they were Israelites before they could regain possession of their family goods. Two tribes in particular had to be most careful in holding to their genealogical tree, the sacerdotal tribe of Levi and the ruling tribe of Juda. And even if we were to accept the statement of Julius Africanus and admit that Herod had all the registers of names and genealogical tables of the noble families destroyed when he came to the throne, in order to hide his own lowly origin, the measure would have reached only the public archives; private documents would not have been touched. To all appearances, however, the story is a fabrication. As a matter of fact, when Josephus in his autobiography sets out to prove the nobility and antiquity of his family, he refers to the Temple archives and recommends them to readers who may doubt him. He informs us elsewhere of the great care taken by the priests to protect themselves against marrying beneath their rank, even in Egypt and Babylon. The members of the royal house of David would have been even more careful. Thus, when Domitian ordered the descendants of David to be put to death, there was no difficulty in discovering them; and we know from Hegesippus that certain relatives of Jesus owed their safety only to their meager fortunes.

It was easy therefore for the Evangelists to procure the geneal-

[36] Cf. Note D: *The Two Genealogies of Jesus.*

ogy of the Saviour. St. Matthew's list descends from Abraham to Jesus and comprises three series of fourteen names each, the first going as far as David, the second up to the captivity, and the third to Joseph, the legal father of Jesus. This arrangement is not haphazard, but quite deliberate, as the final résumé proves. "The summary of the generations: from Abraham to David, fourteen generations; from David to the Babylonian captivity, fourteen generations; from the Babylonian captivity to Christ, fourteen generations." The fateful number of fourteen is a convenient artifice to aid the memory, and also to close the door to all fraudulent additions or subtractions. It may also be symbolic, since the letters in the Hebrew name of David, taken according to their numerical value, give a total of fourteen. To keep within this number, St. Matthew omits some names in each series.

St. Luke goes beyond Abraham to the father of the human race. Adam and Christ are at the extremities of his genealogical list, at opposite poles in the plan of redemption, corresponding to each other as type and antitype, or as sketch and masterpiece. Both of them are representatives of humanity; the one working its destruction, the other bringing about its salvation. Side by side with them are two women; the first instigating the fall, the second co-operating in the restoration. Both Adam and Christ escape the common law of generation and come immediately from the hands of the Creator. Adam is from the slime of the earth, animated by the breath of God; Jesus from the blood of a Virgin made fruitful by the Holy Spirit.

In making up the genealogical table as far as the Babylonian captivity the Evangelists had only to copy the Biblical lists. But from that point on they were forced to rely on documents handed down by memory or kept in family archives. They had no way of testing their accuracy, and, like the authors of Esdras and Paralipomenon, must have transcribed them as they were, taking no care to reconcile them. The ancients were less exacting in matters of genealogy than we are. In St. Matthew, for instance, Joram "begets" Ozias, who is his great-grandson. And it is possible that St. Luke's list, which is much vaguer in expression, is even freer and does not always give the father-son relationship, at least in the order of natural descent.

A comparison of the two lists reveals one serious discrepancy.

From David down, all the names are different except Salathiel and Zorobabel; and the exceptions do not lessen but aggravate the problem. A great number of modern authors, Protestant as well as Catholic, have accepted an apparently simple solution. It is that St. Matthew gives us Joseph's genealogy from Solomon, and St. Luke Mary's from Nathan, David's eldest son. But St. Luke's text fits in badly with this hypothesis, and it is rather strange that before the sixteenth century no Father of the Church or commentator worthy of the name ever hit upon a device that would cut the Gordian knot so easily. The reason is that they were well aware that a Semitic genealogy never ended with a woman. "We would wonder," says St. Ambrose, "why St. Luke gives Joseph's genealogy and not Mary's, if we did not know that it is always the Scriptural practice to trace the male line." St. Augustine goes further: Jesus Christ, he says in substance, is much more the son of Joseph than he would have been had Joseph adopted him, for he is the fruit of the virginal, but very real, marriage between Joseph and his holy Mother; "thus, even if it could be proved that Mary was not of the line of David, Christ would be no less the son of David, for the reason that Joseph is rightly called his father."[37] Moreover the hypothesis is inadmissible from another viewpoint, as the holy Doctor hastens to add, for Jesus is "from the seed of David, according to the flesh, sprung from his loins." These strong expressions would be inexact, if David's blood did not flow in the veins of the Virgin Mother.[38]

From the time of St. Ignatius and St. Justin in the second century, this fact was accepted as uncontroverted dogma.[39] Other Fathers concluded to it from the very marriage of Joseph and

---

[37] St. Ambrose, *In Lucam,* lib. III, n. 3 (ed. Schenkl, p. 99); St. Augustine, *De consensu Evang.,* lib. II, nn. 3 and 4 (ML, XXXIV, 1072).

[38] Rom. 1:3: *ex semine David secundum carnem;* Act. 2:30: *de fructu lumbi ejus sedere super sedem ejus.*

We shall not cite Luke 1:27: "Gabriel was sent to a virgin betrothed to a man of the house of David. And the virgin's name was Mary." St. John Chrysostom connects the words "of the house of David" with "virgin"; others refer them to both Joseph and Mary; but grammar demands that they qualify only the nearest word, Joseph. If St. Luke had intended to apply them to "the virgin," he would not have continued: *"the virgin's* name was Mary," but would have said *"her* name was Mary."

[39] St. Ignatius, *Ad Ephesios,* 18; St. Justin, *Dial. cum Tryph.,* 100.

Mary; for, as we said above, the marriage of a virgin, who was to remain a virgin, has no meaning except in the light of her obligation, as heiress and only child, to unite herself to a member of her own family, or even, according to the interpretation common among the Jews, to her nearest relative.[40] Thus Joseph's genealogy is, by the same token, Mary's.

---

[40] Moses had decided that the daughters of Salphaad, who died without male issue, should be his heirs (Num. 27:1–11); but when the family of Galaad, of which Salphaad was a member, reminded him that, if they should marry strangers, their patrimony would pass to other families, which was contrary to a previous law, it was stipulated that they should marry men of the same tribe as themselves. Consequently, they married *the sons of their paternal uncle* (Num. 36:1–12), hence, *their nearest relatives.* This preserved the spirit of the law. Again, the angel Raphael said to the young Tobias: "Here is one whose name is Raguel, a near kinsman of thy tribe, and he has a daughter . . . he has no son nor any other daughter beside her . . . thou must take her to wife" (Tob. 6:11–12). Raguel is the *brother* of the elder Tobias (Tob. 7:2–4). He yields his daughter willingly, saying to the young Tobias: "Thou art her brother, and she is thine . . . *according to the Law of Moses,* take her and bring her to thy father" (7:11–14). In the context, he is the nearest relative.

CHAPTER II

The Mystery of Bethlehem

1. The Census of Quirinius

"At that time there went forth an edict from Caesar Augustus prescribing a registration of the whole world. This first registration took place under Quirinius, governor of Syria. All went to be enregistered, each in the city of his birth. Since Joseph was of the house and family of David he went up from the town of Nazareth in Galilee to the town of David called Bethlehem, in Judea, to be enregistered with Mary, his spouse, who was with child."[1]

This text of St. Luke has long been the target of Rationalist criticism. It was once held that a decree of Augustus prescribing a census of the whole world was a pure myth; that, if there had been such a decree, it would not have affected an independent kingdom like Palestine during Herod's time; that a census taken by Romans and in the Roman manner would not have required the presence of Joseph, still less of Mary, in Bethlehem; that, in any case, this alleged census could not have been taken under Quirinius, since he became governor of Syria only nine or ten years after Herod's death.

[1] Luke 2:1–2: *ἐξῆλθεν δόγμα ἀπογράφεσθαι πᾶσαν τὴν οἰκουμένην*. "The whole world" *πᾶσα ἡ οἰκουμένη* (all the inhabited world) meant at the time the Roman Empire. There is question here of an *ἀπογραφή* (registration of persons and a settlement of their civil status) and not of an *ἀποτίμησις* (declaration and estimate of taxable goods), but this distinction was not always made. Note that "the registration took place *under* Quirinius"; it is not stated that it was conducted *by* him. Joseph comes to Bethlehem to be registered, but it is not said that this obligation was incumbent on Mary.

Present-day scholarship has scattered much of this mist and has thrown some light on the only point that still remains obscure.

Like all great administrators, Augustus had a passion for statistics. From the moment of his accession he occupied himself with the survey of the Empire begun by Julius Caesar. It was a vast undertaking and entailed a quarter century of work. Augustus took three exact censuses of all Roman citizens in all parts of the world, and put the totals down in his autobiography. At his death a memorandum in his own handwriting was found, which was later described by Suetonius as a *Breviarium totius imperii,* containing "an inventory of the resources of the Empire, the number of citizens and allies in arms, the amount of tributes and revenues, of necessary expenditures and bounties."[2] It is now an admitted fact that in certain countries, such as Egypt, he established a periodical census to be taken up every fourteen years, to supply the place of vital statistics. There are reasons for believing that this measure was universal.[3]

To claim that as an autonomous kingdom Palestine was exempt is completely to misunderstand the true status of those sovereigns who, though called allies, were really only vassals of Augustus. They were phantom-kings, set up or supported by Caesar, docile agents of Roman policy, with no more independence than Rome deigned to allow them. Strabo and Suetonius say expressly that all kings and princes by whatsoever name they were called were an integral part of the Empire and dependent on the Emperor.[4] They were forbidden to declare war or decide important issues or even to meet one another without the consent of their overlord.

---

[2] Tacitus, *Annales,* i, 12. Cf. Suetonius, *Augustus,* 101, and Dion Cassius, *Hist.,* lvi, 31. According to the last named, the *libellus* contained "the number of troops, the state of public resources and expenditures, the sums deposited in the treasury, and finally, everything pertaining to good government."

[3] For Egypt, see Mitteis and Wilcken, *Papyruskunde,* first part, 1912, pp. 192–196. For the rest of the world, cf. Ramsay, *Bearing of Recent Discovery on the Trustworthiness of the N.T.,* 4 ed., 1920, pp. 255–274. Ramsay maintains: (1) that the period of fourteen years was the same everywhere; (2) that the enrollments were simultaneous; (3) that the system was inaugurated eight years before the Christian era. These three points are debatable.

[4] Strabo, *Geography,* XVIII, iii, 25 *ad fin.:* "All the states governed by kings, dynasts, and decarchs are answerable to the Emperor alone, and never depended on anyone but him." Suetonius, *Augustus,* 48: "Nec aliter universos (reges socios) quam membra partesque imperii curae habuit." For example, he appointed tutors for the sons of allied kings and interested himself in their education.

Toward the end of his life, Herod was held in even closer leash than the others: Augustus told him that, though he had treated him as a friend in the past, he would treat him thenceforth as a subject. Herod could not carry out the sentence against his son Antipater without recourse to Rome, or make a valid will without submitting it to Caesar.[5] In this state of servitude, he could hardly have refused to allow a census of his kingdom, if Augustus ordered it or even expressed a wish that it be taken. Indeed, Augustus had already made one very unpopular and vexatious move by exacting from all Jews an oath of fidelity to himself.[6]

To lighten her yoke, Rome made it her policy to respect local customs and to humor the feelings of subjugated nations, especially when they had not yet been officially annexed to the Empire. Thus in Egypt the periodical census brought each citizen back every fourteen years to his birthplace. This system had the double advantage of respecting national traditions and of checking to some extent the scourge of emigration then depopulating the rural districts. We know that it was applied in other lands, and it is only natural that it should have been applied in Palestine from the time of the first registration.[7] Accordingly, Joseph had to go to Bethlehem, the city of his ancestors. Mary went with him, either because of her position as heiress, or to be with her saintly spouse at the moment she was to become a mother, or simply because of an inspiration from heaven which singled out Bethlehem as the cradle of the Messias.

Even those critics most bent on finding St. Luke in error have

[5] All these facts are well known. The texts of Josephus and many others may be found in Schürer, *Geschichte,* 4 ed., 1901, Vol. I, pp. 401–404, 525–529.

[6] Josephus, *Antiq.,* XVII, ii, 4. Six thousand Pharisees suffered penalties because they refused at that time to swear the oath to Augustus. Tacitus (*Annales,* vi, 41) tells of an altogether similar action taken by Archelaus, a king *allied to Rome.* A Roman general had to be sent to stamp out the rebellion.

[7] Vibius Maximus, prefect of Egypt, issued a decree: "Since the registration by houses is about to begin (τῆς κατ' οἰκίαν ἀπογραφῆς), it is necessary that all who, for any reason whatever, are absent from their home, return, each to his own hearth (ἐπανελθεῖν εἰς τὰ ἑαυτῶν ἐφέστια), to complete the usual formalities of registration." There is a phototype of this document and a bibliography in Deissmann, *Licht von Osten,* 4 ed., 1923, p. 234. Other texts are in Mitteis and Wilcken, *Papyruskunde,* first part, Vol. I, 1912, pp. 235–236. The case of Egypt was not unique. The inhabitants of Mesembria in Thrace were summoned to go to their respective cities to be enrolled there according to law and custom (Cagnat, *Inscript. graecae ad res romanas pertinentes,* Vol. I, p. 204).

to bow before these facts. They once held that St. Luke had invented the registration in order to place St. Joseph in Bethlehem.[8] They grant, now, with rather bad grace, that a registration prescribed by Rome may well have taken place in Palestine during Herod's lifetime. However, as the saying goes, the devil loses nothing in the bargain. They claim that St. Luke made use of his knowledge of history to give Joseph's trip to Bethlehem some semblance of probability; and they dig in behind what they consider an unassailable objection: that Quirinius was not governor of Syria at the time of Christ's birth. They should know, however, that Quirinius twice governed Syria as legate of Augustus —once after the death of Archelaus, when he took the census described by Josephus, and at some previous date which has to be determined. It is a simple question of a date, but to establish it requires a detailed study, which would be out of place here.[9]

2. Christmas Night

(LUKE 2:6–7)

So Joseph and Mary set out for Jerusalem. Those four days of walking in the worst part of the rainy season must have seemed very long to the travelers, especially considering Mary's condition.

Jerusalem is only twelve miles from Bethlehem, and the travelers could look down for a moment on both cities from the top of the high hill that separates them.[10] Behind them the capital unfolded the grandeur of its new buildings: the Temple with its golden pinnacle gleaming in the sunlight, its long colonnaded porticoes, and beyond, near the bare rock where one day the Saviour's cross would stand, Herod's sumptuous palace with its lofty flanking turrets. In front of them the modest village of Bethlehem lay along a spur jutting from the central ridge of the

[8] Loisy, *Evangiles synoptiques,* 1907, Vol. I, p. 346.

[9] Cf. Note E: *The Census of Quirinius.*

[10] The average altitude of Jerusalem and Bethlehem is practically the same (2440 and 2476 feet), but the hill that separates them is about 160 feet higher. The spot on the present road where both cities can be seen is about three and a half miles from Jerusalem. The ancient road passed more to the west.

mountains of Judea. The air is so clear that one feels able to touch the town; but to reach it, it is necessary to skirt two deep ravines and pass Rachel's tomb, where the Hebron road turns off.

It was winter. Winter in these countries does not mean that nature is dead. If the vine and fig tree have lost their leaves, and the pale tint of the olive is darkened, there are still groves of evergreens to brighten the landscape. Vegetation quickened by autumn rains carpets the hillside, and in more sheltered spots some early flowers are beginning to sprout. In the years when snow falls, it lasts only a very short while. Freezing weather is even less frequent and of shorter duration. Yet the poor in their loosely built houses feel the cold bitterly on winter nights.[11]

Joseph must have had relatives or acquaintances at Bethlehem. We wonder why he did not knock at their doors, because in the East no home is shut to strangers, still less to friends or relatives. The residents of Bethlehem were not monsters. True, large numbers had come to register; but, whatever the crowding, there would always have been room for two guests with such modest needs. We need only recall the great throngs sheltered in Jerusalem during the Paschal days. There must, therefore, be some other answer to this riddle.

The village dwellings of that time must have been very much like those of Palestine today; a single room, serving as parlor, kitchen, dining room, and bedroom for the entire family, and sometimes also as shelter for domestic animals, for which a space is reserved on a lower level near the entrance. At nightfall light mattresses or simple mats are spread on the floor, and on this bedding the members of the household and their guests retire fully dressed, in the glimmer of the night lamp.[12] For a European there are few torments comparable to this continual intimacy in the presence of eyes which, though perhaps friendly, are too

---

[11] In Jerusalem, where the climate differs little from that of Bethlehem, there are winters without snow or ice. Still 11.81 inches of snow fell there in March, 1892, and in February, 1911; and even 18.11 inches in December, 1879. The thermometer can go down to 5 below or even 7 below (Centigrade), but it is rare for snow or ice to last for more than a few days at a time: this happens only about every ten years. Cf. Vincent-Abel, *Jérusalem antique,* 1912, p. 107.

[12] There is a realistic description, quite trustworthy, however, in Neil, *Everyday Life in the Holy Land,* 1913, pp. 67–73 (with a plate in color).

often prying, when it is impossible to escape and take refuge on the flat roof above. But such was the hospitality Mary and Joseph would have found in a house in the village. They do not seem to have asked for it; at least, the Gospel does not say so.[13] In Mary's condition, if they did not seek comfort, they at least desired privacy.

As Bethlehem was a much frequented stopping place, there was an inn dating from the time of Jeremias just outside the eastern limits of the village.[14] On their way between the country of the Philistines and the other side of the Jordan, travelers used to stop at this inn before entering the desert of Judea or after leaving it.

The inn of those days was much like a modern caravansary: a square area surrounded by high walls through which a single door gave entrance. There travelers and beasts of burden were sure to find water and shelter for the night. Animals spent the night in the open central courtyard, while their owners retired to a sort of platform on one or more sides of the quadrangle. Besides the large common room there were often small alcoves for rent at moderate prices. This was where Mary and Joseph had hoped to find the privacy which they desired; but all the alcoves were occupied and the common room promised all the inconveniences of private houses, and more. Thus, there was no room *for them* at the inn.

They finally found or were directed to one of those natural caves that are quite common in the limestone country of Judea, where country people find a night's lodging for their cattle and sometimes for themselves. The entire furnishing of these caves consists of a movable manger, attached to the wall or even set on the ground, to hold the fodder.

"And it came to pass, while they were there, that the time was fulfilled for Mary to bring forth her child. And she brought forth her first born son and wrapped him in swaddling clothes and laid him in the manger."

A stable became the palace of the Son of David; a crib, the

---

[13] There is not the slightest trace in the Gospel narrative of any search for lodging except at the inn.

[14] Jer. 41:17. The *inn* (גרות) was situated *near* the village (אצל) and not in the village itself, which did not, at that time, go as far down as the present site of the basilica. An inn was needed there because of considerations of topography.

throne of the Son of God! He who wished to be like us, the better to have compassion on our miseries, not only becomes our equal, but humbles himself beneath us. Yet, on second thought, what grandeur in this abasement! Christ does not come into the world like other men, and the curse that strikes all the daughters of Eve does not touch his mother. Mary brings him forth without labor and without the need of anyone's help. Joseph is no more part of the mystery of the Nativity than he is of the Incarnation. There is no question of him in St. Luke's story. It is Mary who takes the newborn Child, wraps him in swaddling clothes, and with her own hands lays him in the crib. Jesus came forth from her womb without the least damage to her virginity, as he was one day to come forth from the sepulcher without breaking the seals. "He comes forth like a shaft of light, like a ray of the sun. His mother is astonished at his sudden appearance. There are no cries at this childbirth, there is no violence. Miraculously conceived, he is yet more miraculously born, and the saints have thought it even more marvelous for him to be born of a virgin than to be conceived of a virgin."[15]

St. Luke indicates the virgin birth with admirable delicacy; then he is silent, as if he were unable to add anything, or preferred to let us contemplate and relish the ineffable mystery. The apocryphal accounts have substituted childish and tactless gossip for this respectful silence. Compared with the simplicity of the Gospel, their fantasies seem insipid and cold, entirely aside from the distasteful episode of Joseph's search for the midwives.[16]

---

[15] Bossuet, *Elévations sur les mystères,* 16 *semaine,* 3me élév.

[16] Pseudo-Matthew, *The Birth of Mary and the Infancy of the Saviour,* XIII–XV. The apocryphal book knows much more about it than the Evangelist: "The third day after the Saviour's birth, Mary leaving the cave went into a stable and placed the child in the crib, where the ox and the ass adored him. Then was fulfilled that which the prophet Isaias had foretold: 'The ox knoweth his Master; and the ass the cradle of his Lord.' The two animals on either side of the Child adore unceasingly. Then was fulfilled what had been foretold by the prophet Habacuc: 'Thou shalt show thyself between two beasts.' Joseph and Mary remained two days in that place and on the sixth day they went to Jerusalem."

The two texts cited by the apocryphal book mean literally: "The ox knoweth his owner, and the ass his master's crib; but Israel is without discernment, and my people without intelligence" (Isa. 1:3). "Make thy work known in the course of the ages" (Hab. 3:2), or, as the Vulgate translates: *Domine, opus tuum, in medio annorum, manifesta illud.* But the Septuagint translates: *ἐν μέσῳ δύο*

Christian piety has always cherished the grotto in which Mary brought her divine Son into the world. To keep the Christians away, Hadrian, in 135, dedicated the place to the cult of Adonis, but this fact only served to authenticate it more surely.[17] Toward the middle of the second century, St. Justin, a Palestinian by birth, testifies that Jesus was born in a grotto near Bethlehem.[18] At the beginning of the next century, Origen writes: "At Bethlehem is shown the grotto where Jesus was born. The fact is well known throughout the whole country. Even pagans know that in this grotto was born a certain Jesus adored by the Nazarenes."[19] Thus, when Constantine and his pious mother wished to erect a basilica over the spot where the Saviour had been born, as they had done at Calvary and on the Mount of Olives, they had only to follow local tradition faithfully handed down from the beginning. "Helena adorned the holy grotto with rich and varied decorations. Sometime later, the Emperor himself, outdoing his mother's munificence, embellished the place in truly royal fashion, lavishing on it gold, silver, and sumptuous tapestries."[20] The superb structure reared at his behest was standing in the year 333, when the Pilgrim of Bordeaux visited Bethlehem, and is still admired today despite dubiously successful restorations and the ravages of time.[21]

ζῴων γνωσθήσῃ "thou wilt be known in the midst of two animals" (or perhaps ἐν μέσῳ δύο ζωῶν "in the midst of two lives"), which gave rise to the legend of the ox and the ass. After all, it is very possible that in the cave that served as a stable there was an ass and an ox (or rather a cow). These animals are often enough found, with or without a goat, in the dwellings of the fellahs.

17 St. Jerome, *Epist. ad Paulinum* (ML, XXII, 581): From Hadrian to Constantine, for one hundred and eighty years the pagans venerated the image of Jupiter at the site of the Resurrection, and the marble statue of Venus at the place of Calvary. "Bethlehem nunc nostram lucus inumbrat Tammuz, id est Adonidis, et in specu ubi quondam Christus parvulus vagiit, Veneris amasius plangebatur."

18 St. Justin, *Dial. cum Tryph.*, 78: ἐν σπηλαίῳ τινὶ σύνεγγυς τῆς κώμης (in a certain cave near the village). This precious text informs us: (1) that Bethlehem was not a town at the time, but a village (κώμη); (2) that the place of the Nativity was a cave (σπήλαιον); St. Jerome says *specus, spelunca;* Eusebius sometimes calls it ἄντρον; (3) that the cave was not in the village, but very near it (σύνεγγυς).

19 Origen, *Contra Celsum,* i, 51.

20 Eusebius, *Life of Constantine,* iii, 43. The basilica was mentioned in A.D. 333 by the Pilgrim of Bordeaux.

21 The basilica had five naves with a single apse at the base of the central nave (the two apses at the extremities of the transept are later additions which mar the form of the edifice). The dimensions, according to the Marquis de

We may regret that Constantine's architects saw fit to enlarge the grotto and make it more regular. We should like to see it in its primitive simplicity, without the marble and the draperies that cover it, just as it was on that Christmas night, when it was seen by the shepherds, the first adorers of the Infant God. Yet despite everything it is a moving experience to walk into this blessed place, and there is comfort in the thought that this matchless sanctuary is now guarded by an almost entirely Christian population, the majority of whom are Catholics.[22]

3. The Shepherds at the Crib

(LUKE 2:8–20)

"In the outskirts of Bethlehem, there were shepherds passing the night in the fields, keeping watch over their flocks."[23]

In Palestine flocks of sheep and goats, called desert flocks, were kept out of doors all year round. As we have seen, the desert of Judea was not far from Bethlehem. Scarcely three miles to the east all cultivated land came to an end, and in this wilderness, sparse in vegetation, desert shepherds let out their flocks to graze winter and summer. Often they would join forces to defend them against marauders and wild beasts. When the night threatened to be chilly they sheltered them in caverns or under ledges of rock, and themselves went off, at need, to the nearest settlements.

Devout Israelites held these men in great scorn. Living as half-savage nomads, far from Temple or synagogue, they naturally found it impossible to conform to the prescribed prac-

---

Vogüé, were: (1) the basilica itself, 165.64 by 86.26 feet (inside); (2) the porch or narthex, 86.26 by 19.68 feet; (3) the atrium (which has disappeared), 131 by 98 feet. The atrium was on the site of the present square. For a detailed study, consult the superb monograph of Frs. Vincent and Abel, O.P., *Bethléem. Le sanctuaire de la nativité.*

[22] Bethlehem suffered a great deal during World War I. Its population dropped from 11,000 inhabitants to 7000, of whom 4000 are Catholics. There are 150 Protestants, as many Armenians, and some Moslems. The rest are Greek Orthodox.

[23] About the desert flocks, cf. *Mishnah,* treatise *Betsah,* v, 7. For their present-day customs, cf. Dalman, *Orte und Wege Jesu,* 1924, pp. 52–53 (English transl. by Levertoff, *Sacred Sites and Ways,* 1935, p. 47).

tices. Abba Gorion said: "Be careful not to choose for your sons the professions of mule-driver, camel-driver, barber, boatman, pedlar, or shepherd; these are the occupations of thieves."[24] Desert shepherds particularly were suspected of not having due regard for private property. Pharisees hesitated to buy wool or milk from them, through fear of co-operating in theft; they were classed with the publicans, and their testimony had no weight in court.

Yet among these outcasts of fortune, hard and lean of body, there were upright souls and pure hearts. It was for them that the Child of the crib, who became humble and little to draw the little and humble to himself, reserved his first call. A group of these poor folk was camping at that time near Bethlehem, on the border between the desert and the last fringes of vegetation. As usual, they were taking turns watching through the night.

Imagine their amazement and fear when they found themselves surrounded with light and when an angel suddenly appeared before them, saying: "Fear not, for I come to bring to you tidings of great joy, for you and all the people. This day is born to you in the city of David a Saviour, Christ the Lord. And this shall be to you a sign: you shall find an infant wrapped in swaddling-clothes and laid in a manger."[25] The sign would not of itself suffice to guide them to the newborn child in the little town of Bethlehem, and the angel must have added more explicit instructions; but it was enough to distinguish the infant from all others and to aid them in recognizing him once he should be found. Scarcely had the angel spoken when a throng of heavenly spirits joined him to intone this song of hope:

"Glory to God in the highest heaven
And peace on earth to men of good will."[26]

How short the hymn, and still how consoling! Whether the

[24] *Mishnah,* treatise *Qiddushin,* iv, 14. Cf. treatise *Baba Qamma,* x, 9.

[25] Luke 2:10–12. "This will be a sign for you," a frequent expression (1 Kings 10:2; Isa. 37:30) to confirm a divine promise. Here the sign is both *distinctive* (to recognize the Child) and *confirmative* (to prove that the angel was telling the truth).

[26] Several Greek Fathers and many manuscripts read ἐν ἀνθρώποις εὐδοκία, which gives this tercet:

Glory to God in the highest heavens
And on earth peace;
Among men, good will (εὐδοκία).

"good will" be God's benevolence or the good will of men, basically it comes to almost the same; for God's benevolence toward men is universal, and it devolves upon men only to put their wills in harmony with his benevolent designs. Thus the angel's prayer involves no restriction; it is addressed to everyone; it lays down only one essential condition, already existent on God's part, and always realizable by men.

The angels vanished as suddenly as they had appeared. Recovering somewhat from their fright, the shepherds took counsel together. "Let us go over," they said, "to Bethlehem and see this thing that has come to pass, which the Lord has made known to us." Those who did not have to guard the flocks hurried to the village to see the miraculous Child of whom the angels had sung.

"So they went in haste and found Mary and Joseph, and the infant lying in the manger. On seeing him, they verified the truth of what had been told them concerning this child. And all who heard the shepherds' story were in amazement at it. Now Mary carefully observed all these things, and meditated on them in her heart."

An infant put into a crib like a castaway, yet surrounded by the solicitude of his parents and the attentive care of his mother, was so exceptional a sight that it could not have been the result of chance. This certainly must be the promised sign, the proof positive that the angel's word was true. And so the shepherds greeted in this tender baby the Master of the world and the Saviour of mankind. They had no treasures to offer him like the Magi, but they prostrated themselves in adoration before him. We may well believe that Mary and Joseph told them more than

---

But the best manuscripts have εὐδοκίας in the genitive, as the Vulgate; and this reading is rightly adopted by editors of critical editions. In fact: (1) this tercet is very clumsy, because the conjunction is placed before the second member instead of before the last, its usual position; (2) the parallelism is broken: *glory* is parallel to *peace; God* to *men; heaven* to *earth.* Hence the following distych:

(*a*) Δόξα	(*b*) ἐν ὑψίστοις	(*c*) Θεῷ
(*b*) καὶ ἐπὶ γῆς	(*a*) εἰρήνη	(*c*) ἐν ἀνθρώποις

The word εὐδοκία can mean the *good will* of men, or the *good pleasure,* the *benevolence* of God. Most Catholic commentators take it in the latter sense. See, however, Lagrange's objections (*Saint Luc,* pp. 77–78).

The Greek has "among men" and not, as the present Vulgate, "to men." But St. Jerome wrote *in hominibus* (cf. the edition of Wordsworth-White). The difference in sense is negligible.

the Gospel narrative indicates, for on leaving the grotto they not only blessed God and sang his praises, but told everyone they met what they had seen and heard, and there was general amazement at their story.[27]

Such were the first worshipers of the Word made flesh. Mary engraved everything that had happened deep in her heart and meditated on the profound meaning of it all. Four times St. Luke mentions the personal, intimate feelings of the Blessed Virgin during her Son's childhood: at Bethlehem, when the shepherds adored him; at Jerusalem, when the aged Simeon took him in his arms; in the Temple, when she found him among the doctors; and at Nazareth, as she watched him grow in stature and advance in wisdom, full of respect and obedience toward herself and Joseph. The Evangelist has not told us the source of his information, but that was not necessary. He could hardly have described the most personal feelings of Mary's heart unless the Blessed Virgin herself or others who had enjoyed her intimacy had confided in him.

---

[27] St. Jerome asserts that the place where the canticle of the angels was sung was Migdal-Eder, a name which means the "Tower of the Flock" (*De nominibus hebraicis;* ML, XXIII, 879, and *Epist. ad Eustochium,* cviii, 10; ML, XXII, 885–886). Up to the middle of the last century, pilgrims who asked to see the Shepherd's Field were conducted to a subterranean excavation in the center of a field called the "Field of Booz," a descent of some twenty steps being then made. Nothing could be less likely than this location. In 1858 some well-planned excavations resulted in the discovery of a much more acceptable place a quarter of an hour distant from the former one. It is a huge cave which the natives call *Siar-el-Ghanem* (enclosure for flocks) and which is still used to shelter sheep and goats.

Guarmani's letter announcing its discovery may be found in full in Mislin, *Les saints lieux,* 3 ed., 1877, Vol. I, pp. 687–693. Here are the essential points: (1) the place is 1.24 miles east-northeast of Bethlehem. St. Jerome says *a mile,* but he never counts fractions of a mile; (2) the site is known in the locality as *Siar-el-Ghanem* (enclosure for sheep, sheepfold); (3) the watchtower on the top of the hill was 16.14 feet square; the base, about 3 feet deep, was cut out of the rock itself; (4) southwest of the tower there is a cave 62.32 by 78.72 feet which is entered at ground level; (5) north of the tower there are the foundations of a three-nave church facing east, measuring 85.28 by 78.72 feet; (6) southwest of the church there is a circular burial cave containing *three* tombs cut into the rock, which seem to have been the object of special veneration, and which are mentioned by ancient pilgrims. For example, in 670, about *one mile* from Bethlehem to the east, Arculf found a church where he venerated the tomb of the *Three Shepherds.* Bernard the Wise, in 865, mentions the monastery of the *Holy Shepherds.* For further details, cf. Guérin, *Judée,* Vol. I, 1868, pp. 214–225.

4. Jesus and Mary in the Temple

(LUKE 2:21–39)

The obligation imposed on the Israelites to have their sons circumcised the eighth day after birth was so strict that it took precedence even over the sacred Sabbath rest. Except in cases of compulsion, or when the child was so weak that his life would be endangered, the ceremony could not be postponed for any reason whatever.[28]

The practice of circumcision is not peculiar to the Hebrews. It existed in Arabia before Mohammed and in Egypt before Abraham. It is found among savage tribes of America and Australia, as well as in central Africa, where it is perhaps a survival of the influence of Islam. But in none of these places has it a marked religious character. It is merely a distinctive sign of clan or race, or a safeguard against certain tropical diseases, or a real or imaginary means of increasing fertility — the very reasons Philo advanced to justify the practice in pagan eyes.[29]

Among the Jews the case was quite different. Circumcision was for them the sensible sign of the covenant between Abraham and God, the effective incorporation of the newborn child into the holy nation, his implicit acceptance of the rights and duties arising from this membership.[30] It was primarily a religious rite, and Jesus wished to submit to it, as to other injunctions of the Mosaic law, "to redeem those who were under the Law." And so, on the eighth day he was circumcised. He who came to pour out all his blood for the salvation of the world wished to shed a drop of it at his birth, and thus begin his life of humiliation and suffering.

At this period, the Jews did not bring the child to the Temple or synagogue. The rite was performed in the family circle, but

[28] *Mishnah,* treatise *Shabbath,* xix, 5. Some curious examples of Rabbinical casuistry (Billerbeck, Vol. IV, pp. 23–26).

[29] Philo, *De circumcisione* (Mangey, Vol. II, p. 211). According to Philo, circumcision, first, gave immunity against a very painful and incurable disease (anthrax); secondly, contributed to hygiene and cleanliness; thirdly, and above all, fostered fecundity (*τὴν πρὸς πολυγονίαν παρασκευήν* or rather *κατασκευήν*).

[30] Gen. 17:9–14. In this passage, *covenant* or *sign of the covenant* occurs six times. St. Paul calls the circumcision of Abraham "the seal of the justice of faith" (Rom. 4:11).

with all possible ceremony. Before the assembled relatives the newborn was given his name. In our Lord's case there was no question of a choice; he was given the name Jesus, as had been intimated to Mary at the Annunciation, and to Joseph at the time of his painful trial.[31]

According to St. Epiphanius, the circumcision took place in the grotto, but there is no reason to believe that the Holy Family stayed there so long. When the strangers had returned to their own homes, Bethlehem took up its normal life again, and the Holy Family would no longer have had the same reasons for wanting privacy. Nor is it likely that the people of Bethlehem would have allowed a compatriot and fellow citizen, of whose presence they must have been aware, to languish in such a wretched shelter.

Joseph was certainly not living as a recluse. He had to go out to earn his bread; for as long as he could work he would never have willingly lived on alms. The rainy season and the tender age of the child did not permit him to return to Nazareth yet, and so he remained in Bethlehem until the day of Mary's purification and the presentation of the child to God in the Temple at Jerusalem.

Every woman conceiving and bearing a male child, says the Law of Purification, shall be (legally) unclean for seven days. After the circumcision of the child, she shall remain in her house for thirty-three days. She shall not touch any holy thing and shall not enter the Sanctuary. When the days of her purification shall be fulfilled, she shall present to the priest at the entrance of the Tabernacle a yearling lamb for a holocaust and a young pigeon or turtledove as a sacrifice for sin. If she has not the means to procure a lamb, let her offer two turtledoves or two young pigeons. The priest shall make expiation for her and she shall be clean.[32] The Immaculate Virgin, who had conceived of the Holy Spirit and become a mother without impairment of her virginity, did not come under the law that touched the other daughters of Israel. If she submitted to it, it was to imitate her

---

[31] For Mary, Luke 1:31; for Joseph, Matt. 1:21.

[32] Lev. 12:2–8. If the mother brought a daughter into the world, these figures were doubled, and the purification took place only at the end of eighty days.

Son and to avoid scandal to her acquaintances, who knew nothing and were to know nothing of her virginal motherhood.

A first-born male child belonged to the Lord by the double title of first-fruit and head of the family. In patriarchal societies heads of families exercise a sort of priesthood. Theirs is the right of offering sacrifice and on them falls the duty of caring for divine worship. It is true that in Israel the priestly tribe of Levi had been given this office, but first-born sons continued nonetheless to be consecrated to God and had to be bought back at a set price.[33] The payment of this ransom was due the thirtieth day after birth and was to be made by the child's father. The place of payment was not prescribed, nor confined to the Temple.

Nor was the mother obliged to go to Jerusalem for the ceremony of purification; she was allowed to offer her sacrifice by proxy. Nevertheless, pious Jews who did not live too far from the Holy City made it a point to appear personally in the Lord's presence; and that is precisely what the Evangelist supposes in Mary's case. "When the time of their purification had been completed according to the Law of Moses, they carried the child to Jerusalem to present him to God, as it is written in the Law: Every male child opening the womb shall be consecrated to the Lord."[34]

---

[33] Num. 3:12–13. "I have set apart the children of Levi from the midst of Israel, to take the place of every first-born who opens his mother's womb. Since the day when I struck all the first-born of the land of Egypt, I have consecrated to myself all the first-born of Israel, both of man and beast. They are mine." Cf. Num. 8:16–17; Exod. 13:12–16; 34:19–21.

[34] Luke 2:22–24. The text of the Vulgate offers little difficulty, since ***dies purificationis ejus*** can refer to Mary, though she is mentioned only in Verse 19. But the Greek text adopted by all the critical editors (even Vogels) has τοῦ καθαρισμοῦ αὐτῶν, "***their*** purification." This cannot refer to both Mary and Joseph (as Godet, Meyer-Weiss, Plummer, etc., think), since there was no law of purification regarding the father. Nor can the word "their" with any better reason be referred to the mother and son, though Lagrange (*Saint Luc*, p. 82) thinks that καθαρισμός as applied to a son can mean "his ransom," for such expressions as "free," "quit of a debt" (καθαρός), are often found in the papyri (Deissmann, *Neue Bibelst.*, p. 24). But in that case the word καθαρισμός would have one meaning when referred to the mother, and another when referred to the son.

Some say that αὐτῶν refers to the Jews, though the Jews are not mentioned in the passage. This is not an impossible explanation; there are several analogous examples in St. Luke.

Our opinion is that "their" is collective and refers to both parents taken as one. This sense is confirmed by what follows: "*They* carried the child to Jerusalem." The purification, strictly speaking, applied only to Mary, but it is ***their*** common

Obviously this law applied no more to Jesus than it did to his mother. He belonged to God by an inalienable right, and did not have to be bought back.

Thus it was at their own choice that Joseph and Mary set out for Jerusalem, carrying the Infant in their arms. Joseph came to pay the five shekels demanded for the Child, a considerable sum considering the slight resources of the Holy Family; and Mary was to offer, in person, the sacrifice of the poor: two turtledoves or two small pigeons.[35] It was not difficult for her to procure these birds. They have always been plentiful in the Cedron valley, east of Bethlehem. Moreover they were sold on the Temple esplanade, and it was sufficient to deposit the price in one of the thirteen boxes provided for that purpose in the women's enclosure.

While the Holy Family was faithfully carrying out these legal prescriptions,[36] a resident of Jerusalem unexpectedly came up to them. He was Simeon, a just man who feared God and firmly hoped that the consoler of Israel was soon to come. The Holy Spirit had assured him that he would not die before seeing the Anointed of the Lord, the Messias promised to the patriarchs and announced by the prophets. It was also by a secret inspiration or some supernatural instinct that he came to the Temple, since he was not a priest, as some have supposed, and was not called there by sacred duties. Some have identified him with Simeon, the son of the great Hillel and father of Gamaliel, the famous doctor who was the first to merit the title of Rabban and was

---

concern. This collective sense is not rare in this Gospel. Harnack singles it out as a defect in St. Luke's style.

[35] The shekel was worth seventy-five cents in our currency, but it is to be noted that the purchasing power of money was much greater in those days. (Cf. Note O in Vol. II, on Jewish money. Translator.)

The Jews took the expression *omne masculinum aperiens vulvam* literally. Thus, if a man married a woman who already had children, he was no longer bound to repurchase his first-born. Secondly, if he married several virgins simultaneously or successively, he was bound to repurchase the first-born child of each of them, if it was a boy. Thirdly, in the case of a miscarriage or a stillborn child, the child who came afterward was the first-born as far as inheritance was concerned, but such a child was not subject to the law of repurchase.

[36] We do not know the usual ceremonial at this period, when the mother came to the Temple in person. It had nothing in common with that of modern Judaism. Cf. Edersheim, *Life and Times,* Vol. I, pp. 194–197.

St. Paul's teacher; but the only thing the two seem to have had in common is the name. In any event, the stranger took the divine Child into his arms and gave expression to his joy in this canticle of thanksgiving:

> Now, O Lord, allow thy servant
> to go his way according to thy word in peace;
> for my eyes have seen the salvation (the Saviour)
> that thou hast destined for all the nations:
> a light to enlighten the Gentiles,
> and glory of thy people Israel.[37]

Simeon had been waiting only for the realization of Israel's hopes and the accomplishment of the divine promises before breathing his last. His language was that of an old man, and tradition must be right in thus describing him. Like the aged Jacob when he found his son Joseph, he said: "Now can I die, since I have lived to see thy face again." But Simeon had seen far more than a beloved son; he had seen him whose face many saintly persons had aspired in vain to look upon. Like the ancient seers of Israel searching the horizon to announce to the world the coming of the Messias, Simeon had seen him and pointed him out. Now his task is done, and he petitions to be relieved from his watch.

Mary and Joseph were marveling at these things. The old man blesses them, either felicitating them upon their lot, or calling down upon them the blessings of heaven. Then he says to the mother: "This child is for the fall and the rise of many in Israel. He shall be a sign of contradiction; and a sword shall pierce thy soul. So shall be revealed the thoughts of many hearts." It is, indeed, the destiny of the Saviour to lay open the secrets of hearts, and to reveal the good and evil dispositions of men. Thus is he to be a sign of contradiction and division, a stone over which many shall stumble through their own fault, an occasion of the

[37] Luke 2:29–32. "Simeon represents himself under the figure of a sentinel stationed by his master on a lofty spot to watch for the appearance of a star, and to announce it to the world. He sees the longed-for star and proclaims its rising, and asks to be delivered from the post he has so long occupied. So too, in the opening of Aeschylus' *Agamemnon,* the sentinel stationed to observe the fire that will announce the capture of Troy, finally espying the impatiently awaited signal, chants at one and the same time the victory of the Greeks and his own deliverance" (Godet, *Saint Luc,* 2 ed., 1872, Vol. I, p. 171).

fall of those who shall refuse to receive him, but a source of glory for all who welcome him. For though he wills to save all men, he will not save them in spite of themselves or without their own co-operation.

Simeon's prophecy, as we have seen, intimately associates the sorrows of Mary with the persecutions which her Son is to undergo. The Passion of Jesus and the compassion of Mary always go hand in hand and reach their peak on Calvary. Mary's sorrows will be solely or principally caused by the sufferings of Jesus, while the most excruciating torment of Jesus will be to see his Mother's anguish at the foot of the Cross. Jesus saves the world by his sufferings; Mary is to be associated in this work of redemption by the sword that pierces her heart.

The aged Simeon was followed by Anna, a prophetess, the daughter of Phanuel of the tribe of Aser.[38] Her husband had died only seven years after their marriage, and she had lived in widowhood until the age of eighty-four, serving God night and day by prayer and fasting, hardly ever leaving the Temple. Her role in the Gospel story is altogether inconspicuous; it is not even stated that she spoke to the Holy Family; but we may assume that she did, for "she rapturously praised the Lord, and spoke of the Child to all who were awaiting the redemption of Jerusalem."

5. The Magi From the East

(MATTHEW 2:1–12)

"When Jesus was born in Bethlehem of Juda in the time of King Herod, Magi came from the East to Jerusalem, saying: Where is the King of the Jews who is just born? We have seen his star in the East and have come to adore him."[39]

---

[38] The gift of prophecy was not an exclusively masculine prerogative. The Rabbis enumerated forty-eight prophets and seven prophetesses: Sara, Mary (the sister of Moses), Debbora, Anna (the mother of Samuel), Abigail, Holda (a contemporary of Josias), and Esther (the liberatrix of the Jews).

[39] Matt. 2:2: "We have seen his star *in the East*" (ἐν ἀνατολῇ); and 2:9: "the star which they had seen *in the East*." The expression ἐν ἀνατολῇ can have three meanings: (1) "while we were in the East"; (2) "we saw the star *over to the East*"; (3) "We saw the star *at its rising*." The first sense is meaningless, for it is obvious that the Magi saw the star from *where they were* before they set

How many minor problems, problems which may never be solved, are brought up by these words of St. Matthew. Were the Magi kings or private persons? Were they Persian, Chaldean, or Arabian? What was the star that guided them, and how did they understand its silent message? Did they reach Bethlehem thirteen days after Christmas, or at a later date? "Who can say," says Bossuet, "and after all, what difference does it make? Is it not enough to know that they came from a land of ignorance, from the midst of the Gentiles, where God was not known, nor the Christ promised and expected? It is commonly believed that they were three, because of the three presents offered. The Church has not decided, and we need not be concerned about it."[40]

The term *Magi* implies an Eastern origin. As far back as we can go in history, the Magi appear as a Median tribe skilled in the art or secret of interpreting dreams. They were also the official sacrificers who immolated all victims.[41] Even after the accession of the Persian Cyrus, who supplanted the Median dynasty, they retained their influence and functions. When Darius introduced the cult of Zoroaster, and when the new worship of Mithra came into vogue, the Magi still remained the priestly caste.[42] They were then very much engaged in the study of astrology, necromancy, and divination by reading goblets, with the result that the name *magus* was finally applied to anyone who devoted himself to the occult sciences. We hear of Magi in Chaldea, Egypt, Armenia, Ethiopia, and Gaul.[43] Simon, St. Peter's opponent at Rome, and Elymas, St. Paul's opponent at Cyprus, were both Magi. St. Jerome rightly says that in everyday language *magus* simply meant magician.[44] In fact, from the beginning of the

---

out on their journey. The third sense is possible and fits in well, for it is the *rising* of stars that is of chief interest to astrologers. Still, the second sense is the most natural, and it is the one we accept. The Magi saw the star rising in *the East;* but we shall see later that it changes its direction.

[40] Bossuet, *Elévations sur les mystères,* 17me semaine, 3me élév.

[41] Herodotus, i, 101, 107, 120, 128, 132; vii, 19.

[42] Strabo, XV, iii, 1; XVI, ii, 39. Cf. Herodotus, vii, 131. Xenophon (*Cyropedeia,* VIII, i, 23) believed mistakenly that Cyrus had established them as a priesthood; they were such long before that time.

[43] Pliny, *Hist. Nat.,* XXV, v, 4 and xcv, 1 (Druids); XXX, i, 16 (Magi of Armenia).

[44] St. Jerome, *In Daniel,* 2:3 "Consuetudo et sermo communis magos pro maleficis accipit."

Christian era, the words *magus,* diviner, sorcerer, astrologer, Chaldean, mathematician, horoscope reader, fortuneteller, enchanter, charmer, and witch were practically synonymous. It is clear however that St. Matthew does not intend the word in any derogatory sense; he uses rather the favorable meaning it had once had. To him, as to Strabo, Magi are sages and wise men, "zealous observers of justice and virtue," eager investigators of heavenly phenomena, who, according to Philo, "searched out the secrets of nature to come to a knowledge of the truth."[45]

Ancient documents of Christian art and literature tell us no more, and the paintings in the catacombs are rather disconcerting in their discrepancies.[46] One, which goes back to the early second century, shows Mary, her hair dressed in the fashion of contemporary Roman matrons, holding in her arms the Child clad in swaddling clothes. The Magi are coming toward her, bareheaded, carrying gifts; there is nothing to indicate either their nationality or their kingly status. Other frescoes present them in a wide variety of garb: sometimes in short tunics, sometimes wrapped in sweeping mantles, with Phrygian caps. When the Blessed Virgin is in the center of the scene, the Magi are divided in twos on either side of her, doubtless for the sake of symmetry; otherwise there are always three. Either for simplicity, or by deliberate intent of the artist, St. Joseph never appears. We find the same diversity on fourth- and fifth-century sarcophagi, as well as in mosaics of a later period, except that in the latter St. Joseph appears occasionally, and the Magi begin to wear crowns. All of which goes to prove that these ancient representations are merely conventional, and that on no point is there a genuine tradition.

The Magi were not kings. If they had been, St. Matthew would not have failed to mention the fact, and Herod would have given them a better reception. If, at the beginning of the sixth century, they were transformed into kings, it was rather to indicate a literal

---

[45] Strabo, *Geography,* XV, iii, 6; Philo, *Quod omnis probus liber* (Mangey, Vol. II, p. 456). St. Jerome (*In Dan.* 2:2) calls the Magi philosophers.

[46] Cf. Wilpert, *Le pitture delle catacombe Romane,* 1923, pp. 176–186. Thirteen representations of the Magi from the second to the fourth century are still visible there, in whole or in part. On the sarcophagi and mosaics, cf. Rohault de Fleury, *L'Evangile. Etudes iconographiques,* 1874, pp. 56–74.

fulfillment of a badly understood prophecy, "The kings of Tharsis and the islands shall offer gifts, the kings of Arabia and Saba shall pay tribute. All the kings of the earth shall adore him."[47]

From what country did they come? Their name suggests Media or Persia. But it is not likely that Persians, who spoke an Indo-European language quite different from Aramaic could have made themselves understood in Palestine, or that they could have found interpreters. Lacking clearer evidence, we should regard Arabia as the land of the Magi. Their gifts suggest this, since incense and myrrh usually came from Arabia, which was also famous for its treasures of gold. The Jews called the country beyond the Jordan and the Dead Sea the East. There lay the kingdom of the Nabateans, known as the Arabian kingdom, whose capital was Petra, and which extended at that time all the way to Damascus. Great numbers of Jews lived there, and the two peoples had frequent commerce with each other. Their idioms were more like two dialects of the same tongue than separate languages.

When they saw a new star rise in the East, the Magi concluded that the king of the Jews had been born. This could not have been an ordinary star. St. John Chrysostom well observes that heavenly bodies are used by astrologers to read the horoscope of a newborn child, but not to discover the time of its birth.[48] The difficulty would be less, but still real, if it were merely a question of those short-lived stars that flare up suddenly in the firmament, shine brilliantly for awhile, and go out as quickly as they appeared. This must have been an extraordinary phenomenon which aroused attention and presaged something unusual.

Several interpreters have suggested that it was an altogether different kind of luminous body, created by God expressly for this purpose, and guided by an angel; this is a very simple explanation that seems to eliminate all difficulties. Certainly, nothing is impossible for God. But even in miracles he ordinarily observes

---

[47] Ps. 71 (72):10. According to Patrizi (*De evangeliis,* Vol. II, p. 321), no author antedating the sixth century said expressly that the Magi were kings, although in referring to them several quote the text from the Psalms. Perhaps the first to call them such was Caesarius of Arles, in a sermon falsely attributed to St. Augustine.

[48] St. John Chrysostom, *In Matthaeum,* hom. vi, 1 (MG, LVII, 62–63).

a certain economy of means, and usually puts secondary causes into play when they can be used for his purpose. Accordingly, this hypothesis of a new creation has few adherents today.

Kepler's explanation enjoyed wide popularity for many years. On May 21, 747 A.U.C., three years before Herod's death, the planet Jupiter went into conjunction with Saturn, and on the following February 15, Mars joined Jupiter, before Saturn had moved a great distance. The three planets thus closely aligned presented a most remarkable spectacle, and it must have been even more striking a short time later when they all disappeared together in the glow of dawn. The dates fit satisfactorily, but a fatal objection against this hypothesis is that the word used by St. Matthew never means a constellation or a sign of the Zodiac or any astronomical grouping, but always an isolated heavenly body: a planet, a star, a comet, or a celestial meteor.[49]

Consequently, present-day scholarship is coming more and more to favor Origen's opinion, that the object was a comet.[50] These luminous bodies, with their capricious paths, bizarre shapes, and changing dimensions, have always stimulated men's imaginations. Prophetic meanings were attributed to them. True, they were usually taken for evil omens, heralding cataclysms, catastrophes, or revolutions. But they were occasionally thought to presage illustrious births, such as that of Mithridates. The reign of Augustus, too, was announced by a comet.[51] It happens also that these fantastic bodies, after disappearing for some months, reappear on the opposite horizon and arouse even greater wonder. Yet if the star of the Magi was a comet, it was certainly not the famous Halley's comet, as was once believed, for that comet blazed up twelve years before our era, too long before the Saviour's birth.

---

[49] Boll, *Der Stern der Weisen* (in *Z.N.T.W.*, 1917, pp. 40–48) has proved this decisively. Ἄστρον can be used of a group of stars or of a single star; but ἀστήρ (which is St. Matthew's word) is never used of a group. The older lexicons had said the same.

[50] Origen, *Contra Celsum,* i, 58 (ed. Koetschau, p. 109). The word κομήτης is an adjective, ordinarily joined to ἀστήρ or used as a noun. It is the long-haired star (from κόμη "head of hair"). There are bearded comets (πωγωνίαι), and those that take the shape of a beam (δοκίδηs), or cask (πίθοι), etc.

[51] Justinus, *Hist.,* xxxvii, 2 (for Mithridates); Servius, on the Aeneid, x, 272 (for Augustus).

If the appearance of a new star, though a very vague symbol in itself, made people think of the king of the Jews rather than of any other, it is because a Messias-King was then commonly expected in Palestine, and this expectation was not unknown among neighboring peoples. Roman historians and Jewish apocalypses could be quoted in proof of this.[52] A more revealing fact, however, is that at the death of Herod three false Messiases arose at almost the same time. One, Judas the Galilean, succeeded in taking possession of Sepphoris, a town near Nazareth, and terrorized the whole neighborhood for a considerable time. Another, a former slave of Herod, and outstanding for his commanding appearance, put the Jordan valley to fire and sword, and eventually met death in battle. The third, named Athrongeus, was a mere shepherd endowed with herculean strength; he was overcome by the Romans, whom he dared to challenge. All three, as Josephus expressly states, aspired to the throne of Judea and had assumed crowns.[53] Besides these, we know that there were many other claimants whose names have not been preserved by history.[54]

To the Jews the coming of the Messias meant the realization of Balaam's prophecy, "A star rises out of Jacob and a scepter is lifted up from Israel."[55] The Messias, it is true, is the Star; but it is only a step from this to say that a star would announce the Messias, and this step had been taken by the Rabbis. The leader of the last insurrection of Jewish patriots, under the Emperor Hadrian, owed a great deal of his amazing success to his surname, Bar-Kokheba, "Son of the Star."

Was the prophecy of Balaam, with its commentaries, known

---

[52] Tacitus, *Hist.*, v, 13; Suetonius, *Vespasian*, 4. For the Jewish Apocalypses, cf. Edersheim, *Life and Times*, Vol. I, pp. 172–179.

[53] Josephus, *Antiq.*, XVII, x, 4–8 and *Bellum*, II, iv, 1–3. According to these passages, Judas the Galilean posed as a king and had himself treated as such. Simon assumed a crown and had himself called king; the shepherd Athrongeus, too, was proclaimed king and wore a crown.

[54] These aspirants to royalty were numerous, according to Josephus (*Bellum*, II, iv, 1: συχνοὺς βασιλειᾶν ὁ καιρὸς ἀνέπειθεν).

[55] Num. 24:17, the targum of Onkelos and the Jerusalem targum translated:

A star shall rise out of Jacob
and the Messias shall rule over Israel.

On Jewish exegesis, cf. Billerbeck, Vol. I, pp. 76–77 and Edersheim, Vol. I, pp. 111–112.

to the Magi? Evidently not, if they lived in Persia or distant Media; but if they came from the Arabian kingdom of the Nabateans, bordering on Palestine, it is not at all unlikely, in view of the similarity of their languages and their frequent contacts with the Jews. By this we do not mean to exclude an interior revelation; God, who called them to his Son's cradle, knew how to make them understand his call.

The capital of Judea was well known, and there was no need of a star to lead them to it. Their arrival stirred the whole city. Herod was frightened when his agents warned him that these strangers were looking for some other King of the Jews; but he had escaped so many plots and foiled so many intrigues, by ruse or violence, that he anticipated no great difficulty in ridding himself of this new secret rival.

He gathered together the princes of the priests, the official guardians of religious traditions, and the Scribes, the authorized interpreters of Scripture. This was not a plenary assembly of the Sanhedrin, whose influence Herod dreaded and whose prestige he was always trying to diminish, but a group of counselors of his own choice, who would be well prepared to tell him where the expected Messias was to be born. They replied unhesitatingly, "In Bethlehem of Juda, for it is written: And thou, Bethlehem, land of Juda, thou art not the least of the princes of Juda, for from thee shall be born a leader who shall rule my people Israel."[56] Herod now knew what he wanted to know. Suspicious by nature and habit, he summoned the Magi secretly to learn from them at what precise moment the star had appeared to them. He dismissed them, saying: "Go to Bethlehem and strive earnestly to find the child, and when you have found him return to tell me, that I too may go to worship him."

"With this assurance they departed, and, behold, the star

[56] Mich. 5:2. The Hebrew is somewhat different:

> And thou, Bethlehem, Ephrata,
> Little among the clans of Juda,
> From thee shall come forth to me
> He that shall rule over Israel.

St. Matthew modifies the text, either citing it as the Scribes consulted by Herod quoted it, or following a variant reading unknown to us, or accommodating it to circumstances. Bethlehem, in itself so lowly, is not such when considered as the birthplace of the Messias.

which they had seen in the East went before them to a place above the spot where was the child. And seeing the star they were filled with a great joy. Having entered the house, they found the child with Mary his mother, and falling on their knees they adored him. Then they opened their treasures and offered him their gifts: gold, incense, and myrrh."[57]

The Magi did not come empty-handed, for Orientals scarcely ever pay a visit to a superior without offering gifts. They brought the most precious products of their country. Incense and myrrh were in fact the principal products of Arabia.[58] These came also from other regions, such as India and Egypt; but the Arabians controlled the market, and thanks to this lucrative commerce, gold too was plentiful among them, so much so that it could be exchanged at ridiculous prices. To their presents the Magi added the homage due to a sovereign and a God. True, it was the usage of the time to prostrate oneself before mere mortals, as a sign of respect and veneration; but the majority of the Fathers see in this attitude of the Magi real adoration, an act of latria. Would they have come from such a distance to pay homage to a mere man, who in no way concerned them? Further-

---

[57] Matt. 2:9–10. Note the details: (1) *Behold* (καὶ ἰδού) indicates surprise. They did not expect it, hence their joy. (2) "They had seen the star in the East" or "over to the East" (ἐν ἀνατολῇ), but they had not seen it afterward; for nothing proves that it guided or followed them to Jerusalem. (3) "The star goes before them" or "leads them." Προάγειν can mean *precede* or *conduct,* but the first sense is more natural, since the route from Jerusalem to Bethlehem is easy to find. (4) "The star stopped (ἐστάθη) above the place where Jesus was." Schanz (*Matthäus,* 1879, p. 105) remarks: "Since Bethlehem is south of Jerusalem, and since no star moves southward, the moving and stopping of the star partakes of the miraculous." (5) "They entered the house." The cave could not be called a house (οἰκία) unless it were certain that the Holy Family was still there; and nothing is less certainly established than that. (6) "They found the child and his mother." The shepherds had found in the cave "the child, Mary, and Joseph" (Luke 2:16). The Magi who had come to find Jesus did not concern themselves with Joseph; or perhaps Joseph was absent at the time, busy at work. (7) "Falling on their knees they adored (or venerated) the child" (πεσόντες προσεκύνησαν αὐτῷ). We prefer the first.

Since the sacred authors are in the habit of describing natural phenomena as they appear to the senses, some commentators think that they are doing so here; but it is difficult to understand the Evangelist's words in this way without doing violence to them. The moving and stopping of the star seem to be miraculous.

[58] On the incense and myrrh, of which the Arabians had a monopoly, cf. Pliny, *Hist. nat.,* xii, 30–35. On the gold, incense, and myrrh of Arabia, cf. Strabo, *Geograph.,* xvi, 18–19.

more, does not the nature of their gifts create the surmise that they intended to honor a superhuman being? Among almost all peoples, incense was reserved for the Divinity, and it was always offered sparingly. The story is told of Leonidas, mentor of Alexander the Great, that when he saw his pupil throwing handfuls of incense on the altars of his gods, he advised him to be less lavish with it until he had conquered the lands that produced it. The Hebrews added an offering of incense to all their sacrifices, except the sacrifice for sin. They also burned it twice a day in the sanctuary on the Altar of Incense.

The symbolism in these gifts is so obvious that we are not surprised to meet it in the most ancient ecclesiastical writers. The poet Juvencus gave it this polished turn, "They offer gold, incense, myrrh, to king, God, and man." Less concisely, St. Irenaeus comments, "They offer myrrh to him who is to die, gold to him whose kingdom will not end, incense to the God of the Jews who now manifests himself to the Gentiles."[59] Myrrh especially was used for burials; the Jews sprinkled it on corpses; the Egyptians, when embalming the bodies of the rich, packed them with myrrh mixed with other substances, but never with incense.[60] In offering to Jesus the best their country could produce, the Magi doubtless did not have in mind any such subtle refinements, but the spirit of God which guided their hand and that of the Evangelist may well have wished to suggest this figurative sense.

Herod had hoped to deceive the Magi by his hypocritical protestations. No scruple would have kept him from ridding himself of a rival, and the idea of a general massacre of the newborn children of Bethlehem held no terrors for him. But he preferred to avoid a slaughter that would make him even more odious, and counted on the Magi to select a single victim for him. Heaven interfered to save the Child. As the Magi were preparing to start back for Jerusalem, an angel warned them to return home by another route. It would be easy to do so. Seven or eight hours'

---

[59] Juvencus, i, 285; St. Irenaeus, *Haer.*, iii, 10. St. Cyprian, St. Justin, Tertullian, Origen, and other more recent writers propose a similar symbolism. The verses of Prudentius are well known (Hymn at Lauds, Feast of the Epiphany).

[60] Herodotus, ii, 86: "The body was filled with powdered myrrh, cinnamon, and other perfumes, *incense alone being excluded.*"

travel would bring them to the Jordan, beyond the Cedron, and by the time Herod learned of their flight they would be safely beyond reach. They probably left that same night before dawn, to avoid arousing suspicion.

Their stay at Bethlehem was not a long one. The distrustful Herod would have been quickly disturbed by any delay, but we have no more data on their departure than on their arrival. St. Augustine thought that they arrived thirteen days after the Nativity, since the Church celebrates the Epiphany on that date; but the mysteries commemorated by the Epiphany did not all take place on the same day, and it cannot be maintained that the Holy Family stayed at Bethlehem and then went up to the Temple at Jerusalem for the presentation of the Child and the purification of his Mother a month after the Magi departed.

6. Flight Into Egypt and Massacre of the Innocents

"An angel appeared in a dream to Joseph, saying: Arise, take the little one and his mother, and flee into Egypt, and remain there until I tell thee further. For Herod is about to seek the child to kill him."[61]

As head of the Holy Family Joseph receives the message and is charged with carrying it out. He rises at once and awakens Mary. The order is peremptory and the danger pressing; there is not a moment to lose. The preparations do not take long; a few belongings, tools, provisions to get together, and before dawn the fugitives are already on the road to Gaza or Hebron. Four or five days' walking would bring them to Rhinocolura, on the Egyptian frontier. There they were safe and had a chance to meet fellow countrymen, for Egypt was the traditional refuge of persecuted Jews.[62] There they might join a caravan to continue their journey.

---

61 Matt. 2:13–14. Their departure was very sudden. St. Joseph was warned in a dream, or rather "during sleep" (κατ' ὄναρ) and departed "during the night" (νυκτός), evidently the same night as the Magi. It must be recalled that Bethlehem is only approximately five miles from Jerusalem, and that Herod could be informed at any moment of the flight of the Magi.

62 Jeroboam fled there (3 Kings 11:40), as did the son of the High Priest

The apocryphal gospels turn this journey into a continuous idyll. Dragons and leopards bow before the Child Jesus; trees bend over to shade Mary from the sun; kindly lions guide the beast of burden with its humble baggage. There would be a certain naïve charm in these legends, if we could forget their lowly origin. One, for example, has attracted the brush of painters. Mary, worn out from walking and the blistering heat, was resting under a palm tree which was loaded with fruit at the top. "I would like," she says, "to taste, if possible, the fruit of this tree." "It is the lack of water," says Joseph, "that concerns me; our water bottles are empty." Then Jesus says to the tree, "Bend over and give my Mother thy fruit." The tree bows to Mary's feet, and when they have plucked the dates, Jesus commands, "Straighten up and open thy roots and let water flow." The tree obeys instantly, and from its roots flows a fresh clear stream. When the pilgrims are again under way the path behind them disappears as though by magic. Arriving in the land of Hermopolis, in a city called Sotinen, where they are complete strangers, they enter a temple containing three hundred and sixty-five idols, which all immediately fall to the ground in a thousand pieces. Thus was accomplished the prophecy of Isaias, "The Lord shall come on a light cloud, he shall enter Egypt, and all the works of the Egyptians shall tremble before his face."[63]

But history is less poetic than legend. Before the building of a railroad during World War I, the journey from Palestine to Egypt held no charms. One index is the account given by a religious of the seventeenth century, who is trying not to paint too black a picture for fear of discouraging future pilgrims: "One must be resigned to twenty-three days on a camel, exposed to the night dews and the excessive heat of sand ablaze in the scorching sunlight. For the hundred or more leagues of the journey you see not a stone, nor a stream of water, nor a spring. . . . Not a bush as tall as your finger, not a blade of grass the size of a hair." And the pious pilgrim concludes, "One bears up

---

Onias III (Josephus, *Antiq.*, XII, ix, 7). According to Philo, there were at this time a million Jews in Egypt.

[63] Pseudo-Matthew, *Book of the Nativity of Mary and the Infancy of the Saviour,* Chap. xx–xxiii (very much abridged). This apocryphal writing is from the sixth century.

patiently under all this discomfort because the Holy Family suffered even more."[64] It is possible that this good Franciscan was not yet sufficiently acclimated or had chosen a bad time for his pilgrimage, but at any season the journey from Jerusalem to Cairo would have been very difficult and oppressively monotonous.

Tradition about the stay of the Holy Family in Egypt is vague and uncertain. In the Coptic chapel in Old Cairo there is a place which is supposed to have served as their refuge. Since the fifth century, legend has made them go all the way to Hermopolis, a city of Upper Egypt near Antinoë. The legend of the sycamore and the well of Matariyeh near ancient Heliopolis seems no older than the thirteenth century.[65]

The Holy Family was not far from Bethlehem when Herod realized that the Magi had duped him. The half-tamed barbarian flew into an epileptic frenzy. He immediately sent his henchmen to massacre all male children of Bethlehem and the vicinity under two years of age. This atrocious measure will not seem incredible if we recall that the cruel despot had successively murdered his father-in-law, the old King Hyrcanus, his first wife Mariamne whom he loved passionately, his mother-in-law Alexandra, his brother-in-law Costobar, and his own sons Alexander and Aristobulus, and that he was even then waiting for permission from Augustus to execute a third son, Antipater. Josephus relates that the bloody tyrant had locked up five thousand prominent men in the theater at Jericho, giving express orders to kill them as soon as he himself should die, in order to forestall general rejoicing at his death. Human life, in Judea as elsewhere, was very cheap. In Rome, in one day, four hundred slaves were led to death to-

---

64 J. Goujon, *Histoire et voyage de la terre Sainte,* Lyons, 1670, pp. 291–293. The distance given by the author (one hundred leagues) is not exaggerated, since it is a good 300 miles between Jerusalem and Cairo. But, exasperating though a camel's pace may be, one wonders how he could have taken "twenty-three days, at the rate of fourteen or fifteen hours a day."

65 Ancient Cairo is a little to the south of the present Cairo. *Matariyeh* is 4 or 5 miles northeast of Cairo near the obelisk of Heliopolis. The sycamore and the spring are very well described by Fr. Jullien (*L'arbre de la Vierge à Matarieh,* Cairo, 1904). Matariyeh is mentioned in the *Arabic Gospel of the Infancy,* xxv; but Fr. Peeters has proved that the passage is an interpolation (*Evangiles apocryphes,* Vol. II, p. xxvii). The Tree of the Virgin has disappeared, and the spring is now lost in the infiltrations of the Nile.

gether, because their master had been found dead in his home; the law on the point was implacable. The life of a newborn child was worth even less; the father was free to dispose of it at pleasure. Suetonius relates that a prodigy occurring before the birth of Augustus made people believe that a king of Rome was soon to be born. To avert this calamity, the senate was bent on decreeing the death of all male children to be born that year; but thanks to powerful intervention, the *senatus-consultus* was not inserted in the archives and remained a dead letter. Though the story is doubtful, it is enough for our purpose that it seemed credible at the time. Later, when the appearance of a comet struck fear into Rome, Nero's astrologer declared that a few striking murders were needed to ward off this evil omen. Consequently Nero had a great number of nobles killed and their sons poisoned or massacred with their tutors. Herod was easily Nero's equal, and the murder of some thirty or forty children was nothing to disturb him.

Popular from earliest times was the feast of the Holy Innocents, those "flowers of the martyrs" cut off in the morning of life by the tyrant's sword, like rosebuds plucked by a tempest. The Church celebrates it today with a poignant commingling of joy and sadness. She exults with the angels who gather these chosen ones to heaven, as innocent as themselves. She mourns with the disconsolate mothers, because they do not know their children's happiness.

> A voice is heard in Rama,
> cries and lamentations unceasing:
> it is Rachel weeping for her children;
> she is inconsolable, because they are no more.[66]

In these words Jeremias deplored the extermination of the northern tribes, but his lamentations were appropriate in all national catastrophes and even in individual tragedies. The prophet had depicted Rachel mourning in Rama, the center of

[66] Matt. 2:17–18, citing Jer. 31:15. Rachel, the mother of Benjamin and of Joseph the father of Ephraim, was buried on the Ephrata-Bethlehem road (Gen 35:19). On the heights of Rama, in the center of the tribe of Benjamin, she mourned over the calamities of Ephraim, whose territory was dominated by Rama.

the tribe of her son Benjamin, over the disastrous fate of Ephraim, another of Jacob's sons. By a sublime personification, the Evangelist represents her as rising from her grave at the gates of Bethlehem to join in the mothers' grief. By allowing the word "Rama" to remain in this quotation, St. Matthew clearly shows that he does not intend a literal application of the text.

The massacre of the Innocents was one of Herod's last crimes: God's patience had been exhausted. The tyrant learned that the heir presumptive to the throne was plotting his death. Antipater, impatient to rule, felt that his father had lived long enough. Voluntary denunciations and cleverly chosen tortures brought the whole affair to light. Herod called an extraordinary tribunal which pronounced the death sentence against this unnatural son, and an embassy was sent to Rome to secure the Emperor's confirmation of the sentence.

Meanwhile the old King was attacked by so strange a malady that everyone saw in it a heaven-sent punishment. An internal fire with no external rise in temperature was slowly devouring him. His entrails became ulcerated, every muscle ached, his feet and belly swelled up and were covered with blood. His genitalia started to decay and breed worms. He was like a putrefying corpse.

In spite of everything, the dying man clung desperately to life. Quacks and astrologers, whose orders he followed blindly, prescribed the waters of Callirrhoe. This famous spring was situated east of the Dead Sea, at the foot of the mountain dominated by the fortress of Machaerus. Herod had himself carried there from Jericho, but the miraculous waters gave no relief. A bath in warm oil almost suffocated him. He was rushed back to the palace at Jericho, and the rumor of his imminent death stimulated revolts everywhere. Two celebrated teachers, Judas and Matthias, followed by a veritable army of disciples, dared in broad daylight to tear down the golden eagle which Herod had placed on the pediment of the Temple in defiance of Jewish Law. The dismal monarch was at a loss to invent a torment to punish this affront. He finally had the two leaders burned alive, with some fifty of their confederates. Shortly afterward he had a moment of gloomy comfort: the reply from Rome was favorable; Augustus allowed him to execute the death sentence against his son Antipater. His own death followed five days later.

In his will Herod assigned Judea, Samaria, and Idumea, together with the title of king, to Archelaus, his son by Malthace the Samaritan. He divided his other states between Antipas and Philip, with the title of tetrarchs, but he had stipulated that his will should be valid only on the approval of Augustus.

It was early in April, in the fourth year before our era. Archelaus had his father's body transported to Herodium, near Bethlehem, and gave it a magnificent funeral. After a week of mourning, he appeared before the great number of people gathered in Jerusalem for the Passover. Without as yet taking the title of king, he had assumed all the powers. From a gilded throne he answered requests, granted pardons and favors, consented to the reduction of taxes. But when the crowds, deceived by his good-natured attitude, began to shout for the death of those implicated in the legal murder of Judas and Matthias, he called their demands extravagant and let loose his bodyguard to kill a great number of the rioters.[67]

Under these unfavorable auspices he started for Rome. Antipas and other members of the family went along, either to march in his retinue or to work surreptitiously for their own advancement. Their departure was the signal for more riots and fresh massacres. A delegate of Augustus, commissioned, it was said, to sequestrate Herod's treasures, was besieged by the aroused populace in the royal palace. Varus, governor of Syria, the man who was one day to perish miserably in the forests of Germany, had to come at the head of his legions to free the delegate. Emerging victorious, he crucified two thousand of the rebels who had most seriously compromised themselves.

Nevertheless Archelaus, assisted by a clever lawyer, Nicholas of Damascus, might have won his cause at Caesar's tribunal, had not a deputation from Jerusalem, supported by the eight thousand

[67] Josephus, no doubt with some exaggeration, says "three thousand" (*Antiq.*, XVII, ix, 3). The history of the last days of Herod and the accession of Archelaus is well summarized by Schürer (*Geschichte,* 4 ed., Vol. I, pp. 411–424) following Josephus, whose *Antiquities* and *Jewish War* are almost our only source for the period. One may also consult F. de Saulcy (*Histoire d'Hérode roi des Juifs,* 1867, pp. 334–380). The author gives a lengthy account of the trial and condemnation of Antipater.

Jews in Rome, come to ask the Emperor to keep Archelaus from the throne and to annex Judea to the province of Syria. After long hesitation, Augustus finally confirmed Herod's will, except on one point: Archelaus received Judea, Samaria, and Idumea, but not the royal crown which he ambitioned and which his father had destined for him. He had to be satisfied with the title of ethnarch. Antipas and Philip shared the other states of Herod, except the cities of Gaza, Hippos, and Gadara, which were returned to Syria. Antipas received Galilee and Perea. Philip occupied the semipagan regions of the north: Batanea, Gaulanitis, Auranitis, Traconitis, and a part of Iturea.

This was the state of things in Palestine in the autumn of the fourth year before our era, when Archelaus returned to Jerusalem.

CHAPTER III

The Mystery of the Hidden Life

1. The Accounts of the Holy Infancy

THE oral instruction given by the Apostles used to begin with the baptism of Christ and end with his Ascension; and it is within this framework that the Second Gospel, the most perfect type of the primitive catechesis, confines itself. Soon, however, the piety of the faithful prompted a desire to go back to the beginning and learn where Jesus came from and what he was before the start of his public life. This desire was satisfied by the two chapters which St. Matthew and St. Luke place as a kind of preface to their Gospels. Their accounts are necessarily alike in the chief threads of which they are woven: the chaste marriage of Joseph and Mary, the virginal conception of Jesus and his birth at Bethlehem, and the return of the Holy Family to Nazareth. But in other respects the two accounts are quite different. And it is readily apparent that, though St. Matthew and St. Luke used the same sources, each independently made from them a selection of those elements which served his distinct purpose.

St. Matthew's attention is focused more on St. Joseph, the scion of David, the legal father of Jesus, head and guardian of the Holy Family. He had sources of information about Joseph, because he had lived in the company of James, the Brother of the Lord, and of Joseph's nephews, Simon and Jude, the sons of Cleophas. His whole account pivots around Joseph. It is to Joseph that God speaks commanding him to take Mary into his home and act as a father to the Son she is going to bear. It is

Joseph whom the angel warns to flee at once to Egypt to save the life of the Child. It is to him again that the heavenly messenger comes to announce the death of the tyrant, when it is time to return from exile. Joseph is the responsible head of the family, who in each case takes the initiative in making decisions.

St. Luke, on the other hand, centers the account of the infancy around Mary, the mother of Jesus. He notes not only her actions and words, but her impressions and most intimate thoughts, as though he were reading her heart. He describes her confusion on hearing the angel's eulogistic greeting and her wonder at the ancient Simeon's valedictory to life. Twice — in the stable of Bethlehem and in the home at Nazareth — he speaks of her gathering into her heart the memories of the marvels wrought in her presence, as if to lay them by, later to nourish her soul on them: *Maria conservabat omnia verba haec conferens in corde suo.*

Surely the intimacies of Nazareth on the day of the Annunciation, and the secrets of Bethlehem on Christmas night, could be known only from the confidences of Mary, and there is universal agreement that St. Luke must have drawn his information directly or indirectly from her. We know how careful he always was to learn from eyewitnesses. Probably he had not conversed with the Blessed Virgin herself, although it is not impossible that he should have, since we are not certain when Mary died or when the Evangelist was converted. But he could have been in contact with several of her companions and other members of her family. He betrays, for example, a very marked interest in the group of generous women who devotedly put their resources at the service of Christ. He tells us that there were many of these heroines; some of them, such as Joanna, the wife of Chusa, and Susanna, are known to us only through St. Luke. He could also have had access to written documents; we think that the *Benedictus* and the *Magnificat* were among them. The Biblical tone of his account of the infancy would seem to indicate that it is a translation from the Hebrew or the Aramaic; but this tone was perhaps deliberately adopted by the author in order that the gracious subject might have as its vehicle a suitable simplicity of style.

Whether he borrows his materials from oral tradition or written documents, in either case St. Luke stamps them with the seal of his own artistry. His two chapters are a diptych in which Jesus and John are placed opposite each other, with Mary as the center and link between them. The two sketches constantly parallel each other, though the colors are different, in keeping with the subject. There is, for instance, the message of Gabriel to Zachary, and his message to the Blessed Virgin; the miraculous conception of John, and the virginal conception of Jesus; the birth of the Precursor, the joy of his family, his circumcision, the canticle of Zachary, and, in parallel fashion, the birth of Jesus, the adoration of the shepherds, the presentation in the Temple, and the canticle of the aged Simeon; finally, there is the growth of the Precursor up to his withdrawal to the desert, and the physical, intellectual, and moral growth of Jesus under the eyes of his happy and wondering Mother. However, on closer examination, most of these comparisons turn into contrasts; but it could not be otherwise, when the two members of the parallel are Jesus and John.

There can be no reasonable doubt that in St. Luke and St. Matthew the account of the infancy was always an integral part of the Gospel. Only an *a priori* denial of miracles and an aversion to the supernatural could have led to a denial of its historical character.[1]

---

[1] Durand's monograph, *L'Enfance de J.-C.* (Paris, 1908), may be read with profit.

J. Gresham Machen, *The Virgin Birth of Christ* (London, 1930), devotes more than half of his remarkable work to an examination of the following questions: authenticity, integrity, characteristics, origin, and credibility of the accounts of Luke and Matthew, and the relations between the two accounts. The author thinks it more probable that Luke used a written source, either Greek or Aramaic, at least for certain sections. This is also the most common opinion. Fr. Médebielle, however (*Dict. de la Bible, Supplément,* Vol. I, col. 268), without altogether rejecting the theory of written documents, finds no proof that they were used. We are inclined to be less positive, at least as regards the *Magnificat* and the *Benedictus.* Dalman (*Die Worte Jesu,* 2 ed., 1930, p. 31) admits the possibility that the *Hebrew style* of the first two chapters of St. Luke comes from Luke himself. The beginning of the Acts offers a similar phenomenon.

The explanation given by Godet (*L'Evangile de Saint Luc,* 2 ed., 1872, Vol. I, pp. 202–203) is worth quoting: "These two narrative cycles emanate from two different environments, one from the circle in which Joseph was the central figure, and of which we may take Cleophas as a representative. . . . The narrative preserved in this circle could easily have come to the ear of the author of the first Gospel. But a cycle of narratives must also have taken shape

2. The Return to Nazareth

"After the death of Herod, an angel of the Lord appeared in a dream to Joseph in Egypt and said to him, 'Arise, take the child and his mother and return to the land of Israel; for they are dead that sought the life of the child.' So Joseph arose and took the child and his mother and returned to the land of Israel. But having learned that Archelaus was reigning in Judea in the place of Herod, his father, he feared to go there. Being warned in a dream, he withdrew into the district of Galilee and came to dwell in a town called Nazareth. Thus was fulfilled the saying of the prophets, 'He shall be called a Nazarene.' "[2]

Joseph obeyed heaven's orders with the same promptness as before; his preparations for the return were no more protracted than those for the departure. Once more he had to cross the desert between Egypt and Palestine, but the joy of seeing his native land soon again helped him to bear cheerfully hunger, thirst, and fatigue. It appears to have been his intention to settle at Bethlehem. Since, by the disposition of Providence, the Heir of David had been born in Bethlehem, was it not in keeping with God's designs to establish there the royal house from which the Messias was to come? Some think, not without warrant, that after the purification of Mary and the presentation of Jesus in the Temple, the Holy Family had gone back to Nazareth, not to take up their abode there, but only to put their affairs in order and then transfer their residence to Bethlehem; and that they had returned to Bethlehem before the arrival of the Magi.

When once more on the soil of Judea, Joseph learned that Archelaus had come into power. Of all Herod's sons, except

---

around Mary in the retreat where she brought her career to a close. These latter must have been of a more intimate kind and must have penetrated more deeply beneath the surface of the events. Without doubt, these are the ones which Luke collected and has preserved."

[2] Matt. 2:19–23. Note: (*a*) "Herod being dead, *behold* (ἰδού)" seems to denote identity of time: "*As soon as* Herod died." And, in fact, after the death of Herod there was no longer any reason to stay in Egypt. (*b*) "*They* are dead." This is what grammarians call a generic plural, designating Herod alone. (*c*) "Take the child and his mother and return to the land of Israel," as in Exod. 4:19, which concerns the return of Moses from Madian to Egypt. (*d*) "Archelaus was reigning." He was commonly called king; actually, as we have seen, he was merely ethnarch.

Antipater, who was a devil incarnate, none had a more hateful reputation. He inherited his father's wild cruelty, his unbridled craving for pleasure, his cunning and deceit. Joseph sensed danger in the neighborhood of this monster, who perhaps shared his father's superstitious fears and obsession with the Messianic peril, at a time when Palestine was unsettled by reason of the appearance of so many false Messiases. It was probably at Gaza that Joseph learned of the change. And so, instead of continuing on the road to Bethlehem, two days distant by easy travel, he turned to the north, through Ascalon, Ashdod, and Caesarea. From there a direct road through the pass of Mageddo and over the plain of Esdrelon led to Nazareth.

It is impossible to determine with any assurance the length of the exile. But events were so precipitous that they may not have been in Egypt more than a few months or even a few weeks. We shall not enter here on a detailed chronological discussion, which would be both complex and tedious. It is enough to know that a body of evidence reaching the point of certitude places the death of Herod in the spring of the year 750 A.U.C. (the fourth year before the Christian era). Various considerations lead us to place the birth of the Saviour toward the end of the year 748 A.U.C. (the sixth year before our era). Hence in this interval of about fifteen months occurred the purification of Mary, the visit of the Magi, the flight into Egypt, and the return to Nazareth. If this be so, the sojourn in Egypt was no longer than a year, and probably shorter; at any rate, a sojourn of seven years, which some defend, is altogether improbable.

In St. Matthew, the sojourn in Egypt and the return to Nazareth are the fulfillment of two prophecies. A prophecy may be said to be fulfilled not only when it is verified in the literal or the typical sense, but also when an event occurs which was contained in the general message of the prophet; and even, in a wide sense, when something happens very much like what the prophet foretold. Speaking in the name of God, Osee had said, "Out of Egypt I have called my son."[3] He was speaking of the

---

[3] *Ex Aegypto vocavi filium meum.* Matt. 2:15 citing Osee 11:1 according to the Hebrew. The Septuagint translates, "I have called from Egypt *her* children" (τὰ τέκνα αὐτοῦ, *the children of Israel*). St. Matthew could draw nothing from the Greek text, even if it were taken in a typical sense.

Hebrew people, which, collectively, is son of God in the theocratic sense. But Israel was the figure of the Messias, or at least the Messias was the highest expression of Israel. Hence St. Matthew applied Osee's words to him in a more excellent sense.

Jesus went to live at Nazareth to fulfill what the prophets had said about him, "He shall be called a Nazarene."[4] These words do not appear in the Bible, and it is altogether arbitrary to suppose that the Evangelist cites from some lost book or from one of the unknown Apocrypha. His allusion to prophets in general shows that he does not mean to quote from any one of them, and that he is expressing the spirit rather than the letter

---

[4] Matt. 2:23: "Quoniam Nazaraeus vocabitur" (ὅτι Ναζωραῖος κληθήσεται).

a) *Orthography of the name Nazareth* — It was certainly written with a *tsadhe* (נצרת) and not with a *zayin*. What proves this is the present Arabic pronunciation (with an emphatic *s*), the Rabbinic and Moslem usage, the transcription of it in the Syriac versions, and the formal assertion of St. Jerome (*Liber interpret. nomin hebr.*): "Scribebatur non per *z* litteram, sed per hebr. sade." The only reason for doubting it would be the Greek form, *zeta* generally corresponding to *zayin* and *sigma* to *tsadhe*. However, Ζόγαρα is found for צער (Gen. 13:10; Jer. 48:34). Cf. Dalman, *Orte und Wege,* 1924, pp. 61–64 (English transl., *Sacred Sites and Ways,* by Levertoff, 1935, pp. 57–60).

b) *Form of the name Nazarene* — Sometimes Ναζαρηνός is found (Mark, four times; Luke, twice), sometimes Ναζωραῖος (always in Matthew, John, and Acts). Ναζαρηνός is the ordinary "gentile name" like Γαδαρηνός, Μαγδαληνός, etc. The termination αῖος suggests rather the name of a sect, as would φαρισαῖος, σαδδουκαῖος, etc. I am inclined to think, therefore, that Jesus was first called Ναζαρηνός from his place of origin, and was called Ναζωραῖος only after that name began to be applied to his disciples (Acts 24:5, τῆς τῶν Ναζωραίων αἱρέσεως). The title was first a sobriquet, like χριστιανός (Acts 11:26), but it was accepted by Jesus' disciples, and from that time on all distinction between the words Ναζαρηνός and Ναζωραῖος disappeared.

c) *How will Jesus be called a Nazarene?* — First, it is necessary to eliminate the sense of *Nazirite* (one who made the vow of a Nazirite), because (1) Jesus was not a Nazirite; (2) he is nowhere called a Nazirite; (3) Nazirite (נזיר) is written with a *zayin,* and has nothing in common with *Nazarene.*

Many authors refer to Isaias 11:1: "A bough shall spring from the stem of Jesse, and a branch (נצר) shall grow from his roots." The prophet calls the Messias *Netser,* a word from the same root as *Nazareth;* but would such a play on words be enough to verify a prophecy? It is as though one were to say: "He will be called a Lyonese because he will be like a lion." If St. Matthew were referring to Isaias, he would use the singular (*prophet*) and not the plural (*prophets*). No other prophet called the Messias *Netser* (*branch*); the word צמח (*tsemaḥ*) "sprout," which is found in Jeremias (23:5; 33:15), is altogether different.

On the other hand, Jesus was actually called a Nazarene, and the prophets give the reason for this derisive appellation in their descriptions of his lowly and humble state.

of the Messianic prophecies, as St. Jerome penetratingly remarks. The prophets had predicted that the Messias would be scorned and despised, a butt of insults and derision: and all that began when he went to live in an obscure village of a rather ill-famed province. His Nazarene origin will be inscribed on his cross. His enemies will call him a Galilean, and give his disciples the sobriquet of Nazarenes, which will become, and is today, their usual designation among the Jews and Moslems. Though he was born in Bethlehem, the cradle of his ancestors, and during his public life made Capharnaum the center of his apostolate, Nazareth was his true home. There he took his first steps; there he lisped his infant syllables; there he grew up under the eyes of his Mother, and worked as a laborer at the side of his foster father. He is, and is called, the carpenter of Nazareth.

No village in Palestine has undergone such radical transformation as Nazareth. Its population has almost trebled in the past fifty years, and the town has grown to such proportions that the early pilgrims would hardly recognize it. The hills that encircle it were once bare; now their slopes are covered with hotels, convents, schools, orphanages, and hospices with their spacious enclosures; and from the beautiful Salesian church crowning the summit of Neby-Saïn the eye can take in a radius of thirty miles.[5] To know it as it once was, one must plunge into the interior of the old quarter and mount the steps along its alleys bordered by tiny, low, flat-roofed houses, that are set back against the hill, and often burrow into the hill itself.

Nazareth cut a poor figure beside the Herodian cities of Tiberias and even Sepphoris, the latter less than four miles away. Its two neighbors, Japhia and Iksal, which guard the southern entrance to the mountainous hills that hide it, have left more important ruins. As Nathaniel's jibe shows, Nazareth could

[5] In 1852, Robinson (*Palestine,* 2 ed., Vol. II, p. 339) estimated the population at 3000 souls; Mislin, in 1868 (*Lieux saints,* 3 ed., Vol. III, p. 525), at 3470; Guerin, in 1880 (*Galilée,* Vol. I, p. 99), at 4950. The census of 1922 gave 9510, of whom 3000 were Moslems. But the town keeps growing rapidly. The many European establishments are responsible for the changing appearance. To mention only the Catholic religious, there are at Nazareth Franciscans, Brothers of St. John, Brothers of the Christian Schools, Salesians of Don Bosco, Fathers of Betharram, Ladies of Nazareth, Sisters of Charity, Poor Clares, Carmelites, and Sisters of St. Joseph.

not be compared even with Cana. Now that it is connected with Jerusalem, Tiberias, and Haifa by highways, and with Sepphoris and Thabor by fairly good roads, it lies along traveled routes. But this was not always so. The road from the East to Egypt divided five or six miles before it reached Nazareth, near a place called Lubieh: one branch headed toward the coast line, by the plain of Asochis; the other, which was more frequented, passed between Thabor and the hills of Nazareth, and crossed the plain of Esdrelon, where it, too, divided again, the left branch leading through Samaria to Jerusalem, the right branch to Egypt by the Mageddo gap and the shore of the Mediterranean. Nazareth was by-passed.

St. Luke summarizes the life of Jesus in his Nazareth retreat up to his twelfth year by saying: "The child grew and waxed strong, filled with wisdom; and the grace of God was upon him."[6] Since the Son of God wishes to be like his adoptive brothers in everything, his tiny body grows like ours, little by little. Gradually his limbs gain strength; held up by Mary he tries his first steps and stammers the words she suggests to him. Later he will help his mother in easy tasks and will wield the tools in Joseph's carpenter shop as if in play. "Lovable infant," says Bossuet, "how happy are they who see you grow out of swaddling clothes, and gain strength in your arms, and hold out your little hands, and caress your holy Mother and the saintly old man who has adopted you, or rather, to whom you gave yourself as a son . . . . I adore you, dear Child, in all your growing years, when you fed at your Mother's breast, or uttered to her who nourished you your infant cries, or slept on her bosom and in her arms."[7] Only the ingenuous and charming pen of a Francis de Sales could describe Mary's joy as she followed the slow progress of this growth and watched a smile break on the face of her dearly beloved Son, and read in it more clearly every day the signs of an awakening mind and heart.

---

[6] Luke 2:40. Note: (1) "He grew and waxed strong" refers to physical development only. (2) "Full of wisdom" is an imperfect rendition of *πληρούμενον*, which is neither an adjective nor a past participle passive, but a present participle middle: "gradually filling himself with wisdom." (3) It is not "*the* grace of God was *in* him," but "*a* grace of God (divine) was *on* him."

[7] Bossuet, *Elév. sur les mystères,* 20me semaine, 1re élév.

God could have fashioned the body of the second Adam as he did that of the first, and could have sent him into the world at a mature age and in the fullness of physical development; but then Christ, not being of our race, would no longer have been our natural representative. It behooved him to be born of a woman, like other members of the human family, and go through the successive phases of our existence, in order to serve as a model for all periods of life. Yet it was fitting that his body, formed by the action of the Holy Ghost in the most pure womb of a virgin, and hypostatically united to the Word, should have a perfection corresponding to his supereminent dignity. It was indeed subject, as ours, to hunger, thirst, fatigue, and the pain caused by the inclemency of the seasons and the ill-treatment of men; but it was exempt from infirmities that are the consequence of the passions, or imprudence, or hereditary predisposition to disease. Not that he must have the keenest eyesight, the most delicate hearing, the most robust body, the most lithe and supple limbs that ever existed. His perfection did not consist in any abnormal heightening of the sense faculties, but rather in the harmonious balance of the whole organism. Though he did not experience any propensity to evil nor any dominance of the senses over reason, he resembled us in everything which did not detract from his moral dignity; and his more delicate organism rendered him more sensitive than we are to both joy and suffering.

Thus in retirement and quiet, the early childhood of Jesus ran its course. Storms from the outside, where tragic events were disrupting the whole world, left Nazareth unruffled in its solitude. The Emperor Augustus had accumulated on his brow all possible titles of honor — so many times consul, so many times *Imperator,* pontifex maximus, god and savior, son of Jupiter — and now he was paying the price of glory by an uninterrupted sequence of domestic misfortunes and national calamities. He had found it necessary to banish his only daughter to the island of Pandataria because of her disgraceful conduct. His two grandsons, the Caesars Caius and Lucius, had died in close succession in the bloom of youth. His only remaining heir was Tiberius, the son of his third wife Livia; and the shifty and suspicious character of this man was a source of great anxiety to Augustus. At the same time, famine was making Rome desolate. Excessive public expenses demanded new taxes, which were burdensome and unpopular. The Temple of Janus, closed for the third time since the founding of Rome, two or three years before the birth of Christ, had not been long in reopening. The barbarians, anxious to throw off the Empire's yoke, were profiting by the critical condition of the times and were stirring up trouble along the Rhine and the Danube. Victorious expeditions brought back only a short-lived peace, and Varus, whom we have seen so brutally suppressing an uprising of the Jews, was soon to be lost forever in the forests of Germany with all his legions.

In Palestine the situation was no better. Archelaus, enraged at his failure to bring back from Rome more than the title of ethnarch, was meditating fierce vengeance on the subjects who had blocked his cause before Caesar. His extortions and cruelties went so far that the people actually sighed for the days of Herod his father; his nine or ten years' rule was nothing but high-handed tyranny. We know few details about it, but we do know that the exasperated Jews finally sent to Rome to demand his removal. Augustus did not deign to write to him, but summoned him as one would summon a flunky, and after hearing him and confronting him with his accusers, exiled him for life to Vienne in Gaul. From that time on, Judea, Samaria, and Idumea were annexed to the province of Syria and governed by procurators, the first of whom was Coponius. Quirinius, the Governor of Syria, who had already taken up a census under Herod, was again charged, ten or twelve years later, with the task of listing properties and persons in this country newly incorporated into the Empire. Such was the state of the world when Jesus reached his twelfth year.

3. The Loss and Finding of Jesus in the Temple

(LUKE 2:41–52)

According to the Mosaic Law, adult Israelites had to appear three times a year before Almighty God to worship and offer sacrifices. Unless legitimately prevented, all those within a day's journey from Jerusalem were required to celebrate there the Passover and Pentecost and the Feast of Tabernacles. Custom had tempered the rigor of the Law for the Jews of the Dispersion and for those living in distant countries, since it was practically impossible to observe the letter of the Law. Galileans, for instance, could not all leave their fields on the eve of Pentecost when harvesting was most needed. But all the Jews in Palestine made it their duty to spend the Passover in Jerusalem, and Joseph, the just man, was naturally among their number.

No legal obligation bound the women and children. Nevertheless, we see in the Gospel that Mary was in the habit of accompanying her holy spouse, and that Jesus joined them when he was twelve years old.[8] In this Eastern land, where children matured early, a youth of thirteen was considered a man. From that time on he was a subject of the Law, and was held to its full observance, even in the matter of its admittedly difficult precepts, such as the annual fast on the Day of Atonement, and the pilgrimage to Jerusalem. But pious parents took pains to introduce their children to these practices a little before the Law enjoined them. When, therefore, St. Luke says that Jesus was in his twelfth year at the time of his presence in the Temple among the doctors, he seems to imply that this was his first pilgrimage to the Holy City.

The distance from Nazareth to Jerusalem by the direct road across Samaria is not more than 110 or 120 kilometers (70 miles), and a good walker could easily cover it in three days; but pilgrims traveling in caravans and constrained to wait for one another could scarcely cover it in less than four stages.[9] The first stage was richest in Biblical associations. Descending from the hills of Nazareth to the great plain of Esdrelon, the traveler put Mount Thabor on his left and skirted Little Hermon, then the heights of Jezrahel, odious dwelling place of Achab and his well-matched consort, and finally Gelboe, the scene of the tragic end of Saul and Jonathan. On the right, as far as the eye could see, stretched the plain, watered by the Cison, that had been im-

---

[8] Luke 2:41. It will be noticed: (1) that Joseph *and Mary* went up each year (κατ' ἔτος) to Jerusalem; (2) that they went there with Jesus when he was twelve years old *according to the custom* of pious folk — no strict obligation bound Mary to go, nor was Jesus bound; (3) that they spent the whole Paschal week (τελειωσάντων τὰς ἡμέρας) in Jerusalem.

[9] The present carriage road is almost 93 miles but it zigzags up and down and around Samaria instead of going directly from Jacob's well to Jenin.

mortalized in the victory song of Debbora. Carmel, forever hallowed by the miracles of the prophet Elias, loomed on the southern horizon. The first stage ended at the Galilean border, so that the pilgrims might avoid spending more than one night in Samaritan territory. They left the capital of Samaria at a distance, and arrived the next day in Sichem, to which they were drawn by memories of Jacob and Joseph. On the evening of the third day they were in Judea, whose northern boundary lay a bit to the north of ancient Silo, where the Ark of the Covenant had found temporary shelter. Thence they passed through the territory of the little tribe of Benjamin, among places whose names are familiar to Bible readers: Bethel, Beroth, Rama, Gabaon, Machmas, Anathoth, Gabaath-Saul. At the end of their fourth day's journey, they finally greeted the high towers and battlements of Jerusalem.

Most of the pilgrims, especially those from distant places, stayed in Jerusalem throughout the Feast, as much to take a needed rest between two fatiguing trips, as to satisfy their devotion. The Feast closed on the twenty-first of Nisan, which was kept like the Sabbath; the return journey was generally begun the next day. The disorder and confusion of a departing caravan can be appreciated only by experience. Relatives, friends, and neighbors seek out and wait for one another, in order to travel as a party. Soon, however, incidents along the way and the uneven pace of the pilgrims break up the ranks and confuse groups in inextricable disorder. People find one another again only at nightfall at a common rendezvous.

According to a likely tradition, the Holy Family had fixed on El-Bireh (the ancient Beroth) as their first stopping-place.[10] Here are found the ruins of a church with three naves, built by the Crusaders on the foundations of an older edifice. El-Bireh might seem too near Jerusalem to have been the end of a day's journey, but caravans were slow in starting and the first stage was usually the shortest.

When the groups were again united according to villages and

---

[10] El-Bireh, a town of a thousand inhabitants, is about nine miles from Jerusalem, and 2930 feet above sea level. The remains of the twelfth-century church, which was 141 by 72 feet, were demolished in 1916.

families, for the evening meal and the night's rest, what was the dismay of Mary and Joseph to discover that Jesus was not with them! They had felt no anxiety during the journey, thinking him to be with neighbors, and it was now too late to go and look for him. What a night of sleeplessness and anguish!

The next day, at dawn, while their companions continued their journey, Mary and Joseph retraced their steps to Jerusalem. In vain did they question all the passers-by, scour all the cross-roads in the city, and knock at all the familiar doors. The whole day passed without the slightest sign of him. Finally, on the third day, they went up to the Temple, doubtless to commit their sorrow to God and ask his guidance in their plight, rather than in any hope of finding Jesus there.

And yet he was there in the midst of the doctors, listening to them and asking questions. The lectures of the Rabbis were familiar and informal; they allowed their hearers to question them on obscure points, and even of their own accord invited free discussion. This method, they found, enabled them to keep their listeners attentive, stimulate thinking, sharpen wits, and combat passivity. The story is even told of a Rabbi who had his pupils ask him questions in order that he might have the occasion to give to a colleague a lesson which, in his opinion, was needed.

Jesus was present, then, at one of these meetings at which the doctors were striving to outdo one another in erudition and subtlety. He was not seated on a high dais in the arrogant posture depicted by some artists; nor was he trying to dazzle the audience with abstruse metaphysical problems or with the intricacies of astrology, as the Apocrypha would have it.[11] This would have befitted neither his character nor his age. He contented himself with listening, asking questions, and when asked, answering them. He fulfilled the ideal of the model pupil as conceived in the teachings of the Rabbis: asking pertinent questions, answering carefully and without anxiety, solving difficulties in an orderly way, keeping within the limits of one's knowledge.[12] His questions and answers on religious and moral matters were so intelligent and so apposite that the doctors marveled, and

---

[11] The *Arabic Gospel of the Infancy,* Chaps. li and lii.

[12] *Mishnah,* treatise *Aboth,* v, 7.

wondered whence came to a child so young such knowledge of heavenly things.

Mary and Joseph witnessing this scene were also astonished, for they had never before seen their Son manifest this divine wisdom, though they knew its source. When the session was over and the onlookers had dispersed, Mary approached Jesus and gently said to him: "My son, why hast thou acted thus to us? Thy father and I have sought thee for three days." Her words are the spontaneous cry of a mother's heart; let us not subject them to cold analysis. What else would a mother say at a time like this? Whether they are a loving complaint or an affectionate rebuke, Mary's words spring, above all, from a desire to know the motive prompting this conduct, so much at variance with the habits of a Son who had been so completely respectful and submissive, and always so anxious to avoid causing them the slightest displeasure. Jesus answered: "How is it that you sought me? Did you not know that I must give myself fully to the things of my Father?"[13] They had done no wrong in anxiously seeking him, and Jesus is not blaming them for it; but, knowing him as they did, they could have remembered that their Son was not entirely theirs, and that his duty was above all to his heavenly Father's interests. This thought would have calmed their fears and moderated their anxiety.

This is the interpretation commonly accepted today, but several Fathers of the Church are perhaps justified in preferring another: "Did you not know that I must be in my Father's house?" From the moment of his unannounced departure from them, the only place he could have been was the Temple, the house of his Father. They could have found him there without the trouble of looking elsewhere. So understood, his answer is, at first glance, less sublime; but how much more natural on the lips of a child, who utters it with a caress and a smile.

---

[13] Luke 2:48–49. Jesus was found again "after three days" (*post triduum, μετὰ τρεῖς ἡμέρας*), which is to be understood, according to the ancient way of reckoning, as *the day after the morrow,* the first and last day being counted, though the interval between them was only one day.

The answer of Jesus "in his quae Patris mei sunt" (*ἐν τοῖς τοῦ πατρός μου*) can be taken in either of two ways: (1) "in the affairs, in the interests of my Father, in that which concerns his glory": this is the ordinary explanation; (2) "in the house of my Father, in the Temple" (Origen, St. Epiphanius, St. Augustine, St. Cyril of Alexandria, etc.).

In any case, his words had a mysterious meaning, whose depths his parents did not at the time reach.[14] Clarified though their minds were by supernatural light, they grasped only little by little the reason and manner of the plan of redemption. Prophetic vision is always part shadow and obscurity, even in the most favored seers. Had Jesus just inaugurated his work? Was he going to leave them, to give himself up completely to the service of his heavenly Father? And if this was his design, was there no way of carrying it out without breaking his Mother's heart? This is what Joseph and Mary did not at once grasp; and perhaps they could not have suspected that Jesus' behavior was aimed more at our instruction than theirs. It teaches us that God's service supersedes all affections, even the most legitimate. How many parents who call themselves Christians do not understand this, even after the lesson the Saviour here gives them!

4. A Life of Obedience and Growth

The story of Jesus' life at Nazareth from his twelfth year to the beginning of his apostolate is summed up in three phrases: "He grew in wisdom and in stature and in grace, before God and before men . . . He was subject to Joseph and Mary . . . His mother kept watch over all these things in her heart."[15]

Having come down from heaven to teach us obedience, Jesus must be a perfect model of it. Thus, at the first instant of conception, he said to his Father, "Thou hast rejected victims and oblations, but thou hast fashioned for me a body. Holocausts and sacrifices displeased thee, but behold, O Lord, I come, to do thy will, O God, as it is written of me at the head of the Book."[16] He will, then, obey all who have a portion of divine authority. He will make himself obedient unto the death of the Cross, and the Apostle will be able to say that he learned obedience in the school of sorrow.

---

[14] Luke 2:50. "They did not understand the word." Some shocked interpreters think this refers to those present; but obviously *they* refers to the parents of Jesus. Others think that, by the figure of synecdoche, the plural is here used for the singular, and that Joseph alone is meant. These are pointless subtleties.

[15] Luke 2:51–52. Physical and moral growth has already been mentioned above (Luke 2:40).

[16] Heb. 10:5–7 citing Ps. 39 (40):7–9; cf. Heb. 5:8; Phil. 2:8.

His whole life at Nazareth is obedience: *"Et erat subditus illis."* What a strange reversal of roles! He whom all things in heaven and on earth obey, himself obeys and does not command. Mary, the most sublime of creatures, commands and obeys, each in turn; but she commands her Creator and obeys a man whose merits are far outshone by her own. Joseph, fully conscious as he is of the infinite dignity of Jesus, and of Mary's incomparable holiness, commands both of them and obeys only God. Mary found all this an inexhaustible subject for meditation. She dwelt on the mystery of the hidden life, but could not sound its depths, and she adored in silence what surpasses human comprehension.

One shrinks from profaning the sanctuary of Nazareth by looking curiously into it. We hardly venture to consider in detail the daily occupations there because there is a certain commonness about them which shocks our delicacy. A person might prefer to contemplate Jesus nourished by angels, and Mary absorbed in an ecstasy of love, impervious to all distractions; but we must not recoil from the sterner reality.

In every Jewish house, the woman's first duty was to grind the wheat needed for the day's consumption, and the strident noise of the millstone, as she set it in motion at daybreak, filled the air. Then she kneaded the flour, lighted the movable oven, and baked her bread on white-hot stones. Preparations for the meal were not arduous, because the menu was simple and usually the same: eggs, milk, cheese, honey, olives, and other fruits, and sometimes fish. These duties done, the mistress of the house did not remain idle. As the valiant woman in the Book of Proverbs,

> She took wool and flax
> and worked it with joyous hands;
> she took hold of the distaff
> and her fingers turned the spindle.

Today hemp and flax are no longer cultivated in Palestine, and wool, cotton, and silk are woven by men. But among the Jews of that time, as in the tents of nomads today, this task fell to the women, and there can be no doubt that Jesus' seamless robe was his Mother's handiwork.

The divine Child rendered Mary all the little services a boy of his age could perform. When his strength allowed it, he joined Joseph in his workshop. Then as now the workshop was always separated from the living quarters, out of consideration for the peace and quiet of the family, which was thus spared constant disturbances such as the gossiping and bargaining of clients and visitors, who were often loud and ill-mannered. We know, moreover, that this arrangement obtained throughout the Greco-Roman world.

Joseph worked in wood. He was doubtless both a carpenter and a joiner, because trades had not yet become so specialized that there was any distinction between these two occupations; both are designated by the same name in Arabic.[17] Though the axiom about "the changeless East" is to be taken with some reserve, we can still learn more from a visit to the workshop of a Galilean carpenter than from any number of learned discussions. We would see one or two saws, a hatchet, a hammer, a mallet, and a plane, rarely a workbench or sawhorse—in short, very primitive equipment.[18] But it is enough for making the usual things: doors, window frames, chests for wardrobes, winnowing forks, harrows fitted with points of flint to beat out corn sheaves on the floor, and above all, yokes and plows in the most antique style. When a new house is to be built, the carpenter is called to square off roughly the beams of poplar and sycamore that are to support the thatched roof and the more or less watertight layer of hard earth spread over it. Arches, now common in Judea, were rare in Galilee until lately.

Joseph's humble position had nothing degrading about it in the eyes of his compatriots. The majority of famous Rabbis had worked with their hands. One of the five principal duties of the

---

[17] He was τέκτων (Matt. 13:55), as was Jesus also (Mark 6:3). Τέκτων means both *carpenter* and *joiner,* sometimes *artisan* in general, rarely *metalworker.* The Latin *faber* means any workman, whether in wood, iron, or stone; a modifier is needed to distinguish their special work: *faber lignarius, ferrarius,* etc. In Hebrew, *naggar,* like the Arabic *najjar,* means both *carpenter* and *joiner.* The tradition about Joseph as a worker in wood is perfectly established. In the second century, the *Protoevangelium of James* represents him with an ax (ix, 1) and St. Justin (*Dial. cum Tryph.,* 88) says that he made plows and yokes. Schneller's opinion that he was a mason (*Kennst du das Land?,* 1920, p. 58) is altogether erratic.

[18] There is still a street of cobblers and a street of smiths at Nazareth, but we did not see any street of carpenters or of joiners.

father of a family was expressed in the maxim of the Rabbi Judah: "He who does not teach his son a trade, teaches him to steal." The point was not only to honor work, but to rout idleness, the most dangerous of vices. "Even if you have a hundred servants," said the Rabbi Eliezer, "you should oblige them all to spin wool; for idleness is the mother of misconduct." St. Paul, himself a Rabbi, invoked a nobler motive: "Put your hands to some honest work, so that you may have something to give to the needy."[19]

Devoting himself to these humble tasks at his foster father's side, Jesus "grew in wisdom, in stature, and in grace before God and before men." His moral and intellectual development kept step with his physical growth. The latter was real and easily perceptible; could the former have been simply an appearance? Was the intellectual and moral progress of Jesus perhaps only the gradual manifestation of immutable perfection, as the sun, which has always the same heat and brightness, sends forth its rays with greater intensity as it rises above the horizon? In a wonderful passage, which unfortunately cannot be cited here in its entirety, St. Cyril of Alexandria says in substance: "The Word Incarnate freely allowed the laws of humanity to keep their full validity in his case that he might resemble us the more, since sudden growth would have had something monstrous about it."[20] It is easy to understand how Jesus gradually grew in stature and grace, but how explain the growth in wisdom and knowledge?

The two natures of Christ should not be pictured as two communicating vessels, one overflowing into the other, nor as two neighboring rooms lighted from the same source. These lame comparisons, based on false theology, only obscure the mystery. Of itself, the hypostatic union leaves the two natures unmixed and inconfused, and adds only the Divine Personality to the human nature. But Jesus Christ, the Son of God, has a title to the possessions of his Father, that is, to sanctifying grace and the light of glory which is its perfection. This right he had from the moment of his conception; and though his redemptive mission

---

[19] Eph. 4:27–28. For the Rabbis, cf. Billerbeck, Vol. II, pp. 10–11 and 745–746.

[20] St. Cyril, *Quod unus sit Christus,* MG, LXXV, 1332. The author concludes: We say that he increased in stature and grace, just as we say that he was hungry or tired or other similar things.

forbade the glory of his soul to overflow upon his body, in such a way as to spiritualize it, there was no reason for withholding from the soul itself the actual possession of the beatific vision. Hence the soul of Jesus, contemplating God face to face, saw in the Word everything produced by the creative activity of the Word. This truth is sufficiently clear in the Gospel, and has been consecrated by Catholic teaching in such wise that it cannot be doubted. But it was also fitting that the Instructor, Legislator, and Supreme Judge of the human race, who came to reveal to the world the mysteries and the wishes of his Father, be endowed with a knowledge more in keeping with his role as Redeemer and second Adam. This is what is called infused knowledge; and its limits are open to free discussion, but its existence cannot be denied without contradicting the common opinion of theologians.[21] For all their perfection, beatific knowledge and infused knowledge are not infinite, because they are the adornment of a created nature; nevertheless, neither one of them is capable of increase, because they were conferred from the beginning in the full measure foreseen and decreed by God. Any progress, therefore, in Jesus' knowledge must have been only in his acquired or experimental knowledge.

Of course, there are some who are reluctant to admit this progress. They fear to make the humanity of Christ less perfect by admitting that it acquired new perfection; they are unwilling to let it be taxed with ignorance in any order of knowledge. Hence they have imagined an infused knowledge of natural things placed by God ready-made, as it were, into Jesus' soul, the function of which in the presence of sensible objects, was simply to recognize them. St. Thomas, who originally shared these scruples, finally dissipated them and formulated this commonsense principle: "We must say that in Christ there was an acquired knowledge, conformed to the human manner of knowing."

[21] Suarez (In 3^{am} part, *Disp.* xxv, sect. 1) says with reference to the beatific vision in Christ: "Existimo opinionem contrariam erroneam et proximam haeresi esse." He would have had even stronger reason for speaking thus after the Decree of the Holy Office of June 5, 1918. The infused knowledge of Christ is not held by theologians as a dogma, but as a theological conclusion. Cf. Vigué, *Quelques précisions concernant l'objet de la science acquise du Christ,* in *Recherches,* Jan.–Feb., 1920.

Certainly the faculty we have of forming ideas with the aid of images perceived by the senses was not inert in him, or without an object. That would be a curious way to conceive the perfection of his humanity. Let us therefore boldly say with the Angelic Doctor, "Since the operation of the active intellect is successive, Christ did not from the beginning know everything according to this knowledge . . . which was always perfect in relation to his age, but not perfect absolutely speaking, and hence it could increase."[22] Thus the apparently diametrically opposed opinions of the Fathers can be reconciled. When they ask whether Christ as man was ignorant of anything, some say "no" and others "yes." Both are right. It can, indeed, be said that even as man Christ was not ignorant of anything, if his human knowledge be considered in all its scope; it can also be admitted that he did not know everything, if the question is confined to this inferior knowledge, acquired by the help of sense impressions.

The acquired knowledge was not redundant as regards the infused and beatific knowledge. It is a matter here of orders of knowledge that are absolutely distinct. The beatific vision created no redundancy, as is obvious. The same must be said for the infused knowledge. Like the knowledge proper to pure spirits, it was formed without the help of sensible images and exercised without recourse to them. Christ had it habitually, and it served him when and to what extent he wished. As an eminent theologian felicitously puts it: "Jesus adapted the manifestation of his higher knowledge to the progress of his acquired knowledge. Consequently his increase in wisdom was at once apparent and real: apparent with respect to his infused knowledge, which could not increase; real, with respect to his acquired knowledge, which was capable of indefinite progress."[23]

The soul of Jesus, hypostatically united to the Word, was the most perfect soul that ever existed. His penetrating intelligence, his quick perception, his tenacious memory, his unerring judgment, and his flawless reasoning were without equal. No hereditary

---

[22] St. Thomas, *Summa,* p. III, q. xii, a. 2 ad 1um and q. ix, a. 4: "Quamvis aliter alibi scripserim." He held the opposite opinion in his commentary on the *Sentences,* p. III, q. iii, a. 3.

[23] Billot, *De Verbo Incarnato,* 3 ed., 1900, p. 221; St. Thomas, *Summa,* p. III, q. xi, a. 5.

defect blurred his mind, no haze of passion hovered between him and truth. He saw effects in their causes and causes in their effects, conclusions in principles and principles in conclusions. Thus he was able to enrich himself quickly with vast stores of knowledge. This is not to say, of course, that he could handle the theorems of celestial mechanics better than Laplace, or speak more languages than Mezzofanti, or apply the theory of sound and light waves better than Edison. To cover the entire span of human knowledge would require a thousand lives, and it is absolutely impossible for a man to know everything. We sometimes hesitate to believe that Christ, even according to his experimental knowledge, was ignorant of anything and that he had to learn. But we must be logical. There are things which no amount of intellectual acumen will discover without a teacher and guide, as, for example, the conventional signs which are employed to embody our thought in speech and writing. No one could decipher the letters of the alphabet and the idiomatic meanings of words without some initial indications. Jesus learned the elements of the Aramaic vocabulary at his mother's knee, and learned the technique of his trade from Joseph; he learned how to read the text of the Bible either in his own home or at the village school; the rest he learned from the book of nature or from contact with life.

It is by the constant application of this acquired knowledge that Christ appears to us as a true man and as a brother; for him as for us, it is the font of feelings and emotions. This knowledge reveals itself instinctively in his conduct and speech. His words and discourses reflect the blue of the Palestinian skies and allow us to breathe the scent of the Galilean hills, and this it is that gives them their charm. Many of his delightful descriptions are of scenes that have been "lived," as we say today. It is impossible to grasp clearly the allegory of the Good Shepherd, the parable of the Sower, or the comparison of the Importunate Friend, to cite only a few examples, unless one is acquainted with local customs.

The use he made of his acquired knowledge reveals, moreover, the delicacy of feeling in the heart of Jesus. It was not in virtue of the beatific vision nor of infused knowledge that he wept at

Lazarus' tomb. It was at the memory of the warm welcome and affectionate attention he had received in the hospitable home of Lazarus, whom he loved as a friend, a sympathetic companion of sure affection and tested loyalty. Jesus is moved at the sight of the widow of Naim sobbing by the bier of her only son, even as our own hearts would be wrung at a similar spectacle. He is touched with compassion when he sees the multitudes wandering aimlessly like sheep without a shepherd. He takes up the defense of the public sinner accused by the Pharisees; he protects the unfortunate adulteress persecuted by the Jews. Nor is it only moral distress that moves him; he has pity on all kinds of suffering. He cannot resist the pleas of the blind, the paralytics, and the lepers who implore his help. Twice he works miracles to appease the hunger of the people following him. All his feelings of pity, fear, disgust, sadness, and joy spring from the same source; they have their explanation in the acquired knowledge of Christ.

"Jesus Christ," as we read in the epistle to the Hebrews, "learned obedience from what he suffered."[24] He knew better than anyone else the nature and moral value of obedience; but it was in the school of suffering that he learned its difficulty, its merit, and its price; and this knowledge is experimental knowledge.

Jesus not only grew in wisdom, in the way we have explained, but more and more he won the favor of God and of men: *Proficiebat gratia apud Deum et homines*.[25] There is no question here of sanctifying grace, for that could not increase in him, since from the first moment of the Incarnation he had received the fullness of grace that God had destined for him from all eternity. St. Luke has already said that "the grace of God was upon him"; the favor of God rested upon him as upon God's only Son, the object of his full complacence. In saying now that he

---

[24] Heb. 5:8. *Didicit ex iis quae passus est obedientiam.* The need of this trial, to become a perfect High Priest: Heb. 2:17; 4:15.

[25] Luke 2:40: χάρις Θεοῦ ἦν ἐπ' αὐτῷ. Note : (1) χάρις without the article; (2) ἐπ' αὐτῷ (on him) and not ἐν αὐτῷ (in him). The difference in meaning and expression is clear in Luke 2:52: προέκοπτεν . . . χάριτι παρὰ Θεῷ καὶ ἀνθρώποις. In the Old Testament, χάρις, which is always without the article, means *favor;* it is used chiefly in expressions such as *to find, to acquire grace* (favor) *before* (ἐναντίον), or, as here, *with* (παρά), *in the eyes of* someone. Cf. Prov. 3:3–4, cited below.

"grew in grace before God and before men," the Evangelist is expressing a different idea which recalls the words of the Book of Proverbs:

> Preserve always goodness and faithfulness,
> Hang them around thy neck, engrave them on thy heart;
> then shalt thou acquire favor (grace) and good renown
> in the eyes of God and the eyes of men.

Such was the boy of Nazareth. Manifesting more and more, as he grew, the treasures of his heart, he constantly gained more and more admiration and affection. Gentle, modest, docile, obliging, without any of the defects that mar the attractiveness of childhood, he pleased everyone who had occasion to see and hear him. More and more, too, in our way of speaking, he earned the complacence of his Father, not by an increase of graces and spiritual gifts, but by the accumulation of acts of virtue. These multiplied acts could not fail to be pleasing to his Father, and St. Paul tells us that they merited a recompense.

5. The Relatives of Jesus[26]

In the sanctuary of Nazareth we never look for more than the three members of the earthly trinity: Joseph, faithful to his position as head of the family; Mary, living only for her divine Son; and Jesus, thoughtful and tender to his mother, grateful and docile to his foster father. We shrink from the very thought of their having to come into daily contact with relatives incapable of understanding them. Instinctively we dismiss these intruders who would trouble the delightful solitude and sweet privacy of the Holy Family.

Nevertheless, our desires must give way before the realities. The Gospel says that Jesus had brethren and that Mary had a sister, also called Mary, who stood at her side at the foot of the Cross. When, after a rather lengthy absence, the Saviour returned to preach in the synagogue at Nazareth, his astonished fellow townsmen said to one another: "Is not this the carpenter's son? Is not his mother called Mary, and his brethren James, and Joseph, and Simon, and Jude? And are not all his sisters living

[26] Cf. Note I: *The Relatives of Jesus.*

in our midst?" Jesus therefore passed as having four "brethren," mentioned by name, and at least three sisters, whose names are not given. His "brethren" followed him to Capharnaum, after the marriage feast at Cana. Later, alarmed at his activity, they tried to bring him back home; six months before his Passion they still did not believe, with a full faith, in his divine mission. After the Resurrection, however, we find them in the Cenacle with Mary, the Apostles, and the holy women. From that time on, their prestige was great in the early Church, and St. Paul says that he could claim their example as justification for permitting himself things from which he prefers to abstain.

Let us try, with the help of tradition and Scripture, to untangle this rather confused maze of Jesus' relatives.

First of all, the brethren and sisters of Jesus are not Mary's children. If there is any dogma which has never for an instant been in shadow, it is that of the perpetual virginity of the Mother of God, before, during, and after the birth of Jesus. When, toward the end of the fourth century, an ignorant monk called Helvidius, who was soon joined by two obscure confederates — one of them another monk named Jovinian, and the second, Bonosus, the Bishop of Sardica in Illyria — dared to question it, a cry of horror and indignation was raised throughout Christendom. St. Jerome seized his pen to refute this presumptuous innovator, and his refutation was so decisive that the apologists following him had practically nothing to do but borrow ammunition from his arsenal of proofs. Helvidius claimed Tertullian and St. Victorinus of Petovia for his opinion. St. Jerome — perhaps too readily — conceded to him Tertullian, but protested vigorously that Victorinus had never subscribed to this heresy. He is worthy of credence, since he knew how to read, and the writings of St. Victorinus were there to refute him, if he were trying to deceive.

Could the brethren and sisters of Jesus have been St. Joseph's children? The Apocryphal Gospels, especially the *Protoevangelium of James,* which enjoyed an undeserved reputation in the early Church, nearly led Catholic tradition astray on this point by making the brethren of the Lord the sons of Joseph by a previous marriage. The Fathers of the first four centuries saw no great difficulty in sacrificing the virginity of St. Joseph, provided that the dogma of the perpetual virginity of Mary remained safe. Clement of Alexandria, Origen, Eusebius, St. Hilary, Ambrosiaster, St. Epiphanius, St. Cyril of Alexandria, and even, at times, St. Augustine and St. John Chrysostom, accepted more or less reluctantly this theory of the Apocrypha. The last two, who seemed at first to be uninterested in the question, soon rallied to St. Jerome's thesis. St. Jerome was not always as positive as when he apostrophized Helvidius in these words: "You claim that Mary did not remain a virgin; but I hold that even Joseph was a virgin through Mary."[27] He could have pushed his advantage and the occasion seemed propitious; but he did not insist, because it was sufficient for his purpose that he had vindicated the virginity of the Mother of God.

A closer study of the Gospel and tradition warrants the assertion today that the "brethren of the Lord" were, beyond the shadow of a doubt, simply his cousins. The word "brother," in the Bible, has a much wider meaning than in our languages; it is used not only figuratively, of compatriots and coreligionists, but also in a proper sense, of near relatives. Lot is called the brother of Abraham, and is his nephew; Laban is said to be the brother of Jacob, and is his uncle. The sons of Oziel and Aaron, the sons of Cis and the daughters of Eleazar are described as brothers, yet they are only cousins.[28] The reason for this usage is that, since Aramaic and Hebrew have no special word for "cousin," it was necessary to use the word "brother" to designate a group of relatives belonging to different families; otherwise paraphrases of intolerable length would have been required. This is exactly the case with the brethren of the Lord: two of them, James and Joseph, were sons of a sister of the Blessed Virgin; and the other two, Simon and Jude, were the sons of Cleophas, St. Joseph's brother.

We owe our information about Cleophas to an authority of the first order. Hegesippus, a native of Palestine, finished his

---

[27] *Adv. Helvidium,* n. 19 (ML, XXXIII, 203); cf. n. 18 (XXXIII, 190).

[28] Gen. 13:8; 14:14–16 (Lot); Gen. 29:15 (Laban); 1 Para. 23:21–22 (the sons of Cis and the daughters of Eleazar); Lev. 10:4 (the sons of Oziel and Aaron). It is probable that the same should be said of the forty-two *brothers* of Ochozias (4 Kings 10:13–14), and of *all the brothers* and sisters of Job (42:11).

Memoirs in the reign of Pope Eleutherius (175–189), when he was an old man. He was born in the first quarter, perhaps at the very beginning, of the second century, and St. Jerome does not exaggerate when he says that he lived close to the time of the Apostles. He was particularly interested in the family of the Saviour, some of whose members he had been able to question for some were still living in the time of Trajan. In historical worth he has few rivals. He has sometimes been called the father of ecclesiastical history, and he would perhaps have greater right to this title than even Eusebius, if his work had come down to us in its entirety.

Hegesippus is therefore better qualified than anyone else to tell us of the relatives of Jesus. What increases our confidence in him is that he draws his information, not from the Gospel, but from personal sources, and delivers it to us just as he had it, with no systematization or attempt at harmony — an attempt that would render it suspect in our eyes.

This unparalleled witness tells us three things of great importance, stating them as well-known facts. First, Cleophas (or Clopas) was the brother of St. Joseph, spouse of the Virgin Mary; secondly, Simeon (or Simon), who succeeded his cousin James in the See of Jerusalem, was the son of this same Cleophas; thirdly, James, the first Bishop of Jerusalem, known everywhere as "the brother of the Lord," was of sacerdotal ancestry and was "another cousin" of Jesus, but was not, like Simeon, the son of Cleophas. He forgets to tell us who were the parents of James himself, but a careful reading of the Gospel supplies for his silence.

"Close by the cross of Jesus," says St. John, "stood his mother, and his mother's sister, Mary of Cleophas, and Mary Magdalene." In keeping with his habit of suppressing all that regards himself and his own, St. John here omits to mention his own mother, but mentions the presence of another Mary whom he calls Mary of Cleophas. While men are usually distinguished from their homonyms by their fathers' names, women are generally distinguished by either their husband's names or by the name of a famous son. Hence it is very probable that Mary of Cleophas was the wife and not the daughter of Cleophas. Now, according to the other evangelists, this other Mary, present on Calvary with the Blessed Virgin and Magdalene, was the mother of James the Less and Joseph, two of the brethren of the Lord. As the wife of Cleophas, she was the sister-in-law of the Blessed Virgin; but there is every reason to believe that there was between them a closer bond of relationship, whose origin we do not know. The insistence with which her son James is designated by the epithet, "the brother of the Lord," seems to show that he was not merely his cousin by marriage.

We know, then, that the mother of two of the brothers of the Lord was Mary of Cleophas, the sister of the Blessed Virgin. We also know that Cleophas, St. Joseph's brother, was the father of a third, called Simon or Simeon. Since the remaining one, Jude, is always connected with Simon and is, like him, of the family of David, it is natural to suppose that he was also a son of Cleophas.

All the points that remain obscure would be cleared up, in our opinion, if two hypotheses are risked. Mary, the sister of the Blessed Virgin, having two sons, James and Joseph, by a first marriage, was married a second time to Cleophas, brother of St. Joseph, who also had two sons, Simon and Jude, by a former marriage.[29] In the light of the customs of the country and the age, there was nothing extraordinary in the marriage of a widow and widower, each with children. The second hypothesis is that the sister of the Blessed Virgin had as her first husband a man of the tribe of Levi, called Alpheus.

In this fashion nine or ten problems would be solved. Thus one could explain why James, Joseph, Simon, and Jude are always named in that order, as brethren of the Lord; why James and Joseph are a pair distinct from Simon and Jude; why Mary, sister of the Blessed Virgin, is called the mother of James and

---

[29] Lagrange objects that, in this hypothesis, James "would have no relationship at all with Jesus; he would be related to him neither by kinship nor by marriage." A surprising statement. If Mary of Cleophas is the sister-in-law of the Blessed Virgin (the wife of the brother of Mary's husband), is she in no way related to her? And if the Blessed Virgin is in some way related to her sister-in-law, why should the Blessed Virgin's son have *no* relationship to the son of that sister-in-law? Besides, we do not exclude, we even expressly admit — as we have said above — a closer bond of relationship between the Blessed Virgin and Mary of Cleophas, though it is impossible to determine what it was.

Joseph and not the mother of Simon and Jude; why, according to Hegesippus, Simon and not James is the son of Cleophas; why, again according to Hegesippus, Simon and Jude are of the family of David; why, according to tradition, James was of sacerdotal ancestry; why the common opinion of Catholics identifies James, son of Mary, sister of the Blessed Virgin, with James the Apostle, the son of Alpheus; why Mary of Cleophas is called in the Gospel sister of the Blessed Virgin, when she was really her sister-in-law, being the wife of St. Joseph's brother; finally, why, after the deaths of Joseph and Cleophas, the two sisters brought their families together, so that thereafter the two families seemed to be but one.

6. The Deaths of Joseph and Cleophas

At the moment when Jesus was to begin his apostolic ministry, his foster father was already dead. His task finished, there was no longer reason for the presence at Nazareth of this faithful servant.[30] It was even fitting that the adoptive father disappear, to let the true Father appear. After his death, Jesus is no longer designated as the son of the carpenter and the son of Joseph, but simply as the carpenter and the son of Mary. Were Joseph still alive, we would see him appear here and there in the Gospel narrative. But he was not at the marriage feast at Cana; he did not go to Capharnaum with the rest of his family; he is not with Mary and her nephews when they try to rejoin Jesus, who seems to forget them in his complete dedication to his divine mission.

Joseph's death was as obscure as his life. We know neither the date nor the circumstances. Let us respect the silence of the Gospels, and not go digging around in the rubbish of the Apocrypha to supply for it. However, in one of these writings, among childish and often ridiculous details, we do by chance discover a moving detail: as Joseph is dying he says to Jesus, standing at his bedside: "The pains and fears of death surrounded me, but my soul found calm when I heard thy voice, Jesus my Protector,

[30] Cf. De la Broise, *La Sainte Vièrge* (in the collection, *Les Saints*), p. 144.

Jesus my Saviour, Jesus my Refuge, Jesus, whose name is sweet to my lips and to the heart of all who love thee."[31] To die in the arms of Jesus and Mary, what a signal privilege! Such was, without any doubt, the lot of the just man, Joseph. It was entirely fitting that the Church should make him the patron of a happy death.

Apparently, Cleophas had preceded his brother Joseph to the grave; for Cleophas, unlike his wife and children, plays no part in the public life of the Saviour. It seems, then, that the two families, each deprived of its protector and head, joined forces and perhaps lived under the same roof. What gives grounds for this conjecture is the fact that after the marriage feast at Cana, when Jesus went to Capharnaum, "his mother, his brethren, and his disciples" went with him; but his sisters, established in Nazareth, did not follow him. This drawing together of the two families naturally made the bonds of relationship closer. The Blessed Virgin and Mary of Cleophas were as sisters to each other; and Jesus and his cousins were as *brothers;* the Gospel and tradition have kept these names.

The brethren of the Lord, at least many of them, were slow to recognize his divine mission. They did not question his miracles, which they regularly saw with their own eyes; but they did not believe in his Messiasship. Soon, however, their eyes were opened, and Ascension Day found them believers. This is not the place to trace their history, but a brief word must be said in conclusion.

Joseph or Joses must have died young. After the brief mention of the Evangelists we hear no more of him.

Simon or Simeon succeeded his half brother James in the See of Jerusalem. Accused of being a Christian and of the family of David, he suffered martyrdom under Trajan in extreme old age.

Jude, like Simon, was the son of Cleophas, St. Joseph's brother. He is the author of the Catholic Epistle which bears his name, and in it he claims kinship with his half brother James, who was

---

[31] *History of Joseph the Carpenter,* xviii. Christ himself is supposed to have told the story to his Apostles. According to this apocryphal writing, which has been translated into French by Fr. Peeters (Paris, 1911, following the Arabic and Coptic versions), Joseph was 90 years old when he married the Blessed Virgin, and died at the age of 111 (Chaps. xiv and xxix).

more famous than himself. Two of his grandsons were prosecuted under Domitian, as members of the family of David; but when the Emperor learned that they jointly owned no more than nine thousand denarii, he concluded that he had nothing to fear from such unimportant persons, and left them in peace. Some descendants of Jude were still living in the reign of Trajan.

By far the most illustrious of the cousins of Jesus, he who was called the "Brother of the Lord" par excellence, was James, surnamed "the Less" or "the Little," either because of his short stature, or to distinguish him from his namesake, the son of Zebedee. His repute for holiness was so great that his rigorous asceticism soon became legendary. "James," it was said, "drank no wine nor strong drink and ate no animal food. To him alone was it permitted to enter the Sanctuary, for his garments were not of wool, but of linen. He was always to be found in the Temple asking pardon for the people. The skin of his knees had become calloused like that of a camel by reason of his constant kneeling in adoration."[32] Up to his death he occupied the episcopal see of Jerusalem which the Apostles had entrusted to him. A faithful observer of the Law of Moses, it was he who counseled St. Paul to offer certain sacrifices in the Temple together with some Nazirites, for the edification of the thousands of Jerusalem neophytes, who were all zealous for the Law.[33] The Jews, who hated him for his apostolic conquests, profited by the Procurator's absence to seize him and hurl him into the valley of Cedron from the height of the Temple esplanade. Still breathing after the fall, he was finished off by blows of a club.[34] The crime did not go unpunished. The invasion of Palestine by Vespasian and the misfortunes then visited on the people were commonly regarded as a chastisement from heaven for the murder of James the Just.[35]

---

[32] Hegesippus, in Eusebius, *Hist. eccl.*, II, xxiii, 5–6.

[33] Acts 21:18–26. The scene is significant.

[34] The martyrdom was mentioned by Clement of Alexandria in the sixth book of the *Hypotoposes* (Eusebius, II, i, 3 and xxiii, 3) and described at length by Hegesippus (Eusebius, II, xxiii, 7–18). It occurred in the year 62, after the sudden death of the Procurator Festus and before the arrival of his successor, Albinus.

[35] Eusebius (*Hist. eccl.*, II, xxiii, 19–20) cites in support of this statement a testimony of Josephus which is no longer found in the writings of that historian, and which was probably an interpolation.

7. The External Appearance of Jesus[36]

Every contemplative soul would love to know what Jesus looked like — what was his cast of countenance, the expression of his eyes, his carriage, his walk, his way of speaking and acting. On all these matters, we must expect the Gospels to be silent. Ancient historians, keen as they were at describing the thoughts and characters of their heroes, scarcely ever depicted their physical appearance. Suetonius and Plutarch were the first to descend to these lesser details, for which we are so avid today, but which the ancients did not consider worthy of record.

Nor has tradition preserved the memory of Jesus' features, and the comment of St. Augustine still remains true: "The representations of Christ in his humanity differ widely from one another, and perhaps any idea we form of it is far from the truth. . . . Nor do we know more of the appearance of the Virgin Mary."[37] This is not to say that images of Christ were entirely lacking in those days. At the beginning of the fourth century, we are told, there was pointed out in Caesarea-Philippi a bronze group representing Christ stretching forth his hand to the woman with the issue of blood as she kneels before him. Eusebius tells us that he had seen paintings of Christ and the Apostles which even then were considered to be ancient, but he does not say that they were faithful likenesses.[38]

We know that the primitive Church did not favor the veneration of images, and she had excellent reasons for this attitude. She feared that recent converts from paganism might pay the same honor to the statues of the saints that pagans gave to those idols of wood, stone, and metal against which the Apologists of the second century inveighed so strongly. On the other hand, the Jewish converts had little taste for practices so contrary to their customs, and it is possible that the prohibition of the Mosaic law against reproducing the human figure was not without influence on Christian circles. The reaction against the Gnostics must also be taken into account. The infamous sect of followers of Carpocrates boasted that they possessed images of Christ, made

---

[36] Cf. Note H: *The Portraits of Christ.*

[37] *De Trinitate,* viii, 4–5, n. 7 (ML, XLII, 951–952).

[38] Eusebius, *Hist. Eccl.,* VII, xviii, 4.

in his lifetime;[39] these they honored publicly, together with those of Plato, Aristotle, and Pythagoras; just as, later on, the Emperor Alexander Severus offered incense and sacrifices to statues of Jesus Christ, Abraham, Orpheus, and Apollonius of Tyana, all placed side by side in his oratory.[40]

With the triumph of Christianity, there was not the same danger. It was easy to explain to neophytes that the worship rendered to images simply passed "through them to go back to their prototypes," as St. Basil puts it.[41] Nevertheless, certain Fathers looked upon them with suspicious eyes. St. Epiphanius relates that once in a village of Palestine, in the neighborhood of Bethel, when he chanced to come upon a curtain on which was painted the figure of Christ or some saint (he could no longer remember which), he tore it to pieces with his own hands and had it replaced by a plain curtain.[42] When the Empress Constantia, sister of Constantine the Great, begged Eusebius to secure for her an authentic image of Christ, the Bishop of Caesarea gave her request a very cool reception.[43]

There is extant no authentic image of Christ. And there is no hope of finding any in the frescoes of the catacombs, some of which go back to the beginning of the second century and even the end of the first. The representations of Christ are not portraits and are not intended to be such. They are idealized figures differing widely from one another. Almost all are youthful, doubtless to symbolize the eternal youth of the Son of God.

What proves that there never was a fixed tradition is the endless variety of iconographical types, and also the fact that even in the early centuries the strange opinion about the physical ugliness of Christ found proponents. In its support, appeal was made to the text of Isaias on the suffering Messias:

> without charm and without radiance to draw the gaze,
> and without beauty to delight . . .

---

[39] St. Irenaeus, *Haer.*, i, 25; St. Epiphanius, *Haer.*, xxxvii, 6.
[40] Lampridius, *Life of Alexander Severus*, 29, in *Augustae Historiae Scriptores*.
[41] Cited by St. John Damascene, *De fide orthodoxa*, iv, 16 (MG, XCIV, 1169).
[42] St. Jerome's translation, *Epist.*, li, 9 (ML, XXII, 522).
[43] *Epist. ad Constantiam*, in Pitra, *Spicil. solesm.*, 1852, Vol. I, p. 383.

> before whom one veils the face;
> despised and, in our eyes, naught.[44]

When Clement of Alexandria is taking the aesthetes of his time to task for their preoccupation with the care of the body and its attire, he follows Isaias and confronts them with the example of Christ, who chose "to be ugly of countenance." Tertullian, with his usual exaggerated rhetoric, thinks that he can prove Christ's ugliness by this odd argument: "Had he been beautiful, no one would have dared touch him with as much as the tip of a finger. If his face was spat on, it was because he invited this treatment by his ugliness."

There is nothing like this in any other Father. Yet one or another of them suggests, on the strength of the Apocrypha, that Jesus sometimes changed appearance, and appeared beautiful or ugly according to the merits or demerits of those who looked at him. Many agree that he was ugly according to the flesh, not in comparison with other men, but because every creature, no matter how perfect, is vile, despicable, and ugly compared to its Creator. Did not St. Paul say that the union of the Word with human nature was for him a descent, a sort of abasement? For the rest, the most distinguished Fathers, and in particular St. John Chrysostom, put the words of the Psalmist on the conquering Messias over against those of Isaias on the suffering Messias:

> Thou art the most beautiful of the sons of men;
> grace is spread upon thy lips.

But St. Augustine has the honor of having suggested the argument most to the point: what proves the beauty of Jesus is the fact that no one was ever more beloved than he.

His power of attraction was extraordinary. One day when he crossed the lake to hold intimate converse with his Apostles, more than five thousand people arrived ahead of him on the opposite bank, and listened to him until evening, forgetting their hunger and fatigue. When night came, the enthusiastic crowd wished to proclaim him king, and he escaped their importunity only by flight. We know too that all the false Messiases whose names or memory have been preserved owed their prestige in great measure to their fine presence and physical gifts.

[44] Isa. 53:2–3 (after Condamin's translation).

Here are some significant facts. While he was speaking at Capharnaum, a woman of the people cried out, "Blessed is the womb that bore thee, and the breasts that suckled thee." It was not his discourse that called forth this cry of admiration from her: she had hardly heard it and could not have understood much of it. No mother could fail to know what she meant.

All the little children ran to Jesus for his blessing. In vain did the Apostles chase them away with gestures and threats; they kept coming back in greater numbers and with greater confidence. There must, then, have been an indefinable attraction about him, which little children, incapable of reasoning, were able to perceive and feel; to it they instinctively succumbed.

The eyes are the light of the body and the mirror of the soul. The Gospel, which leaves us in ignorance of the features of the Saviour, often describes his glance. In Nazareth and in Jerusalem it paralyzed the strength of his implacable enemies; in Gethsemani it made the henchmen of the High Priest fall back. The same glance, that plumbed the depths of Nathanael's heart, fell lovingly on the young man who was aspiring to perfection, made the woman with the issue of blood tremble, filled the soul of Zacheus with joy, melted the guilty Peter into tears, was itself dimmed with tears at Lazarus' tomb, and charged with indignation confronting blasphemers and hypocrites. Let us then conclude with St. Jerome that there was something superhuman in Jesus' face, and particularly in his eyes, that was somehow a reflection of his divinity. Art will always be powerless to depict the expression of a face through which shines forth the soul of Divinity. Many have tried, but with small success. Even *Le Beau Dieu* of Amiens, with its happy blending of "thoughtful serenity, authority, nobility, and gentleness," does not fully realize the desired ideal.

The representations of Christ followed a regular evolution, which had clearly marked stages. At the outset, in the catacombs, Christ is a beardless youth; and this type prevailed long after the Antonines had restored the beard to fashion. Christ is always so portrayed when he is working miracles. The beardless type was succeeded by the bearded and long-haired type. The latter appears from the third century onward, and it becomes general in the fourth, especially in the frescoes portraying Christ as teacher and judge. In the catacombs of SS. Peter and Marcellinus, we see him between the two great Apostles, the one easily recognizable by his pointed beard and bald head, the other by his large face and short thick beard. Here, perhaps for the first time, the head of Jesus is surrounded by a nimbus. His long curly hair is parted in the middle; his hand is lifted in blessing and his lips are open as if to speak. The look in his eyes is arresting. A similar type is often found in the mosaics of the fifth and sixth centuries; the attitude is grave and majestic, but without severity. Then comes the Byzantine type, in which Christ is older, his face framed in a more or less long black beard. "The Christ of the evangelical cycle, in his maturity, does indeed keep his charm and grace, but more and more does this Almighty God, Master of the world, take on a severity of mien, with a touch of sadness and sternness."[45]

What can be called the modern type comes from the legendary descriptions which appeared in the West as in the East from the seventh century on, and were transmitted to us by Andrew of Crete, the monk Epiphanius, the three Eastern patriarchs (in their letter to the iconoclast Emperor, Theophilus), the apocryphal letter of Lentulus, and Nicephorus Callistus. These are its characteristic traits: more than average height, chestnut-brown hair parted in the middle and falling in curls on the shoulders, a serene brow without wrinkle or blemish, a slightly bronzed complexion, a majestic and gentle expression, a beard the color of the hair, fairly thick but not very long, and ending in a double point. The monk Epiphanius adds another touching detail, most likely true of one who had no earthly father: Jesus was the living image of his Mother — in particular, he had her oval face and slightly ruddy complexion.

---

[45] Diehl, *Manuel d'art byzantin,* Vol. I, 1925, pp. 324–325. For the catacombs, consult the monumental work of Wilpert, *Le pitture delle catacombe romane* (Rome, 1903), with many engravings and an atlas of 263 plates. The fresco we have mentioned is reproduced on plate 187, n. 3, and in greater detail in plate 253. For the Middle Ages, cf. Kraus, in the *Dictionary of Christ and the Gospels,* Vol. I, p. 214.

CHAPTER IV

Jesus and John

1. The Preaching of the Precursor

THE narrative of the early years of John is much briefer than the narrative of the boyhood of Jesus. It is contained in two lines: "The child grew and waxed strong in spirit and lived in the wilderness until the day of his manifestation to Israel." Physical development in John, as in Jesus, went step by step with intellectual and spiritual progress. Both lived in retirement, but the adolescence of one unfolded itself by the family hearth, while that of the other was spent in the desert from a very early age, doubtless from the day the child could take care of himself without the help of his parents.[1]

What is pointed out today as the desert of St. John is only relatively a wilderness. From the grotto which is supposed to have been his hermitage, the eye can take in a horizon full of villages, one of them, at least, not more than half a league away. But the real wilderness is not far off. If you trace a line on the map of Palestine, starting at Bethel and ending at Hebron, passing through Jerusalem and Bethlehem, it would nearly follow the course of the mountain range of Judea. From the east, the land slopes imperceptibly at first, then within the space of four or five miles drops abruptly into a chaos of barren rocks gashed by steep ravines, at the bottom of which rushing torrents roar

[1] *Teneris sub annis,* sings the Church. Some say two or three years; others, seven or eight. Let us say, rather, ten or twelve. On the food and raiment of John, cf. Buzy, *Saint Jean Baptiste,* 1912, pp. 97–103, or Lagrange, *Saint Marc,* 4 ed., 1929, pp. 7–8. Lagrange thinks that the ζωνή was a "loin-cloth of skin"; Buzy holds for "leathern girdle" (*Recherches,* 1934, pp. 589–598).

along in winter, tumbling from precipice to precipice down into the gulf of the Dead Sea. There is not a dwelling in sight, not a sign of human activity apart from a few shepherds leading their sheep and goats to pasture among the thorny bushes and aromatic plants that manage to survive the burning heat of this inferno. The Hebrews gave this wilderness a name which in their tongue means "desolation."

Before preaching to others, John was to give the world an example of unparalleled austerity. The winding passages of rock and the caves of this tortuous region were his shelter. His clothing was made of that rough camel skin from which the nomads made their tents. Instead of the silky, colorful cinctures affected by Orientals, he wore around his loins a simple strip of leather. He fed on the honey the wild bees store up in the crevices of the rocks, and on the locusts that abound all year in those regions. Though the natives did not have the same repugnance for these insects which they arouse in us — even today the Bedouins eat them, boiled in salt water and dried in the sun, or roasted on embers and sprinkled with salt — the poorest of the sedentary dwellers of Palestine would find it hard to adapt themselves to such a diet.

This anchoritic mode of existence edified John's contemporaries and gave them no offense. Asceticism was held in high honor among the Jews of that time. The Pharisees boasted that they fasted twice a week; the Rechabites refrained from drinking wine; and the Nazirites abstained from all fermented drinks. Josephus recounts that in his youth he was placed under the care of a solitary named Banus, who dressed in bark and leaves and ate only the wild products of the soil. Banus was twenty years later than the Baptist, and hence was not his predecessor, but at most his imitator or disciple. There were, however, authentic ascetics at that period. To say nothing of the Therapeutae, who were perhaps a figment of Philo's apologetic imagination or at least greatly magnified by him, there was near John's wilderness a group of cenobites who have a place in history. We should say something about these strange people, because it has been asserted that the Baptist and Jesus himself were formed in their school.

The Essenes, numbering around four thousand, were scattered at various places in Palestine, but their principal establishment —

we almost said their mother house — was near Engaddi. Pliny the Elder singles them out as a unique phenomenon: "On the west of the Dead Sea, far enough from the shore to escape its noxious vapors, lives a solitary people, a marvel without equal in the whole world; a people among whom no one is born and who go on forever."[2] The Essenes were celibates and practiced a community of goods. Distrusting the susceptibility and fickleness of youth, they rarely admitted any but mature men into their midst. After a year of noviceship and two more years of trial, the postulants pledged themselves by vow to observe piety toward God, justice toward men, and loyalty to all. They were then initiated into certain esoteric teachings, contained in secret books, which they promised not to divulge, even though threatened with death. Twice a day the Essenes set aside their assigned tasks, took a bath in cold water, put on white clothing, and met for a repast of a sacred nature, to which no outsider was admitted, and at which an impressive silence was observed.[3]

At first glance one might say this was a cloister of Christian monks. Yet nothing was further opposed to the spirit of Jesus and John than Essenism. The Essenes were a schismatic Jewish sect. While priding themselves on a scrupulous observance of the Mosaic Law, they condemned bloody sacrifices; we do not know by what mode of interpretation they explained away the texts in the Pentateuch prescribing and regulating the immolation of victims. On the other hand, their formalism far surpassed even that of the Pharisees. They fancied themselves polluted by the touch not only of a pagan, but of any individual not a member of their sect. Their dietary restrictions were so rigorous that if for some reason one of them happened to be banned from the community, he was reduced to living on roots and wild fruits or dying of hunger. We can find no signs of proselytism among them, nor of Messianic hopes. Their mysticism was directed solely at individual salvation by freeing the soul from the bonds of matter. Jews though they were, Oriental dualism seems to have won them over. Their veneration of the sun, which they invoked at its rising

---

[2] Pliny, *Hist. nat.*, v. 17: "Incredibile dictu, gens aeterna in qua nemo nascitur."

[3] Josephus, *Bellum*, II, viii, 2–13; *Antiq.*, XIII, v, 9; XV, x, 4–5; XVIII, i, 5. Cf. Philo, *Quod omnis probus liber*, 12–13 (Mangey, II, 457–459) and the fragment preserved by Eusebius, *Praepar, evangel.*, viii, 11 (Mangey, II, 632–634).

and whose rays they feared to soil by unseemly conduct, has something rather disturbing about it. "They believe," says Josephus, "that though their bodies are perishable, their souls are immortal. Made of the most subtile ether, the soul is drawn into the prison of the body by a sort of instinctive attraction, and will remain enchained in it until the day when, delivered from the bonds of the flesh, it will joyously fly off toward the celestial spaces. Like the Greeks they believe that the souls of the just pass beyond the seas to a place where reigns eternal springtime, while the souls of the wicked are plunged into a dark and glacial gulf."

In this narrow and hybrid system there was no room for creation, resurrection, a universal Redeemer, or even a national Messias. Satisfied with the Elysian fields of which the Greek imagination dreamed, the Essenes were not natural candidates for the kingdom of God. Had they heard the Sermon on the Mount or the parables on the kingdom, their mysticism would have understood nothing of it. They managed to survive in certain Gnostic sects, but we do not read that they ever furnished recruits to the Church. The occasional claim that John the Baptist and Jesus himself were affiliated with these people, who wrapped themselves in mystery and professed the most intolerant exclusivism, is not only a bold paradox, but the peak of absurdity.[4]

The time had come for the Precursor to leave the desert.

---

[4] On the Essenes and Essenism, see Schürer, *Geschichte,* 4 ed., Vol. II, pp. 651–680 (a copious bibliography and discussion of texts). Lightfoot's dissertation, added as an appendix to his commentary on *Colossians* (3 ed., 1879, pp. 348–419) is still very instructive. The author examines fully the etymology of the name; he refutes Frankel (who repudiates the authority of Josephus and Philo) and studies the relationships, real or supposed, between Essenism and Christianity. He is of the opinion that the Essenes owed nothing either to Buddhism (Hilgenfeld) or to Pythagoreanism (Zeller and the Tübingen school), but admits the influence of Parseeism. He proves that Essenism exerted no influence on newborn Christianity, but that it did influence some of the Gnostic sects of the second century. — The same praise cannot be given to the long article of Bugge: *Zum Essaerproblem* (in *Z.N.T.W.,* 1913, pp. 143–174). [For more recent works see Lagrange, *Le Judaisme avant J.-C.,* pp. 307–330; Bonsirven, *Le Judaisme Palestinien au temps de J.-C.* — cf. references to the word *Esséniens,* Vol. II, p. 338. Note of *J.C.*] Various dictionaries of the Bible (cf. Vigouroux in the *Supplément,* Vol. II, coll. 1109–1132) give the essentials of Essenism, though its history is still obscure.

"In the fifteenth year of the reign of Tiberius Caesar, when Pilate was governor of Judea, and Herod tetrarch of Galilee, and his brother Philip tetrarch of the district of Iturea and Trachonitis, and Lysanias tetrarch of Abilina, during the high priesthood of Annas and Caiphas, the word of God was heard by John, the son of Zachary, in the wilderness; and he went about the whole region of the Jordan, preaching a baptism of repentance for the remission of sins, as it is written in the book of the prophet Isaias:

> 'The voice of him who cries in the wilderness:
> Prepare the way of the Lord,
> make straight his paths.' "[5]

The appearance of the Baptist as a prelude to the appearance of Jesus is an event of capital importance in the Gospel history. It would be very helpful for the chronology of the life of Christ, if we could fix the date with any certainty. Unfortunately, however, the synchronisms provided by St. Luke lead to no definite conclusion. Pilate was for ten years procurator of Judea, and Caiphas was high priest for sixteen years; both of them fell from power only in the spring of the year 36 of our era. Antipas, the son of Herod the Great, was tetrarch until A.D. 39, and his brother Philip, until A.D. 34. Lysanias, as we now know, was tetrarch of Abilina around the same time, but it is impossible to date the beginning or the end of his term of office. Finally, the fifteenth year of Tiberius can be computed in several ways resulting in variations of two or three years. This is not the time nor place to enter into the details of these controversies; suffice it to say that, according to the most authoritative opinion, the Baptist made his appearance in the last months of the year 779 A.U.C., which would be the year 26 of the Christian era.

The Sabbatical year had just begun.[6] It started with the opening of the civil year, after the vintage and the picking of autumn fruits (September-October in our calendar). For twelve months farm work was suspended. There was no labor, no sowing or har-

---

[5] Luke 3:1–4. Cf. Note B: *Chronology of the Life of Christ.*

[6] We know the date of three Sabbatical years: 164–163 and 38–37 B.C., and A.D. 68–69. Cf. Schürer, *Geschichte,* 4 ed., Vol. I, pp. 35–37. If the year 68–69 was a Sabbatical year, the year 26–27 (42 years before) must also have been one.

vesting, no pruning of vines and fruit trees. In an age when chemical fertilization and crop rotation were unknown, the earth demanded a periodical rest under penalty of early exhaustion. The fields lay fallow, and the products which the soil brought forth without cultivation were left for the poor or for travelers, or at least were shared with them. However, since it was forbidden to store anything away, they had to be eaten on the spot. During this time, the Jews added to their stock of tools, built dwellings, and devoted themselves to other occupations. It was a time of rest for the earth, but not for men; Tacitus calumniates the Jews when he says that they consecrated every seventh year to idleness. Nevertheless, work was less pressing than usual, and the people had leisure to go out to the wilderness to hear the Precursor of Jesus.

Oriental sovereigns, when traveling abroad, were in the habit of sending men ahead of them to repair and widen the roads. Vespasian did this on his march to the Holy City; and the heavy labor spent on building a system of roads when the German Kaiser visited Jerusalem has not yet been forgotten there. Such was John's role — to prepare the way for the King of heaven, who was about to manifest himself to the world, and to dispose hearts to receive him. He kept repeating, "Do penance, for the kingdom of heaven is at hand."

For his purpose John employed two rites, baptism and the confession of sins, and their meaning was not obscure. At all times and among all peoples, corporal ablutions have symbolized purification of soul. The preliminary bath imposed on proselytes to Judaism and those to be initiated into the pagan mysteries is well known. Priests of all religions purified themselves before offering sacrifice, and the Essenes did the same before the repast, which was for them a sort of liturgical act. The confession of sins, on the other hand, by reason of the sentiments it expresses and supposes, is a sensible sign of sincere repentance and is its natural accompaniment.

The common people, generally speaking, were moved by feelings of simple piety, and thought only of taking advantage of this means of salvation. Many, following the example of others, submitted without reluctance, but without conviction, to rites which were, in their eyes, if not efficacious, at least harmless. But some, prompted by a desire to spy on the Baptist, came to his baptism in a spirit of hypocrisy; these were the Pharisees and Sadducees. It was to them that John said: "You brood of vipers! Who has given you the secret of escaping the wrath which is ready to fall upon you? Bring forth worthy fruit of repentance and say not: We have Abraham for our father . . . . The axe is already laid to the root of the trees; every barren tree is to be cut down and cast into the fire."[7] The viper, characterized by venom and winding coils, is the image of the Pharisees, whose hypocrisy and malice were so often stigmatized by the Saviour. Their descent from the patriarchs will not save them. A short period is granted them for repentance; should they let it pass, they will suffer the fate of the barren tree. In Palestine, trees are cultivated only for their fruit; every unproductive olive and fig tree is immediately cut down and used for firewood.

Severe to the proud and hypocritical, John has nothing but forgiveness and gentleness for upright and docile hearts who ask only to be told their duty. To them he says, "If you have two tunics, give one to the poor man who has none." Almsgiving was an act of piety much in honor among the Jews. "Redeem thy sins with alms," wrote the prophet Daniel; for, adds the author of Ecclesiasticus, "it blots out sin as water quenches the flame."

When the despised and detested publicans came to John, he did not order them to abandon their profession, dangerous though it certainly was, but still compatible with the observance of justice. He recommended merely that they "exact no more than the taxes." Let them keep within the limits of the law: let them avoid any arbitrary raising of the taxes; let them not take pay for unlawful deals, and the kingdom of God is not closed to them.

To the soldiers of Herod Antipas, who were charged with maintaining public order as police, and whose multiple functions gave many occasions for graft, extortion, false denunciations, and all sorts of other annoyances, John says only: "Molest no one; make no false accusations; be content with your pay."[8] Thus,

---

[7] Matt. 3:7–10; Luke 3:7–9. Instead of *Pharisees* and *Sadducees,* St. Luke says "the multitudes." Otherwise, the variants are almost negligible.

[8] Luke 3:10–14. These texts are peculiar to St. Luke. Three kinds of people ask advice: (*a*) the crowds (the common people); (*b*) the publicans; (*c*) the

on the Jordan, did the Baptist speak in a language adapted to each individual and his specific duties.

2. The Baptism of Jesus

The river that divides Palestine in two down its whole length is one of the swiftest and most sinuous in the world. Seen from neighboring heights, it presents the appearance of a long ribbon of verdure winding at the bottom of a trench cut open in geological times by a powerful earthquake. The jungle of tamarisk, willows, poplars, and clinging creepers was once the lair of lions, leopards, and wild boars. It was called the glory and pride of the Jordan. Along most of its course the borders of the river are uncultivated. Its high, steep banks are unfit for irrigation, and the torrents coursing down the surrounding hills merely carve gullies in the clayey soil, without enriching it. At the opening into the Lake of Tiberias, however, and at the approaches to the Dead Sea, the valley widens out; there is an abundant play of springs, and the desert blooms. The plain extending north of the Dead Sea on both sides of the river over a total of some 12 miles looks like a vast amphitheater, and was called by the Hebrews the Circle or the Circus of the Jordan.[9]

In the days of Christ a forest of palms and balsam trees stood there and made the country famous. Pagan and Jewish historians never cease to extol these fabulous gardens of Herod. Yet the immediate environs of the Dead Sea are so impregnated with salt that they are hardly worth cultivating, and where there is no spring water there is only bareness.

It was at Bethany, beyond the Jordan, that John ordinarily baptized. It was there too that he gave his triple testimony to Jesus. Yet it does not follow that he baptized Jesus there, for he often changed his location, according to the demands of the season and the convenience of his hearers. At all events, from

---

soldiers. These last are not Greeks or Samaritans in the Procurator's service, but Jews in the pay of the Tetrarch, whose territory bordered on the Jordan.

[9] Matt. 3:5; Luke 3:3: *περίχωρος τοῦ Ἰορδάνου* (in Hebrew כִּכַּר הַיַּרְדֵּן). The comparison with an amphitheater is also found in Strabo, *Geog.*, XVI, 41. Strabo says that Herod's gardens were 100 stadia long (11½ mi.). Josephus says that they were 70 stadia long and 20 wide (about 8 x 2¼ mi.).

the fourth century on, the place of the baptism was pointed out on the right bank of the river, four or five miles to the north of the Dead Sea, and a church was rebuilt there in the past century to commemorate it.[10]

The ardent preaching of John, the miracle of his penitential life, and the prestige surrounding him suggested to many that he could well be the Messias; but he energetically denied it:

"I baptize in water to dispose to repentance; but there comes one after me mightier than I, whose shoes I am not worthy to bear. He shall baptize you in the Holy Spirit and fire. He holds in his hand a winnowing-fan to cleanse his threshing floor and gather his wheat into the barn; as to the chaff, he will burn it with unquenchable fire."[11]

For every inhabitant of Palestine, the figure was very expressive. When the sheaves piled up on the threshing floor have been trodden out under the feet of oxen or with flails armed with points, the chief harvester takes his winnowing fan or fork and tosses the mixture of chaff and grain into the air. The grain, which is heavier, falls at his feet. The chaff is scattered by the breeze, and is collected only to feed the fire. This is a picture of what will happen in the days of the Messias, when he comes to separate the good from the evil. In vain will the Jews invoke their descent from Abraham to escape condemnation. Let them make no mistake. If they are found to be too light, they will be fuel for an unquenchable fire.

One winter day, the Carpenter of Nazareth, still completely unknown, appeared on the banks of the Jordan in the midst of the penitents. It is strange, but true, that his cousin John did not know him personally. Having lived in the desert from early youth, John had had no opportunity to meet Jesus, who kept to

[10] In 333, the Pilgrim of Bordeaux gives the distance between the Dead Sea and the place of baptism as five miles (Geyer, *Itinera Hieros.*, 1898, p. 34). This is 5½ English miles, the actual distance of the traditional place. Since then the tradition has not varied either among the Greeks or Latins.

[11] Matt. 3:11–12; cf. Mark 1:7–8; Luke 3:15–18. St. Mark and St. Luke say: "I am not worthy to loose the straps of his shoes," instead of "I am not worthy to bear his shoes." Both expressions have the same meaning: "I am not worthy to be his servant."

the solitude of Nazareth except for the times of pilgrimage to Jerusalem. Of course, John was fully aware of his role as Precursor; he knew that he was preparing the way for the Messias, whose coming was imminent. Moreover, he had been told by revelation that he would know him when he should see the Holy Spirit descend upon him in the form of a dove. But when Jesus came forward to receive baptism from his hands, a supernatural light illumined John's mind, anticipating the promised sign. Thus too, Samuel, searching among the sons of Jesse for the future king of Israel, when he glimpsed the young David, whom he did not know, had heard an interior voice saying to him: "This is he."

When Jesus, separating from the crowd, stood face to face with John and asked to be baptized, John remonstrated with all his might. "It is I," said he, "who have need to be baptized by thee, and comest thou to me!" He knew perfectly — he had, indeed, himself defined — the difference between Jesus' baptism and his own. The baptism of water is only an external ablution symbolizing repentance; the baptism of fire and the Holy Spirit, on the contrary, reaches the soul itself and vivifies it, as fire penetrates to the molecules of a body and communicates to them its own properties. John was powerless to confer that kind of baptism, and wanted to receive it himself. But the Saviour said to him, "Let it be so for the present. It is fitting that we thus accomplish all justice." He does not say, "it is necessary," but, "it is fitting." Actually, he was bound by no legal prescription: John's baptism was not an institution of the Old Law, but a freely embraced work of supererogation. Jesus knew, however, that it was acceptable to God that he be baptized, because the act would edify the people and honor the Precursor.

Straightway after his baptism, without stopping to confess sins like the rest (for he knew himself guiltless), Jesus came out of the Jordan to give himself to prayer. Suddenly the heavens opened, the Holy Ghost descended on him in the form of a dove, and a voice rang out from on high: "This is my beloved son in whom I am well pleased."[12] The theophany was not only

---

[12] Matt. 3:16–17. St. Mark (1:11) and St. Luke (3:22) report the words of the Father as addressed to him whom they concerned: "Thou art my beloved son in whom I am well pleased." These variants are inconsequential. Some

for his sake. John, to whom it had been promised, certainly shared it, as did probably some others of those present, although the Gospel does not say so. This would better explain the eagerness with which the first disciples followed the Saviour when they saw him again forty days later.

It is easy for us now to recognize in this scene the manifestation of the three Divine Persons; but did the spectators plumb this mystery at the time, and did they grasp the full meaning of the words, "This is my beloved son?" Was even John himself more enlightened than the Apostles were after long months in the intimacy of our Lord? We may doubt it. At least those who saw the dove resting on Jesus and heard the words from the sky must have understood that the object of such extraordinary favor was not a man like the rest of them, that he was superior to the Baptist himself, and that faith and obedience were due to him as to a divine messenger. We see, then, the providential purpose in the baptism of Jesus; God wished, in the presence of John and his disciples on the banks of the Jordan, solemnly to authenticate the mission of his Son, and not, as certain exegetes contend, to make him conscious of his mission.

3. The Fast and Temptation of Christ

Opposite and west of ancient Jericho rises steeply the Mountain of Quarantania, named in memory of the fast and temptation of the Saviour. The numerous caves which rise tier upon tier on its sides, once the haunt of anchorites, have become difficult and even perilous to reach nowadays, because the steps cut into the rock from level to level are demolished or very badly worn down, and the slightest misstep would hurl the imprudent climber over a precipice. According to a tradition that has no rival and goes back at least to the seventh century, it was to one of these caves that Jesus retired when he came out of the Jordan.[13] Before

---

manuscripts of St. Luke make the addition: "Thou art my son; today have I begotten thee," which is a citation from Ps. 2:7. On the fantasies of the Apocrypha (the *Gospel according to the Hebrews,* the *Gospel of the Nazarenes,* and the *Gospel of the Ebionites*) regarding the baptism of Jesus, cf. Lebreton, *La vie et l'enseignement de J.-C.,* 1931, Vol. I, pp. 75–76 (English transl., Vol. I, pp. 43–44).

[13] Cf. Guérin, *Samarie,* Vol. i, p. 41.

beginning his active apostolate, he felt the need of extended communion with his Father. The most illustrious Fathers of the Church such as Jerome, Basil, Gregory of Nazianzus, John Chrysostom, as well as founders of religious orders such as Benedict, Francis of Assisi, Ignatius, and many others have followed his example, seeking inspiration and strength in solitude before undertaking the great deeds they planned to accomplish for God's glory.

A providential design directed Jesus thither. St. Mark, who does not intend to recount in detail the Saviour's temptation, gives this summary: "And straightway (after the baptism) the Spirit drove him out into the wilderness. And he was there forty days, tempted by the devil; and he lived among wild beasts, and the angels ministered to him."[14] In other days, lions and leopards would sometimes leave their lairs along the Jordan to scale the steep mountain heights, but today only the yelping of jackals and the occasional snarling of hyenas are heard in the vicinity.

Like Moses on Sinai, and Elias on the road to Horeb, Jesus observed an absolute fast of forty days and forty nights; but he was so absorbed in God, so lost in ecstasy, that the natural process of living was almost suspended, and he seems to have felt the pangs of hunger only at the end of his fast. The devil took advantage of this physical exhaustion to tempt him. Perhaps, however, as a literal reading of St. Mark suggests, the demon did not wait until then.[15]

It was fitting that the Saviour, who had come down from heaven to overthrow the empire of Satan, should at the outset pit himself against the prince of this world, the great enemy of the human race, and should win a signal victory over him. It was necessary, too, in the present plan of redemption, that he be tried in every way, sin alone excepted, the better to have compassion on our weakness. "His sufferings and trials," says the Apostle, "enabled him to come to the aid of those who are

[14] Mark 1:12–13; cf. Matt. 4:1. The spirit which drives (ἐκβάλλει, Mark) or simply leads him (ἀνήχθη, Matt.; ἤγετο, Luke) to the desert is evidently the Holy Spirit; and he leads him there that he may be tried there by the devil (πειρασθῆναι ὑπὸ τοῦ διαβόλου, Matt.).

[15] Matt. 4:2. "Finally he was hungry" seems to imply that the hunger came only at the termination of the fast. On the other hand, St. Mark says (1:13): "He was forty days in the wilderness, tempted by the devil."

tried."[16] He did not act thus merely to serve as a model for us in our fight against devils and to teach us how to overcome them, for there are in him too many perfections that defy imitation. We carry within ourselves the principal source of our temptations, and even when these come from without they are sure to find in us certain things that aid and abet them. But Jesus knew no inclination to evil, and his reason, which was of a perfect rectitude, ruled as master over his lower faculties. In the temptations that assail us, there is always an element of surprise or ignorance or error; on the contrary, there was not so much as a passing shadow on Jesus' intelligence. The balance between his spiritual and his sensible faculties was so perfect that for us it is difficult to understand, not how he overcame temptation, but how he could have experienced it at all.

The word "tempt" is used equivocally in Scripture. God sometimes *tempts* the just to test them, to make them aware of their weakness, or to give them an opportunity for merit. Man *tempts* God by small-souled distrust and by presumptuous pride. The devil *tempts* man to seduce and ruin him.

What, then, did the devil have in mind or hope to gain by attacking Christ? St. Ambrose comes forward with a happy formula: "He tempts him to try him, and tries him to tempt him." He sees in Jesus an extraordinary human being; he suspects that he may well be the Messias and the Son of God. Were he sure of this, he would not wantonly expose himself to certain defeat. Of this he wishes to make trial. If he succeeds in snaring Jesus, he will know that he has nothing further to fear from him. If he fails, he at least counts upon forcing him to declare himself. In either case he will learn what he does not yet know, and certainty seems preferable to doubt.

It is impossible to determine, and useless to inquire, whether the tempter appeared in human form (as is commonly believed and as the Gospel text seems to indicate), or remained invisible and acted toward Jesus as he usually acts with other men.[17] It is more important for us to keep to the words of the account and

---

16 Heb. 2:18; 4:15, etc.

17 Maldonatus on Matt. 4:3: "Quomodo aut qua forma accesserit, Evangelistae non dicunt. Potuit aut invisibiliter accedere, sicut nos quotidie tentare solet, aut sumpta aliqua visibili forma . . . quod est valde probabile."

strive to understand the meaning of the temptation, rather than trouble ourselves with puzzling out its mode.

"At the end of forty days and forty nights of fasting, Jesus was hungry. And the tempter drew near and said to him, 'If thou art the Son of God, command these stones to change into loaves.'

"But he answered and said, 'Not by bread alone does man live, but by everything that happens at the command of God.' "[18]

The first assault of the Evil One is not properly a temptation to gluttony. The term fixed for the fast is passed, and there is no sensuality nor any imperfection in wishing to appease hunger when it has become a torment and there is no further obligation to abstain. Disorder would come from using miraculous power needlessly and at a suggestion prompted by curiosity or malice. But to work a miracle to prove oneself a wonder-worker would be sheer ostentation; to work one merely to satisfy a personal need would be an act of distrust in God. Then is the time to hand oneself over to Providence, which will provide for our needs in unsuspected ways. This is what Jesus means by his answer. The Hebrews in the desert cried aloud for bread; God rained manna down on them, something they did not expect, "in order to prove," as Moses said to them, "that man does not live by bread alone but by everything that happens at the command of God."

This was a double defeat for Satan. He had hoped to exploit the state of starvation in which Jesus found himself after his long fast and get him to perform a useless and inopportune

---

[18] Matt. 4:2–4. St. Luke (4:3–4) has the same text with three variants: (*a*) he leaves out "drew near"; (*b*) he adds "say to this stone," as though Satan pointed to it with his finger, which is more picturesque; (*c*) he shortens the quotation from Deuteronomy, reducing it to "man does not live by bread alone." In St. Matthew this quotation is made according to the Septuagint, with two Hebraisms that make it hard to understand. The Hebrew has: "Man does not live by bread alone, but *by everything that comes forth from the mouth of God,*" i.e., by everything that comes through his command, as did the manna. In the Greek *ἐπὶ παντὶ ῥήματι ἐκπορευομένῳ διὰ στόματος Θεοῦ*, the word *ῥήματι* should be taken in the sense of דבר, "thing," and *διὰ στόματος* then means "by his command."

Some think that Jesus is giving the text an accommodated sense: "Man does not live by bread alone; because there is another life for him, and that life is nurtured by the word of God" (Lagrange, *Saint Matthieu,* p. 60). This would be possible if Jesus had cited the Bible *in Greek,* according to the Septuagint; but he quoted it in Hebrew or Aramaic, and it would be difficult to believe that he departed from the literal sense.

miracle. He was frustrated. He had wanted to find out whether Jesus was Son of God and knew himself to be such. He learned nothing; Jesus kept his secret.

"Then the devil took him to the Holy City, and, placing him on the pinnacle of the Temple, said to him, 'If thou art the Son of God, cast thyself down; for it is written: God has entrusted thee to his angels who shall carry thee in their hands, to prevent thy foot from striking against a stone.'

"Jesus said to him, 'It is also written: Thou shalt not tempt the Lord thy God.' "[19]

The picture here is disconcerting to the imagination and confusing to the mind. It is hard to conceive the devil seizing Jesus around the body and transporting him through space to the Temple, to the stupefaction of all beholders. On the other hand, it is repellent to imagine the Saviour traveling the fifteen or sixteen miles between Jerusalem and the Mount of Quarantania side by side with the devil. If the theory of a vision be rejected, should it not rather be said, as some of the Fathers say, that the Saviour freely and spontaneously takes up the challenge of his antagonist? As an athlete confident of victory he leaves to his adversary the choice of arms, he accepts the terrain chosen by the devil, and betakes himself of his own free will to the place of combat.[20]

---

[19] Matt. 4:5–7. The differences in Luke 4:9–12 are negligible, except that St. Luke inverts the last two temptations. The order followed by St. Matthew is generally preferred by interpreters as presenting a more natural gradation, and above all because Satan could not have returned to the attack after the strong rebuke, "Begone, Satan!" by which he would know himself unmasked. Moreover, St. Luke has omitted these words in the second temptation, which is the third in St. Matthew.

[20] Origen (*In Lucam homil.* xxxi, MG, XIII, 1879): "Sequebatur ut athleta ad tentationem sponte proficiscens," quoted approvingly by St. Thomas (*Summa,* III, q. xli, a. 1, ad 2). Cf. St. John Chrysostom, *In Matth. homil.*, viii, 2 (MG, LVII, 210), who, in the same way, makes a comparison with a fencing master.

A twelfth-century author, Arnold, abbot of Bonneval, in a work formerly attributed to St. Cyprian (*De cardinalibus virtutibus Christi,* v; ML, CLXXXIX, 1637), offers the theory that Jesus was transported to the Temple in spirit, without any change of place, as Ezechiel believed himself transported to Jerusalem without leaving the banks of the Chobar. It is probably to him that St. Thomas refers (*Summa,* III, q. xli, a. 2, ad 3): "Quidam dicunt quod Christus ductus est in sanctam civitatem non realiter sed secundum imaginariam visionem." This opinion has again found favor in our own day: "The narrative wavers between an external reality that is hard to admit, and a psychological and moral reality

The pinnacle of the Temple was not the pylon, a hundred cubits high, that stood between the Sanctuary and the Court of the Priests, but rather the point of juncture of the Royal Porch and the Porch of Solomon, at the southeast corner of the outside perimeter. This point overhung the valley of Cedron, and was a kind of belvedere, looking out toward the mountains of Moab over the gulf of the Dead Sea. It was a dizzying experience to lean over the protective balustrade at the edge and look down into the ravine. This is the height from which tradition says James the Less was hurled to his death.

As before, Satan opens the scene with an ambiguous sentence which is a sort of challenge: "If thou art the Son of God, cast thyself down." If thou art truly what thou pretendest to be, thou hast nothing to fear; angels will receive thee into their hands — God himself assures thee of that. The arch-liar is quoting the Scriptures falsely; the text he uses is not Messianic. Besides, though God promises his protection to the just who have confidence in him, he does not pledge himself to work miracles for the presumptuous. In itself, the trap was obvious. Nevertheless, a brilliant miracle performed at the highest point of the Temple esplanade, before the assembled multitude, might seem to be an effective and ready way to win the people, and avoid long and painful delays. But by taking this short cut Christ would deviate from the line traced out for him by the redemptive plan. Such seems to have been the true purpose of the second temptation, and, as in the case of the first, the Saviour frustrates it with a text from Scripture taken in the literal sense.

"Again, the devil took him to a high mountain, from which he showed him all the kingdoms of the world and the glory thereof, and said to him: 'All these will I give thee, if thou fall down and pay me homage. . . .'

"Jesus said to him, 'Begone, Satan, for it is written: Thou shalt adore the Lord thy God and him only shalt thou serve.' "[21]

---

which suffices to preserve all the importance of the moral teaching given by Jesus" (LeCamus, *Vie de J.-C.,* 1921, Vol. I, p. 276).

[21] Matt. 4:8–10. St. Luke's version (4:5–8) is so different that it must be given in its entirety: "Having led him up (ἀναγαγών), the devil showed him all the kingdoms of the world in the twinkling of an eye (ἐν στιγμῇ χρόνου) and said

An undoubtedly well-inspired tradition saw no need of placing the scene of the third temptation of Jesus on the peak of the lofty Hermon, which raises its majestic head in the north of Palestine, but assigned it to the summit of the Mountain of Quarantania, where the ruins of a Christian oratory can be seen today. The horizon taken in from this point is not vast, for the Mount of Olives hides even Jerusalem from view. But even from the highest point in the Himalayas the most piercing vision imaginable would be unable to see all the kingdoms of the earth. The Evangelist knew this as well as we do, and when he says that Satan showed Jesus "all the kingdoms of the earth," he means to suggest that the devil used his powers to parade the images of these kingdoms before the mind of Jesus.

It all happened in an instant. St. Luke tells us that the vision lasted no more than the twinkling of an eye, and that the Tempter took pains to add: "All this has been given over to me, and I may give it to whomsoever I will." The father of lies is boasting; he is not the absolute master of all this, and cannot dispose of it at will. "The earth is the Lord's and all that it contains." Yet, after the sin of man, the devil has free access to the world and dwells in it as in his fief, and has some title to being called "the prince of this world." He will give it, he says, to the one who bows down before him and renders him homage, as a subject to a king, or a vassal to a suzerain. He deliberately uses an ambiguous word, meaning both adoration and homage, for fear of setting in too violent revolt the conscience of a man whose virtue he well knows. Nevertheless the artifice is so plain that it is difficult to explain it. Perhaps, stunned by his two defeats, the Tempter loses his head and strikes out blindly, risking his all like a gambler angered by bad luck. Perhaps he has ceased to believe in the Messiasship of Jesus and thinks that he is dealing with an ordinary man who cannot fail to be dazzled by such vistas of grandeur. As a matter of fact, this time he does not say, as in the first two temptations: "If thou art the Son of God."

---

to him: I will give to thee all their power and their glory, for it has been delivered to me and I give it to whomsoever I will. Therefore, if thou prostrate thyself before me (ἐὰν προσκυνήσῃς ἐνώπιον ἐμοῦ), this shall belong to thee. Jesus answered him: It is written: The Lord thy God shalt thou adore and him only shalt thou serve." St. Luke omits: (*a*) the high mountain; (*b*) the rebuke, "Begone, Satan!" On the other hand, he adds minor details.

The Saviour rebuffs him by the solemn Hebrew profession of faith in the oneness of God: "Thou shalt adore the Lord thy God and him only shalt thou serve." To cut short any new attack, he adds, "Begone, Satan." The devil withdraws, overcome but not discouraged. The Gospel says that he left Jesus only for a time; he still has hopes of revenge.[22] We shall find him in Gethsemani and on Calvary, but there his rout will be complete and final.

It is an oversimplification to reduce the devil's attack to a triple temptation to gluttony, vainglory, and ambition. This would be to look at the temptation from the wrong side. The devil's purpose was really much more complex, as emerges from the brief account given.

The Tempter's designs are easily grasped. Much less easy is it to understand how Satan's purely external suggestions to Jesus can be called temptations. When we are tempted, the will is drawn in two opposite directions; there is a battle between the attraction of evil and the call of conscience. In Jesus' case, there was nothing similar to this. The proposal of evil could evoke in him only aversion and horror. Yet even within him there could at times be struggle and hence victory and merit. His will was not momentarily suspended between good and evil; but, though the path of duty is laid out clearly before the mind, it is often painful and hard on nature. "The whole life of Christ," says the author of the *Imitation,* "was a cross and a martyrdom." Effort and combat were called for, though there was never any doubt of the issue. Would it not have been desirable to the humanity of Christ to satisfy his hunger by a miracle which he had in his power; to exchange a life of privations, humiliations, and sufferings for a peaceful and glorious existence; to procure the salvation of the world by a brilliant stroke rather than by paying for it the price of his blood?

His submission to his Father's desires and his glorious acceptance of the plan of redemption earned for him an immediate reward. When the devil had disappeared, angels came to serve

---

[22] Matt. 4:11; "Tunc reliquit eum diabolus." St. Luke (4:13) adds "usque ad tempus" (ἄχρι καιροῦ), "until a propitious *occasion.*"

him. But he did not delay in descending again to the plain, where the Precursor was waiting to give testimony to him.

4. The Witness of John

He came as a witness,
to bear witness to the Light,
that all might believe through him.
He was not the Light,
but the witness to the Light.

"And this was the witness of John, when the Jews sent to him from Jerusalem priests and Levites to ask him, 'Who art thou?' "[23]

Moved by John's ardent and inspired words, the crowd looked upon him as a new prophet; they were, in fact, not far from seeing in him the Messias. For their part, the chief priests wished to find out whether he was secretly encouraging the Messianic rumors which were being spread about him. He was preaching a baptism alien to Mosaic legislation and the tradition of the Scribes; and this innovation was the more suspect to the religious authorities because its resemblance to the bath of the proselytes seemed to liken the children of Abraham to recruits from paganism.[24]

And so a delegation set out from Jerusalem to look into the matter. The initiative came from the priests, whose special interest was in religious questions, and not from the Sanhedrin, which was the supreme tribunal for affairs of major moment, especially those of a criminal nature. The delegation, made up of priests and levites, together with several Pharisees, was instructed to bring into the open the aims and pretensions of the

---

[23] John 1:6–7, 19. Only *priests* and *levites* are here referred to, but later on we read: καὶ ἀπεσταλμένοι ἦσαν ἐκ τῶν φαρισαίων, which the Vulgate translates: *Et qui missi fuerant erant ex pharisaeis.* It is unlikely that all the envoys were Pharisees, because most of the priests belonged to the sect of Sadducees. Since ἀπεσταλμένοι has no definite article, these words should be interpreted: "Among the envoys were Pharisees." They were sent "by the Jews," i.e., by competent authority, more probably by the priesthood. The question finally asked by them was precisely the one that was asked of Socrates by the Athenians: Σὺ οὖν τίς εἶ (*Discourses of Epictetus,* III, i, 22, in Arrian.)

[24] This follows from Luke 3:15: "All were wondering in their hearts whether John were the Messias."

Baptist. Unwittingly, it was to furnish him with a magnificent opportunity to give testimony to Christ.

Making a point of courtesy, in order to avoid giving public offense to a man so venerated by the people, the delegates did not put to him the question, "Art thou the Messias?" This would have intimated that they thought he was arrogating that title to himself. They merely asked him, as the Athenians once asked Socrates, "Who art thou?" But John replied to their secret thoughts rather than to their open question, declaring boldly, "No, I am not the Christ." Perhaps in accentuating the "No" he intended to convey the idea that the Messias, about whom they were concerned, was actually in their midst and that it was simply a matter of their recognizing him.

Reassured on the main point, the deputies continued their inquiry. "Art thou, then, Elias?" The marvelous history of Elias was adorned with a thousand legends, that made him easily the most popular of the prophets. He was expected to make an appearance at any moment; even today a glass is reserved for him at the Paschal table in case he should return unexpectedly. Now John had all the appearance of Elias — his rough garment, his leather girdle, his wild and half-savage countenance. He could have asserted himself to be Elias, because he was the one typified in prophecy by Elias, and was performing his functions; but, as he was not in person Elias, he answered firmly, "No, I am not."

"Then," rejoined the delegates, "art thou *the* prophet?" — that prophet, on a par with Moses, who was to be heeded under pain of incurring the divine anger. In Deuteronomy there is question of the prophetic office in general, of the series of prophets qualified to speak in God's name and recognizable by certain signs; but the text was often interpreted as speaking of a prophet greater than all the others, a prophet equal to Moses. It is in this sense that the delegates seem to understand it, since they do not ask John if he is a prophet, but if he is *the* prophet. To the question, thus phrased, John answers with a brusque and flat "No."[25]

[25] On Elias in Rabbinical writings, cf. Billerbeck, Vol. IV, pp. 764–798. The Talmudists did not understand Deut. 18:15 in the Messianic sense; but, since prophecy had long been mute, the first to revive it and verify the promise of Deuteronomy, "Yahweh thy God will raise up for thee a prophet like unto me," must be an extraordinary person comparable to Moses.

The Jews press him. "Who, then, art thou? For we must bring back an answer to those who sent us. What sayest thou of thyself?"

"I am, according to the words of the prophet Isaias, he who cries in the wilderness, 'Make level the way of the Lord.' "

There were some Pharisees among the envoys, subtle and shrewd men, not easily satisfied. They objected: "Why, then, dost thou baptize, if thou art not the Messias, nor Elias, nor the prophet?" Certain passages of the Bible could give grounds for considering baptism as a Messianic function or as at least connected with the work of the Messias; but those texts are to be understood of an abundant outpouring of grace, which is indeed one of the characteristics of Messianic times. John does not pretend to confer grace: "I," he says, "baptize with water (to dispose for repentance), but there is one in the midst of you whom you do not know, one who comes after me, the strap of whose sandal I am not worthy to loose. He will give to you the baptism of fire and the Holy Spirit." This first testimony of the Precursor was so important in the eyes of the Beloved Disciple, that he thought he should record the exact place of it: "This took place at Bethany, beyond the Jordan, where John was baptizing" at the time.[26]

The day after the envoys of the chief priests had returned to Jerusalem, Jesus came down from the Mountain of Quaran-

---

[26] John 1:28. Instead of *Bethany,* some manuscripts have the reading *Bethabara,* due probably to Origen's influence. Cf. *R.B.,* 1895, pp. 510–512. Bethany means *house of the ferry;* Bethabara means *house of passage:* the meaning is practically the same.

Federein (*Béthanie au delà du Jourdain,* 1908) locates Bethany at *Tell el-Medesh,* in the estuary of the *Wady-Nimrin,* 2 mi. north of the present bridge, 10 mi. north of the Dead Sea. Cf. Barrois, art. *Béthanie,* in *Dict. de la Bible, Supplément,* Vol. I, coll. 968–970.

Buzy (*Béthanie au delà du Jourdain,* in *Recherches,* 1931, pp. 444–462) favors Sapsas, in the *Wady el-Kharrar,* opposite the traditional place of Christ's baptism, and hence only 4½ or 5 mi. north of the Dead Sea. *Adhuc sub judice lis est.*

The first testimony of John recounted in detail in the Fourth Gospel (John 1:19–28) is after the baptism of Jesus, as is shown by what follows (John 1:29–35: *the next day*). There is an abridged parallel of it in the Synoptics (Matt. 3:11; Mark 1:7–8; Luke 3:16) who place it *before* the baptism, and do not mention the embassy from the Jews. It must be said either that the Synoptics mention it in anticipation, or that John had spontaneously given the same testimony before the multitudes, then afterward before the envoys.

tania. His fast and temptation were over, and he was going to meet John on the banks of the Jordan. John saw him coming, and said to those around him:

"Behold the Lamb of God, behold him who takes away the sins of the world. This is he of whom I said,

'There comes a man *after* me,
Who has gone *ahead of* me,
because he was *before* me.'

"And I did not know him; but I came to baptize with water that he might be manifested to Israel."[27]

The Lamb of God, or simply, the Lamb, is a favorite expression of St. John the Apostle. In the Apocalypse, it is the immolated Lamb whose blood washes away all stains, who leads the elect to battle and victory, who conducts the choir of virgins, who sits on a throne at the right hand of God, and whose eternal nuptials are celebrated by all the Blessed. What can the word mean on the lips of the Baptist and in the minds of his hearers? The prophets compare the Messias to a gentle and patient lamb which suffers itself to be shorn and led to slaughter without a murmur; but that is only a comparison. On the other hand, the lambs sacrificed in the Mosaic ritual, though in general prefiguring the sacrifice to be offered by Christ on the Cross, are not expiatory immolations. The Paschal lamb had no particular relation to sin, and the lamb sacrificed morning and evening in the Sanctuary was a holocaust, a sacrifice of praise. What then could "Behold the Lamb of God" mean on John's lips?

The lamb is the symbol of innocence, and Jesus, who presented

---

[27] John 1:29–32. Cf. 1:15 and 1:27. Οὗτός ἐστιν ὑπὲρ οὗ ἐγὼ εἶπον·—Hic est de quo dixi: Ὀπίσω μου ἔρχεται ἀνήρ—*Post* me venit vir ὃς ἔμπροσθέν μου γέγονεν—qui *ante* me factus est ὅτι πρῶτός μου ἦν.—quia *prior* me erat. Grammatically, in these three phrases the two adverbs, ὀπίσω, ἔμπροσθεν, *post, ante,* and the superlative πρῶτος (for the comparative πρότερος, *prior*) can be taken either in a temporal sense (*after, before*), or in a local sense (*behind, in front of*), or can indicate a mutual relationship of inferiority and superiority. It is evident, however, that the first phrase ὀπίσω is used in a temporal sense (he who comes *after* me, either by birth or the beginning of his ministry); whereas in the second phrase ἔμπροσθεν must mean superiority, otherwise there would be tautology with the third phrase ("he surpassed me in dignity or in the regard of men," i.e., he has become superior to me; γέγονεν). In the third phrase πρῶτος obviously denotes antecedence (he existed *before me;* note the ἦν opposed to γέγονεν).

himself for baptism in the livery of sin, as one of a crowd of sinners, is innocence itself. That is perhaps what the Baptist meant: Behold the Holy One, the Innocent One, who, far from having anything in common with sin, has the power to take away the sins of the world. Today, we know that he washed sin away in his blood; and the Apostles' preaching after the Resurrection has made this doctrine familiar to us; but it is not necessary to credit the Precursor with a theory on the redemptive death of Christ, which his hearers would certainly not have understood. Not scrupling to repeat himself, John says again:

"I saw the Spirit come down as a dove from heaven, and rest upon him. And I did not know him: but he who sent me to baptize with water said to me, 'He upon whom thou shalt see the Spirit descending and abiding, he it is who baptizes with the Holy Spirit.' That is what I have seen, and I have borne witness that he is the Son of God."[28]

The dove cleaving the air and settling on the head of the Saviour, the voice proclaiming him the beloved Son of the Father, the meeting of the three Divine Persons, which gives a sensible expression to the mystery of the Holy Trinity — this whole superb spectacle is not for Jesus, but for the people present, and especially for the Precursor. Let us leave it to the Rationalists to say that, according to the belief of the first Christians, "Jesus was invested with the Messianic dignity on the day of his baptism, by the coming upon him of the Holy Spirit and by a declaration from heaven which indicated the fact to him."[29] And let us concede nothing to the Protestants who think that he then received "in his innermost consciousness the revelation of his personal relationship with God, of his eternal dignity as Son and, by the same token, of the love of God for him and for the humanity to which such a gift was given."[30] The Word Incarnate had no

---

[28] John 1:32–34. — (*a*) "*I have seen* the Spirit (τεθέαμαι). This word is used in St. John of *sense vision;* besides, we know from St. Luke that the Holy Spirit appeared in a *corporeal form* (σωματικῷ εἴδει). — (*b*) St. John says emphatically that the dove *remained* for some time over Jesus. According to the *Odes of Solomon,* xxiv, it *flapped its wings;* according to Justin and Tertullian (cf. Bernard, *St. John,* p. 50), it *fluttered* and *hovered* above him. This idea seems to be a reminiscence of the Spirit of God moving over the waters (Gen. 1:2).

[29] Loisy, *Les Evangiles synoptiques,* 1907, p. 407.

[30] Godet, *L'Evangile de Saint Jean,* Vol. II, p. 145.

need of any such investiture or of any such revelation. The Precursor it was, that needed such increase of light, to recognize Jesus as the Messias, to proclaim his divine Sonship, and thus to prepare for his coming manifestation.

CHAPTER V

The Gradual Manifestation of Christ

1. The First Followers
(JOHN 1:35–51)

As JOHN stood on the banks of the Jordan with two disciples the day after his solemn testimony to Christ, he saw Jesus passing some distance away. Gazing at him with lingering love in his eyes, he said simply, "Behold the Lamb of God." Forthwith, two of his disciples, leaving him forever, set off to follow Jesus. One of them was Andrew, the brother of Simon Peter; the other was certainly the Evangelist himself, easily recognizable by his care to preserve anonymity and especially by the tone of his account, which betrays the eyewitness throughout. How is it that the words, "Behold the Lamb of God," which they had heard the evening before, could so stir them today? Is it the piercing accents of the Precursor and the expression on his face that move them; is it that the silent workings of grace are just now coming to maturity? That is one of the mysteries of God's dealings with men.

Jesus, sensing that he is being followed, turns to them, and says: "Whom seek you?" They answer, "Rabbi (Master), where dwellest thou?" And he said to them: "Come and see."

His dwelling was probably one of those huts of reeds and leaves that travelers throw up hastily to shield themselves from the night dew and the brisk spring mornings. Thither they went with him and spent the rest of the day and most probably the following night in his company. St. John is anxious that we know the precise moment of this meeting, since it marks a decisive point in the orientation of his own life. "It was about the tenth hour" — four o'clock in the afternoon, according to our reckoning. If only he had given us the briefest sketch of the conversation that brought that memorable day to a close!

Both of them left with hearts aflame to win converts. First Andrew, meeting his brother Simon, said to him, "We have found the Messias, the Christ."[1] He led him to Jesus, who cast upon him a penetrating look and said, "Thou art Simon, son of John. Thou shalt be called Kephas" (which means Peter).[2] The name was prophetic, as the future tense of the verb indicates. Simon will take the name Peter only on the day when he will be designated as the Rock on which Christ founds his Church. As might have been expected, the author of the Fourth Gospel tells us nothing about his own actions; but there is reason to believe that he too brought his brother James to Jesus, because in the list of Apostles James is always ranked among the first adherents.

The next day the Saviour decided to return to Galilee. Meeting Philip, who, like Peter and Andrew, was from Bethsaida, he said to him, "Follow me!" Philip, who was the first to hear this call, eagerly hurried to tell his friend Nathanael: "We have found him of whom Moses and the prophets speak, Jesus of Nazareth, the son of Joseph." But Nathanael disdainfully answered: "Can any good come out of Nazareth?" This was one of those jibes that peasants are fond of directing against another's village. According to all accounts, Nazareth was not as rich nor as large

---

[1] John 1:41. "Andrew first (πρῶτον) found his brother Simon." This seems to indicate that his unnamed companion also looked for and found someone. This would be all but certain, if, with Tischendorf, instead of πρῶτον, we read πρῶτος (the first).

[2] John 1:42. Simon, son of John (ὁ υἱὸς Ἰωάνου); also John 21:15, 16, 17 (Σιμὼν Ἰωάνου). But in Matt. 16:17: Simon Barjona (בר יונא, Hebrew, יונה) "son of Jonas" or "son of the Dove," accordingly as יונה be taken as a proper name (4 Kings 14:25) or as a common noun. Did Simon's father have two names, or is Ἰωνᾶ in St. Matthew a shorter form of Ἰωάνου? Cf. *R.B.*, 1922, p. 339.

Peter's real name was Symeon (in Greek Συμεών), but it is given to him only by St. James (Acts 15:14) and in the title of the Second Epistle of Peter. Everywhere else the Grecized *Simon* (Σίμων) is used. The Synoptics call him Peter, except when they present Jesus as speaking, and once, even then (Luke 22:34). St. John usually unites the old and new names, as Simon Peter. St. Paul almost always uses the name Kephas (except in Gal. 2:7–8). After the Apostolic Age, the name Kephas fell into disuse.

as Cana; and Nathanael, whose opinion of people who came from Nazareth was low, was astonished that the Messias could come from such an out of the way place. But his skepticism did not discourage Philip, who rejoined with a simple "Come and see!" — a phrase which meant, "Do not express yourself lightly; come and judge for yourself." Nathanael, more docile than his outburst would suggest, allowed himself to be led to Jesus.

When he saw him, the Lord said to those around him, in a voice loud enough for Nathanael to hear, "Behold a true Israelite, free of craft and guile." The title of Israelite, proper to the children of Jacob, was in a way more honorable than that of son of Abraham; Nathanael fulfilled its ideal meaning. Flattered by the compliment, he became more tractable, and the following short dialogue ensued between him and Jesus:

"How dost thou know me?"

"Before Philip called thee, when thou wast under the fig tree, I saw thee."

"Rabbi (Master), thou art the King of Israel."

"Because I said to thee: 'I saw thee under the fig tree,' thou believest. Thou shalt see greater things. Amen, amen, I say to thee; thou shalt see the heavens opened and the angels of God ascending and descending upon the Son of Man."

Nothing escapes the eyes of Jesus. From afar he saw Nathanael forming some noble plan or taking some generous resolution, when he thought he was hidden by the fig tree, to whose shade the Rabbis loved to retire to study and meditate on Scripture. That secret of his, which we do not share, could not have been other than a highly honorable one, since it evoked for Nathanael a eulogy from Christ.

But when shall Nathanael and his companions see "the heavens opened and the angels of God ascending and descending upon the Son of Man"? Commentators are at a loss to discover the fulfillment of this promise — at the Transfiguration, the Resurrection, the Ascension, the Last Judgment? No angels appeared at the Transfiguration; at the Resurrection angels were seen only by the holy women; at the Ascension they appeared only after Jesus had disappeared; the Last Judgment is a far-off event; moreover, the vision of angels will then be given to all the elect as well as to the Apostles. Evidently the Saviour is alluding to the mysterious ladder between heaven and earth which angels were constantly ascending and descending in Jacob's vision, as he was sleeping in the neighborhood of Bethel. Something analogous will happen in the life of Christ, and the Apostles will be fortunate enough to witness it. There will be a marvelous exchange of communications between heaven and earth; the angels, God's ministers, will be the intermediaries of this continual interchange, and Jesus Christ will be its center. That, in our opinion, is the meaning of this enigmatic promise.

2. The Marriage Feast at Cana

(JOHN 2:1–12)

If we were to read only the Synoptics, we would get the impression that after his forty days' fast, on which the Baptist's arrest followed closely, Jesus returned immediately to Galilee to begin his apostolate. But the author of the Fourth Gospel, perhaps by design, clarifies the order of events.[3] He speaks of two returns to Galilee, and inserts between them a long series of events which the Synoptics fail to mention at all: the first miracle at Cana, the transfer of residence to Capharnaum, the celebration of the Passover at Jerusalem, the conversation with Nicodemus, the conferring of a baptism like John's, the journey across Samaria and the meeting with the Samaritan woman at Jacob's well, and finally the arrival of Jesus at Cana, where he works another miracle, this time from a distance. Only after all these events should the beginnings of the Galilean ministry recounted by the Synoptics be dated.

Cana, the scene of Jesus' first two miracles in Galilee, is now no more than a little town of a thousand inhabitants. It rests pleasantly on the side of a hill, and a fine spring waters its gardens of fig trees and pomegranates, which are surrounded by gigantic cactus hedges. Nathanael's sneer, and the ruins which extend up to the top of the hill suggest that it was once a much more important place. The chapel commemorating the first miracle occupies the site of a church built in the days of the Crusades, itself erected on the foundations of an edifice of the

[3] Compare John 2:1–4:54 with Matt. 4:12–17; Mark 1:14–15; Luke 4:14–15.

fourth century. The tradition is therefore well established, and bears out the claim of the modern village of Kefr-Kenna that it is descended from the Cana of the Gospel, despite arguments advanced in the last century in favor of a ruin situated three hours away to the north of Nazareth.[4]

"On the third day there was a marriage at Cana of Galilee. The mother of Jesus was there, and Jesus and his disciples were also invited to the marriage."[5]

---

[4] On June 18, 1838, Robinson, the American explorer, looking from the hills of Nazareth at the distant ruins which had been pointed out to him as Khirbet Qana, and which he visited only in 1852, decided that this must be the Cana of the Gospel. There are three reasons in favor of this identification: (1) Cana should be written in Hebrew with a *qoph* (קנה), *Qanah,* and not with a *kaph,* as in *Kefr-Kenna.* (2) St. John always says Cana of Galilee (2:1, 11; 4:16; 21:2) as if to distinguish it from the Phoenician Cana; and there is only one Cana in Galilee known to history, the one north of Nazareth near the place referred to as Khirbet Qana (cf. Josephus, *Vita,* 16–17). Note, however, that these ruins are not called Qanat el-Jalil (Cana of Galilee) as Robinson and others after him maintained. (3) A later tradition beginning in the thirteenth century.

But Kefr-Kenna (*kefr* means village) is more likely, in our opinion, for the following reasons: (1) *The distance* — Khirbet Qana is 8½ mi. north of Nazareth, and is not on the road to any place. Kefr-Kenna is only 3½ or 4 mi. from Nazareth along the road from Capharnaum and Tiberias. This makes Mary's presence at the wedding feast easier to understand, as also the visit of Jesus on his return from Judea. (2) *The site* — No vestige of a Christian edifice has been found at Khirbet Qana; Kefr-Kenna, on the other hand, had a church from the fourth century; and the beautiful spring of which the ancient pilgrims spoke is there, whereas Khirbet Qana has nothing but cisterns. (3) *Ancient Tradition* — St. Jerome writes in his eulogy of Paula (*Epist., cviii,* 13; ML, XXII, 889): "Ideo cito itinere percussit *Nazareth, Cana, Capharnaum.*" Note the order of places. And in the letter of Paula and Eustochium to Marcellus (*Epist.,* xlvi, 12; ML, XXII, 491): "Haud procul inde (from Nazareth) cernetur Cana, pergemus Ithabyrium (Thabor)." Note the proximity of Cana and its position between Nazareth and Thabor. Theodosius (in 530) makes Nazareth and Cana equidistant from Diocaesarea (Sepphoris); the anonymous Pilgrim of Piacenza (570) left Ptolemais (St. John of Acre) and went to Cana by way of Sepphoris, which he said was only three miles from it. All this fits Kefr-Kenna (though the distance of three miles is a little too short), and does not at all fit Khirbet Qana. St. Willibald (eighth century) could also be cited, as well as Phocas and John of Wurtzburg (twelfth century), etc.

For a description of the places, consult Guérin, *Galilée,* Vol. I, pp. 168–182, or LeCamus, *Dict. de la Bible,* Vol. II, coll. 108–118.

[5] John 2:1. *"On the third day,* there was a marriage feast at Cana." In this context there is a series of time indications: John 1:29, "the next day"; John 1:35, "the next day"; John 1:43, "the next day." The "third day" of our text cannot be a continuation of this series, because it would then be, not the third, but the fifth day. Nor can it be the day following the last day of the series, because in both Greek and Latin the "third day" is the *day after the morrow.* Besides, it is highly

Most authors hold that, on leaving Bethany after his conversation with Nathanael, Jesus went along the Jordan valley to Nazareth and arrived there the evening of the third day. Learning that if he had been home he would have been invited to the wedding at Cana, he went there immediately with his disciples, especially since one of them, Nathanael, was from Cana. Bethany is scarcely sixty-five miles from Nazareth by direct route, and Nazareth is only a league and a half from Cana, so the journey could easily have been made in three days. The hypothesis therefore is acceptable.

But there is room for another theory, which does not so hasten events, and seems to fit in better with the data of the Evangelist. It supposes that Jesus left Bethany, as he intended, the day after his meeting with Peter, to go to Bethsaida, the native place of Peter and Andrew. There he found Philip, their fellow townsman, with his friend Nathanael, who was a native of Cana. When it was learned that Jesus was in Bethsaida, an urgent invitation was sent to him to come to the wedding, and in answer to it he arrived at Cana on the third day after his conversation with Philip and Nathanael.[6]

On his arrival he found the town in a festive mood. In patriarchal societies, especially among the Semites, the establishment of a new home is not only a family feast, but an event that concerns the whole clan or the whole tribe. Marriage is consequently celebrated with great pomp and brilliance. Even in recent times, in certain villages of Palestine the newly married couple received something like royal honors. Seated on a sort of rustic throne, they looked on as their fellow citizens filed past

---

improbable that Jesus leaving Bethany for Cana would have arrived there on the following day. Consequently, "the third day" cannot have any reference to the time indications that precede; rather it refers to one of the *events* that have just been mentioned.

[6] Guérin estimates the distance from the starting point to Kefr-Kenna at "75 Roman miles or less by the shortest and most direct route" (*Galilée,* Vol. 1, p. 172), or about 69 mi.; Westcott gives 60 *English* miles, which would be almost the same. But Guérin has Jesus leave from the place of the baptism; and Bethany was perhaps 5 or 6 mi. farther north. Going directly from Scythopolis to Cana without passing through Nazareth would shorten the distance by almost three miles.

them and rendered them homage; thereafter songs, dances, and other country entertainments were organized in their honor.[7]

The Talmudic writers prescribe that the festivities last seven days if the bride be a virgin, and three if she be a widow. The best month for a wedding was March, since it is generally a pleasant season in Palestine, when nature awakens and the farmers have a good deal of leisure. Custom set Wednesday for the beginning of the celebrations. The day was doubtless chosen as being farthest from the Sabbath, which thus would not interfere with the preparations. On Tuesday evening the girl's relatives and friends busied themselves preparing the bride. This was no trifling matter, for the bridal attire included no fewer than twenty-four articles. A crown was set on her head, and rings and bracelets on her hands and feet, and around her neck a necklace of finery or precious stones, as her means allowed. Her cheeks and lips were tinted red and her eyelids were touched with a collyrium to make the eyes seem large and more brilliant. Her fingernails and hair were stained a golden henna. As dusk fell, the groom came ceremoniously with companions to seek her. It was the most solemn moment of the feast, and the whole village took part in it; even the strictest Rabbis had to interrupt their studies to join the procession. In the light of lamps and torches, and to the accompaniment of musical instruments, the procession went slowly forward and, if there was only a short distance to cover, it took a roundabout route. Possibly, too, even in those days, the women raised along the way those strident cries which are the indispensable accompaniment of funerals and weddings, and which always seem so strange to European ears.

Jesus and his new disciples do not seem to have arrived at Cana in time for the opening of the festivities. Mary was already there, either as a friend or relative of one of the spouses, or as a useful helper, whose assistance and advice were appreciated. Her behavior later seems to indicate that she had some part in the arrangements of the feast.

To the Pharisees of their times, who were scandalized at the thought of Jesus and his mother sitting at a marriage feast, the

[7] On modern customs, cf. J. Neil, *Everyday Life in the Holy Land,* London, 1911, pp. 223–260; he gives some interesting details. For ancient customs, cf. preferably Billerbeck, *Kommentar,* Vol. II, 1924, pp. 372–400.

Fathers of the Church replied that Jesus, the perfect model of the ordinary life, as John had been the perfect model of the penitential life, wished by his example to sanction a moderate enjoyment of innocent pleasures, and to honor the celebration of marriage, which he intended to elevate to the dignity of a Sacrament. Besides, his mere presence imposed decency and restraint upon all.

Whether the manager of the feast had miscalculated, or the unexpected arrival of six or seven new guests and of others attracted by the dawning fame of Jesus had set his reckonings awry, the wine gave out before the end of the feast. Mary was the first to notice it, and, anxious to spare her hosts any embarrassment, she whispered to her Son, "They have no wine." It was not a prayer, properly speaking, or even the formal expression of a wish, but the simple exposure of an unfortunate situation, joined to a secret hope that he could remedy it. His answer sounds somewhat sharp to us. "Woman, what wouldst thou of me? My hour has not come yet." Not that the title "woman" has in it anything disrespectful: the Greek tragedies thus addressed princesses and queens, and Caesar Augustus used the title when speaking to Cleopatra. But it does have about it a certain solemnity, and Jesus will use it a second time, when he addresses his mother from the Cross.

The phrase which gives the impression of brusqueness is rather a very much-used Hebrew idiom, which has no exact equivalent in our western languages, its meaning depending on a gesture, the tone of voice, and the expression of the face: "*Quid mihi et tibi?*"[8] In general, it expresses surprise, displeasure, or embarrassment brought on by an unforeseen meeting or unusual turn of events. To translate it, as is often done, by "What is there in common between thee and me?" is to exaggerate its force and to falsify its meaning. The better translation, and one that is applicable to all cases, would be, "What wouldst thou of me?" or,

---

[8] The formula מַה לִּי וָלָךְ is in Judg. 11:12; 2 Kings 16:10; 19:22; 3 Kings 17:18; 4 Kings 3:13; and 2 Para. 35:21. The Greek formula *τί ἐμοὶ καὶ σοι* is in Matt. 8:29; Mark 1:24; 5:7; Luke 4:34; 8:28; John 2:4. Care must be taken not to confuse these formulas with the Arabic *ma lak* (*quid tibi?*), "do not concern yourself with that; it is none of your affair," or with the Greek *τί κοινὸν ἐμοὶ καὶ σοί*; "what is common to me and thee?"

better, "Why ask me that?" As it stands, the answer implies, not a reproach or a reprehension (as several of the Fathers maintain), but a momentary refusal.[9] The expedients thought up by certain exegetes to eliminate this meaning from the phrase seem to us out of place. According to St. John Chrysostom, Jesus wished to show that he was master of his time and yet avoid making his mother blush publicly. Better still, we will say with St. Cyril of Alexandria, "Christ teaches us here what honor is due to one's parents, since for his mother's sake he did what he would not otherwise have done."

In the designs of Providence the hour of his manifestation to the public had not yet sounded, and that is why Christ would not himself have taken the initiative in this miracle. It is the unspoken plea of his mother, whom he could refuse nothing, that prompts him to advance his hour and disturb, in a sense, the divine plan. But is that not true of all persevering prayer? Moses' intercession stayed the arm of God, raised to strike down his wayward people; Abraham's prayer would have saved the guilty

---

[9] Irenaeus, *Haereses,* III, xvi, 7; St. Athanasius, *Contra Arianos,* Sermo iii, No. 41; and especially their commentaries on this passage. St. Augustine (Miraculum exigebat mater. Recede a me, mulier), and St. John Chrysostom (ἐπετίμησε . . . παιδεύων αὐτήν). These extreme views are cited by St. Thomas.

Various explanations have been offered to soften the apparent harshness of Jesus' answer.

a) "Of what concern is it to thee and me? It is no affair of ours. Let them see to it as they are able." See the paraphrase in verse by Nonnus, which reads: τί ἐμοὶ ἠὲ καὶ σοί. Also cited for this interpretation are the Pseudo-Justin (MG, VI, 1889) and Theodore of Mopsuestia (MG, LXVI, 539). This answer would scarcely be charitable or worthy of the Saviour.

b) Mary foresees that the wine is about to fail. She brings this to the attention of her son, who answers: "Leave that to me; my hour has not yet come, but it will come immediately, when the wine shall actually fail." This original solution is exposed at length by J. Bourlier, in *R.B.,* 1897, pp. 405–422. But unfortunately the text says: "And the wine failing" (ὑστερήσαντος οἴνου), and "they have no wine" (οἶνον οὐκ ἔχουσι).

c) "Leave that to me. Is it that my hour has not yet come?" with a question mark. Thus, Knabenbauer in his commentary, Durand, *Recherches,* 1912, pp. 157–159. Cited as authorities for this view are Tatian the Arabian (in Ciasca, *Diatessaron,* Rome, 1888); St. Ephraem, who, as is known, wrote a commentary on the *Diatessaron;* and St. Gregory of Nyssa (MG, XLIV, 1308). But τί ἐμοὶ καὶ σοί does not mean "Leave that to me," and does such a question seem natural?

There are other explanations, even less natural, such as that of Schultz in *Bibl. Zeitschrift,* 1922, pp. 93–96.

We hold to the explanation of St. Cyril of Alexandria and of St. John Chrysostom in their commentaries on this passage.

cities, if he had found in them but five just men; the insistence of the Chanaanite woman finally triumphed over the explicit refusals of Jesus.

When she heard her Son's answer, Mary knew that, far from being definitely refused, her request had actually been granted before it was made. She immediately told the servants to obey his orders, as if she already knew what they would be: "Do whatever he shall tell you to do."

In the vestibule there were six stone urns which were used for the ablutions common among the Jews. The servants were continually drawing from them to pour water over the hands and feet of the guests, and to dilute the wine which was never drunk unmixed. As the feast was drawing to a close, the urns were almost empty. Jesus ordered them to be filled to the brim. The Evangelist says that each held two or three "measures" (together, therefore, between 120 and 190 gallons).[10] It was much more than enough for the needs of the moment, but once the Saviour undertook to perform a miracle, the miracle had to be clearly manifest. When the urns were filled, he said to the servants, "Draw some now, and take it to the master of the feast."

The person whom we thus designate, for want of a better name, was not in the position of the Greek "king of the banquet," a presiding officer chosen by the revelers to have supreme charge of the strength of the wine and the number of cups to be emptied. Nor was he like the trusted slave in a great Roman house, who directed the staff of subordinate servants and saw to it that the guests had all they wanted. He was rather a friend or relative of the family, who generously undertook to organize and direct the service and relieve the groom of these material distractions.[11]

---

10 It may be asked whether St. John is speaking of the Greek measure called μετρητής or of its Hebrew equivalent called *bath.* The content of the Greek *metretes* and the Hebrew *bath* is variously estimated by various authors at between 10 and 10½ gallons. Since each of the urns held two or three measures, the capacity of each was between 20 and 31½ gallons.

11 The Greek *symposiarch* is called in Latin *rex* or *imperator convivii* or *arbiter bibendi.* His role is well described by Plutarch (*Quaestiones conviviales,* i, 4). He was chosen by the guests (Ecclus. 32:1–2: *Rectorem te posuerunt*) or picked by lot (Horace, *Odes,* I, iv, 18: *Nec regna vini sortiere talis*).

The *tricliniarches* (Petronius, *Satyricon,* i, 22) was the slave in charge of the

He had certainly noticed the awkward situation, and not without concern; but he was hoping to be able to reach the end of this meal without untoward incident. Later he would consider what should be done. When the servants offered him the water changed into wine, and he had tasted it and found it good, he wondered whence this stroke of good fortune had come. Perhaps, without his knowledge, wine had been borrowed from neighbors; or perhaps some generous person, made aware of the situation, had offered it as a gift, for near relatives usually contributed in kind to the expenses of a feast. The master of the feast came to the bizarre conclusion that the groom had hidden his best wine, to give his guests a pleasant surprise when they were not expecting any more. He took him aside, therefore, and said to him in a voice that was not meant for other ears, "Every (shrewd) man serves his best wine first, and when the guests are drunk gives them that which is poorer, but thou hast saved the best wine till now," when the feast is almost over.

Piqued because he had not been told, but still glad of the relief, he allowed himself a rather broad pleasantry which was permissible in the circumstances and could, to his way of thinking, be taken as a compliment. It would be wrong to take his quip seriously; for there was never anything like a common practice of serving the poorer wine near the end of a feast; in fact, not one example of it can be cited from the whole of pagan antiquity.[12]

This was "the first sign" Jesus worked to prove that his mission was divine, and it had to be striking, to preclude any possible suspicion of error or fraud. That is why the changing of the water into wine took place in stone jars standing in plain view, which were too heavy to have been brought from any place else,

---

service at table. Cf. Marquardt, *Vie privée des Romains,* transl. Henry, Vol. I, p. 172.

In St. John, ἀρχιτρίκλινος (a very rare word, found only in Heliodorus, *Aethiop.,* vii, 27) is neither the Greek symposiarch, nor the Latin tricliniarch. He is a free man who has charge of the direction of the feast, being either a relative or a friend or someone hired for the occasion.

[12] Windisch (in *Z.N.T.W.,* 1913, pp. 248–255) has taken the trouble to look for one, and has not found a single perfect parallel. Instances are found of Amphitryons serving their guests dishes and wines inferior in quality to those reserved for themselves (Martial, *Epigr.,* iii, 60; Pliny the Younger, *Epist.,* ii, 2; Pliny the Elder, *Hist.,* xiv, 14).

which had never contained wine before, and which the servants in the sight of all had just filled to the brim with water. Seeing this miracle, the disciples believed in him, not yet with a perfect faith, but with faith lively enough to attach themselves to him and follow him everywhere. In St. John, as everyone knows, faith develops by imperceptible stages from the first rays to full light.

"After this Jesus went down to Capharnaum, with his mother and his brethren and his disciples, but he remained there only a few days," because the Passover was near and he intended to spend it in Jerusalem.[13]

It has been suggested that his intention was not to settle at Capharnaum, but merely to wait there for a caravan going to the Holy City. That would have been a very strange itinerary indeed! He did not have to go back a day's journey to join a caravan; in fact, each little Galilean village made up its group of pilgrims, and experience shows that overnumerous bands make the journey neither more pleasant nor more convenient. We think, then, that his departure for Capharnaum was final. From the moment the Saviour began his public life (and he began it by the miracle at Cana) he had to leave Nazareth. The insignificance of the place and the prejudices of its inhabitants made it ill-suited to be the first center of the Gospel. The two capitals of Galilee, Sepphoris and Tiberias, founded by Herod Antipas, were half-pagan. Capharnaum, as we shall see later, offered several advantages. It is true that St. Matthew does not mention this change of residence until after the imprisonment of John the Baptist; but it could not be otherwise, since he omits the whole period between the temptation and the start of the public life. On this point, as on many others, the Fourth Gospel corrects the impressions given by the Synoptics.

---

[13] John 2:12. *After this* does not in itself indicate an immediate departure; but since Jesus left with his new disciples, it is probable that he did not delay. From Nazareth to Capharnaum there is a *descent* of more than 1640 feet.

3. The First Passover at Jerusalem

(JOHN 2:13–25)

The Paschal solemnities drew a great number of merchants to the Holy City. Many pilgrims preferred to buy on the spot the victims destined for sacrifice — lambs and goats for the Paschal feast, cattle and sheep for the holocausts and for peace-sacrifices, pigeons and turtledoves for the purification of the poorer women, and wine, oil, salt, and flour, which were obligatory complements to certain sacrifices. In paying the poll tax of a half shekel, which every adult male Israelite had to put once a year into the Temple treasury, it was necessary to go to the money-changers, because this tax was paid in the currency of Tyre, whose tetradrachma was equal in weight to the Sanctuary shekel.

The Temple and its accessory buildings covered an enormous amount of space, not all of which however was equally sacred. Around the Sanctuary proper, protected by a balustrade through which only Israelites were entitled to pass, stretched a vast rectangular court, bordered on its four sides by colonnaded porticoes. This was called the Court of the Gentiles, because pagans were allowed to enter it; but it was not a purely profane place. A well-known passage of the Mishnah forbade anyone to enter it with a staff or purse or burden of any kind, or to use it as a short cut. Normally not much credit is to be put in the artificial legislation of the Talmud, but it does seem that this prohibition was in force among the Jews at the time of Christ, although it was naturally impossible to impose it on pagans. It proves that the whole esplanade of the Temple was regarded as consecrated by its nearness to the Sanctuary. But when the feasts were in progress it was invaded by merchants, thanks to the complicity of the priests, who made a profit out of this toleration. Every abuse tends to strike roots and spread. In our own country, do we not sometimes see sellers of pious objects, who were first tolerated on the porch, penetrating gradually into the basilica itself? If unchecked, they would soon go up as far as the foot of the altar. At the approach of the Passover, the Temple courts took on the appearance of a bazaar, littered with the excrement of thousands of animals. At the most solemn moments of the sacred liturgy the bleating of sheep, the lowing of cattle, and the shouts and arguments of the tradesmen and customers could be heard.

It was the first time Jesus had entered the Temple with the authority of a divine envoy. At the sight of the profanation, his anger flared up. From a bundle of cords that came to hand he made a whip, and with it drove men and beasts before him in every direction, overturning as he passed the little tables that the money-changers used as counters, and ordering those selling doves instantly to carry away the piled-up cages. "Take all this away and do not change my Father's house into a market." The disciples watched him, perhaps not without some trepidation, and the words of the Psalmist came to their minds: "The zeal of thy house, O my God, devours me!"[14]

This action of the Saviour seemed to St. Jerome a greater miracle than the cure of the man born blind, the resurrection of Lazarus, and even the Transfiguration. "His eyes must have darted flames," he says, "and his face must have shone with a divine majesty." But let us not forget that, in setting himself up as a judge to extirpate an intolerable abuse, Jesus was within his rights and could count on the approval of all right-minded people.

The priests, whose duty it was to keep public order in the Temple, abashed and staggered by this bold stroke, do not seem to have interfered at once. But soon they recovered themselves. "What miracle dost thou show us to justify acting thus?" They did not reproach him for what he did, but asked him his title for arrogating to himself a power that belonged to them. Since he said that he was sent by God, let him give some proof. Jesus answered: "Destroy this temple, and in three days I will rebuild it."[15] He was referring to the temple of his body. The Jews did not understand him, and they could not have understood him unless he made a gesture, pointing to himself. The disciples were

---

[14] John 2:13–17. The Synoptics report the same event, or one like it, during the week of the Passion: Matt. 21:12; Mark 11:15–19; Luke 19:45–48. Cf. Lagrange, *Saint Jean,* pp. 64–65.

[15] John 2:19: *Solvite templum hoc*. This is equivalent to a conditional proposition: "If you destroy this temple, I will raise it up again." The Greek word ἐγείρειν means to *raise* a building *up again* from its ruins (Ecclus. 49:15) or to bring back the dead to life (John 5:21).

no nearer understanding him at the time, but they kept a respectful silence, and when, after the Resurrection, they saw that the prophecy had been fulfilled, their faith was thereby increased. The Jews, on the other hand, without seeking an explanation (which Jesus would not have refused, had they asked), chose to twist his words and ridicule them. They shrugged their shoulders in pity, as though they had just listened to the prattlings of a madman. "This temple has taken forty-six years to build, and thou speakest of rebuilding it in three days!" What extravagant presumption!

Herod had begun to build the Temple twenty years before our era, the same year Augustus visited Syria. The heavy work on the Sanctuary was speedily finished, owing to preparation of the material beforehand; but the interior ornamentation, the colonnaded porches, and the entirety of the immense edifice were completed only on the eve of the revolution of the year 66. Thus forty-six years had been spent on it at the time of the Gospel scene; this would bring us to the year 27 of our era — a bit of information that is most important in fixing the dates of the birth and death of Christ.[16]

4. Nicodemus

(JOHN 3:1–21)

Jesus had refused the sign that the chief priests had so imperiously demanded, and had contented himself with alluding to the miracle of his Resurrection. He did not acknowledge any right on their part to exact an account of him, and reserved to himself the choice of prodigies to support the authenticity of his mission.

Yet, during the course of the Feast, he worked so many brilliant miracles that all witnesses with open minds recognized the finger of God, and several months later the prodigies were still fresh in the memories of the Galileans. Many of the people believed in him, but with a timid and wavering faith, which was incapable of resisting the shock of self-interest or passion.

Jesus knew all this. He had no need to learn what was going

[16] For the calculations, cf. Note B: *Chronology of the Life of Christ.*

on in the depths of men's consciences, for he "knew what was in man." That is why he "did not trust himself to them"; he entrusted to them neither his person nor his teaching, though he was ready to instruct them when they should show any desire to learn.[17]

Among those whom his miracles had affected, without however working any complete conversion in them, was one of the most influential and wealthy men in Jerusalem. Nicodemus was one of the lights of the Sanhedrin and one of the pillars of Pharisaism. He wanted very much to meet the young Galilean doctor, but he belonged to that countless number of timid souls who are enslaved by a sect or party, and are paralyzed by group opinion and human respect. He decided, therefore, to meet Jesus at night, to hide his actions from the members of his caste. The interview was not, however, entirely secret. Some of the disciples were present, and one of them has given us a rather summary account of what was said — it fills only a page, although the conversation must have gone on well into the night. It is not surprising that some obscurity should result from this conciseness.

Nicodemus greeted Jesus deferentially, as he would a teacher whose lectures he wished to follow. "Rabbi, we know that thou comest from God to instruct us, because no one can work the miracles which thou workest unless God is with him." He uses the plural, as though speaking on behalf of a group. Perhaps he actually was spokesman for other fearful souls like himself, who wished to satisfy their curiosity without running the risk of compromising themselves. He did not give the reason for his visit, but it may easily be divined. He wanted to know the object and nature of the kingdom whose coming John had announced and whose actual presence Jesus was now preaching.

---

[17] John 2:23–24. The miracles took place during the week of the Paschal solemnity (ἐν τῷ πάσχα, ἐν τῇ ἑορτῇ); the Latin *in pascha in die festo* would give the impression that they took place on the 15th of Nisan, the *day* of the solemnity itself.

Note the play on words (multi *crediderunt* in eum . . . ipse autem non *credebat* semetipsum eis) built on the two meanings of *credere* (πιστεύειν). "Many *believed* in him, but he did not *believe* in them." Is the meaning "He did not trust himself to them" or "he did not confide in them"? Probably both: to *trust himself to them* has reference to his Person; to *confide in them* refers to his doctrine.

The impression produced by the miracles upon the Galileans (John 4:45) and men like Nicodemus (John 3:2) was deep and lasting.

Christ, who reads the innermost recesses of hearts, answers Nicodemus' tacit question. "Amen, amen, I say to thee, no one can see the kingdom of God unless he be born again." These purposely solemn words invite a search for a spiritual meaning under their material covering. Nicodemus certainly went beyond any grotesque notion of a physical rebirth, but he pretends to misunderstand, in order to force the Saviour to explain further: "How can a man when he is old be born again? Can he enter again his mother's womb and be born a second time?" Ignoring the captious note in the question, Jesus gravely answers: "Amen, amen, I say to thee, no one can enter the kingdom of God unless he be born of water and the Holy Spirit. What is born of the flesh is flesh, and what is born of the Spirit is spirit." This time there is no ambiguity. There is no question here of carnal birth, but of spiritual regeneration, a true creation requiring the intervention of the Spirit. In the beginning the sensible world issued from the waters quickened by the breath or spirit of God hovering over the abyss. For the future, man will be born to supernatural life in the water of Baptism vivified by the Spirit of grace.

Even though the action of the Spirit eludes any test of the external senses, it is nonetheless real. It manifests itself by its effects. We do not doubt the existence of the wind, though we do not see it and know only imperfectly where it comes from and where it goes. Why doubt the fact of supernatural regeneration just because it happens mysteriously? "Do not wonder to hear me say, 'You must be born again.' The wind blows where it will (and we cannot stop or direct it); thou hearest its voice, but knowest not where it comes from or where it goes. So it is with everyone that is born of the Spirit." In the case of a regenerated soul, we can be aware of the effects of grace without knowing its intimate nature, just as we can be sure of the presence of the wind by the movement of the air, the rustling of the leaves, and the swelling of the waves.

"How can this be?" objects Nicodemus, with an ignorance more feigned than real. He draws this biting answer: "Thou art the teacher of Israel and understandest not these things! Amen, amen, I say to thee, we speak what we know and bear witness of what we have seen, and no one wishes to accept our witness! If I have told you of earthly things and you do not believe me, how shall you believe me when I tell you of heavenly things?"[18] Nicodemus, a teacher in Israel, should have known of the outpouring of graces which was to characterize the Messianic age, and should have recalled these words of Ezechiel: "I will give them a new heart and I will put a new spirit in their breast. I will take away their heart of stone and give them a heart of flesh." What does all this mean, if not a renovation of the moral being?

It was not fitting for the Saviour to begin a fruitless discussion of texts. Besides, it was not the place for discussion, but for belief in the testimony of him who speaks of what he has seen. So far he has taught only of things that have the earth as their setting — spiritual regeneration, the efficacy of grace and of the sacraments. What will it be like when he reveals mysteries of which heaven keeps the secret — the Trinity of Divine Persons, the eternal generation of the Word, the procession of the Holy Spirit?

Only the Son of God is qualified to teach such things, because he comes from heaven, abides there, and returns there:

> No one has gone up into heaven,
> but he who has come down from heaven,
> the Son of Man who is in heaven.

---

[18] John 3:1–12. The solemnity of this dialogue is accentuated by the thrice-repeated formula, "Amen, amen, I say to thee" (verses 3, 5, and 11).

a) *The regeneration* — Is this "to be born from on high" or "to be born again"? The Greek word ἄνωθεν can mean either. But no ambiguity is possible in the Aramaic, and Jesus must have said one *or* the other, so that we must make a choice. Origen, St. Cyril of Alexandria, and St. Thomas prefer to take ἄνωθεν in the sense of "from on high" (*desursum, caelitus*), and they refer to passages in which this is the meaning (John 3:31; 19:11, 23). But the other meaning "again" is preferable for three reasons: (1) Nicodemus would have no reason to misunderstand or pretend to misunderstand, if Jesus had said, "It is necessary to be born *from on high*." (2) The regeneration is represented as a *second birth* (παλιγγενεσία, Titus 3:5; ἀναγεννάω, 1 Peter 1:3, 23) in Scripture and the Fathers. (3) The old Versions (Latin, Coptic, and Syriac with the exception of the Syro-Palestinian) suppose this meaning.

b) *The action of the Spirit* — "Spiritus ubi vult spirat . . . sic et omnis qui natus est ex spiritu." In Hebrew, Greek (πνεῦμα), and Latin (*spiritus*), the same word can mean *wind* or *spirit*. In the first part of the text quoted, almost all modern authors agree in translating "The *wind* blows where it will." We are not the ones to direct its course and, even when we can discover its actual direction, we do not know where it comes from or where it is going. This is a comparison, a kind of parable applicable to the Holy Spirit in regenerated man. If, with many ancient authors, the first member is understood of the Holy Spirit, there would be no comparison; and yet the comparison is formally expressed (οὕτως ἐστίν — "so it is").

He descended from heaven to unite himself to human nature. He goes back to heaven, where he has always abided with the Father. If he came down from heaven, it was only to lead men to heaven, saving them by the blood of the cross. "As Moses raised up the serpent in the desert, so must the Son of Man be raised up, that whoever believes in him may have eternal life." The Israelites who looked with confidence on the brazen serpent raised by Moses were healed of their incurable illness; in the same way whoever turns toward the Crucified on Calvary with faith and love acquires a right to eternal life.

There is no longer question of Nicodemus; one wonders, indeed, whether he is still present. In any case, Jesus continues to instruct his disciples, unless it be that the brief and sublime exposé of the whole plan of redemption that follows is the Evangelist's own commentary on the Master's teaching.

"God so loved the world that he gave his only Son, that whoever believes in him may not perish, but may have eternal life.

"For God did not send his Son into the world to judge the world, but to save the world.

"He that believes in him is not condemned. He that does not believe in him is already condemned, because he has not believed the only Son of God.

"Now the judgment consists in this: when the Light came into this world, men loved the darkness more than the Light, for their works were evil.

"Whoever works evil hates the light and flees from the light, for fear his works be unmasked. But whoever does the truth comes to the light, in order that it may be manifest that his works are done in God."[19]

5. The Disciples of Jesus Baptize

(JOHN 3:22–36)

The animosity of the Levitical priesthood, the underhand hostility of the Pharisees, the uncertain attitude of the common people, and the kind of terrorism exercised by the Sanhedrin, all indicated

[19] John 3:13–21. These beautiful lines, rich in theological meaning, would require long explanations which would be out of place here. Such explanations may be found in any good commentary, such as that of Maldonatus or Toletus.

that Jerusalem was not yet a favorable field for the spread of the Gospel. Time must be allowed for passions to calm down, and men of good will to become stronger. Hence Jesus left the capital and went to some spot in Judea which it is now impossible to determine. A word which St. John uses leads us to suspect that it was not too far from the Holy City, and that it lay near the northern frontier in a section readily accessible to the crowds.[20]

Those secretly interested in him, but paralyzed by the nearness of the Sanhedrin, came to join him there; and in order to attach them to himself by an external rite, he instituted a baptism, which he did not administer himself, but charged his disciples to administer. Was this Christian Baptism, or only a prelude and prophecy of the Sacrament? To attempt to answer the question by recourse to authorities would result only in confusion, because they are about equally divided. It does, however, seem difficult to advance the institution of the Sacrament to so early a date. We would not urge that Baptism supposes the death and Resurrection of Christ, of which, according to St. Paul, it is the efficacious sign and the mystical realization; for the Sacrament could confer the fruits of the redemption by anticipation. But the decisive point, in our opinion, is that the disciples were not aware at that time of the mystery of the Trinity, or of the divinity of Christ, or even, in any distinct way, of his Messianic dignity. If the Sacrament was instituted so early, how is it that the Evangelists make no slightest allusion to it in the course of the public life of Christ, and no least trace of it appears before the Resurrection?[21] Nevertheless, this preliminary baptism is not to be confused with the baptism of John; the latter was only a preparation for the kingdom of God; the former was in a way an entrance into the kingdom, because it put the recipient in direct contact with the Head and Founder of the kingdom.

---

[20] To go from there to Galilee it was necessary (ἔδει, John 4:4) to cross Samaria. Hence the scene would not be on the banks of the Jordan, but perhaps at Bethel, where there is a large reservoir in the town and two plentiful springs in the neighborhood; or at some other point in northern Judea well provided with water.

[21] John 3:22–24. This rite was a prelude to Baptism, just as the anointing performed by the Twelve (Mark 6:13) was a prelude to Extreme Unction. The Council of Trent (Sess. VI, can. 1) leaves the question open, and the most conservative exegetes (Schanz, Knabenbauer, following St. John Chrysostom) follow the same opinion that we do.

For his part, John had moved to a place called Ennon (the Springs), where there was an abundance of streams. Possibly at that season (it was the beginning of April) the fords of the Jordan, swollen by the late winter rains and the melting snows from Hermon, were hardly suitable for his work; but it seems rather that the Baptist, fearing treachery from the Pharisees and the vengeance of Antipas, in whose territory eastern Bethany lay, was looking to his own security in establishing himself between Samaria and the Greek city of Scythopolis, some six or seven miles south of the latter town. There was a remarkable group of springs there within the radius of half a league, some of which grew into rivulets and flowed into the near-by Jordan.[22]

To some ill-disposed souls, Jesus seemed to be setting himself up as the Baptist's rival, and his baptism could be taken as a counterfeit of John's. One day an argument broke out between John's disciples and a certain Jew "on the subject of purification." Perhaps, in comparing the two baptisms, the Jew showed a preference for that of Jesus; at least this would be a likely explanation of this obscure episode. John's disciples, rallying to their master's defense, went to him, saying, "Rabbi, he who was with thee beyond the Jordan and to whom thou hast borne witness, is himself baptizing and all are running to him." To these over-zealous informers, blinded by spite and anger, John preaches moderation and calm: "Man has nothing but what he has received from heaven. You bear me witness that I said, 'I am not the Christ, but his forerunner.' He is the bridegroom; he must increase, and I must decrease." Noble words, from a soul of which envy does not even touch the surface. John is satisfied with the subordinate role that has fallen to him. He must efface himself before him of whom he is only the forerunner. This is as it should be: the morning star disappears at sunrise.

"He must rise, and I must sink." This was John's last word. The considerations that follow seem to be a commentary, in the Beloved Disciple's own style and with his signature:

"He that comes from the earth is earthly and such also is his speech. He that comes from heaven is above all. He bears witness

---

[22] For the identification and description of the places, cf. Abel (*R.B.*, 1913, pp. 220–223) or, in more detail, Buzy (*Saint Jean-Baptiste*, 1922, pp. 221–229).

to what he has seen and heard, but no one receives his witness. To receive it is to confess that God is true.

"He whom God has sent speaks the words of God, for (God) does not give him the spirit by measure. The Father loves the Son and has given all things into his hands. He that believes in the Son has eternal life. He that does not believe in the Son shall not see life: the wrath of God lies heavy upon him."[23]

In these short phrases, pregnant with meaning and without any apparent interconnection, the master ideas of Johannine theology are easily recognizable. The subject of the discourse is the Son, raised in dignity above all and the universal representative of the Father who loves him. Coming from heaven, he speaks of what he has seen and heard; he delivers the message entrusted to him by his Father. To accept his testimony is to honor the Father and to be assured of a title to eternal life. To reject him is to lose all rights to life and incur the anger of God. These theological dicta are in St. John's usual antithetic and sententious style.

Not all of the Baptist's disciples imitated their master's abnegation. Several chafed at seeing him fall into second place in popular esteem and favor. With chagrin they watched his adherents decrease, and with a jealous eye they followed the continual growth of the other camp. Jesus might have decided at this point that it was high time he put an end to the seeming rivalry by returning to Galilee. But before any decision was taken an unforeseen event occurred to hasten his departure — John was thrown into the prison at Machaerus. Here is the story.

Two sons of Herod the Great, Antipas and Philip, had been ruling as tetrarchs for the past thirty years; the former over

---

[23] John 3:31–36. Among modern commentators, Schanz, Knabenbauer, and Zahn think that the Baptist is still speaking; Patrizi, Calmes, Belser, Tillmann, and Lagrange take these words as the Evangelist's own reflections. The latter seem to be right.

Verse 34 is difficult: "He whom God sends proclaims the words of God; for he does not give the Spirit by measure." The pronoun *he* can mean the envoy of God, Christ, who "gives without measure," without counting, the entire message which he has received; or God, who "gives without measure" to his representative the gifts of the Spirit. We prefer the latter meaning, which links much better with the following verse: "The Father loves the Son and has *given* him (into his hands) everything."

Galilee and Perea, and the latter over Iturea and Trachonitis. A third son, also named Herod, but called Philip by St. Mark (probably because that was his name among the people), had had no share in his father's inheritance and was living as a private person, we do not know where. In accordance with a very common practice in the Herod family, this prince had married his niece, Herodias, and had had a daughter by her, the infamous Salome. A little before the time with which we are concerned, Antipas, on his way to Rome, visited a while with his brother, Herod Philip. He made use of his sojourn to seduce Herodias, Philip's wife, and to prevail upon her to join him as soon as he returned from Rome. She agreed to everything, but on the express condition that Antipas first divorce his lawful wife, the daughter of Aretas, king of the Nabateans. The wife got wind of the matter, but gave no hint of her discovery, the better to escape the impending insult. When the tetrarch had arrived home again she asked his permission to spend a few days at Machaerus, which was famous for its pure air and the efficacy of its hot springs. The unsuspecting Antipas readily gave his consent; but Machaerus was near the Nabatean border, and Aretas' daughter fled to her father as soon as she got there. Everything was working out for the best. Antipas was free of his wife without having to repudiate her; Herodias could step into the vacant place, according to their agreement. With her daughter Salome, who was about fifteen years old, she left her husband and went to live at the court of Antipas, her uncle as well as brother-in-law.

However indulgent public opinion was toward the affairs of the Herod family, this incestuous union, cynically publicized, could not fail to arouse universal indignation. John became the mouthpiece of the public conscience and the defender of outraged morality. He told the voluptuous tetrarch in so many words that he was not allowed to live with his brother's wife. Not content with denouncing the scandal to the people and sending a rebuke by an intermediary, he went before Antipas personally, to signify to him the *non licet* of the Law of Moses and the natural law. He is not to be pictured as proudly appearing before Herod, like Elias before Achab; such a theatrical scene would only have exasperated the guilty man and anchored him more deeply in his adultery. Although the Herods had been educated for the most part in Rome and were complete skeptics in religious matters, they made it a point not to flout public opinion, and, as far as possible, they even respected the prejudices of their subjects. There was, therefore, some hope of leading the tetrarch around to a sense of honor and duty.[24]

This time the courageous protests of the Baptist fell on deaf ears; nevertheless, the crafty tetrarch let him go without touching him. He was too clever a politician to seem to give in to personal feelings; he preferred to hide his private revenge under the mask of the common good, by representing his accuser as a hot-blooded demagogue, a dangerous agitator, whom it was imperative at all costs to hinder from making trouble. This is the historian Josephus' version, which complements the Gospel account: "Herod, fearing that (John's) eloquence would incite revolt (for the people followed him in everything), judged it advisable to make the first move and silence him, before a possible revolution which he would later on have cause to regret. Because of this suspicion of Herod's, John was sent off as a prisoner to Machaerus."[25] This place, which is visible on a clear day from the Mount of Olives and the heights of Bethlehem, was a strategic spot of the first order. Antipas had made of it a fortress, a prison, and a palace. It was situated on a mountain east of the Dead Sea, over which it rose more than four thousand feet, and was surrounded by deep ravines, except on the eastern side where a narrow passage, easily defended, connected it with the plain of Moab.

Herod had to use a trick to catch his prisoner. John was no longer in his territory, but was baptizing at Ennon, between Samaria and the free city of Scythopolis. The Synoptics make it clear that he was "delivered up" by his enemies, but we do not know the details of the plot. Who were the Baptist's enemies? The only ones we know of are the Pharisees; for the sacerdotal class, after the questionings which they had made him undergo,

---

[24] Mark 6:18: "It is not permitted thee to have thy brother's wife." The same in Matt. 14:4: "John *was* saying these things to Herod"; St. Luke (3:19) says that Herod *"was rebuked* by John because of Herodias."

[25] Josephus, *Antiq.*, XVIII, v, 2. Machaerus is almost on the same parallel as Bethlehem. It is about 3700 ft. above the level of the Dead Sea. The Dead Sea is no more than 6½ mi. (Josephus says 60 stadia) distant in a straight line, but because of the winding road it takes three hours to reach it.

no longer showed signs of hostility. This fact aids us in understanding a statement in the Fourth Gospel which at first reading is puzzling. "When the Lord learned that the Pharisees had heard that he was making more disciples and was causing more people to be baptized than John, he left Judea and returned again to Galilee."[26] If the Pharisees betrayed the Baptist and handed him over to Herod, would they not treat Jesus in the same way, now that they knew of his success, and the growing number of his disciples? Prudence suggested that he escape their designs by taking flight. The Synoptics connect this departure with the arrest of the Baptist; St. John, with the suspicions and fears of the Pharisees. It is less a case of two distinct motives than two facets of the same motive.

6. The Samaritan Woman
(JOHN 4:1–45)

To get to Galilee, "Jesus had to pass through Samaria."[27] Those who have him coming from the banks of the Jordan endeavor

---

26 John 4:1. The correlation between the departure of Jesus and the feelings manifested by the Pharisees at the news of his progress is very explicitly marked. It is to be remembered that the Pharisees were the ones who had shown the greatest animosity to the Baptist (John 1:24–25).

Note here: (*a*) "When he learned" (ὡς ἔγνω) marks a relationship of cause and effect. (*b*) "He abandoned (ἀφῆκεν) Judea" is stronger than "he left." (*c*) "He came *again* (πάλιν) into Galilee," emphasizing that he *twice* returned, which detail is not mentioned by the Synoptics.

It is necessary to compare the Synoptic texts. "Learning that John *had* been delivered up (παρεδόθη) he withdrew to Galilee" (Matt. 4:12). "After John had been delivered up (παραδοθῆναι) Jesus withdrew to Galilee" (Mark 1:14). The Gospels say "to deliver to the tribunal, to the judge, to the executioner, to death," but "deliver up" taken without a complement always means to deliver by treason or violence, and the deliverer in that case is a traitor (ὁ παραδούς, ὁ παραδιδούς — Judas). That the expression is used in this technical sense is proved by more than twenty examples which cannot lightly be dismissed. It must, therefore, be concluded that John was betrayed to Herod by his enemies.

27 John 4:4: Ἔδει δὲ αὐτὸν διέρχεσθαι διὰ τῆς Σαμαρείας . . . *"It was necessary* that he cross Samaria." Curiously, Josephus uses the same expression (*Vita,* 52): "Anyone who would go quickly from Galilee to Jerusalem *had necessarily* (πάντως ἔδει) to cross Samaria." He gives elsewhere (*Antiq.,* XX, vi, 1) a point of information which has been too much overlooked by interpreters: "It was the *custom* of the Galileans (ἔθος ἦν), when they were going to Jerusalem for their feasts, to take the road across Samaria." He notes this with reference to the scuffle that he mentions later on. According to the *Bellum,* II, xii, 3, only one Galilean was killed.

without success to explain such a long detour, but they could spare themselves the trouble. There is nothing to suggest that he is coming from the Jordan, and St. John's text actually implies the contrary.

The historian Josephus expressly states that pilgrims going from Galilee to Jerusalem usually passed through Samaria, even at the times of the great Jewish feasts. It was the shortest route, and offered no particular danger. Samaria as well as Judea was at the time subject directly to Rome. The result was that under the Procurators, especially Pilate, who was very keen about keeping order, the hostility of the Samaritans rarely went as far as physical violence. Two or three exceptions are indeed always cited, but they were exceptions, and happened at troubled periods. It seems that the Samaritans sometimes amused themselves by lighting fires on the hills to trick the Jews, who used this method to announce the first day of the month to their coreligionists in outlying districts. It was a very bad joke, but did not result in any deaths. Another time, profiting by the interregnum following the removal of Archelaus, they made bold to scatter some human bones in the Temple courts, on the morning of the Passover, to prevent the celebration of the feast. The third case was more serious. In the year 52 there was a quarrel between Samaritans and Galileans near Engannim (Jenin), on the border between the two provinces. The Galileans lost a few men, and later inflicted terrible reprisals on the Samaritans. The Governor of Syria soon restored order, and the incompetent Procurator, who had failed to foresee or quell the conflict, was removed and sent into exile.

The worst to which the Jewish pilgrims were exposed was that kind of insult which Christian travelers until lately experienced in Moslem territory. A fanatical village would close its gates to them, or refuse to sell them provisions. Generally, however, it came down to a discourteous reception and uncivil words. The following anecdote is told in several ways in the Talmudic writings, and gives a fair idea of conditions. At Sichem one day, a Samaritan asked the Rabbi Ismael where he was going. "I am going," answered the Jew, "to adore God at Jerusalem." "Would you not do better," said the other, pointing to Garizim, "to worship God on that mountain, instead of going to adore him on a dunghill?" By that he meant Jerusalem. Ismael answered: "You people are like dogs that delight in carrion. You love Garizim because Jacob buried there the idols of his wife Rachel." After this exchange, the Rabbi thought it prudent to make a hasty departure, and left Sichem during the night.

The feud, ten centuries long, between the Jews and Samaritans went back to the death of Solomon. When the tribes of the north separated from the tribe of Juda, the political schism involved a religious schism as well. Jeroboam did all in his power to encourage the frequentation of the sanctuaries he had erected at Dan and Bethel, in order to keep his subjects from going to the Temple in Jerusalem. After the fall and destruction of Samaria in 722, Sargon, passing over the peasants and common people, sent twenty-seven thousand Samaritans of the higher classes into captivity — artisans, priests, and nobles — and replaced them with Babylonian colonists, who imported their own national deities with them. The strangers were soon absorbed into the native population and finally adopted the cult of Yahweh, with which they mingled some of their own superstitions. From this amalgam arose a mixed race, which the Jews pointedly called Cuthites, after Cutha, a Babylonian town from which many of the settlers came. The mutual animosity was heightened when the Jews, on their return from captivity, refused the help of the Samaritans in rebuilding the Temple at Jerusalem. It reached its climax when the Samaritans built a rival sanctuary on Mount Garizim. John Hyrcanus wrecked it completely, but to no avail, because the Samaritans continued to sacrifice on Garizim; and even today the small community of Nablus, which numbers less than a hundred and fifty members and is dying out, moves out each year to the holy mountain for the immolation of the Paschal lamb.

The Samaritans were as much monotheists as the Jews. They held Moses in great veneration and accepted the Pentateuch as a sacred book. To believe Josephus, they observed the Torah even more strictly than the Jews, but without the additions and interpretations with which the Scribes and Pharisees had overloaded it. The hybrid character of the Samaritans, in religion as well as in blood, explains the differences in relations noticeable at various times between the two peoples. At times the Jews treated the Samaritans as separated brethren; at other times they likened them to *Goyyim,* objects of aversion and contempt. The Samaritans, for their part, willingly admitted their Israelitic origins when Jewish affairs were going smoothly; otherwise they denied all relationship with them — a change of attitude which led to their being compared to the bat in the fable.

It took two days to cross Samaria, and Sichem was usually the stop at the end of the first stage. It was May, and the journey of seven or eight hours across a series of valleys reflecting the rays of the summer sun was an unpleasant experience. The travelers, starting at dawn so as to make a halt before the most oppressive heat of the day should arrive, did not reach the entrance to the gorge between Hebal and Garizim before noon.[28]

---

[28] John 4:5–6: "He comes to a city of Samaria called Sichar, near the field that Jacob gave to his son Joseph. The spring of Jacob was there. . . . It was about the sixth hour (noon)." One could not ask for anything more precise. Today Joseph's tomb is shown five or six minutes distant from the well of Jacob. The monument has nothing ancient about it; but, even if it is not authentic, Joseph's real tomb cannot be far away, because Jacob's well has not changed its site.

This well of Jacob is 105 feet deep. It is cut in the rock, but the upper part, which narrows as it nears the opening, is masonry. As far back as the fourth century there was a church there in the shape of a Greek cross, with the well at the center. It was replaced in the time of the Crusades by a three-nave church, lately rebuilt by the Orthodox Greeks who own the land. The well itself is now in a crypt located under the main altar. It is sometimes called *well* (φρέαρ, John 4:11–12), sometimes *spring* (πηγή, John 4:6 *bis*), because it is fed by a subterranean spring. The three nearest springs are, from south to north: the spring of Daphneh, five or six minutes away at the foot of Garizim; the spring of Balatah, almost the same distance away; the spring of Askar, a quarter of an hour away at the foot of Hebal.

Until recently, Sichar, or Sychar, was identified with the wretched hamlet Askar. There were two difficulties against this: (1) *Askar* is written in Arabic with an *ayin,* which is a very rough consonant. It was answered that the primitive name had undergone this transformation to give it a meaning (*askar* in Arabic means *soldier*). (2) Why should a woman of Askar, which has a fine spring of its own, go to Jacob's well to draw water, and also pass by the stream which was fed by the spring of Balatah? It was said in answer that special power may have been attributed to the water of this well, and that the inhabitants considered it better for the digestion (Smith, *The Historical Geography of the Holy Land,* 6 ed., 1898, Chap. xviii, *The Question of Sychar,* pp. 367–379). This may be so. We did not find the water either fresher or better than the water of the neighboring springs.

The question has recently entered a new phase. The site of the ancient Sichem has been found. It is an isolated hillock on the eastern entrance of the valley that separates Garizim from Hebal, only five or six minutes away from Jacob's well. Wisely directed excavations which have been completed there in recent years

Near the road skirting the foot of Garizim was Jacob's well, dug in a field which the Patriarch had bought from the sons of Hemor and bequeathed to his son Joseph to serve as his place of burial. The pilgrim is surprised to find such a deep well here, since there are at least three copious springs within a radius of a mile. But the Patriarch probably had it dug on his own land to avoid any dispute with the always suspicious and often hostile native population among whom he dwelt. The well was doubtless sheltered by a small pavilion which offered shade and comparative coolness to the passer-by. Weary from his journey, Jesus went in and sat on the curb of the well, or simply leaned against it, while his disciples went to near-by Sichar to get some provisions.

An unexpected visitor soon disturbed his solitude. It was a woman of Samaria, not from the village, which was five or six miles away, but from the province of that name. She carried her pitcher on her head, and on her arm the gear still used in these countries for drawing water — a long cord of goat's hair with a leather bucket hanging at the end. Did she come from Askar, as is generally supposed? If so, she would have had to disregard the beautiful fountain in that village and cross, without stopping, another stream which she would have met along the road. This would hardly seem likely, above all at the hottest hour of the day. The question, however, has recently entered into a new phase, and St. Jerome, whose opinion was once judged erroneous, may well have been right when he identified the Sichar of St. John with the ancient Sichem. Excavations on a little hill covered with ruins, a few minutes west of Jacob's well, seem to prove that Sichem, though abandoned after Nablus was built,

---

have shown that the mound was inhabited two thousand years before the Christian era, and was surrounded by a rampart about 820 yds. in circumference. This is large enough for a Chanaanite city comparable to Jericho. Under the Seleucids, Sichem moved 2 mi. westward, to the interior of this very fertile and well-watered valley. The new town was named by Vespasian, *Flavia Neapolis,* which name it still bears with a slight modification (Naplus, in Arabic *Nablus*). But excavations seem to show that the old site was not entirely abandoned, and that it was still inhabited in the time of Christ. It seems, too, that Sichem, was then called *Sichora* (cf. *Die Ausgrabungen von Sichem,* in *Zeitschr. d. deutschen Palästina-Vereins,* Vol. XLIX, 1926, pp. 229–236 and 304–320). And so we come back to the identification proposed by St. Jerome: Sichar = Sichem. And all the difficulties collapse at once.

was still inhabited at the time of Christ, its name having been changed for some reason or other to Sichora. It is from there, and not from Askar, that the Samaritan woman would have come, and there would have been nothing strange about her going to Jacob's well.

Tormented by thirst, Jesus asked her for a drink, a trifling kindness never refused a stranger. His thirst was real and not feigned; nevertheless his asking was somewhat unusual, since the Jews never spoke to an unescorted woman, especially a Samaritan, except in extreme necessity; and Jesus could have waited for the Apostles to return. His object, therefore, in opening this conversation must have been to gain a soul rather than to quench his thirst.

The dialogue between him and the woman would lose some of its charm by the change of a word, and its savor would be spoiled by commentary:

Jesus — "Give me to drink."

The Woman — "Thou who art a Jew, dost thou ask of me to drink, of me who am a Samaritan?"

Jesus — "If thou didst know the gift of God, and if thou didst know who he is that asks of thee to drink, thou thyself, perhaps, wouldst ask it of him, and he would give thee living water."

The Woman — "Lord, whence wouldst thou draw this living water? Thou hast not even the means of drawing it, and the well is deep. Art thou greater than our father Jacob, who gave us this well, and drank of it himself, he and his sons and his flocks?"

Jesus — "Whoever drinks of this water shall thirst again; but he that drinks of the water which I will give him shall never thirst again. And the water which I will give him shall become a fountain of water springing up for life eternal."

The Woman — "Lord, give me of this water, that I may no longer thirst, and no longer have to come here to draw."

Jesus — "Go, call thy husband and return here."

The Woman — "I have no husband."

Jesus — "What thou sayest is altogether true; for thou hast had five of them, and he whom thou hast now is not thy husband."

The Woman — "Lord, I see that thou art a prophet."

The scene is extraordinarily true to life. The Samaritan woman, who has long since forgotten how to blush, is not embarrassed by this conversation, nor is she intimidated by this encounter with a Jew, whom she recognizes as such by his dress and accent. Her manner is slightly captious and her tone somewhat ironical; nevertheless she affects a certain politeness and uses the title, Lord, in speaking to one whom she feels to be no ordinary man. But she does not take his overtures seriously. Where will he find living water, this man who has not even the wherewithal to draw it? Water that will quench thirst forever; that is too good to be true! And so she does not believe; her evasive answers should not mislead us.

The quiet dignity of Jesus is in complete contrast with the elegant persiflage of the woman. The Saviour has divined a natural fund of sincerity and honesty in this soul, and he wishes to win it. First he piques her curiosity by using language full of mystery. Ah! If she only knew the gift of God! If she only knew who was speaking to her! The living water he promises quenches thirst once for all, and springs up toward eternal life. She does not understand and does not try to understand; she turns it all into a joke. He must, then, change his tactics and deliver a telling blow. When the woman finds herself unmasked and pierced to the quick, she suddenly makes a volte-face. There is no place for guile with a man who reads hearts and can reveal the most intimate secrets. She cries out, "Thou art a prophet!" Not yet *the* prophet par excellence, the Messias, but at least an envoy from heaven, qualified to speak of heavenly things. The dialogue then assumes a different tone.

The Woman — "Lord, I see that thou art a prophet. Our fathers worshipped (God) on this mountain, and you say that it is in Jerusalem one must worship Him." (Who is right, you or we?)

Jesus — "Woman, believe me, the hour is coming when neither on this mountain nor in Jerusalem shall the Father be worshipped. You worship what you know not: we worship what we know; for salvation comes from the Jews. But the hour is coming — it is already here — when true worshippers shall worship the Father in spirit and truth. For the Father seeks such worshippers. God is spirit, and those who worship him must worship in spirit and truth."

The Woman — "I know that the Messias is coming. When he comes, he shall declare unto us all things."

Jesus — "I that speak with thee, I am he."

With Samaritans and Jews things are not the same. The Jewish worship alone is legitimate, it alone is sanctioned by God. The Jews worship with full knowledge, because they guard the treasure of revelation, preserved and enriched by the Prophets, whom the Samaritans refuse to accept. Salvation comes from the Jews, because the Messias is to arise from their midst, and the light of the Gospel is to radiate from Jerusalem. So much for the past. In the future, the differences shall disappear together with the privileges. God will be no more worshiped on Mount Moriah than on Garizim or any other place, for God wishes to be worshiped in spirit and in truth.

The New Law, which is spirit and truth, is to replace the Old Law, as light puts darkness to flight and reality supplants figure. The spirit is not tied down, like matter, to narrow temporal and spatial limits. The new worship, the spiritual worship, will not be a temporary, changing, provisional institution, restricted to one race and confined to a single place, but a perfect, absolute, definitive institution, embracing all humanity and reaching all over the world, reflecting in a way the immutability and immensity of God, who is Spirit.

The Samaritan woman, now subdued, listens attentively, striving to understand, perhaps without too much success. She was counting on the Messias to explain these mysteries. The Samaritans were, in fact, expecting a Messias, whom they called "Taheb," that is, *He who comes,* or *the Restorer* (the meaning of the name being no more certain than the description of the person). "I know," she says, "that the Messias is coming." The Messias? "I am he," Jesus answers, "I that speak to thee." As he said the words, the disciples came up. The woman, amazed and as one distracted, fled, leaving her full pitcher and gear near the well, and ran toward the town.

The disciples for their part were not a little surprised to find their Master talking alone with a woman. The Pharisees were scrupulous about talking to strange women, and pushed their circumspection so far as to avoid speaking to their own wives in public. In his dealings with the other sex, Jesus had himself always given his followers an example of extreme reserve. The respect they felt for him by that time closed their lips, and they did not dare put the question which might have sounded censorious: "Why speakest thou to this woman?" But when they begged him to partake of the food they had brought, and he, absorbed in thoughts of higher things, answered, "I have food to eat which you do not know," they wondered whether someone had brought him food in their absence. It was unlikely. There was therefore some mystery that had to be clarified. It soon was.

"My food is to do the will of him who sent me, in order to accomplish his work. Do you not say yourselves, 'Yet four months and the harvest comes'? I say to you, lift up your eyes and see these fields; they are white for the harvest. The reaper is already receiving his wages and gathering his fruit for eternal life, so that the sower and the reaper may rejoice together. The proverb has this much of truth, that one sows and another reaps. I have sent you to reap that for which you have not labored. Others have labored and you gather the fruit of their labor."

It was a habit with Jesus to use the activities of nature to lift men's minds to an understanding of heavenly things. With a sweeping gesture he pointed to the magnificent plain of Makhnah, which unrolled before their eyes as far as they could see, covered with already whitening harvests, swaying in the noonday breeze and shimmering like silver. In our colder countries we speak of a golden harvest, but in Palestine that figure would suit only a barley harvest. Wheat takes on a beautiful silver tint under the fires of the summer sun, beckoning to the harvesters to take up their sickles.

Jesus was speaking of a different harvest than the one he pointed to, as the disciples readily understood — a harvest of souls, "which bears fruit for eternal life." This harvest, already ripe, has been sown for them by others, but they are the ones called to reap it. Who, then, is the sower? Is it not the Sower of the parable helped, if you wish, by the prophets who announced him to the world, and the Precursor who opened the way for him? "The Sower is the Son of Man." It is just four months since his baptism on the banks of the Jordan, when he began to sow the good seed. Now the seed is coming to maturity and calls for reapers. These will receive the recompense due them, and the Sower will rejoice with them.

Most authors before Maldonatus, who here relies on Origen,

conceive the scene differently. They suppose that while Jesus was teaching the disciples the sublime doctrine of a heavenly food, they were looking at the surrounding fields, and, instead of listening to the Master, were making in an aside the trite observation that "in four months it will be harvest time." This would date the scene at the beginning of February or the end of January. On this hypothesis they construct a whole chronology of the Gospel history, which is full of difficulties, not to say impossibilities.

When the sowing is over toward the end of December, the Palestinian peasant has before him four months of rest. He goes back to work only toward the end of April to reap the barley, and a month later to harvest the wheat. He could therefore say by way of a proverb: "Yet four months and the harvest comes." It may be objected that there is no historical proof of the existence of such a proverb; but there are hundreds and thousands of farmers' proverbs in Palestine today of which history would have preserved no record, had not a painstaking scholar spent a lifetime collecting them on the spot.[29]

Besides, it is hard to believe that Jesus spent eight or nine months in Judea with disciples whom he had not yet called to the apostolate, before beginning the Galilean ministry which the Synoptics link so closely with his baptism. When he returns to Galilee, the memory of the miracles wrought by him at the last Passover in Jerusalem is still very fresh in the minds of the people, which would hardly allow for an absence of eight or nine months. But if his return is placed during the month of May, his fatigue and thirst are better explained, as well as the presence of the Samaritan woman at Jacob's well at an unusual hour. In that case, the parable of the whitening harvest becomes very realistic and its application strikingly apposite.[30]

---

[29] Dalman, *Arbeit und Sitte in Palästina,* 5 vols. divided into 2 parts, Gütersloh, 1928–1937.

[30] On this text, cf. Note B: *The Chronology of the Life of Christ.*

In Palestine, sowing takes place only when the heavy autumn rains permit first plowing. These rains do not come until November, and are sometimes delayed until December (in 1908 in Jerusalem, they did not come until the 18th of December; Dalman, *Arbeit und Sitte in Palästina,* 1928, Vol. I, p. 261). Normally, sowing begins in November and can go on up to the end of December.

On the seacoast and in the Jordan valley, the barley harvest begins around the

Meanwhile the Samaritan woman was not idle. Her excitement attracted a crowd around her. "Come," she said, "come and see a man who has told me all that I have ever done. Would not he be the Messias?" She dares not speak positively, because it is not proper for a woman to make dogmatic statements; but her manner shows that she is personally convinced.

Her fellow townsfolk came down in crowds to Jacob's well. We do not know what Jesus said to them, but they were well enough satisfied with it to beg him to stay with them. And he did stay for two days, and many of them believed in him. And when he had gone, they said to the woman: "No longer do we believe only because of what thou hast said. We ourselves have heard him, and we know that he is truly the Saviour of the world."

Was their initial faith brought later on to the completeness that was lacking to it, or did the good seed that Jesus had sown during his brief stay finally wither away? The Gospel is silent on the point, and we must refrain from conjecture.

7. The Return to Galilee

(JOHN 4:46–54)

After spending two days with the Samaritans, Jesus returned to Galilee. The Galileans, who had witnessed his miracles in Jerusalem at the last Passover, which was not so far away, received him with transports of joy. They were proud of the exploits of their young fellow countryman, and for once gave the lie to the proverb: "No man is a prophet in his own country."

We may say of anyone that he has three fatherlands: the locality where he first saw the light of day, the province in which

---

15th of April, and the wheat harvest in May. At Jerusalem, Bethlehem, and Hebron, it is two or three weeks later. On the 12th of May, 1838, Robinson found the people of Jericho occupied in threshing the grain; on the 4th of June, the wheat harvest began at Hebron; on the 17th of May, 1852, he could not find guides in Beisan and the valley of Jezrael, since everybody was occupied with the harvest (Robinson, *Biblical Researches in Palestine,* 1856, Vol. I, p. 431 and Vol. III, p. 336). In 1928, all the harvesting in Samaria was finished by the 15th of June. In the outskirts of Nazareth we saw asses and camels carrying the last sheaves to the threshing floors, which were then in full operation.

In the episode of the Samaritan woman, the text speaks of the *whitening* harvest, which could only mean the wheat harvest. It is therefore either the month of May or, at the latest, the beginning of June.

he lives, and the nation of which he is a member. As a matter of fact, the Evangelists give Jesus three such fatherlands: *Bethlehem,* the cradle of his ancestors and his own birthplace; *Nazareth,* his ordinary home during the greater part of his life; and *Capharnaum,* the city of his choice and the principal theater of his apostolate.

St. John knew that Jesus had lived at Nazareth and preached in Capharnaum, but he regards Bethlehem and Judea as his real country.[31] It was Jerusalem and Judea that received the first fruits of his teaching. There, too, his career was to end, and there he would have stayed longer were it not for the intrigues of his enemies. The schemings of the Pharisees forced him to leave first the capital, and a little later Judea. Thus "Jesus returned to Galilee, for he had himself said that a prophet is not honored in his own country." His reception by the inhabitants of Jerusalem and his compatriots of Judea, despite the miracles he had worked in abundance, was proof of the saying.

Before reaching Capharnaum, he stopped a few days at Cana, for some reason which we do not know. The report of his return spread speedily over the whole region and came to the ears of a royal official whose son was seriously ill.[32]

This man knew from hearsay of the miracles of Jesus, and set out for Cana immediately in hope of meeting him. It takes about six or seven hours of difficult walking across a steep and rocky mountain pass to reach Cana from Capharnaum.[33] As soon as the

---

[31] Those who, in St. John, understand Nazareth as the "country" of Jesus are forced to add it to the Gospel text: "Jesus went into Galilee (*but not to Nazareth*), for he said that no one is honored in his own country." In that case the Evangelist would have omitted precisely the point to which the proverb was intended to be applied, and would have given not an inkling that it was implied.

[32] This personage is a βασιλικός, someone attached to the person or service of the *king,* the Tetrarch Antipas, who is called *king* in Matt. 14:9; Mark 6:14, etc. The author of the Vulgate translates *regulus,* as though he read βασιλίσκος. Yet St. Jerome writes (*In Isaiam,* 65:1): "Regulus, qui Graece dicitur βασιλικός, quem nos de aula regis rectius possumus interpretari *palatinus.*" Fundamentally, the βασιλικός can be a *courtier* (St. Jerome's *palatinus*) or a relative of the king (Lucian, *Dial. deor.,* 20), but he is more probably a functionary or royal dignitary (Plutarch, *Solon,* 27). Whether a civil or military functionary, we cannot say.

[33] From Capharnaum to Cana is about 14 miles. The road through the Valley of Pigeons (*Wady el-Hamam*) is almost impassable today.

official arrived there, he hurried to find Jesus, to ask him to go back to Capharnaum with him and there to cure his son. Although a Jew by birth and religion, his faith was not as lively and bright as the centurion's whose story the Synoptics relate. For him Jesus was neither the Son of God nor the Messias, but a prophet and wonder-worker. He had, besides, no notion of a cure from a distance, of which the Old Testament offers few instances.

To test and strengthen his faith, the Saviour gave him an answer which is addressed less to him than to all his coreligionists. "Unless you see signs and wonders, you do not believe."[34] The father, however, is not discouraged by this seeming refusal and reproach, but says, "Lord, come down, I beg thee, before my son dies." Moved by this cry of paternal anguish and touched by his faith, sincere though yet imperfect, Jesus says to him, "Go, thy son lives."

It was the seventh hour of the day, one o'clock in the afternoon. It was too late to return to Capharnaum. After the rough morning trip men and beasts needed rest. Besides, the father, heartened by the Saviour's words, had become calm, and a precipitous departure would have betrayed distrust. So he waited until the next day and was met on the road by servants, who had come to tell him the good news. The natural question was at what time his son had begun to improve. They replied, "Yesterday, at the seventh hour, the fever left him." It was the very time that Jesus had said to him, "Thy son lives."[35]

Struck by this marvel and touched by grace, the royal official was converted, together with his whole family. Of his further life we know absolutely nothing. Many think that he may be Chusa, the steward of Herod Antipas, whose wife Joanna accompanied Jesus on his apostolic journeys. Others think he is

---

[34] John 4:48: ἐὰν μὴ σημεῖα καὶ τέρατα ἴδητε, οὐ μὴ πιστεύσητε. *Signs* (σημεῖα) are miracles worked in support of a doctrine or a prophecy; *wonders* (τέρατα) are miracles of an extraordinary kind. The phrase would perhaps be more forceful and more natural if followed by a question mark or an exclamation point: "Unless you see signs and wonders, will you not believe!"

[35] The meeting place is clearly indicated. It is where the road begins to *descend* into the Valley of the Pigeons after passing the Horns of Hattin (John 4:51: ἤδη δὲ αὐτοῦ καταβαίνοντος). The hour of the cure is also given: it was the *seventh hour* (John 4:52), one o'clock in the afternoon.

Manahen, the foster brother or boon companion of the same Herod, whom the Acts represent as one of the most influential members of the Church of Antioch. Since this unidentified person is to be sought for in the tetrarch's entourage, each of these conjectures has a certain likelihood.

"This was a second miracle," says St. John, "that Jesus worked on his return from Judea to Galilee."[36] The Evangelist makes a special note of this apparently trivial detail, perhaps because the Synoptics' account leaves the impression that nothing happened between the baptism of Jesus and the beginning of the Galilean ministry, which started with the call of the four great Apostles. St. John restores events to their proper perspective, and informs us that before preaching in Galilee the Saviour had already announced the Gospel at the center of the Judaic theocracy, at Jerusalem and in Judea.

---

[36] John 4:54. It is *a* second miracle worked by Jesus on his return from Judea, but not absolutely *the* second. He had worked many miracles in Jerusalem (John 2:23) and perhaps elsewhere.

There is no cogent reason to identify this miracle with the cure of the servant of the centurion (Matt. 8:5–13; Luke 7:1–10). In both, it is true, the invalid is at Capharnaum, and the miracle is worked at a distance; but everything else is different. In St. John, it is a *Jew,* a royal dignitary (βασιλικός), who comes in person to intercede for his *son.* In the Synoptics, it is a *pagan,* a centurion, who sends others to request Jesus to cure his slave or servant (δοῦλος in St. Luke, παῖς in St. Matthew, meaning the same).

BOOK TWO

THE GOSPEL IN GALILEE

CHAPTER I

The Choice of the Apostles

1. The Lake of Tiberias

JUST before starting out for Jerusalem to celebrate the first Passover of his public life, and after the miracle at Cana, Jesus had gone down to Capharnaum with his family and his new disciples. Nazareth was too far removed from the chief highways to be the center of his apostolate. Besides, the obtuse Nazarenes, used to seeing the carpenter's son share their work and live as they lived, were too much dominated by prejudice to admit that this compatriot and fellow laborer of theirs was one sent from heaven. On the other hand, the two capitals of Galilee, Sepphoris and Tiberias, recent creations of Herod Antipas, were half pagan. Tiberias in particular aroused strong revulsion in the Jews because it was built on a necropolis.

And so on his return from Jerusalem and Judea, where he had spent several weeks, perhaps even months, Jesus made Capharnaum his headquarters. This town is on the north bank of the Lake of Genesareth, two or three miles from the mouth of the Jordan. Today it is entirely deserted, but then it was a rather lively mart and a very busy stop on the route which linked Damascus to Egypt and the Mediterranean. It was never (and could not have been) a stronghold; there are no vestiges of towers or ramparts in its ruins. The bulk of its heterogeneous population were fishermen and shopkeepers with a sprinkling of businessmen and fiscal agents, as well as a small garrison of Herod Antipas' soldiers to watch the frontier, keep order, and back up the tax collectors.[1]

Isaias had foretold a glorious future for this corner of the earth. "The land of Zabulon and the land of Nephthali, way of the sea, country beyond the Jordan, district of the nations" — this land shall see happy days when "a great light shall shine upon the people that walk in darkness and the shadow of death."[2] Capharnaum formerly belonged to the tribe of Nephthali. The little tribe of Zabulon, which included Nazareth, was locked in between the plain of Esdrelon, occupied by the tribe of Issachar,

---

[1] It may now be taken as certain that *Tell Hum* marks the site of the ancient Capharnaum. (*a*) There are in this territory no other ruins as important as these, which stretch to the north of the lake for a length of about 800 yds. and a width of 400 yds. On the other hand, at *Khan Minyeh,* which many have considered to be the site of Capharnaum, there are apparently no ruins antedating the Arab occupation. (*b*) St. Jerome says that Corozain was two Roman miles from Capharnaum (Eusebius says the same; cf. Klosterman's critical edition of the *Onomasticon,* 1904). Now Corozain was certainly at *Kerazeh,* which is, as a matter of fact, two miles from *Tell Hum.* (*c*) Josephus (*Vita,* 72), when seriously wounded on the east bank of the Jordan near Julias, was carried to the other side of the river and came to Κεφαρνωμή, before arriving at Seven Fountains (*Et Tabghah*) which is east of *Khan Minyeh.* (*d*) The pilgrim Theodosius (about 530), coming from the west, passed through Seven Fountains before arriving at Capharnaum.

The best descriptions of the site are those of Masterman (*Studies in Galilee,* Chicago, 1909, pp. 71–89) and Dalman (*Orte und Wege Jesu,* Gütersloh, 1924, Chap. viii, pp. 141–171; English transl., 1935, pp. 133–159). Guérin's *Galilée* (Vol. I, 1880, pp. 226–239), which was very good for its time, antedates the excavations.

It was the American explorer, Robinson, who made the fortunes of *Khan Minyeh.* On May 18, 1852, the ruins of *Kerazeh* seen from a near-by eminence seemed to him to be too insignificant to be those of Corozain. He decided, then, that Corozain ought to be at *Tell Hum,* and Capharnaum at *Khan Minyeh.* If he had taken the trouble to climb the steep slope of *Kerazeh,* he would have seen ruins almost as extensive, and the remains of a synagogue almost as large as those of *Tell Hum.* His authority has carried along several English-speaking authors, among them Sanday, who, however, has since retracted (*Dictionary of Christ and the Gospels,* 1906, Vol. I, p. 315), and some French writers of the Life of Christ (Fouard and LeCamus). Fillion makes no pronouncement.

Protestants persist in writing *Kapernaum;* but the true spelling of the name is Καφαρναούμ, as the oldest texts and versions prove. The spelling Καπερναούμ does not appear until the beginning of the fifth century.

[2] Matt. 4:15–16, quoting Isa. 9:1–2. The beginning of the text of Isaias, which is abbreviated by the Evangelist, runs thus: "In the past he (God) has humiliated the land of Zabulon and the land of Nephthali; in the future he will cover with glory the way of the sea, the land beyond the Jordan, district of the nations" (after Condamin's translation).

and the shore of the Mediterranean, allotted to the tribe of Aser. These four tribes made up the province of Galilee, called sometimes "Galilee of the Gentiles" because it was encircled by pagan peoples. Together they did not take up more territory than a medium-sized French *département,* and the apostolate of Jesus was to embrace only a limited section of it. The Lake of Tiberias with its circle of hills was the principal theater of the preaching of the kingdom of God, and within its horizon most of the miracles narrated in the Gospel were accomplished.[3]

The modern pilgrim would believe himself to be dreaming, if he were to read on the spot the dithyrambic descriptions of the country in Josephus and the Talmud. If we are to believe them, it was a land of milk and honey, an enchanted place, an earthly paradise. "God created the seven seas," said an ancient Rabbi, "but he reserved the Sea of Galilee for himself." According to Josephus, countless towns and villages adorned its banks — Hippos, Sennabris, Tarichea, Tiberias, Magdala, Capharnaum, Bethsaida, and others less famous. The air was the purest in the world, the waters the most limpid, the climate the healthiest. Fruit trees of all lands found there a meeting place. Tropical palms lifted their heads deep in the valleys. The olive, the fig, and the vine of the temperate zones carpeted the hillsides. The oak and walnut of the north crowned the summits of the mountains.[4] Today this splendor is no more. Only one city, Tiberias, remains, and a scattering of miserable hamlets. In place of the hundreds or thousands of sails that dotted the waters, we see only a handful of poor fishing craft. Under Ottoman rule the hilltops lost their ornament of oaks and walnuts, and the hills themselves, stripped of their sustaining walls and terraced gardens, disclose gashes of black basalt and grayish limestone. There are no longer any palm trees on the plain. Thickets and gigantic thistles choke the scanty crops. Would that a farsighted and liberal administration could bring this desert to bloom again

[3] The Lake of Tiberias, or the Sea of Galilee, is 13 mi. long, 7½ mi. at its widest point, and some 38 mi. in circumference. Its area is about 66 sq. mi. It is much larger than Lake Como (42½) and much smaller than Lake Garda (139). The ancient Hebrews, like the Arabs, called any body of water of medium size a sea.

[4] Josephus, *Bellum,* III, x, 7–8.

someday, without in the least depriving it of its religious features and its sacred character!

And still the vandalism and carelessness of man have not succeeded in killing the charm of this privileged spot of nature. The graceful, oval lake, which the Hebrews compared to a harp (from which it got its name *Kinnereth*), still reflects the same bright sky.[5] This liquid mirror, which can all be taken in at a glance, and encircled by a good walker in a dozen hours, is so foreshortened by the clear air that you feel you could talk to someone on the other bank. The impression of calm, the hush, and the austere serenity created by this panorama is, of course, largely due to the memories it awakens, but if one is fortunate enough to see it around Paschal time, when spring is flowering the plain and greening the hills, it is truly enchanting. The pilgrim can enjoy it as well as the tourist, without forgetting that he came in search, not of a charming and picturesque country, but of the footprints of the Master he adores, the memory of whose miracles and teachings is brought back to him in every fold of the ground, every inlet of the shore.

Here a pile of columns and broken capitals marks the site of the synagogue where Jesus promised his faithful the gift of the Eucharist. There under a heap of rubble is all that remains of ancient Capharnaum, where he brought Jairus' daughter back to life, healed the woman with the issue of blood, and Peter's mother-in-law, and the paralytic whom four men had carried to him, and a man born blind, and a leper, and crowds of other stricken people whom the Gospel mentions only in groups. Everything on the lake and along its banks brings back the kindnesses of the Saviour: two tempests stilled, three miraculous draughts of fish, two multiplications of loaves, the freeing of the Gerasene

---

[5] Lortet (*La Syrie d'aujourd'hui*, in *Tour du monde*, 1882, Vol. I, pp. 210–212) writes: "The water of the lake is ordinarily a very beautiful blue. . . . During a storm, I have sometimes seen the water turn a dark violet. In the evening, it wonderfully reflects the sky, becoming a brilliant blue. During the daytime, one often notices varicolored patches . . . owing to currents or light breezes that ripple the surface and make the water sparkle in a special way. . . . Almost everywhere the banks are bordered by magnificent clumps of oleander, forming enormous thickets covered with thousands of flowers. Nothing could be more delightful than this rosy girdle reflected in the transparent blue waters, where it is superimposed on the beautiful azure of the sky."

demoniac, the cure of the blind man of Bethsaida. From here can be seen the summit of Thabor where Jesus was transfigured; and hidden behind the holy mountain is the little town of Naim. Two thirds of the Gospel miracles were enacted within this blessed horizon.

The Lake of Tiberias teems with fish. Schools of them can be seen sometimes swimming at the surface, so packed together that they look like reefs at water level. Countless flocks of fish-eating birds — white pelicans, silvery grebes, dark-feathered cormorants — swoop down onto the lake and enliven its deserted banks. Even today they tell of catches that would sound fabulous were they not vouched for by trustworthy witnesses.[6]

2. Preaching in the Synagogues

The three Synoptics begin the public life of Jesus only after the arrest of St. John the Baptist. But before this event, the Fourth Gospel depicts him expelling the vendors from the Temple, giving instruction to Nicodemus, baptizing in Judea, preaching in Samaria, and working two miracles at Cana.[7] All this, however, was but a prelude, and it was only after his return to Galilee that Jesus inaugurated and organized his active apostolate. Never-

---

[6] The most accurate description of the lake, from the viewpoint of climate, flora, and fauna, is that of Dom Biever, *Conférences de Saint-Etienne,* 1910 and 1911. Interesting also are: Lortet, *La Syrie d'aujourd'hui,* (1884); Masterman, *Studies in Galilee* (Chicago, 1909); and Dalman, *Itinéraires de Jésus* (Paris, 1930).

Forty-three species of fish have been counted in Galilee; those which have some commercial value belong to three families: the Chromidae, the Siluridae, and the Cyprinidae (to which latter class the carp belong). The principal table fish is the Chromis (St. Peter's Fish), which is unknown in Europe. Characteristic of it is a dorsal fin equipped with sharp bristles which can inflict rather painful wounds on rash or inexperienced fishermen. The Arabs call it *musht* (the comb). This excellent fish rarely reaches the length of 12 inches. The most curious fish in the lake is a silurus (the *Clarias macracanthus,* in Arabic *barbut*) which can live out of water for several hours. When out of water, it emits a sound very much like a mew, hence its name, "catfish." Since it has no scales, the Jews consider it unclean. Consequently it is sold at a very cheap price. As a matter of fact, all fish were cheap, even up to a short time ago. At the end of the last century, seven pounds of fish could be bought at Tiberias for about 29 cents. Later on, of course, things changed greatly.

[7] The changing of water into wine, and the cure of the son of the royal official (John 2:1–11; 4:46–54).

theless the reading of the Synoptics leaves an unavoidable impression that before definitely associating the Apostles with himself, the Saviour preached by himself in the synagogues of Galilee, from which his fame spread over the whole country; and St. John's account does not contradict this.[8]

A preacher of the Gospel must have an audience. Jesus was sure of finding one every Saturday in the smaller synagogues, three times a week in the more important localities, and every day in towns large enough to guarantee at least ten people for divine service. The synagogue was not only a house of prayer; it was also a meeting place, a school, and a courthouse; but above all it was a place dedicated to the reading and explaining of the Bible. Everyone could have his turn to speak, depending on the invitation or consent of the heads of the synagogue, and we are told that these voluntary and sometimes prolix speakers went far into the morning.

All the Galilean synagogues whose ruins have been exhumed in recent times were built along the same pattern. They were of freestone put together without cement or mortar, carefully trimmed outside, and covered inside with a layer of stucco as a base for appropriate decorations. They were divided into three naves by two rows of columns, and presented the appearance of pagan or Christian basilicas, though they were unlike the latter in the absence of chevets or apses, and differed from both in that the two rows of columns turned to meet at the end opposite the entrance instead of running the whole length of the building. The colonnade often supported on its three sides a tribune or gallery for women. In the façade was a large portal, surmounted by a richly decorated pediment, and flanked on both sides by smaller doors.[9]

---

[8] Mark 1:14: "After John was delivered up (to the Tetrarch Antipas), Jesus came to Galilee, preaching the Gospel of the kingdom of God and saying: 'The times have been fulfilled and the kingdom of God is near. Do penance and believe in the Gospel.'" St. Matthew (4:17) and St. Luke (4:14) both insert this statement between the imprisonment of John the Baptist and the call of the first four Apostles. St. John entirely omits the preaching in Galilee up to the next-to-last Passover.

[9] In the district which was the principal theater of Jesus' preaching, may be seen the ruins of a dozen synagogues, none of which is more than six hours'

The synagogue at Capharnaum is by far the largest and most sumptuous yet explored. It was built on a foundation higher than the level of the adjacent streets, and its three entrances opened to the south directly onto a terrace which looked down upon the beautiful panorama of water-side towns and hills surrounding the lake. While the other synagogues were of black basalt, a stone common in this volcanic region, the one at Capharnaum was built entirely of blocks of white limestone, gleaming like marble, which had to be hauled from a considerable distance. We would like to believe that this magnificent edifice, which could be criticized only for excessive ornamentation, existed at the time of Christ, but archaeologists consider it a work of the end of the second century or the beginning of the third. Though yielding to the verdict of these competent judges, we think it certain that this monument, whose ruins are so worthy of admiration, stood on the site of the less sumptuous synagogue where Jesus preached his first sermons.[10]

---

journey from Capharnaum. All present the same architectural features, and several bear Hebrew inscriptions. They have been excavated by Kohl and Watzinger, who have given a detailed description of them (*Antike Synagogen in Galilaea,* Leipzig, 1916). A very clear sketch of them is to be found in Masterman, *Studies in Galilee* (Chicago, 1909), Chap. vi.

[10] There is an excellent monograph of the lamented Fr. Orfali, O.F.M., on the excavations carried on under his direction from 1906 to 1921 (*Capharnaüm et ses ruines,* Paris, 1922). It has several engravings and 12 plates.

All the land around the ancient synagogue now belongs to the Franciscans, who have enclosed it within a wall and have built there a beautiful convent. From now on, the place is secured from vandalism and from the rapacity of the natives who used the ruins as a quarry.

The interior of the synagogue of Capharnaum measured 80 by 61.17 feet. The colonnade supported a balcony, access to which was had by an outside stairway. The entrance doors faced south, like those of all the other Galilean synagogues except that of Arbela (*Irbid*), where the nature of the soil made another orientation necessary. In front of the entrance facing the lake, stretched a porch reached by steps (four at the west and fourteen on the east). This porch was supported by columns (as may be observed also at *Kefr Bir 'im*) and was a sort of lookout embracing a beautiful panorama.

Fr. Orfali thought that this is the synagogue which the Centurion of Capharnaum built as a gift for the Jews, "doubtless with military manual labor." Masterman (*op cit.,* p. 76) gives as his opinion that "nothing in the architecture or ornamentation makes this date *impossible,*" but he thinks it *less likely;* and this is the more common opinion today (cf. *R.B.,* 1923, pp. 317–318). Yet no one will contradict Masterman when he says: "And even if the greater part of the present structure belongs to a later time, it is likely that the site and at least some of the masonry go back to the time of Jesus, for there are clear indica-

The Saviour's preaching here, at the beginning of his ministry, is not much different from John's message on the banks of the Jordan: "Do penance, for the kingdom of God is at hand." John said these words when he pointed out the Messias, and Jesus repeats them when he reveals himself. His very presence was an invitation to a reform of life, according to the saying of the prophet:

> Keep ye the right, do justice:
> for my salvation is soon to come,
> and my justice soon to be revealed.[11]

Christ's contemporaries knew that the best preparation for Messianic salvation was a change of heart. Many even made this an essential condition for the appearance of the Messias and the establishment of the kingdom of God.[12]

The expressions "kingdom of God" and "kingdom of heaven" are altogether synonymous, for among the Jews "Heaven" was one of the names proper to God. St. Matthew speaks generally of the "kingdom of heaven," as did his compatriots and probably Jesus himself. The other Synoptics prefer the "kingdom of God," which was more intelligible to readers unfamiliar with Jewish traditions.[13]

In Hebrew, Greek, and Latin the one word has three meanings which modern languages distinguish. Sometimes it expresses the sovereign power of God, sometimes the exercise of this power, and sometimes the domain in which it is exercised. Since we cannot remain satisfied with an indeterminate meaning, we must choose between these three, and the choice is the more difficult

---

tions that an earlier building of great architectural pretensions stood there." Cf. also the *Supplément* to the *Dict. de la Bible,* Vol. I, cols. 1055–1063, the article by Abel, O.P.

[11] Isa. 56:1. Here Messianic salvation is offered to all peoples.

[12] Billerbeck, *Kommentar,* Vol. I, pp. 163–172.

[13] The kingdom of heaven (Matthew, 33 times); the kingdom of God (Matthew, 3 times; Mark, 14 times; Luke, 32 times; John, twice). But frequently the phrase *my kingdom,* or *the kingdom of my Father* occurs; and sometimes simply *the kingdom* (Matt. 8:12; 13:38: the children of the kingdom).

It is to be noted: *first,* that in the expression "kingdom of heaven" (*malkuth Shamaïm*) the word *Shamaïm* never has the definite article, because it is a proper name, a synonym for God; secondly, that in Hebrew *Shamaïm,* which has no singular form, means simply *heaven,* and one cannot imagine a plurality of heavens.

the more closely the ideas are associated and in certain cases subtly overlap.[14]

God is the King of the universe, King of Israel, and King of hearts. He rules in heaven, he rules in Sion, and he should rule over the individual soul. Hebrew monotheism and the dogma of creation necessarily imply God's sovereignty over the world, the work of his hands, but it does not follow that this universal sovereignty should have been expressed from the first under the figure of royal power, and indeed it seems that the title "King of Israel" was applied to God before that of "King of the World." It is read for the first time in the canticle of Moses, at the moment God came "to possess his people" by freeing them from the Egyptian bondage.

"Thou shalt plant them on the mountain of thy inheritance in the place which thou hast prepared for thy habitation, in the sanctuary which thy hands, O Lord, have established. Yahweh shall reign for ever and ever."[15]

When the ratification of the covenant on Sinai made the children of Israel the chosen people, the priestly race, the domain of Yahweh, they were unique among all the surrounding nations in having only God as their king. It was a true theocracy, to use the word which Josephus so aptly coined.[16] God governed his people through his representatives, the prophets, judges, and chiefs of his choosing. Isaias admirably expresses this relationship when he says:

> Yahweh is our Judge,
> Yahweh is our Chief
> Yahweh is our King.[17]

The institution of royalty left the theocratic regime completely unchanged. The visible king was looked upon as the delegate, the lieutenant, and the understudy, as it were, of the invisible King. This is what David means when he addresses the assembled

[14] *Regnum, βασιλεία,* מלכות (*malkuth*). The Hebrew word means, "royalty," "reign," and "kingdom"; but if territory is meant ממלכה (*mamlakah*) is used, and for the royal dignity, מלוכה (*melukah*).

[15] Exod. 15:17–18.

[16] Josephus, *Contra Apionem,* ii, 17: "Moses, *to use a new word, θεοκρατίαν ἀπέδειξε τὸ πολίτευμα.*"

[17] Isa. 32:22.

people, "The God of Israel has chosen me from all the house of my father to be king of Israel . . . and he has chosen my son Solomon to sit upon the throne of the royalty of Yahweh."[18] Thus the throne of David and Solomon is in reality the royal throne of God. But the kings of Juda did not live up to this ideal any more than the kings of Israel, so that all the hopes and all the aspirations of the prophets looked toward a better time to come. A descendant and heir of David, glimpsed by the seers of Israel in a more or less distant, more or less distinct perspective, will embody the ideal of their dreams. He will reign in the name of God and his reign will be God's reign on earth.

When the Messias comes, the descendant and heir of David, the Chosen One, the Anointed of the Lord, God will not have him reign in his place; He will reign with him and by him. In the Prophetical and Sapiential books Yahweh was the King of glory, the King of heaven and earth, the King of the nations, the King of kings, the King eternal: and this is exactly what the Messias will be. The center of the theocracy will always be Jerusalem but it will not be shut up within the narrow confines of Palestine. It will embrace all the peoples of the world, and the kingdom of the Son of Man will be limited no more in space than in time. Then will begin the era of peace, justice, and happiness sung by Isaias. The centuries of long silence that followed the period of prophecy lived in this hope, and the apocrypha of the Old Testament — the *Book of Henoch,* the *Book of Jubilees,* the *Sibylline Oracles,* the *Apocalypse of Baruch,* the *Psalms of Solomon* — were its echoes. If the seventeenth *Psalm of Solomon* were not so long it might be cited in full:

> Lord, thou art our king for ever and ever. . . .
> Lord, raise up for them the son of David, their king. . . .
> He shall have the nations submissive under his yoke. . . .
> The peoples shall come from everywhere to see his glory.
> In his time there shall be no longer any injustice among
> them, for all shall be holy: Christ the Lord is their king.[19]

---

[18] 1 Para. 28:5.

[19] The Greek text may be found in Gebhardt (*Die Psalmen Salomos,* pp. 126–135) which is reproduced by Lagrange, *Le Messianisme,* pp. 332–337.

The study of Messianism presents considerable difficulty, since the concept of it differs so much in different authors and at different periods. Schürer

Thus the sovereignty of God over Israel and the world is affirmed with the same force in the extracanonical books as in the Bible. But the actual expression "kingdom of God" appears only two or three times in the Old Testament.[20] It is rare in pre-Christian writings, and when it becomes common, among the Rabbis of the second century, it corresponds but little to the Gospel meaning. To take "the kingdom of God" or "the yoke of the kingdom of God" on oneself then meant to embrace in practice all the details of the Torah. Thus, after the disasters and blighted hopes of the two great revolts in 70 and 135, which brought almost complete ruin on the nation, Messianic longings had undergone an evolution. The devout Jew, turning in upon himself, henceforth dreamed less of a national restoration than of his individual salvation; the social reign of the Messias concerned him less than did the rule of God over the individual conscience. Even before the revolt in the year 70 a number of Scribes and Pharisees had refused to take part in the agitations of the frenzied patriots, and Vespasian had sent them away to Jamnia and Lydda, far from the scene of military operations. Though matters had not gone that far at the beginning of the Christian era, these tendencies began to manifest themselves from the time of the Roman occupation of Judea.

It is therefore difficult to say precisely what the hearers of Jesus had in mind when they spoke of "the kingdom of God" or heard it mentioned, especially since the notion varied with each one's personal aspirations. Nor is this surprising, for how many Christians could give the exact import of the second petition in the Our Father, "Thy kingdom come!"? What is certain is that

---

(*Geschichte,* 4 ed., Vol. II, pp. 579–651) offers a very complete treatment of it, with a copious bibliography up to 1907. Cf. also Lagrange, *Le Messianisme,* 1909, and *Le Judaisme avant Jésus-Christ,* 1931; Billerbeck, *Kommentar,* Vol. IV, 1928, pp. 799–1015; Gressmann, *Der Messias,* 1929; Bonsirven, *Le Judaisme palestinien* (cf. *Messianisme, Messie, Règne du ciel,* Vol. ii, pp. 351 ff. and 365 ff.).

[20] Except for 1 Para. 28:5 (cited above) and three or four other texts where God says "my kingdom," the complete expression "the kingdom of God" is not found at all outside of Wisd. 10:10, where it has a meaning that is difficult to ascertain:

> "The Lord will show Jacob the *kingdom of God*
> and make known to him the holy things."

the contemporaries of Christ conceived the kingdom of God as some sort of divine intervention which would make Israel worthy of its mission. In the beginning Jesus did not explain its nature; that would be the work of the Day of the Parables, and also the starting point of the misunderstandings between him and his audience. At first he merely held it out as something desirable and prepared hearts to receive it.

The words of the first discourse made a profound impression on the crowds. "They were struck with astonishment, never having heard the like; for he did not teach like the Scribes." The Scribes never dared propose anything as their own, but always entrenched themselves behind some famous name and usually lost themselves in a labyrinth of subtle questions or puerile casuistical jousts. But this man spoke with the authority of a prophet. He grappled straightway with the deepest moral problems and solved them like a master, offering no authority except his own.

3. The Call of the Four Great Apostles

One morning a larger crowd than usual pressed around the Saviour, reluctant to lose a single word. Not far away moored to the bank were two boats whose occupants had disembarked and were busy on the shore repairing or cleaning their nets after a fruitless night of fishing. One of the boats belonged to Simon Peter, and the other to Zebedee, the father of the future Apostles, James and John.

From time immemorial, the people living on the lake had made their livelihood by fishing.[21] Often several families worked together, for many arms were needed to handle the fishing gear

[21] At one time the town of Tarichea, south of Tiberias, pickled these fish in abundance, and they were exported to distant places and considered a delicacy, according to what the ancients tell us. Tarichea owes its name to this industry, for the Greek word ταραχεύειν means to salt fish or meat, to prepare pickled foods. Even in our own day the catch of fish is extraordinary. Lortet wrote in 1884 (*La Syrie d'aujourd'hui*, p. 506): "The lake is so full of fish that everyday within a few minutes we had our boat filled to the brim with thousands of them of all sizes." In 1896, the fishermen on Lake Tiberias banded together to clear the southern shore of heaps of large rocks, and they hauled 9260 lbs. of fish to shore with two large nets tied together. Some years later, a fishing expedition organized on the eastern bank by two brothers brought in 3970 lbs. These catches are, obviously, unusual, but catches up to 660 lbs. are not rare (Biever, *Conférences de Saint-Etienne*, 1911, pp. 291–292). Can the same be said today?

which they used. Thus it happened that two pairs of brothers, Peter and Andrew, and James and John, were together when they heard the Saviour's call. Crowded by the ever increasing multitude, Jesus climbed into Peter's boat and asked him to push off a little from the shore. There, seated on the rowers' bench, he continued his instructions to the people.

When he had finished, he said to Peter: "Launch out into the deep and lower your nets into the water for a catch." "Master," answered Peter, "we have toiled all night and have caught nothing, but at thy word I will lower the net." Now, this was no trifling matter, considering the size of the trammel net used for night fishing. It was made up of three nets of the same length, suspended from a single rope and held at the surface by cork floats. When it was played out full length, the fishermen circled it several times, beating the water with their oars to drive the fish into it. The fish readily passed through the two outer nets, but were blocked by the close-meshed net in the middle, and the more they struggled the tighter they were caught in the treacherous trap. If the first try did not succeed, the net was let down in a different place and the maneuver was repeated until dawn, when operations normally ceased for the time being.

Peter had tried those waters all night long, and felt sure that another attempt would yield nothing, especially in the daylight, which was less favorable for that kind of fishing. Humanly speaking, it was so much useless extra labor. But his act of meritorious faith was rewarded by quick success. No sooner had the long net been strung out than it weighed down in the middle and was in danger of breaking under the load of captured fish. Peter and his companions signaled to their associates in the other boat to come and help them hoist their net aboard or at least gradually lighten its contents. They all worked together and the two boats were finally so full that they threatened to sink straight to the bottom.

Such a result as this, at a designated point, in a spot vainly tried a few hours earlier, evidently partook of the marvelous. Peter was the first to recognize it. He had witnessed other miracles of the Saviour — at least the one at Cana — but they had not struck him as forcibly as this one, because they did not affect him personally. Falling down at Jesus' feet, he said: "Depart from me, O Lord, for I am a sinful man." It was not the kind of religious fright which is often inspired by a manifestation of the supernatural that made him speak thus. It was the sense of his own unworthiness. And at the sight of the marvelous catch, all who had helped, particularly James and John, who were in the other boat, felt the same shock. Jesus said to Peter, "Fear not! From now on thou shalt be a fisher of men." And the partners brought their craft back to shore, left everything, and followed him.[22]

It will have been noticed that this account of St. Luke's gives Peter a leading role. It is Peter whom Jesus addresses, and it is he whom he specially calls to follow him. But the others also feel themselves to have been called, and immediately leave everything to follow the Master — which is evident proof that the call was not given to Peter alone. It can scarcely be doubted that Andrew was in the boat at the time with his brother, and was called at the same time, although St. Luke does not mention him.

The first two Evangelists have a different version of the vocation story:

"Walking along the shore of the sea of Galilee, Jesus saw two brothers, Simon, surnamed Peter, and Andrew, casting their nets into the sea; for they were fishermen. He said to them 'Come, follow me, and I will make you fishers of men.' And straightway they left their nets and followed him.

---

[22] Luke 5:1–11. To be noted are: (1) *The fishing method* — St. Luke uses the generic term for net (τὰ δίκτυα) meaning neither a *cast net* (ἀμφίβληστρον) nor a *seine* (σαγήνη), but a *dragnet,* which is proved by the following: (*a*) They put out into the open sea; but the cast net is thrown from the bank or near it. (*b*) The net is *dropped,* let down into the water (χαλᾶν), while the cast net is thrown. (*c*) The net is emptied into the boat out on the water; but the seine is dragged to the shore. (*d*) Finally, there is question here of night fishing, when neither the cast net nor the seine was used.

The three dragnets are each between 100 and 200 yds. long. There is a good description of the whole operation in Biever, *Conférences de Saint-Etienne,* 1911, p. 305, and by Masterman, *Studies in Galilee,* 1909, p. 41.

(2) *The crew* — There are two boats of *associates* (v. 7, μέτοιχοι, *socii,* and more precisely κοινωνοί, v. 10, *socii Simonis*). The boat of Zebedee was manned by at least five men: the father, two sons, and hired *men.* Simon Peter was not alone in his boat, because Jesus says to him: "launch out into the deep and let down (χαλάσατε in the plural) *your* (in the plural) nets. He could not have been able to do this by himself. There can be no doubt that his brother Andrew and others were with him.

"A little further on he saw two other brothers, James and John, the sons of Zebedee, mending their nets in the boat with Zebedee their father, and he called them. And leaving their father Zebedee in the boat with the hired men they followed him."[23]

The best commentators are agreed that, despite the obvious differences in the accounts, all three Synoptics are reporting the same event.[24] How can we think that after leaving everything to follow Christ the Apostles needed a new call? To justify a second call, Cajetan supposes that the first time the Apostles left only their nets, their boats, and their father, and the second time they left *absolutely everything*. But this smacks of Rabbinical subtlety and is a rather desperate subterfuge.

You may, if you choose, harmonize the two accounts by tortured dovetailings. You could distinguish, for example, the two successive scenes by having St. Luke's precede or closely follow the one we have outlined from the other two Synoptics. Perhaps it is better to say with St. Augustine that "Mark and Matthew give a brief résumé of the event, and are interested only in its outcome, while Luke develops it and clarifies it with a description of the miraculous catch." In other words, St. Luke writes as an

---

23 Matt. 4:18–22; Mark 1:16–20. The only noteworthy difference between the two accounts is that according to St. Mark, James and John leave *their father in the boat with the hired men*. These latter are not domestic servants, but laborers hired (μισθωτοί) by the day or week.

Peter and Andrew are described as throwing the cast net (Matt. 4:18, βάλλοντες ἀμφίβληστρον; St. Mark has ἀμφιβάλλοντες, which means the same). After a fruitless effort with the dragnet, the men, returning to shore sometimes threw out cast nets, hoping for better luck.

The other two brothers are *mending* their nets (καταρτίζοντες). After each catch the nets were stretched out on the beach, to mend the mesh that had been broken by sharp rocks or the cutting fins of certain fish. They were also cleaned by picking out stones and pieces of wood. This is the operation mentioned by St. Luke (5:2), ἔπλυνον τὰ δίκτυα.

24 To begin with St. John Chrysostom and St. Augustine: the latter writes (*De consensu Evang.*, ii, 16, n. 37; ML, XXXIV, 1095): "Matthaeus et Marcus breviter haec perstringunt quemadmodum gestum sit, quod Lucas apertius explicavit, commemorans ibi etiam miraculum super captura piscium." St. Augustine is somewhat embarrassed by the fact that, according to St. Luke, Jesus says to Peter *in the boat:* "I will make thee a fisher of men," while in St. Matthew and St. Mark, Peter and Andrew are called *on the shore*. He offers this answer: "Potuit utique prius hoc Petro dicere quod Lucas insinuavit; et ambobus postea quod illi duo commemorant." But the first solution is satisfactory.

historian, careful to bring out the chain of causes and effects. The others are speaking as catechists and are not concerned with the details.

There is something surprising about the disciples' immediate response to Jesus' call. There is no resistance, not a moment of hesitation. The reading of St. Mark and St. Matthew might give the impression that this was the first time Jesus had met them; but St. John and St. Luke make clear that they had already seen his miracles, shared his weariness, and lived in his company. There is nothing psychologically improbable, therefore, in their ready answer to his call.[25]

But how is it that Jesus now invites them to follow him when they had already followed him so long? This difficulty did not escape the astuteness of St. Augustine, who offers two possible solutions, though of unequal merit. Either the disciples who followed Jesus across Judea and Samaria were not the future Apostles, but supernumeraries who disappeared without a trace, or the Apostles had been called after the miracle at Cana during the first sojourn at Capharnaum, though the Synoptics, since they omit this whole period, report the call only after the arrest of the Baptist.

The first hypothesis would need very strong evidence, which is however entirely lacking. We cannot believe that the companions of Jesus in Judea and Samaria, who conferred baptism in his name and were promised a rich harvest of souls and were commanded to prepare themselves to reap it, are unknown characters or chance acquaintances, soon left to a commonplace destiny.

The second hypothesis we originally found rather attractive. The Saviour would have called the Apostles before leaving for Jerusalem to celebrate the first Passover of his public life, and the Synoptics, beginning the story of Jesus' preaching only after John's arrest, would here be mentioning in retrospect an event which they were unable to report in its proper chronological place. But this solution, though satisfying at first glance, runs counter

---

[25] John 1:37–4:4–5. St. Luke reports the deliverance of the Capharnaum demoniac and the cure of Peter's mother-in-law before the call of the Apostles. Certain features of the miraculous draught of fish (Luke 5:3–5) show that Peter already had some association with the Saviour.

to the positive data of St. Luke and even some fairly clear indications in the other Evangelists. At the moment when Jesus calls his Apostles, he is surrounded by a densely packed crowd and has difficulty getting away from them: evident proof that the preaching of the Gospel has already been inaugurated. Several other signs point in the same direction.

It is therefore preferable to settle on another harmonization in order to reconcile more satisfactorily the divergent data. The first six Apostles (Peter, Andrew, James, John, Philip, and Nathanael or Bartholomew) had met Jesus on the banks of the Jordan, and from that time on had accompanied him everywhere. This was not yet a call to the Apostolate, but a sort of novitiate or probation. This preliminary stage would have been rather long if it lasted nine or ten months, as the common opinion has it. It would seem more natural that it lasted only a few weeks, or at most a couple of months, as we believe we have shown.

After the arrest of the Baptist, Jesus led his disciples back to Galilee; but before definitively associating them with his work he wished to prepare the ground, and for a certain period he preached by himself in the synagogues, as the Synoptics tell us.[26] Then it was that the disciples of yesterday went back to their boats, from which our Lord again summoned them to make them fishers of men.

"You will be fishers of men!" How often through the centuries has that call echoed in the hearts of other disciples, who have not counted the cost but have left all, friends, relatives, and native land, to go to preach the Gospel to savage peoples, possibly only to be repayed for their devotedness by persecution and martyrdom. After sacrificing everything — the joys of the present and the dreams of the future — in the service of their Master, they will die happy in the thought that the testimony of their blood is the most fruitful of apostolates.

No symbols were dearer to the first Christians than those of the fisherman and the fish. Christ was often portrayed in the catacombs as a fisherman, and the faithful as little fish born in the waters of Baptism. When the faithful discovered that the

---

[26] Matt. 4:12–17; Mark 1:14–15; Luke 4:14–15. Jesus is preaching alone in Galilee *before* the call addressed to the Apostles: he is teaching in the synagogues (Luke), and his fame has spread throughout the country (Luke).

Greek word for fish is written with the first letters of the words *Jesus Christ, Son of God, Saviour,* they used it as a way of proclaiming their faith without drawing the attention of the pagans. They took to engraving the image of a fish on tombstones, sarcophagi, signet rings, and pieces of wood or metal which they hung around their necks as Baptismal tokens and carried to the grave with them as symbols of hope.[27]

4. The Choice of the Twelve

A period of trial intervened between the call of the Twelve and their election. We do not know how long it lasted. St. Matthew lists the Twelve on the occasion of their temporary mission, but it appears even from his account that the election had already been made by that time. St. Mark and St. Luke connect it with the Sermon on the Mount, or rather with the night of prayer that preceded it. What better hour for setting apart the heralds of the Gospel than that in which the Saviour was to trace in bold strokes the program of the kingdom of God!

The report of Jesus' miracles attracted large multitudes around him. They came from Judea and Galilee, Jerusalem and Idumea, from the countries beyond the Jordan and the neighborhood of Tyre and Sidon.[28] They were nearly all Jewish by race or religion. Idumea had to accept Judaism under the Hasmonean princes, willingly or by compulsion. Perea, despite its Greek enclaves, was for the most part Jewish, and Phoenicia, of which Tyre and Sidon were the capitals, numbered a great many Jewish colonies.

---

[27] The acrostic for 'Ιησοῦς Χριστὸς Θεοῦ 'Υιὸς Σωτήρ is ΙΧΘΥΣ (fish). St. Augustine writes (*De civitate Dei,* xviii, 23; ML, XLI, 580): "Graecorum quinque verborum . . . si primas litteras jungas erit ἰχθύς, id est, Piscis, in quo nomine mystico intelligitur Christus." On this symbolism in the literature, painting, and plastic arts of the early Church, see the five-volume work of Doelger, 'Ιχθύς, *Das Fisch-Symbol in frühchristlicher Zeit,* Münster, 1928–1932.

The fish, the ordinary food of the lake people of Tiberias and the symbol of Christ, became also the emblem of the Eucharist, the celestial Food of our souls and the real partaking of the Body of Christ. Suffice it to recall the famous inscriptions of Abercius and Pectorius.

[28] Mark 3:7–10; Matt. 4:23–25; Luke 6:17–19. St. Mark speaks of the great concourse of people on the *eve* of the Sermon on the Mount; St. Matthew mentions it *before,* and St. Luke *after* the sermon. These differences are easily reconciled; the multitude does not disperse all at once.

Never had the Saviour strewn his miracles with such a lavish hand. One day the sick and possessed whom he had cured, and those expecting a cure, pressed around him with such frantic enthusiasm that he ordered his disciples to hold a boat ready for him in case he should need it to withdraw.[29] He does not seem to have used it, however, and the day apparently passed without another incident. But when evening came, wishing to get off alone to spend the night in prayer, he climbed one of the hills overlooking the Lake of Genesareth.[30] According to instructions, the disciples were to meet him there in the morning, and a comparison of the Gospels reveals that a great multitude went with them.

"In those days," says St. Luke, "Jesus retired into the mountain to pray, and he spent the whole night in prayer to God. And when day was come, he summoned his disciples and chose twelve of them, to whom he gave the name Apostles: Simon, whom he surnamed Peter, and his brother Andrew, James and John, Philip and Bartholomew, Matthew and Thomas, James (the son) of Alpheus and Simon called Zelotes, Jude, the brother of James, and Judas, who was to betray him."

This list, reproduced by the three Synoptics and the author of the Acts, with interesting variants, seems almost to follow the order in which the Apostles were called, and there is in it a certain hierarchy which does not seem to be the result of chance. The Twelve are always divided into three groups of four, which are always made up of the same members, with Peter, Philip, and James of Alpheus respectively at the head of each group. Peter always heads the whole list with the express designation of *first;* Judas is always last, branded with the infamous epithet of *traitor*. The number *twelve* is symbolic. There will be twelve foundations of the Church, as there were twelve patriarchs, and

---

29 According to St. Mark, Jesus has the boat made ready, that the crowd *may not crush him* (ἵνα μὴ θλίβωσιν αὐτόν), for the sick were *hurling themselves on him* (ὥστε ἐπιπίπτειν αὐτῷ). St. Luke says the same in less vivid style.

30 Mark 3:13; Luke 6:12; Matt. 5:1. Jesus climbs *the* mountain; but the mountain (τὸ ὄρος) is the whole group of hills surrounding the lake, either on the western side (Matt. 5:1; 8:1; 15:29; Mark 3:13; 5:11; 6:46; Luke 6:12; 8:32; 9:28–37) or on the east (John 6:3, 15).

St. Luke adds that he went there to pray, and that he spent the whole night in prayer. The retirement of Jesus to the mountain in order to pray there is mentioned in other texts (cf. Matt. 14:23; Mark 6:46; Luke 9:18).

twelve tribes of Israel.[31] Hence, after the Saviour's Resurrection the Apostles hastened to fill the post left vacant by the defection of Judas, in order to complete the prophetic number. Although Jesus called them Apostles, the Evangelists usually designate them as the Twelve, when not including them in the general group of disciples, from which the context alone aids in distinguishing them.[32]

We are inclined to think of the Apostles as rough, simple-minded men whose ignorance is equaled only by their destitution.

---

[31] Here are the four lists:

Matt. 10:2–4	*Mark 3:16–19*	*Luke 6:14–16*	*Acts 1:13*
1. *Simon called Peter*	*Simon Peter*	*Simon named Peter*	*Peter*
2. and Andrew	and James	and Andrew	and John
3. James	and John	James	and James
4. and John	and Andrew	and John	and Andrew
5. *Philip*	*and Philip*	*Philip*	*Philip*
6. and Bartholomew	and Bartholomew	and Bartholomew	and Thomas
7. Thomas	and Matthew	and Matthew	Bartholomew
8. and Matthew	and Thomas	and Thomas	and Matthew
9. *James* (son of) *Alpheus*	*and James of Alpheus*	*and James of Alpheus*	*James of Alpheus*
10. and Lebbeus (Thaddeus)	and Thaddeus	and Simon the Zealot	and Simon the Zealot
11. Simon the Cananean	and Simon the Cananean	and Jude of James	and Jude of James
12. and Judas Iscariot	and Judas Iscariot	and Judas Iscariot	

NOTE: (*a*) St. Matthew, listing the Apostles on the occasion of their mission, enumerates them in pairs, perhaps in the order in which they were sent out *two by two*. He is careful to put himself last in his own group; and, not content with placing St. Peter at the head of the list, expressly states that he is the first (πρῶτος). (*b*) St. Mark puts Matthew in the seventh place, the place which belongs to him, and places the sons of Zebedee ahead of St. Andrew, perhaps to link more closely together the three Apostles who seem to have enjoyed greater intimacy with our Lord. (*c*) St. Luke, in his Gospel, lists the Apostles of the first group in pairs. Judas is naturally omitted in the Acts. John, who had become inseparable from Peter after the Saviour's Resurrection, takes the second place; and Thomas, who had become conspicuous because of his profession of faith, occupies the sixth position.

[32] The word *Apostle* is found only once in St. John (13:16) and in the general sense of *one sent*. The Twelve are called *Apostles* only once in St. Matthew (10:2), twice in St. Mark (3:14 and 6:30), and five times in St. Luke. They are usually spoken of under the name of *the Twelve* (8 times in Matthew; 12 in Mark; 7 in Luke; and 5 in John; and also in Acts 6:2, and 1 Corinthians 15:5).

The lower we put them in the social scale, the more we seem to enhance the work of Jesus, who knew how to make the best of such mediocre material and accomplish such great things with such lowly instruments. But this elaborately darkened picture labors under the difficulty that it contradicts the facts.

Even if they were not Scribes and Doctors of the Law, the Apostles were not necessarily illiterate. It is highly probable that they could all read and write, for education was at that time much more widespread among the Jews than is generally believed. Each synagogue had its school and there were synagogues in all villages of any importance. The *ḥazzan,* or sacristan, acted as instructor where no other teacher was available, and from the time of the later Hasmonean kings, a half century before the Christian era, all young Israelites were obliged to attend school. The general decline of studies came only later, at the time of the great upheaval before and after the national catastrophe in A.D. 70. Why, then, should we suppose that the Jewish contemporaries of Christ were more ignorant than the Moslem of today?

The Apostles may have been poor, but they were not indigent. They worked for a living, as did the great majority of their compatriots. They belonged to that middle class among whom riches were rare but penury almost unknown. The four great Apostles had a sufficiently remunerative occupation. Peter and Andrew found it possible to dedicate themselves to Christ without leaving their family in need. They had a house, a boat, and fishing nets. Many of the lake dwellers of today do not have as much. Zebedee, the father of James and John, even enjoyed a certain affluence, since he had hired servants, and his wife Salome was one of those women who assisted the Saviour with their resources and their devoted service. The Apostles in the second group apparently had been members of liberal professions — certainly Matthew, who was a tax collector, and probably Philip, who was the one whom the Greeks approached when they wished to speak to Jesus. There are indications that the same was true of Thomas and Bartholomew. As for the Apostles in the last group, James and Jude were certainly educated, if they composed the Epistles bearing their names; and Judas, charged with the humble finances of the Apostolic college, was not unlettered. The conclusion from all this is that ignorance and poverty were neither reason for exclusion from nor a special title to inclusion in the Saviour's selection.

Among these elect what variety was there of tastes, what diversity in talents, what difference in characters! Peter, the first among them, by the express will of Jesus, was probably also outstanding by reason of his richly gifted nature. Impulsive, fiery, loyal and devoted, prompt to conceive and ardent to execute, he seemed born to command others and to carry through great enterprises; but his occasionally blind impetuosity easily turned into presumption, and the mortification which hard experience inflicted upon his optimism exposed him to discouragement and diffidence. That was the price he had to pay for his superior qualities. When Jesus saw him for the first time on the banks of the Jordan, he presaged his glorious future by promising him a symbolic name, Kephas or Peter. When making him an Apostle, he gave him the name, and confirmed it when he appointed him to rule his Church after himself. In molding him he employed gentleness tempered with some severity, and unflagging patience. And Peter, after his fall and repentance and solemn rehabilitation, takes the role of chief and fills it without the slightest embarrassment. He speaks, answers questions, makes decisions, and acts at all times as master in the name of his colleagues; and it never enters anyone's head to contest his pre-eminence. Almost everything the Gospel tells us about him comes from St. John and St. Matthew. St. Mark is the one who says the least about him, and never praises him. The Rationalists are surprised at this: rather should we be surprised at their surprise. Is not this reserve of St. Mark to be expected, if, as tradition tells us, he was Peter's interpreter? Would anyone have the Prince of the Apostles profit by his own catechetical instruction to preach his own panegyric?

Andrew, the brother of Peter, is his living opposite.[33] He is a quiet, modest man, devoid of ambition or pretentiousness, self-effacing and gladly retiring into the background; effortlessly and unaffectedly making himself inconspicuous. His is the honor so much extolled by the Fathers of having been the first to seek

---

[33] The Synoptics record only the call and choice of Andrew; St. John adds three characteristic details: John 1:41–44; 6:8; 12:21.

and find Jesus, and it is he that led his brother Peter to him. Nevertheless, his role in the Gospel is an obscure one. He is lost in the crowd, and is not one of the circle of privileged Apostles. Andrew is the wise man, the man of good counsel, to whom others have recourse in case of difficulty. On the day of the first multiplication of loaves, he is the one who takes it upon himself to verify that there are on hand as provisions only five barley loaves and two little fishes; it is to him that Philip comes on a certain day to ease his own responsibility (John 12:22). But under his apparent calm there is intrepid courage and indomitable strength. God, who is pleased to exalt the humble, reserves for him the most glorious of martyrdoms.

Except for Peter, who must always be considered apart, none of the Apostles were more intimate with Jesus than the sons of Zebedee.[34] They are the only ones who, with Peter, are permitted to climb the mountain of the Transfiguration. They alone are brought into the room where Jairus' daughter sleeps the sleep of death, and they are the only ones allowed within a few paces of the place of the Agony. Though their ambitious mother's request that they might sit on the right and left of Christ in glory was refused, they were given to drink his chalice. A premature martyrdom ended James's life. John's was so prolonged that the belief grew that he was immortal, but his life was in reality a protracted martyrdom. We have said all there is to say about St. John when we recall that he was the disciple whom Jesus loved, that he reclined on Jesus' breast at the Last Supper, and took his place finally at his mother's side. Guardian of the Virgin Mary, himself a virgin, his was the honor of revealing to the world the virginal tenderness of the Heart of Jesus. John is the herald of fraternal charity and the Apostle of divine love.

---

[34] The call (Matt. 4:21; Mark 1:19–20; Luke 5:10); at the raising of the daughter of Jairus (Mark 5:37; Luke 8:51); on the Mount of Transfiguration (Matt. 17:1; Mark 9:2; Luke 9:28); the indiscreet request of their mother (Mark 10:35–41; Matt. 20:20–24); in Gethsemani (Mark 14:33); on the shore of the lake after the Resurrection (John 21:2). The two *sons of thunder* (Mark 3:17) demand the punishment of the inhospitable Samaritans (Luke 9:54). This is practically all that concerns the two brothers together. John's role at the Last Supper, during the Passion, and after the Resurrection is known to us by what he says of himself in the third person under the anonymous title of "the beloved disciple" of Jesus.

But in the effeminate features and languorous poses certain artists give him, I fail to recognize the man whom Jesus called the *son of thunder,* the man who would have called down fire from heaven on the inhospitable Samaritans, and who hurled against the heretics of his time the fulminations of the Apocalypse. John became what he was only by changing his nature and taking as his pattern him who proclaimed himself meek and humble of heart.

Outside the four great Apostles, St. Matthew is the only one whose call is reported in the Gospel, and that briefly. Matthew, or Levi, the son of Alpheus, was a publican. At Rome that name was applied to wealthy persons, generally knights, who acquired by lease the right to levy taxes in a town or province — something like the revenue farmers or the partisans of the *ancien régime.* The title was extended, however, to include subordinate employees who collected certain taxes or rents. Besides the land and poll tax, there was, then as today, a great deal of indirect taxation: fees on sales and purchases, customs duties and transfer taxes, as well as toll charges on bridges and roads. We have no accurate idea of the organization of the fiscal system in the tetrarchies of Antipas and Philip, but presumably it was modeled on that of Rome. Since the tariffs were often vaguely defined and recourse against arbitrary impositions practically nonexistent, the publicans were tempted to commit many injustices and annoyances. The result was that they were loathed everywhere, and, though Jews by race, they were put in a class with pagans.

Jesus was walking along the lakeside of Capharnaum when he noticed Matthew seated at his desk. He said to him merely, "Follow me," and Matthew rose at once to follow him, leaving his money, accounts, and registers where they were. The Gospel offers no details. The only thing judged worth telling us is how promptly the publican obeyed. His decision was sudden, but not imprudent or thoughtless. He certainly knew of Jesus' miracles by hearsay, and may even have seen some of them. Although it is impossible to date this episode exactly, it seems to belong to the first days of the Saviour's preaching.[35] And in the list

[35] Matt. 9:9; Mark 2:13–14; Luke 5:27–28. This very brief account is identical in all three, except that the first Evangelist calls the publican *Matthew,* the

of Apostles Matthew comes immediately after the six who were at the marriage feast at Cana.

In the second group of Apostles, as in the first, a certain hierarchy of honor is noticeable; at least the order does not seem to be haphazard.[36] Philip, who is always named first, had met our Lord immediately after the great Apostles and had heard from his lips the call, "Follow me." Everything leads to the supposition that he obeyed unconditionally. The Gospel depicts him as a frank and practical-minded though somewhat timid person. He loves to be able to account for things, and his words to Nathanael, "Come and see," are characteristic. Asked by Jesus how they are going to feed more than five thousand people in the desert, he figures it up and ends in confusion, and our Lord seems to have enjoyed his embarrassment. In the Cenacle he poses a naïve question which the Master takes up with gentle good humor. When the Gentiles ask him to lead them to Jesus, he does not dare take the responsibility on himself until after he has consulted Andrew.

Bartholomew, if he is the same as Nathanael, was Philip's conquest, and is appropriately listed after him. The identification of the Nathanael of St. John with the Bartholomew of the Synoptics is the result of several concordant facts, nor is it weakened

---

name which reappears to the exclusion of any other in the lists of the Apostles: St. Luke calls him *Levi,* and St. Mark, *Levi, the son of Alpheus.*

People often had two names, one Greek, the other Aramaic; not infrequently they had two Semitic names. Each of the five Machabee brothers had two Aramaic names (1 Mach. 2:2–5).

Matthew's call apparently took place a short distance outside Capharnaum; because, after the cure of the paralytic carried by four men, "Jesus went forth and beheld Levi" (Luke), "went forth toward the sea . . . and as he was passing along, he beheld Levi" (Mark).

[36] Philip, Thomas, Bartholomew-Nathanael, and Jude are no more than named in the Synoptics. All that we know of them comes from St. John.

Philip — His conversation with Jesus and Nathanael (John 1:44–49); Jesus asks him a question (John 6:5–7); he consults Andrew about some Gentiles who wish to see Jesus (John 12:21–22); "Show us the Father" (John 14:8–9).

Thomas — "Let us go and die with him" (John 11:16); "We do not know where thou goest" (John 14:5); he is incredulous and then believing (John 20:24–28); on the Lake of Tiberias (John 21:2).

Nathanael — He is brought to Jesus by Philip (John 1:45–49); on the lake with a group of the Apostles (John 21:2).

Jude — He asks Jesus a question after the Last Supper (John 14:22).

by any contrary data. St. John, who has something to say about almost all the Apostles, does not even mention Bartholomew, any more than the Synoptics mention Nathanael. On the other hand, every time he speaks of Nathanael he puts him in the company of the Twelve. Bartholomew is a patronymic (son of Tholmaï or Ptolemy) and its bearer must have been known also by another name. Despite his brag of being a citizen of Cana and his lack of esteem for mere Nazarenes, Nathanael was a true Israelite, free of guile or cunning. Nothing need be added to the Saviour's eulogy.

Thomas (in Hebrew) and Didymus (in Greek) means the *Twin*. The salient trait in his character seems to have been a tendency to pessimism. When Jesus speaks of returning to Judea to bring Lazarus back to life, Thomas believes that he is walking to his death, and to give himself courage says, "Let us go and die with him." He stubbornly refuses to believe his colleagues who have seen the risen Christ. That would be too good to be true, he thinks; one of those wonderful things that never happen. But, once convinced, he gives himself over to the Saviour body and soul in an outburst of faith and love, "My Lord and my God."

Three of the Apostles of the last group have the same names as three of Jesus' cousins; but that fact is without special significance, since the names in question were so common that each of them appears twice in the list of the Twelve. We explain elsewhere our reasons for thinking that James, the son of Alpheus, is the James who is called the Brother of the Lord, par excellence, and who died a martyr's death after governing the Church of Jerusalem for more than thirty years.[37]

The uncertainty of tradition about Jude, called also Thaddeus or Lebbeus, recommends adherence to the common opinion of the Latin Church, which sees in him the half brother of James the Less and the author of one of the seven Catholic Epistles.

As for the Apostle Simon: there is no reason to identify him with Simon or Simeon, that other cousin of the Lord who succeeded to James in the see of Jerusalem and suffered martyrdom under Trajan. His surname, Zelotes (or the Cananean, which in Hebrew means the same thing), does not prove that he belonged

---

[37] Cf. Note I: *The Relatives of Jesus.*

to the revolutionary sect that went under that name. It should rather be taken in the sense of "The Zealous" or "The Enthusiast."[38]

The presence of Judas in the apostolic college is always somewhat disconcerting. It may be that Jesus, though foreseeing his treason, still chose him to give an example to superiors who, since they do not know the future, ought to make their decisions according to the actual dispositions of candidates. We must believe that when he was chosen Judas was not unworthy. It was the demon of avarice, ambition, and envy that seized his soul later and, through fall after fall, plunged him into the abyss.

Judas the traitor has found admirers and apologists in our day; which is not surprising, since Satan too has his. They say that the Iscariot, more discerning than his colleagues, saw that Jesus' popularity was waning, and wished to precipitate events in order to force him to some glorious deed while there was still time. The rehabilitation is pointless and too late! Judas has already been judged and condemned by the infallible Judge: "Better for that man that he had never been born."

[38] St. Luke (Luke 6:15; Acts 1:13) calls him Zelotes (Ζηλωτής); St. Matthew (10:4) and St. Mark (3:18), the Cananean (Καναναῖος).

CHAPTER II

The Divine Mission of Christ

1. Miracle Upon Miracle

EVERY extraordinary messenger from God to men should produce his credentials, and the miracle is the seal of God. After inaugurating his work with two miracles at Cana, Jesus Christ scatters miracles everywhere along his way.

The Gospel calls them acts of power (δυνάμεις) because they require supernatural power, and also signs (σημεῖα), inasmuch as they serve to authenticate the mission of the Saviour, who appeals more than once to their unimpeachable testimony. He cures a paralytic to prove to the Pharisees that he has power to forgive sins. He answers the disciples of the Baptist, who come in their master's name to ask him if he is really the Messias, by saying, "Go tell John what you have seen and heard: the blind see, the lame walk, the deaf hear, lepers are cleansed, the dead rise, and the poor have the Gospel preached to them."

Whether they are worked from a distance or not, the miracles of Christ are all characterized by their leaving no room for doubt. Neither the disciples nor the indifferent — nor even his enemies — dispute their reality. In well-disposed souls they engender spontaneous faith. In the merely curious they awaken surprise, astonishment, amazement, a kind of religious fear, and an instinctive feeling that the finger of God is here. In his sworn enemies, determined in advance to shut their eyes to the light, they inspire hate and fright. Unable to deny them, the Scribes and Pharisees pretend to take them for the work of Satan, whereas in their heart of hearts they see in them a threat to their own standing and influence. They tell their confederates: "This man works too many miracles. If he be allowed to continue everyone will flock to him."[1]

A single miracle thoroughly certified, if done by a wonder-worker as a proof of his mission, is enough to authenticate that mission; but the demonstration gains much more probative force when the divine envoy possesses this superhuman power to be used at will, when and as often as he wishes. That was the case with Christ's miracles. Several times the Evangelists mention a number of them together.[2] Not counting groups of miracles and all the marvels which have the person of Jesus himself for their object, such as the Transfiguration, the Resurrection, and the subsequent apparitions, thirty-three miracles are described in detail. Among them there are eight contraventions of the laws of nature, six expulsions of devils, sixteen cures of various diseases, and three raisings from the dead. Six of these prodigies, with the two miracles at Cana, belong to the beginning of the Galilean ministry.[3]

The Demoniac at Capharnaum

The first miracle reported by the Synoptics took place on a Saturday in the synagogue at Capharnaum. There was a man possessed by an unclean spirit, who kept crying out in a strident voice, "What have we to do with thee, Jesus of Nazareth? Thou hast come to destroy us. I know who thou art — the Holy One of God." The devil speaking through this man's mouth may have wished simply to distract the crowd and prevent them from listening, or he may have been trying, by flattering Jesus' self-love, to force the Saviour to declare himself, if he was more than a man. Whatever the devil's intention, Jesus cannot accept from the father of lies the honorable title, "The Holy One of God." He therefore silences him: "Hold thy peace, and go out of this man." And the devil with a terrible cry throws his victim violently to the ground, without, however, injuring him, and then abandons him.

---

[1] John 11:48. Cf. 12:19.
[2] Mark 1:32–34; 6:56, etc.
[3] Cf. Note L: *The Gospel Miracles.*

Those who had not yet become too accustomed to the sight of miracles were dumbfounded.[4] They may have been present at exorcisms before, but they had never seen anything like this. Jewish exorcists used to practice rites and employ formulas reputedly handed down from King Solomon, mixed in the course of time with all sorts of superstition and charlatanism. To draw the devil out of the body of a possessed person, they employed a kind of magic ring and the root of a plant called *baaras,* gathered in the neighborhood of Machaerus and endowed, they said, with marvelous power.[5] Instead of making use of such affectation as this, which often provoked only ridicule, Jesus pronounced but a single word of command, "Hold thy peace, and go out of this man." The witnesses of the scene said to one another, "What is this! Here, indeed, is a word powerful above all others! This man commands unclean spirits and they obey him." This time he found no Pharisees present to indict his actions, and the fame of the event spread over the whole country.

Peter's Mother-in-Law[6]

When Jesus left the synagogue, he went to the house of Simon Peter, whose mother-in-law was suffering from a burning fever. When they told him about it, discreetly suggesting that he apply a remedy (since he certainly could), he leaned over the sick woman's bed, took her by the hand, and rebuked the fever, as he had just rebuked the unclean spirit. The sick woman felt herself suddenly cured, without any of the prostration a violent attack of fever always leaves behind it. Immediately she arose and busied herself with her household duties, serving the guests at table, because it was just about noontime, the hour when the first meal was usually taken on the Sabbath after leaving the synagogue.

---

[4] Mark 1:23–28; Luke 4:33–37.

[5] Cf. in Josephus, *Antiq.,* VIII, ii, 5, the account of the solemn exorcism performed by Eleazar in the presence of Vespasian and Titus. On the marvelous plant used, cf. Josephus, *Bellum,* VII, vi, 3. For an exorcism with an unfortunate result, cf. Acts 19:13–16. St. Justin, *Dial cum Tryph.,* 85, mentions some of the procedures of Jewish exorcists and their lack of success. Cf. *Apol.,* II, 6.

[6] Mark 1:29–31; Luke 4:38–39; Matt. 8:14.

These two miracles, one after the other, had aroused the whole city. This became evident as soon as the Sabbath rest was over. "When the evening had come, and the sun had set, they brought to him all the sick and possessed. And the whole city was gathered around his door. He healed many who were sick and afflicted with various diseases and cast out many devils."[7] Possibly the Evangelists are outlining a comprehensive picture of the Saviour's thaumaturgic activity, by linking it to a single event. They have familiarized us with the abridgements by which they summarize a whole situation, which, indeed, are fully justified in the style of catechesis. This explains why St. Luke, in order to avoid coming back to the subject, here places in the mouths of the devils the words which St. Mark reports only later on: "The devils departed crying, 'Thou art the Son of God.' But he would not permit them to speak, because they knew he was the Christ."[8] And St. Matthew takes this occasion to draw a moral from the many cures, "Thus was fulfilled the word of the prophet Isaias:

> 'He has taken upon himself our sufferings,
> He has burdened himself with our sorrows.' "[9]

The importunity of the crowd would not allow the Saviour an hour's rest. "One morning before dawn he withdrew to a solitary place to hold converse with God. Simon Peter and his companions hurried after him, and when they found him, said to him: 'Everyone is seeking thee.' He answered: 'Let us go into the neighboring hamlets to preach there also, for I have come for that.' And he went throughout all Galilee preaching in their synagogues and casting out devils."[10]

---

[7] Mark 1:32–34. Cf. Matt. 8:16; Luke 4:40.

[8] Luke 4:41. Cf. Mark 3:10–11.

[9] Matt. 8:17 quoting Isa. 53:4. "The special significance of the quotation lies in this, that it is literally applicable to the situation in terms which contain a thought still more profound. In assuming the penalty, the servant (of Yahweh) also expiates the fault in such a way that to him is given to deliver his brethren from both the one and the other. It was this deliverance that Jesus inaugurated by casting out devils and curing sicknesses" (Lagrange, *Saint Matthieu,* 1923, p. 169).

[10] Mark 1:35–39; Luke 4:42–44.

The Leper

One of the most sensational miracles of this opening period was the instantaneous cure of an unfortunate man afflicted with leprosy. This horrible disease was once common in Palestine, and is still not altogether rare there.[11] Under the name of leprosy were included at that time several skin troubles of various degrees of malignity. True leprosy, which is not of its nature contagious, at least by simple contact, has so far resisted all cures, though it can sometimes be arrested for so long that it seems to be completely cured. The most common type attacks the extremities first, gradually gnawing away the nose, ears, lips, toes, and fingers. Then it invades the rest of the body, covering it with purulent, fetid sores, and rots away the flesh, strips the bones, and loosens the joints. A visitor to a leprosarium is haunted for a long time by the nightmare of these hideous and repulsive shreds of humanity. The poor leper has to watch with living eyes while his body decomposes as it would in the grave, and death after a lingering agony is his only hope of release.

The Law of Moses made the leper an outcast from society. He had to live outside inhabited places, go bareheaded so that he could be recognized from a distance, and if he happened to meet anyone he had to cover his mouth with the folds of his garment and cry out, "Unclean! Unclean!" He was in a state of perpetual legal impurity, and to touch him brought defilement, like touching a corpse. There was no attempt made to cure leprosy. It was an affliction from God, and only he who had sent it could cure it. Properly speaking, Jesus does not cure lepers, he *purifies* them.

The leper in the Gospel was attracted by the Saviour's fame and ventured to come near him and throw himself at his feet, saying, "Lord, if thou wilt, thou canst make me clean." Moved by compassion the Saviour stretched out his hand and touched

---

[11] There are still lepers in Jerusalem (in the suburb of Siloe and the hospital of the Moravian Brethren), at Ramleh and Nablus. The number of lepers in Palestine may be estimated at about 200, counting those cared for in the leprosarium of Damascus. At the hospital of the Moravian Brethren in 1903, the 60 lepers came from 36 different localities, which proves that the malady is not epidemic. On the various kinds of leprosy, cf. Hastings, *Dictionary of Christ and the Gospels,* 1909, s.v. "Leprosy."

him, accompanying his gesture with the words: "I will it, be made clean!" And the leprosy that covered his body from head to foot vanished immediately.[12]

In dismissing him Jesus made two recommendations. "See to it that thou tell no one, but go show thyself to the priest and offer the sacrifices which Moses prescribed for purification as testimony to them." When a leper was cured, or thought that he was, he had to present himself before the priest whose duty it was to pronounce on the disappearance of the symptoms of the disease. If after a long and minute examination the verdict was favorable, he must go through several purificatory rites, a complicated ceremonial which is described in a whole chapter of Leviticus.[13] Finally he became legally clean, was declared so by the competent authority, and re-entered the current of life with others.

We may well believe that the leper of the Gospel promptly presented himself before the priests to obtain a certificate of his cure, since this was his duty and a matter of self-interest. But he paid no attention to the injunction to say nothing about it. He spread the news of what had happened far and wide. His disobedience has been strongly censured, but it seems to us that he should benefit by several extenuating circumstances. He doubtless believed in all good faith that a miracle worked in public could not be kept hidden for long, and that the Saviour's prohibition was dictated by modesty and did not dispense him from showing gratitude. Perhaps, too, the command not to talk about it was only temporary, until the leper had fulfilled the legal requirements and proved by facts that Jesus was not contemning or attacking the Mosaic Law, as had been charged. Christ's words lend themselves to this interpretation and many commentators have understood them so.

Nevertheless his indiscretion had troublesome consequences. Jesus could no longer go out in public without being beset by a crowd of cripples and sick begging for cures. This led him to

---

[12] Matt. 8:1–4; Mark 1:40–44; Luke 5:12–14. St. Matthew records the miracle immediately after the Sermon on the Mount. The others offer no indication either of time or place. In all accounts the Evangelists always use the term *cleanse* instead of *cure*.

[13] Leviticus, Chapter xiii, has the law for lepers and a diagnosis of leprosy. The

take refuge in desert places, though in the end his hiding place was always found.[14]

The Paralytic Carried by Four Men

When time had somewhat cooled the enthusiasm of the populace, Jesus returned to Capharnaum, but to avoid noisy demonstrations entered secretly under cover of darkness. Once his return was reported, the crowd closed in on his dwelling place and did not hesitate to invade it with the Oriental unrestraint which allows anyone to enter another's home as though it were his own. Soon the house was full to overflowing and the door was blocked, so that the tide of late arrivals was forced to flow back into the surrounding streets.

While Jesus was instructing those fortunate enough to get near him, four men carrying a paralytic on a litter tried to push through. But the crowd was so dense that their efforts were fruitless. Then they bethought themselves of an unusual stratagem. Most Galilean houses had only a ground floor, and flat roofs like terraces, which were generally accessible from the outside. The roofs were made of roughly squared beams covered with reeds or branches. Over these was spread a layer of clay which was rolled flat from time to time to keep the winter rains from flooding the interior. It was easy to lift this up and put aside the reeds and to slide a human body through the gaps in the beams. Resorting to this method, the men carrying the paralytic ascended to the terrace from outside, made a hole in the roof, and with the aid of ropes lowered the sick man wrapped in his matting down in front of Jesus, showering dirt on everybody in the room.

This bold maneuver, difficult for the actors as well as the spectators in the scene, implied strong faith in the litter bearers and the patient. Our Lord rewarded it on the spot by saying to the paralytic, "Courage, my son, thy sins are forgiven thee." Believing with most of his compatriots that incurable sickness was a punishment for sin, the afflicted man must have sensed in those words a sure sign of a coming cure, and his faith increased. But the Scribes and Pharisees in the crowd were scandalized. They

---

rites employed in the purification of lepers are described in the following chapter.

[14] Mark 1:45; Luke 5:15–16.

asked themselves, "Why is he speaking thus? He is blaspheming. Who can forgive sins except God alone?" They were right in assigning to God the exclusive power to forgive sins; for it belongs only to the one offended to pardon the offense; a man arrogating this power to himself would be claiming a divine attribute and would be guilty of blasphemy. Their mistake was in thinking Jesus was nothing but a man.

Reading these unspoken murmurs in their hearts, Jesus put this question to them: "Which is easier, to say to this paralytic, 'Thy sins are forgiven thee,' or to say, 'Arise, take up thy pallet, and go away'?" To cure an incurable disease by a single word and to forgive sins are equally easy to say and difficult to do, for they suppose infinite power. He who can do one can do the other, but the first can be immediately verified, and can serve as a proof of the second, which cannot be perceived. "Now," continued, the Saviour, "that you may know that the Son of Man has power on earth to forgive sins, Arise (he said to the paralytic), I command thee. Take up thy pallet and go back to thy home." And immediately the man stood up, shouldered the mat he had been lying on, and went home glorifying God.[15]

Terrified amazement seized the onlookers, and they cried aloud, "We have seen something very strange and very wonderful

---

[15] The episode is recorded by the three Synoptics: Matt. 9:1–8; Mark 2:1–12; Luke 5:17–26. We follow the more circumstantial account of St. Mark. The scene is laid in Capharnaum (Mark 2:1; cf. Matt. 9:1). St. Luke, marking the beginning of the Pharisees' attacks against Jesus, notes that "Pharisees and doctors of the Law came from Galilee, Judea, and Jerusalem."

The scene is well described by St. Mark. Those carrying the sick man *uncovered the roofing* (ἀπεστέγασαν τὴν στέγην) by lifting up the edges of the branches packed with clay, thus making *an opening* (ἐξορύξαντες) large enough to let down a human body; then they lowered the pallet (χαλῶσι τὸν κράβατον), naturally with ropes (as the word χαλᾶν indicates), unless the people below received the body in their outstretched hands.

The expression of St. Luke (διὰ τῶν κεράμων καθῆκαν αὐτὸν σὺν τῷ κλινιδίῳ, 5:19) would suggest that the layer of clay was covered with brick paving, which was sometimes the case. But it may be that, since he was writing for readers unfamiliar with Palestinian customs, he uses the term to indicate the roof itself, without attempting to describe it. The Greek for "living on the tiles" (ἐπὶ τῶν κεράμων διατρίβειν) means to *live on the roof*.

Examples of such breaking in of roofs are not rare. It was thus that Herod managed to circumvent many of his enemies who had barricaded themselves in their homes (Josephus, *Antiq.*, XIV, xv, 12). Slanting roofs covered with tile were also broken through (Thucydides, I, 134, iv, 48, etc.).

this day. Never have we seen the like." The dismayed Scribes and Pharisees were silent, fearing to alienate the people; but the rest, perceiving the import of the miracle and the meaning which Jesus wished to impart to it, glorified God for having "given such power to men."

In curing the paralytic Jesus' direct purpose was not to prove his divinity nor his Messiasship, but rather the power which belongs to the *Son of Man* — perhaps this is the first time that he gives himself this title — to forgive sins. It was for his audience to follow this out to its logical conclusion, and discover who he must be that dared claim this extraordinary power, proving by a miracle that his claim was no mistaken arrogance. He had stated the premise himself when he conceded to the Pharisees that no one but God could forgive sins.

The Centurion's Servant

Capharnaum was the scene of yet another prodigy. It is impossible to fix the date but it seems to belong to the beginning of the public life. There is question here of a centurion, one of whose servants, a slave to whom he was greatly attached, was at death's door. The centurion was undoubtedly the commandant of the small garrison which Herod Antipas maintained there to keep order and to watch the port. Though in the service of the Jewish tetrarch, he was himself a pagan; for the Herods enlisted men of all religions and all nationalities in their cohorts, which were organized along Roman lines. This man belonged to that very large class of Gentiles who professed monotheism, observed the Sabbath, and frequented the synagogues, without going so far as to receive circumcision, and without assuming the whole burden of the Mosaic Law. Since the promotion of centurions to the rank of military tribune was very unusual, they often grew old at their posts and had every reason to seek the friendship of the population. There are many examples of such men in secular history. The one at Capharnaum had a special claim to the gratitude of the Jews, since out of his own money he had built for them a house of prayer.

The servant to whom he was so attached — either because the man was very valuable to him, or because he had for him an affection that was not unheard of between master and slave — was *paralyzed* and suffering bitter agony. To the ancients paralysis was a vague term, covering afflictions of widely different kinds, like tetanus, articular rheumatism, meningitis in its final stages, or even an accidental lesion of the spinal column. Whatever was wrong with the servant, he seemed beyond help and was dying in intense pain. His master had perhaps heard of the royal functionary who had gone to Jesus in a similar crisis, and had the idea of going himself for assistance to the great healer; but afraid that a stranger's request might displease him, he entrusted the pleading of his cause to some prominent Jews who were under great obligation to him. They acquitted themselves of their task with zealous concern. "He deserves to have thee grant his request," they said, "for he loves our nation, and it is he who has built a synagogue for us." Jesus followed them without the slightest objection.

As he drew near the house, the centurion, learning of his coming and knowing how reluctant pious Jews were to enter a pagan's house, sent his friends to say, "Lord, come no further, for I do not deserve that thou shouldst enter under my roof. That is why I did not count myself worthy to go to find thee myself; but say only one word and my servant shall be healed." Thou hast only to command, for art thou not Master? "As for me, I have only the authority of a subaltern, and yet when I say to a man, 'Go,' he goes at once; or to another, 'Come,' he straightway runs up; and if I say, 'Do this,' to my servant, he does it."

"I am not worthy that thou shouldst enter under my roof." A beautiful expression of humility for a pagan dignitary; words that the Church has made sacred by putting them on the lips of the priest at the moment he is to receive the Body of the Lord into his breast or distribute it to the faithful. When Jesus heard them he allowed his admiration to show forth. This was the spontaneous reaction of his sense faculties in contact with the external reality received by his experimental knowledge. It was expressed in the exclamation, "Truly I have not found such faith even in Israel!" After this eulogy the sequel was no longer in doubt. The centurion's messengers found the sick man in perfect health when they got back to the house.[16]

Jesus takes the strong and humble faith of the centurion as an occasion to predict the call of the Gentiles and the rejection of the Jews. "I say to you, many shall come from the east and the west, and shall take their places in the kingdom of heaven, while the children of the kingdom (those who seemed to be its heirs by right of birth) shall be cast forth into the outer darkness, where there shall be weeping and gnashing of teeth."[17] The Jews loved to picture the reign of the Messias as a lavish feast set out for the children of Israel, which the pagans would watch from a distance, consumed with envy, shame, and rage. Sweet revenge for the years of oppression under pagan regimes! Now Jesus reverses the roles: Gentiles of good will are invited to the celestial banquet, and the children of Israel are excluded through their own fault.

The Son of the Widow of Naim

Some time later Jesus was passing through the country districts of Lower Galilee, followed as usual by his disciples and a multitude unwilling to miss a word. He was crossing the plain of Esdrelon at its eastern border where the hills of Nazareth run into the plain. From the foot of Thabor, to the south, a jumble of little houses in ruins can be seen clinging to the northern slope of Little Hermon. They are the remains of the ancient Naim, which no longer possesses any of the attractions and charms its name would suggest. But the silos, wells, and tombs scattered here and there are testimony to a nobler past. A little white chapel recently erected and visible from a distance commemorates one of the most touching of the Saviour's miracles.[18]

---

[16] Luke 7:1–10; Matt. 8:6–10. We are following the more complete account of St. Luke. The two narratives, despite differences in detail, are certainly concerned with the same event, as almost all interpreters agree. The principal difference is that St. Matthew puts in the mouth of the centurion the words which St. Luke attributes to the messengers. Matthew frequently attributes the action of the instrument to the cause, and usage allows this.

[17] Matt. 8:11–12. This prophecy fits in well with the praise of the centurion. St. Luke (13:29–30) less appropriately puts it in a different context.

[18] Luke 7:11–17. This miracle, which is of uncertain date, comes after the cure

Jesus was drawing near the gate on the plain side of the town, when shrill cries, more like shrieks than sobs, came to his ears. It was a funeral procession on its way to the cemetery. First came the mourners and flute players, then four men carrying on a stretcher or in an open coffin a corpse wrapped in a shroud; finally almost the whole village, come to express their sympathy with a poor widow who was mourning her only son.[19] It is impossible to attend Oriental funerals without an emotion which custom itself does not entirely dull, even if there be a suspicion that the grief is a little artificial. But the sorrow of the widow, who in losing her son had lost everything, was so harrowing that the heart of Jesus was stirred. His first word, "Weep not!" was one of consolation and hope for the mother.

He immediately made his way through the crowd and touched the coffin with a gesture of authority. The bearers understood and lowered the lifeless body to the ground. This was the signal for a new outbreak of sighs and lamentation. Custom demanded it. Jesus silenced the mourners and turned to the youth stretched out on the bier, his body tightly bound with bandages and his face covered with the winding sheet. "Young man," he said to him, "I command thee, arise!" The dead man sat up and began to speak. His mother stood by motionless and speechless with amazement, as in a dream, gazing upon the scene, not daring to believe it. Before leaving, the Saviour took thought of her.

---

of the centurion's servant (*deinceps*, ἐν τῷ ἑξῆς, understanding χρόνῳ). The less probable reading (ἐν τῇ ἑξῆς, understanding ἡμέρᾳ) would indicate the *next day;* but it is unlikely that such a large multitude would have traveled the 28 mi. between Capharnaum and Naim in one day.

In Hebrew, *Nain* means beautiful, lovable, delightful. The miserable present-day Naim, with its population of 150 Moslems, hardly bears out this etymology. See the description of Guérin, *Galilée,* Vol. I, 115–117. Near the fountain, there are ruins marking the site of a church which was later transformed into a mosque. The Franciscans acquired the property in 1880 and built the chapel which is to be seen there now.

19 The dead were carried to the burial place on a stretcher or bier, or in an open coffin used for all the deceased. Today, among the Jews, the face of the dead person is covered during the funeral procession. About funerals among the ancient Jews, cf. Billerbeck, *Kommentar,* Vol. IV, pp. 579–592. In smaller localities everybody attended the funerals. Even the Rabbis assisted; for accompanying a dead man to his last resting place even took precedence over the study of the Law. Sometimes the women preceded the coffin and the men followed; sometimes this order was reversed. The bearers relieved one another at intervals, and each pause was a signal for fresh laments.

To make her realize her happiness, he presented to her her son fully alive, doubtless with some words of encouragement which the Gospel leaves to our imagination.

None of Christ's previous miracles had produced such an impression on the multitude. The raising of Jairus' daughter took place only later and before a small group of chosen witnesses. This one was worked in broad daylight, before a whole town, and in circumstances unequaled for evidence and publicity. And all the spectators were struck with that kind of religious fear that is inspired by a divine apparition. "They praised God, saying, a great prophet has risen in our midst, and God has visited his people."

There is nothing like this miracle in the Old Testament. There is no comparison between the miracles worked of old by men of God and those done with such consummate ease by the God-Man himself. When, on the other side of Little Hermon, hardly an hour away from Naim, Eliseus wanted to call the son of the Sunamite woman back to life, he shut himself up alone with the dead boy, and after long prayer stretched out over him, mouth on mouth, eyes on eyes, hands on hands, as though trying to bring warmth once more into the little body. But there was no stir of life. The prophet goes down the stairs and comes up again, walks back and forth in the house, goes through the process several times, until finally he sees a light, fluttering breath hovering on the cold lips of the child. Elias acts the same way in raising the son of the widow of Sarepta from the dead.[20] "It is obvious," says Massillon, "that he is calling upon a power other than his own, that he is summoning from the realms of the dead a soul which is not subject to his call, that he himself is not the master of life and death. Jesus Christ brings the dead back to life as though it were the most ordinary of actions. He speaks as master to those resting in eternal sleep. It is clear that he is the God of the dead as well as of the living, never more calm than when he is working the greatest of miracles."[21]

The report of the miracle at Naim spread rapidly, not only in

---

[20] For Elias, cf. 3 Kings 17:2–22; for Eliseus, cf. 4 Kings 4:25–37.
[21] Massillon, *Sermon sur la divinité de J.-C.,* 1re partie.

Galilee, but also "in the whole of Judea and all the country roundabout."[22]

2. The Message of the Baptist

The news of these marvels soon reached St. John in the prison at Machaerus, where he had been languishing some months. Though the Tetrarch wished to keep him under lock and key, and put a stop to his propaganda, he did not forbid him all intercourse with his disciples. But not all of these latter shared the noble feelings of their master. Many of them followed the growing prestige of the Galilean teacher with jealous eye. Some even came close to considering him a dangerous rival. Twice already they had shown an unfriendly attitude toward him, and perhaps the report they had just made on his recent miracles sprang from the same uneasiness and ill will.[23]

The Baptist chose two of them to deliver a message to Jesus, which they repeated word for word with Homeric fidelity. "John sent us to ask thee if thou art he who is to come or if we should wait for another."[24] A question such as this at John's behest and in his name is somewhat startling. Could John have been ignorant that Jesus was the Messias? Had he not been sent like Elias to open up the road for him? Had he not heard the voice from heaven which proclaimed him to be the Son of God, the Beloved of the Father? Had he not himself recognized him at the Baptism and pointed him out in public as the Lamb of God who takes away the sins of the world? Would his faith now undergo an eclipse, and would doubt invade his soul? Quite the contrary; for if it were true, as Tertullian imagined, that the prophetic spirit had left him once his mission was over, the glowing eulogy Jesus is about to speak of him would make no sense. How is it

---

[22] Luke 7:17. Here *Judea* is used in the wide sense for all of Palestine, as in Luke 1:5; 23:5; Acts 2:9; 10:37; 11:1, etc.

[23] It is John's disciples who come to tell him of the miracles of Jesus (Luke 7:18). One gets the distinct impression that they regarded Jesus as their Master's rival (John 3:25–26). They join the Pharisees in asking him why his disciples did not fast (Matt. 9:14; cf. Mark 2:18; Luke 5:33).

[24] Matt. 11:2–3; Luke 7:18–20. According to Tertullian, the spirit of prophecy had left John: "Itaque Joannes, communis iam homo et unus iam de turba,

possible to conceive of a waning of the prophetic spirit, on an essential point in his mission, in him whom Christ calls the greatest of prophets and even more than a prophet?

Some Fathers think that John, foreseeing his own coming death, sent to Jesus to ask, "Art thou he who is to come to Limbo, to console and deliver the souls of the just, or is that mission reserved for someone else?" But can such a puzzling question reasonably be attributed to John, especially when the phrase *he who is to come* so clearly and unmistakably designates the Messias?[25]

We must therefore concur with the common interpretation. John addresses the question to Jesus less for his own sake than for his disciples. They are the ones who need strengthening in faith, and it is for their benefit that Jesus works several miracles before dismissing them. "In their presence he healed many sick, cast out devils, and restored sight to the blind."[26] Then he sent them back, saying, "Go tell John what you have seen and heard: the blind see, the lame walk, lepers are cleansed, the deaf hear,

---

scandalizatur quidem qua homo" (*Adv. Marcion.*, iv, 18; ML, II, 402). A singular and unimportant opinion.

The frame of mind of the Baptist has been variously interpreted:

a) *He is beginning to suspect* that Jesus is the Messias (Strauss, Renan, Weizaecker, Loisy, and the Rationalists generally).

b) *He is beginning to doubt* that Jesus is the Messias (Tertullian and a certain number of Protestants).

c) *He asks, not for his own information,* but for the sake of his disciples (Catholics for the most part).

d) *He asks also for himself:* (1) to know whether he will go to Limbo (the Fathers cited below); (2) to obtain more light (St. Ambrose and others); (3) because he is somewhat impatient at the slowness of Jesus' revelation. Consult Buzy (*Saint Jean-Baptiste*, 1922, pp. 286–306) who gives the various opinions and stoutly defends the thesis that "John did not ask this question for his own sake, because he had no need to do so, and could not ask such a question" (p. 303).

[25] In favor of this opinion are cited: Origen, *Homily on the Witch of Endor* (MG, XII, 1011); St. Cyril of Jerusalem, Catech., iv, 11 (MG, XXXIII, 469); St. Gregory of Nazianzus, *Orat.*, xliii, 75 (MG, XXXVI, 597); St. Jerome, *In Matth.*, 11:3 (ML, XXVI, 70). St. Ambrose has something similar in *In Lucam*, 720 (ML, XV, 1661).

But "he who is to come" is a consecrated expression to indicate the Messias (Matt. 21:9; 23:39; Mark 11:9; Luke 13:35; 19:38; John 11:27, etc.); and the Baptist has used it himself (John 1:15–27).

[26] Luke 7:21: "At that very time" (ἐν ἐκείνῃ τῇ ὥρᾳ).

the dead rise. And blessed is he who shall not be scandalized in me."[27]

It is not to be thought, however, that Jesus' statement was entirely unnecessary for John. All prophetic vision has its obscurities; it is never as clear as seeing things directly. How often did Christ foretell his death and Resurrection to his Apostles without succeeding in giving them an exact idea of it? Prophet though he was, John could have conceived the plan of redemption differently from its reality in Jesus. He may have been surprised at its slow progress and the obstacles which had to be overcome. The graceful or imposing figures he had used — the baptism of the Spirit and fire, the Winnower setting to clean his threshing floor, the Spouse coming to take his bride — all seemed to promise a more rapid and brilliant fulfillment.

His imperfect comprehension of the plans of Providence — supposing that such obscurity had existed in his case — would not have been capable of unsettling his faith or impairing his confidence. But he had disciples who needed instruction and strengthening. It is for them, more than for himself, that he turns to Jesus. However, since the question comes from him, it is to him that the answer will go. The last words, "Blessed is he who shall not be scandalized in me," may sound like a personal warning; but they are general and there is no reason to think that they were directed to the Baptist in particular. The unqualified praise that follows is a certain proof that they implied no censure nor admonition. Jesus waits for the departure of the messengers before delivering the magnificent panegyric which, since the death of the Baptist was so near, may be called a funeral oration:

"What went you out into the wilderness to see? A reed swayed by the wind?" (Surely not; for no one makes a journey for any such reason as that.)

"What, then, went you out into the wilderness to look upon? A man clothed in soft garments? (Not that either, for) they that

[27] Matt. 11:4–6; Luke 7:22–23. This is the fulfillment of several prophecies in Isaias: the dead raised to life (Isa. 26:19); the blind, the deaf, the dumb, the lame cured (Isa. 35:5–6); the poor evangelized (Isa. 61:1).

are clothed in rich garments live (not in the wilderness, but) in the palaces of kings.

"What, then, went you out into the wilderness to see? A prophet? Yes, and I say to you, more than a prophet; for this is he of whom it is written: Behold I send my messenger before thee, who shall prepare thy way for thee.

"Amen, I say to you, among those born of woman there has not risen a greater than John the Baptist; yet the least in the kingdom of heaven is greater than he."[28]

Others in the Old Testament may have equaled his sanctity, but none have surpassed him in dignity. Let us not confuse the two. Holiness is measured by the amount of sanctifying grace, which at death is changed into glory. Dignity has for its measure the relationship, more or less close, which unites us to the Person of the Word Incarnate. The priest may be on a much lower level than the laity in the practice of virtues which produce saints; but he is always above them by the fact that he is a minister of Christ and dispenser of the divine mysteries. In the same way, an ordinary Christian may be inferior in sanctity to the just men of the Old Law; yet he is superior to them in dignity, because the Baptism which incorporates him into Christ makes him another Christ. Holy though the just of the Old Law may have been, they were still the children of bondage (the old economy compared to the new was always, as the Apostle says, a state of slavery), while the least Christian is the son of a free mother, the Church, the glorious spouse of Christ.

John is the link between the two Testaments. He stands at the end of one and the beginning of the other. Properly speaking, he belongs to neither. He has the advantage over the prophets and the other spokesmen of the ancient revelation — Abraham, Moses, Elias, Isaias — in having pointed to the Messias in the

[28] Matt. 11:7–11; Luke 7:24–28. There is a notable difference between the two texts. St. Luke says: "Among the children of women there is no prophet greater than John." And St. Matthew: "There has not risen anyone greater than John." Fundamentally, both come to the same thing, since the prophets were the greatest of the great; Abraham, Moses, and Jacob were prophets. St. Matthew's expression: *οὐκ ἐγήγερται μείζων*, "there has not risen (there has not *been raised up*) anyone greater," brings to mind the prophets *raised by God.*

Evidently Jesus does not place John above *all men* in general. This follows from the contrast: "the greatest (in dignity) of the Old Testament is the least in the New," or better, "less than the least in the New."

flesh. They had only foretold or prefigured him. Prophet from his mother's womb, he proclaimed by a mysterious leap of joy the presence of him whom the Virgin was to bring forth. He closes the phalanx of prophets as a witness to Christ. "The Law and the prophets go as far as John (and no further). Thenceforth the kingdom of God is preached and the first to come can force an entry into it. The violent alone carry away this kingdom,"[29] since courage and energy are demanded to overcome obstacles and to carry it by assault.

Men of good faith had already acknowledged John's special mission and his consequent greatness. The common people and the publicans had listened to his words, received his baptism, and thus had given glory to God; whereas the Pharisees, puffed up with their pretended knowledge, stood apart and rejected the gift of God.

"To what shall I compare this (perverse) generation? To children sitting in the market-place and calling to one another, 'We have piped and you have not danced; we have intoned a funeral chant and you have not beaten your breast.'

"John came neither eating bread nor drinking wine, and you said, 'He is a demoniac.' The Son of Man came eating and drinking (like everyone else) and you say, 'He is a glutton and a drinker, a friend of sinners and publicans.'"[30]

Children of all lands love to play games imitating spectacles from real life that catch their imagination. In Palestine, wedding processions and funeral trains would be among such spectacles.

---

[29] Luke 16:16. This verse of St. Luke is found in a collection of disparate maxims. St. Matthew places the thought in a better context (11:12–15), but he does not express it as clearly, though fundamentally the meaning is the same: "From the days of John the Baptist up to this hour, the kingdom of heaven is being taken by violence (βιάζεται) and the violent (βιασταί) are carrying it away; for all the prophets and the Law have prophesied up to John (and not beyond, because John is the Precursor); and, if you are willing to understand it, he is himself Elias who is to come. Let him hear that has ears."

The reconcilation of the two texts is easy. (*a*) The Old Law ceases with John; (*b*) the kingdom of God begins with him; (*c*) the kingdom is *to be taken* by force or assault (βιάζεται in the passive sense in St. Matthew), or each one *takes it* by force or assault (βιάζεται in the middle sense in St. Luke). The two senses, passive and middle, are both legitimate and warranted by convincing parallels. Cf. W. Bauer, *Wörterbuch,* 1928, and Moulton-Milligan, *Vocabulary.*

[30] Luke 7:31–34; Matt. 11:16–19. The texts are almost identical.

As soon as some lively member of the group suggests one of these little dramas, they assign roles and do a marvelous piece of improvisation. But there are always glum spirits who cannot be satisfied. Be the scenes gay or sad, they refuse to take part. It is to these cross-grained and discontented characters that Jesus compares the perverse generation of Scribes and Pharisees. John came preaching penance and leading his disciples along austere paths; they treated him like a fanatic, a wild man, a being possessed. Then Jesus comes, affable and universally approachable, with nothing forbidding or repellent about him, and they censure him for the lack of rigor in his asceticism, and for his predilection for the lowest of the low.

There is no point in asking who are represented by the children in the parable who are inviting their companions to play. They are not Jesus or John, nor the disciples of Jesus or John. The comparison bears only upon the sulky children who stubbornly reject all their comrades' proposals. To these the cursed generation is compared. The other children are introduced only to complete the picture, and have no special meaning.

"Thus," concludes the Saviour, "has divine wisdom been justified by its works (or by all its offspring)."[31] Whichever reading is adopted, the meaning is the same. In St. Matthew, the works of God bring to light, proclaim, and vindicate his wisdom. In St. Luke, all the children of wisdom, all men who are truly wise, have *justified* — vindicated and demonstrated — divine wisdom in the eyes of this incredulous generation, by conforming their conduct to the laws of wisdom.

---

[31] Luke 7:35; Matt. 11:19. This conclusion presents a striking variation. St. Luke has the reading: *Καὶ ἐδικαιώθη ἡ σοφία ἀπὸ πάντων τῶν τέκνων αὐτῆς.* The best manuscripts have *Καὶ ἐδικαιώθη ἡ σοφία ἀπὸ τῶν ἔργων αὐτῆς.* The reading of St. Matthew offers no difficulty, nor is there any in the reading of St. Luke, if the shade of difference between *ἀπό* and *ὑπό* be taken into account. To give the real meaning without ambiguity, the passive verb should be changed into an active verb. The works of God have been justified, i.e., have caused it to be recognized as just, and have vindicated his wisdom (Matthew). All the children of wisdom have justified (in the sense above) the wisdom of God.

Maldonatus thinks that the "children of wisdom" designates all the Jews, believers or unbelievers; but this would be hard to admit. The children of wisdom are the truly wise who have believed in the words of John and of Jesus.

CHAPTER III

The Sermon on the Mount

1. The Beatitudes

THE Sermon on the Mount follows closely upon the call of the Twelve. St. Matthew and St. Luke have preserved different versions of it, but, despite variants, the same discourse is easily recognizable in both. There is the same exordium and the same conclusion; the same subject is developed in the same order and often in the same terms; the circumstances of time and place are the same. The fact that in St. Matthew the sermon is three times as long as in St. Luke is explained by the methods of composition of the two Evangelists. The first is fond of blocking together teachings of the same kind belonging to different periods, while the second prefers to distribute them according to the occasions that gave rise to them, leaving out whatever his Greek or Latin readers may misunderstand. Of course, our Lord could have repeated himself, and the two versions, despite their striking resemblances, may represent two different discourses. But, since the only reason for distinguishing them is that one was given on the mountain and the other on the plain, and since this discrepancy can be resolved, the majority of commentators after St. Jerome and St. John Chrysostom have with good reason held that they are one discourse.[1]

Nowadays, pilgrims are shown the "Mount of the Beatitudes" on the road from Nazareth to Capharnaum, at a point where rise twin peaks called by the inhabitants the "Horns of Hattin." The place is a melancholy reminder of the bloody disaster of July 4,

[1] Cf. Note J: *The Sermon on the Mount.*

1187, when the true Cross fell into the hands of the infidel and the Frankish rule over Palestine came to an end. But ancient tradition gives no warrant for this localization, for even in St. Jerome's day the memory of the true locale was so confused that the common people thought of the Mount of Olives, and he himself proposed Thabor. The Horns of Hattin are quite far away from the Lake of Tiberias. Would Jesus have sought quiet ten or eleven miles away from Capharnaum when he could have found it at the gates of the town? All the circumstances before and after the discourse indicate that it must have been delivered not far from Capharnaum, and so we are inclined to set the scene on the isolated promontory that separates the plain of Capharnaum from the valley of Seven Fountains, or on one side of the near-by hillocks.[2]

The Sermon on the Mount is only a brief résumé of Jesus' actual discourse. Even in the more extended form which is found in St. Matthew, twenty minutes' leisurely speaking would have been ample for its delivery. The Evangelists have preserved only its substance. No public orator bent on instructing an ignorant group would ever have condensed so many ideas into so few phrases. There are abrupt transitions, and thoughts obscured by reason of abbreviated expression; there are absolute maxims which require explanation not to be found except in the general

[2] The place is still undetermined, for the Mount (τὸ ὄρος, Matt. 5:1; 8:1; Mark 3:13; Luke 6:12) designates no particular mountain, but the circle of hills around the Lake. St. Jerome rightly says that it is not to be looked for in Judea, but in Galilee (*In Matth.*, 5:1; ML, XXVI, 33–34): "Putamus vel Thabor esse vel *quemlibet alium* excelsum montem." The ancient pilgrims do not mention its location. In the twelfth century, Peter the Deacon and John of Wurzburg, and in the thirteenth Burchard, indicated that it was near Seven Fountains (Et Tabghah). The Gospel text shows clearly enough that it could not have been far from Capharnaum. Cf. Dalman, *Orte und Wege Jesu,* 1924, pp. 107–108 (English transl., Levertoff, 1935, pp. 114–115).

In view of this lack of knowledge, a more picturesque site could not be selected than the Horns of Hattin (*Qarn Hattin*). These are twin elevations rising about 1800 ft. above the lake, "which have been aptly compared to the pommel and cantle of an Arab saddle" (Lortet, *La Syrie d'aujourd'hui*). They do give that impression when seen at a distance. Pilgrims were able to reach this place very easily from Nazareth, which circumstance may have made it a popular choice. Considerations of convenience have also caused the multiplication of loaves to be localized not far from there, in contradiction to the text of the Gospel.

Heidet has a detailed study of the variations in the tradition, in the *Dictionnaire de la Bible, Supplément,* Vol. I, 1928, cols. 940–950.

teaching of the Gospel. The discourse has sometimes been called the charter of Christianity, but it is not a code applicable to a political or even a religious government. Neither is it a summary of the Christian faith, because it has nothing about the doctrine of the Redemption, the Sacraments, the Church, or the Last Things. Nor is it a treatise on morals, for the limits of justice and duty are not clearly defined, and precepts are not distinguished from counsels. It is simply a rule of ideal perfection, proposed to all aspirants to the kingdom of God and to all who wish to catch its spirit.

Since it is not a simple collection of scattered maxims, the Sermon on the Mount should have a purpose, a plan, a conclusion. What is the master idea? Some have thought that it is found in the saying "I have not come to destroy the law, but to perfect it." It would follow in that case that St. Luke, who does not record these words, understood nothing of the discourse; that the Beatitudes, which are placed at the beginning, are a sort of appetizer, and that the entire discourse is nothing but an apologia. The central theme is rather the Christian spirit as opposed to the Jewish. Jesus defines the Christian spirit by a double contrast: he opposes it first to the Old Law, which is corrected, completed, and transformed by the Law of Grace; then to the ideal of perfection that satisfied the Pharisees, who passed as perfect models of Jewish piety. The Beatitudes can be considered as an introduction or a program. The discourse ends with a short conclusion in the form of a parable.

Seated as a master instructing his pupils, Jesus addresses his disciples: not only the Twelve, but all the rest from whom the Twelve had been chosen. Chance hearers are not, however, excluded. They will understand what they can and, however little it will be, it will give birth to a desire to learn more.[3] After lifting his eyes to heaven, to show that his doctrine comes from on high, he lowers them on his disciples and speaks:

"Blessed are the poor in spirit, for theirs is the kingdom of heaven. Blessed are the meek, for they shall possess the land. Blessed are the afflicted, for they shall be consoled. Blessed are

[3] Jesus speaks especially to his disciples, but it is evident from the discourse that the multitude is also present (Matt. 7:28; Luke 7:1).

they that hunger and thirst for justice, for they shall have their fill. Blessed are the merciful, for they shall receive mercy. Blessed are the pure hearts, for they shall see God. Blessed are the peacemakers, for they shall be called children of God. Blessed are they that suffer persecution for justice, for theirs is the kingdom of heaven.

"Blessed shall you be when they shall insult you, and when they shall persecute you, and speak all kind of evil against you falsely, because of me. Rejoice and be glad, because your reward is great in heaven. Thus did they persecute the prophets before you."[4]

It matters little whether we count eight Beatitudes with St. Ambrose and the great majority of interpreters, or only seven with St. Augustine, who compares them to the seven gifts of the Holy Ghost. They are all only different aspects of a single Beatitude, and Jesus could easily have increased or lessened their number.

The Beatitudes are roads of entry into the kingdom of God, which is presented in its two phases, its earthly realization and its final consummation. The first four embrace it in all its amplitude, from its establishment on earth to its fulfillment in heaven. They give both the conditions for entrance and the dispositions necessary to remain in it. The rest envisage it rather in its consummation, as a reward and a crown. That a man be called blessed, he need not presently possess the object that is to make him happy. It is enough that he be on the road to it as a goal assured, for the certain hope of future happiness is a source of true joy. The disciples, familiar with this manner of speaking from their reading of Scripture, would understand what Jesus meant.

BLESSED ARE THE POOR. Though the Beatitudes may seem transparently clear, they are actually somewhat diffi-

[4] Some succeed in finding nine or ten Beatitudes, counting as one or two the special assurance given the disciples (Blessed are you . . . rejoice). A fruitless controversy.

For a more detailed explanation of the Beatitudes and a bibliography on the subject, cf. Pirot, *Béatitudes évangéliques,* in *Dict. de la Bible, Suppl.,* Vol. I, cols. 927–937.

cult for us to understand, less because of their consciously paradoxical turn than because of their allusions to the Old Testament. Several are direct citations. No one will be able to understand the first Beatitude without keeping in mind the Biblical notion of the "poor man." The poor mentioned here are not the indigent: the Bible has other words to designate destitution and distress. The *poor* man of Scripture, especially in the Psalms and the Prophets, is the man without defense, the victim and toy of powerful tyrants, who accepts his pitiful lot without a murmur and turns toward God alone as his only hope. God protects the poor man. He is his refuge and support. The Messias will have the same concern for him. He will console him and announce the good news preferably to him. Actually, it is in this class of the weak and oppressed that God always found his most faithful worshipers, and from among them Jesus recruited his best disciples. In the course of time, the poor man had become for the Hebrews almost synonymous with the pious man, resigned, abandoning himself to Providence, and prompt and ready to obey the commandments of God. The words "in spirit" were added by the Evangelist or his translator to indicate these moral dispositions. The poor in spirit enter the kingdom of God on the ground level, so to speak, for their condition prepares them for it. But it would be absurd to think that Jesus beatifies indigence and canonizes pauperism. If fortune and power are a danger from the supernatural point of view, they are not insurmountable obstacles.[5]

BLESSED ARE THE MEEK. This second Beatitude, which is almost a doublet of the first, is a quotation from the text of the Psalms, "The meek shall inherit the land." The Hebrew words for "poor" and "meek" come from the same root,

---

[5] The word *'ani* (עני) does not properly mean "poor" or "indigent," but *oppressed, humiliated, helpless, without resources. Poor* as opposed to rich (*'ashir,* עשיר) is *rash* (רש), *'ebion* (אביון) or *dal* (דל). The *poor man* of the Bible, in the prophets and the Psalms, is usually actually poor, but what sets him apart from others is his resignation and submission to the will of God; and this is what makes him the object of divine complacence. Penitent Israel is *poor,* and God has pity on it (Isa. 41:17; 49:13). God protects the *poor* (Ps. 9:13–18; 33 [34]:7; 34 [35]:10, etc.); the Messias will deliver him (Ps. 71 [72]:2–4; 12–13, etc.).

and differ only by a letter. They are often used interchangeably and are distinguished only by a very subtle shade of meaning: the poor man is the one who submits without complaint to his sad lot; the meek man is the man who, penetrated by the conviction of his own nothingness, adores the inscrutable designs of Heaven. The meek, distrustful of themselves and relying upon God alone, "shall inherit the (promised) land," like Caleb and Josue, who were models of patience and submission. The Promised Land was a type of the Messianic kingdom and a symbol of the heavenly kingdom. Nothing disposes for it better than patience and meekness, which are two halves of the same virtue.[6]

BLESSED ARE THE AFFLICTED, FOR THEY SHALL BE CONSOLED. Isaias has the Messias saying: "I come to console those that weep," by teaching them to sanctify their sufferings, and by holding up before their eyes the shining hope of endless happiness. The wise men and the just of the Old Testament had learned the value of sorrow: "It is better," says Ecclesiastes, "for a man to go to the house of mourning than the hall of feasting, for the house of mourning recalls to him the memory of his destiny."[7] In itself suffering has no moral value. It is not the diamond, but only its setting. The diamond is resignation, by which suffering is embraced in union with the suffering Christ. Being sorrowful in God, whether it come from the realiza-

[6] The second Beatitude (the third in the Greek text) is a citation from Ps. 36 (37):11. *Mansueti autem hereditabunt terram.* The words *'ani* (עָנִי) and *'anaw* (עָנָו) are derived from the same root *'anah* (עָנָה), *to be oppressed, humiliated, afflicted.* They are interchangeable and are treated as synonyms in poetic parallelism. What proves that they mean nearly the same thing, or are even identical, is that the Septuagint translates *'ani* by πτωχός 34 times, by πραΰς 46 times, by πένης 12 times, by ταπεινός 9 times. It translates *'anaw* by πραΰς 7 times, by πτωχός 4 times, by ταπεινός 3 times, and by πένης twice.

After God's promise to Abraham to give him the land of Chanaan (Gen. 15:7–8), the expression "to inherit the land" in the rest of the Pentateuch means *to take possession of the Promised Land;* in the following books it means *to obtain that of which the Promised Land was the type,* the kingdom of the Messias, the kingdom of heaven. In the text cited, the expression occurs four times: those who *hope* in God, the *meek* (πραεῖς), those who *bless* God, and the *just* shall inherit the land (Ps. 36 [37]:9, 11, 22, 29).

[7] Eccles. 7:3. The Messias is to come to console the *afflicted* (Isa. 61:2: *abelim,* πενθοῦντας, *contritos corde*).

tion of our miseries or be caused by the injustice of men or the blind forces of nature, carries in itself the germ of consolation and becomes a source of joy to us.

BLESSED ARE THEY THAT HUNGER AND THIRST FOR JUSTICE, FOR THEY SHALL HAVE THEIR FILL. The old economy was powerless to satisfy our inborn ideal of justice and sanctity; but the prophet had foretold that in Messianic times each man would be able to allay his hunger and slake his thirst. We experience this even here below to a certain degree, if we make the precepts and evangelical counsels our rule of life. And we shall be fully sated when we contemplate the glory of God face to face. Such is the beatitude promised to those who hunger and thirst for justice. They have a foretaste and an anticipated possession of it by the very fact that they aspire to it, with the certain hope of gaining it some day.[8]

The last four Beatitudes, unlike the others, directly envision the eternal Kingdom of Christ. On the last day the merciful shall obtain mercy, the pure of heart shall see God face to face, the peacemakers shall be treated as cherished children of the God of Peace, and the persecuted shall receive the crown for their courage and patience. The prospect awaiting them should fill them with immense joy.

The object of these last Beatitudes is clear. It remains to determine their subject. The *merciful* are not only those who give generous alms, nor those who feel compassion for the unfortunate, but also those who forget personal offenses and pardon injuries, and thus strive to imitate one of the essential attributes of God, his mercy: "Misericors et miserator Dominus." Pardoning others, they shall in turn be pardoned by the Sovereign Judge.[9]

---

[8] Isa. 55:1; Ecclus. 51:33; Apoc. 22:17. The just man of the New Covenant "shall not hunger nor thirst" (Isa. 49:10), because God shall refresh every thirsty soul and satiate every hungry soul" (Jer. 31:25).

[9] The word *merciful* (ἐλεήμων) occurs in only one other place in the New Testament (Heb. 2:17), where it is applied to Christ made like unto us, so that he may be *merciful* and may *compassionate* our miseries. It could well be taken here in the same sense, if it were not necessary to harmonize the subject and the object of the Beatitude: the *merciful* shall obtain *mercy*.

Is the *pure heart* the virginal heart, never tarnished by the slightest breath of the demon of pleasure? Nothing darkens the vision of heavenly things more, or puts a thicker veil between God and ourselves, than the surrender of the soul to carnal pleasures. But Christ is alluding here to a saying of the Psalmist: "Who shall ascend the mountain of the Lord, and who shall stand in his holy place? The man with innocent hands and clean heart." The pure heart is, therefore, not simply the chaste heart, but the innocent heart, the heart in which God dwells by His grace.[10]

The *peacemakers* are undoubtedly the lovers of peace, but above all they are the creators of peace, those who establish its sway around them and make it radiate far and wide. The celebrated Hillel is credited with this beautiful maxim: "Be ye disciples of Aaron, who loved peace, who pursued peace." Aaron is not the only one that the peacemaker imitates. It is God himself, who is the God of Peace;[11] it is Jesus Christ, who came to bring peace to all things in heaven and on earth. Reproducing in themselves the image of God, the peacemakers shall be called the children of God.

Is it necessary to explain who they are who suffer persecution for justice? They are all those who suffer for the name of Christ or for the cause of the Gospel. They are proclaimed blessed even before they receive the final reward, the assurance of which they already possess.

To render the Beatitudes as they are proposed to the Jews by St. Matthew intelligible to his own readers, St. Luke would have had to interpret them. He therefore omits everything that would suppose a knowledge of the Biblical allusions they contain, and retains only the contrast between the present unenviable position of the just in the eyes of the world and their future happiness. Then he adds four maledictions which are the exact counterpart of his four Beatitudes:

---

[10] Ps. 23 (24):4. The explanation given is by far the most common one because of the obvious allusion to the text of the Psalmist.

[11] God is a God of Peace (Rom. 15:33; 16:20; 1 Cor. 14:33, etc.). The principal role of Christ is to be peacemaker (ποιῶν εἰρήνην, Eph. 2:15; εἰρηνοποιήσας, Col. 1:20). The Latin *pacifici* does not exactly correspond to εἰρηνοποιοί. *Pacificatores* would be better. Hillel's dictum, cited in our text, is in the *Mishnah*, treatise *Aboth*, i, 12.

"Blessed are you who are poor, for yours is the kingdom of God. Blessed are you that hunger now, for you shall have your fill. Blessed are you that weep now, for you shall laugh one day. Blessed shall you be when men hate you and excommunicate you and insult you and cast out your name as infamous, because of the Son of Man. Rejoice in that day and exult, for your reward is great in heaven. In the same way did their fathers treat the prophets.

"But woe to you rich, for you have already received your comfort. Woe to you that are sated now, for you shall hunger one day. Woe to you that laugh now, for you shall lament and weep. Woe to you when all men shall applaud you, for in the same way did their fathers act toward the false prophets."[12]

Jesus does not indiscriminately bless all the poor and starved and afflicted and persecuted. He is speaking expressly only to his *disciples,* who suffer or will suffer all this with the moral dispositions demanded of them as Christians. The promises made to them are all of a religious and spiritual kind, although two of them are expressed by a metaphor. It would be absurd to think that Jesus' hearers or St. Luke's readers did not go beyond a crude idea such as "You that hunger now shall one day make good cheer and sit down to a sumptuous banquet."

Most of the disciples were of moderate means. Zacheus, Nicodemus, Joseph of Arimathea, and others like them came only later and were never very numerous. Almost all those who were rich and powerful and blessed in a worldly way stayed outside. The Saviour addresses them in turn, although they are not necessarily present. He may have lifted his gaze over the crowd which surrounded him and with a sweeping gesture included the fictitious audience to whom the four maledictions applied. Those rich men, those pleasure seekers, those idols of the world — Christ declares them to be unhappy, because the momentary satisfaction of their carnal appetites is a sorry compensation for the frightful lot awaiting them in eternity.

---

[12] Luke 6:20–25. There is no good reason for supposing that St. Luke transposes to this place maledictions from another discourse, or that he makes them up himself, seeing that they are virtually contained in the corresponding Beatitudes. St. Matthew may have omitted them because he places this discourse at the beginning of the Galilean ministry and, as yet, has not said anything about the opposition which Jesus encountered from the blessed of this world.

The ideal proposed to the disciples, and especially to the Apostles, is not to remain dead theory. It has to be woven into the texture of their lives:

"You are the salt of the earth. If the salt has become insipid, how give back to it its taste? It is good for nothing but to be cast outside to be trampled under foot.

"You are the light of the world. A city built on the mountain cannot stay hidden, and when one lights a lamp it is not to place it under a bushel measure. It is placed on a lampstand to give light to the people of the house. Let your light shine before the eyes of men, that they may see your good works and glorify your Father who is in heaven."[13]

The Apostles, and, proportionately, also the simple faithful, are the salt of the earth and the light of the world. Salt seasons food and preserves perishable substances from corruption. If it should happen to lose its savor it is utterly useless and cannot even be used as fertilizer. It is thrown out under the feet of the passers-by, as sheer waste matter. Such is the sad picture of the Apostle who fails his calling.

Like a city built on the hills, the disciples of Christ are in open view and cannot flatter themselves that they go unnoticed. Their example is powerful for both good and evil. Woe to them if they ever forget it! If a lighthouse beacon is extinguished, there follow deaths and shipwrecks. If the Apostle is faithless to his role, bewilderment and ruin follow after.

---

[13] Matt. 5:13–16. "If the salt becomes insipid." Chemically pure salt does not lose its active qualities, but our Lord is referring to the salt mixed with foreign substances, which was to be found (and still is) southwest of the Dead Sea in a cliff several miles long called Jebel Usdum. The rock salt of this immense deposit is of a bluish color, and often contains a mixture of gypsum and chalky marl. When this is the case, it must be thrown out into the street, since it is not fit to be used as a seasoner.

Every Christian, especially every apostle, should be a *light* (Eph. 5:8, φῶς), the *son of light* (1 Thess. 5:5, υἱὸς φωτός), and a *luminary* (Phil. 2:15, φωστήρ). In Palestine, the poorest people keep a lamp lit all night to light their only room. They are very careful not to hide it under a bushel measure or under some piece of furniture.

Many think that, in mentioning the *city built on a mountain,* Jesus made a gesture toward Safed, which is so high that it is visible from afar, and, as a matter of fact, can be seen from the shore of the Lake of Tiberias.

2. The Old Law and the New

After outlining the Christian ideal in the Beatitudes, Jesus goes on to oppose it first to the Mosaic legislation, then to the practices of the Pharisees, who were the contemporary norm of Jewish piety. In presenting himself as a reformer, he does not play the part of a revolutionary. He does not erase the past. He builds a new structure on the old foundations:

"Think not that I have come to destroy the Law and the prophets. I have come not to destroy but to fulfill. Amen I say to you, as long as heaven and earth shall remain, not one iota, not one tittle of the Law shall pass away without being fulfilled in every point. He, therefore, that shall violate one of these least commandments and teach others to do the same shall be the least in the kingdom of heaven; but he that observes them and teaches others to keep them shall be great in the kingdom of heaven."[14]

The Law and the Prophets are the whole Bible, although in his discourse Jesus considers especially and almost exclusively the Mosaic code. Viewed under its different aspects, the Old Testament was a revelation, a prophecy, a system of morality, and a ritual. The Son of God does not come to overturn all this,

---

[14] Matt. 5:17: Οὐκ ἦλθον καταλῦσαι ἀλλὰ πληρῶσαι. The word καταλύειν means to *untie* (an animal), to *annul* (a contract), to *abolish* (a law), to *destroy* (a town), to *overturn* (a power), to *disband* (an army); and in general to *put an end to* something. The word πληροῦν means to *fill up, complete, finish;* and, figuratively, to *fulfill* (a promise, a duty), to *accomplish*, to *realize* (a prophecy, a Biblical type), to *complete*, to *perfect* (a legislation, an institution). The two words chosen are applicable to the four aspects of the Old Testament; but it is perhaps better to take them in their absolute sense, as we have done, without understanding any complement such as "the Law and the Prophets." I have come to *perfect*, not to *destroy*.

Verse 19, which has a pronounced Semitic flavor, means simply: "The teacher, the preacher, who is faithful to the best of his ability in observing and enforcing the least precepts, will receive a high place in heaven; he that does otherwise will receive a low place." The "kingdom of heaven" here evidently means Heaven, for here on earth rank is not always assigned according to distributive justice.— Some good authorities understand *solvere* (λύειν) in the sense of *abolish, abrogate* (like καταλύειν above); but what teacher will undertake to abrogate the precepts of Christ, or to induce others to abrogate them? And, if he does, should he be admitted to heaven even in the lowest place?

but to fulfill it, with the same sovereign authority that had established it. He illumines and completes the old revelation of shadows and twilight. He verifies the prophecies announcing his coming and his reign. He rounds out the moral law and breathes a new spirit into it. Finally, he makes real the figurative element in the old rites and ceremonies, putting in their place a more august liturgy, one more worthy of God. In this sense, the perishable world will not end until the least fragment of Scripture, be it the smallest letter, like an *iota* in Greek or a *yod* in Hebrew or even a simple stroke of the pen that distinguishes letters otherwise alike, is entirely fulfilled, in the measure God intends. Thus there is no question of abolishing the moral law summed up in the Decalogue, but of bringing it to perfection.

In saying that the Law is dead, broken to pieces, nailed to the cross, St. Paul does not contradict the Master's teaching, nor does he any more than Jesus present the Gospel as a break with the past, or its antithesis, as Marcion fancied. For him it is a new starting point. The Mosaic Law contained an accumulation of prescriptions and rites which were only types. They now exist only in fulfillment of type, supplanted as they are by better institutions. The moral element of the Law is definitely sanctioned by Christ; but it is no longer the Law of Moses; it is the Law of Christ, and from him has its obliging force. It can therefore be said that it is entirely abolished, and it can be said that some of it remains. Everything lies in the explanation given.

The Mosaic legislation had three grave deficiencies. Since it was political as well as religious, it subordinated the happiness of the individual to the well-being of society, and the recompense it promised hardly went beyond the earthly horizon. It looked above all to the external act, seeming to neglect the interior disposition: so much so that the heads of the schools wondered whether it ever touched the intention. Finally, it was restricted to obligatory precepts and left out of consideration the counsels of perfection. It said, "Do this, avoid that," and one could consider himself acquitted of further obligation once he had materially fulfilled its orders.

The Gospel is the transformation even more than the continuation of the Mosaic legislation. To make clear the contrast, Jesus chooses five articles where the superiority of the New Law stands out with full clarity: the prescriptions regarding murder, adultery, perjury, revenge, and the attitude toward one's neighbor.

"You know that it was said to the ancients: 'Thou shalt not kill: Whoever kills shall be liable to the Tribunal.'

"And I say to you: 'Whoever shall become angry with his brother shall be liable to the Tribunal; and whoever shall call his brother harebrained (*Raca*) shall be liable to be called before the Great Council; and whoever calls him fool (*Nabal* — impious) shall be subject to the fire of Gehenna.'

"You know that it was said: 'Thou shalt not commit adultery.'

"And I say to you: 'Whoever looks on a woman with lust is already an adulterer in his heart.'

"You know that it was said to the ancients: 'Thou shalt not forswear thyself, and thou shalt fulfill the vows made to the Lord.'

"And I say to you: 'Swear not at all. Neither by heaven, for it is the throne of God; nor by the earth, for it is the footstool of his feet; nor by Jerusalem, for it is the city of the great King.'

"Neither swear by thy head; for it is not within thy power to make a single hair white or black.

"Let your speech be: 'Yea, yea; Nay, nay!' All that is more than this is from the spirit of evil.

"You know that it has been said: 'Eye for eye and tooth for tooth.'

"And I tell you not to resist the evil-doer. But if anyone strikes thee on the right cheek, turn to him the left; and if anyone calls thee to law to have thy tunic, give up to him thy cloak. And if anyone compels thee to go one mile with him, accompany him the distance of two miles. Give to him that asks of thee, and lend to him that would borrow of thee.

"You know that it was said: 'Thou shalt love thy neighbor and thou shalt hate thine enemy.'

"And I say to you: 'Love your enemies and pray for your persecutors, that you may be children of your heavenly Father, who makes his sun to rise upon the evil as upon the good, upon the just and the unjust.' For if you love them that love you, what reward do you deserve? Do not the pagans the same? And if you greet only your brethren, what are you doing more than others? Do not the Gentiles the same?"[15]

All Jews were acquainted with the Mosaic Law from hearing it read on Saturday in the synagogue, and the Decalogue was especially familiar to them. Jesus takes this as the basis for the moral structure he intends to build. His way of speaking, "It was said to the ancients . . . and I say to you," is sign enough that he is setting himself up as a legislator superior to Moses.

The Law punished willful homicide with death.[16] The Gospel goes much farther. It likens to murder the anger that leads to murder. There is a wrath that is just and holy, inspired by zeal for God or for the neighbor's amendment. This is not what is meant here, but the anger of which St. John speaks: "Whoever hates his brother is a murderer in his heart." If, when wrath explodes, scornful and contemptuous words are used, corresponding to the Aramaic word *raca* (harebrained, empty-headed), the fault becomes graver.[17] It reaches its peak, if the scorn and contempt are joined by insult and that cruelest of offenses, which would be to accuse someone of the kind of madness that is real impiety: "The fool has said in his heart: 'There is no God.' "[18] The increasing gravity of the sin is expressed by a gradation in the penalties, phrased in a parabolic language which none of the hearers would be likely to take literally. The man who becomes angry with his brother is liable to the ordinary Tribunal. This was an assembly of twenty-three judges who, in cities of secondary rank, judged criminals and were empowered to hand down death sentences. The man who treats his brother with contempt will be brought before the Sanhedrin, that formidable council to which

---

[15] Matt. 5:21–47. The literal translation would be: "You have heard that it has been said to the ancients." The formula is repeated five times. In Verse 31, on divorce, it is shortened to: "It has been said"; but this verse occurs again later (19:9) in its proper historical context. We shall explain it then.

[16] Exod. 20:13; Deut. 5:17; Lev. 24:17 (the penalty).

[17] *Raca,* in Hebrew *req* (רק), and in Aramaic *reqa* (ריקא), means literally *empty* (κενός). The metaphor is common everywhere; we would say "empty-headed."

[18] *Fool* (μωρός, *nabal,* נבל) is used particularly of one with no sense of moral obligations or religious ideas; of one who denies the existence of God (Ps. 13[14]:1), who insults God (Ps. 73[74]:22) or the saints (Ps. 38[39]:9), who is unmindful of God's favors (Deut. 32:6).

the most serious crimes were referred and which delivered only the death sentence. Finally, if in anger one accuses his brother of impiety, he is judged and condemned in advance, and his lot is Gehenna.[19] Gehenna was the name of a valley south of Jerusalem where rubbish and the carcasses of animals were burned. The flames constantly crackling there made it a symbol of hell. The Saviour does not say what will be the penalty for homicide, perhaps because he would not have them think that such a crime could be committed under the Law of Grace.

Animosity, resentment, bitterness, rancor, are all banished by the Christian spirit. The duty of fraternal charity is so imperious that it comes before all others. "If thou be before the altar in the act of offering thy sacrifice, and dost remember that thy brother has a grievance against thee, leave thy sacrifice there and go to be reconciled to thy brother." Urgent though sacrifice be, reconciliation is even more urgent. It matters little whether the grievance be real or imaginary. Clear up the misunderstanding and re-establish concord as soon as possible. Jesus Christ does not say, "If thou hast wounded or offended thy brother," but, "If thy brother has a grievance against thee." Obviously, however, this is a counsel of perfection rather than a strict obligation.

The superiority of Christian morality is manifest in the question of marriage and sexual relations. The Old Law forbade adultery and punished the two accomplices with death; but it was silent on the impure intention.[20] At least in appearance, it likened lust for another's wife to covetousness for his goods.[21] The Gospel has

---

19 There is a gradation in the sin and in the punishment:

1. Anger — any tribunal
2. Contempt — the Sanhedrin
3. Insult — Gehenna

But the style is parabolic, and it is not necessary to determine what corresponds to the Tribunal and the Sanhedrin. Only the last term, Gehenna, borders on allegory; it seems directly to signify hell.

20 Exod. 20:14; Deut. 5:18; Lev. 20:10 (the penalty).

21 Exod. 20:17: Desire for the wife, the ox, or the goods of another is expressed by the same word (לא תחמד). In Deut. 5:18 different words are used, but the desire for another's wife is expressed by the word that in Exodus is used of the desire for an ox or an ass. Among the Jews, the ninth and tenth commandments were one commandment: a prohibition against coveting the goods

further refinements. It condemns impure desires, not only because they lead to evil acts, but because of their intrinsic malice. We do not go so far as to say that the Jews did not know the malice of impure desires. The natural law supplies for the silence of the written law, which, being a civil and a criminal code as well as a rule of morality, was concerned with the act and its repression rather than with the internal dispositions.[22] Much less could the Old Law be expected to teach the value and merit of virginity. And it had still other imperfections which the Gospel came to correct, by restoring marriage to its primitive holiness, by proclaiming the indissolubility of the conjugal bond, and by proscribing divorce, which had been tolerated with certain safeguards by the lawgiver of the Hebrews.

The Old Law forbade perjury, false witness, and any abusive employment of the name of God, but the casuists among the Rabbis did wonders with this prohibition.[23] There is nothing stranger than the two treatises of the Talmud on Vows and Oaths. All oaths were taken to be licit unless they were contrary to the truth. Conversation was so coated with them that they were introduced almost unconsciously. One would say, for example: I swear that I slept or that I did not sleep, that I will sleep or will not sleep. Swearing by creatures, even when they were closely related to the Creator, was considered quite indifferent, provided the name of God was not used. To invoke God's name in vain meant to invoke it in attestation of something evident, such as

---

or the wife of another. To get the number ten, Josephus and Philo divide the first commandment into two, and modern Jews make of the preamble the first commandment.

22 The rule was this: "For an Israelite, a good intention, but not a bad one, is counted by God as the act itself; for a non-Israelite, the opposite is true." There are, however, many texts condemning carnal covetousness, but many of them are recent and may have been written under the influence of Christianity. It will suffice to quote a text from the treatise *Kallah:* "The man who looks upon a woman with an (unchaste) intention is like the one that has had relations with her." What follows is untranslatable.

23 The Old Law expressly forbids false witness (Exod. 20:16; Deut. 5:20), false oaths (Lev. 19:12: לשקר), and useless oaths (Exod. 20:7; Deut. 5:11: לשוא), as well as the breaking of a vow made to the Lord (Num. 30:3; Deut. 23:21; Ps. 49[50]:14).

two and two are four, or something absurd, such as two and two are five.

Jesus had to oppose this spirit of laxity. He forbade swearing by creatures; they are the work of God, and man has no absolute rights or power over them. He proscribes the idle oath, since it is at least an irreverence. "Yes" and "No" in his affirmations and denials ought to be enough for a Christian. Jesus does not forbid oaths absolutely, for they can be demanded by the higher interest of the individual or of society. But if it had not been for original sin, oaths would be superfluous, for they always carry a suspicion of a lie in the one taking them, and a feeling of distrust in the one exacting them.[24] From this viewpoint it can be said that the oath derives from a bad principle.

"Eye for eye, tooth for tooth, wound for wound, life for life": such was the maxim universally accepted in the Semitic world two thousand years before our era.[25] Moses wrote it into his code; but to cut at the roots of individual acts of vengeance, which multiplied and ramified beyond all conceivable lengths among the Arabs of the desert, Moses reserved the application of this maxim to regular tribunals. Furthermore it is doubtful whether it was ever applied in all its rigor except in the case of false witnesses, who had to undergo the penalty of talion (retaliation) unless the offended party agreed to accept some compensation.[26]

---

[24] There are examples of oaths in the New Testament (Rom. 1:9; 2 Cor. 1:23; Gal. 1:20; Phil. 1:8). Jesus says (Mark 5:37): "Sit sermo vester est, est: non, non; quod autem his abundantius est, a malo est." Though the general sense is clear, the meaning of the details is controverted. Should *est, est: non, non* (ναὶ ναί, οὒ οὔ) be understood as a simple repetition to strengthen an affirmation or a denial; or is there an ellipsis, so that the meaning is: Say yes (if it is) yes; say no (if it is) no? The dictum of St. James favors the second interpretation (5:12): Ἤτω δὲ ὑμῶν τὸ ναὶ ναί, καὶ τὸ οὒ οὔ, "Let your yes be yes, and your no be no." In the phrase *ex malo est* (ἐκ τοῦ πονηροῦ ἐστιν), the adjective can be masculine (comes from the *Evil One,* the devil) or neuter (comes from an evil *principle*). The latter is more natural and seems better, but it differs very little from the first; for, after all, it was the devil who brought about the deterioration of our nature. — St. John Chrysostom is known to have condemned all oaths; and St. Jerome, the swearing by creatures. These two doctors have not been followed except by some heterodox sects.

[25] Exod. 21:24; Lev. 24:20; Deut. 19:21. The same is found in the Code of Hammurabi and in the Law of the Twelve Tables, which gave us the word *talion* (Si rupit membrum . . . talio est).

[26] Josephus says (*Antiq.*, IV, viii, 35) that the plaintiff fixed the amount of

Despite these mitigations the *lex talionis* smacked of primitive barbarity. How different is the Christian spirit! It teaches us not only to avoid harshness in claiming our due, but even, if need be, to sacrifice something of our rights for the sake of peace. Of course the precept to turn the left cheek when struck on the right, or to give up a cloak to the man who has seized one's tunic, or to do twice as much thankless work as is arbitrarily demanded, is not to be taken literally. Jesus means that a true Christian meets violence with gentleness, cupidity with disinterestedness, and unjust demands with a surrender of his own rights when circumstances counsel it, in order to overcome evil by good, as St. Paul puts it. What is required is the interior disposition rather than the literal execution, as St. Augustine well observes. And if our renunciation would be likely to exasperate the aggressor and make him even more intractable instead of softening him and leading him back to reason, charity would then dictate the contrary course. Giving or lending everyone everything he asks would only too often encourage laziness and extravagant spending. Here is a case where the letter killeth and the spirit quickeneth. The spirit of this precept is to seek peace even at the price of sacrifices and to refuse to meet violence with violence. Still we should not forget that a rule of perfection, given solely for the individual, is not applicable to society, since society is the natural protagonist of justice and rights.

Love of enemies is the height of the paradoxical — or of the sublime. In the Old Law the injunction to love the neighbor concerned only compatriots. Kindness to strangers was prescribed, but a stranger meant a *metic* (resident foreigner, *ger*), a proselyte in the broad sense, living among the Israelites. It is true that there was an article of the law forbidding injury to enemies and commanding that they be denied none of the ordinary services granted to all. But here again the law meant an Israelite, enemy by deed or circumstances, but by right a friend, since a fellow

---

the pecuniary compensation, as in Moslem law. This must have been the current practice. According to the *Mishnah* (*Baba Qamma,* viii, 1), a slap with the palm of the hand was fined 200 *zuz,* a slap with the back of the hand 400 *zuz,* because of the greater insult (*ibid.,* vii, 6). The *zuz* was worth a Roman denarius.

citizen.[27] If there is no passage in Scripture allowing personal and private hate, there are still many texts that authorize and sanction national hates against all neighboring and rival peoples except Egyptians and Idumeans.[28] But the comparative silence about love of enemies could be taken as permission to hate them, and the Rabbis actually did come to that conclusion.[29] It was forbidden to charge interest in making a loan to other Jews, but it was allowed with the *Goyyim,* and it was easy to persuade oneself that there need be no consideration for strangers.[30] The ferocious intransigent hostility of the Jews against the Gentiles had become proverbial in the Greco-Roman world.[31] It is to an audience imbued with these prejudices that Jesus says, "Love your enemies, do good to those that hate you, pray for those that persecute you or calumniate you, that you may be children of your Father who is in heaven."

Surely he does not ask the impossible. He does not order us to love our enemies as much as our friends, or those who have done favors for us, or those near to us. He wants us to love them with that love of charity that depends on the will alone and will prompt us to desire their spiritual good, to pray for their salvation, and to bestow on them those marks of interest and good will to which all members of the human family are entitled. Such is the precept, but the practice of the saints is an indication that the field of the counsels has a much broader scope. God himself, who makes the sun shine on the evil as well as the good, and generous rain to fall equally on the fields of sinners and the just, is here proposed to us as a model: "Be ye perfect as your heavenly Father is perfect."

There is then a very deep abyss between the legislation promulgated by Moses from the summit of Sinai and the ideal

[27] In Lev. 19:18, a neighbor is a *re'* (רֵעַ), a companion, a fellow citizen; in Lev. 19:33–34, a neighbor is a *ger* (גֵּר), a stranger residing in Israel, as can be seen from a parallel passage in Deut. 22:1–2. In Exod. 23:5, the *enemy* (*sona'*) is clearly an Israelite.

[28] Exod. 17:16; Deut. 25:17–19 (Amalech); Num. 23:18 (Madian); Deut. 7:15 (Chanaan); Deut. 23:2–6 (Ammon and Moab); Deut. 23:7 (Egypt and Edom).

[29] Cf. Billerbeck, *Kommentar,* Vol. I, pp. 353–370.

[30] Deut. 23:19–20. Here the stranger properly so called is the *nokri, alienigena.*

[31] Tacitus, *Hist.,* v, 5; Juvenal, xiv, 103–104. Cf. Th. Reinach, *Textes d'auteurs grecs et romains relatifs au judaisme* (Paris, 1895).

proposed by Christ on the Mount of Beatitudes. The Old Law forbade murder, the New prohibits even those feelings of bitterness and animosity which lead remotely to it. The Old Law punished adultery, the New punishes unchaste looks and impure thoughts that open the door to it. The Old Law forbade perjury, the New bans all idle oaths. The Old Law seemed to allow vengeance under the name of retribution; the New, not content to prescribe forgetfulness and pardon of injuries, even counsels that we raise our patience and abnegation to heights of heroism. Finally, the Old Law commands love of those near to us, but the New commands love of the neighbor without any distinction, including even our enemies.

If we now descend from speculation to everyday life, the contrast between Jewish piety and Christian piety will be just as great. Almsgiving, fasting, and prayer passed among the Jews as the touchstones of the true worshiper. The Pharisees prided themselves on their excellence in these three virtues, but they spoiled their practice of them by artifices and selfish affectations which the Saviour goes on to stigmatize as hypocrisy.

"Take heed not to perform your acts of virtue before men, to be seen by them. Else you shall have no reward before your Father who is in heaven.

"When, therefore, thou givest alms, sound not the trumpet before thee as the hypocrites do in the synagogues and in the streets, that they may be honored by men. Amen, I say to you, they have received their reward. As for thee, when thou givest alms, let not thy left hand know what thy right hand is giving, that thy almsgiving may be secret, and thy Father, who sees in secret, will requite thee.

"When you set yourself to pray, imitate not the hypocrites who love to pray standing in the synagogues and on street corners, to be seen by men. Amen, I say to you, they have received their reward. But thou, when thou wouldst pray, enter into thy oratory and shut the door, to pray to thy Father in secret, and thy Father, who sees in secret, will requite thee.

"When you fast, wear not a wasted look, as do the hypocrites who make their faces wan to show men that they are fasting. Amen, I say to you, they have received their reward. But thou, when thou art fasting, anoint thy head and wash thy face, that thou mayest not seem to be fasting for men, but for God, and thy Father, who sees in secret, will requite thee."[32]

The evil does not consist in doing good works before men (edification can counsel it sometimes, and even exact it), but in doing them in view of men in order to draw their attention, to gain their esteem and ingratiate oneself with them. Secret though this anxious quest for human approbation may seem, it does not escape God's eyes. It vitiates a good act, deprives it of merit, and eliminates the reward. It is its own reward, as worthless as the feeling which inclines one to ambition it.

The Talmud gives an exaggerated eulogy of almsgiving: "A penny given in alms," says a Rabbi, "merits the vision of the face of God." And it was in almsgiving that the Pharisees strove to distinguish themselves from the mob. There were plenty of occasions for it. There were door-to-door collections, the public distribution of the "poor tithes," offerings for the indigent which could be dropped in one of the thirteen poor boxes in the Women's Court. The Pharisees indulged in their usual ostentation when they did their part. No document warrants the assertion that they actually had trumpets blown to announce the time and place of their distribution of charity. This is possibly only a metaphorical way of speaking. But the fact is that they were always very careful to proclaim aloud even their smallest contributions. The true Christian, on the other hand, acting only for God, does not let his left hand know what his right hand has given. The figure means that he takes pains to hide his acts of virtue from other men, and so to speak, even from himself.

The Pharisees put the same kind of ostentation into their prayers. They deliberately chose the busiest places, letting themselves be caught in public at the hour of prayer, so as to fulfill their obligations in the full view of all. The large phylacteries,

---

32 Matt. 6:1–6, 16–18. *Attendite ne justitiam vestram faciatis coram hominibus.* It may be asked whether justitia (δικαιοσύνη) in this text means "act of virtue" or "almsgiving"; many Greek manuscripts read ἐλεημοσύνη. In later Hebrew, almsgiving was called "justice" (צדקה, *tsedaqah*), because beneficence was regarded as the characteristic virtue of the just man, and this derived sense has passed into Syriac and Arabic.

which they wore on their brows and wrapped around their left arms, marked them out to all as exact in prayer.

Only one day in the year, the Day of Atonement (*Kippur*), was prescribed by the Mosaic Law as a fast day. In the course of time, custom introduced several others. But they were not enough for the devout Pharisees. "I fast twice a week (Monday and Thursday)," says the haughty Pharisee of the parable, crushing with scorn the publican who does not fast. Always the same smugness and the same pride! After the death of Christ, when his disciples fasted in their turn, as he had foretold, they chose Wednesday and Friday to distinguish themselves from the hypocrites. They made the distinction even more pronounced by being careful to avoid boastfulness and vainglory.[33]

3. The Golden Rule and the Conclusion

To love God with all one's heart and one's neighbor as oneself is the epitome of Christian morality. The same was not true of the Old Law, in which the precept of love of neighbor was not clearly enunciated. For the Jew, the neighbor was a relative, a friend, someone living close by, his fellow townsman, his fellow countryman; not a stranger, a foreigner, a national or personal enemy. For the disciples of Christ, the neighbor is man himself, without exception or restriction. Thus understood, the love of neighbor includes the love of God and is inseparable from it. The two loves are but one, and St. Paul could say of fraternal charity that it is the end, the sum, and the fulfillment of the law of grace.

Christian altruism has found its highest expression in what is called the Golden Rule: "All that you would that men do to you, do you also for them; in this is the (whole) Law and the prophets." Or: "Do unto others as you would have them do unto you."[34] A search through the whole hotchpotch of the Talmud is rewarded with only a single maxim like it, which is attributed

[33] *Didache*, vii, 1: "Fast not with the hypocrites; they fast on Mondays and Thursdays; fast ye on Wednesdays and Fridays." This is an allusion to Matt. 6:16. Cf. the note in Funk, *Patres Apostolici,* 2 ed., 1901, Vol. I, p. 19.

[34] Matt. 7:12; Luke 6:31. St. Matthew concludes the discourse with this maxim. St. Luke inserts it in the passage about the love of enemies.

to the great Hillel. Looking on his rival Shammai browbeating a proselyte, he is supposed to have said, "What displeases you to have done to you do not to another." But Hillel was not the first to invent this formula, for it is in the Book of Tobias, and similar sayings may be found in profane writers.[35] It has however only a distant likeness to the Golden Rule; for, though it forbids doing evil, it does not prescribe doing good to all men, whether friends or enemies. The gap between the two is very wide.

To put others in our own place and to treat them always and in every way as we would like to be treated ourselves is a very difficult and rare practice, for it presupposes that selfishness has been killed. To aspire to it and attain it we must be deeply anchored in the conviction, based on faith, that God will treat us as we have treated others:

"Judge not, and you shall not be judged; condemn not, and you shall not be condemned. Pardon, and you shall be pardoned. Give, and it shall be given to you; a full measure, pressed down, shaken together, running over, shall they pour into your lap. For you shall be served with the same measure wherewith you yourselves serve."

We know from experience that we often fall into the same faults we have thought others prone to, and we are unjustly suspected of things of which we have suspected others. But it is not to this immanent justice that our Lord alludes when he says: "Judge not, that you be not judged." He is speaking of the terrible sentence in store for those who judge without authority or without good will. Have we been appointed judges of those who are better than we are?

"Why dost thou see the straw which is in thy brother's eye, and dost not consider the beam which is in thine own eye? And how shalt thou dare say to thy brother: 'Let me take out the straw which is in thine eye,' when there is a beam in thine? Hypocrite! First take out the beam which is in thine eye, and then thou shalt think of taking out the straw from thy brother's eye."[36]

---

[35] For the Talmud, cf. Edersheim, *Life and Times,* I, p. 535 and II, p. 236. The maxim cited as coming from the Talmud is in reality from Tobias 4:16.

[36] Matt. 7:3–5; Luke 6:41–42 (identical).

Our words and actions have their roots deep in our thoughts. That the former be charitable, our thoughts must become charitable. No good tree bears bad fruit, and no bad tree bears good fruit, for it is by the fruit that the nature of the tree is known. "Figs are not gathered from thorns, and grapes are not gathered from brambles." The criterion by which one distinguishes the prophet from the impostor, the saint from the hypocrite, is as follows: "By their fruits you shall know them."[37] Not that this is an absolutely infallible index — a wolf can be concealed for some time under sheep's clothing — but the norm is good enough in practice; for hypocrisy at length drops the mask, and the real personality finally shows through the disguise.

The Sermon on the Mount is over. The hearers who have lent an attentive ear are full of wonder. How could they help admiring this teaching, so beautiful, so sublime, so different from the narrow and prosaic formalism of the Scribes? But it is not enough to hear, not enough to applaud. The lesson learned must be put into practice. Hell is paved with good intentions, and good intentions never saved anyone.

"Not all that say to me, Lord, Lord, shall enter into the kingdom of heaven, but they only that do the will of my heavenly Father."[38]

"Whoever hears my words and puts them into practice is like the wise man who builds his house upon a rock. The rain falls, the torrents come, the winds blow and beat against that house; but it holds firm, because it is built upon the rock.

"And he that hears my words and does not put them into practice is like the fool who builds his house upon sand. The rain falls, the torrents come, the winds blow and beat upon that house, and it falls, and its ruin is complete."[39]

---

[37] Matt. 7:15–20; Luke 6:43–44 (summarized).

[38] Matt. 7:21; Luke 6:46.

[39] Matt. 7:24–27; Luke 6:47–49. St. Luke has the same parable with some variants, which, though they affect only the style, are of interest inasmuch as they reflect the method of the two authors. St. Matthew, faithful to Hebrew parallelism, proceeds by short, incisive, co-ordinated phrases, and expresses in identical words the members that are contrasted, changing only the mutually opposed words: "rock" — "sand," "wise man" — "fool," etc. St. Luke varies the expression and

The parable needs no explanation. Daily experience is its best commentary. When the idea was conceived of building an imperishable monument of French gratitude to the Sacred Heart of Jesus on the Mount of Martyrs, it was decided to sink down to live rock, whatever its depth, as many shafts as the Basilica was to have pillars. These shafts filled with a cement masonry of hydraulic lime, were intended to sustain the mighty arcades that were to support the edifice. It was a matter of changing a mountain of earth into a mountain of stone.[40] It would require years and it would cost millions, but no time was to be lost, and no one could tell just then whether the millions would be forthcoming. Many criticized the boldness of the pious Cardinal Guibert who had signed the project. Nevertheless, he was acting as a wise man; he was imitating Him who chose the Rock whereon to build his Church. He that builds for eternity must give to his work a foundation that is unshakable.

As has been said: "The Sermon on the Mount is not our Lord's last word; rather it is an introduction to the teaching of the Gospel. In this account of Christian morality, with its ideal, its duties, and its rewards, Christ, as yet, makes no mention of his Church, and keeps even himself in the background almost all the time. Only by the authority of his words does he reveal himself, but that authority is sovereign, and to the upright and attentive mind a revelation in itself."[41]

The Sermon on the Mount, reread by chance after long years of forgetfulness, evoked the following reflections from a celebrated

---

introduces a subordination of phrases. Since he makes everything converge toward the idea of the *foundation,* he indicates only one cause of ruin: the flooding waters, which attack especially the foundations.

"Whoever comes to me, hears my words, and puts them into practice, I will show you to whom he is like. He is like to a man building a house, who digs deep and lays the foundations upon the rock. When the flood comes, the stream beats upon that house without being able to shake it, for it is solidly built upon the rock.

"But he that hears (my word) and does not put it into practice is like to a man who builds a house upon the ground without (any) foundation. The stream beats upon it, and straightway it falls."

40 There are 83 shafts, of which 25 are 5 ft. 5 in. broad; some 45,780 cu. yds. of masonry underground.

41 Lebreton, *La Vie et l'enseignement de J.-C.,* 1931, Vol. I, p. 251 (English transl., Vol. I, p. 198).

critic of the past century: "It may be said that on the day when that discourse was uttered on the top of a hillock in Galilee, something new and unforeseen was produced and revealed in the moral teaching of mankind. Moses, on descending from the heights of Sinai, had by promulgation of the Decalogue established the dogma of the unicity of the living God and had regulated the severe prescriptions that attach to it; he had declared and imposed the first principles of divine worship and of human society. But on that other day, when, in a province of Judea far from Jerusalem, on a verdant hillock near the Sea of Galilee, in the midst of a population of the poor and sinners, of women and children, the Nazarene then aged about thirty years, a private individual, without visible authority and in no sense a national leader, but deriving from within himself alone the conviction of that divine mission whereof he made himself the inspired organ as a son sent by his father; when this man set himself to speak with so much sweetness and strength, such tenderness and daring, such innocence and courage, then truly a new moral era came into being."[42]

This page from a notorious freethinker cannot, of course, be taken without due reservations. We quote it only as a feeble echo of the enthusiasms and admiration which the Sermon on the Mount awakened in its first hearers.

---

[42] Sainte-Beuve, *Nouveaux lundis,* 4 ed., 1884, Vol. iii, pp. 246–247.

CHAPTER IV

First Assaults of the Enemy

1. The Scribes and Pharisees

HENCEFORTH we shall meet the Scribes and Pharisees hounding Jesus at every step. Something, therefore, should be known about these men who will play a leading role in the struggle launched against the Saviour, up to the day when the Sadducees will enter upon the stage to hasten the drama to its denouement.

At first, the interpretation of the Law devolved upon the priesthood. "The lips of the priest," says the prophet Malachias, "are the guardians of knowledge; at his mouth shall they seek the understanding of the Law." But in proportion as the sacred literature was augmented by the encroachments of the unwritten law upon legislation, as the latter attached itself by spurious links to the written law, the study of the Bible became an extremely complex matter; for the Bible is at once a history, a theology, a system of morality, and a civil and criminal code. The full knowledge of any science calls for the concentration of the whole man; but the sacerdotal caste could no longer devote itself to it, absorbed as they were by the duties of divine worship, by anxiety about their fortunes, and by the preoccupations of politics. As a consequence, it was the Scribes who devoted all their attention to the study of the Torah, that became the acknowledged interpreters of the Law and of its traditional accretions. Since these traditions were not fixed in writing before the end of the second century, but were transmitted orally, they had to be memorized in their entirety for long years at the feet of a master.

To believe the *Sayings of the Fathers,* the Scribes were the direct heirs of Moses. Josue was supposed to have received the Torah with all its redundancies from Moses and to have handed it down to the ancients; they in turn handed it down to the prophets, and the prophets to the members of the Great Synagogue, the last member being Simon the Just, who was succeeded by Antigonus of Soko. After Antigonus came the five famous "pairs" succeeding one another without interruption down to Hillel and Shammai.[1]

It is hardly necessary to remark that this genealogy of men handing the torch of sacred tradition on to one another for fifteen centuries is a fantastic illusion. It owed its origin to the anxiety of the Scribes to dignify their beginnings and to enhance their authority and impose it on the common people, from whom they loved to distinguish themselves by the gravity of their demeanor and the amplitude of their apparel. Predestined to responsibility and honors — for the study of the Bible fitted one for all posts — the Scribes were simultaneously or in succession, judges and lawyers, teachers and preachers, statesmen and churchmen, directors of consciences and counselors of the great, physicians of body and soul. Places were reserved for them in the Sanhedrin of Jerusalem beside distinguished men and the chiefs of the priesthood. They were the ones that usually commented on Scripture in the schools and synagogues, and their decisions, when unanimous, had the force of law.

In the Gospel, the Scribes and Pharisees are closely associated. This is perfectly natural, for, though not all the Pharisees were Scribes, nearly all the Scribes were Pharisees. The Pharisees appear in history for the first time under the name of "The Pious" (*Ḥasidim*) as supporters of the Machabees. The name "Pharisee" which means "Separated" or "Separatist," is probably a soubriquet which they decided to adopt because it expressed their policies so well. They spoke of one another as "Companions" (*Ḥaberim*), and were a real sect, though not a community like the Essenes.

Their history emerges from obscurity about a hundred and ten or twenty years before our era, at the time of their violent break with the Sadducees. The affair is recorded in Josephus and

[1] *Mishnah,* treat. *Aboth.,* Chap. I. The text and a commentary are to be found in the edition of Marti and Beer (Giessen, 1927). The last pair, Hillel and Shammai, lived in the time of Herod, a little before the birth of Christ.

the Talmud somewhat as follows. John Hyrcanus (135–104 B.C.), the first of the Hasmoneans to wear the royal crown, was giving a great banquet, to which he invited the leading Pharisees, who were then in his high favor. Toward the end of the feast, smitten with that ready sense of devotion so often born of wine and good cheer, he asked his guests what he should do to please God fully, and to be acceptable to them. They expostulated, vehemently protesting that the King was a finished model of all virtues. One alone kept silent. Pressed with questions, he finally said that the King would do well to be satisfied with his kingdom and to relinquish the High Priesthood. "And why?" demanded Hyrcanus. "Because," answered the other, "it is said that your mother was a slave under Antiochus Epiphanes." The story was a calumny, and the King was highly indignant. A Sadducee, named Eleazar, fed fuel to his wrath by remarking that in their hearts all the Pharisees thought the same. And they, when asked what punishment the insulter deserved, said that he deserved merely flogging and imprisonment. The prince thought the punishment too lenient, and from that time on he turned to the Sadducees, and his two successors followed his lead.

Whether the story be legend or fiction, it proves the existence, more than a hundred years before our era, of two parties between whom smoldered a latent antagonism which could be fanned into open hostility by any minor incident. The Pharisees and Sadducees differed in everything: social status, religious ideas, and political views. While the Pharisees recruited their ranks from the middle class, as did the Scribes, the Sadducees were the aristocracy of the nation, an aristocracy of rank, birth, and fortune. Happy in a state of affairs which assured to them honor and privileges, the Sadducees asked only that the *status quo* be preserved, and they feared any popular movement that threatened to change it. The Pharisees were essentially a religious party and kept aloof from politics. Opportunists in the sense in which the prophets had been opportunists, they regarded the rule of the foreigner as a punishment from heaven; they accepted any government which left them free to practice their religion as they understood it. Still, being instinctively nationalistic, they were more resigned than submissive, and would gladly have availed themselves of any favorable opportunity to throw off the odious yoke.

Compared to the Sadducees, the Pharisees were the representatives of Jewish orthodoxy. They believed in the immortality of the soul, eternal punishment and reward, the resurrection at least of the just, the existence of angels and devils. They admitted Divine Providence and man's free will, and held that divine initiative destroys neither merit nor responsibility. Rabbi Aqiba, the famous leader of the last revolt, said: "God has foreseen everything, and yet there is free will; divine goodness will judge the world, but according to the works of each one." The Sadducees, on the contrary, denied the existence of spirits, and their principles logically led to fatalism.[2]

Three vices spoiled the very real qualities of the Pharisees: a narrow formalism, unbridled pride, and scorn for the masses.

Under the pretext that tradition was the protective hedge of the Law, they went so far as to prefer the former when there was a conflict between the two, and even said that it was more culpable to violate the oral tradition than to violate the written Law itself. Justly did the Saviour ask them: "Why do you transgress the precepts of God for the sake of your traditions?"

The prayer of the Pharisee of the parable paints Pharisaic pride to the life. "O God, I thank thee that I am not like the rest of men, thieves, unjust, adulterers. I fast twice a week, I pay the tithe for the least fruits of the soil." The Pharisee regards himself as God's creditor for having done some works of supererogation, to the neglect of his essential duties. And this self-esteem filled him with a limitless scorn for the common people (*'am-ha-arets*), that is to say for everyone who was not a Pharisee. These ignorant boors — and for the Pharisee an *ignorant* person was anyone who did not devote his time to the study of the Law and the observance of its traditional practices — did not deserve to live or eat the fruits of the earth. The real Pharisee did not invite such people to his table nor deign to share theirs. Mere contact with them was defilement.

[2] Our principal and almost only source of information on the teaching of the Pharisees and Sadducees is Josephus, who describes them at considerable length and compares the doctrines of the two sects, though he likens them to the Greek schools of philosophy. Cf. especially, *Bellum,* II, viii, 14; *Antiq.,* XIII, v, 9; x, 6; and *Antiq.,* XVIII, i, 2–4. He compares the Pharisees to the Stoics (*Vita,* 2).

The high opinion which the Pharisees had of themselves, their *esprit de corps,* the lofty ideal which they proposed, the asceticism they paraded, their dignified bearing, their independence of public authority — all helped to elevate them in the eyes of the masses. Their preponderant influence is attested by Josephus, perhaps with some exaggeration, for, though of sacerdotal rank, Josephus was also a Pharisee. According to him, their authority among the people was so great that the Sadducees were often forced by public opinion to follow their views even in matters of liturgy and worship.[3]

2. The Feast Given by Matthew

The Scribes and Pharisees being what they were, their hostility to the Gospel was inevitable. They reproached Jesus for his dealings with sinners and people of evil repute, for his violation of the Sabbath and the traditional observances, and for his claim to forgive sins. But their chief, though unexpressed, complaint was his increasing popularity, which could be construed as a lowering of their own importance and a lessening of their influence.

Above, in the story of the paralytic carried by four men and let down through the beams of the roof, how scandalized the Scribes and Pharisees were when they heard Jesus say to the sick man, "Thy sins are forgiven thee"! Not daring to protest aloud, they muttered under their breath: "This man blasphemes; who can forgive sins except God alone?" The joyous and enthusiastic acclamations of the crowd silenced them that time. Perhaps, too, the miracle had made an impression on them, for they had not yet conceived the truly diabolical idea of attributing Christ's miracles to the intervention of the devil.

The conflict broke out on the occasion of the feast which Matthew gave in Jesus' honor after he had been called to follow

[3] The texts on the Pharisees and Sadducees, with a bibliography concerning them up to 1907, may be found in Schürer, *Geschichte,* 4 ed., II, pp. 447–489. For the Talmud and the ancient Jewish sources, cf. Billerbeck, *Kommentar,* Vol. IV, 1928, pp. 334–352. Among the most important modern works are Abrahams, *Studies in Pharisaism and the Gospels,* Cambridge, 2 vols., 1917 and 1924; J. M. Lightley, *Jewish Sects and Parties in the Time of Christ* (London, 1925). There is a substantial summary in Edersheim, *Life and Times,* 11 ed., 1901, Vol. I, pp. 310–324.

him.[4] A great number of publicans or very disreputable people had been invited, and Jesus and his Apostles were seated at table with them. The Scribes and Pharisees, who had secretly slipped into the room to spy on him, or were watching the arrivals, were gravely scandalized. Still they did not dare lay the blame on Jesus himself. Toward his disciples, however, they were more courageous. "What!" they said. "Does your master eat and drink with publicans and public sinners?" In their eyes this was more than an impropriety; it was the worst of infamies. The embarrassed disciples relayed their remarks to Jesus. He answered simply: "It is not they that are well that need a physician, but they that are sick. Go, learn what this means: 'I will have mercy and not sacrifice.' I have not come to call the just, but sinners."

Some of John the Baptist's disciples were also present. They were as gravely scandalized by the Saviour's conduct as were the Pharisees, but for a different reason. Together with the Pharisees they asked Jesus this insolent question: "Why do the disciples of John and the disciples of the Pharisees fast, and thy disciples do not fast?"[5] John's neophytes understandably imitated their master's austerity, and we know that the Pharisees followed the custom of their sect and ostentatiously fasted twice a week. Jesus refuted their insidious criticism in one word: "Do those invited to a marriage fast as long as the bridegroom is with them? No; as long as the bridegroom is in their midst they cannot fast. But a day shall come when the bridegroom shall be taken away from them, and then they shall fast in turn."[6]

John's disciples, as well as the Pharisees, were able to understand this language. Had not John called Christ the Bridegroom and compared himself to the *paranymph*, the intimate friend of the bridegroom?[7] The Pharisees were equally aware that the days

[4] Matt. 9:10–17; Mark 2:15–22; Luke 5:29–39. The three accounts are so close to one another that they evidently go back to the same source, written or oral. Some slight differences will be mentioned later on.

[5] In St. Matthew, the disciples of John are the ones that ask the question; in St. Luke, the Pharisees. In St. Mark, both ask it.

[6] "The guests of the wedding-feast": literally, "the sons of the bridechamber" (*οἱ υἱοὶ τοῦ νυμφῶνος*), a Hebraism translated by *filii sponsi* in St. Matthew and St. Luke, and by *filii nuptiarum* in St. Mark.

[7] John 3:29: *sponsus* (*νυμφίος*) and *amicus sponsi* (*ὁ φίλος τοῦ νυμφίου*). The latter is the paranymph to whom John compares himself.

of the Messias had been represented under the figure of a nuptial banquet which would realize the prophecy of Osee: "I will espouse thee forever," and of Isaias, "Thy Bridegroom is thy creator."[8] Fasting and mourning are out of place at a marriage feast. Numberless passages in the Talmud recommend to the guests, as a duty of good manners, an expansive and boisterous joy, even dispensing them from certain legal obligations for this purpose.[9] Jesus does not condemn fasting. He approves of it and supposes its practice; but for his disciples he postpones it until another day.

The Pharisees attached to fasting an intrinsic value independent of the intention. This amounted to mistaking the setting for the diamond, and subjecting the spirit to the letter. Jesus was constrained to correct such a pernicious error. The matter of fasting serves as an introduction to a more general teaching:

"No one tears a patch from a new garment to sew it on old clothing; else he spoils the new garment and disfigures the old. Likewise, no one pours new wine into old wineskins; else the new wine will burst the old wineskins and so both wine and wineskins will be lost. Rather pour the new wine into new wineskins."[10]

It was once customary, and is even now in some European countries, to put wine into goatskins or sheepskins turned inside out and tarred inside to keep the liquid from seeping through. Care is taken not to pour fresh, still fermenting wine into skins that are worn out by friction or lengthy service. Nor does anyone cut a piece from new garments to patch up old clothing. That would be to sacrifice the new at a total loss, without fittingly repairing the old. The allegory is clear. The new garment and new wine are the Gospel. The old clothing and old skins are the Old Law. The two do not go together; they are not complementary; they are mutually exclusive. To attempt to mix or associate

---

[8] Osee 2:19; Isa. 54:5.

[9] Texts in Billerbeck, *Kommentar,* Vol. I, pp. 500–518.

[10] Luke 5:36–38. This is a *parable* (παραβολήν) which is presented by the other Synoptics in a slightly different form. "No one sews a piece of crude cloth (ἄγναφον) on an old garment, otherwise the new piece which is added takes something from the old garment (by shrinking at the first washing) and the rent becomes worse" (Mark 2:21). Matt. 9:16 has the same. In the language of parable, this difference is negligible. With regard to the wine and the wineskins, there is no divergence among the Evangelists.

them would be to spoil the one without benefit to the other. The new spirit calls for new legislation. Old-fashioned, decayed observances are not to be imposed on the disciples of Christ. The Saviour does not formulate this conclusion in so many words, but he distinctly suggests it.

To benefit by the new regime, it is necessary to sacrifice the old. The Pharisees were not ready for this sacrifice, and it will always be a stumbling block for converts from Judaism. Jesus points this out in a final maxim. "No one, when he has drunk old wine, wants new wine; for he says: 'The old is better.' "[11] It is true that old wine is generally preferable to new, but the comparison does not bear upon the quality of the two wines. Jesus is using a kind of parable to throw into relief the difficulty that every man experiences in changing his habitual attitudes, good or bad. The Pharisees are accustomed to the thin wine of the old traditions; they have no taste for the strong wine of the Gospel. The teaching of the Scribes seems better to them; they stagnate in their old routine.

3. The Unnamed Penitent Woman

At this period of Christ's life, the hostility of the Pharisees had not yet become universal, and one of them, less prejudiced or less fanatical than the rest, felt that he might invite him to his table without compromising himself too much in the eyes of his confreres.[12] Nevertheless this man's motives are somewhat ambiguous. He does not seem to have had any ill will or treacherous intentions, but rather a certain curiosity and a desire to see for himself. He forces himself to be correct and courteous, but remains cold and reserved about it.

The guests had placed themselves at table in the posture then in use, reclining on slightly raised couches and supporting themselves on the left elbow, their bare feet almost touching the floor,

---

[11] Luke 5:39: "Et nemo bibens vetus statim vult novum; dicit enim: Vetus melius est." The word *statim* does not correspond to anything in the Greek. Instead of the comparative *melius,* the Greek has the positive χρηστός, but the meaning is the same. The old wine to which we are accustomed is *good;* it is enough for us; we do not want any other.

[12] This episode is peculiar to St. Luke (7:36–50). The Pharisee is named Simon. The woman is a *sinner* who has *learned of* Jesus' presence in the Pharisee's house.

and their faces turned toward the entrance through which the service was brought. Suddenly a woman carrying a vessel of perfume came into the banquet hall and slipped stealthily into the open space between the wall and the guests. Stopping behind Jesus, she fell at his feet. The guests were somewhat disconcerted for she was known, not certainly as a courtesan — the servants would have barred her entrance if she were — but as one of these women of light morals who in the midst of their disorderly lives still keep up a semblance of respectability. What she was about to do shows that she was under the influence of grace and determined to break with her past. She had heard of Jesus, and knowing his compassion for physical and moral miseries and his indulgence toward repentant sinners, had only waited for a favorable occasion to come and ask his pardon. Her move is not accidental. She comes at a set time to the house of the Pharisee who, she has heard, is to entertain Jesus.

She was about to pour the contents of her alabaster vase on the Saviour's feet, when a sudden burst of sorrow prompted her to wash those adorable feet with her tears, and kiss them with great emotion. She unbound her abundant hair to dry his feet before anointing them with the perfume: a great gesture of humility and supreme homage, for every Jewish woman considered it a disgrace to appear in public with her hair in disorder.

Meantime, Jesus, to all appearances unaware of what was happening around him, did not interrupt her. The scandalized Pharisee was saying within his heart: "If this man were a prophet, he would know that the woman who is touching him is a sinner." Our Pharisee is satisfied. He knows now what he wanted to know. His companion at table is not a prophet, but an ordinary man. The lesson which he is about to receive is a hard one, but it is well deserved.

"Simon," Jesus says to him, "I would say something to thee."

"Speak, master," the Pharisee frigidly replies.

"Two men were in debt to a creditor; one owed five hundred denarii, and the other fifty. Since they had not wherewith to pay, he forgave the debt to both. Which one will love him more?"

"He, I suppose, to whom he forgave more."

"Thou hast answered well," says Jesus. And then, pointing to the woman, who was benumbed with fear, he said: "Thou seest this woman? When I came into thy house, thou didst not pour water on my feet (as was customary when a guest came from a journey); but she has washed my feet with her tears and has dried them with her hair. Thou gavest me no kiss of welcome (the custom between friends upon meeting, the courtesy accorded an honored guest); but, from the moment I came in,[13] she has not ceased to kiss my feet. Thou didst not anoint my head (an attention always shown persons of consideration); but she has anointed my feet with precious ointment. And therefore, I say to thee, her many sins are forgiven her because she has loved much. He who has been forgiven little, loves little."[14] And turning to the woman he said to her: "Go, thy sins are forgiven thee."

The application of the parable does not seem to fit its general tenor. One would expect the conclusion to be: "She will love much, because much has been pardoned her." Instead, the Saviour concludes in reverse: "Much has been pardoned her because she has loved much." It is true that both conclusions are legitimate, for love can be the cause as well as the effect of pardon. The love of charity gains pardon, and pardon evokes the love of gratitude. In the parable Jesus restricts himself to the latter point of view, for it is rare that a creditor remits debts because

[13] The Vulgate has "since she came in" (ex quo intravit); but the Greek has, "Since I came in" (ἀφ' ἧς εἰσῆλθον). The difference is slight. The sinner, who had thought over her action beforehand, waited only for Jesus to enter and then entered herself.

[14] Luke 7:47: Οὗ χάριν, λέγω σοι, ἀφέωνται αἱ ἁμαρτίαι αὐτῆς αἱ πολλαί, ὅτι ἠγάπησεν πολύ· ᾧ δὲ ὀλίγον ἀφίεται, ὀλίγον ἀγαπᾷ.

The meaning is: "*This is the reason* (because of the acts I have enumerated as expressive of ardent love), *I declare to you, that her many sins have been forgiven* (ἀφέωνται, have been and remain forgiven), *because she has loved much.*" If the comma is omitted before *I declare to you,* the meaning is not appreciably changed, and love would still be the cause and not the effect of the pardon. *Much* has been forgiven her, because she has loved *much.*

The second part: "He to whom little has been forgiven loves little" can be understood in two ways. If we take only the material presentation of the parable, the explanation will be: "He who has been forgiven little will love little; he will love in proportion to the benefit received." But if we take the application which Jesus draws from the parable, we will prefer the following meaning: "If anyone receives little pardon, it is because he loves little. The pardon given is in proportion to the love."

of his debtors' affection for him; but the case of the sinful woman is entirely different. Doubtless the pardon which she received will increase her gratitude; but her love, inspired by faith, a generous and ardent love of which she has just given open proof, has won pardon for her, even before the fact is solemnly declared to her. This is the truth that Jesus wants to emphasize when he adds for the benefit of his host and the others present, "He who has been forgiven little, loves little." In the relations between God and man, if one receives little pardon, it is that he loves little; or rather, he who loves little does not love enough, and the lack of love, at least of initial love, draws no pardon. Charity, on the other hand, as St. Peter says, effaces a multitude of sins. Turning for the last time to the poor woman, who was lingering there in trembling confusion, Jesus reassures her and dismisses her saying: "Thy faith has saved thee; go in peace."

A certain number of interpreters, Catholic as well as Protestant, doubtless wishing to spare Christ a supposed slip in logic, attempt to establish a perfect balance between the tenor of the parable and its application. They construe thus: "This is why I declare to you that her numerous sins have been pardoned, because she has loved much." The sensible proof that numerous sins have been forgiven is that she has given great signs of love. Our objection to this translation is not that it begs the text; there are graver objections against it. "If the parable is to be applied strictly, the conclusion must be that the penitent gave greater signs of love because she had been pardoned more and she knew it. But she did not know this, because Jesus goes on to declare it, not only to the others, but also to the woman herself. And as a matter of fact, the parable could not be applied mechanically to divine matters. The man who has offended God is not certain of pardon and can only trust to the mercy of God and ask for it. So it is with the sinful woman. The parable had brought matters to this point, that he who has sinned more can love more. The sinful woman had proved that. Then Jesus crosses over into the realm of divine realities, and, not as a teacher who works from ordinary norms and by means of conjecture, but in virtue of his full knowledge and authority, pronounces that her sins, her many sins, are forgiven. Thus his kindness to the sinful woman finds its justification. Knowing herself to be greatly in debt, she had loved much."[15]

A shadow of mystery hovers over this episode, and many think, though without advancing any proof, that the mystery is intentional. The author leaves us in ignorance of the date and place of the event, although it seems likely that it happened along the shores of the lake and should be placed in the Galilean period of Jesus' teaching. The Evangelist tells us that the scene was the house of a Pharisee named Simon, but this name was so common among the Jews of the time that it is of no real help.

Was the unnamed sinner Mary of Magdala or Mary of Bethany, or are all of them but one and the same person? It is not absolutely impossible that they are the same; but it must be agreed that St. Luke does not seem to have suspected it. At any rate, he does not establish any relationship between them. Immediately after the story which we have just read, he enumerates the holy women who accompanied Jesus in his apostolic journeys, and he mentions, among several others, "Mary Magdalene, from whom he had cast out seven devils." Magdalene is here introduced as an unknown person, one of the women whom Jesus had cured of various maladies and freed from unclean spirits.

This fact does not seem to fit in with the story of the unnamed sinner of whom St. Luke has just spoken. The same is to be said about Mary of Bethany, mentioned two chapters later. "Jesus entered a certain village, where a woman named Martha welcomed him into her house. And Martha had a sister named Mary." Here again Mary is introduced as a new figure, and no indication is given that she has ever left her pious family and her peaceful village. Of course, it may be said that the Evangelist is simply placing before us his documents as he found them, not concerning himself with establishing identifications that are not indicated in his sources. Doubtless this can be held, and the dogma of inspiration does not forbid it; but is it not somewhat

[15] Lagrange, *Saint Luc,* 1921, p. 232. Fr. Buzy, who defends the opposite opinion, cites in favor of his view Toletus, Salmeron, and Sainz (*Las Parabolas del Evangelio,* etc., 1915, p. 533). The Protestant partisans of this opinion are numerous.

bold to fancy oneself better informed on the facts of the Gospel story than the Evangelist himself?

4. Plucking Grain on the Sabbath

The chief complaint of the Scribes and Pharisees against Jesus was his alleged violation of the Sabbath. One Saturday Jesus was leading his disciples along a path which bordered or cut across a field of ripe grain.[16] On that day it was allowed and even counseled to walk in the country, provided that the prescribed limits were not transgressed: two thousand cubits (about 1000 yards) from the walls or the last houses of the town. The disciples, who had left the synagogue around noon, had not yet taken their first meal.[17] To allay or beguile their hunger they plucked some ears of grain as they went by, and shelled them with their fingers before eating them. The Mosaic Law expressly sanctioned the Oriental custom permitting travelers to pick and eat figs, grapes, olives, and other fruits they chanced upon in their journey: "If thou goest into thy neighbor's vineyard, eat of the grapes as many as pleases thee, but take not any away with thee. If thou goest into his field, thou mayest pluck the ears with thy hand, but thou mayest not reap them with a sickle."[18]

The Apostles were therefore within the law on this point. But the Pharisees tried to pick a quarrel with them on a double infraction of the Sabbath rest. It was forbidden to reap or to thresh grain on the Sabbath, and the Pharisees made plucking the ears and shelling them equivalent to harvesting and threshing the crop. The Jerusalem Talmud, in agreement with Philo, is explicit on the point: "To pick a piece of fruit or some grain is to harvest; to sift rice or barley is to winnow: two works forbidden on the Lord's day."[19]

---

[16] Matt. 12:1–8; Mark 2:23–28; Luke 6:1–5. The three versions agree except that Matthew alone adds the example of the priests working in the Temple without violating the Sabbath, and St. Mark alone gives the maxim, "the Sabbath is made for man, and not man for the Sabbath."

[17] Josephus, *Vita,* 54: "On the Sabbath, it is customary to break the fast at the sixth hour," i.e., at noon, or between eleven o'clock and noon, after leaving the synagogue.

[18] Deut. 23:24–25.

[19] *Mishnah,* treat. *Shabbath,* vii, 2; *Jerusalem Talmud,* in Schwab, Vol. IV, p. 967; Philo, *Vita Mosis,* ii (Mangey, Vol. II, p. 137).

Since the Master was responsible for the misdeeds of his disciples, he was the one the Pharisees challenged: "Why are thy disciples doing what it is not permitted to do on the Sabbath?" It was not for the Saviour to bicker with them on the merits or demerits of their Rabbinical interpretations. He therefore raises the question to a higher issue and proves by two examples that the observance of the Sabbath is a matter of positive law, and therefore admits of exceptions, and should yield in many cases to necessity and more important needs. "Have you not read what David did, when, pressed by hunger, he entered the house of God, and took the loaves of proposition which the priests have the right to eat, and with them fed himself and his companions?"

This story was known to all readers of the Bible. David, fleeing with a band of faithful partisans from the jealous anger of King Saul, came to Nobe where the Tabernacle was kept at the time, and begged the High Priest Achimelech to give him some badly needed food.[20] The Pontifex had at hand only some flour cakes, called loaves of proposition, which he had just taken from the altar. Yet he did not hesitate to give them to David, once he was assured that he and his companions were legally pure. There are, then, cases in positive law in which the law ceases to hold, and that on the testimony of the inspired Books. The moral which Jesus draws is this: "The Sabbath was made for man and not man for the Sabbath."[21] If then, in a particular case, the Sabbath worked to the detriment of man, an exception was in order. The Jews themselves had understood this in the war against Antiochus, when they decided not to let themselves be massacred defenselessly to avoid infringing the Sabbath rest.[22]

The priests in the Temple materially violate the Sabbath both by offering the daily sacrifice, which is doubled that day, and by

[20] 1 Kings 21:1–6. St. Mark (2:26) says "under the High Priest Abiathar." Abiathar, the son of Achimelech, was present at the time (1 Kings 22:20), but he was not yet the High Priest. It is probable that the Evangelist calls him High Priest *by anticipation,* or that he uses the title in the wide sense that it sometimes had, of a member of a high-priestly family. The event is dated by Abiathar rather than by Achimelech because Abiathar, the faithful follower of David, was much better known than his father.

[21] Mark 2:27.

[22] 1 Mach. 2:33–42. From that day forward, the Jews fought battles on Saturday when necessary (Josephus, *Antiq.,* XII, vi, 2).

performing other manual works entailed in divine worship. Jesus claims as his own the right to exempt himself from the Sabbath rest, and vindicates for his disciples the same privilege enjoyed by the priests in their Temple service: "I say to you there is one here greater than the Temple. Ah! If you understood what means this word of the prophet Osee, 'I desire mercy and not sacrifice,' you would not have condemned the innocent."[23]

The Law of the Sabbath allows exceptions, because its reason for existence is not only the worship of God, but also the physical and moral good of man. It is subordinated to the Temple service, it yields to charity, which is preferable to sacrifice itself. And here is the decisive argument: "the Son of Man is Lord even of the Sabbath."[24] He is therefore not himself subject to it and can dispense others from it. In calling himself Lord of the Sabbath, Jesus Christ proclaims his divinity, for the power of abrogating or modifying the Law belongs only to him who formulated it.

Seven of the Gospel miracles were cures on the Sabbath: the Capharnaum demoniac, Peter's mother-in-law, the paralytic of Bethesda, the man born blind at Jerusalem, the man with dropsy, the woman sick for eighteen years, the man with the withered hand. It would seem that the Saviour deliberately chose that day for his miracles.

In a certain synagogue — we do not know where or when — Jesus was instructing the people assembled there for the Sabbath service, when he noticed an unfortunate man whose right hand was withered.[25] The *Gospel according to the Hebrews* puts in the man's mouth words which may well be the echo of an authentic tradition: "I was a mason, I gained my living by the work of my hands. Jesus, I beseech thee, give me back my health,

---

23 Matt. 12:6–7, citing Osee 6:6. Elsewhere in St. Matthew, the same text of Osee has an entirely different application.

24 Matt. 12:8; Mark 2:28; Luke 6:5. It is St. Mark that adds the word *even* (καὶ τοῦ σαββάτου).

25 Matt. 12:9–14; Mark 3:1–6; Luke 6:6–11. The accounts are basically the same, with some variety in the details: (*a*) St. Matthew names as adversaries only the Pharisees; St. Luke adds the Scribes; and St. Mark, the Herodians. (*b*) In St. Matthew, the adversaries of Jesus question him; in St. Mark and St. Luke, Jesus questions them. (*c*) In St. Luke the enemies of Jesus deliberate on what to do to him; in the other two they plot his death. (*d*) The comparison of the sheep fallen into the pit is peculiar to St. Matthew.

that I may not beg my bread in shame." His pleadings were unnecessary. Jesus had already decided to perform a miracle, because the Pharisees or legalists, his adversaries, had flocked in to spy on him and indict his conduct. These rigid moralists forbade the practice of medicine on the Sabbath except in danger of imminent death. Taking medicines and applying remedies were both banned; but there was an ingenious twisting of the Law to allow taking a potion provided that it was not taken as a remedy but merely as a beverage. In the eyes of these cunning casuists, the intention purified the act.

It has been suggested that the Pharisees brought this man to the synagogue expressly to see what Jesus would do, but that is hardly likely. In any case, the sick man was not in collusion with them. Jesus would not have countenanced such an intrigue without unmasking it, and would not have cured a man so ill-disposed. He first commanded the man to rise and stand forth plainly in the midst of the assembly. Then, turning to his adversaries, he asked them: "Is it permitted to do good rather than evil on the Sabbath, to save a life rather than lose it?" They kept their peace, because they were well aware of the implications of the question, but were at a loss for an answer. Jesus continued: "Who of you, if one of his sheep falls into a pit on the Sabbath day, does not pull it out? Is not a man worth more?" Then, looking around upon them with indignation in his eyes, but also with sadness, because they were so blind, he said to the sick man: "Stretch forth thy hand." He obeyed, and the withered hand became as supple and strong as the other.

Far from stripping the scales from their eyes, this miracle only blinded them more. They plotted with the Herodians to do away with Jesus at the earliest occasion. The Herodians were the partisans of the Herods, who dreamed of a return of national unity under a prince of that family, and a consequent liberation from the foreign yoke. They were more interested in politics than religion, but were disposed to join the Pharisees in a temporary alliance, the more surely to destroy their common enemy. For the Scribes, the support of the Herodians was a guarantee of impunity. We shall see them again, on the eve of the Passion, plotting with the Pharisees and Sadducees and all the other enemies of the Saviour.

5. The Sin Against the Holy Spirit

The underhand schemings and intrigues of the Pharisees had not succeeded in cooling the enthusiasm of the multitudes nor their eagerness to follow Jesus. The house at Capharnaum to which he was fond of retiring was forthwith so beleaguered by the curious that the Apostles, whose task it was to stem or at least control the tide of arrivals, had hardly the leisure to eat in peace.

Those concerned about the life and health of the Saviour, his relatives, were finally alarmed at the situation. They came down from Nazareth, determined to put an end to this excess of zeal, which, to their minds, was sheer extravagance putting the whole family in a compromising position. Have there not been in modern times well-intentioned people who said of a Curé of Ars or a Don Bosco, "He has no common sense; he is going to foolish extremes; he is going to kill himself"? Jesus' relatives knew the evil intentions of the Pharisees, and that they were capable of anything; they may therefore have feared a bold stroke or a campaign of defamation which could not but besmirch the name of the whole family. Briefly, under the pretext of serving him, they came to take hold of him and force him, willingly or not, to prudence and moderation, to silence and retirement.[26]

"Piety," says Maldonatus, "makes an explanation of this

---

[26] Mark 3:20–21. Literally: "And he comes into a house (ἔρχεται εἰς οἶκον and not ἔρχονται), and the multitude gathers again so that they could not even eat bread (μηδὲ ἄρτον φαγεῖν). And his own (οἱ παρ' αὐτοῦ), having learned this, went out to lay hold of him, for they said: He is beside himself (ὅτι ἐξέστη)." There are several obscure points.

a) Who are "his own"? — The words οἱ παρ' αὐτοῦ, "his own people," do not designate fellow townsmen or compatriots, much less the disciples; but rather, his relatives in the widest sense; they alone are authorized to watch over him and to bring him home, if there is anything excessive in his conduct. Still, the expression "his own" does not exclude more or less numerous exceptions.

b) What does ὅτι ἐξέστη mean? — The Vulgate translates, *quoniam in furorem versus est*. This is much too strong. Ἐξίσταμαι does not mean "to be mad," "deranged," "crazy," but "to be beside oneself" from emotion or passion. It is the feeling experienced by the witnesses of Jesus' miracles (Mark 2:2–12; 5:42; 6:51; Matt. 12:23, etc.). Only in a very improper sense can it be said that they were "crazed" with admiration or amazement.

c) Who said this of Jesus? — Many good interpreters attribute this scarcely charitable remark, not to Jesus' relatives, but to others around him. "Jesus'

distressing episode more difficult; for the mind shrinks from believing, or even from thinking, that the relatives of Christ treated him as a madman or looked upon him as such." Maldonatus is right, but he aggravates the difficulty by forcing the meaning of the word used by St. Mark. It is clear that those who came to check Jesus are not, as claimed, his friends or disciples, nor the Scribes and Pharisees; but members of his family, his cousins or the husbands of his cousins in Nazareth. Of course this plot could be the work of certain individuals and not necessarily the work of the whole group — the Evangelists have accustomed us to this collective way of recounting things. Nor should we exaggerate the pretext which they advance, nor yet make them say, as the translation of the Vulgate might suggest, "He is mad, he is crazy." The corresponding Greek word means simply, "He is beside himself," under the influence of emotion or violent passion. The expression is ordinarily used to indicate the admiration and amazement that seized the crowds when they beheld the miracles of Christ. Nonetheless, this feeling of Jesus' relatives, or at least several of them, shocks and revolts us. To understand, if not to excuse, this sentiment, we must remember "that our Lord's first thirty years were spent in the obscure life of a small community, and that His kinsmen and fellow-villagers looked upon Him as one of themselves, an unlettered artisan. When they suddenly saw Him traversing the country as a miracle-working prophet, they were seized with astonishment that, in many cases, became disgust; and to readjust their judgment concerning Him, to sit humbly at His feet after despising Him for so long, was more than most of them could do. From this point of view, faith found far less obstacles among strangers."[27]

When Jesus' relatives arrived at Capharnaum, he was at grips

---

relatives come to take him, because *they* said (ἔλεγον, i.e., it was being said about him)." Grammatically, this interpretation is possible, and such indeterminate use of the plural is quite frequent, as Turner has shown in *J. T. S.*, Vol. XXV, pp. 378–386. Still, it is natural to attribute these words to our Lord's relatives, and to see in them the reason of their conduct: "They came to take him, *for they said:* He is beside himself." One would shrink from this conclusion, perhaps, if ὅτι ἐξέστη necessarily meant "He is crazy"; but the depreciatory sense of this expression should be proved and not supposed *a priori*.

[27] Lebreton, *La vie et l'enseignement de J.-C.*, 1931, Vol. I, p. 286 (English transl., Vol. I, p. 229).

with the Pharisees, helped by reinforcements of Scribes who purposely had come from Jerusalem to lend their support. He had just liberated a blind and dumb demoniac, whose double affliction was not due to congenital defect or any organic injuries, but to the control exercised over him by an evil spirit. Once the devil was expelled, the unfortunate man had immediately recovered his sight and speech. Now, while the crowd was applauding and noisily manifesting its joy, the Pharisees began whispering to one another or slyly suggesting to the people, "He is possessed by the devil. It is by the power of Beelzebub, the prince of devils, that he casts out devils."[28]

The absurd calumny collapsed under its own weight. Jesus meets it only with a common sense argument which shows, at the same time, that the charge may be retorted on his detractors:

"Every kingdom divided against itself shall be destroyed; and every city or house divided against itself shall not endure. Now if Satan casts out Satan, he is at war against himself; how then shall his kingdom endure? And if I cast out devils by Beelzebub, by whom do your children cast them out? Let them be your judges.

"But if I cast out devils by the spirit of God, then the kingdom of God has come upon you. Who can enter a strong man's house and plunder his goods if he has not first bound the strong man? Then only shall he plunder his house. He that is not with me is against me, and he that does not gather with me scatters."[29]

---

[28] Matt. 12:22–23. In Luke (11:14–16; cf. Matt. 9:32–34) the man is only dumb, as St. Augustine remarks (*De consensu evang.*, ii, 37): "Lucas mutum dicit tantum non etiam caecum; sed non ex eo quod aliquid tacet, de alio dicere putandus est." St. Matthew (9:32–34) reports elsewhere a miracle in which the possessed person is only dumb, as in St. Luke, but the reflections of the bystanders are the same as here; which suggests that he is narrating the same event, first inserted in an artificial grouping of miracles (Matt., Chaps. 8 and 9), and then repeated in its proper chronological place as an introduction to the discussion with the Pharisees.

[29] Matt. 12:25–30; Mark 3:23–27. The name which we have translated as Beelzebub is written in Greek βεελζεβούλ, and in some manuscripts βεεζεβούλ. The Vulgate has *Beelzebub* because St. Jerome thought that the reference was to the god of Accaron (4 Kings 1:2–6: *Baal* = "lord" and *Zebub* = "fly": apparently the god who protects against flies). But the origin of this word, which is not found in the Talmud or in any other Rabbinic writings, is cloaked in mystery. Cf. Billerbeck, *Kommentar,* Vol. I, pp. 631–635, and Nestle, in the *Dict. of Christ and the Gospels.* That the Jews performed exorcisms is an established fact. Cf. Josephus, *Antiq.,* VIII, ii, 4, and *Bellum,* VII, vi, 3. The

The expulsion of the devil was the sensible sign of his defeat and the fall of his empire. If the prince of this world ceases to be master in his own house, it is because someone stronger than he has overcome him and bound him. This is, therefore, the dawning of the Messianic era. But instead of drawing this conclusion, the Pharisees took Jesus for a henchman and confederate of Beelzebub, who gave him his power over the devil's forces. They had formerly given rein to their hostility in jibes, abuse, and threats of death. This time the measure is full:

"I say to you, every sin and blasphemy shall be forgiven men, but blasphemy of the Spirit shall not be forgiven. And if anyone speaks against the Son of Man, that shall be forgiven him, but if he speak against the Holy Spirit, that shall not be forgiven him either in this world or in the world to come."[30]

To blaspheme Christ, says St. Jerome, to refuse to recognize him as God because he presents himself under the appearance of a mere mortal, is a sin which circumstances may excuse or lessen. But to know with certainty that something comes from God, and through envy to attribute to Satan the manifest work of the Holy Spirit, that is a crime which shall not be forgiven in this world or in the next.

---

plant they used, mentioned above on p. 238 was a species of rue (πήγανον). Cf. the dissertation of Billerbeck on Jewish demonology, *Kommentar,* Vol. IV, pp. 527–535.

[30] Mark 3:28–29; Matt. 12:31–32. St. Luke says, in another context (12:10): "Whoever says a word against the Son of Man will be forgiven; but he that blasphemes against the Holy Spirit will not be forgiven."

The problem of the sin against the Holy Spirit would require a long dissertation, and this is not the place for it. Knabenbauer has published one in *R.B.,* 1892, pp. 161–170, in which he gives the various opinions. The two principal ones are the following:

a) The sin against the Holy Spirit is *unpardonable* in that it *will never actually be forgiven,* either because God foresees that those who have committed it will never repent, or because he decides not to give the efficacious graces needed for conversion. This is Knabenbauer's opinion, and he cites in favor of this view Jansenius of Ghent, St. Jerome, St. Athanasius, and even St. Augustine.

b) The sin against the Holy Spirit is unpardonable *not absolutely but from its own nature* (St. Cyril of Alexandria, St. Thomas, Maldonatus, Bellarmine, etc.). This is the opinion which we follow. "Dicitur irremissibile secundum suam naturam, in quantum excludit ea per quae fit remissio peccatorum; per hoc tamen praecluditur via remittendi et sanandi omnipotentiae et misericordiae Dei, per quam aliquando tales quasi miraculose spiritualiter sanantur" (St. Thomas, *Summa,* II, ii, q. 14, a. 3).

Absolutely speaking, every sin can be forgiven; for, though repentance is an essential condition of pardon, there is no heart, no matter how hardened, that cannot be softened by grace. On the other hand, we know that death is the term of the time of trial, and a man is never to be despaired of as long as there remains in him the breath of life. This is why certain authors reduce the sin against the Holy Spirit to final impenitence or something equivalent: despair, presumption, obduracy at the last hour. But the Evangelists give another idea, if we read them carefully. The sin against the Holy Spirit is the sin of the Scribes and Pharisees who knowingly and deliberately attribute the manifest workings of grace to the source of evil, and while they watch Jesus liberating demoniacs, say: "It is by the power of Beelzebub that he casts out devils. He is possessed by an unclean spirit." In saying this, they certainly blaspheme against the Son of Man, but, what is more serious for them, they blaspheme against the Spirit of grace and holiness.

All other sins are lessened to some extent by error, ignorance, surprise, inadvertence, or even passion; but the sin of pure malice is inexcusable. It is peculiarly the sin of Satan, the more so because, instead of being buried in the depths of one's conscience, it is propagated by scandal, thus blocking the expansion of the kingdom of God.

It is not absolutely irremissible — for the power and mercy of God have no limits — but of its nature it is irremissible, because, as far as in it lies, it precludes all access to divine grace. The sin of pure malice is the only one that creates in us something like a second nature, of which man cannot possibly strip himself except by a miracle of grace:

"If the tree is good, the fruit shall be good. If the tree is evil, the fruit shall be evil. The quality of a tree is known by its fruit. Race of vipers, evil as you are, how can you say anything good? From the abundance of the heart the mouth speaks. The good man brings forth good things from the good treasure (of his heart); the wicked man brings forth only evil things from his evil treasure."[31]

---

[31] Matt. 12:33–35. The allegory of the good or bad tree has already appeared in the Sermon on the Mount (Matt. 7:16–20; Luke 6:43–45); it may have been repeated in the Saviour's teaching.

To the axiom that the mouth speaks from the abundance of the heart, as in the case of the blasphemers of the Spirit of God, the Evangelist attaches another saying which was undoubtedly pronounced on another occasion and before another audience. "I say to you, that every idle word that men shall speak, they shall render an account of it on the day of judgment. For by thy words shalt thou be justified (declared innocent)."[32] "The idle word," says St. Jerome, "is the useless word, useless to him that says it and to him that hears it." If we must render an account before the tribunal of God of every vain and thoughtless word, what of slander, calumny, and blasphemy against the Holy Spirit!

Jesus has finished with the Scribes and Pharisees, and now his relatives come back upon the stage. It is not at all certain that this is a continuation of the same drama, or even that we are dealing with the same actors. However, since St. Mark has been careful to bring together the two episodes about the Saviour's relatives, it is likely that he intended to establish more than a purely literary connection between them.[33]

During the violent altercation of which we have just spoken,

---

[32] Matt. 12:36–37. "Otiosum verbum est, quod sine utilitate loquentis dicitur et audientis" (St. Jerome). — "Omnis otiosi, id est inepti et inutilis dicti, ratio est Deo reddenda" (St. Hilary). Both, in their commentaries on St. Matthew.

[33] Mark 3:31–35 (cf. Matt. 12:46–50; Luke 8:19–21). The reasons for separating the two incidents are serious but not decisive.

a) Those who wish to check Jesus are "those with him, his own" (οἱ παρ' αὐτοῦ); those who wait at the door are "his mother, his brethren." The difference in expression seems to indicate a partial difference of persons involved.

b) "Those with him" are motivated by selfish and not very friendly intentions; there is nothing similar insinuated about the second group.

c) So rapid is the sequence of events that it would seem at first glance that everything narrated here happened on the same day; however, upon examination it becomes apparent that the episodes must have been separated by a considerable interval: (1) the choice of the Apostles (3:15–19); (2) the entry into the house surrounded by the crowd (3:20–21); (3) the incursion of his own when they hear of it (3:21–22); (4) the conflict with the Scribes from Jerusalem (3:23–30); (5) the arrival of his mother and his brethren, who wait at the door (3:31–35); (6) the Day of Parables (4:1). This accumulation of events without any indications of time seems somewhat artificial, for the Day of Parables did not follow so closely after the choice of the Apostles. It may be that the episodes in No. 5 and No. 2 are brought together in the same context because the relatives of Jesus are involved in both of them. What makes this likely is that the incident told in No. 4 is reported in Luke 11:14–16, and the episode in No. 5, in Luke 8:19–21, in an entirely different context.

the relatives of Jesus stayed at the door, either because they were waiting for the end of the dispute, or because they found it impossible to get inside on account of the crowd. Whatever their purpose, the presence of Mary in their midst is easily explained at a time when her Son's life seemed to be in danger. Someone said to Jesus: "Thy mother and thy brethren are outside waiting for thee." And Jesus answered: "Who are my mother and my brethren?" Then, looking around on the audience encircling him and pointing to his disciples, he added: "Behold my mother and my brethren; for whoever does the will of my Father who is in heaven, he is my brother and my sister and my mother."

Jesus, the perfect model of filial piety does not disown his mother. God forbid! Nor does he disown those united to him by family ties. He wishes only to show that there is a spiritual relationship nobler and more intimate than relationship according to the flesh. All the Fathers who have commented on this passage are unanimous in affirming this. Let us hear St. Ambrose: "The Teacher of morals, in order to serve as an example to his disciples, is the first to practice what he commands them; he himself submits to the rule he has formulated. He does not reject the duties of filial piety, but he knows that he owes more to the service of his Father than to affection for his Mother. He has no hurtful disdain for his kin, but he wishes to teach that spiritual ties are more sacred than the ties of the body."[34]

He who unites himself to God by faith and love becomes the son of God and the brother of Jesus Christ. If by zeal he engenders Christ in the souls of others, he becomes "the mother of Christ," as St. Jerome makes bold to say. And if he engenders Christ in himself, he becomes one with him. It is no longer he that lives, but Christ lives in him.[35] Such is the new birth and the new kinship created by the Gospel.

---

[34] St. Ambrose, *In Lucam.* 8:21 (ML, XV, 1678). St. Jerome (ML, XXVI, 84): "Isti sunt mater mea qui me quotidie in credentium animis generant." St. Hilary (ML, IX, 993) and St. John Chrysostom (MG, LVII, 466) have something similar.

[35] Gal. 2:20; 4:19; "Filioli mei, quos iterum *parturio,* donec *formetur Christus* in vobis." It is the spiritual childbirth of which St. Jerome speaks.

CHAPTER V

The Day of Parables

1. The Gospel Parable

SHORTLY after his open break with the Scribes and Pharisees, Jesus came forth from his house in Capharnaum and went to the lakeshore. The inhabitants of the city followed him thither, and before long so great a crowd had gathered that he entered a boat with his Apostles and pushed off somewhat from the shore. All that side of the lake is intersected with shallow coves surrounded by semicircular banks. In the Valley of Seven Fountains, west of Capharnaum, there are no less than four or five such retreats within the space of half a league. Experience proves that from the center of these inlets the voice can carry without effort to all points of the opposite bank; and the lake is usually so calm in these little bays that there is hardly a ripple on the surface of the water.

Seated at the prow of a large fishing boat, Jesus could thus take in his whole audience at a single glance. From this improvised rostrum he began to speak in parables.[1] It was not the first time he had used parabolic language; yet on that famous

---

[1] Matt. 13:1–3; Mark 4:1–3; Luke 8:4. St. Luke does not describe the scene; the other two describe it in almost the same terms, but here St. Matthew is, by exception, the more circumstantial and the more precise: "On that day, Jesus went out of the house (where he was living in Capharnaum) and sat down by the sea. And great multitudes gathered around him, so that he entered a boat and sat there, and the whole multitude stayed on the beach. And he spoke many things to them in parables." Before the Day of Parables, he had often used *parabolic language* (cf. Mark 2:17–22; 3:23; Luke 4:23; 5:36) but not the parable properly speaking, as we define it here.

day he inaugurated a kind of teaching that surprised the multitudes and even the Apostles.

The Gospel parable is a fictional story based on customs or the facts of everyday life. Its purpose is to bring to light some moral lesson or dogmatic truth. As we see, the parable is akin to the fable. They are two types of the same literary form. But, whereas the fable plays with the unreal, making animals think and fish talk, and whereas it teaches mere human prudence and everyday wisdom, the Gospel parable keeps close to probabilities and always has a religious purpose.[2] The fable can, of course, be a vehicle of supernatural teaching — there are two examples of it in the Old Testament[3] — but Jesus did not choose this less noble type of expression, because the parable as he conceived it was adapted to all kinds of hearers.

The parable is sister to the allegory, as the comparison is to the metaphor. The parable is merely a comparison developed in the form of a story, and the allegory is nothing but a succession of connected metaphors. Every comparison can be turned into a metaphor, and every metaphor can be turned into a comparison, by expressing or suppressing, as the case may be, the statement of the relationship of similarity which both of them contain; but the result would often be an obscure metaphor or a lifeless comparison. In the comparison and the parable two similar objects are brought side by side; in the metaphor and the allegory the object spoken of is hidden behind another which is like it. Hence to understand a parable it is enough to place it beside the object of comparison and to recognize the analogies; but to understand an allegory, all the metaphors need to be translated and changed into the proper terms that correspond to them.

If the Gospel parables were all pure parables — like the Good Samaritan, for example — there would be no difficulty in explaining them; but many of them, particularly those dealing with the kingdom of God, contain a mixture of allegorical features, and the interpreter must determine the number of these and their purport. The difficulty is increased by the fact that the parables are often introduced by some inexact formula such as: "The

---

[2] Cf. Note K: *The Gospel Parables.*

[3] Judg. 9:8–21; 4 Kings 14:9–10 [Note of J. C.].

kingdom of God is like a sower, a king, a merchant," and so forth. It is not precisely the kingdom of God that has this likeness; rather the parable in its entirety represents some aspect of the kingdom of God, and the meaning is this: things in the kingdom of God are proportionately like those in the parable. Another source of obscurity peculiar to the parables of the kingdom is that, as has been pointed out, in Hebrew, Greek, and Latin the same word is used for *reign, royalty,* and *kingdom.*

The Old Testament, which is so rich in allegories, gives but little space to parables properly so called. In fact, the parable scarcely appears in any writings before the Christian era, for the Similitudes of the Book of Henoch are of an altogether different kind. The Rabbis of the second century affected a mixed type derived from the parable and the allegory; but no literature has anything equal to the Gospel parables in their simplicity, naturalness, freshness, nobility, and charm.[4]

So far the Saviour had been concerned chiefly with conveying to his hearers the spiritual nature of the kingdom of God, which is entered only by a sincere conversion. In the Sermon on the Mount, he had emphasized the interior dispositions which assure its conquest. The parables on the lake are to define its intimate nature.

The ideas which the Jews had formed of the kingdom of God were as vague and fluctuating as their longings and dreams. Almost all of Christ's contemporaries were waiting for a national king of the line of David, who should deliver Israel, exterminate her oppressors, and inaugurate in Jerusalem an era of justice, peace, and unalloyed happiness. Had not the prophets spoken of another David, who would one day rule over all nations, with Sion as his capital? It was difficult before the event to draw the line of demarcation between what was symbolic and what literal in these dithyrambic promises. To prepare the hearts of men for the kingdom, some sort of flashing intervention of heaven was

[4] It is said that Rabbi Meir knew three thousand fables in which the fox was the hero. When he died, the parable was said to have died with him, no doubt to indicate that he had a monopoly. Cf. Fiebig, *Altjüdische Gleichnisse und die Gleichnisse Jesu,* 1904; Buzy, *Introduction aux paraboles évangéliques,* 1912, pp. 135–169.

counted upon, which would change the face of things and by a dramatic stroke introduce a magical state of affairs from which all evil would be excluded. Even the wise Philo allowed himself to be lulled by these dreams. He wrote: "If the children of Israel are in captivity at the ends of the earth, they will escape their stunned masters on that day . . . they will be drawn together to the same place under the guidance of an apparition which will be more divine than human, and visible only to them. . . . They will rebuild their ruined cities, and cultivate their wasted fields, and the long sterile soil will recover for them its pristine richness. . . . Everything will be suddenly transformed," and the happiness enjoyed by their fathers will be as nothing in comparison with their own beatitude.[5] The writers of the Jewish Apocalypses cannot find words vivid enough to describe this idyllic felicity. Under their plans the kingdom of the Messias takes on a strong resemblance to Mohammed's paradise. One of their chief errors was the failure to distinguish clearly enough the two phases of the kingdom of God; they put it either entirely on earth, or entirely in heaven. Either way, the role of the Messias was distorted, and God's part in it was sometimes so predominant as to leave no room at all for the action of his envoy.[6]

It is against these and similar errors that the parables of the kingdom are directed. The Sower throws into relief the universal destination of the Gospel and the need of human co-operation to establish it in souls. The Darnel and the Net show the two phases of the kingdom and the mixture of good and evil in the first phase. The Mustard Seed, the Leaven, and the Growing Grain depict the more or less slow and hidden, but infallible and marvelous growth of the kingdom of God. The Treasure and the Pearl teach that no price is too high to purchase the happiness of being admitted to it.

---

[5] Philo, *De execrationibus,* 8–9 (Mangey, II, 435–436); *De praemiis et poenis,* 15–20 (Mangey, II, 421–428).

[6] "If dangerous animals will cease to harm, if peace is to reign all over the world at the time of the Messias as in the time of Adam, if nature is to be at last fruitful in unheard of miracles, it is because the innocence of Messianic times is to surpass that of Eden. This picture had been outlined in ancient prophecy with symbolic import (e.g., in Isa. 11:6–10). In the Apocalypses it is grotesquely exaggerated and surcharged with the desires of crass realism" (Lagrange, *Judaisme avant J.-C.,* 1931, pp. 77–78).

It is unlikely that all these parables were given on the same day. As is his wont, St. Matthew gathers them into one chapter, but St. Luke puts in this place only the parable of the Sower. The statements of the Saviour and of the Evangelists on the purpose, the frequency, and the failure of the parables are better understood, if this type of preaching was spread over a certain length of time. However the scene described by the three Synoptics is not a mere literary fiction, and there certainly was a Day of Parables.

2. The Parables of the Kingdom

(1) The Sower; (2) The Darnel; (3) The Net; (4) The Mustard Seed and the Leaven; (5) The Growing Grain; (6) The Treasure and the Pearl.

Seated in his boat, in the center of the natural semicircle of the shore crowded with his audience, Jesus asks for silence by the simple word, "Hear!" Then, without any other preamble and without even announcing the subject of his discourse, he begins with these words:

"Behold the sower went forth to sow. And while he was sowing, a part of the grain fell along the wayside and the birds came and ate it up. Another part fell on rocky ground, where there was not much soil, and shot up immediately; but because the roots were not deep, it dried up quickly under the heat of the sun. Another part fell among thorns which grew up and choked it. But other grains fell on good soil, and brought forth fruit: thirty, or sixty, or a hundred-fold, He that has ears to hear, let him hear!"[7]

In other countries, Jesus might have mentioned other causes of infecundity: prolonged dry spells, late frosts, heavy destructive rains, hailstorms. Those he picks out would not fit the plains of the Beauce region or the valley of the Nile, but they were well adapted to the land of Palestine.

---

[7] Mark 4:1–9; Matt. 13:1–9; Luke 8:4–8. Though briefer, St. Luke offers two interesting details. The grain that falls along the road is eaten by the birds and *crushed under the feet of the passer-by*. That which falls on stony ground dries up *for lack of moisture*. Otherwise the differences are slight. In St. Luke, all the grain that falls on good soil is multiplied *a hundredfold;* St. Mark has an *ascending* gradation of fecundity (thirty, sixty, a hundredfold), and St. Matthew a descending gradation (a hundred, sixty, thirty).

When, after the first autumn rains, usually in November, a cursory plowing has more or less loosened up the soil, the farmer begins his sowing. Although he scatters seed with a sparing hand, some grains always fall on the paths lining or crossing the fields. This grain is lost beyond recovery, for if, by a miracle, it is not trampled on by the passer-by, it will not escape the greedy fledglings and wild pigeons. The sparrows particularly are so voracious that they can often be seen flying around the sower and snatching the grain before it reaches the ground.

Though not as stony as the plain of Judea, the Galilean hills are sometimes only a thin layer of humus pierced by black basalt or gray limestone. On this shallow ground the seed grows quickly, but because it has no roots it soon dries up in the midday sun.

There is still another danger always to be feared. Among the flora of Palestine are many thorny plants; briars and brambles are designated by some twenty words which are not synonyms. The most redoubtable scourge of the farmer is a huge thistle which a light plow is powerless to root out. Cut down to the level of the soil or destroyed by fire, it grows back worse than before, choking the plants in its vicinity before they mature.

In good soil, on the other hand, the seed multiplies as abundantly as anyone could wish. Although, owing to the primitive methods of the fellahs and the lack of fertilizer, the present yield of grain in Palestine is scarcely more than twelve or thirteen times the amount of seed planted, the fields that are well cultivated yield much more. At all events, the question in the Gospel is not the total yield of the crop, but the fruit of this or that grain. Hence it is not necessary to characterize this feature as hyperbole. Modern travelers in Syria as well as Egypt have often counted more than a hundred grains on the same ear, and have verified that several ears come from a single grain.[8]

[8] "It is not rare to find five or six ears grow from one grain of wheat or barley" even today (Biever, *Conférences de Saint-Etienne,* 1911, p. 274). A trial sowing at Seven Fountains (*Et Tabghah*) in well-prepared soil produced fifty times more than was sowed (*ibid.,* p. 275). The hundredfold harvested by Isaac (Gen. 26:12) could be nothing more than a round number or hyperbole, but Varro (*De re rustica,* I, 44) mentions places in Italy and Africa where the wheat produced a hundred to one. According to Herodotus (i, 193), Babylon was so fertile that it yielded 200 and even 300 to one in the best years. Pliny (*Hist. Nat.,* XVIII, xxi, 1) says that Augustus was given an ear that carried 400 grains, and that Nero received a culm divided into 360 stalks from the same grain. *Vix credibile!*

The story, therefore, was perfectly clear to the dwellers around the Lake of Tiberias. The one obscurity is this, that Jesus — purposely no doubt, and to force his hearers to question him — failed to give the key to the story by indicating the term of comparison. As soon, therefore, as the Apostles were alone with him, they did not fail to ask him what it meant. He answered them: "If you do not understand this parable, how will you understand the others?" for there are others that are not as simple. He is not reproaching them; it is his vivid way of making them understand that they are not sufficient unto themselves and that in such matters they would be mistaken to rely on their own natural cleverness.

The Sower is Christ, the seed the Gospel. The soil is the soul of the hearers. These words are enough to explain all. The Sower remains in the background; all attention is concentrated on the effects which the Gospel produces in souls more or less disposed to receive it. The seed, which is in itself fruitful, is often made sterile by the nature of the soil; thus the word of the Gospel is rendered unfertile on account of the inadequate dispositions of those that hear it. And just as the grain sometimes does not grow, and sometimes grows but does not last, or lasts but bears no fruit, so the word of God sometimes does not go so far as to produce faith, sometimes produces only a short-lived faith, and sometimes a faith that lasts but is inoperative. And just as the grain of wheat yields more or less, according to the varying richness of the soil, so the word of God is more or less fruitful according to the more or less active co-operation which the hearers give. This is the meaning of the parable, but the Saviour gives to his explanation a more concrete and less pedantic turn:

"The Sower sows the word. The grains that fall along the wayside are they that hear the word but do not understand it; Satan straightway comes and tears out the word sown in their souls.

"The grains that fell on rocky ground are they that hear the word and receive it with joy, but not having it rooted in them-

---

But, if the newspapers can be believed, a farmer of Saône-et-Loire reaped from three grains of wheat 84 ears which had altogether 3140 grains! (*Echo de Paris*, Nov. 28, 1926). Take it with due reserve! The point of the parable, however, is not so much the fecundity of the grain as the fertility of the soil.

selves, they have no resistance; when trials and persecutions come, they are straightway scandalized.

"The grains that fell among thorns are they that have heard the word; but the cares of the world, the deceitfulness of riches, and other passions choke the word, and it remains unfruitful.

"And the grains sown on good earth are they that hear the word, and receiving it (in their hearts) produce fruit; the one thirty-fold, the second sixty-fold, and the third a hundred-fold."[9]

The word of God is always rich in life and energy, but there are many external causes that destroy its natural fruitfulness. Jesus enumerates three of them, encountered most frequently in Palestine. They are enough for him to present in symbol the three states of soul which most frequently paralyze the action of the divine word.

There are indifferent or surfeited souls who lend to the word only a distracted attention, or listen to it only as one listens to music falling pleasantly on the ear. This word does not penetrate; it stays on the surface; the most insignificant matter effaces it from the memory.

Others hear the word with interest, joy, and admiration, because they find it beautiful, consoling, sublime; but they do not dream of making it the rule of their lives. Characters without depth and stability, the truth skims the surface of their minds without disturbing their wills. If they experience any feelings, they are "languishing affections, feeble imitations of true feelings, desires ever sterile and unfruitful which are dispelled in an instant."[10] The slightest trial obliterates these superficial impressions, as the sun in one day withers the plant that has no roots.

Those who not only esteem the word and cultivate and love it, but also try to put it into practice, give more promise. But un-

---

[9] Mark 4:14–20; Matt. 13:19–23; Luke 8:11–15. In all three accounts, especially in St. Mark, there is a certain negligence of style. It does not interfere with the thought and has not been reproduced in our translation. Instead of saying as the exact explanation of the parable would require, "the road, the stony soil, the thorny ground on which the good seed falls represent such and such hearers," they say, "that which fell in the road, on stony soil, on thorny ground are those, etc." A purist may be shocked at such carelessness; but usage allows us to say "to sow a field" or "to sow wheat"; and the fecundity depends both on the soil and the seed. They are interconnected, and this justifies the transition from one to the other.

[10] Bossuet, *Sermon sur la prédication,* third point.

fortunately they would reconcile the spirit of the world and the spirit of God, Belial and Jesus Christ. Their soul lies open to every suggestion from the outside. The love of pleasure, luxury, and human glory stifles their good desires. They are flowers that never bear fruit, or bear fruit that never ripens.

The application could be varied, all within the limits of the parable. But we should go no further, for fear of changing the parable into an allegory. It would be vain, for example, to try to find out what is the meaning of the road or the birds of the air or the rocky ground or the burning sun or the brambles and thorns. These are comparisons and not metaphors. Interpreters once saw in the different yield of the seed — thirty, sixty, or a hundred each — married people, widows, and virgins; or the simple faithful, religious, and martyrs; but this is to go too far beyond the literal sense, the only sense that Jesus intended to teach us here.

The parable of the Darnel continues that of the Sower and completes it.

"The kingdom of heaven is like a man who had sowed good seed in his field. While people were asleep, the enemy came to sow darnel amid the wheat. When the blade shot up and brought forth an ear, the darnel also appeared and the servants came to the owner of the field and said, 'Didst thou not sow good seed in thy field? Whence comes it then that there is darnel?' He answered, 'An enemy has done this.' 'Wilt thou that we go,' they said to him, 'and gather it up?' 'No,' he answered, 'for fear that in gathering up the darnel you tear up also the wheat. Let them grow together until the harvest. Then I shall say to the harvesters: First gather up the darnel and bind it into bundles and throw it into the fire, but gather the wheat into my barn.' "[11]

---

[11] Matt. 13:23–30 and 13:36–43. This parable and its explanation are proper to St. Matthew. The darnel (in Arabic *zawan,* in Greek ζιζάνιον), *zizania,* is the *lolium temulentum* of the botanists. The French word *ivraie* comes from the low Latin *ebriaca,* since the darnel or tare produces symptoms like those of intoxication (*ivresse*). It is one of the *graminaceae* growing in fields sown with wheat and ripening at the same time as the wheat. The Jews looked upon it as a degenerate grain, and the Arabs took it to be a wheat that was bewitched. Biever (*Conférences de Saint-Etienne,* 1911, pp. 279–280) thus describes the sorting: "Since the wheat ordinarily reaches a height greater than that of the tares, the peasants cut the grain with their sickles above the tares so that the

Darnel is a plant that usually grows between harvests and ripens at the same time as the cereals with which it grows. Its grain is poisonous to men and herbivorous beasts, possessing toxic properties that bring on vertigo and nausea and have won for it the nickname of "drunkard's plant." It is a fierce plague for the farmer, because it can scarcely be distinguished from the wheat by the most experienced eye until it develops the ear. Then it is easily recognized by its thinner stalk and smaller fruit, but it is too late to remedy the evil, because its roots are so entwined with the roots of the wheat that any attempt to root it up entails the risk of tearing up the wheat. It is better to wait until the harvest time, when the sorting is easier. This is what the master recommends to his servants. The darnel will be bound into sheafs, and it will be prudent to throw them into the fire to prevent the seed from scattering and infesting the field again.

It is surprising that the Apostles did not immediately grasp the meaning of a parable which seems so simple to us today. The reason is that there is here a greater admixture of allegory than in the preceding, and hence there was still greater need to translate the parable into plain language. Thus, as soon as they were alone with Jesus, the Apostles asked him the meaning, and he explained to them the allegorical terms. The field is the world. He who sows the good seed is the Son of Man. The sower of the darnel is Satan. The wheat and the darnel symbolize respectively the good and the bad. The harvest signifies the end of time, and the harvesters, the angels.

"At the consummation of the world, the Son of Man shall send his angels, who shall sweep from his kingdom all subjects of scandal and the workers of iniquity, and cast them into the burning furnace where there shall be weeping and gnashing of teeth. Then the just shall shine like stars in the kingdom of my Father."[12]

---

ears of the tares are not touched. . . . Ordinarily the reapers first root up the darnel gradually, as the work of the wheat-cutting goes forward, throwing the darnel into little piles behind them." Dalman (*Les Itinéraires de Jésus,* 1930, pp. 250–251) seems to say that the sorting is often done after the harvesting, when the wheat is being sifted. The grains of darnel being smaller pass through the sieve, and may be used as chicken feed; for, though they are poisonous to men and ruminants, they are harmless to fowls.

[12] Matt. 13:36–43. This explanation is given only to the disciples and at their express request.

We have, then, seven allegorical terms in all: the sower, the field, the wheat, the enemy, the darnel, the harvest, and the harvesters. All the rest — the men sleeping, the inquiry of the servants, the binding of the darnel into bundles, the good grain gathered into the barn — belongs to the category of parable and has no special application. The fire, however, into which the darnel is thrown to be burnt, is clearly symbolic of the inextinguishable fire into which the issue of Satan shall be hurled.

The three lessons which the Saviour gives us here are transparently clear. The kingdom of God as it exists here on earth will always be a mixture of good and evil. The good and evil live side by side, and it will not always be easy to tell them apart. This mingling does not come from the divine Sower, nor from the seed, which is essentially good. It comes from the darnel slyly scattered by the great enemy. It will come to an end on the last day, but deadly as it is, it must be suffered whenever there is risk of tearing up the good grain in an effort to root out the darnel.

The parable of the Net is identical in meaning with that of the Darnel, and this time Jesus interprets it as he tells it:

"Again the kingdom of heaven is like to a great net which is cast into the sea and gathers fish of all kinds. When it is full, the men drag it to land, and sit down and do the sorting; they keep the good fish in vessels, and the bad they throw away. Thus shall it be at the consummation of the world: the angels shall go forth to separate the wicked from the midst of the good and shall cast them into the burning furnace, where there shall be weeping and gnashing of teeth."[13]

[13] Matt. 13:47–50. The net mentioned here is the σαγήνη (*sagena,* from which the word *seine* is derived). The Arabs call it *jarf*. It is as much as 400 or 500 yards long, and six or seven men are needed to handle it. It is held vertical by cork floats on the top and lead weights on the bottom. When it has been stretched in a semicircle facing the bank, one or two men harness themselves to each of the extremities and draw the ropes to haul it to shore, while the others push it or watch that it does not get caught on the rocks. Masterman (*Studies in Galilee,* 1909, pp. 40–41) and Biever (*Conférences de Saint-Etienne,* 1911, pp. 302–304) give good descriptions of the maneuver.

The adjective used by St. Matthew to designate *bad* fish is σαπρός, which means specifically "rotten," "moldy," "spoilt." We do not know the Aramaic term which the Evangelist used, but σαπρός fits the catfish (*clarias macracanthus*) because of its legal uncleanness. Besides, this silurid, whose meat is considered a delicacy, seems to live in the slime at the bottom, and should taste of mud.

Fishermen on the Lake of Tiberias still use equipment which, as Egyptian and Babylonian monuments prove, existed from the earliest times. It is a net of large dimensions which they let out in a semicircle with the aid of a boat, the two ends of it resting on the bank. When the operation is completed, the men combine their efforts and pull it carefully to shore, full of whatever fish it has picked up in the process. All the fish in the Lake of Tiberias are edible; the distinction between good and bad is to be understood only from the legal viewpoint. The fish regarded by the Mosaic Law as bad were those without scales. The *silurid* or *clarias macracanthus,* popularly known as the catfish, fell into this class. When it was caught with others, it had to be thrown back into the water, since it was banned for eating. This fish, impure in the eyes of the Jews, is made the figure of the reprobates whom the angels will separate from the elect on the last day, to be cast into the dark gulf of hell.

It will have been observed that the kingdom of God is presented under two aspects. In the parable of the Darnel, it is social; in the parable of the Sower, it is individual. In the first we are members of the kingdom of God which is organized as is every social body, with a hierarchy and a government, tending to a common end, made up in its earthly phase of good and bad, but characterized in its final phase by the absolute triumph of good. In the second, the kingdom is rather the reign of God within us. It is our personal affair, as though we were all alone in the world. But though the two points of view can be separately considered, it must not be concluded that they are independent of each other, for God reigns in us only to the extent that we are members of his kingdom, which he came to found on earth.

Two pairs of parables follow. The first illustrates the growth and power of expansion of the kingdom of God, the other the incalculable happiness there is in becoming part of it, no matter what price is demanded.

"The kingdom of heaven is like to a mustard seed which a man has taken and sowed in a field. It is the smallest of all seeds; but when it has grown up it is greater than the vegetables and becomes a tree, so that birds of the air come and take shelter under its branches.

"Again, the kingdom of heaven is like unto leaven which a woman hides in three measures of flour, until the whole mass is fermented."[14]

The mustard plant, whose seeds are used in making mustard, abounds in Palestine. There are several species of it, but the one in question here is the black mustard which is cultivated in gardens. The smallness of the seed was proverbial, and to indicate "practically nothing at all" they would say, "as large as a mustard seed." All the more remarkable is the plant's vigor, because in good earth it can grow more than six feet high. It was easily the largest of the vegetables, among which it was classed because its young shoots were eaten as a salad and its seed served as a condiment. Its stalk, woody at the base, and its wide-spreading branches give it a treelike appearance and the natives call it a tree. When its fruit is ripe, legions of sparrows and goldfinches swoop down on its branches to pilfer its seeds, of which they are very fond.

If Christ had wished to present a figure of the future grandeur of the Church, he would undoubtedly have chosen other symbols: the indefinitely expanding vine stock, or the oak tree with its enormous branches, or the cedar enthroned on the mountaintop. But such was not his intention. His purpose was to emphasize the humble beginning of his work, comparable in size to the grain of mustard seed, and to show that such modest beginnings do not preclude further developments.[15] What, as a matter of fact, in profane eyes, was the Church in its cradle? Twelve Galilean fishermen gathered around a village carpenter. The first Christian assembly after the death of its Founder numbered no more than one hundred and twenty members. And yet, before the death of the last Apostle, Christianity will have overleaped the frontiers

---

[14] The mustard seed, Matt. 13:31–32; Mark 4:30–32; Luke 13:18–19 (in another context); the leaven, Matt. 13:33. On the mustard seed, cf. *Dict. de la Bible,* Vol. V, cols. 1600–1602. Mustard (*σίναπι, sinapis*) has "an extremely small seed; not absolutely the smallest of seeds, but the smallest of those that are usually planted" (*ibid.,* col. 1601). Maldonatus says the same. Actually, the poppy seed, for example, is much smaller.

[15] Loisy says well (*Les évangiles synoptiques,* I, 770), "Like the mustard-seed when it is cast into the ground, the Kingdom of God is at first almost imperceptible in its growth; but it grows, and its marvelous expansion is altogether out of proportion to its small beginnings."

of the civilized world. Three centuries of persecution are powerless to check its progress. All the powers of this world league together to block its passage, but in vain; it continues its triumphal march. What a contrast between its humble origin and its prodigious growth! The grain of mustard seed has become a tree in the shade of which all the nations of the whole world seek shelter.

As mysterious as the growth of the seed is the action of the leaven. Everywhere else in Holy Scripture, leaven is represented as an agent of corruption, but here its good or bad properties are not involved. The only feature emphasized is its energetic and rapid action, a very apt figure of the great change which the Gospel produces in souls. In Palestine, where each morning the women cook the bread for the day, a little leaven is set aside at night and mixed into the freshly kneaded dough; the amount of leaven in the mass being so negligible, the result is all the more surprising.

Something similar happens in human society when the Gospel appears. The parable of the Mustard Seed shows us the gradual expansion and unexpected progress of the Gospel. The parable of the Leaven calls our attention to the interior work of grace in regenerated souls. Christianity with its moral code and its ideals reacted forcefully on the terribly degraded pagan religions; and the spring of heroism which wells up from it over the world, far from spending itself, flows ever more abundantly. What century has been richer in miracles of holiness than our own?

Christianity's power of expansion and its interior vitality are symbolized even more expressively in a delightful parable which, contrary to his usual practice, St. Mark is alone in recording. "Thus is the kingdom of God, as if a man should cast seed in the earth. Whether he is asleep or awake, day and night the seed sprouts and grows, and he knows not how. For the earth fructifies of its own accord (producing) first the blade, then the ear, then the grain that fills out the ear. And when the fruit is ripe, the sickle is straightway put to it, for it is the time of harvest."[16]

---

[16] Mark 4:26–28. The precise meaning of the parable is controverted. Maldonatus seems to have grasped it: "Voluit Christus docere verbum Dei semel praedicatum etiam eo qui praedicavit nihil agente praeterea, per se crescere fructusque

St. Mark is right in grouping this little parable with that of the Sower; it is but another aspect of the same subject. We know already that the Sower is the Son of Man, and that the seed is the word of God. The Sower is necessarily introduced whenever there is question of a sowing, but the point of the parable is not directed toward him. The point is rather the fecundity of the Gospel seed: not the fecundity that depends upon the good or bad quality of the earth, as in the parable of the Sower, but its intrinsic fecundity, the fecundity inherent in its nature. In Palestine the cultivation of grains makes perhaps the most modest demands on the time and labor of the farmer. Once he has sown his field, in November or December, he may sleep when he cares to, and may quote the proverb: "Four months to wait, and the harvest will come." The winter rains and the spring sunshine take care of the irrigation of the soil and the ripening of the ear. It is the same with the word of the Gospel. After sowing the seed, the Sower may fade out of sight without jeopardizing his work; the good seed will grow and bring forth the fruit by its own inborn power. There are, however, two great differences between the farmer of the parable and the divine Sower. The latter knows how and why the seed he has sown in the furrow grows and fructifies. He may appear to sleep, but his invisible activity is unceasing.

This particular parable is not a pure allegory, and not all its features are symbols. The Sower, however, who is identical with the Harvester, is clearly Christ, and the considerable lapse of time between the sowing and the harvest seems to be mentioned as

---

proferre." But he gives too large a place to allegory. Buzy (*Enseignements paraboliques,* in *R.B.,* 1917, pp. 180–184) excludes the allegorical element almost entirely: "The parable is nothing but a parable" (p. 181). We believe that he is right in regarding the role of the Sower here as accessory. Fonck (*Die Parabeln des Herrn im Evangelium,* Innsbruck, 1902) and Sainz (in *R.B.,* 1916, pp. 406–422) both allow too much, perhaps, to allegory. Lagrange takes a middle position (*Saint Marc,* 4 ed., p. 117). He approves of Loisy's explanation (in the *Evangiles synoptiques,* Vol. I, p. 764) that we have here pure parable, but adds with regard to the Sower: "He has sowed and he shall reap. It is hard to believe that he is mentioned only as a detail needed for the comparison. Though needed as the sower, it would not have been necessary for him to reappear as reaper, if Jesus had wished to speak solely of the development of the Kingdom." Goebel (*The Parables of Jesus,* 1900, pp. 80–93) and Wohlenberg (*Das Evangelium des Markus,* 1910, pp. 140–142), who both relate this parable to that of the mustard seed and find exactly the same meaning in both, do not take sufficiently into account the differences in the details.

a sedative for the impatience of those who were expecting an immediate and glorious manifestation of the kingdom of God.

Two lightly sketched parables show the inestimable value of the kingdom.

"The kingdom of heaven is like to a treasure buried in a field. The man who finds it hides it again; and goes full of joy to sell all that he possesses to buy that field.

"Again, the kingdom of heaven is like to a merchant who is in search of fine pearls. When he has found one of great price, he sells all that he possesses to buy it."[17]

During periods of political or social instability, at times of civil or foreign wars, when no one is sure of tomorrow, many people bury their silver or gold to save it from pillage. After Titus took Jerusalem, the idle Roman soldiers spent their time digging out many of these hiding places in the environs of the city. When a landslide or some other accident happened to expose one of these forgotten, unclaimed treasures, Roman law — and probably also Jewish law — granted the whole to the one discovering it, provided it was on his property or in a public place. The man in the parable acts on this principle. He does not want to seize upon a treasure found in another's field, but he considers that he can have it if he gains a title to the field. Whether he is right or wrong is a matter for casuists to decide. Jesus neither approves nor blames. He makes no judgment on his act, but proposes for our imitation only the man's readiness to undergo any sacrifice to gain a priceless treasure.

The man with the pearl teaches exactly the same lesson. We can imagine one of those bric-a-brac merchants, who are so numerous

[17] Matt. 13:44–46. *The treasure* — Paulus says in the *Digesta:* "Thesaurus est vetus quaedam depositio pecuniae, cujus non exstat memoria ut jam dominum non habeat. Sic enim fit ejus qui invenerit cum non alterius sit." The finder took it with a clear conscience. Cf. Horace, *Sat.,* II, vi, 10–13. For the Jewish custom, see Billerbeck, Vol. I, p. 674.

The pearl — Pliny (Hist. Nat., IX, liv, 1) writes: "Principium culmenque omnium rerum pretio margaritae sunt." We need not take him at his word when he tells us that Cleopatra's pearl was worth ten million sestertii, and that the pearls with which Lollia Paulina was covered were worth forty million. But in modern times (in 1500), Charles the Fifth had a pearl which sold for eighty thousand ducats — almost two hundred thousand dollars; and a necklace of pearls belonging to Mme. Thiers brought, on the 15th of June, 1924, a much higher price, even considering the depreciation of the franc.

in the East, selling everything conceivable, including jewels. The one in the parable knows that his fortune is made if he can get his hands on a choice pearl. After the diamond, Pliny tells us, the pearl is the queen of jewels. The passion for beautiful pearls raged more intensely in ancient times than it does today and rose at times to frenzy. Cleopatra's pearl was said to have cost ten million sesterces. Those adorning the head and neck of Paulina, the wife of Caligula, were said to be worth four times that sum. The man in the parable, then, is looking for an unblemished pearl with all the qualities most valued by connoisseurs — limpidity, depth of luster, polish, size, perfect roundness. If he succeeds in finding it, he does not hesitate to convert all his possessions into money to make himself master of it, certain that by reselling it he will become rich. The Semites never had any idea of a just price, which was especially difficult to determine in a case like this; and we could involve the man with the pearl in the same kind of case of conscience as the man with the hidden treasure. But that is not the question. What the Saviour wishes us to learn is that the kingdom of God can never be bought at too high a price. Whether it be offered to us without any search on our part, or come as the fruit of long and laborious seeking, we should be ready to sacrifice everything to gain entrance to it. To break with the past, with our environment or families; to sever the closest bonds; to vanquish the stiffest opposition: all this requires, at times, heroic courage. The story of great converts of all ages is a proof of it.

When he had ceased speaking, Jesus said to his disciples: "Have you understood all these things?" When they said, "yes," he added: "Well then, every scribe initiated into the teaching of the kingdom of heaven is like to the master who brings forth from his storehouse things new and things old." Instructed as they are in the mysteries of the kingdom of God, it is theirs now to instruct others, teaching each one what is appropriate to his case.

3. Christ's Reason for Teaching in Parables

Obviously surprised by this new method which their Master was using, the Apostles asked him one day, "Why dost thou speak to them in parables?" Before hearing Jesus' answer, we might be tempted to answer for him, "Because it is the most popular and familiar kind of teaching, the best fitted to hold attention and impress the memory, the most appropriate for the understanding of children and simple minds, the most worthy, finally, of him who has deigned to have pity on our infirmities and stoop to our ignorance." St. Mark seems to give the reason when he writes: "He spoke to them in many such parables so far as they were able to understand him; and he did not speak to them without parables, but privately explained everything to his disciples." Is this not a way of saying that he adapted his discourses to the capacity of his hearers and clothed them in the language of parables to bring them within the reach of all? And he would have explained them to his hearers, as he explained them to his disciples, if they had taken the trouble to ask him. But the answer which the Evangelists attribute to Jesus has a different ring. In St. Luke, he says:

"To you has been given to know the mysteries of the kingdom of God; but to the rest in parables, that seeing they may not see, and hearing they may not understand." For, as St. Matthew specifies, "in them is fulfilled the prophecy of Isaias: You shall hear and shall not understand, you shall see and you shall not perceive. The heart of this people is become heavy. They have hardened their ears and closed their eyes, for fear of seeing with their eyes, and hearing with their ears and understanding in their hearts and being converted, so that I may heal them."[18]

---

[18] Matt. 13:10. And the disciples coming to him said: Why dost thou speak to them in parables?	Mark 4:10. And when he was alone, his disciples with the Twelve questioned him concerning the parables.	Luke 8:9. And his disciples asked him what the parable (of the Sower) meant.
11. He answered them: To you it has been given to know the mysteries of the kingdom of heaven; to them it has not been given.	11. And he said to them: To you has been given the mystery of the kingdom of God;	10. He said to them: To you it has been given to know the mystery of the kingdom of God.
12. For he that has, to him shall be given, and he shall abound; but he that has not, even what he has shall be taken away from him.	(25. for he that has, to him shall be given; and he that has not, even what he has shall be taken away from him.)	(18. For he that has, to him shall be given; but he that has not, even what he seems to have shall be taken away from him.)

It was not on the Day of the Parables, but quite a long time afterward, when they had learned what little fruit and efficacy the parables were having, that the Apostles asked their question. Unknowingly, they were touching upon the eternal and insoluble problem of the difference in the distribution of graces; sufficient for all, but efficacious for those only that accept them. A grace given to one at the moment when God knows that he will accept it is a greater benefit than the same grace made inefficacious by the resistance of free will. The Apostles are privileged. To them it has been given to know "the mysteries of the kingdom of God." But this favor would not have been denied others, if they had desired it and asked for it. If they have not obtained it, they have only their own stupid indifference to blame.

---

13. Wherefore I speak to them in parables, because seeing they do not see, and hearing they do not hear and do not understand. 14. And the prophecy of Isaias is fulfilled.	but to those without, all things come in parables, 12. that seeing they may not see and may not perceive, and hearing they may hear and not understand, for fear that they be converted and be forgiven.	but to the rest (I speak) in parables, that seeing they may not see, and hearing they may not understand.

a) ***The questions*** are not the same. According to St. Luke, they ask only for an explanation of the parable of the Sower; in St. Mark, they ask a general question about parables; in St. Matthew, they wish to know why Jesus speaks in parables. There is no difficulty in reconciling the three accounts, the answer elicited will naturally correspond to the way the question is put.

b) ***The answers*** are not the same: relatively easy in St. Matthew, difficult in St. Luke, more difficult in St. Mark. The *mystery* (or *mysteries*) of the kingdom is its secret, its intimate nature, which it has been granted to the disciples to learn, but not to the mass of hearers. Thus far there is no difficulty, for ordinary correspondence with grace prepares and disposes for the reception of new graces. Note that the disciples are not only the Apostles, but also listeners of good will who come to Jesus as soon as he is alone, in order to question him (Mark 4:10).

The difficulty comes from the final particles, or those that appear to be final (ὅτι, *because;* ἵνα, *in order that;* μήποτε, *for fear that, lest*). Let us eliminate the first; ὅτι in St. Matthew can mean "that" and not "because"; εἶπεν ὅτι, "he answered them (that) the mysteries, etc." and not "he answered them (because) the mysteries, etc." This idiomatic *that* should be omitted in translation.

As to the final particles ἵνα (in St. Mark and St. Luke) and μήποτε in St. Mark, there is a clear allusion to the text of Isaias which St. Matthew quotes in full, and the interpretation should be the same; either of a finality on the part of man (in μήποτε) or of a finality on the part of God (ἵνα), who, foreseeing man's obstinacy, plans to draw from it the occasion for the accomplishment of his hidden designs.

Christ's teaching is not an esoteric doctrine reserved for a few initiates, as were the Eleusian mysteries and the mysteries of Samothrace; nor is it a philosophy clouded in mist and imposing secrecy on its adherents to make it seem more venerable, like the philosophy of Pythagoras. The Apostles received the command to proclaim in the full light of day what they had heard in the shadows, and to cry from the housetops what had been whispered in their ears. Jesus never enjoined secrecy except about the glorious facts that concerned himself, or about those truths the revelation of which was premature; but that was not the case with the teaching of the kingdom of God; this was precisely his concern at this time.

It is useless to ask whether the teaching in parables was a punishment or an act of mercy. It was an act of mercy for men of good will who profited by it, and a punishment for those who through their own fault failed to do so. The reasons why the Saviour adopted this type of teaching at a certain period were many. Let us examine some of them. The extreme sensitiveness of the Roman authorities who were quick to sound the alarm at the mere mention of a Jewish kingdom had to be treated with caution. It was the accusation that Christ was aspiring to kingship that finally put an end to Pilate's long hesitations; and it was the fear of a Jewish restoration that decided Domitian to persecute the distant relatives of Jesus. Again, Jesus must avoid arousing the ardent nationalism of the Galileans, who were always ready to rise in revolt in support of any claimant to the throne of David. What happened on the evening of the first multiplication of loaves is proof that this was not an imaginary danger.

Another reason, perhaps, for teaching in parables was to separate those hearers who sought instruction from those who were drawn by mere curiosity or ill will. Actually, the two categories are neither exclusive nor definitive. The disciple of today may turn back tomorrow; the unbeliever of today may be tomorrow's believer. The line of demarcation is not concerned with the future; it is traced only for the present. But to maintain that the Saviour deliberately made himself obscure and unintelligible in order to punish the indifference, the fickleness, or the inconstancy of the multitudes seems to us utterly unreasonable. For, besides the fact that the complete change of attitude which was so noticeable among the Scribes and Pharisees was not yet clearly apparent among the mass of the people, if Jesus wished to punish them — this is St. John Chrysostom's remark — he had only to be silent, instead of propounding undecipherable enigmas. Let us put it down as a principle that his hearers could have understood him if they had wished to. St. Augustine and St. John Chrysostom, who, at first glance, differ so much in their interpretation, are at one on this point. Why then did his hearers fail to understand? One of Chrysostom's disciples, Theophylactus, tells us: "By speaking to them in parables, Jesus accommodates himself to the capacity of his audience . . . . he stimulates them to come and question him, so that by their questions they may learn what they do not know. Thus it was that he explained everything to the disciples, because they came and questioned him."

Is the parable then of its nature obscure? Yes and no. The moral parable usually is not: the mere telling of it is enough to make its lesson understood; for example, the parables of the Good Samaritan, the Pharisee and the Publican, the Importunate Friend, or the Unjust Judge. It is otherwise, however, in the case of the parables that are either wholly or partially allegorical, like the parables on the Kingdom. To us who have precise notions of the reign of God, there is in them little obscurity; but this was not true of the Jews of that time. They had not merely inexact but entirely erroneous ideas on the kingdom of God. How could they understand the parable of the Darnel, for example, if they did not ask for an explanation of it? The Apostles themselves did not — indeed, could not — understand it. What distinguishes them from the crowd is that they asked questions about it. Then they learned that the kingdom of God was not some corner of the earth, like Palestine, but the entire universe; they learned that the Sower was the Son of Man and that his completely spiritual role consisted in conquering souls, the children of the kingdom. They learned, above all, something of which the Jews were not aware, that the Messianic kingdom would be a mixture of good and bad and that the good and the evil would be separated only at the end of the world. That is what the crowds could have learned if they had wanted to, as did the Apostles, and, like the

Apostles they would have been initiated into the mysteries of the kingdom of God. Let us be careful not to reduce the whole question to this dilemma: "justice or mercy." The alternative is so far from being exclusive that most ancient and modern commentators mix the two elements in unequal doses, and, if sometimes they make one element predominate to the detriment of the other, they never completely suppress either. Practically all of them see in the parables an act of mercy joined to punishment, or a punishment tempered with mercy.[19]

---

[19] The opinions of the heads of schools of thought on the purpose of the parables are as follows:

a) St. John Chrysostom and his disciples. — "If Jesus had not wished to instruct and save them, he had but to keep silent and not speak to them in parables; but he did speak to them obscurely, to stimulate their curiosity. . . . They could have come to him and questioned him, as did his disciples; but through sluggishness and carelessness they did not care to do this" (*In Matth. hom.* xlv [or xlvi]; MG, LVIII, 473). Maldonatus says that this was the common opinion of his contemporaries. Likewise, regarding the blinding of the Jews: "They could not believe because they did not wish to believe. They were not unbelieving because Isaias had predicted it: Isaias had predicted it because they were to be unbelieving" (*In Joann. hom.* lxvii [or lxviii]; MG, LIX, 375–376).

b) St. Augustine. — On the blinding of the Jews: *Non poterant credere quia dixit Isaias: Excaecavit oculos eorum.* "Quare non potuerunt si a me quaeratur, cito respondeo: quia noluerunt. Malam quippe earum voluntatem praevidit Deus et per prophetam praenuntiavit ille cui abscondi futura non possunt" (*In Joann. tract.* liii; ML, XXXV, 1777).

With respect to the parables according to Matt. 13:15 compared with Mark 4:12: "Ubi intelligitur peccatis suis meruisse ut non intelligerent; et tamen hoc ipsum misericorditer eis factum, ut peccata sua cognoscerent et conversi veniam mererentur" (*Quaestiones xvii in Matth.,* q. xiv; ML, XXXV, 1372). A punishment for the present, a mercy for the future.

c) St. Thomas, *Summa,* III, q. xliii, a. 3; "Christus turbis quaedam loquebatur in occulto, parabolis utens ad annuntianda spiritualia mysteria, ad quae capienda *non erant idonei vel digni;* et tamen melius erat eis, vel sic sub tegumento parabolarum spiritualium doctrinam audire, quam omnino ea privari." But the *ad tertiam* offers this variation: "Turbis Dominus in parabolis loquebatur, quia *non erant digni vel idonei* nudam veritatem accipere quam discipulis exponebat."

There is something worth while in each of the three explanations and, though one may not succeed in reconciling them, they may be brought close together. Cf. among others, Durand, *Pourquoi J.-C. a-t-il parlé en paraboles?* in *Etudes,* 1906, Vol. CVII, pp. 256–271 (*i.* The demands of justice; *ii.* the dictates of prudence; *iii.* the feeling of mercy); Lagrange, *Le but des paraboles* according to the Gospel of St. Mark, in *R.B.,* 1910, pp. 5–35; Buzy, *Introduction aux paraboles évangéliques* (Paris, 1912), pp. 233–400; Prat, *Nature et but des paraboles évangéliques,* in *Etudes,* 1913, Vol. CLXXXV, pp. 198–213. Fr. Skrinjar (*Le but des paraboles sur le règne et l'économie des lumières divines d'après l'Ecriture sainte,* in *Biblica,* 1930, pp. 291–321 and 426–449; 1931, pp. 27–40) defends skillfully and with conviction the blinding purpose of the parables. On the opposite

For us Occidentals the great difficulty is with the text of Isaias, to which not only the Synoptics refer, but also St. John and St. Paul: "Go say to this people: Hear and do not understand, see and do not perceive. Harden the heart of this people, shut its ears, close its eyes." After receiving this heartbreaking order, Isaias made a supreme effort to avert its effect. And Jesus, exactly like St. Paul, recalls this text at the moment when he is multiplying his exhortations in an attempt to overcome the obstinate resistance of the Jews. The text cannot therefore express an absolute decree of the divine will to tear away from men all hope of conversion. Rather, it prophetically announces their positive blindness. The Semites do not distinguish as we do the different modalities of the first cause and the divine will. For them "to will, to desire, to order, to permit," and on the other hand "to do, to have done, to let be done, to give occasion for doing" are often expressed by the same word. In accordance, then, with this manner of speaking, inexact if you will, but familiar to the Hebrews, everything that happens, even misuse of the human will, is considered to be willed and caused by God, because he permits it when he could have prevented it. Several Fathers have remarked that God ordinarily blinds by flooding with light, and hardens by multiplying invitations which should soften hearts.[20] If man obeys the appeals from on high, it is a mercy and a gift

side, cf. Holzmeister, *Vom angeblichen Verstockungszweck der Parabeln des Herrn,* in *Biblica,* 1934, pp. 321–368, with an abundant bibliography.

[20] This was the case in the hardening of Pharaoh's heart cited in Exodus and the blinding of the Jews in St. John's Gospel. Origen, *Periarchon,* III, i, 10–11; also St. Irenaeus, *Haeres.,* IV, xxix, 1; MG, VII, 1063; "Unus et idem Deus his quidem qui non credunt, sed nullificant eum, infert caecitatem, quemadmodum sol, qui est creatura ejus, his qui propter aliquam infirmitatem oculorum non possunt contemplari lumen ejus; his autem qui credunt ei, et sequuntur eum, pleniorem et majorem illuminationem mentis praestat." The same comparison is found in St. John Chrysostom (*In Joann. hom.,* lxvii or lxviii, 2; MG, LIX, 376).

On his part, St. Augustine writes (*In Joann. tract.,* liii; ML, XXXV, 1777): "Sic excaecat sic obdurat Deus deserendo et non adjuvando, quod occulto judicio facere potest, iniquo non potest." But it must be added, as he himself adds, "Etiam hoc eorum voluntatem meruisse respondeo." It is always man himself, and never God, who takes the initiative in the blinding or hardening of hearts. St. Augustine's theory is perfectly correct from a theological viewpoint, and God can blind by withholding his graces; but in Scripture God ordinarily blinds by a multiplication of graces. God hardens Pharaoh's heart while seeking to soften it; Isaias blinds his compatriots by his passionate preaching; Jesus blinds the Jews of his time by lavishly multiplying his miracles.

of God; if he resists all appeals, he brings upon himself deserved punishments, the most immediate of which is his very refusal of grace. Scripture therefore says that God wills the hardening and the blinding, because he does not prevent it, because he provides the occasion for it by his repeated appeals, finally because he intends to order the very malice of man to a higher good. Let us, however, remember that he never hardens or blinds any except those that have begun to harden and to blind themselves through their own fault. The text of Isaias: "Go say to this people: Hear and understand not," is only a use of that figure of speech which seems to incite someone to excessive evil in order to inspire horror of it. Who with common sense would take literally the apostrophe of Agrippina to Nero, which suggests the very contrary of what it expresses:

> Go forward, O Nero! With ministers such as these,
> You will distinguish yourself by glorious exploits.
> Go forward! You have not taken such a step only to recoil, etc.

To return to the parables. Of themselves, they do not blind any more than do miracles. But parables, like miracles, may be the occasion of a blinding which God, in his wisdom, permits for good reasons. The light of the sun is always a blessing from heaven, yet, though it gives light to healthy eyes, it can also blind eyes that are diseased. This comparison is made by several of the Fathers, particularly St. Irenaeus, who makes this application: "One and the same God strikes blind the unbelievers who despise him and who rate him as nothing; but to those that believe in him and follow him, he gives a livelier and brighter spiritual light."

CHAPTER VI

New Miracles Around the Lake

1. The Gerasene Demoniac and the Calming of the Storm

After these discourses, there followed yet more striking miracles. Four of these prodigies — the calming of the storm, the freeing of the Gerasene demoniac, the cure of the woman with the hemorrhage, and the raising of Jairus' daughter from the dead — are grouped in inseparable pairs, which St. Mark links closely with the Day of Parables.

No class of miracles is more abhorrent to materialistic criticism than the casting out of devils. If, to spare oneself the need of furnishing proofs, one assumes as axiomatic that the world of spirits is a myth, one should logically hold that the belief in possession is a superstition, and that the deliverance of possessed persons is an illusion or a piece of trickery. We are told that these possessed persons were merely sick people afflicted with cerebral diseases or bizarre nervous maladies which, in the centuries of ignorance, were attributed to supernatural beings. "The pathological character of possession consists in the total or partial, continuous or intermittent, eclipse of personality. It is a particular form of insanity or mental debility, in which the consciousness of one's individuality happens to be smothered or impeded by the *idée fixe* of an outside and malevolent individuality which substitutes itself for, or is superadded to, that of the subject. Not only madness but nervous diseases in general, notably epilepsy, were considered as cases of diabolical possession."[1]

If this be true, one of three things follows: either Jesus shared in the errors of his contemporaries and believed, in good faith, that he was working expulsions, which were, in fact, only imaginary; or, more enlightened than the rest, he adapted himself to their ignorance, the better to influence them, just as a doctor pretends to believe the fancies of a sick person, the better to work on his imagination; or, finally, the confusion is due to the Evangelists, who have attributed to Jesus their own errors.

Let us not make the Evangelists more simple-minded than they were. They knew very well how to distinguish possession from sickness. Jesus *cures* the sick and *delivers* the possessed; and if, in some cases, he is said to cure the possessed, it is because in such cases the possession is complicated by some morbid affliction; for it is a remarkable fact, well established by experience, that the ordinary — we do not say essential — condition of Satan's seizure of a human being is some physical or moral debility. Just as there are people who are resistant to suggestion and hypnotism, so there are natures that are more rebellious than others to the invasion of the Evil One. As a matter of fact, diabolical possession is usually accompanied by organic or functional disturbances, either because these disorders are caused by the presence of the enemy or because they furnish a favorable field for his entry and activity.

It is undeniable that the Evangelists and Jesus himself believed in the reality of diabolical possession and obsession; but we do not rely on vocabulary to prove it. They could have spoken of lunatics, energumens, and demoniacs, without guaranteeing the meaning implied in the etymology of these words; just as we speak of someone being bewitched, petrified, moon-struck, born under a lucky or unlucky star, without believing in astrology or occult influences. But the case of the Gospels is altogether different. Jesus proclaims aloud his power to cast out devils; he delegates this power first to the Apostles, then to the seventy-two disciples; he promises the same power in the future to those that believe in him and says that he has come to "cast out" the prince of this

---

[1] Loisy, *Les évangiles synoptiques,* 1907, Vol. I, p. 452.

world. To these facts must be added Christ's positive teaching, inasmuch as "he both describes the power and tactics of the devil and explains the way to fight him, and displays in his whole Messianic labor the triumphant counterpart of the enterprise of the Evil One. This last series of texts leaves no semblance of probability to the opinion that interprets the attitude of Jesus as a deliberate accommodation to errors that were widespread at the time and which he thought harmless."[2]

Still, even for one who admits the possibility and existence of diabolical possession, its frequent occurrence in the time of Christ is somewhat surprising. Six such cases are reported in the Gospel in some detail, three of them — the Capharnaum demoniac, the lunatic at Thabor, and the Gerasene energumen — being cases of possession properly so called, the devil identifying himself with the sufferer and speaking in his name. In three others, which could be called obsessions were it not an ambiguous term, there was no absorption of the personality, and everything was reduced to a kind of inhibition, or to various molestations produced by the spirit of evil. But in addition to these particular cases, the following formula recurs as a refrain: "Jesus cured the sick and cast out devils."[3]

These phenomena seem to have been rarer in Judea and Perea; but how explain their extraordinary frequency in Galilee? Since Jesus had come to destroy the empire of the prince of this world, he must match himself against him in the lists and not only vanquish him but make his own victory undeniably evident. Now, Galilee was the first and chief battlefield. It is here that Satan before yielding is making his supreme effort, and God, without whose permission he could do nothing, gives him free rein, in order to make his defeat more evident and the triumph of Christ more striking. When the disciples returned, proud of having cast out the demon by the power of his name, he said that he "saw Satan fall, from the heights of heaven, swift as a flash of lightning." From that moment, as a matter of fact, the power of Satan was broken; the sequel but hastened his rout. In our day, in coun-

---

[2] L. De Grandmaison, *Jésus-Christ,* 1928, Vol. II, p. 347 (English transl., Vol. III, p. 135).

[3] Mark 1:34; Luke 13:32, etc. This power is delegated to the Twelve (Matt. 10:8), to the Seventy-Two (Luke 10:17), to the faithful (Mark 16:17).

tries where Christianity holds sway, his external activity is very much weakened and practically annihilated.[4]

The Day of Parables was coming to a close. Jesus, having landed with his Apostles, answered their questions and resolved their doubts on the meaning, nature, and use of parabolic language. Since the crowd was besieging the house to which they had retreated, giving them not a moment's respite, they decided to hurry back on board without any preparations. When this was seen, other boats that happened to be there cast off their moorings, and accompanied them toward the eastern shore.

Worn out with fatigue, Jesus sat down in the stern, near the helmsman, not on the rough rug fixed to the rower's bench, but on a movable cushion which was reserved for passengers of distinction. Resting his head on this pillow, he was soon sleeping a profound sleep. Nothing indicated that the crossing would be difficult until a squall abruptly beat down upon them. The Lake of Tiberias is famous for these sudden gusts of wind. It lies more than 600 feet below sea level at the bottom of a perpetually torrid basin, and is surrounded by high hills and dominated on the north by the Great Hermon, which lifts its snowy summit almost 9000 feet in the air. These differences of altitude and temperature quite often stir up violent wind currents, which rush down into the Jordan valley or through the deep ravines along the northern shore. Many a modern pilgrim has experienced these sudden squalls. You may set out on motionless water, smooth as a mirror, under a calm and serene sky, without enough breeze to fill a sail. Suddenly the horizon is blanketed by thick clouds and the wind begins to blow a gale. Then the boatmen's faces grow somber, their gaze becomes restless, they intone a doleful chant, and, since for fear of capsizing they must clew up the sails, they take to the oars and make for the nearest shelter.[5]

[4] J. Smit (*De daemoniacis in historia evangelica,* Rome, 1913) divides his work into two parts: I. General questions (the possibility and nature of possession, Jewish demonology, Christ's attitude toward possession). II. An exegesis of four particular cases (the demoniac of Capharnaum, the Gerasene energumen, the daughter of the Chanaanite woman, the lunatic of Thabor). We refer the reader to this monograph; cf. also the article, *Possession diabolique,* in the *Dict. apologetique de la foi Catholique,* Vol. IV, 1928, cols. 53–80.

[5] Reminiscences of a crossing in March, 1908. The storm in the Gospel was a violent gust of wind accompanied by rain (*λαῖλαψ μεγάλη ἀνέμου*, Mark 4:37; Luke 8:23) that cut the water like an earthquake (*σεισμός*, Matt. 8:24).

The waves stirred up by a wind of incredible violence were crashing against one another as if by the effect of an earthquake. Caught on the side by the squall, which was blowing in the direction of the Jordan, the boat threatened to sink, and it was very difficult to bail out the water that kept pouring in from the heavy seas. Fully aware of their danger, the Apostles still did not dare to disturb Jesus' sleep, which, in the circumstances, may have seemed to them to have in it something mysterious. Finally, however, they decided to wake him by that cry of alarm in which there was a thinly veiled tone of reproach: "Lord, we are lost, save us! Does it not concern thee to see us perishing?" In answer to their appeal, Jesus rebuked the wind and spoke to the sea as one would speak to a shrieking madman broken loose from his bonds: "Be quiet! Silence!"[6] Immediately the wind fell and there was a great calm. Turning to the Apostles, the Master said to them, "Why are you afraid? Where is your faith? Can it be that you do not yet believe?"

If they fancied that Jesus while sleeping did not know their danger and could not come to their help even in his sleep, their faith was still very imperfect. The excitement of the moment was doubtless some excuse, for fear does not reason; but their faith had to be strengthened by this test and this lesson. Does it not seem, too, that in giving the command to depart at a late hour, despite the foreknowledge of imminent danger, and in surrender-

---

About storms on the Lake of Tiberias, consult the interesting account of Biever (*Conférences de Saint-Etienne,* 1909, pp. 120–122). They rise very suddenly, "sometimes within the space of a quarter of an hour in calm weather," and their suddenness and violence are always very striking. According to Biever, however, they cause more fright than damage: "Despite the frailty of the craft that plow the lake, no serious accident has happened within the memory of man. During the seventeen years I spent there, no barque has ever foundered, and no member of a crew has ever been drowned" (*ibid.,* p. 121). It must be added that the natives never embark when storms threaten, and they have certain ways of telling their approach: the rolling of the "Big Drum" from Cape Naqura announces a strong west wind, and the "lightning from Banias" at the foot of Hermon presages a wind from the north.

[6] Joüon (*L'Evangile de N.-S. J.-C.,* 1930, p. 207) translates: "He forcefully commanded the wind, 'Be still!' and said to the sea 'Silence!'" referring σιώπα to the wind and πεφίμωσο to the sea. To justify his translation, he refers to *Biblica,* 1926, p. 439, and to *Recherches,* 1928, p. 350. An evident tautology is thus avoided. Still, πεφίμωσο (perfect imperative passive) literally means "be muzzled" (from φιμός, "muzzle") and is stronger than σιώπα, "be still," so that there is a gradation in the Greek.

ing himself up to a sleep so deep that natural causes hardly explain it, our Lord was providing a lesson for future ages? How often in the course of centuries has he renewed the miracle of Tiberias in favor of his Church! Heresy, schism, and impiety have constantly broken loose against it. All the powers of the world and of hell in unison have plotted its ruin, and he seemed to sleep. Fear not, ye men of little faith! Christ's Church has been promised immortality. He will remember her at the opportune moment; he will not be deaf to your cries of distress.

The Apostles were not alone. Some boats had followed them, and the boatmen who manned them, astonished at this miracle, said to one another: "What manner of man is this, who commands the winds and the waves and they obey him!"[7]

Upon disembarking, the Apostles were met by an extraordinary person who had seen them coming from a distance and had run down to meet them. This man had chosen as his living quarters one of the many caves cut practically everywhere into the sides of those hills, which at that time served as tombs and even now are sometimes used by the inhabitants of the country as dwellings. Completely naked and repulsive to look at, this unfortunate creature was living the life of a beast. Often he would turn his fury upon himself and gash his body with stones. In the East, lunatics and possessed persons are allowed to wander at will and live as they please; but the howlings and sudden attacks of this man had terrorized the passers-by, and several attempts had been made to chain him down. But this had to be given up, because, endowed with superhuman strength, he would quickly break his

[7] Mark 4:35–41; Luke 8:22–25; Matt. 8:23–27. St. Matthew makes the episode a part of a series of miracles that really belong to various periods; St. Luke places it *after* the Day of Parables but does not explicitly link it with that day; St. Mark does so expressly: "That same day when evening had come" (*ἐν ἐκείνῃ τῇ ἡμέρᾳ, ὀψίας γενομένης*). The departure is abrupt; they take Jesus *ut erat* (*ὡς ἦν*), "without any preparation"; they make him sit on the cushion, "the pillow" (*προσκεφάλιον*) reserved for travelers of distinction, and distinct from the heavy rug (*ὑπηρέσιον*) fixed on the rowers' bench. The variants in the dialogue between Jesus and his disciples have already been noted in the Introduction (p. 32).

The Apostles' boat, when it set out, was accompanied by other craft (Mark 4:36) and it is not said that the wind dispersed them. It would be strange to attribute to the Apostles the exclamation, "What manner of man is this, who commands the winds!"

bonds and fetters and go back again to his savage way of life.[8]

When he came near to Jesus, as though driven by an irresistible force, he prostrated himself before him, crying out with all his might: "What is there between me and thee, Jesus, son of the most high God? I adjure thee in the name of God, do not torment me!" Borrowing the tongue of the possessed man, the devil adjures Christ by one of those magical formulas that were supposed to have greatest efficacy. Thus it is not to the demoniac but to the devil himself that Jesus answers, "Go out of this man, unclean spirit!" The order was not immediately obeyed. That the miracle be made very clear, it was necessary to expose what a powerful enemy was being dealt with.

"What is thy name?" asked Jesus.

"My name is Legion, for we are many."

The legion, the principal factor in the victories of Rome and visible symbol of her hegemony, was five or six thousand strong, but the word of the Father of Lies is not an article of faith. The devil was doubtless bragging, either to impress the witnesses of the scene or because he enjoyed mystifying them, lover that he is of burlesque and buffoonery. But he was well aware that he was not deceiving Jesus. Thus he begged as a favor not to be expelled beyond the limits of this territory.

Some distance away on the side of the mountain a large herd of swine was grazing, as many as two thousand of them. They belonged either to private individuals who had banded together to cut down the expense of watching and keeping them, or else to the whole town as collective property. The raising of these

---

[8] Mark 5:1–20; Luke 8:26–39; Matt. 8:28–34. St. Matthew's account is very summary; we prefer to follow that of St. Mark, which is more circumstantial. The name of the city differs in the three Synoptics: the most probable reading in Matthew is Γαδαρηνῶν, in Mark Γερασηνῶν, and in Luke Γεργεσηνῶν. This reading is a variant due perhaps to the influence of Origen, who adopted it for reasons other than textual (cf. Lagrange, *Saint Marc,* 4 ed., 1929, pp. 132–135). There remain to be considered Gerasa (*Jerash*) and Gadara (*Umm-Qeis*). Neither of these names is possible for geographical reasons, if they are to be taken to indicate the two well-known cities of the Decapolis, for it is improbable that either one of them extended to the place where the miracle could have taken place. It may be conjectured that St. Mark, speaking of the coastal region, calls it the "country of the Gerasenes," and that the translator of St. Matthew thought he should substitute "country of the Gadarenes" because Gadara was much nearer to the lake than Gerasa. But the textual question is, so far, without a definite answer.

animals was forbidden in Palestine, but here we are in half-pagan territory where the Jews were probably in the minority. Such, then, was the asylum that the devils craved, if they must leave their victim. Nor could any refuge have been more appropriate for these unclean spirits. No sooner were they given the permission they had asked than they passed into the bodies of these animals. The swine, seized with terror and panic, went tumbling en masse down the side of the mountain, and, unable to stop their headlong rush in time, hurled themselves into the sea and perished by drowning. Their bewildered custodians fled in every direction and carried the news of the disaster to the neighboring hamlets and as far as the town, which seems to have been a considerable distance away.

The Evangelists do not mention the name of the city, nor do they indicate the precise place of this dramatic drowning. They tell us only that the scene was on the eastern bank, in the country of the Gadarenes, or the Gerasenes, or the Gergesenes, for the texts vary in the three Synoptics, and it is impossible to say with certainty what the true reading is. In any case, it cannot have been Gadara, an important town of the Decapolis situated six or seven miles south of the lake, and separated from it by the Hieromax (*Yarmûk*) river,[9] which is as wide as the Jordan. Nor may we place it at Gerasa (*Jerash*), the famous capital of the Decapolis, which is at least thirty-six miles from the lake as the crow flies. Origen knew a place in the district called Gergesa — his influence is probably responsible for the reading *Gergesenes* passing into a great number of manuscripts.[10]

In default of documentary proofs, a direct inspection of the places themselves furnishes us with enough clues. The hills on the east side of the lake are always several hundred yards away from the bank. At only one point, directly across from Magdala, there is a promontory which breaks off from the mountain and advances toward the lake, almost reaching the level of the water. If the swine were feeding on the top or on the sides of this

---

[9] Or perhaps *Hieromices;* cf. Schürer, *Geschichte*, Vol. II, p. 158.

[10] Smit, who treats the question of place at considerable length (*De daemoniacis* [Rome, 1913], pp. 241–354) cites all the pertinent texts and documents on the subject.

steep spur and stumbled down its slope, carried by their furious onrush, they would have fallen into the water because of their momentum. To the south, this promontory borders on a valley (the Wady-es-Semak) through which runs a torrent that is dry three quarters of the year, where it would be easy to land. The hill is tunneled with caves which, after being used as tombs, could have given asylum to the demoniac. It is true that in the immediate vicinity there are no considerable ancient ruins to be seen, but the city may well have been some distance away from the place where the miracle took place, and the Evangelists do not say that it was an important place. Besides, this region has been little explored, and how many cities of considerable importance have left not the slightest trace of their existence on the soil of Palestine! Of no country may it be more aptly said that the very ruins have perished.[11]

Informed by the swineherds of what had happened, the inhabitants of the town ran to the spot. Imagine their astonishment and fright at the sight of the demoniac, whose madness they had all experienced or at least known to be genuine, tranquilly seated at Jesus' feet and, a fact which seems to have struck them even more, decently clothed in borrowed garments. The prospect of being finally delivered from a curse that had terrorized the whole countryside was partial compensation in their eyes for the loss of their swine. Besides, since it was obviously a miracle, they were afraid of estranging a wonder-worker endowed with such power.

---

[11] Many years ago, Guérin proposed this identification (*Galilée,* 1880, Vol. I, p. 323): "A sort of promontory stretches in a continuous slope to within some yards of the beach; it is very probable that from this place the herd of swine cast themselves into the sea." Masterman (*Studies in Galilee,* 1909, p. 33) and Dalman (*Orte und Wege,* 1924, p. 193 [English transl. by Levertoff, 1935, p. 178]) are of the same opinion. Lagrange once characterized this as an *impossible* opinion (*R.B.,* 1905, p. 519), but after a new inspection accepted it without difficulty (*Jésus-Christ,* 1928, p. 185; *Saint Marc,* 4 ed., p. 136).

The distance between the foot of the mountain and the sea is variously estimated. Guérin says *some paces;* Masterman, *forty feet* (twelve meters); Lagrange, *thirty meters;* Dalman, *forty*. This last estimate is exaggerated, but everything depends upon the starting point selected, because the slope runs down almost to the water's edge.

What is the real name of the place? It is variously pronounced Kursi, Kersi, Kersa, Gersa. Of course vowels, especially in proper names, are indistinct in the mouth of an Arab. The Moslems, who in June, 1928, carried me around the lake, called the promontory *Jebel el-Khanazir* (Mountain of the Swine), probably because they had heard it called so by the Christians.

Hence, desiring him to be neither a neighbor nor an enemy, they courteously asked Jesus to leave their country. He agreed to do so.

When the demoniac saw Jesus climbing back into the boat, moved by a feeling of gratitude, or perhaps by fear of falling again into the power of Satan unless he himself should leave this infested region, he begged Jesus to take him with him, but the favor was refused. "Go home to thy people and tell them what the Lord in his mercy has done for thee." Reassured by these words the man hurried to go and publish in his native city and the rest of the Decapolis what had happened to him, thus preparing the country for the preaching of Jesus, who would be returning to that territory a few months later.

There are some sentimental souls who pity the lot of the poor swine condemned to death en masse, or sympathize with their owners in the loss of their unlawful gain. By what right, they ask, was this loss inflicted on them? Would it not have been better for Jesus, if he could, to prevent the devil from doing this injury? It would be as much to the point to ask why God permits physical evil, sickness, epidemics, fires, earthquakes, floods, and all the scourges that lay waste the world and afflict humanity. God has his purposes, of which we are in ignorance; and Jesus could have had his: it is not ours to judge. Perhaps the Saviour wished to prove the reality of diabolical possession and to make the malice of the devil apparent to the senses and something to be feared. Does not such an important moral teaching make up for the loss of dumb animals? And do the owners of the swine deserve so much sympathy when they were violating the Law of Moses which forbade the raising of swine in any part of Palestine?

2. The Daughter of Jairus and the Woman With the Issue of Blood

When the Apostles' boat touched the western bank, the crowd, impatient to see Jesus again, ran down to meet him. Among them was one of the heads of the synagogue, a man called Jairus, whose twelve-year-old daughter was at death's door.[12] He must

[12] Mark 5:21–43; Luke 8:40–56; Matt. 9:18–26. For a comparison of the three accounts, see the Introduction, pp. 22–24.

have been among those present at the miracles which had as their scene the synagogue of Capharnaum. As soon as he learned of the Wonder-Worker's return, he went to meet him and, falling at his feet, said, "Lord, my daughter is about to die. Come, please, and lay thy hands on her and restore to her life and health." He had doubtless seen Jesus lay his hands on sick people whom he had cured, and thought this gesture necessary.

He who had not been proof against the tears of the weeping widow of Naim could not be insensible to the earnest pleas of a father threatened with the loss of his only child. Without losing a minute, Jesus followed him, accompanied by his Apostles and a great number of curiosity seekers. The farther he went, the more dense the crowd became and it was only with great difficulty that he made his way through the waves of this human flood.

Lost in the confused mass was a woman who had been afflicted for twelve years with an obstinate flux of blood which had defied the skill of physicians and the power of all remedies. Yet there was no lack of specifics prescribed for this disease. According to the Rabbis, it would have been enough for her to carry on her person the ashes of an ostrich egg, wrapped up in a piece of cotton or wool, according to the season, or else to eat a grain of barley found in the dung of a white mule, to be perfectly cured at the end of three days. It is doubtful whether recipes of this kind and others like them — of which there was quite a list[13] — would have been very effective. The poor woman had vainly tried every sort of remedy and spent her whole fortune without experiencing the slightest relief. On the contrary, her affliction had only become worse. Tired of the struggle she had finally lost hope in all medicines. She could still turn to the one about whom such marvels were being told, but she recoiled before the shame of exposing publicly an illness that was generally regarded as the price of misconduct. It was possible also that she was afraid of seeing the empty space that would form around her, for her malady was one of those which brought legal uncleanness by ordinary contact.

Here, then, is the expedient that she devised. Imagining that a kind of magical power emanated from the body of Jesus, she

---

[13] It can be found in Billerbeck, *Kommentar,* Vol. I, p. 520.

said to herself, "If I succeed only in touching the hem of his garment, I shall be made safe." The difficulty was in reaching him. She slipped furtively through the dense crowd that was slowing down the pace of the procession, and, gaining ground little by little, she finally grasped from behind one of the multicolored tassels which Jesus, like all pious Jews of his time, wore on the four corners of his robe. Instantly she realized that she was completely cured. Whence came to her this certainty? Those miraculously cured at Lourdes could answer that question. They have been sure of the recovery of their health even before they had any experience of it.

Jesus, however, cast a searching look upon the crowd as though seeking a culprit, and asked: "Who touched my cloak?" He knew; because the miracle was not accomplished without his knowing it. But he asked because he wished to evoke from the woman an avowal, however painful, which would be a proof of her lively faith as well as a lesson to the bystanders. But the crowd was so dense and the question seemed so strange even to the Apostles that they could not help showing their astonishment. "Lord, the crowd is pressing upon thee from every side, and dost thou ask, 'Who touched me?' " There was a moment of silence and Jesus stood motionless. He seemed to be searching for a certain face.

Then, seeing that she was discovered, and determined moreover to make the humiliating admission which she now considered a debt of gratitude, the woman threw herself trembling at his feet and publicly proclaimed her whole sad story; how she had suffered for twelve years from this incurable malady, and how she had been instantly cured by touching Jesus' cloak. As he dismissed her, the Saviour said to her: "My daughter, thy faith has saved thee. Be cured of thy infirmity." Here was a double favor; health of body and of soul.

An ancient legend, somewhat doubtful, however, in its origin, tells us that the woman's name was Veronica, identifying her with the woman who wiped the bloodstained face of Jesus on Calvary. An old author, once wrongly believed to be St. Ambrose, even took her to be Martha, the sister of Lazarus. God alone knows her real name; but her simple faith, and the eulogy which it won for her from Jesus, have made her memory imperishable.

The procession started on its way again, but in the interval the daughter of Jairus had died. When they came near the house, the sad news was brought to the chief of the synagogue. "Thy daughter has just died. Why trouble the Master further?" Evidently these people considered the Wonder-Worker powerful enough to restore health to the sick, but not to recall the dead to life. The father, however, was hoping against hope. To console him, Jesus said to him: "Fear not. Only believe; nothing is impossible to faith."

They found the house of death already invaded by the mourners and flute players who were a necessary accompaniment of all Jewish funerals. As the end approached, friends and neighbors flocked in, and as soon as death was established they began singing their plaintive traditional chants. The house was full of disorder and uproar. Jesus imposed silence on all saying: "Why this uproar and this weeping? Weep not. The child is not dead but sleeps." Those present, knowing how things stood, ridiculed him, not knowing that he was comparing this momentary death to a peaceful sleep which was soon to be broken by a sudden awakening.

Indifferent to their mockery, Jesus pushed back the crowd and made the mourners and flute players leave the house, keeping with him only the father and the mother of the dead girl, and Peter, James, and John, the three privileged souls who would be allowed to contemplate his glory on Thabor and his agony in the Garden of Olives.

Together they went to the upper room where the little body was lying in state. Jesus took the child by the hand, saying the words which Mark later heard from Peter's mouth and has preserved for us in the original, *Talitha, kumi,* which mean "Maiden, arise." The dead child immediately arose and began to walk. The Saviour told her parents, too distracted with joy to think of anything else, to give their daughter something to eat, because her cure was so complete that she was beginning to feel hungry. Then he left them, charging them that they say nothing to anyone about it. The miracle could not remain hidden, but it was not for them to publish it, as though seeking credit for a favor for which they were not responsible.

When Jesus had come out of Jairus' house, two blind men who had heard that he was there began to follow him crying out: "Son of David, have mercy on us!" It was quite common for the afflicted to travel together to offer one another mutual aid and company. Even today it is not rare to see pairs of blind men traveling about in Palestinian towns arm in arm. Those in the Gospel cried out in vain, because Jesus went his way without seeming to hear them. By putting their faith to the test, he wished to make them more worthy of the favor he had in store for them and had already granted in his heart. And so they went with him to the house to which he was going. Then it was that he asked them: "Do you believe that I can do this that you desire?" "Yes, Lord," they answered with one voice. Jesus placed his fingers upon their eyes, saying: "Be it done to you according to your faith," and their eyes were immediately opened to the light.

Without giving them time to thank him, Jesus added in a serious tone: "Take care that no one learn of it." Now, their blindness was a matter of public notoriety, and their sudden cure could not fail to become known. They had been seen to enter the house blind and to come out having sight. How could anything so patent remain hidden? Perhaps, after all, Christ's injunction concerned less the cure itself than the words they had made use of in making their plea. The title "Son of David" was Messianic, and it was still too early to spread it about in public, especially among Galileans who were imbued with very crude notions about the Messias.

At all events, the blind men did not believe that they were bound by this prohibition, and they published far and wide what had happened to them. Protestants in general are scandalized at their disobedience, but the Fathers of the Church do not hesitate to absolve them on the ground of their simplicity and their good faith.[14]

[14] Matt. 9:27–31. The prohibition against talking about the miracle is expressed by a very strong word ἐνεβριμήθη (he enjoined upon them), the fundamental meaning of which is "to groan, to rumble." According to Maldonatus, all the ancient authors (St. John Chrysostom, St. Jerome, etc.) excuse them for publishing the miracle everywhere (διεφήμισαν), despite the express injunction, which perhaps referred to something other than the miracle itself. St. Jerome writes (ML, XXVI, 59): "Dominus, propter humilitatem fugiens jactantiae gloriam, hoc praeceperat, et illi, propter memoriam gratiae, non possunt tacere beneficium."

CHAPTER VII

Supreme Effort in Galilee

1. Martyrdom of John the Baptist

THREE episodes in the Galilean ministry are so closely linked in the Gospel narrative that they must belong to the same period: the martyrdom of John the Baptist, the mission of the Twelve, and the visit to Nazareth. But the martyrdom of John is a little before the other two.[1]

We have seen how Herod Antipas, exasperated by the rebukes of the man who had reproached him for his doubly incestuous marriage to Herodias, his niece and sister-in-law, had John thrown into the dungeons of Machaerus. The tetrarch wanted to stifle the importunate voice, though he was unwilling to go as far as assassination. He was not bloody by nature, and though he had no more respect for human life than the other tyrants of his time, he would at least have recoiled before the thought of a wanton murder, especially since he knew of the veneration which surrounded the Baptist, and realized how unpopular the author of his death would be. Besides, whether he liked it or not, he was himself undergoing the influence of his prisoner. He enjoyed seeing

[1] St. Mark narrates the facts in the following order: (*a*) the visit to Nazareth (6:1–6); (*b*) the mission of the Twelve (6:7–13); (*c*) Herod's fears (6:14–16); (*d*) the martyrdom of John (6:17–29); (*e*) the return of the Twelve (6:30). But it is plain that John's martyrdom occurred earlier, for it is reported on the occasion of the fears of Herod's taking Jesus for John risen from the dead. On the other hand, the Twelve accompany Jesus to Nazareth but do not stay there. Indeed, the three Synoptics give the impression that Jesus is alone at Nazareth and that he is still alone when he leaves that town (Mark 6:6). It is therefore probable that upon arriving at Nazareth, or when he was about to arrive there, he sent the Twelve on their mission.

him and talking with him, perhaps in the hope of cajoling him by these marks of respect; but he always came away from these conversations full of perplexities and superstitious fears.

John had a much more implacable enemy in the court of Antipas than the weak and voluptuous tetrarch. For a long time now, Herodias had been trying to have him done away with; she was waiting only for the favorable occasion. A word of St. Mark takes us behind the scenes of this intrigue and throws light on the pyschology of the actors. Herodias was the one who was pulling all the strings in the drama and preparing its denouement. The chief obstacle to overcome was the indecisive character of the tetrarch and his wish to humor public opinion, which he knew to be favorable to his captive.[2]

A favorable occasion presented itself in the spring of the year 28, when Antipas was celebrating his birthday.[3] Ever since he had repudiated the daughter of King Aretas in order to marry his own niece Herodias, he could expect reprisals from the Nabateans, and it may have been to guard his southern frontier, which was exposed to surprise attack, that he was then residing at Machaerus. This reputedly impregnable fortress was at the same time a splendid castle, with a view reaching far out over the mountains of Judea, and particularly pleasant in the springtime for anyone coming from the furnace of Tiberias. The tetrarch had summoned all his nobility thither, having a mind to treat them to a truly royal feast.

Modern custom imposes a certain restraint on banqueters, but the official banquets of those days almost always degenerated into orgies. When Herod's guests were made giddy by the fumes of a heady wine and were incapable of savoring any pleasure except the grossest sensations, the dancers were introduced. As a general

[2] St. Matthew mentions the mission of the Twelve by anticipation (10:1 — 11:1). St. Luke, who has similarly anticipated the imprisonment of John (3:19–20) and had not mentioned his martyrdom, also mentions the visit of Jesus to Nazareth by anticipation.

[3] He was celebrating his *γενέσια*. Sovereigns were accustomed to celebrate the anniversary of their birth, and the anniversary of their accession to the throne; but in several inscriptions the first in contrast with the second is called *γενέσια*. *Γενέθλια* was also used. Cf. the very erudite note in Schürer, *Geschichte*, Vol. I, pp. 441–442.

rule, they were women of evil life and of the lowest station, whose reputations were beyond further loss; but this year a princess of the royal blood, the stepdaughter of the incestuous tetrarch, stepped into the role of the courtesans. Her name was Salome, and she was at the time hardly more than fifteen or sixteen years old. Shameless as we may suppose the women of that house to have been, the girl would never have taken the initiative in an act of this kind at her age, if she had not been inspired and urged by her mother.

Salome charmed all present, more perhaps by her provocative attitudes than by her youthful grace, so much so that Antipas, not knowing too well what he was saying, promised to give her whatever she asked for, be it half of his kingdom; and he accompanied his promise by one of those oaths which the Jews of the time used with such prodigal folly.

The girl immediately went out to tell her mother what had happened, for her mother, like the other women of the court, was not present at a banquet at which the men surrendered themselves to every sort of license. The news was no surprise to Herodias; it was what she was waiting for. "Ask," she said without hesitation, "that they bring thee upon a dish the head of John the Baptist." Salome returned to the banquet hall and presented her strange request. "I will that thou give me forthwith upon a plate the head of John the Baptist."

Shocked out of his torpor and drunkenness by this startling request, Herod hesitated to answer. He saw now the foolhardiness of his promise, and he was greatly dismayed. But his regret had come too late. He had given his word, the word of a king — the tetrarch was very fond of hearing that title — and all the guests had their eyes fixed upon him, curious to see how it all would end. Accordingly he ordered one of his bodyguards, who in Oriental courts filled the office of executioners, to go and fetch the head of the Baptist. The prison at Machaerus was part of the palace, and they did not have long to wait. The henchman soon returned with the bloody trophy; the tetrarch offered it to the girl, and she in turn gave it to her mother. St. Jerome tells us that Herodias, transported with joy and fury, pierced the tongue of the Baptist with a bodkin. The incident of Fulvia piercing the tongue of Cicero may have given rise to this legend, but the drama of Machaerus is horrible enough without surcharging it with apocryphal details.[4]

The implacable hatred of Herodias, the precocious perversity of Salome, the vacillating character of the tetrarch and his superstitious fidelity to an impious oath, the servile and stupid indifference of the courtiers all conspired to consummate the crime and to make the Precursor the last of the martyrs of the Old Law on the threshold of the New. John's still numerous disciples carried away his remains and buried them with honors. No one could dispute the body with them. The vengeance of Herodias was sated, and perhaps the weak tetrarch believed that thus he was offering to his victim a sort of posthumous reparation.

The martyrdom of the Baptist did not go unpunished. Aretas, king of the Nabateans, outraged by the affront to his daughter, after a war of skirmishes and surprise attacks finally inflicted upon Herod a bloody defeat which might have turned into a catastrophe had not Rome intervened. Herod's contemporaries saw it as a punishment from heaven for the assassination of a man who was hearkened to as a prophet and venerated as a saint. The divine vengeance did not stop there. After the death of the Emperor Tiberius, Caligula had conferred the royal power on Agrippa the First, the brother of Herodias. Jealous of his nephew and driven on by his ambitious concubine, Antipas asked for the same favor, but in vain. Instead of a crown he received a decree of exile. He was banished to a city of Gaul, called *Lugdunum*, probably *Lugdunum Convenarum* (Saint Bertrand de Comminges today), then a rather important town not far from the Spanish border. There he died unknown and forgotten by all. The haughty Herodias, in a characteristic burst of pride, chose to share the exile of her accomplice whose evil genius she had been.[5]

---

[4] St. Jerome, *Apol. adv. Rufin.*, iii, 42; ML, XXIII, 488.

[5] Josephus (*Antiq.*, XVIII, v, 2): "It seemed to many that God Himself had brought about the destruction of Herod's army and had justly punished him for putting to death John who was called the Baptist." Josephus says that Antipas was exiled to Lugdunum in Gaul (*Antiq.*, XVIII, vii, 2: Λούγδουνον, πόλιν τῆς Γαλλίας), but he also says (*Bellum*, II, ix, 6) that he died in Spain. However, *Lugdunum Convenarum* was not far from Spain. The same Josephus tells us that the daughter of Herodias was called Salome, and that she married

The daughter of Herodias soon married her uncle, Philip the Tetrarch, some forty years older than herself. Philip died in the year 34, and the young dancer of Machaerus married another near relative, called Aristobulus: marriages between blood relations were almost the rule in the family of the Herods. The active part Salome took in the murder of John assures her a gloomy niche in history and the fantasies of modern dramatists shall never succeed in exonerating her memory.

2. The Mission of the Twelve

John's disciples brought the sad news to Jesus when he was about to send his disciples out to preach in the villages of Galilee. Diligent witnesses of his actions and his miracles, depositories of his teaching, initiates in his apostolic methods, the Twelve were able henceforth to try their own strength and to learn to fly with their own wings.

Hence Jesus took them aside and, after giving them the most ample powers, sent them out two by two and commissioned them to exhort men to penance and to announce the coming of the kingdom of God. Emissaries of the synagogue usually had a companion on their journey as a confidant of their thoughts, a witness of their activities, and a safeguard of their good conduct; and this custom seems to have been adopted by the early Church. Peter and John were sent out together to Samaria to strengthen the neophytes; Silas and Jude were dispatched as delegates to promulgate to the Christian communities of Syria and Cilicia the decrees of the Apostolic assembly; Paul and Barnabas were charged with carrying to Jerusalem the alms of the community of Antioch, and later to defend there the rights of the Gentiles. We know that St. Paul was always faithful to this practice, not only because, to his mind, it provided mutual help, but also because it was a protection for the good name of which he was so jealous. The Twelve were therefore sent two by two, and perhaps St. Matthew gives the basis for guessing the order: Peter and Andrew, James and John, Philip and Bartholomew, Thomas and

---

in succession her great-uncle Philip the Tetrarch (who died in 34) and her cousin Aristobulus, the son of Herod, king of Chalcis, who was the brother of Herodias (*Antiq.*, XVIII, v, 4).

Matthew, James and Jude, Simon Zelotes and Judas the traitor, of whose disloyalty there had not yet been any hint.[6] These are the instructions Jesus gave to them before leaving them:

"Go not in the direction of the Gentiles and enter not into the cities of the Samaritans, but go rather to the lost sheep of the house of Israel. Proclaim everywhere on your journey that the kingdom of Heaven is near.

"Heal the sick, raise the dead, cleanse the lepers, cast out devils; what you have freely received, freely give.

"Take not gold nor silver nor small coins in your girdles, nor wallet for the journey, nor two tunics, nor shoes, nor a staff, for the laborer has a right to his maintenance.

"In whatever village or town you enter inform yourselves who is worthy to shelter you and stay with him until you leave. On entering into the house, wish it peace; and if the house be worthy of it, your peace shall descend upon it; if not, it shall return to you.

"If a town or a house refuses to receive you and listen to your words, leave it and shake off (against it) the dust from your feet. Amen, I say to you, on the day of judgment Sodom and Gomorrah shall be less severely treated than that town.

"Behold, I send you forth as sheep into the midst of wolves; be, therefore, prudent as serpents and guileless as doves."[7]

First of all, the Saviour assigns to the Apostles the field of their apostolate and traces for them a summary of the program of their preaching. Let them not go among the Gentiles and the Samaritans, for it is not yet the turn of pagans and foreigners. The Jews as heirs of the divine promises enjoy, as far as the Gospel is concerned, a right of priority which it is proper to respect, and which St. Paul, the Apostle of the Gentiles, will

---

[6] Matt. 10:2–4. In St. Matthew's list, the Apostles sent on the mission are grouped in pairs, each pair of names being joined by the conjunction *and*.

[7] Matt. 10:5–16; Mark 6:7–11; Luke 9:2–5. In St. Mark and St. Luke (who follows Mark step by step), the discourse is very much abbreviated. They reduce it to the three following recommendations: (1) to take nothing special for the journey; (2) not to change lodgings; (3) to shake the dust from their feet against an unbelieving town. St. Luke (10:3–11), in the discourse given later to the seventy-two disciples, inserts several items placed by St. Matthew in the discourse to the Apostles. On his own part, St. Matthew adds to the discourse a prediction of persecutions which seems to have been given in another set of circumstances.

always respect. The Twelve are to announce to the Jews whom they meet on their journey that the kingdom of God is at hand. It is an invitation to the repentance which disposes hearts for the reception of the Gospel.

As ambassadors of Christ, the Apostles sent out on their mission are fortified with the amplest powers to cure the sick, to cleanse lepers, to expel devils, and to raise the dead. These *charismata* are not given to them for their own personal advantage; gratuitous by nature, they are to be used gratuitously in the service of their neighbor.

Being absolutely disinterested, the Apostles should be free from all earthly concern. They are not to take provisions for their journey, nor any kind of viaticum, nor gold nor silver nor small coins. Nor are they to take two tunics nor footwear nor even a staff. It is unlikely that Jesus forbade the Apostles the use of a staff if they needed one for their journey, or that he forbade the sandals that all travelers, rich or poor, usually wore on the rocky paths of Palestine. That is why St. Mark allows the staff and sandals which St. Matthew seems to forbid. We must admit, then, either that the staff and the sandals do not mean the same thing in the two Gospels, or that St. Matthew reproduces the letter of Jesus' discourse and St. Mark keeps its spirit. That kind of staff would be forbidden, for example, which pilgrims of the time used for carrying their light bundles, as they still do today, and the footwear denied them would be those held in reserve for appearing with greater decency before persons of quality. Surely no one would accept St. Augustine's solution. He thought that the staff St. Matthew forbade was a material object, and the staff St. Mark allowed is the apostolic authority of which the staff is the emblem.[8]

---

[8] St. Matthew says (10:9–10): "*Procure not* (μὴ κτήσησθε) gold . . . nor wallet for the journey, nor two tunics, nor *shoes*, nor a *staff* (μηδὲ ὑποδήματα, μηδὲ ῥάβδον)." St. Mark says: "*Carry nothing for the journey* (μηδὲν αἴρωσιν) *save a staff;* no bread, nor wallet, nor money in your girdles; but go shod with sandals (σανδάλια), and do not wear two tunics." The shades of meaning are to be noted:

a) St. Matthew says, μὴ κτήσησθε, "do not procure"; κτάομαι has the extended meaning "to possess," but in its proper sense it means "to acquire," "to procure" something that one has not. St. Mark and St. Luke say, "do not take," "do not carry."

b) St. Matthew forbids *shoes* (ὑποδήματα); St. Mark allows *sandals* (σανδάλια). The words are different; the objects indicated may also be different.

In any case, the precept imposed on the Twelve does not touch their successors or imitators unto the end of time, for the conditions are different. The Apostles were sent on a temporary mission among their fellow countrymen to whom hospitality was a sacred duty and who would allow them to lack nothing. They will have to admit this on the day when the Lord will ask them, "When I sent you without a purse or wallet or shoes did you need anything?" The purpose of the prohibition imposed on the Twelve was to teach them confidence in God and also to inculcate a lesson too often forgotten by those whom it concerns: that the beneficiaries of the Gospel have the duty of contributing to the support of the apostolic worker, for the minister of the altar should live by the altar.

The Apostles will go across the world as sheep among wolves. To escape hostile intrigue and avoid suspicions and calumnies they need the prudence of the serpent as well as the guilelessness of the dove, which is often the best and the surest qualification. Let them then be careful of what they do and what they say. Before knocking at a door for hospitality let them carefully find out

---

c) All three formulate the prohibitions εἰς τὴν ὁδόν, "for the journey," or "in view of the journey"; but St. Matthew and St. Luke forbid the staff that St. Mark allows, noting that it is the *only* exception (εἰ μὴ ῥάβδον μόνον); for the sandals on the feet are not *carried*.

St. Augustine writes with regard to the staff (*De consensu evang.,* II, 30, n. 74; ML, XXXIV, 1111): "Potuit sic breviter dici: *Nihil necessariorum vobiscum feratis, nec virgam, nisi virgam tantum;* ut illud *nec virgam* intelligatur nec minimas quidem res; quod vero adjunctum est *nisi virgam tantum* intelligatur quia per potestatem a Domino acceptam, quae virgae nomine significata est, etiam quae non portantur non deerunt." This is oversubtle: would the Apostles have been able to decipher this enigma, incapable as they were of understanding things which were much simpler?

Fr. Power (*Biblica,* IV, 1923, pp. 241–266) proposes another solution. The shepherds in Palestine carry two staffs: an *iron-shod* staff like a club, which hangs from their girdles and is used as a defensive weapon; and a *long, hooked staff,* a crook, used to lead back their fractious goats and sheep. Jesus forbade them to take a club, but allowed the crook, and thus St. Matthew and St. Mark are in agreement.

Without having recourse to any such subtleties, we believe the meaning to be: "Procure nothing in view of the journey (St. Matthew), and carry nothing for the journey (St. Mark and St. Luke), except what is *indispensable:* neither a spare tunic, nor a mendicant's wallet, nor shoes nor a traveler's staff for carrying bundles; but you may have sandals which everyone wears and carry a staff in your hand, *if you need it* for the journey." The Evangelists suppose that we have common sense.

whether the family that is to receive them has a good name. Once installed there, they are not to look for another domicile. Should they leave they would offend their hosts and open themselves to the accusation of fickleness and inconstancy, and perhaps to an even less enviable charge.

If any place rebuffs them or refuses to hear them, they will shake upon it the dust from their feet, to indicate by this symbolic gesture that they disclaim all responsibility and are leaving the faithless city to its lot. We shall later see Paul and Barnabas doing this very thing to the unbelieving Jews of Antioch in Pisidia. Paul will tell the blasphemous Jews of Corinth, as he shakes his garments, "Let your blood be on your own heads! As for me, I am innocent of it; henceforth I go to the Gentiles."

The Apostles carried out the Lord's commands exactly. "They exhorted men to penance, they cast out devils and anointed the sick with oil and healed them."[9] What was the meaning of this anointing? The Jews used anointings with oil to soothe pain and to dress wounds, but they also knew that it was not a panacea for all physical ills. Since, before healing the sick, the Saviour had the practice of using gestures as well as words, in order to arouse the faith of the sufferer, he undoubtedly suggested this rite to them to accustom them little by little to the efficacious action of the Sacraments, which he was to institute later on. This rite was not yet Extreme Unction. The Apostles were not yet priests, and therefore they were not qualified to administer that Sacrament; nor were the sick fit subjects to receive it, since they had not received Baptism. This anointing was a kind of prelude to the

[9] Mark 6:13: ἤλειφον ἐλαίῳ πολλοὺς . . . καὶ ἐθεράπευον. The use of the imperfect indicates customary action, but there is no connection between the two acts of anointing and healing. Maldonatus vigorously defends the sacramental character of this anointing and almost censures those who hold the opposite opinion on the ground that they are favoring the heretics. "Ubi sacramentum est, si hic non est? Aut cur hic non, si alibi est?" One may answer him that there is a Sacrament where there is an external rite performed by a qualified minister and producing *ex opere operato* the grace that it signifies; and such is not the case here. The contrary opinion maintained by Bellarmine has become the commoner opinion today. According to Bellarmine, the anointing performed by the Apostles was *adumbratio quaedam sacramenti futuri,* and according to the Council of Trent (Sess. XIV, Chap. i), the Sacrament of Extreme Unction is only *insinuatum* here; and that is the exact word.

Sacramental rite; just as the baptism conferred by the Apostles during the lifetime of Jesus was a prelude to Christian Baptism.

3. The Visit of Jesus to Nazareth

While the Apostles were traveling through the Galilean countryside, Jesus went once more to visit the humble village where he had grown up under Mary's eyes and lived the life of a laborer at Joseph's side.[10] He betook himself there from Capharnaum, after he had raised the daughter of Jairus from the dead. The Apostles had accompanied him at the start, but he soon left them on the road in order to visit without escort or display his fellow townspeople to whom he was about to make an urgent and last appeal. The first two Evangelists record this episode in concise and almost identical terms; St. Luke narrates it in more detail, but he places it at the beginning of the Galilean ministry, even before the call of the four great Apostles. But it is easy to see that he here abandons the chronological order, since he refers to many miracles performed at Capharnaum although as yet he has spoken neither of Capharnaum nor of miracles. All told, his account has too many points in common with that of the other Synoptics not to refer to the same event; and the event itself is not the sort to happen twice with the same characteristic circumstances. Most authors since St. Augustine are of this opinion, and Maldonatus goes so far as to say that any other seems impossible. Those, however, who hold the contrary opinion, would perhaps be right, had Jesus' visit to Nazareth been as brief as is generally supposed.

---

[10] Matt. 13:53–58; Mark 6:1–6; Luke 4:16–30. St. Luke's account follows immediately after the baptism and the temptation, but the allusion in Verse 23 shows that this is too soon. St. Matthew dates the episode after the Day of Parables by a formula of transition which can have no chronological value; St. Mark is more precise: "Leaving that place (Capharnaum, where he had raised the daughter of Jairus from the dead), he came into his own country."

The identity of the three accounts, which is regarded by Maldonatus as evident, is unhesitatingly accepted by St. John Chrysostom (MG, LVIII, 187–188) and by St. Augustine, who studies the question *ex professo* (ML, XXXIV, 1120–1122). There are, however, several authors who hold that there were two visits, one reported by St. Luke, the other by St. Mark and St. Matthew. Knabenbauer, Fillion, etc., maintain this, and, among Protestants, Godet, Edersheim, and Plummer.

Like all places of any importance, Nazareth had a synagogue, but it was doubtless not a large enough town for three meetings a week — on Monday, Thursday, and Saturday. The Nazarenes were almost all artisans or farmers, and could therefore gather in the synagogue only on feast days and the Sabbath. Then only could the Saviour hope to reach his compatriots, since they were too absorbed in their daily labors the rest of the time.

We do not know to the last detail the regulations of the Sabbatical liturgy in the time of Christ, for the historian Josephus is almost silent on the point, and Philo's pompous descriptions are designed rather for literary effect than for accuracy. On the other hand, the ritual recorded in the Mishnah at the end of the second century had had time to evolve since the dispersion of the Jews, and the perfect uniformity it implies is more a matter of theory than practice. Yet we can say without fear of error that at this time the long ceremony on the Sabbath already comprised essentially three parts: prayer, reading of the Bible, and moral instructions.[11]

They began with the *Shema'*, which was a profession of religious faith made up of three passages from the Pentateuch, in which the oneness of God was avowed together with Israel's obligation to acknowledge it. All adult Jews of free station were obliged to repeat this formula at least twice a day, but in the public recitation in the synagogue it was encompassed by certain doxologies to heighten its solemnity. After the *Shema'* came the prayer par excellence (*Tephillah*), the *Eighteen Benedictions* which everybody, men, women, and slaves, had to say at least three times a day. The *Tephillah* underwent various modifications in the course of time, and was enriched later with a special *benediction* directed against the Christians; but in substance it is anterior to Christianity. The whole assembly recited the *Shema'* together, everyone knowing it by heart; but it was enough to say *amen* to the benedictions of the *Tephillah*, which was recited by the officiating minister.

[11] Cf. Billerbeck, *Kommentar,* Vol. IV, 1928, on the Sabbath service in the synagogue (pp. 153–188), on the *Shema'* (pp. 189–207), and on the "Eighteen Blessings" (pp. 208–249); or Schürer, *Geschichte,* 4 ed., Vol. II, pp. 497–544. The classic work on the liturgy in general is by Elbogen, *Der jüdische Gottesdienst in seiner geschichtlichen Entwicklung* (Leipzig, 1913); there is also an excellent sketch in Bonsirven, *Sur les ruines du Temple* (Paris, 1928), pp. 220–226.

The prayer was followed by reading from the Holy Books. First of all the Torah was read in Hebrew, out of respect for the original text, though Hebrew was not understood by very many; it was then translated into the vernacular; into Aramaic in the synagogues of Palestine, and into Greek in those of the Diaspora. The Pentateuch was thus read in its entirety, either in the course of a single year, or in a cycle of three or three and a half years, depending on the locality and the period. The Talmud is full of minute regulations about the reading and interpretation of the Torah, many of which doubtless remained in the realm of theory. Greater latitude was allowed to the one who read the prophecies, and it would seem that he was free to choose the passage he wished to read and also to pass from one context to another.

The most striking feature of the liturgical service is that none of the functions seems to have been vested in any particular minister. The only exception was the final benediction, which was the exclusive prerogative of the priests, if one was to be found in the assembly. All other offices — the prayer, the reading, and the sermon — could be filled by any Israelite, provided that he was decently clothed and was recognized by the local authorities as capable of the task. It was the head of the synagogue that passed judgment on the capability of the various officiants, choosing them in advance, or approving of them on the spot. The meetings of the Christian communities in the beginning, before a stationary hierarchy was established, give us some idea of the freedom of procedure. At Corinth, for example, all the men were thought capable of improvising exhortations and prayers under the impulse of inspiration. It must be added, however, that at the time when St. Paul wrote to the Church of Corinth, it was at most four or five years old, and that it was born in the synagogue, from which it may have borrowed some customs when it was transferred to the house of Titus Justus.

On the first Sabbath after his arrival at Nazareth, in accordance with his former practice, Jesus went to the synagogue. Curious eyes were immediately turned on him, for it had been a year since they had seen him. On the floor of the synagogue, fronting toward the entrance, there was a kind of stage where the principal personages of the place sat facing the people.

Behind them was a chest for the sacred books, and on one side a pulpit or ambo for the reader of the Law and the Prophets. On other occasions, Jesus had modestly kept his place in the midst of the crowd as a young and unknown artisan; but now his name was famous throughout Palestine, and his fellow townsmen, though taking little interest in his work, were proud of him, because his renown reflected on themselves. He was probably invited to ascend the platform and to comment on the Prophets. We know that in later times the one who read the selection from the Prophets was charged with conducting the ritual, but it is doubtful whether this custom prevailed at the beginning of the first century.

When the time came to read and comment upon the Prophets, Jesus received from the hands of the *ḥazzan* or minister of the synagogue the book of Isaias, and either by design or providential chance opened to these words:

> The spirit of Yahweh is upon me,
> for Yahweh has consecrated me with anointing:
> He has sent me to bring the good news,
> to heal the contrite hearts,
> to proclaim to the captives liberty,
> and to the prisoners deliverance;
> to proclaim a day of grace of Yahweh,
> and a day of vengeance for our God.[12]

When he had finished, he rolled up the volume again, gave it back to the *ḥazzan,* and reseated himself, since the one giving the explanation to the people assumed this posture.

We do not know what was the content of his discourse. St. Luke sums it up in one line: "Today is fulfilled the prophecy which you have just now heard." What it must have been may be judged from the impression produced upon the audience, who with eyes fixed upon him did not grow weary listening to him. The inspiration of his tone, the strength and nobility and charm of his words drew from all the exclamation: "Never has man spoken as he!" Their astonishment was increased when they reflected that he had not attended the schools of the Scribes. They asked themselves in wonderment: "Whence comes to him this knowledge, and who

[12] Isa. 61:1–2 (after Condamin's translation).

has given him the power to work such marvels?" Harking back in memory, they compared the past with the present, and the contrast provoked this question: "Is not this the carpenter's son; is he not himself a carpenter. Do we not know Mary his mother, and his brethren, James, Joseph, Simon, and Jude? And are not all his sisters living among us?"[13] They were profoundly astonished when they compared his present greatness with the lowliness of his origin.

But their astonishment soon gave way to scandal, for weak natures are scandalized by what they cannot understand. Their initial enthusiasm and admiration gradually yielded to skepticism and distrust. Their abrupt change of front is easily explained. The Nazarenes expected to see their fellow townsman use his widely known gifts as wonder-worker for their own benefit. They were disappointed, and therein lay the source of their discontent and irritation. Jesus did not perform a single notable miracle at Nazareth, and St. Mark goes so far as to say that he could not, because of their incredulity. Yet he did heal several sick by laying his hands on them, which shows that this was not real powerlessness, but unwillingness. He deliberately placed barriers to his power as a punishment for their lack of faith. Nowhere had he met such apathy and indifference, and he sadly repeated the proverb, "A prophet is not without honor except in his own country, among his own and in his own house." He had made it a rule to exact faith from the sick whom he meant to cure. Not finding this disposition among the Nazarenes, he could not perform many miracles among them.

Those who restrict Jesus' visit to Nazareth to the limits of a few hours, or a single day, raise a psychological problem very difficult to solve. How explain in so short a time such a sudden change of feeling? Has one ever seen an assembly pass, at one sitting, from the liveliest enthusiasm and most generous admiration to coldness, then to mute hostility, then open attack, and

[13] St. Luke has simply: "Is not this the son of Joseph?" (4:22); St. Matthew has the Nazarenes saying: "Is not this the carpenter's son?" (13:55); and St. Mark: "Is not this the carpenter?" (6:3). The first two Evangelists then enumerate Mary his mother, his four brethren, and his sisters. But St. Matthew says "all his sisters," which suggests that there were more than two. About these "brethren and sisters" of the Lord, see Note I: *The Relatives of Christ.*

finally homicidal rage? The opposition must have increased gradually and animosity reached its peak with an accumulation of complaints. At the start the Nazarenes are proud of their compatriot and charmed with his eloquence; but reflecting on his obscure beginnings, they refuse to recognize him as an envoy from God. Accustomed to treating him as an equal, they are shocked and humiliated by the superiority to which he lays claim. The absence of the miracles upon which they had counted seems to them to be a sign of contempt.

An occasion soon occurred which made their rancor flare up. We are still in the synagogue but, according to all indications, it is another Sabbath than the one of which we have just spoken. Jesus was answering the grievance which they took most to heart, and which some of them had perhaps expressed openly: "No doubt you will quote me the proverb, 'Physician, cure thyself.' All the miracles that thou hast wrought at Capharnaum and of which report has come even unto us, do them here in thy own country."[14] The proverb was one of frequent application. It was naturally applied to a doctor more skilled in curing the sickness of others than his own, and also to a man prolific of good advice which he does not allow to influence his own personal conduct. If Jesus would have them to believe in him, why did he not work the miracles that would gain their faith? If they remained incredulous, it was his own fault. The Saviour answered their insolent insinuations:

"Amen, I say to you, there were many widows in Israel in the time of Elias, when heaven was closed for three years and a half; yet he was not sent except to the widow of Sarepta in the country of Sidon. There were also many lepers in Israel in the time of the prophet Eliseus, but none was cleansed except Naaman, the Syrian."

---

[14] Luke 4:23. The Hebrew proverb was: "Physician cure thine own lameness." Plummer gives similar proverbs in Greek and Latin. Its application in the present context is disputed. Some give this interpretation: "Before curing the people of Capharnaum thou shouldst cure thy fellow townsmen of Nazareth, who are closer to thee." Others propose the following explanation, and it seems to be the better: "If thou wouldst have us believe thee and take thee for what thou claimest to be, do first what is necessary; work miracles such as those that have been told of thee at Capharnaum. Otherwise is will be said of thee: Others he advised; himself he could not advise."

Exasperated by being discovered and exposed, the inhabitants of Nazareth can contain themselves no longer. They were demanding miracles. They were convinced that they had a right to them as compatriots and fellow townsmen. But Jesus points out how the prophets went to strangers and preferred a poor woman in the country of Sidon and a leper of Damascus. This allusion they understood only too well, and it raised their fury to a high pitch. On leaving the synagogue, as though at a given signal, they hurried him out beyond the group of houses to the brow of the hill on the side of which their town was built. According to a tradition that goes back to the time of the Crusades and may be even older, they carried him a mile and a half farther. To the south of Nazareth, there is a ravine wide enough to carry off the winter rains. This wretched path leads to a little esplanade that rises more than 300 feet above the plain of Esdrelon, facing Thabor and Little Hermon. The Tarpeian Rock is nothing compared to this precipice, and the place would have been admirably suited to a dramatic execution; but it is hardly likely that the Nazarenes would have gone so far away when they had so many steep crags in the neighborhood. Two or three hundred paces from the Greek church, where the ancient synagogue is said to have been, a rock is pointed out which would have served their purpose well.[15]

But Jesus' hour had not yet struck. "Passing through the midst of them, he went his way" calmly, either because the Nazarenes had finally recoiled before the enormity of the crime, or because the Saviour had overawed them by the majesty of his person and the power of his look, or because God had blinded his enemies and paralyzed their arms. With a heart full of sadness, Jesus left Nazareth, and while he waited for the return of the Apostles, "he went through Galilee preaching everywhere round about."

[15] Luke 4:29: "They pushed him up a steep peak (ἕως ὀφρύος, *usque* ad supercilium) of the mountain on which their town was built." 'Ὀφρύς properly means "eyebrow, *supercilium*," and as a geographical term, *a steep rock, a jagged peak.* Note that there is no definite article; therefore it is not *the* peak, but *a* peak. The precipitous rock near the Maronite church some 200 yds. from the Greek Uniate church (the ancient synagogue) is, according to Stanley (*Sinai and Palestine*, 1881, p. 367), 30 or 40 feet in height; but the base is so littered with debris that it is impossible to get a real estimate of its height. The place now pointed out to pilgrims is very picturesque, but it can by no means be called ὀφρύς, a *precipitous rock.*

CHAPTER VIII

The Bread of Life

1. The First Multiplication of the Loaves

THE growing fame of Jesus was beginning to disturb the suspicious tetrarch of Galilee. Since the death of John, the soul of Antipas had been obsessed by the image of his victim, and he now thought he saw him come back to life again in Jesus. He lent an eager ear to popular talk. Some were saying, "It is John risen from the dead," or "He is Elias, the forerunner of the Messias." "No," said others, "he is one of the ancient prophets returned to the world." Herod kept collecting all these rumors, so perplexingly different from one another, and his foolish fears disturbed his sleep. He imagined that he saw John's ghost standing before him again to reproach him for his incest. "I have cut off the head of the Baptist," he said. "Well then, here he is again, risen from the dead!" He was keenly anxious to see Jesus and to converse with him. This desire of his was a matter of public knowledge, and it was not the kind of thing to reassure the Apostles, who knew that the crafty tetrarch's intentions were open to suspicion.[1] They hurried to rejoin their Master in order to give him an account of their mission and to ask for new instructions. They told Jesus everything they had done and said in his name; they

[1] Luke 9:7–9; Mark 6:14–16; Matt. 14:1–2. We follow here the more precise and more complete account of St. Luke. St. Matthew gives only a colorless summary. In St. Mark (6:14) the *dicebat* of the Vulgate supposes the Greek ἔλεγεν, but the correct Greek reading is ἔλεγον (*dicebant*), according to the best Greek manuscripts and the parallel in St. Luke. Herod was perplexed because *people were saying*. St. Luke alone tells us that the Tetrarch *was seeking to see Jesus* (9:9).

told him of the sick they had cured, the devils they had cast out, the sinners they had brought to repentance.

When they were all together again, Jesus had them embark and commanded them to sail to a deserted spot on the opposite shore. What was urging him thither was not so much anxiety to escape the reach of Herod, whose territory he was to re-enter the next day, as the desire to steal away from the importunate demands of the multitude and to talk heart to heart with his Apostles, while securing for them a little rest after the taxing labors of their mission. The loving heart of the Master was sensitive to such refinements. "Come," he said to them, "let us go apart to a lonely spot and rest awhile." The Passover was drawing near and pilgrim caravans were already forming around the lake, making ready to start the trip to Jerusalem as soon as the latecomers should arrive. The crowds pressing around the Saviour, of whom they had lost sight for some time, were becoming enormous. Such was the eagerness of the visitors that the Apostles, who were busy welcoming them and dismissing them, were on their feet night and day, scarcely having time to eat. St. Mark says succinctly: "They had not even the leisure to eat in peace."[2]

On the eastern bank opposite Capharnaum rose Bethsaida, which Herod Philip had enlarged and made one of his two capitals. He had named it Julias in honor of Julia, the notorious daughter of Augustus. Twelve or fifteen towns were dependencies of this city, and its rather extensive territory took in a low plain running along the lake for about three miles, furrowed by many watercourses, but today become a marsh for lack of drainage. On the southern extremity of this plain the hills sloped down to the bank, and this place, which today is entirely a wilderness, offered even then almost complete solitude. Hither the Apostles directed their way. But the multitude seeing them depart guessed their purpose and started to follow them by the land route. Circling the northern bank of the lake and fording the Jordan a little above its mouth, many of them covered the distance of six or seven miles with

[2] Mark 6:31: *Requiescite pusillum . . . nec spatium manducandi habebant* (a good translation of εὐκαίρουν, which means "to have leisure," "to be at one's ease"). St. Matthew says (14:13): "When he learned (of the death of the Baptist), Jesus withdrew from there," the territory of Antipas. The two motives are not mutually exclusive, but, since the death of the Baptist had occurred some time before this, St. Matthew's phrase may be merely transitional.

such speed that they outstripped the Apostles to their rendezvous. The sea route is shorter, but in the morning before the breeze comes up, it takes longer for a boat that has to be rowed than for a good walker.

When the Apostles came to land, they saw that the lengthy privacy they had dreamed of was impossible, for the crowd kept swelling with new arrivals. Touched with compassion at the sight of these people, who suggested to his mind the picture of a flock without a shepherd, Jesus first cured some of the sick among them, and then going up a little from the shore, sat down on the slope of a hill and spoke to the gathering until twilight about the kingdom of God.[3]

It may have been four o'clock in the afternoon, and though his audience had fasted since morning, they gave no sign of becoming weary or impatient. Still, the Apostles, presuming on the liberty their Master allowed them and even seemed to encourage, said to him: "Lord, the hour is late, and the place a desert. Dismiss the multitude that they may buy something to eat in the neighboring villages before nightfall." "There is no need of that," Jesus answered them. "You yourselves give them something to eat." Respectfully the Apostles held their peace, not understanding this extraordinary command. After a moment of silence, Jesus turned to Philip, as if asking his advice, though actually to test him. He said to him: "Where can we buy bread enough to feed so many?" Philip replied with the good sense and candor characteristic of him: "Two hundred denarii would not be enough to give each one a morsel of bread." The estimate was only too accurate. Cheap though food was in those days, two hundred denarii would certainly not have been enough to give half a pound of bread to each of five thousand guests, even without considering the fact that the Apostles probably did not have that much money in their purses.

Meanwhile, the practical man in the group, Peter's brother,

[3] Matt. 14:13–21; Mark 6:30–44; Luke 9:10–17; John 6:1–15. It is interesting to compare the four accounts of the first multiplication of the loaves. It will be seen that, while the Evangelists are in agreement on the essential points of place and time, the number of persons fed, the number of loaves and fishes, and of baskets filled, they still preserve their independence on secondary details. We are following here the versions of St. John and St. Mark.

Andrew, had gone to find out whether some of the people present had anything that they might contribute to the common need; but no one had thought of making any provision for this unforeseen trip. One youth, however, more provident or shrewder than the rest, had brought with him five barley loaves and two fishes. It was too much for him alone, but he was sure of disposing of them at a profit. Andrew came back and reported the result of his inquiry, adding in a downhearted way, "What is this for so many?" It may seem surprising that the Apostles, with their experience of the Saviour's power, had not from the beginning thought of a miracle; but a miracle did not seem to them to be necessary, since in the end there was still time to send the crowd home. Besides, they may have thought that miracles are not performed for the sake of purely material needs.

Up to that point Jesus had hardly ever worked a miracle without being asked for it. This time he takes the initiative, for he wishes to give an unmistakable sign of his omnipotence, symbolizing and making credible the even more marvelous multiplication of the bread of the Eucharist. At his command the Apostles made the people sit down. "There was much grass in this place," says St. John; and this grass "had a light green tint," adds St. Mark. It was then the end of March, during the season in which even today the plain is bedecked with flowers and has the appearance of a fairyland. After the winter rains, under the hot rays of the springtime sun, rich vegetation springs out of the earth, as though by magic. The grass grows so thick and so high that it sometimes impedes travel on foot or on horseback.

Obedient to the orders they had received, the Apostles divided the people into separate groups, and, as much to avoid disorder as to make it easier to serve them, had them sit in symmetrical rows of fifty or a hundred. This purple and emerald carpet, overlaid with wide patches of white where the people were seated, must have looked from a distance like flower beds in a garden. And this is the picture that spontaneously flowed from the pen of the Evangelists. The arrangement also made it easy to give an approximate estimate of the numbers. There were around five thousand, not counting women and children.[4]

---

[4] The grass was *light green* in color (Mark 6:39: χλωρός); it was *high* and

When all were seated, Jesus asked for the five loaves and, raising his eyes to Heaven, blessed them and broke them, then gave them to his Apostles with orders to distribute them to the crowd. He did the same with the fishes. This gesture of Jesus is reminiscent of the father of the family at the beginning of every meal. The Jews never sat down to table without pronouncing this formula of blessing over the bread and the wine: "Blessed be thou, Lord our God, King of the World, who makest bread come from the earth," or "who dost produce the fruit of the vine."[5]

At what precise moment and in whose hands were the loaves and fishes multiplied? It is as impossible to answer as it is superfluous to ask. Every miracle, be it a creation or a change of substance, or a multiplication of an already existing thing, has in it something mysterious that evades the observer. Is this not often true even of natural phenomena? The evolution of a grain of wheat from the growing seed to the ripening of the ear is unfolded before our eyes in successive phases, and yet all is as mysterious as if it had happened in an instant.

When all were satisfied, Jesus gave the order to collect what was left over so that nothing should be lost. The Jews had the custom of collecting the crumbs scattered on the table. Bread, the chief sustenance of human life, was in their eyes a sacred thing, and they would have scrupled to lose a morsel of it. The Apostles filled twelve large baskets with the remains of the miraculous feast.

The first multiplication of loaves is recounted by all four of the Evangelists. This unusual agreement allows us to compare St. John with his predecessors and to draw several conclusions about the peculiar character of his Gospel. St. John, as usual, is outstanding here in his precision of detail. He gives the exact date,

---

thick (πολύς), for the Passover was drawing near (John 6:4); the multitude was seated on this grassy carpet *in companies* of fifty and a hundred (Mark 6:39: συμπόσια, συμπόσια), and when seated looked like *flower beds* in a garden (Mark 6:40: πρασιαί, πρασιαί). These details would all be true of the lakeside only from mid-March to mid-April.

[5] Jesus *blesses* the bread (Matthew, Mark, Luke, εὐλογήσας), or *gives* thanks (John, εὐχαριστήσας). But in the second multiplication, Matthew and Mark use the word "give thanks." It follows that εὐλογεῖν and εὐχαριστεῖν are synonyms, and that they designate the ordinary blessing given before a meal.

the approach of the Passover; he tells the part played by Philip and Andrew, which the Synoptics attribute to the Apostles as a group. But the figures are the same: five thousand people, five loaves of bread and two fishes, and twelve baskets of fragments. There is no trace of any farfetched symbolism at the expense of historical truth. True it is that St. John would probably not have mentioned the multiplication of loaves and the walking on the water, both being well known from the accounts of his predecessors, had he not wished to make of them a preface to the Eucharistic discourse. This bread which is multiplied by a simple act of the will, and this body which defies the laws of gravity after the manner of a spirit, are they not suitable to render more credible the sacramental presence of Christ in the consecrated Host? The mention of the Passover has, without doubt, the same symbolic purpose, the date of the promise coinciding with the date of the institution. But the account of St. Mark had already made it clear that the Passover was near; and if St. John were straining for symbolism at any price, would he be the only one to note with emphasis that the multiplied loaves were barley loaves? This circumstance lends itself very awkwardly to Eucharistic symbolism.[6]

2. Jesus Walks on the Water

When evening came, Jesus went down to the beach with his Apostles and ordered them to go and wait for him at Bethsaida while he dismissed the crowd.[7] Nothing less than a formal command would have constrained them to comply, for they were loath to leave him after enjoying his company so little throughout the day, and at a moment when the enthusiasm of the people presaged

---

[6] John 6:9 and 6:13. Loisy correctly observes (*Le quatrième évangile,* 2 ed., 1921, p. 221): "The entire sixth chapter is dominated by the idea of Christ the bread of life." But he sees everywhere a symbolism that exists only in his own imagination. Thus, p. 225: "It is not as bread of the poor, but as seasonal bread, bread recalling the Paschal festivities, that the barley loaves are types in our Gospel." But nowhere in Palestine did the harvest occur before the Passover; the barley loaves could not in any way "recall the Paschal festivities." The loaves made from the first fruits were offered only the day after Pentecost. Loisy trusts too much to the simplicity or ignorance of his readers.

[7] Matt. 14:22–36; Mark 6:45–56; John 6:14–21.

serious developments. Finally, at nightfall, despairing of seeing him come back, they cast off in the direction of Bethsaida.

The crowd did not seem any more disposed to withdraw so soon. They had concluded that such a great wonder-worker was no ordinary man. They kept saying, "This is truly the Prophet" foretold by Moses. The spirit of prophecy had been dead for centuries in Israel, and the one who would bring it back to life must be the Messias or his forerunner. All that Theudas and the Egyptian impostor will have to do later to collect an army of blind supporters will be to claim the gift of prophecy. Is it surprising, then, that the Galileans, easily aroused as they were, and at the moment thrilled by the miracle they had just seen, conceived the idea of proclaiming Jesus king? But, divining their design, he fled into the mountain and there passed the night in prayer.[8]

All this time the Apostles were carrying on a bitter struggle with the heaving waves. It often happens after a calm day that a violent wind rises at sunset and grows in intensity up to dawn. This was what happened on that particular night. The wind blowing from the north and the northwest was against them. In such conditions the sails were more dangerous than useful; to make any progress they were forced to take to the oars. But despite their greatest efforts, they could scarcely hold their course and avoid being swept away by the waves.[9]

---

[8] They believed that he was the prophet foretold by Moses (Deut. 18:15). Under Cuspius Fadus, Theudas misled the people by calling himself a prophet (Josephus, *Antiq.*, XX, v, 1); under Felix, an anonymous Egyptian achieved the same success by making the same claim (Josephus, *Antiq.*, XX, viii, 6 and *Bellum*, II, xiii, 5).

When Jesus was threatened with being proclaimed king, "he withdrew *again* into the mountain (John 6:15, πάλιν). The *again* is an allusion to John 6:3, where it is said that Jesus ascended the hill after landing. St. John does not say, but implies that he had come down again to the shore to dismiss the multitude and to *compel* the Apostles to embark (Matt. 14:22; Mark 6:45, "he constrained them," ἠνάγκασεν).

[9] Thomson (*The Land and the Book,* Part II, Chap. 25) cites a personal experience. His rowers, struggling all night against an east or northeast wind, were able to land only at dawn. The sea, he says, was like a boiling kettle.

The Apostles had made only 25 or 30 stadia when Jesus came to them. (The Roman *stadium* was one furlong, or 607 English feet.) Their speed had slackened because of the storm and their decision to wait until dawn before landing; for it is always dangerous to land at night in a rough sea.

At the fourth watch of the night, toward three o'clock in the morning, they were still only twenty-five or thirty stadia (about three or four miles) from their starting point. At that moment, in the uncertain glimmer of the cloudy sky, which was not yet lighted by the full Paschal moon, they saw an indistinct human form coming toward them. Haunted by stories of spirits and ghosts, their imaginations took this at first for a phantom. But soon their vision became clearer and they recognized Jesus, who made as if to pass on as though he did not see them. At their cry of distress, he turned reassuringly, "Have confidence! It is I. Fear not!"

When Simon Peter heard the voice of his beloved Master, he promptly cried out, "Lord, if it be thou, command me to come to thee upon the water." There is not the slightest trace of hesitation in these words, though perhaps there is discernible in them, besides a sincere love of Jesus, a little self-seeking. When the Master said just the one word, "Come!" Peter unhesitatingly stepped out upon the water. But at the sight of the clashing waves making valleys and mountains around him, threatening to engulf him, he was seized with fright and cried out, "Lord, save me!" Jesus held out his hand and raised him above the waves for a moment, saying, "Oh man of little faith, why didst thou doubt?" Then he went into the boat with them, and the storm calmed down. Swiftly they came to their destination, though we cannot say whether this was the result of another miracle.

Those in the boat, seized with religious fear, fell at the Saviour's feet, saying: "Truly, thou art a son of God."[10] On the

---

The Romans divided the night into four watches of three hours each; the fourth watch would therefore extend from 3 to 6 a.m., that is to say, to sunrise. The Jews in ancient times divided the night into three watches, but we know that St. John follows the Roman usage.

[10] Matt. 14:33: Οἱ δὲ ἐν τῷ πλοίῳ προσεκύνησαν αὐτῷ, λέγοντες· Ἀληθῶς Θεοῦ υἱὸς εἶ. "They that were in the boat" suggests that there were others besides the Apostles; large fishing boats could hold more than a dozen people. Those in the boat prostrated themselves before Jesus (προσκυνεῖν does not necessarily mean "to adore," to honor with the worship of latria). They said, "Thou art a son of God," but not *the* Son of God, which would mean the Word Incarnate, the Messias. St. Thomas (on Matt. 16:17) aptly remarks that there is a great difference between the title given to Christ by these people and by others, and the confession of St. Peter. "Quia alii filium adoptivum confessi sunt, hic autem filium naturalem; ideo hic prae ceteris beatificatur, quia primus confessus est divinitatem."

previous evening they had seen an altogether astonishing miracle, the multiplication of the loaves; but this miracle which saved them from grave danger touched them more closely. As a matter of fact, even believers do not readily become accustomed to such striking supernatural manifestations. Though the marvels of Lourdes are repeated hundreds of times, they always awaken the same enthusiasm and arouse the same acclamations.

The Apostles came to land in the country of Genesareth.[11] This region, which owed its fabulous fertility to its many watercourses and its soil made up of alluvial deposits mixed with volcanic rock, comprises not only the plain which the inhabitants called the Ghor (*Ghuweir*) between Magdala and Khan Minyeh, but also the neighboring slopes and the delightful Valley of Seven Fountains, which from a distance seems to be a continuation of it, though the two are separated by the spur of Oreimeh.

We do not know at what precise spot the Apostles landed, but we know the direction in which they were headed and the destination which they succeeded in reaching. On the eastern bank the Lord had told them to sail toward Bethsaida on the other

---

The parallel text of St. Mark (6:51) may very well be understood of the Apostles alone: "They were utterly (λίαν ἐκ περισσοῦ) astonished, for they had understood nothing concerning the loaves, but their heart was blinded." They were unable to draw the conclusion from the miracle of the loaves.

[11] Matt. 14:34; Mark 6:53. Josephus says that the region of Genesareth extended 30 stadia along the shore and had a width of 20 stadia (about 3½ by 2¼ mi.). It is irrigated from the hills of Galilee by three watercourses called, from north to south, Ravine of the Pigeons (*Wady el-Hamam*), the *Wady el-Rabadiyeh,* and the Valley of the Column (*Wady el-Amud*); and three rich springs, again from north to south, the Round Fountain (*Ain el-Madawarah*), *Abu Shusheh,* and the Fountain of the Fig Tree (*Ain et-Tin*).

The measurements given by Josephus suggest the inclusion in the plain of Genesarth of the Valley of Seven Fountains which is adjacent to it. This name "Seven Fountains," in Arabic, *et-Tabigha* or *et-Tabghah,* corresponds to the Greek *Heptapegon* (Ἑπτάπηγον) corrupted in the Arabic pronunciation. It derives its name from the springs of warm water (32° Cent.) to which the natives have given fantastic names: the Fountain of Job (*Ain Ayyub*), which is enclosed in an octagonal basin 262 ft. in circumference, *Hammam Ayyub* (Job's Bath), *Tannur Ayyub* (Job's Furnace), both of these surrounded by a round tower, etc. This valley, which is about a mile and a half from Capharnaum, is famed for its fertility. With many others we place the western Bethsaida here. Excavations carried on in 1932 have revealed the plan of a basilica built in the fourth century on the spot where it was erroneously thought that the first multiplication of loaves took place. Cf. *Dict. Bib., Supplément.,* Vol. III, col. 415.

side of the lake, and the next day "They disembarked at the place to which they were going." This could not be Bethsaida–Julias, which is situated on the same side of the lake where they were the evening before, and almost on the same meridian. In that case they could not be said to cross the lake and go to the opposite shore. We must, therefore, admit the existence of a second Bethsaida, which cogent reasons oblige us to locate in the Vale of Seven Fountains about a mile and a quarter west of Capharnaum.

That there should have been on the north shore of the lake two towns or hamlets called Bethsaida, belonging to two different provinces, Galilee and Gaulanitis, presents no difficulty. We could cite a number of localities in France just as close to each other that are called by the same name. Bethsaida means "House of Fishing," and it is not surprising to find this name in two places which were always the favorite rendezvous of fishermen, because for various reasons fish are abundant there. Two such places are the plain of Bateihah, east of the Jordan, where the Bethsaida enlarged by the Tetrarch Philip was situated, and the Vale of Seven Fountains west of Capharnaum. This valley owes its name to the hot-water springs whose heat attracted masses of fish. Even today the people of Tiberias set themselves up there in huts of leaves each year for several months, and devote themselves to fishing. The little bay of Seven Fountains, which takes in a view of the whole lake, provides easy landing everywhere, and offers a safe anchorage for the fishing boats, having a gently sloping beach which is not obstructed as elsewhere by blocks of rock. It is there that we place the home of Peter, Andrew, and Philip — and perhaps of the sons of Zebedee.[12]

---

[12] The principal reasons for admitting the existence of another Bethsaida west of the Jordan are the following:

a) While on the eastern shore, Jesus ordered the Apostles to go and wait for him *on the other side* (εἰς τὸ πέραν) *toward* Bethsaida (Mark 6:45). And, in fact, they landed *at Genesareth* (Matt. 14:34; Mark 6:53); nor was it the storm that drove them there, since they landed *where they were going* (John 6:21).

b) The next day, the people who had seen the Apostles sail in the direction of Bethsaida went to look for Jesus, not in Bethsaida-Julias, but in the neighborhood of Capharnaum (John 6:22–24), and actually found him there. The place indicated should therefore be the Bethsaida of Seven Fountains a mile and a quarter west of Capharnaum.

3. The Promise of the Eucharist
(JOHN 6:22–71)

After the departure of the Apostles and the sudden disappearance of Jesus, the crowd on the eastern bank gradually dispersed. Most of them had gone to their homes or taken refuge in near-by dwellings, but several remained on the shore, still expecting the return of the man they wanted to make king. Passing a beautiful starlit night at the beginning of spring in the soft atmosphere of the lakeside had nothing frightening or unusual about it for these hardy Galileans.

When they awoke the next day, they looked in vain for the Saviour. Certain that he had not embarked with his Apostles the night before in the only boat that was moored at the time near the bank, but not knowing his place of refuge, they were at a loss where to go. However, as morning came on, they saw some boats from Tiberias coming toward them, for they were at one of the spots on the lake where fish were plentiful, and the morning

---

c) John says (12:21) that Philip was from *Bethsaida in Galilee.* This supposes that there is another Bethsaida not in Galilee, and this applies to Bethsaida-Julias, which is in Gaulanitis.

d) All the Apostles except Judas were Galileans (Act. 1:11; 2:7) and Peter was noticeably such (Mark 14:70; Luke 22:59). Now, if there were no other Bethsaida but Bethsaida-Julias, at least three of the Apostles (Peter, Andrew, and Philip) would not be Galileans, since Bethsaida-Julias was not in Galilee, but in Gaulanitis. It is an empty quibble to object that Judas the Zealot was called a Galilean (Acts 5:37; Josephus, *Antiq.,* XVIII, i, 6; XX, v, 2; *Bellum,* II, viii, 1), yet he was a native of Gamala in Gaulanitis. The reason why he was called a Galilean was that he lived in Galilee, and his exploits took place in Galilee. "Galilean" was for him a *surname* (Josephus, *Bellum,* II, xvii, 8), and Josephus knew very well that he was a *Gaulanite* (*Antiq.,* XVIII, i, 1) and that his native city, Gamala, was in *Gaulanitis* (*Bellum,* II, xx, 4 and 6) as also was eastern Bethsaida (*Bellum,* II, ix, 1).

e) Stewart (*Dict. of Christ and the Gospels,* Vol. I, p. 199) adds an argument which is not devoid of weight. The accursed towns, Capharnaum, Corozain, and Bethsaida are contrasted with the pagan towns, Tyre and Sidon (Matt. 11:21–22; Luke 10:13–14). This implies that they were by religion Jewish towns, and were situated in the theater of Christ's miracles. Now, eastern Bethsaida, which is separated from Galilee by the Jordan, was more than half pagan, and Jesus seems to have worked no miracle there, since he led a blind man who was a native of the place outside the town to cure him (Mark 8:22–23).

There is a tendency today to admit the existence of only one Bethsaida, the one which Philip enriched and called Julias; but the proponents of this opinion are far from equaling those of the contrary opinion, either in number or weight.

hours were considered best for fishing, especially when calm seas follow a stormy night. Those who despaired of finding Jesus again availed themselves of these boats to get ferried to the opposite bank, toward the spot to which they had seen the Apostles sail.[13] Finally they found Jesus in the town, or in the outskirts, of Capharnaum. When they met him they asked him this banal question: "Rabbi, when camest thou here?" What a thing to ask him! Of what importance was the time and manner of the Master's return? His answer was dry and severe:

"Amen, Amen, I say to you, you seek me, not because of the signs you have witnessed, but because of the loaves with which you were filled. Gain not for yourselves the food which perishes but that which endures for life eternal, which the Son of Man will give you, for it is he that God, the Father, has marked with his seal."[14]

---

[13] John 6:22–24. This sentence is long and involved, but not ambiguous. The principal proposition encloses two incidental details which for the sake of clearness could be placed in parentheses. *The principal proposition* is this: the next day, the multitude that had remained on the other side of the lake, on the eastern bank . . . this multitude, seeing that Jesus was not there, nor his disciples, themselves (the people) got into boats and came to Capharnaum, seeking Jesus. *First incidental detail:* they had seen (instead of ἰδών read εἶδον with a pluperfect sense) that there was only one boat there, and that Jesus had not entered it with his disciples, but that the disciples had gone off without him. *Second incidental detail:* However (read ἀλλά instead of ἄλλα which would be superfluous), some boats came from Tiberias, near the place where they had eaten the bread blessed by the Lord.

[14] John 6:27: Ἐργάζεσθε τὴν βρῶσιν. The verb ἐργάζεσθαι with an accusative means "to work so as to have," "to procure by labor." Thus ἐργάζεσθαι τὸν βίον "to work for one's living" (Andocides, xviii, 49); ἐργάζεσθαι χρήματα "to procure supplies" (Herodotus, I, 24). Ἐργάζεσθαι τὴν βρῶσιν could mean "to prepare one's food," but this would imply that one already had it, which is not true of the food promised by the Son to those who believe. The nourishment, therefore, is not the *effect* or the *direct result* of labor, but the reward promised to those who obtain it on the condition of believing. The commentary of St. Thomas is excellent: "operando quaerite, seu operibus mereamini." The work required is faith.

The meaning of σφραγίζειν in the final phrase (τοῦτον γὰρ ὁ Πατὴρ ἐσφράγισεν ὁ Θεός) is disputed. Some, referring to John 3:33 (Qui accipit testimonium *signavit* quoniam Deus verax est), explain it thus: "God has stamped him with his seal by the testimony he has rendered to him; the miracles are the *seal* with which God has stamped him" (cf. 1 Cor. 9:2 and Rom. 4:11). Others paraphrase it thus: "God has stamped his human nature with the divine nature, so that his divinity is like the *seal* of his humanity." Perhaps, without attempting to be more precise, it is enough to say with St. Augustine: "Proprium quiddam

These words are the *clue* of the whole discourse. If they are lost to view or neglected, the reader will lose himself in a labyrinth without light and without exit. The imperishable Food which we should strive to obtain is placed well above our efforts. It cannot be the immediate fruit of our own activity. It is necessary that the Son of Man give it to us; but he will give it — he formally commits himself to give it — to anyone who shall, on his own part, fulfill the conditions which he demands. Nor is his an empty promise; he has the power to carry it out; for the Father in sending him into the world has not only invested him with the fullness of power, but has marked him with the seal of his divinity.

The Jews certainly did not grasp the nature of this divine imprint, but they must have suspected that it was a distinctive mark authorizing him to speak and act in the name of God. They also understood — and this was the essential point — that Jesus was promising them a food much different from what they had eaten the day before, and that if they were to share it, there was a condition to be fulfilled on their part. Therefore they asked him: "What are we to do in order to work the works of God" and to make ourselves worthy of this food? Doubtless they are thinking of acts of piety or supererogation, such as fasting, almsgiving, and prayer. They do not dream of faith. Our Lord's answer goes on to enlighten them: "The work of God is to believe in him whom he has sent." The only thing that Jesus demands of them, that he may give them the promised Food, is that they believe in him.

---

illi dedit ne ceteris comparetur hominibus." This distinctive mark is the seal with which the Father has stamped him.

But what is this mysterious Food (βρῶσιν) which we should strive to procure from our Lord? Let us say immediately, with St. Cyril of Alexandria, Toletus, Cornelius a Lapide, Corluy, and many others, it is *Jesus Christ in the Sacrament of the Holy Eucharist*. Those interpreters who do not admit the unity of the discourse think that up to Verse 48, or even to Verse 51, there is question of the *physical Person of Christ* which we can assimilate to ourselves in a certain way by a living faith. Thence comes the strange expression "the eating of Christ by faith," which admits of a correct theological explanation, but which is not scriptural and would not have been sanctioned by St. John. It probably owes its origin to a well-known saying of St. Augustine: "Ut quid paras dentes et ventrem? Crede et manducasti" (*In Joann. tr.*, xxv, n. 12; ML, XXV, 1601). And later on: "Panem de coelo desideratis: ante vos habetis et non manducatis" (*ibid.*, n. 14). We shall say later what is to be thought of this "eating by faith."

But this was precisely what they were not disposed to do. If he wishes them to believe in him, let him produce his titles; let him prove his mission, as Moses and the other prophets proved theirs. "What sign dost thou work that obliges or permits us to believe in thee? What are thy works? Our fathers ate the manna in the desert, as it is written: 'He gave them the bread of angels to eat.' " Without adding it, they imply: "Do the same and we will believe." His former miracles counted for nothing, even the multiplication of the bread which they had benefited by the day before. They must have signs from heaven of their own choosing, such as the manna falling from heaven.

"Amen, amen," Jesus answered them, "Moses did not give you the bread from heaven, but my Father gives you the bread from heaven, the true bread; for the bread from heaven is that which comes down from heaven and gives life."

The manna fell from the air that surrounds us and which we improperly call the heavens. Not only did it not give life to the soul; it did not even sustain the life of the body except for a very short time. And far from giving life to the world, it benefited only a small group of men lost in a vast universe. How different from this truly heavenly Food, universal and divine, of which the manna was but the shadow and the pale figure!

Then was heard a cry of good will, or words, at least, that sounded like it: "Lord, give us always this bread!" Is this an expression of sincere and considered feeling? Would they have aspired with such ardor for the Bread from heaven, if they had understood its nature? The answer that Jesus gives seems to imply that, as they speak, they are thinking only of a more delicate, more tasty food than they are in a position to obtain for themselves:

"I am the bread from heaven. He that comes to me shall not hunger, and he that believes in me shall not thirst. But I have said to you that having seen me you do not believe . . . . It is the will of my Father that whoever sees the Son and believes in him possess eternal life, and I will raise him up on the last day."

Up to this point Jesus has been speaking to the multitude; that multitude which had followed him yesterday to the other side of the lake, which was seeking him this morning and had finally found him at Capharnaum. Now new interlocutors come upon the scene: the Jews. For St. John, "the Jews" always means those implacable enemies who spy upon the Saviour and persecute him, who clamor against him and seek to kill him. While he is speaking, these Jews are murmuring and railing against him. He, the bread from heaven! What foolishness, what extravagance! Is there anyone that does not know who he is? Do we not know his mother, Mary, and his father, Joseph? How can he dare pretend that he has come down from heaven? Without descending to an argument with them, our Lord affirms with still greater force what he has just said:

"I am the bread of life. Your fathers ate the manna in the desert and they died. This is the bread which came down from heaven. Whoever eats of it shall not die. I am the living bread which came down from heaven. If anyone eats of this bread, he shall never die. And the bread which I will give you is my flesh for the life of the world."

The superficial reader will, perhaps, find that Jesus is merely repeating himself. Actually, up to now, he has only been bordering on the mystery. He penetrates it now, and leads us into it with him. When he said that he was the Bread of Life, the living Bread, the Bread which had come down from heaven, it was clear that he was speaking of his own person; but it was not yet known how he would serve as food. He now says that the Bread is his own flesh, and that his flesh is to be eaten. It is impossible any longer to mistake the meaning of his words. The preceding dialogue was only a prelude. His purpose in it was to lead the minds of his hearers gradually to a belief in the most consoling of all our mysteries, and to bring them little by little to a notion of the true Bread of Life without too direct an affront on their preconceived ideas and stubborn prejudices. Thus had he dealt on a former occasion with Nicodemus, to show him the need of a new birth by water and the Spirit; thus too with the Samaritan woman, to explain to her the nature of that living water which quenches forever our thirst for happiness. The notions are first general and, by the same token, obscure; they provoke a series of questions and answers, and by degrees all the details come to full light.

"I am the bread of life": such is the theme of the whole discourse. If these words were left to themselves, without explanation or commentary, though better adapted to designate the Eucharistic Christ, they could strictly be understood of Christ in his natural state. Between these two there are, in fact, many analogies. The Person is the same, the same God made man; the only difference is in the manner of being. The one no less than the other comes from heaven and is a gift of the Father; the one no less than the other feeds the soul and nourishes it with virtue and appeases the hunger and thirst for the divine. But whereas Christ in his natural state is immolated for us on the Cross, the Eucharistic Christ, mystically immolated in the Eucharist, gives himself to us in the form of nourishment and beverage, as true Bread and true Drink of which the manna in the desert and the miraculous waters of Horeb were the prophetic figures. This Eucharistic Bread we really eat. It satiates our soul and regenerates our body, implanting in it the seed of immortality for its glorious resurrection. On the other hand, in no idiom, be it Greek or Hebrew, Latin or French, does usage permit us to speak of eating or drinking Christ in his natural state.[15] We must therefore draw the conclusion that in calling himself the Bread of Life, Christ was

[15] The metaphorical sense of "eat," "devour someone" is limited to certain poetical expressions, the meaning of which is never ambiguous because it is prepared for by the context.

Thus Prov. 30:14 (cf. Hab. 3:14):

> It is a race whose *teeth* are swords
> and whose *molars* are knives
> *to devour* the unfortunate upon the earth
> and the poor from among men.

In such fixed expressions, the choice of words is not arbitrary; it is regulated by usage. In the metaphorical sense, *comedere* or *devorare* are used, and not *manducare;* in Greek κατεσθίειν is used, not ἐσθίειν nor, a fortiori, τρώγειν. Thus 2 Cor. 11:20: "Sustinetis si quis vos in servitutem redigit, si quis devorat (κατεσθίει)."

An even bolder figure occurs in poetry, Ps. 26(27):2: "Evil men have drawn near against me to *devour my flesh*" (cf. Job 19:22). This forceful figure has become common in French. We say "s'acharner (derived from the word *chair*) sur quelqu'un, contre quelqu'un," like a wolf or a vulture on its prey.

But it is plain that this metaphorical meaning (the *only* metaphorical meaning used) is impossible in the sixth chapter of St. John. (1) It is always *depreciatory;* (2) it is poetical, and must be prepared for by the context; (3) it is not used in Greek with the verb ἐσθίειν, especially if it is parallel to πίνειν; (4) it is still more impossible with the word τρώγειν, which St. John uses four times (John 6:54, 56, 57, 58) and which means "to graze," "to nibble," "to crunch," and simply "to eat" (still in a proper sense) when joined with πίνειν in the expression "to eat and drink."

from the beginning referring implicitly to his sacramental state, which alone legitimizes and authorizes such a manner of speaking.

Is it probable, is it even possible, that in the same discourse, before the same audience, in treating of such a fundamental doctrine, Jesus used these words in two different senses, as though wishing to create ambiguity and thus give the Jews an excuse for misunderstanding him? Did he not know beforehand, at the beginning of his discourse, whither he wished it to tend and what he intended to teach? Is it credible that he changed the theme in mid-course, like some extemporizer who forgets his original purpose and slips into a new topic without being aware of it? Has not St. John recounted two miracles which were already known from the Synoptic account, precisely as an introduction to the promise of the Eucharist? No, the Bread of Life, the heavenly Bread that is food for the soul and a pledge of immortality for the body does not stand for two disparate or at least different objects in this discourse; It stands for one and the same thing, described by more and more precise traits — communion with the Body and Blood of Christ in the Sacrament of the Altar. St. Cyril of Alexandria, the most profound if not the most eloquent of St. John's interpreters, is surely right in affirming that when Christ said, "Obtain the imperishable food which the Son of Man will give you," he was already thinking of this Eucharistic nourishment whose nature he intended soon to explain.[16]

The Jews now clearly grasp what Jesus means to say: he is offering them his flesh to eat, if they have faith in him. But since their minds turn to thoughts of cannibalism, the proposal seems to them absurd, immoral, and scandalous. "How can this man give us his flesh to eat?" This is not the time to explain the *how;* Jesus is now asking only for faith, and after what they have seen him do, he has every right to it. He will tell them, therefore, only of the need and the effects of his heavenly Food.

"Amen, amen, I say unto you; unless you eat the flesh of the

---

[16] St. Cyril of Alexandria, *In Joannem,* Bk. III, Chap. 4 (MG, LXXIII, 481): "He is here alluding to the spiritual and mystical nourishment whereby, sanctified in body and soul, we live in him. But he speaks more clearly later, and it is there that we shall explain it." Toletus, who follows St. Cyril attributes the same interpretation to St. Augustine.

Son of Man and drink his blood, you shall not have life in you.

"He that eats my flesh and drinks my blood has eternal life; and I will raise him up on the last day. For my flesh is true food, and my blood is true drink.

"He that eats my flesh and drinks my blood abides in me and I in him. As my father the living (God) has sent me, and as I live by my Father, so he that eats me shall live by me.

"Behold the bread that came down from heaven. Not as your fathers, who ate (manna) and died; he that eats this bread shall live forever."

Could Jesus have chosen clearer, more precise, more emphatic — I was going to say more realistic — terms to teach the Catholic dogma of the Real Presence? And if he had in mind merely a virtual or symbolic or mystical presence, could he have used more obscure, more inappropriate terms; terms more contrary to accepted usage, more likely to lead well-disposed souls astray? To eat his flesh and drink his blood, this is what he repeats as many as nine times in four verses, even using a synonym which is untranslatable in our language, and even more impossible to understand in a metaphorical sense. The terms employed by Jesus can be understood only of the real action expressed by the words. And to put an end to all doubt, if doubt were still possible, he says that the flesh of the Son of Man is a true food, comparable to the manna with which the Israelites nourished themselves in the desert, and that his blood is a true drink, as were the miraculous waters of Horeb.

"To eat the flesh of Christ," say the Protestants, "is to contemplate the holy life of our Lord, to receive his life through the Holy Spirit in order to reproduce it in our own lives. To drink his blood is to contemplate with faith his violent death, to make it one's own ransom, and to appropriate to oneself its expiatory efficacy."[17] Wishing to suppress the mystery, they drift into word-riddles still more mysterious and incomprehensible, which the Jews may well be excused for failing to understand. But, it is objected, if the Eucharist had not been instituted, we would have to content ourselves with the figurative meaning; that meaning is therefore possible. An imaginary hypothesis and

[17] Godet, *L'Evangile de S. Jean,* 4 ed., Neuchâtel (no date), Vol. II, p. 495.

a puerile sophism! If Jesus Christ had not instituted the Eucharist, he would not have promised it, and we would not have to interpret the meaning of the promise. But once the Eucharist was instituted, what new clarity flooded the words of the promise made a year before! Thus when our Lord in the Cenacle, holding in his hands the bread or the chalice, pronounced the sacramental words — surely astonishing words — the Apostles manifested no astonishment; they asked for no explanation. The reason was that, knowing Christ to possess the words of eternal life, they had firmly believed the promise, that promise of which they were now happily witnessing the fulfillment.

Those few writers of the sixteenth century who were unable or unwilling to accept the Eucharistic sense, however evident, of Jesus' discourse at Capharnaum must be given the benefit of an attenuating circumstance. John Huss and other heretics had misused the words to support their contention that Communion under both species and Communion for little children were of divine right, and they accused the Catholic Church of contradicting the formal teaching of the Saviour on these points. A very convenient method of defense was to answer that the sixth chapter of St. John did not treat of the Eucharist. Cajetan adopted this method, and his reputation drew in his train several theologians and even a renowned exegete, Jansenius of Ghent. They soon formed a minority important enough to attract the attention of the Council of Trent.[18] Finally, however, they fell into such disrepute that very few if any would be disposed to follow them today.

Since the Eucharist is food it is as necessary for the health and life of the soul as material food is for the body. Without food our body would quickly waste away. How, then, without a miracle, could our soul keep alive for long if deprived of the Eucharistic Bread? "Unless you eat the flesh of the Son of Man,

[18] Cavallera, *L'interprétation du chapitre VI de saint Jean: Une controverse exégétique au concile de Trente,* in *Revue d'histoire ecclésiastique,* Vol X, 1909, pp. 686–709. The Council declared that Communion under both species does not follow from Chapter VI of St. John, "utcumque secundum varias sanctorum Patrum et Doctorum sententias intelligatur" (Sess. xxi, Chap. 1), and this is strictly true. Cajetan's opinion could still be held, but the gradual adherence of the faithful and of theologians to the Eucharistic sense has altered the situation.

you shall not have life in you." Assuredly the necessity of the Eucharist is not as absolute as that of faith and Baptism. This is not the place to study the nature or extent of its necessity. Let us only say that the actual reception of the Eucharist or the desire of it is indispensable for the perfection of the Christian life, because without it the Mystical Body of Christ would not have its full completion.[19] Is not the bond that intimately unites the faithful among themselves and with Christ, and constitutes the Mystical Body, an effect of the Eucharist? "Because there is but one (Eucharistic) bread," says St. Paul, "we are all one (mystical) body, all of us who partake of this same bread (of the Eucharist)." And Jesus Christ himself says in St. John, "He that eats my flesh and drinks my blood abides in me and I in him. As my Father, the living (God), has sent me and as I live by my Father, so he who eats me shall live by me."[20]

It is impossible to conceive a more intimate union with Jesus Christ than this. In an effort to give some idea of it the Fathers resorted to surprisingly realistic expressions. St. Cyril of Alexandria says, "It is as if two pieces of wax are fused together," so that, after the joining, the molecules of the two bodies are no longer distinguishable. A less imperfect comparison would perhaps be that of iron heated to a white heat in the furnace; the incandescent iron then acquires the properties of fire, heat, and light, so that it can be said that the fire is in the iron and the iron in the fire. Something analogous happens in the communicant. This divine Food has the effect of divinizing him. The food we take abides in us in a certain way by the nutritive elements which it imparts to us, but in no way can we be said to abide in it.

---

[19] How the necessity of the Holy Eucharist is to be understood is discussed in P. de la Taille's *Mysterium Fidei,* 1921, pp. 587–617. [Very brief résumé in the author's *Mystery of Faith and Human Reason,* pp. 30–31. *Translator.*]

[20] John 6:58. The Latin *propter* could suggest another meaning: "As I live *for* my Father who has sent me, so he that eats me lives *for* me." The thought in itself is correct: the envoy should promote the interests of him that sent him and labor *for* him, and it is proper that the communicant nourished by the body of Christ live and spend himself *for* Christ. But in the Greek the preposition διά with the accusative designates cause or means, and Latin commentators are right in explaining the *propter* of the Vulgate as if it were *per*. Cf. 1 Cor. 10:16–17.

Some are of the opinion that in saying, "I live *by* my Father," Jesus is thinking of his eternal generation, but in that case he would have said, "I live by my Father who has begotten me," and not, "I live by my Father who has sent me." These last words show that the allusion is to the Word Incarnate.

On the contrary, when the Eucharistic Bread has transformed us into It, we can say in full truth: "I live; no, it is no longer I that live; it is Christ that lives in me."

I live by him as he himself lives by the Father who sent him. The Son of God lives the life of the Father who eternally begets him, but here there is question of the Word Incarnate. By virtue of the Hypostatic Union in which the Father has the initiative and of which he is by attribution the efficient cause, the humanity of Christ lives a divine life; not only has it sanctifying grace, but it also possesses substantial sanctity rendering it worthy of adoration. The same holds true, in due proportion, in the marvelous union between Christ and the communicant. Not only is the soul vivified by grace, but the body itself receives the seeds of a glorious immortality.

The long dialogue on the nature, effects, and necessity of the Eucharist is divided into three acts. The first takes place on the beach before the multitude which has been looking for Jesus and finally finds him. The second develops in the synagogue of Capharnaum before the captious and hostile Jews. The third is enacted somewhere outside the synagogue before the crestfallen disciples and the almost wavering Apostles.[21]

Among the disciples who were following in Jesus' footsteps many were tempted to turn back. The mystery of the Eucharist was too strong for these neophytes. They were scandalized and said: "This is a hard teaching. Who can so much as listen to it?" Aware of their timid objections and their secret murmurings, Jesus said to them: "Does this scandalize you? When you see the Son of Man ascend again to where he was in the beginning, what shall you say? Will your scandal still endure?"[22]

---

[21] The three parts are as follows: *First part* (22–40), those who are looking for Jesus find him on the western side of the lake (25) near Capharnaum, and speak with him. *Second part* (41–59), the hostile Jews murmur, and Jesus answers them. This takes place in the synagogue of Capharnaum (59). *Third part* (60–61), conversation with the Apostles and other disciples, probably outside the synagogue and on another day.

[22] John 6:63. This question, to which the reader must supply the answer, can be understood in either of two opposite ways. The first explanation, which is that of St. Cyril, St. Augustine, St. Thomas, and many other commentators, ancient and modern, supplies this answer: "Your scandal will cease" or "You will be less scandalized." This is the interpretation which we have adopted. The

Our Lord demands from his disciples an act of faith without reserve. He refers them for a moment to the triumph of his Ascension; then they shall understand — if they are capable of understanding anything — that he who ascends to the heaven whence he has come down, is qualified to speak to them of heavenly things and to propose to their faith doctrines full of mystery. They will also understand that the eating of his body glorified and spiritualized, has nothing in common with a cannibal feast. Let them elevate their thoughts higher, above the flesh, for "it is the spirit which gives life." The flesh by itself, apart from the spirit, is worth nothing and "is of no avail."

The demoralized disciples listened no further. They began to leave one after the other, and though his heart was broken at seeing them depart he did nothing to stop them.[23] If he had meant to speak only of a purely spiritual eating, if to communicate in his body and blood was simply to think about it or to meditate on his redeeming death, a single word would have been enough to undeceive them and lead them back to him. He did not say that word. "Ah!" cries Bossuet. "That is not your way, my Saviour, that is surely not your way; you do not come to trouble men's minds with great words that come to nothing."

The steady desertion of the disciples left a void around Jesus, and it was possible to fear for a moment that discouragement might win over even the Apostles. "You also," he said to them one day, "do you wish to go away?" Certain that he was expressing the sentiments of all his colleagues, Simon Peter answered without a moment's hesitation: "Lord, to whom shall we go? Thou hast the words of eternal life. We have believed and we know that thou art the Holy One of God." Peter does not yet make the confession of faith which will win him the dignity of head of the

---

second supplies the answer: "You will be even more scandalized." It too has a great number of defenders: Maldonatus, Toletus, Corluy, Lagrange, etc. The reader may take his choice.

[23] John 6:61–72. Note that these words: "Jesus said these things teaching in the synagogue of Capharnaum" (John 6:60), mark the termination of the discourse in the synagogue. All that follows — words and actions — up to the end of the chapter, may have happened elsewhere and much later. A certain amount of time was needed to take note of the void growing around Jesus.

Church, "Thou art the Christ, the Son of the living God." But today he gives his master an equivalent title: for since the Holy One of God shares in a unique and incommunicable way in infinite sanctity, the title places Jesus in the realm of divine realities.

Was Peter mistaken in making himself the spokesman of the Twelve? One of them, still remaining in body at Jesus' side, is one day to betray him, if he has not already betrayed him in his heart. Our Lord tries to hold him back from the slope down which he is slipping by showing him that he is not deceived. "Have I not chosen all of you, the Twelve? And yet one of you is a devil!" The Son of Perdition is wantonly running to his own ruin. Nothing is any longer able to move him.

CHAPTER IX

The Paralytic of Bethesda

1. The Incidents of the Cure
(JOHN 5:1–19)

THE war declared on Jesus by the Pharisees of Galilee was about to flame up still more violently in southern Palestine. The cure of the paralytic on the Sabbath was what finally let loose their hatred.

The Saviour was in Jerusalem on the occasion of a feast of uncertain date. If we read in the text of St. John "the feast of the Jews" with some of the good manuscripts, the feast referred to can be only the Passover, the principal solemnity of the liturgical cycle, or perhaps the feast of Tabernacles, which was celebrated at that time with such brilliance that many considered it the Jewish feast *par excellence*. If, on the contrary, with other authorities we read "a feast of the Jews," it will be some feast of secondary rank such as Pentecost, which was not so well known to the pagans, or the feast of the civil New Year, which fell around the end of September, or finally the Feast of Lots (*Purim*), which was celebrated a month before the Passover to commemorate the deliverance of the Jews under Esther and Mardochai. But there are serious reasons, which we explain elsewhere, for transposing this episode to a position after the first multiplication of the loaves, though St. John narrates it before that event.[1]

[1] John 5:1. Should we read ἑορτή, "*a* feast," or ἡ ἑορτή, "*the* feast"? Tischendorf accepts the definite article; Hort rejects it; Vogels and Von Soden put it in brackets as doubtful. The Coptic versions have the article. The Latin versions throw no light on the subject, since *dies festus* can mean either *the* feast or *a* feast. The same is true of the Syriac versions. The reasons for accepting or rejecting the article seem to us to be of about equal weight.

In that case, the feast in question would have to be the Passover which was near at hand at the time of the multiplication of the loaves, and which Jesus would have no reason for avoiding, since his prolonged absence from Jerusalem is to be motivated precisely by the attempts of the Jews to put him to death after the cure of the paralytic.[2]

"There is at Jerusalem, near the Probatic Gate, a pool called in Hebrew Bethesda, which has five porticoes. Under these porticoes lay a multitude of the sick, blind, lame, and crippled (awaiting the bubbling up of the water)."

The Probatic Gate or the Sheep-Gate was located north of the Temple, and it is thought to have been named so because it afforded passage to the numerous flocks of sheep destined to sacrifice. Outside the gate, in the northern suburb, which was not yet included within the walls, was a pool called Bethesda (House of Mercy), the remains of which have recently been discovered near the French church of Sainte-Anne. It is interesting to find that the plan of the edifice corresponds exactly to Origen's description of it. It was a vast reservoir, rectangular in shape, bordered on its four sides by porticoes, with a central portico cutting through and dividing it into two distinct basins. The spring or aqueduct that supplied it with water is unknown.[3]

St. John Chrysostom and St. Cyril of Alexandria think that the unnamed feast is Pentecost. St. Irenaeus (*Haer.*, II, xxii, 3) thinks that it is the Passover; but since he counts only three Passovers in the public life of Christ, the Passover of John 5:1 had to be identified with that of John 6:4.

[2] Cf. *Concord of the Gospels,* at the end of the volume.

[3] The pool of Bethesda. Up to recent times it was identified with an immense reservoir (*Birket Israil*) 387 ft. in length by 125 ft. in width, the bottom of which, full of earth and debris, is 69 ft. below the Temple esplanade. This basin is in the ancient moat of the city between the Temple and Mount Bezetha.

The real pool of Bethesda was a little farther north, inside the present enclosure of the White Fathers, who have conducted some very interesting excavations there, though they are often impeded by the proximity of property which they do not own. There is a detailed description (with plates) in Abel-Vincent, *Jérusalem,* Vol. II, 1926, pp. 685–698.

The name *Probatica* comes from the *present* Vulgate: "Est autem Jerosolymis Probatica piscina quae cognominatur Hebraice Bethsaida." St. Jerome had written: "Est autem Hierosolymis, super Probatica (*porta* understood), piscina, quae etc." (Wordsworth-White, *Nov. Test. latine,* Vol. I, p. 532), which agrees exactly with the Greek: Ἔστιν . . . ἐπὶ τῇ Προβατικῇ (πύλῃ understood) κολυμβήθρα, etc. It was the gate, and not the pool, that was called Probatica. The existence of this Probatic gate is historically proven; it was north of the Temple (2 Esdr. 3:1, *porta gregis,* πύλη Προβατική; 3:21; 12:38).

What caused the bubbling up which periodically agitated the surface of the water? The present Vulgate says explicitly: "From time to time the angel of the Lord came down into the pool and the water was troubled; and the first to step into the pool after the troubling of the water was cured of his disease, whatever it was." But this verse is lacking in the original text of St. John, and it was very probably lacking in the Vulgate as it came from St. Jerome's hands. If the text is authentic, this infallible cure, coming at a set moment, always limited to a single beneficiary, and devoid of any apparent moral reason would be the most extraordinary miracle in Scripture. But what is certain is that the people believed in the healing power of this water and attributed the periodical agitation to a supernatural agency.[4]

Miracle or not, the bubbling up of the pool, happening perhaps at rather regular intervals, as still happens in the modern Jerusalem's only spring, called by the Christians the Spring of the Virgin, attracted a great number of sick under its porticoes. Among them was a paralytic whose affliction went back thirty-eight years. When Jesus saw him stretched out on his mat, he was touched with compassion and said to him, "Dost thou truly wish to be cured?" Not that he had any doubt about the matter, but he asked the question to arouse the man's faith, by presenting him with the prospect of a cure which would depend solely upon

---

The name of the pool has numerous variants in the Greek manuscripts and in the versions: *Bethesda, Bethzetha, Belzetha,* etc. *Bethsaida* is certainly incorrect. We uphold *Bethesda* (House of Mercy) with Vogels, Weiss, and other critics.

[4] The critical editions usually omit Verse 4 because: (*a*) it is lacking or obelized in the best Greek manuscripts (A B C D, etc.) and the most ancient versions (Sur-Cur., Sah., Lat., d f l q); (*b*) in other witnesses it appears with numerous variants, omissions, and inversions, which are ordinary signs of spuriousness.

The English editors of the Vulgate omit it for the same reasons; because it is lacking from two of the oldest manuscripts, and those that have it offer it in three different forms, each with secondary variants. An addition of the verse is easier to understand than its omission. It was natural to supply for St. John's silence, and to explain the movement of the water and justify the popular belief. St. Augustine, who certainly did not read our Verse 4, has done exactly that (*In Joann. tract.,* xvii, n. 3): "Subito videbatur aqua turbata et a quo turbabatur non videbatur. *Credas hoc angelica virtute fieri solere.*" The last words of Verse 3, which are much better attested than Verse 4, are retained by the English editors of the Vulgate.

his will. The sick man hastened to reply: "(Yes), Lord (but) I have no one to cast me into the pool at the first movement of the water. While I am going, another goes down before me." Jesus said to him, "Rise, take up thy pallet and walk." The crippled man felt himself healed and immediately departed, taking with him the mat that served him as a bed, as Jesus had commanded him.

By this action the man had unconsciously broken the Sabbath rest, as the Scribes and Pharisees had defined it in detail. On their list of thirty-nine works forbidden on the Sabbath was a prohibition against carrying a burden from one place to another, and everything not used for clothing or attire was regarded as a burden. Thanks to a weird misuse of logic, it was permitted to carry a sick man in his bed because the bed was then considered a personal accessory, which explains the paralytic's presence near the pool; but to carry merely the bed was forbidden. The miraculously healed man, with no suspicion of this law, was leaving in all peace of conscience when the rigoristic Jews peremptorily rebuked him. "Today is the Sabbath. Thou art not allowed to carry thy bed." Since he naturally gave as an excuse the explicit command of the man who had cured him, they asked who that was; but he did not know, for, eager to avoid any noisy and untimely demonstrations, Jesus had straightway lost himself in the crowd.

On the same evening, to all appearances, Jesus met the man in the Temple as if by chance and gave him this grave advice, "Behold thou art cured; sin no more, lest something worse happen to thee." Physical evil is not always a punishment for sin — we will find the Saviour opposing this false notion of his contemporaries — but sometimes it is, and it seems that it would have been so in the present case.

Since the beneficiary of the miracle had not been forbidden to speak, he hastened immediately to tell it all to the Pharisees, perhaps imagining in his simplicity that if Christ's supernatural power were proclaimed openly, the fury of his enemies would be disarmed. He did not know them well enough. They redoubled their rage under the pretext that, not content with violating the law himself, Jesus was making others violate it.

What Jesus said to justify himself was not calculated to appease them. "My father works up to the present (without making any exception for the Sabbath) and I also work (like him)."[5] The Sabbath rest was instituted to commemorate God's rest on the seventh day of Creation.[6] God, said the Rabbis, is the first to give us an example in this matter; he is not like those rulers who impose laws on others without restricting themselves. But common sense refutes their quibbling.[7] It is evident that God's rest after the work of creation is not absolute. He preserves the world from annihilation by a continuation of the act of creation, and governs it by his providence. "God does not cease to act," wrote Philo, "for action is as essential to him as heat is to fire, the more so since he is the principle of activity for all beings."[8]

When, on other occasions, the Scribes reproached him for violating the Sabbath rest, Jesus defended himself with the common-sense maxim that the Sabbath was made for man, and not man for the Sabbath; and that consequently the service of God or the higher law of fraternal charity supersedes the obligation of the Sabbath rest. On one occasion, he has even said that the Son of Man is Master of the Sabbath. Today he draws the conclusion of this principle, claiming the right to act with complete independence, regardless of the Sabbath, as his Father acts. The Scribes understood very well that by calling God his Father he was setting up between God and himself an unique and incommunicable relationship founded on community of nature, and very different from the relationship of which the children of Israel could boast. Thus they knew that in claiming the right to act on an equality with his Father he was proclaiming himself God. "For if he were not truly God," St. John Chrysostom aptly remarks,

---

[5] John 5:17: Ὁ πατήρ μου ἕως ἄρτι ἐργάζεται, κἀγὼ ἐργάζομαι. "My Father works up to now (it matters not when) without being hindered by the institution of the Sabbath, which commemorates God's rest on the seventh day of creation (Gen. 2:2), and I also work." The parallelism demands that we understand "in like manner," or, better still, that we refer ἕως ἄρτι to both clauses. Note that it is not, "I work *with* my Father," I share his activity, which would necessarily be understood of the *divine nature,* but, "I also work," which can be understood of the Person of the Word acting through the *human nature* in the work of Redemption.

[6] Gen. 2:1–3; Exod. 20:11; 31:17.

[7] Billerbeck, *Kommentar,* Vol. II, p. 462.

[8] Philo, *Legum alleg.,* 1, 3 (Mangey, Vol. II, p. 44). Likewise Aristobulus, in Eusebius, *Praepar. evang.,* XIII, xii, 11, and Clement of Alexandria, *Stromata,* vi, 10 (ed. Staehlin, p. 504).

"his claim would be as impious as it would be extravagant." To make such a claim one would need the madness of a Caligula.

The exasperation of the Jews increased to such an extent that they sought means to kill Jesus, because, not content with breaking the Sabbath, "he was calling God his Father, making himself equal to God." Hate gave them insight, and they reasoned better than will the followers of Arius later on.

2. The Activity and Role of the Son of God
(JOHN 5:19–30)

Jesus took the occasion of the incident of the paralytic to explain his relationships with God and the world, and to appeal to his Father's testimony. It is possible, however, that these somewhat disparate teachings were not all given on the same day or before the same audience.

"Amen, amen, I say to you, the Son can do nothing of himself, but only what he sees his Father doing. What the Father does, the Son does in like manner; for the Father loves the Son and shows him all that he does, and will show him even greater works to make you marvel. For as the Father raises the dead and gives life, so the Son gives life to whom he will.

"The Father judges no one; he has given all judgment to the Son, in order that all may honor the Son as they honor the Father. He that does not honor the Son does not honor the Father who has sent him.

"Amen, amen, I say to you, he that hears my word and believes in him who sent me has eternal life and is not sent to judgment, but passes from death to life.

"Amen, amen, I say to you, the hour is coming, it has already come, when the dead shall hear the voice of the Son of God, and they that hear it shall live. For as the Father has life in himself, so he has given to the Son to have life in himself, and has given him all power to judge, because he is the Son of Man.

"Be not astonished (to hear me say) that the hour is coming when they that are in their tombs shall hear his voice and shall come forth, the good to go to the resurrection of life, the evil to the resurrection of judgment.

"Of myself I can do nothing; according to what I hear I judge; and my judgment is just, because I seek not my own will, but the will of him who has sent me."[9]

The three great Doctors of the Church who have commented on the Fourth Gospel — John Chrysostom, Cyril of Alexandria, and Augustine — anxious above all else to combat Arianism which was still a redoubtable menace, saw here only the Word receiving from the Father, by virtue of the eternal generation, knowledge and power with the divine nature, and having but one and the same operation with the Father. Bossuet sums up their thought in a few terse sentences. "If the world has come into being, it is because the Father made it; and I also. If the world continues to exist, it is because the Father conserves it; and I also. He has done and he does everything by his Son. 'The Son does nothing of himself, and does only what he sees his Father doing.' Is there a world which the Father has not made? God forbid! the Father does all that he does by his Son, and the Son does nothing but what he sees his Father doing, just as he says nothing but what he hears him say. But how does he speak to him? By begetting him. Because for the Eternal Father, to speak is to beget; to pronounce his *Verbum*, his Word, is to give him being. Likewise to show him all that he does, to reveal to him the essence of his being and his power, in a word, to open his heart to him is to beget him. . . . The Son says nothing but what he hears; he does nothing but what he sees done. But to hear his Father and to see what he does and what he is, is to be born of him. 'What the Father does, the Son does likewise. The Father raises whom he

---

[9] A life of Christ can give no more than a summary idea of a text so rich in doctrine, especially since so many of the details are subjects of controversy. The controversies bear upon two principal points:

a) "The Son does only that which he *sees* the Father doing." Is there question here of the Word *as Word* (St. Augustine, St. Cyril, St. Thomas, etc.)? Or of the Word *made Man* (Maldonatus and other interpreters)?

b) "The Son *gives life* to the dead as does the Father." Does this refer to the life of the body (St. John Chrysostom, St. Cyril, St. Hilary, and the majority of commentators), or to the life of the soul (St. Augustine and several moderns, Catholics as well as Protestants), or now to one, now to the other: the life of the soul especially in Verse 21, where "to give life" is used in a general sense; the life of the body in Verse 25, where there is question of the *resurrection* of the dead? It would take too long to develop the reasons pro and con.

will, and the Son also raises whom he will,' with equal authority; because his authority, like his nature, is that of the Father."[10]

Not all interpreters would be disposed to follow Bossuet to the last detail, despite the support he may claim from the Fathers. They would not readily admit that when God *shows* a thing to his Son, it means that he begets him, nor that when the Son *sees* a thing *done* by his Father, it means that he is *begotten* by him. It has always been a question with them whether Jesus is here speaking as God or as man, or now as God and again as man. But between these alternatives there is a middle term. Between the divine nature and the human nature there is the Person of the Verbum, who is the bond of union between the two natures; between the divine action and the human action there is the theandric action, in which the two natures co-operate. The Incarnate Word would not be Saviour, if he were not at once God and man, and if he did not act at the same time as God and as man.

If the general statement, "My Father works up to the present, and I also work," must be understood of the Word independently of the Incarnation, and indicates the community of operation of Son and Father in this wise, that the Son does nothing without the Father and the Father nothing without the Son, almost everything else in the passage clearly refers to the Word Incarnate, the Son of God made man. For Jesus Christ here presents himself, repeatedly and insistently, as the envoy of God, the agent of the resurrection, him to whom judgment has been entrusted *because he is the Son of Man.* When he affirms that he does nothing but what he sees his Father doing, is this assertion to be extended to the creation and conservation of the world? Is it not restricted by the context to the work of redemption? The explanation appended to it warrants this interpretation: "For the Father loves the Son and shows him all that he does and will show him even greater works, in order that you may believe." He will not show him works greater than the creation and conservation of the world, but works that are more excellent in the execution of the plan

10 Bossuet (*Méditations sur l'évangile,* 87me jour) inspired especially by St. Augustine (*In Joann. tract.,* xviii–xxii).

of redemption. By virtue of the eternal generation, the Father does communicate to the Son power and intelligence as well as nature; but the phrase "to show," meaning "to beget," would be a very unusual expression, the more so because it is not because he loves the Son that the Father begets him. On the other hand, without forcing the text and without exegetical subleties, all this can be understood of the Word Incarnate. The Hypostatic Union is an effect of the love of the Father, who directs in all things the activity of Christ, and has made him execute great things in the past and will grant to him to accomplish still greater in the future.

On sending his Son into the world to redeem the world, the Father who loves him places everything into his hands. *Pater diligit Filium et omnia dedit in manus ejus*. He gave him the power to raise the dead, the power to communicate supernatural life which he possesses in his own right, and the power to judge all mankind.

There are two resurrections: that of the soul, and that of the body. The first is limited to those who on earth shall hear the voice of the Son of Man; the second extends to all who, whether they wish it or not, shall hear his call at the end of time. The Incarnate Word is the agent of both these resurrections. "As the Father has life in himself, so he has given to the Son to have life in himself." He is not a mere channel or stream, but the source of supernatural life, for by the fact of the Incarnation he possesses all the fullness of divinity. "Because he is the Son of Man, the Father has given him the power to judge." It was indeed fitting that the head of humanity, its Saviour and Redeemer, its representative before God, be constituted its supreme judge. From him no injustice nor arbitrariness is to be feared, for "he can do nothing of himself, and he does not his own will, but the will of him who sent him." He is the author of life inasmuch as he is God, and he is judge inasmuch as he is man; but he is both the one and the other because the Incarnate Word unites the two natures in one and the same Person.

3. The Witnesses of His Divine Mission

(JOHN 5:31–47)

The place which Jesus claims beside his Father and the role which he attributes to himself in the redemption of the world require proofs. Who answers for him? Where are his guarantees? Let him produce them, if he wishes to be believed, for his word alone is not enough. The Saviour anticipates this objection and answers it in advance. There is no lack of witnesses, but he will produce a witness to take the place of all others.

"If I bear witness to myself, my witness is not true (it is not acceptable as valid testimony). So be it! There is another who bears witness to me, and I know that the witness which he bears to me is true.

"You sent (on a previous occasion an embassy) to John, and he bore witness to the truth. Not that I appeal to the witness of a man, but this I say for your salvation. John was the torch that burns and gives light; and for a moment you rejoiced in his light.

"For myself, I have a higher witness than (that of) John. The works which my Father has given me to accomplish, these works that I do bear witness to me, that the Father has sent me.

"And the Father who has sent me also bears witness to me. (But) you have neither heard his voice nor seen his face; and his word does not abide in you, because you do not believe him whom he has sent.

"You search the Scriptures, because you think that they contain eternal life. So be it! It is they that bear witness to me. And you are not willing to come to me to possess life.

"I do not seek glory from men, but I know you, that you have not the love of God in you. I have come in the name of my Father, and you have not received me. If another comes in his own name, you will receive him.

"How can you believe, you who receive glory one from another, and do not seek the glory that comes from God alone?

"Think not that I will accuse you before the Father. He that accuses you is Moses, in whom you have placed your hope. If you believed Moses you would believe in me, for he has written concerning me. But if you do not believe his writings, how shall you believe my words?"

In other passages, Jesus appeals to seven witnesses: his word, his miracles, John the Baptist, the Scripture, God the Father, the Apostles, the Holy Spirit. But the testimony of the Holy Spirit and of the Apostles is still premature; he reserves it for the future. He does not wish here to invoke his own testimony; not that it would be valueless, for he will rely on it in other circumstances; but today his adversaries refuse to accept it on the basis of the legal axiom that no one is admitted as a witness in his own case. Nor will he rest his case upon the testimony of John. Doubtless he could do so, because John was a torch lighted by God to illumine men with his light — a truth that the Jews themselves had understood a short while ago. But he has no need of that testimony, since he has a testimony worth inestimably more, one that is enough for him — his Father's.

The testimony of the Father is not that which he gave of his Son on the banks of the Jordan at the time of the Baptism; still less is it that which he will give later on the summit of Thabor at the Transfiguration. There is question here of an abiding testimony, which every man can verify and check at all times and which bears within itself the seal of divinity. His miracles and, in a more general way, the works which his Father gives him to accomplish are his credentials signed by the hand of God; they are the seal which authenticates his mission. This is a testimony which no one can reject unless he wishes to close his eyes to the evidence. It would be useless for the Jews to object that they had not heard the voice of God as Moses had, and that they had not seen his face, a favor which even Moses could not obtain. That is not needed for faith. It is enough that the word of God, recorded in the Scriptures, be alive and active in their souls. But that is precisely what is lacking to them.[11]

---

[11] John 5:37–38: "The Father who sent me has borne witness to me. You have neither heard his voice nor seen his face, and you have not his word abiding in you, because you do not believe him whom he has sent." The reasoning is difficult to grasp, but it seems to be this. You could receive the testimony of the Father only by the external senses (hearing and sight) or by an internal inspiration. But you have neither seen nor heard God — you make no claim to that, nor do I reproach you for that — nor have your minds been illuminated by the light of God, for that could happen only if you gave credence to his

They search the Scriptures; they count its words, letters, and accents; they pay homage to it in their own way and profess that it teaches the way of salvation.[12] Nor does our Lord blame them for this. But they do not bring to their study the required dispositions: simplicity and humility. Jesus knows them well; he knows that they have not in their hearts the love of God. But in the matter of faith, the mind without the heart gives but an imperfect light. In their interpretation of the inspired word, they seek rather the esteem and praise of men than the glory of God. This it is that prevents them from believing truths which would upset their expectations or their dreams. And thereby the mystery of their unbelief is solved: they do not believe Christ, because they do not believe Moses.

---

envoy. Therefore the divine testimony, real though it is, is for you as though it had never been given.

[12] John 5:39: *Scrutamini Scripturas* (Ἐραυνᾶτε τὰς γραφάς). The question is whether the verb (in Greek and in Latin) is to be taken in the indicative ("You study the Scriptures") or in the imperative ("Study the Scriptures"). The Fathers, with the exception of St. Cyril of Alexandria, are generally for the imperative. Almost all modern authors, however, prefer the indicative, which fits in better with the reason given: "Because you think to find in them eternal life." The imperative would rather require: "Because in them *is found* eternal life."

CHAPTER X

In the Environs of Galilee

1. Departure to the Country of Tyre and Sidon

AFTER the miracle of Bethesda and the discourse which followed it, Jesus withdrew for a time from Jerusalem to wait for the excitement to calm down. "He went about in Galilee," says St. John, "since he was unwilling to go to Judea, because the Jews sought to put him to death."[1] Galilee itself was not a very safe place for him. The feelings of Herod Antipas toward him were ambiguous, and some emissaries from Jerusalem were following him into his own country. They had no hope, of course, of seizing Jesus by force so far away from their confederates, but they came to spy on him and to try to alienate minds and hearts from him. Having nothing more serious to level at him, they fell back on a petty complaint. They had noticed that his disciples neglected to wash their hands before sitting down to meals.

This charge was obviously made by the Scribes from Jerusalem, since the Galileans were generally not so scrupulous. But the Pharisees, particularly the Judean Pharisees, were always faithful to this practice, which they regarded as sacred, and whose origin they attributed to Solomon. Water was poured twice on each hand, the second ablution completing the first; for the first, having contracted an impurity from the hands, must itself be purified. At that rate, logically, the purifications should never have ended. The quantity of water necessary, the portion of the hand the ablu-

---

[1] John 7:1. All this is very natural, if the transposition of Chapters V and VI is admitted. Chapter VII would then follow Chapter V.

tions were supposed to reach, everything was provided for and regulated in the minutest detail. When a devout Jew came in from a walk, during which he was exposed to unclean contacts, this summary ablution was not enough. He had to plunge his hands into running water or into a receptacle containing at least thirteen gallons of pure water. Such was the theory, which was impossible to put into practice in a country so poor in water as was Judea. The purification of vessels of metal, leather, wood, and clay was elaborated into a science so complex that it took up a whole treatise in the Talmud.

The Scribes and Pharisees were scandalized at the unceremoniousness of the Apostles and said to the Saviour: "How is it that thy Apostles transgress the traditions of the ancients and do not wash their hands before eating?" Jesus answered:

"And you, how is it that you trangress the divine precept, 'Honor thy father and thy mother'? This is what you teach: When a man has said to his father or mother: 'All the goods that you can hope for from me are *Corban* (that is, consecrated to God),' that man may do nothing more to come to the aid of his father or his mother. In this and in many other things, you violate the law of God by your traditions. Hypocrites! It is of you that Isaias the prophet speaks: 'This people honors me with their lips, but their hearts are far from me. The worship which they give me is vain, for they teach doctrines which are nought but the traditions of men.' "[2]

The Pharisee had a very subtle and truly Rabbinical means of freeing himself from the duties of filial piety. To bar his parents from the use of his goods, it sufficed for him to pronounce a bizarre vow. If in a moment of irritation or bad humor he happened to say to them, "Whatever you could expect from me is consecrated to God," he was powerless thereafter to lend them any further aid or to do anything for them. This oracular formula is

---

[2] Matt. 15:1–9; Mark 7:1–13. This dispute took place with the *Scribes* (St. Matthew adds *and the Pharisees*) *from Jerusalem*. St. Mark, writing for non-Jews, explains to his readers the kind of purification in use among the Pharisees and *all the Jews* who imitated them. On the ablutions of the Jews, and also the peculiar vow which permitted children to deprive their parents of all assistance, all the details that may be desired are to be found in Billerbeck, *Kommentar,* Vol. I, pp. 691–718. Whoever has the leisure may also read the following treatises of the *Mishnah* and the *Gemara: Tohoroth, Nedarim, Shebu'oth.*

clear enough in itself, but it is often wrongly interpreted, so incredible does its natural meaning appear to be. Thus, it is supposed that the son offers to God everything that could be of advantage to his father or mother. As a matter of fact, however, the unnatural son does not offer to God anything at all, for in that case he would deprive even himself of it. He merely declares that everything belonging to him is to be considered by his parents as consecrated property which they are forbidden to touch. In other words, he vows that he will give nothing to his parents, and, according to the Talmud, the oath is valid, though it is subject to dispensation. In this way a man succeeds in harming his parents with no loss to himself. How could the notion of a vow so contrary to the natural law and to filial piety ever have entered a human brain? Is not the Saviour right when he accuses the Scribes of overturning the law of God by their so-called traditions?

His adversaries were silent, with confusion and rage in their hearts. The Apostles were troubled and said to Jesus: "Thou seest how shocked the Pharisees are at hearing thee speak thus." But without concerning himself longer with the Pharisees, Jesus says to the crowd surrounding him: "Hear me all, and understand well. It is not what enters into the mouth that defiles a man; it is what comes out of the mouth that defiles him." There is nothing mysterious about this sentence; yet at the request of his Apostles he consents to explain it to them:

"Are you then without understanding? Do you not know that what enters into the mouth and passes through the stomach and comes out by natural ways cannot defile a man? But what comes out of the mouth comes from the heart, and that is what defiles a man; for from the heart come forth wicked thoughts, murders, adulteries, fornications, thefts, false witnesses, and blasphemies. These are what truly defile a man; but to eat without washing the hands does not defile a man (from a moral point of view)."

As though he had previously formed the project, Jesus left the territory of Herod Antipas for a short time and went into Phoenicia, whose most celebrated cities were Tyre and Sidon.

2. In Phoenicia and the Decapolis

For the first time since the flight into Egypt, Jesus goes beyond the borders of Palestine into infidel territory.[3] He is not drawn there by thoughts of the apostolate, for the hour of the Gentiles has not yet struck. Rather he is looking for a refuge from the treacherous intrigues of his enemies, a place to rest and take a breath after so many trying experiences, and above all he is seeking the isolation necessary to complete the instruction of the Apostles.

He did not find what he was seeking. His fame as a wonder-worker had preceded him there, and as soon as they had wind of his arrival, curiosity seekers and petitioners for favors were besieging the house where he was hiding. A woman of that land, who was a pagan by religion and a Syro-Phoenician by race (which means that she belonged to the old substratum of the native population called Chanaanites to distinguish them from the Israelites who were very numerous in those localities), was among the first to find him. She cried out in distress: "Have pity on me, Lord, Son of David! My daughter is frightfully tormented by a devil." But, indifferent to these titles of honor heaped upon him, and to all appearances untouched by the mother's tears, Jesus answered not a single word. Perhaps he wished to test and strengthen her faith, or to teach his disciples the sovereign power of a humble and persevering prayer. The woman was not discouraged, but redoubled her cries and pleadings.

The impatient Apostles finally decided that it was time for them to step in and put an end to this painful scene. "Lord," they said, "dismiss this woman (by giving her what she wants), for she is wearying us with her cries." Their compassion was not unmixed with selfishness. Surely they wished to see the intruder go away satisfied, but they wanted even more to get rid of her. Jesus answered them: "I have not been sent except to the lost sheep of Israel." The pagans will have their turn. That will be the work for you. But the time has not yet come either for me or for you.

[3] Matt. 15:21–39; Mark 7:24–8:10. St. Luke passes over this whole journey in silence, as also the incidents preceding it after the return to Genesareth (Matt. 14:34; Mark 6:53).

Meantime the Chanaanite woman, ignoring the Apostles, prostrated herself at Jesus' feet. "Lord," she said, "please come to my help. Free my daughter!" Jesus finally answered her, but how sharply and how severely! "Wait until the children have had their fill, for it is not proper to take bread from the children and throw it to little dogs."

Among the Semites, dogs are looked upon as repulsive and contemptible creatures. They are allowed to wander uncared for, shelterless and without a master. Here, however, the reference is to domestic animals, the sort of family pets allowed in the house and fed with scraps and leftovers. The allegory is clear. The children are the Jews, the sons of the Covenant and the promise. By virtue of their contract with God, they should be served first; later the Gentiles will receive what is left. The Chanaanite woman understands exactly what is meant, and, taking up the allegory, she turns the argument with a retort as witty as it is pertinent. "Yes, Lord. Thou speakest the truth, and I do not ask for more, for the little dogs under the table eat the children's crumbs." She wants only the lost scraps that content the curs while they wait for their food. Overcome by such humility and patience, our Lord, who wanted nothing more than to allow himself to be overcome, said to her kindly: "Oh, woman, great is thy faith. Be it done to thee according to thy desire. Go, the devil has gone out of thy daughter's body."

Great indeed was the faith of the Chanaanite woman, and the Fathers of the Church do not weary of singing her praises. Nothing rebuffs her, neither the ungenerous attitude of the Apostles nor the icy silence of Jesus nor his categorical and apparently definitive refusal. She hopes against hope and the outcome proves her right. Returning home, the happy woman finds her daughter stretched out on her bed and sleeping tranquilly. The devil has fled.[4]

This miracle, in a way wrested from the Saviour by the stubborn prayer of the Syro-Phoenician woman, as the miracle of Cana had been drawn from him by the silent plea of Mary, is not the opening move in the evangelization of the Gentiles. It

---

[4] Matt. 15:22–28; Mark 7:25–30. According to the *Clementine Homilies* (ii, 19; iii, 73), the mother was named Justa and the daughter, Berenice. A very weak authority!

is rather a presage than a prelude. The Saviour had no intention of settling in pagan territory. Failing to find the calm and seclusion he wished for, he will not stay there long. "Again leaving the country of Tyre, he went by way of Sidon to the Sea of Galilee, across the country of the Decapolis."[5] Tyre was only a day's journey from Sidon, its ancient rival; but instead of going into the pagan village of Sidon, Jesus probably crossed through the territory. An easy road would bring him to the farthest of the Jordan springs. Going thence around Hermon and turning to the south, he would come to the Decapolis.

The Decapolis was a confederation of Greek cities, originally ten in number, united by the bonds of a common race, language, and religion, as well as by commercial intercourse and considerations of mutual defense. After the death of Alexander the Great, the Macedonian veterans had come to settle to the south of the Lake of Tiberias and founded there two towns, Pella and Dion, names which recalled to them memories of their fatherland. Pella of Macedonia boasted of being the birthplace of Alexander, and Dion, at the foot of Olympus, enjoyed an equal celebrity. Later other towns of the Hellenic type sprang up in the same region, and, although the charmed number of Ten did not remain unchanged, the name Decapolis persisted for a long time. All these towns were to the east of the Jordan except Scythopolis, which was wedged in as a strip of land between Galilee and Samaria. From Scythopolis these towns spread out fanwise into Transjordania, with Damascus as the northernmost and Philadelphia as the farthest south. Since the more or less vast territories they

---

[5] Mark 7:31: *καὶ πάλιν ἐξελθὼν ἐκ τῶν ὁρίων* Τύρου *ἦλθεν διὰ Σιδῶνος εἰς τὴν θάλασσαν τῆς Γαλιλαίας ἀνὰ μέσον τῶν ὁρίων Δεκαπόλεως.* (*a*) The starting point is the territory of Tyre (*ὅρια* can have no other meaning); (*b*) he went *by way of Sidon,* but the question here is whether the town or the territory is meant; (*c*) the destination is the *Sea of Galilee,* the eastern shore of the lake; (*d*) the only difficulty is in the phrase "across the Decapolis." Many see in it a new destination; but either it is the same as the other, defining it by apposition (which is impossible, because no city of the Decapolis is on the lake), or it is different, and in that case the two should be joined by a conjunction. The sense is therefore: "He went *from the country of Tyre,* passing *by way of* (the town or territory of) *Sidon,* and came to the Lake of Tiberias *across* the region of *the Decapolis.*" This would be a detour, but nothing proves that Jesus must have taken the direct route. St. Matthew (15:29) says only: "Departing thence (from the country of Tyre), he came near to the Sea of Galilee, and going up a mountain he sat down there." There is no allusion to the Decapolis.

occupied were not contiguous, they formed so many enclaves in the states of Antipas. The population of these towns was for the greater part Greek, but in the rest of the country it was mixed with a large share of indigenous elements and numbered a great many Jews.[6]

It was apparently in this half-pagan environment that there occurred the miracle described in the picturesque and lively narrative so characteristic of St. Mark. "They brought to Jesus a man deaf and stammering, and asked that he lay his hands upon him," to cure him, of course, of his double infirmity. He was not a deaf-mute from birth, for he was not entirely dumb. He babbled inarticulately, almost unintelligibly, because of a congenital defect of speech which had become more aggravated by an early deafness. Up to this, we have seen Jesus cure the sick either by a simple touch, or by the imposition of his hands, or by a word of command. Sometimes the cure occurred gradually in successive phases, oftener it was instantaneous. Sometimes it was done at a distance, sometimes it seemed to require the presence of the miracle-worker. Since Jesus had at his command a supernatural power, he used it in accordance with his wisdom and divine inspiration for reasons regarding which he was accountable to no one.

Today we see him adopt a new mode of action. Taking the deaf-mute aside, apart from the crowd, he put his fingers into the man's ears after having moistened the stammerer's tongue with spittle; then, lifting his eyes to heaven, he sighed and said to the sick man, "Ephphata!" — that is to say, "Be opened!" Commentators have always wondered at the sigh and the reason for the air of mystery. They have supposed that when he took the sick man aside he did so in order to find a solitude more favorable to prayer, or that he wished to avoid all appearance of ostentation, or that he feared to have his gesture interpreted by the pagans as the performance of magic. They could, perhaps, have added that he intended above all to arouse in the man the faith that was still lacking to him, since this was the normal condition of a miracle. He could not suggest this necessary faith in words, because the deaf man could not hear. He therefore

[6] On the Decapolis, see Schürer, *Geschichte,* 4 ed., Vol. II, pp. 148–193; or Van Kasteren in Vigouroux's *Dictionnaire de la Bible.*

undertook to arouse it in him by a solemn ceremony and symbolic actions well calculated to bring it into being. He put his fingers into the man's ears as if to open them; he moistened his tongue with spittle as though to give or restore to him all his vocal flexibility. And in fact "the ears of the deaf-mute were opened, and his tongue was loosed, and he spoke distinctly."[7]

All of Christ's miracles are theandric actions, which means that they are operations in which the two natures meet, the divinity supplying the omnipotence without which a miracle is impossible, and the humanity actively concurring after the manner of an instrument, by a prayer, a word of command, or a symbolic gesture. But the cure of the deaf-mute of the Decapolis is peculiar in this, that it somehow takes on a sacramental character, the words corresponding to the gestures, and the two combined producing the favor which they symbolize. Thus it is that the Church borrows these rites in the administration of Baptism. Is not the state of fallen man comparable to that of the deaf-mute of the Gospel? When the priest, with his fingers moistened with saliva traces the Sign of the Cross on the ears and mouth of the neophyte, while pronouncing the sacramental word *Ephphata,* he disposes him to hear and to profess supernatural truths.

Jesus had enjoined upon the cured man and his guides the most absolute silence. The injunction was serious and not feigned. He had wrought this miracle out of pure condescension; it was a work of mercy which he wished to be kept secret, as an example for us to follow on similar occasions. But the people ignored the command. They hastened to publish everywhere what had happened. Gratitude may be their excuse. They may have attributed the command to their benefactor's modesty, and missed seeing in it an express prohibition. At all events, the report of the miracle was so widespread throughout the whole country that, despite the fact that Jesus withdrew from the Decapolis and climbed the mountain that dominates the Sea of Galilee on the

[7] Mark 7:32–36. The sick man is deaf (κωφός), but not dumb; he is μογιλάλος, "stuttering," "speaking with difficulty." A "bond" (δεσμός) prevents his tongue from articulating. When cured, he speaks correctly (ὀρθῶς), giving letters and syllables their true value. Jesus looks up to heaven to pray: "His sighing is also an insistent though silent prayer" (Lagrange). Others think that he sighed over the miseries of humanity: a somewhat forced explanation.

east, the multitude followed him there. From every side they brought to him the lame, the blind, the deaf, the crippled, and a great many other sick. They laid them all at his feet, and he cured them. The admiration of the people went beyond all bounds, and they applied to the young Wonder-Worker the words of Isaias: "He does all things well; the deaf he makes to hear, and the dumb to speak."[8]

It was also on the eastern shore, and about the same period, that the second multiplication of loaves took place. About four thousand people — not counting women and children — had followed the Saviour for three days. The supply of food, which Orientals never fail to provide for themselves on a journey, was exhausted, and the people were far from any habitation. Touched by so much patience and good will, Jesus said to his Apostles: "If I send them away fasting, they will faint on the road, for many have come from afar off." He seemed to be asking their advice on how to take care of this difficulty, but they could find no remedy. They had certainly not forgotten the first multiplication, but they doubtless supposed that the Master would not have recourse a second time to such an extraordinary means of caring for physical needs.

As on the first occasion, the inventory of their resources was not encouraging. They had on hand altogether only seven loaves and a few small fishes. Jesus took the loaves in his hands and, after pronouncing over them a formula of blessing, gave them back to the Apostles to be distributed to the multitude. He did the same with the little fishes. Everyone ate until satisfied, and seven baskets of fragments were collected.[9]

The two multiplications are alike, but it could not have been otherwise. Whenever there is question of a meal, a blessing must be pronounced, guests must be fed, food must be distributed, and the fragments must be collected. But all the rest of the details are different. There are four thousand people instead of five thousand; seven loaves and some small fishes instead of five loaves and two fishes; seven baskets of fragments instead of twelve panniers. The first multiplication took place in the territory of the

[8] Matt. 15:30–31; Mark 7:37.

[9] Matt. 15:32–38; Mark 8:1–10. There is no difference between the two accounts.

Tetrarchy of Philip, and the multitude came from Capharnaum. Here we are in the Decapolis, and the multitude has been following Jesus for three days. It is hard to satisfy the critics. If the second multiplication were not reported by two Evangelists who had already reported the first, would they not say that this is the same event differently distorted by legend?

As soon as the multitude had been dismissed, Jesus and his Apostles embarked and made their way to a place called Magedan or Dalmanutha, which topographers have not yet succeeded in identifying. Do these two names designate the same place or two different places, or does one designate a town and the other a district? In any case, we are on the western shore of the lake, in the plain of Genesareth or its immediate vicinity.[10]

---

[10] Matt. 15:39: ἦλθεν εἰς τὰ ὅρια Μαγαδάν, "He came into the region (or into the confines) of Magedan." Mark 8:10: ἦλθεν εἰς τὰ μέρη Δαλμανουθά, "He came into the country of Dalmanutha." On this enigma, cf. Nestle, in the *Dict. of Christ and the Gospels,* 1906, Vol. I, p. 406; or Dalman, *Orte und Wege,* 1924, p. 136 (English transl., Levertoff, 1935, p. 128). There is an exposé of the various opinions in Lagrange, *Saint Marc,* 4 ed., 1929, pp. 504–505. The riddle is still unsolved.

CHAPTER XI

The Church Founded on Peter

1. On the Road to Caesarea Philippi

SCARCELY had Jesus set foot on Galilean soil than he found the Pharisees and Sadducees in league against him. This is the first time that we find these quarrelsome brothers conspiring together. The pact which they are sealing on this day will have its final outcome on Calvary. "Master," they said to him, "we wish to see from thee a sign from heaven."[1] They are not asking for one of those miraculous cures which they considered too easy and of too little probative value, but for a truly celestial prodigy such as the appearance at a given moment of a new meteor or an eclipse of the sun or moon outside the periods of conjunction. Moses had caused manna to rain down in the desert; Josue had stopped the course of the sun; Elias had opened the cataracts of the sky which had been closed for three years. If Jesus should declare that he was unable to imitate them, he would be acknowledging himself inferior to these prophets, and would be forced to renounce his Messianic pretentions.

The devious maneuvers of these willfully blind men plunged Jesus into a sadness that wrested from him a deep sigh. Never before had sadness reacted so forcefully upon his sense faculties.[2] He answers by taking the offensive.

---

[1] Matt. 16:1–4; Mark 8:11–13. St. Matthew has already spoken of the demand for a sign (12:38–39). St. Luke places it elsewhere. The demand may have been made more than once.

[2] Mark 8:12: "Sighing deeply in his spirit." The sigh during the cure of the mute (Mark 7:34) was rather a prayer than an expression of grief.

"When evening has come, you say: 'It will be fair weather, for the sky is the color of fire,' and in the morning, you say: 'To-day there will be rain, for the sky is threatening and turning red.' If you know to read the face of the heavens, why can you not read the signs of the times?"[3]

In Palestine, a sun sinking at evening in a blazing horizon presages fair weather for the next day, while the same rosy tint at dawn threatens rain. It is different in Egypt, where rain is rare and the sky is almost perpetually serene. Thus it is that a certain number of manuscripts, all of which, or almost all, have undergone Egyptian influence, suppress these two verses so apt in their observation and so perfect in their local coloring. St. Luke gives the same thought a different turn, either reporting a saying of the Saviour uttered on some other occasion, or varying the expression to make the thought intelligible to those of his readers who were less familiar with the climate of Palestine. "When you see the clouds rise in the west, you say: 'The rain comes,' and so it happens; and when the wind blows from the south, you say: 'It will be hot,' and so it happens." As a matter of fact, in most Mediterranean regions rain comes from the west and heat from the south. But in whatever way Jesus formulated this fact of experience, the conclusion he draws against his adversaries is the same. "Hypocrites! You know how to judge the face of the sky and of the earth. How is it then that you do not judge the face of this time?" Forecasts made from the appearance of the sky are worth noting, but they are by no means infallible. On the other hand, the signs of the Messianic times, the accumulation of works authenticating Christ's divine mission, and the prophecies which are having in him their fulfillment are signs that do not deceive. They are clearer and more certain than the best established meteorological forecasts. To one who would refuse to see them, a celestial miracle would bring no light.

The Jews were not wrong in asking for a sign. For four centuries the role of prophet had disappeared from Israel, but there

[3] Matt. 16:2–3. "The red glow in the western sky in the evening is frequent in summer when the weather is fair and settled. In the morning, this red glow is in the east, coloring the thick clouds that give a menacing look to the sky" (Lagrange, *Saint Matthieu,* p. 317). On the authenticity of this passage cf. *ibid.,* pp. 315–316. St. Luke, in another context (12:54–56), modifies the presentation of these signs, which are peculiar to Palestine.

was hope of the return of the prophetic era, and they were waiting for the coming of a prophet like to Moses, a legislator and liberator of his people. When, in the year 163 B.C., the Altar of the True God, which had been profaned by idolatrous sacrifices, was destroyed, the materials were preserved for a destiny that was to be determined by the Prophet. Later, the hereditary dignity of High Priest was entrusted to Simon, the brother of Judas Machabeus, on condition that it should have the sanction of this same Prophet.[4] As an ambassador from God to man, a prophet is obliged to produce his credentials. In this Jesus Christ did not fail; but the more he multiplied his miracles, the more did the unbelieving demand new and more startling signs. To convince them, there remained only the miracle of his Resurrection. "This perverse and adulterous generation seeks a sign, and no other sign shall be given it, except the sign of Jonas," who after three days came from the belly of the sea monster that had swallowed him.

Without delaying longer to confound his enemies, Jesus embarked and gave the order to sail to the eastern shore. So abrupt was the departure that the Apostles did not have time to lay up stores for the journey. There was nothing but a single loaf of bread in the boat, perhaps left there by an oversight. The Apostles were disturbed by their lack of provisions and were pondering means of supplying them, when they heard the Master say to them: "Take heed to beware of the leaven of the Pharisees and Sadducees, as well as the leaven of Herod." They did not in the least understand this admonition. Why did he speak of leaven when they did not even have bread? Reading the depths of their hearts, Jesus added:

"Why do you concern yourselves about the bread that you have not brought? Are you heedless and without understanding? Are your eyes incapable of seeing, and your ears of hearing, and your memory of retaining? When I broke five loaves for five thousand

---

[4] The *profaned altar* (1 Mach. 4:46): "They laid up the stones in the mountain of the Temple in a convenient place, awaiting the coming of a prophet who should give a decision concerning them." *Simon the High Priest* (1 Mach. 14:41): "The Jews and their priests agreed that Simon should be their ethnarch and High Priest forever, till there should rise a prophet worthy of faith."

people, how many baskets of fragments did you gather? Twelve. And when I distributed seven loaves to four thousand, how many panniers of fragments did you collect? Seven. Do you not yet understand?"

Jesus offers them in passing a motive for confidence, but his main purpose is to inculcate another lesson. He therefore explains himself more clearly. "How is it that you do not see that when I warned you against the leaven of the Pharisees and Sadducees, I was not speaking of bread?" The leaven of the Pharisees is hypocrisy and narrow formalism. The leaven of the Sadducees is ambition and worldliness. The leaven of Herod is craftiness and unbridled love of pleasure. The metaphor is so simple that the Apostles should have understood it from the first.

They disembarked at Bethsaida, a coastal village which the Tetrarch Philip had made into a town by increasing its size and moving it a mile or more inland to a higher and healthier site.[5] But the old village still had a population of fishermen whose livelihood attached them to the borders of the lake. Jesus had just entered the town when they brought to him a blind man, pleading with him to touch him. Doubtless they had observed that he often cured the sick by a simple touch, and it may have been the common persuasion that this touch was necessary. Without saying anything the Saviour took the blind man by the hand and led him outside the town. Since the miracle he was about to perform was an act of merciful compassion, and not a proof of his divine mission, he wished to have no other witnesses than the Apostles. Once outside the town, he put spittle on the eyes of the blind man, and laying his hands upon him he asked him

[5] There is agreement now in locating Bethsaida-Julias in a place called by the Arabs, *et-Tell,* a natural or artificial hillock covered by ruins, which rises some 65 ft. above the plain, 2 mi. north of the lake, and 300 yds. east of the Jordan. The original hamlet of Bethsaida (House of Fishing) must have been on the lake, either at *el-Araj* near the Jordan, or at *Mesadiyeh* more to the east. The ancient Bethsaida must have continued in existence as a suburb or port of Julias, a name which never came into common use. On the history of Bethsaida and its location, cf. Guerin, *Galilée,* 1880, Vol. I, pp. 329–338; Masterman, *Studies in Galilee,* 1909, pp. 101–106; Dalman, *Itinéraires de Jésus,* 1930, pp. 215–247. We have already exposed the reasons for distinguishing this Bethsaida from the native place of the Apostles Peter, Andrew, and Philip (cf. Dalman, *Sacred Sites and Ways,* tr. of Levertoff, 1935, pp. 161–164).

whether he saw anything. The man answered: "I see men, for I see, as it were, walking trees." Blind from birth, at first he saw objects only in a confused way and on the same plane; for the eye perceives only form and color; it is habit and education that brings the appreciation of dimensions and distances. Things floating in the air seemed to the man larger than they were, and he distinguished men from trees only by the fact that he saw them walking. To complete the cure, Jesus lays his hands upon him again, and his vision of objects far and near becomes entirely distinct.[6]

The whole setting is mysterious. The spittle of a fasting man was considered a remedy against eye trouble, but surely no one ever imagined that it could cure complete blindness.[7] What, then, did Jesus' action mean? Apart from the symbolic meaning which we mentioned in the preceding chapter when speaking of the deaf-mute of the Decapolis, Jesus undoubtedly wished to arouse the faith of the sick man by working his cure by degrees, as if, to be complete, it required a supplement of faith. At first, the man sees objects in a confused way and without perspective, like fantastic beings coming out of a thick fog. At our Lord's second gesture, he clearly distinguishes everything, and no longer takes men for walking plants.

From there Jesus went northward to go to Paneas, which the Tetrarch Philip had enriched and embellished and named Caesarea in honor of Caesar Augustus. It was two days' journey distant. If, as is probable, he went along the east bank of the Jordan, he crossed through territory inhabited by Jews and pagans, though the pagans had the advantage in numbers, at least in the more important localities. Caesarea, which was outside of Palestine, since the northern border of Palestine was at Dan, almost three miles west, had always been a thoroughly pagan town. Its picturesque site at the foot of high mountains, in the midst of murmuring waters and lavish vegetation, had always occasioned its consecration to nature divinities such as Baal and

---

[6] Mark 8:22–26. Some phrases of the Vulgate differ somewhat from the Greek text, which we have followed. Consult a good commentary.

[7] *Talmud of Jerusalem,* Treat. *Shabbath,* xiv, 14 and 18; Treat. *Abodah Zarah,* xi, 10 and 19.

Astarte. From the bottom of a deep grotto, which was surmounted by a steep rock, gushed the most famous, if not the most abundant, of the headsprings of the Jordan. When the Greeks settled there in the third century B.C., they dedicated the place to the rustic god Pan and to the Nymphs, as can still be seen in the numerous inscriptions carved into the rock. The sanctuary of Pan earned for the city the name Paneas or Panias, which it still keeps in a form slightly modified by the Arabic pronunciation of Banias.

At the summit of the cliff which overlooks the source of the Jordan, Herod had built in honor of Augustus a temple covered with gleaming white marble, visible from afar in every direction: without doubt the finest monument of Emperor worship erected on the Palestinian border. Jesus does not seem to have entered the more than half-pagan town of Caesarea, but he must have taken note of the famous cliff crowned by the Temple of Augustus, lifting its silhouette upon the lofty esplanade as on a gigantic pedestal. Some have thought that this spectacle suggested to him the image of the Church built on the unshakable rock of Peter, and this hypothesis, when tested on the spot, is not lacking in likelihood.[8]

2. St. Peter's Confession

Toward the end of the journey, Jesus went aside to be alone with his Father. This was his habit on the eve of great enterprises

[8] This is the impression we had a long time ago when we visited the famous rock for the first time, not suspecting then that others had or would later have the same thought. Cf. Immisch in *Zeitsch, f. neut. Wissenschaft,* 1916, pp. 18–20; but the author spoils his theory by identifying the cavern from which the Jordan rises with the "gates of hell." Banias was built on the last spur of Great Hermon. The rock dominating the grotto of Pan was estimated by Ebers and Guthe to be 98 ft. high; by Smith, to be 150 feet. The effect is less striking nowadays, because the upper wall of the grotto has sunk and the ground level has risen, and the Jordan wells up all around under a heap of large stones. Nothing remains of the Temple of Augustus, described by Josephus (*Antiq.* XV, x, 3; *Bellum,* III, x, 7 and I, xxi, 3). About its probable site, cf. Immisch, *loc. cit.,* and Guerin, *Galilée,* II, 315. Trusting to Eusebius' statement (*Chronicle*), it has been repeated that Caesarea was so called in honor of Tiberius. This is incorrect. Philip founded it in the year 2 or 3 B.C., while Augustus was alive. Banias is 2½ or 3 mi. east of Dan, which marked the northern border of Palestine (Dan to Bersabee). Dan, which in Hebrew means *judge,* was situated at *Tell el-Qadi* (Hill of the Judge). At the foot of the hillock, which was the site of Dan, rises the most copious of the Jordan springs.

and grave decisions. The Apostles rejoined him in the environs of Caesarea Philippi. As he was walking along with them, he asked them a question: "What do people say about the Son of Man, and what am I in their eyes?" Questioned together the Apostles naturally would not all have the same answer to give. Each reported what he had heard, and the feelings of the multitude about Jesus were greatly varied. Some said, "He is John the Baptist"; others, "He is Elias"; still others, "He is Jeremias or some one of the prophets of olden times."[9] The appearance of the Baptist had been very brief. Outside of Judea scarcely more than his name was known. Many may have thought that he had escaped Herod's clutches or, as Herod himself thought, that he had risen from the dead. The great wonder-worker Elias was generally regarded as the precursor of the Messias. And Jeremias, according to the expectation of the times, was to come to the aid of Israel at a time of national crisis. It was he "who prayed much for his brethren and for the Holy City," and it was he who had placed the liberating sword into the hands of Judas Machabeus.[10] Those who refused to identify Jesus with any of these three illustrious personages could not but recognize in him a prophet the like of whom had not been seen for centuries. Finally, though all agreed that he might well be one of the forerunners of the Messias, none took him for the Messias himself.

"But you," continued Jesus, "whom do you say that I am? You who are living my life, who have shared my confidences and seen my works; what think you of me?"

Simon Peter hastened to reply: "Thou art the Christ, the Son of the living God."

After all that the Apostles had seen and heard in their long and intimate companionship with their divine Master, they would have needed to be remarkably unintelligent to think that he was no more than a mere son of God by adoption, as are other just men. Yet, were they all as enlightened as St. Peter? It may be doubted. At all events, Peter anticipated them, not so much

[9] Matt. 16:13–14; Mark 8:27–28; Luke 9:18–19. The scene took place in the *region* (Matthew, *μέρη*) or in the *villages* (Mark, *κώμας*) of Caesarea-Philippi, on the road (Mark, *ἐν τῇ ὁδῷ*) when Jesus rejoined his Apostles (Luke 9:18) after his prayer.

[10] 2 Mach. 15:15–16 (cf. 4 Esdr. 2:17). On Elias, cf. Billerbeck, *Exkurs.*, 28, Vol. IV, pp. 764–798.

because of his habit of taking the initiative, not so much because of his impetuous temperament, as that he was conscious of an interior light which the others, perhaps, did not possess to the same degree. "When Jesus asked them the opinion of the people, they all made answer," says St. John Chrysostom. "When he asks them what they themselves think, Peter alone breaks in and forestalls the rest." It may well be thought that he considers himself their interpreter and spokesman; but he has not consulted them, he has not made inquiry about their belief; he is giving expression to his own conviction. And it is to him, and him alone, that Jesus is about to direct his answer. It is Peter alone that he congratulates; him alone he rewards, and him alone among all of them he proclaims blessed.

"Blessed art thou, Simon Bar-Jona, because flesh and blood have not revealed this to thee, but my Father who is in heaven. And I say to thee, thou art Peter, and upon this Rock I will build my Church, and the gates of hell shall not prevail against it. I will give thee the keys of the kingdom of heaven; and whatsoever thou shalt bind upon earth shall be bound in heaven, and whatsoever thou shalt loose upon earth shall be loosed in heaven."[11]

Peter is proclaimed blessed because his confession is not dictated by flesh and blood, by nature left to itself. It is not a conclusion of reason, but an act of faith, and therefore a grace given to him by the heavenly Father. It could not come to him from any other source, for no one knows the Son but the Father and those to whom the Father deigns to reveal him. "If he had not recognized him as born of the Father himself," again says St. John Chrysostom, "he would not have had a revelation; if he had thought that he was merely a son among other sons, his confession would not have merited such praise." Indeed, this was

---

[11] Matt. 16:17–19. This text is peculiar to Matthew. Here Peter's patronymic is *Bar-Jona* (Son of Jonas). In Hebrew יוֹנָה, in Aramaic יוֹנָא, is the name of the prophet Jonas, which means *Dove*. In St. John (1:42), the Vulgate also has *Simon filius Jona*, but the Greek has Σίμων ὁ υἱὸς Ἰωάνου (son of John). There is some resemblance in Hebrew between יוֹנָה (Jonas) and יוֹהָנָן (Ἰωάνης), and many think that the first must be an abbreviation of the second (Chase, in *Dict. of the Bible,* Vol. II, pp. 676–677). It is more probable that, according to a widespread custom of the times, Peter's father bore two names that were somewhat alike, Jonas and John.

not the first time that Jesus had heard himself called Son of God. The demoniacs, Nathanael, and the disciples whom he had saved from the storm had already accorded this title to him; but by the name "Son of God" the Jews did not mean to express the unique and incommunicable relationship uniting the Word to his Father by virtue of the eternal generation; nor did they intend to designate the Messias, who was never commonly called by that name. They were thinking only of someone favored by God, the depository of his authority, of his power, or of his favors.

It is impossible to read this passage, which is found only in St. Matthew, without being struck by the Semitic coloring of the language. Everything about it reveals a Jewish hand and a Palestinian origin. There is not a single phrase, scarcely a single word that does not have a native tang. The "living God," the patronymic appellation *"Simon Bar-Jona,"* the "gates of hell," the "keys of the kingdom," the metaphor of "loosing and binding," and above all the play on words in "Peter" which is so natural in Hebrew and Aramaic and so awkward to translate into other languages: all bear the mark of their origin. The other Synoptics have reduced Peter's confession to this phrase: "Thou art the Christ," or "the Christ of God"; and they have omitted the answer given by Jesus. To explain this silence, it has been suggested that Peter, in giving the catechesis collected by his disciple Mark, readily told everything that might lessen his stature, but was silent on whatever would magnify him in the eyes of the faithful. This is possible. But I am inclined to think that the too Semitic tone of the passage contributed to its omission. We know that this was St. Luke's ordinary practice in like cases, and that when St. Mark occasionally inserts bits of this kind he feels the need of explaining them.

To checkmate what they termed Roman pretensions, the early Protestants maintained that, when saying these words, "Thou art Peter, and upon this rock I will build my Church," Jesus pointed to himself, as though to say, "True, thou art Peter, but I will found my Church upon another Rock, the rock that I am now showing to thee." Not even among the most rabid enemies of the papacy would there be one to defend this ridiculous interpretation today. It has not even the merit of being a poor joke.

Neither would they be likely to say, with the estimable author of the *Gnomon:* "The Church was founded on the Apostles inasmuch as they were the first converts and the first to convert others. It is in this that Peter's prerogative consists without prejudice to the privilege of the others: that he was the first to preach the Gospel to the Jews and to the Gentiles."[12] But the commentators who remain faithful to the spirit of primitive Protestantism continue to say that the Church was founded on the faith of Peter or on the divinity of Christ proclaimed by Peter; and this can be said quite truly, provided that we understand, with all the Fathers and Catholic Doctors, that it was founded on the person of Peter because of and by reason of his faith, or on the faith which Peter teaches, which does not at all exclude the person of Peter.[13] If they object that, according to St. Paul, no one can lay any other foundation than that which he has himself laid, namely, Christ Jesus, who will fail to see that the text of St. Paul and that of St. Matthew are entirely different from each other? The Apostle is speaking of a doctrinal monument, whose foundation can be none other than the primordial dogma of Christianity. The Evangelist is speaking of a religious society to which a head is being given, and this head can be nothing else but a person. Simon, who has received for this purpose the symbolic name of Peter, will become the foundation of the Church, represented under the image of a temple or a house that is to be built, and he will give to the whole edifice its solidarity and cohesion.[14]

---

[12] Bengel, *Gnomon Novi Testamenti* (Stuttgart, 1892), p. 102. The author adds: "Quid haec ad Romam? . . . Videat Petra Romana ne cadat sub censura versus 23." Always the same obsession with "papistry"! Another Protestant, Kuinoel, commenting on the same passage, adds this frank reflection: "Many understand the Rock as Christ himself, or Peter's confession of faith. They would never have had recourse to such forced interpretations, if the papists had not misused this text to attribute to the successors of Peter, that is to say, to the Roman pontiffs, a singular and divine prerogative and authority."

[13] Cf. Bellarmine, *Controvers. de Summo Pontifice,* lib. I, cap. 10–14; or Palmieri, *De Romano Pontifice* (Rome, 1877), p. 246 ff. What impresses one most in reading these texts of the Fathers is that the older they are the more explicit they are on the literal sense of "Thou art Peter and upon this Rock I will build my Church." Once the primacy of the Roman pontiff was well established, the Fathers did not hesitate also to use these words of Christ in an accommodated sense.

[14] 1 Cor. 3:9–15. Cf. Prat, *Theologie de Saint Paul,* Vol. I, pp. 110–112 (English transl., Vol. I, pp. 94–95).

Could Jesus have expressed himself with greater clearness? In Greek and in Latin, where the word "rock" differs in gender accordingly as it is a proper name or a common noun, Jesus' words could provide prejudiced minds with matter for quibbling; but in the idiom which our Lord used, this is not the case. In Aramaic the word *Kepha* means "rock." It is the name which our Lord has chosen expressly for Simon Bar-Jona, and he now brings home to him the significance of the name by saying to him, "Thou art Rock, and upon this Rock I will build my Church."[15] None of his hearers could mistake his meaning, and if he had meant to convey something else, he would have grossly deceived them.

Let no one be surprised that here the name "Church" is read for the first time. How could the Church be mentioned before there was question of founding it by giving it a head? And indeed, properly speaking, the Church does not have its birth until Pentecost. Only then does Peter enter upon the possession of his title and his functions, and it is from that day forward that the name "Church" recurs so often under the pen of St. Paul, of St. Luke in the Acts, and of the author of the Apocalypse.

In the Old Testament the Church designated the children of Israel as a religious society; but when Christ says *my Church,* he very clearly indicates that he intends to found an entirely new and distinct society, though it be built on the substructure of the old.[16] The metaphors of "foundation" and "building," which are

---

[15] In Hebrew *keph* (כֵּף) means "rock," either as a place of refuge (Jer. 4:29), or as a dwelling place. In Aramaic, *Kepha* (כֵּיפָא) has the same meaning (Num. 20:8, where it translates *sela'*), though it can also mean "stone," especially in the feminine. This is also the meaning of the Assyrian (ka-a-pe shashade-e, "the rocks of the mountains"). In Syriac, *kepha* (כאפא) becomes feminine, with the meaning "stone," and it is less suitable as a man's name, but fits in better with the play on words, like the French, "Tu es Pierre et sur *cette* Pierre."

When it became necessary to translate *kepha* into Greek, there was a choice between πέτρα and πέτρος. Πέτρα would be more exact, because it means "rock," as does *kepha;* but Πέτρος is more suitable as a man's name. However, with Πέτρος the play on words is sacrificed, and the meaning suffers; for πέτρος which is a synonym for λίθος, means "stone" or "pebble," but not "rock." It is worse still in Latin, where *petrus* as a common noun does not mean anything. French is better equipped, for *pierre* can be taken in the sense of "rock," and the play on words is still found in French, as in the phrase pronounced by our Lord.

[16] In the Septuagint, the word ἐκκλησία (Matt. 16:18 and 18:17 bis) is

more applicable to an edifice than to an assembly, were suggested to him by the symbolic name, Peter. Besides, the minds of his hearers were prepared for it by a phrase used to designate the Chosen People as a group: the assembly of the *House of God.*

Contemporary Rationalists and Protestants who have freed themselves from denominational prejudices are coming back of their own accord to the Catholic explanation of St. Matthew's text. Many of them even force its meaning in the direction of "Roman pretensions" in order to deny its authenticity. "Simon Peter," writes one of them, "is not only the historical foundation of the Church; he is its present and permanent foundation. In the eyes of St. Matthew, he still lives in a power which binds and looses, which holds the keys of the kingdom of God, and which is the authority of the Church itself; not a diffuse authority, but an authority which is general and distinct, which is to particular authorities what Simon Peter is to the disciples and to St. Paul himself. . . . Simon Peter is the prime apostolic authority in all that regards faith, since to him by preference the Father has revealed the mystery of the Son; in all that regards the government of communities, because Christ has entrusted to him the keys of the kingdom; in all that regards ecclesiastical discipline, because he has the power of loosing and binding. Not without reason has Catholic tradition founded upon this text the dogma of the Roman primacy. Consciousness of this primacy inspires the entire development in Matthew, who has in view not only the historical person of Simon, but also the traditional succession from Simon Peter."[17] Loisy here speaks like Bossuet, though not as eloquently. "That which must serve as the support of an eternal Church can never have an end. Peter shall therefore live in his

ordinarily the translation of *qahal* (קהל), which designates the people of Israel as a religious assembly. A synonym for *qahal* was *'edah* (עדה), which the Septuagint usually translates by συναγωγή. But συναγωγή in the time of Christ meant the *building* where the Jews gathered, and the Christians appropriated the name ἐκκλησία to designate either the entire body of Christ's followers, or the collection of the faithful of a particular town or region, or, later, the place where they met. It is curious to find that the Jewish Christians continued to use the name "Synagogue" instead of "Church" (St. Epiphanius, *Haeres.*, xxx, 19: συναγωγὴν αὐτοὶ καλοῦσι τὴν ἐκκλησίαν ἑαυτῶν καὶ οὐχὶ ἐκκλησίαν).

[17] Loisy, *Les évangiles synoptiques,* Vol. II, pp. 9–10 and 12–13.

successors. Peter shall always speak in his See."[18] Here then Rationalism is in agreement with the Fathers and the Councils; but, as the saying goes, the devil loses nothing by the bargain. Loisy goes on to conclude that Matthew's text cannot go back to Jesus, for Jesus taught the imminence of the Parousia and had no intention of founding the Church.

Others find a mythological flavor in our text.[19] The "gates of hell" remind them of the legend of Ishtar. They find in the "keys of the kingdom" an allusion to the belief in many heavens which need special keys to open them; and the metaphors of binding and loosing are found to be borrowed from Egyptian papyri or cuneiform tablets. They therefore conclude that the text cannot be traced to Jesus, but they agree that it is perhaps due to Matthew, whom they consider to be the better archaeologist. But there are found in our time scholars bold enough to deny, without the shadow of a proof, that the text is Matthew's,[20] or to maintain that its first form was simply this: "Thou art Peter, and the gates of hell shall not prevail against thee."[21] These excesses of hypercriticism have generally had the reception they deserve. We mention them only to show how inevitable is the Catholic exegesis, once one intends to explain the text of St. Matthew as it stands; for of its authenticity there can be no doubt.[22]

In the words, "the gates of hell shall not prevail against it," many heterodox writers and some Catholics see only a promise

[18] Bossuet, *Sermon sur l'unité de l'Eglise,* 1re partie.

[19] Dell, in *Z.N.T.W.*, 1914, pp. 1–49; cf. *ibid.*, 1916, pp. 18–26.

[20] Resch, *Texte und Untersuchungen,* 10 (Leipzig, 1893), pp. 187–196; Schnitzer, *Hat Jesus das papsttum gestiftet?*, 3 ed., 1910. The latter attributes the interpolation to the second century, the former, to the third.

[21] Σὺ εἰ Κηφᾶς καὶ πύλαι ᾄδου οὐ κατισχύσουσί σου.

So Harnack, in the reports of the Prussian Academy of Sciences, 1918, pp. 637–657. The rest of the text would be a later addition, with σου (*against thee*) changed into αὐτῆς (*against it*). Harnack has been refuted by Schepens, *Recherches,* 1920, pp. 269–303; Fonck, *Biblica,* 1920, pp. 240–264; Kneller, *Zeitschrift f. kathol. Theologie,* 1920, pp. 147–169.

Without denying the authenticity of the text, Allen (*Saint Matthew,* 1907, p. 179) suspects that the whole passage could well be the work of the Evangelist. Plummer (*Saint Matthew,* 1910, p. 227) asks whether St. Matthew could not have attributed to Peter in particular what Jesus said to all the Apostles. Always the same fear of "papistry"!

[22] On questions of authenticity and historicity, cf. Y. de la Brière, in *Dict. Apologetique de la foi Catholique,* Vol. III, cols. 1339–1366.

of immortality. That it surely is; but it is much more than that. According to the tenor of the text, the Church is indefectible because it has received an assurance that it will victoriously resist the furious assaults of its enemies. Hell (the Hades of the Greeks) is not here merely the dwelling place of the dead; as in the Apocalypse and the Gospel of Nicodemus, it is a hostile power, an *aggressive* force which will be unleashed in vain against the Church of Christ. Just as the house built upon a rock stands firm against storms, torrential rains, and overflowing rivers, so the Church founded on Peter, by virtue of the divine promise, defies and shall defy up to the consummation of the world the conspiring efforts of schism, heresy, and impiety.[23]

To Peter are entrusted "the keys of the kingdom of heaven." He that possesses the keys of a house opens and closes it as he wills. As master he disposes of all that it contains. The keys of a conquered city are delivered to the conqueror in token of allegiance and submission. Peter does not receive the keys of the kingdom of heaven as if he were a mere guardian whose office

---

[23] It is true that "to be at the gates of hell," or "to go to the gates of hell" (*sheol*), i.e., of the tomb, means to be at the point of death; but it does not follow that "the gates of hell" means death outside this expression, and that we must translate, "Death shall not prevail against it."

a) Here Hell is personified, as in the Apocalypse (1:18; 20:13–14) and in the *Gospel of Nicodemus* (Tischendorf, *Evang. apoc.*, 2 ed., p. 399: "Haec videns Infernus et Mors").

b) The personification comes from the words "shall not prevail against it." The word *κατισχύειν*, which is very common in the Septuagint, where it occurs more than a hundred times, has a very precise meaning. Governing the genitive, and sometimes the accusative, it always means "to get the better of," "to prevail against," and it implies the idea of *aggression*. According to Maldonatus, who admits elsewhere that he is alone in his opinion, the sense is that the Church, not content with defending herself, victoriously *attacks:* "Hoc enim multo majus est." This would, no doubt, be more glorious for the Church, and yet not all agree. The aggressors are not specifically heresies (Athanasius) or vices (Ambrose) or persecutors (Euthymius), but hostile powers in general, human or diabolical.

At first thought, the "gates" suggest the defensive rather than the offensive; but it must be remembered that "gates" often mean the city itself (Gen. *22:17*: "Thy race shall possess the gates of their enemies"; also Gen. 24:60; Exod. 20:10; Deut. 5:14, etc.), because in the Oriental world, the gate summed up the life of the city. It was there that contracts and treaties were concluded and justice administered. The "gate of the king" meant the royal court, and we say the *Sublime Porte* for the Ottoman Empire. "The gate, from its importance and defensive strength, became the synonym for strength, power and dominion" (Warren, in the *Dict. of the Bible,* Vol. 2, p. 113).

it is to shut out the unworthy and to admit those who have been invited. All the keys belong to him; nothing escapes his control.

To Peter is also given, without restriction and without exception, the power of "binding and loosing." This expression is very often used in Rabbinical writings to signify "to inflict or lift a penalty," "to forbid or permit." Obviously the Rabbis could not claim for themselves the power to make or abolish laws; they were interpreters and not legislators. But the right given to Peter has no such limitation. Everything that he decides is sanctioned in heaven. Armed with the universal power of binding and loosing, he will exercise in the Church a triple power: legislative, judicial, and administrative. The collective power given later on to all the Apostles and to their successors, far from limiting Peter's privilege, is itself limited by it.

3. The First Prediction of the Passion

As this day was coming to a close, Jesus confided to his Apostles a secret which he had hidden from them up to now, or to which he had made only passing allusions which they had not understood. "Then he began to disclose to his disciples that he must go to Jerusalem to suffer much from the notables and the high priests and the scribes, and to be put to death, and on the third day rise again."[24]

This revelation came at the proper moment. Before this, it would have been too early; the disciples were not yet able to face the scandal of the Cross. Later it would have come too late; from the moment that they recognized Jesus as the Messias, they must grow accustomed little by little to the idea of a suffering Messias, an idea which was always repellent to the Jews because it was so much opposed to their national preconceptions. That Christ should suffer was necessary; not with an absolute necessity, but as a consequence of the plan of redemption freely accepted by the Son and ratified from all eternity by the Father, who knew of his acceptance. And this plan of redemption was to be carried out at Jerusalem, in full daylight, at the center of religious unity,

---

[24] Matt. 16:21; Mark 8:31; Luke 9:22. Identical texts, except that Mark and Luke add that Christ was to be rejected (ἀποδοκιμασθῆναι) by the Sanhedrin, and Mark notes that Jesus spoke *clearly,* without circumlocution (παρρησίᾳ).

and in the very place where so many prophets had preached and died. St. Mark clearly distinguishes the three acts of the drama: first the ill-treatment on the part of the Sanhedrin, then the sentence of death passed by the proper authority, and finally the Resurrection on the third day.

It is difficult to imagine how stunned the Apostles must have been at this unexpected revelation. The Messias, the Saviour of Israel, the Redeemer of the world, the Son of God — denied by his people, put to death by the supreme tribunal of his nation! Was this credible, was it possible? The most scandalized of all was the very man whose faith had just been eulogized so highly. Peter, taking Jesus a little to one side to avoid being overheard by the rest, said to him: "God forbid! Lord, this shall not be." But Jesus, turning to the group of Apostles to give them a timely lesson, severely reproved Peter: "Get thee behind me, Satan! Thou art a scandal to me. Thou hast not the thoughts of God but of men."[25]

The prediction of the Passion and the severe lesson given to Peter were the starting point of a teaching which our Lord gave on a certain day, not only to his Apostles, but to all who would habitually accompany him or would desire to walk in his footsteps:

"If anyone will come after me, let him renounce himself; let him carry his cross and follow me.

"For whoever would save the life (of the body at any price) shall lose the life (of the soul); and who ever shall lose the life (of the body) for me and for the Gospel, shall save the life (of the soul).

"For what profit would a man find in gaining the whole world, if he should lose his soul? And what ransom could a man give in exchange for his soul?

"Whosoever shall be ashamed of me and of my words, of him shall the Son of Man be ashamed when he comes in company with the holy angels, in the glory of his Father."[26]

---

[25] Matt. 16:22–23; Mark 8:32–33. Literally: "Get behind me, Satan" (*ὕπαγε ὀπίσω μου, σατανᾶ*).

[26] Matt. 16:24–27; Mark 8:34–38; Luke 9:23–26. The triple meaning of the Hebrew *nephesh* (נפשׁ) and of the Greek *ψυχή* makes the play on words

To grasp the full force of the expression "to renounce" we need only apply it to others. To renounce someone is to desert his cause, to lose interest in him, to count him for nothing, and to deny him. To renounce oneself in order to follow Christ is, therefore, to become nothing in one's own eyes, to be oblivious of one's own interests, honor, and aspirations, in order to embrace the interests of Christ, to live only for his service and glory, and to be ready if necessary to sacrifice oneself for his cause.

The imitators of the Crucified must be ready to suffer everything, to carry the Cross with him, and to accompany him to Calvary. The punishment of crucifixion was very common in Palestine under the rule of the Romans. Varus had caused two thousand Jews to be crucified at the same time; and Quadratus had done the same to all the revolutionaries he was able to capture alive. Gessius Florus had inflicted the same punishment upon a considerable number of people of all ranks. After the capture of Jerusalem, Titus will crucify such an enormous number that there will be no wood left for crosses. Nor has history recorded all the hecatombs. Many of Christ's hearers may well have been present at such bloody spectacles. All knew *de visu* or by hearsay that the condemned man had to carry his cross to the place of execution. They therefore knew, when Jesus said to them, "Carry your cross and come after me," that he was inviting them to share his lot.

The paradoxically turned maxim: "Whoever would save his life shall lose it, and whoever shall lose it for me and for the Gospel shall save it," does not ring true in our language, because it is built on a play of words which is untranslatable in our tongue. But there was nothing obscure in it for Jesus' hearers, knowing, as they did, that the same Hebrew word meant at once "life," "the soul," and "the person." They understood very well that the loss of the life of the soul, which would come about if one wished to save the life of the body at any cost, would be an irreparable loss. In Oriental legislation, a murderer condemned

---

untranslatable in French, except to say "Qui veut *se* sauver, *se* perdra, et qui *se* perd *se* sauvera" ("He that wishes to save himself shall be lost, and he that loses himself shall be saved").

We shall explain later (Vol. II, pp. 8–10 and 112–113) what it means to "follow Jesus."

to die to satisfy the penalty of the *lex talionis* could sometimes buy back his life for a sum of money; but it is plain that the whole universe would not be enough to pay the ransom for the soul. On the last day, when the Son of Man shall come escorted by his angels, to render to each according to his works, he shall say to those who have denied him or have been ashamed of him, "I know you not." And from this verdict there shall be no appeal.

A mysterious saying, which was perhaps spoken on another occasion, terminates this discourse. "There are some here present who shall not taste death until they see the Son of Man coming in his kingdom," or "until they see the kingdom of God coming in power."[27] Of what coming is Christ speaking?

Some have thought of the Transfiguration, which was to occur in six days, or the Ascension of Christ, or the descent of the Holy Ghost at Pentecost, or the Parousia and the Last Judgment. It must be admitted that none of these explanations is satisfactory. Just as God in the Old Testament was considered to "come" to his people each time that he intervened to punish them or to deliver them, so now why cannot every striking manifestation of justice and mercy within the Church be considered as a coming of Christ, the Saviour and avenger of his own? If such be the case, the destruction of Jerusalem, which many of the disciples will witness, that collapse and, in a sense, obliteration of the Judaism which was the principal obstacle to the growth of the newborn Church, will satisfy well enough the idea of "the kingdom of God coming in power."

---

[27] St. Luke (9:27) says merely: "Until they see the kingdom of God." St. Mark (9:1): "Until they see the kingdom of God coming in power." St. Matthew (16:28): "Until they see the Son of Man coming in his kingdom." Durand (*Verbum Salutis, Saint Matthieu*, p. 318) notes: "These divergences require comment. They inform us that there is no longer question, as there was in the previous verse (of St. Matthew), of a visible and personal return of the Son of Man, but of that very special assistance which he promises to his own and to his work in the sixteenth chapter of St. John."

What confirms this explanation is the language of Jesus when he says to the Apostles, as he predicts his death: "I am coming to you again" (John 14:3; 14:18, 28). There is not always question of a visit after the Resurrection.

CHAPTER XII

Last Days in Galilee

1. The Transfiguration

THE announcement of Jesus' coming Passion and death had plunged the Apostles into dismay. They had been waiting for a brilliant manifestation of the kingdom of God shortly to come, and were already counting on the place of honor they were some day to occupy in it, and now they saw their dreams collapsing. Grim reality suddenly took the place of their dazzling prospects. All they now heard was abnegation, renunciation, a cross to carry, death to be undergone to earn the true life. These austere teachings, for which they were somewhat unprepared, completed their confusion.

The Master saw the need of reviving their courage by offering a prevision of his glory to those among them whose preponderant influence set the tone, so to speak, of the Apostolic College. For this reason, he chose the very ones who were one day to be the witnesses of his agony: Peter, his vicar here below and the foundation of his Church; James, the first of the Apostles to bear witness to him with his blood; John, the confidant of his most intimate thoughts. He took them aside onto a high mountain where he had decided to spend the night in prayer.[1] This was six full days, or, what comes to the same, about eight days after the scene of Caesarea Philippi.[2] The synchronism of the two events, which the three Synoptics take pains to indicate, marks a deliberate correlation between the confession of Peter and the

[1] Matt. 17:1–13; Mark 9:2–13; Luke 9:28–36.

[2] Matthew and Mark: "Six days"; Luke "about eight days."

momentary glorification of the Son of God on the holy mountain.

The Gospel does not name the mountain, but a very well-established tradition, dating from the fourth century, has always identified it as Thabor. St. Cyril of Jerusalem and St. Jerome, who both lived in Palestine, call it Thabor without the slightest hesitation. Among the Greeks, as well as among the Latins, this tradition has persisted uninterrupted up to our own time, when the enlightened piety of American Catholics has rebuilt the ancient Church which commemorated the mystery.

A certain number of contemporary scholars wish to substitute Great Hermon, arguing that Thabor is not a mountain, and that in the time of our Lord a town crowned its summit. It is true that Hermon is a marvelous prospect point at which the whole of Palestine, from Dan to Bersabee, unrolls before the eye as on a relief map, but if its defenders ever tried to climb it (it is a more laborious climb than the ascent of the Pyrenees) without any of the helps put at the disposal of tourists by modern industry, their enthusiasm would soon cool. Certainly for altitude Thabor cannot rival Hermon, but everything is relative. Thabor is the high point of Lower Galilee. Seen from the floor of the valley of the Jordan and the plain of Esdrelon, from the edge of which it rises in a harmonious curve, it gives the impression of being higher than it is. Its isolation, which distinguishes it from the neighboring summits, is well marked by the Evangelists.[3]

---

[3] Thabor rises about 1840 ft. (Guérin says 595 m.; Socin, 562 m.) above the Mediterranean, and almost 2600 ft. above the Lake of Tiberias. The plateau which crowns the summit running from east to west, measures about 800 by 400 yds. The summit of Great Hermon is 9166 ft. high. There is a description of Thabor in Guérin, *Galilée,* Vol. I, pp. 143–164, and of the ascent of Great Hermon, *ibid.,* Vol. II, pp. 290–295.

St. Cyril of Jerusalem (*Catech.,* xii, 16; MG, XXXIII, 744) and St. Jerome (*Epist.* xlvi, 12, and cviii, 13; ML, XXII, 491 and 889) affirm that Thabor is the mountain of the Transfiguration; but Origen (MG, XVII, 1548) and Eusebius (MG, XXIII, 1092) should not be quoted, because they confine themselves to citing Ps. 88 [89]:13: *Thabor et Hermon in nomine tuo exsultabunt.* Nicephorus Callistus says that St. Helena had a church built there (*Hist. eccles.,* viii, 30). In the sixth century, the anonymous Pilgrim of Piacenza saw three churches on Thabor (*Itiner.,* 6). In the following century, Arculf found a large monastery there (in Adamman, *De locis sanctis,* xi, 27). From that time on, tradition has not varied, and there exists no rival tradition, since the strange mistake of the Pilgrim of Bordeaux (333), who designates the Mount of Olives, cannot be called a tradition.

In times of disturbance and civil war, Thabor was often turned into a place of refuge and an improvised citadel. In 218 B.C. Antiochus the Great built a rampart around it. Josephus did the same in A.D. 66, but the way he speaks of it shows that the mountain was not inhabited at that time. Appointed chief by the rebels of Galilee, Josephus put into a state of defense eight cities which he enumerates; he also fortified Mount Thabor, which he distinguishes from these cities. The ruins of the wall which he built, a mile and four fifths in circumference, can still be seen. There was never any question, therefore, of a town on the mountain, and Vespasian thought it superfluous to take possession of it. The lack of drinking water in the place did not favor the establishment of a settled population there. Even supposing that in the time of Jesus there were some families of woodcutters or shepherds living there, the plateau of Thabor was large enough to offer the completest quiet to lovers of solitude.[4]

The journey from Caesarea Philippi to Thabor was a walk of two or three days, but it may well be that the Saviour, to avoid the crowds, made a detour by way of the seacoast, which at that time belonged to the Tyrians, and down the plain of Esdrelon, possession of which was disputed by Samaria and Galilee. Going that way, he would have reached the foot of Thabor only at the end of six full days. The beautiful mountain was ascended by a steep, twisting path of steps, through a thicket choked with oak, mastic, carob, and turpentine trees. At the end of an hour of difficult climbing, they came to a rather wide and bare plateau from which could be seen almost the whole theater of Jesus' Galilean apostolate and the scenes of his principal miracles: Naim, Cana, Capharnaum, and the edge of the Lake of Tiberias, and close by the circle of hills where Nazareth was hidden.

What strikes the onlooker most about Thabor is its isolation and its graceful sweep. Polybius (*Hist.*, v, 50) compares it to a woman's breast. "Even if there were no tradition, how could the pilgrim fail to be impressed by this magnificent mountain, whose abundant flora and great trees offer a singular contrast to its vast surroundings. Even today, no one who visits it will escape its allurement" (Dalman, *Les Itinéraires de Jesus,* trans. Marty [Paris, 1930], p. 255; cf. Dalman, *Sacred Sites and Ways,* trans. Levertoff, 1935, pp. 189–191).

[4] Cf. Josephus, *Bellum,* II, xx, 6; IV, i, 1 and 8. Josephus is always careful to distinguish the towns which he fortified from the Mountain called Thabor (τὸ Ἰταβύριον καλούμενον ὄρος), where he never mentions any particular locality.

Day was coming to a close when the Saviour arrived there with his three disciples. Fatigued by the journey and the heat of a long summer day — it was most probably in the month of August — they gradually grew drowsy, while a short distance away their Master prolonged his prayer. Their sleepiness was excusable, and we do not find our Lord rebuking them for it. When they awoke, they saw before them a spectacle so strange that they must have wondered whether they were still dreaming. Jesus appeared to them enveloped in a dazzling cloud. He was not gleaming with borrowed light, like Moses on Horeb reflecting the divine splendor. His whole person flashed forth light. His face shone like the sun, and his garments were resplendent with a whiteness which no fuller's art could imitate. Near by at his right and left stood the two greatest figures of Israel, the two illustrious representatives of the Law and the Prophets: Moses, the lawgiver of the Hebrews, and Elias, the forerunner of the Messianic times. Yielding the place of honor to Jesus, they were conversing with him about the things that were to happen soon in Jerusalem, especially his redemptive death which would put an end to the Old Covenant and replace the Synagogue by the Church.[5]

Peter, when he saw that they were about to depart, too moved to weigh the meaning of his words, cried out: "Master, it is good that we are here.[6] If thou wilt, we shall make three tents,

---

[5] St. Luke here has several details omitted by the others: (1) Jesus ascends *the* mountain (no other qualification) *to pray there;* (2) Moses and Elias converse with Jesus *about his approaching Passion;* (3) during the time, the Apostles slumber.

St. Luke describes the Transfiguration itself very summarily: "As he prayed his appearance (or *face, τὸ πρόσωπον*) altered, and his garments became dazzlingly white." The others say: "He was transfigured before them (*μετεμορφώθη ἔμπροσθεν αὐτῶν*)." St. Matthew adds: "His countenance shone as the sun and his garments became as white as light." And St. Mark more realistically: "His garments became brilliant and very white, white as no fuller on earth could have made them." Contrary to his practice, St. Mark's account is briefer, but it is the most vivid.

[6] Καλόν ἐστιν ἡμᾶς ὧδε εἶναι. The phrase is the same in all three Synoptics, except that St. Matthew prefixes it with the word Κύριε (Lord), St. Mark with the word 'Ραββί (Master), and St. Luke with 'Επιστάτα (Praeceptor or Master). The usual translation is: "It is good *for us* to be here." It is a natural enough sentiment, though somewhat egotistical; but to derive that meaning from the text, we should read: καλόν ἐστιν ἡμῖν ὧδε εἶναι (bonum est *nobis* hic esse). Peter is happy to be able to be useful and to render service, forgetful of himself. It is the sign of a loving and generous soul.

one for thee, one for Moses, and one for Elias." Surprise mingled with religious fear confuses his mind. He is thinking that he may perpetuate this vision of glory, or at least prolong it into the next day by preparing three leafy huts like those in which the watchers at harvest and vintage time shelter themselves for lack of better protection against the night dews. Peter's offer came from a generous impulse, since he was not thinking of himself or his companions; but it was as ill-timed as it was superfluous. While he was still speaking, a luminous cloud enveloped them all, and a voice came forth from it saying: "This is my beloved Son in whom I am well pleased. Hear ye him."

Three times only did the voice from heaven make itself heard to give solemn testimony to the Beloved Son: immediately after the Baptism when Jesus was about to inaugurate his ministry; on the Mount of the Transfiguration; and on the eve of the crowning of his work when he sacrificed himself for our salvation.

The Apostles, trembling with fear, had thrown themselves face downward on the ground and would have remained thus prostrate for a long time, had not Jesus brought them back to themselves by touching them and saying: "Arise; fear not." Straightway lifting themselves up and looking around them, they saw no one except their Master, looking the same as always. Whether it lasted for hours or only minutes, the vision produced an indelible impression on them and Peter kept a lively memory of it to the end of his life. "It is not on the credit of ingenious fables that we have announced the power and coming of our Lord, Jesus Christ, but as eyewitnesses of his majesty. He received honor and glory from God the Father when there came down from the heights of heaven a voice which said, 'This is my beloved Son, in whom I am well pleased,' and we ourselves, we heard this voice coming from heaven when we were with him on the holy mountain."[7]

As they were coming down from Thabor the next day, Jesus enjoined them: "Tell no one what you have seen until the Son of Man be risen from the dead."[8] Why this prohibition? St. Jerome is of the opinion that it did not refer to the other Apostles;

[7] 2 Peter 1:16–18.

[8] Matt. 17:9; Mark 9:9–10. Cf. Luke 9:36.

but it is general, and St. Luke says expressly that the three witnesses of the Transfiguration did not reveal their secret to anyone. A premature publication of such a great marvel would have awakened untimely hopes in the multitudes, increasing even more the scandal of the Cross. Again, did not the other Apostles have to be spared the temptation to envy which might have been born in them by the favor accorded the three privileged ones? In a few days, we shall see them debating which one among them was superior to the others.

Satisfied to obey the command without questioning its reason, the three disciples went down the mountain in silence, wondering in their hearts what could be the meaning of the saying, "until the Son of Man be risen from the dead," but they did not dare to ask for any light upon the subject. Hoping, perhaps, to get an answer by a roundabout method, they asked this question, which was no doubt suggested to them by the recent appearance of Elias: "Why do the Scribes and Pharisees say that Elias must come first?" that is, before the Messias, to prepare the way for him. The thought of the Apostles seems to have been: "Since, according to the teaching of the Scribes, Elias must restore all things and make smooth the way for the Messias, how can his role be reconciled with the Resurrection of Christ, because to rise again Christ must of necessity first die?" The answer of the Saviour comes to this: "Yes, Elias is to restore all things and to prepare the way for the Messias, but in reality Elias has already appeared in the person of John, and his role as forerunner did not shield him from persecution; no more will it shield the Christ from suffering and death, because it is so written."[9] This was not at all what the Apostles expected, but they understood that under the name of Elias their Master was speaking of John the Baptist. It would have been difficult to misunderstand.

---

[9] Mark 9:12–13. This rather difficult text is rendered as follows by Joüon (*L'Evangile de N.S.J.-C.*, 1930, p. 133): "Elias is to come first and restore all things. But how is it written of the Son of Man that he must first suffer and be dishonored? Well, I say to you: Elias has (already) come, and they have done to him all that pleased them, as it is written of him." For details, see a good commentary.

About Rabbinical opinions on Elias, consult the long dissertation in Billerbeck, ***Kommentar,*** Vol. IV, pp. 764–798; and on Moses, *ibid.*, Vol. I, pp. 153–158.

2. The Cure of the Lunatic[10]

A spectacle altogether different from that which they had seen on the summit of the mountain was waiting for the Apostles at the foot of Thabor: a striking contrast which Raphael has powerfully depicted in his masterpiece, though death prevented him from putting the finishing touch to it. Above in the light everything breathes peace, calm, serene joy, confidence in the company of the radiant Christ who showers his brilliance on everything about him. Below in the shadow there is trouble, disorder, confusion, obscure and powerless striving.

Pressing around the nine Apostles who had been left in the plain, a curious and amused crowd were witnessing a debate between the Scribes and the disciples, probably about the reasons for the failure the disciples had just experienced in their vain attempt to deliver a poor demoniac. As soon as they saw Jesus, whom they had lost sight of for a rather long time, they ran up to him with their usual demonstrations of enthusiastic homage. He asked them the object of the dispute which he had noticed from a distance and snatches of which he had perhaps heard. But all, disciples and onlookers alike, kept silence, held back either by reverential fear or by shame at having to admit their failure. Then a man dragging a young child by the hand broke through the crowd and said to Jesus:

"Master, I bring to thee my son, who is possessed by a dumb spirit; and whenever it seizes him, it makes him stamp, and makes him become rigid and shrink, foaming at the mouth and gnashing his teeth. Often it throws him into the fire and plunges him into water. It makes him shriek and twists him into convulsions, and leaves him only after breaking him with fatigue. I brought my child to thy disciples, but they could neither cure him nor expel the evil spirit."

In this case are discernible several symptoms of epilepsy complicated by attacks of hysteria: violent convulsions, inarticulate cries, foaming at the mouth, contraction of the muscles, rigidity of the limbs, and finally a complete prostration after the onset.

---

[10] Matt. 17:14–20; Mark 9:14–29; Luke 9:37–43. The narrative of St. Mark is the most lively and circumstantial. We are following it while taking the others into account.

The attacks occur at regular intervals, a phenomenon which the ancients attributed to the influence of the moon. But in the lunatic of the Gospel there is something more than epilepsy. There is the presence of a malevolent spirit which paralyzes the will, momentarily deprives the patient of hearing and speech, and suggests the idea of suicide. We have said elsewhere that the evil spirit works most frequently in a diseased organism, either because he finds it such or renders it such; and it may be asked whether the affliction provides the occasion for his presence or is its effect. Here it seems rather to be the occasion, since these disorders had existed in the child from a very tender age.

A circumstance very apt to touch the heart of Jesus was that the poor possessed child was an only son. Yet at first he welcomed the father's request only with the exclamation of grief: "O unbelieving and perverse generation, how long shall I be with you? How long shall I suffer you?" He was speaking to the multitude, indifferent rather than hostile; but there were Scribes and Pharisees mixed in with them, who were triumphing at the failure of the Apostles. He was also speaking to the Apostles, who were discouraged by their recent failure and whose faith was beginning to waver. He was speaking, finally, to the father himself, whose deferential language scarcely concealed his lack of confidence and his skepticism. And yet Jesus added in a softened tone: "Bring the child to me." The father obeyed, but for the unfortunate child this was the signal for a paroxysm of rage. As soon as he was in the presence of Jesus, he felt himself violently shaken by the evil spirit and falling down rolled upon the ground whitening it with foam. The bystanders groaned with horror before the stricken father. To open the man's soul to faith Jesus said to him gently: "How long has he been in this state?"

"Since his childhood, but if thou canst do anything, come to our aid. Take pity on us."

"If I can! What sayest thou? All things are possible to him that believes."

No. It is not the power of the Wonder-Worker that is lacking; rather it is the faith of others, the faith which is the normal, if not the essential, condition for a miracle. This time the father understands, and at the same instant grace begins to become active in his soul. "I do believe, Lord," he cries, "but come to the aid of my little faith." He sincerely believes, but he is afraid that he does not believe enough to gain the favor which he so much desires.

He was soon reassured. The crowd, which, tired of waiting, had begun to disperse, reassembled. And now, before that multitude of spectators Jesus commands the spirit of evil to depart. "Deaf and dumb spirit, I command thee, go out of this body and never return." The boy uttered a terrible shriek, twisted convulsively, and then lay still as though dead, and many thought that he had really expired. But they were mistaken. At one and the same moment the child was delivered from the devil and forever cured. Jesus took him by the hand and, restoring him to his senses, made him stand up. Then he gave him back to his father, cured also of his own unbelief. Less than this would have aroused the admiration of the multitude, as ready to be enthused as it was to fall back into its ordinary torpor.

When the Apostles were alone again with their Master, they questioned him:

"Why were we unable to cast out this unclean spirit?"

"Because of your little faith. Amen, I say to you, if you had faith as much as a grain of mustard-seed, you would say to this mountain, 'Remove from here,' and it would change its place, for nothing would be impossible to you. As for this kind (of devil), it can be cast out only by prayer and fasting."[11]

The Apostles had never hitherto encountered so frightening a manifestation of diabolical power. Before this new obstacle their faith had reeled, and yet faith alone works miracles. There is no question here, be it understood, of the theological virtue by which we adhere with heart and mind to revealed truth, but of a charism which adds to faith a special confidence, with the

---

11 Mark 9:29. *Τοῦτο τὸ γένος ἐν οὐδενὶ δύναται ἐξελθεῖν εἰ μὴ ἐν προσευχῇ καὶ νηστείᾳ*. This kind (*τοῦτο τὸ γένος*) designates not devils in general, but a particular class of demons like the one which possessed the lunatic. Several critical editors omit or bracket the words *and by fasting* (*καὶ νηστείᾳ*), but Vogels and Von Soden, rightly, it would seem, retain them. On the other hand, Matt. 17:21 (Hoc autem genus non ejicitur nisi per orationem et jejunium) seems to be borrowed from Mark 9:29.

certainty of being heard when God's glory is at stake. This faith would be able to move mountains; which is a hyperbolic way of saying that it can achieve the impossible.[12]

The more a miracle contravenes the ordinary laws of nature, the less frequent it is: such a miracle is the raising of the dead. Certain exorcisms fall into this category of exceptional miracles which suppose, in general, more holiness in him who works them, or at least present dispositions of greater perfection. The words of Jesus teach us that prayer and fasting are among the preparations which are the most effective assurance of God's aid.

The Galilean apostolate was coming to an end. Jesus wished to save the last moments of his sojourn in this country exclusively for the instruction of his Apostles. He therefore traveled through without preaching and, as it were, incognito in order to keep apart from the multitude of casual disciples who were everywhere clinging to his footsteps.[13] From the foot of Thabor to Capharnaum was only a good day's journey, but he did not go there by a direct route.

On the way Jesus renewed to the Twelve the prediction of his Passion: "Impress this well upon your minds: the Son of Man shall be delivered into hands of men who shall put him to death, but he shall rise again on the third day." By what marvel of incomprehension did the Apostles fail to understand? St. Luke says that "they had over their minds, as it were, a veil which prevented them from seeing." The sudden prediction of a great calamity, which nothing has hinted at, often leaves us incredulous. The Apostles knew that there are conditioned prophecies whose effect one can avert. They suspected that the Master's words had some mysterious meaning which the future would reveal to them. In a word, any hypothesis seemed more credible to them than the death of the Messias, the Son of God. Jesus would have settled their doubts if they had had the courage to ask him; but they

---

[12] Matt. 17:20. This assurance is placed by St. Luke in another context (17:6), and it is repeated by Jesus on the occasion of the cursing of the fig tree (Matt. 21:21; Mark 11:23). It fits very well into St. Matthew's context in this place.

[13] Matt. 17:21. "Gathering again in Galilee" (*συστρεφομένων αὐτῶν*). The Latin *conversantibus illis* has the same meaning, if the prefix *cum* is given its full force.

Mark 9:30: "They passed through Galilee without stopping" (*παρεπορεύοντο, praetergrediebantur*), "and he did not wish anyone to know it."

kept a respectful silence, or perhaps they were afraid to learn the bitter truth.[14]

On the road to Capharnaum an odd dispute arose among them about which one of them was the greatest. Beyond doubt, they were not so silly as to claim, each for himself, the first place; but they were urging the merits of their favorites and discussing the claims of the others. They deserved the lesson in humility which was to be given them without delay.

3. A Stop at Capharnaum

Since he wished to escape notice during his short stay in the city, Jesus retired to the friendly home which was his customary refuge. But his return became known to the agents charged with levying the contribution which all adult Israelite males paid every year. At the time of the exodus from Egypt, Moses had imposed upon the Hebrews a tax of a half shekel of silver for the building of the Tabernacle where the Ark of the Covenant reposed. Joas exacted the same sum for the restoration of the Temple which had been neglected and despoiled by the impious Athalia. From the time of Nehemias, custom had made this tribute payable by all male Jews from their twentieth year on.[15] Everywhere, in the Diaspora as well as in Palestine, there were special functionaries appointed to collect the tribute and to send the proceeds to Jerusalem for the needs of the Temple.

Jesus had not paid his personal tax at the ordinary time, since

[14] Matt. 17:22–23; Mark 9:31–32; Luke 9:44–45. St. Luke says merely: "The Son of Man shall be delivered into the hands of men," but in the other two Evangelists the prophecy is blindingly clear. And yet, says St. Mark, "They did not understand the thing (τὸ ῥῆμα) and were afraid to ask."

[15] Exod. 30:11–16; 2 Esdr. 10:32–34; Josephus, *Antiq.,* XVIII, ix, 1; *Bellum,* VII, vi, 6. The *Mishnah* (treat. *Sheqalim,* i, 3) decreed: "Those bound to pay the half-shekel are Levites, simple Israelites, neophytes, freedmen; but not slaves, women, or children (though it is accepted from them): but it is not accepted from pagans or Samaritans." About the didrachma, cf. Schürer, *Geschichte,* 4 ed., Vol. II, pp. 314–315; Juster, *Les Juifs dans l'empire romaine,* 1914, Vol. I, pp. 377–385; F. Nau, *Le denier du culte à Eléphantine au cinquième siècle avant Jésus-Christ,* in the *Revue de l'Orient Chrétien,* XVII, 1912, pp. 100–104.

The right of all the Jews to send the proceeds of this collection to Jerusalem was universally recognized. Flaccus the Praetor of Asia, who was accused of violating this privilege by confiscating the sums destined for the Temple, was defended by Cicero.

he had been absent for several weeks. Thus, when he returned, the collectors meeting Peter asked him whether his Master was going to pay the half shekel or didrachma. Fiscal agents, whether collecting for the Tetrarch Antipas or for the Romans, would not have put the question with such civility and consideration, but the greatest reserve was recommended to the collectors of this personal tax. While its payment was considered a strict religious duty, it still remained voluntary and could not be exacted by compulsion. Despite this, the Saviour, like the pious Jews of his time, had never dispensed himself from it, and Peter being aware of this, answered in the affirmative.

When he returned to the house, he was on the point of telling how he had committed himself in his Master's name; but Jesus forestalled him, saying: "What thinkest thou, Simon? From whom do the kings of the earth receive tribute and taxes? From their sons, or strangers?" In ancient times, taxes were not so much funds destined for public services, as a personal revenue of the ruler, who disposed of them as he pleased. The matter was therefore clear, and Peter answered without hesitation: "They receive them from strangers." "Then," replied Jesus, "are the sons exempt?" The conclusion was evident. Never had a king imposed taxes on the members of his own family, and much less upon his own children. The implication was equally evident, and Jesus left it to be drawn by the Apostles. Since the duty levied for the Temple is a tax paid to God, the natural Son of God is certainly exempt from it. But up to that time, outside the intimate circle of the Apostles, Jesus had kept his divine sonship a secret. There was therefore danger of scandalizing the Jews who did not know it.[16]

---

[16] Matt. 17:24–27. The episode is peculiar to St. Matthew; the readers of St. Mark and St. Luke would not have understood it without an explanation. To grasp our Lord's reasoning, it is to be remembered that the tax of the half shekel which was owed to the Temple was a *tribute paid to God*. Josephus expressly affirms this (*Antiq.*, XVIII, ix, 1: τὸ δὲ δίδραχμον ὃ τῷ Θεῷ καταβάλλειν ἑκάστοις πάτριον), as does the Scripture (Exod. 30:12–13: *Dabunt singuli pretium pro animabus suis Domino . . . dimidium sicli juxta mensuram templi*). The didrachma was to be paid *according to the weights of the sanctuary,* i.e., in the coin of Tyre, which had kept the ancient weight of the shekel.

Jesus says: "In order that *we* may not scandalize them," as though to indicate that the reason for avoiding scandal was the same for the Apostles as for himself. Naturally, the servants attached to the person of the royal heir

Even if the common purse had been empty at the time, the Saviour could easily have found in his retinue the modest sum exacted from him (equal to 37 cents in our money); but he preferred to work a miracle to affirm for the last time to the Galileans, whom he was about to leave, his power as divine Envoy. He therefore said to Peter: "That we may not scandalize the people, go to the sea, cast in a hook, and thou shalt find a stater in the mouth of the first fish that thou shalt catch. Take it and give it to them for me and thee." Peter's prompt obedience appears very natural to us who know who Jesus was; but it must have seemed to the bystanders as strange as was the order he received.

Even in our own day the lakeside people often employ for line fishing an ordinary cord to which are fixed several fishhooks without bait. The lake is so full of fish that a man handy with this primitive contrivance can finally hook some victim. The miracle was in foreseeing that the first fish captured would have a stater in its mouth. In the Sea of Galilee there is an extraordinary fish about which naturalists who have observed it closely tell marvelous stories. It gathers in its mouth the eggs laid by the female, sometimes as many as several hundred, and when they are hatched, it keeps the young there until they are able to fend for themselves. Then its enormously enlarged jaws stay open and can swallow objects much larger than a mere piece of money. In memory of the Gospel miracle, these fish are called, rightly or wrongly, St. Peter's fish.[17]

---

share his immunity. However, if this text should be cited as authority for maintaining the exemption of the clergy from taxes, the argument would limp in two ways: because taxes are not paid to God, but to a temporal ruler; and because the relation of the clergy to Christ is not the same as that of the Apostles to their Master.

[17] *Chromis Simonis* (Gunther). Lortet, who named it *Chromis paterfamilias,* thus describes it in his *Syrie d'aujourd'hui,* 1884, p. 506: "The majority of the species of the genus Chromis incubate their young in the interior of the mouth. Frequently there are found in the jaws of a fish scarcely eight inches long more than 200 embryos of a silvery color. These young fish, who remain for some weeks in this singular haven of protection, do not emerge therefrom until they are strong enough to escape from their numerous enemies and to provide for their own existence. One of these species has a jaw which is enormous in comparison with the size of the body." Page 507: "The female lays about two hundred eggs in the rushes and reeds in a small hollow formed by rubbing her body in the slime. The male afterward takes the eggs in its jaws. . . . The

The silver stater which was the outcome of this miraculous cast was worth exactly one shekel; just enough to pay the tax for Christ and his Apostle. The new favor accorded to Peter in such close association with the person of the Lord himself was remarked by his colleagues. There could be no further doubt. Peter was, indeed, the chief of the Twelve. He is the one who will continue Jesus' work on earth, when the Son of Man shall have gone to rejoin his Father. And still it seemed to some of them that others might have as many claims as he to this honor, because of close family relationships or sacrifices shared or services rendered. Such thoughts as these were tossing about in their confused minds, never, however, formulated in this crudely jealous shape. Reading their hearts and saddened to see so much imperfection in those whom he wished to be so perfect, Jesus looked at them with sorrowful eyes. "What were you conversing about on the road?" he asked them. Ashamed at being exposed and yet remembering their recent discussion, they did not know how to answer and were silent. However, one of them found courage and asked the question: "Who is the greatest in the kingdom of heaven?" He meant, no doubt, to speak, not of the kingdom of the elect, where disputes on the subject of rank and precedence are out of place, but of the religious society which the Son of Man had just founded here below and was soon to deprive of his visible presence. Who would be its guide and head?

Jesus seated himself as though to begin a discourse, and the Apostles grouped themselves around him. Then he had a little child come to him, probably a member of the family whose guest he was.[18] He took him in his arms and placed him in the midst

young emerge only when they are about four fifths of an inch long." Dom Biever, who lived a long time on the shores of the lake, adds some details: "The young, which soon make up a considerable volume, stay pressed against one another like the seeds of a pomegranate. The mouth of the foster father is by this time so distended that the jaws cannot be closed" (*Conférences de Saint-Etienne,* Paris, 1911, p. 296). Masterman (*Studies in Galilee,* Chicago, 1909) has the same. Like Biever, he attributes the phenomenon especially to the species called *Hemichromis sacra.* There are sketches in Vigouroux, *Dictionnaire de la Bible,* s.v. *Poisson.*

[18] A late and poorly supported tradition says that this child was Ignatius, the future Bishop of Antioch. The conjecture that makes him a child of St. Peter is hardly better founded, though Clement of Alexandria (*Strom.,* III, vi, 52) and St. Jerome (*Contra Jovin.,* I, ii, 261) assure us that St. Peter had children.

of the Twelve and gave them their answer. It was not at all the answer they expected, but it held a lesson in humility valid for all times and especially apt under the circumstances.

"Amen, I say to you, unless you become again like little children, you shall not enter the kingdom of heaven.

"He then that shall humble himself as this little child, he is the greatest in the kingdom of heaven.

"And whoever receives one such little child in my name receives me."[19]

The child, like the grown man, has his faults and may be said to carry within himself the germ of all the vices, which will one day grow unless grace prevents it. But the child possesses an aggregate of lovable qualities which are often wanting in mature age. He is simple and docile, free from ambition and pretense, eager to learn and quick to believe what he is told. These precisely are the dispositions which open the door to the kingdom of heaven, whether it be considered in its earthly realization or in its final consummation. It is of the latter that the Lord is thinking when he says: "If any one would be the first (in heaven), let him be (on earth) the last of all and the servant of all. . . . He that makes himself little (on earth) like this little child, he shall be the greatest in the (heavenly) kingdom." Without directly answering their question, he says enough to show that it deserves no answer. "You are concerned to know who will be the most esteemed, the most looked up to within the Church, upon whom shall devolve the authority and primacy. You miss the point. Instead of thinking of the life that passes away, think rather of the life that has no end. There matters shall be reversed."

4. Caring for the Little Ones of the Flock

At that moment an interruption from John changed the subject

[19] Matt. 18:3–5; cf. Mark 10:15; 9:35; and 9:37; Luke 18:17; 9:48. According to St. Matthew, Jesus answers the Apostles, who *question* him to know who will be the greatest in the kingdom of heaven. According to St. Mark, he answers on his own accord, because the Apostles, who have been discussing this question on the road, do not dare admit it (Mark 9:33–34). St. Luke, who has not mentioned this dispute before, speaks of it now (Luke 9:46–47). These are differences in wording which are worth noticing, without attaching too much importance to them.

of the conversation. These words of the Saviour, "Whoever receives one of these little ones in my name, receives me," reminded him of a recent incident. During their mission, the Apostles had met an exorcist who did not belong to the group of the disciples, but he was casting out devils in the name of Jesus. They had forbidden the man to appropriate a name of which they thought they had a monopoly; thus they thought, in good faith, that they were safeguarding both their own privileges and their Master's honor. John had certainly not been the last to silence the interloper, for patience and gentleness were not at that time his crowning virtues. But now some scruples beset him, and he candidly sets forth his case of conscience. "Master, we saw one who was not one of us casting out devils in thy name and we hindered him because he is not following us."[20]

John wrongly supposes that the power to cast out devils is an exclusive prerogative of the Apostles, and that the name of Jesus is efficacious only in their mouths. Jesus corrects this error by saying: "Do not hinder him in the future, for no one who has wrought a miracle in my name can straightway speak ill of me. For whoever is not against us is for us." The power of miracles is a gratuitous gift, which does not necessarily demand an explicit adherence to the true Church, if one is not separated from it through his own fault. Besides, to invoke the name of Jesus is to be already on the road to finding him. This is the making of an initial act of faith which needs only a little more light to reach the goal. For the man of good faith, the invocation of the name of Jesus will be the ray to enlighten his soul. At least, it is morally impossible after this experience that he straightway turn against Jesus. With such dispositions a man is already on his side, won over, so to speak, in advance. Of him Jesus can say, "Whoever is not against us is for us," and this in no way contradicts his former statement, "He that is not with me is against me, and he that does not gather with me scatters." There are circumstances in which an explicit confession of faith is

---

[20] Mark 9:38–39; Luke 9:49–50. If the incident took place during the time when the Apostles were preaching in pairs, the sons of Zebedee, who were sent out together, were the ones who silenced the exorcist. Jesus gives them for the future this piece of advice: "Do not hinder him further" (*μὴ κωλύετε αὐτόν*, the present of duration).

demanded, because simple silence would be a kind of apostasy; but, except for such unusual cases, one who is not hostile is rather favorable, for Christ has been set up as a sign of contradiction, and absolute neutrality in his regard is all but impossible.

Once the incident of the exorcist has been settled, the conversation resumes its course; but little by little the discourse becomes more elevated and more general. First there had been question of children who were small in stature and young in age. Other children are now brought upon the stage: the humble folk who believe in Jesus and who are so close to him that in receiving them we receive him. The good done to these little ones is done to Christ himself.

"But if anyone scandalize one of these little ones who believe in me, it were better for him that a millstone be tied to his neck and he be cast into the waves of the sea. Woe to the world because of scandals! It is necessary that scandal come; but woe to that man through whom it comes! If thy hand or thy foot scandalize thee, cut it off and cast it far from thee; for it is better for thee to enter into life with one hand or lame than to be cast with two hands or two feet into eternal fire. And if thine eye scandalize thee, pluck it out and cast it far from thee. It is better for thee to enter into life with one eye than to be cast with two eyes into the flaming Gehenna."[21]

Drowning was not a capital punishment written into the Mosaic code or introduced by custom, but this kind of death must have appeared to the Jews more frightful in that it deprived the drowned man of the honors of burial. In themselves, the millstone and the abyss of the sea do not increase the punishment, but they symbolize the horror of a death which the guilty person has no hope of escaping. If in the present state of man, the world being

---

[21] Matt. 18:6–9; Mark 9:42–48; cf. Luke 17:1–2 in another context. The only difference between St. Matthew and St. Mark is that the latter, instead of speaking of the foot and the hand together in the same sentence, mentions them separately.

The change from *children* to *little ones* is noticeable in Matt. 18:6 (these little ones who believe in me), and especially in Matt. 18:10 and 14. In all three cases the Evangelist uses the word μικροί (little ones), while in speaking of the children 18:2, 3, 4, 5) he uses παιδία. Many commentators make a point of this distinction, following the lead of Origen, St. Jerome, and St. John Chrysostom; but there are texts in which the meaning of the word *little* remains doubtful.

what it is, scandal is inevitable, this does not in the least lessen the gravity of the evil or the responsibility of the giver of scandal. To avoid it one should be ready to sacrifice what he holds most dear, a foot, a hand, or an eye. To scandalize the little ones, or simple souls, is such an enormous crime that there is no torment severe enough to punish it.

5. Advice to the Apostles as Pastors of Souls

"See that you do not count as nought one of these little ones; for I say to you that their angels behold the face of my Father who is in heaven. What think you? If a man has a hundred sheep and one of them strays, does he not leave the ninety-nine others upon the mountain to run in search of the sheep that has strayed? And if he find it, I say to you, he feels more joy over it than over the ninety-nine others that were not lost. Thus it is not the will of my heavenly Father that a single one of these little ones perish."[22]

The possibility that we may regard scandal given to the little ones as a matter of small importance makes it the more odious. To plumb the depths of its malice, we must know what price God sets upon a soul. If a man with a hundred sheep happens to lose one of them, he immediately goes to search for it, and he greatly rejoices at having found it. This is a picture of God running, as it were, in pursuit of stray souls, or watching over them to keep them from straying.

St. Matthew and St. Luke present this parable from two different points of view. St. Luke insists more on the joy of the Good Shepherd, while St. Matthew emphasizes more his solicitude, because Jesus has just recommended to the Apostles respect and care for the little ones who are the more deserving of concern because of their weakness. "How great is the dignity of a soul," says St. Jerome, "when God has given to each an angel to protect him!" If by your negligence you contribute to the loss of the soul

---

[22] Matt. 18:10–14. Christ here extends to all men the Old Testament teaching on the Guardian Angel for cities, provinces, and kingdoms. It does not follow, however, that there is a special angel appointed to guard each individual soul, since the same angel can fill this office for several souls. St. Luke places the parable of the Lost Sheep in another context (15:3–7).

of one of these little ones, the angel who is charged with the care and, in a sense, the responsibility for him will be your accuser before the sovereign Judge.

It is still to the Apostles, the depositories of ecclesiastical authority, that the following recommendations are addressed:

"If thy brother has sinned, go and reprove him between thee and him alone. If he listens to thee, thou shalt have gained thy brother. If he does not listen, take with thee one or two others, that the whole matter be settled in the presence of two or three witnesses. And if he refuses to listen to them, speak of it to the Church; but if he refuses to listen to the Church, let him be to thee as a heathen and a publican.

"Amen, I say to you, all that you shall bind upon earth shall be bound in heaven, and all that you shall loose upon earth shall be loosed in heaven.

"Again, I say to you, that if two among you agree upon earth, in asking for anything at all, it shall be granted to them by my Father, who is in heaven. For where two or three are gathered together in my name, there am I in the midst of them."[23]

A superior's duty is paternally to admonish the delinquent so that he may return to himself and recognize his fault. This he will do more easily if he is spared the humiliation of a public rebuke. When this first attempt yields no results, then recourse must be had to a more energetic remedy, a correction made before witnesses, and thereby resembling the first step of a judicial process. Finally, if the culprit stubbornly holds to his misguided

---

[23] Matt. 18:15–20. The Vulgate has, "si peccaverit *in te* frater tuus"; but there are strong reasons for thinking that the words *in te* do not belong in the text. (*a*) The authentic Greek text seems to be Ἐὰν ἁμαρτήσῃ ὁ ἀδελφός σου (without εἰς σέ). For an examination of the testimony, cf. Lagrange, *Saint Matthieu,* p. 353. (*b*) The omission of εἰς σέ would be inexplicable; the addition of it would be easily explained by the proximity of a text (Matt. 18:21) wrongly taken as a parallel. (*c*) There is question here of the conduct of pastors of souls in dealing with sinners; the fault referred to is, therefore, a public sin, and not a personal offense. The case of a personal offense is treated later (Matt. 18:21); it is solved, without the intervention of the Church, through forgiveness by the offended party. "The context is so much against it (the addition of *in te,* εἰς σέ) that even those who have retained the addition, such as Augustine and Thomas, have understood the entire passage as dealing with fraternal correction, and Schanz understands it the same way. But this cannot be the case unless the shorter reading is adopted" (Lagrange).

ways, the affair will be brought to the tribunal of the Church; and if he is still obstinate and refuses the satisfaction demanded, he will be officially separated from the community of the faithful. It is clear that Jesus is here legislating for the future. For, though founded in principle, the Church has not yet its constitution, nor will it have it until after the descent of the Holy Ghost on the day of Pentecost.

The Church is not an aggregate of individuals, nor is it a pure democracy, but a society governed by heads and represented by them. On them falls the duty of excommunicating rebels. The Church has received from her Master the power of binding and loosing, a power which in no way diminishes Peter's privileges, but confirms and completes them.

The power of loosing and binding, of remitting sins or retaining them, is given without restriction; all depends upon the dispositions of those who have recourse to the ministry of the Church. God, on his part, is always disposed to pardon the sincerely repentant sinner and to sanction the sentence of absolution pronounced by his ministers. But to be able to count on his mercy, must we always be ready ourselves to pardon without any limit to our indulgence? This is the question which Peter naïvely puts to Jesus: "Lord, if my brother sin against me, how many times should I pardon him? Up to seven times?" The Rabbis said that God pardons a fault three times, but not more. Peter therefore thought that he was being generous by doubling the number of pardons in a case of personal offense. How little did he understand the inexhaustible riches of the divine mercy! Jesus answers him: "I do not say up to seven times, but up to seventy times seven times."[24] These two sacred numbers multiplied together give the picture of an indefinite number. And, indeed, if we always have need of pardon from God, is it not our duty always

---

[24] Matt. 18:21–22; cf. Luke 17:3–4: "Take heed! If thy brother sin, rebuke him, and if he repent, forgive him. And if he sin against thee seven times a day and yet seven times a day turn to thee saying: 'I repent,' forgive him." St. Luke's text is extremely condensed, and can be well understood only if compared with St. Matthew's. In the first instance (v. 15) there is question of a sin against God; the Apostle (as the minister of God) should rebuke the delinquent and forgive him, if he repents. In the second instance, the matter is one of personal offense (si peccaverit *in te*); the Apostle (as an individual) should forgive the offender who shows his repentance, even though it be seven times a day.

to pardon our brothers? The following parable brings this truth to light:

"A certain king wished to settle his accounts with his servants. While he was engaged in this, one was brought to him who owed him ten thousand talents. Since this man had not the means to pay the debt, the king commanded him to be sold, with his wife and children and all his goods, to pay the debt. But the servant falling at his feet prostrated himself before him, saying: 'Have patience with me and I will pay thee all.' Moved with pity the master set him free and forgave him his debt. Upon going out, this servant met a fellow servant who owed him one hundred denarii, and taking him by the throat, he said to him: 'Pay me what thou owest.' That servant fell at his feet, saying: 'Have patience with me and I will pay thee.' But the other refused and had him cast into prison until he should pay his debt. Seeing this, the other servants were greatly distressed, and they went to tell the master what had happened. Then the master summoned the culprit and said to him: 'Thou wicked servant! I forgave thee all thy debt because thou didst pray me. Shouldst not thou have had pity on thy fellow servant, as I had pity on thee?' And the king in his anger delivered him to the torturers until he should pay his debt. So shall my Heavenly Father do to you unless each of you pardons his brother from his heart."[25]

A servant who owes his master the enormous sum of ten thousand talents (more than twelve million dollars in American money); a creditor who, without any legal process, has his debtor sold together with his wife and children — all this seems altogether

[25] Matt. 18:23–35. The talent was worth 6,000 drachmas or denarii. The denarius was worth 20.65 cents; therefore 10,000 talents would amount *in round numbers* to $12,380,000, and 100 drachmas would be $20.65. To find the value in present-day money it would be necessary to multiply these numbers by five. But in parables, the exact value matters little. Many Jewish parables have for their hero a king who symbolizes God, and this symbolism floating before the author's mind often impinges upon the language of the parable at the expense of realism. The king in this parable is all-powerful; he is magnificent in his liberality, terrible in his justice. His debtors, who are unable to pay their debt to him, have need of his pardon, but he does not pardon those who will not pardon others.

incredible. But to keep the parable probable there is no need of making an inventory of Roman or Jewish law. Rather we should think of Oriental potentates, the absolute kings of Persia, Egypt, or Babylon, all of whose subjects, no matter how high and honorable their position, were still servants, whose goods and persons could be disposed of at will. The kind of servant who would owe ten thousand talents would be, for example, a satrap or governor of a large province, and his debt would represent the total amount of the taxes of a vassal kingdom. The meaning of the parable, however, does not depend on these details, and they could well be different. It bears upon two points alone: the unworthy conduct of the servant who, though pardoned himself, cannot pardon in turn, and the severity of the punishment which he receives from his indignant master. We should stop there, unless we are going to transform a parable into an allegory, for example, by asking whether God ever takes back the pardon he has once given. We know that God repents none of his gifts, and that, though lost merits can revive, sins washed away by penance or remitted by mercy never revive. What can be said is that God will treat more severely the ungrateful man who does not pardon the slightest offenses after having himself experienced the infinite liberality of divine pardon.

Such was the last teaching that Jesus gave to his compatriots before going to preach the Gospel in Judea and the countries beyond the Jordan.

6. Final Farewell to Galilee

Jesus was leaving Galilee, never to return until after the Resurrection. From the spring of the year 27 to the autumn of the following year, for about fifteen or sixteen months, he had traversed Galilee in every direction, sowing everywhere the Good Word and profusely scattering miracles. If occasionally he went beyond the frontier into Phoenicia and the Decapolis and the tetrarchy of Philip, he always came back soon. But the triangle, whose points were Capharnaum, Bethsaida, and Corozain, was the chosen field of his apostolate; a very confined theater, if compared to that of Paul or Xavier. And what proves how much the historians of Jesus have left unsaid, is the fact that Corozain, one of the cities where he displayed the greatest activity, is not even mentioned in the Gospel except in the curse leveled against it.

At first, the enthusiastic welcome by his compatriots seemed to give the lie to the proverb that no one is a prophet in his own country. They ran from afar to hear him; they followed him into the wilderness; they allowed him no rest either day or night. But little by little, indifference and apathy followed infatuation. The "Galilean Idyll" had ended. The inconstancy and fickleness of a crowd is not enough to explain this change of attitude. The calumnies and intrigues of the Pharisees from Judea surely contributed; but there were for it more direct and more personal reasons. Souls gradually surfeited by the sight of miracles began to experience a sense of disappointment which they had not felt at the beginning. This Messias was so different from the one that they had expected! This man who called the poor blessed, who praised renunciation and sacrifice, who demanded that they render to Caesar the things that are Caesar's, this man did not correspond to their gross ideal. So they had been mistaken when they had hailed him as Saviour and Liberator of Israel. The longer this continued, the deeper became the gulf between the spirituality of the Gospel and the selfish aspirations of Galilean nationalism. And so, as he left these guilty cities forever, Jesus hurled against them this terrible anathema:

"Woe to thee, Corozain! Woe to thee, Bethsaida! For if the miracles which were wrought in your midst had taken place in Tyre and Sidon, those cities would long ago have done penance in sackcloth and ashes. And I say to you, Tyre and Sidon shall be treated less severely than you on the day of judgment.

"And thou, Capharnaum, shalt thou be exalted to heaven? No, thou shalt be lowered down to hell. For if the miracles wrought in thee had taken place in Sodom, it would have remained to this day. And I say to thee, Sodom shall be treated less severely than thou on the day of judgment."[26]

---

[26] Matt. 11:20–24: "Then he began to upbraid the cities in which most of his miracles had been wrought, because they had not done penance." St. Luke, who places this passage in another context (10:13–15), omits the preamble and abridges the rest. St. Matthew inserts this passage *before* the end of the Galilean ministry; St. Luke places it a little *after* the departure from Galilee. It seems to us to be most appropriately placed at the time when Jesus bade adieu to his ungrateful fatherland. This is also the opinion of Maldonatus and other good authorities.

Guilty towns and nations must suffer a double punishment, proclaimed solemnly at the Last Judgment, but inflicted well before that term: an individual punishment which, at the hour of death, overtakes each of the inhabitants in the measure in which they have shared in the general infidelity; collective punishment striking the city itself, to be inflicted in this world beyond whose horizon the city as a city does not go.

From this last point of view the curse pronounced by the Saviour has been only too effective. The accursed towns have disappeared from the face of the earth, leaving no more trace than Sodom or Gomorrah. Only Bedouins come to pitch their tents among the ruins buried in the ground. Scarcely fifty years ago, even the true sites of Capharnaum and Corozain were unknown; and the site of Bethsaida, whence came Peter, Andrew, and Philip, is still disputed.

And so Jesus goes to carry the Gospel to other countries; but what immense sadness must have filled his heart as he addressed this final and poignant farewell to the three cities he had loved so much!

SUPPLEMENTARY NOTES

NOTE A

The Country of Jesus

Even if we did not have the witness of St. Jerome, we would readily conjecture that a view of the scene where the earthly life of Jesus unfolded would help much to an understanding of the Gospel. To supply for personal knowledge, some summary notions may be useful.[1]

1. The Extent and Contour of Palestine

"I am ashamed," writes St. Jerome to Dardanus, "to indicate the dimensions of the Promised Land for fear of providing pagans with an occasion for mockery." Still, he gives them: 160 Roman miles (less than 147 miles) at the greatest length from Dan to Bersabee. But the Jews never fully occupied this restricted territory; the Philistines on the south and the Phoenicians on the north always disputed it with them.

The surface of Palestine, including Transjordania, is ordinarily

[1] Most of the authors who have studied the Land and the Book put their attention on the entire Bible (Robinson, *Biblical Researches;* Thomson, *The Land and the Book;* Stanley, *Sinai and Palestine;* Smith, *Historical Geography of the Holy Land,* etc.). Dalman, *Les Itinéraires de Jésus, Topographie de la Palestine,* 1939, restricts his study to the Gospel, but the translation of this work by Marty seems to us less clear than the German text, which is none too lucid. Stapfer, *La Palestine au temps de Jésus-Christ,* describes especially the manners and customs. Masterman, *Studies in Galilee* (Chicago, 1909), is instructive. For the ordinary reader, the Guides to Palestine and the Dictionaries of the Bible are enough. Legendre, *Le pays biblique,* 1928, though overburdened with superfluous details, is useful. Dalman, *Arbeit und Sitte in Palästina* (Gütersloh, 1928–1932), is interesting but very specialized. The most recent and pertinent work is *Syrie-Palestine, Iraq, Transjordanie* (Paris, 1932). The *Aperçu Général* and the section on Palestine were put together by Abel, O.P., and printed after 1929.

estimated at about 9700 square miles.[2] This is nothing like the extent of Switzerland, or even that of Belgium or Holland; Portugal is three times as large. But a nation's importance and its influence on the world are not measured by its size. Egypt and Chaldea were no more extensive than Palestine; Thebes and Athens, the famous rivals, were much smaller; Tyre and Sidon ruled the sea from the height of a rock. The small size of Palestine was, therefore, no obstacle to its brilliant destiny and to the designs that God had upon it.

There is probably no corner of the earth where so many contrasts are brought together in such a restricted space. To get any idea of them, it is necessary to traverse, from west to east, the maritime coast, the central ridge, the course of the Jordan, and the high plateaus of Transjordania, all so varied in appearance, climate, and produce.[3]

The *Palestinian coast line,* from the borders of Egypt to the promontory of Carmel, follows a straight line inclining a little to the east, without gulfs or indentures, without as much as a sentinel islet to break the monotony. It is, indeed, the *littus importuosum* of the ancients. The treasures of Herod were needed to create a port at Caesarea, and only the tenacity of the Crusaders could make anything out of the rock of Athlit. Jaffa with its semicircle of reefs at water level and its narrow channels swept by ocean winds is often impassable, even to modern steamers. How different from Greece, bristling with capes, haloed with peninsulas, jagged as an acanthus leaf. While the Greeks and Phoenicians, used from childhood to manning the oars, sallied forth far and wide to sow the world with their colonies, the Jew of the Mediterranean littoral was confined at home, so to speak, by the nature of his coast line. In compensation, he possessed a very wide and very rich plain along the sea. The lowlands, changed into deserts and swamps under Ottoman rule, were in other days fertile enough to root the children of Israel in their soil.[4]

---

[2] English engineers estimate the whole of Cisjordanian Palestine, within the limits described by us, at 6038 square miles, and Transjordania at 3660, for a total of 9698. Belgium, before the small annexations of 1919, had an area of 11,358 square miles; Holland, about 12,738; Switzerland, 15,960; Portugal, 35,573. Reclaimed Alsace-Lorraine, with its 5597 square miles, is almost as large as Palestine on this side of the Jordan.

[3] To anyone wishing to have a clear idea of the relief map of Palestine we recommend R. Koeppel, S.J., *Palästina. Die Landschaft in Karten und Bildern* (Tübingen, 1930) (195 maps, sketches, and photographs). Dalman's publication, *Hundert deutsche Fliegerbilder aus Palästina* (Gütersloh, 1925), is interesting; but these photographs, taken from the air during the war, almost always at an angle, distort the landscape.

[4] Between the maritime plain and the mountains of Judea stretches a kind of

The *mountain chain* which makes up the skeleton and, so to speak, the backbone of Palestine may be considered as a continuation of Lebanon. Seen from a distance it presents the appearance of a uniform barrier dipping in the middle and rising again at both ends. In reality it is divided into three sections which present very different characteristics and which once bore different names. In the south are the mountains of Juda, with a mean height of some twenty-five hundred feet; in the middle, the mountains of Ephraim, whose peaks never reach this altitude; in the north, the mountains of Nephthali, which are much more lofty.[5]

The marvel of Palestine is the *depression of the Jordan.* Geologists agree in saying that this formidable dislocation of the earth's crust extends from the Taurus chain to Central Africa, almost following the direction of the meridian.[6] A little beyond the meeting of the three sources of the Jordan, the river begins to run below sea level, and when it empties into the Dead Sea, reaches a depth of almost 1300 feet. It is a phenomenon unique in all the world; no other earth depression approaches it.[7]

Transjordania is, in a sense, the counterscarp of this gigantic trench.

---

stage or tableland which is uniformly fertile, called Shephelah; it is described by Legendre in *Le pays biblique,* pp. 35–39, or better in Smith's *Histor. Geog. of the Holy Land,* pp. 199–236, where Shephelah is rightly distinguished from the maritime plain.

[5] In Judea, north of Hebron, one peak rises 3369 feet; another north of Bethel, 3316 feet. The two highest points in Samaria, Garizim and Hebal, are respectively 3076 and 2847 feet high. No summit in Lower Galilee reaches 968 feet; Thabor is only 1837 feet. In Upper Galilee, several peaks reach above 280 feet. Jebel Jermak reaches 3936. The Transjordan levels are as a rule higher at equal latitudes than the level of the corresponding terrain on the opposite side of the Jordan. In Hauran, the highest point of the Mountain of the Druses is 6035 feet, and Great Hermon, the northern barrier of Palestine, reaches a majestic 9166 feet.

[6] The articles published in the *Revue Biblique* by A. de Lapparent (*L'origine et l'histoire de la mer morte,* 1896, pp. 570–574) and Laferiere (*La faille du Jourdain et le fossé syro-africain,* 1924, pp. 85–106), following the labors of Lariet, Blanckenhorn, Hull, and Suess, give an accurate idea of this immense fissure.

[7] The most distant source of the Jordan is in the Anti-Lebanon, near Hasbeya, at an altitude of 1847 feet; the most picturesque bubbles up in the grotto of Pan at Banias (Caesarea-Philippi) at 1079 feet; by far the most abundant springs up from the foot of Tell el-Qadi (the ancient *Dan,* meaning in Hebrew "judge" as *qadi* does in Arabic). This third spring, about 2½ miles from the second, is at an altitude of no more than 502 feet. These three streams come together a little farther down to form the Jordan. The river shortly afterward traverses Lake Huleh, which at low tide is a triangular marsh with sides measuring four miles. Its surface is only seven feet *above* sea level. By the time it reaches Lake Tiberias, the Jordan is 682 feet *below* sea level, and when it reaches the Dead Sea, 1286 feet below the level of the Mediterranean.

The two parts of Palestine, now separated by the Jordan, "in primitive times formed a continuous plateau slightly tilted in the direction of the Mediterranean, composed of layers of volcanic rock, carboniferous terrain, Nubian sandstone, Cenomanian and Senonian limestone covered with marine deposits . . . (but) while the earth strata on the eastern side kept their horizontal position, those on the western side inclined toward the depression so far as to cover under the Cenomanian limestone the Nubian sandstone and the earlier rock."[8] The result is that the corresponding strata on the two sides of the trench are now not always parallel, and the level of the eastern side is generally higher than that of the side facing westward.

2. Climate, Fertility of the Soil

Given the differences of altitude and exposure, Palestine, despite its limited area, is bound to present a great variety of climates. The temperature of the maritime plain is like that of the Egyptian seacoast; the Jordan Valley, sinking from seven hundred to thirteen hundred feet below the level of the Mediterranean between Tiberias and the Dead Sea, possesses a tropical or subtropical climate; the highlands of Judea, of Samaria, and of Upper Galilee enjoy a climate comparable to that of southern Italy. The climate of Lower Galilee, where Nazareth is, is a mean between that of the Ghor and that of the mountains. As to the plateau of Transjordania, which the ancients called "Palaestina Salubris," it experiences cold in the wintertime. The hereditary ability of the Jewish race to adapt itself to the most diverse atmospheric conditions may be attributed to this continual passing from one climate to another.

The most characteristic trait of the Palestinian climate, and of the Syrian climate in general, is the division of the year into two clearly marked seasons: the rainy season, which begins about the 15th of October and practically ends about the 15th of April; and the dry season, which goes from the 15th of April to the 15th of October. Rain is a rare phenomenon during the four months of June, July, August, and September.[9] Still, the amount of annual rainfall is quite sufficient.

At Jerusalem, over a period of fifty years (1861–1910), there was an average rainfall of 21.78 inches, and even more than that at Nazareth. Thus Jerusalem receives annually less rain than Constan-

[8] L'egendre, *Le pays de Jésus,* 1928, p. 124.

[9] However, a light rain fell at Jaffa on the 15th of August, 1899. The phenomenon is less rare on the seacoast than in the interior.

tinople or Rome, but notably more than Paris or London, and very much more than Vienna or Athens.[10] The Jordan Valley has a smaller share, but abundant dews compensate for the lack of rain.

Abrupt changes in temperature, the fertility of the soil, and the healthiness of the climate depend to a great extent on the wind flow. During the rainy season the southwest wind prevails. It arrives charged with moisture from the Mediterranean, which condenses on contact with the mountains. While the rains from December to February are useful for feeding the springs and cisterns, those that the Scripture calls "early" and "late" (*matutinae* and *serotinae*) have greater influence on the harvests. The "early" rains, which are expected from the beginning of October, make possible the softening of the soil and its preparation for the sowing, which would be jeopardized if rain did not fall before December. The late rains of March and April contribute to a good yield of grain by hardening the stalks and filling out the ears.

In summer, the wind veers to the northwest. It regularly blows from the seacoast in the morning, and around eleven o'clock reaches the mountains of Judea, where its stimulating breeze is felt, and it does not cease until sunset. This is why the summer months in Jerusalem, despite the heat registered on the thermometer, are less uncomfortable than those which immediately precede and follow.

But if the west wind is helpful to the cultivation of the fields and to health, the southeast wind is dreaded by the inhabitants of the country. The Assyrians represented it as a hideous monster, a sort of hybrid vampire. The Egyptians and Syrians called it *Khamsin,* a word meaning "fifty" in Arabic, because it blows for a period of fifty days, with, fortunately, numerous interruptions. "It dries up and parches the atmosphere, burns up vegetation, paralyzes all energy, and, when prolonged, induces a state of discomfort and enervation."[11] And this east wind comes back in autumn to retard the rainy season, to com-

---

[10] Vincent-Abel, *Jérusalem,* Vol. I, 1912, pp. 98–103 and Plate XV. At Jerusalem, a year is considered wet if the quantity of rainfall is above 75 centimeters, and dry, if it does not reach 50 centimeters. The wettest winter on record was that of 1877–1878, with 109 centimeters; the driest was that of 1869–1870, with 31 centimeters.

[11] Vincent, *Jérusalem antique,* fasc. I, 1912, p. 104. The mean annual temperature at Jerusalem is 15.9 deg. Centigrade; in January 7 deg.; in July and August, 22.9 deg. At Beirut the average for January is 14.5 deg., and for August, 28.5 deg. The highest temperature recorded in Jerusalem over a period of fifty years was 44.4 deg. Centigrade (August, 1881); the lowest, −4 deg. Centigrade (January, 1864).

plete the baking of the soil and dry up the springs, and to produce a kind of marsh fever. When there is no rain in October, it is the most unhealthy month of the year.

The Bible describes the Promised Land as a "country rich in watercourses, fountains, and bubbling springs; as a fertile soil producing in abundance wheat, barley, vines, fig trees, pomegranates, oil, and honey." The description is exact, though perhaps somewhat embellished by the contrast with the desert from which the Hebrews emerged when they entered into the land of promise. "Yet the traveler passing through today gets the impression of a bare, rocky, parched country, whose present desolation compared with its ancient wealth would almost seem to indicate a divine curse. Let us say at once that the entire country is often judged by certain regions like Judea which are more frequently visited, and by the appearance that it presents in certain seasons, when, because of lack of rain, nature has begun to die or is already dead."[12] But the nature of the terrain has not changed, and the course of the winds has not been modified in two thousand years. The gradual deforestation may have had some influence on the impoverishment of the soil, but that is not the full explanation. The principal cause is to be sought in the neglect of the soil during twelve centuries of Moslem rule. It is not nature, it is man that has ruined this excellent land, and it rests with man to restore to it the fruitfulness of other days. Even today, the sections which are given over to agriculture produce fine harvests, despite the primitive methods of the present-day peasant farmers and the absolute lack of fertilizer.[13]

To be sure, the desert of Juda never furnished more than meager pasture lands, but the desert of Juda is only an inferior part of Palestine. The neighborhood of Jerusalem was always rocky and arid, as the geographer Strabo, a contemporary of Jesus, remarks, and not a dozen springs were to be found within a radius of two leagues.[14] Still, even in that disinherited region, the olive, the vine, and the fig tree used to thrive. Proof of it are the numerous wine and oil presses found almost everywhere in the countryside. Elsewhere the hills and mountains were cultivated up to the top, thanks to the sustaining walls

---

[12] Legendre, *Le pays biblique,* 1928, p. 197.

[13] Especially to be mentioned is the region cultivated by the Zionist Jews with the aid of very modern improvements [Note by J. Calès, S.J.].

[14] Strabo, *Geography,* XVI, ii, 36: "In the vicinity the terrain is poor and dried up, and the rest of the country within a radius of sixty stadia, to tell the truth, is nothing but a stone quarry." This is an exaggeration, because 60 stadia (7½ miles) would go beyond Aïn Karim and Bethlehem, and there are some fine valleys within that radius.

which prevented fertile land from being washed away by rainstorms, as one sees in Maronite Lebanon and in certain sections of Italy. Southern Judea — the part called Negeb — has now the appearance of a steppe, but the considerable ruins which have been discovered there prove that at one time it was inhabited by an active and very dense population. If the plain of Jericho, which the ancients regarded as prodigiously fertile, is today a wilderness, it is because the aqueducts and irrigation canals have long since disappeared, and the springs there produce only marshland. Without depending upon the testimony of Josephus, who was overpartial to his own country, here is how a foreigner, the serious Tacitus, with his *imperatoria brevitas,* describes Palestine: "The men are healthy and robust, rain is infrequent, the soil is fertile. The produce of our climates abounds there, and in addition, the balsam and the palm-tree."[15]

A scholar who knew this country well, after traveling through it in every direction to make a map of it, asserted that it could provide nourishment for a population ten times as large, if it were well cultivated. It is true that he wrote at a time when Palestine numbered perhaps no more than five or six hundred thousand inhabitants.[16] (Today the population has vastly increased, as our footnote indicates.)[17] The census made in the time of David, if the figures that have come down to us are not corrupt, would give a population of six and a half million for the whole of Palestine, and there are competent critics who do not think this an exaggerated estimate. In any case, several Jewish colonies and certain domains exploited by religious orders, like the Trappists of Latrun, the Benedictines of Abu-Ghosh, and the German Lazarists of Seven Fountains, abundantly demonstrate the fruitfulness of the soil of Palestine.

---

[15] Tacitus, *Histor.,* v, 6. According to Strabo, a contemporary of Jesus, the Joppa (Jaffa) district was so populous that 40,000 soldiers could be recruited from Jamnia (now Jabneh) and its environs. Today perhaps not 400 could be levied.

[16] Conder, *Tent Work in Palestine* (London, 1880), p. 368. Conder surveyed more than two thirds of Cisjordania for the large map of Palestine published by the *Palestine Exploration Fund.*

[17] In 1919, Palestine numbered 687,850 inhabitants (exclusive of Transjordania); in 1926, 752,269, and with Transjordania 887,000; in 1931, 1,035,821; in 1932, 1,151,000. According to *Palestine économique* (Paris, 1936), the population in 1935 would have been as high as 1,360,000 souls, 375,000 of them Jews; but one may always be skeptical of Oriental statistics. [The estimated population in 1946 was 1,912,000; that of Transjordania, 400,000. *Translator.*]

3. Political Divisions – Countries Visited by Jesus

Palestine, within its natural limits — the Mediterranean on the west, the Egyptian desert on the south, the Syrian desert on the east, and the last spurs of Great Hermon on the north — at that time was under the rule of five different administrations. There were:

1. The little Roman province of Judea, governed by a procurator and comprising Idumea on the south, Judea properly so called in the center, Samaria in the north. This was the territory willed by Herod to his son Archelaus. It passed under Roman rule in A.D. 6.

2. The Tetrarchy of Herod Antipas, comprising Galilee, north of Carmel, and Perea, east of the Jordan. Antipas governed it from the death of Herod (4 B.C.) until A.D. 39.

3. The Tetrarchy of Philip, separated from Galilee by the Jordan and from Perea by an undetermined border. Philip died in A.D. 34, and his states were given by Caligula to his nephew Agrippa I.

4. The Decapolis, a federation of Greek cities (originally ten), all except Scythopolis situated east of the Jordan and forming as many enclaves in Perea.

5. Phoenicia, then a dependency of the Roman province of Syria, and stretching along the seacoast as far as Ptolemais (Saint-Jean-d'Acre), perhaps as far as Carmel.

Jesus made only one rapid excursion into Phoenicia. It is improbable that he entered the pagan towns of Tyre and Sidon. No other town of this country is named in the Gospel.

Jesus traversed the Decapolis several times and worked more than one miracle there, but the Gospel does not mention by name any of the towns in that region. The country of the Gadarenes or Gerasenes can scarcely mean the territories of Gadara and Gerasa, which were well-known cities of the Decapolis.

Oftener he had occasion to enter the Tetrarchy of Philip, which was separated from Galilee only by the Jordan. We find him at Caesarea, the ancient Banias, and at Bethsaida, the name of which the Tetrarch had changed to "Julias." These were the two principal cities of Philip; and since they were half pagan, it is open to speculation whether the Saviour ever passed through their gates. No other town of this Tetrarchy is named.

In Judea, Jesus does not seem to have gone much beyond the outskirts of Jerusalem and the road leading from Jerusalem to Jericho through Bethphage and Bethany. We would like to believe that he preached the Gospel at Bethlehem, his native town, and we know that he awaited the hour of his Passion at Ephrem. The towns of Emmaus and Arimathea are also in Judea.

Frequently he had to pass through Samaria to go to Jerusalem and to return to Galilee; but only one town is named, Sichar near the Well of Jacob. Ennon near Salim, the last place wherein John baptized, must have been in Samaria or in the region of Scythopolis.

Though he preached for a long time in Perea, the Gospel mentions only one locality in that region, Bethany beyond the Jordan.

Even in Galilee the Gospel mentions only six towns or villages; three in the hill country: Nazareth, Cana, and Naim; three in the valley: Capharnaum, Corozain, and the western Bethsaida. Mary Magdalene recalls for us the name of Magdala, near the lake. The lake itself is called the Lake of Genesareth in St. Luke, the Sea of Tiberias in St. John, and the Sea of Galilee or simply the Sea in St. Mark and St. Matthew. These last two also mention a country of Dalmanutha or Magedan, not yet identified with certainty.

We have described all these places in the respective passages where the Gospel story offered us the opportunity of doing so. It must suffice now to refer the reader back to them.

For special study one may consult the *Géographie de la Palestine,* by Fr. Abel, O.P.: Vol. I, *Géographie physique et historique,* 1934; Vol. II, *Géographie Politique, Les villes,* 1938. For a long time, there will probably not be any work more complete and more to the point.

[Cf. *The Westminster Historical Atlas to the Bible,* Wright and Filson, 1945. *Translator.*]

NOTE B

Chronology of the Life of Christ

The long and erudite dissertation of Patrizi on the principal dates of Christ's life shows clearly that there is no real Patristic tradition on the subject, except, perhaps, for the date of the Passion.[1] It is therefore necessary to go the Gospel texts themselves and to complete their information from the data of profane history.

We shall examine: (1) the date of Christ's birth; (2) the date of his baptism; (3) the length of his public life; (4) the date of his death. These four questions are not independent; they exercise mutual control and are to be solved as functions one of another.

1. Date of Christ's Birth

Jesus was born during Herod's lifetime and at the time of the census taken up under Quirinius. But, whereas the date of Herod's death is now known with certainty, the date of the census of Quirinius is not. It is well known that in A.D. 527 Dionysius Exiguus calculated the date of the Incarnation as the beginning of the Christian era, and placed it in the Roman year 754. Herod died in the spring of the year 750. It is therefore necessary to put back the date of Christ's birth at least four years.[2]

1. *The date of Herod's death.* (*a*) According to Josephus, Herod died a little before the Jewish Passover,[3] after reigning for thirty-four years in Jerusalem, of which he had made himself master in the year 717.[4] If we count the years from the month of Nisan to the month of Nisan, taking fractions of years as whole years, after Josephus' method of calculation, Herod must have died in the Roman year 750 (4 B.C.)

b) A little before Herod's death, there was an eclipse of the moon.[5]

[1] Patrizi, *De Evangeliis,* lib. III, dissert. xix (Vol. II, pp. 171–277).
[2] Schürer, *Geschichte,* 4 ed., Vol. I, pp. 415–417 and 444–449.
[3] Josephus, *Antiq.,* XVII, ix, 3, and *Bellum,* II, i, 3.
[4] Josephus, *Antiq.,* XVII, viii, 1, and *Bellum,* I, xxxiii, 8.
[5] Josephus, *Antiq.,* XVII, vi, 4.

This could only be the eclipse which took place on the 12th or 13th of March in 750 (4 B.C.), since no other eclipse was visible at Jerusalem during the two years following, and the eclipse of the 15th of September, 749 (5 B.C.), was too far away from the Passover to enter into the computation.

c) The Ethnarch Archelaus, Herod's son, was deposed by Augustus during the consulship of Lepidus and Arruntius (Roman year 759), and Josephus says that this was the ninth or tenth year of his rule.[6] (The slight discrepancy is explained by the fact that Josephus distinguishes between Archelaus' accession and his effective taking possession of power, because he was not recognized by Augustus for several months.) In any case, this points to the year 750 as the date of Herod's death.

d) Antipas, another of Herod's sons, was Tetrarch of Galilee for at least forty-three years, since we have coins of his forty-third year. He was exiled by Caligula in the summer of 792 (A.D. 39). Thus we again arrive at the year 750 for the date of Herod's death.

If, therefore, Herod died in the spring of the year 750 (4 B.C.), Christ was born *at the latest* in the beginning of that same year. But there are other considerations which oblige us to go back still farther. On this point see Note E: *The Census of Quirinius.*

In the West, the anniversary of our Lord's birth was always celebrated on the 25th of December. In the East, up to the end of the fourth century, it was either celebrated on the 6th of January together with his baptism, or there was no special feast for it. Patrizi has collected and discussed all the texts of the Fathers on this subject in his *Dissertatio* xxi (*De Evangeliis,* Vol. II, pp. 280–291: *De die natali Christi*). He notes in the beginning: "We do not claim that the date of December 25th is absolutely certain, but we maintain that it is the most probable date." A modest and warranted claim.

2. Date of Christ's Baptism

1. ***The appearance of the Baptist.*** The synchronisms furnished by St. Luke (3:1–2) are of little assistance in fixing a precise date, for Caiphas was High Priest from A.D. 18 to 36, Pilate was Procurator of Judea from 26 to 36, Antipas was Tetrarch of Galilee up to 39, Philip was Tetrarch of Trachonitis up to 34; and we know nothing about Lysanias, except that he died or was deposed in 37, since in that year the tetrarchy was given by Caligula to Agrippa I.

There is only one date, "the fifteenth year of Tiberius," that gives

[6] Dion Cassius, LV, 27; Josephus, *Bellum,* II, vii, 3; *Antiq.,* XVII, xiii, 3.

promise of less uncertain results. Since the death of Augustus occurred on the 19th of August, 767 (A.D. 14), the fifteenth year of Tiberius would go from the 19th of August, 781, to the 19th of August, 782. The interval between accession and the beginning of the following year was often counted as a year. According to this method of computation, the fifteenth year of Tiberius could go up to January 1, 781 (A.D. 28), for the Romans, and up to October 1 of the same year for the Orientals. But it is entirely gratuitous to suppose that St. Luke computes the years of Tiberius from the *death* of Augustus. The Roman emperors counted their years of rule from the day of their investiture with tribunician power. This day most often coincided with the death of their predecessor, but it could be different. Thus Titus counted the years of his reign from the day when his father made him an associate in the Imperial rule, and at his death he was in the eleventh year of his tribunician power, though he had reigned only twenty-six months.[7] In January, 765 (A.D. 12), Tiberius, who had been made an associate in the Imperial rule by Augustus, had received, not in Rome but *in the provinces,* an authority equal to that of his foster father. According to the computation of the people of the provinces, his reign began at that time, and St. Luke may well have dated it from that time. If counted thus, the fifteenth year of Tiberius corresponds to the year A.D. 26. The date is that of the appearance of the Baptist, but it seems that, according to the Evangelist's account, the baptism of Jesus followed very soon after. The date of Christ's baptism can therefore be fixed at the end of the year 26 or the beginning of the year 27.

2. *The age of Jesus at the time of his baptism.* He was about thirty years old (Luke 3:23: ἀρχόμενος ὡσεὶ ἐτῶν τριάκοντα). The word ἀρχόμενος does not indicate the entrance of Jesus into his thirtieth year, but the opening of his public ministry; ὡσεί does not mean "almost," but "about" (thirty years, more or less). At the time of the Passover following his baptism, the Jews said to Jesus (John 2:20): "Forty-six years have been spent in building this Temple, and thou speakest of rebuilding it in three days." The Temple was not finished until A.D. 66, and at that time it was still in the process of construction; it had been begun in the Roman year 734 (20 B.C.), since the laying of the foundations coincided with the visit of Augustus to Syria.[8] If we add forty-six years, we come to the Roman year 780 (A.D. 27). This makes an excellent synchronism.

This result fits in admirably with our other calculations: the end

---

[7] Cf. Cagnat, *Epigraphie latine,* p. 186; Goyau, *Chronologie de l'empire romain,* p. 151; Ramsay, in Hastings, *Dict. of the Bible,* Vol. V, p. 481.

[8] Cf. citations and discussions of the texts of Josephus, in Schürer, *Geschichte,* 4 ed., Vol. I, pp. 369–370.

of the year 26 for the appearance of the Baptist, the beginning of the year 27 for the baptism of Jesus and the first Passover, the year 28 for the second Passover and the promise of the Holy Eucharist, the year 29 for the third Passover and the death of Christ.

3. Duration of the Public Life[9]

According to various authors, the duration of the public life was: (1) a single year; (2) two years and some months; (3) three years and some months.

Since the first opinion has no solid probability, the choice lies between the other two. Those who restrict the public life of Christ to a single year depend upon reasons drawn from mysticism. Clement of Alexandria invokes the text of Isaias: "The Spirit has sent me to preach *the year of grace* of the Lord." Gaudentius of Brescia says that "the Victim of Calvary is a lamb of one year because one year elapsed between his baptism and his death." The Gnostics claimed that Christ was baptized in his twenty-ninth year, and by adding the year of his preaching they arrived at the number *thirty,* the fateful cipher of the aeons. St. Irenaeus peremptorily refutes them by observing that John expressly mentions three Passovers in the course of the public life, which therefore must have lasted two years at the very least. But the Bishop of Lyons places a considerable interval between the baptism and the beginning of Christ's preaching. According to him, Jesus should not have started to preach before reaching the age of a teacher, that is, his fortieth year. For he must serve as a model and exemplar for children, for youths, for grown men, and for old men; and therefore he must approach old age. The Jews said to him on one occasion: "Thou art not yet fifty years old." One does not speak thus to a man who is less than forty. These reasons have convinced no one.

One thing that is absolutely certain is that the public life of Christ from his baptism to his death lasted more than two years. After Christ's baptism and fast, and the marriage feast at Cana, St. John mentions the proximity of a Passover which Jesus was about to celebrate at Jerusalem (John 2:13, 23). A second Passover is mentioned in the middle of the public ministry, on the occasion of the first multiplication

---

[9] For details cf. *Recherches,* 1912, pp. 82–104: *La date de la passion et la durée de la vie publique de J.-C.* The bibliography given on pp. 82–84 is no longer complete. Cf. Holtzmeister, *Neuere Arbeiten über das Datum der Kreuzigung Christi,* in *Biblica,* 1932, pp. 93–103, and especially the scholarly *Chronologia vitae Christi* (Rome, 1933), by the same author. [Add also: E. Levesque, *Abrégé chronologique de la vie de N.-S. J.-C.* (Paris: Beauchesne, 1941). The author resolutely sustains a ministry of three and a half years. Note of J.C.]

of bread (John 6:4). The third Passover is that of the Passion. Should a fourth Passover be inserted? Neither the Synoptics nor St. John warrant it.

1. *Data of the Synoptics.* All agree that the account of the Synoptics does not give the impression of a long period. The events compressed into compact groups do not require any considerable time. St. Matthew in the first part of his Gospel gathers together events and discourses from all periods of the ministry without giving any clear chronological indications to clarify his progress. St. Luke gives almost two thirds of his Gospel to the story of the last six months, and the rest fills only five or six chapters. In St. Mark, the next-to-the-last Passover falls in the sixth chapter, and a year seems more than enough for what precedes. If we had to depend on the Synoptics alone — save for two small details of which we shall now speak — the theory of a single year of ministry would be defensible.

The Synoptics do not *directly* furnish any chronological information, but St. Mark tells us that the place of the first multiplication of loaves was carpeted with green grass (Mark 6:39: ἐπὶ τῷ χλωρῷ χόρτῳ, *soft green, bright green*). Consequently it is springtime and, considering the climate, the month of March. We would already know this from reading St. John (6:4), since the Passover was near at hand. The reference is to the next-to-last Passover of the public life.

Another indirect piece of information is the episode of the disciples plucking the ears of grain, which is found in all three of the Synoptics (Matt. 12:1–8; Mark 2:23–28; Luke 6:1–5). On the lake shore, grains of wheat are scarcely edible until April, and, if there is question of barley, until toward the end of March. Although this episode is placed before the multiplication of loaves, it would not furnish an argument for introducing another Passover between the first and the next-to-last Passover, unless the Evangelists always followed strictly the order of events, and if this episode did not belong to a series of alleged infractions of the Law.

Nothing can be drawn from the "second-first sabbath" of St. Luke (6:1); first of all, because no one knows what is the meaning of "second-first," and above all because the δευτεροπρώτῳ in St. Luke's text is not authentic. Conjectures on the origin of the reading and an account of the attempts made to find a meaning for it may be found in Plummer.

2. *The data of St. John.* We have already spoken of the most important point: the mention of three Passovers, one at the beginning, another in the middle, and a third at the end of the public life of Christ. We have also seen how valuable for the chronology was the

information about the time taken to construct the Temple from its foundation up to Christ's first Passover.

The unnamed feast of Chapter 5 is less important because of two uncertainties: it is not known whether the text should read "a feast" or "the feast" of the Jews; secondly, it is uncertain whether Chapter 5 should not be placed chronologically after Chapter 6. We have examined these two questions elsewhere, and may disregard them here. At all events, whichever reading be adopted, and whatever be the decision on the inversion of chapters, no change in the chronology is involved. If the inversion is admitted, the unnamed feast will be the Pentecost following the next-to-last Passover (with the reading ἑορτή), or better, that Passover itself (with the reading ἡ ἑορτή). If the inversion is not admitted, the unnamed feast will be the feast of Lots (with the older explanation of John 4:35), or the feast of the New Year (with the explanation of that text which we have adopted). In any case, there would be no reason to prolong the public life of the Saviour beyond two years and some months.

There remains, then, the text of St. John (4:35): "Do you not say: Yet four months and the harvest comes? And I say to you: Lift up your eyes and see the fields, how they are white for the harvest." The ordinarily accepted explanation of the phrase οὐχ ὑμεῖς λέγετε ὅτι ἔτι τετράμηνός ἐστιν καὶ ὁ θερισμὸς ἔρχεται is this: "While I speak to you, are you not saying to one another, as you look at the fields in the vicinity: Yet four months are needed before the ripening of the harvest?" According to this interpretation the time would be the month of *January*. For although the date of the harvest varies a great deal according to the altitude, in the plain of Sichem, where they were at this time, it does not begin before the month of May. Accordingly, Jesus, setting out for Jerusalem a short time after the marriage feast of Cana (John 2:12) in order to celebrate the Passover, would have spent *nine full months* in Judea. But this seems improbable for several reasons:

a) When he returns to Galilee, the memory of the miracles wrought by him in Jerusalem is still very vivid (John 4:45): "Cum ergo venisset in Galileam, exceperunt eum Galilaei, cum omnia vidissent quae fecerat Jerosolymis in die festo; et ipsi enim venerant ad diem festum." This manner of speaking indicates a recent event, the enthusiasm over which has not been allowed to cool by the passage of time.

b) Not only do the Synoptics fail to mention this long sojourn in Judea, but they identify the return of Jesus into Galilee after the baptism with his return after the imprisonment of the Baptist: "Cum autem audisset Jesus quod Joannes traditus esset secessit in Galileam"

(Matt. 4:12; Mark 1:14). If a lapse of nine months had intervened between these two events, such silence would be hard to explain.

c) The narrative of St. John does not give the impression of a long sojourn in Judea. Only one incident is reported to explain the abrupt departure of Jesus. He does not seem to have preached, but only to have baptized through the instrumentality of some disciples who had followed him from Cana, but whom he had not yet called in any decisive way (John 3:22–4:3). One or two months would amply suffice to justify the expression: "Post haec venit Jesus et discipuli ejus in terram Judaeam et illic demorabatur (διέτριβεν) cum eis et baptizabat" (John 3:22).

d) Arriving at Sichar, Jesus is tired and thirsty, and a long halt is made at Jacob's well. This episode is evidently more natural in the month of May, when the early heat is very distressing, than in the month of January, the season of rain and cold.

e) Is it not somewhat childish to suppose that, while Jesus was speaking to them of a supernatural food with which he nourished himself, the Apostles were diverting themselves by gazing at the fields and exchanging this banal reflection, "Yet four months and the harvest will be ripe"? The narrative of St. John shows them to be attentive and respectful, and Jesus' answer gives no license to suppose any such unseemly side remark!

For all these reasons, and others which we shall see later, it seems preferable, after the lead of Origen and Maldonatus, to regard our text as a sort of proverb current among the farmers after the work of sowing. "Yet four months of rest and respite, and then we shall have to think of the harvest." Thus understood, the proverb is literally applicable. In Palestine, sowing takes place in November, after the first rains and autumn labors, and continues in December. The barley harvest begins in April and continues during the next two months, depending on the kind of grain and differences in climate. The farm calendar of Gezer, published in the *Revue Biblique* (1909, pp. 243–269), puts an interval of four full months between the sowing and the harvest. The formula used by St. John, "Do you not say" (οὐχ ὑμεῖς λέγετε) is exactly the one used for proverbs and for constantly repeated formulas (Luke 12:54–55; Matt. 16:2; Mark 7:11): λέγετε, "you say," i.e., "you are in the habit of saying."

If it be objected that this proverb has not yet been found in Hebrew literature, the objection is futile, since that is the case with thousands of other proverbs. Besides, it would be easy to find analogous proverbs in various languages. Ovid, for example, writes (*Heroid.* xvii, 263): "Sed nimium properas et tua messis in herba est." In Dalman's *Arbeit und Sitte in Palästina,* 1928–1932, are to be found hundreds and thousands of country proverbs in use at present, which no one had recorded before.

From these facts and considerations the following conclusions may be drawn:

a) The theory limiting the public ministry of Christ to one year is devoid of solid proof, and seems to be in opposition both to the chronological data of the Synoptics and to the formal text of St. John. It appears to be of Gnostic origin.

b) The arguments for and against two or three years of public life are not altogether decisive. Still, since a duration of two years and some months is enough to satisfy all the data of the problem, the *onus probandi* falls on those who are not content with this estimate. They bring forward no valid proof for their opinion; for we have shown that neither the unnamed "feast" (John 5:1), nor the τετράμηνος (John 4:35), nor the so-called σάββατον δευτερόπρωτον favors their views. On the other hand, the compact and rapid narrative of the Evangelists cannot easily be accommodated to a duration of three years and more.

c) There exists no tradition, properly so called, for or against either of these two opinions. It will be remarked, however, that the medieval interpreters and even modern commentators up to our time quite commonly admit a duration of three years and some months, while the ecclesiastical writers of the first five centuries, with the exception of Eusebius, hold to a duration of less than three years.

d) After duly weighing everything, the opinion of the Fathers wins our adherence, the more so because it fits in better with the date of the Passion.

4. Date of Christ's Death

This date must fulfill three conditions: (*a*) It must fall *on a Friday:* Wescott's opinion placing the Passion on a Thursday has not been considered. (*b*) It must fall within the time of *Pilate's rule:* Pilate was Procurator from A.D. 26 to 36. (*c*) It must fall at the time of the *full moon of Nisan,* that is to say, it must be either the 14th or 15th of Nisan.

The problem therefore presents itself thus: what are the years between A.D. 27 and 35 in which the Jewish Passover could have fallen on a Friday? The answer is easy and accepted by morally all: the years 29, 30, and 33 are the only ones filling these conditions. Now it seems that the year 33 may be excluded as being too late; because this would make Jesus thirty-five years old or more at the time of his baptism, and this would not fit in well with the text of St. Luke; and again, at the time of the first Passover of the public life, the Temple would have been under construction for forty-nine or fifty years, contrary to the text of St. John (2:20). See above, on the date of Christ's birth.

If, therefore, we eliminate the 3rd of April, 33, the choice remains between the 18th of March, of the year 29, and the 7th of April, of the year 30. The choice between them is the more difficult because the dates are so close together.

In favor of the year 29 tradition is cited: (*a*) Many of the Fathers, in order to date the Passion, name the consuls of the year 29: L. Rubellius Geminus and C. Fufius Geminus, or the *two Gemini.* Thus Tertullian, Hippolytus, the *Acts of Pilate,* the *Catalogue of the Popes* of the year 360, St. Augustine, Prosper of Aquitaine, Sulpicius Severus, etc. (*b*) Despite the indications of St. Luke apparently to the contrary, they place the Passion in the 15th or 16th year of Tiberius, which, according to various methods of computation, would correspond to the year 29. Thus Julius Africanus, Tertullian, Lactantius, and the *De Pascha computus* of the Pseudo-Cyprian. (*c*) The *fasti consulares* of the year 354 fix the Passion in the year 782 of Rome (A.D. 29); the *Legend of Abgar* (cited by Eusebius, *Hist. eccl.,* I, 13) places it in the Greek year 340, i.e., from September, A.D. 28, to September, A.D. 29. (*d*) Several Fathers say that the destruction of Jerusalem occurred forty years (Chrysostom) or forty-two years (Origen, Clement of Alexandria) after the Passion. This brings us always to A.D. 29.

Against the 18th of March, A.D. 29, it is objected that the Passover would in that case fall before the spring equinox; but this is no real objection, as we think we have abundantly proved elsewhere.[10]

One serious difficulty is that, in the year A.D. 29, the conjunction of the sun and moon occurred at 3:15 a.m. on the meridian of Jerusalem. Patrizi supposes that if the moon was seen on that evening *before* sunset, the new moon would have occurred on the 4th of March, and the 18th of March would have been the fifteenth day of the moon. That seems very improbable, and the 18th of March could only be the fourteenth day. Let us rather say that it is unknown whether the fixing of the new moon depended solely on observation, and whether the priesthood upon whom devolved the fixing of the calendar did not, at that period, follow more or less arbitrary rules.

---

[10] *Recherches,* 1912, pp. 96–97. We may add a fact which had escaped us at the time. For the Jews of the Elephantine, the two extreme dates for the Passover were the 14th of March and the 6th of May. Cf. *R.B.,* 1907, p. 271. The article by Fotheringham (*Astronomical Evidence for the Date of the Crucifixion,* in *J.T.S.,* Vol. xii, Oct. 1910, pp. 120–127) may be consulted. But it must be remembered that the Jews did not regulate these matters exclusively by astronomy. And if we may judge from the *Book of Jubilees,* they were well advised, since their knowledge of astronomy was very rudimentary.

This difficulty does not exist for the 7th of April, A.D. 30, which was certainly a Friday and the fifteenth day of the moon in the month of Nisan (the fourteenth according to Schoch). But this date is completely devoid of Patristic support.

Let us propose the following dates with all reserve, while admitting that the birth of Christ could have been one or at most two years earlier, and his death a year later, accepting also the traditional dates as the *days* of his birth and his baptism.

Birth of Christ	December 25	748	year of Rome (6 B.C.) (or 8 B.C.)
Baptism	January 6	780	(A.D. 27)
First Passover	April	780	(A.D. 27)
Return to Galilee	May	780	(A.D. 27)
Second Passover	March	781	(A.D. 28)
Feast of Tabernacles	October	781	(A.D. 28)
Feast of Dedication	December	781	(A.D. 28)
The Passion	March 18 or	782	(A.D. 29)
	April 7	783	(A.D. 30)

If, for the dates of the birth and death of Christ, the dates which are nearest to each other be selected (6 B.C. and A.D. 29), Christ would have been thirty-three years old plus some months. If his birth be placed earlier and his death later, his age would be that much more.

For the sake of comparison we subjoin the dates proposed by other authors.

	Birth	*Baptism*	*Public Life*	*Passion*	*Day of the Moon*
Patrizi (1853)[11]	Dec. 25, 7 B.C.	Jan. 6, A.D. 26	3 years	Mar. 18, 29	15th
Turner (1898)[12]	7 or 8 B.C.	A.D. 26 or 27	2 or 3 yrs.	Mar. 18, 29	14th
Masini (1917)[13]	Nov. 28, 5 B.C.	A.D. 26	3 years	Mar. 18, 29	
Pfättisch (1911)[14]		A.D. 28	2 years	Apr. 7, 30	
Gerhardt (1930)[15]	7 B.C.	A.D. 27	3 years (?)	Apr. 7, 30	15th
H. von Soden (1899)[16]	4 B.C.	A.D. 28 or 29	1 or 2 yrs.	Apr. 7, 30	15th
Mémain (1886)[17]	Dec. 25, 9 B.C.	Jan. 9, A.D. 29	4 years	Apr. 3, 33	15th
Lévrier (1905)[18]	Dec. 25, 5 B.C.	Jan. 6, A.D. 23	3 years	Mar. 22, 26	
Chaume (1918)[19]		Sept., A.D. 30	4½ years	Apr. 8, 35	
Levesque (1917–1941)[20]	Dec. 25, 5 B.C.	Sept. 10, A.D. 26	3½ years	Apr. 7, 30	

[11] Patrizi, *De Evangeliis,* 1853. This is perhaps the most fully documented study on the chronology of the life of Christ. Many have exploited it without mentioning it.

[12] C. H. Turner, in Hastings, *Dictionary of the Bible,* Vol. I, 1898, pp. 403–415. The Date of the Passion proposed by Patrizi and Turner (March 18, A.D. 29) is

accepted by Hitchcock (*Dictionary of Christ and the Gospels,* Vol. I, pp. 415–416), Mangenot (*Dict. de la Bible*), and many others. Dittrich proposes the 15th of April, A.D. 29.

[13] Masini, *When was Jesus Christ born?* in the *Expositor,* 1917, Vol. II, pp. 178–192. The author has apparently been influenced by Clement of Alexandria for the date of the Nativity.

[14] J. M. Pfättisch, *Die Dauer der Lehrtätigheit Jesu* (Freiburg-im-Br., 1911).

[15] O. Gerhardt, *Das Datum der Kreuzigung Christi,* in *Astron. Nachrichten,* Oct., 1930, and previously in a thesis of the same title (Berlin, 1914).

[16] H. von Soden, in *Encycl. Biblica,* 1899, p. 809.

[17] Mémain, *La connaissance des temps évangéliques,* 1886, passim.

[18] Lévrier, *Clé chronologique des dates exactes de la vie de Jesus-Christ,* Vol II, (Poitiers, 1905). The author, aiming at an exactness which is impossible in these matters, goes constantly astray.

[19] Chaume, *Recherches sur la chronologie de la vie de Notre-Seigneur,* in *Revue Biblique,* 1918, pp. 215–243 and 506–549 (separately bound). Apr. 8, A.D. 35, is certainly a Friday, but in this hypothesis, Jesus would have been about forty years old at the time of his death.

[20] Levesque, *Abrégé chronol. de la Vie de N.-S. J.-C.* [Note of J.C.].

NOTE C

The Word As Life and Light

1. The Johannine Concepts of Life and Light

In the Gospel of St. John and in the First Epistle, which is like a preface to his Gospel, *life* is always the supernatural life of grace and glory; for St. John does not regard grace and glory as two different states, any more than does St. Paul; rather he takes them as two phases of the same state, grace being transformed into glory at the termination of the time of trial. St. John speaks of *life eternal* (ζωὴ αἰώνιος, with or without the article, 23 times) or simply of *life* (ζωή, with or without the article, 25 times), with no change of meaning.

The Word is *Life,* by a figure of speech which places the cause for the effect, because he is the principle of all supernatural life (John 11:25; 14:6; 1 John 1:2; 5:12, etc.). This title does not belong to him solely by *attribution,* as creation is attributed to the Father and sanctification to the Holy Spirit; because in the present order of Providence, which binds the salvation of man to the work of satisfaction of the Incarnate Word, all supernatural life, both before and after the Incarnation, is derived from Christ. The Son is not only the author of the supernatural life as its efficient cause equally with the other Divine Persons, but also by the special title of meritorious cause. The Redemption belongs to the Word because of the merits of his humanity, but it also belongs to him as a *Person;* for the Word, both before and after the Incarnation, is always the same Person: "Jesus Christ was yesterday, he is today, he shall be forever" (Heb. 13:8), always Saviour, always Redeemer, ever since there has existed a guilty humanity which he is charged to lift up again. It is by no means necessary to hold, with a great number of the Fathers of the Church, that all the theophanies of the Old Testament were apparitions of the Son of God; it is enough to say that all the graces accorded to fallen humanity are the anticipated fruits of Calvary and pertain therefore to the Son of God as to their meritorious cause.

Whereas *life,* in St. John, is always the supernatural life (the life of grace, or the life of glory, or both together), *light* is sometimes used in the ordinary sense of physical brightness; usually, however, light corresponds to life, with which it has close relationships, and considered in their cause they are both identified with the Word Incarnate. Jesus Christ says of himself: "I am the light of the world" (John 8:12; 9:5), "I have come into the world as Light" (John 12:46), just as he says: "I am the resurrection and the life. I am the truth and the life" (John 11:25; 14:6). He is also called the *True Light* (John 1:9; 1 John 2:8), and this is to distinguish him from the Baptist, who is only a *torch,* λύχνος (5:35); or from the light *of this world* (John 11:9) perceived by the eyes of the body.

The effects of *Light* and *Life* in the regenerated soul are inseparable, for man cannot be illumined by the Word without being vivified by him; but the concepts differ. Light considered as coming from the Word is revealed truth; considered as received by man it is faith. But it is important to remember that, in St. John as well as in St. Paul, to *believe* is not solely an intellectual act, a simple adherence of the soul to revealed truth; it is an act of submission entailing an abandonment of the whole self to the divine will. This living and active faith *informed* by charity produces what St. Paul calls "justification" and St. John calls "life."

Logically, light comes before life and leads to it. "While you have the Light (Christ, the Light of the World), believe in the light (the word of Christ, the truth he reveals), that you may become children of light (by faith)" (John 12:36). Believers become the children of light υιοὶ φωτός, when they pass from the darkness of error and ignorance into the light of truth (Eph. 5:8–9); when they are no longer sons of the night and the darkness, but sons of the light and the day (1 Thess. 5:5).

The intimate connection between light and life emerges clearly from the following texts: "I am the Light of the world. He that follows me does not walk in darkness, but shall have *the light of life,* τὸ φῶς τῆς ζωῆς" (John 8:12). Grammatically this can be understood: "the light that comes from the Life, i.e., from the Word," but the more common interpretation is much more natural: "the light that produces life, that is somehow identified with life." And this interpretation is confirmed by the concluding words of St. John: "These things are written that you may believe that Jesus is the Christ, the Son of God, and that *believing* you may have life" (John 20:31).

It is very truly said that "light is at one and the same time the effect and the cause of *life*,"[1] but only if light and life be taken in two different senses. Thus we arrive at the following definition of τὸ φῶς τῆς ζωῆς: "the light which both springs from life and issues in life; of which life is the essential principle and the necessary result."[2] In other words, the Word Incarnate is Life and Light, the principle of life and light in the regenerated soul; but if life and light as they are in man are compared, light logically precedes life, and life results from light.

2. In Him Was (the) Life

(ἐν αὐτῷ ζωὴ ἦν)

The third and fourth verses of St. John's opening chapter contain the following words: χωρὶς αὐτοῦ ἐγένετο οὐδὲ ἓν ὃ γέγονεν ἐν αὐτῷ ζωὴ ἦν, which are susceptible of the following punctuations:

a) ἐγένετο οὐδὲ ἕν. Ὃ γέγονεν, ἐν αὐτῷ ζωὴ ἦν (*factum est nihil. Quod factum est, in ipso vita erat*)
b) ἐγένετο οὐδὲ ἕν. Ὃ γέγονεν ἐν αὐτῷ, ζωὴ ἦν (*factum est nihil. Quod factum est in ipso, vita erat*)
c) ἐγένετο οὐδὲ ἓν ὃ γέγονεν. Ἐν αὐτῷ ζωὴ ἦν (*factum est nihil quod factum est. In ipso vita erat*).

We have not taken into consideration the eccentric reading: ἐγένετο οὐδὲ ἓν ὃ γέγονεν ἐν αὐτῷ. Ζωὴ ἦν since it is too poorly attested and results in an inadmissible tautology: *sine ipso factum est nihil quod factum est in ipso.*[3]

It is well known that in ancient Greek manuscripts words were not separated, and punctuation is either entirely lacking or very sparse, at least up to the fifth century A.D. Greek particles lavishly used by the Classical authors supplied to some extent the lack of punctuation in their writings, otherwise the division of phrases was left to the intelligence or caprice of the reader. It is certain that the autograph of St. John bore no punctuation marks in this passage, and therefore the

[1] Frey, *Biblica,* 1920, p. 234 (*Le concept de la "vie" dans S. Jean*).

[2] Westcott, *The Gospel according to St. John,* 14 ed., 1902, p. 128.

[3] A list of the defenders of each of the readings is to be found in Zahn, *Evang. des Joh.,* 4 ed., Leipzig, 1912, Excursus i, pp. 706–709, or in Lebreton, *Orig. du dogme de la Trinité,* 4 ed., 1919, Note I, pp. 386–389 (English transl., Algar Thorold, 1939, Note VI, pp. 444–446), or in Lagrange, *Saint Jean,* 1925, pp. 6–9. The critics disagree. Tischendorf and Vogels adopt reading 3; Von Soden and Hort, reading 1 or 2; but the latter puts reading 3 in the margin and admits that it "has high claims to acceptance on internal grounds," and that the punctuation in the manuscripts, versions, and Fathers "has no *textual* authority." *Introduction, Appendix,* p. 74.

manuscripts and versions and the writings of the Fathers are not, properly speaking, witnesses of the original text in this respect. Rather they are evidence of the interpretation which it pleased each writer to give to the text. The punctuation adopted must, therefore, be judged on its intrinsic merits, i.e., according to the more or less acceptable meaning it gives to the text.

It must be admitted that, as far as can be judged at present, most authorities of the first three centuries linked together the words ὃ γέγονεν ἐν αὐτῷ ζωὴ ἦν (*Quod factum est in ipso vita erat*). In favor of this division it may be said that thus a more perfectly balanced rhythm is obtained, since there are two phrases more equal in length; thus, also, is avoided the apparent pleonasm which would result if ὃ γέγονεν were linked with the absolute negative οὐδὲ ἕν which immediately precedes. But rhythm is not all-important, nor is St. John here writing in verse or in strophes; and the alleged pleonasm rather has the effect of adding greater emphasis. The question, then, to be decided is whether this division of words, with the comma placed either before or after ἐν αὐτῷ, gives to the text a more acceptable meaning.[4]

The heretics — Manicheans, Arians, Eunomians, and Gnostics of all types — placed the comma after ἐν αὐτῷ, all of them reading: ὃ γέγονεν ἐν αὐτῷ, ζωὴ ἦν (What was made in him was life). The Manicheans drew these conclusions: first, that all things made *in* the Word, that is to say, *by* the Word, were animate beings; secondly, that inanimate beings such as matter were not the work of the Word. The Gnostics saw in the phrase "what was made in him" *spiritual men,* those alone who are in possession of the true life, and they classed all others in the category of *material men,* destined to eternal death. The Eunomians, interpreting

[4] Since St. Jerome formally pronounces in favor of the division: *In ipso vita erat* (though he once ends a quotation of the text with: *et factum est nihil,* at the beginning of the *Quaestiones hebr.* in *Genesim,* ML, XXIII, 939), it is generally thought that the original Vulgate had the same reading as the present Vulgate: *sine ipso factum est nihil quod factum est. In ipso vita erat.* But Wordsworth and White hold that this was not so. The majority of the older and better manuscripts have: *Quod factum est in ipso vita erat.* This was also the most widespread reading in the Old Latin, with the interesting peculiarity that this version read *est* instead of *erat,* as Origen's explanation would require. See the collation of six of the principal codices in ML, xii, 353–354.

Even in the sixteenth century Maldonatus wrote: "Tres apud graves auctores lectiones invenio. Prima est quam quotidiano sequimur usu, ut post illud *nihil* sententia claudatur, deinde sequatur alia *Quod factum est, in ipso vita erat.*" This was the punctuation adopted by Sixtus V in his Bible, while the Clementine edition seems to wish to leave the matter undecided: *nihil, quod factum est, in ipso vita erat.* The well-known opinion of St. Augustine may well have had great influence on the Latins. Of the punctuation spoken of by Maldonatus, Toletus says: "Ita legit major pars Latinorum," though he himself prefers, as more coherent, the punctuation of the present Vulgate.

the words "what was made in him" as applying to the Holy Spirit, concluded that the Holy Spirit was a creature, since he was made by the Word. Even the Arians attempted to make subtle misuse of a text in which they clearly saw their condemnation. But what is still more extraordinary is that Origen succeeds by his subtlety in giving an orthodox meaning to the text so punctuated. His thought is not crystal clear, but, if we understand him correctly, this is the substance of what he holds: the Word alone is the true life, and only those that are united to him share that life. Now, the just man was not only *made by him* but *has become in him* (ὃ γέγονεν ἐν αὐτῷ); he therefore shares the life of the Word, he is *life in him:* all others are in death. Origen perceives that if ὃ γέγονεν ἐν αὐτῷ designates the just man precisely as united to the Word by faith and charity, the reading ζωὴ ἐστιν in the present tense is demanded. He remarks that some copies have this reading, but he does not dwell on this difficulty, which, moreover, is not the only one in his system.

The Catholic authorities who adopt the division ὃ γέγονεν ἐν αὐτῷ ζωὴ ἦν generally place the comma before ἐν αὐτῷ and arrive at the following meaning: "What was made was life in him"; but they differ in their interpretation. According to St. Cyril of Alexandria, the Word gives a kind of life to all things by keeping them in existence and by preventing them from falling back into the nothingness from which the creative act has drawn them. But in this there is nothing special to the Person of the Word; and again, it is necessary to take ἐν αὐτῷ as if it were δἰ αὐτοῦ. Besides, life understood in this sense has no relationship to the light of the world. Over and above this, St. Cyril is obliged to give to "life" the altogether unusual meaning of "existence," and this gives the finishing blow to his explanation.

Has St. Augustine been more felicitous? At least he bases his hypothesis on firmer ground. He considers the Word as the eternal Exemplar according to which God created the world. The workman who proposes to fashion a piece of furniture first conceives an image of it, for how else could he fashion it? The piece of furniture has itself no life, but it lives in the vital act produced by the soul of the workman; and thus creatures, even inanimate things, live in the Word, who is Life itself. If it were a matter of interpreting Philo or some neo-Platonist, this explanation would be acceptable; but exegetes of all schools now agree that it is hardly suitable in interpreting John, the Theologian, who, even more than St. Paul, confines himself within the horizon of supernatural realities. Besides, there is no relation between the life that creatures have in the Word as exemplary cause, and the light of men, in whatever way it be understood.

M. Loisy, while keeping to the punctuation of St. Augustine and St.

Cyril, is dissatisfied with their exegesis. He suggests the translation: "What was made, in that was life," or in other words, "In that which had become there was life." He finds this interpretation very clear and "very natural," but many will disagree with him. To refer ἐν αὐτῷ to ὃ γέγονεν and not to the Word, which is dominant in the whole passage, is an extreme choice which no one has ever thought of. How can we believe that the Evangelist has had recourse to such a tortuous construction in order to express a notion so simple in itself and yet so foreign to the present subject, namely, the notion that there was life in the world? (Loisy, *Le Quatrième évangile,* 2 ed., 1921, p. 92.)

The punctuation to adopt is, therefore, that of St. John Chrysostom, of St. Jerome, and of the present Vulgate. St. Jerome informs us that it was the punctuation of the Alexandrians and the Egyptians, and that the majority of the instructed faithful of his time read it so, although he personally saw no difficulty in keeping the other punctuation. The latter does, in fact, offer a philosophical meaning which is very beautiful and very attractive; however, it is doubtful that it is the meaning of the Theologian, and to defend it, it is necessary to change the text to read: *"Quod factum est in ipso vita est,"* as St. Augustine does and also St. Ambrose, and many copyists of the Old Latin and the Vulgate.[5]

3. Why the Word, and Not the Son?

Whence did St. John derive the notion and the term "Logos," unknown elsewhere in the New Testament? Why does he use it in preference to that of Son, with which he himself identifies it at the end of his

[5] St. John Chrysostom is very insistent, and suspects the heretics of having thought up the reading *Quod factum est in ipso vita erat* in order to propagate their errors (*In Joan. hom.,* v, 1; MG, LIX, 53). St. Jerome (with the exception of one sole passage) always cites the text thus: *sine ipso factum est nihil quod factum est,* stopping there (e.g., *In Ezech.,* 37:10, and *In Amos.,* 6:12; ML, XXV, 347 and 1065). St. Ambrose writes: "Alexandrini quidem et Aegyptii scribunt *sine ipso factum est nihil quod factum est* et, interposita distinctione, subito *In ipso vita erat.* Salva est fidelibus ista distinctio. Ego non vereor legere *Quod factum est in ipso vita EST,* et nihil habet quod teneat Arianus" (*In Psalm.,* 36:18–19; ML, XIV, 984, or Petschenig, p. 98). The same remark is found in *De fide* (iii, 6, n. 43; ML, XVI, 598). St. Ambrose, like St. Augustine, always supposes that St. John had the present tense, *vita est,* a reading which is found in many manuscripts of the Old Latin version (cf. ML, XII, 34–35) and of the Vulgate. And, indeed, the present tense is necessary for the Platonistic exegesis of St. Augustine and St. Ambrose. But St. John certainly put ἦν in the imperfect. Codex Bezae alone has ἐστίν, which Origen said he had found in some rare manuscripts; Origen, however, does not himself adopt it (*In Joann.,* 1:4, Preuschen's edit., p. 76). Far from favoring the "exemplary cause" explanation, the imperfect rules it out.

Prologue? How is it that he then drops it, seeming almost to forget it, except at the beginning of his First Epistle? Delicate questions, indeed, and perhaps unanswerable, but they cannot be ignored.

In the Classical period the word λόγος has a great variety of meanings: a spoken word, a speech, a narrative in prose as opposed to a narrative in verse (ἔπος), reason, intelligence, judgment, opinion, a definition, the intimate reason of something, an account to be rendered, a relation of proportion or of analogy. But the primitive meaning in Homer and Hesiod is "the spoken word, a speech," after the etymology (from λέγειν, *to say, to speak*); such also is the basic meaning of *verbum* (from εἴρειν, for ϝείρειν *to speak, to say*). The learned Tertullian translates the Λόγος of St. John by *Sermo*.

The Stoics gave the name λόγος to the world-soul which has so much affinity with the *fire* of Heraclitus, though the abstruse Heraclitus would probably not have availed himself of the term λόγος. The Stoic world-soul is not only the principle of all activity, but also universal Reason, of which our intelligence is only a spark; it is likewise the law of the universe which draws all beings by an irresistible force to the fated terms of their destiny.

To the Jew imbued with the purest monotheism, nothing was more repugnant than the pantheistic Logos of the Stoics. The personality and transcendence of God and the distinction between God and the world are written in the first lines of the Bible in unforgettable characters. Far from being attracted by monistic theories, the Jews could not even have conceived them. Stoicism, however, is more than a cosmogony. The disciples of the "Porch" were the first to distinguish between the λόγος ἐνδιάθετος (internal word, *verbum mentis*) and the λόγος προφορικός (externalized word, speech); and this distinction was to bear fruit. For in Classical Greek, λόγος meant reason, and not thought; intelligence as a faculty of the soul, and not intelligence in act, or rather the act of intelligence.[6] This is the first step toward a grasp of the Johannine Logos.

A second and more decisive step is due to the Platonism of Philo. It is well established that Plato has, in his authentic works, no theory of

---

[6] These terms will be sought for in vain in the philosophers before Socrates (cf. H. Diels, *Die Fragmente der Vorsokratiker,* Vol. III, 1910, Index). Nor are they found in Plato or Aristotle. Still, Aristotle has something approaching them: Οὐ γὰρ πρὸς τὸν ἔξω λόγον ἡ ἀπόδειξις, ἀλλὰ πρὸς τὸν ἐν τῇ ψυχῇ, ἐπεὶ οὐδὲ συλλογισμός. Ἀεὶ γάρ ἐστιν ἐνστῆναι πρὸς τὸν ἔξω λόγον, ἀλλὰ πρὸς τὸν ἔσω λόγον οὐκ ἀεί (*Anal. post.*, I, x, 7; Didot, I, 131). But this distinction between ὁ ἔξω λόγος and ὁ ἔσω λόγος, ὁ ἐν τῇ ψυχῇ is, perhaps, to be found nowhere else before the Stoics. The terms ἐνδιάθετος and προφορικός are found in Philo and Plutarch. Zeller, in my opinion, has proved that the Stoics invented the terms (*Die Philos. der Griechen,* 4 ed., 1909, Part III, pp. 68–69).

the Logos; but he has a theory of the intelligible world, the world of ideas which serves as the principle and model of the sensible world. For Plato, ideas "are independent substances, and not thoughts conceived by God, and consequently intermediaries between him and the world. For Philo, on the contrary, they are the ideal models which God has constructed in his mind before the creation of the world, just as an architect draws up beforehand the plan of the city that he wishes to build. This modification of the Platonic theory is, certainly, very remarkable, but Philo is not its first exponent; Plato was thus understood in his day."[7] To this Platonic entity so transformed, Philo gave the name, Logos: "If we must speak in clearer terms, we shall say that the intelligible world is none other than the Logos of God in course of creating the world." If man, as Moses says, was made to the image of God, how much more is the universe made to that image, for it is as much greater than man as the whole is greater than a part. "And so it is clear that what we call the intelligible world is the exemplar, the archetype, the idea of ideas, the Word of God."[8] This is all that can be found in Philo which can throw light on the doctrine of the Prologue. All the other titles with which Alexandrian philosophy adorns its Logos — high priest, mediator, divider, demiurge, instrument of God in creation, son of God — all do nothing but obscure the very simple and very beautiful idea of the exemplary cause.

Not all the critics subscribe to Harnack's judgment that "the Logos (of the Fourth Gospel) has hardly more than the name in common with the Philonian Logos"; but everyone should agree that the differences are great.[9] The Philonian Logos is an abstract notion, vague and

---

[7] Lebreton, *Les origines du dogme de la Trinité,* 5 ed., 1927, p. 202 (English transl., Note VII, p. 151). We can do more than refer to the excellent Note: *"The Doctrine of the Logos in Philo and in Saint John"* (English transl., pp. 440–443).

[8] *De mundi opifico* (Mangey, I, 5). In this passage the Logos is: (1) the Logos of God (ὁ Θεοῦ λόγος — the word of God); (2) the intelligible world (ὁ κόσμος νοητός), as opposed to the sensible world; (3) the original exemplar (τὸ ἀρχέτυπον παράδειγμα), in so far as it is in the mind of God; (4) the original seal (ἡ ἀρχέτυπος σφραγίς), in so far as it is imprinted on created beings to make them like the archetype; (5) the idea of ideas (ἡ ἰδέα τῶν ἰδεῶν), the seat of ideas, the universal idea which comprises all particular ideas. The Logos is also the *image* of God, in such a way that the world made to the image of the Logos is the image of an image (εἰκὼν εἰκόνος) or the imitation of an image.

[9] *Dogmengeschichte,* 4 ed., 1909, Vol. I, p. 109. Cf. Cremer, *Biblisch-theol. Wörterbuch,* 9 ed., p. 646. Loisy more recently shifted his ground. In 1903 (*Quatrieme évangile,* p. 154) he wrote: "The influence of Philonic ideas on John is not controvertible." In 1921 (2 ed., p. 88) he writes: "It is not over probable that there is a literary dependence of the Johannine Gospel upon Philonic writings." There is there more than a *nuance.*

fluid, an idea constantly personified without ever attaining personality. Philo never identified his Logos with the Messias; the "Word made flesh" would have been meaningless to him. On the other hand, the Logos of St. John is a concrete being, the Incarnate Son of God, Jesus Christ, a personality unique throughout his twofold existence. But there are resemblances between the two notions. In both, the Word plays a role in the creation of the world; and, in both, he is mediator between God and man. But upon closer examination most of the analogies are to be explained by community of origin, viz., the Biblical source from which both authors drew.

In the important passage cited above, Philo expressly refers to Moses, and claims to do no more than set forth his teaching.[10] The Sapiential Books apply to personified Wisdom almost all the titles Philo assigns to the Logos. She is a vapor (ἀτμίς) of the power of God, an emanation (ἀπόρροια) of his pure glory, an effulgence (ἀπαύγασμα) of the eternal light, a spotless mirror (ἔσοπτρον) of the divine activity, an image (εἰκών) of His goodness. She was brought forth before the hills, she works to prepare the heavens and to set the foundations of the earth, she is the delight of the Almighty.[11]

This is all, of course, only personification, but is it otherwise in Philo? It is also true that *Wisdom* is not styled the divine Logos, but she could not be. Although in Greek λόγος means both "word" and "reason," in the Septuagint it has only the first meaning, where it translates the Hebrew *dabar* (by exception *'omer* and *millah*) corresponding to the λόγος προφορικός of the Stoics. Nevertheless, the Word is also personified in the Bible and presented as the agent of creation and revelation, and, again, as the instrument of divine vengeance. From on high in heaven God sends his Word; by his Word he saves and heals, and creates the world and makes firm the heavens.

The poetic tone of this section leaves no room for misunderstanding the meaning of the vivid presentation. But it seems that little is now lacking to make out the Word of God as a real Person. Exegetes and theologians almost up to our time have maintained that the Rabbis had, in fact, taken this step and attributed personality to God's word. As a matter of fact, the Targum frequently treats of the *Memra* — sometimes its synonym *Dibbura* is used — which speaks and acts as a person in those circumstances in which God deals with the world. But the *Memra* is not a hypostasis; if it were, the Targums would have used it in those passages of the Old Testament in which the word of God

---

10 Philo, *De mundi opifico* (Mangey, I, 5): Μωσέως ἐστὶ τὸ δόγμα οὐκ ἐμόν.
11 Wisd. 7:25–26; Prov. 8:22–29.

is personified and approaches most nearly to a hypostasis, and it is precisely there that they avoid it. The fact that the *Memra* appears only in the Targums and is never mentioned in the old Rabbinical writings, such as the *Mishnah* and the *Tosephta,* proves that it was not part of the teaching of Judaism. In reality the Memra of Yahweh (pronounced Adonai) is nothing else than a simple paraphrasis used to cloak an anthropomorphism or to avoid pronouncing the divine tetragrammaton in the public reading of the Bible. Several other synonyms for God: the name (*shem*), the place (*maqôm*), heaven (*shamaïm*), the brilliance or the presence (*shekinah*), all have a similar origin.[12]

Arrived at this stage of its evolution, "Logos" was well adapted to the use which the Evangelist wished to make of it. As λόγος ἐνδιάθετος it meant not only the intelligence but the thought of God, the perfect image of God Himself; as divine Exemplar it expressed a twofold relation, to the worker who produced it, and to the work for which it served as a model; as λόγος προφορικός it recalled the creative and revealing Word of the Old Testament. It had the advantage of being understood by contemporary Jews as well as by the Greeks; and, not being the exclusive property of any philosophical school, it did not necessarily carry in its train a troop of compromising ideas. It could be purified and transformed while having as its basis meanings which were consecrated by usage. St. John causes it to make three great progressive steps: he presents it as true Person, and not as a simple personification; he attributes to it the divine nature in the strict sense; he identifies it with the Messias of the Jews and the Saviour of all mankind, Jesus Christ.

But, it will be objected, in that case it is no longer the Logos of the Greeks nor the Logos of the Hellenistic Jews; both will easily see that their Logos has been changed; in trying to satisfy everyone, the Evangelist will succeed in satisfying no one. But we have proof that he did satisfy them. St. Basil tells us that "many men, unsympathetic to our beliefs and proud of their worldly wisdom admired the Prologue of St. John, and did not hesitate to use it to embellish their own works." What repelled them, according to St. Augustine, was "the Word made

---

[12] Cf. Weber, *Jüdische Theologie,* 2 ed., 1897, Chap. xiii; *Mittlerische Hypostasen, pp.* 177–190; Billerbeck, Vol. II, 1924, *Exkurs: Memra Jahves,* pp. 302–333. The last author numbers 179 occurrences of *Memra* in the Targum of Onkelos, and altogether 420 in the two Targums of Jerusalem. It is, perhaps, well to note that *Memra* is a masculine noun as are *shem* and *maqôm. Shamaïm* is a plural, but when it designates God it is considered as a proper name and does not take the definite article.

flesh."[13] St. John had a profound reason for presenting the pre-existent Christ first of all as the Word of God rather than as the Son of God. For the pagans, hearing the name "Son of God," would straightway think of those demigods who were born of carnal intercourse between immortals and mortals. And as far as the Jews are concerned, the name "Son of God" was not to them a Messianic title: they understood "sons of God," but not "the Son of God." Origen informs us that when the Christians spoke to them of the Son of God, they asked what it meant.

These were only reasons of expediency. There are also other reasons which the Fathers of the Church bring to light. "Why the Word?" says St. Basil. "That it might be manifest that he proceeds from Mind. Why the Word? Because he was engendered impassibly. Why the Word? Because he is the image of him who engendered him, manifesting in himself the entire Engenderer."[14] St. Gregory of Nazianzus and St. Cyril of Alexandria say almost the same, though less succinctly.

4. Division and Paraphrased Translation of the Prologue

We have considered it necessary to indicate double translations wherever possible; our preferences have been indicated either in this note or in the course of the book:

a) v. 5: The darkness did not receive (does not impede) the light.

b) v. 9: He enlightens every man coming (when he comes) into the world.

c) v. 16: We have received grace upon grace (grace for grace).

d) v. 18: The only-begotten Son, μονογενὴς υἱός (the only-begotten God, Θεός).

1. The Word (*a*) in his inner life, (*b*) in his relationship with creation, (*c*) and with the human race.

---

13 St. Basil, *Homilia,* xvi, 1 (MG, XXXI, 479); St. Augustine, *De civit. Dei,* X, xxix, 2 (ML, XLI, 309). Cf. *Confessions,* VIII, ii, 14.

14 St. Basil, *op. cit.,* n. 3 (MG, XXXI, 472). To understand the Greek Fathers, it should be noted that, before St. John Damascene, in general they compared the Word not to the λόγος ἐνδιάθετος but to the λόγος προφορικός. The reason was that, in current speech, λόγος meant reason, and not thought (ἔννοια, νόησις). They argue, as does St. Basil in the passage quoted: "Our word (λόγος) proceeds from our thought, and is its image; in like manner, the Word of God, etc." He adds: ὁ ἡμέτερος λόγος τοῦ νοοῦ γέννημα, "our λόγος is the product of the understanding"; but the context shows that he is referring to the word *produced by the intelligence* through the intermediary of thought. The Latins, who considered the *internal word* not as a faculty, but as a *fetus mentis,* would be nearer to the thought of St. John.

a) *In the beginning* of time, which measures created things, *was the Word;* he is therefore eternal. *And the Word was with God,* and is therefore personal and distinct from the Father. *And the Word was God;* he was not the Father (ὁ Θεός), but he had the divine nature (Θεός).

b) *He was in the beginning with God,* before co-operating with the Father in the work of creation. *All things were made through him, and without him was made nothing that was made.*

c) *In him was* (the) *life,* the source of all supernatural life, comprising grace and glory. *And the Life was the Light of men, and the Light shines in the darkness, and the darkness received it not* (belonging to the nature of the light is to shine in the darkness, and the darkness cannot impede it, extinguish it).

2. Progressive manifestation of the Word, the Light of the human race (7–15).

a) John, the witness of the Light — *There was a man sent from God, whose name was John. He came as a witness, to bear witness to the Light, that all might believe through him* (through his witness and his ministry). *He was not himself the Light, but* (his mission) *was to bear witness to the Light.*

b) The Word was the Light of men from the beginning of humanity — *He existed* (he who is) *the true Light which enlightens every man coming into the world* (which enlightens every man when it comes into the world). *He was in the world, and the world was made through him, and the world knew him not.*

c) The Word as the Light of men after the Patriarchal and Mosaic revelations — *He came into his own domain* (among the people who were his possession and heritage) *and his own received him not* (neither as a people nor in the aggregate); *but to as many as received him, he gave the power to become the sons of God, to those who believe in his name, who were born not of blood, nor of the will of the flesh, nor of the will of man, but of God.*

d) The Word as the Light of men after the Incarnation — *And the Word was made flesh, and pitched his tent among us, and we have beheld his glory* (the glory of his life, of his miracles, his Resurrection, his Ascension), *glory such as an only-begotten son, full of grace and truth, can receive from his father.*

e) The testimony of John — *John bears witness concerning him and cries: He who comes after me has gone before me* (has been preferred to me), *because he was before me.*

3. Conclusion — Reflection of the Evangelist (16–18).

Of his fullness we (Christians) *have all received, and grace upon grace* (grace for grace), *for the law was given through Moses; but grace* (supplanting and abrogating the Law) *and Truth* (the fulfillment of ancient type and figure) *have come through Jesus Christ.*

No one has at any time seen God: the only-begotten Son (the only-begotten God), *who is in the bosom of the Father, he has revealed him to us.*

NOTE D

The Two Genealogies of Jesus

1. The Genealogy According to St. Matthew (1:1–17)

The genealogy in St. Matthew descends from Abraham to Jesus and comprises three series of fourteen names each: the first from Abraham to David, the second from Solomon to the Captivity, the third from the Captivity to Joseph and Jesus himself. This division, which was perhaps chosen by the author as an aid to the memory (1:17), is in part artificial, because, to construct it, it was necessary to omit certain names. (*a*) Between Joram and Ozias, three well-known kings, Ochosias, Joas, and Amasias are omitted. A good reason for this omission has been brought to light by Heer, namely, that Scripture condemns their memory.[1] (*b*) Josias was not the father of Jechonias but his grandfather: Josias begot Joakim, and Joakim begot Joachin (or Jechonias). The omission may have been accidental: because of similarity of names, the reader may have passed from Josias to Joachin, omitting Joakim. But then, to have a third series of fourteen names, it was necessary to repeat Jechonias. (*c*) Between Phares, who was born before the sojourn in Egypt, and Naasson, chief of the tribe of Juda at the time of the Exodus, there was an interval of 430, or at least 215, years. This is too much for three successive generations; some intervening generations must have been omitted (*d*) Between Salmon, who was born in the desert of Sinai, and Jesse, the father of David, there are likewise only three names, and the same conclusion is to be drawn. (*e*) Between Zorobabel and Jacob, St. Matthew counts only eight generations, whereas St. Luke counts seventeen. Since the Captivity goes back to the year 538, eight generations do not seem to be enough to fill in the interval.

Besides the reason of aiding the memory, it has been thought that a motive for these omissions may have been the desire to have three

---

[1] Heer, *Die Stammbäume Christi Jesu nach Matthäus und Lukas,* 1911, pp. 134–153 and 204–214.

series of *fourteen* names for "the genealogy of Jesus Christ, the son of David." The numerical value of the letters of David's name in Hebrew is fourteen (דוד , 4 + 6 + 4).

St. Matthew names in this list only four women: Thamar, Rahab, Ruth, and the wife of Urias (Bethsabee). St. Jerome in his commentary writes with reference to this: 'Notandum in genealogia Salvatoris nullam sanctarum assumi mulierem, sed eas quas Scriptura reprehendit, ut qui propter peccatores venerat, de peccatoribus nascens, omnium peccata deleret." But Ruth was not a sinner, and Thamar was in good faith and the Scripture does not censure her. What these women had in common was that they were foreigners and not Israelites: Rahab was a Chanaanite; so also, very probably, was Thamar; Ruth was a Moabite, and Bethsabee must have been a Hethite like her husband.

2. The Genealogy According to St. Luke (3:23–38)

The genealogy in St. Luke is ascending and goes back to Adam and even to God. It comprises four series, each containing three groups of seven names, with the exception of the third series which has only two groups. The first series ends at the Captivity, the second at Nathan, the son of David, the third at Abraham, and the fourth at God.

This distribution into four series does not appear to be intentional, since the number of members is not certain. If the names of Adam and Jesus be included in the list, following Biblical usage, but the name of God be left outside the series, there are 77 names in the Greek text, 76 in the Vulgate, 75 in the Sinaitic-Syriac, and 72 in six manuscripts of the Old Latin version. Between Sale and Arphaxad will be remarked the name of Cainan, which is not found either in the Vulgate or the Hebrew Old Testament genealogy: a proof that St. Luke is making use of the Septuagint version. The numerical differences lend themselves ill to symbolism; still, St. Irenaeus, who counts 72 names in his list, and St. Augustine, who counts 77, adding to the 76 names of the Vulgate the name of God, have sought out symbolical meanings which are quite forced and derived from entirely opposed principles.

St. Luke's introduction to the genealogy deserves careful examination.

Καὶ αὐτὸς ἦν Ἰησοῦς ἀρχόμενος ὡσεὶ ἐτῶν τριάκοντα, ὢν υἱὸς ὡς ἐνομίζετο, Ἰωσὴφ τοῦ Ἡλὶ κτλ. No matter how it be twisted, this text will never yield any other meaning than this: "And Jesus was beginning (his ministry) at the age of about thirty years, being, as was thought, the son of Joseph, son of Heli, etc." Those who propose the translation: "being the son, (not) as was thought, of Joseph, (but in reality) of

Heli (the father of Mary)," admit that this is not the natural meaning, but they maintain that it is admissible. This is certainly not the case. The τοῦ before Ἡλί and the following names is not the definite article (which would not be used before a proper name), but a demonstrative pronoun referring to the name that precedes it: "Jesus, son of Joseph (without any article), who is (son) of Heli." This is true to such an extent that, if Ἰωσήφ were in the nominative, the reading would have to be Ἰωσήφ ὁ Ἡλί, τοῦ Ματθάτ: "Joseph, who is son of Heli" (Ἰωσήφ ὁ Ἡλί), which Heli (in the genitive and represented by **τοῦ**) is son of Ματθάτ.

3. Reconciliation of the Two Genealogies

The real difficulty is that from David to Joseph all the names are different — except for Salathiel and Zorobabel, which, far from lessening the difficulty, only increases it. To say that all these persons bore two names, and that St. Matthew has selected one of the names and St. Luke the other, is a desperate solution, the very unlikeliness of which is its sufficient refutation. To tell the truth, the difficulty should not unduly preoccupy us. It is clear that, in going back from David to Abraham and to Adam, the Evangelists have drawn up their genealogical tables according to data furnished by Scripture; but for the names from David to Joseph they have transcribed a trustworthy family document perhaps without any concern to reconcile discrepancies, if, indeed, they were aware of them. For us, therefore, it is all the more difficult to account for their lack of agreement.

First Solution — This consists in assuming that Matthew gives the genealogy of Joseph and Luke that of Mary, or vice versa. According to this theory, Joseph and Mary were both descendants of David, one of them through Nathan and the other through Solomon. The names of Salathiel and Zorobabel, which are common to the two lists, create a difficulty. The answer given is that they do not designate the same persons; these two names are not rare, and it is quite natural that a father named Salathiel, living after the Captivity, should call his son Zorobabel.

Because of its simplicity, this solution enjoyed a wide vogue from the sixteenth century on. Vogt enumerates 82 Catholic authors and 84 Protestant who sponsor it, without counting a score or more others who more or less favor it.[2] The first in point of time was Giovanni

[2] Vogt, S.J., *Der Stammbaum Christi bei den heiligen Evangelisten Matthäus und Lukas,* 1911. On this monograph, and that of Heer above referred to, cf. Lagrange, in *R.B.,* 1911, pp. 434–451.

Nanni (Annius of Viterbo) who died in 1502, but he has little to recommend him as an historian or theologian.

If it is objected that the traditional name of the Blessed Virgin's father is Joachim and not Heli, the sponsors of this theory answer that Heli or Eli is an abridged form of Eliachim, the whole difference being in the interchangeable divine name (*El* or *Jo*): so much so that in the Book of Judith the same High Priest is sometimes called Eliachim (Judith 4:5, 6, 10), sometimes Joachim (15:9).

But there are graver objections against this theory. First, its *novelty*. How is it that up to the sixteenth century no one ever thought of this very simple way to solve the discrepancy? Secondly, the *authority of the Fathers,* who agree in saying that a Jewish genealogy cannot end with a woman. Thirdly, the impossibility of explaining in this way the text of St. Luke, as we have shown above, and *a fortiori* the text of St. Matthew.

Second Solution — This solution goes back to Julius Africanus, who states that he had it from some relatives of Jesus whose trustworthiness he does not doubt.[3] It is based on the Levirate Law (Deut. 25:5–10), according to which, when an Israelite died without male issue, his brother must marry the widow in order to perpetuate the line of the deceased. The son born of this union had two genealogies: one the *natural* one through his real father, the other a *legal* one, which gave him the same ancestors as the deceased. This solution would be simple, were it not for the complication introduced by the presence of both Salathiel and Zorobabel in the middle of the genealogical tables of both Matthew and Luke. Cf. Cornely, *Introductio,* 1897, Vol. III, p. 199, and my article, *Généalogie,* in the *Dictionnaire de la Bible.*

4. Conclusion

1. We admit, with all the Fathers and with the unanimous opinion of the commentators up to the sixteenth century, that St. Luke as well as St. Matthew is giving us the genealogy of St. Joseph, and we are of the opinion that St. Luke's text, according to the reading accepted by all the critical editors, cannot be understood as a genealogy of Mary.

2. Since the Evangelists give us their documents as they found them, without informing us how to reconcile them, it is perhaps impossible today to attempt a reconciliation which will give certainty; but any probable solution is enough.

---

[3] Julius Africanus, *Letter to Aristides,* reproduced in part by Eusebius (*Hist. eccl.,* I, 1), and in part by Routh (*Reliquiae sacrae* [Oxford, 1846], Vol. II, pp. 228–237).

3. The problem resolves itself into a search for causes that could have brought about a deviation in a genealogy, producing side by side with a *natural* line of descent, a *legal* line of descent. One of such causes, as we have seen above, could be the Levirate Law, but this was not the only one. Though adoption after the manner of the Greeks and Romans was unknown among the Hebrews, another sort of adoption was familiar to them. The Scripture tells us that Mardochai adopted Esther (Esth. 2:7). Josephus (*Antiq.,* I, vii, 1) affirms that Abraham, who at the time had no children of his own, adopted Lot. When Jacob was dying, he said to Joseph (Gen. 48:5–6): "The two sons who were born to thee in the land of Egypt before my coming shall be mine: Ephraim and Manasses shall be to me as Reuben and Simeon. But the children whom thou hast begotten after them shall be thine; they shall be called by the name of their brethren in their inheritance." Is not this a real adoption? By virtue of this act: (1) the two eldest sons of Joseph are regarded as the sons of Jacob and like them will receive their share of the inheritance; (2) Joseph's younger sons are called by the names of Ephraim and Manasses, i.e., are considered as their descendants from the legal point of view. Outside the priestly tribe, there were in reality only twelve tribes, and all Israelites had to belong to one of these tribes and have for eponymous ancestor one of the twelve patriarchs. Proselytes were inscribed in one of the tribes and their genealogy went back legally to one of the sons of Jacob, just as the freedmen of Rome became by law members of one of the *gentes.* They had two genealogies, one natural, the other legal.

A more usual case must have been that of Sesan (1 Para. 2:34–35). Having no male child, he married his daughter to an Egyptian slave named Jeraa, and they had a son called Ethei, and thus his line was perpetuated. The daughters of Salphaad married their first cousins (Num. 27:3) for the purpose, it seems, of continuing their father's line.

Another reason for the deviation of the genealogies was the following: the people of Israel were divided into families (*mishpaḥah*), the families into houses (*beth-ab*), and the houses into hearths. Though the number of the twelve tribes was unchangeable, that of the subdivisions was not. Families once numerous could be reduced to a single house whose members had one genealogy according to natural descent, another (this one legal) according to the family to which they were associated. We have an example of this in 1 Para. 23:11, but a closer study of the genealogies in the Books of Paralipomenon would perhaps furnish others.

NOTE E

The Census of Quirinius

1. Accurate Statement of the Question

Jesus Christ was born in the time of King Herod, but not long before Herod's death, which occurred in 4 B.C. He was about thirty years old at the time of his baptism, which took place, at the earliest, in the beginning of the year A.D. 27. It does not therefore seem that his birth, which coincides with the Census of Quirinius, can be placed earlier than the year 7 B.C. Now in the year 7 B.C. it was not Quirinius that was governor of Syria, but C. Sentius Saturninus, and the successor of Saturninus was P. Quintilius Varus, who governed Syria until after the death of Herod. It seems impossible, therefore, that St. Luke can be right when he writes: "This first registration occurred when Quirinius was governor of Syria" (Luke 2:2).

Quirinius is not an unknown personage. Tacitus devotes a paragraph to him in his *Annales* (iii, 48): "Impiger militiae et acribus ministeriis, consulatum sub divo Augusto, mox, expugnatis per Ciliciam Homonadensium castellis insignia triumphi adeptus, datusque rector Caio Caesari, Armeniam obtinuit." Quirinius was consul in the year 12 B.C. and died in A.D. 21, at an advanced age. From A.D. 1 to 3 he was adviser to Caius Caesar, who died on the 21st of February in A.D. 4. Strabo tells us (XII, vi, 5) that King Amyntas, who was killed by the Homonadenses, brigands of Cilicia, was avenged by Quirinius; he must therefore have been governor of Syria at that time, since Cilicia was a dependency of Syria. Finally, an inscription found in 1764 at Tivoli (Tibur) can refer only to Quirinius, and proves that he was *twice* governor of Syria. A facsimile of it may be found in the *Dictionnaire de la Bible,* s.v. Cyrinus, with Mommsen's restoration. The date of Quirinius' second legateship in Syria is known: it was at the time of the death of Archelaus (A.D. 6) when he was charged with taking a census (ἀποτίμησις) of Palestine, recently annexed to the Province of Syria, for the purpose of establishing the assessment of taxes. We do not know the date of his first legateship, but it is generally agreed that Saturninus was governor of Syria from 8 to 6 B.C., and that his successor was Varus, who was still functioning at the time of Herod's death. There is, therefore, an open period between the year 12 B.C., the date of the consulship of Quirinius, and the year 8; but it seems impossible to date the birth of our Lord as early as that, for, if he was born in the beginning of 8 B.C., he would have been about thirty-four years old at the time of his baptism.

2. Various Solutions

The first solution, proposed by Hervart in 1612 and afterward adopted by many exegetes, both Protestant (Olshausen, Tholuck, Wieseler, Ewald, Caspari, etc.) and Catholic (Calmet, Wallon, Lagrange, etc.), cuts the difficulty at the root. Luke's text (2:2): αὕτη ἡ ἀπογραφὴ πρώτη ἐγένετο ἡγεμονεύοντος Κυρινίου is translated: "This registration was *previous to that* of the governor Quirinius," i.e., previous to the well-known registration by Quirinius in A.D. 6, at the death of Archelaus. According to this translation, the first census could have occurred at any time previous.

The translation cannot be said to be impossible, since many good philologists accept it, but it is somewhat forced and unnatural, and it would doubtless not have come to anyone's mind except for anxiety to solve the difficulty of chronology. The word πρῶτος has, indeed, the meaning of πρότερος and even of πρό. In St. John, for example, there is the phrase πρῶτός μου ἦν (1:30) and πρῶτον ὑμῶν (15:18), and a papyrus has σου πρῶτος εἰμι, but in such cases the word in the genitive corresponds exactly to the word to which πρῶτος is joined. It is true, there are examples in which the second term of the comparison is "understood": e.g., Ὁ λόγος μου πρῶτος τοῦ Ἰούδα (4 Kings 19:23), "My cause prevails over (that of) Juda."

2. The second solution is suggested by Tertullian's statement: "Sed et census constat actos sub Augusto tunc in Judaea per Sentium Saturninum apud quos genus ejus inquirere potuissent" (*Adv. Marcionem,* iv, 1). According to this solution, the census would have been begun by Quirinius and completed by Saturninus, who was governor of Syria from 8 to 6 B.C., and St. Luke attributes it to Quirinius, the more important of the two. This is admissible; the year 6, and even, if necessary, the year 7 B.C., would be suitable for the Saviour's birth.

3. However, a third solution seems to us to be preferable. It is certain that there were sometimes two imperial legates in the same province. Thus in Africa in the year A.D. 75 we find two governors, one *charged with taking the census,* the other in command of the troops,

and both styled *Legati Augusti* on a milestone, which is an official document. Josephus, too, mentions two men who were simultaneously legates in Syria, Sentius Saturninus and Volumnius, whom he several times calls "governors" (*ἡγεμόνες*). The same could very well have been true at the time of Christ's nativity, if Quirinius was at that time occupied in fighting the Homonadenses. If this expedition took place between the years 7 and 5 B.C., which is probable, several points would be explained. First, the presence of a second legate charged with the administration of Syria and the registration in Palestine; secondly, the mention by Tertullian of Sentius Saturninus as the official charged with the registration; finally, the statement of St. Luke attributing the registration to Quirinius, who was the principal personage. Note that St. Luke does not say: "This registration was carried on *by* Quirinius, the legate of Syria," but "under Quirinius" (*ἡγεμονεύοντος Κυρηνίου*). The Vulgate "facta est a praeside Syriae Cyrino" is too specific.

We shall not have a more precise solution until some document permits us to fix the exact date of the first legateship of Quirinius in Syria. The great explorer of Asia Minor, W. Ramsay, has attempted to make the matter more precise, first in his work *Was Christ Born in Bethlehem?* (1898), then in the work entitled *The Bearing of Recent Discovery on the Trustworthiness of the New Testament* (1914), but without arriving at decisive results. Two inscriptions recently discovered at Antioch in Pisidia inform us that P. Sulpicius Quirinius was (honorary) duumvir of that Roman colony, from which it may be concluded that he was then or had been governor of Syria. This was certainly *after* 12 B.C., because he was consul in that year, and he could not have been governor of Syria before his consulate. But the arguments that Ramsay brings forward to prove that the registration of Judea must have occurred in the year 8, or perhaps 6 B.C., are only probable. The year 6 would suit very well, the year 8 would be much less suitable.

NOTE F

The Dynasty of the Herods

1. Abridged Table of Herod's Descendants

HEROD THE GREAT († 4 B.C.) m—

- Doris
  - *Antipater* († 4 B.C.)
- *Mariamne I*
  - *Aristobulus* († 17 B.C.)
    - Herod († A.D. 48)
      - Aristobulus m—SALOME
    - Agrippa I
      - Agrippa II
      - Berenice
      - Drusilla
  - *Alexander* († 17 B.C.)
- Mariamne II
  - HEROD PHILIP m — HERODIAS
    - SALOME
- Malthace
  - ARCHELAUS m — Mariamne; m — Glaphyra
  - HEROD ANTIPAS († A.D. 39) m — Daughter of Aretas; m — HERODIAS
- Cleopatra
  - PHILIP († A.D. 34) m — SALOME

In this table the names of persons mentioned in the Gospel are in capitals; the names of Herod's victims are in italics. The brace indicates descent; (m —) designates marriage; (†) designates date of death. Herod had, in all, ten wives; omitted from the table are the names of those who were without issue, or without importance in history.

The origin of the family is uncertain. Nicholas of Damascus maintained that it was of Jewish stock; Josephus (*Antiq.*, XIV, i, 3) says that it was from Idumea; others, e.g., Justin and Julius Africanus, assert that it was from Ascalon in the country of the Philistines. The founder of the family was a certain Antipater, who was named ruler of Idumea by King Alexander Janneus. His son Antipater under Hyrcanus II became the most important man in the kingdom. He died by assassination in 43 B.C., leaving two sons, Phasael and Herod, the first of whom he named ruler of Jerusalem, the other, ruler of Galilee.

Some time later, Aristobulus, the younger brother of Hyrcanus II revolted against him, conquered him, and had him ignominiously mutilated. He also put to death Phasael, Herod's brother; but Herod escaped him and took refuge in the fortress of Masada, from which he fled to Rome under the pretext of pleading there the cause of the younger Aristobulus, son of Hyrcanus II. As a result of some intrigue or other he had himself declared king and supplanted the dynasty of the Hasmoneans.

A much more complete genealogical table of the entire family may be found in the work of F. de Saulcy, *Histoire d'Hérode roi des Juifs,* 1867, and in Hastings, *Dictionary of the Bible,* Vol. II, p. 354, where a very complete chronology of the history of the dynasty may also be found.

2. Members of the Family Mentioned in the Gospel

Seven members of the family are mentioned in the Gospel: Herod and four of his sons (Archelaus, Herod Antipas, Philip, Herod Philip), and Herodias and Salome. The descendants of Aristobulus, the son of Herod, play a certain role in the history of Apostolic times, but none in the Gospel.

1. *Herod the Great* — Herod was named King of the Jews in 40 B.C. by Anthony and Octavius, but it took him three years to conquer his kingdom with the support of the Romans, and still a dozen years more to consolidate his rule. Only three events of Herod's life have any bearing on the Gospel: (*a*) the date of the rebuilding of the Temple (20 or 19 B.C.) referred to in John 2:20: "This Temple has been forty-six years in building"; (*b*) the date of the death of Herod (the spring of 4 B.C.) close to the birth of Jesus; (*c*) the massacre of the Innocents (Matt. 2:16–17).

2. *Archelaus* — The will of his father Herod, whose son he was by Malthace the Samaritan, conferred upon him the title of King, together with the rule of Judea, Samaria, and Idumea. Augustus confirmed this will except for the title of King, for which he substituted that of Ethnarch, while promising Archelaus the royal dignity later, if he should show himself worthy of it. Archelaus was even crueler than his father. Before leaving for Rome, he had three thousand of his

subjects massacred by his soldiers because of a pretended uprising. His reputation was detestable. Thus when St. Joseph, upon returning from Egypt, learned that Archelaus was ruling in Judea, he did not go to Bethlehem, as he had intended, but retired to Nazareth in Galilee (Matt. 2:22–23). At the end of nine or ten years, Archelaus was exiled to Vienne in Gaul, and nothing further is heard of him. Cf. Josephus, *Antiq.*, XVII, viii, 2–4; ix, 3–7; xi, 1–4; xiii, 2, and the corresponding places in the *Bellum*.

Several authors have thought that in the parable of the King who went into a far country to receive a kingdom (Luke 19:12–27) allusion is made to the journey which Archelaus made to Rome in order to secure confirmation of his father's will.

3. *Herod Antipas* — Like Archelaus, this Herod was a son of Herod and the Samaritan Malthace. By virtue of his father's will he was only *Tetrarch* of Galilee and Perea, but the title of King was accorded him by flattery, and he is thus designated in the Gospel (Matt. 14:9; Mark 6:14, 27). Scarcely anything is known of him except what the Gospels record: his incestuous marriage with Herodias, the murder of the Baptist (Matt. 4:12; 14:3–12; Mark 1:14; 6:17–29; Luke 3:19–20), his fears, and his wish to see Jesus (Matt. 14:1–2; Mark 6:14–16; Luke 9:7–9). Jesus warns his disciples against "the leaven of Herod" (Mark 8:15), whose cunning he had stigmatized (Luke 13:31–32). The *Herodians* are adversaries of Jesus (Mark 3:6; 12:13; Matt. 22:16). The odious role of Antipas during Christ's Passion is well known (Luke 23:7–12).

Josephus tells us of the war waged by Antipas against Aretas, the King of the Nabateans whose daughter Herod had repudiated, of his humiliating defeat, his exile and miserable end at Lugdunum in Gaul (Josephus, *Antiq.*, XVIII, v, 1–3; vii, 1–2; *Bellum,* II, ix, 1 and 6).

4. *Herod Philip* — Philip, another son of Herod the Great by Mariamne II, daughter of the High Priest Simon, had no share in his father's last will. He lived in retirement, perhaps in Rome, and would have been entirely unknown if he had not married Herodias, who, together with her daughter Salome, left him in order to marry another uncle, Herod Antipas. This Herod, who has no other name in Josephus, is called Philip by St. Mark (6:17) and probably by St. Matthew (14:3). All the princes of this family, whatever their distinctive names, were called Herod. Archelaus and Antipas put no other name on their currency.

5. *Philip the Tetrarch* (Luke 3:1) — This prince enlarged and embellished ancient Paneas and renamed it Caesarea (Mark 8:27; Matt. 16:13). Late in life he married his grandniece Salome.

6. *Herodias* — This woman was the granddaughter of Herod the

Great and of Mariamne I, the daughter of Hyrcanus. Her father Aristobulus was put to death by Herod. She married her paternal uncle Herod Philip, and deserted him to marry another uncle, the Tetrarch Antipas. She is famous for her part in the murder of John the Baptist (Matt. 14:3–6; Mark 6:17–22). In the year A.D. 39 she chose to share the disgrace of her concubine husband Antipas and accompanied him into exile in Lugdunum in Gaul.

7. *Salome* — Daughter of Herodias and Herod Philip, she went with her mother to the court of Antipas. She made the demand for the head of John the Baptist (Matt. 14:4–6). She married her granduncle Philip the Tetrarch, who died in A.D. 34; then she married a certain Aristobulus, the son of Herod of Chalcis, great-grandson of Herod the Great.

The best documented work on the dynasty of the Herods is that of W. Otto in the *Real-Encyclopädie* of Pauly-Wissowa, *Supplement,* fasc. ii, cols. 1–202.

NOTE G

The Magi, History and Legend

1. Opinions and Theories

There exists no tradition properly so called about the country of the Magi, about their names, their number, their rank, the date of their coming to Jerusalem, or the nature of the star that appeared to them. This thesis has been abundantly proved by the learned dissertation of Patrizi, and recent studies have done nothing but confirm it.[1]

1. *The Country of the Magi* — The following countries have been credited with being the place from which they came: (*a*) *Persia,* because the ancient *Magi* were Medes, and the Medes made up one country with the Persians; also because of the name Magi, since in Persian the word means "great" as does μέγας in Greek. Thus Clement of Alexandria, St. John Chrysostom, and the author of the *Opus Imperfectum.*[2] (*b*) *Chaldea,* because of the reputation of the Chaldeans as astronomers and astrologers. In the Greek Book of Daniel, the Babylonian *ashshaphim* (astrologers) is translated eight times by μάγοι, and the name Rabsaces (Rebmag, Jer. 39:3–13) is often interpreted "prince or chief of the Magi." Thus Origen, Maximus of Turin, etc.[3] (*c*) *Arabia,* which opinion is the most ancient and widespread, because of the nature of the gifts offered, and because of the nearness of Arabia and the similarity of languages. Thus St. Justin, Tertullian, St. Epiphanius, etc.[4]

2. *Names of the Magi* — Here, most of all, free rein has been given the imagination. The Magi are given names for the first time in a

---

[1] Patrizi, *De Evangeliis,* Lib. iii, dissert, xxvii, Vol. II, pp. 309–354.

[2] Clement of Alexandria, *Stromata.,* i. 15; Chrysostom and Pseudo-Chrysostom in the Commentaries on Matthew.

[3] Origen, *Contra Celsum,* I, 58; St. Maximus of Turin, *Homil.,* 21.

[4] St. Justin, *Dialog.,* 77–78; Tertullian, *Contra Judaeos,* 9; St. Epiphanius, *Expos. Fidei,* 8.

manuscript in the *Bibliothèque Nationale* dating from the seventh or eighth century: Bithisarea, Melchior, Gataspa. In the ninth century, they are called Gaspar, Balthasar, and Melchior on a mosaic in Ravenna.[5] In the twelfth century, Zacharias of Besançon affirms that their Greek names were Appellius (*fidelis*), Amerus (*humilis*), Damascus (*misericors*); their Hebrew names were Magalath (*nuntius*), Galgalath (*devotus*), and Saracin (*gratia*).[6] The Armenian Vardapet Vardan attributes to them names which he calls Chaldean or Hebrew: Kaghda, Badadilma, Badadakharida.[7] The Syrians, who count *twelve* Magi, are not at a loss to give them names. According to Solomon, Bishop of Bassora, here are the names of the first four, the ones who brought the gold: Zarvandad son of Artaban, Hormizd son of Sitruq, Gushnasaph son of Gunaphar, Arshaq son of Mihruq.[8] That is enough, and perhaps too much.

3. *Number of the Magi* — No Father before the end of the fourth century or the beginning of the fifth says that the Magi were three in number. The author of the *Opus Imperfectum* (wrongly attributed to St. John Chrysostom) enumerates twelve, and this is the common opinion of the Syrians, not to mention the claims of Cologne. The paintings of the catacombs represent them sometimes as two, sometimes as four, but oftenest as three, one carrying gold, another incense, and another myrrh.[9] From the time of St. Leo and St. Maximus of Turin, the Latins usually speak of *the three Magi;* but, in the ninth century, Strabo notes in the *Glossa Ordinaria:* "Etsi tria munera obtulisse dicuntur non ideo non plures quam tres esse probantur." True, the three gifts are not an argument, but they offer an indication which justifies the practice of artists and the accepted manner of speaking.

4. *Rank of the Magi* — Patrizi, who has made the most serious study of this subject, affirms that before the sixth century no ecclesiastical author says expressly that the Magi were kings.[10] Several Fathers, it is true, say that the adoration of the Magi fulfilled the prophecy: "Reges Tharsis et insulae . . . reges Arabum et Saba dona adducent"; but this prophecy would be fulfilled even if the Magi were

---

[5] Muratori, *Rerum italic. scriptores,* Vol. II, p. 114; ML, CVI, 620. The authority is Agnello, in his life of his predecessor in the See of Ravenna. The unknown author of the *Collectanea* (ML, XCIV, 541) informs us that Melchior had a big beard and long white hair, that Gaspar was young, beardless, and florid, and Balthasar was dark-skinned and bearded.

[6] *Concordia evangelist.* (ML, CLXXXVI, 83.)

[7] *Journal ascetique,* 1867, p. 160.

[8] Assemani, *Biblioth. orient.,* Vol. III, Part I, p. 316.

[9] Wilpert, *Le pitture delle catacombe Romane,* 1923, pp. 176–186.

[10] Patrizi, *De evangeliis,* Vol. II, p. 321.

not kings, and kings of Tharsis and Saba. The first to style the Magi kings is apparently St. Caesarius of Arles in the sixth century, for the three sermons of St. Augustine in which they are so called are not the work of the Bishop of Hippo.

5. *The Star of the Magi* — We know nothing of this star except what the Gospel tells us; hence opinions vary greatly. (*a*) Origen assumed that the star was a comet, and many agree with him.[11] (*b*) Kepler held out for the conjunction of the planets Saturn, Jupiter, and Mars, which occurred in the Roman year 747 (7 B.C.), around the time of the Nativity of Christ.[12] (*c*) Estius was for an ephemeral star like the one which appeared and disappeared in the year 1572. "Anno 1572 his oculis vidimus stellam novam durantem toto anno, non cometis sed stellis perpetuis similem, clare et pulchre lucentem. . . . Quae ita torsit ingenia omnium naturaliter philosophantium, ut exitum difficultatis non reperirent, nisi manifestum agnoscendo miraculum aut fatendo generationes et corruptiones fieri in caelo."[13] Estius has had few followers. (*d*) Knabenbauer thinks that it was a meteor expressly created by God in our terrestrial atmosphere which disappeared after filling its purpose. Schanz seems to share this view. The Fathers in their anxiety to combat the astrologers, likewise say that the star of the Magi was not like other stars, but of a different nature.

2. Formation and Evolution of Legend

At the beginning of the second century, St. Ignatius of Antioch thus describes the star of the Magi (*Ad Ephesios,* xix, 2): "A star shone in the sky more brightly than the other stars, and its indescribable light struck men with astonishment by reason of its novelty. All the other stars, with the sun and the moon, formed a retinue for this star, whose splendor eclipsed all the rest." The χορὸς ἐγένετο τῷ αστέρι seems to be an allusion to Gen. 37:9. In the course of the same century, the *Protoevangelium* of James (xxi. 2) has the Magi speaking thus: "We have seen an enormously large star eclipsing all the other heavenly bodies, so much so that they were no longer visible. Thus we have learned that a King was born in Israel, and we have come to adore him." Toward the end of the same century, Clement of Alexandria, in his *Excerpta ex Theodoto,* lxxiv, 2 (ed. Staehlin, Vol. iii, 1909, p. 130), has something quite obscure on this "unusual and new star."

---

11 On this point see Roth, *De stella a magis conspecta* (Mayence, 1865).

12 Münter, *Der Stern der Weisen* (Copenhagen, 1826), and Mémain, *Connaisance des temps évang.,* 1886, pp. 464–470 (with four plates).

13 Estius, *Annotationes,* etc., on Matt. 2:4.

The real inventor of legend about the star seems to have been the author of an apocryphal writing with the suspicious name, *The Book of Seth,* which is mentioned by St. Hippolytus (*Philosopheumena,* v, 22: παράφρασις Σήθ) and by St. Epiphanius (*Haereses,* xxvi, 8 and xxxix, 5). According to St. Hippolytus, this book contained all the secrets of the Gnostic sect of Sethites. The author of the *Opus Imperfectum* (a commentary on St. Matthew wrongly attributed to St. John Chrysostom but dating from the end of the fourth century or the beginning of the fifth) extracted from it all that referred to the Magi (MG, LVI, 637–638). Here in brief is what was contained in the *scriptura inscripta nomine Seth* — the Greek text of the commentary is lost: Twelve learned astrologers, called Magi in the tongue of that country, were wont every year to climb a mountain to watch for the star which was expected to appear. Finally "it appeared coming down from that Mount of Victory in the form of a little child surmounted by an image of the Cross. It spoke to them, gave them instructions, and commanded them to go to Judea. When they set out, the star accompanied them for two years, and they lacked neither food nor drink." And after the Resurrection of Christ, Thomas went to find the Magi, baptized them, and made them his fellow workers.

In the ninth century accurate information was provided on the names of the Magi, who are only three in number, and on their dress. The mosaic of San Apollinare at Ravenna, of which we have spoken above, dates from well into the sixth century, but Agnello describes it as he himself saw it in the ninth. It had, however, been retouched or redone and the names of the Magi in particular are in a writing which must be dated after the sixth century. See Rohault de Fleury (*L'Evangile, études iconogr. et archéol.,* 1874, Vol. I, p. 70) for a good description and a facsimile of the mosaic in its present condition.

Latin opinion seems to have crystallized in the ninth century with the *Glossa Ordinaria* of Wilfred Strabo (ML, CXIV, 575): (*a*) The Magi are Arabian kings coming from Persia. Notice this original geography: "Fuerunt de terra Persarum, ubi est Saba fluvius a quo regio nominatur juxta quam est Arabia, ubi Magi fuerunt reges." (*b*) They are three, but accompanied by a large retinue. (*c*) They arrive at Bethlehem on the thirteenth day: "Non post annum quia tunc non inveniretur in praesepio sed in Aegypto, sed decima tertia die." (*d*) The star was expressly created: "Numquam prius apparuit, sed eam tunc puer creavit et Magis deputavit, quae mox, peracto officio, esse desiit." (*e*) The Magi adore Christ, and in him the Holy Trinity. (*f*) St. Joseph is not with Mary, in order to eliminate all evil suspicion.

Peter Comestor (The Eater) at the end of the twelfth century found still more to add (ML, CXCVIII, 1541–1542), but it is time to stop.

NOTE H

The Portraits of Christ

1. The Holy Face

The leading work on the paintings in the catacombs, superseding all others, is that of Wilpert, *Le pitture delle catacombe* (Rome, 1903), with an atlas of 267 plates. Cf. especially Chapter XIII (*Pitture cristologiche,* pp. 171–234) and the chapters following, on Baptism, the Eucharist, the Resurrection.

In the *Dictionary of Christ and the Gospels* (London, 1906), Vol. I, pp. 309–316, may be found an article entitled "Christ in Art," which admirably sums up the iconographic evolution of the representation of Christ.

The learned work of Dobschütz, *Christusbilder* (Leipzig, 1889, in the collection *Texte und Untersuchungen,* Vol. XVIII), gathers together all the documents on the subject and gives a critical edition of the principal texts. It is primarily from this source that we have drawn the following points of information.

1. Antoninus of Piacenza (circa 570), *Itinerarium,* 23 — In Jerusalem, in the Basilica of Santa Sophia, which was built on the supposed site of the Praetorium, the pilgrim saw the stone on which Christ stood before Pilate, and also a tableau depicting him. On this stone the Saviour had left the imprint of one of his feet, "pedem pulchrum, modicum, subtilem," and this imprint corresponds to the picture. He continues: "nam et staturam communem, faciem pulchram, capillos subanellatos, manum formosam, digita longa imago designat, quae illo vivente picta est et posita est in ipso praetorio" (cf. Geyer, *Itinera Hierosolymitana* [Vienna, 1898], p. 176).

2. Andrew of Crete (circa 726) — In a fragment attributed to this author, a tradition is retailed which says that St. Luke painted the pictures of Jesus and Mary preserved in Rome, and that the figure of Jesus agrees with the one which Josephus the Jew saw depicted in

Jerusalem: *σύνοφρυν, εὐόφθαλμον, μάκροψιν, ἐπίκυφον, καὶ εὐήλικα.* In this picture, therefore, Jesus has "eyebrows which meet (a mark of beauty and an index of strength for the Orientals), beautiful eyes, a long (oval) face, the head slightly inclined, a commanding height." This fragment, appended to the *De fide orthodoxa* (iv. 16) in some of the Greek manuscripts, and translated into Latin (around 1150) by Burgundio of Pisa, is later cited as St. John Damascene's (MG, XCIV, 1175, note). The author of the *Golden Legend* and St. Vincent of Beauvais popularized it in the West. The *Golden Legend* (Feast of SS. Simon and Jude, 157) links this description with the portrait reputed to have been sent by the Saviour to Abgar, King of Edessa: "One sees there the image of a man with large eyes, and slightly stooped shoulders, which is a sign of maturity."

3. Around the year 800, the monk Epiphanius (*Vita Mariae Virginis,* MG, CXX, 204; more fully in Dobschütz, p. 302) traces a portrait of Christ of which the following are the essential features: height, six feet; arched eyebrows; beautiful eyes; large nose (*ἐπίρρινος*); slightly stooped stature; oval face like that of his mother; complexion the color of wheat (*σιτόχρους*); long, curly hair, the color of which it is difficult to name; the eyebrows would be called black, the hair and beard tending to red (*πυρράκης*, like David), the eyes (*ἐπιξανθίζοντας καὶ χαρόπους*) tawny and blue (?). He resembles his mother.

In the fourteenth century, Nicephorus Callistus (*Hist. eccl.,* I, 40; MG, CXLV, 748–749) copies the monk Epiphanius, adding nothing of his own. However, instead of "six feet" he puts "seven spans" (*ἑπτὰ σπιθαμῶν*).

4. *Letter of the Three Patriarchs* of Alexandria, Antioch, and Jerusalem to the Emperor Theophilus, around 835 (MG, XCV, 349) — According to this document ancient historians represented Christ as *σύνοφρυν, εὐόφθαλμον, ἐπίρρινον, οὐλόθριξιν, ἐπίκυφον, εὔχρονον, γενειάδα μέλανα ἔχοντα, σιτόχρουν τῷ εἴδει κατὰ τὴν μητρῷαν ἐμφάνειαν, μακροδάκτυλον.*

In this portrait one can recognize the arched eyebrows, the beautiful eyes, the head inclined forward, as mentioned by Andrew of Crete; the large nose, the curly hair, the wheat-colored complexion, the resemblance to Mary mentioned by the monk Epiphanius, and the long fingers mentioned by Antoninus of Piacenza. I conjecture that instead of *εὔχρονον* should be read *εὔχρουν, εὔχροον,* according to the reading which the Latin translator must have followed (*eleganti colore*).

5. The *Letter of Lentulus* to the Roman Senate — The author of this letter, who lived in the twelfth or thirteenth century, calls himself *prefect* of Judea under Augustus (!) or under Tiberius. This apocryphal piece enjoyed great repute in the fourteenth and especially the fifteenth centuries. Since it is often referred to and is not readily accessible to most

readers, we shall quote it here after the critical edition of Dobschütz (*op. cit.,* p. 319). "Apparuit temporibus istis et adhuc est homo magnae virtutis, nominatus Jesus Christus, qui dicitur a gentibus propheta veritatis, quem ejus discipuli vocant filium Dei, suscitans mortuos et sanans (omnes) languores, homo quidem statura procerus mediocris et spectabilis, vultum habens venerabilem, quam possent intuentes diligere et formidare, capillos habens coloris nucis avellanae praematurae, planos fere usque ad aures, ab auribus (vero) circinos, crispos, aliquantulum ceruliores et fulgentiores, ab humeris ventilantes, discrimen habens in medio capitis, juxta morem Nazaraeorum, frontem planam et serenissimam, cum facie sine ruga et macula, quam rubor (moderatus) venustat; nasi et oris nulla prorsus (est) reprehensio; barbam habens copiosam capillis concolorem, non longam sed in mento (medio parum) bifurcatam; aspectum habens simplicem et maturam, oculis glaucis variis et claris existentibus, in increpatione terribilis, in admonitione blandus et amabilis; hilaris servata gravitate; aliquando flevit sed nunquam risit; in statura corporis propagatus et rectus, manus habens et brachia visu delectabilia; in colloquio gravis, rarus et modestus."

6. It may be interesting to compare with this the portrait traced in the fourteenth century by St. Bridget supposedly at the dictation of the Blessed Virgin: "Anno vicesimo aetatis suae in magnitudine et fortitudine virili perfectus erat. Inter medios moderni temporis magnus, non carnosus sed nervis et ossibus corpulentus; capillus ejus, supercilia et barba crocee brunes erant, longitudo barbae palmo per transversum manus, frons vero non prominens vel mersa sed recta; nasus aequalis, non parvus nec nimis magnus; oculi vero ejus tam puri erant quod etiam inimici ejus delectabantur eum aspicere; labia non spissa sed clare rubentia; mentum non erat prominens nec nimis longum sed pulchro moderamine venustum; maxillae carnibus modeste plenae; color ejus erat candidus claro rubeo permixtus; statura ejus recta et in toto corpore suo nulla macula erat, sicut et illi testabantur qui eum totaliter viderunt nudum et ad columnam alligatum flagellabant, nunquam super eum vermis venit, non perplexitas aut immunditia in capillis." There is a very enjoyable French translation by Ferraige, Doctor of Theology, who does not seem always to have grasped the meaning, as when he has St. Bridget say: "He was tall, not plump like the men of the present time" (*Revelations de Sainte Brigitte,* Lyon, Bk. IV, Chap. lxx, at the end).

2. The Supposed Ugliness of Christ

If one were to believe certain critics, the champions of the physical ugliness of Christ would be legion. N. Müller (*Encycl. protestant. Theol. und Kirche,* article, *Christusbilder,* Vol. IV, 1928, p. 64) lists

Clement of Alexandria, Tertullian, Origen, St. Justin, St. Cyprian, St. Basil, St. Isidore of Pelusium, Theodoretus, and St. Cyril of Alexandria. This list betrays a too rapid and too superficial reading of the texts. The following note proposes to show this.

We admit the guilt of Clement of Alexandria and Tertullian. The former writes: "The Holy Spirit testifies through Isaias that the Lord himself was ugly of countenance": Τὸν Κύριον αὐτὸν ὄψιν αἰσχρὸν γεγονέναι διὰ Ἐσαΐου τὸ Πνεῦμα μαρτυρεῖ (*Paedagog.*, III, 1; cf. *Stromat.*, II, 5; III, 1). Tertullian is still more explicit: "Tacentibus apud nos prophetis de ignobili aspectu ejus, ipsae contumeliae loquuntur: passiones humanam carnem, contumeliae inhonestam probarent. An ausus esset aliquis ungue summo perstringere corpus novum, sputaminibus contaminare faciem nisi merentem?" (Tertullian, *De carne Christi,* 9; ML, II, 772. Cf. *De pallio,* 3; *Contra Marcionem,* iii, 7; *Adv. Judaeos,* 14; ML, I, 252; II, 330, 630). Tertullian's argument is worthless. History speaks of martyrs who were ferociously attacked by their executioners precisely for the purpose of disfiguring them and so lessening the sympathy of the spectators. See the Fifth Lesson in the Office of the Blessed English Martyrs, Campion and his companions.

Origen reports without disapproval a strange opinion, according to which Jesus appeared differently to men, depending on the merit or demerit of those who looked at him, beautiful to some, ugly to others. There are inklings of this opinion in the *Refutation of Celsus,* and it is clearly formulated in the Commentary on St. Matthew, of which we have only a Latin translation: "Venit traditio talis ad nos de eo, quoniam non solum duae formae in eo fuerunt, una quidem secundum quam omnes eum videbant, altera quidem secundum quam transfiguratus est coram discipulis suis in monte . . . sed etiam unicuique apparebat secundum quod fuerat dignus (as the manna tasted differently to different persons) . . . et non mihi videtur incredibilis traditio haec."[1]

This so-called tradition, which without doubt comes from the Apocrypha in which we see Christ taking the form of Andrew, Thomas, etc., seems to have momentarily attracted St. Augustine, who combines it with Tertullian's idea: "Nisi foedum putarent (Judaei) non insilirent, non flagellis caederent."[2] But it is known that St. Augustine elsewhere maintains the physical beauty of Christ.

As to the other Fathers involved in the charge, they are surely innocent of any such allegation.

---

[1] Origen, *In Matth. series,* n. 100 (MG, XIII, 750). In *Contra Celsum,* vi, 77, there is something similar about the different forms of Jesus (τῶν διαφόρων τοῦ Ἰησοῦ μορφῶν).

[2] Augustine, *In Psalm.,* 127:6 (ML, XXXVII, 1781).

St. Justin repeats time and time again that there are two comings of Christ: one when he appears mortal (θνητός), passible (παθητός), without glory (ἄδοξος), without honor (ἄτιμος), and without beauty (ἀειδής); the other when he shall appear glorious, impassible, immortal, etc. Thus, when he is called ἀειδής, there is no question of any *special* ugliness in him as compared to other men, but merely of a contrast between the two states and the two comings.[3]

St. Cyprian does no more than quote *without commentary* the text of Isaias; but he quotes it mixed in with other texts from Zacharias, the Epistle to the Philippians, etc., which have reference to the abasement of Christ in the Incarnation. The "non est species neque decor" of Isaias has no more to do with the physical ugliness of Christ than St. Paul's "formam servi accipiens," and it proves only to what extent the Divine Word abases himself.[4]

Several Greek Fathers, St. Basil, St. Isidore of Pelusium, and St. Cyril of Alexandria, it is true, apply the text of Isaias to the whole of Christ's mortal life, and not only to his Passion, and interpret the "Speciosus forma" of the Psalmist of the beauty of Christ's soul, or of his divine nature. The value of their interpretation is open to discussion, and it does not agree with that of the Latins and of St. John Chrysostom; but these Fathers do not thereby conclude to any *physical ugliness* of Jesus Christ.

Saint Isidore of Pelusium is perfectly clear on this point: "Jesus is without charm and beauty for two reasons: first because he has hidden the form of the master, in order to clothe himself with that of the slave; and again, because during the Passion, which he suffered of his own free will, he endured every kind of outrage."[5] By what sort of perverse logic can one go so far as to draw from this an argument for the physical ugliness of Christ in comparison with other men?

With regard to Cyril of Alexandria, Müller enjoys a triumph: "Cyril," he says, "attributes to Christ a *very ugly countenance* (ein sehr hässliches Aussehen)." St. Cyril would have saved him from this blunder if he had had the patience to read a not overlong text to the end. "Compared to the glory of the divinity, the flesh is of no worth. The Son appeared in a form quite devoid of beauty, for being by nature God, he became like unto us. Now man is an immeasurable distance below God."[6]

---

[3] Justin, *Apol.*, i. 52; *Dial. cum Tryph.*, 14, 49, 85, 110, 121 (MG, VI, 405, 503, 584, 675, 757).

[4] Cyprian, *Testim. adv. Judaeos*, ii, 13 (ML, IV, 707).

[5] Isidore of Pelusium, *Epist.*, III, 130 (MG, LXXVIII, 829).

[6] Cyril of Alexandria, *Glaphyra in Exod.*, i, 4 (MG, LXIX, 395).

This is also the teaching of St. Basil.[7] The human nature of Christ, however beautiful, has no charm or beauty when compared to the divine nature. *Exinanivit semetipsum formam servi accipiens.*

---

[7] Basil, *In Psalm,* xliv (MG, XXIX, 396).

NOTE I

The Relatives of Jesus

1. Scriptural Data

1. Several times the Gospel mentions the "brethren" and "sisters" of Jesus: (*a*) after his baptism, when he went down to Capharnaum with "his mother, his brethren, and his disciples" (John 2:12); (*b*) while he was preaching in a house of that town, "his mother and his brethren standing without called for him" (Mark 3:31; Matt. 12:46; Luke 8:19); (*c*) six months before the Passion, "his brethren did not believe in him" (John 7:3–5); (*d*) after the Ascension, the Apostles persevered in prayer "with the (holy) women, and Mary the mother of Jesus, and his brethren" (Acts. 1:14); (*e*) from that time forward, these persons enjoyed great authority, and St. Paul claims the right to conduct himself "as the other Apostles, and the brethren of the Lord, and Kephas" (1 Cor. 9:5); (*f*) the Galileans, when they saw Jesus, said: "Is not this the carpenter, the son of Mary, and the brother of James and Joses and Jude and Simon? And are not his sisters here with us?" (Mark 6:3; cf. Luke 4:22). St. Matthew's variant (13:55) is interesting: "Is not this the carpenter's son. Is not his mother called Mary, and his brethren James and Joseph and Simon and Jude? And are not all his sisters here with us?"

Jesus is therefore supposed to have *four* "brethren," listed in the following order: James, Joses, Simon, and Jude, and at least three sisters whose names are not given.

The group of the "brethren of the Lord" is several times distinguished from the group of the Apostles. Thus Acts 1:14; 1 Cor. 9:5.

Nowhere is it said that these "brethren" are Mary's children, nor Joseph's. On the contrary, the Gospel everywhere gives the impression that the Holy Family is made up of only three persons. At Bethlehem the shepherds and the Magi find only Jesus, Mary, and Joseph; these three alone fly to Egypt and live there for a time; they live together in Nazareth and together they make the pilgrimage to Jerusalem. The Gospel never gives us leave to associate anyone else with them, at least during the lifetime of Joseph.

2. Mary of Cleophas, the sister of the Blessed Virgin:

Εἱστήκεισαν δὲ παρὰ τῷ σταυρῷ τοῦ Ἰησοῦ ἡ μήτηρ αὐτοῦ καὶ ἡ ἀδελφὴ τῆς μητρὸς αὐτοῦ, Μαρία ἡ τοῦ Κλωπᾶ, καὶ Μαρία Μαγδαληνή.	There were standing by the Cross of Jesus his mother, and his mother's sister, Mary of Cleophas, and Mary Magdalene. (John 19:25)

Most authors see here only *three* women: the Blessed Virgin, her sister, Mary of Cleophas, and Mary Magdalene. But Zahn, for frivolous reasons, counts four, distinguishing the Blessed Virgin's sister from Mary of Cleophas. The following are his arguments. (*a*) It would be strange for both of two sisters to be named Mary. *Answer:* Perhaps, if both were sisters with the same mother and father, but not if they were half sisters, stepsisters, or sisters-in-law as is here the case. (*b*) The word "sister" as a qualification should come *after* the name Mary; it should be "Mary of Cleophas, his mother's sister." *Answer:* The rule is an illusion and a creature of Zahn's imagination. One need only to open a Concordance to be convinced of this. Such a qualification is placed either before or after the name: v.g., τῆς μητρὸς αὐτοῦ Μαρίας (Matt. 1:18), Μαρίας τῆς μητρὸς αὐτοῦ (Matt. 2:11), etc. (*c*) In such lists the groups are *often* divided into pairs: here, therefore, there are two pairs: his mother and his mother's sister, and Mary of Cleophas and Mary Magdalene. *Answer: Often,* no; this happens only once: in the list of the Apostles according to St. Matthew, where the Apostles are enumerated in pairs *because they are sent out on their mission two by two* (Matt. 10:2–5). But in other lists of the Apostles it is otherwise (Mark 3:16–19; Luke 6:14–16; Acts 1:13), and also in the list of the brethren of Jesus (Matt. 13:55; Mark 6:3), despite the fact that they are two distinct pairs. Hence all of Zahn's arguments are fallacious and unworthy of him.

3. The women present at the death of Jesus according to the Synoptics:

Matt. 27:56: Among them Mary Magdalene, and Mary the mother of James and of Joseph, and the mother of the sons of Zebedee.	Mark 15:40: Among them Mary Magdalene, and Mary the mother of James the Less and of Joses, and Salome.	Luke 23:49: The women who followed him from Galilee.

The Synoptics do not make note of the presence of the Blessed Virgin, doubtless because they thought it unnecessary to mention it. On the other hand, they note the presence of Salome, the wife of Zebedee, omitted by John, who always discreetly screens anything referring to himself and his family. Otherwise they are the same persons: Mary Magdalene, and Mary the mother of James the Less and of Joseph. It follows that this second Mary is Mary of Cleophas, sister of the Blessed Virgin. To deny it would require very strong proofs, which, however, do not exist except in the imagination of critics yielding to preconceived ideas.

2. The Data of Tradition

It is important to distinguish carefully the dogmatic tradition from the historical tradition: the latter is wavering, the former never varies.

1. *The Dogmatic Tradition.* This maintains the perpetual virginity of Mary, before, during, and after the birth of her divine Son. On this point there is not a discordant voice up to the end of the fourth century, except for Tertullian, who is without authority in matters of orthodoxy. It follows that the "brethren of the Lord" were not and could not have been the sons of Mary. Origen affirms this without hesitation: "Et filii, qui Joseph dicebantur, non erant orti de Maria, neque est ulla Scriptura quae ista commemoret."[1] It was not fitting, Origen says again, that the body of Mary submit to the contact of man after the Holy Spirit had entered into her and the power of the Most High had overshadowed her; she must be among women the first-fruits of virginity, as Jesus was among men.[2] St. Basil expresses the same thought even more strongly: "Those who love Christ cannot bear to hear it said that the mother of God ceased to be a virgin."[3] This sentiment is not dictated by piety alone; it is founded on the Gospel. Would Christ have entrusted his mother to St. John, if she had other children? Would she herself have said to the angel: "I know not man," if she had not resolved to remain always a virgin? And would the Evangelist have recorded this saying of hers, if she had violated her promise? The thing is so clear that Loisy is prompted to say: "The assertion of Mary is so absolute that the common opinion of Catholic exegetes, who see in it an intention of keeping perpetual virginity, cannot be said to be arbitrary. No passage of the Gospel or of the Acts contradicts it; for if there is question of the brothers of Jesus, they are never presented as sons of Mary, and it is to be noted that not one of them, not even James, is named individually as a brother of the Lord."[4]

---

[1] Origen, *In Lucam, homil.,* vii; MG, XIII, 1813. Cf. *Contra Celsum,* i, 47.

[2] Origen, *In Matthaeum series,* MG, XIII, 876–877.

[3] Basil, *Homilia in sanctam Christi generationem,* 5; MG, XXXI, 1468. The authenticity of this fine discourse, admitted by Combefis and Dupin, and attacked by Garnier, has been recently vindicated by Usener, who shows in particular that the use of *θεοτόκος* by St. Basil has in it nothing surprising. Cf. Bardenhewer, *Altchrist. Literatur,* Vol. III, p. 152.

[4] Loisy, *Evangiles synoptiques,* 1907, Vol. I, p. 290. In the *Evangile selon Luc,* 1924, p. 89, without making a formal retractation, he is a little less incisive.

In the year 380, an obscure Roman named Helvidius, soon followed by the monk Jovinian and by Bonosus, Bishop of Sardis in Illyria, dared to attack the perpetual virginity of Mary and to maintain that after the birth of Jesus she bore sons to Joseph, whom the Gospel calls the brethren of the Lord. St. Jerome in 382 refuted Helvidius, and St. Ambrose attacked Jovinian, whose error was condemned by several Councils.[5] St. Jerome had no difficulty in showing that the word "brother" is often taken in a wider sense in Scripture and is not restricted in use to blood brothers; again, that the title "first-born" is given to a newborn child before it is known whether there will be any brothers; and that when the Gospel says that Joseph had no carnal relations with Mary *before* the birth of Jesus, it does not follow that he did *afterward*. Jerome even boldly takes the offensive against his adversary: "Tu dicis Mariam virginem non permansisse; ego mihi plus vindico, ipsum Joseph virginem fuisse per Mariam." He does indeed see in the Gospel that James, the "brother of the Lord," was the son of Mary's sister; but he does not pursue his advantage, and having proved the perpetual virginity of Mary, seems to lose interest in the question of the brethren of Jesus, as does St. Ambrose, who writes in his refutation of Jovinian: "Potuerunt fratres esse ex Joseph, non ex Maria. Quod quidem si quis diligentius prosequatur inveniet. Nos ea prosequenda non putavimus, quoniam fraternum nomen liquet pluribus esse commune."[6] St. Jerome himself, ten years after his refutation of Helvidius, writes modestly: "Jacobus, qui appellatur frater Domini, ut nonnulli existimant Josephi ex alia uxore, ut autem mihi videtur Mariae sororis matris Domini, cujus Joannes in suo libro meminit, filius."[7] On the other hand, St. John Chrysostom and St. Augustine never seem to have said, when these controversies arose, that the brethren of the Lord were sons of St. Joseph. Theodoretus, who usually follows Chrysostom, is very precise on this point: "James was not a son of Joseph by a previous marriage, as some have held, but he was the son of Clopas and a cousin of the Lord, for his mother was the sister of the Virgin."[8]

From that time on the question advanced no farther. It was admitted that the brethren of the Lord were not the sons of St. Joseph, but no special effort was made to discover their parentage. Strabo, the author of the *Glossa Ordinaria,* has not a word on the subject. The

[5] St. Jerome, *Adversus Helvidium de Mariae virginitate perpetua,* ML, XXIII, 183–206. St. Epiphanius, in his *Panarion,* had refuted Helvidius and his followers in advance, *Haeres,* lxxviii, MG, XLII, 700–740.

[6] St. Ambrose, *De institutione virginis et sanctae Mariae virginitate perpetua,* ML, XVI, 305–384.

[7] St. Jerome, *De viris illustribus,* 2; ML, XXIII, 609.

[8] Theodoretus, *In Galat.,* 1:18; MG, LXXXII, 468.

Abbot Rupert confines himself to the statement that they are *propinqui vel consanguinei* of the Saviour. St. Thomas does no more than cite in passing the words of St. Jerome in order to answer an objection.[9]

A certain Papias — not the bishop of Hierapolis, but a little-known personage of the twelfth century — made an attempt to solve the problem. This is his solution: "Maria mater Domini; Maria Cleophae, sive Alphaei uxor, quae fuit mater Jacobi episcopi et apostoli et Symonis et Thadei et cujusdam Joseph; Maria Salome, uxor Zebedei, mater Joannis evangelistae et Jacobi; Maria Magdalena. Istae quatuor in evangeliis reperiuntur. — Jacobus et Judas et Joseph filii erant materterae Domini. Jacobus quoque et Joannes alterius materterae Domini fuerunt filii. — Maria, Jacobi minoris et Joseph mater, uxor Alphei, soror fuit Mariae matris Domini, quam Cleophae Joannes nominat, vel a patre, vel a gentilitatis familia vel alia causa. — Maria Salome vel a viro vel a vico dicitur; hanc eamdem Cleophae quidam dicunt, quod duos viros habuerit."[10]

Except for a confusion about Maria Salome, Papias gives proof of an uncommon perspicacity. The same cannot be said of the author of the *Golden Legend,* who sees the facts as follows: "Tradition tells us that Anna (the mother of the Blessed Virgin) had successively three husbands: Joachim, Cleophas, and Salome. By Joachim she had a daughter, the Virgin Mary, whom she gave in marriage to Joseph. Then after Joachim's death, she married Cleophas, Joseph's brother, by whom she had another daughter likewise called Mary, given later in marriage to Alpheus. This second Mary had four sons by Alpheus: James the Less, Joseph the Just, Simon, and Jude. Finally, from her third marriage with Salome, Anne had still another daughter, also called Mary, who married Zebedee. And it is from the union of this third Mary with Zebedee that James the Greater and John the Evangelist were born."[11]

Thus according to the dogmatic tradition, the brothers of the Lord are certainly not the sons of Mary, who remained perpetually a virgin; and according to pious belief, strengthened more and more by the Catholic sense, neither were they the sons of Joseph.

2. *The Historical Tradition.* Let us remark that the Fathers, whatever their opinions, never based them on historical tradition. St. Jerome and St. Ambrose expressly refrained from doing so, as did the adversaries they attacked. The controversy revolved exclusively around

---

[9] St. Thomas, *Summa Theol.,* p. III, q. xxviii, a. 3, ad 5.

[10] In Routh, *Reliquiae sacrae,* Vol. I, 1846, p. 16.

[11] Jacopo de Voragine (of Viraggio near Genoa), *The Golden Legend,* for the 8th of September, trans. Wizewa, 1911, p. 494.

questions of exegesis. The opinion that makes the brethren of Jesus the sons of St. Joseph, born of a previous marriage, rests on the authority of the Apocrypha alone — the *Protoevangelium of James,* the *Gospel of Peter,* the *Gospel of the Pseudo-Matthew,* the *History of Joseph the Carpenter* — a weak authority, if indeed any authority at all.[12] In the absence of authentic tradition, a certain number of Fathers accepted the opinion with varying degrees of assurance: Clement of Alexandria, Origen, Eusebius, St. Hilary, St. Epiphanius, the author of a sermon falsely attributed to St. Gregory of Nyssa, Ambrosiaster, St. Cyril of Alexandria, and even St. John Chrysostom and St. Augustine in their earlier writings.

There is however an ancient testimony, isolated, it is true, but of the first importance. It is that of Hegesippus, a well-informed historian, born in Palestine around the beginning of the second century, who interested himself especially in the relatives of Jesus. This is what he has to say:

a) After the martyrdom of James, it was unanimously decided that Simeon, the son of Clopas, was worthy to occupy the see of Jerusalem. "He was, it is said, a cousin of the Saviour; Hegesippus recounts in fact that Clopas was *a brother of Joseph*" (Eusebius, *Hist. eccl.,* III, 11).

St. Epiphanius (*Haer.,* LXXVIII, 7) says the same and adds (*ibid.,* 14) that this Simeon, the son of Clopas, was a cousin of James the Just, as Hegesippus says in another passage.

b) "After James the Just was martyred, like the Lord and for the same reason, Simeon, the son of Clopas, uncle of Jesus, was made bishop. All preferred him because he was a cousin of the Lord" (Eusebius, IV, xxii, 4, expressly citing Hegesippus). This text is perfectly clear, except for a word "second" which we have omitted: *ὃν προέθεντο πάντες, ὄντα ἀνέψιον τοῦ Κυριοῦ δεύτερον.* Some authorities make *δεύτερον* refer to *ἐπίσκοπος* mentioned in the preceding clause: "All preferred him (as the *second* bishop) because he was a cousin of the Lord." This is possible, but somewhat oversubtle. Others refer *δεύτερον* to the nearer word *ἀνέψιον*: "All preferred him because he was a *second* (another) cousin of the Lord." If we adopt this translation, and it is more natural, it follows that James himself was *also* a cousin of the Lord. But we prefer to prescind from this controversy. In any case, the testimony states that Simeon was a cousin of the Lord, and that his uncle Clopas was an *uncle* of Jesus, being Joseph's brother.

c) Hegesippus says of James, the "brother" of the Lord: "He alone was allowed to enter into the Holy Place, for he wore not wool but

[12] St. Jerome, *In Matthaeum,* 12:49–50; ML, XXVI, 84: "Quidam fratres Domini de alia uxore Joseph suspicantur, sequentes deliramenta apocryphorum."

linen" (Eusebius, III, xxiii, 6). He was clad in linen like the priests, and could enter into the part of the Sanctuary called the Holy Place to which only priests had access. He therefore belonged to the priestly class,[13] and whatever the tribe of his mother may have been, his father must have been a descendant of Aaron. But this would not be St. Joseph's brother, Clopas.

d) Finally, Hegesippus tells us that Jude was, like Simon, of the family of David. His descendants were persecuted under Domitian as relatives of Jesus (Eusebius, III, xx, 1–5). It is therefore natural to believe that he was, like Simeon, a son of Clopas.

The information furnished by Hegesippus, combined with the Gospel data, leads to the following conclusions:

1. The sister of the Blessed Virgin, also called Mary, was the wife of Cleophas or Clopas, St. Joseph's brother. She was, therefore, a sister-in-law of the Blessed Virgin; but very probably there existed between them a closer relationship which we cannot determine.

2. Simon or Simeon, who was Bishop of Jerusalem after James the Less, was a son of Cleophas or Clopas. He was a cousin of the Lord, but not a brother of James, who was of priestly race.

3. James the Less was a son of the sister of the Blessed Virgin; Joses seems to have been a blood brother of James, just as Jude, who was of the family of David, was probably a blood brother of Simon, son of Cleophas.

4. The brethren of the Lord, therefore, belonged to two distinct families, which, however, were closely united and perhaps lived at one time under the same roof. This is why the names of each of the two groups (James and Joses who were sons of Mary, and Simon and Jude who were sons of Cleophas) are always found together.

5. Mary, the wife of Cleophas, had children who were not his; her husband Cleophas also had children who were not hers. Only one hypothesis seems able to explain this curious fact, viz., that the Blessed Virgin's sister, having children by her first marriage, perhaps to Alpheus of the priestly race (James the Less and Joses), later married St. Joseph's brother Cleophas, who already had children by a first wife. If we were to suppose that this Mary was the mother of Simon and Jude by her marriage with Cleophas, we could not explain why St. Mark attributes to her only two sons: James the Less and Joses.

---

[13] Rufinus, the translator of Eusebius, and St. Epiphanius make of him a high priest, supposing that he went into the Holy of Holies, but Hegesippus does not say that.

3. Were Any of the Brethren of the Lord Among the Twelve?

Similarity of names proves absolutely nothing, for at that time James, Simon, and Jude were such common names that each of them appears twice in the list of the Apostles (Simon Peter and Simon Zelotes; James the son of Zebedee and James the son of Alpheus; Jude Thaddeus and Judas Iscariot). Still there are strong reasons for identifying James "the brother of the Lord," the first Bishop of Jerusalem, with the Apostle James, son of Alpheus.

1. When St. Paul returned to Jerusalem three years after his conversion, he saw, apart from Peter, "no other Apostle save James the brother of the Lord: ἕτερον τῶν ἀποστόλων οὐκ εἶδον εἰ μὴ Ἰάκωβον τὸν ἀδελφὸν τοῦ Κυρίου" (Gal. 1:19). (*a*) If James were not one of the Twelve, he would have no right to the title "apostle" in the wide sense of the word, for, according to tradition, he never left Jerusalem. (*b*) It is *as an apostle* (ἕτερον) that he is placed in opposition to the Prince of the Apostles; his apostleship is, therefore, of the same order. (*c*) The expression "none other among the Apostles" (ἕτερον τῶν ἀποστόλων, and not simply ἕτερον ἀπόστολον) can scarcely be understood except of another member of the group of the Twelve. As to the translation: "I saw no other Apostle (apart from Peter), *but* (εἰ μή) I saw James (who was not an Apostle)," it is not very natural, to say the least.

2. Antiquity knew only two Jameses in the Apostolic circle. Thus Clement of Alexandria says: "There are two Jameses: one surnamed the Just, who was hurled down from the pinnacle of the Temple, and beaten to death, they say, by a fuller (about A.D. 62); and another who was decapitated (about A.D. 42 by order of Agrippa I)." To prove that there were only two, we ought not to seek authority in the use of the Latin surname *minor*, corresponding to the appellative ὁ μικρός (Mark 15:40). Still, the argument that St. Jerome draws from it is not a sophism, since in the papyri ὁ μικρός and ὁ μέγας are found distinguishing the smaller of two brothers from the larger when both have the same name (see examples in Moulton-Milligan, *Vocabulary*, p. 412).

3. According to the three Synoptics, the Apostle James was the son of Alpheus. Since James, the brother of the Lord, was the son of Mary of Cleophas, it was supposed that he was also the son of Cleophas, and those who sustained the identity of the two Jameses taxed their ingenuity to show that Alpheus in Hebrew is the same name as Cleophas or Clopas. Thus, Cornely in the *Introductio*. But Alpheus and Cleophas have nothing in common. Alpheus in Hebrew is Halpai (הלפי); and Clopas stands for Cleopas, abridged from Cleopater or Cleopatros. It

could be said that the father of James (the Apostle and brother of the Lord, supposing that they are one and the same) had two names, one Hebrew and the other Greek, which was a common thing in those days. But Hegesippus suggests to us another solution: James the brother of the Lord was not the son of Cleophas; and his mother, Mary of Cleophas, could have borne him to a first husband named Alpheus. In that case, nothing stands in the way of identifying the two Jameses.

In favor of the identification, see Maier, in *Bibl. Zeitschrift*, 1906, pp. 164–193 and 255–266. On the reasons for doubting it, see Malvy, in *Recherches*, 1918, pp. 122–131. The Greeks celebrate the feast of James the son of Alpheus on the 9th of October, and that of James the brother of the Lord on the 23rd of the same month. The old Latin Martyrologies put the feast of the former on the 22nd of June, and that of the latter on the 28th of December.

4. Works to Consult

1. Cornely, *Les frères de N.-S.J.-C., in Etudes Religieuses,* 1878, Vol. I, pp. 5–21 and 145–169. The four brothers of Jesus are sons of Cleophas and Mary, the sister of the Blessed Virgin. "It is almost certain that James was one of the twelve Apostles. . . . It is also highly probable that Judas, the son of Cleophas, is the same as the Apostle Thaddeus. As for Simon, the brother of Jesus, the reasons for according to him the title of Apostle and those for denying it to him are almost of equal weight" (p. 169).

2. Durand, *Les frères du Seigneur,* in *L'Enfance de J.-C.,* 1908, pp. 210–276. The author insists above all on the perpetual virginity of Mary, which excludes the opinion of Helvidius. He also defends the virginity of St. Joseph, but without pronouncing upon the degree of certainty; still, he apparently approves the position of Cornely. This author, basing his view on "the Catholic sense," holds that "henceforth it would be temerarious to call into doubt the perpetual virginity of the spouse of Mary." On the question, whether there was one or more Apostles among the brothers of the Lord, Durand gives no opinion.

3. Lagrange, *Note sur les frères du Seigneur,* in his *Saint Marc,* 4 ed., 1929, pp. 79–93. The author examines: (*a*) what the expression can mean; (*b*) what it means in the present case according to the Biblical texts; (*c*) what it means according to tradition (p. 79). In the first edition of *Saint Marc,* he concluded (p. 89): "We do not claim that it is historically demonstrated that the brethren of the Lord were his cousins. We say only that absolutely no objection can be brought against the perpetual virginity of Mary, which is suggested in

many passages of Holy Scripture and affirmed by Tradition; moreover, that it is very probable, according to Scripture combined with Tradition, and according to the historical tradition of Hegesippus, that the brethren of the Lord were not sons of St. Joseph." In his *Saint Jean,* 1925, p. 493, with Zahn, he distinguishes Mary of Cleophas from the sister of the Blessed Virgin (John 19:25). The latter is Salome, the wife of Zebedee, and mother of the Apostles James and John, who are consequently first cousins of the Saviour. In his *Saint Marc,* 1929, p. 93, the Blessed Virgin's sister is no longer Salome, but "another Mary, the wife of Alpheus, who was, perhaps, of a Levitical line of descent."

4. Lightfoot, *The Brethren of the Lord,* in *Epistle to the Galatians,* 1892, pp. 252–391. The author conscientiously studies the texts of the ecclesiastical authors without entering into discussions of exegesis. He distinguishes three opinions which he associates with the names of the principal proponents of each: Epiphanius, Helvidius, and Jerome. For Epiphanius, the "brothers of the Lord" are sons of Joseph, born of a previous marriage. This is the opinion which Lightfoot himself embraces. He refutes the opinion of Helvidius, who makes them out to be children of Joseph and Mary, born after the birth of Christ. However, he admires the courage of Helvidius, Bonosus, and Jovinian. "They endeavored to stem the current which had set strongly in the direction of celibacy; and, if their theory was faulty, they still deserve the sympathy due to men who, in defiance of public opinion, refused to bow their necks to an extravagant and tyrannous superstition" (p. 287). St. Jerome's opinion, which regards the brethren of the Lord as cousins of Jesus, is not taken into consideration. Many Anglicans, among them Harris in the *Dictionary of Christ and the Gospels,* Vol. I, pp. 232–237, follow Lightfoot, often doing little more than summarizing his opinion.

5. Zahn, whose tremendous erudition is not matched by his critical and historical sense, is the principal champion of the opinion of Helvidius (*Brüder und Vettern Jesu,* in *Forschungen,* Vol. VI, 1900, pp. 225–363). He advances no arguments in addition to those proposed by Helvidius himself: (*a*) The natural meaning of the word "brother." (*b*) Jesus was Mary's *first-born* (Luke 2:7); this implies that Jesus had younger brothers; (*c*) Mary knew not Joseph *before* bringing forth Jesus (Matt. 1:25); this implies subsequent intercourse. These sophisms had been thoroughly refuted by St. Jerome in his answer to Helvidius. Zahn's conclusions are these: (*a*) Every time there is mention of the brothers of the Lord, four brothers are meant; namely, James, Joseph, Simon, and Jude, who were born after the birth of Jesus, of the marriage of Joseph and Mary; Joseph was of the family

of David, while Mary probably belonged to the tribe of Levi (*b*) Mary's sister was Salome, wife of Zebedee and mother of the Apostles James and John. (*c*) None of the brothers of the Lord was an Apostle. (*d*) Mary, the mother of James the Less and of Joseph (Mark 15:40; 16:1; Matt. 27:56), is probably the same as the Mary of whom St. Paul speaks (Rom. 16:6), and her son Joseph is perhaps Joseph Barsabas (Acts. 1:23). It is obvious that Zahn has given free rein to his imagination. His notions, at least in their essentials, are embraced by many Protestant authors. We need mention only the *Encyclopedia Biblica* and Hastings, *Dictionary of the Bible.*

NOTE J

The Sermon on the Mount

1. A Comparative Analysis of the Sermon

	Matthew I	*Luke I*	*Luke II*	*Mark*	*Matthew II*
A. The Beatitudes	5:3–12	6:20–23			
B. Maledictions		6:24–26			
C. The Salt of the Earth	5:13		14:34–35	9:50	
D. The Light of the World	5:14–16		11:33 8:16	4:21	
E. Jesus Fulfills the Law	5:17–20		cf. 16:17		
F. Murder — Injuries	5:21–24				
G. Reconciliation	5:25–26		12:57–59		
H. Adultery — Impurity	5:27–28				
I. Occasion of Scandal	5:29–30		17:1–2	9:42–47	18:8–9
J. Divorce Condemned	5:31–32		16:18	10:11–12	19:9
K. Perjury — Oaths	5:33–37				
L. The Lex Talionis	5:38–42	6:29–30			
M. Love of Enemies	5:43–48	6:27–28 6:32–33			
N. Gratuitous Loans		6:34–36			
O. Almsgiving	6:1–4				
P. Prayer	6:5–8				
Q. The Lord's Prayer	6:9–13		11:2–4		
R. Pardoning Offenses	6:14–15			11:25–26	
S. Fasting	6:16–18				
T. Treasures for Heaven	6:19–21		12:33–34		
U. The Eye the Lamp of the Body	6:22–23		11:34–36		
V. Serving Two Masters	6:24		16:13		
W. Confidence in God	6:25–34		12:22–31		
X. Judge Not	7:1–2	6:37			
Y. The Mote and the Beam	7:3–5	6:41–42			
Z. Pearls Before Swine	7:6				
a. The Efficacy of Prayer	7:7–11		11:9–13		
b. The Golden Rule	7:12	6:31			
c. The Narrow Gate	7:13–14		13:23–24		
d. As the Tree so the Fruit	7:15–20	6:43–44			
e. Not Words but Deeds	7:21–23	6:46			
f. Closing Parable	7:24–27	6:47–49			
g. Give and You Shall Receive		6:38			
h. The Blind Leading the Blind		6:39			
i. The Disciple Less Than the Master		6:40			
j. From the Abundance of the Heart		6:45			

2. Primary and Secondary Parts*

In the table on page 511, the column *Matthew I* contains the whole sermon in order according to St. Matthew; the column *Luke I,* the entire discourse according to St. Luke; the column *Luke II* contains the parts that are put in other contexts by St. Luke; the column *Mark* has the parallel passages in St. Mark; the column *Matthew II* contains St. Matthew's doublets, i.e., the passages which he repeats and places in a different context.

An examination of the Sermon on the Mount yields the following results: (*a*) the sermon has 107 verses in St. Matthew, only 30 in St. Luke; (*b*) 40 verses of Matthew are parallel to 20 of Luke in the same context; (*c*) 42 verses of Matthew are parallel to 36 of Luke in other contexts; (*d*) 23 verses are peculiar to Matthew; (*e*) 10 verses are peculiar to Luke.

Four principles may be formulated about the constitutive parts of the Sermon on the Mount:

1. The parts common to Matthew and Luke in this same context must be regarded as belonging to the Sermon.

2. The parts that are special to Matthew also belong to the Sermon except 7:6 and perhaps parts of some of the others.

3. The passages of Matthew which have parallels in *other* contexts of Luke are not part of the Sermon, but are inserted into it by the first Evangelist because of similarity of subject.

4. Of the ten verses of Luke which are without parallels in Matthew, three (Luke 6:24–26) present the reverse of the Beatitudes and are, so to speak, the negative side of the same idea. Two (Luke 6:39–40) seem to contain disparate matter unrelated to the subject of the Sermon; another (6:45) agrees well enough with the subject, but the idea is found in Matthew in another context.

There is naturally a great deal of hypothesis in these reflections, since it is quite possible that Christ repeated the same teachings, almost in the same words, on other occasions. Yet it is unlikely that the disciples would have asked our Lord, about six months before the Passion, "Teach us to pray," if he had taught them the Lord's Prayer in the Sermon on the Mount, almost at the outset of his preaching.

In Hastings, *Dictionary of the Bible,* there is a lengthy article by Wotaw (extra volume, 1904, pp. 1–45) in which can be found useful references and a very copious bibliography. Naturally, the theories and hypotheses of the author are not to be blindly accepted. It is clear that he has seldom consulted Catholic commentaries outside the Fathers. It is to be regretted that there is not an entirely satisfactory Catholic monograph on this subject.

* This Note has been edited (*Translator*).

NOTE K

The Gospel Parables

1. Definition and Number

1. *Definition* — In the Old Testament the *mashal,* translated παραβολή by the Septuagint and *parabola* by the Vulgate, has a wide variety of meanings. It is applied to the *oracles* of Balaam, to the *allegories* of Ezechiel, to *proverbs* or popular sayings, to *sarcastic* thrusts, to moral *maxims.* See Buzy, *Introduction aux paraboles,* 1912, pp. 52–124.

In the New Testament (except in the Epistle to the Hebrews, where παραβολή is used twice in the sense of *type,* prophetic figure), the word occurs only in the Synoptics, who use it 48 times for 33 different cases. The Vulgate generally translates it as *parabola,* but eight times, in St. Luke, as *similitudo,* though there is no difference in meaning to justify the difference in translation.

The word παραβολή means *comparison,* and, in fact, at the base of every parable there is an expressed or latent comparison. Understood in the usual way the Gospel parable may be defined as *a fictional but plausible narrative, the purpose of which is to illustrate by comparison a moral lesson or dogmatic truth.*

a) *Narrative* — every apologue (of which the parable is a species) entails, short though it be, a complication and a *dénouement.* If the narrative is merely outlined, it is called a *similitude.*

b) *Fictional.* A factual narrative could be as instructive as a fictional story, but in fiction the narrator is freer to make a choice of details apt for instruction, and to eliminate superfluous details. As a matter of fact, all the Gospel parables are fictional.

c) *Plausible.* This is not a necessary condition, but, lacking plausibility, the parable would turn into a fable, and that literary form is not found in the New Testament, though there are two instances of it in the Old.

d) *Illustrating a moral lesson or dogmatic truth.* Here it is necessary to understand "in the supernatural order." The parable, like the apologue, is designed to instruct, and in that way it differs from a *tale,* whose sole aim is to amuse and please. But the Gospel parable is the vehicle of *Revelation,* and in this it is distinguished from the fable, which is concerned with inculcating practical wisdom and common truths.

2. *Number.* The variety of concepts and definitions of the parable in various authors results in a variety of enumeration of the Gospel parables. Steinmeyer enumerates 23 (or 24), Goebel 26 (or 27), Trench 30, Bruce 33, Lisco 37, Jülicher 53 (28 similitudes, 21 parables, 4 examples), Bugge 71 (of which 37 are parables properly so called), Fonck 72, Van Koestwald 80 (or rather 79, one of them being counted twice), Von Wessenberg 101, Buzy 33, in *Les Paraboles* (*Verbum Salutis*), 1932. In the tables that follow, we keep to 30 parables and 32 similitudes. A certain number of comparisons remain in the Gospel which may be called parables.

2. The Nature of the Gospel Parables

Jülicher (*Die Gleichnisreden Jesu,* 2 ed., 1910) and his faithful disciple Loisy (*Etudes èvangeliques,* 1902) have proposed about the parables a theory which must be challenged. Here, briefly, is a summary of it in five points:

1. The parable and the allegory are two incompatible literary forms; they differ as night and day. A parable mixed with allegory would be a hybrid, a monstrosity.
2. The parable, like the comparison, is always clear; the allegory, like the metaphor, is always obscure; thus the allegory often requires an explanation, but the parable never needs one.
3. The allegory piques the curiosity, sharpens the wit, flatters the reader by its half-light and shadow, where there is always something to guess; it is an aristocratic *genre;* the simple and easy parable is a popular *genre.*
4. Jesus, being a popular orator who aimed at being understood by everyone, could not have propounded allegories. The Evangelists are the ones who attribute them to him under the pressure of theological reflection, anxious, as they were, to explain the blindness of the Jews.
5. Hence, to arrive at the true thought of Jesus in the Gospel parables, it is necessary to reduce them to their native purity and to set aside all allegorical elements.

The postulates of Jülicher and Loisy are contradicted by the experience of all countries and all periods of time. The parable and the allegory have such close affinity that it is almost impossible for an allegory to be long sustained without accumulating features of the parable, and the parable is often colored by allegory. In the very two examples given by Aristotle as types of the fable — Stesichorus' "The Horse and the Stag" and Aesop's "The Fox and the Leeches" — the intention of both authors was allegory. Quintilian finds a supreme elegance in this mixture: "Habet usum talis allegoriae frequenter oratio sed raro totius: plerumque apertis permixta est. . . . Illud vero longe speciosissimum genus orationis, in quo trium permixta est gratia: similitudinis, allegoriae et translationis" (*Instit. orat.* viii, 6); provided always that the metaphors do not clash.

It is maintained that the comparison is popular and the metaphor aristocratic. That is a graceful turn, but nothing more. The common people use as many metaphors as comparisons. Primitives and savages have a special taste for allegory, and employ it more than the savants of civilized peoples. Let us hear Quintilian again, in the passage cited above: "Metaphora . . . ita est ab ipsa nobis concessa natura ut indocti quoque ac non sentientes ea frequenter utantur. . . . Allegoria parvis quoque ingeniis et quotidiano sermone frequentissime servit." But, say they, the allegory is obscure. Not always; and, on the other hand, the parable is obscure when the term of comparison is unknown. Multiply comparisons as much as you will, you will not succeed in making a blind man understand what light or color is. David did not understand Nathan's apologue, though it was clear enough, until the prophet said to him: *Tu es ille vir.*

Jülicher's theory is therefore baseless and perhaps already too antiquated to need refutation. Cf. Buzy, *Introduction,* pp. 2–51 and 173–230.

3. Rabbinic Apologues

Jewish literature offers us almost nothing, either in the first century of our era or in the two preceding centuries, that could be compared with the parables of the Gospel. The Parables or Similitudes of the Book of Henoch are neither parables nor allegories. The stories written in the form of allegory by some of the self-styled prophets belong to a quite different literary form. The parables of the Talmud are closer to the Gospel parables. The elements of the question may be found in Lagrange, *Les paraboles en dehors de l'Evangile,* in *R.B.,* 1909, pp. 342–357; Buzy, *Introduction aux paraboles évangeliques,* 1912, pp. 135–182; Fiebig, *Altjüdische Gleichnisse,* 1904, and *Die Gleichnisreden Jesu in Lichte der rabbin. Gleichnisse,* 1912; Abrahams, *Studies in Pharisaism and the Gospels,* 1917, Vol. I, pp. 135–182; Bacher, *Die Agada der Tannaiten,* Vol. I, 2 ed., 1904; Vol. II, 1890.

The *Mishnah,* compiled at the end of the second century, has very few parables; the *Tosephta* at the beginning of the next century has more; the more recent parts of the Talmud, the *Midrashim* and the *Gemara,* have many. True, the attribution of this or that parable to such and such an author, dead now several centuries, is always open to error. Those attributed to contemporaries of Christ are exceedingly rare and so much the more interesting. In Billerbeck, *Kommentar,* Vol. I, pp. 654–655, can be found a parable or quasi-parable attributed to the great Hillel by an author of the seventh century. The thought is beautiful, but the parable itself, or whatever it should be called, would be an enigma, if it were not followed by an explanation. Pearls of this value are rare in the Talmud, and it requires a good deal of time to discover others like them. Almost all are cold and childish. Fiebig, who made a special study of them, does not rate them very highly. Abrahams defends them, while admitting that many are banal and handled in a trivial way. I do not think that it has occurred to anyone to prefer them to, or even to compare them with, the Gospel parables.

4. Division

A. *Parables Properly So Called*

Dogmatic Parables

	Matthew	*Mark*	*Luke*
1. The Sower	13:3–23	*4:3–20	
2. The Darnel	*13:24–30	8:4–15	
3. The Mustard Seed	*13:31–32	*4:30–32	13:18–19
4. The Leaven	*13:33		13:20–21
5. The Treasure	*13:44		
6. The Pearl	*13:45–46		
7. The Net	*13:47–50		
8. Growing Grain		*4:26–29	

Moral Parables

	Matthew	*Mark*	*Luke*
9. Houses Built in Sand and on Rock	7:24–27		6:47–49
10. The Two Debtors			7:41–42
11. The Good Samaritan			10:29–37
12. The Importunate Friend			11:5–8
13. The Miser			*12:16–21
14. The Barren Fig Tree			*13:6–9
15. The Lost Sheep	18:12–14		*15:4–7
16. The Lost Drachma			15:8–10
17. The Prodigal Son			15:11–32
18. The Faithless Steward			16:1–13
19. Lazarus and the Rich Man			16:19–31
20. The Importunate Widow			*18:1–8
21. The Pharisee and the Publican			*18:9–14
22. The Unmerciful Servant	18:21–35		

* We have marked with an asterisk those parables and similitudes which are called such in the Gospel. Although we distinguish the parable of the Talents from

Prophetic or Eschatological Parables

	Matthew	*Mark*	*Luke*
23. The Laborers in the Vineyard	*20:1–16		
24. The Two Sons	21:28–32		
25. The Wicked Vinedressers	*21:33–46	*12:1–12	*20:9–19
26. Guests at the Banquet	22:1–10		14:15–24
27. The Wedding Garment	*22:11–14		
28. The Ten Virgins	25:1–13		
29. The Minas			19:12–27
30. The Talents	25:14–30		

B. *Parables in Outline or Similitudes*

	Matthew	*Mark*	*Luke*
1. Physician, Cure Thyself			4:23
2. The Salt	5:13	9:49–50	14:34–35
3. The Lamp on the Stand	5:14–15	4:21	8:16; 11:33
4. The City Built on a Mountain	5:14b		
5. Accuser and Judge	5:25–26		12:57–59
6. The Eye, Light of the Body	6:22–23		11:34–36
7. The Two Masters	6:24		16:13
8. The Child Begging His Father	7:9–11		11:11–13
9. As the Tree Such the Fruit	7:16–20 12:33–37		6:43–45
10. Need of a Physician	9:12–13	2:17	5:31–32
11. The Bridegroom and His Friend	9:14–15	2:18–20	5:33–35
12. Old and New Garments	9:16	2:21	5:36
13. Old and New Wineskins	9:17	2:22	5:37–38
14. New Wine and Old Wine			5:39
15. Secrets Preached on the Rooftop	10:26–27	4:22	8:17; 12:2–3
16. The Pupil and the Master	10:24–25		6:40
17. Children Playing in the Marketplace	11:16–19		7:31–35
18. The Divided Kingdom	12:25–27	*3:23–26	11:17–18
19. Assaults of the Unclean Spirit	12:43–45		11:24–26
20. The Wise Scribe	13:52		
21. True Defilement	*15:10–20	*7:14–23	
22. The Blind Led by the Blind	15:14		6:39
23. The Children and the Dogs	15:26–27	7:27–28	
24. First Places at the Feast			*14:7–14
25. Building a Tower			14:28–30
26. Undertaking a War			14:31–33
27. Servants Awaiting Their Master		13:34	*12:35–38
28. The Faithful and the Negligent Stewards	24:45–51		12:41–48
29. The Duties of a Good Servant			17:7–10
30. The Corpse and the Vultures	24:28		17:37
31. The Thief	24:43–44		12:39–40
32. The Fig Tree, Harbinger of Summer	*24:32–35	*13:28–29	*21:29–31

that of the Minas, and the parable of the Wedding Garment from that of the Guests at the Banquet, we have not intention of pronouncing against their identity.

NOTE L

Gospel Miracles

1. Nomenclature of the Gospel Miracles

It is worthy of note that the word corresponding to "miracle" (θαῦμα) is not used in the Gospel, although the feeling of *wonder* and astonishment awakened by a miracle (according to its etymology) is often mentioned by the Evangelists.

The words in the Gospel which designate miracles are: *acts of power, signs, works, prodigies,* and, by exception, an *extraordinary thing* (παράδοξον, Luke 5:26).

1. *Acts of Power* (δυνάμεις) — This is the favorite word of the Synoptics, and it is generally translated by *miracles*. In fact, a miracle requires superhuman power; it is a participation of divine power. Men of good faith seeing it say: "The finger of God is there." The multitude of disciples praised God in a loud voice "super omnibus, quas viderant, *virtutibus*" (Luke 19:37). The towns of the lakeshore are inexcusable for having failed to understand this language (Matt. 11:20–23 and parallels).

2. *Signs* (σημεῖα) — St. John prefers to use this word. A *sign* is the seal affixed by God to Christ's mission. The miracle of Cana is the first of the *signs* wrought by Jesus. The Jews demand a *sign* from him (John 2:18; Matt. 12:39, etc.); they invite him to produce his credentials. If they are sincere, they are obliged to avow with Nicodemus that no man could work the *signs* which Jesus wrought unless God were with him (John 3:2). John reports only a few of the *signs* wrought by Jesus, but this small number suffices as a motive of credibility (John 20:30–31).

2. Miracles Related in Detail

	Matthew	*Mark*	*Luke*	*John*
1. Water Changed Into Wine at Cana				2:1–11
2. The Son of the Royal Official				4:46–54
3. First Miraculous Draught of Fish			5:1–11	
4. The Possessed Man at Capharnaum		1:23–28	4:31–37	
5. St. Peter's Mother-in-Law	8:14–15	1:29–31	4:38–39	
6. The Leper at Capharnaum	8:1–4	1:40–45	5:12–16	
7. The Paralytic Carried by Four	9:1–8	2:1–12	5:17–26	
8. The Servant of the Centurion	8:5–13		7:1–10	
9. The Son of the Widow of Naim			7:11–17	
10. The Man With the Withered Hand	12:9–14	3:1–6	6:6–11	
11. The Cripple at Bethesda				5:1–15
12. The Calming of the Tempest	8:23–27	4:35–41	8:22–25	
13. The Gerasene Demoniac	8:28–34	5:1–20	8:26–39	
14. The Woman With an Issue 15. of Blood and Raising of Daughter of Jairus	9:18–26	5:21–43	8:40–56	
16. Two Blind Men at Capharnaum	9:27–31			
17. First Multiplication of Loaves	14:13–21	6:30–44	9:10–17	6:1–13
18. Walking on the Water	14:22–23	6:45–52		6:17–21
19. The Daughter of the Chanaanite	15:21–28	7:24–30		
20. Second Multiplication of Loaves	15:32–39	8:1–10		
21. The Deaf Stammerer		7:32–37		
22. The Blind Man of Bethsaida		8:22–26		
23. The Lunatic at Thabor	17:14–21	9:14–29	9:37–43	
24. The Tribute Money	17:24–27			
25. The Man Blind From Birth				9:1–38
26. The Mute Demoniac	12:22–23		11:14	
27. The Woman Infirm for Eighteen Years			13:10–17	
28. The Man With Dropsy			14:1–6	
29. The Raising of Lazarus From the Dead				11:1–44
30. The Ten Lepers			17:11–19	
31. The Blind Men of Jericho	20:29–34	10:46–52	18:35–43	
32. The Accursed Fig Tree	21:18–22	11:12–14		
33. Healing of Malchus' Ear			22:51	

This list does not include: (*a*) the miracles which concern the Saviour's person; (*b*) the miracles of his glorious life; (*c*) the probably miraculous happenings which are not presented as such by the Evangelists, for example the expulsion of the vendors from the Temple, the falling backward of the men at Gethsemani, Jesus withdrawing himself from the rage of his enemies; (*d*) the countless miracles numbered *en bloc* in the Gospels.

3. Miracles Mentioned Collectively

It would be a grave mistake to think that the thirty and some miracles narrated in detail by the Evangelists represent the entire thaumaturgic activity of Jesus. They are only specimens of various prodigies — the dead restored to life, demoniacs delivered, lepers cleansed, blind, deaf-mutes, paralytics, and other sick cured — giving not even an approximate idea of them and in no way explaining the wild enthusiasm of the multitudes. St. John informs us that Jesus wrought a great number of signs (20:30: σημεῖα) which are not included in his Gospel, and that an infinity of books would be needed to contain the narrative of all that the Saviour did (21:25).

The Beloved Disciple is amazed that after so many and such great miracles the Jews remained incredulous (12:37). Here are some instances of the collective mention of miracles:

1. At the time of the first Passover of the public life (John 2:23; cf. 4:45).
2. The evening of the Sabbath when Jesus had cured Peter's mother-in-law (Mark 1:34): "he cured many sick afflicted with various diseases." Cf. Luke 4:40 and 5:15.
3. Before the Sermon on the Mount (Matt. 4:24–25; Mark 3:10–11; Luke 6:17–19).
4. In the presence of the messengers from the Baptist (Luke 7:21): "he cured many sick of various diseases and afflicted with evil spirits, and restored sight to many blind."
5. During his visit to Nazareth (Mark 6:5): "He could work there no miracle" because of the unbelief of his fellow townsmen; still, "he healed a few sick by laying his hands upon them." Cf. Matt. 13:58.
6. After the first multiplication of loaves (Mark 6:54–56; Matt. 14:35–36).
7. Before the second multiplication of loaves (Matt. 15:30–31).
8. He delegated to the twelve Apostles the power of working miracles (Matt. 10:8; Luke 9:1–2; cf. Mark 6:13); also to the seventy-two disciples (Luke 10:9) who were sent out on a mission.

APPENDIX

CONCORD OF THE GOSPELS

The text of the four Gospels, or only of the three Synoptics, arranged in chronological order and presented either *in extenso* or by means of simple reference is called a Harmony or Synopsis or Concord or Concordance.

Around the year 175, Tatian put together the text of the four Gospels so as to make of them one continuous narrative. His work, which enjoyed great favor in the Syrian Church and was commented upon by St. Ephraem, had the serious drawback that it cut up and mixed together the sacred text.[1]

At the beginning of the fourth century, Eusebius of Caesarea, inspired by an idea conceived by Ammonius of Alexandria, created the *Canons* which bear his name and whose structure he explains in a letter to Carpianus. The text of each Gospel is divided into a great number of fragments numbered in order. These numbers, arranged in an ingenious table, make it possible to discover immediately what is special to each Evangelist, what he has in common with one or more of the others, and to find parallel passages without groping.[2]

Nowadays it is preferable to have the text *in extenso* before the eyes. There exist a great number of synopses in Greek, Latin, and

---

[1] The *Diatessaron:* ἐν διὰ τεσσάρων: *unum* (Evangelium) *per quatuor*. The word διατεσσάρων meant, in medicine, a remedy made up of four ingredients; in music, a chord of four notes.

[2] The *Canons of Eusebius,* with the *Letter to Carpianus* (in Greek) and St. Jerome's explanation in his letter to St. Damasus, may be found at the beginning of the *Novum Testamentum graece et latine* of Nestle. Ammonius had divided the Gospels into very small fragments: 355 for St. Matthew, 241 for St. Mark, 342 for St. Luke, and 232 for St. John. The numbering was inscribed in the margin of each Gospel. Beside each of these numbers Eusebius wrote another number: (I) for passages common to the four Gospels; (II) for passages common to the three Synoptics; (III) for Matthew, Mark, and John; (IV) for Matthew, Luke, and John; (V) for Matthew and Luke; (VI) for Matthew and Mark; (VII) for Matthew and John; (VIII) for Mark and Luke; (IX) for Luke and John; (X) for passages proper to each Gospel. A special table listed them all together. Even today, when Students' Aids abound, the *Canons of Eusebius* have their usefulness.

even French. The best one is always the one to which the reader has become accustomed.[3]

These synopses are not all alike. Some (Mechineau, Fillion) are content to present the text in parallel columns without giving reasons for the order adopted; others (Camerlynck, Lavergne) accompany the text with notes justifying the order chosen; a few (Rambaud, Azibert), in order to facilitate the comparison of the Gospels, take in each column the special features so as to form a consecutive and complete narrative, a sort of "Diatessaron," which they print in Roman characters, while the rest is printed in italics.

It would be interesting to have a harmony which, by some typographical process or by the use of various colors, would present to the eye the resemblances and differences of the Synoptics both in ideas and style; such a work, which would be difficult to construct, does not yet exist.

---

[3] *Greek Synopses:* Tischendorf, 4 ed. (Leipzig, 1875); Rushbrooke, (London, 1880); Wright (London, 1885); Huck, 6 ed., 1922; Lagrange, 1926. *A Greek-Latin Synopsis:* Patrizi, 1853. *Latin Synopses:* Fillion, 1892; Rambaud, 2 ed., 1898; Mechineau, 1896; Azibert (Albi, 1897); Brassac, 1913; Bover (Madrid, 1921); Camerlynck, *Synopsis,* 4 ed. (Bruges, 1932), etc. *French Synopsis:* Lavergne (following Lagrange), 1927. We have not mentioned the English and German synopses.

[*English Synopses:* Hartdegen, O.F.M., *A Chronological Harmony of the Gospels,* (St. Anthony Guild Press, 1942); Steinmuller, *A Gospel Harmony* (Sadlier, New York — Chicago, 1942). Both of the harmonies use the "Confraternity" edition. *Translator.*]

PART ONE

THE CHRONOLOGICAL ORDER OF EVENTS

To facilitate the examination, it is well to divide the Gospel narrative into several sections. The distribution and number is indicated in the following table.

1. Period of Preparation

Section I. The Hidden Life up to the Baptism
Section II. From the Baptism to the Second Miracle at Cana

2. Apostolate in Galilee

Section III. Up to the Sermon on the Mount
Section IV. From the Sermon on the Mount to the Parables
Section V. From the Parables to the Bread of Life
Section VI. In Phoenicia and the Decapolis
Section VII. Last Days in Galilee

3. Apostolate in Judea and Perea

Section VIII. Part Peculiar to St. John
Section IX. Part Peculiar to St. Luke
Section X. Part Common to the Three Synoptics

4. The Passion, Death, and New Life

Section XI. The First Days of Holy Week
Section XII. Holy Thursday. The Last Supper
Section XIII. Good Friday. The Passion
Section XIV. Jesus Christ Risen from the Dead

The following notes have as their purpose to indicate the *order* but not the *date* of the events. On the dates, consult Note B: *Chronology*. It is understood that for the year and the day no date can be fixed with full certainty. The mention of *feasts* by St. John and some indications furnished by the Synoptics allow only the determination sometimes of the month or the season.

1. Period of Preparation

Section I. The Hidden Life Up to the Baptism

The message of Gabriel to Zachary precedes the Annunciation and the Visitation by *six months.* Mary sojourns with Elizabeth *three months,* probably until the birth of John (Luke 1:26 and 1:56), and it is upon her return to Nazareth that the painful ordeal of Joseph occurs (Matt. 1:19). Jesus is adored by the shepherds *on the night of his birth* (Luke 2:8–9); he is circumcised on the *eighth day* (Luke 2:21) and is presented in the Temple on the *fortieth day* (Luke 2:22). After the arrival of the Magi (Matt. 2:13), the Holy Family flees into Egypt and remains there until after the death of Herod.

The only two doubtful points are the date of the coming of the Magi and the duration of the sojourn in Egypt. The Magi cannot have arrived at Bethlehem *before* the Purification, nor *very long after it.* If they had arrived before the Purification, the presentation of Jesus in the Temple would be inconceivable, owing to fear of the suspicious Herod; they cannot have arrived long after that event, because in that case the date of the Saviour's nativity would have to be pushed back too far. The baptism of our Lord could not have occurred before the year A.D. 27 (the Roman year 780), and if he was born only fifteen months before the death of Herod, he would have completed his thirty-first year at the time of his baptism. Herod, it is true, massacred all the children who were *under two years old,* "secundum tempus quod exquisierat a Magis"; but we do not know the date of the apparition of the star, and whether that date coincided with the conception or with the birth of Jesus. Besides, Herod may have raised the age limit to make sure of reaching his victim. Since the return of the Holy Family to Nazareth followed close upon the death of Herod (Matt. 2:19), the sojourn in Egypt cannot have been longer than a year, if that long.

Section II. From the Baptism to the Second Miracle of Cana

St. Luke (3:1–2, 23) gives the same date for the inauguration of John's ministry and the baptism of Jesus. "Immediately afterward" (Mark 1:12, cf. Matt. 4:1; Luke 4:1) followed the *forty-day* fast. The testimony of the Baptist given on *three consecutive days* (John 1:29–35) must have followed soon after, and also the miracle of Cana (John 1:37; 2:1), and the transfer of residence to Capharnaum (John 2:12), the Passover being near. Between the baptism and this

Passover, when Jesus cast the sellers out of the Temple, about three months intervened.

We have given elsewhere (*Chronology*) our reasons for reducing the Saviour's sojourn with his new disciples in Judea to two months. He must, then, have returned to Galilee, across Samaria, around the month of May (John 4:35).

The Synoptics mention the imprisonment of the Baptist immediately after the baptism and fast of Jesus (Matt. 4:12; Mark 1:14; cf. Luke 3:19–20), but the Fourth Gospel tells us that John was baptizing at Ennon while Jesus' disciples were baptizing in Judea (John 3:22–24). John's arrest must have coincided with the Saviour's *second* return to Galilee, and not with the *first,* as the Synoptic account, by passing over this whole period in silence, would lead us to believe.

2. Apostolate in Galilee

Section III. Up to the Sermon on the Mount

St. Luke here follows St. Mark except in three details: he places the visit to Nazareth *at the very beginning;* he recounts the cure of Peter's mother-in-law *before* the call of the Apostles; he places the call of the Twelve *before* the arrival of the multitudes. In all three cases, St. Mark's order seems preferable. (*a*) St. Mark and St. Matthew agree in placing the visit to Nazareth at the approach of the next-to-last Passover, and St. Luke himself mentions numerous miracles already worked by Jesus at Capharnaum (Luke 4:23). Besides, there is no warrant for admitting two distinct visits, one at the beginning and the other at the end of the Galilean ministry; the accounts have too many points in common not to be identical. (*b*) It is much more likely that Jesus entered St. Peter's home *after* calling him to the Apostolate, as St. Mark and St. Matthew say. It is also more likely that Jesus chose the Twelve *from the midst* of the multitudes of disciples who had flocked to him.

Yet we do not maintain that St. Mark's order is rigorously chronological. This section includes: (*a*) a miracle that makes a profound impression upon those present (1:21–28); (*b*) a series of miracles (1:29–45) which arouse still greater admiration and enthusiasm; (c) a group of four occasions of recrimination provoking accusations by the Pharisees (2:1–3:6): about the remission of sin in the case of the cured paralytic; on the subject of fasting and consorting with sinners on the occasion of the feast tendered by Matthew; about violation of the Sabbath with reference to the plucking of the grain and the cure of the man with the withered hand on a certain Saturday. All this suggests an artificial arrangement, explained and warranted by the demands of Mark's catechesis.

Section IV. From the Sermon on the Mount to the Parables

Here we have no data to establish a chronological order. St. Luke has six more episodes than St. Mark, three of which he has in common with St. Matthew. When we speak of *a day* of parables, we do not mean to say that they were all delivered on the same day. St. Luke assigns an entirely different place to the parable of the Mustard Seed and the Leaven (Luke 13:18–21), and it is quite probable that our Lord did not explain the reason for the failure of the parables on the same day on which he propounded them.

Section V. From the Parables to the Bread of Life

Here again St. Luke follows St. Mark, except for the visit to Nazareth, which he has already recorded by anticipation. Less careful of chronological order, St. Matthew distributes the events in different contexts. St. John rejoins the Synoptics at the first multiplication of the loaves, reports the miracle of Jesus walking on the water, and adds the long discourse on the Bread of Life.

Four miracles make up an inseparable group: the calming of the tempest, the Gerasene demoniac, the raising of Jairus' daughter, and the cure of the woman with the issue of blood. St. Mark clearly seems to say that Jesus embarked for the country of the Gerasenes the *evening of the day of parables* (Mark 4:35). Yet some think that "on that day" is equivalent to the vague expression "at that time," or that it relates, not to what immediately precedes, but to the parable of the Mustard Seed, which St. Luke presents in another context (Knabenbauer). This last hypothesis, however, is somewhat forced. The return to Capharnaum and the restoration to life of Jairus' daughter occurred on the same day as the cure of the demoniac.

The reasons for inserting the cure of the paralytic of Bethesda between the discourse spoken in the synagogue of Capharnaum and the journey to Phoenicia, in other words, the reasons for inverting the order of the fifth and sixth chapters of St. John are as follows:

1. The end of Chapter V (where Jesus is in Jerusalem) fits in badly with the beginning of Chapter VI (where he crosses over to *the other side* of the Jordan): which implies that he is in Galilee.

2. On the contrary, the end of Chapter V (where the Jews in Jerusalem seek to kill Jesus) fits in perfectly with the beginning of Chapter VII: "After that Jesus went about through Galilee, not wishing to go to Judea, because the Jews were seeking to put him to death."

3. The discourse in Chapter VII is a continuation of the discourse of Chapter V, and it is hard to imagine any very long interval between the two, for Jesus alludes to the first as to something recent (John 7:21–23, an allusion to 5:8; likewise 7:25, an allusion to 5:18).

4. The multiplication of loaves recounted in Chapter VI follows close upon the death of John the Baptist (according to Matt. 14:13 and Mark 6:29–30). Now, by Chapter V the Baptist has long since disappeared from the scene (5:35).

5. With the present arrangement, it is difficult to identify the unnamed feast of John 5:1. According to the commonly accepted explanation of John 4:35, which places the return of Jesus into Galilee in the month of January, this feast could only have been the carnival-like feast of Lots (*Purim*). With our explanation of that passage, the unnamed feast could be Pentecost or the Feast of Trumpets. But these feasts, after which the Passover of John 6:4 must be placed, are very far from the Feast of Tabernacles (John 7:2). On the other hand, once the inversion is admitted, everything arranges itself naturally. At the time of the multiplication of the loaves, the Passover is near at hand (John 6:4). Jesus goes up to Jerusalem (John 5:1) to the Pentecost that follows, if the reading is ἑορτή without the article; to the Passover itself, if the reading is ἡ ἑορτή with the article. The second alternative is preferable, since it is hard to see what could have prevented the celebration of the Passover by the Saviour at Jerusalem *before the plot* which was hatched against him, the plot mentioned at the end of Chapter V.

This inversion is now accepted, at least as probable, by a great number of interpreters, both Catholic (Olivieri, O.S.B., Meinertz, Lagrange, Durand, Lebreton) and Protestant (Norris, Bernard, etc.). See Meinertz (*Bibl. Zeitschrift*, Vol. XV, 1917, pp. 239–249) who gives a brief history of the hypothesis, and Bernard (*Gospel according to St. John* [Edinburgh, 1928], pp. xvii–xix) who treats the question from an exegetical point of view.

Sections VI and VII. In Phoenicia and the Decapolis — Last Days in Galilee

These sections present no difficulty, since the Evangelists agree on the order.

3. Apostolate in Judea and Perea

Only St. John and St. Luke record this period, which comprises the last six months of Christ's life, from the departure from Galilee to Holy Week. The two other Synoptics rejoin St. Luke only at the approach of the Passion (Luke 18:15), and in what precedes they have nothing in common with him except the discussion on divorce (Matt. 19:1–12; Mark 10:1–12).

Section VIII. Part Peculiar to St. John

This section escapes controversy, for the Evangelist carefully indicates the order and the dates of Jesus' movements. The Saviour arrives at Jerusalem in the middle of the octave of the Feast of Tabernacles, near the beginning of October (John 7:14), and then goes to Perea (John 10:40); he returns to Jerusalem for the Feast of Dedication, toward the middle of December (John 10:22), and then goes back again to Perea (John 10:40). The death of Lazarus draws him to Bethany (John 11:17), after which he takes refuge in Ephrem, a little before the last Passover (11:54–55). See in Vol. II, pp. 3–5, the reasons for considering independently, during this period, the section special to St. John and that special to St. Luke.

Section IX. Part Peculiar to St. Luke

(Cf. Table, pp. 538–539)

We shall divide this section into three groups of texts in order to facilitate comparison.

1. In the *first group,* which includes several passages placed by St. Matthew in other contexts, St. Luke's order seems better almost throughout.

The framework is a journey from Galilee to Jerusalem. Repulsed by the Samaritans (*a*), Jesus sends the Seventy-Two out on a mission (*c*), arrives at Jericho (*h*), at Bethany (*i*), and at the Mount of Olives (*j*), where it is probable that he taught the Lord's Prayer.

It is quite possible that the requests of the three candidates (*b*) were not all made at the same time; in any case, they are in place at the time when Jesus leaves Galilee, not to return again. The curse leveled against the Galilean cities (*d*) also comes very naturally after his definitive departure from Galilee. The words "I praise thee, Father" (*e*) and "Blessed are you" (*f*) are linked very closely in St. Mark with the return of the Seventy-Two, whereas in St. Matthew the connection with the context is much more vague ("at that time"). In St. Luke, the precept of charity (*g*) serves as an introduction to the parable of the charitable Samaritan, but the context in St. Matthew is also good, and it has the support of St. Mark. It would seem that our Lord enunciated the precept twice; once in answer to the question of the lawyer (Luke), once again in answer to the question of the Scribes (Mark) and the Pharisees (Matthew).

The parable of the Importunate Friend (*k*) and the instruction on the efficacy of prayer (*l*) can be placed nowhere better than after the Lord's Prayer. The *Our Father* was taught to the Apostles at their express request (Luke 11:1); St. Luke does not give it a definite place (ἐν τόπῳ τινί), but since he reports it immediately after the scene at Bethany, it may be conjectured that it was near the Mount of Olives, not far from the place where the church of the Pater Noster now stands.

2. The *second group* has the appearance of an accumulation of diverse elements linked by an association of ideas or reminiscences, or by some other connection which we cannot determine. We agree in general with the following judgment of Maldonatus: "Quia materia similis erat, Evangelista res diverso loco gestas uno loco posuit. Solent Evangelistae hoc facere." However, we do not go so far with him as to say that Judea was the theater of Chapter XI, and Galilee that of Chapter XII. We should rather be inclined to think that St. Luke is following his source, without concerning himself about topography or chronology.

In the Judean period, that is, in the last half year of Christ's life we list all the passages peculiar to St. Luke (*f, k, n, q, r*), except perhaps *b*, for lack of a better place to assign to them. We would prefer St. Matthew's order when it has the support of St. Mark (*a, c, i, j, o*). About the rest, it is difficult to decide. The lamp (*d*) is introduced better in St. Matthew; the Eye the Light of the Body (*e*) is placed better in St. Luke. The indictment of the Scribes and Pharisees (*g*) is better located in St. Matthew than in St. Luke, where Jesus pronounces it at the table of a Pharisee whose guest he is; but the Saviour may have stigmatized the hypocrisy of the Pharisees more than once. On the other hand, the instruction on confidence and detachment (*l* and *m*), inserted by St. Matthew into the Sermon on the Mount, comes very appropriately after the parable of the Foolish Miser (*k*). As for the exclamation "Beatus venter" (*b*), though it is peculiar to St. Luke, it is so closely linked with what precedes that it seems to belong to the Galilean period (like *a*).

3. The *third group* contains seven beautiful parables of St. Luke (*a, l, m, n, q, x, y*) and three miracles (*b, g, v*) which he alone reports. It is a disputed question whether the parable of the Invited Guests in St. Luke (*h*) is the same as that of St. Matthew (cf. Vol. II. pp. 217–218). The apostrophe "Jerusalem, Jerusalem" (*f*) is doubtless more appropriately placed by St. Matthew on the eve of the Passion, but the section on the Parousia can very well remain where St. Luke has placed it, for St. Matthew gathers everything relating to this subject into Chapter XXIV. As to the three disparate maxims (*p*), it

requires a miracle of ingenuity to find a place for them. However, cf. Knabenbauer, *In Lucam*, pp. 469–471.

Section X. Part Common to the Three Synoptics

Here the three Evangelists keep pace with one another, except that St. Matthew inserts the parable of the Laborers in the Vineyard before the arrival at Jericho, and St. Luke places the episode of Zacheus after the entry into the city. St. Luke also links the parable of the Minas very closely to the episode of Zacheus, while St. Matthew uses this parable as a kind of introduction to the description of the Last Judgment, if we suppose that the parable of the Talents is identical with that of the Minas.

4. The Passion, Death, and New Life

Section XI. The First Four Days of Holy Week

St. Mark informs us with more precision than the others that when Jesus went up to the Temple on Palm Sunday, he stayed there only a short time because of the lateness of the hour (Mark 11:11), and then took the road back to Bethany with his Apostles. If it were not for this information, we would have placed on that Sunday evening the attempt of the Gentiles to see Jesus, which is related by St. John immediately after the triumphal entry into Jerusalem; and also the episode of the expulsion of the buyers and sellers from the Temple, which St. Matthew reports in the same place.

It was therefore on Monday morning, when he was coming back from Bethany, that the Saviour cursed the barren fig tree. The curse had its effect suddenly, and the tree immediately withered (Matt. 21:19), but the Apostles did not notice it until the next day (Mark 11:20). The buyers and sellers were also driven out of the Temple on Monday. No other event is mentioned on that day.

On Tuesday the Scribes and Priests demand to know by what right Jesus had done these things. The battle is joined and lasts all that day. First the Saviour propounds three parables (the Two Sons, the Wicked Vinedressers, the Guests Refusing to Come to the Banquet) symbolically representing the reprobation of Israel. He then sustains the successive attacks of the Herodians urged on by the Pharisees, the attacks of the Sadducees, and those of the Pharisees themselves. Then he takes the offensive and reduces them all to silence. At this point St. Matthew introduces the great indictment of the Scribes and Pharisees (Chapter XXIII) which St. Mark (12:38–40) and St. Luke (20:45–47) both mention briefly, St. Luke having reported it on another occasion. For a while there follows a pause. Jesus rests in the

Women's Court, where he sees the poor widow bringing her alms. He leaves there to go forth to the Mount of Olives, and, with only his Apostles as audience, describes the destruction of Jerusalem, the end of the world, and the Last Judgment.

Wednesday is signalized by only two incidents: the conspiracy of all the enemies of Jesus, and the treason of Judas. The first two Evangelists seem to put the feast at Bethany on this same day, since they recount it between the conspiracy of the Jews and the bargain of the traitor. But, since this repast is evidently identical with the feast which St. John dates with precision (John 12:1: "six days before the Passover"), it must be concluded that the Synoptics simply intend to indicate a relationship between the anointing at Bethany and the death and burial of Jesus. Mark 14:8 — "she has anointed my body beforehand for burial." Likewise Matt. 26:12.

Section XII. Holy Thursday. The Last Supper

The first two Synoptics proceed here, as in the whole narrative of the Passion, step by step, and are obviously reproducing a catechesis already molded in set form. In his usual way, St. Matthew abridges what concerns the preparation of the Passover, while St. Mark inserts details which seem to be personal memories. The harmony between them is much closer in the denunciation of the traitor, the institution of the Holy Eucharist, and Jesus' conversation with his Apostles on the road to Gethsemani. They seem to be drawing from the same oral or written source.

In this section, St. Luke and St. John go each his own way, except that St. Luke, in what concerns the preparation for the Passover, unquestionably depends on St. Mark both for facts and expression (*κεράμιον ὕδατος, βαστάζων, οἰκοδεσπότης, τὸ κατάλυμα, ἀνάγαιον μέγα ἐστρωμένον*). Since St. Luke omits the conversation on the road to Gethsemani, everything in his account takes place in the Cenacle, and in the following order: (*a*) desire to celebrate this last Passover with the Apostles; (*b*) blessing of the wine of the feast (22:17–18); (*c*) institution of the Eucharist under two species (22:19–20); (*d*) denunciation of the traitor (22:21–23); (*e*) the dispute among the Apostles and the lesson in humility (22:24–30); (*f*) prediction of Peter's temptation and denial (22:31–34); (*g*) recalling the past and the incident of the two swords (22:35–38); (*h*) going out to the Mount of Olives (22:39). It would seem that St. Luke does not intend a strict chronological order, since he combines what happened in the Cenacle and what happened on the road to Gethsemani, and he puts the consecration of the chalice, which took place after the repast

(22:20: μετὰ τὸ δειπνῆσαι), before the denunciation of the traitor, which occurred during the meal (Matt. 26:21; Mark 14:18).

St. John's precise recollection will help us to arrange events. At the beginning, the washing of the feet with an instruction on humility coinciding with the one which, in St. Luke, is provoked by the dispute among the Apostles; then, during the meal, the denunciation of the traitor, who goes out after swallowing the morsel dipped in sauce, which is certainly not the Eucharistic Bread (John 13:30). Since the chalice was consecrated *only at the end of the meal,* and since there is no reason to separate the two consecrations, Judas cannot have been present at the institution of the Eucharist. The only doubtful point is the place for the prediction of Peter's denial. The first two Evangelists clearly place the prediction on the road to Gethsemani, and if the other two seem to indicate the Cenacle, it is because they have no place else to insert it, since they do not relate what occurred on the walk from the Cenacle to the Garden.

Section XIII. Good Friday. The Passion

St. Matthew and St. Mark go hand in hand here, but while the latter does no more than add descriptive details and the incident of the youth who escapes naked from the hands of the servants (Mark 14:51–52), the former inserts various episodes: the end of Judas (Matt. 27:3–10), the dream of the Procurator's wife (Matt. 27:19), Pilate washing his hands (Matt. 27:24–25), the dead coming forth from their tombs (Matt. 27:52–53); after which he rejoins St. Mark, and they continue their way together.

St. Luke is influenced at several points by a different tradition. He omits the conversation that took place on the way to Gethsemani and reports the substance of it in the Cenacle (the prediction of the denial by Peter, and the incident of the two swords). He abridges the account of the Agony in the Garden, but adds the apparition of the consoling Angel and the sweat of blood. He mentions the healing of Malchus, who was wounded by St. Peter (Luke 22:51). But it is especially in the narrative of the trial of Jesus that he separates himself from the others. The triple denial by Peter and the scene of mockery are reported before the interrogation, and this takes place in the morning, the meeting at night in the palace of Caiphas being passed over in silence. St. Luke alone mentions the sending of Jesus to Herod; on the other hand, he omits the crowning with thorns and the mock enthronement in the court of the Praetorium. The meeting with the women of Jerusalem, the absolution of the Good Thief, and the prayer of the Saviour at the moment of death, all show that he is drawing from an independent tradition.

St. John has scarcely anything in common with the Synoptics except the general framework and the principal lines. He supposes their account to be well known, but he completes and clarifies it in passing. Everywhere he reveals himself to be an eyewitness. The detachment of Roman soldiers is commanded by a *tribune;* it is Peter that cuts off the right ear of *Malchus,* the *manservant* of the High Priest; there is a parley at the *gate of the house of Annas* to introduce Peter, who is recognized by a kinsman of Malchus. The questioning by Pilate revolves about the *kingship* of the Saviour, and this is finally the motive of the condemnation after the dramatic scene of the *Ecce Homo.* On Calvary, four points hold John's attention: the title on the Cross affirming the Saviour's kingship; the testament by which he entrusts his mother to the beloved disciple and his disciple to his mother; the piercing of Jesus' side by the lance and the flowing forth of blood and water; and the "consummatum est" which fulfills the prophecies.

For Section XIV, see Note X: *Apparitions of the Risen Christ.*

The narrative of the apparitions in St. Mark and St. Luke could lead one to think that there were no apparitions outside Judea, and also that the Ascension followed very shortly after the Resurrection. But in the Acts of the Apostles (1:3), St. Luke tells us that forty days elapsed between these two events; and St. Mark himself alludes twice (14:28; 16:7) to apparitions in Galilee.

PART TWO

SYNOPSIS OF THE FOUR GOSPELS

The life of Jesus Christ is here divided into four periods corresponding to the four books of this work. Each period is divided into several sections, as indicated in the preceding notes, to which we refer the reader for justification of the order adopted.

[The asterisks indicate departure from the French edition in order to supply missing texts or to correct apparent errors or misprints. *Translator.*]

1. Period of Preparation

Section I. The Hidden Life Up to the Baptism

	Matthew	*Mark*	*Luke*	*John*
Prologue of St. John				1:1–18
Preface of St. Luke			1:1–4	
Genealogy of Jesus	1:1–17		3:23–38	
Gabriel's Message to Zachary			1:5–25	
The Annunciation			1:26–38	
The Visitation—Birth of John			1:39–80	
The Ordeal of St. Joseph	1:18–25			
The Nativity — Adoration by the Shepherds			2:1–20	
The Circumcision — Presentation of Jesus in the Temple			2:21–38	
The Adoration by the Magi	2:1–12			
The Flight Into Egypt — Massacre of the Innocents	2:13–18			
The Holy Family at Nazareth	2:19–23		2:39–40*	
Jesus in the Temple Among the Doctors			2:41–52*	

Section II. From the Baptism to the Second Miracle at Cana

	Matthew	*Mark*	*Luke*	*John*
Preaching of John in the Desert	3:1–12	1:1–8	3:1–18	
Baptism of Jesus in the Jordan	3:13–17	1:9–11	3:21–22	
The Fast and Triple Temptation of Jesus	4:1–11	1:12–13	4:1–13	
Witness Rendered to Jesus by John the Baptist				1:19–34
The First Five or Six Disciples				1:35–51
The Wedding at Cana — Transfer to Capharnaum				2:1–12
The First Passover — The Driving of the Vendors From the Temple				2:13–25
Visit of Nicodemus by Night				3:1–21
Sojourn in Judea — Jesus Baptizes				3:22–36
Imprisonment of the Baptist	(14:3–4)	(6:17–18)	(3:19–20)	4:1–3
The Samaritan Woman — Return to Galilee				4:4–45*
Cure of Son of Royal Official				4:46–54*

2. Apostolate in Galilee and the North of Palestine

Section III. Up to the Sermon on the Mount

	Matthew	*Mark*	*Luke*	*John*
The Kingdom of God Is Near	4:12–17*	1:14–15	4:14–15	
Call of the Four Great Apostles	4:18–22	1:16–20	5:1–11	
The Demoniac in the Synagogue		1:21–28	4:31–37	
Cure of Peter's Mother-in-Law	8:14–15	1:29–31	4:38–39	
Many Miracles — Enthusiastic Acclaim	{ 8:16–17* 4:23–25	1:32–39	4:40–44*	
Cure of a Leper	8:1–4	1:40–45	5:12–16	
The Paralytic Carried by Four	9:1–8	2:1–12	5:17–26	
Call of Matthew — Feast at Matthew's House	9:9–17	2:13–22	5:27–39	
The Grain Plucked on the Sabbath	12:1–8	2:23–28	6:1–5	
The Man With the Withered Hand	12:9–14	3:1–6	6:6–11	
Concourse of Crowds — Choice of the Twelve	{ 4:23–25 12:15–21*	3:7–19	6:12–19	
Sermon on the Mount. Cf. Note J.	5:1–7:29		6:20–49	

Section IV. From the Sermon on the Mount to the Parables

	Matthew	*Mark*	*Luke*	*John*
The Relatives of Jesus Seek to Lay Hold of Him	(12:46–47)	3:20–21	(8:19)	
Controversy With the Pharisees	12:24–32	3:22–30	11:15–22	
The Servant of the Centurion	8:5–13		7:1–10	
The Son of the Widow of Naim			7:11–17	
The Embassy From John the Baptist	11:2–6		7:18–23	
Eulogy of John the Baptist	11:7–19		7:24–35	
The Sinful Woman Anoints the Saviour's Feet			7:36–50	
Holy Women in the Saviour's Retinue			8:1–3	
The Spiritual Relatives of Jesus	12:48–50	3:31–35	8:20–21	
The Parables of the Kingdom. Cf. Note K.	13:1–52	4:1–34	8:4–18 13:18–21	

Section V. From the Parables to the Bread of Life

	Matthew	*Mark*	*Luke*	*John*
Calming of the Tempest — The Gerasene Demoniac	8:23–34	4:35–5:20	8:22–39	
The Daughter of Jairus — The Woman With the Issue of Blood	9:18–26	5:21–43	8:40–56	
Cure of Two Blind Men and a Dumb Man	9:27–34			
A Visit to Nazareth	13:53–58	6:1–6	(4:16–30)	
Mission of the Twelve — Discourse	9:35–11:1*	6:7–13	9:1–6	
Herod's Anxiety About Jesus	14:1–2	6:14–16	9:7–9	
Martyrdom of the Baptist	14:3–12	6:17–29		
First Multiplication of Loaves	14:13–21	6:30–44	9:10–17	6:1–13
The Multitude Wishes to Proclaim Jesus King				6:14–16
Jesus Walks on the Water	14:22–33	6:45–52		6:16–21
Discourse on the Bread of Life at Capharnaum				6:22–71
The Paralytic of Bethesda and Discourse				5:1–47

Section VI. In Phoenicia and the Decapolis

	Matthew	*Mark*	*Luke*	*John*
Miracles in Genesareth	14:34–36	6:53–56		
Denunciation of the Pharisees	15:1–20	7:1–23		
Around Tyre and Sidon — The Chanaanite Woman	15:21–28	7:24–30		
The Decapolis Deaf-mute	15:29–31*	7:31–37		
Second Multiplication of Loaves	15:32–39	8:1–10		
Leaven of the Pharisees	16:1–12	8:11–21		
The Blind Man of Bethsaida		8:22–26		

Section VII. Last Days in Galilee

	Matthew	*Mark*	*Luke*	*John*
The Confession of Peter	16:13–20	8:27–31	9:18–20	
First Prediction of the Passion	16:21–23	8:32–33	9:21–22	
The Following of Christ	16:24–28	8:34–9:1	9:23–27	
The Transfiguration	17:1–8	9:2–8	9:28–36	
Descent From Thabor	17:9–13	9:9–13		
The Lunatic Boy at Thabor	17:14–21	9:14–29	9:37–42*	
Second Prediction of the Passion	17:22–23	9:30–32	9:43–45	
The Tax of the Didrachma	17:24–27			
The Simplicity of Little Ones	18:1–5	9:33–37	9:46–48	
The Stranger Exorcist		9:38–41	9:49–50	
Warning Against Scandal	18:6–10	9:42–49	(17:1–2)	
Fraternal Correction	18:15–22		(17:3–4)	
The Unmerciful Servant	18:23–35*			

3. Apostolate in Perea and Judea

Section VIII. Part Peculiar to St. John

	John
At Jerusalem for the Feast of Tabernacles	7:1–13
Opposition and Conspiracy of the Pharisees	7:14–52
The Adulteress	7:53–8:11
Relation Between the Son and the Father	8:12–30
Sons of Abraham, Sons of Satan	8:31–59
Cure of the Man Born Blind	9:1–41
The Good Shepherd	10:1–21
At Jerusalem for the Feast of Dedication	10:22–42
The Raising of Lazarus From the Dead	11:1–53
Retirement to Ephrem	11:54–57

Section IX. Part Peculiar to St. Luke

Group 1	*Luke*	*Matthew*	*Mark*
a) The Inhospitable Samaritans	9:51–56		
b) The Three Petitioners	9:57–62	8:19–22	
c) The Mission of the Seventy-Two	10:1–12	10:7–15*	
d) Woe to Thee, Corozain	10:13–15	11:20–24*	
e) I praise Thee, Father	10:16–22	11:25–27 11:28–30*	
f) Blessed Are You	10:23–24	13:16–17	
g) The Great Precept of Charity	10:25–28	22:34–40	12:28–31
h) The Good Samaritan	10:29–37		
i) At the Home of Martha and Mary	10:38–42		
j) The Lord's Prayer	11:1–4	6:9–13	
k) Parable of the Importunate Friend	11:5–8		
l) The Answered Prayer	11:9–13	7:7–11	

Group 2	*Luke*	*Matthew*	*Mark*
a) The Agent of Beelzebub	11:14–26	12:22–45	3:22–27
b) Beatus Venter Qui Te Portavit	11:27–28		
c) The Sign of Jonas. The Ninivites	11:29–32	(12:38–42)	8:11–12
d) The Lamp and the Lampstand	11:33	5:15	
e) The Eye, the Light of the Body	11:34–36	6:22–23	
f) Repast at the House of a Pharisee	11:37–38		
g) Indictment of the Scribes and Pharisees	11:38–54	23:4–36	
h) Fear Not Men but God	12:2–9	10:26–33*	
i) The Sin Against the Holy Spirit	12:10	(12:31–32)*	3:28–29
j) Haled Before Tribunals	12:11–12	10:16–20	13:11
k) The Foolish Miser	12:13–21		
l) Confidence in God	12:22–32	6:25–34*	
m) Lay up Treasure in Heaven	12:33–34	6:19–21	
n) Blessed Is the Watchful Servant	12:35–38		
o) You Know Not the Hour the Thief Comes!	12:39–40	24:43–44	13:35–36
p) The Conscientious and Careless Steward	12:41–46	24:45–51	
q) Punishment of the Wicked Servant	12:47–48		
r) Kindling the Fire. Baptism of Sorrows	12:49–50		
s) I Come to Bring War and Discords	12:51–53	10:34–36	
t) Signs of the Times	12:54–56	16:2–3	
u) The Duty of Reconciliation	12:57–59	5:25–26	

Group 3	*Luke*	*Matthew*	*Mark*
a) The Barren Fig Tree. Penance!	13:1–9		
b) The Stooped Woman	13:10–17		
c) The Mustard Seed and the Leaven	13:18–21	(13:31–33)	4:30–32
d) The Narrow Gate	13:22–30	(7:13–23)	
e) Go, Tell That Fox (Herod)	13:31–33		
f) Jerusalem! Jerusalem!	13:34–35	(23:37–39)	
g) Cure of the Man With Dropsy	14:1–6		
h) Parable of the Guests Invited to the Feast	14:7–24	(22:1–10)	
i) Requisite of the True Disciple	14:25–26	(10:37–38)	
j) Take Thought of the Cost!	14:27–35		9:50
k) Parable of the Lost Sheep	15:1–7	(18:11–14)*	
l) Parable of the Lost Drachma	15:8–10		
m) Parable of the Prodigal Son	15:11–32		
n) Parable of the Unjust Steward	16:1–13		
o) Denunciation of the Avarice of the Pharisees	16:14–15		
p) Three Disparate Maxims	16:16–18	(11:12–13)	
q) Lazarus and the Evil Rich Man	16:19–31		
r) Woe to Givers of Scandal	17:1–2	18:6–9	9:42–48
s) Fraternal Correction	17:3–4	(18:15, 21–22)	
t) Lord, Increase Our Faith	17:5–6	(17:20)	
u) The Servant's Duty	17:7–10		
v) The Ten Lepers	17:11–19		
w) The Coming of the Son of Man	17:20–37	(24:26–41)	(13:1–37)
x) Parable of the Unjust Judge	18:1–8		
y) The Pharisee and the Publican	18:9–14		

Section X. Part Common to the Three Synoptics

	Matthew	*Mark*	*Luke*
The Question of Divorce	19:1–12	10:1–12	(16:18)
Blessing of the Little Children	19:13–15	10:13–16	18:15–17
If Thou Wilt Be Perfect	19:16–22	10:17–22	18:18–23*
The Danger of Riches	19:23–26	10:23–27	18:24–27
And They That Have Left All?	19:27–30	10:28–31	18:28–30
The Workers Coming at the Eleventh Hour	20:1–16		
Third Prediction of the Passion	20:17–19	10:32–34	18:31–34*
Aspiration of the Sons of Zebedee	20:20–23*	10:35–40	
Exhortation to Humility	20:24–28	10:41–45	(22:24–27)
The Blind Bartimeus at Jericho	20:29–34	10:46–52	18:35–43
Zacheus the Publican			19:1–10*
Parable of the Talents or Minas	25:14–30		19:11–27

4. The Passion, Death, and New Life

Section XI. The First Days of Holy Week

	Matthew	*Mark*	*Luke*	*John*
Saturday, Banquet at Bethany	(26:6–13)	(14:3–9)		12:1–11
Palm Sunday	21:1–16	11:1–10	19:28–38	12:12–19
Prediction of the Ruin of Jerusalem			19:39–44*	
The Gentiles Desire to See Jesus				12:20–36
Return to Bethany	21:17	11:11	(21:37–38)	
Monday. Cursing of the Fig Tree	21:18–19	11:12–14		
Expulsion of Sellers From Temple	21:12–13	11:15–18	19:45–48*	
Return to Bethany		11:19		
Tuesday. The Withered Fig Tree	21:20–22	11:20–25		
By What Authority?	21:23–27	11:27–33	20:1–8	
The Two Sons (Jew and Gentile)	21:28–32			
The Wicked Vinedressers	21:33–46	12:1–12	20:9–19	
Guests Invited to the Wedding	22:1–14		(14:16–24)*	
Tribute to Caesar	22:15–22	12:13–17	20:20–26	
Whose the Wife Married to Seven?	22:23–33	12:18–27	20:27–40	
Which Is the Greatest Commandment	22:34–40	12:28–34	(10:25–28)	
The Christ, Whose Son Is He?	22:41–46	12:35–37	20:41–44	
Denunciation of Scribes and Pharisees	23:1–36	12:38–40	{ 20:45–47* 11:39–54	
Woe to Jerusalem!	23:37–39		13:34–35	
The Widow's Mite		12:41–44	21:1–4	
Prediction of the Ruin of the Temple	24:1–3	13:1–4	21:5–7	
Eschatological Discourse	24:4–51	13:5–37	21:8–36	
Parable of the Ten Virgins	25:1–13			
The Last Judgment	25:31–46			
Wednesday. Conspiracy of the Jews	26:1–5	14:1–3	22:1–2*	
The Bargain of Judas	26:14–16	14:10–11	22:3–6	
The Mystery of the Unbelief of the Jews				12:37–50

Section XII. Holy Thursday. The Last Supper

	Matthew	*Mark*	*Luke*	*John*
Preparation of the Passover	26:17–19	14:12–16	22:7–13	
The Washing of the Feet				13:1–11
Example of Humility	(20:25–28)	(10:42–45)	22:24–30	13:12–17
With Desire Have I Desired			22:14–18	
Denunciation of the Traitor	26:20–25	14:17–21	22:21–23	13:18–19
Departure of Judas				13:30–31
Institution of the Eucharist	26:26–29	14:22–25	22:19–20	
Discourse After the Supper				13:32–17–26
On the Road to Gethsemani	26:30–35	14:26–31	(22:31–39)	18:1

Section XIII. Good Friday. The Passion

	Matthew	*Mark*	*Luke*	*John*
The Agony in the Garden	26:36–46	14:32–42	22:40–46	
Consoling Angel. Sweat of Blood			22:43–44	
The Arrest of Jesus	26:47–56	14:43–50	22:47–53	18:2–11
Episode of the Youth		14:51–52		
Jesus at the House of Annas				18:12–23
Jesus at the House of Caiphas	26:57	14:53	22:54	18:24
Triple Denial by Peter	{ 26:58 { 26:69–75	{ 14:54 { 14:66–72	22:55–62	{ 18:15–18* { 18:25–27
Trial and Condemnation	26:59–66	14:55–64	22:66–71	
Insults and Ill-Treatment	26:67–68	14:65	22:63–65	
Jesus Led to Pilate	27:1–2	15:1	23:1	18:28
First Questioning by Pilate	27:11–14*	15:2–5	23:2–5	18:29–38
Jesus Sent to Herod and Back			23:6–16	
Barabbas or Jesus?	27:15–23	15:6–14	23:17–21*	18:39–40
Pilate Washes His Hands	27:24–25			
The Scourging	27:26	15:15	23:22	19:1
The Crowning With Thorns	27:27–31	15:16–20		19:2–3
Ecce Homo!				19:4–5
Sentence of Condemnation	27:26	15:15*	23:23–25*	19:6–16
The Road to Calvary	27:32	15:21	23:26–32	19:17
The Crucifixion. Division of Garments. Mockery	27:33–43	15:22–32*	23:33–38*	19:18–24*
The Good and the Bad Thief	27:44	15:32*	23:39–43*	
Mary and John at the Foot of the Cross				19:26–27*
My God, My God! . . . I Thirst	27:45–49*	15:33–36*		19:28–29
Death of Jesus. Prodigies	27:50–54	15:37–39	23:44–48*	19:30
The Women From Galilee	27:55–56*	15:40–41*	23:49*	19:25
The Pierced Side				19:31–37
The Burial of Jesus	27:57–61	15:42–47	23:50–56	19:38–42*
Guards Placed at the Tomb	27:62–66			
Despair and Death of Judas	27:3–10		Act. 1: 16–19	

Section XIV. *Jesus Christ Risen from the Dead*

	Matthew	*Mark*	*Luke*	*John*
The Resurrection of Jesus	28:2–4			
The Holy Women at the Empty Tomb	28:1, 5–10	16:1–8	24:1–11	20:1
Peter and John at the Sepulcher			24:12*	20:2–10
Apparition to Mary Magdalene		16:9–11		20:11–18
The Guards Suborned by the Priests	28:11–15			
The Two Disciples at Emmaus		16:12–13	24:13–35	
Apparition of Christ in the Cenacle			24:36–43	20:19–23
Another Apparition Eight Days Later				20:24–29
First Epilogue of John				20:30–31
On the Shore of the Lake of Tiberias				21:1–23
On a Mountain in Galilee	28:16–20*	16:14–18		
The Ascension		16:19–20	24:44–53	
Second Epilogue of John				21:24–25

Partial synopses will be found in the Supplementary Notes. Thus: Note J: *Analysis of the Sermon on the Mount;* Note K: *List of Parables and Similitudes;* Note L: *List of Miracles Recounted in the Gospel;* Note X: *Apparitions of the Risen Christ* (see Vol. II).

An examination of the *doublets,* i.e., discourses or narratives occurring twice in the same Gospel, is of interest in the study of the Synoptic Question. We have treated this subject in the *Revue Biblique,* 1898, pp. 541–553. A remarkable and more recent work is that of Hawkins, *Horae Synopticae* (Oxford, 1909), pp. 80–107.

VOLUME II

BOOK THREE

THE GOSPEL IN PEREA AND JUDEA

CHAPTER I

Toward Jerusalem

1. Departure for Judea and Perea

THE period upon which we are now entering is the richest in divine teachings and the poorest in outward events. The theater of action, the staging, the scenery, and the actors are all abruptly changed. The Gospel is shifted from the hills of Galilee and the lake shore of Bethsaida to the mountain country of Judea and the plains of Perea. St. Mark and St. Matthew, who have so charmingly told the story of the first phase of Jesus' preaching, are now silent; they do not rejoin the third Evangelist until the approach of the Passion. St. Luke and St. John will henceforth be our guides. The latter, as is his wont, restricts himself to a few of the more striking episodes, never passing beyond the horizon of the Holy City, while St. Luke, more indifferent than ever to details of time and place, continually orients Jesus toward Jerusalem without bringing him to the end of the journey. The two accounts are complementary and mutually enlightening, but if any attempt were made to bring them forcibly together, it would be at the risk of distorting the perspective. Better to let them enjoy their independence.

Not that we can afford to neglect the hints they offer. St. John informs us that Jesus left Galilee and reached Jerusalem during the Feast of Tabernacles, at the beginning of October. Seeing that the Pharisees have designs upon his life, he retires to Perea but reappears in Jerusalem for the Feast of Dedication toward the middle of December. He then returns to Perea and remains there until the day when the death of Lazarus draws him back to

Bethany. Thereafter he takes refuge in Ephrem, a town situated not far from the northern border of Judea. Apparently the Passover is near at hand, and he does not wish to withdraw too far from Jerusalem, where the Cross awaits him. Such in brief are the last six months of the Saviour's life, according to St. John: two visits to Jerusalem, not counting the visit of the Passion; two sojourns in Perea, before and after the Feast of Dedication; one visit to Bethany to raise Lazarus from the dead; one brief stay at Ephrem on the eve of his death. These pieces of information provide a very firm chronological framework.[1]

We expect no such precision from St. Luke. True, on three occasions, without taking into account the journey that is to end on Calvary, he indicates a progress of Jesus toward Jerusalem. The temptation is strong to see here three distinct journeys, which would be identified with the three visits mentioned by St. John. But such rigid harmonizing cannot be effected without difficulty, so different are the viewpoints of the two Evangelists. The best that can be said of it is that it is not impossible.[2] Others hold that St. Luke is recording throughout only one journey, which proceeds by short stages, with extended interruptions and many detours, to carry the Gospel to groups of people who had not yet received it. In that case, Jesus, bearing constantly toward Jerusalem, would have spent about six months in arriving at his goal.[3] But the

---

[1] The movements of Jesus during these last six months:

In St. Luke	*In St. John*
a) Toward Jerusalem (9:51)	*a*) Jerusalem, Feast of Tabernacles (7:10)
b) At the home of Martha and Mary (10:38)	*b*) Sojourn in Perea (10:40)
c) Toward Jerusalem (13:22)	*c*) Jerusalem, Feast of Dedication (10:22)
d) Presence of Jesus in Perea (13:31)	*d*) Another Journey to Perea (πάλιν, 10:40)
e) Toward Jerusalem, coming from the North (17:11)	*e*) Bethany, Raising of Lazarus (11:17)
f) At Jerusalem, for the Passion (19:28)	*f*) Retirement to Ephrem (11:54)
	g) Jerusalem, for the Passion (12:12)

[2] The principal champion of this hypothesis is Wieseler, followed by Ellicott, Caspari, and others. Luke 9:51 would correspond to John 7:10; Luke 13:22 would correspond to John 10:22; Luke 17:11 would correspond to John 11:55. Levesque (*Revue Apol.*, Aug., 1929, pp. 132–140) has taken up this hypothesis and modified it.

[3] Godet, *Saint Luc,* 2 ed., Vol. II, pp. 5–6: "We find here (in Luke 9:51–19:28)

hypothesis does not stand up under examination. Besides the fact that it does not fit in well with the data of St. John, it leaves unexplained how Jesus, almost at the beginning of his journey, is at Bethany, less than two miles from the Holy City. He would then have marked time at the gates of Jerusalem, where he knew that the Pharisees were plotting his death.

From the day when he bids his last adieu to Galilee, Jesus keeps his gaze constantly fixed upon Jerusalem; and it is in that direction that St. Luke ceaselessly guides his steps, perhaps, as has been said, to seal the whole period with the seal of the Passion. Into this very elastic framework left vacant by his predecessors, St. Luke fits the documents which his researches have furnished him, without anxiety to classify them in any rigorous order. It is to this inspiration that we owe the charming pages which put the finishing touches to the intellectual and moral portrait of Christ. But since the minor details of time and place, which so disproportionately preoccupy us, were of little interest to the Evangelist, we must admit with St. Augustine that this or that episode or discourse may have been put in one place rather than another simply by anticipation or in retrospect.[4] St. Luke tells us only what we already know from the other Evangelists, that during this period the principal theater of Jesus' preaching was Perea.

The name Perea was applied to the country across the Jordan, and more particularly to a stretch of land bordering the river for about sixty-five miles, from the Lake of Tiberias to the Dead Sea. It was bounded on the east by steep wooded hills ending in a bare plateau adjacent to the wilderness. This region, which in ancient times had been allotted to the tribes of Ruben and Gad, was at this time occupied by a predominantly Jewish population hemmed in by pagan nations. On the north and east were the cities of the Decapolis; on the south lay the country

---

the sketch of a lengthy and prolonged journey. Jerusalem is and continues to be the constant goal of the journey; but Jesus advances only by short stages, stopping in each locality to preach the Gospel." So also Plummer and others.

[4] *De cons. evang.*, II, 23, n. 54: "Sed ille (Lucas) post plura, nec ipse sane expresso ordine temporum, sed recordantis modo, utrum quod prius omisit, an quod posterius etiam factum quam sunt ea quae sequuntur praeoccupavit, incertum est."

of Moab belonging to the king of the Nabateans. Not as rich nor as populous as Galilee, Perea was an agricultural region in which the towns were few and far between. The capital, an ancient city enlarged and fortified by Herod Antipas, faced Jericho on the opposite bank of the Jordan; but the customary residence of the tetrarch when he visited Perea was the fortress of Machaerus, where his father had built a splendid palace.[5] Perea was separated from Judea only by the river, which was fordable in several places. It was, however, far enough from Jerusalem to offer the Saviour a shelter from sudden attack.

St. Luke announces the change of scene with a solemnity of tone which is further heightened by the Biblical coloring of the language: "Now it came to pass that the days of his taking up being fulfilled, Jesus set his face steadfastly to betake himself to Jerusalem."[6] That is to say, "as the time approached when Christ must quit the world to go to his Father, he directed his steps firmly toward Jerusalem, where he knew that he must die."

The shortest and most traveled road from Galilee to Jerusalem crossed the entire width of Samaria. The Samaritans ordinarily

---

[5] Josephus, *Antiq.*, XVIII, ii, 1. The ancient name was Betharamphtha. Herod named it Livias in honor of Livia, the wife of Augustus. This name was changed to that of Julias when Livia, adopted into the *gens Julia* by the will of Augustus, became Julia Augusta.

[6] Luke 9:51. The *taking up*, that is, the departure of Jesus from this world for heaven, comprising his death, Resurrection, and Ascension. The word ἀνάλημψις is not found elsewhere in the Bible, but the corresponding verb frequently occurs to designate the Ascension (Mark 16:19; Acts 1:2, 11, 22). References in Plummer at Luke 9:51.

Set his face is a Semitic mode of expression for "firmly envisage a difficult and painful enterprise." The time has come to act, cost what it may; "the days are accomplished"; the final period is about to begin.

The first two Synoptics also mark very clearly the change of scene. St. Matthew says (19:1): "Having brought these discourses to a close, Jesus withdrew from Galilee and came to the confines of Judea beyond the Jordan." Instead of "*to the confines* of Judea" one might translate "into the *country* of Judea," for ὅρια means either, but this would involve a conflict of data. Being *in Perea* is not being *in Judea,* but on its boundaries, since the Jordan is the natural boundary of these two provinces. St. Mark says (10:1): "Jesus leaving there (the Lake of Tiberias) came into the region of Judea *and* beyond the Jordan." He is not contradicting St. Matthew. He is simply mentioning the *two* fields of apostolic labor (the *et,* omitted in the Vulgate, is critically certain: καὶ πέραν τοῦ 'I). If the *et* is omitted, ὅρια must be translated, as in the Vulgate, "in *fines* Judaeae ultra Jordanem," in order to avoid the contradiction.

allowed free passage; but sometimes at the approach of their great feasts, which more often than not coincided with the feasts of the Jews, their fanaticism flared up, and they refused hospitality to pilgrims from Galilee. Travelers, therefore, did not linger overlong in Samaria, and used to plan their journey so as not to pass any more than one night there. However, in the rainy season it was necessary to make sure of a shelter, and so Jesus had sent forerunners to arrange for lodgings for his numerous following. In the village where they presented themselves the messengers saw all doors close in their faces. James and John, the "sons of thunder," said to our Lord: "Wilt thou that we make fire come down upon them to consume them?" In their desire to call down lightning upon this inhospitable people, the sons of Zebedee doubtless had in mind the horrible vengeance which, in other times and not far from here, the prophet Elias had drawn down upon his persecutors.[7] But they were forgetting that the spirit of the New Testament is not that of the Old. Our Lord recalls this to them in severe terms.[8] The very natural indignation of James and John would be even more understandable if, as some authors think, they had personally met with the rebuff.

Jesus and his escort directed their steps to some less fanatical village, apparently without immediately quitting the territory of the Samaritans.[9]

---

[7] A certain number of manuscripts add: "As Elias did." The scene to which allusion is made took place near Samaria, where King Ochosias fell sick (4 Kings 1:1–16).

[8] Luke 9:55: "Turning to them he rebuked them" (στραφεὶς δὲ ἐπετίμησεν αὐτοῖς). The Vulgate adds: *dicens: Nescitis cujus spiritus estis.* But the critics (even Vogels) reject the addition. The following addition: *Filius hominis non venit animas perdere sed salvare,* is even less well attested. Both, however, are an exact commentary on *increpavit illos.*

[9] Generally the hospitality of the Samaritans was not asked except when a halt was made in their territory, and it is difficult to suppose that the caravan could have left the borders of Samaria the same day. The words εἰς ἑτέραν (instead of ἄλλην) κώμην favor the sense that we have adopted without, however, demanding it.

2. The Three Aspirants[10]

Those who were desirous of following Jesus to share his labors were becoming more and more numerous, but some among them were inspired by calculated self-interest or by ephemeral enthusiasm which needed to be put to the test. Three such aspirants were encountered when our Lord was on his way to Jerusalem. It is not said that they arrived together or on the same day. St. Luke may very well have grouped them together to sketch with one stroke of the pen the various imperfect dispositions which the Master censures in those who wish to follow him, and the sacrifices he demands of them.

The first is an educated man — a Scribe, says St. Matthew — and he speaks with assurance: "Master, I will follow thee wherever thou goest." He has not seriously reflected on the breadth and the consequences of the offer he is making. The Master neither accepts nor rejects it. "The foxes have their lair and the birds of the air a place of refuge, but the Son of Man has not where to lay his head." These words, true as they were during the whole course of our Lord's public life, had become more literally true ever since he had quit Galilee; the incident of the Samaritans had just now proved that he was never sure of a shelter for the night. The bold aspirant is invited to estimate his own strength. Has he enough courage and abnegation to follow Jesus *wherever* he goes, even though it be to Calvary? He must sound the depths of his own soul: the decision is in his own hands.

We would like to know what that decision was. The Gospel does not inform us. The moral lesson has been given; all else is accessory. Still, we do not see on what grounds certain writers impute to the Scribe a wrong intention or compare him to the rich young man who was so taken aback and saddened by the prospect of quitting his fortune.[11] Granted that a little conceit and some lack of reflection had precipitated the step he took, his

---

[10] Luke 9:57–62. St. Matthew relates the first two requests, but in an altogether different context (8:19–22). Two differences of wording, interesting for the interpretation, will be noted later on.

[11] Among others, St. Jerome (on Matt. 8:19 ff.) and St. John Chrysostom.

offer seems sincere and devoid of hidden design. No more in this than in the following cases does the silence of the Gospel offer any basis for prejudgment.

Jesus does not wait for the second petitioner to formulate his request: he forestalls him and addresses to him the words, "Follow me." It is the same invitation that once before had transformed a Publican into an Apostle. Taken by surprise, the candidate asks for a delay: "Lord, permit me first to go bury my father." But the Master answers with a refusal: "Leave the dead to bury their dead; as for thee, come, preach the kingdom of God." Now, the request seemed legitimate and the refusal seems somewhat harsh. Harsh indeed, in the view of many interpreters, since the man was only asking the favor of going to attend his aged and sick father whose death was expected in a very short time. Jewish customs would seem to demand this explanation. In Palestine, then as now, burial followed shortly upon death. As soon as a sick man breathed his last, relatives and friends invaded the house of death to conduct the funeral ceremonies, which ordinarily took place the same day. Can it be thought that during so short an interval the son of a man who had already died had left the funeral bier to go to meet Jesus?

But the majority of Catholic interpreters, and also some Protestants, are of a different opinion. Jesus, they say, wishes to give us a lesson applicable to all ages, and to teach us that the service of God takes precedence over all other obligations, even the most sacred. The Old Law had before this forbidden the High Priest and the Nazirite to bury their father or mother with their own hands, in order to avoid contracting the legal uncleanness which would be communicated by contact with a dead body. This duty should be left to persons less specially consecrated to God. And does not the safety of the nation sometimes impose similar sacrifices? Can the soldier desert his post to go and embrace his dying brother or father? So it is with this man. Others will fulfill for him the duties of filial piety: let him answer without delay the voice of God calling him! The *dead,* the children of this world, will bury their *dead,* those who have breathed the same atmosphere with them. The soldiers of Christ have more pressing, more imperious duties. The battle is joined:

they must follow their leader to the end, to victory. This is what may be said in support of this explanation.

But the text of St. Matthew, if carefully read, suggests an explanation which, while not suppressing the difficulty, greatly lessens it.[12] Mark well, there is no question here of a stranger or of a chance meeting with someone previously unknown. Here there is question of a *disciple* already admitted into the Master's retinue, who receives the news of his father's death in the course of the journey and asks permission to go and bury him. Upon this disciple, whose generosity is known to him, Jesus imposes the painful and heroic sacrifice: "Leave the dead to bury their dead; as for thee, come (with me), preach the kingdom of God." Time is pressing, the occasion offers itself but once; perhaps Jesus has selected this disciple to be one of the Seventy-Two who are to be sent on a temporary mission after the fashion of apostles.

The third candidate offers himself spontaneously as did the first, and asks for a delay as did the second, but under different conditions. "I will follow thee, Lord, but suffer me first to go bid farewell to those of my family" or "to put in order the affairs of my house."[13] Before committing himself, this man lays down conditions: a circumstance which may throw doubt upon his sincerity. If he had fully decided to follow Jesus, he should have regulated his affairs and taken leave of his family. The maxim, "Do not today what can be put off until tomorrow," may be valid in diplomacy, but it is open to censure in the ordinary conduct of affairs. Tomorrow the Master will be far away, and a thousand

---

[12] Matt. 8:21: "Another of his disciples said to him: 'Lord, permit me, etc.'" Here therefore there is a question of a *disciple* who has already voluntarily given himself to Jesus and who is among his followers. It may well be that the imperative call, "Follow me," recorded by St. Luke on the occasion of the present scene, was actually given before this. But this last point is not important. Clement of Alexandria asserts that the name of this disciple was Philip (*Stromata,* III, 4). How does he know?

[13] Luke 9:61–62. The present Vulgate reading: *Permitte mihi primum renuntiare his quae domi sunt,* should be translated: "Permit me first to go to take leave of my family affairs." But the best manuscripts have *qui* instead of *quae,* meaning "to go to announce the affair to my family." This is also the meaning of the Greek, for ἀποτάξασθαι τοῖς εἰς τὸν οἶκόν μου does not mean "to regulate, put in order affairs (τοῖς, neuter) at my house," but rather, "to take leave of those (τοῖς, masculine) of my house."

difficulties may arise. "Whoever puts his hand to the plow and looks back is unworthy of the kingdom of God." This proverb, parallels of which are to be found in profane literature, needs no explanation.[14] The plowman who looks behind him will trace but a tortuous furrow; the runner of a race who takes his eye from the goal is renouncing the crown; the worker in the apostolate who aspires to do a work worthy of God must, like St. Paul, forget the past, to think only of the present and the future.[15] Jesus does not absolutely repel this aspirant with his too worldly views, but admonishes him to bring his dispositions into harmony with his desires, and to lift his soul to the level of his ambitions.[16] The Old Testament was not so insistent. When Elias spread his mantle over Eliseus to consecrate him as a prophet, the young disciple begged to be allowed first to embrace his father and mother; and his aged master consented. But the Law of Grace and the movement of the Holy Spirit disclose to us a much loftier ideal of perfection.

It will be recognized that among the disciples of Christ some content themselves with believing in him and putting his teachings into practice, while others attach themselves to him personally and follow in his footsteps. All bear the name of disciple, but the distance between them is that between the commandments and the counsels. The vocation of the first does not sever family ties or change outwardly their way of life, and thus their conversion may pass unnoticed. Others, responding to a special appeal of the Saviour, leave everything, property, parents, and fatherland, in order to follow him effectively in his apostolic journeys. The

---

14 Hesiod, *Works and Days,* 443; Pliny, *Hist. nat.,* XVIII, xix, 49. The Pythagoreans said: Εἰς τὸ ἱερὸν ἐπερχόμενος μὴ ἐπιστρέφου (If thou goest to the temple, turn not thy head); it is the axiom, *age quod agis,* applied to religious matters.

15 Phil. 3:13. "Forgetting that which is behind me and directing all my effort to what is before me, I press on toward the goal." It is clear from the context of St. Luke that the words "is not fit for the kingdom of God" do not mean "is incapable of entering into the kingdom of God," but "is not a useful worker or collaborator for the preaching of the kingdom of God." This is what the Greek εὔθετος accurately expresses, being said of an instrument which is *suitable, proper for its purpose,* and consequently *useful.*

16 Some have fancied that St. Luke is here recounting the story of his own conversion. The hypothesis is without foundation or likelihood.

appeal may assume the form of an imperative, "Follow me!" Thus did the call come to the four great Apostles and to Philip and Matthew, as it came to the candidate whose story we have just been recalling. But oftener the call is expressed in a simple counsel: "If thou wilt be perfect, sell thy goods and give the profit of them to the poor — and thou shalt have treasure in heaven — and then come, follow me"; or "If anyone will come after me, let him deny himself, let him take up his cross and follow me." This effective enlistment is offered to volunteers alone, for it demands total self-surrender without restriction, without reserve.[17] "If anyone come to me (to live my life, to share my work) and hate not his father, his mother, his wife, his brothers, and his sisters, he cannot be (in the strict sense of the word) my disciple." For such a one the love of God and zeal for souls will take the place of all other affection.

3. The Mission of the Seventy-Two

(LUKE 10:1–24)

It is from this chosen group that Jesus selects seventy-two pioneers to prepare the way for him. Were they seventy, or seventy-two? Authorities for and against (manuscripts, Fathers, versions) are almost equally divided.[18] What tips the scale in favor of seventy-two (the reading of the Vulgate) is that no reason can be assigned for introducing this reading were it not authentic, and several reasons can be conjectured to explain its being changed. Moses was assisted by a council of seventy elders,

---

[17] Matt. 19:21. To these volunteers is addressed the counsel to reflect well before committing themselves, Luke 14:25–33. This last text will be studied later.

[18] Luke 10:1. The reading ἑβδομήκοντα is adopted by the majority of critics (Tischendorf, Von Soden, Vogels, Scrivener); Lachman and Hort place δύο in parentheses; the Fathers (Tertullian, Eusebius, Basil, Ambrose) compare the Apostles to the *twelve* fountains and the disciples to the *seventy* palm trees of Elim (Exod. 15:27). On the other hand, many excellent Greek texts (note the agreement of *B* with *D*), the most ancient versions (Latin, Syriac, Sahidic), and a number of Fathers (Augustine, Epiphanius) sponsor the reading *seventy-two;* and the testimony of the other Fathers is impaired by their searching after symbolism. It was very easy to pass from *seventy-two* to *seventy:* the Seventy of the Septuagint, despite the name consecrated by usage, were in reality seventy-two, six from each tribe, according to legend (*Letter of Aristeas,* 46: ἀφ' ἑκάστης φυλῆς ἕξ, in Swete, *Introd. to the O.T. in Greek,* p. 528).

the Sanhedrin numbered seventy members, the nations of the earth enumerated in Genesis come to the total of seventy, the Pentateuch was said to have been translated into Greek by the Seventy. This number could easily have been substituted for seventy-two, which was much less usual and less susceptible of variations of symbolic interpretation. Let us therefore say seventy-two, without attributing to this detail more importance than it deserves.

When he sent forth the new missionaries two by two, Jesus gave them their instructions, just as on another occasion he had instructed the Twelve:

"The harvest is abundant, but the laborers are few; pray therefore the Master to send forth laborers to (collect) his harvest. Go: I send you forth as lambs into the midst of wolves.

"Carry neither purse, nor wallet, nor sandals, and greet no one on the way.

"Whatever house you enter, first say: 'Peace to this house': and if a son of peace be there, your peace shall rest upon him; if not, it shall return to you. Stay in that house, eating and drinking what they have with them, for the laborer has a right to his hire.

"Whatever town you enter, if they receive you, eat what is served you, cure the sick, and say to all: 'The kingdom of God is near.' If in the town that you have entered they do not receive you, go forth into the streets, saying: 'We shake off upon you even the dust of your town that has clung to our feet; yet know you that the kingdom of God is near.' I say to you, that on the day of judgment Sodom shall be less ill-treated than that town."

By force of circumstances, the instructions now given to the disciples are very much like those given on a previous occasion to the Apostles, for the situation is almost the same. They shall carry with them nothing but what is strictly needed, because the people who are to be evangelized should provide for their sustenance and see to their needs. Totally intent upon the work of God, they shall not tarry by the way, and shall not waste time in superfluous visits and salutations. They are sent out two by two either to offer mutual protection and assistance as occasion demands, or to bear witness to each other's actions, or to add weight and authority to their words. To the homes and cities that receive them they shall bring blessings and peace; they shall call down the vengeance of God upon those that reject them. The twelve Apostles had been invested with the power to cast out devils, and had been commanded to bring the Gospel only to the children of Israel. These two details are not expressly formulated in the mandate given to the seventy-two disciples; but we shall immediately see that they did cast out devils, and, though the Gospel does not so inform us, it is unlikely that they exercised their apostolate in pagan territory or in Samaria. The field of activity has simply shifted from Galilee to Judea and the country beyond the Jordan.

Their mission over, the Seventy-Two returned to their Master doubtless at a prearranged rendezvous. They could scarcely contain their joy. "Lord," they said, "in thy name even the devils are subject to us." Their pride in having been the instruments of these marvels is genuine and legitimate, for they attribute their success to its true cause: the power of the name of Jesus. With neither praise nor blame Jesus indicates to them a worthier and nobler motive for joy: "I beheld Satan fall from heaven like a flash of lightning. Behold, I have given you power to tread upon serpents and scorpions, and to render powerless all the might of the enemy. Yet rejoice not so much in having devils obey you as in having your names written in heaven."[19]

While the disciples were putting to flight the great adversary by the sole power of the Saviour's name, Jesus was contemplating in spirit Satan dispossessed of his empire and falling from the heights to which the sin of man had raised him. His fall is basically consummated at the moment when the Son of God, about to die, delegates to his Apostles and disciples the power to cast him out, and it continues with the precipitous rapidity of a thunderbolt.

---

[19] Luke 10:18–20: ἐθεώρουν τὸν Σατανᾶν ὡς ἀστραπὴν ἐκ τοῦ οὐρανοῦ πεσόντα. The imperfect (ἐθεώρουν) marks coincidence of time: "*While* you were expelling demons, *I was seeing* Satan fall." According to grammar, the translation could be: "I saw Satan fall as lightning falls from heaven" (joining ἐξ οὐρανοῦ with ἀστραπήν), but it is much more natural to understand it: "I saw Satan fall from heaven." The metaphor "fall from heaven," meaning "fall from an elevated rank," is a common one (cf. Matt. 11:23; Luke 10:16). Cicero employs it: "Collegam de coelo detraxisti" (*2 Phil.*, 42).

It is surprising that some of the Fathers of the Church and many commentators have thought that the Saviour is here calling to mind the revolt of Lucifer and his accomplices, with the purpose of humbling the pride of his disciples by reminding them of the fall of the rebel angels.[20] But the words of Christ, far from being a reproach, are, on the contrary, the expression of an intense joy. The disciples have every reason to rejoice at their victory over the infernal serpent; they are only forgetting that there is for them a source of more intimate joy, that is to say, the fact that their names are written in the Book of Life. There are two books in which the names of the friends of God are written: the book of predestination, from which no name shall ever be erased, and the book of knowledge of the present, which is always subject to revision. In what way are the names of the disciples written in the book of the just? Do all the disciples there present receive the assurance that their names shall never be erased? That is God's secret.

"In that same hour he thrilled with joy in the Holy Spirit, and said:

I praise thee, Father, Lord of heaven and earth,
for having hidden these things from the wise and clever
and for having revealed them to the little children.
Yes, Father, for such was thy good pleasure.
All things have been given me by my Father:
and no one knows who the Son is except the Father,
nor who the Father is except the Son,
and him to whom the Son chooses to reveal him."[21]

---

[20] Cf. Knabenbauer, *In Lucam,* p. 338. The Fathers suppose that our Lord is thinking of Isa. 14:12: "Quomodo cecidisti de coelo Lucifer?" It is possible that he is making an allusion to this passage, but that does not change the meaning. He is not speaking of the first fall of Lucifer, but of a new fall which presents some similarity to the first.

[21] Luke 10:21–22; Matt. 11:25–27. St. Matthew places this passage immediately after the cursing of the cities, with a vague transition which does not indicate precisely either the occasion or the audience: "At that time, Jesus answering said." St. Luke places it after the return of the seventy-two disciples. When he welcomes them, Jesus allows his joy to break forth (ἐν αὐτῇ τῇ ὥρᾳ ἠγαλλιάσατο).

The texts are identical in almost all details. In place of οὐδεὶς γινώσκει τίς ἐστιν ὁ υἱός . . . ὁ πατήρ (No one knows *who* the Son . . . the Father is, i.e., of what kind, what he is), St. Matthew has: οὐδεὶς ἐπιγινώσκει τὸν υἱόν . . . τὸν πατέρα

This thrill of joy of our Lord is unique in the Gospels. Having taken upon himself our nature, the Saviour must have experienced all feelings of which sin is neither the beginning nor the term: joy and sadness, fear and sorrow, satisfaction, displeasure, tenderness, indignation. But this is the first and only time that the Gospel depicts his joy by the expressive word which the news of the Incarnation suggested to Mary, and which the nuptials of the Lamb suggest to the Elect in the Apocalypse. Why this thrill, this sudden explosion of overflowing joy? Let us picture to ourselves the scene. Jesus has just cursed the three ungrateful cities for whose benefit he had expended so much, only to have his efforts and his zeal and love repaid by indifference and unbelief. The Scribes and Pharisees, not content with rejecting his message, have conspired together to neutralize his activity, and have succeeded in alienating from him all the people. And now the seventy-two disciples, simplehearted and obedient men, have accepted their mission with joyfulness; they make converts and work miracles and cast out devils; and far from being puffed up with their triumphs, conscious that they are powerless except in the strength of his name, they place at his feet the fruit of their labors, deeming themselves unprofitable servants. A baffling contrast which St. Paul frequently emphasizes, seeking the reason for it in divine Providence: "Brethren," he writes to the Corinthians, "consider that there are not among you many wise according to the flesh, not many mighty, not many noble. God has chosen what was foolish according to the world to confound the wise, what was feeble to confound the mighty, what was base and despised and, so to speak, nothing to destroy what was (something), that no one may glory in the sight of God."[22] And now

---

(No one *comprehends, knows perfectly,* the Son . . . the Father). The meaning is the same.

Instead of "I praise thee, Father, *for having hidden* this from the wise, etc.," it may be translated: "I praise thee, Father, *that, having hidden* this from the wise, thou hast revealed it to the humble." There are in Scripture numerous examples of this Hebrew construction (Matt. 23:25; cf. Isa. 12:1: Confiteor tibi Domine, quoniam iratus es mihi, conversus est furor tuus et consolatus es me), where the expression of praise refers only to the second member of the sentence. But here the first translation is acceptable and more generally admitted, because the blinding of the supposedly wise is on the part of God an act of wisdom.

[22] 1 Cor. 1:26–29; cf. 2 Cor. 4:3–4; Rom. 1:22.

Jesus seeing the "wise" who were puffed up with pride blinded by their own fault, and the simple and humble illuminated by divine light, praises the Father of mercies almost in the terms employed by Mary in her *Magnificat.*

Jesus recollects himself for a moment to meditate the mysterious ways of God in the salvation of the world. The initiative in it always belongs to the Father, but the Son is charged with the task of accomplishing it. The Word Incarnate is appointed universal Mediator between God and men; it is he that has the mission of revealing to men his Father, for he alone knows the Father perfectly. "My Father has delivered all things to me, and no one knows what the Son is except the Father, nor what the Father is except the Son, and him to whom the Son deigns to reveal him." A perfect knowledge, one that is adequate to its object, needs an intelligence that measures the object that is known. To know God in this way it is necessary to be God. "For," says St. Cyril of Alexandria, "he that is known by the Father alone is above all that can be conceived or spoken of; and the same is true of the Father, who is known by the Son alone. The holy and consubstantial Trinity, which is above all that can be conceived or expressed, can alone know itself."[23]

This passage of St. Luke and St. Matthew is, in the picturesque phrase of a Protestant exegete, like "an aerolite from the Johannean heavens."[24] It must be admitted that it has a Johannine flavor; hence the Rationalists, in order to get rid of a text which obstructs their theories, do not hesitate to mutilate it or declare it entirely apocryphal.[25] But since, according to the most elementary principles of sound criticism, it is impossible to deny

---

[23] St. Cyril of Alexandria, on Luke 10:22 (MG, LXXII, 672–673).

[24] Hase, *Geschichte Jesu,* p. 527, cited by Plummer.

[25] On this question we can do no better than refer the reader to the learned monograph of Schumacher, *Die Selbstoffenbarung Jesu bei Mt. xi, 27* (*Lk. x. 22*) (Freiburg i. B., 1922). Consult also Lebreton, *Histoire du dogme de la Trinité,* 6 ed., 1927, Vol. I, Note D, pp. 591–598 (English transl., 1939, Vol. I, pp. 433–435); Lagrange, *Saint Luc,* 1924, pp. 300–301; De Grandmaison, *Jésus-Christ,* Vol. II, Note Q, pp. 60–62 (English transl., 1938, Vol. II, pp. 331–334). Among the Rationalists who attack the text some (Renan, Loisy, Norden) simply reject its authenticity; others (Wellhausen, Harnack, Bultmann) mutilate it, since they will not admit that Jesus could have said: "No one knows the Father except the Son."

its authenticity, it must be agreed that St. Luke and St. Matthew, who reproduce it with variants which rule out any mutual dependence, know how to speak on occasion the language of St. John, just as St. Paul had done before them.

Turning then to the disciples, among whom the Apostles must be numbered, Jesus adds:

"Blessed are the eyes that see what you see! I say to you that many prophets and kings have desired to see what you see and did not see it, to hear what you have heard and did not hear it."[26]

The Father has revealed to the little ones and the lowly, mysteries that have remained hidden from the mighty, arrogant in their own knowledge and supposed wisdom. These lowly and little ones are the seventy-two disciples. After the episode that we have recounted they go back into the shadows and disappear from the scene. Eusebius informs us that in the fourth century there existed no authentic list of their names. The lists fabricated later, linking them with famous names, are devoid of all historical value.[27] Still it is natural to number among them St. Matthias who was destined to fill out the number of the Twelve, and also his competitor Joseph Barsabas surnamed Justus, for both of them had followed the Saviour from the beginning. And, considering the role that he played in the history of the primitive Church, the name of Barnabas may be added to these. All else is empty conjecture.

4. The Good Samaritan

(LUKE 10:25–37)

It was apparently after the return of the Seventy-Two and on the road to Jerusalem that a certain lawyer approached the Saviour and proposed to him this question: "Master, what must

---

[26] Luke 10:23–24. In Matt. 13:16–17, the discourse is addressed to the Apostles, who were doubtless with Jesus when the Seventy-Two returned, so that it could have been addressed to both groups. St. Matthew has simply taken it out of its proper place.

[27] Eusebius, *Hist. eccl.,* I, 12, cites some curious theories of Clement of Alexandria. On the lists falsely attributed to St. Hippolytus, St. Epiphanius, and Dorotheus, cf. Scherman, *Propheten-und Apostellegenden, nebst Jüngerkatalog,* 1907, in *T.U.,* XLII, 3.

I do to gain eternal life?"[28] His intention was not precisely to set a trap for Jesus, but to test him, to discover whether or not the reputation of this young teacher from Galilee was overrated.[29] The answer to his question was easy. All that was needed was for him to open the Bible, and to this authority Jesus refers his questioner: "What is written in the Law? How readest thou?" The Scribe has his answer ready: "Thou shalt love the Lord with thy whole heart, with thy whole soul, with thy whole strength, with thy whole mind, and thy neighbor as thyself."

The precept of the love of God was written at the beginning of the profession of faith that every Israelite had to recite twice a day; but when the Bible prescribed the love of neighbor it could be asked whether it envisioned mankind in general, or solely the Jew. At any rate, the two precepts are never placed side by side in the Old Testament or in the writings of the Rabbis. We must therefore suppose that this lawyer already had some idea of Christ's doctrine, and that he was completing the text of his profession of faith by the teachings of Jesus, in order to pave the way for the question he was holding in reserve on the true meaning of the word *neighbor*. However that may be, his answer was perfect and merited this commendation: "Thou hast answered

---

[28] The part of the Gospel peculiar to St. Luke comprises two sections very different in character. In the second (11:14–18:14) it is impossible to establish a chronological order, precise indications of time and place being lacking. In the first section (9:51–11:13) it is otherwise. Without doing any violence to the text, an itinerary may be found of a journey from Galilee to Jerusalem, passing through Samaria and coming to Perea when the Samaritans object to a transit through their country:

1. Definitive departure from Galilee in the direction of Jerusalem (9:51);
2. Attempt to pass through Samaria (9:52–56);
3. Mission of the Seventy-Two to prepare the way in Perea (10:1–24);
4. On the Jericho road. Parable of the Good Samaritan (10:25–37);
5. Halt at Bethany at the house of Mary and Martha (10:38–42);
6. The *Our Father* on the Mount of Olives, according to tradition (11:1–13).

It is here that the entry into Jerusalem must be placed, during the festivities of Tabernacles and the events recorded by St. John (7:1–10:21). It would be surprising that, coming so close to Jerusalem, the Saviour should not have entered the city. That St. Luke does not mention such entry is due to the fact that no visit to Jerusalem before the Passion enters into the plan of the Synoptics, any more than it came into the Apostolic catechesis.

[29] The lawyer is represented as *tentans eum* (ἐκπειράζων), but both the Greek and the Latin word mean to *test* or to *make trial of a person* or *thing* as well as to *tempt*.

well: do this and thou shalt live." But the Scribe feels the need of *justifying* himself, of showing that he has not spoken frivolously, that his question was neither otiose nor naïve, and that it was not to be settled in a word. He therefore answers in the self-sufficient tone of a man touched to the quick: "But who is my neighbor?" This is what he is expecting to hear from the Master.

As a matter of fact, for the Jew the neighbor was a friend or relative, someone close to him, a compatriot, but not a stranger nor an enemy, much less a heretic or an idolater.[30] It is certain that the Talmud applies the divine command of love of neighbor only to Israelites. As late as the twelfth century, Maimonides makes bold to affirm that the Sanhedrin may not condemn to death the murderer of a pagan, because the Mosaic law which punishes murder takes into consideration only the murderer of one's neighbor, that is to say, the Jew.[31]

Jesus answers the lawyer by telling him the parable of the Good Samaritan, which at the same time contains a precious moral lesson.

"On the road which leads from Jerusalem to Jericho a certain man fell into the hands of robbers who, after having stripped him and beaten him, left him half dead. A priest going down that way saw him and passed by on the other side. Likewise a Levite coming to the place saw him and passed by on the other side. But a traveler, a Samaritan, noticed him and, moved with compassion, approached him and bandaged up his wounds after pouring upon them wine and oil, and placed him upon his own beast and brought him to an inn and took care of him. The next day, taking two denarii (from his purse) he gave them to the innkeeper, saying: 'Take care of him, and on my return I will repay thee for whatever thou spendest over and above.' "

---

[30] Deut. 6:5; Lev. 19:18. On the Rabbinical notion of *neighbor,* cf. Edersheim, *Life and Times,* Vol. II, p. 237; Bonsirven, *Le Judaisme Palestinien,* Vol. II, pp. 198 and 239.

[31] Lightfoot (*Opera Omnia,* Leusden ed., 1699, Vol. II, p. 523) cites another text of Maimonides more odious still, if it is authentic: "If a pagan falls into the water, draw him not out, for he is not thy neighbor" (עין זה רעך). It is superfluous to say that this is perverse exegesis of Biblical texts.

Everything leads to the assumption that the parable was suggested to our Lord by the scene which lay before his eyes. There is not in Palestine a spot more suited to the exploits of highwaymen and bloody dramas of vengeance. On the rapid descent from Jerusalem to Jericho, for the space of ten or twelve miles, the country bears a sinister aspect. As soon as one passes Bethany there are no more houses or farms, and the only vegetation are clumps of asphodel and thorny thickets. Farther on the desolation becomes still more pronounced. On the right and on the left are bare hillocks which seem to have fallen from some other planet. The road runs along a ridge flanked by deep ravines and intersected by trenches which form an inextricable labyrinth. Here and there slabs reddened by the mixture of manganese in their composition impart to the landscape the color of blood. In ancient times everything contributed to render the place fearsome to the traveler, who knew that every rocky protuberance and every fissure of the soil might conceal a brigand or an enemy. Indeed, scarcely a century ago the lone traveler would not have dared venture along this road without an escort.[32]

What often happened to defenseless travelers in those days happened to the man in the parable. He was captured and despoiled by the robbers who infested these parts. He was beaten down with blows and left for dead, no doubt because he had put up some resistance, since such gentry would have designs upon his purse rather than upon his life. The Priest and the Levite who did not deign to dismount to give succor to the poor wounded man are introduced to lend realism to the story, since Jericho was a priestly city and their duties would often oblige them to pass along that road, and their enforced relations with the brigands would tend to assure them safe-conduct. But these two are also purposely mentioned in order to contrast the hardheartedness of

---

[32] St. Jerome, in the annotated translation of the *Onomasticon* of Eusebius, writes at the word *Adommim:* "Ubi et castellum militum situm est. Ejus cruenti et sanguinarii loci dominus quoque in parabola descendentis Jerichum de Jerusalem recordatur." A short distance from Khan-el-Hatrur, called by the Christians "The Inn of the Good Samaritan," can be seen the ruins of an ancient stronghold known by the name *Qala'at-ed-Damm* (Castle of Blood). It is surrounded by a moat dug into the rock, about twenty feet in width and about the same in depth. This stronghold, supposing that it existed at the time of Christ, would not have provided effective protection to travelers along the entire route.

men consecrated to the service of the altar with the compassionate charity of a Samaritan. He it is who forgets national antipathies and racial hatreds to obey a natural sentiment of humanity. Immediately he sets to work on the victim's most urgent need; he bandages his wounds, after having carefully bathed them with wine and oil according to a recipe of ancient medicine still used in the country regions of Palestine.[33] That done, he places the wounded man on his own beast, which he leads by a halter as far as the inn. About half the way along the road from Jerusalem to Jericho there is now, and always has been, a caravansary where man and beast may find a little shelter and some water from a cistern. To this place, for lack of a better, the Good Samaritan conveys his wounded charge. He passes the night close to him, and being unable to tarry longer, he gives the innkeeper two denarii, the wage for two days' work, and promises to pay on his return any extra expense.

"Which of these three," asks Jesus in conclusion, "showed himself to be a *neighbor* to the man fallen into the hands of robbers?" The lawyer unhesitatingly answers: "It was he that took pity on him." "Very well," answers Jesus. "Go thou and do likewise." In other words: "Thy neighbor is not only a friend, a relative, a fellow-countryman: he is man without distinction, without exception; he is anyone at all that has need of thy help and to whom thou canst be of assistance." For all that it lacks Aristotelian form, the definition is nonetheless clear.

The parable of the Good Samaritan belongs to the class of parables that are called "examples." Such are the Pharisee and the Publican, Lazarus and the Rich Man, and also, though in a lesser degree, the Prodigal Son. Whether fiction or fact, the moral is the same. It may even be said that a fictional narrative can be more instructive and more moving, since the narrator is at liberty to choose and arrange the features to his own taste without being constrained by historical fact. In such parables

---

[33] On the oil and wine used to dress wounds, cf. Billerbeck, *Kommentar,* Vol. I, p. 248, n. 2. A tract brought to light by Fr. M. Julien (*L'Egypte* [Lille, 1895], p. 276) proves that the Arabs used this recipe with full confidence. Furthermore it is recommended by Hippocrates: "Bind up the wound covered over with leaves boiled in oil and wine." By itself the alcoholic wine of Palestine cauterizes the wound and the oil, preventing contact with the air and dust, contributes to antisepsis.

there is no trace of allegory. A typical situation is proposed as a model for all analogous situations. Hence there is no need to look for any special significance in the descent from Jerusalem to Jericho, or the robbers and their victim, or the Priest and the Levite and the Samaritan, or the oil and wine poured on the wounds, or the two denarii given on account. Of course, preachers are not forbidden to draw for the benefit of their hearers a symbolism from such details, provided that it flows naturally from the text. But to see in the oil and wine, the blood of Christ and the anointing by the Holy Spirit; or in the inn and the innkeeper, the Church and St. Peter, would be to trail off into allegories which are scarcely any longer in accord with our tastes.

Many ancient writers believed that the Good Samaritan represents Jesus Christ. Were they justified? Certainly, if correctly understood. Though no particular feature of the parable has a mysterious meaning, still the moral lesson that emerges is susceptible of innumerable applications. If we are seeking the literal meaning, Christ did not intend to point exclusively to himself under the figure of the Good Samaritan. That is quite plain. But, though the parable is applicable to all who have imitated the Good Samaritan — to saints like Camillus of Lellis and Vincent de Paul, for example — it applies with greater force to the One who has realized in himself the ideal of a heart compassionate for our humanity, a humanity more sorely wounded by the original Fall than the man fallen among robbers.

5. At the Home of Martha and Mary

(LUKE 10:38–42)

On his journey from Jericho to Jerusalem, Jesus encountered Bethany on his way. There "a woman named Martha welcomed him into her house. She had a sister called Mary, who seated herself at the Lord's feet and was listening to his word."[34] It is thus that St. Luke introduces to us the two sisters as persons unknown, without seeming to suspect that Mary of Bethany may be identified with either of two women of whom he has already

34 St. Luke, who mentions neither Bethany nor Lazarus, gives the two sisters exactly the same traits that we recognize in them in St. John.

spoken, the unnamed sinner who anointed the feet of Jesus after bathing them with her tears, and Mary Magdalene, from whom he had cast out seven devils and who used to accompany him on his apostolic journeys. He does not mention Lazarus, either because of his youth or because his sickly condition rendered him inactive. It is Martha, doubtless the eldest in an orphaned family, that acts as mistress of the house, thus effectively living up to her name; for Martha means "mistress." In this capacity the duty and honor of receiving and caring for guests devolves upon her.

She acquits herself of the charge with a somewhat unquiet zeal. Since this was not the first time that she was receiving our Lord and his escort under her roof, she must have known that neither he nor his followers were overexacting, but it may be that, on that particular day, the unexpected arrival of a larger than ordinary group distracted her. Over and above that, she was chagrined and vexed to see her sister hold aloof from serving, to seat herself at the feet of the Master, drinking in avidly every word that fell from his lips. She too was lending an ear, eager to miss nothing of his divine teachings; but every moment she was distracted by the multiple occupations of housekeeping. Finally, unable any longer to contain her feelings, she came and took her stand in front of Jesus, and with the familiarity that long-established relationship excuses said to him: "Lord, art thou not concerned that my sister is leaving to me all the worry of serving? Tell her, then, to help me." She receives a serious answer, but the tone of it must have tempered the gentle rebuke: "Martha, Martha, thou art anxious and troubled about many things: now, one thing alone is necessary. For Mary has chosen the best part."[35]

---

[35] Luke 10:42: *Porro unum est necessarium*. There are three readings:
a) Ἑνὸς δέ ἐστι χρεία (Tischendorf, Scrivener, Vogels);
b) Ὀλίγων δέ ἐστι χρεία (Von Soden);
c) Ὀλίγων δέ ἐστι χρεία ἢ ἑνός (Hort, Weiss).

Reading *b* is so poorly attested that it is surprising to find it preferred by Von Soden. It is the work of a copyist who could not understand how one thing could be enough for a meal. It is doubtless for the same reason the clause has been omitted from a small number of manuscripts (*D* and some manuscripts of the Old Latin).

Reading *c* is that of five Greek codices (א *B L 1* and *33*), of two versions (Bohairic and Ethiopian), and of Origen. This seems to indicate a common Egyptian origin.

Reading *a* is that of the rest of the Greek manuscripts, of the Syriac versions, of the Vulgate, and of three codices of the Old Latin. St. Jerome was acquainted

The masters of the spiritual life like to see in the two sisters of Bethany the image of the active and the contemplative life. There is no reason for decrying the allegory. Why could not a real happening have a symbolic meaning? And why has the Evangelist, who had so many other facts to record, chosen by preference to report this fact — charming, if you will, but still quite insignificant — unless he wished to transmit to us a moral lesson? Mary, detached from all earthly cares, all attentive to the care of her soul, has chosen for herself the *good part,* which turns out to be the *best part,* because instead of ending with time, as does the active life, it perpetuates itself and has its consummation in eternity. Still, for all that it is the best part, the part of Mary is not the only good part. God does not inspire all souls with the same desires and he does not lead all by the same way. Can we imagine a world peopled only by contemplatives? And could Mary have given herself without distraction to the things of heaven, if Martha had not occupied herself with the things of earth?

The defect would be found in excessive preoccupation with earthly matters, because at bottom one thing alone is necessary, the care of the soul. The ancient and modern commentators who see in the *unum necessarium* only a maxim of popular wisdom, and who interpret thus: a few dishes or only one are needed to appease hunger, seem to us to be substituting a puerile idea for a sublime teaching. Jesus is not reproaching Martha for preparing too many dishes, but for being too preoccupied with material cares; it is for this reason that Mary, who is all absorbed in a more excellent occupation, has chosen the best part.

---

with reading *c* but retains *a* in the Vulgate. St. Basil cites reading *a* and comments on *c*. Briefly, reading *a* is by far the best attested, and it alone gives a meaning worthy of the Saviour. If it is adopted (ἑνὸς δέ ἐστι χρεία, *unum est necessarium*), "it is impossible," as Lagrange remarks, "to understand the *one thing* as referring to the meal; the meaning is evidently spiritual" (*Saint Luc,* p. 319). If *c* is accepted, it must be interpreted with St. Basil (MG, XXXI, 973: Ὀλίγων μέν, δηλονότι τῶν πρὸς παρασκευήν, ἑνὸς δὲ τοῦ σκόπου). "*Few things* are needed if there is question of the meal; *one thing alone* is necessary if there is question of the end" to be attained. But this interpretation is farfetched. St. Augustine has a fine discourse on the *unum necessarium* (ML, XXXVIII, 615–618).

CHAPTER II

The Lord's Prayer

1. The Six Petitions of the Our Father

ONE day Jesus was at prayer, motionless, with his eyes fixed upon heaven. The disciples, who were used to seeing him in this attitude, did not disturb his recollection. But when he had finished, one of them said to him: "Master, teach us to pray as John taught his disciples." And he taught them the Lord's Prayer: "When you pray, pray thus." Not that this is the unique and obligatory formula of all prayer — neither the Apostles nor the Church ever understood it to be such — but it is the ideal pattern upon which all our prayers should be modeled if they are to be effective. It is called the Lord's Prayer, not because our Lord made use of it for himself — the Incarnate Word would never ask pardon for his sins, nor could he call upon his Father together with us or in the same way as we do — but because it is the only prayer that our Lord himself taught us.

It has been handed down to us in two Gospels with some variants.[1] Though it is notably shorter in St. Luke than in St.

---

[1] The form of the *Our Father* differs somewhat in the two Evangelists:

Matthew 6:9–13	*Luke 11:2–4*
Our Father who art in heaven,	Father,
Hallowed be thy name,	Hallowed be thy name,
Thy kingdom come,	Thy kingdom come.
Thy will be done, on earth as in heaven.	Give us each day our daily bread,
Give us this day our daily bread,	And forgive us our sins
And forgive us our debts	For we also forgive whoever is our debtor,
As we also forgive our debtors,	And lead us not into temptation.
And lead us not into temptation,	
But deliver us from evil.	

We see that St. Luke omits the third petition and the last part of the sixth. He reduces the opening invocation to one word, Father. In the fourth and fifth petitions, he has variants which will be examined later.

Matthew, St. Luke's omissions are quite naturally explained by the class of readers for whom he was writing, and everything leads to the conclusion that St. Matthew has reproduced with greater fidelity the Saviour's very words. His version is also the one that has been adopted in the sacred liturgy and in the everyday use of the faithful. One of the most ancient documents of Christian literature after the canonical writings — perhaps the most ancient of all — gives this precept: "Pray not as the hypocrites (the Jews) pray, but as the Lord himself has commanded in the Gospel." And after transcribing the text of St. Matthew, it adds: "Thus pray three times a day."[2]

Though the wording of St. Matthew is to be preferred, the same cannot be said of the place that he assigns to the Lord's Prayer. He inserts it in the Sermon on the Mount, in the middle of a passage of studied composition ruled by the laws of Hebrew parallelism, where its insertion too obviously disturbs the harmony and equilibrium of the whole. St. Luke, on the contrary, places it in the second period of our Lord's teaching, after his visit to the sisters of Bethany. And there is little likelihood that Jesus taught it earlier than this, for in that case, what reason would there be for the Apostles' request that he should teach them to pray? We think, therefore, that tradition was rightly inspired in placing the origin of the Pater Noster on the Mount of Olives, between Bethany and Jerusalem, at the spot now occupied by the cloister of Carmel where the divine prayer carved in marble may be read in all the principal languages of the world. St. Mark, while not reporting the Lord's Prayer, seems to allude to it when he places in the mouth of our Lord these words pronounced on the road from Bethany to Jerusalem, exactly where the Our Father was taught: "When you pray pardon those against whom you have any grievances so that your Father who is in heaven may pardon your faults."[3]

The introduction is thus expressed in St. Matthew: "Pray you, therefore, thus." In St. Luke it is: "When you pray, say." It is to be noted that the third petition merely adds precision to the second, and that the second member of the last petition has as its purpose to complete and generalize the first member. This may explain St. Luke's omissions.

[2] *Didache,* or *Doctrine of the Twelve Apostles,* viii.

[3] Mark 11:25. Words pronounced by Jesus on Tuesday of Holy Week, while returning from Bethany to Jerusalem.

Prayer formulas were abundant among the Jews. They had them ready for all the circumstances of life — before and after meals, when confronting any extraordinary phenomenon or any beautiful natural spectacle, when receiving either good or bad news — not to mention the *Shema,* which was their profession of faith, and the *Eighteen Blessings,* which constituted their official prayer. A religious inspiration frequently animates these formulas, but who will dare compare them to the prayer of our Lord? The efforts spent to find its elements in the Talmud have been a pure waste of time. Many expressions taken out of their context may offer analogies, but it is easy to recognize either that they are borrowed word for word from the Old Testament or that in their proper setting they have an altogether different sound.[4]

The Lord's Prayer is only a few lines, and it is within the reach of every mind, but what grandeur there is in its simplicity, what richness of meaning in its conciseness![5] From the time of St. Augustine, writers in the Latin tongue have divided it into seven petitions; the majority of modern commentators, in agreement with the Greek Fathers, number only six because the last two petitions are so closely connected that they are in reality only one.

---

[4] Billerbeck (*Kommentar,* Vol. I, 406–425) gives *in extenso* all the passages of the Talmud which present some similarity to the *Our Father.* See also Abrahams, *Studies in Pharisaism and the Gospels,* 1924, Vol. II, Chap. 12: *The Lord's Prayer;* and Dalman, *Die Worte Jesu,* 2 ed., 1930: *Das Vaterunser,* pp. 283–365.

[5] In addition to commentators who are often very brief (St. Jerome, St. John Chrysostom, Pseudo-Chrysostom, St. Cyril of Alexandria), the Fathers of the first five centuries who have explained the *Our Father* are Tertullian (Migne's text being very defective, see the Vienna edition, 1890, pp. 180–200), St. Cyprian (ML, IV, 519–544, the title of the opusculum is omitted from the Index through an error), Origen (MG, XI, 415–462; critical edition of Koetschau [Leipzig, 1899]), St. Augustine in his explanation of the Sermon on the Mount (ML, XXXIV, 1275–1287), St. Gregory of Nyssa (MG, XLIV, 1119–1194, five discourses). In addition to his commentary St. John Chrysostom has a homily on the *Our Father* (ML, LI, 41–48), and St. Cyril of Jerusalem has a brief explanation in his last *Catechesis* (MG, XXXIII, 1117–1124).

Cf. Chase, *The Lord's Prayer in the Early Church* (Cambridge, 1891) (*Texts and Studies,* I, 3); G. Walther, *Geschichte der griechischen Vaterunser-Exegese,* 1914 (*T.U.,* XLIII, 3); J. Hensler, *Das Vaterunser* (Münster-i-W., 1914) (abundant bibliography).

There are very numerous modern explanations of the *Our Father.* From an oratorical standpoint, Monsabré, *La prière divine,* 1909; the second part of St. Theresa's *Way of Perfection* is a mystical explanation. [Cf. *The Complete Works of St. Theresa of Jesus,* translated by E. Allison Peers, Vol. II, Chap. XXX–XLII, pp. 123–186. *Translator.*]

The prayer is made up of two tercets, the first of them having as its object the praise of God, the second, the needs of man. The three members of the first tercet are wishes as well as prayers. We wish that the thrice holy name of God be honored everywhere as it deserves, that the reign of the King of Kings be everywhere established in individual souls as in societies, and that the will of the sovereign Master be accomplished on earth among creatures gifted with reason, as it is accomplished in heaven among the angels and the Elect. After the honor to God, the needs of men are presented, needs of the body and needs of the soul. We beg God to grant us, for the present, what is needed to maintain life; for the past, pardon for our sins, and for the future, preservation from sin.

The Pater Noster is above all a social prayer. When we recite it even as individuals we say "Our Father" in the name of the whole Church. In the words of St. Cyprian, "it is essentially a public and common prayer. We do not recite it for ourselves alone, but for the whole Christian people, since the whole Christian people is one." Doubtless the Lord's Prayer would not be discordant upon the lips of a pagan, because God as creator and conserver of all things is also Father, and because he has made man to his image and likeness; but it cannot have its full significance as Christ taught it except on the lips of a Christian.

In saying *Our Father* we think of him who has made of us a new creation, divinizing us by Sanctifying Grace, of him whose adopted sons we have become as brothers of his only Son. Such also were the saints of the Old Testament, because the grace of Christ flowed upon them by anticipation; still they did not dare call God their Father except in a collective and inferior sense, as members of the Chosen People. Only at the approach of the Christian era in the deuterocanonical books do we find the first, we may say, timid adumbrations of the use of the name Father addressed to God in an individual sense, and upon closer inspection it is not yet altogether the Christian formula.[6]

The phrase *who art in heaven* at the beginning of the Pater Noster recalls to us the grandeur of God, his sanctity and his

---

[6] Cf. Lagrange, *La Paternité de Dieu dans l'Ancien Testament,* in *R.B.*, 1908, pp. 189–199, and Dalman, *Die Worte Jesu,* 2 ed., 1930, pp. 150–159 (*Der Vater in Himmel*).

power; it invites our reverence and recollection, and at the same time inspires us with confidence and hope.

HALLOWED BE THY NAME. In Holy Scripture the "name" of God is God himself, made manifest to man in the voice of creation, revealed to Christians through the instrumentality of Christ. In this first petition we wish that God may receive from every rational creature the honor that is due him. To hallow or to keep holy the name of God is not only to refrain from pronouncing this fearsome name in vain; it is to proclaim it holy, as do the Seraphim of Isaias, who mutually re-echo their adoration; it is to acknowledge his holiness still more by our actions than by our words; it is to honor him, to venerate him, to love him; it is to wish that all men may join us in fearing him as their sovereign Lord and in loving him as the best of fathers.

THY KINGDOM COME. The kingdom of God is at once individual and social: it is in us, and we are its members. Under this twofold aspect we wish, not, properly speaking, its coming — for God has always reigned in the souls of the just, and the visible kingdom founded by Christ already exists — but its progress and development in breadth and depth up to its final consummation, when God will be all in all and we shall reign with Christ the King.[7] The reign of God is not established by an irresistible intervention of Heaven without the co-operation of men, as the Jews imagined. And therefore we pray God almighty and the Father of all mercies to complete his work, to level the obstacles that impede the expansion of Christianity, to inspire with zeal the preachers of the faith, to give to hearers the will to believe, and to increase in all the faithful the true Christian spirit. Thus the reign of God and Christ is envisioned in all its amplitude; in individual souls and in societies, in the struggles of the Church militant and in her final triumph.

Many of the Fathers restrict their attention to the reign of God in the souls of the just, a reign which is sketched on earth and consummated in heaven, or they think that in reciting the Our Father we express our longing for the triumphal return of

---

[7] St. Jerome comments as follows on the text: "Vel generaliter pro totius mundi petit regno . . . vel ut in unoquoque regnet Deus." Yes, but why the *vel?* Only by ruling individual souls does God rule the world.

Christ, when he shall have exterminated all hostile powers and set all his enemies under his feet.[8] These various explanations are by no means mutually exclusive, and it seems that a petition so universal may very well embrace them all.

THY WILL BE DONE ON EARTH AS IT IS IN HEAVEN. God, who has created us free, respects our freedom, for to do violence to it would destroy it. It follows that man's will can oppose itself to the will of God. In this third petition we pray God to remedy this anomaly and disorder. According to the happy dictum of St. Cyprian: "We do not beg that God do his will — what would ever prevent that? — but that he make our will conformed to his." He can by his grace solicit our will without doing violence to it, and can rectify it without suppressing it. There is here much more than an acceptance of the will of God, more than an act of resignation comparable to the *Dominus dedit, Dominus abstulit* of the saintly Job; this is a prayer that all men — and we ourselves first of all — may obey God along the road

[8] Tertullian, *De oratione,* 5: "Optamus maturius regnare et non diutius servire," alluding to Apoc. 6:10. St. Cyprian, *De orat. domin.,* xiii: "Nostrum regnum petimus advenire a Deo nobis repromissum, Christi sanguine et passione quaesitum, ut qui in saeculo ante servivimus, postmodum Christo dominante regnemus." He also admits the eschatological meaning. — For St. Augustine the reign of God which we ask for is the striking *manifestation* of his reign which will take place at the time of the Parousia (*De sermone in monte,* ii, 6, n. 20): "Nulli autem licebit ignorare regnum Dei, cum ejus Unigenitus non solum intelligibiliter, sed etiam visibiliter, in homine Dominico de caelo venerit judicaturus vivos et mortuos." In the *Retractationes* (I, 19, n. 8) the saintly Doctor withdraws the expression *"homo Dominicus"* which he would prefer not to have used, but maintains his explanation. — On the contrary Origen sees only the rule of God in individual souls. This reign is susceptible of indefinite increase, and when we say: "Thy kingdom come," we ask God that he reign always more and more, until that day when we shall reign with him who shall reign in us completely. — St. Cyril of Jerusalem in his concise way seems to draw inspiration from Origen: "He whose thoughts and words and works are pure will say to God with confidence: Thy kingdom come." — For St. John Chrysostom also there is question of the reign of God in the souls of the just: "We have need that God reign in us, that sin may not reign in us" (MG, LI, 45). — St. Cyril of Alexandria has his own exegesis. When we say "Thy kingdom come," we are wishing for the return of Christ to excite us to live correctly. The wicked cannot pronounce these words except with terror. The saints petition the complete reign of God because they have suffered so much, and they aspire to receive the recompense of their good works. — The thought of St. Gregory is not easy to grasp, for he makes the reign of God consist in God's sovereignty, to which is opposed the reign of evil or sin. — The brief commentary of St. Jerome has been transcribed above.

of trial, as the angels and the elect obey him at the end of the road in glory.

GIVE US THIS DAY OUR DAILY BREAD. This fourth petition, which seems the simplest, is, on the contrary, the most widely discussed. St. Augustine gives a choice of three explanations: the word of God, the Eucharist, and material bread. The word of God is indeed the nourishment of the soul. Our Lord had said: "My nourishment is to do the will and to accomplish the work of him that sent me." But it is hard to believe that the disciples, without further indication, would have thought of this heavenly nourishment. The idea of the Eucharist was, perhaps, less remote from their thoughts. Some months earlier Jesus had proclaimed himself the Bread of Life, and had promised to give his followers his body as food and his blood as drink. Nevertheless, before the institution of the Blessed Sacrament and before the established usage of the faithful in the East to partake of it daily, the Eucharist could scarcely be recognized under the figure of daily bread. Hence it is now agreed that *bread* should keep its natural meaning, always remembering that in Scriptural usage bread represents all that is needed for existence. Do we not ourselves use the expression "to gain his bread" for gaining a livelihood? If our Lord forbids us to be preoccupied about material bread, he does not forbid us to be occupied about it; much less does he forbid us to ask it of God. Perhaps it may also be admitted that the daily bread indicates, implicitly and by extension, all that is necessary for the life of the body and the life of the soul. The Holy Eucharist would not be excluded, for it is truly *our bread,* since Christians alone are allowed to partake of it; it is also our *daily bread,* since the wish of the Church is that we should partake of it daily.

We have quoted the fourth petition according to the usual text, that of St. Matthew. St. Luke presents a variant which is not negligible: instead of *give us this day,* he says: *"Give us each day* our daily bread."[9] Both are petitions for only one day's bread,

---

[9] Matt. 6:11. *τὸν ἄρτον ἡμῶν τὸν ἐπιούσιον δὸς ἡμῖν σήμεραν.*
Luke 11:3. *τὸν ἄρτον ἡμῶν τὸν ἐπιούσιον δίδου ἡμῖν τὸ καθ' ἡμέραν.*
There are two interrelated divergences. St. Matthew uses the aorist imperative *δὸς ἡμῖν* (*give us, this time*), and he says *σήμερον* (*today*). St. Luke uses the

but the request of St. Luke is general and takes in the future; St. Matthew's looks only to the present day, supposing that the Pater Noster is recited morning and evening. Such was in fact the original practice of the faithful.

PARDON US OUR OFFENSES AS WE PARDON THOSE WHO HAVE OFFENDED US. The literal translation is: "Forgive us our debts as we also forgive our debtors"

---

present imperative δίδου ἡμῖν (*give us habitually,* cease not to give us), and says τὸ καθ' ἡμέραν (*every day*).

The precise meaning of ἐπιούσιος is much disputed. Origen (*De oratione,* xxviii, 7) had never met the word any place else; and it is only recently that another example of it is believed to have been unearthed (cf. Bauer, *Wörterbuch,* 1928, p. 462).

The etymology is uncertain. (*a*) The majority of authorities believe it to be derived from the present participle feminine of ἔπειμι (to come) used as a noun, ἡ ἐπιοῦσα (with ἡμέρα understood), meaning "the coming day" and being applicable not only to the morrow (the ordinary sense) but also to the day which is about to begin or which has begun. In our opinion this is the simplest derivation and the one best adapted to the petition of the Our Father. (*b*) Others refer it to the neuter of the same present participle of ἔπειμι; τὸ ἐπιόν meaning "the time to come" (like ὁ ἐπιὼν χρόνος); ἄρτος ἐπιούσιος would thus mean "the bread of the future." But how does that fit in with the "this day" of St. Matthew? (*c*) Many derive ἐπιούσιος from ἐπὶ τὴν οὖσαν, with ἡμέραν understood, "for the present day." This meaning would be acceptable but no example of ἐπὶ τὴν οὖσαν meaning "today" can be cited. (*d*) Certain others following Origen take it as ἐπὶ and οὐσία, "for existence," or "superior to substance." But against this derivation is the fact that it fails to make the elision demanded in ἐπὶ, which would result in ἐπούσιος. Again, the philosophical sense here attributed to οὐσία is not to be found in usage outside the Schools, the ordinary meaning of οὐσία being "fortune," "goods." The dissertations on this subject are so numerous and so disparate that it would be difficult to select the most useful.

The same variety is to be found in the versions. St. Jerome puts *supersubstantialem* in St. Matthew, and keeps the *quotidianum* of the Old Latin in St. Luke. In his translation *supersubstantialem* he was certainly thinking of the derivation ἐπὶ τὴν οὐσίαν suggested by Origen, which favored application to the Holy Eucharist. We do not know to what Aramaic word the Greek ἐπιούσιος corresponds. The Hebrew text which S. Jerome believed to be the original of St. Matthew had מחר (*maḥar*), the bread "of tomorrow." St. Jerome himself thought that ἐπιούσιος is synonymous with περιούσιος which in the Septuagint corresponds to the Hebrew סגלה (*segollah*) "excellent, special bread": "Quando ergo petimus ut peculiarem vel praecipuum nobis Deus tribuat panem, illum petimus qui dicit: Ego sum panis vivus" (Commentary, in ML, XXVI, 43). Again in the text published by Morin (*Anecdota Maredsolana,* III, ii, 262): "Panem nostrum supersubstantialem da nobis hodie, hoc est, qui est de tua substantia. In hebraeo evangelio secundum Matthaeum ita habet: Panem nostrum crastinum da nobis hodie, hoc est, panem quem daturus es nobis in regno tuo da nobis hodie." The opinion of St. Jerome has exercised great influence, but it has not prevailed in the Church.

(Matthew), or "Pardon us our sins for we also forgive whoever is our debtor" (Luke).[10] But in translating thus, one would run the risk of being misunderstood by those who are unaware that in Scriptural language an offense is a debt contracted by an offender with the one offended, and that to pardon the offense is to forgive a debt. God in his goodness promises pardon to those who pardon. So great is the obligation of pardon that it seems to take precedence over all other duties. "When thou offerest thy sacrifice at the altar, if thou rememberest that thy brother has something against thee, leave thy offering upon the altar and go first to reconcile thyself with thy brother, and then thou shalt come to offer thy sacrifice." In any case it is an essential condition for obtaining pardon for ourselves. "If you forgive, your heavenly Father will forgive you; but if you do not forgive, neither will your heavenly Father forgive you." The one reciting the Pater Noster is considered to have done so, for he says with confidence: "Forgive me, *for* I also forgive" (Luke), or "Forgive me *as* I also forgive" (Matthew). Between the forgiveness which we receive and that which we accord to others there is only a distant likeness, enough however to justify the comparison. Even though one be free of all debt to divine justice — for example, after Baptism, or after an act of love so intense as to efface even the temporal punishment due to sin that has been forgiven — he could still address to God this petition, for the Pater Noster, as we have said, is not solely a personal supplication but a public and collective prayer.

LEAD US NOT INTO TEMPTATION BUT DELIVER US FROM EVIL. Conscious of our own feebleness and fragility we pray God to remove from us the occasions of sin, or if he allows secondary causes to have their natural play, to make us emerge unharmed from the perilous crossing. The deliverance from evil which we then implore is, so to speak, the positive side of the same petition, and it is, perhaps, for that reason that, as Origen surmises, St. Luke thought he could omit it. "Bring it about, O Lord, by Thy fatherly providence that we fall

[10] Matt. 6:12; Luke 11:4. The difference is insignificant if it be observed that offense and debt are synonymous. In St. Matthew, the one reciting the Our Father has already forgiven; in St. Luke, he forgives while he recites it. The *as* in St. Matthew and the *for* in St. Luke both indicate that the condition for being forgiven has been fulfilled by the one praying.

not into the occasions of sin or yield to temptation; preserve us from every evil whether it come from Satan, or the world, or our own evil nature." There is question of moral evil, the only true evil for man, without, however, excluding physical evil, which can be the source of merit for us, but also the occasion of a fall. If there were question of physical evil without relation to moral evil, this would really be a seventh petition.

Souls inflamed by the love of God are but little disquieted by physical evil. "I am very certain," says St. Theresa, "that the perfect do not beg God to deliver them from suffering, nor temptations, nor persecution, nor combat. These trials are, in their eyes, the most certain sign that their contemplation and the graces they receive proceed from the Spirit of the Lord. Far from fearing them, they desire them and ask for them and love them, like soldiers who much prefer the hazards of battle to the indolence of peace. . . . But for them there are more redoubtable enemies, more treacherous foes who do not reveal themselves to us until after devastating our souls and ravaging our virtue. . . . These enemies are the ones; fear them; pray the Lord; insistently supplicate Him, in reciting the Our Father, to deliver us from them."[11] Thus, however different the dealings of God with souls, he makes all of them find in the Lord's Prayer the satisfaction of their desires and of their needs.

The final *Amen* is a liturgical addition, like the *Gloria Patri* which ends the Psalms.

2. Efficacious Prayer

Prayer well said is all-powerful with the heart of God; Jesus Christ himself assures us of this: "Ask and you shall receive; seek and you shall find; knock at the door and it shall be opened to you. For everyone that asks receives; and everyone that seeks finds; and to him that knocks it is opened."[12]

If our prayer is not always answered it is because we pray badly or with improper dispositions or because we ask for what

---

[11] St. Theresa, *The Way of Perfection,* Chap. XXXIX. [Cf. Complete Works of St. Theresa of Jesus, trans. E. Allison Peers, Vol. II, pp. 163–164. *Translator.*]

[12] Luke 11:9–10; Matt. 7:7–8.

is evil, for things that are harmful or less profitable to our souls. *Aut male, aut mali, aut mala:* the sharply chiseled formula of St. Augustine. How could it be otherwise, since God is our Father and the best of fathers?

"If one of you asks his father for a loaf, will he give him a stone? And if he asks for a fish, will he give him a serpent? And if he asks for an egg, will he give him a scorpion? If, therefore, you who are evil (in comparison with God who is goodness itself) know how to give good things to your children, how much more will your Father who is in heaven give, to those that ask for it, the spirit of sanctity?"[13]

Even among men the axiom "Ask and you shall receive," while not infallible, has enough truth in it to justify the proverb. But we are here on the supernatural plane of relationships between God and man. There without possible exception, the persevering prayer always obtains its object. A parable briefly outlined aids us to grasp this. If a guest arrives unexpectedly in the middle of the night, and you have nothing to offer him and go to a neighbor to borrow from him, you will doubtless hear him answer from within: "Leave me in peace; the door is locked and I with my little ones am in bed. I cannot get up to give thee what thou askest." But continue rapping on the door: he will finally get up and give you all you ask for.[14]

This scene of village life should be clearly envisioned. The peasants of Palestine bake their bread from day to day, not expecting any visitors at night-time. People of the East, as though haunted by a superstitious fear of the dark, are loath to travel after twilight. The man of the parable is, therefore, caught unprepared, and has no other recourse than to run to a neighbor whom he knows to be better provided. But the situation is delicate. Houses were locked at nightfall and the only room in the house was transformed into a bedroom. All the members of the household, stretched out side by side on mats or rugs, slept under the feeble glimmer of a night lamp. It was impossible to get up to look for anything, or to open the door, or to get back to one's place, without disturbing everyone else and waking them all up.

[13] Luke 11:11–13; Matt. 7:9–11.

[14] Luke 11:5–8. Peculiar to Luke. The parable is only sketched; it is presented under the form of a hypothesis and not a story, but its meaning is clear.

The unsympathetic neighbor has, therefore, a good excuse, and it is easily understood that he needs some urging. But for the sake of peace and quiet he finally yields to the insistence of his friend. Importunity wrests from him what friendship would never have been able to gain. Hence is proved the truth of the proverb: "Knock without wearying, and they will open to you."

The parable of the Widow and the Wicked Judge is another illustration of the same idea.[15] The Saviour proposed this parable one day to give a readily intelligible form to the maxim: It is necessary to pray always, never growing weary.[16]

There was a judge so given to evil as to dread neither the menace of divine justice nor discredit in the eyes of men. Self-respect and the fear of public censure can to a certain extent take the place of conscience; but the judge in the parable was no longer susceptible to such feelings, and he allowed himself to be led only by self-interest, passion, and caprice. A poor defenseless widow without resources had come to him to demand justice against an oppressor. Since she had no powerful patrons to defend her cause, nor treasure to dispense to buy a favorable verdict, she received at first only scorn and rebuffs at the tribunal of the wicked judge. But strong in the consciousness of her rights, she returned again and again to the charge with all a woman's obstinacy. And finally the judge, beset by her importunities which left him neither truce nor rest, said to himself: "It is useless for me to hold out despite God and man: if I do not look to it this woman will end by assassinating me."[17] Better to do justice to be rid of her. And he acts accordingly.

---

[15] Luke 18:2–5. This parable is peculiar to St. Luke, who has placed it in another context where it more properly belongs. We have thought well to link it with the parable of the importunate friend with which it has special affinity.

[16] Luke 18:1: *Oportet semper orare et non deficere* (μὴ ἐγκακεῖν — *not to weaken, not to slacken*). Compare the formulas of St. Paul: *Sine intermissione orate* (1 Thess. 5:17); *orationi instate* (Col. 4:2: προσκαρτερεῖτε, i.e., *attach yourselves to, be intent upon prayer*).

[17] Luke 18:5: ἵνα μὴ εἰς τέλος ἐρχομένη ὑπωπιάζῃ με, *ne in novissimo veniens sugillet me*. The word ὑπωπιάζειν, like the Latin *sugillare,* means properly "to strike under the eye" (ὑπώπιον), "to blacken someone's eye." Pliny says *oculi sugillati,* "blackened eyes." Many moderns take the expression literally: the judge was afraid that the woman would leap at his face and give him a black eye. But it is better to hold to the figurative meaning corresponding to our familiar

Of course the wicked judge is not a symbol of God, nor is this an allegory. It is a parable with a very simple meaning. If persevering prayer succeeded in triumphing over the perverse will of the wickedest of judges, what power will it not have with the heart of the most loving of fathers? "There is," says Bossuet, "one way of forcing God and of wresting from him his graces, and that is to keep asking without growing weary."[18]

---

phrase "to break or split my head," i.e., "to worry me to death." *Sugillo* or *suggillo* is also often used in a figurative sense.

[18] Bossuet, *Méditat. sur l'Evangile. Sermon sur la Montagne,* fortieth day.

CHAPTER III

The Feast of Tabernacles

1. Unexpected Arrival in Jerusalem

(JOHN 7:1–36)

FOR several months Jesus had been traveling through Galilee, the Decapolis, and the tetrarchy of Philip, while avoiding the approaches to Jerusalem. He was aware that the cure of the paralytic at Bethesda and the discourse in which he had declared himself the Son of God equal to the Father had aroused enemies in the city who were resolved to destroy him; but his hour had not yet come, and his work in the north of Palestine was not yet accomplished.

Meanwhile the Feast of Tabernacles was approaching. This feast was celebrated on the 15th of *Tishri,* the first month of the civil year which began toward the end of September after the grain harvest and the vintage and the gathering of the autumn fruit crop. It was originally an agricultural festival, instituted to give thanks to God for the fruitfulness of the soil; later on, it included also the commemoration of the sojourn of the Hebrews in the wilderness. In memory of that event, all Jews of free status, except the sick and women and children, lived for a week in huts of leaves which called to mind the tents pitched in the wilderness of Sinai, when the miraculous cloud had given them shade in the daytime and light by night during their journey. An entire treatise of the Mishnah regulates with childish minuteness the shape, dimensions, and materials of these leafy cabins in which all the Israelites had to live for seven days, except in case of rain, which was very rare at that season.

In the splendor of the public ceremonies, the pomp of the festivities, and the heavy influx of pilgrims, this feast so eclipsed all the other solemnities of the liturgical cycle that it was called "The Feast" par excellence.[1] Great multitudes of Jews from the Dispersion, and strangers also, came to the city, since the time of year was very favorable to travel by land or sea.

At the approach of the feast, all Galilee pushed forward the preparations. The inhabitants of Capharnaum and the neighboring localities set out upon the road, leading the animals destined for sacrifice and the beasts of burden laden with provisions for the journey. But Jesus seemed to have decided not to join the caravan. His near relatives, those who are commonly called his "brethren," gave voice to their surprise and displeasure. "Leave this country," they said to him, "and go to Judea, that thy disciples may be witnesses of the works which thou dost. He that wishes to be known does not work in the dark. Since thou dost such great things, show thyself to the world"; appear upon a stage worthy of thee! Such was the reasoning of some who were not enlightened by the Spirit of God; for at that period, says St. John, even his brethren did not believe in him.[2] The Evangelist is speaking of the group in general, disregarding exceptions; it is not necessary to include in this unbelieving mass St. James, the first bishop of Jerusalem, surnamed "the brother of the Lord."

Undoubtedly, Jesus' relatives believed in his miracles — they were too evident to be denied — but they were mistaken about the nature of his divine mission. Like the majority of their contemporaries, they were dreaming of a national liberator, and they judged him capable of filling this role, the luster of which would reflect glory upon the whole family. But for such a role decisiveness and boldness were required, and they regarded him as timorous and irresolute. In their opinion, all that was needed to

---

[1] According to Josephus, it is the holiest and greatest of feasts (*Antiq.*, VIII, iv, 1: ἑορτὴ ἁγιωτάτη καὶ μεγίστη). Its Greek name was σκηνοπηγία (from σκηνοπηγεῖν, *to pitch a tent*). It lasted from the 15th to the 22nd of Tishri, the first month of the civil year, corresponding to September-October. The treatise of the Mishnah entitled *Sukkoth* deals with this feast. The texts of the Talmud are brought together in the long dissertation of Billerbeck, *Das Laubhüttenfest,* Vol. II, pp. 774–812 of the *Kommentar.*

[2] John 7:1–5. On the meaning of "believe" in St. John, cf. Abbott, *Johannine Vocabulary,* 1905, "Believing," pp. 19–102.

stir up enthusiasm and to arouse the multitude was that he should show some of his gifts as a wonder-worker and some of his natural eloquence. Numerous adherents in Jerusalem could be counted upon who would be disposed to support him. Besides, the occasion was eminently favorable. The lesson of history was clear. The Feast of Tabernacles, more than any other, was suited to foster any great movement that caught the popular fancy.

To these ill-inspired counselors, who so strangely misunderstood the spiritual nature of the kingdom of God, Jesus replies: "My time is not yet come; but yours is always at hand. The world cannot hate you; but it hates me, because I bear witness concerning it, that its works are evil. Do you go up to this feast; but I do not go up, for my time is not yet fulfilled."[3] A day will come when he will go up to encounter the hosannas of the populace, but the commands of his Father do not permit him to anticipate that day, which will be little in advance of the day of his death. He does not say: "I will not go up to this feast," but, "I do not go up to it" now, with you, in the way you expect. Strictly speaking, he does not go up to the feast at all, since he deliberately allows the solemn inauguration of the feast, its essential part, to pass by. But he wishes to avoid above all, as premature and untimely, a showy entrance in the midst of the caravan of Galileans many of whom would be sure to create a noisy manifestation in his favor. Such a demonstration could provoke a quarrel with his adversaries and could readily give umbrage to the Roman authorities.

Great was the disappointment of the multitude waiting for the appearance of the one about whom so many marvels had been told. Their feelings about him were sharply divided. "He is a

---

[3] John 7:6–8. It is not without hesitation that we follow the difficult text of the Vulgate, *non ascendo* (οὐκ ἀναβαίνω) instead of *nondum ascendo* (οὔπω ἀναβαίνω) which offers no difficulty. The reading οὔπω ἀναβαίνω is much the commoner reading of the Greek manuscripts (16 uncials and almost all cursives) and of the versions, except the Vulgate and five or six codices of the Old Latin; it is adopted by Hort, Weiss, and Vogels against Tischendorf, Scrivener, and Von Soden. On the other hand, it seems that if the easier reading οὔπω ἀναβαίνω were the original, the more difficult οὐκ ἀναβαίνω would never have been substituted for it. When Porphyry quotes the latter reading to the Christians as a decisive argument against the veracity of Christ, St. Jerome seems to have no suspicion of any other reading (*Cont. Pelag.*, II, 17). But the difficulty is more apparent than real, as we believe we have shown.

good man," said some. And others answered, "No, he is a seducer." The most firmly convinced of his supporters did not dare to express their thoughts aloud, paralyzed as they were with fear of the hostile Jews.

When this effervescence had somewhat died down, and while the Feast in full swing was drawing attention elsewhere, Jesus unexpectedly made his appearance. He knew that the greatest peril lay in a tumultuous arrival during which an ambush could be so readily organized in the midst of the crush of pilgrims. The stay itself in Jerusalem would be relatively safe, thanks to Roman supervision which was even reinforced at the time of feasts. Jesus therefore began to preach in the outer courts of the Temple and under the surrounding porticoes.

This was the first time that the Saviour taught publicly in the Temple enclosure, and he was soon surrounded by a motley crowd. In the gathering were members of the Sanhedrin, anxious to be on hand when this new teacher should present himself; Pharisees, who had not forgiven him for his cure of the paralytic on the Sabbath some months before; the curious, always ready to swell any kind of a crowd without very well knowing why; the indifferent, rather sympathetic than hostile; and, finally, some timid supporters lost in the mass. This medley must be borne in mind if we are to fill out the true features of the scene so briefly sketched by the author of the Fourth Gospel. The change of interlocutors is manifest without always being clearly indicated.[4]

Many, when they heard Jesus speak, were surprised to discover such great learning in a man who had never studied in the schools. He was constantly quoting the Scriptures and explaining them with an ease that implied long years spent at the feet of a master. Now it was well known that he had never attended the

---

[4] John 7:15–32. Five or six groups of questioners appear one after the other: the Jews, leaders hostile to Christ (v. 15), the crowd of strangers who know nothing of his antecedents (v. 20), the inhabitants of Jerusalem, sympathetic but somewhat skeptical (v. 25), well-disposed hearers (v. 31), the Pharisees, and members of the Sanhedrin (v. 32). Bernard (*Gospel according to St. John,* 1928, pp. 259–265) places Verses 15–24 immediately after Chapter V. The reasons he gives for the displacement are attractive, but the transposition does not seem to be necessary.

school of the Scribes. "The Jews were astonished," says St. John.[5] If we consider the depreciatory meaning that this Evangelist generally associates with the name "the Jews," we will be convinced that this astonishment sprang from envy rather than admiration. These ill-disposed men, without denying the knowledge of the young teacher, regarded him as self-taught in a somewhat unsafe learning, as the propounder of ideas that were personal and hence open to suspicion. His answer is a proof of this:

"My teaching is not mine, but his who sent me. Do what he commands you, and you shall know that my teaching comes not from myself. He that speaks in his own name seeks to assert his own worth; but he that speaks only to honor him that sent him is truthful and does not commit the injustice of glossing over or altering the truth."

Every docile and well-disposed soul opens itself spontaneously to the divine light, just as a trusting disciple readily enters into the mind of his master. Unfortunately the Pharisees whom Jesus was addressing did not share these feelings. Faithful in observing the minutiae of the Law, they neglected its essential points: justice and charity. "Moses gave you the Law; and none among you keeps the Law." (If you kept it, would you seek the life of an innocent man?) "Why do you seek to put me to death?" Hearing Jesus say this, many in the audience, ignorant of the plot of the Pharisees or refusing to believe it, thought that he was speaking irrationally, and that a persecution mania was dictating these words of his. "Truly, thou art possessed," they cried. "Who is thinking of killing thee?" Allowing the insult to pass, Jesus continues to answer his accusers:

"Moses gave you circumcision — not that it is from Moses, but from the Patriarchs — and you practice it even on the Sabbath. If, then, a man is to be circumcised on the Sabbath lest the Law of Moses be broken, are you angry with me because I restore health to a whole man on the Sabbath?" A positive law such as the law of the Sabbath may be suspended. It may yield to another positive law such as the law of circumcision, as you

[5] John 7:15: *Mirabantur Judaei.* The Greek word θαυμάζειν means "to be astonished" as well as "admire."

all agree; much more is it superseded by the higher law of charity.

When he had finished speaking, his more or less zealous disciples and his intractable enemies and those who may be called the neutrals interchanged their views. These last were the inhabitants of Jerusalem who were acquainted with the conduct of the Scribes. They said: "Is not this the man they are seeking to put to death? Well, he is speaking with full freedom, and no one says anything against him! Can it be that the rulers have come to recognize that he is the Christ? Not that. For we know whence he is; but when the Christ comes, no one will know whence he is." There was at the time a very widespread opinion that the appearance of the Messias would be so sudden that it could not at all be foreseen. There was a proverb which said: "Three things come unexpectedly: the Messias, a piece of good luck, and a scorpion." The Jews who disputed with St. Justin raised this objection: "If the Messias has come, no one knows anything of it; when he manifests himself, everyone will know who he is." And again, "If he is born and if he exists somewhere, he is unknown and does not even know himself. He will have no power until Elias has consecrated him with anointing and made him known to the world."[6] These faulty logicians argued in the same way. Knowing that Jesus had been born at Bethlehem and was living at Nazareth or Capharnaum, they concluded that he was not the Messias. Our Lord answers them in a voice loud enough to allow all to benefit by his answer: "Yes, you know me and you know whence I am." (But this external and superficial knowledge is nothing.) "What you do not know is that I did not come of myself, and you know not him who sent me. But I know him, because I am from him and he has sent me."

Still, many in the multitude believed in him; at least they were making their way toward faith. These said: "When the Messias comes, will he work greater miracles?" This observation, springing from the common sense of the people, exasperated the authorities, and they resolved to put an end to the affair by seizing Jesus. But after some reflection the Sanhedrin preferred to have him arrested by the police who were at their disposal, in order

[6] Justin, *Dial. cum Tryph.*, 8 and 110.

to give their act some semblance of legality. We shall soon see how their plan miscarried.

2. The Adulteress[7]

During his stay in Jerusalem at the time of the feast, Jesus withdrew every evening from the noise and crowding of the city to seek, on the Mount of Olives or at Bethany, the pure air and the calm and silence; but he used to come back very early in the morning to the Temple and spend the whole day instructing the people.

One morning, upon returning from the Mount of Olives, he seated himself upon one of the stone benches arranged along the porches, and a crowd of listeners formed a circle around him. Suddenly the Scribes and Pharisees broke into the group, dragging with them a woman accused of adultery. The charge was probably not without foundation, for the Feast of Tabernacles, with its diversions and promiscuous meetings and long night sessions, was all too favorable to license. Placing the unfortunate creature, confused and trembling, in front of Jesus, they said to him: "Master, this woman has just been taken in the very act of

---

[7] John 7:53–8:12. Abbé P. Martin has devoted enormous labor to defending the Johannine authenticity of this episode (*Introd. à la Critique textuelle du N.T.*, Vol. IV [lithographed], Paris, 1886). Scrivener (*Introd. to the Criticism of the N.T.*, 4 ed., 1894, Vol. II, pp. 364–369), who carefully cites all the authorities (manuscripts, versions, Fathers) for and against authenticity, also admits that the episode can belong to St. John, supposing that it was added to the Gospel already published, but with this reservation (p. 464): "On all intelligent principles of pure criticism the passage must needs be abandoned; and such is the conclusion arrived at by all the critical editors." In fact, all the critical editors do reject it; only Vogels (Catholic) puts it in double brackets to indicate that he considers it very doubtful. The critics' reasons are the following: (1) the absence of the episode from a great number of authorities; (2) the unusual number of variants in documents which carry it; (3) the considerable number of expressions foreign to the language of St. John; (4) the fact that it interrupts the natural sequence of the narrative. These arguments, which greatly impress specialists, are not decisive for nonspecialists.

The examination of this question is outside our sphere. It is enough for us that the episode is *canonical* and hence an authoritative source for the life and teaching of Christ. Whether it belongs to St. John or another *inspired* author is something outside our present purpose. The reasons favoring authenticity may be found in Corluy's Commentary (pp. 206–213).

adultery. Moses in the Law commands us to stone such a one. But thou, what is thy opinion?" The Law of Moses did in fact punish with death a wife guilty of adultery, and even a betrothed woman, since the betrothal was a true marriage; but it had been a long time since the legislation had been applied or even applicable. It had been necessary to moderate the rigor of the law in the course of centuries because of the slackening of morals, and no longer were wives suspected of infidelity forced to undergo the ordeal of the "bitter water." The Talmud attributes the initiative in this moderation to Johanan-ben-Zakkai, a contemporary of Christ, and, over and above that, it recognizes that stoning was not countenanced by the Romans.[8]

The tone of the questioners was deferential, but their intentions were anything but pure. They were anxious to place Jesus in the position of contradicting either the Law of Moses or his own principles of mildness, and perhaps to set him in conflict with the Roman authority. Whatever his answer should be, they had high hopes of using it against him.

Without attending to what they were saying, Jesus bent down toward the ground and wrote on the sand with his finger. Some exegetes with fruitful imaginations have thought that he wrote upon the ground the sins of the accusers and their condemnation. The conjecture is unfounded. To trace signs or characters in the sand in the middle of a conversation is the gesture of one who shows no interest in what is being said, or of one who refuses to answer an ill-timed or impertinent question. The crime of adultery came under the authority of the Sanhedrin; that was the tribunal they should have approached. In the case of a flagrantly evident crime, they could have proceeded to the execution without any

[8] The *betrothed* and her seducer should be stoned (Deut. 22:23–24). The adulterous *wife* and her accomplice were punishable by death (Deut. 22:22; Lev. 20:10), but the kind of death was not specified. According to the Rabbis, criminals condemned to capital punishment could be strangled, decapitated, burned alive, or stoned. Stoning was, in their eyes, the most severe penalty; and they held that when the law did not specify the kind of death, the least severe penalty should be applied, i.e., strangulation. The strange conclusion followed, that the adulterous wife would be punished less severely than the betrothed who was unfaithful. But Ezechiel implies (16:40) that the adulterous wife is stoned. The violator of the Sabbath also (Num. 15:32–35), though the law (Exod. 31:14) did not specify the kind of death. Hence there is no reason to conclude, as Billerbeck does, that the woman brought before Jesus was a betrothed woman (*Kommentar,* Vol. IV, p. 520).

formal process, if the Roman Procurator would tolerate it. From no viewpoint did the affair have any reference to the Saviour, and he had no opinion to give.

When the Scribes and Pharisees still insisted, Jesus finally rose and, directing at them a stern gaze, said to them: "Let him that is without sin among you cast the first stone at her." And then sitting down again he leaned once more toward the ground and began to write. Feeling themselves pierced through and through by his searching glance, whose penetration had perhaps been brought home to them by a swift examination of conscience, the Scribes and Pharisees began one by one to take their leave, beginning with the oldest. Soon Jesus found himself alone with the woman and doubtless also a group of sympathetic onlookers. Standing erect before her, he said to her: "Woman, where are thy accusers? Has no one condemned thee?" The poor bewildered creature could only answer: "No one, Lord." "Neither do I," replied Jesus. "I will not condemn thee. Go, and henceforth sin no more." Such mercy could not be an encouragement to crime. The sinner never obtains pardon except on condition of repenting, and repentance would not be sincere unless accompanied by a firm purpose of amendment.

3. Christ the Source of Life

(JOHN 7:37–52)

Two commemorative ceremonies added to the gaiety of the Feast of Tabernacles: the procession to the Fountain of Siloe, and the illumination in the Women's Court.

Every morning, the multitude, organized into a procession, descended the Tyropoeon Valley as far as the Pool of Siloe, from which the officiating priest drew water in a golden ewer and returning poured it out in libation before the altar of the Most High. Both going and returning, those assisting at the ceremony held in the left hand a citron fruit (*ethrog*) and in the right a palm branch twined with shoots of myrtle and green willow (*lulab*). The Levites chanted the great Hallel, and the whole multitude, keeping time with the refrain, vigorously waved the *ethrog* and *lulab* in token of joyfulness and triumph. It was, on the word of the Rabbis, an indescribable spectacle of popular joy. This liturgical act was a symbol and a dramatized prayer. It commemorated the miraculous water that gushed forth from the rock of Horeb beneath the rod of Moses, and it was a figure of the outpouring of graces proper to Messianic times. When the priest performing the functions drew the water of Siloe, while the choir repeated the verses of Isaias: "You shall draw water with gladness from the fountains of salvation," every thoughtful soul among them must have dreamed of the blessings promised for the days of the Messias.

The Feast properly so-called lasted only seven days, but it was closed with a great solemnity, free from work after the manner of the Sabbath. This, from the time of the Machabees, was considered an integral part of the Feast. The people, leaving the leafy huts, gave themselves over unrestrainedly to rejoicing and diversions.

The daily rite of libation had, in all likelihood, ceased on the eve of the eighth day, but it is probably not without significance that Jesus chose that particular day to draw from the rite its mystical meaning. As long as the people were living in the leafy shelters, they asked of God only fruitful dews; on the eighth day they asked that God should send early and copious rains. As the Feast of Tabernacles ordinarily fell at the beginning of October, the arrival of the first rains was impatiently awaited, since they would further the lightening of the soil and allow timely application to the work of autumn planting. Standing on the Temple esplanade in the midst of an immense crowd, Jesus cried out:

" 'If any one thirst, let him come to me and drink! He that believes in me, as the Scripture says, torrents of living water shall flow from his bosom.' — This he said of the Spirit that believers were to receive, for the spirit had not yet been given, because Jesus had not yet been glorified."[9]

[9] John 7:37–39. Several remarks may be made about this text rich in doctrine: *a*) "If any one thirst, let him come to me and drink." This is the traditional division of the phrase. The sense is complete. Jesus is the Spring from which anyone who thirsts may quench his thirst (1 Cor. 10:4; cf. Joel 3:18; Ezech. 47:1–12). Still, some divide otherwise: "Let him drink who believes in me." A good but unconvincing plea in favor of this division is made by Turner (*J.T.S.*, Oct., 1922, pp. 66–70).

To be sure, the Holy Spirit had guided the Patriarchs, inspired the Prophets, and lived in the souls of the just; but he had not yet received the mission to sanctify souls by the sensible manifestation of his Person. The theophanies of the Old Law did not have as their direct purpose the conferring of grace; this is the privilege of the New Law inaugurated on the day of Pentecost by the descent of the Holy Ghost. Then the disciple of Christ, receiving in its fullness the outpouring of the Spirit, should not only draw from the source of life, but should also become capable himself of pouring out its fruitfulness, and of quenching the thirst of those who thirst after justice. The prophets had predicted this effusion of grace:

> Fear not, my servant Jacob,
> And my well-beloved whom I have chosen;
> For I will pour forth waters upon the thirsty places,
> And streams upon the parched soil.
> I will pour forth my spirit upon thy posterity,
> And my blessings upon thy descendants.
> And they shall sprout as grass on the brink of the water,
> As the meadows by the river banks.[10]

---

b) "He that believes in me" is a sort of nominative absolute, completed after "as the Scripture says." These words do not belong to what precedes, but to what follows. The citation is not word for word. The same idea is found prophetically in Isa. 58:11 and Zach. 14:8. According to these texts, the true Israel, the believing Israel, will become in time a spring: "Thou shalt be a fountain whose waters do not fail" (Isa. 58:11).

c) The expression "torrents of living water shall flow from his bosom" (ἐκ τῆς κοιλίας αὐτοῦ) is surprising. What was the Aramaic word corresponding to κοιλία? Some think of the Syriac *karsa* (כרסא) "belly," "womb" (the meaning of κοιλία) and by extension "body." Others, of *m'ay'* (מעא), plural *m'in* (מעין) "the intestines," "the interior" (cf. *J.T.S.*, 1922, Vol. XXIV, p. 70). Billerbeck suggests the Rabbinical *guph, gupha* (גופא), which means "body," "person" (*Kommentar*, Vol. II, 492). But how could κοιλία be a translation of this word?

d) "This he said of the Spirit . . . for the spirit had not yet been given." In the first member, τὸ Πνεῦμα (with the article) designates the Person of the Holy Spirit; in the second, πνεῦμα (without the article) designates the sanctifying action of the Holy Spirit, as frequently in St. Paul. The visible mission of the Holy Spirit begins on the day of Pentecost, according to the repeated promise of the Saviour in the discourse after the Last Supper (John 14:16; 15:26; 16:7).

[10] Isa. 44:2–4, after the translation of Condamin, who adds: "Magnificent promises in favor of Israel."

The Israelites in the desert cried aloud for water; Moses struck the rock with his rod and made a spring gush forth from which all quenched their thirst. This water, says St. Paul, came not from the inert rock, but from Christ, who thus preluded the work of redemption. The true Rock from which gushed forth springs of living water was Christ himself: *"Petra autem erat Christus."* And the typical sense of this miracle prefiguring the Redemption was not unknown to the Children of Israel. Witness this passage of Isaias:

> Yahweh redeems his servant Jacob.
> They thirst not in the desert where he leads them;
> He makes the water to flow forth from the rock for them;
> He cleaves the rock and the water gushes forth.[11]

Jesus' discourse was certainly not confined to the brief and enigmatic statement transcribed by St. John, for it brought conviction to certain well-disposed souls. Many were saying: "This is truly the prophet of whom Moses speaks, the forerunner of the Messias." Others with deeper penetration went so far as to say: "This is the Messias." And still others voiced this objection, which they considered unanswerable, but which was in fact only a product of their ignorance: "Can the Messias come from Galilee? Does not the Scripture teach that he is of the line of David and therefore comes from Bethlehem?"

Meantime the menials sent to seize Jesus dared not lay hands on him, either because they were afraid of a popular uprising or because their own consciences had been stirred by what they had just heard. When the chief priests and Pharisees rebuked them for their inaction, they answered: "Never has man spoken as this man." "What then!" retorted the Pharisees. "Are you too bewitched by him? Has any one of the rulers or important people declared in his favor? He has no supporters except among the common people, that accursed breed ignorant of the Law." On the lips of the Pharisees, this was the supreme insult. "The rustic man has no fear of sin," we read in the *Sayings of the Fathers,* "and there is not among the vulgar a single God-fearing man."

---

[11] Isa. 48:21 (Condamin's trans.). The allusion of Isaias to the waters of Horeb is plain (Exod. 17:5–6; Num. 20:11).

This time, one of the members of the Sanhedrin, Nicodemus, found courage to say: "Does the Law permit a man to be condemned without hearing from his own mouth what he has done?" It was the language of reason and justice, but these fanatics were not disposed to listen to it. They rudely turned on him: "Art thou also a Galilean? Ponder the Scripture; thou wilt see that no prophet comes from Galilee." Strange mistake for men who piqued themselves on their Biblical erudition! Not to mention several others whose place of origin is disputed, no one was unaware that Jonas came from Gath-Hepher, a village near Nazareth.[12] But passion robs one of memory as well as of reason.

4. Christ the Light of the World

(JOHN 8:12–20)

Illuminations and nocturnal festivities were also characteristic features of the Feast of Tabernacles. They took place in the Women's Court, which was a vast quadrangle to which all Israelites, without distinction of sex, had access. Here is a very much abridged description of these night festivities according to the Talmud, whose figures should be received with all reserve. On the evening of the first day huge golden candelabra one hundred cubits high (about 150 feet) were set up, surmounted by enormous lamps the light of which was so intense that the whole city was illuminated as if by daylight. Levites stationed on the fifteen steps separating the Women's Court from the Court of Israel chanted canticles, accompanying themselves on all sorts of musical instruments, harps, lyres, cymbals, trumpets; and the sound of the music resounded for eight leagues, as far away as Jericho. This was the signal for the festivities. The most popular of these

[12] Westcott is a little too positive, when he writes, with reference to John 7:52: "Jonas, Osee, Nahum and perhaps Elias, Eliseus and Amos were Galileans." Osee was certainly from the Northern Kingdom, but there is nothing to prove that he was a Galilean. An ancient tradition affirms that Nahum was of the tribe of Issachar, and St. Jerome names the Galilean village of which he was a native; but neither tradition nor authority is decisive. The fact that Elias and Eliseus were often in Galilee does not prove that they were natives. As to Amos, Judea justly claims him. The Galilean origin of Jonas is not open to doubt (4 Kings 14:25).

was the dance with torches, requiring agility as well as skill. The dancers, all the while executing rhythmical evolutions, threw flaming torches high into the air, catching them before they fell to the ground. These amusements and others like them lasted sometimes up to cockcrow. It was said of them, as of the libations: "He that has not seen them has seen nothing."

It would be a mistake to consider these amusements solely under their profane aspect. The Feast of Tabernacles, as we have said, commemorated the sojourn of the Israelites in the wilderness; and, though the Rabbis did not emphasize this point, the illumination was intended to recall to all the luminous cloud that guided their ancestors in their nightly marches across the solitudes of Sinai, an event the recollection of which was engraved on the memory of the Hebrew people. All the Jews had heard the story of the exodus from Egypt read in their synagogues; when the Lord "went before them during the day in a pillar of cloud to direct their steps, and at night in a pillar of fire to give them light, thus enabling them to pursue their march by night as by day. Neither the pillar of cloud abandoned them by day, nor the pillar of fire by night." The Psalmist, when he sings of the guiding providence of God over Israel, does not forget this feature:

> He spread out the cloud to cover them
> And the fire to give them light by night. . . .
> He opened up the rock and the waters gushed forth,
> Flowing like a river across the desert.[13]

It was precisely in the Hall of the Treasury, which was part of the Women's Court where the great candelabra were set up for the illuminations, that Jesus spoke to the Jews still filled with the impressions aroused by these symbolic spectacles:

"I am the Light of the world. He that follows me walks not in darkness, but shall have the light of life."[14]

---

[13] Ps. 104 (105):39–41. A poetical version of the narrative of Exod. 13:21–22.

[14] John 8:12. "Light of the world" is a Messianic title (Isa. 42:6; 49:6; Mal. 4:2; cf. Luke 2:32). The "light of the Messias" is a common expression in the Talmud, where the Messias is called simply "Light" (*Nehirah*). Cf. Billerbeck, *Kommentar,* Vol. I, p. 67, and Vol. II, p. 428. On the meaning of the text itself, see Note C: *The Word As Life and Light.*

The illumination in the Women's Court was no more than an ephemeral glimmer, spreading no farther than the horizon of Jerusalem; the luminous cloud of the desert was no more than a local phenomenon from which one small nation alone derived benefit. Here present is the Sun which is to illumine the entire universe. It was promised many centuries ago, when God said to his Servant through the instrumentality of the prophet Isaias:

I have given thee for a covenant to the people,
a light to the nations,
to open the eyes of the blind,
to bring forth captives from prison. . . .
I will make thee Light of the nations,
to carry my salvation
even to the farthest parts of the earth.[15]

So well did the Jews know what Jesus meant by applying to himself these Messianic texts that they cried out with one voice: "Thou bearest witness to thyself; thy witness is worthless." From the legal standpoint one isolated testimony is insufficient, and a personal testimony to oneself is null and void as open to the suspicion of partiality. Jesus could indeed have answered that the light is a proof of itself by its own evidence and has no need of other proof; but he accepts their battleground:

"If I bear witness to myself, my witness is valid, because I know whence I come and where I go. But you know neither the one nor the other. Your judgments are according to the flesh. As for me, I do not judge anyone; but if I judged, my judgment would be conformed to truth, because I am not alone, but with him who sent me. In your law it is written that the witness of two men is acceptable: now, when I bear witness to myself, the Father who sent me bears witness to me."

To the question: "Where is thy Father?" he answers: "You know neither my Father nor me. If you knew me, you would know my Father." The reason — he has often given it before — is that his Father and he are but one, and therefore to know him is to know his Father. Once more the Scribes and Pharisees plot against his life, but his hour has not yet come, and the plot fails.

---

[15] Isa. 42:6–7 and 49:6 (Condamin trans.).

5. Children of Abraham — Children of Satan

(JOHN 8:21–59)

Open war has now been declared. More caution is to be observed with those who on three or four occasions have sought to seize the Saviour and who are now more than ever thinking of putting him to death.

One of the things that had shocked them most was the saying: "Where I go you cannot come." Jesus intensifies their irritation by giving the reason: "I go away, and you shall seek me in vain, and you shall die in your sins." He is alluding to the day of crisis and anguish when the Jews shall cry aloud for a deliverer and shall find none. On the day when there shall sweep down upon them the catastrophe that is to annihilate their national aspirations, they shall invoke heaven and earth in vain; they shall be abandoned by God and man, and shall die in their unbelief, because they have declined the aid of him who alone could have saved them.

His hearers make a show of treating these terrible threats with derision: sarcasm is the weapon of the weak and the vanquished. What does he mean by these words: "Where I go, you cannot come"? Does he intend to go into pagan territory and to preach his doctrine to idol worshipers? Could he, by any chance, be entertaining the notion of doing away with himself? If he is meditating such a dark crime, his virtuous adversaries decline to follow him. The Jews rightly regarded suicide as a crime against nature and an impious thing in the sight of God, who plunges the one guilty of despair into the darkest place of hell.

Without taking up these grave insults, Jesus answered solemnly: "You are from below: I am from above. You are of this world: I am not of this world. Therefore have I said to you that you shall die in your sins. Yes, verily, if you do not believe that *I am he,* you shall die in your sins."[16]

---

[16] John 8:23–24. The affirmation *ego sum* (ἐγώ εἰμι) is placed on the Saviour's lips some twenty times by St. John. When it is followed by a complement, or when one can be understood, there is no difficulty: *"I am* the bread of life, the Light of the world, the door of the sheep, the good shepherd, the resurrection and the life, the way, the truth, and the life" (John 6:35; 8:12; 10:7; 10:11; 11:25; 14:6; 15:1). — *Ego sum* means "I am he," in the answer to the Samaritan woman (4:26); "It is I," in the address to the Apostles when they think they are

The only way to escape ruin is to believe that *"I am he"*: mysterious expression, which is to recur immediately, and once again in the discourse after the Last Supper. So spoke Yahweh when he wished to assure his people of his fatherly protection, and to recall to them the role of liberator which he had taken upon himself by oath: "See you that I am he. . . . Understand that I am he. . . . I am he; I am he, I say to you, who will deliver you." Jesus puts himself in the place of the God of Israel, and adopts his very words to affirm his role of Saviour.

"Who, then, art thou?" asked the astonished Jews.

"Precisely what I say to you," answered Jesus.[17]

---

seeing a ghost (6:20); "I am he," in the address to the cohort seeking him (18:5). But four times the phrase is used absolutely (John 8:24–28; 13:19; and 8:59). The last case is special, and will be examined later on. In the other three cases there is no complement to be understood: comparison is to be made with the cases in the Old Testament where God says "I AM HE" (אני הוא); as in Deut. 32:39; Isa. 43:10 and 46:4.

[17] John 8:25: Τὴν ἀρχὴν ὅ τι (ὅτι) καὶ λαλῶ ὑμῖν. The present Vulgate: *Principium QUI et loquor vobis* is scarcely intelligible. St. Jerome wrote *Principium QUIA et loquor vobis.* Some manuscripts, but not the best, substituted for *quia* either *quod* or *qui.* Cf. Wordsworth-White, *N.T. Latine,* 1898, p. 565, note. St. Augustine attempts to find a meaning in St. Jerome's version: *Quasi dixerit, PRINCIPIUM me credite; et addit: QUIA ET LOQUOR VOBIS, id est: quia humilis propter vos factus ad ista verba descendi.* The commentary needs another to explain it.

The Greek text is not easy, because the adverbial phrase τὴν ἀρχήν and the word ὅ τι (or ὅτι) have several meanings.

a) St. John Chrysostom and his followers understand it as an interrogative phrase: "First, why do I speak to you at all?" And the holy Doctor explains: "You are not worthy that I should speak to you, much less that I should tell you who I am." It is a refusal to answer an impertinent question. Grammatically this meaning is admissible, because τὴν ἀρχήν means "first," and ὅ τι (or ὅτι) can be interrogative. But this exegesis seems to have something unsatisfactory in it.

b) Others translate, as does Maldonatus: "I am what I have told you from the first," but this translation presents several difficulties. "From the beginning" in St. John is ἐξ ἀρχῆς and not τὴν ἀρχήν. And a verb in the *past* would be required, ἐλάλησα, and not the present, λαλῶ. Nor can we see how Christ defined his nature *from the first.*

c) The most acceptable translation seems to be that of Godet: Précisément ce qu'aussi je vous déclare ("Precisely what I also declare to you"), or that of Crampon: Absolument ce que je vous déclare ("Absolutely what I declare to you"). That of Bernard (*Internat. Crit. Comment.,* 1928, p. 302) comes to the same: "Primarily, I am what I am telling you." That of Westcott is close to it: "Altogether, essentially, I am what I even speak to you." But the celebrated Anglican exegete adds an explanation which is not clear: "My Person is my teaching."

"When you have lifted up the Son of Man, then you shall know that *I am he*. I do nothing of myself, but I say what my Father has taught me. And he who sent me is with me; he does not leave me alone, for I do what is pleasing to him."

For us, nothing can be as moving as these words, revealing to us the Cross lifted above Calvary, inviting all men to recognize their Redeemer. But what touching significance could they have for those to whom the allusion meant nothing? Still, merely from hearing them, many of his listeners believed in him. Perhaps they saw something miraculous in the protection with which God surrounded this man, the object of so much hatred. Was he not right in saying that his Father watched over him always, never abandoning him? It is to be added that these last words were but the conclusion of a long discourse which contained many motives for belief. To strengthen the faith of these recent initiates, Jesus says to them:

"If you persevere in my word, you shall truly be my disciples, and you shall know the truth and the truth shall make you free."

There was an axiom among the Stoics: "Only the wise man is free; any man deprived of wisdom is a slave." The Jews for their part were ready to say with Philo: "Every virtuous man is free"; and they did not fail to count themselves among the virtuous.[18] And so these words, "the truth shall make you free," aroused energetic protests in the crowd. "We are the race of Abraham," they cried, "and we have never been slaves of anyone." From whom did these protests come? From the new believers whose wavering faith staggered under the slightest shock? Or from the unbelieving Jews mixed in among them?[19]

It does not seem that any objection can be raised to this translation, for *τὴν ἀρχήν* does mean "altogether," "absolutely," especially in negative phrases, but also in affirmatives; and *λαλεῖν* is often employed in St. John for *λέγειν*: John 3:11 (*ὅ οἴδαμεν λαλοῦμεν*); 3:34, etc.

To what *word* is the Saviour alluding? Perhaps to what he has just said: "I am from above," or "I am he"; more probably he is referring to the entire discourse where he has several times defined himself as "sent by God" and "Son of God."

[18] The Stoic axiom is quoted by Cicero (*Parad.* 5): *Μόνος ὁ σοφὸς ἐλεύθερος καὶ πᾶς ἄφρων δοῦλος*. Similar texts are to be found in Epictetus, Seneca, and other disciples of the Porch. Philo entitled one of his treatises: *"Quod omnis probus* (*σπουδαῖος*) *liber."*

[19] Schanz lines up a very long list of authorities for each of the two opinions;

The text of St. John indicates no change of questioners; but, on the other hand, would Jesus call those who had just believed in him "children of Satan," and would he reproach them for plotting against his life? Whatever is to be said about this obscure point, which is of secondary importance, a violent dispute followed which we shall simply transcribe:

Jesus — "Amen, amen, I say to you, whoever abandons himself to sin is the slave of sin. The slave does not always abide in the house (of the master, who can sell him or cast him out), but the Son abides always in the house (of his Father, whose full power he has). If then the Son restores to you your freedom, you shall be truly free.[20] I well know that you are children of Abraham, but you seek to kill me, because my word does not penetrate into you. But I teach what I have seen with my Father, and you do what you have seen with your father."

The Jews — "Our father is Abraham."

Jesus — "If you are the children of Abraham, do the works of Abraham. But now you seek to kill me, me who tell you the truth which I have heard from my Father. This Abraham would not have done. You are doing the works of your father."

The Jews — "We are not illegitimate children. We have but one father, God."

Jesus — "If God were your father, you would love me, for I have

---

many other names could be added on both sides. Some distinguish two classes of believers: those who believe *in him* (v. 30: *crediderunt in eum, ἐπίστευσαν εἰς αὐτόν*), and those who believed *him* (v. 31: *crediderunt ei, ἐπίστευσαν αὐτῷ*). Cf. Bernard, *St. John,* 1928, p. 305.

[20] John 8:34–36. The general meaning is clear: "The sinner is the slave of sin, and the Son of God alone has the power to deliver him." But the proof given, because of its laconic form, remains obscure. It should be developed in an orderly way.

a) *To do sin* (ὁ ποιῶν τὴν ἁμαρτίαν) is not simply to commit sin casually, but to give oneself over, to abandon oneself to sin, just as *to do the truth* (John 3:21: ὁ ποιῶν τὴν ἀλήθειαν) is to practice it, to live it. Cf. 1 John 3:4–8. This habitual sin is truly a servitude, a slavery.

b) The slave is in the *service* of his master, and he is a *stranger* to his master, not being part of his household or his family. But if there is question of a sinner, he is in the *service* of sin, the master to which he has given himself, and he is a *stranger* to God, his legitimate master, who never loses his rights over him.

c) How will he be liberated? By enfranchisement. If he is enfranchised and enters into the house and the family of God, he will by that very fact be delivered from the yoke of sin. But who can enfranchise him? The Son of God alone, to whom God gives full power, and who has received as his inheritance all the goods of his Father (Heb. 1:2).

come forth and come from God. . . . I have not come of myself; he it is that sent me. . . . Why do you not understand my speech? Because you cannot hear my word.[21] You have the devil for your father, and you will to do the desires of your father. He was a murderer from the beginning and did not stand in the truth, because there is no truth in him. When he lies he speaks from his own proper nature, for he is a liar and the father of lies.[22] But me, who tell you the truth, you do not believe. Which of you can convict me of sin? If I tell you the truth why do you not believe me? He that is of God hears the words of God, but you do not hear them, because you are not of God."

The Jews — "Do we not rightly say that thou art a Samaritan and one possessed by the devil?"

Jesus — "I am not possessed by the devil, but I honor my Father, whom you dishonor.[23] For my part, I do not seek my own glory; another seeks it and judges. Amen, amen, I say to you, if any one keep my word he shall never see death."

The Jews — "Now we know that thou art possessed by the devil. Abraham is dead, and also the prophets; and thou sayest: If any one keep my word he shall never taste death. Art thou greater than

---

[21] John 8:43. At first sight, the sentence seems tautological, but it is not. To *understand* it is necessary to *listen* calmly and patiently, but their hatred and their prejudice render them incapable of that. As is said later on (v. 47): They do not hear God's words, *because they are not of God,* because they are ill-disposed.

[22] John 8:44. This verse is open to misinterpretation.

a) The devil was a murderer (ἀνθρωποκτόνος) from the beginning of the world, when he caused the fall of the first man. "It is through the envy of the devil that death came into the world" (Wisd. 2:24).

b) *In veritate non stetit.* The common Greek reading is ἐν τῇ ἀληθείᾳ οὐχ ἕστηκεν, the word ἕστηκεν being the perfect with present sense from ἵστημι, but the best manuscripts and modern critics are for the reading οὐκ ἔστηκεν, imperfect of στήκειν, "to stand up." The meaning, therefore, is very simple. When he caused the death of the first man, he was not in the truth; he lied; he deceived Adam by his lie; and there is nothing extraordinary in that, for "there is no truth in him"; after his defection he is essentially a liar.

c) The phrase *cum loquitur mendacium, ex propriis loquitur, quia mendax est et pater ejus* can be understood in two ways: "because he is a liar and the father of the liar," and also "because he is a liar and the father of the lie." The word *ejus* (αὐτοῦ) could belong to *mendax* (ψεύστης) or to *mendacium* (ψεῦδος). The second is more generally received, and appears to us to be better; but in favor of the first, there are reasons which may be found in Schanz. Hilgenfeld held that the translation should be: "He is a liar as well as his father," and this father of the devil would be Ialdabaoth, demiurge and god of the Jews, according to the Ophite Gnostics. Corluy (*Comment. in Joann.,* 2 ed., 1880, pp. 229–230) has taken the trouble to refute Hilgenfeld.

[23] Note that the Gospel text reads: "I honor my Father, and you dishonor me" (Translator).

our father Abraham, who is dead, as the prophets also are dead? What, then, dost thou claim to be?"

Jesus — "If I glorify myself, my glory is nothing; it is my Father who glorifies me, he of whom you say that he is your God, though you do not know him. But I know him. If I were to say that I do not know him, I would be a liar like you. But I know him and keep his word. Abraham, your father, thrilled with the desire of seeing my day: he saw it and rejoiced."

The Jews — "What! thou art not yet fifty years old, and thou has seen Abraham?"

Jesus — "Amen, amen, I say to you: before Abraham was I exist."

The rage of the Jews rose to a paroxysm. This man was saying that he was superior to their father Abraham; he was claiming to be the only one who knows God; he was promising eternal life to those who believed in him. What fatuousness! What blasphemy! They seized stones to stone him as a blasphemer, but he escaped from their hands, if not by a miracle at least by an effect of that providence which watched over him. He quit the Temple leaving his enemies more firmly fixed than ever in their willful blindness.

CHAPTER IV

The Man Born Blind

(JOHN 9:1–41)

1. Circumstances of the Cure

IN THE environs of the Temple there was a man blind from birth who used to come to beg alms together with other beggars. Everyone knew that he had been blind from birth, for that was the refrain of his plaintive song, repeated throughout the whole day to move the pity of passers-by.

Jesus fixed upon him a glance so attentive that the disciples took note. "Master," they said, "who sinned, this man or his parents, that he should be born blind?" Ezechiel had, of course, written that the child does not bear the responsibility for the crimes of his father, and the Book of Job had developed the theme that suffering is sometimes a trial permitted or sent by God; still, many of the Jews persisted in believing that physical evil is always the punishment of sin. On the other hand, though the pre-existence and migration of souls haunted the brains of some steeped in Greek philosophy, this idea certainly had not penetrated to the mass of the people, any more than the curious notion of the Rabbis that Esau, by kicking his brother Jacob, had gone astray from his mother's womb! Still they wondered whence came this poor man's congenital infirmity.

Jesus could have answered that God, for reasons for which he does not have to account to anyone, allows secondary causes to have free play; that since the original Fall man is no longer protected against physical ills by a special providence; that the case of this unfortunate man was sufficiently explained by his membership in guilty humanity. But without entering into such speculations, he brought to their attention that they were neglecting another hypothesis. "Neither he nor his parents have sinned, but that God may manifest in him his power." Neither his personal sins nor the sins of his parents are the cause of this misfortune. Among other purposes worthy of his wisdom, God has permitted it to happen in order to cause the merciful power of his Son to shine forth. This time Jesus will work a miracle without being asked for it, and this miracle will be a *sign* proving his divine mission. "I must do the works of him who sent me while it is day. The night is coming when no one can work. While I live in the world, I am the light of the world."

The day is given to man to accomplish his daily tasks; the night is the time for rest: such is the law of nature to which the Incarnate Word has willed to submit. For him the day is the duration of his earthly life. He will act well beyond those limits with his unseen grace, but that will not be the same labor, the labor incumbent upon him as Messias. As long as the day lasts, this day to which death will put an end, he must prove to all that he is the Light of the World. He is about to show this by a symbolic act in giving the faculty of sight to a man who has never yet seen the light of the sun.

Not only does Jesus work this miracle spontaneously, without even requiring in advance the faith of the beneficiary of the miracle; but, instead of curing him by a word or simple touch, he makes use of a kind of sacramental rite and subordinates the cure to the fulfillment of an external condition. "He spat upon the ground and made clay with the spittle and rubbed the eyes of the blind man with it, saying: 'Go, wash in the Pool of Siloe (which means *Sent*).' "[1]

---

[1] The name Siloe was first given to the tunnel of Ezechias, then to the pool which received the waters of the fountain of Gihon, then to the whole region. On the other side of the Brook Cedron there is today a village named Siloe. This word *Shiloah* (from שלח, "to send") probably means overflow channel (the overflow of a lake or basin), a very appropriate name for the underground channel which diverted the water from Gihon into the pool. The Pool of Siloe measures only 52.4 by 19 feet. It was once a square, 23 yards on all sides, as is proved by the excavations carried out in the ruins of the basilica erected in this place by Justinian. Some 50 yards lower down there was a much larger basin. Today it is dry and transformed into gardens.

The saliva of a fasting man was, in those days, considered to be a specific against inflammations of the eye; not so, however, clay, which never passed as an eye salve.[2] Far from curing, it would rather have had the effect of aggravating the trouble, were it not already incurable. Before curing the blind man, Jesus blinds him still more, if that were possible; and the command to go wash in the Pool of Siloe could have had no other purpose than to prepare him for the cure by a trial of his faith and obedience.

The Pool of Siloe is situated in the Tyropoeon Valley outside the present city. It receives its water from the Virgin's Fountain (*Gihon*) by means of a subterranean channel, reputedly dug by order of King Ezechias. To go there, the blind man, with the help of a guide, we may suppose, followed the long sloping road which led down to it. There he washed his eyes and came back cured.

Great was the stir among the people upon his return. His habitual companions and the people of the neighborhood had no doubt about his identity; but those who had only seen him in passing had trouble in recognizing him, for nothing changes a face as does the look of the eyes. They said: "This cannot be he; without doubt it is someone who looks like him." But the man himself kept telling his story in the selfsame words to anyone who would listen to him: "The man who is called Jesus rubbed my eyes with clay, saying: 'Go to the Pool of Siloe to wash.' I went, I washed, and I see." "Where is this man?" they asked him. "I know nothing of that."

It was a Sabbath day, and Jesus had committed two infractions of the Sabbath rest as it was regulated by the Scribes. He had molded clay — servile work in the highest degree — and he had practiced medicine, which was permitted only to care for someone in danger of death. The case was judged grave enough to be brought to the Pharisees, who plumed themselves on being the most authoritative and most faithful interpreters of the Law of Moses.

---

[2] Tacitus, *Histor.*, iv, 81. A blind man begs Vespasian to rub his eyes with his saliva: *oculorum globos dignaretur respergere oris excremento*. Clay was not employed except against inflammations and tumors: *Turgentes oculos vili circumline caeno* (Serenus Sammonicus, second-century doctor).

2. Intrigues of the Pharisees

On being interrogated by the Pharisees, the man who had been cured could only repeat what he had already said: "He put clay on my eyes, I washed, and I see." The miracle was undeniable, but the majority of the Pharisees were determined to listen to nothing. "No," they said, "a man who thus violates the Sabbath is not from God." Still, those among them who had not yet closed their minds to all conviction — they made up but a small minority — timidly objected: "How can a man that is a sinner work such signs" where the finger of God is so manifest? But their protests were lost in the hostile clamor. The idea suggested itself of asking, perhaps in derision, the opinion of the man himself who had been cured: "And thou, what sayest thou of the man who has opened thy eyes?" Without hesitation comes his answer: "He is a prophet."

Rather than believe in the miracle, the Pharisees preferred to believe in a hoax. The pretended blindness was nothing but a fraud, a sham. The man's parents were summoned for questioning: "Is this man here your son, the one you say was born blind? How is it, then, that he now sees?" We all know the instinctive fear which rises in the hearts of little people in the presence of the agents of authority and justice. And the parents of the blind man had a special reason to fear, for the Sanhedrin had decided to exclude from the Synagogue anyone who would recognize Jesus as the Christ (Messias).[3] This penalty, more feared than the thirty-nine strokes with the lash, brought with it a certain infamy in the public eye and condemned the culprit to live in temporary exile from society almost like a leper. Hence the answer of the man's parents was cautious and reserved: "We know that he is our son, and that he was born blind. How it comes about that he now sees, and who has opened his eyes, we do not know. Ask him. He is old enough to answer." The blind man is again summoned for an attempt at intimidation, and the dialogue resumes:

---

[3] John 9:22: "Jam enim conspiraverant Judaei, ut si quis confiteretur eum esse Christum, extra synagogam fieret." On Jewish excommunication, major and minor, its causes, formalities, effects, and duration, see Billerbeck, *Kommentar,* Vol. IV, pp. 292–333.

Pharisees — "Give glory to God (by confessing the truth). We know that this man is a sinner (thy denials will not be worth anything)."

The Man — "Whether he is a sinner I do not know; I know only that I was blind, and that I now see clearly."

Pharisees — "What did he do to thee? How did he open thy eyes?"

The Man (in a bantering tone) — "I have already told you and you have heard it enough. Why do you wish to hear it again? Can it be that you wish to become his disciples?"

Pharisees — "Be thou accursed! Become his disciple thyself, if thou wilt. As for us, we are the disciples of Moses. We know that God spoke to Moses, but as for that man, we know not whence he is."

The Man (still laughing) — "What a marvel! You know not whence he is, and he has opened my eyes! Yet we know that God hears, not sinners, but those that honor and obey him. Has it ever been heard that anyone has opened the eyes of a man born blind? If this man were not from God, he could not do any such thing."

Pharisees (carried away by anger) — "Thou art nothing but sin, and wilt thou give us a lesson!"

Seeing that they could get nothing out of this simple fellow whose common sense confounded their sophistry, they drove him out loading him with insults.

The man's courageous confession and the affront he had received merited a reward. Shortly afterward Jesus met him, and it may be taken for granted that the encounter was not accidental. The blind man who had never seen Jesus recognized him without doubt by his voice, and here, without the change of a word, is the dialogue:

Jesus — "Dost thou believe in the Son of God?"[4]

The Man Born Blind — "Who is he, Lord, that I may believe in him?"

Jesus — "Thou seest him, and he it is who speaks to thee."

The Man (prostrating himself) — "Lord, I believe."

Jesus — "I have come into this world to bring about a discrimination.[5] Those who do not see shall receive sight, and those who see shall become blind."

---

[4] John 9:35. Tischendorf and Hort (but not Von Soden and Vogels) prefer the reading: *Believest thou in the Son of Man?* which is in codex ℵ and *B*. The formal act of faith would be the same: the beneficiary of the miracle is prepared to believe all that Jesus tells him.

[5] John 9:39: Εἰς κρίμα εἰς τὸν κόσμον τοῦτον ἦλθον. He does not say κρίσις (the

During this short dialogue, the curious had gathered around. The Pharisees, feeling themselves referred to in these final words, asked: "Are we blind, we too?" They expected an affirmative answer: the one they got was more crushing. "If you were blind, you would have no sin; but because you are conscious of seeing, your sin remains." There are two kinds of spiritual blindness: that of the simple who lament their ignorance and wish to emerge from it, and that of the proud who willfully close their eyes to the light of truth. The first kind of blindness is easily curable, whereas the other has no remedy. The coming of Jesus brings about the discrimination between the two classes of blind, but the discrimination is less the personal work of Jesus than of the men themselves because of him.

The cure of the man born blind is a *sign* and a *symbol:* a sign expressly chosen as such to engender faith in the most biased minds, and a symbol vesting in sensible form a divine teaching.

The sign is striking and manifest. The man born blind has never seen the light; his blindness is complete and, humanly speaking, incurable, so much so that neither he nor his parents dream of calling upon the miraculous power of Jesus. The man is known to all, because he is always in the neighborhood of the Temple, in the most frequented quarter, surrounded by beggars in the midst of whom his plaintive cry sets him apart. His cure is effected publicly in full daylight with a certain show calculated to call attention to it. When he comes back from Siloe cured, the crowd gathers around him, the Pharisees intervene, they question his parents, they question the man himself; and their inquiry results in their confusion. Finally, they do not deny the material fact; they only refuse to draw from it the conclusion and to say: "The finger of God is here!"

The symbolic character of the miracle is no less evident. According to the Prophets, the Messias was to restore sight to

---

act of judging) but κρίμα (the result of judgment, discrimination). The discrimination happens because of him, for he is set up as a sign of contradiction (Luke 2:34); but it is not he who makes the discrimination. Though he would have the right to judge and condemn (John 8:15), he is sent into the world to save and not to judge (John 3:17). The exercise of judgment concerns the future (John 5:22).

the blind. This can be understood in a proper and in a figurative sense. In the miracle of the man born blind, Jesus Christ verifies the prophecy in two ways: he gives to the eyes of the body the faculty of sight, and he illuminates the eyes of the soul by a ray of supernatural faith. He does not work either of the two prodigies without the consent and the concurrence of the interested party; and it is here above all that the symbolism is apparent. To be cured, the blind man must carry out a command the reason for which he does not know; to be delivered from spiritual blindness he must confess that Jesus is the Son of God. The lesson is easy to grasp. The Pharisees will not be delivered from their spiritual blindness unless they wish to emerge from it; but since they boast of their clearness of vision, their blindness has no remedy. Better is the condition of those who, being blind, know it and avow it. Such humble and docile people will be the first to be received into the kingdom of God.

CHAPTER V

The Good Shepherd

1. One Flock and One Shepherd

(JOHN 10:1–21)

THE parable of the Good Shepherd is linked with the cure of the man born blind, and is a continuation of the discourse pronounced during the Feast of Tabernacles. All indications of time and place are lacking, but there are several hints that allow us to conclude that we are still in the presence of the same audience, made up of enemies, indifferent listeners, and some more or less zealous disciples.

"Amen, amen, I say to you, he that does not enter by the door into the sheepfold, but lets himself in by another way, is a thief and a robber. He that enters in by the door is the true shepherd. To him the gatekeeper opens, and the sheep recognize his voice, and he calls them by name and leads them forth. And when he has brought out all his own sheep, he goes before them, and the sheep follow him, because they recognize his voice. But they do not follow the stranger, because they do not recognize the stranger's voice."[1]

Two thousand years ago in Palestine conditions were almost the same as they are today. Shelter is provided for the flocks of

[1] The words *"Amen, I say to you"* never begin a new discourse and always serve to justify what has just been said. In the preceding chapter we see that the Pharisees boast of being the disciples of Moses (John 9:28) and the spiritual guides of the people; they wish to exercise control over Christ's miracles; they threaten his followers with excommunication (v. 22); but they are blind guides, and willfully blind (vv. 39–41), who cannot but mislead instead of leading. They are evil shepherds, and the parable is directed to them.

sheep, which always remain outdoors, by penning them at nighttime in an open-air enclosure built of loose stones and surrounded by hedges of brambles and cactus. At one corner of the fold is a narrow gate through which the sheep enter and leave one by one, and thus they may be counted both going out and returning. If several flocks are together in the same enclosure, the shepherds take turns in watching, to scare away thieves and robbers. In the morning, when one of the shepherds comes to take his flock, the man on guard lets him in, and his sheep recognizing his voice immediately gather around him. When he has driven them outside, he places himself at their head and, obedient to his call, they follow him in a long file.[2]

These animals are gifted with marvelous instinct. In parts of the country where watercourses are scarce, one often sees ten or twelve flocks gathered around a cistern or spring, in the sweltering "time of the Dog Star." The sheep huddle together and lie down in the shade of a tree or rock, if there is one in the neighborhood, and patiently wait their turn. At the opportune moment the shepherd gives them warning by a kind of guttural cry, and all together they move to the trough that serves as a watering place. Another signal gives them notice to yield their places to others, and they again set themselves in motion behind the shepherd.[3]

This little pastoral scene of the Gospel is not an allegory pure and simple, and we should not try to translate each term into plainer language as though it were a string of metaphors. Certain elements that have no special significance are introduced simply to fill out the picture. For example, we should not ask whether

---

[2] Cf. J. Neil, *Everyday Life in the Holy Land,* 1913, pp. 31–38. A water color shows the door of the sheepfold from which are emerging sheep mixed with goats. A short-kirtled shepherd walks in front of them, carrying the ordinary gear: the shepherd's crook, the club, and the sling.

[3] Impressions of Upper Galilee, between Banias and Tyre (June, 1887). Cf. Jaussen, *Coutumes Palestiniennes,* 1927. The flocks, generally made up of white sheep and black goats, are guarded by a boy fourteen or fifteen years old who gives a name to each of his animals and makes them obey him. To prove it, a young shepherd cries out in a shrill voice: *Ya Bayda!* (Eh, Whitey!) "In the middle of the flock about fifty yards away, a magnificent ewe, white all over, lifts her head and, at a second call, comes trotting to the shepherd who caresses her" (p. 306).

the guard of the sheepfold is Moses, or John the Baptist, or the Archangel Michael, or Christ, or the Holy Spirit, or God without making distinction of Persons. The variety of theories such as these should have warned the interpreters that they were on the wrong track. The "similitude" of the Good Shepherd — as St. John calls it — is a mean between allegory and parable.[4] It is not in itself obscure, but it is figurative in the measure intended by its author, and hence the key to its understanding must be given by Christ himself.

"Amen, amen, I say to you, I am the Door of the sheep. All who came before are thieves and robbers, and the sheep have not heard them. I am the Door; he that enters through me shall be safe. He shall come in and go out (as he pleases) and shall find (good) pastures. The thief comes only to rob and kill and destroy, but I come to give life and abundant life."

Christ is the Door of the sheep as well as of the shepherds, because he is the only way that leads to the Father; but here there is question only of the shepherds.[5] Strangers, intruders, marauders, who seek only to injure the flock, make their way into the sheepfold by fraud or by climbing over the wall; the sheep flee at their approach, because they do not know them. Only the true shepherd enters by the door that is Christ. "All that came before are thieves and brigands." In the Fourth Gospel, "he who comes" is a sort of technical expression to designate the Messias.[6] Here, therefore, Jesus is speaking of the false Messiases who have preceded him. Three of them, whose names are known, appeared shortly after his birth; we know also that there were several others at the same period. These impostors succeeded in recruiting some partisans, but, after a short series of murders and acts of

[4] *Similitude* (παροιμία). St. John does not use the word *parable* and the Synoptics do not use *similitude,* but the meaning of the two terms is almost the same. Both correspond to the Hebrew *mashal,* which is susceptible of several meanings: apologue, allegory, proverb, enigma.

[5] J. H. Bernard (*Gospel according to St. John,* 1928, p. 365) gathers the texts of the Fathers to prove that Christ is the Gate of the sheep. No one denies it; but that is not the question. The point at issue here is the sense intended by Christ in this similitude.

[6] John 10:8: "Art thou *he who comes* (ὁ ἐρχόμενος — the Messias), or must we wait for another?" (Matt. 11:3; Luke 7:19; cf. John 1:15; 3:31; 6:14, etc.) — The difference between *fur* (κλέπτης) and *latro* (λῃστής) is that *fur* is an ordinary thief, and *latro* is a highwayman, a robber, a brigand.

brigandage, the fire which they had lighted was quenched in blood. On the contrary, the shepherds to whom Christ will open the gate of his sheepfold will be there as in their own domain; they will enjoy complete security, and Providence will bring about that they find rich pastures for their flocks.[7] All these elements are appropriately applied only to the shepherds. The sheep do not come and go as they please, and it is not upon them, but upon the shepherd, that the task falls of finding the best grazing land.

Christ is not only the Door through which the shepherds must pass to avoid being treated as intruders; he is also the Good Shepherd and, indeed, the only Shepherd, for the others are such only in a lower order. These disparate images of door and shepherd would clash in an allegory; they are in place only in a literary *genre* where diverse comparisons may follow one another to clarify the same object.

"I am the Good Shepherd. The good shepherd lays down his life for his sheep, but the hireling and he to whom the sheep do not belong takes flight and abandons them when he sees the wolf coming; and the wolf seizes them and scatters them. The hireling flees because he is a hireling and has no care for the sheep.

"I am the Good Shepherd. I know my sheep and my sheep know me, as I know my Father and my Father knows me; and I lay down my life for my sheep.

"I have yet other sheep that are not of this sheepfold. Them also must I gather; and they shall hear my voice, and there shall be but one flock and one shepherd."[8]

---

[7] John 10:9. If *salvabitur* (σωθήσεται) is understood of eternal salvation it fits both sheep and shepherds equally well; but the sense "he shall be safe" is more in harmony with the parable and with the context. The shepherd who enters by the gate shall be safe and sound; he shall have nothing to fear from dogs or other shepherds, for he is at home. He comes in and goes out as he pleases; he busies himself with searching for good pasturage for his sheep.

It is thus that the Bible describes the office of the shepherd. Moses asks God to choose someone who "may *go in* and *go out* before the people, who may make them *go in* and *go out,* that Israel may not be like a flock without a *shepherd* (Num. 27:17). Ezechiel also, in the well-known allegory of the Shepherd: "I will make them *go out* from the midst of peoples to lead them into their own ground. . . . I will *lead them to good pastures* upon the mountains of Israel" (Ezech. 34:14).

[8] John 10:11–16. Details to be noted:

Three characteristics distinguish the Good Shepherd from the hireling and the intruder: he knows his sheep and is known by them; he risks his life to defend them; he watches over the well-being and increase of the flock. These three characteristics fit Christ in such an eminent degree that to understand them it is necessary to lay aside the symbol and pass straight to its application. He knows his sheep and they know him, as he knows his Father and his Father knows him. The knowledge which the faithful have of him cannot be adequate and comprehensive; but it is so intimate that it may be compared to the mutual knowledge of the Father and the Son. St. John purposely uses this hyperbole to bring out more feelingly the close bond which unites Christ and the Christian in the communion of the Mystical Body.

The Good Shepherd lays down his life for his sheep. Shepherds have been known to risk their lives in defense of their sheep; but recklessly to sacrifice one's own life to save irrational beings would be neither proper nor reasonable. A human life is worth more than that. But what an ordinary shepherd cannot and should not do, this the Good Shepherd has literally done. He has given his life for his sheep that they may live, for, in the present plan of divine Providence, they could not have life except at that price.

"I offer up my life to take it up again: that is why my Father

---

a) The hireling is not an intruder; he takes an interest in the sheep, but it is natural that he flees before the wolf, because the sheep do not belong to him. He is introduced to set forth the devotedness of the shepherd to whom the sheep belong, and who defends his property, even at the peril of his life.

b) The comparison *As my Father knows me, etc.*, does not bear upon the nature of knowledge of the Father and the Son — that would be a very strong hyperbole — but upon the reciprocity of that knowledge, which is *mutual*.

c) In the last verse the Vulgate has *et fiet unum OVILE et unus pastor*. But all the other versions, all the Greek manuscripts, and all the Fathers (apart from those who made use of the Vulgate) have *flock* in place of *sheepfold*. Could St. Jerome have had before him a copy reading αὐλή instead of ποίμνη, or was he distracted at this point? In any case, *flock* fits in better than *sheepfold*, since a sheepfold can contain many flocks, whereas a single flock necessarily supposes a single sheepfold.

Jesus says: *I have other sheep who are not of this sheepfold* (the only one which exists, the Jewish theocracy to which the Church succeeds). These sheep are his, not in virtue of predestination, but because all who believe, and will believe in him, belong to him and are given to him by his Father. He must *conduct* them and *lead* them, for ἀγαγεῖν has both meanings, and also the meaning *to draw to himself*.

loves me. No one takes it from me; I offer it up of myself. I have the power to offer it up, and the power to take it up again: such is the command that I have received from my Father."

This is not the place to explain how the freedom of Christ is reconciled with his obedience, and perhaps this is a mystery which transcends human understanding. Still, it is true that he receives from his Father the command to die, and it is true that he dies freely. He offers up his life because he wills it, but he does not sacrifice it without the intention of taking it up again; for our Redemption would be incomplete, if the Resurrection did not follow his death.

In all the literatures of the world since the time of Homer and even before him, kings are the shepherds of the people. God did not disdain to call himself shepherd of Israel, and in the prophecies the Messias has the same title.[9] No symbol was dearer to the early Christians, and the image of the Good Shepherd is profusely scattered among the frescoes of the catacombs. The prophecy of Ezechiel is well known: "Woe to the shepherds of Israel, who feed themselves instead of feeding the sheep. . . . It is I who will feed my sheep: I will search for the one that is lost; I will bind up the wounds of the one that is wounded; I will care for the one that is sick. . . . I will raise up for them one only shepherd, my servant David. It is he who shall bring them to pasture, and he shall be their shepherd."[10]

Before the coming of the Messias, there was only one shepherd and one sheepfold, a closed sheepfold, reserved to the chosen race. When the Church succeeded to the Synagogue and put an end to Jewish exclusiveness, it recruited its members from every country, as the prophets had announced by saying that the kingdom of the Messias should have no limits but the confines of the world. "I have yet other sheep that are not of this sheepfold; them I must gather, and there shall be but one flock and one shepherd." These strange sheep that are to be sought out are evidently the Gentiles. They must not be considered as belonging

---

[9] God, the Shepherd of Israel, Ps. 22(23):1–6; Mich. 7:14; Zach. 10:3, etc. — The Messias Shepherd, Isa. 40:11; Ezech. 37:24; 34:23, etc. — Christ is the Chief of Shepherds (ἀρχιποιμήν), 1 Peter 2:25; 5:4.

[10] Ezech. 34:2–23.

to another sheepfold; the fold, both before and after, is one. Rather the pagans are wandering sheep which Christ wishes to lead into his sheepfold, and then there will be truly only one flock and one shepherd. There will also be only one sheepfold: that goes without saying; but Jesus avoids the use of this term because, in the minds of his hearers, the same fold can contain several flocks belonging to several shepherds. The fusion of Jews and Gentiles in the unity of the Mystical Body — that pivot of Pauline theology — finds here a new expression as happy as it is picturesque.

2. The Feast of Dedication

(JOHN 10:22–39)

The apologue of the Good Shepherd had vividly impressed a part of the audience. Christ's implacable enemies kept saying: "This man is possessed by the devil; he is mad." But others replied: "These discourses are not those of a man possessed by the devil. Can the devil open the eyes of a man born blind?" Jesus came back to Jerusalem two months later for the Feast of Dedication and resumed the subject, in order to explain how the Son is equal to the Father, and how their activity is inseparable.

The Feast of Dedication began on the 25th of Kislew, the month corresponding almost to our month of December. It had been instituted by Judas Machabeus in 164 B.C. to commemorate the restoration of the altar of the true God, which had been profaned three years before by Antiochus Epiphanes. It lasted eight days and was celebrated with great pomp and splendor, above all in Jerusalem. The ceremonial, partially modeled on that of the Feast of Tabernacles, included grand illuminations, which had gained for it the name of Feast of Lights.[11]

---

[11] The institution of the feast (1 Mach. 4:59); celebration of the feast "with green branches and palms" (2 Mach. 10:7). Josephus, after having described it, says: "They made a law that their descendents should celebrate every year for eight days the restoration of the Temple. From that time, up to the present day, we celebrate this feast which we call the feast of Lights, a name which was given to it, I believe, because liberty had shone forth for us in a way unhoped for" (*Antiq.*, XII, vii, 7). A more extended description according to the Talmud may

Since it was at the height of the rainy season, Jesus had taken refuge in the Porch of Solomon and was walking along the colonnade which overhung the ravine of Cedron toward the east.[12] The people who wanted to hear him were accompanying him as he walked up and down, after the fashion of the peripatetics. On that particular day the attendant crowd was far from sympathetic. Of a sudden the Jews crowded around him, calling upon him to answer their question: "Why dost thou still keep our soul in suspense? If thou art the Christ, tell us so frankly and openly." Jesus had, before this, given a clear enough manifestation on this point to anyone who was willing to reflect. If he had not openly claimed the title of Messias, outside the circle of the Apostles, it was to avoid furnishing fuel for popular passions, so ready to be inflamed, and to avoid giving occasion to disorders which the Roman authorities would have pitilessly repressed. But he had shown that he was such by his teaching and miracles.

"I have told you and you do not believe me. The works which I do in the name of my Father bear witness to me. But you do not believe, because you are not of the number of my sheep. My sheep hear my voice: I know them and they know me; and I give them eternal life. They shall never perish and no one shall be able to snatch them out of my hands. What my Father has given me is greater than all; and no one can snatch (anything) out of the hands of my Father. (Now) I and my Father are one."

Abstracting from variants, the argument is presented thus: "No one can snatch my sheep out of the hands of my Father, and consequently out of mine, for I and my Father are one."[13]

---

be found in Billerbeck, *Kommentar,* Vol. II, pp. 539–541. The Hebrew name of the feast is *Hanukkah* (חנכה), Dedication, Consecration.

[12] Josephus, *Antiq.,* XX, ix, 7. "This Porch, the work of Solomon, was situated on the outside of the Temple and overhung a deep valley (the Cedron) for a distance of 400 cubits. The wall is built of very white, rectangular stones each one of which is 20 cubits in length by 6 in height." No objection can be taken to the length of the wall, 400 cubits (about 600 ft.), but stones 20 cubits in length by 6 in height (30 by 9 ft.) were certainly rare.

[13] John 10:29. In our translation we have followed the Vulgate. The Greek manuscripts offer three variants:

a) ὁ πατὴρ ὃς δέδωκέν μοι πάντων μείζων ἐστίν.

b) ὁ πατὴρ ὃ δέδωκέν μοι πάντων μεῖζον ἐστίν.

c) ὁ πατὴρ ὃ δέδωκέν μοι πάντων μείζων ἐστίν.

The reading *c* (with the neuter of the pronoun and the masculine of the

It is plain that, to be conclusive, this reasoning supposes the perfect equality of the Son and the Father, equality of nature as well as of power. Thus orthodox writers have always depended upon this text to prove the dogma of the consubstantiality of the Father and Son.

The Jews understood very well what Jesus wished to say. They understood it better than the Arians of the fourth century, better than certain commentators of our own day. They cried out "Blasphemy," and seized stones to stone on the spot the blasphemer who made himself equal to God. But in those sunny countries there is some distance between cries of "Death" and the execution, between gestures and blows. The most violent storms sometimes subside as rapidly as they break out. Then, too, they were under the eyes of the Roman garrison, which looked down from the height of Antonia upon the crowd massed in the

---

adjective), which is preferred by Von Soden, is very feebly attested and conveys no meaning; it defies translation.

The reading *a* (pronoun and adjective both masculine) is that of all the Greek manuscripts, both cursives and uncials (except four), of the Syriac versions, and of the Coptic-Sahidic version. It is adopted by Vogels. The meaning is perfectly clear: No one can take my sheep away from me. "My Father who has given (them) to me is greater than all and no one can snatch them from the hands of my Father: I and my Father are one." The only difficulty about this reading is that it is too easy. To state that God is greater than all seems a truism.

The reading *b* (pronoun and adjective both neuter) has for it only four uncials (among them *B* and *L*), but it is that of the Latin versions, and naturally of the Latin Fathers, except perhaps Tertullian. It has certainly the merit — if it be a merit — of being a difficult reading. First of all the inversion is very awkward: "My Father, what he has given me is greater than all," instead of "What my Father has given me is greater than all." Secondly, one wonders: what is it that the Father has given him? The context suggests the answer: "the flock." But can it be said that it is "greater than all" and that for that reason nothing can take it from the Father? It is necessary, then, to introduce an idea alien to the context: "divine power, divine nature." Even in this hypothesis, the phrase: "the divine nature which the Father has given me by eternal generation is greater than all," although incontestably true, does not fit in with what follows: "and no one can take from the hands of my Father." One still wonders what: the sheep? the power which I have from my Father?

But, it must be repeated, the variants do not weaken the reasoning, and the phrase could be omitted without disturbing the general sense.

The text is quoted according to the Vulgate in the Fourth Lateran Council (Denzinger, 432); but, as is known, a Scriptural proof is not defined together with the doctrine it supports; and Catholic authors understand the *quod dedit mihi* of the Vulgate either of the sheep, or of the Church, or of the power conferred on Christ, or of his function as Redeemer, or of the divine nature which he has from the Father. Both questions, the critical and the exegetical, are open.

Temple courts. Jesus tranquilly replied: "I have shown you many good works done in the name and by the authority of my Father. For which of these works do you wish to stone me?" "It is not for good works," they howled in fury, "but because being only a man thou makest thyself God." He answered:

"Is it not written in your law: 'You are gods'? If those to whom God speaks are called gods — for the witness of the Scripture is unimpeachable — why do you accuse of blasphemy him whom God has consecrated and sent into the world because he has said: I am the Son of God? If I do not the works of my Father, do not believe me; but if I do them and you refuse to believe me, believe at least my works, and thereby know and acknowledge that my Father is in me, and I in my Father."[14]

The answer can be paraphrased as follows: It is not the use of the name of God that is a blasphemy, since the Scripture applies it in a figurative sense to certain magistrates who had but a small share of divine authority. For a much stronger reason the name would suit him "whom the Father has consecrated and sent into the world." Has not such a one the right to call himself "Son of God"?

To those who had no suspicion of the mystery of the Trinity there was no other answer to make. If he had said, "I am God," he would have been understood as wishing to substitute himself for the one God of Israel, and the Jews would have had reason to cry, "Blasphemy." In saying, "I am the Son of God, but my

---

[14] John 10:34–39. The citation is taken from Ps. 81(82):6, where God applies to the judges the name *elohim* (god) in a non-proper sense, as in Exod. 7:1: "I have constituted thee *god* of Pharao and thy brother Aaron shall be thy prophet." It is an *ad hominem* argument to which the Jews, according to their principles, can have nothing to answer.

The discourse pronounced on the Feast of Dedication contains a complete Christology:

1. "I and my Father are one" proves the consubstantiality of the Father and the Son and the distinction of the two Persons (v. 30).

2. "My Father is in me and I am in my Father" is the most exact formula of *circuminsession* (v. 38).

3. "I am the Son of God," with the relation of Father to Son, expresses the eternal generation of the Word (v. 36).

4. "He whom the Father has sent into the world" (v. 36) designates the temporal mission of the Incarnate Word.

5. "He whom the Father has sanctified" (v. 36) would remain to be explained; but it is impossible to exhaust a teaching so rich in doctrine.

Father and I are but one," he affirms the oneness of the divine essence and at the same time the distinction of Persons. The plural verb and the relation of Father to Son mark the distinction, and the singular attribute designates the oneness. But he does not wish them to believe merely his word; he makes an appeal to his works, which are divine.

Far from appeasing or convincing Jesus' enemies, this discourse irritated them still more. Again they sought to seize him. By what miracle did he escape from their hands? The Gospel does not tell us.

The Saviour left these fanatics and returned to the other side of the Jordan, to the place where John had baptized at the beginning of his ministry. There he was joined by a great number of people who were attracted by the fame of his miracles, and also, it would seem, by the witness of John. For they said: "John worked no miracles, but everything that he said about this man is fulfilled." Thus the Baptist even after his death was gaining recruits for the Saviour.

The Porch of Solomon, the scene of the drama we have just outlined, enjoyed special veneration in the primitive Church. It was there that Peter, after the cure of the beggar at the Beautiful Gate, addressed an immense multitude with such great success that, despite the furious opposition of the Sadducees, the number of the faithful increased to five thousand. It was there that the Apostles established their headquarters when the multitude of believers, men and women, augmented beyond measure. Nowhere else could the first preachers of the faith have found so spacious a basilica. The Porch of Solomon surpassed in length St. Peter's in Rome.

CHAPTER VI

Against the Pharisaic Spirit

APART from the short visit to Jerusalem for the Feast of Dedication, Jesus spent in Perea the four or five months elapsing between the Feast of Tabernacles and the raising of Lazarus. St. Luke has preserved for us a series of miracles belonging to this period, into which he has inserted some of the most beautiful of the parables: the Prodigal Son, Lazarus and the Rich Man, the Faithless Steward, the Pharisee and the Publican; but he is so reticent on indications of time and place that it is impossible to follow the march of events and to reconstruct the historical framework.

After his departure from Galilee, Jesus preaches scarcely at all in the synagogue. Either because of the hostility of the religious leaders, or because of the immense crowds which no edifice would have been able to hold, we shall find him in such a place only once during this period. He teaches in the open, before a generally sympathetic audience. Sometimes he addresses himself specially to his disciples, for, although his teaching has in it nothing of the esoteric, still it requires some initiation to understand its full bearing. Often he attacks the Scribes and Pharisees, denouncing their vices and errors.[1]

---

1 The part peculiar to St. Luke — called in English "The Great Interpolation" — comprises about nine chapters (Luke 9:51–18:14). Elsewhere we have given an analysis of it, together with indications of parallel passages. See the Appendix: *Concord of the Gospels,* Vol. I, pp. 528 ff.

The first part (9:51–11:13), in which a certain sequence of events is noticeable, and which seems to belong to the beginning of the sojourn in Judea and Perea, has been studied above at the beginning of Book III. For the rest we make no attempt to establish a chronological order.

1. The Question of Divorce[2]

One day a group of Pharisees proposed to him this case of conscience: "Is it allowed that a man repudiate his wife for any reason?" The question, which was purposely ambiguous, could mean: "Is the least pretext enough to repudiate a wife?" or "Is there any valid reason for repudiating her?"

Moses, finding divorce prevalent in neighboring nations, and doubtless among his own people also, had confined himself to regulating it. He had restricted it to a case where the wife had committed a shameful act, and had obliged the husband repudiating her to place in her hands in the presence of witnesses a writ declaring her entirely free of the conjugal bond.[3] This formality, while it gave the husband time for reflection and repentance, was also a safeguard for the wife. Dealing with a gross and carnal people, who would not have accepted any constraint unknown in neighboring nations, Moses had learned that essentials must be saved, and primordial principles of morality must be safeguarded: time and the progress of revelation would do the rest.

The wife was not sacrificed to the arbitrary whim of her husband. The euphemism "something shameful" clearly enough indicated misconduct, and this was exactly what the disciples of Shammai understood by it. But, for the rival school of Hillel, any physical or moral defect, a spoiled sauce or a burned roast, or even less, if that is possible, was justification for divorce. The

---

[2] Matt. 19:1–12; Mark 10:1–12. This is the only incident that the first two Synoptics report between the departure from Galilee and the events immediately preceding the Passion. Of this episode St. Luke has retained only our Lord's saying about the indissolubility of marriage (Luke 16:18), and has placed it in the midst of various maxims directed against the Pharisees.

[3] Deut. 24:1–4. If the repudiated wife remarries and the second husband also repudiates her or dies, it is absolutely forbidden for the first to take her back.

On all that concerns the "book of divorce" (βιβλίον ἀποστασίου), cf. Billerbeck, *Kommentar,* Vol. I, pp. 303–321. In Lightfoot, *Horae Hebr.,* Vol. II, 291, may be found the Hebrew text of the usual formula. After the date, the name of the place, and the husband's name, the text continues: "Cum summo animi consensu, atque absque ulla coactione urgente, ego repudiavi, dimisi atque expuli te (name of the wife and her country) ita ut libera et de jure tuo sis, nuptum iri cuicumque placuerit, etc."

The controversy between the Rabbis revolved around the meaning of **ערות דבר** (*'erwath dabar,* ἄσχημον πρᾶγμα, *propter aliquam foeditatem*), which the Hebrew legislator gave as the sole reason for divorce.

famous Rabbi Aqiba in the second century went one better still: it would be enough that a man should find his wife uglier or less attractive than another woman; in such a case he would have the right to dismiss her. It would seem that these laxist principles were current in Palestine at the time of Christ. Josephus blithely tells how he had repudiated his wife, the mother of three children, because her way of acting displeased him; which would seem to amount to "incompatibility of temperament."[4]

The intention of the Pharisees was to lead Jesus to make a pronouncement on the liceity of divorce, about which they themselves, strong in the authority of Moses, had no doubt at all. Disdaining to engage in Rabbinical quibbles, Jesus went straight to the basic consideration:

"Have you not read that in the beginning God made man and woman different in sex and said to them: A man shall leave his father and mother, and cleave to his wife, and they shall be one and the same flesh. Since they are but one flesh, let not man separate what God has made one."

By creating only one human couple in the beginning, and by uniting the man to the woman in a way that made them but one moral person, God had sufficiently manifested his intention of founding marriage on the basis of unity and indissolubility; hence it is not in man's power to undo what God has done, to separate what he has united. These conclusions were not contested by the Jews, who did not admit divorce for other nations. They saw in this only a privilege for Israel, a privilege of which they were proud. From this arose their objection: "Why did Moses enjoin upon us to give (to the woman who is repudiated) the writ of divorce and to dismiss her?" The permission given by Moses was only a temporary tolerance which was to cease with the Gospel. Such is the meaning of the answer which St. Matthew ascribes to Jesus:

"Moses permitted you to dismiss your wives because of the hardness of your heart; but in the beginning it was not so. And

---

[4] Josephus, *Vita,* 76 (426): *τὴν γυναῖκα, μὴ ἀρεσκόμενος αὐτῆς τοῖς ἤθεσιν, ἀπεπεμψάμην τριῶν παίδων γενομένην μητέρα.* The true reason was that he wished to marry another woman, nobler and more to his taste. Polygamy was permitted by Jewish law, but it was severely frowned upon at Rome where Josephus had settled.

I say to you: Whoever repudiates his wife — outside the case of fornication — commits adultery."[5]

The apparently restrictive phrase must be interpreted in the light of Gospel teaching about the indissolubility of marriage,

[5] Matt. 19:9: μὴ ἐπὶ πορνείᾳ (*nisi ob fornicationem*). In Matt. 5:32, the restrictive phrase is presented thus: παρεκτὸς λόγου πορνείας (*excepta fornicationis causa*).

1. The ordinary solution, which may be called the classic one, goes back to St. Jerome (in Matt. 19:9; ML, XXVI, 135). It amounts to this: (*a*) "fornication" here means adultery; (*b*) the divorce is only a bodily separation; (*c*) neither husband nor wife could marry again, because the conjugal bond is not broken. — But there are three difficulties: (*a*) fornication (πορνεία) is not adultery (μοιχεία); (*b*) to "repudiate" (ἀπολύειν) is not the same thing as to part company (χωρισθῆναι), and the Jews had no idea of a divorce that did not break the conjugal bond; (c) for a bodily separation there are several other reasons besides adultery.

2. The second solution is based upon the authority of St. Augustine (*De Conjugiis adulter.*, i, 9, ML, XL, 456). Jesus does not answer the insidious question of the Pharisees. He does not state that divorce is permitted because of adultery: he abstracts from such a case, and this is not a concession, but a preterition. Bellarmine, *De Matrimonio,* lib. I, cap. i, finds St. Augustine's opinion very probable. The teaching of St. Matthew, in itself true but incomplete on this point, is completed by St. Mark, St. Luke, and St. Paul. Among moderns, Zahn follows the same explanation.

This explanation is not to be confused with the opinion according to which Jesus took his stand upon the ground of the Mosaic Law, on which the Pharisees who were interrogating him also placed themselves. In this explanation he would only be giving a provisional decision: "As long as the law of Moses remains, there is no other cause for divorce than fornication."

3. The third solution keeps to the proper sense of the words. *Dimittere* (ἀπολύειν), when used of marriage, does not mean "to send away," but "to repudiate," and the Jews to whom Jesus was speaking could not have understood it otherwise. Πορνεία (fornication) is always distinct from μοιχεία (adultery), but the word πορνεία can also mean "concubinage," "marriage between relatives" forbidden by the Mosaic Law (Lev. 18:1–17), a law which was retained and strengthened by the Church. The concubinage of the Corinthian who had married his stepmother is qualified by St. Paul as πορνεία and could not be designated in any other way, for the Greeks had no special word for concubinage. Cf. Cornely on 1 Cor. 5:1. This *matrimonium attentatum* was evidently null and void, and the man who has attempted it not only can but must dismiss his companion. Keeping rigorously to the terms, the texts of St. Matthew become very clear; "Whoever repudiates his wife (πᾶς ὁ ἀπολύων) — *outside the case of concubinage* (παρεκτὸς λόγου πορνείας, Matt. 5:32), or *not because of concubinage* (μὴ ἐπὶ πορνείᾳ, Matt. 19:9) — and marries another is an adulterer." Thus Jesus answers the Jews who interrogate him about *divorce* and not about a bodily separation, and teaches that marriages between blood relations are invalid under the Law of Christ as they were under the Law of Moses. For this explanation, may be cited: Döllinger, Schegg, Patrizi (*De Interpret. Bibl.,* 2 ed.[Rome, 1886], n. 281), Aberle, Cornely, etc. For other explanations cf. Vosté (*R.B.,* 1918, pp. 569–579) and Colson (*Expositor,* June, 1916).

and in harmony with the context of St. Matthew which supposes a return to the primitive sanctity of marriage as God announced it in the terrestrial Paradise. Hence, in whatever way the phrase "outside the case of impurity" is understood, there is no real exception. Christ explains this beyond the shadow of a doubt as soon as he is alone with the Apostles: "Whoever repudiates his wife and marries another commits adultery; and he that marries the repudiated wife commits adultery." No subterfuge, no escape; the rule is absolute and does not admit of any exception. St. Mark is still more explicit: "Whoever repudiates his wife and marries another, makes himself an adulterer with regard to the first; and if the wife repudiates her husband and marries another, she makes herself an adulteress."

Among the Jews, only the man could initiate divorce proceedings, but Roman women sometimes arrogated this right to themselves, with the sanction or the tolerance of the public authorities, and it seems that this abuse had already penetrated into Palestine, at least in the royal family. Witness the case of Salome, Herod's sister, who abandoned her husband Costobar; and Herodias, who left her uncle Philip to marry another uncle Antipas. St. Mark, writing at Rome for readers who were acquainted with such usages, could comment upon the Saviour's thought and add by way of explanation the sentence: "If a wife repudiates her husband to marry another, she makes herself an adulteress." The teaching of Jesus on the indissolubility of Christian marriage is so clear, both in St. Paul and in the Gospel, that the Catholic Church has never had any doubt on this point, despite the apparent exception formulated by St. Matthew.[6]

[6] 1 Cor. 7:10. "To those who are united in marriage, I command — not I, but the Lord — that a wife is not to depart from her husband (μὴ χωρισθῆναι); and in case she has departed, that she is not to contract a new marriage or that she be reconciled to her husband; and that a husband is not to send away (μὴ ἀφιέναι, *not to repudiate*) his wife." As is plain, St. Paul expressly refers to a *command* of the Lord such as is transmitted to us by St. Mark (10:11–12) and St. Luke (16:18). The clause forbidding the husband to repudiate his wife is absolute and without exception (μὴ ἀφιέναι); the case of a bodily separation is envisioned, but then the woman cannot remarry, which evidently supposes that the marriage persists.

The exegesis of the Fathers has been studied by Max Denner (*Das Ehescheidung im N.T.*, Paderborn, 1910). His conclusion is that *all* the writers of the first three centuries, and the Latin Fathers with very few exceptions, are for the indissolubility of Christian marriage, even in the case of adultery. Cf. Ott, *Die*

But the disciples, imbued with Jewish ideas, hearing it announced for the first time, were so surprised that they cried out: "If such be the case of a man with his wife, it is not expedient to marry." Jesus replies: "Not every one takes in this saying, but only those to whom God gives (to take it in): there are eunuchs who are born such from their mother's womb; and there are eunuchs who have become such by the deed of men; and there are those who have made themselves eunuchs for the sake of the kingdom of heaven. Let him that is capable of taking it in, take it." This parabolic language would have scandalized the Pharisees, if they had heard it. It is still a rock of scandal for many Christians separated from the Church of Rome; but it was not such for the Apostles whom Jesus was addressing. By that time, they had been enough enlightened to know and appreciate the excellence of virginity. The *Qui potest capere capiat* is not aimed simply at a speculative understanding of this counsel of the Gospel; it is a discreet invitation to make it pass into life's practice.

2. Hypocrisy of the Pharisees

At this period not all the Pharisees were equally hostile to Jesus, and one of them invited him one day to share his midday meal. Ordinarily an invitation would be given to the evening meal, but the Pharisee, desirous of entertaining him, had taken advantage of his passing through, perhaps to take his measure and to assure himself personally whether his merit corresponded to his renown.

Since there was no question of a ceremonial dinner, the servants had not poured water on the hands of the guests, and Jesus went to take his place at table without making the usual ablutions beforehand. Now, he had been in contact with all kinds of people and was probably returning from a journey; he should, therefore, according to the maxims of the Rabbis, have washed his feet and

Auslegung der neutest. Texte über Ehescheidung, Münster, 1911. Many Protestants of the present day agree that this was the teaching of Jesus (see a list of names in Vosté, *R.B.,* 1918, p. 575). But they hold, at least some of them, that Matthew has introduced the restrictive clause *on his own authority* to avoid certain practical difficulties. So Kirsopp Lake, *Expositor,* Nov., 1910, p. 427. W. P. Paterson, *Expositor,* Oct., 1910, pp. 289–305, is more reasonable.

his hands. The Pharisee, who was observing him, was interiorly scandalized. But, whether through courtesy or deference, he did not dare manifest his astonishment. Our Lord, divining his thoughts, said to him, "You Pharisees, you purify the exterior of the cup or dish, but your interior is full of rapine and malice. Foolish men! Did not he who made the outside make the inside also? Give alms according to your means and all will be pure for you."[7]

Logic would seem to call for this conclusion: "Purify yourselves inside, and the outside will be pure." But Semitic thought does not proceed with such rigor. Christ is opposing moral purity, the true purity, to legal, or rather Rabbinical purity. It is as though he said: "Acquire purity of heart — to which almsgiving greatly contributes — and thus possessing essential purity, the only kind that matters, you need not be anxious about the multiple purifications prescribed by your Doctors." He names beneficence in preference to any other virtue because he knows the rapacious instincts of these men, and also because Scripture frequently commends the efficacy of almsgiving for the remission of sin.

After this charitable advice, Jesus passes without transition to a vehement indictment of the Scribes and Pharisees. This sudden change of attitude was occasioned, no doubt, by some special circumstance which St. Luke does not record:

"Woe to you Pharisees, who pay the tithe on mint and rue and the smallest herb, and who neglect justice and the love of

---

[7] Luke 11:39–41. The general meaning of the text is clear, but there are some difficulties of detail: (*a*) "He who made the *outside* (the vessels, the body) has also made the *inside* (the soul)." If it is reasonable to purify material beings, how much more to watch out for the purity of spiritual creatures? — (*b*) *Verumtamen quod superest date eleemosynam.* The *quod superest* of the Vulgate has been understood in three ways: (1) *what remains to you* after you have restored the fruit of your rapine; (2) *what remains to you* after providing for your subsistence, *your superfluity;* (3) *the only means that remains to you.* None of these meanings is satisfactory, if compared with the Greek: πλὴν τὰ ἐνόντα δότε. Many think that τὰ ἐνόντα means *what is within* (give in alms the *contents* of the dishes and cups and you will be quite pure); others think that τὰ ἐνόντα means *what is in your possession,* your goods, your resources (as in Plato's *Republic,* p. 488c), or that κατά is understood with it, *according to your means* (as in Demosthenes 312, 20: ἐκ τῶν ἐνόντων). This last meaning seems the best: "Give alms to the poor *of your goods,* or *according to your means.*"

God. Those things it behooved you to do, and not to omit these others.

"Woe to you Pharisees, who strive for the first places in the synagogues and for greetings in the streets.

"Woe to you, who are like hidden sepulchers which men tread upon without perceiving them."

One of the Scribes present gathered quite clearly that the grievances pronounced against the Pharisees were also directed against people of his own kind. Almost all the Scribes were Pharisees, and they formed with the latter but one body of which they were the soul. This man therefore believed himself authorized to intervene in favor of his confreres. "Lord," said he, "speaking thus you insult us also." The answer proves that he has hit the mark:

"Woe to you also, doctors of the law, because you load men with insupportable burdens, which you yourselves do not deign to touch with the tip of your finger.

"Woe to you, who build the sepulchers of the prophets killed by your fathers; you are witnesses to them and you co-operate in the deeds of your ancestors: they killed them, and you build their tombs.

"Woe to you, doctors of the law, who take away the key of knowledge: you yourselves do not enter, and you prevent others from entering."[8]

We can well believe that our Lord had often stigmatized the conduct of the Scribes and Pharisees. St. Matthew has an analogous indictment couched in still stronger terms. It may be

[8] Luke 11:42–52; Matt. 23:1–36. St. Luke has three *woes* against the Pharisees and the same number against the Scribes. We transfer the explanation of obscure points in St. Luke to the examination of the seven *woes* of St. Matthew.

The ending of Verse 48, in whatever way it is explained, is difficult. Fr. Lagrange translates: "You are, then, witnesses! And you give your assent to the works of your fathers, for they have killed them, but you build." The translation is literally exact, but what does it mean? Maldonatus is of the opinion that the sentence is ironical: you claim to honor the prophets in raising tombs to them; in reality you are continuing the work of your fathers; they have killed them; you bury them. See Maldonatus on Matt. 23:31. He takes care to add: "Non quod Christus judicaret eos eo animo sepulchra prophetarum aedificare, ut patrum suorum homicidiis consentirent, sed quod factum ipsum in eam etiam partem non minus quam in contrariam posset aliquis interpretari."

that the Evangelists, to avoid repetition, have gathered all the grievances in the same discourse, which is placed on the eve of the Passion by one of them, and left in its historical setting by the other.

In St. Luke's version the Scribes are treated more severely than the Pharisees, whose spiritual guides they were. Jesus reproaches the Pharisees for three things: a narrow formalism, which made them cleave to minutiae, to the prejudice of essentials; a puerile ostentation and vanity in striving for places of honor; and finally a hypocrisy which likens them to concealed sepulchers. But the Scribes are still less pardonable. They crush others with burdens, which, by a perverted casuistry, they manage to shift from their own shoulders; they erect sumptuous tombs to the prophets, as though to repair the misdeeds of their ancestors, while they themselves show the same hostility toward the successors of the prophets; they arrogate to themselves a monopoly of knowledge, and make of it a sort of reserved domain, to prevent others from following the way of salvation which they themselves desert.

From this day on, the Scribes and Pharisees swore against the Saviour a sullen hatred which awaited only an occasion to break out into the worst excesses. They spied malignantly on his every movement, and exerted every effort to draw from him, by their insidious questions, some compromising word. Their blindness was equaled only by their foolishness. These men, who boasted that they held the key of knowledge, had learned nothing from the preaching of the Baptist or the miracles of Jesus: "When you see the clouds massing in the west, you say: 'The rain is coming.' And so it happens. And when the wind blows from the south, you say: 'It will be hot.' And so it is." Jesus does not reproach them for their more or less accurate prognostications, but he is astonished that they close their eyes to much more important signs, signs which are altogether infallible. "Hypocrites! You know how to discern the face of the sky and of the earth; why then do you not discern the signs of the present times?"

And yet, the case of the Scribes and Pharisees is not hopeless, and Jesus exhorts them to repentance. Debtors to divine justice, and debtors who cannot pay, there always remains for us up to the fatal day the hope and the possibility of softening our creditor. "While thou art going with thy adversary before the magistrate, strive to come to an agreement with him before arriving. Otherwise he shall drag thee before the judge, and the judge shall deliver thee to the officer, who shall cast thee into prison. And thou shalt not come out from there, I say to thee, before thou hast paid the last mite."[9]

An event that had happened recently gave a practical turn to this interview. Some pilgrims from Jerusalem were telling how Pilate had ordered the massacre of certain Galileans while they were in the act of offering their sacrifices in the Temple. The people were wondering what could have drawn down such a misfortune upon these men; for the belief prevailed that every calamity, whether public or private, was always the punishment of crime, and that the more unfortunate a man, the greater must be his guilt.

"Do you think," said Jesus, "that these Galileans were the greatest sinners in Galilee? No, I say to you. But unless you do penance, you shall all perish in like manner. And the eighteen men whom the tower of Siloe crushed in its fall, do you think that they were the guiltiest in Jerusalem? No, I say to you. But unless you do penance, you shall all likewise perish."[10]

Neither the murder of the Galileans nor the accident at Siloe has left any other trace in history. At a time when mass killings were so frequent, such a massacre would be only one more incident of local interest. Perhaps the Galileans, who were famous for turbulence, had raised some disturbance which Pilate, with characteristic brutality, had straightway suppressed, "mingling

---

[9] Luke 12:58–59. There are five persons: the pursued debtor, his adversary or creditor (ἀντίδικος), the magistrate or governor (ἄρχων), the judge (κριτής), and the officer or bailiff (πράκτωρ). It is a parable, and not an allegory: two analogous situations are compared, but we are not to search for what corresponds to the various persons. In reality, as Godet remarks (*Saint Luc.*, Vol. II, p. 148), "in the application, God is at once adversary, judge, and bailiff: the first by His sanctity, the second by His justice, the third by His power."

St. Matthew (5:25–26) has a similar parable, but the application is altogether different; it treats of avoiding the judgment of God, but by effecting a reconciliation with the neighbor.

[10] Luke 13:1–5. The incident must be recent, because *it is announced* to Jesus while he is speaking to the people. The Vulgate, *aderant quidam,* would allow us to think that they were already there, but παρῆσαν here means *came,* not *were present.*

their blood with their sacrifices." These last words need not be taken literally, since it is unlikely that the Procurator's soldiers had invaded the Sanctuary. Perhaps they struck down the Galileans in the Temple courts, while the victims offered by them were being slain inside.

The parable of the Barren Fig Tree, proposed on this occasion, had for its purpose to engrave more deeply in the minds of all the need of penance for peoples as well as for individuals.

"A man had a fig tree, planted in his vineyard, and having come to seek fruit on it and finding none, he said to the vinedresser: 'Behold, for three years I have come to seek fruit on this fig tree and have found none. Cut it down. Why does it drain the soil without profit?' The vinedresser answered: 'Lord, let it alone this year too, so that I may dig a trench all around it and manure it. Perhaps it will then bear fruit; otherwise thou shalt cut it down.' "[11]

For the inhabitant of Palestine, to rest in the shade of his vine and fig tree was the image of peace and security and perfect contentment. In the hierarchy of trees, the fig tree held the second place, after the olive but before the vine.[12] It owed this esteem as much to its prodigious fecundity as to the sweetness of its fruit. With its two flowerings and successive ripenings, each within six months of the year, it bears fruit capable of long preservation. The man in the parable is astonished and grieved

---

[11] Luke 13:6–9 — *a*) 13:6: *Arborem fici habebat quidam plantatam in vinea sua.* The meaning is not, "he had planted a fig tree," but, "he had a fig tree, planted in his vineyard." Hence, we are not to think, with Maldonatus, that he has come to look for the fruit *the first year* after the planting, nor, with Knabenbauer, *after the third year*. The master was reasonable, and knew that while vines can give fruit from the third year, the fig tree is not productive until the fourth or fifth year, and the olive tree after the eighteenth or twentieth.

b) 13:8: *Ut quid etiam terram occupat?* The Old Latin versions have *detinet, evacuat, intricat*. None of these translations comes up to the Greek καταργεῖ, which means "render the soil unprofitable" (ἀργός).

c) 13:9: *Siquidem fecerit fructum, sin autem.* "If it bears fruit (well and good); otherwise, thou shalt cut it down." This is the figure called "ellipsis." The Greek adds εἰς τὸ μέλλον, which can be translated, "if it bears fruit in the future" or "if it bears fruit next year," understanding ἔτος, year. In any case the reprieve is only for one year.

[12] Judg. 9:8–13. Apologue of Joatham to the Sichemites.

to find his tree obstinately barren. An unfruitfulness of three successive years is not to be explained by late frosts or torrential rains or prolonged droughts; it must be considered final and beyond remedy. There is only one thing to do: to rid the soil of this parasite which encumbers and exhausts it. The fig tree does harm by the sole fact that it is useless. Its wide branches, twice as great as the height of the tree, and its thick foliage intercept the sun's rays so much that nothing can grow in its shade. Its deep roots suck up the juices from the soil far and wide at the expense of neighboring plants, which die or waste away. Marauders, drawn by the deceptive promise of fruit, end up by trampling down everything around it. As soon as it ceases to be fruitful, it becomes a real scourge. Still, the vinedresser suggests one last effort. Who knows whether exceptional care may not restore to the tree its former fruitfulness? The master agrees to try, but only for one year.

Though the fig tree may not be a symbol of Israel, as was the vine, still such symbolism would here be suggested by the context, which is a pressing appeal addressed especially to the Jewish nation. The history of Israel was one long series of infidelities. God has never ceased, through the instrumentality of the prophets, to require the fruits of salvation. He has obtained none. His patience is now exhausted; the reprieve that he now accords is the last. The sentence of death is about to bear down upon this ungrateful people. Let us travel no farther along the road of allegory. There is no need to seek the meaning of the three years of waiting, of the compassionate vinedresser, of the care he proposes to give to the barren tree, and of the delay of one year which he requests in order to make the attempt. Not that the preacher is forbidden to apply all these details to the individual soul and to draw from them practical conclusions for the conduct of life — this has been done with both eloquence and unction — but the interpretation of the thought of Jesus ought not to pass beyond the literal meaning.[13]

---

[13] Those fond of allegory see in the *three* years of unfruitfulness either the periods of Abraham, Moses, and John the Baptist; or the times of the Judges, the Kings, and the Prophets; or the times of the Law, the Prophets, and the Gospels; or the three years of Christ's teaching. What then would the year of reprieve mean?

Another day the Saviour was preaching in a synagogue. As far as we know, this was the first time he preached in such a place after his departure from Galilee — and the last time in his life. In the synagogue there was a poor woman who was bent over double and who was unable, despite her best efforts, to straighten up completely.[14] This infirmity of hers, which had already lasted eighteen years, was not due to an accident, nor was it the result of a gradual paralysis; it was the effect of the action of an evil spirit. Properly speaking, the woman was not possessed by the devil, for she retained the free use of her faculties; but she was his unfortunate victim. We know that God sometimes permits Satan to afflict sinners, and even the just, either to test some and punish others, or for other purposes worthy of his divine wisdom, but not to be fathomed by our shallow reason.

Before working a miracle Jesus was almost always careful to prepare the subject for it by arousing in him faith and confidence; but today the miracle he is meditating is less an act of mercy than a lesson for those present. The afflicted woman was some distance away, perhaps in the part of the synagogue reserved for women. Jesus had her come near and placed his hands upon her, saying: "Woman, thou art delivered from thy infirmity." Immediately straightening up, she gave thanks to God. This spontaneous movement of gratitude shows that her present dispositions were good, whatever may have been the disorder of her past life.

---

[14] Luke 13:10–17 — *a*) "He was teaching in one of their synagogues on the Sabbath (ἐν τοῖς σάββασιν). The reference is to a particular incident, and not to a custom. The plural τὰ σάββατα has often the sense of the singular (Luke 4:16; Mark 2:23; Matt. 12:1, etc.).

b) The woman had "a spirit of infirmity" (πνεῦμα ἔχουσα ἀσθενίας), that is to say, she had an infirmity caused by an (evil) spirit. In the same way, "a deaf and dumb spirit" was the expression for a spirit causing deafness and dumbness (Mark 9:24).

c) She was "bent over on herself" (συγκύπτουσα). It is natural to refer the adverbial expression εἰς τὸ παντελές to the nearest word ἀνακύψαι (she could not raise her head *altogether, entirely*), rather than to the words μὴ δυναμένη (she could not *at all* raise her head). Knabenbauer objects that the former reading would detract from the miracle, but that is no reason for doing violence to the text.

d) St. Luke (vv. 12 and 16) uses *loosen, unbind,* instead of *cure,* because the woman was *bound* by the demon, and the metaphor is suggested by the comparison with an animal that is loosed to allow it to drink.

But the head of the synagogue was indignant on seeing Jesus work a miracle that was not on the program, and which seemed to him to be a violation of the Sabbath rest. In fact, the rigid Pharisees prohibited the practice of medicine and the administering of remedies on the Sabbath, except in case of danger of death. And Jesus' gesture of imposing hands could pass for the application of a remedy. Not daring to approach the Wonder-Worker himself, the head of the synagogue reprimands those present: "There are six days in the week when servile work is allowed: come and be cured on one of those days, and not on the Sabbath." In his comical embarrassment, this head of the synagogue is talking nonsense. The afflicted woman had not come to the synagogue to be cured, and no one had brought her there for that purpose. What, then, was the trouble? Still, his ludicrous sortie found some supporters, and it is to them that Jesus now addresses himself:

"Hypocrites! Does not each one of you on the Sabbath day loose his ox or his ass from the manger to lead them out to the watering-place? And this daughter of Abraham, whom Satan has held chained for eighteen years, should she not have been loosed from her bonds on the Sabbath day?"

The argument was to the point. The most rigid of the Pharisees, who counted among the thirty-nine servile works forbidden on the Sabbath the acts of tying and untying, making a knot and loosening it, did not hesitate to loose domestic animals to permit them to drink. If the daily care of a beast of burden warranted this derogation of law, should less be done for a human being, for a poor Israelite who had been waiting eighteen years for her liberation? While the Pharisees, finding nothing to answer, could scarcely disguise their annoyance, the common people whom their sophistry had not yet captured noisily manifested their joy and applauded without restraint.

About the same period, the Pharisees of Perea bethought themselves of a stratagem to induce the Saviour to cross the frontier of Judea, where it would be easier to lay hold on his person. As though they had suddenly become anxious about his safety, they came to him and said: "Leave this place where Herod wants to kill thee." The Gospel lets it be clearly understood that Antipas was conniving with them. The voluptuous tetrarch was not cruel by nature. He had put the Baptist to death reluctantly, and the specter of his victim was haunting his disordered imagination. The fame of Jesus, in whom he believed he saw the Baptist come to life again, disquieted him. But though he was as anxious as the Pharisees to see Jesus leave his territory, he preferred stratagem to force. Still, the danger evoked by Jesus' enemies to draw him into Judea, where a surprise attack seemed easier, was not altogether chimerical. Machaerus, where the tetrarch resided, was only a few miles distant, and from this eagle's nest Herod could at any moment send his myrmidons to seize him. It was to the tetrarch himself, and not to the Pharisees — who were only emissaries — that Jesus sent his answer:

"Go and say to that fox: I cast out devils and heal the sick today and tomorrow: the third day shall be the end. I must go my way today, tomorrow, and the next day; (I will then depart for Judea), for it is not fitting that a prophet perish outside Jerusalem."[15]

The fox, often confused with the jackal, was the symbol of weakness armed with cunning. Nothing could better characterize Herod Antipas. Conscious of his powerlessness, he counted on diplomacy. But this time his craft is baffled. The Saviour will not leave until his work is done. He does not say at what moment, but he makes it plain that the time is not far distant. The popular expression "today, tomorrow, and the day after tomorrow" means the future; just as "today and yesterday" means the past, an undetermined space of time, but not a long one.

3. A Dinner With the Pharisees

(LUKE 14:1–24)

Despite the recent differences of Jesus with the Pharisees, an influential member of their party, immune to the prejudices of his fellows, or moved by a feeling of curiosity stronger than his prejudices, received him at his table on the Sabbath. Saturday was a day of prolonged feasting for the Jews. All work was for-

[15] Luke 13:31–33. Amasias, the priest of the golden calf of Bethel, in connivance with King Jeroboam II had used the same strategem to drive the prophet Amos away from the Kingdom of Israel, but with no greater success (Amos 7:10–17).

bidden, and the meetings of the synagogue left time to spare, no small part of which was devoted to the usual three meals. The dishes were prepared beforehand, because a fire might not be lighted or even kept going; but, for all that, they were not reduced to cold meals. The recipes for keeping dishes hot all day, without violating the Sabbath rest, make up one of the most curious chapters of the Talmud.[16]

The meal to which the Saviour was invited was probably the one that followed immediately after the service in the synagogue, toward midday. The welcome extended to him was polite but not too cordial. Some uneasiness was felt among the guests. All eyes were fixed on Jesus, in expectation of what he would say or do. In front of him, as if by chance, there was a man afflicted with dropsy. How came this sick man to be there? Had he furtively introduced himself into the gathering with true Oriental disingenuousness, impelled by a vague hope of cure; or had ill-wishers placed him there purposely, to see whether Jesus would dare to cure him on the Sabbath? The Saviour's conduct and the tenor of the text would favor the second supposition. Jesus, surveying the doctors of the law who were attentively observing him, posed this question: "Is it permitted to heal someone on the Sabbath day?" To say "no" was to defy common sense; to say "yes" was to deny the principles of Rabbinism forbidding the practice of medicine on the Sabbath, except in the case of a mortal sickness. The Pharisees to whom the question was addressed kept silent. Then Jesus, taking the hand of the man with dropsy, cured him without a word and sent him out of the hall, where he had no further business. Though the Gospel says nothing, we would like to believe that this man's dispositions were good; in any case, he was not in connivance with the Pharisees. The Saviour would not have rewarded any such treacherous complicity with a miracle.

This is the seventh cure worked by Jesus on the Sabbath.[17] On other occasions the Pharisees had violently protested; today they

---

[16] *Mishnah,* treat. *Shabbath,* Chap. III and IV, with the corresponding *Gemara.*

[17] Luke 14:1–14. The others are: the Capharnaum demoniac (Luke 4:32), Peter's mother-in-law (Luke 4:38, also Matthew and Mark), the man with the withered hand (Luke 6:6, also Matthew and Mark), the crippled woman (Luke 13:10), the paralytic of Bethesda (John 5:10), and the man born blind (John 9:14).

kept silence. Could they do otherwise after refusing to answer the question proposed to them? But though they were silent, the plain signs of their disapproval could be read in their faces and in their looks. The Saviour's answer is aimed at an unspoken objection: "If your ass or your ox has just fallen into a cistern on the Sabbath day, which of you does not hurry to pull him out?"[18] Accidents such as this are not rare in Palestine, where there are so many cisterns with caved-in vaults. In such circumstances the most rigid Pharisees did not hesitate to bring aid to their beasts of burden without fear of violating the Sabbath rest. Now, could the saving of an animal be compared with the saving of a man?

The guests deserved still another lesson. The Saviour had noticed upon entering how adroitly many of them had managed to take possession of the best places. In ceremonial banquets the master of the house assigned to each guest the place he was to occupy, and the story brings out how delicate this task could be when one was dealing with punctilious people. At an ordinary meal this was left to the chance of arrival and the discretion of the guests. It was then that rivalries born of self-love were given full play. To reprimand this irregularity without naming any names, Jesus describes a fictitious case, which St. Luke calls a parable because its application is indirect. He imagines a wedding feast, where etiquette was most strictly observed and questions of precedence were ruled by a protocol which no one could disregard without obliging the master of the house to intervene.

"If thou art invited to a wedding feast, do not take the first place, for fear that someone more distinguished happen to arrive and the host of both of you come to say to thee: 'Yield to him this place,' and then thou shalt go in confusion to take the last place. When thou art invited, go and put thyself in the last place. Then he who invited thee shall come to say to thee: 'Move up higher,' and this shall bring thee honor in the eyes of the other guests. For he that exalts himself shall be humbled, and he that humbles himself shall be exalted."

---

[18] Luke 14:5. Many manuscripts have υἱός (son) instead of ὄνος (ass). If this reading is adopted the translation is: "If your son or *even* your ox falls into a cistern."

Something a little like this is to be found in the Talmud; but, whereas the Talmud restricts itself to counsels of ordinary prudence, the Gospel means to inculcate by a vivid example a lofty moral lesson.[19] It is doubtful whether the listeners understood it. None of them felt that he himself was meant. If they sought the places of honor at feasts and in the synagogue, it was because they judged themselves worthy, and were shocked only by the excessive pretensions of their rivals. At all events, they were not disposed to place themselves in the school of Christ. They were waiting only for an occasion to press the attack.

Jesus turns from them to address his host, whose correct attitude had not betrayed any ill will. He treats him with consideration, and the counsels that he suggests are given in a friendly tone, and have in them nothing bitter or wounding.

"When thou givest a dinner or supper, do not invite thy friends, or thy brethren, or thy relatives, or rich neighbors, for fear that they invite thee in return and thou be repaid. When thou givest a feast, invite rather the poor, the sick, the lame, and the blind. Thou shalt be blessed, for they have not the means of repaying thee, and thou shalt receive thy recompense in the day of the resurrection of the just."[20]

This far surpasses the morality of the Commandments. Jesus is not formulating a rule of social conduct, but a counsel of perfection. The paradoxical appearance of the maxim and the lively tone of the language permit no misunderstanding. "Take care," Jesus seems to be saying, "If you invited your friends or rich people they would return it in kind, and this would be to your injury. If you invite the outcasts of life and fortune, you are storing up treasures for heaven, and the hundredfold awaits you on the day of the glorious resurrection."

On hearing the word "resurrection," one of the guests, seized with a fit of artificial fervor, which was perhaps only one of those pious effusions aroused in certain natures by a feeling of comfort

---

[19] Luke 14:7–11. Cf. *Recherches*, 1925, p. 522, *Les places d'honneur chez les Juifs contemporains du Christ;* the Talmud parable in Billerbeck, *Kommentar*, Vol. I, p. 916, and Vol. II, p. 204.

[20] Luke 14:12–14. Note the μήποτε (*for fear* that they return it to you, which would be a loss from a supernatural viewpoint); also the μακάριος ἔσῃ (you *will be blessed* in having received nothing here below and in awaiting your recompense in heaven).

and good cheer, cried out all of a sudden: "Blessed is he that shall partake of the banquet of the kingdom of God!" Isaias had depicted the happiness of the Messianic times under the image of a sumptuous feast, and the Jews were very fond of this figure, which many among them were tempted to take too literally. But, whatever the nature of this mysterious banquet, the Pharisees were all very sure that they would share in it, whether as children of Abraham or as the elite of the chosen people. The purpose of the following parable was to combat this assurance. Its meaning may be summarized thus: it is by no means enough to be invited to the banquet: it is necessary to accept and honor the invitation, and this many of the Jews refused to do.

A certain rich man had invited a great number of people to a grand feast. On the day chosen, following a custom which persists even today in the East, he sent a servant to notify the invited guests that everything was ready and that they had only to come. As though word had been passed around, they began to excuse themselves under various pretexts. One said: "I have bought a field and need to go to see it; please excuse me." Another: "I have acquired five yoke of oxen and I am going to try them out; I pray thee to excuse me." A third: "I have taken a wife, and therefore I cannot come." The last excuse is the most discourteous in form, but the reasons given by all three, even if true, are no less frivolous. The man who has just bought a field — very likely through a go-between, as is often the case in those countries — is naturally anxious to visit it to make sure that he has not been cheated; the one who has just bought the five yoke of oxen is no less anxious to try them out to assure himself of their quality, good or bad; but, for all that, a delay of a few hours does not dispense them from keeping their pledged word.

Among ancient peoples, especially among the Semites, failure to honor an invitation after it has once been accepted is a deadly affront. Among the Arabs it would be a *casus belli*. Hence, when the servant returned to report the failure of his mission, the master, greatly incensed, said to him: "Go out quickly through the streets and lanes of the city and gather here the poor, the crippled, the blind, and the lame." The servant punctually carried out the order and, finishing his circuit, came back and said: "Lord, I have done what thou hast commanded me and there is still room." "Well then," answered the master, "go out to the roads and along the hedges (where travelers and beggars are to be found) and bring here by force (all that you meet) so that my house may be filled." And addressing those present he adds: "I say to you that none of those men who had been invited (in the first place) shall taste my dinner."[21]

This parable would be clearer had fewer commentaries been written about it. The best way to misunderstand it is to transform it into pure allegory. There is no need to ask whom the servant represents: his role is a necessary part of the story itself; and manifestly he does not represent either John the Baptist or Christ. Nor should we look for something that corresponds to the reasons given by the guests who refuse to come. The Evangelist is only presenting them by way of example; he could have changed them or multiplied them without changing the meaning of the parable. The enumeration of the poor, the crippled, the lame, and the blind who replace the originally invited guests is likewise of no special significance. As to the *compelle intrare* (force them to enter), about which such a battle has raged, it evidently means nothing more than moral pressure, an insistent invitation, since it is clear that a single servant would have been powerless to gather recalcitrants into the banquet hall by force. The host who has prepared everything so lavishly has a natural desire of attracting a large number of banqueters, to prevent his efforts from being wasted and to justify the expense, and also to avenge himself for the insult he has received. The guests originally invited have spurned his friendly advances; he now openly shows them that he prefers to them the unknown and the miserable.

---

[21] Luke 14:15–24. St. Matthew has a similar parable (22:2–14). We shall examine at the proper time whether it is the same. Cf. note p. 218.

a) In that of St. Luke there is only *one* servant who is charged with reminding the guests of the time of the feast. This slave is called in Latin *vocator* (Pliny, XXXV, x, 36 et 89; Suetonius, *Caligula,* 39; Seneca, *De Ira,* III, xxxvii, 3). In Egypt, where the invitation was given by letter specifying the place, the day, and the hour, the sending of a *vocator* was unnecessary. For modern Palestinian usage see Tristram, *Eastern Customs,* p. 82.

b) The guests refuse, not *at the same time* (*simul,* Vulgate), but *in unison, unanimously* (ἀπὸ μιᾶς, understand γνώμης). But nothing indicates that there was a previous understanding or conspiracy.

To grasp the true meaning of the parable and the moral lesson drawn from it, we need only go back to the circumstance which called it forth. One of Christ's fellow banqueters was waxing enthusiastic about the felicity of the Messianic banquet to which he knew that he himself, as a son of Abraham, was invited, and the delights of which he was savoring in advance. The Saviour answered him that to enjoy a feast it is not enough to be invited; it is necessary to prepare for it and to attend. The Jews were in undeniable possession of a priority of call, as St. Paul frequently recognizes. The Gospel goes "to the Jews first, then to the Gentiles." And when the Jews will refuse to answer the call, the Apostle will say to them: "It was necessary to announce the word of God to you first of all; but since you reject it, judging yourselves unworthy of eternal life, we turn to the Gentiles, as the Lord commanded us."[22]

The call comes to nought unless it is answered. You same Pharisees who flatter yourselves that you have a sure title to eternal life will be forced to admit this "when you shall see Abraham and Isaac and Jacob and all the prophets in the kingdom of God whence you shall be excluded; while they shall come from the east and the west, from the north and the south, to sit down (to the feast) in the kingdom of God. And the last shall be first and the first last."[23]

Before leaving the Pharisees, whom we shall meet again in Jerusalem during the week of the Passion, let us give one more parable which paints to the life their pride and their foolishness. It is addressed to "those who boasted of being the only ones to practice justice and from this took occasion to despise all the rest."

4. The Pharisee and the Publican[24]

"Two men went up to the Temple to pray," doubtless at the time of the official prayer, at the third or the ninth hour of the day, about nine o'clock in the morning or three in the afternoon.

[22] Acts 13:46–47. On priority rights for the Jews, Rom. 1:16.

[23] Luke 13:28–30. Cf. Matt. 8:11–12.

[24] Luke 18. 9–15: *Dixit autem et ad quosdam* (εἶπεν δὲ καὶ πρός τινας). This introduction does not link the parable either with what precedes or with what

One of them wore on his forehead and attached around his left arm by a broad thong those little square boxes called phylacteries, in which was written the profession of the Jewish faith. At the four corners of the mantle with which he was draped floated the tassels of two-colored wool which distinguished the strict observer of the Law. He walked with a slow pace, with a grave and composed mien, answering only by a condescending nod of his head the greetings of his admirers. This was the Pharisee.

The other hurried his steps and brushed along the wall as though afraid of being recognized. Though nothing in his clothes or his external appearance set him apart from the anonymous crowd of passers-by, yet he met on his way hostile looks in which could be read the distrust for a stranger and hatred for the tax office. This was the Publican.

The two men crossed the Court of the Gentiles and penetrated into the part of the Temple where access was permitted only to Israelites. The Publican arrested his steps at the very end of the Women's Court, while the Pharisee ascended the steps that led to the Court of Israel and pushed on to the balustrade that separated it from the Court of the Priests. Standing there in a conspicuous place before the Sanctuary, he prayed in a low voice:

---

follows. It is addressed to certain proud people or is directed *against* them (πρός has both meanings).

a) The Pharisee's Prayer. He is *standing erect;* and conspicuously (σταθεὶς) he prays *within himself* (εἰς ἑαυτόν), not having the effrontery to say aloud everything that he is thinking. He flatters himself in general for not being like other men, for forming a class apart, and in particular for performing two works of supererogation: (1) He fasts twice a week (*sabbatum,* σάββατον, has here this meaning). We know from the *Mishnah* and the *Doctrine of the Twelve Apostles* (viii, 1) that the days were Monday and Thursday. (2) He pays tithes on everything he *acquires* (πάντα ὅσα κτῶμαι). If he were speaking of all that he *possessed* he would say κέκτημαι.

b) Prayer of the Publican. He kept at a distance, perhaps prostrate on the ground (ἑστὼς does not indicate a standing position); he lowers his eyes and strikes his breast; he says: "Have mercy on me, *the* sinner" (τῷ ἁμαρτωλῷ), as though he would thus distinguish himself from all the others.

c) Conclusion: "The publican went away more justified than the other," or better: "justified rather than the other" (παρ' ἐκεῖνον) who was not at all justified. The moral of the parable is found in the last sentence. It teaches us humility, not the way to pray. Prayer is the framework, and not the background of the picture. But perhaps this accessory idea brings it closer to the parable of the Widow and the Unjust Judge which has as its subject the efficacy of persevering prayer.

"O God, I thank thee that I am not like the rest of men, thieves, rogues, adulterers, such as that publican down there. I fast twice a week; I pay tithes for everything that I acquire." It may well be that the Pharisee is not exaggerating when he speaks of his fasts and his scrupulous observance. Not only does he pay tithes for the smallest products of the soil, even those that grow without cultivation, such as mint, rue, and cummin, but also for those he buys in the market, for fear that the vendor has not paid the tithe. Nor does he confine himself to the exact observance of the only fast prescribed by law, the Day of Atonement; he adds, as do the more fervent among his colleagues, the fasts of supererogation on Monday and Thursday of every week. He is contented with himself withal, and from the height of his pride he contemplates with pity the rest of the human race. He could readily believe himself God's creditor. His prayer is nothing but a personal panegyric and an indictment of his neighbor. It is so extravagant as to have the appearance of a caricature; but similar ones are found in the Talmud. To show the lengths to which the foolishness of these self-styled just men could go, it will be enough to quote the words of the famous Simeon-ben-Jokkai: "If there are but two just men in the world, they are myself and my son: if there is but one, it is myself."[25]

Meantime the Publican, prostrate in his corner, not daring to lift his eyes to heaven, strikes his breast, and from his penitent heart more than from his lips this brief prayer goes up to God: "O God, have mercy on me who am nothing but a sinner." It is the avowal which costs our self-love so dearly and assures for us the favor of God; it is the cry of David weeping over his sin to obtain forgiveness; it is the cry of the Prodigal abhorring his past wanderings and finding again his place at the paternal hearth; it is the cry of all great converts whom God has sometimes drawn from such great depths to lift them to such lofty heights.

"I say to you," concludes the Saviour, "the Publican went down to his house justified more (or *rather*) than the other; for he that exalts himself shall be humbled; and he that abases him-

[25] Cf. Billerbeck, *Kommentar,* Vol. II, p. 240, and Edersheim, *Life and Times,* Vol. II, p. 291. Billerbeck concludes (p. 241): "The prayer placed in the mouth of the Pharisee is not a tendentious invention: it reflects strict reality."

self shall be exalted."[26] This is the general law which we see strikingly verified at the beginning of creation and at the birth of the Church: Lucifer, the dazzling archangel, dares to aspire to the throne of the Most High and is precipitated into the lowest depths of the abyss; Mary, the most pure and most holy Virgin, humbles herself and makes herself little, and God exalts her to heights to which the Seraphim scarcely dare to lift their gaze.

---

[26] Luke 18:14–15. The *Textus Receptus* has ἤ γαρ ἐκεῖνος which supposes a question: "*For* do you think that he (the Pharisee) could have been justified?" (Godet and Plummer.) The text adopted by critics (except Tischendorf) is παρ' ἐκεῖνον, which can mean "more than the other" or "rather than the other." Fr. Buzy (*R.B.*, 1917, p. 206) sponsors the first sense: "The Pharisee has his legal justice, the Publican obtains interior justice." As St. Augustine remarks (*Ep.*, XXXVI, 4, n. 7; ML, XXXIII, 139), the Gospel does not say that the Pharisee was condemned. It does not say so expressly, but leaves it to be understood, and so the majority of Catholic and Protestant interpreters understand it.

CHAPTER VII

Characteristics of the Christian Spirit

1. Confidence in God and Watchfulness

THE Christian spirit could be defined as the direct antithesis of the Pharisaical spirit: fear of God in place of the fear of men, simplicity and self-forgetfulness in place of ostentation and self-love, genuine virtue in place of sham, substance in place of shadow. In conversation with his Apostles, our Lord often had occasion to call attention to this contrast.

Upon leaving the house of the Pharisee whom he had so grievously scandalized by sitting down to table without washing his hands, Christ finds himself surrounded by an immense throng. "Thousands of people," says St. Luke, "were treading upon one another to get near him."[1] But, instead of addressing this confused multitude, ill-prepared to understand him, he speaks first of all to his Apostles:

"Beware the leaven of the Pharisees, I mean hypocrisy. There is nothing hidden that shall not be revealed, and nothing secret that shall not become known. What you say in the darkness shall re-echo in full daylight, and what you whisper in the ear, in the most secret chamber, shall be published on the house-tops."[2]

Jesus had already put them on their guard against the teachings of the Pharisees; today it is their hypocrisy that he denounces under the figure of a corrupting leaven. Hypocrisy is the conscious and willful opposition between outward conduct and inward senti-

---

[1] Luke 12:1. The language is perhaps hyperbolical, as in Acts 21:20.

[2] The same thought in Matt. 10:26–30, but in another context and for a different case.

ments; it is ambition concealing itself under the mask of zeal; it is vice that puts on the trappings of virtue in order to deceive others and to deceive oneself. However, this disguise, unworthy of an honorable man, is useless; for sooner or later hypocrisy unmasks itself. If it could lay claim, not to an excuse, but to an explanation, it would be the desire to please men, or the fear of displeasing them. Shabby motives indeed, in the eyes of faith.

"I say to you, my friends, fear not those who, after killing the body, can do no more. Fear him who, after having killed, has the power to cast into Gehenna. Yes, I repeat, fear him," but with a filial fear allied to confidence. Is not God your Father, and can you doubt his fatherly kindness: "Are not five sparrows sold for a double-as? Well, not one of them is forgotten before God. Fear not; you are worth more than many sparrows"; and you are a thousand times more worthy of God's solicitude. "All the hairs of your head are numbered," and not one of them falls without his permission.[3]

While Jesus was preaching to his disciples abandonment to God who so solicitously watches over the least creatures that come forth from his hands, a young man from the middle of the crowd brusquely asked him: "Master, please tell my brother to divide the inheritance with me." The request may have been justified. Apparently the elder brother holding the whole patrimony was refusing to yield to his younger brother his legal share in the inheritance. In such cases, instead of going to court, the parties to the dispute often chose some illustrious Rabbi as arbitrator. But the young man was on the wrong road. The Son of God had not come down from heaven to settle such petty legal disputes, and it was a strange misunderstanding of his role to submit such a quarrel to him. Jesus brings this home to the young man rather dryly: "Man, who has appointed me your judge to distribute your shares?" This said, he leaves him to his reflections; and to draw a lesson from the homely incident, he adds: "Guard yourselves from all avarice, for however wealthy a man may be, his life does not depend upon what he possesses."[4]

---

[3] Luke 12:4–7. Also Matt. 10:28–31, almost word for word. In St. Matthew, two sparrows for one *as;* in St. Luke, five sparrows for a double-*as*. Naturally enough, the more one buys, the cheaper the price. The *as* was worth about one cent.

[4] The episode is found only in St. Luke (12:13–15). The last phrase presents

It is evident that riches do not give to life its meaning and its value; it is no less evident that they cannot prolong it. The following parable goes on to set forth this truth in full light.

One year the land of a certain rich landowner was so fertile that his granaries were bulging with produce. If he had been wise, this abundance would not have troubled him. He had around him plenty of unfortunates to aid, plenty of misery to relieve. This would have been a good investment which he would have recovered later on a hundredfold. But avarice locked his heart against every sentiment of humanity. He said to himself: "What shall I do, since I have not enough room to store my crops? I shall pull down my granaries and build larger ones and I shall say to my soul: 'Thou hast goods for many years; rest thyself; eat, drink, and be merry.' " He was speaking to his animal soul, the seat of sensations and pleasures, unfolding before it a limitless perspective of gross pleasures, the ideal of the epicurean of all ages. Now while he was dreaming of this eternity of sensual happiness, a voice whispered to him: "Fool! This very night thy soul shall be required of thee, and what thou hast amassed, whose shall it be?"

It is out of place to speculate whether God made himself heard by the rich man through an internal inspiration, or in a prophetic dream, or by the brutal and eloquent voice of facts. This circumstance is outside the purpose of the parable, which tends entirely to this conclusion: "Such is (the fate of) the man who stores up treasure for himself and is not rich according to God."[5] To store up treasure for oneself is to listen solely to the appetite of egoism

---

some difficulty: *ὅτι οὐκ ἐν τῷ περισσεύειν τινὶ ἡ ζωὴ αὐτοῦ ἐστιν ἐκ τῶν ὑπαρχόντων αὐτῷ*. Godet paraphrases it thus: "Although or *because* a man has superfluity he is not thereby assured of life." But note that it is *ἡ ζωή*, "life in general," and not *ὁ βίος*, "physical life, existence." The meaning therefore is: "Human life (its duration, its moral value) does not depend on wealth"; in other words, "there is no equation between wealth and life." The possession of wealth does not increase either the duration or the value of life, and privation of wealth does not diminish either the one or the other. The thought is general, but the parable of the Rich Miser brings into relief the duration rather than the value.

[5] Luke 12:16–21. St. Ambrose says to the rich man embarrassed by his fortune: "Inopum sinus, viduarum domus, ora infantium . . . istae sunt apothecae quae manent in aeternum."

The language of the reveler of the parable may be compared with Isa. 22:13–14: "Comedamus et bibamus; cras enim moriemur"; Wisd. 2:7–8: "Vinis pretiosis et unguentis nos impleamus . . . coronemus nos rosis." On the uncertainty of tomorrow, cf. Ecclus. 11:19–20; James 4:13–15.

and the thirst for pleasure; to be rich according to God is to make that use of riches which God proposes in giving them to us. He that is rich according to God escapes the curse fulminated against riches, and may partake of the blessedness promised to the poor in spirit.

The parable of the Rich Miser was a subject of salutary reflections for the multitude. Meantime Jesus addresses his disciples, who are capable of grasping a more elevated teaching:

"Be not anxious about the nourishment that is to sustain your life, nor the clothing that is to protect your body. Life is more than nourishment, and the body is more than clothing. (God who has given you the one will not refuse the other.)

"See the birds of the sky. They sow not, neither do they reap, and God provides for their subsistence. Are not you of much more value than they?

"Which of you, by thinking of it, can add one day to his life or one inch to his height? If then the least things are beyond your power, why are you anxious about the rest?

"Consider the lilies of the field. They spin not, neither do they weave. And yet, I say to you, Solomon in all his glory was not clothed as one of them. If, then, God thus clothes the grass, which today grows in the fields and tomorrow shall be cast into the fire, what will he not do for you, men of little faith?

"Therefore, be not troubled about what you shall eat, and what you shall drink; be not agitated by these cares as the pagans are; for your heavenly Father knows your needs. Seek (first) the kingdom of God, and all these things shall be given you besides. Fear not, then, little flock, for it has pleased God to give to you the kingdom."[6]

---

[6] St. Matthew, who places this instruction in the Sermon on the Mount (6:25–33), does not differ from St. Luke except in *nuances*. "Birds of the sky" instead of "ravens"; "lilies of the field" instead of "lilies." In both there is an ambiguous phrase. It can be translated: "which of you can add a cubit to his height?" or "a cubit to the length of his life?" for the Greek word ἡλικία signifies both *height* and *age,* duration of life. But to add a cubit (about eighteen inches) to one's height would be no small thing. On the other hand, since a cubit meaning duration would be a strange figure in French, we have rendered the idea by an equivalent. In Hebrew, on the contrary, the figure has nothing surprising about it: "Thou hast given to my days (the length of) few palms" (Ps. 38 [39]:6). The palm is the breadth of the hand.

If the disciples believe themselves forgotten by God, let them learn from the spectacle of nature. Galilee is a country of birds and flowers. You cannot traverse its hills and valleys without starting hundreds of flying creatures; and the number, splendor, and variety of the flowers that embellish the plains in the spring-time are a marvel for the eye. Now, who is it that makes it his concern to feed these little birds, five of which are sold for two small coins in the village market? Who is it that clothes the lilies of the field and the superb purple anemone with a fabric silkier and more richly colored than the mantle of a king?[7] It is God; do you not know it?

The Saviour does not forbid his disciples to be occupied about sustenance and clothing, but to be preoccupied about them. He does not wish the children of God to let themselves be buffeted about by fear and doubt, or, like derelict ships tossing adrift, to be swept along by cupidity and the love of gain.

"Do not heap up treasures on earth, where rust consumes and thieves steal them. Store up treasure for heaven, where neither rust nor thieves penetrate. Where your treasure is, there will your heart be also."

In the affairs of the soul, confidence will be presumption if it is not allied to watchfulness; for death comes unexpectedly, like a robber:

"If the master of the household knew the hour when the thief would come, he would watch, I assure you, and would not allow his house to be entered. Therefore, hold yourselves always ready. For the Son of Man will come at the time you least expect."[8]

"Have your loins always girt and your lamps always lit, as

---

[7] In many a spot in Palestine, in particular in the Plain of Genesareth, "turtle-doves are found in really prodigious numbers. At every step they rise in flocks and sometimes they touch one another on the trees where they go to perch" (Lortet, *La Syrie d'aujourd'hui,* 1884, p. 526).

The richness of the spring flowers in Galilee has struck all travelers, and everyone remarks the purple anemone (*anemone coronaria*) which is generally identified with the "lilies of the field." The word "lily" in Hebrew (*shûshân*), as in Arabic, is applied to a number of different species. The white lily exists in Lebanon and has been found in Upper Galilee, but not in the rest of Palestine. At any rate it has never been common and the characteristics of the "lily of the field" do not fit it. Cf. *Les lis de la Bible,* in *Études,* Vol. LXXXVII, 1901, pp. 390–396; a color picture of the purple anemone in *Dict. de la Bible,* Art. *Anémone.*

[8] Matt. 24:42–43; Luke 12:39–40.

servants who are awaiting the return of their master, ready to open to him as soon as he knocks at the door. Happy the servant whom the Master, on his arrival, finds watchful! Amen, I say to you, he will make him sit at his table and will himself gird his loins to serve him."[9]

Earthly masters, to be sure, show no such kind attentions to servants who have merely done their duty; but it must be remembered — and this saves the verisimilitude — that the master of the parable is the figure of him who came down from heaven, not to be served, but to serve.

The reward promised to the good servant seemed to St. Peter to be so extravagant that he intervened in the name of his colleagues to find out whether this was the reward of all the faithful, or only of the privileged elite: "Lord, is it for us that thou sayest this, or for all?"[10] The answer of our Lord comes to this: "There is a gradation among the servants, a kind of hierarchy of duties and responsibilities. The reward and punishment will be proportioned to each one's fidelity or infidelity in the different conditions in which he is placed."

Here we have a confidential servant whom the master has established as head of his household to distribute to the others their allowance and their tasks. If he acquits himself zealously in his employment, the master on his return will entrust him with the administration of his property. If, on the contrary, counting on the master's delay in returning, he starts to beat the servants and maids, and spends his time in eating and drinking, the master, coming back unexpectedly, will cleave him asunder as an untrustworthy slave.[11] The punishment will be proportioned

---

[9] Luke 12:37.

[10] Luke 12:41.

[11] Luke 12:41–48; Matt. 24:45–51. St. Matthew does not mention the intervention of Peter; otherwise the texts are almost identical.

a) The servant or slave placed over the others was called by the Greeks οἰκονόμος, by the Latins *dispensator*, sometimes *actor*. He was in charge of all domestic concerns (θεραπείας, Luke), or the whole household (οἰκετείας, Matthew).

b) One of his functions was to distribute rations, especially grain. This distribution of grain which took place daily, weekly, or monthly, according to circumstances, is expressed in St. Luke by the technical word σιτομέτριον, from σιτομετρεῖν, "to measure out grain."

c) The master on his return has this wicked servant "cut in two": διχοτομεῖν cannot mean anything else. This punishment was usual in the East (Herod., II, 39, n. 5; II, 139, n. 2: διατέμνειν). Caligula applied it frequently in Rome and

to the crime. The servant who, knowing his master's will, directly disobeys his orders will be severely punished; the one who unknowingly commits reprehensible acts will be less severely punished. As a general rule: "Much will be required of those to whom much has been given; much will be demanded from those to whom much has been entrusted."

Peter had wished to know whether all the vigilant and faithful servants would be treated in the same fashion. Our Lord proposes to him the case, not of an ordinary servant, but of a steward upon whom the master has shifted the care of his house: such will be the role of the Apostles and their successors in the Church of Christ. The reward or punishment that awaits the servant is proportioned to his responsibility. If he abuses the master's confidence; if he profits by his lengthy absence to tyrannize over his underlings and to live a disorderly life, he will undergo the punishment of treacherous slaves. But if, without going as far as that, he is guilty of negligence, his fault will not go unpunished.[12] Nothing could be fairer. As to the reward of the faithful and diligent servant, this had been treated before, and there was no occasion to bring it up again.

2. The Narrow Door, the Way of the Perfect

The Christian spirit — especially if it is lifted to its perfection — supposes effort, sacrifice, renunciation, heroism.

One day, when Jesus was preaching about watchfulness, without which confidence in God would be a snare, he abruptly inter-

---

aggravated it by the use of a saw: "Multos honesti ordinis . . . medios sera dissecuit" (Suetonius, *Caius,* 27).

d) The following clause, "and shall mete out to him the lot of the unfaithful" (Luke) or "of hypocrites" (Matthew), merely explains the preceding, "he shall have him cut in two"; but St. Matthew abandons the parabolic meaning to pass to its application when he adds, "there shall be weeping and gnashing of teeth."

12 Luke 12:47. This verse contains the general principle of retribution. "He that knew the will of his master and did not act accordingly shall receive a great number of strokes; and he that did not know it and does reprehensible things shall receive *few strokes,"* in comparison with the former. In the Vulgate, *plagis* is to be understood after *fecit digna* (ποιήσας ἄξια πληγῶν). The first servant transgressed a *formal* will; the second, an *unspoken* will which he could and should have divined.

rupted himself, as though he had lost sight of his audience and were speaking to himself: "I have come to cast fire upon the earth, and what would I but that it be already enkindled? But I must (first) be baptized with a baptism the waiting for which fills me with anguish."[13] In this passage, the fire that he brings to the earth is neither the ardor of zeal nor the flame of charity; it is the brazier of purifying trial. The prophets had foretold that the Messias would come to purify the sons of Levi as the refiner purifies gold and silver, and to purify the children of Israel as the crucible purifies precious metals of their dross.[14]

Christ's life offered as a holocaust upon the altar of the Cross will be the devouring fire purifying the world of its iniquities, and the persecutions to be undergone by his disciples for his sake "will complete what is wanting to the passion of Christ." The anticipation of this dolorous baptism through which he must of necessity pass to complete his work is, in some sense, a prelude to the agony in the Garden of Olives; for though truly God, he is nonetheless man, and the approach of the Passion wrests from him this cry of anguish.

All who live piously in Christ Jesus, says St. Paul, will suffer persecution and must undergo the fire of purifying trial.

"Think you that I have come to bring peace upon the earth? No, I say to you, not peace, but discord. Hereafter, in one family five persons shall be divided, three against two, and two against three: father against son and son against father, mother against daughter and daughter against mother, mother-in-law against daughter-in-law and daughter-in-law against mother-in-law."

---

[13] Luke 12:49–50. *"Et quid volo nisi ut accendatur?"* The Greek is difficult: καὶ τί θέλω εἰ ἤδη ἀνήφθη. Word for word: "And what do I will if it is already kindled?" But the meaning is not clear, though both the Anglican versions are content with it.

Some translate: "And *how* I desire that it should already be kindled!" The meaning is clear, but it is difficult to see how it is reached according to grammar. Origen proposes to divide the phrases: καὶ τί θέλω; Εἰ ἤδη ἀνήφθη! "And what do I will? May it be already kindled!" The particle εἰ gives the optative sense to the verb: "Isn't it yet kindled!" This approaches the interpretation of the Vulgate, and is the one we have adopted.

Coarctor (συνέχομαι) is said of someone who is the victim of a burning fever (Luke 4:38; Acts 28:8), or of a violent passion (Luke 8:37; 2 Cor. 5:14). For the feeling expressed compare John 12:27 and the prayer in Gethsemani.

[14] Mal. 3:1–4; Isa. 1:25. The figure of the winnower (Matt. 3:12; Luke 3:17) has the same meaning.

It will be necessary to take sides for or against Jesus, and this choice will not be made without struggles and heart-rendings. What a sorrowful drama is the history of a conversion! What obstacles to surmount; what resistances to overcome in order to answer the divine call! A crisis of this kind was about to flare up in Palestine, and it was proper to prepare minds and hearts to meet it. This somber future had within it something frightening for pusillanimous souls, something to make them doubt about salvation. One of these timorous spirits asked him: "Lord, shall they be many that are saved?" Jesus could not satisfy his indiscreet curiosity. The number of the elect, as also the date of the Judgment was the Father's secret. Without attending to the questioner, he says to the bystanders:

"Strive to enter by the narrow door; for many, I say to you, shall seek to enter and shall not be able. When the master of the house has shut the door, and you cry from without: 'Lord, open to us,' he shall answer you: 'I know you not.' In vain shall you say: 'Lord, we ate and drank with thee; thou taughtest in our streets.' He shall answer you: 'I tell you, I know not whence you are. Depart from me, workers of iniquity.' Then there shall be weeping and gnashing of teeth, when you shall see Abraham, Isaac, Jacob, and all the prophets in the kingdom of God, from which you shall be excluded. They shall come from east and west, from north and south, and shall take their places (at table) in the kingdom of God. And many of the last shall be the first, and many of the first shall be the last."[15]

---

[15] Luke 13:22–30. (*a*) To understand this passage it should be noted that there are two doors. First, the door of entry into the terrestrial kingdom of Christ, which is relatively *narrow* as compared with the wide door of perdition (Matt. 7:13–14). One should always strive to enter through the narrow door, for this is always possible (ἀγωνίζετε εἰσελθεῖν, the present imperative). Secondly, there is the door of the celestial Kingdom, which when once closed is not opened again: "You shall seek to enter and shall not be able," with the verbs in the future. That door is closed at death for each one of us; after the Last Judgment it is closed for all humanity. It may be asked whether a period or a comma should be placed after "they shall not be able" (οὐκ ἰσχύσουσιν). It makes little difference. Either way, the thought is continuous, and there is no longer question of the *narrow* door of this life, but of the *closed* door of the future life. Cf. Matt. 7:21–23.

b) The celestial Kingdom is a banquet (Luke 14:15; Apoc. 19:9), but to have a share in it, it is not enough to be invited; entry into it must be made through the vestibule of the terrestrial kingdom. The Gentiles who enter thus

The Gentiles, who were formerly the last, shall now be treated as the first, and shall be seated as such at the heavenly banquet; in contrast, the Jews, who heretofore rightly believed themselves to be the first, shall be placed in the last rank and shall be likened to unbelievers.

This austere language was called for. Perhaps never before had there been among Jesus' hearers more outward eagerness joined to a more profound apathy. Formerly, the Galilean crowds were accustomed to follow him up the Mount of Beatitudes, along the borders of the Lake of Tiberias, and beyond the Jordan; but their enthusiasm had been short-lived. Once their curiosity was satisfied, they had dispersed as if by magic, leaving Jesus alone with the Twelve. Now they were traveling with him, forming a constant retinue. In proportion as the end approached, they were expecting the speedy coming of the kingdom of God, in which, like the sons of Zebedee, they were anxious to have a place of honor. What kept them close to the Master was less a personal attachment to him and devotion to his cause than a vague hope prompted by self-interest and ambition. On the eve of every revolution, as soon as a new star appears on the political horizon, numerous satellites are sure to swing into its orbit. Such calculations had to be refuted; such illusions had to be destroyed. Jesus, turning to the multitude doggedly pressing upon his footsteps, addressed to them these grave words: "If anyone come to me and hate not his father and mother, and wife and children, and brothers and sisters, and even his very life, he cannot be my disciple. And he that comes to follow me without carrying his cross cannot be my disciple."

Ordinary Christians must be prepared for any sacrifice, if duty demands it. They must be ready to break away from the most legitimate affections, if these be in conflict with the law of God. But Jesus is here addressing his *real disciples* and those who aspire to become such. There are disciples and disciples. Our Lord does not demand of all believers the practice of absolute abnegation and the total abandonment of their goods and families.

---

will be admitted; the Jews who refuse to do so will be excluded. A fine statement of Rabbi Joseph may be quoted: "This world is like the vestibule to the future world. Prepare yourself in the vestibule to be able to enter into the banquet hall" (*Mishnah,* treat. *Aboth,* iv, 16; ed. Marti and Beer, 1927, p. 107).

At Bethany, Capharnaum, Jerusalem, and elsewhere he had believers who had never left either parents or property.

Upon the young man who questions him about the way of salvation he imposes no other obligation than the way of the commandments, but he adds: "If thou wilt be perfect, sell thy possessions and give the proceeds to the poor, then come and *follow me*." There is, then, the way of salvation, and there is the way of perfection; the road of the commandments, and the road of the counsels. He that wishes to follow Jesus like the twelve Apostles, like the seventy-two disciples, must renounce his goods, his family, his country, and even his own person, *adhuc autem et animam suam*. No reserves, no delay! To one Jesus refuses permission to go to take leave of his family; to another, the permission to go bury his father; to a third he says that he that looks back after putting his hand to the plow is not worthy of the kingdom of God.

The ambitious among them who aspire to be his auxiliaries in the apostolate and his collaborators in the work of God, he warns not to decide thoughtlessly: he recalls to them that he has not a stone whereon to lay his head. He adjures them to sound their souls, to make sure that they are able to rise to the heights to which they aspire.[16]

---

[16] Two points are to be clarified: the meaning of *disciple*, and the meaning of *following Jesus*.

a) The term *disciple* is applied indifferently to simple believers, to those who habitually accompanied our Lord, and to the twelve Apostles. Oftener than not, only the context allows us to distinguish. St. John uses the term *apostle* only once, and in the very general meaning of *envoy* (John 13:16). He rarely says *the Twelve* (John 6:67–71; 20:24). The Synoptics employ these terms a little oftener; but the Apostles, even when they are by themselves, are almost always designated under the name *disciples*.

b) To *follow* Jesus can be said in a moral sense (to imitate) and in a physical sense (to accompany). St. John is the only one to employ it in a moral sense. "He that follows me walks not in darkness" (8:12); "if anyone serve me, let him follow me" (12:26). But in St. John, it is to be understood *almost* always in the physical sense, and *always* in the other Evangelists.

When reference is made to the crowds which follow Jesus, it is only a transitory act: they follow him to the Mountain of Beatitudes, along the borders of the lake, on the other side of the Jordan (Matt. 4:25; 13:2; 14:13 and parallel passages) soon to abandon him. Toward the end, however, they form a constant retinue (Luke 14:25, συνεπορεύοντο αὐτῷ ὄχλοι πολλοί, the crowds *were traveling with* him). But in most cases *to follow Jesus* does not mean an imitation of Christ or an occasional escort, but an *effective* and *constant* following.

"Which of you, proposing to build a tower, does not pause at the beginning to calculate whether he has the means to complete it? If he has laid the foundations without being able to continue, all the passers-by will ridicule him, saying: 'Here is a man who began to build and was unable to finish.' And what king going to engage in battle with another king does not pause at the beginning to consider whether with ten thousand men he can attack one who has twenty thousand? Otherwise, while his adversary is still far away, he sends an embassy to treat of peace. He among you that does not renounce all his possessions cannot be my disciple."[17]

Our Lord had never given such instructions to ordinary believers; but these words were addressed to a chosen few. The desertion of such volunteers, once they have enlisted, would be a misfortune for the Church. "Salt is good; but if it becomes insipid, who shall give it back its savor? It is thrown out, for it is no longer good even to fertilize the ground. He that has ears to hear, let him hear!"

---

1. Every time that Jesus says to anyone "Follow me" the words mean, not "Believe in me" or "Imitate me" or "Observe my commandments," but "Come with me to live my life and to share my work." This appeal was addressed to Philip (John 1:44), to the four chief Apostles (Matt. 4:20–22; Mark 1:18; Luke 5:11), to Matthew (Matt. 9:9; Mark 2:14; Luke 5:27), and to an anonymous petitioner (Matt. 8:22; Luke 9:59).

2. Every time that Jesus gives anyone the counsel to *follow him* (ἀκολουθεῖν) or what comes to the same, to *come after him* (ὀπίσω μου), he orders him to sell his property, giving the proceeds to the poor, to quit all immediately and to join his retinue (the rich young man, Matt. 19:21; Mark 10:21; Luke 18:22; the three petitioners, Luke 9:57–62; Matt. 8:19–22). Compare Matt. 19:27; Mark 10:28; Luke 18:28.

3. The Apostles are surprised that a man who *does not follow them* (οὐκ ἀκολουθεῖ ἡμῖν, Mark 9:38), who does not follow Jesus with them (Luke 9:49: οὐκ ἀκολουθεῖ μεθ' ἡμῶν), that is to say, who "is not part of the habitual retinue of Jesus," expels devils in the name of Jesus.

4. Upon those who wish to *follow* in this way the Saviour imposes an absolute renunciation and the obligation of taking up their cross in his train (Matt. 16:24; Mark 8:34; Luke 9:23); but it is always in the conditional: "*If* anyone wishes to *follow* me." At the same time he warns them to reflect and to weigh well the difficulties (Luke 14:25–35), something which he never does for the simple believers. He is content to say to them, "Believe in me" with a lively and active faith.

[17] Luke 14:28–33. *Disciple* in the full sense of the word.

CHAPTER VIII

The Parables of Mercy

1. The Strayed Sheep and the Lost Drachma

(LUKE 15:1–10)

THE compassionate kindness of Jesus to the poor, the lowly, and all the outcasts of society profoundly scandalized the Scribes and Pharisees, who had nothing but scorn for the ignorant common people. What irritated them even more was the interest he seemed to take in publicans, the refuse of Jewish society, and the indulgence he showed to public sinners, whose mere approach was considered a defilement.

The various collectors of taxes formed a very numerous caste, more closely bound together by the sullen hatred and affected disdain directed against them by their compatriots. These men were attracted to Jesus by his sweetness, and were coming around seeking from him the signs of sympathy which everyone else denied them. The Saviour did not repel their advances; had he not admitted one of their number into the group of his Apostles? When they invited him to sit down with them at table, he did not disdain to do so. Notorious sinners mingled with them, in the hope of obtaining pardon and restoration. The meetings with these unfortunates went on increasing in number, and it was said that they made appointments to meet him. Strange court for the divine King! This preference of his for physical and moral misery was the complaint oftenest phrased against him by his declared enemies. In vain had he told them that he had not come to call the just, but sinners. They did not understand such language. By reproaching him with being the friend of publicans and people of evil life, they thought they were doing him a mortal injury.[1]

To reveal to them the marvels of God's mercy, and to teach them at the same time the value of one soul in the eyes of God, Jesus propounded to them three of the most touching of the parables: the Strayed Sheep, the Lost Drachma, and the Prodigal Son. The first two are not so much parables as appeals to common experience and the natural feelings of his hearers. They serve as an introduction to the third, which has justly been called the pearl of the Gospel parables.

"Who among you, if he possesses a hundred sheep and happens to lose one of them, does not leave the ninety-nine others in the country, to run in search of the strayed sheep? And when he has found it, he lays it upon his shoulders, and, upon coming home, calls together his friends and neighbors to tell them: Rejoice with me because I have found my lost sheep.

"I say to you that there shall also be more joy in heaven for one sinner that does penance than for ninety-nine just who have no need of penance.

"And what woman possessing ten drachmas, if she happens to lose one of them, does not light her lamp and sweep her house, to search for it carefully? When she has found it, she calls friends and neighbors to tell them: Rejoice with me, because I have found my lost drachma.

"Such, I say to you, is the joy among the angels of God even for one sinner that does penance."[2]

In what is called the Wilderness of Juda, it is not unusual for a sheep to fall behind the flock, either because it gets tangled in a thicket of thorny bushes, or because it falls to the bottom of an old cistern, or rolls down an embankment and cannot climb up again. At evening, when the flock is counted as it is being let into the sheepfold, its absence is easily detected. But the watchful shepherd of the parable does not wait until evening to notice that one of his sheep has disappeared, and he sees in a flash which

[1] Luke 15:1: "All the publicans and sinners were drawing near him, to listen to him; and the Pharisees and Scribes murmured, saying: 'He welcomes sinners and eats with them.' " The imperfect is the imperfect of *custom,* or perhaps of *simultaneous action,* alluding to some particular circumstance.

[2] Luke 15:2–10. The parable of the Lost Sheep is found also in Matthew (18:12–14), but in another context and with a different application.

one is missing. Immediately he leaves the others in the pasturage common to several flocks, where they will run no risk, and goes off in search of the lost sheep. If it spends the night outside the sheepfold, it will almost inevitably be the prey of wild beasts: wolves, hyenas, or leopards. As soon as the shepherd finds it he lifts it up on his shoulders; this is the best and the only practical way of bringing a lone sheep back to the fold. On his return he gives vent to his joy and wants to share it with his companions. It is this openhearted and overflowing joy that is the essential trait of the parable. It symbolizes the joy of the angels and the elect at the conversion of a sinner.

Still, this joy in heaven, easier to imagine than describe, has less often been the inspiration of sacred orators and Christian artists than the search for the lost sheep and its conveyance back to the sheepfold. No scene from the Gospel was dearer to the painters of the catacombs. From the end of the first century, they profusely multiply the images of the Good Shepherd in the frescoes of the burial chapels. The sheep is the emblem of the soul which the divine Shepherd carries to the heavenly sheepfold, represented by a clump of verdant trees, in the midst of which leaps up a spring of living water. The Good Shepherd has the conventional symbols of the classical shepherd: the short tunic tucked up at the waist, the leggings, and sometimes the flute and shepherd's crook. He is young with eternal youth, and joy and happiness radiate from his countenance.

The parable of the Lost Drachma has the same meaning. The drachma was a Greek coin almost equal to the Roman denarius, a quarter of a Jewish shekel, or about twenty-one cents. The poor woman who has lost it hurries to light the lamp in order to dispel the darkness of her humble lodging, where only a feeble daylight penetrates. She carefully sweeps the chinks of the floor filled with straw and miscellaneous objects. When at last she finds her little treasure, she calls her neighbors to share her demonstrations of joy: a character stroke which is perfectly true to life.

Basically the parable of the Lost Drachma adds nothing to that of the Strayed Sheep. They are not so much two distinct parables as two aspects of the same. Two facts of common experience show us that we can neither lose without regret something that is precious, nor find it again without joy; and this sentiment is so universal that it is found even in heaven. God cannot remain indifferent to the fate of a human soul upon which he has stamped his image, which he has marked with his seal, and purchased with the blood of his Son.

We might be tempted for the sake of climax to invert the order, putting in the first place the lost drachma whose value is less; but we should remember that its loss is more painful to the poor woman who has only ten of them; hence we see that the order of climax really has been observed.

The third parable, whose object is incomparably more elevated, completes the two preceding ones without being strictly linked to them. It may have been spoken on another occasion and before another audience. Having justified his love for publicans and sinners, our Lord no longer occupies himself with the Scribes and Pharisees, who retire into the background; he now effaces himself and brings his Father upon the scene, the better to expound the infinite treasures of divine mercy.[3]

2. The Prodigal Son

(LUKE 15:11–32)

Even from a mere literary standpoint, the parable of the Prodigal Son is a marvel of exquisite feeling and pure inspiration. It is impossible to tell it in other words than those of the Evangelist, and one fears to spoil it by comment, just as an unskilled lapidary would fear to ruin a diamond given him to cut and set.

Three persons appear in the story: the father, the prodigal, and his elder brother, representing respectively God, the sinner, and the just man; a sinner who comes back to the right path, and a just man who is not free of all imperfections. There the allegory ends; the rest must be interpreted according to the rules of the parable. The drama unfolds in three acts, in which each actor in turn takes the center of the stage: the wanderings of the

[3] The transition *ait autem* (εἶπεν δέ) is very vague. Frequently it does no more than establish a material link with what precedes. It is the idea common to the three parables that constitutes the link here.

Prodigal, the joyous welcome by the father, and the complaints of the elder brother leading to the concluding moral.

"A certain man had two sons. The younger said to him: 'Father, give me the part of the inheritance that is coming to me.' And he divided his fortune between them. A few days later, the younger son, converting all his possessions into money, set out for a far country, and there squandered all his wealth living in debauchery. And when he had consumed all, a great famine came upon that country, and he began to suffer want. And he went to hire out his services to an inhabitant of that country, who sent him to his farm to feed his swine. The unhappy youth longed to fill his stomach with the carob pods which were the food of those animals, but no one gave him any."[4]

This first tableau depicts for us the young man's misery rather than his wickedness; it presents to our minds rather his misfortune than the shame of his conduct. His youth — for youth is the age of thoughtlessness and impulsive acts — while it does not excuse his faults, to a certain degree extenuates them. The Gospel does not speak of his premeditation, perhaps to allow us to keep some sympathy for him. He may have had valid reasons for asking for an advance of his inheritance, and he does not claim it as a right, since he is well aware that during his father's lifetime nothing is owing to him except his maintenance. And so his father, without weakness or imprudence, immediately yields to his wish. But as soon as he is in possession of his part of the inheritance, the prodigal hurries to set out for a distant country, and there he soon squanders it all in foolish spending. Was he suddenly befuddled by the sight of the gold and the prospect of the pleasures he could buy with it? That is possible; but it would seem more probable that it was all a plan nurtured in advance.

[4] Luke 15:11–16. We follow the Vulgate in two cases where the precise meaning of terms is open to discussion: (*a*) *Vivendo luxuriose* (ζῶν ἀσώτως). The adverb ἀσώτως is very rare, but ἄσωτος means "lost to morality," "a libertine," and ἀσωτία means "orgy," "debauch." Many think that there is question here of prodigality rather than debauchery, but these two vices generally go together, especially in a young man; and prodigality had already been mentioned (*dissipavit*, διεσκόρπισεν). (*b*) *Cupiebat implere ventrem suum* (γεμίσαι τὴν κοιλίαν αὐτοῦ). The reading *satiari* (χορτασθῆναι) is almost equally well attested, but it is open to suspicion of *euphemism*, and the realistic reading appears to us more probable because it better depicts the miserable and abject state of the prodigal.

His intentions were not pure. He wanted to enjoy his freedom, to live independently, to leave his father whose presence thwarted him, to flee a country where too many familiar faces imposed constraint upon him. The Gospel insinuates all this without laying stress upon it, since the purpose is less to depict the sin of the prodigal than his misfortune.

In what somber colors are his extreme misery and his abject servitude depicted! When a providential famine makes desolate the country where he has taken refuge, he finds himself alone, without resources, without relatives or friends — for he cannot count upon the comrades of his debauches — and he sinks so low as to become a keeper of swine. Among the ancients, and especially the Jews, this was, of all occupations, the most ignoble. In Egypt, according to Herodotus, swineherds were excluded from all the temples, and were doomed to perpetual celibacy, at least to marriage with those of their own class.[5] Beset by hunger and forgotten by all, the prodigal is reduced to envying the fodder of the unclean beasts whose guardian he is. This fodder was the fruit of the carob tree, a very common evergreen producing pods or seeds of unsavory taste, which even the poorest refused to eat, except for lack of finer or more substantial fare.[6] Such was the food that the unfortunate youth would gladly have eaten; but the keepers of the keys of the granary would give him none, and the only thought that raised his spirits was to vie for it with the swine. Why, then, does he not break his chains and flee far from this foul hole? He is held back by habit, shame, and human respect. To return to his father's hearth, he must retrace his steps through places that had witnessed the parade of his folly; he must encounter the bantering laughter and the offensive compassion of his former servants; he must sustain, perhaps, reproaches and coldness from his father. He has not the courage; and that is the peak of his misery.

The story of the prodigal is that of every prodigal. When he abandons himself to awakening passion, he flatters himself that he can stop in mid-course, or at least avoid excess. But once he

---

[5] Herodotus, II, 47. The raising of pigs was forbidden to the Jews (*Baba Qamma,* vii, 7).

[6] The *siliquae* (κερατία) are certainly carob pods, the fruit of the carob tree. Description and pictures in *Dict. de la Bible* of Vigouroux.

slips on the fatal slope, he falls from one abyss to another. The dizziness which seizes him sweeps him farther and farther from God, lower and lower in the mire. This sort of fascination and this insatiable need of change of which the Scripture speaks has been wonderfully described by Bossuet: "Reason, once delivered to the allurement of the senses and captured by that heady wine, can no longer answer for itself or know where its intoxication will carry it. . . . What else is the life of sense than a fluctuating movement from appetite to disgust and from disgust to appetite, the soul constantly floating uncertain between ardor slackening and ardor renewing itself?"[7] In vain! The "something bitter" sung by the poet rises suddenly in the midst of the flowers and grasps him by the throat,[8] and that aftertaste of bitterness does not appease the hunger for pleasure; just as the salty water of the sea, which the shipwrecked mariner carries to his lips to quench his thirst, does but increase its intensity.

Slave of passion, the prodigal deplores its tyranny and groans under its yoke, without being able to take the resolution to break his bonds. To grasp the strength of the ties which habit forms, the heart-rending plaints of St. Jerome in his desert of Chalcis must be read, or the intimate disclosures of St. Augustine on the agony of the struggle which preceded his final victory.[9]

Still, the excess of his misery finally drew the unfortunate prodigal from his torpor.

"The young man entering into himself said: 'How many hired servants in my father's house have bread in abundance, while I die here of hunger? I will arise: I will go to find my father and will say to him: "Father, I have sinned against heaven and against thee. I am no longer worthy to be called thy son; treat me as one of thy servants." ' And rising he went to his father.

"When he was still a long way off, his father saw him and, moved with compassion, ran to him and fell upon his neck and

---

[7] Bossuet, *Sermon sur l'enfant prodigue,* first point. Bossuet comments on the *fascinatio nugacitatis* and *inconstantia* in the Sacred Books.

[8] Lucretius, *De Rerum Natura,* iv, 1133–1134.

"Medio de fonte leporum
Surgit amari aliquid quod ipsis in floribus angat."

[9] St. Jerome, *Epist.,* xxii, *Ad Eustochium,* 7 (ML, XXIII, 398–399); St. Augustine, *Confess.,* Bk. VIII, Chap. 11 (ML, XXXII, 760–761).

tenderly embraced him. The son said to him: 'Father, I have sinned against heaven and against thee. I am no longer worthy to be called thy son.' But the father said to the servants: 'Quickly bring the finest robe and put it on him; put the ring on his finger and shoes on his feet. Bring out the fatted calf and kill it and let us make merry, because my son was dead and behold he is alive; he was lost and behold he is found again.' And they began to make merry."[10]

The second scene, where the father comes upon the stage, is painted with extreme delicacy of touch and consummate art, suggesting to the reader's mind much more than the words can express. If the father sees his son when he is still far off, it is not the result of mere chance; it is because he has never become resigned to his loss and has always cherished the hope of seeing him soon again. Like the mother of the young Tobias, morning and evening he climbed the hill near his house, searching the horizon on every side as far as his eyes could carry. Finally he descries a wan and tattered traveler, enfeebled by fatigue, one would say a beggar. But no, his heart has recognized him. It is his son. He runs forward to meet him; he wishes to cover at least half of the distance. Divining his son's repentance or reading it in his face, he falls upon his neck, tenderly embracing him and covering him with his tears, without leaving him any time to offer a word of excuse or regret. The prodigal has prepared a confession, a model of sincerity, humility, and firm resolve, in which he fully acknowledges his faults, proclaims his own unworthiness, and accepts in advance all obligation of atonement. "Father, I have sinned against heaven and against thee. I am no longer worthy to be called thy son; treat me as one of thy

---

[10] Luke 15:17–24. Some details: (*a*) *Entering again into himself* (*in se reversus*), a classical phrase (Epictetus, III, i, 15: Diod. Sic., xiii, 95; Horace, *Epist.*, II, ii, 138; Lucretius, IV, 1020; Terence, *Adelphi,* V, iii, 8). Passion makes a man go out of himself; reflection and remorse make him enter into himself again.

b) On Verse 21, St. Augustine correctly remarks: "Non addit quod in illa meditatione dixerat: *Fac me sicut unum de mercenariis tuis*" (*Quaest. Evang.*, ii, 39). This addition is rejected by all the critical editors of the Greek text except Hort, who adopts it because it is in the *Vaticanus*.

c) The presents given by the father, *the finest robe,* the ceremonial robe (1 Mach. 10:20; cf. Ezech. 27:22); the *ring* of persons of quality (James 2:2; Gen. 41:42; Esther 3:10; 8:2); the *fatted calf* (killed by the witch of Endor in honor of Saul, 1 Kings 28:24).

servants." But he does not finish. He stops before the last phrase, either because his father cuts him off, or because, after the welcome he has received, he understands that this humble formula is no longer in place, and that in proffering it he would seem to doubt his father's heart.

But his father, all busy with the preparations for the feast, is not listening to him. Bring out quickly the finest robe, the ring, the shoes! He wants to see his son as he was before. Kill the fatted calf, reserved, perhaps, for a solemn occasion or for the unexpected visit of some distinguished guest. What visitor more worthy of being feasted than a cherished son who was believed to be lost?

In almost all the countries of the East rich families had on hand apparel for show and ceremony, of such style that all the members of the family, young and old, could wear it when occasion required. It is a cloak of this kind, the finest that could be found, that the father orders to be brought to attire his son. The shoes are put on his feet, that he may no longer look like a beggar or a vagabond, and the ring is placed on his finger as the sign of nobility or of a freeman's quality. It is known that in Rome the ring was the distinctive insigne of the knight, and in the Bible the ministers of Assuerus and of Pharao received the royal ring as a mark of the dignity with which they were invested.

All these kind attentions and marks of preference seem to be contrary to all likelihood. Is there in the world a father so tender and compassionate, so forgetful of insult, and so ready to forgive, so generous to the ingrate? But it must be remembered that the father in the parable is the image of the Father of Mercies, and that he is withal a very imperfect image. It is then seen that the portrait, far from being too highly colored, is in fact rather dim and pale. The father of the parable waits for his son, but does not go in search of him; perhaps because he does not know where he is. But God, who knows all, never loses sight of the sinner; he follows him in all his wanderings, he solicits him by his grace, he leaves nothing undone to bring him back. The sinner would not seek God, if God had not first sought him. Nothing can be more touching than the father's welcome to his son, his urge to run to him, his emotion, his tears, his caresses, his fatherly embrace. But how much more touching is the welcome which God has reserved for the penitent sinner, and which he commands his servants to provide for him? What are the gifts of the father in the parable compared with the gifts that God prepares for the repentant sinner? He clothes his soul again with innocence; for Confession, if accompanied by a very intense contrition, is a second Baptism which restores to him everything that he has lost by sin, adding to it the grace of the Sacrament. He contracts with him a new alliance eternal in its nature, which he will not be the first to break. God guarantees for him the aids which will prevent him, if he but makes use of them, from being wounded or soiled along the path of life. And finally, having no more to give, he gives himself immolated in the Eucharist, sealing and consummating the reconciliation in the Sacred Banquet. The welcome given by God to prodigals who return to him would make the angels jealous, were they capable of envy.[11]

"Meantime, the elder son was in the fields. On his return, as he drew near to the house, he heard music and dancing and, calling one of the servants, he asked him what this meant. And he answered him: 'Thy brother has come back, and thy father, happy in finding him again safe and sound, has had the fatted calf killed.'

"Indignant, he refused to enter. And when his father came out to beg him to do so, he said to him: 'Behold, for so many years have I been serving thee without transgressing any of thy commands, and never hast thou given me a kid with which to make merry with my friends. And when this one comes, who has consumed thy property with harlots, thou hast killed the fatted calf!'

"'My son,' answered his father, 'thou art always with me and all that I have belongs to thee; but it behooved us to make merry and rejoice, because thy brother, he who was dead, lives again; he was lost and is found again.'"[12]

---

[11] We do not say that the first robe, the ring, the shoes, and the fatted calf *signify* sanctifying grace, the divine alliance, actual graces derived from the sacrament, the Eucharist: that would be to forget the nature of parabolical language. We say only that, if the parable is transposed to apply it to God, these things come naturally to mind, and that no other explanation is more satisfactory. The Council of Trent (Sess. VI, ch. vii) gives an example of such accommodated application.

[12] Luke 15:25–32. (*a*) The elder son is coming back from the fields, probably

Many would be inclined to regard this third scene as a digression, whereas, on the contrary, it gives the parable its significance. The elder brother, occupied in the fields, had not been informed of his brother's return, because it was thought that he would not be long in getting back to the house. This circumstance, together with his surprise at finding the house making festival without his knowing anything about it, contributed to his irritation. Certainly it was wrong for him to sulk and to reprove his father for not having given him a kid, to make merry with his friends. His father would have given him that and much more, had he known his wish. But he had not dreamt of it because, as he goes on to say, everything in the house belonged to both of them.

This defect does not prevent him from being a good son, industrious and obedient. He tells no lie when he asserts that he has never knowingly transgressed his father's wishes. But he belongs to the same category as certain Christians of exemplary conduct but narrow views, who come to grasp only with difficulty the mystery of God's mercy; who are surprised, as Jonas was, that God should pardon guilty and repentant Nineva; who are almost scandalized at the indulgence shown by the Church and her ministers toward sinners most heavily laden with crime. Let them meditate, these narrow souls, on the parable of the Prodigal Son.

The majority of Latin commentators have seen in the elder son a figure of the Jewish people, or of the Pharisees. The Greek Fathers were better inspired. For them, without any hesitation, the two brothers are symbols of the sinner and the just man. Would God say to the Jews, and above all to the Pharisees:

---

from supervising some agricultural improvement, for the father is rich. He hears the noise of the music and dancing (*symphonias et choros*); this was to liven up the feast (Suetonius, *Caligula,* 37; *discumbens de die inter choros et symphonias*). While the servants played the flute, the others danced; or else the players themselves marked time swaying and tapping their feet.

b) He accuses his brother of having dissipated his fortune with harlots. Though this fact has not been mentioned, it is likely and could have been known by report.

c) Note in these parables the literary effect of the refrains (Verses 7 and 10, 24 and 32), the Homeric repetition, and the strict parallelism of the narratives.

"You are always with me, and all that I have belongs to you"? Could they themselves say, without raising a protest: "We have never transgressed thy orders"? Would God treat with such gentleness those whom Jesus and the prophets loaded with such stinging reproaches?[13]

Preachers who describe with such eloquence the ingratitude of the prodigal, his misery and abjection, his slavery, his repentance, and his humble avowal, his pardon and rehabilitation, generally neglect the last sentence, which nevertheless contains the moral of the parable. "My son, thou art always with me, and all that I have belongs to thee, but it behooved us to make merry and rejoice, because thy brother was dead and he is now alive, he was lost and is found again." Perhaps there are not in human language terms strong enough to express the feelings suggested to the pious soul by this parallel and this contrast. The penitent sinner becomes the favorite of God, the object of divine complacence and predilection: what a subject of admiration; what a marvel! But what happiness for the just man to hear the words: "My son, thou art always with me, and all that I have belongs to thee"! If a free choice were given, who would not prefer innocence preserved to innocence recaptured? Rightly do we admire, and rightly does the Church enthusiastically extol Mary

---

[13] Though the commentary of Origen is lost we have the excellent explanation of Titus of Bostra (MG, LXXII, 801–809; critical edit. of Sickenberger in *T.U.*, XXI [Leipzig, 1901], a good summary in the *Catena in Lucam* of Cremer [Oxford, 1844], pp. 117–121). There is also the commentary of St. Cyril of Alexandria, who thinks, as Titus does, that the two brothers symbolize sinners and just, and he refutes the opposite opinions. We know the thought of St. John Chrysostom from his *De Paenitentia* (MG, XLIX, 282–284); it is in conformity with the preceding two.

The sermons and homilies on the Prodigal Son are innumerable. Migne's collection, *Orateurs sacrés,* contains twenty-seven of them in French. We could add Ventura, Olivier, Félix, Monsabré, Grépin (*Entretiens sur les paraboles,* 1900), Pichenot (*Les Paraboles expliquées,* 1901), Buzy (*Les Paraboles,* 1902). Five of the better-known authors give an idea of the moral applications of which the parable is susceptible: Bossuet's first sermon on the Third Sunday of Lent (pleasure the source of sorrow, and sorrow the source of pleasure); Bourdaloue's Spiritual Retreat, fifth day (conversion), Massillon's Friday of the Second Week of Lent (against impurity); Félix, *Le Prodigue et les prodigues,* 1891 (six conferences); Monsabré, *Retraite de Notre-Dame,* 1896 (four conferences). None of them dwell on the third scene, the most interesting in our opinion, but also, perhaps, the most difficult to develop.

Magdalene, St. Paul, St. Augustine, and all the great converts of either sex; but has not the Catholic liturgy accents more moving still to chant the glory of those pure souls who will follow the Spotless Lamb wherever he goes, and will form the retinue of the Immaculate Virgin before the throne of God?

CHAPTER IX

The Proper Use of Wealth

1. The Unfaithul Steward

(LUKE 16:1–18)

Two parables on the proper use of wordly goods follow without transition after the three parables of mercy. Lacking all indications of time and place, we may conjecture that the scene and also the audience remain unchanged. Jesus addresses himself directly to his disciples, but he knows that there are Pharisees present whose carping remarks he will soon hear. Before this mixed gathering he proposes the parable of the Unfaithful Steward.[1]

A very rich man had entrusted the management of his entire fortune to an official whom the Greeks called an *econome* and the Latins a *procurator*. He was not a slave put in charge of other slaves; rather he was an important personage enjoying absolute liberty in his functions, and disposing of his master's property practically without control. Such freedom in the exercise of his charge was a constant temptation to fraud and peculation. One day he was accused of squandering the fortune of which he had charge. Was it by theft properly so called, and by fraudulent

[1] Luke 16:1–9. The introductory formula, "Now he said to them" (ἔλεγεν δέ), authorizes the supposition of a change of place and audience, but does not demand it. This steward (οἰκονόμος) can be an important personage (Josephus, *Antiq.*, XII, iv, 7). The Vulgate has *villicus;* it should rather be *procurator*. Cicero (*De orat.*, I, 58) clearly distinguishes the two words: the *villicus* is a slave placed in charge of other slaves in farm work (Horace, *Epist.*, i, 14). The *procurator* administers a large estate such as that of the Emperor, or even a small province like Judea or Egypt.

misappropriation; or by bad management and foolish spending? At any rate, the charge was well founded, since he makes no attempt to clear himself. His master said to him: "What is this I hear about thee? Render an account of thy administration, for thou canst no longer keep thy place." It is not a mere threat; it is a fixed decision, a categorical dismissal.

The discharged steward said to himself: "What shall I do, now that my position has been taken away from me: I am too weak to till the ground, and I am ashamed to beg. This is what I will do so that, when I am relieved of my duties, people may take me into their homes." What he intends to do his conduct will show. Until he turns in his accounts and his dismissal becomes an accomplished fact, he still keeps authority over his subordinates and can conclude or cancel contracts. Summoning his master's debtors into his presence, he says to the first: "How much dost thou owe him?" — "One hundred measures of oil." — "Take thy note, sit down and quickly write fifty." Then to the second: "And thou, how much dost thou owe him?" — "One hundred measures of wheat." — "Take thy note and write eighty."[2]

The steward gives back to each of them the note in which he acknowledges his indebtedness, bidding him to write out another one, and to do so quickly, for time is pressing. A simple change of figures, with rewriting and erasures, would too readily betray the fraud. Whether their debt results from a loan in kind, as is more probable, or from rents to be paid by farmers or lease-

[2] The βάτος (Hebrew, *bath*) was the tenth of a κόρος (Hebrew, *kor*). Benzinger (*Hebräische Archäologie,* 1894, p. 185) places the measure of the *bath* at 36.44 liters; Kennedy (Hastings, *Dict. of the Bible,* Vol. IV, p. 912) places it at 36.92 liters. These are the older measurements. More recently somewhat higher values have been assigned (40.5 liters by Kennedy, 39.55 liters in *Jewish Encycl.,* Vol. III, p. 489). The values assigned to the *kor* by Josephus (*Antiq.,* VIII, ii, 90), if the text is not corrupt, are misleading and contrary to all the other data.

Changing these values into gallons and bushels, the hundred measures of oil would be 951 and 977 gal. (1057 in the more recent measurements); the hundred measures of grain would be 1022 or 1050 bu. (perhaps 1135). According to the estimates of Lagrange (cf. *Saint Luc,* p. 433), the 951 or 977 gal. of oil would have been worth approximately $1,284 or $1,389 in equivalent values, on the Palestinian market; the 1022 or 1050 bu. of grain at $1.50 to the bushel, equivalently $1,533 or $1,575. Thus in remitting 50% of the oil and 20% of the grain, the dishonest agent made to the debtors a gift of between $940 and $1,009, and a much more considerable sum considering the purchasing power in those days.

holders matters little, for such rents falling due are true debts. These first two debtors are mentioned by way of example, but it is clear that the steward acts in the same unscrupulous way with the others. He no longer takes pains to dissemble, since he has nothing more to lose, and he has made all those who are under obligation to him his accomplices, interested in keeping silence. This final swindle provides him with shelter against want for the future: how can the people whom he has enriched at the expense of his master refuse him an asylum?

When the owner learned of the affair he could not help admiring the cleverness of his steward, who had played his hand with a skill worthy of such a rascal. He pays him this eulogy: "He is a *clever* thief and a *skillful* swindler." It may surprise us that he resigns himself so readily to his loss, but we already know that he was very rich and not overcareful. Then too, the advantage of being rid of a dishonest manager may have seemed to him sufficient recompense.[3]

The man of the parable, concludes Jesus, was not mistaken in admiring the guile of his steward, "for the children of the world are shrewder with those of their own kind than the children of light." It is a fact of experience that worldlings following the maxims of their perverse environment display more cleverness, more versatility, and more patience, to preserve and increase their fortunes than Christians with the principles of the Gospel to guide them often show in safeguarding their spiritual interests. The faithless steward who, in desperate case, finds the means of making sure of his future is a proof of it, and can give them a lesson in foresight. It is not his way of proceeding that should serve as an example but his decisiveness and his skillfulness.

"And do you," concludes Jesus, "make friends for yourselves with the money of iniquity, so that, when it shall fail you, these friends may welcome you into everlasting dwellings."[4]

---

[3] Luke 16:8: "The master praised the unjust steward for having acted prudently." The master (ὁ κύριος) is certainly the man of the parable and not our Lord, who simply records the fact. Jesus speaks in his own name in the following verse: "And I say to you." He does not say *how* the children of this world are wiser ***in relation to those of their own kind*** (*in generatione sua*) than are Christians, but it is clear that the reference is not to the same sphere of interests.

[4] Luke 16:9. Mammon (Μαμωνᾶς) is the Aramaic *Mâmôna* (מאמונא), which properly means "deposit," or, by extension, "gain," "riches." St. Augustine

Wealth is called the *money of iniquity,* less because it is the fruit of injustice — which it too frequently is — than because it is the stimulant and the frequent occasion of injustice. Far from being evil in itself, it has a useful role in the moral life, just as it has in the social life; everything depends upon the use that is made of it. Employed for the relief of the poor, or spent for the worship of God, it prepares friends for us in heaven who will open the gate for us when it quits us together with all things else.[5] The Protestants are mistaken: they cannot destroy the merit of almsgiving and good works, at least without erasing this page of the Gospel.[6]

The proper use of earthly goods is not only a guarantee for the future life, it also disposes the Christian soul to receive in this life spiritual goods in larger measure. The horizon is changed, and the parable of the Wicked Steward is no longer in perspective:

"He who is faithful in little things will be faithful also in great: and he who is unjust in little things is unjust also in great. If you have not been faithful in the riches of iniquity, who will entrust to you the true good? And if you have not been faithful in managing another's goods, who will entrust to you your own?

---

tells us that the word had passed into the Punic language (*Sermo in Monte,* II, 14, n. 47). The expression "riches of iniquity" (9) or "wicked riches" (11) is found in a passage of the Book of Henoch (LXIII, 10) before the Christian era, and in Euripides in a fragment of the tragedy *Alexander* (ed. Nauck, p. 377) which may serve as a commentary on our text: *Ἄδικον ὁ πλοῦτος, πολλὰ δ'οὐκ ὀρθῶς ποιεῖ* (Wealth is wicked; it does much wrongfully).

5 The Latin has *cum defeceritis* (when you die), as also the Greek Textus Receptus. The better attested reading is *ὅταν ἐκλίπῃ*, "when it (riches) shall fail," that is to say, at death. Those who will welcome the rich benefactor into heaven are, naturally, the poor aided by him, whom he has made his friends (St. Augustine, *Quaest. Evang.*, ii, 34).

6 The dissertations on this parable are numberless. The monograph of Rücker, *Uber das Gleichnis vom ungerechten Verwalter,* 1912 (in *Bibl. Studien,* XVII, 5) gives a survey of them. Many of them go off in a wrong direction, by wishing to turn into an allegory a parable whose details are inconsistent with allegory. Others believe (or pretend to believe) that Jesus approves the guile of the dishonest steward; hence they are scandalized. But it is very clear that the one of whom is said, *laudavit dominus villicum iniquum,* is the rascal's master and not Jesus, who speaks for himself only in the verse following: "And I say to you."

You cannot at the same time serve God and Mammon," the idol of riches.[7]

Let us not forget that Jesus is addressing his disciples, or those who wish to become such; his collaborators, or those who are to continue his work. When he speaks of spiritual goods it would seem that he means the charisms which are related to the government of the Church and ecclesiastical functions, rather than actual graces and the gifts of the Holy Ghost. To share in these true riches of the Christian community, the only ones which count, in contrast to perishable goods, one must first give proof of fidelity in the use of goods of an inferior order. Experience, which is subject to but few exceptions, proves that the man who is faithful in the least things will acquit himself with the same conscientiousness in affairs that are loftier; and if he has shown himself unscrupulous in subordinate duties, he will be no better in the highest offices. And much more, the slave of Mammon is unfit for the service of God, for these two masters are opposed, the one to the other, and both of them demand the whole man.

Hearing these words the Pharisees could not keep from laughing.[8] For their part, they saw no incompatibility between the worship of God and that of money, and they knew very well how to reconcile the two. Far from fearing riches as a danger,

---

[7] Luke 16:10–13. Verse 12 presents difficulty: "Si in alieno fideles non fuistis, quod *vestrum* est quis dabit vobis?" In the Greek there are two readings almost equally attested: τὸ ἡμέτερον (Hort and Weiss) and τὸ ὑμέτερον (Tischendorf, Von Soden, Vogels). We prefer the latter which is that of the Vulgate, but basically both give the same meaning: "If you are faithless in the management of *temporal* goods, who will entrust to you *spiritual* goods?" Temporal goods are called "another's" because they are external to our own selves; spiritual goods are the true goods, *our own goods*. In speaking to his disciples about these true goods, Jesus can say indifferently *our* goods or *your* goods.

[8] Luke 16:14. "The Pharisees sneered." The Greek is more picturesque: ἐξεμυκτήριζον, "they wrinkled their noses" (μυκτήρ, *nostril*), or pushed up their noses with the finger as a sign of mockery. Jesus, the poor man, exhorting to poverty seemed grotesque; he reminded them of the old fable of the fox with his tail cut off. Their teaching is very different. "There is no sorrow in the world like poverty. Our Doctors have said: Put all evils on one scale of a balance and on the other side poverty (they will balance)." Cf. Billerbeck, *Kommentar*, Vol. I, 818–826.

they regarded them as a blessing of heaven and a sure gauge of God's friendship. Poverty appeared to them more odious than the ten plagues of Egypt, and the eulogy of it spoken by Jesus seemed to them comical in the extreme. They draw upon themselves this severe and well-merited lesson: "You make a parade of your justice before men, but God knows your hearts. He that exalts himself before men is an abomination before God." To support his teaching about the proper use of worldly goods he goes on to propose to them a parable which unfolds partly on earth and partly in the life to come.

2. The Wicked Rich Man and Lazarus

(LUKE 16:19–31)

There was once a rich man who was used to tasting all the refinements of luxury and all the enjoyments of life. His tunic was of fine Egyptian linen and had that softness of texture and dazzling whiteness for which the ancients paid its weight in gold. His mantle was made of the Tyrian purple which was the raiment of kings and emperors. Every day a Sardinapalian banquet attracted reveling guests around his table, where the most exquisite dishes were served, and the dances of courtesans and the play of jesters enlivened the feast.

Meantime, in front of the great gate of his palace there lay a beggar in rags: his name was Lazarus. He was used to hearing these wild orgies from afar, and he would have longed to gather the crumbs which fell from the sumptuous board to fill himself with them. But no one ever paid any attention to him; no one even took the trouble to chase away the house dogs which kept coming and licking the blood from the sores with which his body was covered.

Now it came to pass that one day the poor man died and was carried by the angels to Abraham's bosom. The rich man also died, and his body was buried, doubtless with the pomp and magnificence of which his whole life had been a spectacle. But what became of his soul?[9]

[9] Luke 16:19–22. (*a*) The *nemo illi dabat* is not in the Greek. It comes from Luke 15:16. If no one had ever given him anything, he would not always have

In the earthly destiny of these two men there is a revolting inequality and disorder which cries for vengeance. Such a thing could not endure. Of a sudden comes a reversal. The poor man passes from extreme misery to supreme happiness. The rich man sees his life of ostentation and debauchery come to an end in the tomb, to begin beyond this earth a life of endless retribution. This sudden change was not a mere reversal of social situation; it shows forth the moral law of retribution. The rich man is not represented to us as miserly and cruel. He does not mistreat the poor Lazarus; he does not drive him away. He passes him by without bothering about him, without looking at him. He is the type of the self-centered pleasure seeker. Instead of thinking of the misery which his immense riches could relieve, he thinks of nothing except varying his amusements to escape the cloying monotony of pleasure. He is rightly characterized as the *wicked* rich man, because he makes an evil use of his fortune. Lazarus, on the other hand, is the type of the resigned and patient poor man. If the parable fails to bring his virtues into relief, it is because that was not to the point. Forgotten, neglected, and despised by all, he has not a word of complaint or blame. His silence speaks for him eloquently enough. And the fact that he is carried by the angels to Abraham's bosom shows well enough that he has made good use of his poverty, as the other had made bad use of his riches. Both find themselves together again in the abode of the dead, but how changed now are their roles!

The ancient Hebrews had very indefinite notions about the conditions of the future life, and their imaginations, working on such data, in the course of time gave rein to fancies which it is difficult to reduce to any system. The Sheol of the Jews — like the Hades which is its Greek translation — was the abode of the dead, the

---

come back again, but they had never given him enough to appease his hunger.

b) Many think that the sympathy of the dogs licking Lazarus' sores is contrasted with the hardness and insensibility of men, but, on the contrary, this is the ultimate feature of his helplessness: *even* the dogs (ἀλλὰ καὶ κύνες) set themselves to torment him.

c) The Vulgate has *sepultus est in inferno. Elevans autem oculos.* The Greek is divided differently: καὶ ἐτάφη. Καὶ ἐν τῷ ᾅδῃ, "and he was buried. And in Hades (or Sheol) raising his eyes." The detail of his burial is not otiose. If he had not been buried, his good fortune on earth would not, according to Jewish notions, have been complete. The reversal of fortune must not take place except in the next life.

kingdom of the shades, but with this difference, that the Greek Hades was properly the king of this subterranean region, while the Sheol of the Hebrews designated the place itself, and was not personified except by poetic license. These vague ideas became more precise with the progress of Revelation. Belief in the resurrection made of Sheol a temporary abode, and the dogma of reward and punishment made it necessary to establish a barrier between the good and the bad, represented sometimes as a wall, sometimes as a ditch. Sinners were plunged into Gehenna, and the just lived in a place called Eden or Paradise and sometimes, though rarely, Abraham's bosom. The origin of this last expression is obscure. It probably came from the image under which the future life of the just was commonly represented. "The present world," says Rabbi Jacob, "is the vestibule of the world to come. Prepare thyself in the vestibule to enter one day into the banquet-hall." The just man, after death, was introduced into this banquet at the right of his father Abraham, that is to say, in his bosom. This is the place of honor which the new guest, the poor man Lazarus, now occupies. The wicked rich man sees him from afar. Immediately he raises his voice to make himself heard from a distance, and there follows this dialogue with Abraham:

The Wicked Rich Man — "Father Abraham, have pity on me and send Lazarus to dip the tip of his finger in water to cool my tongue, for I suffer cruelly in this furnace."

Abraham — "My son, remember that during life thou didst receive thy share of good things, and Lazarus his share of evil. Now he is comforted here, whereas thou sufferest. And withal, between you and us there is an abyss which prevents us, should anyone wish it, from passing hence to you, and thence to us."

The Rich Man — "I pray thee, then, Father Abraham, to send Lazarus to my father's house, where I have five brothers, to tell them how it is, for fear that they also may come to this place of torment."

Abraham — "They have Moses and the prophets: let them hear them!"

The Rich Man — "No, Father Abraham, if someone from the dead should go to them, they would do penance."

Abraham — "If they hear not Moses and the prophets, neither will they believe one risen from the dead."

Some among the older authors believed that this was a historical narrative; and Tertullian makes use of it to prove that the soul is corporeal, since reference is made to the bosom of Abraham, the finger of Lazarus, and the tongue of the reprobate. Today it is generally admitted that it is simply a parable which should be interpreted according to the rules of parabolic language. Still, many, while agreeing that it is a fictional narrative, assign much too large a share to allegory, and derive from it conclusions that pass beyond the sacred text.

It cannot be repeated too often that in a parable a distinction must always be carefully drawn between the dogmatic or moral lesson, which is the kernel, and the material details, which are only the shell. How could the dialogue between Abraham and the wicked rich man be introduced without bringing them together in the same place, whether this be conformable to reality or not? In order to describe to another or to represent to ourselves the state of souls separated from the body and the relationships between them, do we not have to materialize, to introduce symbols, to make use of metaphors? Thus it is that the wicked rich man is represented as raising his eyes from the bottom of the abyss, as seeing Lazarus in Abraham's bosom, as raising his voice to be heard at a distance, as wishing his tongue to be cooled by a drop of water from the finger of Lazarus, a wish which cannot be realized because a wide and deep gulf separates him from the other side. To speak without figures: the sentence which has struck him is irrevocable; he cannot expect any assuagement of suffering; even the saints can do nothing for him. Such is the first truth which the parable teaches us.

The wicked rich man wishes that Lazarus may return to the world to inform his brothers of his unhappy fate to save them from it. It must not be concluded that the damned are aware of what is going on in the world, or that they interest themselves in the happiness of others, or that they experience feelings of sympathy and compassion. This setting was necessary to draw out Abraham's answer, which is the second moral of the parable. The light of Revelation is enough to make the Jews inexcusable. If they contemn the Scriptures or disregard them, one risen from the dead would not convert them. The history of the Gospel is a striking demonstration of this. To believe, the Pharisees call for a miracle. Jesus offers them the miracle of the resurrection of Lazarus of Bethany, and soon his own Resurrection, and they persist in their obstinate unbelief.

CHAPTER X

The Resurrection of Lazarus

1. The Family of Bethany
(JOHN 11:1–37)

FIFTEEN stadia or about a mile and three quarters from Jerusalem, on the road to Jericho, there was a village called Bethany, pleasantly situated on the eastern slope of the Mount of Olives. The nearness of the wilderness offered a contrast which heightened its charm. Today there is only a heap of poor ruins which the Moslems who live there call El Azariyeh, in memory of Lazarus. The present-day village, attracted to the celebrated tomb which was a goal of pilgrimages from the fourth century, has retreated little by little toward the east. Ancient Bethany was situated two or three hundred paces away, on the incline of a hill which is now crowned by the Convent of the Passionists. In this place have been found tombs dating back to the Chanaanite period, and coins from the two centuries before and after the birth of Christ.[1]

During his several sojourns in Jerusalem, the Saviour often went to pass the night at Bethany, far from the noise and tumult, in the home of the hospitable family whose three members, Martha and Mary and Lazarus, are so well known to us. Their parents, who do not appear at all in the Gospel story, must have been

[1] About the site of the ancient Bethany, between the Passionist Convent and the Tower of Melisenda, cf. Vincent in *R.B.*, 1914, pp. 438–441. In the fourth century a church was erected over the tomb of Lazarus. St. Jerome speaks of it, and also the pilgrim Etheria. It was called *Lazarium,* from which came the name of the modern village El Azariyeh. Lazarus is a shortened form of Eleazar, a name very common among the Jews.

dead, and Martha the elder of the two sisters held the position of mistress of the household. As for Lazarus, either because of his youth, or because of an early illness, he yielded all authority and initiative to his sisters.

Some time after the Feast of Dedication, Lazarus' condition became alarming, and his sisters had the news of it brought to Jesus, who had gone back to Perea and was staying at the other Bethany, where John had started his work of baptizing. The message was brief: "Lord, he whom thou lovest is sick." Nothing could be imagined more delicate and more discreet than this prayer; for it is a prayer, though its object is insinuated rather than openly expressed. "He whom thou lovest is sick." After saying that, would it be proper to add: "Come quickly and cure him," as some strangers like the Centurion and the dignitary of Capharnaum had done? Is not his affection for Lazarus the most pressing of reasons and the most effective of arguments?[2]

In the presence of the messenger, who certainly brought his words back to Bethany, Jesus is content to reply: "This sickness is not to death but for the glory of God, and the glorification of his Son."[3] Indeed the sickness of Lazarus did not tend to death as its final term, since death is so soon to be forced to release its prey; it tended to glorify God by offering to his Son the occasion to work a marvelous miracle. But the intentionally obscure answer lent itself to another interpretation, and the disciples gathered that Lazarus was not to die. They were confirmed in this impression upon seeing their Master remain two days in the same place, either to carry on without interruption a work already begun, or to put the faith of Martha and Mary to the test. What

---

[2] St. Augustine says of this text: "Sufficit ut noveris; non enim amas et deseris."

[3] John 11:4: "This sickness is not *for* death (πρός), but in view of (ὑπέρ) the glory of God, in order that (ἵνα) the Son may be glorified." We think that all three particles express purpose. The purpose (or one of the purposes) of God in permitting this sickness is not to have Lazarus die, but to make his own glory shine forth in glorifying his Son. By itself, *non est ad mortem* (οὐκ ἔστιν πρὸς θάνατον) could very well mean, "will not end in death," but the context seems to require the sense of purpose (in God's view, the sickness is not allowed for that reason). The preposition πρός with the accusative admits of this meaning: πρὸς ἡδονήν (Thucyd., II, 65) "to be agreeable"; μήτε πρὸς ἔχθραν μήτε πρὸς χάριν (Demosth.) "neither for hate nor favor."

must have been the disappointment and desolation of the two sisters when the messenger came back alone, with an answer so full of hope, and so cruelly belied by the fact! For Lazarus was dead when the messenger returned to Bethany.

After two days of waiting the Master announced that they would go back to Judea. Had he, then, forgotten that he had just quit the Holy City to escape the ambushes of the Pharisees who were plotting his death? The disciples could not keep from remonstrating with him. "Master, just recently the Jews were again seeking to stone thee; and art thou now going to thrust thyself again into their hands?" Jesus reassures them:

"Has not the day twelve hours? If anyone walks in the daytime he runs into no obstacle, because the light of the world illuminates him; but if he walks by night, he stumbles, because he lacks the light."

This language, though figurative, is not obscure. The Incarnate Word is sent into the world as a laborer who must complete his task, as a traveler who must pass through the stages of his journey before nightfall. As long as his work is unfinished, as long as the day endures, he has nothing to fear. Providence watches over him. It will be otherwise when the end, symbolized by the night, comes. But that hour has not yet struck. He can therefore continue his earthly pilgrimage without fear.

Their imaginations haunted by real or fancied perils, the disciples scarcely heard him and did not understand. They understood still less when he said: "Our friend Lazarus is asleep, but I go to wake him."[4] — "Lord," they said, "if he sleeps he is safe." A refreshing sleep was considered by ancient medical science as one of the six symptoms presaging the end of a crisis and the beginning of convalescence. Even today, in certain sections of Palestine, there is a current proverb: "He that sleeps is cured." Since Lazarus was sleeping, he was out of danger; consequently, to what purpose a journey to Bethany? As the Apostles, obsessed with fear, persist in misunderstanding him, Jesus speaks to them

[4] John 11:12. "Sleep" for "die" is a euphemism common to all languages, especially when speaking of dear ones. It has been calculated that the metaphor is employed thirteen times in the New Testament, while the word in its proper sense occurs only three times. The Apostles therefore could and should have understood it.

without figures: "Lazarus is dead, and I am glad for your sakes that I was not there, so that you may believe." Indeed, the Apostles believed in him after the miracle of Cana;[5] they had believed with a livelier and more illumined faith after the promise of the Eucharist; but we know from St. John that faith is susceptible of perpetual ascents. The resurrection of Lazarus will be a new steppingstone which will lift their faith to a higher stage.

If Jesus had been present in Bethany before the death of Lazarus, he would probably not have resisted the tears of the two sisters, and one of those cures to which they had become habituated would have made but little impression on them. But they had not yet become casually indifferent to raisings from the dead. When Jesus proposed to them to go to Bethany to waken Lazarus from the sleep of death, they did not dare draw back. Thomas cried out in the name of all: "Let us also go and die with him!" Beyond all doubt, the sentiment was generous and sincere. Still the abrupt and trembling proposal of Thomas seems to be the effort of a timid man encouraging others to give himself heart, rather than the expression of a calm and resolute bravery.

When Jesus finally came to Bethany, Lazarus had been buried for several days. Among the Jews burial generally took place the same day as death. According to a belief of the Rabbis which goes back, perhaps, to Gospel times, the soul of the dead hovered for three days about the tomb, as if it hoped to regain possession of its former dwelling place; but on the fourth day, seeing the work of decomposition going forward, it lost all hope and retired, never to return. Meanwhile the visits of condolence occasioned by the grief of the bereaved lasted all week. Relatives and friends succeeded one another in the house of death without intermission, and the coming of new arrivals was always marked by new outbursts of tears and sobs. The visitors crouched upon the ground, remaining silent for a longer or shorter period according to the degree of their relationship or friendship.[6] Since the family of Lazarus was very well known in the environs of Jerusalem and

---

[5] John 2:11, "his disciples *believed* in him"; John 6:69, "We have *believed,* and we know that thou art the Holy One of God"; John 11:15, "that you may *believe.*"

[6] About these customs, according to the Talmud, cf. Lightfoot, Vol. II, pp. 648–649. The great mourning lasted for thirty days, but visits ceased at the end of seven days; the mourning was strictest during the first three days.

in the city itself, less than two miles distant, there was a considerable gathering of people present when the approach of Jesus was announced.

Leaving her sister in the house to receive condolences, Martha immediately hurried to meet the divine Master, and said to him: "Lord, if thou hadst been here my brother would not have died." But what she adds seems to show that she keeps even now a ray of hope. "I know well that whatever thou shalt ask of God he will grant thee." Still, she does not dare to ask for the return to life of a corpse already in the process of decay. It was an unexampled prodigy; and had not Jesus by his voluntary delay shown clearly enough his refusal to work a miracle on this occasion? Some such attitude of mind caused her to place a wrong construction on the Master's formal assurance:

"Thy brother shall rise again."

"Yes, I know that he shall rise again on the last day at the time of the resurrection (the general resurrection of the just)."

"I am the resurrection and the life. He that believes in me, even if he be dead, shall live; and he that lives and believes in me shall never die. Dost thou believe this?"

"Yes, Lord, I believe that thou art the Christ, the Son of God, he who comes into this world."

Magnificent confession of faith, worthy of the Apostle Peter! Martha gives to Jesus his two Messianic names — the Christ, and he who comes — and if she is not yet initiated into the mystery of the eternal generation of the Word, she recognizes at least that his unique and incommunicable sonship is very different from ours. Still, it may be doubted that she had penetrated the profound significance of the words, "I am the resurrection and the life." I am the source of supernatural life, the agent of the resurrection; this twofold power belongs to me by right of birth and by right of conquest, so that I have no need of asking it of anyone whatsoever. He who believes in me possesses in his soul a life which death is unable to take away, and he has in his body the seed of glorious immortality.

Martha, returning to the house, found Mary still sitting in the midst of a group of visitors. In a low voice, so as not to be overheard, she said to her: "The Master is here, and is calling for thee." Without waiting to know whether her sister was carrying out a commission or speaking of her own accord, Mary immediately rises and goes to meet the Saviour. Surprised at her abrupt departure and not knowing its cause, but thinking that without doubt she is going to mourn at the tomb, the visitors also rise and follow her to the place where Jesus is staying, for he has not yet entered the village. Mary falling at his feet repeats word for word what her sister had said. "Lord, if thou hadst been here my brother would not have died." How many times, when Lazarus was near death, had they said over and over again those words of regret and hope: "Ah, if the Master were only here!" Recalling those days of anguish and disappointment, Mary broke out into sobs, and all the Jews present, infected by her sorrow, set to weeping.

At this sight, "Jesus groaned in spirit and troubled himself." He asked: "Where have you laid him?" He knew: but in the ordinary conduct of life he allowed himself to be guided, as others are, by his experimental knowledge. "Lord," someone said to him, "come and see." Not one there present had any thought of a resurrection. And then Jesus, again groaning, approached the sepulcher; and for the first time he was seen to shed tears. The Jews, surprised at this, said to one another: "See how he loved him!" But others among them, inclined to be critical, still complained: "He who opened the eyes of the man born blind, could he not have prevented this man from dying?"

Jesus weeps, Jesus groans, Jesus is troubled; in a God-Man what a mystery is this! We yield, despite ourselves, to instinctive movements of fear, of pity, of indignation, of anger. But he does not yield to them, except in the measure he judges to be appropriate. "He troubles himself," else nothing could trouble him. He allows himself to be touched by compassion in the presence of another's sorrow. Does not St. Paul recommend as an act of Christian charity to weep with those who weep, and to rejoice with those who are joyful? Why should not the divine Master give the example to his disciples?

This twice repeated groaning of our Lord has much intrigued commentators, both ancient and modern. As groaning generally implies a movement of displeasure or anger, many have supposed that Jesus was showing his indignation against death, the cause of so many tears, or against sin, through which death entered into the world, or against Satan, first author of sin and death. One of them, subtler than the others, has fancied that the groaning of Jesus was due to the incredulity of the Jews who, to believe, needed the resurrection of Lazarus, and consequently his death. But why search so far afield, when the text of the Gospel is so explicit? "Jesus seeing Mary weeping, and the Jews who accompanied her weeping with her, groaned in spirit and troubled himself and shed tears."[7] The groaning, the troubling, the tears, have all the same cause: the contagious sympathy with sorrow. Who of us, at the sight of a family in tears, of an inconsolable mother, has not felt his heart torn, his whole being agitated, and tears come to his eyes? Compassion is the most universal and the most human of sentiments. Jesus has willed to experience it. He yields himself to it without shame. He takes an active part in the grief of the beloved family. His emotion, real and not feigned, betrays itself outwardly in gestures, perhaps in an exclamation of pity, and also in tears. But this groaning, this troubling, these tears last only a brief time, because, as they come near to the tomb, Jesus resumes his air of serene majesty.

2. Lazarus, Come Forth!

(JOHN 11:38–44)

To follow in detail the scene that is about to unfold before us, some words of explanation are indispensable. Jewish tombs were generally cut out of the rock, the soft limestone of the Palestine soil lending itself marvelously to such use. They belonged to two

[7] Jesus groaned (vv. 33 and 38). The verb ἐμβριμάομαι is well translated in the Vulgate by *fremere* or *infremere,* for in βριμ and *frem* the same Indo-European root is recognized. The primitive meaning is to *sigh* or *rumble,* but the cause may be of various kinds. There is the murmur of anger (ἐμβρίμημα ὀργῆς, Lam. 2:6), of indignation (Mark 14:5: ἐμβριμῶντο αὐτῇ); the disciples grumble at the prodigality of Mary of Bethany; the murmur of impatience (Aesch., Theb, 461, speaking of warhorses snorting to go into battle). But often the meaning is attenuated as in Matt. 9:30 and Mark 1:43, when Jesus forbids (*comminatus est*) the two blind men and a leper cured by him to say anything to anyone. There, the murmuring consists of a prohibition given with a severe manner and in a sharp tone. Here, the groaning of Jesus in the presence of the spectacle of the common sorrow of the sisters and their friends is the organic reaction to the compassion he feels. Nothing more mysterious is to be sought.

principal types. Some were cut out of the vertical face of the rock, sometimes fronted by a vestibule which gave access through a narrow low opening to the tomb itself, which could be entered only by bending over. Such was the sepulcher of Christ; such also the sumptuous sepulchers shown in the environs of Jerusalem under the names of the Tombs of the Kings, the Judges, and the Prophets. In flat terrain or on a gentle slope, the burial vault was at a lower level than the vestibule, and descent was made to it by steps carved into the rock. A slab placed horizontally over this stairway sealed the vault. The tomb of Lazarus, according to indications furnished by St. John, and as far as the examination of the place allows us to judge after changes undergone in the course of centuries, belonged to this latter type. It was a vault on which a rock was placed.[8]

Jesus commanded the people who were standing around to lift this rock. They were setting themselves to the task in obedience to his orders, when Martha felt a start of fright. In what condition would the corpse be found? What sight and smell would be encountered? Even if the aromatics spread on the body at the time of burial could neutralize or lessen the evil smell, they had not arrested the decomposition of the body. In that hot country, death had done its work swiftly. Martha, who knew this only too well, could not keep herself from saying: "Lord, by this time he stinks, for he is now in the fourth day." — "Have I not told thee," answered Jesus, "that if thou believest, thou shalt see the glory of God?" It was the scarcely veiled announcement of the miracle and an invitation to believe in preparation for it.

The slab laid flat over the entrance was soon lifted away. Jesus, raising his eyes to heaven, made this brief prayer, one of the few ejaculatory prayers that the Gospel has preserved for us: "Father, I give thee thanks that thou hast heard me. I know that thou hearest me always, but because of those that stand around me have I said this, that they may believe that thou hast sent me." Then, in a tone of irresistible command, he cried out in a loud voice: "Lazarus, come forth!" Immediately at the narrow entrance of the vault a head covered by a shroud is seen emerging; then a human body bound in bandages like an infant in swaddling

---

[8] Cf. Note V: *Jewish Burial.*

bands stands erect on the steps and rises like a specter to the vestibule, where the stupefied bystanders were crowding around. Jesus says only: "Unbind him and let him go."

The transports of joy of the two sisters, the thanksgivings of Lazarus, astonished at seeing again the light of day, the stupefaction of the crowd, the serenity of Jesus in the midst of all this tumult; what a picture to tempt the brush of an artist! But the Evangelists are not aiming at literary effect, and no one of them tells a story for the sake of telling it. And so St. John stops short at the most moving point of the story.[9]

The story in itself is a marvel of naturalness, of grace, of exquisite feeling. Nowhere else is the twofold physiognomy of Jesus, divine and human, depicted in features so vivid and so harmonious. Without intending to do so, the eyewitness discloses himself in every line by the accumulation of precise details, by the animated and concise delineation of feelings, and by the sustained truth to life of the characters. In short, everything, including those omissions and transpositions of minor details which a stylist would certainly have avoided, carries the sign and seal of a man who is writing his memoirs without studied effort and without affectation, in the order in which they come back to mind.

The resurrection of Lazarus is a serious embarrassment to the Rationalist critics. We generally spare the reader the tiresome exposition of these ephemeral and contradictory systems; but it is well to show, once for all, the sophisms to which the *a priori* denial of miracles and the phobia of the supernatural can lead. But no surprises are to be expected. However little one may be acquainted with the ideas professed by the various authors, one knows in advance what their interpretation of the miracle is going to be.[10]

---

[9] The Synoptics, who all record the raising of the daughter of Jairus, do not mention the raising of Lazarus, because, with the exception of the Passion, they tell scarcely anything of what took place in Jerusalem or its neighborhood.

[10] See Godet, *L'Evangile de saint Jean,* Vol. III, pp. 158–164, on the various Rationalist explanations of his time. Strauss judges very severely the *natural* explanation of Paulus, in his *Vie de Jésus,* Vol. II, pp. 154–165 (trans. Littré). His own *mythical* explanation is scarcely better, though at first glance it appears less childish.

The *natural* explanation of Paulus is the first in date. Lazarus was not dead at all. He had been buried by mistake. It was simply a syncope or torpor, and Jesus suspected this. When the tomb was opened, the outside air revived the supposedly dead man, and Jesus, noting in his countenance some signs of life, did not hesitate to command him to come forth. Everything is conveniently reduced to a lucky coincidence.

After the natural explanation came Strauss's "myths," those spontaneous creations of popular imagination; then Baur's "tendencies," under the urge of which the Evangelists gave body to what they had in their minds, without bothering about objective reality. We pass over these old and outmoded theories to come to one of the more recent representatives of criticism. M. Loisy derives inspiration from his predecessors and strives to surpass them. According to him the resurrection of Lazarus was not an invention, but an intuition of the author of the Fourth Gospel. "The author really saw what he recounts to us; but he did not see it of old and as a companion of Jesus. He sees it in his mind, as a mystical contemplation of the Gospel. . . . There is no reason to be surprised at this, since the author is a great mystic. That is not too much to say; we must in addition say that he was a prophet. The Fourth Gospel may well be nothing else than a vision like the Apocalypse and in the same measure."[11]

Some still hark back to the bizarre expedient once fancied by Renan. If we take his view, Lazarus was already cured when Jesus came to Bethany, but the two sisters, ashamed of having bothered Jesus to no purpose, wished nevertheless to provide him with a miracle. Lazarus allowed himself to be wrapped in bandages and covered by a shroud, and to lie as if dead in the family vault. Jesus, having ordered the tomb to be opened, had no difficulty in raising from the dead one who was so much alive. But how could the Saviour have lent himself to such a comedy? Ah, says Renan: "Jesus was no longer himself. Not by his own

[11] Loisy, *Le Quatrième Evangile,* 1903, p. 659. In the new edition, 1921, p. 335, he seems to revert purely and simply to Baur's explanation: "The material of the narrative is seen to be constructed (with the aid of elements furnished by the Synoptics) to serve as an illustration of the principle formulated by Jesus: 'I am the resurrection and the life.' " When one quotes a theory of Loisy, one never knows whether he still holds it. Many are misled by this, and this is why we seldom quote him.

fault, but by the fault of men, his conscience had lost something of its primitive limpidity. Despairing and pushed to extremes, he was no longer master of his own actions. He was drifting with the stream. As always happens in great divine careers, he submitted to the miracles which public opinion demanded of him, rather than worked them himself."[12] The day came when Renan perceived that he was taking advantage of the simplicity, or say rather, the stupidity of his readers, and he veered to a hybrid system which borrowed its elements from two opposite schools. "Jesus' friends," he now wrote, "were desirous of a great prodigy which would vigorously strike at the incredulousness of Jerusalem. A raising from the dead must have seemed to them best suited to carry conviction." The proposal was made to Jesus, but he confined himself to telling the story of the poor man Lazarus, adding: Now, even if Lazarus should rise from the dead, they would not believe. The miracle came into being. Here again it becomes necessary to quote the text. "Later on, some singular misunderstandings became current with regard to this subject. Hypothesis was changed into fact. There was talk about Lazarus raised from the dead, about the unpardonable obstinacy required to resist such a testimony. When one knows of what inexact statements and of what cock-and-bull stories the gossip of Oriental towns is made up, one does not regard it as impossible that even a rumor of this kind should have spread in Jerusalem during Jesus' lifetime, and should have had for him such dismal consequences."[13]

Nowadays the critics are glad to retreat behind a barrier of silence; the miracle of Bethany is treated as though it had never happened. This is the cleverest tactic, if not the most honest. It dispenses with the need of furnishing an explanation of a fact which is unexplainable for anyone who will not admit the reality of miracles.

---

[12] Renan, *Vie de Jésus,* 1863, pp. 359–360.

[13] *Ibid.,* 13 ed., 1867, pp. 372–374. Still he does not completely reject his first hypothesis, and the informed reader can rediscover it by reading between the lines: "One is occasionally tempted to suppose that the family of Bethany committed some imprudence or fell into some excess of zeal." And he still holds that Jesus had lost "the primitive limpidity of his conscience." It is, in brief, a return to the mythical theory of Strauss, to which is added complicity on the part of the Saviour, who allows things to go on without remonstrance.

3. Plot of the Jews and Retirement to Ephrem

(JOHN 11:45–57)

In view of such a marvelous prodigy, the spectators could not but recognize the supernatural power of the Wonder-Worker, and, in answer to the request that Jesus had made of his heavenly Father, the majority believed in his divine mission. Still, there were some among them, perhaps those who had not been eyewitnesses of the miracle, who made haste to inform the Pharisees. The fact that they addressed themselves to the mortal enemies of Jesus is enough to prove their hostile intent. The Pharisees went into conference with the chief priests, without whom they could do nothing. This was not a regular assembly of the Sanhedrin, but a simple private meeting.

The more excited in the group were saying: "This man works too many miracles. If we let him alone, everyone will believe in him; then the Romans will come and ruin our (holy) place and our whole nation." They did not deny the reality of the miraculous facts; on the contrary, it was there precisely that they saw the danger. The popularity of this Wonder-Worker is growing beyond measure; it is urgent that he be checked. Otherwise, sooner or later, perhaps tomorrow, he will put himself at the head of an insurrectionist movement, and the Romans will stifle it in blood. That will be the end of the Jewish people and the Holy City and the Temple of the true God.

These prophets of evil received a sympathetic hearing, but no one knew what plan to adopt, until Caiphas, the High Priest then in office, took up the question. In a tone penetrated by the arrogant insolence of the man, he said: "You know nothing at all. You do not reflect that it is to our interest that one man should die for the whole people, that the nation may not perish." He was speaking in covert terms, but everyone there understood very well what he meant. He wished to say that it was necessary to sacrifice Jesus to the good of the country. What is the life of one man, when there is question of the safety of a whole people?

God used him without his suspecting it, in order to teach us a loftier truth. "He did not say this of himself," says St. John, "but, being pontiff of that year, he prophesied that Jesus was to die for his people, and not only for his people, but for all the children of God" scattered throughout the world. St. John was not unaware — no Jew could be unaware — that the office of High Priest was not an annual one, though at that time it was at the mercy of the Roman Procurator. But he was prompted to remark that Caiphas was pontiff that memorable year, and that in this capacity he prophesied without knowing it and without wishing it. God, who can attach to words and things a significance that they would not have of themselves, places in the mouth of the High Priest, the authorized representative of the Jewish nation, words which could be understood of the redeeming death of Christ.

The advice of Caiphas received general assent, and from that day all the conspirators resolved to put Jesus to death as soon as a favorable occasion should present itself.

The Saviour was unwilling to make use of his divine power to defeat their schemes. In order to teach us how to act in like circumstances, he withdrew from Bethany, which was too near Jerusalem, and retired to Ephrem or Ephraim, a village situated fifteen or sixteen miles to the north, on the borders of the wilderness. Thence, in less than two hours he could pass over into the territory of Samaria, or go down by an easy road to the fords of the Jordan. Ephrem, under the modern name of Taiyibeh, is today a very flourishing Christian town, and the hill which it tops has one of the most beautiful prospects of northern Palestine.[14] Such was the place of refuge where the Saviour remained in the company of his Apostles, from the raising of Lazarus up to the approach of the Last Passover.

[14] Ophra, Ephron, Ephraim, Ephrata, Ephrem, etc., are variants of the same name. In the division of Palestine this town was assigned to the tribe of Benjamin (Josue 18:23). The present town, situated on a hill 2700 feet high, 4 or 5 miles north of Bethel, numbers 1000 inhabitants. History and description in Guérin, *Judée,* Vol. III, pp. 45–51.

CHAPTER XI

Last Apostolic Journey

1. The Ten Lepers

(LUKE 17:11–19)

"THEREAFTER Jesus no longer went about in broad daylight among the Jews, but departed into the region near the desert to a town called Ephrem, and he abode there with his disciples. Now, the Passover of the Jews was approaching, and many were going up to Jerusalem before the feast to purify themselves."[1]

The Saviour's private sojourn with his disciples in the peaceful village of Ephrem lasted only a short time, scarcely three or four weeks. It was only a day's journey from Ephrem to Jerusalem, but he did not go there directly, because we find him at Jericho on the eve of Holy Week. To explain this detour, some think that he intended to join the caravan of Galilean pilgrims coming that year by the valley of the Jordan. Others, on the contrary, think that he wanted to avoid a meeting with his fellow countrymen who were following the ordinary route through Samaria; and this because he feared that by joining them he might make a showy entry into Jerusalem.

A text of St. Luke mentions his presence in the north of Palestine a short time before the Passion. "Jesus going to Jeru-

---

[1] John 11:54–55. This text permits the conclusion that he *sojourned* some time at Ephrem (ἔμεινε); that he soon left this village because of the *proximity* of the Passover; but not that he went *directly* to Jerusalem. In fact, he is at Bethany six days before the Passover (12:1) and at Jericho a little before that, according to the Synoptics (Mark 10:46–11:1 and parallels).

salem was passing between Samaria and Galilee";[2] or perhaps, since the meaning is not altogether certain, "across Samaria and Galilee." In the perspective of the Evangelist this was apparently the last pilgrimage to the Holy City. Did the Saviour wish to extend a last appeal to his ungrateful country? This is hardly probable, after the solemn and apparently final farewell he had addressed to it on leaving for his new field of apostolic labor. May we not conjecture that St. Luke is mentioning in retrospect this journey between Samaria and Galilee, as the setting of the cure of the ten lepers, among whom was found a Samaritan?

The ten lepers were traveling together, doubtless to lend one another assistance. These unfortunates, banished from the society of men, readily forgot national antipathies and religious rivalries in order to pool their misery. So it is that in our own day Jews and Christians and Moslems mingle freely in the lazarets of Damascus and Jerusalem. Jesus was approaching a village which the Gospel does not name; but a tradition, not very ancient and not very authentic, identifies it with Jenin (the ancient En Gannim),[3] a pleasant little town seated on a hill in the midst of orchards and watercourses. What can be said in its favor is that it verifies an essential topographical detail that is mentioned, for En Gannim, nestling in the southern depression of the Plain of Esdrelon, was situated just on the frontier of Samaria and Galilee, and could have belonged by turns to one province or the other.

---

[2] Luke 17:11: Ἐν τῷ πορεύεσθαι εἰς Ἱερουσαλήμ, καὶ αὐτὸς διήρχετο διὰ μέσον Σαμαρείας καὶ Γαλιλαίας. We read with the critical editions διὰ μέσον, instead of διὰ μέσου of the Textus Receptus, but the meaning is certainly the same.

Were is not for the topographical difficulty, it could be translated "across Samaria and Galilee" (Wieseler, Olshausen, and others so understand it); but to go to Jerusalem traversing Samaria and Galilee is a bizarre itinerary, as though a traveler should go from Turin to Rome passing through Lyons and Paris. It should therefore be translated "between Samaria and Galilee" (note the absence of an article before the two nouns), having Samaria at the right and Galilee at the left and consequently traveling toward the Jordan. There are instances of this meaning, not for διὰ μέσον which is poetic, but for its equivalent διὰ μέσου.

[3] Jenin is a large Moslem town of about 3000 souls. It certainly corresponds to En Gannim (Spring of Gardens) which was first assigned to the tribe of Issachar and then became a Levitical village. Since it is about equally distant (about 19 miles) from Nazareth and Sichem (near Nablus), Jesus must have stopped there quite often to pass the night. The lepers knew him by sight or from reputation; they call him by name. In this locality the shapeless ruins of an ancient Christian church are still to be seen.

Just at the time when Jesus was about to enter the town, the ten lepers ran up to him and, standing at the respectful distance prescribed by law and custom, cried out with all their might: "Jesus, Master, have mercy on us!"[4] It is known that lepers' voices become hollow and hoarse, and that they must make a real effort to be heard. The condition of these unfortunate men and the humility of their plea had touched the heart of the divine Master. "Go," he said to them, "show yourselves to the priests," as the law enjoins on anyone who claims to be cured of leprosy. For the priests had to examine the case and give the final decision whether the sick man could or could not resume association with others.

The lepers hastened to obey, and their obedience, a sure token of their faith, was immediately rewarded. Scarcely had they started when they felt themselves cured. The signs of a cure were too palpable to leave any room for doubt. Seeing this the Samaritan retraced his steps, and thanking God in the clear and distinct voice which he had just recovered, prostrated himself at Jesus' feet. He rightly thought that, before carrying out the command the execution of which would require several days, it was proper to give thanks to his benefactor, whom he might not have occasion to meet again. His gesture met with the approval of our Lord, and he said to those present: "Were not all ten cured? And where are the other nine? Has none other, then, returned, save this stranger, to give glory to God?" In saying these words, he may have been thinking of his own faithless country and the three accursed towns that he had showered with benefits. He then dismissed the Samaritan, still prostrate before him, with this comforting assurance: "Rise and go; thy faith has saved thee."

Selfishness is so natural to man that it makes him quickly forget a benefit and a benefactor. Hence it is that gratitude, triumphing over selfishness, is so pleasing to God.[5] Of ten lepers cured by

---

[4] They cry *from afar* (πόρρωθεν). The distance is not indicated in the Pentateuch (Lev. 13:46; Num. 5:2). The Rabbis fixed a minimum of four cubits (about six feet), and when the wind was coming from the direction of the leper, one hundred cubits (about fifty yards), or even more. The principal Rabbinical texts concerning leprosy and lepers can be found in Billerbeck, *Kommentar,* Vol. IV, 745–763.

[5] St. Bernard (*In Cantic.,* LI (ML, CLXXXIII, 1027): "Ingratitude is a

Christ only one feels the need of giving thanks; and he is a Samaritan. Did the others think that their being Jews gave them a kind of right to the miracle? Or did they think that the most urgent need was to present themselves before the priests, to accomplish the formalities and offer the sacrifices prescribed by law? At least, by putting off the expression of their gratitude to a future so full of chance, they were lacking in delicacy and called forth the Saviour's sorrowful exclamation. Still, since they had yielded a ready faith to his words, we may believe that with the health of the body they received also the cure of their souls, and that they did not entirely forfeit its fruit.

We have neither the means nor the right to pass judgment on the gravity of their fault. The Evangelist is silent on this point. He centers all his attention upon the action of the grateful Samaritan, who had deserved to hear the words spoken before this to the woman with the issue of blood and to the penitent sinner, words which will soon be heard by the blind man of Jericho: "Go, thy faith has saved thee." This privileged man is a Samaritan, a heretic, an excommunicate from Judaism. In anticipation of the call of the Gentiles, the barrier separating the chosen people from foreign nations is being lowered; it is beginning to fall.

2. The Two Comings of Christ

(LUKE 17:20–37)

In St. Luke an instruction about the end of the world follows the episode of the ten lepers; no chronological relationship, however, can be established between the two. A group of Pharisees was proposing to Jesus this burning question: "At what period shall the reign (or the kingdom) of God arrive?" Their previous attitude does not for a moment allow us to suppose that they had any intention of receiving instruction. Were they thinking of the reign of a national hero raised up by God to restore the throne of David and to break the foreigner's yoke? One would think rather that they were asking in ironical tone at what date the

searing wind which dries up the springs of pity, the dew of mercy, the streams of grace."

kingdom of God would finally appear, that kingdom of which he was ceaselessly talking, and which he said was close at hand.

"The kingdom of God does not come," answered the Saviour, "as a phenomenon subject to observation. There shall be no occasion for saying: 'It is here' or 'It is there.' The kingdom of God is in the midst of you."[6]

The kingdom of God is not observable like a meteor, whose apparition and whose phases can be described. It is a spiritual phenomenon which the eyes of the body do not perceive. To perceive it, reasoning clarified by the interior sense of faith is required. One cannot trace its progress or follow its evolution. It germinates and grows insensibly and without noise, like a seed which one casts into the ground. It is the hidden leaven, which will cause the whole batter to rise; it is the grain of mustard seed, which will become a tree. You do not see it, though it exists and acts. It is in the midst of you, and, if you will, it is in you.

Whether they were satisfied or not, the Pharisees no longer insisted. Then Jesus turns to his disciples, and his discourse, with the change of audience, changes also its theme. He has been speaking to the Pharisees of the kingdom founded here below by the Messias at his first coming; in the presence of his disciples he proceeds to lift a corner of the veil that hides the second coming of the Son of Man, to judge the living and the dead.

"A time shall come when you shall long to see one of the days of the Son of Man, and you shall not see it. They shall say: 'He is here' or 'He is there.' Go you not forth, do not stir. As the

---

[6] Luke 17:20–21. *Regnum Dei non venit cum observatione* (μετὰ παρατηρήσεως). Παρατήρησις, a rare word, comes from a much-used verb, παρατηρεῖν, which means "to observe attentively" the stars or auspices or the symptoms of a sickness. The coming of the kingdom of God is not subject to that kind of observation, because its beginnings are humble and its progress hidden. It is not a phenomenon appearing all of a sudden, like an eclipse or a comet, or suddenly flaring up, like a political revolution.

Regnum Dei intra vos est (ἐντὸς ὑμῶν). According to grammar, one could translate "in the midst of you," "among you," or "in you," "inside of you." But the latter meaning, acceptable in itself, does not at all fit, considering the context. Jesus is answering the *Pharisees* who have interrupted him, and the Evangelist expressly remarks that, after having answered the Pharisees, he turns to his disciples. Would he say to the Pharisees that the kingdom of heaven is in them, that they possess it? Since the kingdom of God is in their midst, it is within their reach, it is *for them* in some way, but this is a *derived* meaning.

lightning shines and flashes in the twinkling of an eye from one point of the heavens to another, so shall appear the Son of Man on the day of his coming. But first he must suffer many things and be rejected by this generation.

"As in the days of Noe, so shall it be in the days of the Son of Man. They were eating, they were drinking, they were marrying, they were giving in marriage, up to the day when Noe went into the Ark; then came the deluge and engulfed them all. So also in the days of Lot. They were eating, they were drinking, they were buying, they were selling, they were building, they were planting. But when Lot went forth from Sodom, a rain of fire and brimstone beat down upon them and caused them all to perish. A like thing shall happen in the days of the Son of Man.

"Then he that is on the housetop, let him not go down into his house to take anything away; and he that is in the field, let him not turn back. Remember Lot's wife. He that shall seek to save his life shall lose it; and he that is willing to lose it shall save it. I say to you, in that night, of two that shall be in the same bed, one shall be taken and the other shall be left; of two women busy grinding at the same millstone, one shall be taken and the other shall be left; and of two men working in the fields, one shall be taken and the other shall be left.

"The disciples asked: 'Where shall this be, Lord?' And he answered: 'Wherever the body is, the vultures shall be gathered around it.' "[7]

The second coming of Christ is distinguished from the first by three characteristics: its suddenness, the irresistible surprise, and the instantaneous gathering of all men into the same place. The

---

[7] Luke 17:22–37. Almost the entire passage is read word for word in the Eschatological Discourse in St. Matthew, but sometimes in a different context and with a different application:

a) The Parousia, sudden as lightning (Luke 17:23–24; Matt. 24:26–27);

b) It will surprise men, like the Deluge (Luke 17:26–30; Matt. 24:37–39);

c) One will be taken, another left (Luke 17:34–36; Matt. 24:40–41);

d) General assembly, as of vultures around a corpse (Luke 17:37; Matt. 24:28).

It is interesting to compare the little collection of texts in Luke 17:31–33 with Matt. 24:16–18 and Matt. 10:39, to see how the Evangelists apply the same words of our Lord to different circumstances. We should note, however, that it is made up of proverbial expressions susceptible of various applications: "He that is on the housetop, let him not go down into the house" for such and such a reason; "He that seeks to save his life (or his soul) shall lose it" in such and such a way.

apparition of the glorious Christ will have the splendor and the speed of lightning which in a moment rends the sky in two and sets it ablaze. Those who would say, "He is here," or "He is there," do not deserve to be listened to, because at his coming he will manifest himself at once to all eyes.[8]

There will be in the history of the Church periods of great distress when the despairing faithful in their bewilderment shall call Christ to their aid. They shall long to "see one day of the Son of Man, and they shall not see it." They will not wish to see Jesus again in the humility of his mortal life, were it only for a single day — such a wish would be as strange as it is incapable of realization — they will sigh for his glorious return. The day of the Parousia is unique; it is *par excellence* the day of the Lord; but according to his promise, he preludes it by coming to the aid of his Church in hours of tribulation and trial. It is an intervention of this kind that the faithful will call for in their plea, when they see themselves destitute of all human succor; but they will not always obtain it as soon as they would wish.[9]

The Parousia will be a surprise for all men, as the deluge was for the contemporaries of Noe, and the rain of fire and brimstone for Lot's contemporaries. The sudden apparition of Christ will draw them out of their torpor and carelessness, but it will be too late. All their efforts to save their lives and their goods will

---

[8] Luke 17:23: "He is here. He is there." The same expressions have been seen above, but the application varies greatly accordingly as the first or the second coming is meant. When the *Messianic Kingdom* appears, there will be no occasion to say (οὐκ ἐροῦσιν) "He is here, he is there," because a precise spot cannot be marked; a kingdom is not an indivisible point. Shortly before the apparition of Christ in glory, they will, perhaps, say: "He is here, he is there," but it will certainly be a mistake, for the apparition will be instantaneous and simultaneous. Hence, those who spread this false news must not be listened to.

[9] Luke 17:22. Many ancient commentators thought that the desire of the disciples looks to *the past:* they will desire to see Jesus as he was in his mortal life. But almost all the moderns, Catholic and Protestant, believe that the wish looks to the future: they will desire to see the second coming of Christ. But what is the meaning of "one of the days of the Son of Man," since there is but one day of Parousia? It may be supposed that, by analogy with "the days of Noe," "the days of Lot," this expression comprises the whole period immediately preceding the Parousia; but is it likely that the disciples will ever wish to be present, even for one day, in those calamitous times? We retain, therefore, the explanation given in the text: they will wish to see *a day* when Christ shall manifest his presence and his role as savior and judge *as on the day of the Parousia.*

be useless. The eternal destiny of everyone of them will be irretrievably fixed. Of two people living together, working at the same task, one will be counted in the number of the elect, the other will be abandoned to the fate of the reprobate.

The disciples want to know where the division of the good and bad will take place. The Saviour's answer is not such as to satisfy their untimely curiosity: "Wherever the body falls the vultures shall gather around it." What difference does it make to know in advance at what spot of the world the Son of Man will appear? The survivors of the last generation and the dead awakened by the archangel's trumpet will surely find their way to it. An irresistible force will drive them on, as instinct gathers the vultures from the four quarters of the heavens to a corpse. In the African and Arabian deserts travelers often see clouds of these rapacious birds, coming from one knows not where, to wheel around in the air and swoop down on their prey, which has scarcely been laid low in the sand. This phenomenon, observed by Job, may well have originated the proverb.[10]

Far from fearing the return of Christ coming to judge mankind, the first Christians asked for it in all their prayers. To the impatient who complained of the long delay St. Peter replied that a thousand years are as one day in the sight of the Eternal. The persecutions to which they were exposed by Jews and Gentiles must have whetted their desires. The Evangelist invites them to pray and be patient; and on this occasion he proposes to them

---

[10] Luke 17:37: Ὅπου τὸ σῶμα, ἐκεῖ καὶ οἱ ἀετοὶ ἐπισυναχθήσονται. Matt. 24:28 substitutes πτῶμα (*corpse*) for σῶμα (*body*), but this does not alter the meaning. We have here a sort of proverb, which goes back to Job's description of the *nesher* (vulture): "Wherever there are corpses, there is he found" (Job 39:30). *Nesher* in Hebrew, as also ἀετός in the Septuagint, means both "eagle" and "vulture." Many exegetes hold that it here refers to the eagle; for the eagle, they say, also feeds on carrion. It makes but little difference. Note that the language here is that of parable, and that Christ is not compared to a corpse, nor are the faithful compared to vultures. Two analogous situations are simply placed side by side: as vultures fly at full speed and straight to their prey, so the just go to judgment. Still, the comparison of Christ to a corpse did not shock the ancients: they even dwell on it at times with an insistence that is shocking to us. The essential point is that they agree on the true meaning, for which certain modern authors substitute the most bizarre explanations. For example, the corpse and the vultures would be the Jewish nation and the Roman standards (Calmet after Lightfoot), or sinners and avenging angels (Schanz), and so on.

the parable of the Wicked Judge who, despite his bad will, finally yielded to the insistence of an obstinate widow. "Will not God avenge his elect who cry to him night and day? . . . I say to you that he will avenge them without delay. Yet, shall the Son of Man at his coming find faith upon the earth?"[11]

3. The Little Children. The Rich Young Man

The first two Evangelists, who have passed in silence over the apostolate in Judea and Perea, here rejoin St. Luke almost on the eve of the Passion. The point of meeting is the charming episode of the blessing of the little children by Jesus. They were being brought to him from all sides, some led by the hand by their parents, others carried in their mothers' arms. The elders were begging Jesus to touch the little ones and to pronounce over them some words of blessing. The disciples — we would like to think that this does not mean the Apostles — were viewing with baleful eyes this multitude closing in and constantly increasing their importunity; but Jesus seemed to be encouraging them and even to have started it all. The disciples were of the opinion that the zeal of the people was indiscreet and Jesus' patience really excessive. All day long blessing creatures incapable of appreciating this benefit and profiting by it: what an unworthy occupation for the Master, what sterile labor, what hours of time

[11] Luke 18:6–8. We omit a phrase variously translated: *καὶ μακροθυμεῖ ἐπ' αὐτοῖς*. It is commonly admitted that *ἐπ' αὐτοῖς* refers to those who pray night and day, and not to their persecutors, who are not even mentioned. The verb *μακροθυμεῖν* means properly "to have patience," "to be patient"; but Plummer remarks that it is sometimes almost synonymous with *βραδύνειν* and means "act slowly," "draw out," "retard," as in Ecclus. 35 (32):22: *Ὁ Κύριος οὐ μὴ βραδύνῃ οὐδὲ μακροθυμήσει ἐπ' αὐτοῖς*. We adopt this meaning and translate it as a question: "Will he be slow in acting in their behalf?" which fits very well with "I say to you, he will avenge them without delay." If, following the Vulgate, we read: *καὶ μακροθυμῶν*, it could be translated: "though he act with mercy toward them," but this does not fit in well with what follows (cf. *Expos. Times*, 1913, Vol. XXV, p. 71).

We have commented elsewhere (Book III, Chap. ii) on the parable of the Wicked Judge, which is placed here by St. Luke, and also on the parable of the Pharisee and the Publican (Book III, Chap. vi), which follows immediately after.

lost to the apostolate! They began to disperse the multitude, parents as well as children, with indignant gestures and threatening words.

Grievously disturbed by such lack of comprehension, Jesus severely reproved them. "Suffer the little children to come unto me, and see to it that you send them not away, for the kingdom of heaven belongs to such as are like to them. Amen, I say to you, he that does not receive the kingdom of heaven like a little child shall never enter it." Speaking thus he drew them to him, clasping them in his arms and blessing each one of them singly, placing his hand upon their heads. What he loves about children is the simplicity, the docility, the candor which predestines them to the kingdom of God.[12]

The Saviour's affability and unwearied kindness exercised an irresistible attraction over hearts. One day a rich personage, reckoned despite his youth among the notables of his country, came to meet him, and falling down at his feet said to him: "Good Master, what am I to do to inherit eternal life?"[13] Perhaps because of the impression produced upon him by the scene with the little children, he couples with the title "Master," customarily given to the Rabbis, the epithet "good," which was reserved to the Author of all good. Such an epithet, frowned upon by custom, had an air of flattery in the mouth of a stranger. It drew from Jesus the answer: "Why dost thou call me good? No one is good save God." Either avoid this unusual method of address, or confess my divinity.[14] "But if thou wilt enter into (true) life,

---

[12] Mark 10:13–16; Luke 18:15–17; Matt. 19:13–15. The narrative, which is fundamentally the same in all three, is more vivid in St. Mark. Jesus is indignant at the disciples (ἠγανάκτησεν); he enfolds the children in his arms (ἐναγκαλισάμενος); he blesses them by placing his hand on their heads. Note that the text speaks of very little children (παιδία) and even infants at the breast (βρέφη).

[13] Matt. 19:16–22; Mark 10:17–22; Luke 18:18–23. This personage is a *leader* (ἄρχων, Luke), a *youth* (νεανίσκος), but not a child, since he has observed the law from his youth (ἐκ νεότητος). He comes before Jesus and falls on his knees before him (προσδραμὼν καὶ γονυπετήσας); Jesus looks upon him with love (ἐμβλέψας αὐτῷ ἠγάπησεν αὐτόν, Mark); he goes away sad (περίλυπος), which proves, says St. John Chrysostom, his first good intentions. The Fathers who think otherwise may have confused him with the lawyer of Luke 10:25.

[14] The young man's question and Jesus' answer differ in the three Synoptics.

keep the commandments. They are known to thee: avoid adultery, homicide, theft, false witness: honor thy father and thy mother; love thy neighbor as thyself."

The young man, leaving aside the epithet that had been the cause of displeasure, answered: "All this have I done since my childhood. What is still lacking to me?" If he had been boasting, the Saviour would not have cast on him that penetrating and gentle look which so much impressed those present, nor would he have experienced that awakening feeling of tenderness mentioned by St. Mark. The keeping of the commandments is the gauge of eternal life. And yet there is something still better. "If thou wilt be perfect, go sell thy goods, give the proceeds to the poor, and thou shalt have treasure in heaven; then come and follow me." At these words the young man's face became somber and his heart was saddened, for he possessed great riches. The mere thought of renouncing them made him shudder. What would become of him without his gold and the prosperity it procured? St. Mark notes in passing the sign of vexation that creased his countenance; but the Apocryphal Gospel of the Hebrews, wishing to dramatize the scene, robs it of much of its naturalness and pathos. It pictures the young man as scratching his head, while Jesus apostrophizes him thus: "Thou makest the claim to observe the law and the prophets; but is it not written in the law: 'Thou shalt love thy neighbor as thyself'? Thou hast under thy eyes

---

Mark and Luke	*Matthew*
"*Good* Master, what am I to do to inherit life eternal?"	"Master, what *good* am I to do to have life eternal?"
"Why dost thou call me *good?* No one is *good* save God."	"Why askest thou me about what is good? God alone is *the Good* (by essence)."

The Vulgate, by writing *Magister bone* and by adding *Deus* to *unus est bonus,* makes the text of Matthew conform partially to that of the other two. As it is in the Greek, the text of Matthew is difficult, and no very clear explanation has been found. Perhaps the meaning is: "You ask me about what is *good,* but it belongs to the author of all good, to Him who is *good* by essence (ὁ 'Αγαθός), to teach you that. Confess, then, my divinity or cease questioning me on this point." This would come close to the meaning in the other Synoptics, which presents no serious difficulty. "In declining this title Jesus does not wish to say that God alone is morally good, but that only He is essential Goodness" (Dalman, *Die Worte Jesu,* 2 ed., 1930, p. 277). Billerbeck (*Kommentar,* Vol. II, p. 25) fully agrees, and cites the texts of the Talmud where God is designated simply as *the Good.*

many brethren, children of Abraham like thyself. While thy house was overflowing with good things, never did anything come forth from it to relieve their misery."

The majority of the ancients, misled by a false analogy or by a faulty memory, crush this poor young man, because they confuse him with the doctor of the law who came to set a trap for the Saviour. The young man of our story is rather weak than culpable, and St. Basil and St. John Chrysostom do him justice. His respectful attitude, his thoroughly deferential tone, the seriousness of his questions, the witness that he truthfully renders to himself, the benevolence of Jesus toward him, and the affection that he begins to feel for him — all speak in favor of his uprightness and sincerity. He belonged to that legion of enthusiastic souls who dream of sacrifices and renunciation in the chapel, but are disconcerted and cast down by brutal reality. They would like to be perfect, on condition that it costs nothing. They could for a time create an illusion and delude even themselves, but the moment of action unveils them to the eyes of others and to their own eyes. The young man of the Gospel aspired to great things, and the Saviour's words opened up the road for him. For lack of courage, he recoils, and if he goes away sad, it is because he has missed his destiny and perhaps compromised his salvation.

Without occupying himself further with him, Jesus surveyed with his look the compact group of faithful disciples and addressed to them these grave words: "With what difficulty shall they that possess great riches enter into the kingdom of God!" The Apostles listened to him in consternation. "My children," he repeated, "it is easier for a camel to pass through the eye of a needle than for a rich man to enter into the kingdom of God." — "But then," said the Apostles, "who can be saved?" He fixed upon them a deep look that pierced the secret heart and replied: "That is impossible to men, but all is possible to God."[15]

---

[15] Mark 10:23–27; Matt. 19:23–26; Luke 18:24–26. St. Mark, who is more circumstantial than the others, describes in this passage three *looks* of Jesus: (*a*) a look of kindness upon the young man (10:21, ἐμβλέψας); (*b*) a look cast around about the crowd of disciples (10:23, περιβλεψάμενος); (*c*) a penetrating look upon the disciples when saying to them: "Nothing is impossible to God" (10:27). St. Matthew mentions only the last; St. Luke mentions none of them.

A camel passing through the eye of a needle, that is something that never has been and never will be seen. Shocked by this hyperbole, certain interpreters have substituted for the camel a sort of cable, which in Greek bears almost the same name, or have fancied that the needle's eye denotes the narrow little door fixed at the base of large gates, which allows passage to a stooping man, but not to a camel. Superfluous hypotheses. An altogether similar hyperbole is found in the Talmud to express something very difficult and humanly impossible.[16] Let us allow the Orientals to use their own speech without trying to accommodate it to our modern taste.

Riches are often the instrument of passion and the food of vice. Therein lies their danger. They feed pride, ambition, unbridled love of pleasure and amusement, scorn of right and of justice. To immunize the rich against this virus requires a miracle of grace. But history teaches us that the miracle is not infrequent. To possess wealth without becoming its slave, to regard it as a loan from God, to employ it for almsgiving and for honorable purposes, to hold it without infatuation and to lose it without despair; this is to be truly poor in spirit, according to the utterance of Clement of Alexandria in his fine homily on the salvation of the rich.[17]

Doubtless it was the incident of the young man captivated by his riches that provoked the question raised by St. Peter in the name of his colleagues. "Behold, we have left all things to follow thee. What shall come to us in return?" — "Amen, I say to you," answered Jesus, "when the Son of Man shall take his place upon the throne of his glory on the day of the (universal) renewal, you shall be seated upon twelve thrones to judge the twelve tribes

[16] Cf. Billerbeck, *Kommentar,* Vol. I, p. 828. There are things which no one ever thinks or dreams of, for example that an elephant should pass through the eye of a needle. A Rabbi of the third century said to one of his confreres who was a bit oversubtle: "Thou art indeed from Pumbeditha where they make an elephant pass through the eye of a needle." It was a sort of proverb to denote something humanly impossible. It is therefore unnecessary to weaken the hyperbole by conjecturing that κάμιλος, "cable," "rope," should be read instead of κάμηλος, "camel." G. Aicher has written a monograph on the question (*Kamel und Nadelöhr,* Munster, 1908) with the purpose of *reconstructing the primitive text*. Labor lost.

[17] Clement of Alex., *Quis Dives Salvetur?* (MG, IX, 620).

of Israel. And everyone who shall leave his house, or his brothers, or his sisters, or his father, or his mother, or his wife, or his children, or (even) his fields, for my name, shall receive a hundredfold (in this world) and life everlasting." Wonderful promise, but conditional and not exclusive. Among the Twelve there will be a Judas whose place shall be taken by another. Similar reversals, for good or evil, can always happen up to the end of life. That is what is to be hoped for or feared; that is what is expressed by this proverb, enigmatic in its conciseness: *Many of the first shall be last, and of the last, first.* The following parable is proof of it.

4. The Eleventh-Hour Laborers

The master of a household had gone out in the morning into the public square to hire laborers. After coming to an agreement with them about the wage of one denarius a day he sent them into the vineyard. Going out again at the third hour, and once more at the sixth and then the ninth hours, he saw there other unemployed laborers, and them too he sent into his vineyard, saying to them: "I will give you what shall be owing to you." And around the eleventh hour he found still others unemployed and said to them: "Why stand you there all the day doing nothing?" And they answered: "Because no one has hired us." To whom he said: "Go you also into my vineyard."

"When evening came the master of the vineyard said to the steward: 'Call the laborers and pay them their wages beginning with the last.' The laborers of the eleventh hour coming up received each one denarius. When it was the turn of the first, they hoped to receive more; but they received one denarius each. They began to murmur against the householder, saying: 'These have worked but one hour, and thou hast made them equal to us who have borne the burden of the day and the heat.' But he answered them: 'Friend, I do thee no wrong. Didst thou not agree with me for one denarius? Take what is thine and go. I wish to give to this last one as much as to thee. Am I not allowed to dispose of what belongs to me? Is thine eye evil because I am good?' So the first shall be last, and the last first."[18]

[18] Matt. 20:1–16. The parable is framed by the maxim: "Many of the first shall be the last and of the last first" (Matt. 19:30: Πολλοὶ δὲ ἔσονται πρῶτοι

One might think that the parable was written yesterday, so perfectly does it reflect present-day customs in Palestine. In the spring, the care of the vineyards calls for many hands, and the proprietor is sure to find them in the market place, where the laborers come at dawn to wait for someone to hire them. A friendly agreement is made about the daily wage which at that time was usually one denarius. The man of the parable, either because time was pressing, or from charitable motives, goes out several times: in the morning at nine o'clock, at midday, then at three in the afternoon, and finally at the eleventh hour, i.e., an hour before sunset, to gather all the unemployed laborers. He makes a contract with the first; he promises the others a just recompense; the last he hires without any promise.

The proprietor of the vineyard, so liberal and so just, evidently represents God; the laborers are men, whom he calls to his service; the denarius is the recompense which he dispenses to them at the end of their labors; the evening is, as often, the approaching judgment at the hour of death. There is no occasion to assign special signficance to the householder's excursions to the market place in such a way as to make of them either special epochs of history or the various ages of human life.[19] Such precision is foreign to the purpose of the parable, namely, to show that the call of God makes itself heard at all epochs of history and all ages of life, and that it is never too late to answer the call.

The delicate point is to show how the proverb, "the first shall be last, and the last first," which frames the parable, is justified by it. The circumstance that the last to come are the first to be paid has no special importance, because this order is imposed by

---

ἔσχατοι καὶ ἔσχατοι πρῶτοι), or more clearly: "So shall the first be last and the last first" (Matt. 20:16: Οὕτως ἔσονται οἱ ἔσχατοι πρῶτοι καὶ οἱ πρῶτοι ἔσχατοι). The last words added in the Vulgate: *Multi enim sunt vocati, pauci vero electi,* are rejected from the Greek text with reason by critical editors, as borrowed from Matt. 22:14. If they are retained, as they are in the Textus Receptus, we must say, with St. John Chrysostom, that they have no link with the parable.

[19] For Origen (MG, XIII, 1337–1361) the different hours, to which he attributes an undue importance, are the different ages of the world, or, if we find this interpretation too abstruse, the different ages of life. St. Jerome (MG, XXVI, 140–142) admits both explanations but in inverse order, in the first place the ages of life. St. Hilary accepts only the first (ML, IX, 1629–1630). On St. John Chrysostom, see next note.

the need of having the workers who were engaged in the morning present at the paying of those who were engaged at the eleventh hour. The paradox is found rather in this, that, contrary to all expectation, the last are treated like the first, and the first like the last.

We know from other sources that God will render to each according to his works, that there are in heaven many dwellings, that the elect differ from one another in splendor and brilliance as do the stars in heaven; but here the reward is considered with respect to something that it has in common and equally for all.

How can so many keen minds see in the laborers of the first hour a symbol of the reprobate? These laborers have faithfully accomplished their task, they have received their wage, the master declares that it is owing to them, and they do not go so far as to refuse it. They are, therefore, in possession of beatitude, which, as all agree, is symbolized by the denarius. If statements as clear as these are not to retain their natural meaning, all interpretation must be given up. But, it may be objected, their murmuring has deprived them of the reward that was destined for them. But why? Can one fall from beatitude when once in possession of it? These murmurings, which fit in very well with the narrative that serves as dressing for the parable, have no bearing on its application. We may appropriately repeat the very apt statement of St. John Chrysostom, made precisely with reference to the present subject: "In parables not everything is to be taken literally. The purpose must be adhered to without quibbling about the rest." Here the purpose is to bring out this primary lesson: "Friend, I do thee no wrong. Take what is owing to thee. I wish to give to this other one, just as to thee."[20]

[20] Chrysostom, *In Matth. Hom. LXIV* (al. LXV), no. 3 (MG, LVIII, 613). Adhering strictly to the literal sense, he admits together with everyone else that the denarius represents *beatitude,* or what comes to the same thing, *salvation* (ἡ σωτηρία, Origen), *happy immortality* (ἡ ἀφθαρσία, Irenaeus, *Haer.*, IV, 36). He then examines three difficulties: (*a*) How can it be said that the first ones *murmur?* (*b*) How does the equal reward given to all verify the adage: *The first shall be the last?* (*c*) How have the laborers of the eleventh hour the right to say: *No one has hired us?* Here are his answers to the three questions:

a) This feature is *parabolical.* It is what would happen on earth, and it is necessary for drawing forth the answer of the master justifying himself, but it has no possible application to the elect.

So too, the murmurings of the martyrs of the Apocalypse, complaining about the delays of God's justice, have no other purpose than to draw the answer: "Be patient yet a little while until the number of your martyr brethren is complete." So too, the elder brother of the Prodigal, just man that he is, is surprised and becomes sulky, in order to give his father occasion to say to him: "My son, thou art always with me, and all that I have belongs to thee; but it behooved us to rejoice at the return of thy brother who was lost and has been found again."

If the laborers of the first hour typified the damned, the final sentence would be meaningless. The elect and the reprobate belong to two entirely different categories. They cannot be compared in worth. The elect are not the first among the reprobate, nor are the reprobate the last among the elect. All the elect, despite differences in individual glory of which there is no question here, receive the denarius of the beatific vision. Where there is equality between first and last, there is in reality neither first nor last; and it can be said by way of a proverb that the first are last, and the last first.

In the Rabbinical writings there is a parable which is often compared to ours; but it is altogether different. A king who had engaged a great number of laborers noticed one who was working much more than the others. He took him aside and walked with him all the rest of the day. When evening came, he paid him as much as the others, and said to his discontented companions: "This man has done in two hours as much as you have done the

---

b) The reward is the same for all, but the laborers of the eleventh hour receive it first. We see such reversals (τὰς τοιαύτας μεταβολάς) in the history of the Jews and Gentiles. Also, the good thief, the last convert of Jesus, is the first to share his glory. But the adage is verified in the parable in the sense that, *contrary to all expectation,* the last are treated like the first, and the first like the last.

c) The third difficulty is easily solved. There is reference to the *efficacious* call, the answer to the divine call. Why did he not call them all in the morning? As far as he is concerned, he did call them all, and if not all have obeyed at the same time, the difference comes from their wills.

The Pseudo-Chrysostom, a Latin author of the fifth century, who has read St. Irenaeus, Origen, St. Hilary, and St. Jerome, combines two explanations: *Judaei et in primo loco vocati sunt ante Gentes, in secundo autem loco vocati sunt per Gentes. . . . Aut ideo dicit primos novissimos futuros, et novissimos primos, non ut novissimi digniores sint quam primi, sed ut coaequentur* (*Opus imperfectum,* 35, MG, LVI, 822). The real Chrysostom had said the same.

entire day."[21] A diligent laborer achieves his task in less time than a lazy one; that is quite evident. But this is not the implication of the Gospel parable. The master does not reprove those that were called first for any laziness; when they make the point that they have borne the burden of the day and the heat, they are not lying. The moral of the parable is consequently this: priority of call and of response to the call does not give anyone an exclusive right to the heavenly heritage. In other words, it is never too late to answer the call of God, though willful delay may be extremely dangerous.

---

[21] Jerusalem Talmud, *Berakoth,* ii, 8 (Schwab, 1871, pp. 48–49). Surprisingly Maldonatus, who is ordinarily better inspired, gives this meaning to the Gospel parable. According to him, the last receive the same wages as the first, because they have done in one hour as much work as the others in twelve, and they become the first in that they are paid first. The Gospel says nothing like that. Polemic against the Protestants who hold, on the basis of this parable, that celestial beatitude is equal for all, because it is a pure gift of grace without regard to merits, has made Maldonatus deviate from the straight path. Lifting a weapon against his adversaries, he has himself gone astray.

Sanday (in the *Expositor,* first series, Vol. III, pp. 81–101) proves very well: (1) that celestial beatitude is a reward; (2) that it is unequal among the elect; (3) that the murmuring of the first-hour laborers cannot mean their exclusion from heaven. But many Anglicans are not of his opinion. The old Protestant dogma of faith saving without works still persists among them.

CHAPTER XII

The Passion Draws Near

1. On the Road to Jerusalem

In the first days the month of Nisan in the year 29 of our era (782 years after the foundation of Rome), Jesus descended the Valley of the Jordan, directing his steps to Jerusalem where the Cross awaited him.

Silent and pensive, he walked before his disciples like a chief who is leading his soldiers to the assault, or rather like the champion of a noble cause who hastens to confront the danger in order to ward it off from his followers. The Apostles were in a daze, surprised at his unusual attitude and conscious of the gravity of the hour, knowing well the animosity of the Scribes, the implacable hatred of the Pharisees, the sullen hostility of the chief priests, and the murderous purposes of the Sanhedrin. Not long ago, at the mere mention of a journey that would lead them closer to the Holy City, Thomas had felt the need of lifting his courage with the energetic protestation: "Let us go and die with him!" And now that Jesus was, so to speak, rashly throwing himself into the jaws of the wolf, was there not reason to tremble? The mixed multitude that followed — disciples of yesterday and pilgrims casually encountered — had also a vague impression that tragic events were impending.[1]

---

[1] This little drama is admirably described by St. Mark, 10:32: *Ἦσαν δὲ ἐν τῇ ὁδῷ ἀναβαίνοντες εἰς Ἱεροσόλυμα, καὶ ἦν προάγων αὐτοὺς ὁ Ἰησοῦς, καὶ ἐθαμβοῦντο, οἱ δὲ ἀκολουθοῦντες ἐφοβοῦντο.* Jesus walked *first,* by himself (*ἦν προάγων* — he *led them forward,* preceding them); the Apostles follow, full of astonishment and *stupor* (*ἐθαμβοῦντο*); then comes the crowd, filled also with *fright* (*ἐφοβοῦντο*). Some link the last member with the Apostles, but this forces the meaning of

The Saviour does not wish to expose his secret to the crowds, but it is important that the Apostles should be instructed about it. Twice before, at Caesarea Philippi after the confession of Peter and upon the descent from Thabor after the Transfiguration, he had prepared them for the scandal of the Cross by revealing to them some circumstances of his Passion. He now goes on to describe to them the details, with a precision which more resembles history than prophecy. Taking them aside he said to them: "Behold, we go up to Jerusalem, and the Son of Man shall be delivered to his enemies, and they shall condemn him to death, and shall deliver him to the Gentiles, who shall scoff at him and spit upon him, and shall scourge him and put him to death; but the third day he shall rise again."[2]

The six acts of the great drama — the treason of Judas, the capital sentence pronounced by the Sanhedrin, the recourse to the Roman authorities who alone can carry it into execution, the insults and maltreatment by the soldiery, the crucifixion to which the scourging is but a prelude, and finally the resurrection on the third day — all are enumerated clearly and in order. Nothing is lacking but the proper names. All this had been predicted in veiled terms before; the only new item in the present confidential disclosure is the intervention of the Roman authority, which carries with it, in case of condemnation, the torment of the cross.

Nothing could have been more explicit; and still the Apostles did not understand.[3] They understood well enough the words and the phrases — a child would have grasped the meaning of them — but they did not succeed in persuading themselves that all this

---

οἱ δὲ ἀκολουθοῦντες and mars the effect of the marvelous summary. All that can be said is that the Apostles shared the fears of the crowd, but this detail, which goes without saying, is not expressed.

[2] Mark 10:33–34. The other Synoptics (Matt. 20:18–19; Luke 18:31–33) differ little. They agree in saying that Jesus *had taken the Twelve aside,* παραλαβὼν τοὺς δώδεκα (Mark adds κατ' ἰδίαν). To rise again *after three days* (Mark) or *on the third day* (Matthew and Luke) are synonymous expressions. Matthew says more expressly: he will be delivered to the Gentiles *to be* mocked, scourged, and *crucified;* but crucifixion is implicitly contained in the scourging and the *putting to death by the Gentiles.*

[3] Luke 18:34. "They understood nothing of these things, and this saying was hidden from them, and they did not know what was being said to them." Note with what insistence St. Luke expresses the Apostles' lack of understanding.

must be taken literally. The idea of a suffering and crucified Messias entered only with difficulty into the Jewish mind; and the Apostles, accustomed to the figurative and parabolic language of the Saviour, imagined that there was here a mystery to which the future would give them the key.

What they could not ignore was the imminence of the final unraveling of events, so frequent were the allusions of Jesus to his approaching death becoming. Was he, then, about to inaugurate his reign and keep his promises about seating them on twelve thrones to judge the twelve tribes of Israel? So they thought, beyond a doubt, for they multiplied their questions on the subject of his glorious return. In every change of rule, intriguing and ambitious people turn readily toward the rising sun to salute its first rays.

The wife of Zebedee believed the moment opportune to make an attempt on behalf of her sons. Prostrating herself at Jesus' feet in the attitude of humble suppliance, she said to him softly: "Master, I have a favor to ask of thee." It may be that she hoped that our Lord would immediately make one of those vague promises which are half an engagement beforehand. She had a right, she thought, to count upon it more than anyone else. To say nothing of the bonds of kinship which may have related her to the Saviour, she had given her two sons to him, and was devoting to him her own time and her own resources. When the Saviour invited her to state her wish, she said to him: "Command that these two sons of mine may sit one at thy right and the other at thy left, in thy kingdom."

James and John, who were standing beside their mother, were surely in accord and connivance with her. Thus it is not to the mother, but to the sons, that Jesus directs his answer: "You know not what you ask. Can you drink the chalice that I drink, and undergo the baptism wherewith I am baptized?" The chalice and baptism were two metaphors familiar to the Jews, imbued, as they were, with the language of the Scriptures. The chalice was good or bad fortune, but especially bad. This depreciatory sense probably came from the cup of anger and vengeance which, according to the Prophets, God gave his faithless people, and also impious nations, to drink. In any case, the chalice was a symbol of affliction and bitterness. The Hebrews also represented tribulations under the figure of torrential waters into which one was plunged. In the same sense we say an abyss of sorrow, a deluge of evils.

The chalice which Jesus will drain to the last drop and the baptism wherewith he must be baptized are not so much his sanguinary death as his life of suffering and humiliation. Hence he speaks of them as things of the present. "The chalice that I drink, the baptism wherewith I am baptized." The sons of Zebedee understand him without difficulty, and in a burst of sincere generosity they answer with one voice: "Yes, we can!" "Ah well," Jesus continues, without further attending to their mother who had been their agent, "you shall drink the chalice that I drink, and you shall be baptized with the baptism wherewith I am baptized; but as to sitting at my right and at my left, it does not belong to me to grant it; that is for those to whom my Father has destined it."[4]

The initiative in salvation and predestination is always attributed to the Father, though it is a work common to the three divine Persons. God, who sees the future as we see the present, from all eternity reserves for those who show themselves worthy the places that they merit; for in heaven there is neither caprice nor favoritism, as too often happens here below. The sons of Zebedee shall drink the chalice of bitterness and undergo a baptism of tribulation. James will fall beneath the sword of Agrippa. John will suffer exile to Patmos and will pass through a series of trials that may well be compared to a dolorous baptism.

---

[4] Matt. 20:20–28; Mark 10:35–45. The variants do not affect the meaning. (*a*) In St. Mark the sons directly make the advance; in St. Matthew their mother makes it for them; but in both Jesus directs his answer to the sons. (*b*) St. Matthew has only the metaphor of the *chalice:* "Can you drink the chalice that I shall drink?" (ὃ ἐγὼ μέλλω πίνειν); St. Mark adds the metaphor of the *baptism,* and he puts both verbs in the present: "that I *drink,* that I *undergo.*" (*c*) The present Vulgate has "non est meum dare *vobis,*" but *vobis* is lacking in the Greek and the better Latin manuscripts. The sentence is general, and it is useless to ask to whom the first two places are reserved: Peter and Paul (St. Hilary) or Moses and Elias (Euthymius). Such conjectures are vain.

Some recent authors (Schwartz, J. Weiss, Loisy, etc.) hold that the prediction of Jesus implies the violent death of John, and that according to Papias John actually was martyred together with his brother James. We cannot pause to refute these fantastic theories which lead nowhere. Cf. *Recherches,* 1923, pp. 370–373.

Both will receive the crown of justice promised to good laborers; but let them cease aspiring after arbitrary preferments.

It may be said in defense of the two brothers that in asking this favor of a supernatural order they were not so much obeying the promptings of ambition and selfishness as the desire to be more closely united to their beloved Master. But still it must be admitted that their venture involved something of an offense to their colleagues. The latter were not yet so firmly grounded in humility as not to feel in their turn a lively indignation, which they translated into noisy protests. The lesson which they deserved, both the one and the other party, was not slow in coming:

"You know that among the Gentiles the rulers govern imperiously, and that the great of the earth make their rule press heavily. Let it not be so among you. Whoever wishes to become great shall make himself your servant, and whoever wishes to be the first shall be the servant of all. For the Son of Man has not come to be served, but to serve, and to give his life for the ransom of many."

It is in this spirit that the successor of Peter uses the title of "Servant of the Servants of Christ." And St. Paul, who so strongly adjures the faithful not to make themselves the slaves of men, does not fear to call himself the slave of the brethren for the love of Christ. It is true that among the Hebrews, where the slave was part of the family, the term did not arouse the idea of abasement, abjection, or infamy, which slavery implied among the pagans.

Not content to clothe himself in the form of a slave, the Incarnate Word comes to offer his life for our ransom. This doctrine of the redeeming death, which St. Peter and St. Paul and St. John have made so familiar to us, we find here too, just as surely and just as clearly expressed under the pens of the Synoptics. Jesus Christ has come "to give his life as a ransom for many."[5]

---

[5] Matt. 20:28; Mark 10:45: *δοῦναι τὴν ψυχὴν αὐτοῦ λύτρον ἀντὶ πολλῶν*. Compare 1 Tim. 2:6: *ὁ δοὺς ἑαυτὸν ἀντίλυτρον ὑπὲρ πάντων*. "On this fundamental utterance rests the whole primitive tradition of the redemptive death of Jesus, like an ear of wheat within the blade, a tradition explicitly mentioned by St. Paul as existing before his own reception into the Christian community" (L. de Grandmaison, *Jésus-Christ,* Vol. II, p. 268; English transl., Vol. III, p. 47). The allusion is to 1 Cor. 15:1–11. See our *Théol. de St. Paul,* Vol. I, pp. 507–508 and Vol. II,

In instituting the Holy Eucharist he will say still more clearly that "his blood is shed for the remission of the sins of a great number," in order to seal the "covenant" between God and man. He gives his life for all, and his blood is shed for all. These words "for many, for a great number," far from implying any limitation, only insinuate that not all will actually profit by his redeeming death; or rather, they mean that the blood of one victim is sufficient to redeem the whole sinful mass, however great it may be; and this does not exclude, but rather supposes, its universal effectiveness.

2. A Halt at Jericho

Seven or eight days before the Passion, Jesus passed through Jericho with a large escort of disciples and pilgrims. The City of Palms had changed its site since the days of Josue. From the hillock which it had then occupied near the Fount of Eliseus, and where its shapeless ruins are still to be seen, it had moved to the south along the road from Jerusalem to the Jordan ford. Herod and Archelaus vied with each other in beautifying the city. At great expense, they had built an amphitheater, a hippodrome, and a sumptuous palace, with pools fed by conduits carrying water from a great distance. At this time, Jericho was the second most important city in Palestine, and in area it equaled the capital. The miserable village which has fallen heir to its name and site has retained nothing of its splendors. Even its ruins have perished. Of its balsam groves, its forests of pine trees, and its rose gardens there remains no trace.[6]

The passage of Jesus through Jericho was marked by two con-

---

pp. 231–232 (English transl., Vol. I, p. 432; Vol. II, pp. 191–194); also the exposé and refutation of some Rationalist theories by Fr. Médebielle, in *Biblica,* Vol. IV, 1923, pp. 3–40: *"La vie donne en rançon."*

[6] The present village is called *Riḥa,* abridged from *Eriḥa,* in which it is easy to recognize the name Jericho. The Chanaanite city situated farther to the north has been excavated several times. Cf. *R.B.,* 1910, pp. 404–417 and 1930, pp. 403–433. It was surrounded by two walls but was very small, as were all the cities of that epoch, covering no more than fourteen or fifteen acres. Herod's city, the fame of which was ephemeral, was a mile and a half distant, near the place where the Wady el-Qelt emerges into the plain. St. Epiphanius (MG, XLI, 157) gives it a circumference of twenty stadia (4155 yards), almost the same as Jerusalem at the time of Christ and modern Jerusalem within the ramparts.

quests: that of Bartimeus the blind beggar, and of Zacheus the rich publican.

The son of Timeus was crouching in a rut of the road to solicit charity from the passers-by, in a place where he ran no risk of being jostled or crushed by them. At any time, but especially at the time of great feasts, such blind beggars are to be seen in the outskirts of Palestinian cities, lying along the side of the road, chanting their plaintive refrain all the day long. The blind man of Jericho, hearing an unusual commotion, asked the reason for it. He was told that the celebrated Galilean Wonder-Worker, Jesus of Nazareth, was passing that way. This name, which he knew by reputation, brightened his soul with a ray of hope. He began to cry out at the top of his voice to overcome the noise of the crowd: "Jesus, son of David, have mercy on me!" In vain did they try to silence him. Heedless of the reproofs of those whom he was disturbing by his shouts, he cried out even louder: "Son of David, have mercy on me!" Son of David was the current title of the Messias, and this is apparently the meaning that the blind man gave to the name.

Jesus commanded that he should be brought to him. Nothing more than that was needed to change the sentiments of the volatile crowd. They pressed about the sick man, encouraging him with words of kindness. "Come, friend," they said to him, "get up! The Master is calling thee." The blind man needed no urging. He immediately rose, and, hastily throwing aside his cloak which might impede his progress, he leaped forward to Jesus' feet. Their conversation was brief:

> "What dost thou wish that I do for thee?"
> "Lord, that I may see."
> "Go. Thy faith has saved thee."

Instantly the blind man recovered his sight and began to give thanks to God, the enthusiastic crowd joining in. But he did more than that, and better. From that time on he attached himself to Jesus' footsteps, never to leave him again. The care that St. Mark has taken to preserve his name for us is a good indication that he was a member of the first Christian community.[7]

---

[7] Mark 10:46–52; Matt. 20:29–34; Luke 18:35–43. St. Mark, whose text we are following, places the cure at the *departure* from the city; St. Matthew does

Jericho, as a frontier city and an important center of commerce, possessed a numerous personnel of Treasury agents: customs officers, collectors of tolls and other taxes, leviers of fees for sale and transfer, and the like. The whole system seems to have been arranged in an orderly hierarchy. The person whom the Gospel calls the chief of the publicans doubtless exercised the office of supervisor or controller. At any rate, he enjoyed some sort of jurisdiction over the other employees. Though a publican, he was Jewish by race, and his name was Zacheus, that is to say, the Pure or Just; a name in no degree justified by his profession. He was a rich man, and, in view of the unscrupulousness and rapaciousness of the people belonging to his caste, we might be tempted to believe that the greater part of his fortune was the income from fleecings and extortions. What gives us a better idea of him, however, is that, after distributing half his goods to the poor, he still can feel himself in a position to give fourfold compensation for the wrongs he has inflicted. Hence he has not acquired by unjust means more than one eighth of what he has. In short, he is the good publican.

Zacheus was consumed with the desire to see Jesus close at hand, but this was a difficult thing for a man so short of stature, since a dense crowd was blocking every approach of the road. There was a row of sycamores on the route along which Jesus

---

the same, but instead of *one* blind man, he mentions *two;* St. Luke notes expressly that Jesus was *approaching* Jericho. The word conflict is famous. The solution would be easy if ἐν τῷ ἐγγίζειν αὐτὸν εἰς Ἰεριχώ in St. Luke could be understood as "when he *was near* to Jericho," whether entering or leaving; but ἐγγίζειν does not seem to bear this interpretation. After all, there could have been two blind men both of whom were cured, one at the entry to, the other at the departure from the city; St. Matthew, as is his wont, would have combined them into one account.

Blind men would not be lacking in Jericho. In that low-lying region, with humid nights followed by tropical days, where the atmosphere was charged with fine torrid dust and infested with flies, cases of purulent ophthalmia, resulting in complete blindness, were not rare.

Still, as Maldonatus remarks, the Gospel accounts resemble one another so much that it is very difficult to admit two and especially three distinct miracles; but his hypothesis that Bartimeus asked for a cure at Christ's entrance into the city, and obtained it only at his departure, does not seem very satisfactory. Still it is accepted by Schanz (on Matt. 20:29).

For what two recent Catholic commentators have written in different directions, cf. Knabenbauer, *In Matth.,* 1893, Vol. II, pp. 191–194, and Lagrange, *Saint Luc,* pp. 484–485.

was to pass. This tree, very different from the false plane-tree related to the maple that we call sycamore, was more like the mulberry. In the springtime it is covered with innumerable wild figs, from which it got the name of sycamore or mulberry fig. Since the branches grow almost at ground level, it was easy to climb, even for a dwarf. Such was the ideal observation tower that struck Zacheus' fancy. Forestalling others, he clambered out on a limb that overhung the road and installed himself there. Anyone may have seen the clusters of human fruit that hang from the chestnut trees in the Champs Élysées when foreign royalty is passing through. It is, then, quite probable that Zacheus was not the only one on that lookout of his. But he was the only one honored by a glance from Jesus. Raising his eyes to him and addressing him like an old acquaintance, Jesus said to him in a familiar tone: "Zacheus, come down quickly, for today I must lodge in thy house." A favor unique in kind. Jesus accepted invitations, but he was not accustomed to invite himself, especially to the homes of those whom he did not know.

Zacheus nimbly leaped down from his sycamore and hastily made off to see to the preparations for receiving such a guest. Jesus followed closely after, despite the whisperings of the crowd, murmuring and scandalized to see him cross the threshold of the publican. "He is going to lodge with a sinner!" No one suspected that the glance of Jesus had transformed the man. "Lord," said the happy Zacheus, "I am going to give half my goods to the poor and, if I have done wrong to anyone, I am making fourfold amends." He cheerfully despoils himself of his fortune, ready to give even himself if the Saviour calls him to follow, as he had called his confrere, Matthew. With what joy he must have heard the word of absolution, addressed to those present certainly as much as to him: "Today salvation has entered into this house, for this man is a true child of Abraham. The Son of Man has come to seek and to save what was lost."[8]

Nowhere more than in the story of Zacheus may we observe the hidden work of grace. To a feeling of admiring curiosity, in which one might think that nature alone had a share, succeeds the desire of coming near to Jesus, of seeing him, of hearing him, of

---

[8] Luke 19:1–10. The very clear narrative needs no explanation.

serving him. Then as soon as Jesus has spoken, it is the activity of faith that revolutionizes, conquers, and transfigures the man. Finally comes the disposition to give away all to please the Master, not excepting the gift of self.

What became of Zacheus? An uncertain tradition makes him Bishop of Caesarea in Palestine, or sends him to our own faraway Quercy. He is, however, in possession of a more certain glory: the glory of being canonized during his lifetime by him whose word can never be mistaken.

3. Parable of the Minas and Talents

The passage through Jericho had been a triumph for Jesus. Many who were escorting him followed him into Zacheus' dwelling. What had just happened awakened in them fantastic hopes, and their overheated imaginations were opening up to all kinds of illusions. They were thinking that the Messianic crisis was about to blaze up, that the kingdom of God as they conceived it would manifest itself at an early date, and that this dramatic event would be enacted in Jerusalem, the religious center of the nation. To calm these impatient expectations, and at the same time to teach them a useful lesson, Jesus proposes the parable of the Minas.

"A certain man of noble race went away for a time into a far country to seek the royal dignity. Having summoned ten of his servants, he gave to each of them one mina, saying: 'Turn this to account until I return.' But his fellow citizens who hated him sent an embassy after him with this message: 'We will not have this man reign over us.'

"When he returned, invested with royalty, he called his servants to find out from them how they had used his money. The first to present himself said: 'Lord, thy mina has earned ten more.' — 'Well done, thou good servant,' answered the master, 'because thou hast been faithful in small things, receive the rule of ten cities.' The second came and said: 'Lord, thy mina has earned five others.' — 'Thou too,' answered the master, 'receive the rule of five cities.'

"The third came in his turn and said: 'Lord, behold thy mina, which I have kept hidden in a linen cloth; for I feared thee, because thou art an exacting man. Thou takest up what thou hast not laid down, and thou reapest what thou hast not sown.' The master answered: 'By thy own word I judge thee, thou wicked servant. Thou knowest that I am an exacting man, taking up what I did not lay down and reaping what I did not sow. Why then didst thou not place the money in the bank, so that on my return I would have drawn it out with interest?' Then he said to the bystanders: 'Take his mina away from him and give it to him that has ten.' — 'But, Lord, he has already ten of them.' — 'It matters not. I say to you, to him that has shall be given, and from him that has not, even what he has shall be taken away.'

" 'As for my enemies, who would not have me to be their king, let them be brought here and put to death in my presence.' "[9]

The aspirant who goes away to a distant land to seek the royal investiture is evidently Jesus Christ. He is, indeed, already reigning; but he has not yet received the official consecration of his royalty, and to receive this he goes away to his Father. The irreconcilable enemies are, no less clearly, those who in a few days will say to Pilate: "We will have no other king than Caesar." The allegory contained nothing obscure for Christ's contemporaries. At that epoch, the kings allied to Rome, who were in reality nothing more than vassals, had to solicit the permission of the Emperor to ascend the throne. Archelaus, Herod's heir, had his claims rejected, and he brought back from Rome nothing but

---

[9] Luke 19:11–27. The parable is closely related both to the Zacheus episode and to the journey to Jerusalem: "To those who were listening to these words (addressed to Zacheus) he proposed this parable because it was near Jerusalem, and it seemed to them that the kingdom of God was straightway to manifest itself." We are therefore still at Jericho. Matt. 25:14–30 should be compared.

a) The heir of a throne certainly has more than ten servants or subjects. Ten is an indeterminate number. But only three, as in St. Matthew, have any role to play.

b) The history of Archelaus, heir of Herod, can be compared with the king who goes far away to seek investiture and who on his return takes vengeance on his rebel subjects (Josephus, *Antiq.*, XVII, ix, 3; *Bellum*, II, i, 3).

c) In St. Luke, as in St. Matthew, the master prolongs his absence. This could be to leave the servants time to derive the advantage from the money entrusted to them, or else to emphasize that the Parousia is not imminent.

the title of ethnarch, instead of the crown which his father had willed him dependently upon the Imperial assent. We know well the pitiless vengeance he wreaked on his subjects who had petitioned the Emperor to refuse him the throne, even up to the day when Augustus, incensed at his acts of violence, sent him into exile in Gaul.

The man of the parable is sure of the justice of his cause. He will return sooner or later with the trappings of royalty, and then he will treat everyone according to his deserts. He will severely punish his rebellious subjects, and will royally reward his faithful servants. He has entrusted to ten of them a modest sum, equal to a little less than twenty-one dollars of our money, not to draw profit from them, but to make trial of their zeal, their loyalty, and their skill, thus to estimate the services which they can some day render him in administering his state.

St. Matthew gives this parable a different turn without changing the essential meaning:

"A man setting out on a journey summoned his servants, and entrusted to them his goods. To one he gave five talents, to another two, and to a third only one — to each of them according to his ability; then he went away. Immediately he that had received five set himself to lay them out at interest, and gained five more. Likewise, he that had received two gained two more. But he that had received only one went and dug in the ground and buried his master's money.

"A long time afterward, on his return, the master had an accounting made by his servants. He that had received the five talents brought back five more, saying: 'Lord, thou didst entrust to me five talents. I have gained five more.' The master answered: 'Well done, thou good and faithful servant; because thou hast been faithful in small things, I will place thee over greater. Enter into the joy of thy master.' Then he of the two talents came forward and said: 'Lord, thou didst entrust to me two talents; behold, here are two more that I have gained.' The master answered him: 'Well done, thou good and faithful servant; because thou hast been faithful in small things, I will place thee over greater. Enter into the joy of thy master.'

"In his turn, he that had received only one talent came forward and said: 'Lord, I knew that thou art an exacting man, reaping where thou didst not sow, and gathering where thou didst not scatter anything. I was therefore afraid and hid thy talent in the earth. Behold then, take thy property.' The master answered him: 'Thou wicked and slothful servant. Thou knowest that I reap where I did not sow, and gather where I did not scatter anything. Thou oughtest therefore to have placed my money in the bank, so that on my return, I would have drawn out the capital with interest. Take the talent away from him and give it to him that has ten; for to him that has, shall be given, and he shall abound; but from him that has not, even what he has shall be taken away. As to the useless servant, let him be cast forth into the outer darkness, where there shall be weeping and gnashing of teeth.' "[10]

It was not a rare thing among the ancients, as Egyptian and Assyrian monuments attest, for a rich man starting on a long journey to entrust to tested servants the administration of his property. The man of the parable entrusts to three of his servants his entire fortune, which was considerable. The talent was worth sixty minas, or six thousand drachmas, a sum equal to $1,239 in our American money; but to estimate its value in purchasing power, relatively to our present money, it should

---

[10] Matt. 25:14–30. St. Matthew adds this parable to that of the Ten Virgins, as an introduction to the scene of the Last Judgment, with this purely literary transition: "As a man setting out on a journey." There is nothing to fix the time or place.

a) In the Greek a period can be placed either after or before εὐθέως (*immediately*). If it is placed after it, we have, as in the Vulgate, "he went away immediately." If it is placed before it, we have, "Immediately the one who had received five talents, etc." This latter division is better, since it places emphasis on the diligence of the good servant, whereas a hasty departure of the master would be of no particular importance.

b) In vv. 24 and 26: "Thou gatherest where thou didst not scatter" (ὅθεν οὐ διεσκόρπισας) there is probably allusion to the Jewish method of winnowing grain. By means of a shovel or pitchfork it was thrown into the air and the mixture of chaff and threshed grain was separated or scattered (διασκορπίζειν) by the wind over the threshing floor. The exact translation, then, would be: "Thou reapest what thou didst not sow and thou gathered what thou didst not winnow" (cf. Ezech. 5:2–10). St. Luke, whose readers were unacquainted with Palestinian customs, replaces the last metaphor by the colorless expression: "you take up what you have not put down" (19:21–22).

be multiplied several times. However, the master takes care to proportion the amount of the deposit to the ability of each of his servants, for not all are equally capable of managing a large fortune. The two good servants who have both doubled their holdings receive the same reward, because they have displayed the same zeal and have expended the same amount of labor, each according to his means. The bad servant, who adds insolence to laziness, is justly punished.

It is clear that this just and liberal man represents God. The talents may be symbols of natural and supernatural goods, qualities of mind and body, graces sanctifying oneself or given for the benefit of others; in a word, everything that we owe to God and of which we must render an account before his judgment seat. But, as often happens, the application compenetrates the parable. God hands over to his diligent servants the interest as well as the capital, something which is scarcely to be met with in masters here below; he has them enter into the joy of their Lord, and this is not a mere invitation to a joyful feast; he commands the evil servant to be cast into outer darkness, where there shall be weeping and gnashing of teeth, and this does not mean solely that he excludes him from a banquet. Thus the Evangelist, as he develops the parable, gives us at the same time its explanation.

In the parables of the Minas and Talents, the lesson — the same in both — is twofold. First, every man, born servant as he is of the sovereign Master, is bound to make the goods received by him bear fruit, and the mere fact of forgetting or neglecting this is a dereliction of duty. In the second place, the reward is measured, not by the results obtained, since abilities and resources differ, but by the zeal employed and the labor expended. All the other elements — the rank of the master, the circumstances of his departure and return, the number of servants, the larger or smaller sums entrusted to them, the way in which they exploit them, the nature of the reward and punishment — all are accessory, and may be varied without in any degree changing the bearing and meaning of the parable. In St. Luke, the master being a legitimate king speaks, acts, and rewards regally. In St. Matthew, the master being only a private individual must not step out of his role. He does not dispose of the rule of cities, and he recognizes according to his ability the services rendered. This the laws of verisimilitude demand.

Should the two parables be identified? Nothing opposes it in principle, provided that the parable of St. Luke be left in the historical setting which he assigns to it. St. Matthew, who links it with the Last Judgment, simplifies it and retains only the traits that fit his theme, whereas St. Luke maintains its complexity. The parable of the Talents can be extracted from that of the Minas by leaving aside all that has to do with the rebellious subjects. But the parable of the Minas could not be drawn from that of the Talents without adding an essential point, a point which could be the subject of another parable.[11]

---

[11] Maldonatus, following St. Ambrose and St. Jerome, admits the identity of the two parables and affirms that "all recent authorities" are of the same view. Still, many authors of our day, following St. John Chrysostom, are of a contrary opinion. Among Catholics may be cited Schanz, Knabenbauer, Fillion, and among Protestants, Plummer and Godet. It is certainly possible that Jesus proposed the same parable twice with variants, but it is equally possible that the Evangelists, while retaining the moral lesson which is the essence of the parable, have modified its presentation. We do not wish to say that St. Luke *arranges* St. Matthew's version to his taste, nor St. Matthew that of St. Luke. Each follows his own bent in conformity with the tradition at his disposal.

BOOK FOUR

DEATH AND NEW LIFE

CHAPTER I

The Triumph of a Day

1. The Banquet at Bethany

THE Passover of the year 29 was approaching. From the remotest parts of Palestine and even from the confines of the Roman world Jews and proselytes were pouring into Jerusalem en masse. The roads were crowded with pilgrims, traveling sometimes singly, oftener in family groups or by villages, all driving before them the victims destined for sacrifice. Though the duty of celebrating the Passover at Jerusalem was not incumbent on those who lived too far from the Holy City, still all the inhabitants of the country considered it their duty to perform the pious pilgrimage once a year, and all the Jews of the Dispersion took it to heart to appear at least once during their lifetime in the Temple of the true God, just as devout Moslems of the present day dream of venerating the sanctuary of Mecca and the tomb of the Prophet before they die.

Large numbers of pilgrims used to arrive quite a long time before the Paschal festivities. Those who came from a distance, fearing accidents along the route and unforeseen delays, made their plans accordingly in advance. Others deliberately anticipated the date fixed, in order to submit to the legal purifications and to fulfill vows, some of which, such as that of the Nazirites, required several days of attendance.[1] Still others, inspired by more utilitarian motives, were anxious to make sure of lodgings with people of their acquaintance. The area of Jerusalem at that time was not appreciably larger than at present and, though

[1] John 11:55. Those who were not in a state of legal purity could not eat the Passover until the following month (Num. 9:10; 2 Para. 30:17–18).

the ancients did not require comforts in the modern sense, still it was a real problem to provide shelter during the night for such a huge multitude of strangers. Even if the figure of three million visitors given by Josephus be regarded as greatly exaggerated, we know from other sources that the influx was enormous.[2] When all the houses of the city were filled to overflowing and there remained no more room even on the roof terraces, the pilgrims flowed back on the neighboring villages or encamped outdoors in the valley or on the hillsides in the neighborhood.

In this swarming and motley crowd many eyes were searching for Jesus and they were surprised at not seeing him. He had come up only secretly to the feasts of Tabernacles and Dedication; for six months he had been living in hiding beyond the Jordan or in an obscure village in the north of Judea. What did this obstinate silence mean, this deliberate self-effacement after the brilliant manifestations at the beginning? The Galileans, above all, when gossiping under the colonnades of the Temple, were expressing to one another their wonderment. "What do you think? Is he not coming to the feast?" As for the most influential members of the Sanhedrin, Pharisees and leaders of the priestly caste, they were not forgetting their declared enemy, and time had only sharpened their rancor. If many of them were entertaining the fond hope that Jesus might abandon the struggle, the majority were harboring no such illusions and were counting on his return among them soon. Expecting this eventuality, they had given orders to all their satellites to notify them of his arrival as soon as it should become known, so that his arrest could be arranged either by craft or violence as circumstances should permit.

At the very time that they were hatching their plot against him, Jesus was at Bethany. He had arrived six days before the Passover. However, precise as it may appear to be, this indication does not furnish us with an absolutely sure date. The most natural calculation would lead us to select the Saturday before the Passion; but it cannot be thought that Jesus covered on the

[2] Josephus, *Bellum,* II, xiv, 3: In the year 65, the Jews in Jerusalem numbered 3,000,000. — *Bellum,* VI, ix, 3: Cestius, the Governor of Syria, requested the High Priest to have the number of lambs slain for the feast counted. There were 255,600 of them; and since the eating of each lamb required a minimum of ten persons, the number reaches or even surpasses 3,000,000. *Credat Judaeus Apella.*

Sabbath day the distance of seven or eight leagues which separates Jericho from Bethany. He therefore arrived either on Friday before nightfall or on Saturday evening after the expiration of the Sabbath rest.[3] The first hypothesis is the more probable and more generally accepted. In that case, Jesus would have passed the whole of Saturday at Bethany. This minor uncertainty does not seriously affect the chronology of the Passion. It is certain that the Saviour died on Friday and that he instituted the Holy Eucharist on the day before. Similarly, it is extremely probable that he made his entrance into Jerusalem on Sunday, that he taught in the Temple on the two following days, and that he spent Wednesday in private with his Apostles.

Witnesses as they had been of the raising of Lazarus, which had happened one or two months before, the inhabitants of Bethany enthusiastically welcomed the divine Wonder-Worker and gave a lavish feast in his honor. On Saturdays the Jews partook only of foods cooked in advance and kept hot by methods described in careful detail in the Talmud.[4] It may well be that the people of Bethany, warned of the Saviour's coming, had prepared everything beforehand, or that they put off the banquet to the evening following the end of the Sabbath.[5] The repast took place in the house of Simon the Leper, a person otherwise un-

---

[3] John 12:1. Three points of uncertainty: (1) Should the *Passover* be understood as the 14th of Nisan, the day of the slaying of the Paschal lamb; or the day of the Paschal solemnity, the 15th of Nisan? (2) Was the Passover solemnized that year on Friday or Saturday? (3) Should the day of arrival and the day of departure be included or excluded (in counting the six days)?

[4] *Mishnah*, treat. *Shabbath*, Chap. IV. Cf. *Jewish Encycl.*, Vol. X, pp. 503–504.

[5] The feast was a supper (δεῖπνον, John 12:2), an evening meal. We admit that the meal described by St. John (12:1–8) is identical with that of St. Matthew (26:6–13) and St. Mark (14:3–9). The differences are slight and easy to reconcile. Besides, (*a*) *the place and the time are the same:* Bethany during the week of the Passion. St. John gives the precise date, six days before the Passover. Though the others seem to link the episode with Wednesday of Holy Week, this is simply because they wish to connect the complaints of Judas, which were the index of his venal soul, with his treason. (*b*) *The guests invited are the same.* The Synoptics say that the feast took place at the house of Simon the Leper; St. John, noting that Lazarus was one of the guests and that Martha was serving, indicates clearly enough that they are not in their own home. (*c*) *The perfume is the same.* It is genuine nard (πιστική, Mark and John). St. Mark and St. John give the same estimated value, 300 denarii. St. John adds that its weight was one pound. (*d*) *The anointing is the same.* The Synoptics mention only the

known. He may have owed his cure to Jesus, since the natural cure of leprosy, if not altogether unknown, was extremely rare. Lazarus was among the guests, which proves that the feast did not take place in his house. Martha's experience and skill had been enlisted to supervise and direct the service. Mary too was present and, if she had been overlooked in the assignment of duties, she was about to assume for herself the most honorable role of all.

They had taken their places at table in the posture then in use, the body reclining on a sloping couch covered with a mat and cushions. The left elbow supported the breast, leaving the right hand free; the bare feet almost touched the ground on the outer side. Women were not ordinarily present at banquets, and when they were, they were placed at the ends of the table. Of a sudden Martha's sister was observed entering the hall carrying one of those alabaster phials in which the ancients used to keep precious perfumes, under the impression that this material possessed the quality of preserving the aroma indefinitely.[6] Mary glided along the wall behind the guests until she came to the place where Jesus was reclining, facing the entrance. Then, instead of opening the cover of hardened wax that closed the mouth of the *alabastrum,* she broke the slender neck of the vase with a sharp blow and poured all the contents, first on the Saviour's head and then on his feet. Then — act of homage supreme — she bowed down over his adorable feet and wiped them with her abundant hair.

The witnesses of the scene looked on without too much surprise. The anointing of the head was an ordinary courtesy in the case of such a distinguished guest. The anointing of the feet was out of the ordinary, but the public sinner had already given the example, and no mark of honor seemed too great for the man who had raised Lazarus from the dead. What must have caused surprise was that all the perfume was poured out at once to the

---

anointing of the head; St. John omits it as taken for granted and mentions specially the anointing of the feet, which was unusual. (*e*) *The complaints are the same.* St. Matthew, as is his wont, attributes the grumbling to the guests as a whole. St. Mark mentions the Apostles. St. John specifies the principal culprit, Judas. (*f*) *Our Lord's answer is the same:* praise of Mary for an act which will render her famous for all time.

6 Pliny, *Hist. nat.,* xxxvi, 12, and xiii, 3.

last drop, since the vase, containing not less than a pound, would have been enough for several anointings.[7] And when the sweet and penetrating scent of the spikenard had perfumed the entire room even the least qualified judges among them understood the worth of the sacrifice offered by Mary. If they were unaware that genuine nard was imported from the Himalayan regions of India, they well knew that every part of the plant, the root, the stalk, the leaves, the corymb of flowers, and the clustered fruit, all reached a very high price; they knew, too, that liquid nard — the essence of nard — was considered the queen of perfumes.[8] There was no mistaking that this was genuine nard and not one of those fraudulent imitations placed on the market by speculators. True nard was distinguished from counterfeits by its lightness, its golden color, its agreeable taste, its delicious aroma, and, above all, by its price.[9]

The pound of liquid nard poured on the head and feet of Jesus was estimated to be worth three hundred denarii, and this estimate was in no way excessive. Three hundred denarii was the average wage of a laborer for a whole year. Philip had calculated that two hundred denarii would be enough to provide a morsel of bread for each of more than five thousand people. How much misery could have been relieved with the price of this spikenard! The onlookers were astounded at this prodigal and, in their eyes, useless expenditure. Many of them murmured in whispers, and the discontent seems to have spread even to some of the Apostles. But is was Judas who had the boldness to voice aloud what others were thinking in their hearts: "Why was this perfume not sold for three hundred denarii, which could have been distributed to the poor?" He was hiding his avarice under the mask of charity, for Judas, St. John tells us, was a thief, and since he had charge

---

[7] John 12:3. The Roman pound weighed 11.53 oz.

[8] Pliny, *Hist. nat.*, xii, 26: *Principale in unguentis.* He is speaking of Indian nard, for there were other kinds of inferior quality: Cretan, Syrian, Gallic, or Celtic nard.

[9] The Evangelists agree in saying that the nard was of great price (*βαρυτίμου*, Matthew; *πολυτελοῦς*, Mark; *πολυτιμοῦ*, John). St. Mark and St. John qualify it by a word (*πιστικῆς*) that the Vulgate translates by *pistici* (Mark) and *spicati* (John). The probable meaning of the Greek word is "authentic," "unadulterated," from *πιστός*, "faithful," "sincere." The derivation from *πίνω*, "to drink," to indicate *potable* nard, is altogether inadmissible. For other hypotheses, cf. Bernard, *Saint John,* 1928, pp. 416–417.

of the common purse, he was accustomed to abstract a part of its contents.[10] The greater the amount put into it, the greater the chance for his thievery to pass unnoticed.

Mary, still prostrate at the Saviour's feet, was little moved by these criticisms. Her conscience was tranquil; she had merely obeyed her faith and her love. But what must have been her joy to hear Jesus come to her defense! "Why molest her? The poor you have always, and you may aid them when you will. But me you have not always. She has anointed my body beforehand for burial. Amen, I say to you, wherever this gospel is preached in the whole world, what she has done for me shall be published to her praise."

The prophecy has been literally fulfilled. There is not in the whole world a Catholic house of prayer where the praise of this woman does not resound from year to year. The exploits of kings and emperors — battles won, nations subdued, cities conquered — are obliterated by all-effacing time, but Mary has today achieved immortal glory. In her praise the Church chants and will chant to the end of time the verses composed in her honor by the saintly Cardinal, Robert Bellarmine:

Mary, with kisses chaste,
Caresses the feet of God;
With tears she bathes them,
With her tresses dries them,
And anoints them with the precious nard.[11]

2. Triumphal Entry Into Jerusalem[12]

Jesus' presence at Bethany was announced in Jerusalem by

---

10 John 12:6: τὸ γλωσσόκομον ἔχων, τὰ βαλλόμενα ἐβάσταζεν. "He had the purse and he took out what was put into it." The γλωσσόκομον was, properly speaking, a casket in which were kept the reeds or tongues (γλῶσσαι) of wind instruments, and by derivation it designated a little case in which jewels or precious metals or money were kept. The word βαστάζειν means "to carry" or "carry away" (*ferre* and *auferre, portare* and *asportare*), but it is clear that only the second meaning fits in here, since it justifies the *fur erat:* he was a thief, seeing that he carried away the money. The first sense would be a truism: having the purse he carried the money.

11 Hymn at Matins, feast of St. Mary Magdalene.

12 The episode is reported by the four Evangelists (Matt. 21:1–9; Mark 11:1–10; Luke 19:28–38; John 12:12–19), with variants which will be mentioned later.

the pilgrims who had accompanied him from Jericho. And so, at the expiration of the Sabbath, the visitors flocked there, both to meet again the Master, who for several months had seemed to be keeping out of sight, and to see Lazarus, whose recent resurrection had caused such a stir. The sight of a man who had been raised from the dead was in itself more eloquent than any number of discourses, and many who had come out of curiosity returned believing. These evidences of interest and sympathy could not fail to exasperate the leaders of the priests, who felt their own credit declining in proportion as the renown of the Saviour increased. For a time they had thought of doing away with Lazarus whose nearness was an embarrassment to them, but they now understood that the much more redoubtable adversary was the man who had raised him from the grave. They were awaiting only a favorable occasion to press the attack.

The day after the Sabbath, Jesus left Bethany to repair to Jerusalem. He could travel there by either of two roads: one of them, corresponding very closely to the present route from Jericho, skirted the Mount of Olives and entered the city by the Fountain Gate; the other, which was shorter and more frequented, climbed the hill directly and then descended at a slant to lead to the northeast corner of the Temple. This was the road taken by the Saviour, accompanied by his disciples and a considerable crowd which was perceptibly increasing. Arriving midway up the eastern slope, the Saviour, as if seized by a sudden inspiration, pointed out to two of his disciples a village called Bethphage,[13] saying to them:

---

[13] Bethphage is mentioned only by the three Synoptics and only in this text. "When they drew near to Jerusalem and came to Bethphage on the Mount of Olives" (Matt. 21:1). — "When they draw near to Jerusalem and Bethphage and Bethany on the Mount of Olives" (Mark 11:1). — "When he drew near to Bethphage and Bethany on the mountain called Olivet" (Luke 19:29). It follows, (*a*) that Bethphage was situated near Bethany and near Jerusalem; (*b*) on the road or near the road from Bethany to Jerusalem; (*c*) on the slope of the Mount of Olives. According to the Talmud, Bethphage (בית פאגי = *the house of green figs*) was considered in certain cases as a suburb of Jerusalem, because, in part, the Sabbath limits of the two were common. Hence it was no farther from Jerusalem than a mile and a half or so. Compare Neubauer, *Géographie du Talmud,* 1868, p. 149. The Talmudic texts may be found in Billerbeck, *Kommentar,* Vol. I, pp. 855–856.

In 1876, a stone was accidentally unearthed adhering to the soil. It was cut into the form of a cube 3.28 ft. high, 4.26 ft. long, and 3.61 ft. wide. On the lateral faces were half-effaced paintings representing the raising of Lazarus, the

"Go to the village which is in front of you. On entering it you will see an ass which no one has yet ridden. Loose it, and bring it to me. And if anyone ask you what you are doing, answer: 'The Master has need of this animal; he will immediately send it back.'" The messengers punctually carried out their instructions, and everything happened as the Lord had predicted. On arriving at the village, they saw a foal tied near a door at a turning of the road and they started to loose it. The people who were there said to them: "Why are you loosing it?" They answered as Jesus had told them and were not molested.

St. Matthew tells us that the foal was tied near its mother, and the disciples, carrying out Jesus' orders, brought both animals, a natural precaution to make the still untamed foal more docile. The other Evangelists have omitted this detail as too insignificant to mention, but St. Matthew probably felt prompted to give it because it verifies more literally the prophecy of Zacharias. At all events, according to St. Matthew, as well as the others, it is the foal and not its mother that serves as a mount for the Saviour.

Upon the return of the messengers, a breath of enthusiasm stirred through the ever increasing multitude. Mass enthusiasm is as contagious as mass fury, and often in popular tumults the "vivas" and the cries of "death" are shouted loudly by people who do not know the reason for them. A procession was spontaneously organized. Some of them covered the foal with their garments, by way of a saddle, and made Jesus sit upon it. Others strewed their mantles under his feet along the road, or went into the field to collect armfuls of leafy branches and flowery herbage to scatter them along the route. Still others plucked the greening young sprouts from near-by palms and olive trees and waved

---

meeting of Jesus with Martha and Mary, and a group of men with a she-ass and a foal. These words of a four-line inscription may still be deciphered: BETHPHAGE . . . CUM ASINA DUCTUS AD HIEROSOLIMAM. On the same spot were found the foundations of an ancient church. The Franciscans who own the ground have erected a chapel there. It was at this place that Bethphage was localized at the time of the Crusades. This localization cannot have been far wrong, though the exact site is hard to determine. The traditional site is about ½ mile from the tomb of Lazarus, on the route leading directly from Bethany to Jerusalem by the Mount of Olives.

them in token of joyfulness, acclaiming with unanimous voice the king of peace who was making his entry into his capital:

> Hosanna to the Son of David!
> Hosanna in the highest heaven!
> Blessed be he who comes in the name of the Lord!
> Blessed be the king of Israel![14]

Ten centuries before, a procession of a different kind had been formed very near to that spot to enthrone one of Jesus' ancestors, like him a son of David. The High Priest Sadoc, assisted by the prophet Nathan, poured the holy anointing over the head of Solomon at the Fountain of Gihon at the foot of the Mount of Olives, and the new king, mounted on his father's mule, entered Jerusalem to the sound of trumpets amid triumphal chants which reverberated through the whole Valley of Cedron.[15]

Display and show are not appropriate for him whose kingdom is not of earth, and his triumph will be more modest. Certainly the robust and agile ass of the Orient, bright-eyed and proud in carriage, has little resemblance to its degraded relative of our countries, undernourished, mangy, ill-groomed, and refractory. Still, it never was a royal mount; and the prophet Zacharias emphasizes that fact:

> Rejoice greatly, O daughter of Sion;
> Shout for joy, O daughter of Jerusalem;
> Behold, thy king will come to thee, the just and victorious.
> He is humble and riding upon an ass, upon the foal of an ass.[16]

A victorious king mounted upon an ass! What a strange spectacle; what a violent contrast! To explain this anomaly the Jews

---

[14] The acclamation is taken from Psalm 117 (118):25–26. It differs a little in the four Evangelists. All have: "Hosanna! Blessed is he who comes in the name of the Lord." But St. Luke omits the Hosanna; St. John adds, "and the King of Israel"; St. Matthew says, "Hosanna to the Son of David." He ends, as does St. Mark, with, "Hosanna in the highest." St. Mark inserts in the middle the phrase: *Benedictum quod venit regnum patris nostri David.* The multitude acclaiming Jesus does not adhere to the text of the Psalm, borrowing only the well-known words which correspond to our "Viva": "Hosanna" (הושיעה נא) hoshi'annah, "save us" and "Blessed is he who comes in the name of Yahweh."

[15] 3 Kings 1:38–40. The scene takes place at Gihon, the Fountain of the Virgin.

[16] Zach. 9:9. On the Messianic applications of this text in the Rabbinical books, cf. Billerbeck, *Kommentar,* Vol. I, 842–844.

maintained that the Messias would come upon the clouds, according to the word of Daniel, if the people were worthy of him; otherwise he would come mounted upon an ass, according to the word of Zacharias. The Apostles, deafened and distracted by the clamor, did not dream at the time that one of the most manifest of the Messianic prophecies was being fulfilled before their eyes. It was only after the Resurrection that they marveled at the way God had imperceptibly directed the hands and hearts of men to execute his own designs.

Up to that time, Jesus had always slipped away from noisy manifestations of popular enthusiasm. When they had wished to make him king after the first multiplication of the loaves, he had fled into the mountains. He had laid upon the Apostles who were witnesses of his Transfiguration a command of absolute silence until the day of his victory over death, and he ordinarily laid the same injunction upon the sick whom he cured. He had revealed only gradually and with a certain mysteriousness his dignity as Messias and Son of God. But today the time has come to claim these titles aloud before the whole assembled people. The hour approaches when he will answer without any evasion to Pilate's question: "Yes, I am a king."

When he reached the crest of the hill the acclamations redoubled. The Valley of Cedron lay below like an immense amphitheater, its tiers occupied by a numberless multitude encamping there to await the Feast. This whole multitude, without very well knowing why, joined their plaudits to those of the procession. It was an astonishing spectacle. Some of the Pharisees who happened to be in the crowd could not hide their vexation. "Master," they said to Jesus, "impose silence on thy disciples." Jesus answered them: "If they should be silent, I assure you, these stones would cry aloud!" It was a figurative way of saying that the truth would shine forth in full daylight whatever the efforts to stifle it in the shade. The Apostles had done nothing to inflame the multitude; they had simply followed the course of events; even had they wished, they would have been powerless to arrest the ovation. Meantime the very children, with the imitative instinct of their age, began to play their part. Louder than the rest, they cried out: "Hosanna to the Son of David!" In vain did the Pharisees exert themselves to silence them. A complaint was made to Jesus about this clamor, which he did not seem to hear. But he answered: "Yes, I hear them. Have you never read in the Book of Psalms:

'Out of the mouths of children and sucklings
Thou hast established thy praise, to confound thy adversaries,
To silence the enemy and the envious'?"[17]

The procession was coming down the Mount of Olives on the slope directly facing the Temple. Jesus had before his eyes that magnificent edifice, one of the wonders of the world, the palaces of Herod and the Hasmoneans, and the ramparts of the city, flanked by lofty towers which seemed to defy the shock of catapults and the efforts of centuries. And now he was seen to be weeping over Jerusalem, as he had wept at the tomb of Lazarus.[18] But these were tears whose bitterness was not sweetened by any perspective of the future. And these are the plaints he was heard to utter:

"Ah, that thou hadst known, even in this day, what would have brought thee peace. A day shall come when thy enemies shall throw a rampart about thee, and surround thee and encompass thee (as in a vice), and shall beat thee to the ground, thee and thy children, and shall not leave in thee a stone upon a stone, because thou hast not known the time of thy visitation (the hour when the Lord came to offer thee grace and salvation)."

The whole city was being thrown into commotion by various movements which the Evangelists strikingly depict for us in a few lines.[19] The disciples were rejoicing and praising God; the common people in general were testifying their joy and heartily joining in the spontaneous ovation; the priests were uneasily wondering how it would all end; the Pharisees were seething with rage, and were testily saying: "All our efforts are in vain. Behold the entire world is running after him."[20] The

---

17 Matt. 21:14–16. The answer of Jesus is taken from Ps. 8:3.

18 Luke 19:41–44. "The Lord wept (ἔκλαυσεν) over Jerusalem." Κλαίειν is "to weep over" (a death), "to lament"; thence κλαῦμα, "lamentation." On the contrary, as St. John says, for Lazarus "he shed tears" (ἐδάκρυσεν), John 11:35. There is more than a shade of difference.

19 Feelings of the disciples (Luke 19:37), of the common people (John 12:18), of the priests and Levites (Matt. 21:15).

20 John 12:19. "The Pharisees said to themselves (πρὸς ἑαυτούς, i.e., *to one*

situation was becoming clear to them. There could be no more temporizing: the least delay could compromise everything.

The crowd was too noisy and too turbulent for Jesus to break in with a discourse. This was impossible at the moment. Besides, the day was waning and it was time to think of retirement. The Saviour considered attentively all that was happening around him, as if planning his campaign of the next two days. Then he went forth with the Twelve to retire to Bethany, where they spent the night.[21]

---

another): 'You see well that you come to nought' (*οὐκ ὠφελεῖτε οὐδέν*, i.e., *you are useful for nothing*)." One would say that the more ardent are chiding the lukewarm.

[21] Mark 11:11. "He entered into Jerusalem, into the Temple: and having examined all things, since it was now late, he went out with the Twelve to return to Bethany." Very important details for the harmonizing of the Gospels.

CHAPTER II

Monday of Holy Week. Rejection of the Jewish People

1. The Cursing of the Fig Tree

ON MONDAY morning Jesus returned very early to the Temple. Since yesterday had been for him a day of great fatigue and he had left Bethany fasting, he felt the pangs of hunger on the way. It was not a feigned hunger, nor yet a miraculous one exactly timed to serve as a setting for the scene which was to follow, as some commentators would like to believe. The Saviour, having taken to himself a nature like to ours, assumes also its feebleness, its infirmities, and its needs.

Some distance from the road was seen a premature fig tree, already covered with thick foliage. Jesus went up to it to see if it had any fruit, but he found upon it only leaves. It could not have been otherwise, for, as St. Mark says, "it was not the season for figs." Still, the Saviour cursed the barren tree. "May no one ever eat fruit of thee henceforward forever."

This story of the Evangelists astonishes the reader, scandalizes the critics, and embarrasses the exegetes. Even abstracting from his divine and his infused knowledge, Jesus knew very well — what no Palestinian peasant was ignorant of — that premature fig trees never bear fruit in Jerusalem before June; that autumn figs, if they happen to stay on the branches throughout the winter, always fall off before the first sprouts of springtime, and that if a few have by chance clung to the tree, they would be no longer edible at the end of March or the beginning of April. What, then, is the meaning of this gesture of the Saviour, seeking fruit where he knows beforehand with certainty that he will find none? What sense is there in the curse pronounced against an irrational and nonresponsible creature?

Our Lord's gesture is an acted allegory. The Old Testament prophets and even the New Testament offer us several like it. When the Apostles saw him approaching the solitary tree on which he had no hope of finding fruit to appease his hunger, they should have understood that this useless attempt had something mysterious about it. But when they heard him complain against the barren fig tree, as if it were responsible for its own unfruitfulness and were bound to give fruit at a time when other trees could not produce, they had no doubt that his action was symbolic. For people used to the language of the parables, the meaning was easy to divine, and it is to be noted that, in this instance, the Apostles did not ask for an explanation. What moral lesson is to be drawn from this allegorical action? It is that the entire life of man in the service of God is the fruit-bearing season, and that the sovereign Master can demand the fruit at any time. What he demands of us are not good intentions, symbolized by the foliage, nor good desires only, of which the flowers would be the emblem, but the tasty fruit of good actions and good works. Woe to the man whom the Master will find lacking these at the time of his visitation! For him there will be neither merciful reprieve nor delay in execution. The sentence of condemnation, straightway followed by eternal death, will be the price of his lack of foresight.

This the Apostles understood immediately. But when in the course of this day and the next they heard the Saviour announce the rejection of Israel, linking that rejection with the hypocrisy and false virtue of the spiritual guides and responsible heads of the nation; when in the parable of the Wicked Vinedressers, he showed them the representatives of the chosen people obstinately refusing fruit to the Master of the vineyard, they understood that the allegory had been intended to go much farther, and that the accursed fig tree, concealing its real barrenness under the deceptive promise of luxuriant foliage, was the symbol of rejected Judaism.

The cursed fig tree withered away on the spot, but the Apostles, passing that same way again at a late hour, did not notice it.

They remarked it early on the following day, and they were surprised, since they did not expect a miracle of that kind. "Master," cried St. Peter, "behold, the fig tree that thou didst curse is withered up." Without replying to this artless observation, Jesus made to the Twelve a promise of miraculous power still more astonishing. "Have faith in God. Amen, I say to you, if anyone full of firm and lively faith unhesitatingly commands this mountain to rise and cast itself into the sea, it shall be done." With an accompanying gesture he indicated the Mount of Olives whose summit hid from view the city of Jerusalem, and the Dead Sea stretched out in the distance, at a depth of almost 4000 feet. And then he added: "All that you ask for in your prayers, if you have faith, you shall receive." Jesus has just been speaking of a special faith, the "faith of miracles," able to move mountains. Now he is speaking of the confidence which must accompany every prayer well said, to assure its effectiveness, on condition, of course, that the prayer tends to God's glory and the spiritual good of him who prays.[1]

2. The Buyers and Sellers Expelled From the Temple

Since Jesus is to spend the last two days of his public ministry in the Temple, it will not be inappropriate to give a brief description of that edifice.

The Temple of the true God, which the Mosque of Omar has replaced, was erected in the middle of a vast esplanade, much greater in area than the Acropolis of Athens or the Capitol of Rome or the sacred wood of Olympus; greater even than our Place de la Concorde.[2] The threshing floor of Ornan, bought by

---

[1] Matt. 21:18–22; Mark 11:12–14 and 11:20–24. St. Mark's account is more circumstantial and more picturesque. According to St. Matthew, the cursed fig tree withers immediately, and the impression is given that the disciples make their remark at the same time. St. Mark tells us that this happened on the following day.

The fig tree bears twice a year. The first fruit, the fig flowers, appears at the end of March, always before the leaves, at the ends of the sprouts of the preceding year. It ripens in June or toward the end of May. The new sprouts then produce fruit that begins to ripen in August or September. This fruit can stay on the tree until the winter, since the ripening is gradual. That *edible* fruit should remain until March would be miraculous. The naturalist Post, who lived in Syria more than thirty years and who paid special attention to this point, had never heard of such a thing happening (Hastings, *Dict. of the Bible,* II, 6).

[2] The present esplanade is a rectangle, or rather, a trapezoid. The longer sides

David to serve as the base of the future Temple, was not one-fiftieth part of it. It was enlarged by the enormous substructions to which the names of Solomon and Herod were always attached, but which, in reality, were the work of centuries. The basements of the Temple thus erected resembled at a distance a mountain of rock pierced within by a multiplicity of galleries, conduits, sewers, and cisterns, making up an inextricable labyrinth. Nowadays the total effect is much less imposing, because the retaining walls have crumbled under masses of ruins. In some places it is necessary to dig down ninety feet or even more to reach the first layer fitted into the rock.[3]

From whatever direction the Temple was approached, except from the north, where there was no entrance open to the public, it was necessary to *go up* to the Temple. It was reached either by long and wide staircases, or by viaducts spanning the Tyropoeon Valley, or by gently sloping avenues leading to the middle of the courts. On arriving there, one was dazzled by the multicolored flagstones and, above all, by the interminable files of Corinthian columns surrounding the immense platform on all four sides. The Royal Porch on the south, with its four rows of one hundred and sixty-two monolith columns, so great in

measure: on the west 1608 ft., and on the east 1555 ft.; the smaller sides: on the north 1050 ft., on the south 928 ft. Hence a perimeter of some 5141 ft., for exact measurements are hard to obtain. We believe that in the time of Christ the area was less, since the Antonia extended farther south than is allowed for in these measurements, and the northeast corner did not then belong to the Temple area. The northeast limit was, in our opinion, a wide moat, now fallen to pieces, which extended east and west, a little to the north of what is called the Golden Gate.

We have a treatise of the Mishnah entitled *Middoth* (*Measurements*) on the dimensions of the various parts of the Temple and two long descriptions by Josephus (*Antiq.*, XV, xi and *Bell.*, V, v). Despite that, there remain several points of obscurity. The Mishnah often refers to the ideal Temple of Ezechiel, citing it five times and having it in view elsewhere without citing it. With Ezechiel, it makes the outer courts a square of 500 cubits, the cubit probably being that of seven palms (20.67 in.) rather than six palms (18.90 in.). On the other hand, Josephus often gives his measurements at a guess. For him the entire area of the Temple of Herod was a rectangle two stadia in length (641 ft.) by one in width (607 ft.). This last measurement is plainly too small, referring to the south side which extended from one valley to the other, and at the time of Herod, as now, this side was 328 ft. more than that.

[3] At the southeast corner the wall is 155 ft. high, of which 79 ft. are below the soil. At the northeast corner it was necessary to dig down 118 ft. below the present level to reach the base of the wall.

circumference that three men with arms outstretched could scarcely encompass the shaft, gave the impression of the most monumental of basilicas.[4] The ceiling was of carved cedar and lavishly covered with ornamentation in silver and gold.

Everyone, without distinction of race or religion, had free access to the outer courts, but only Israelites and circumcised proselytes could enter the Sanctuary itself. This was encompassed by an elegant balustrade upon which at regular intervals were placed inscriptions in Greek and Latin forbidding strangers to go beyond it under penalty of death.[5] Beyond the balustrade a stairway of fourteen steps led to a landing on which was built the wall of the sacred enclosure. This was a lofty structure of great stones polished like marble, its monotony relieved by nine richly decorated gates. The principal entrance for both men and women was at the east, toward the Mount of Olives. This was the Beautiful Gate, or Gate of Nicanor, celebrated for its facing of Corinthian brass.

The various parts of the Temple reserved to Jews mounted one above another in elevation. From the Court of the Gentiles an ascent was made to reach the Women's Court, and again to reach the Court of Israel. The Court of the Priests, the altar of sacrifice, and the Sanctuary properly so called were on still higher levels. The Jews must have drawn their inspiration from the Greek architects, whose temples, rising from a flat coping as from a pedestal, reached up solitary into the blue of heaven, giving the impression of greater height than they really had, whereas our churches, with their entrances on the ground level, are often overwhelmed by high neighboring buildings.

The dimensions of the Sanctuary properly so called were fixed by immutable tradition. The Holy of Holies, which the High Priest entered once a year, measured only 20 cubits (about 36 feet) square. The Holy Place, where stood the golden candelabrum, the Altar of Incense, and the table for the showbread,

---

[4] Josephus, *Antiq.*, XV, xi, 5. A monolith column left in the stoneyard, perhaps because of some defect in the stone, shows that Josephus is not exaggerating (photograph in the *Jewish Encyc.*, XII, 89).

[5] One of these inscriptions, discovered by Clermont-Ganneau, is in the Museum of Constantinople. It reads in Greek: "Let no stranger enter within the balustrade surrounding the holy place. Whoever is caught there must attribute solely to himself his death which will ensue."

was the same as the Holy of Holies in width but twice as long. These dimensions would have been out of proportion to the rest of the edifice had not this disharmony been remedied by raising the height of these buildings and by enclosing the Holy Place and the Holy of Holies in a group of much more stately constructions. In front of the Sanctuary properly so called stood a monumental pylon, a sort of triumphal arch 100 cubits in height and the same in width. Through the opening of this pylon the faithful could see the veil that covered the entrance to the Sanctuary, and on its pediment the decoration of the famous golden vine.

On Monday morning, when Jesus arrived, he found the outer courts of the Temple invaded by a noisy crowd of merchants and money-changers. They had not forgotten that he had expelled them two years before, at the time of the first Passover of his public life. But nothing is harder to extirpate than an abuse, especially when the powers who ought to suppress it have become accomplices. With the connivance of the priests interested in this unbecoming traffic, the vendors of pigeons had again piled up their cages under the porticoes, and the money-changers had reinstalled the little tables behind which they carried on their lucrative trade. Perhaps, too, the lambs and young bulls were defiling the sacred precincts as before. The approaches of the Temple had again assumed the appearance of an Oriental bazaar with its uproar and clamor and disputes.

Jesus pushed these sacrilegious traffickers before him, overturning with his foot the desks of the money-changers, upsetting the piled-up cages of the dove vendors, and turning back the people who were crossing the courts with their burdens to make a short cut. No one dared to resist him, such was his flashing look of indignation, and such their consciousness that all the people were on his side. Finally, to justify his action, he addressed himself to the principal culprits, the heads of the priesthood, who were favoring the profanation of the holy place where they were in duty bound to keep order and decorum. "Is it not written: My house shall be called a house of prayer for all the nations? And you have made it a den of thieves."[6]

---

[6] Matt. 21:12–13; Mark 11:15–17; Luke 19:45–46. If only St. Matthew and St. Luke are read, it could be thought that the expulsion of the vendors took

Struck dumb by such boldness, the leaders of the priests, upon whom was incumbent the duty of policing the Temple, said nothing at the time. But the next day, surrounding themselves with Scribes and notables to give greater weight to their censure, they came and demanded of him by virtue of what authority he had done this, and who had given him the power thus to act. Yesterday the attitude of the people had kept them respectful; today, strong in the support of the Scribes and Pharisees, they speak up with assurance. Still, they assume a pretense of calmness, as people sure of their rights. They want to know why this lay person, this stranger, this Galilean, interferes in their office and usurps their functions.

"I also," said Jesus, "will ask you one question, and if you answer me this, I in turn will tell you by what authority I do these things. Whence was the baptism of John? From heaven, or from men?" The members of the Sanhedrin must take sides. If they admit the divine mission of the Baptist, Jesus will be sure to say to them: "Why, then, did you not believe him?" If they claim that the baptism of John was a purely human institution, all the people, who regarded John as a prophet, will turn against them. Irresolute and nonplused, they finally answered that they did not know. "Well then," said Jesus, "neither do I tell you by what authority I do these things" that you reproach me for. It is probable that the question of the priests regarded not solely the expulsion of the vendors from the Temple, but the solemn entry into Jerusalem as well, together with the incidents which had signalized it. During these two days, Jesus had clearly affirmed his office of Messias, and the acclamations of the populace had aroused the fears of his enemies and had revived their hatred.

---

place on the same day as the triumphal entry; but St. Mark informs us that it was on the following day. The text cited by Jesus to justify his action is a composite borrowed partly from Isa. 56:7, and partly from Jer. 7:11.

The majority of Catholic authors and many Protestants (Godet, Plummer, etc.) are of the opinion that the expulsion recorded by St. John (2:13–16) on the occasion of the first Passover is different from that which the Synoptics report here. The different versions can be reconciled; and it may be said that the Synoptics were forced to insert the episode here if they saw fit to preserve it, since they record only one Passover. Still, the identification of the two seems to be somewhat forced. It cannot be objected that an episode of this kind could happen only once, or that the first expulsion would have been enough to end the abuse. On the contrary, inveterate abuses are almost ineradicable.

We shall see the reverberations which the triumphal entry was causing in men's minds.

3. The Greeks Wish to See Jesus[7]

Among the strangers present in Jerusalem at this time were some Gentiles who professed monotheism and frequented the synagogue. While not assuming the entire burden of the Mosaic Law, they accepted certain of its practices, such as prayer, almsgiving, the Sabbath rest, and the annual pilgrimages. Inasmuch as they had not submitted to circumcision, they were forbidden access to the Sanctuary, but they freely circulated, like all the rest, in the outer courts of the Temple, and everyone admitted that they had the right to offer sacrifices, at least holocausts, on the altar of the true God.

Some among these half proselytes, noting the reception given to Jesus on Palm Sunday, and knowing by hearsay of the miracles which he had wrought, were keenly desirous of meeting him and conversing with him. Hence they begged the Apostle Philip to arrange an introduction. Why Philip rather than one of the others? Perhaps, simply because they had met him before or because they knew him personally or because Philip, whose name is Greek, spoke their language. They said to him: "We wish to see Jesus." If there was question merely of seeing him, all they had to do was to open their eyes; but they wanted to hear him, to observe him at their ease and close at hand, and doubtless also to ask him questions. Their unexpected request perplexed Philip. Rather timid by nature, he remembered that the Master, on sending them out to preach, had commanded them not to turn aside to the Gentiles, and he wondered whether the petition of these strangers would be favorably received. In his perplexity Philip consulted Andrew, the man of experience and good counsel,

---

[7] John 12:20–36. The episode of the Gentiles, together with the incidents associated with it, is related by St. John immediately after the triumphal entry into Jerusalem. But we know from St. Mark (11:11) that Jesus did not linger in the Temple that evening, because of the advanced hour, and it is evident that the whole ending of this chapter is a summary of the last preaching of Jesus, when he takes leave of the multitude (12:36): "Having said these things, he went away and withdrew from their sight."

whose age and the fact that he had been the first to follow in Jesus' footsteps gave him great authority in the Apostolic group. Andrew calmed his scruples, and they went together to expose to Jesus the wish of the Gentiles.

We do not know the result of their venture. We like to believe that it was crowned with full success. Jesus never repulsed anyone. He affably gave instruction to the Samaritan woman; he heard the prayer of the Centurion and praised his faith; he did not resist the repeated request of the Chanaanite woman; he cured the Samaritan leper and received affably his expressions of gratitude. True, he does not present himself to the Gentiles, for their hour has not yet come; but why should he turn his back on them? There is, however, no further reference to these Gentiles who wished to see him, and it is not to them, but to Andrew and Philip, that the Saviour's answer is addressed:

"The hour has come for the Son of Man to be glorified. Amen, amen, I say to you, unless the grain of wheat fall into the ground and die, it remains alone (and without fruit). But if it die, it brings forth much fruit.

"He who loves his life loses it; and he who hates his life in this world keeps it unto eternity.

"If anyone serve me, let him follow me; and where I am, there also shall my servant be, and my Father will honor him."[8]

The apparently disparate and unconnected sentences find their unity in the idea of meritorious and fruitful sacrifice. It is through the Passion and death that God proposes to glorify his Son; and the hour of his death is so near at hand that it may be said to have come already. In the plan of divine Providence, as St. John and St. Paul have exposed it to us, the redeeming death is a principle of life and a seed of glory for Christ and for us, as the death of the grain of wheat is a condition of its fecundity. Without the redeeming death there is no Resurrection; without the Resurrection, no sending of the Holy Ghost, no Mystical Body of Christ. If the blood of martyrs is the seed of the elect, the blood of Christ opens heaven to millions of souls. But to be meritorious, the sacrifice must be voluntary; the merit of Christ is in his obedience; it is because he was obedient to death that

---

[8] John 12:23–26.

God has exalted him. So too will those be exalted who serve him and serve their brethren. Imitating his obedience, they will share his glory and will be with him always.

Here Jesus pauses for a moment. All the horror of the Passion, the treason of Judas, the agony in the garden, the abandonment by the Apostles, the ascent of Calvary, the immobility of the Cross, passes before his mind: a sorrow-filled drama which moves his heart. And then he is heard to pronounce these words as if speaking to himself:

"Now my soul is troubled, and what shall I say? Father, save me from this hour? But (no, for) it is just for this that I have come. Father, glorify thy name!"[9]

This anguish of Jesus should surprise us no more than his agony; but it would be very shortsighted psychology that would present the two scenes as comparable. The situations are entirely different. The feelings of the soldier on the eve of battle, in the midst of his comrades, are not the same as at the moment when, alone on the field of carnage, at a post which he cannot quit, he sees the rain of fire and steel beat down upon him. In Gethsemani, facing the frightful reality, and feeling himself abandoned by all, Jesus says to his Father: "If it is possible, let this chalice pass away from me. Yet not my will but thine be done." In the Temple, when the prospect is remoter, this conditional prayer comes to his mind only to be immediately put aside. "Shall I say: 'Father, save me from this hour'? But (no, for) it is just for this that I have come. Father, glorify thy name."

And then from the heights of heaven a voice resounded: "I have both glorified it (that name), and I will glorify it again."

---

[9] Commentators, Catholic and Protestant, are divided on the punctuation of the sentence. Some, with the Vulgate, put only one interrogation point: "Nunc turbata est anima mea. Et quid dicam? Pater, salvifica me ex hac hora." Others, with St. John Chrysostom, put two: "What shall I say? Father, save me from this hour?" We prefer the latter, which harmonizes better with what precedes and what follows. If Jesus wished to make to the Father an absolute petition (Save me), he would not have deliberated (What shall I say?). On the other hand, what he adds explains why he will not make this petition. Those who hold the opposite opinion are forced to say that he makes the petition but immediately withdraws it. At all events, no basis for this view can be found in the prayer in Gethsemani, which, being conditional, had no need of being withdrawn.

Some of those present, hearing the voice without distinguishing the words — as had happened to many of the witnesses of Jesus' baptism, and would happen again to Paul's companions on the Damascus road — thought that it was the sound of thunder. Others thought that an angel had spoken to him. But it was God promising to glorify his own name in glorifying his Son, for the glory of the Son necessarily redounds to the Father. Even to those who had not caught its meaning, the voice from heaven was a testimony in favor of Jesus.[10] He could say to them: "Not for me did this voice come, but for you. . . . Now is the judgment of the world; now will the prince of the world be cast out. And I, when I shall be lifted up from the earth, will draw all men to myself." He was alluding, as the Evangelist tells us, to the kind of death he was to die.

The lifting up upon the cross, supreme ignominy, will be for the Son of Man the beginning of his glorification here below. From the height of his gibbet, he will draw all the world to himself. But the Jews know nothing of such language, and for them it is an enigma. "We know from the Scripture that the Christ abides forever. And how canst thou say, 'The Son of Man must be lifted up'? Who is this Son of Man?" Manifestly the title "Son of Man" is unfamiliar to them. And yet they should have known that Jesus appropriated it to himself as king, and savior, and judge, for he had very clearly explained it before. Today he is content to answer:

"Yet a little while the light is among you. Walk in the light, that darkness may not overtake you. He who walks in the darkness does not know where he goes. While you have the light, believe in the light, that you may be sons of light."[11]

---

[10] The voice from heaven is heard at the baptism of Christ (Mark 1:11), at the Transfiguration (Mark 9:7), on the eve of the Passion (John 12:28), speaking to Peter (Acts 11:7), and speaking to John (Apoc. 10:4). This voice from heaven has no affinity with the *bath qol* (daughter of the voice) of the Rabbis, which was a sort of oracular utterance sent from heaven to decide doubtful cases, and to take the place of the prophetical spirit, of which Israel was no longer worthy. Cf. Weber, *Jüd. Theologie,* 2 ed., p. 190.

[11] John 12:31–36. The Cross is the principle of the Saviour's glorification for two reasons: because it overturns the empire of Satan "the prince of this world," and because it is the pedestal from which the Word Incarnate, the work of Redemption completed, raises himself to the Father to sit at his right hand. The expression employed by Jesus: "When I am lifted up from the earth"

Such was his word of farewell. "These things Jesus spoke and he went away and hid himself from them." In these words St. John closes the apostolic career of the Saviour, before embarking upon the story of the Passion. The other Evangelists add to this history a final page, the tragic struggle of the Tuesday of Holy Week.

(*above the earth, far from the earth,* ἐκ τῆς γῆς), carries the twofold meaning of elevation upon the cross and departure from the earth. The Jews understood it in the second way, and this explains their objection: "The Messianic kingdom of the Son of David lasts forever, according to the Scripture (Isa. 9:7; Dan. 7:13; 2 Kings 7:16, etc.); how then can he go far from the earth?" The Jews of course suspected that the title "Son of Man" in the mouth of Christ was equivalent to "Messias," but Jesus in the whole passage had not designated himself by the title "Son of Man." This seems to indicate that the dialogue is given in abridged form by St. John.

CHAPTER III

Tuesday of Holy Week. Conspiracy of the Enemy

1. Herodians, Sadducees, Pharisees

EARLY as Jesus had risen, on his return from Bethany the crowd had forestalled him, for, as St. Luke says, "everyone rose at dawn and ran to the Temple to hear him."[1] As the mornings are quite cold in Jerusalem near the spring equinox, he walked back and forth under the porticoes while he taught the people.

His enemies were not sleeping. When they had demanded of him his title to set himself up as a reformer, he had baffled their guile by proposing to them a question to which they had no answer. But they were not admitting defeat: they were preparing a new offensive. It was the Pharisees who opened the attack. First of all they put their auxiliary troops on the march, their allies of recent date, the Herodians, mixed in with some of their secret disciples who would inspire no mistrust.

The Herodians were not a religious sect but a political party. They were supporters of the dynasty of the Herods, perhaps courtiers of Herod Antipas who was in Jerusalem at the time. At bottom, they loved the Romans no more than did other Jews; but knowing well that open resistance would only prejudice their situation, they bowed to facts and openly proclaimed loyalty, seeking to ingratiate themselves with the Emperor, from whom they hoped some day to obtain complete autonomy. For a brief moment their hopes will be realized under Caligula and Claudius,

[1] Luke 21:38: "Omnis populus manicabat ad eum in templo audire eum."

only to decline again under the yoke of the Procurators. Did they look upon the movement started by Jesus as a fantasy, dangerous in itself, and prejudicial to their plans; or did they see in him a pretender to the throne of Herod? At any rate, they were opposed to him from the beginning of his preaching;[2] and today they enter with full zest into the conspiracy of the Pharisees and Sadducees and undertake to set the first trap.

"Master," they said, "we know that thou art truthful and sincere, and teachest the way of God in truth, and that thou carest nought for any man; for thou dost not regard the person of men. Tell us, therefore, what dost thou think: Is it lawful to give tribute to Caesar or not?" The question, polite in form and presented with an air of candor, was a very insidious one. It must be answered without evasion, yes or no, and in either case the reply was sure to alienate part of Jesus' audience. By saying yes, he would, in the opinion of the people dreaming of a national liberator, renounce his claim to be the Messias. By saying no, he would, from the viewpoint of the Romans, be calling for revolt, and that would be the crime of *laesa maiestas*. The Pharisees were hoping for a negative answer; for their intention was to denounce him to the Roman authorities and to turn him over to the Procurator as guilty of conspiracy. Divining their malice, Jesus said to them: "Why do you tempt me, you hypocrites? Show me the coin of the tribute." They handed him a denarius. It was in official Roman denarii that the Romans demanded payment of taxes; other coins were accepted only at a discount. Now, the Roman denarius always bore the image and name and titles of the reigning Emperor. This fact explains the Saviour's question and their answer. "Whose is this image and inscription?" They answer: "Caesar's." And Jesus said: "Render, therefore, to Caesar the things that are Caesar's, and to God the things that are God's." From the moment that the Jews make use of this money, they recognize Caesar as the *de facto* sovereign. What comes from Caesar must return to Caesar. Jesus does not say: "You must obey God *or* man; there is no middle course"; but: "You must obey God *and* man; there

[2] Mark 3:6. After a cure wrought by Jesus on the Sabbath, "the Pharisees took counsel with the Herodians how they might do away with him."

is no conflict." Both authorities are legitimate, each in its own sphere. If human authority does not encroach upon the rights of God, there will never be a conflict. Taken aback by this answer of wisdom and a bit confused at the imprudent venture to which they had lent themselves, his assailants beat a retreat.[3]

Seeing the Herodians discomfited, the Pharisees sent the Sadducees to the rescue, reserving to themselves the final charge. The Sadducees were a religious sect and at the same time a political party. Almost all of them belonged to the priesthood, whereas the Pharisees were recruited from all classes of society. Holding the highest posts and desirous of retaining them, the Sadducees were supporters of the established order. To them the Pharisees were suspect as democrats, and the Zealots, as revolutionaries. Not without reason, the Sadducees were accused of rationalism; for while they professed faith in the one true God, their God, like the God of the Epicureans, remained indifferent to things here below. They denied divine Providence, the future life, the immortality of the soul, and, *a fortiori,* the resurrection of the body. The question they are about to ask takes its inspiration from their teaching.

Among the Jews, when a man died childless, his brother living in the same place was bound to espouse the widow in order to perpetuate the name and lineage of the deceased. The Sadducees propose a question rising from this law, which was called the Levirate. Seven brothers successively espouse the same woman and all die without children. To whom will the woman belong on the day of the resurrection? It was one of those fanciful questions which intrigued the subtlety of the Rabbis. Cases more ridiculous than this can be found in the Talmud.[4] To the Sadducees this

[3] Matt. 22:15–22; Mark 12:12–17; Luke 20:20–26. The three accounts differ very little. It is the Pharisees who start the attack (Matthew); they enlist the services of the Herodians but join to them some of their own disciples, as though not sure of the auxiliary troops (Matthew and Mark). The assailants, animated by treacherous intentions (Matthew, Mark, Luke), affect an air of innocence (Luke 20:20); on hearing the answer of Jesus, they are struck with admiration (Matthew, Mark, and Luke) and keep silent (Luke).

[4] Matt. 22:23–33; Mark 12:18–27; Luke 20:27–39. A more ridiculous case is the following: thirteen brothers were married; twelve of them died childless. What must the surviving husband do? Should he espouse the twelve widows? See solution in Billerbeck, *Kommentar,* Vol. III, p. 650.

argument against the resurrection appeared unanswerable, and they were curious to see how Jesus would extricate himself from it. The seven successive husbands all had the same rights over the wife, and it was impossible for her to belong to all seven of them at the same time.

"You are altogether mistaken," the Saviour replied to them. "You understand neither the Scriptures nor the power of God. In the day of the resurrection there will be neither marriage nor espousals. The risen are to be like the angels of God in heaven. (They will change neither their nature nor their sex, but there will be no carnal commerce.) As to the resurrection, have you not heard what God said to Moses: I am the God of Abraham, the God of Isaac, and the God of Jacob? God is not the God of the dead, but of the living."

Punctilious minds, habituated to the subtleties of the schools, might object that God could be the God of Abraham even though Abraham were not still living, at least living the life of the body, and that there is no necessary connection between the immortality of the soul and the resurrection of the body. Jesus could easily have found in the prophets more convincing texts.[5] But the Sadducees could have declined to accept them, since they regarded the authority of Moses as the sole foundation of dogmatic and moral teaching. Besides, they denied the resurrection solely because they denied the immortality of the soul and the providence of God. Now, the text quoted by Jesus proved both. God concluded with Abraham an eternal alliance confirmed by oath. Being good, faithful, and just, he never abandons those who have known, loved, and served him. He is not only the God of Abraham's soul, but of his whole person, and will always be such. Sooner or later, the body of Abraham will share in his reward as it shared in his merits. Thus the principle of retribution comes to the same conclusion which faith, in accord with reason and religious feeling, teaches us.

All the people applauded this manner of speaking. Even some Scribes could not keep from admitting that the Master had spoken well, while the discountenanced Sadducees found nothing to reply.

The Pharisees, seeing that Jesus had closed the mouths of their

---

[5] For example Isa. 26:19; Dan. 12:2.

allies whose clumsy attack had just ended in failure, now gathered to deliver the final assault. A Scribe versed in the knowledge of the Scriptures makes himself their spokesman, but with such moderation that he falls short of their purpose. "Master," he says, "which is the great commandment in the Law?" In the 613 articles of the Mosaic code the Rabbis made a distinction between *heavy* precepts and *light* precepts, and they established in each a certain hierarchy which was a subject of discussion. Jesus does not enter into such controversies. He contents himself with referring his questioner to the Jewish profession of faith, written on his phylactery and which he was bound to recite at least twice daily: "Thou shalt love the Lord thy God with thy whole heart, and with thy whole soul, and with thy whole mind, and with thy whole strength. This is the greatest and first commandment. And the second is like to it: Thou shalt love thy neighbor as thyself. On these two commandments depend the whole Law and the Prophets."

The Scribe, whose intentions had not at first been altogether pure, declares himself fully satisfied: "Well answered, Master, thou hast spoken the truth. God is one and there is no other God but he. He should be loved with the whole heart, and with the whole understanding, and with the whole soul, and with one's whole strength. To love one's neighbor as oneself is more excellent than all holocausts and sacrifices." In this language there is still some self-sufficiency and a slight suspicion of patronage. Despite this, the Scribe had spoken sensibly, and Jesus congratulates him for it: "Thou art not far from the kingdom of God."[6]

---

[6] Matt. 22:34–40; Mark 12:28–34; cf. Luke 10:25–28, in different circumstances. The difference in attitude of the Scribe in the three Synoptics is very worthy of note. In St. Matthew, as also in St. Luke, he *tempts* (*πειράζων*); in St. Mark he proposes a question, "seeing that Jesus had answered the Sadducees well"; and St. Mark's addition is all in praise of him (Mark 12:32–34). The answer ordinarily given is that the Scribe, animated at first by bad intentions, changed his attitude on hearing Jesus' answer. It is better to say that *πειράζειν* has not always the depreciatory meaning of *tempt;* it also means to *make trial of*. The Scribe, hearing Jesus' answer to the Sadducees, wants to sound him out, to see what side to take. The Saviour's answer satisfies him and then they are in agreement. This implies at first an imperfect but not necessarily evil disposition.

The Jewish profession of faith (Deut. 6:4–9: "Hear Israel, the Lord thy God is one," etc.) contains only the precept of love of God. The precept of love of

The Pharisees had chosen their man badly. They had thought to embarrass the Saviour by having him questioned by a disciple who would arouse no suspicion. Caught in their own trap, they abandoned the fray.

In his turn Jesus now takes the offensive. Since they ask no more questions, he goes on to ask a question himself. The Messias promised by the prophets and expected by the Jews, is he not the son of David? How is it, then, that David, under God's inspiration, calls him his Lord, according to what is written in the Book of Psalms: "'The Lord said to my Lord: Sit thou at my right hand, till I place all thy enemies as a stool beneath thy feet.' David himself, therefore, calls him his Lord: how is he his son?"[7]

The Scribes and Pharisees did not know what to answer. They never doubted that the text concerned the Messias. In no other text of the Bible is the Messianic sense more manifest. No other is oftener cited in the New Testament, no other was more confidently exploited by Christian apologists: the Church has taken from it one of the articles of the Creed. It is like an abridged Christology: the Person and the function of Christ, his eternal generation, his victory over all his enemies, his priesthood according to the order of Melchisedech, his office of universal judge, his endless reign at the right hand of the Father, are

---

neighbor is, indeed, formulated in Leviticus (19:18), but the Jews understood by "neighbor" a friend, one close to them, a compatriot. Still, Philo combines the two precepts when he writes *man* instead of *neighbor* (*De Septenario,* Mangey, II, 282): "Of the two principal precepts one regards God (who must be honored) by piety and holiness; the other concerns men (who must be treated) with humanity and justice." But Jesus was the first to give to the word "neighbor" its true value, and to make the love of God and of neighbor two phases of the same precept.

[7] Matt. 22:41–46; Mark 12:35–37; Luke 20:41–44. Psalm 110 (Vulgate, 109) is cited more than fifteen times in the New Testament (cf. Dittmar, *Vetus Testamentum in Novo,* Göttingen, 1903, pp. 51–52, 243–244, and 338), above all in the Epistle to the Hebrews. It is evident that this psalm was then universally regarded as Messianic, and as the work of David. Neither Jesus nor the Apostle supposes that these two points can be contested by the Jews. Still, we must wait until the middle of the third century to find the Talmud actually applying the psalm to the Messias. St. Justin's antagonist (*Dial c. Tryph.,* 33) maintains that the reference is to Ezechias, but this eccentric opinion is found nowhere else. The Rabbis of the first two centuries after the Passion say that the subject of the psalm is Abraham or David himself. See Billerbeck, Vol. IV, pp. 452–465.

described in terms which very patently do not fit a mere mortal. By citing this text, the Saviour silences his adversaries; on the day of Pentecost, St. Peter quotes it to the assembled multitude as a decisive proof of the Resurrection of Christ; the Epistle to the Hebrews employs it without fear of contradiction to prove the cessation of the Levitical priesthood. But when St. Justin, in the second century, wishes to use it against the Jews, he is surprised to hear his antagonist answer that the psalm was about King Ezechias!

What had happened in the interval? Something quite natural. When the Jews perceived that the Christians were turning the words of the psalm victoriously against them, they ceased to apply it to the Messias. The conspiracy of silence, easy to organize in a Judaism reduced to a school of thought, lasted for almost two centuries.

2. The Parables of Rejection

Pharisees and Sadducees, Herodians and doctors of the law, priests and notables, the whole Jewish aristocracy and the whole ruling class are now in coalition against the Saviour. The people in general still remain favorable, but they are changeable and fickle; they look on and remain inactive; their platonic sympathy is incapable of action and resistance. Thus the Jewish nation as a whole is ripe for rejection. Jesus announces this to them in three parables tending to the same conclusion: the Two Sons, whose actions belie their words; the Wicked Vinedressers; and the recalcitrant guests invited to the Marriage Feast. The first is addressed to the members of the Sanhedrin who had declined to say whether the baptism of John was from heaven or from men:

"A father said to one of his two sons: 'Son, go work today in my vineyard.' But he answered: 'I will not.' Afterward, moved by remorse he went. The father having given the same command to the second, this one answered: 'I go,' but he went not. Which of the two did the father's will?" All present answered: "The first." Jesus said to them: "Amen, I say to you, the publicans and harlots shall enter the kingdom of God before you. For John came to you to preach justice, and you did not believe him.

But the publicans and fallen women believed him. And you, despite their example, have persisted in your unbelief."[8]

The Two Sons evidently represent Judaism and Gentilism, but it does not follow that all the details are allegorical. Because they forgot this, certain copyists have thrown the story into confusion by putting in the first place the son who said yes and did not obey, interpreting him as a type of the Jews who were the first to be called. The purpose of the parable, however, is to show that true obedience consists not in words, but in deeds; the order of the call is an indifferent circumstance.

The chief priests and Pharisees pretended not to recognize themselves in the foregoing parable. To these willfully deaf ones Jesus must speak more loudly and more plainly:

"Hear another parable. A man planted a vineyard, and put a hedge about it, and dug a ditch around it, and built in it a watch-tower; and having let it out to some vinedressers, he went on a journey. And when the time of vintage drew near, he sent his servants to claim the fruits coming to him. But the vinedressers laid hold of them, and one they beat, and another they slew, and a third they stoned. Again he sent other servants more numerous than the first; and they suffered the same fate. Finally he sent his own son to them, saying: 'They will surely respect my son.' But the vinedressers, on seeing the son, said among themselves: 'Come, let us kill him, and we shall have his inheritance.' They therefore laid hold of him, and cast him out of the vineyard, and killed him. When the master of the vineyard comes, what will he do to those vinedressers?

"Those present answered with one voice: 'He will destroy those wretches and will entrust his vineyard to other vinedressers, who will render to him the desired fruit.'

"Jesus said to them: 'Have you never read in the Scriptures: "The stone which the builders rejected, the same is become the cornerstone; this is the Lord's doing and it is wonderful in our eyes"? Wherefore I say to you, the kingdom of God shall be taken from you, and shall be given to a nation that will yield its fruits.'

---

[8] Matt. 21:28–32. On the textual criticism, cf. Lagrange, *S. Matthieu*, 409–410.

"And when the chief priests and Pharisees heard these words, they understood that they concerned them. And they would have seized him, if they had not feared the people, because these held him as a prophet."[9]

It would be surprising if those concerned had not understood, for the parable needs no explanation. The numerous variants which it shows in the three Synoptics in no way alter its meaning. The number and kind of servants sent by the master, the varieties of evil treatment inflicted on them — insults, wounds, stoning — are descriptive elements which have no influence on the general meaning. The same is to be said of the various acts of care lavished on the vineyard; all together they mark God's solicitude for the chosen people, without requiring the particular application of single details. The allegorical elements are clear. The wicked vinedressers evidently represent the Jews and especially the responsible heads of the Jewish nation. It may seem strange that they deceive themselves into thinking that they will come into possession of the inheritance by putting the heir to death, but did not Caiphas use almost the same reasoning when he said to his colleagues: "It is expedient that this one man die, that the nation may not perish"?

A final parable, that of the Invited Guests who have promised to come to the banquet and do not come, completes the cycle of instructions on the rejection of the Jews and the call of the Gentiles. We have already met this parable in St. Luke, but St. Matthew gives it so different a turn and makes so new an application that we cannot neglect his version.

A king, celebrating the marriage of his son, sent forth his servants to summon those who had been invited to the feast, and

[9] Matt. 21:33–46; Mark 12:1–12; Luke 20:9–19. The principal interest of the variants is that they show the freedom enjoyed by the sacred writers when telling the same fact, especially when they are relating a parable. The most noteworthy variant is the following: All three have Jesus proposing the question: "How will the master of the vineyard treat the vinedressers?" In St. Mark, without waiting for any answer, he immediately adds: "He will destroy them and will give the vineyard to others," whereas in St. Matthew it is the listeners who give this answer. In St. Luke, on the contrary, the hearers, understanding that there is reference to themselves, cry out: "God forbid!" We follow the version of St. Matthew.

they refused to come. He sent other servants to tell them: "I have had my beeves and fatted poultry killed; the feast is ready. Come to the wedding." But without heeding him they went their way, one to his field, another to his business; and others seized his servants, and loaded them with outrages and killed them. Angered at the news of this, the king sent his armies with orders to exterminate the murderers and to burn their city. Then he said to his servants: "The marriage-feast is ready, but those invited were not worthy. Go to the crossroads, and whomsoever you shall meet, summon to the wedding." The servants went out into the streets and gathered together indiscriminately all whom they found, so that the festive hall was full of guests. And the king went in to see the guests at table, and noticed a man who was not wearing a wedding garment. He said to him: "Friend, how didst thou come in hither without a wedding garment?" But the other could make no reply. And the king said to the servants: "Bind his hands and feet and cast him forth into the outer darkness; there shall be weeping and gnashing of teeth. For many are called, but few are chosen."[10]

The Messianic banquet is the wedding feast which God celebrates in honor of his Son. Those who answer the call with an insulting refusal are the Jews; those who are substituted for them are the Gentiles, called last and arriving first. Invited guests do not ordinarily aggravate the affront of a refusal by putting to

[10] Matt. 22:1–14; cf. Luke 14:16–24. Is it the same parable? The question is controverted. Many interpreters, following Maldonatus, regard the identity as more probable; many others, with St. Augustine, hold that the parables are not the same. That the master of the house is in one case a king and in the other an ordinary person; that the meal given by him is a dinner or a supper; that he sends out the same servant or different servants to summon the guests; that the fractious guests decline on this or that pretext; these are inconsequential variants in a parable. St. Matthew, however, has two essential parts which are lacking in St. Luke: the presence at the feast of a guest without a wedding garment, which introduces a new moral; and the murder of the servants charged with carrying the summons, a murder justifying the king's vengeance and the destruction of their city. In St. Matthew, the Jews are not only excluded from the Messianic banquet for having repelled the call of God; they are exterminated as a nation. Hence there is reason to distinguish the two parables as we have them. Still, it may be said that St. Luke has simplified the parable of St. Matthew, omitting the elements which did not suit his purpose; or that St. Matthew has combined two parables originally distinct. On this question the reader may consult Buzy, *Y a-t-il fusion des paraboles évangéliques? R.B.*, 1932, 31–49.

death the ones sent to invite them; nor would a king ordinarily reduce their capital to ruins to avenge himself for their refusal. Here, as often happens in allegorical parables, the historical reality envisioned by the author leaves its mark on the figurative representation and lends to it its own coloring. There is, then, no point in asking what happens to the wedding feast during the period of negotiations. The Messianic feast has no limits either in time or space. It continues up to the consummation of the ages and is perpetuated in heaven.

At the moment when the earthly phase of this banquet closes, the king enters the hall to see whether all his guests are worthy to stay. He notices one who has no wedding garment. If we put aside figurative language, this man has faith which has made him a Christian, but he lacks the charity and good works which would render him worthy of continuing in heaven the feast begun on earth. Hence he is cast out and relegated to the darkness outside, where there will be weeping and gnashing of teeth. As in the parables of the Darnel and of the Net, admission into the Church and exclusion from heaven apparently follow each other so closely that they make up only one scene.

The man excluded from the final feast because he has not the wedding garment, which he could and should have provided for himself, is brought in only as an example. It is not said how many will find themselves in a similar condition. The parable does not allow any conclusion, either to the small number of the elect in proportion to the mass of the human race, or, *a fortiori,* to the proportion of Christians reprobated in comparison with those who are saved. These abstruse questions, which divine Providence has kept to itself, do not enter into the perspective of the parable story.[11]

---

[11] Some points need clarification.

a) From the fact that the recalcitrant guests are exterminated and their city burned, some have drawn the conclusion that St. Matthew composed his Gospel *after* the destruction of Jerusalem. But this is an altogether mistaken deduction. Without bringing in Christ's divine knowledge, it may be said that burning was at that time the fate of any rebellious city, indeed, of any city taken by assault. There are more than thirty examples of it in the Bible, and the phrase *abbul, aqqur, ina ishati ashrup* (I have ruined it, destroyed it, burned it) recurs some hundred times as a refrain in the Chronicles when the Kings of Assyria tell of the conquest of enemy cities.

3. Indictment of the Scribes and Pharisees

(MATTHEW 23:1–39)

The Saviour had more than once stigmatized the hypocrisy of the Scribes and Pharisees, their love of gain, their strait formalism, their pride, and their love of display. At the moment when they have just delivered their final assault, he again unmasks these cunning foes. St. Matthew, faithful to his own literary procedure, assembles here all the charges leveled against them and makes of them a vigorous indictment, which can be divided into three parts: a sketch of the Pharisaic character, seven maledictions pronounced against them, and the prediction of the catastrophes due to overtake the Jews for having followed these blind guides.[12]

"Upon the chair of Moses have sitten the Scribes and Pharisees. Observe, therefore, what they say to you, but do not as they do. For they say, and they do not. They lay heavy burdens upon the shoulders of men, and not with one finger of their own do they choose to move them.

"Anxious in all things to attract the attention of men, they widen their phylacteries and enlarge their tassels immoderately. They strive for the first places at suppers and in the synagogues. They love to be saluted in the street and to receive the title, 'Rabbi.' "

Without concerning himself with the Pharisees who were present, Jesus addresses himself directly to the people to put

---

b) The king invites to his feast the *good* and the *bad* (Verse 10: πονηρούς τε καὶ ἀγαθούς) without distinction. But to enter, it is necessary to have a wedding garment; that is to say, a decent garb. It has been inferred that the author of the invitation provided each of his guests with a robe of honor, but no such unlikely custom finds support in history. As a matter of fact, the mode of acquiring and keeping the wedding garment is outside the purpose of the parable. We are only told that it was indispensable.

c) The conclusion, "Many are called but few are chosen," is applied to the whole of the parable and not merely to the last part. The one guest who did not have a wedding garment is the representative of a category the size of which we do not know. It would be wrong to conclude that all Christians with very few exceptions will be saved, and just as unfounded to think that the proportion of the reprobate is greater than that of the saved. Let us respect the mystery of God's designs.

[12] First part, Matt. 23:1–12; second part, 23:13–31; third part, 23:32–39.

them on their guard against these blind guides. They are, indeed, the authentic interpreters of the Law of Moses; as long as they stay within their province, it is necessary to follow them; the common people cannot do otherwise. But as to imitating their example, that is quite another affair. They are evil models. Our Lord reproaches them for their hardheartedness, their ostentatiousness, and their childish vanity. They are accustomed to pile upon the backs of others crushing burdens which they themselves would not touch with the tip of their finger. Artful casuists that they were, the Scribes and Pharisees had learned how to evade the more troublesome prescriptions of the law. Was not a whole treatise of the Mishnah devoted to moderating the rigor of the Sabbath rest as they themselves had regulated it? Conversely, they were faithful to the minutest observances, provided that they could thereby attract the notice of men without too much effort. They immoderately increased the size of those little cubes called phylacteries, containing the profession of the monotheistic faith and which they wore attached to their forehead and left arm during prayer. These they kept on for long periods to give the impression that they were always praying. They also exaggerated the dimensions of the two-colored tassels which pious Jews used to sew to the ends of their garments.[13] Always the same ostentation! At banquets and in the meetings at the synagogues they took the places of honor by assault or maneuvered ways and means of getting into them.[14] But what most flattered their vanity was the title of "Rabbi" (my Master), which they loved to hear fall from the lips of numerous disciples.

Nor were the Apostles exempt from such petty vanities. Among them also there had been competitions, intrigue, and disputes about rank. Our Lord profits from circumstances to give them a lesson: "As for you, do not have yourselves called 'Rabbi,' for you have but one master, and you are all brethren. And do not have yourselves called 'Father' here on earth, for you have but

---

[13] The use of *phylacteries* is based on Deut. 6:8 (cf. Exod. 13:9) taken literally. That of *fringes* (κράσπεδα — *fimbriae*) on Deut. 22:12; Num. 15:38–39. On the *tephillin* and the *tsitsith* see *Dict. de la Bible* in articles *Phylactères* and *Franges* (with pictures). The two long dissertations of Billerbeck (*Kommentar,* Vol. IV, pp. 250–292) offer curious details, but not of great use for interpretation.

[14] On this point one may recall Book III, Chapter II.

one Father, who is in heaven. Do not have yourselves called 'Teacher,' for you have but one Teacher, Christ. Let the greatest among you be your servant. He that exalts himself shall be humbled, and he that humbles himself shall be exalted." Being all brothers, and all equal — the hierarchy announced for the future is not yet organized — the disciples should treat one another as such. Future generations, while not directly envisioned in this instruction, must at least follow its spirit.

After this short *aside* to the Apostles, Jesus returns to the Scribes and Pharisees and pronounces against them the seven following maledictions:

"Woe to you, Scribes and Pharisees, hypocrites, who shut the kingdom of heaven against men. You yourselves do not enter, and you prevent others from entering.

"Woe to you, Scribes and Pharisees, hypocrites, who traverse land and sea to make a single proselyte; and when he has become one, you make of him a son of hell even worse than yourselves.

"Woe to you, blind guides, who say, 'If anyone swear by the Temple, it is nothing; but if he swear by the gold of the Temple, he is bound,' and 'If anyone swear by the altar, it is nothing; but if he swear by the gift placed on the altar, he is bound.' Blind fools! Which is greater, the gold, or the holy place that sanctifies the gold? And which is greater, the gift, or the altar that sanctifies the gift? He that swears by the altar swears also by that which is placed on the altar. And he that swears by the holy place, swears also by the throne of God, and by him who sits upon the throne.

"Woe to you, Scribes and Pharisees, hypocrites, who pay the tithes on mint and dill and cummin, and neglect the weightier matters of the law: justice, mercy, and faith. Those things it behooved you to do, and not to omit these others. Blind guides, who strain out the gnat, but swallow the camel!

"Woe to you, Scribes and Pharisees, hypocrites, who clean the outside of the cup and of the dish, while the inside is full of extortion and uncleanness. Blind Pharisees! Clean first the inside of the cup, that the outside may also become clean.

"Woe to you, Scribes and Pharisees, hypocrites, who are like whited sepulchers, which without are beautiful, whereas within they are full of bones and rottenness. Thus without you appear just to the eyes of men, but within you are full of hypocrisy and iniquity.

"Woe to you, Scribes and Pharisees, hypocrites, who build tombs to the prophets and adorn the sepulchers of the just. You say: 'If we had lived in the days of our fathers, we would not have shed, as they did, the blood of the prophets.' You confess, then, that you are the sons of those who slew the prophets."[15]

This terrible indictment may be summarized under three headings: false zeal, formalism, and hypocrisy.

The fever of propaganda which was devouring Judaism subsided for a while after the catastrophe of the year 70, but at the epoch with which we are occupied it was at its height. Scribes and Pharisees engaged in fierce rivalry to increase their following. During Herod's reign, two celebrated Doctors drew into their train a veritable army of disciples. This fury of proselytizing throughout the Roman Empire is sufficiently known to us through Jewish authors and through satirists and profane historians. Few pagans accepted circumcision, but a great number of them, disgusted with a religion without beliefs and without morality, frequented the synagogue, professed the unicity of God, and bowed to certain Jewish practices such as the observance of the Sabbath. When, at the same time, they kept their pagan morals and superstitions — as often happened — the only result of their conversion to Judaism was to make them sin with more light and thus to render them "twofold the sons of hell." Since the prime effort of the Pharisees was to inspire in their disciples the most profound contempt for any teaching other than their own, the principal obstacle to the spread of Christianity was the ascendency of the Pharisees over souls, alienating them from the Gospel by calumny and threats of anathema. It is thus that they closed the door of the kingdom of heaven; not that they had its keys, but because they forbade access to it and obstructed the avenues to it. It often happened, if we may believe St. Justin,

---

[15] Matt. 23:13–31. On the Jewish customs to which reference is made in this passage, information may be found in Billerbeck, *Kommentar,* Vol. I, pp. 923–929, or in any other similar work (Lightfoot, *Horae Hebraicae,* Meuschen, Wetstein, etc.); more recently, Bonsirven, *Le Judaïsme palestinien.* See the alphabetical table, Vol. II, p. 359 f., under the word *Pharisiens.*

that the half proselytes were more fanatical and more hostile to the religion of Christ than were Jews by race.[16]

We have had occasion more than once to point out the formalism of the Scribes and their ludicrously subtle casuistry. A whole book would scarcely be enough to give a complete idea of it. The Jews of the time had a mania for binding themselves by vow to do or not do this or that. The validity of these inconsiderate oaths, according to the teaching of the Pharisees, did not depend upon the intention of the one pronouncing them, nor upon the legitimacy of the act in question, but solely upon the formula employed. The least omission, the least change in the consecrated form, whatever be the intention, rendered the vow invalid. No examples identical with those that the Saviour brings forward are found in the Talmud, but there are some which are altogether similar. The following one is much to the point: To promise something by swearing by the Torah creates no obligation, but to promise the same thing by the content of the Torah imposes an obligation. Whence comes the difference? In the opinion of the casuists, it is in this, that in the first case one could be swearing by the parchment of the Torah, which had no special holiness, but in the second case one swears by the content of the Torah, which is something especially holy.

The law commanded the payment of the tithe for grain, wine, and wood, and in general for all the products of the soil that served for the nourishment of man. The Pharisees observed this faithfully and even to scrupulosity. They made no exception for mint and dill and cummin, which are plants growing without cultivation and serving to season the food. The formalism of certain ones went still farther; they maintained that even if one plucked an ear of corn to eat the grain, it was necessary to pay the tithe. What the Saviour blames in the Pharisees is not so much the adherence to these minutiae as the neglect of things a thousand times more important: fidelity, justice, and mercy. To act in this way, was it not to strain out a gnat and swallow a camel?

---

16 On Jewish propaganda, there is a monograph of Weill, *Le Prosélytisme chez les Juifs selon la Bible et le Talmud,* Strasbourg, 1880. Schürer (*Geschichte,* 4 ed., III, 150–188) and Juster (*Les Juifs dans l'empire romain,* 1914, I, 253–337: *Prosélytisme*) give the essentials for the period we are interested in.

The Pharisees used to clean the kitchen utensils with such scrupulous care that the rules on purifying vessels of wood, copper, clay, and metal filled a whole treatise of the Mishnah. But they were less anxious to assure themselves whether the contents were the product of theft or rapine. Still the same distortion: taking great account of externals and accidentals, and counting as nothing the internal and essential.

To paint to the life the hypocrisy of the Pharisees, our Lord has recourse to a singularly expressive comparison: whited sepulchers. At the approach of great feasts, the Jews used to whitewash the stones of tombs to warn pilgrims to avoid them, since an uncleanness was contracted by merely treading upon them, even unawares. These stones, now gleaming white, nonetheless covered heaps of bones and rottenness, a striking image of the Pharisees whose exterior belied their interior. Their hypocrisy expressed itself in a still more cunning way. They affected to honor the prophets; they adorned their tombs; they proclaimed that had they lived in the time of their fathers they would not have treated them so shamefully. And still, when a prophet like John the Baptist appeared, or the king of the prophets, Christ, they meted out to them the same treatment that their ancestors had forced the ancient seers of Israel to undergo.

"Fill up the measure of your fathers!" cried Jesus. "Serpents, brood of vipers, how are you to escape the fire of hell? I send you prophets and wise men and scribes; some of them you slay and crucify, and some you scourge in your synagogues and hunt from city to city. It must be that there fall upon you all the innocent blood shed upon the earth, from the blood of Abel the just unto the blood of Zacharias, son of Barachias, whom you slew between the sanctuary and the altar. Amen, I say to you, all these things shall come upon this generation."[17]

---

[17] Matt. 23:32–36. The individual is responsible only for his own acts, but the nation as one moral person is responsible for all the national crimes, and must sooner or later be punished for them. The Jewish people (this generation, i.e., this race) will have to render an account for all the blood spilled by it, from the blood of Abel (Gen. 4:10) to the blood of the High Priest Zacharias (2 Para. 24:22). The murders of these two just men are cited as examples not only because

"Fill up the measure of your fathers!" This rhetorical permission, which is apparently an exhortation to crime in order to inspire greater horror of it, is, in every literature, the most energetic expression of indignation and anger. God's justice is patient, because it is eternal; but a time comes, for peoples as well as for individuals, when the measure is heaped up, and then the might of God presses down upon the guilty. The Jewish people, murderer of the prophets, is tending toward that limit. It will reach it when it has steeped its hands in the blood of the Son of God, and when it treats as malefactors the ministers whom he will send to continue his work. Then the vengeance of God will pour down pitilessly upon this deicide race, and will demand a reckoning for all the blood it has iniquitously shed.

"Jerusalem, Jerusalem; thou that slayest the prophets and stonest those who are sent to thee by God! How often would I have gathered together thy children, as a hen gathers together her chicks under her wings, and thou wouldst not! Behold, your house will be left to you a desert. I say to you, you shall not see me henceforth until you say, 'Blessed is he that cometh in the name of the Lord.'"[18]

---

they are known to all, but because, according to the Scripture, the blood of Abel and Zacharias cries to heaven for vengeance.

The difficulty about Zacharias, *son of Barachias,* is well known. The reference is certainly to Zacharias, *son of Joad,* who was killed by order of Joas *in atrio domus Domini* (2 Para. 24:21). This cannot be the prophet Zacharias, son of Barachias, in whose case no violent death is reported; much less Zacharias, the son of Baruch (Josephus, *Bellum,* IV, v, 4), who fell by the sword of the Zealots in A.D. 68 or 69. Why, then, is the son of Joad called the son of Barachias? One can hardly suppose that, at a time so far back, the same person had two such different names as Joad and Barachias, inasmuch as the Scriptures know only one name, Joad. Some Catholic authors admit a lapse of memory in St. Matthew, causing him to mistake the prophet Zacharias, son of Barachias, for the High Priest, son of Joad; but this hypothesis cannot be reconciled with the correct notion of Inspiration. There is reason to think that the addition, *son of Barachias,* is the work of a copyist or of the Greek translator of Matthew. It is lacking in the parallel passage of St. Luke (11:51) and also in some manuscripts of Matthew (such as *Sinaiticus*). The Gospel of the Nazarenes, which St. Jerome regarded as the original of Matthew, had here *son of Joad.* The question remains unsolved. On the meaning of *this generation* (i.e., *this race*), see *Recherches,* 1927, pp. 316–324.

[18] Matt. 23:37–39. Certain critics omit the word *desert* (ἔρημος), which is lacking in many Greek manuscripts. The meaning would then be: "Your house

Frightening menace, and yet consoling promise! Their house — not the Temple, which is the house of God, but the Holy City, which is their dwelling place — will soon be deserted, above all by those whom the Romans will expel from it with an absolute prohibition against returning. The Saviour is to leave them, but he will return on that day when they shall say: "Blessed is he who comes in the name of the Lord." The promise can, indeed, be interpreted as dependent upon a condition that is not to be fulfilled; but everything leads us to the belief that it is to be realized at the end of time, and that then "all Israel will be saved."

---

is left to you," abandoned to your own devices, destitute of divine aid, destined to ruin.

We believe that the final words refer to the ultimate conversion of the Jews predicted by St. Paul (Rom. 11:25). The repentant Jews will say on the eve of the Parousia equivalently this: "Blessed be he who comes in the name of the Lord." Cf. Prat, *Théologie de S. Paul,* 320–321 (English transl., I, 264–266).

CHAPTER IV

The End of a World and the End of the World

1. The Widow's Mite

ANXIOUS to get a little rest at the close of this long and fatiguing day, the Saviour had retired to the Women's Court. This was a vast rectangular courtyard surrounded on three sides by a colonnade supporting the gallery where women could be present at the liturgical ceremonies. Two monumental doors faced each other, one on the east and the other on the west. The latter was reached by a wide semicircular staircase of fifteen steps which led to the Court of Israel. Jesus had seated himself, probably on one of these steps, in the midst of the twelve Apostles. In front of him, across the eastern door, he could see the panorama of the Mount of Olives, and below him to the left, the Hall of the Treasury, along which were arranged thirteen trumpet-shaped alms boxes where the faithful deposited their offerings. At the time of feasts the concourse of people was enormous, because it was especially at such times that they paid their overdue assessments and made voluntary offerings or fulfilled vows. These transactions very often required the intervention of a priest, whose duty it was to determine rates and to certify the genuineness of coins. Thus the public was able to take note of each one's liberality.

In the midst of this swarming crowd a poor widow was timidly approaching, anxious to contribute to the upkeep of divine worship according to her means. We often hear of the widow's *obolus* or *denarius,* but the woman of the Gospel was not rich enough to offer such a sum. She was holding in her hand two minute bronze coins worth together one quarter of an *as,* about one third of a cent in our money. The destination of the voluntary alms was clearly written on each of the boxes of which we have spoken, but the poor woman, not knowing how to read, had to approach the priest on duty. In a loud voice he announced the amount of the offering and threw it into the receptacle provided for it, no doubt provoking in the bystanders a pitying smile.

From the height of the steps where he was seated, the Saviour followed with his eyes the poor woman, who was retreating in confusion under the contemptuous glances of the crowd. Here was a lesson for the Apostles which he did not wish them to miss. "Amen, I say to you, this poor woman has given more than all the rest. For the others have given out of their abundance, whereas she has deprived herself of necessities in giving all that she had." The wonderful power of almsgiving! This mendicant, making a loan to God, assures for herself in heaven a capital more enviable than all treasures here below.[1]

Jesus came out from the Women's Court and crossed the Court of the Gentiles. He then descended the Valley of Cedron to climb the lower slopes of the Mount of Olives. There he turned to gaze once more upon the Temple which he would not visit again. "Look, Master, what great stones and what a beautiful monument!" said one of his disciples, pointing to the layers of stone placed one upon another without cement, and so artfully that the eye could scarcely distinguish the joinings. The whole structure presented the appearance of a fairy palace carved out of rock. The Temple of Jerusalem, resting on its gigantic substructures, seemed built for eternity.

Jesus answered sadly: "The day will come when of this fine

---

[1] Mark 12:41–44; Luke 21:1–4. Mark's account is livelier: "Jesus sat down opposite the Treasury and observed." On the Treasury, see Billerbeck, *Kommentar,* Vol. II, pp. 37–45. Josephus speaks sometimes of several halls of the Treasury, sometimes, as does St. Mark, of one (*Antiq.*, XIX, vi, 1), doubtless the principal one situated in the Women's Court. The widow offered "two *lepta* which are the quarter part of an as" (λεπτὰ δύο ὅ ἐστιν κοδράντης). The λεπτόν was a little bronze coin called *perutah.* The Roman *as* was worth a little more than six centimes of old French money.

edifice there shall not remain a stone upon a stone."[2] The prophecy has been fulfilled to the letter. Whoever today traverses the esplanade, where the Mosque of Omar has replaced the Temple of Herod, can prove it with his own eyes. Imposing ruins remain of the most famous temples of Egypt, Greece, and Rome; but here, even the ruins have perished. Everything has conspired to annihilate them. When one of Titus' soldiers, guided by an unseen hand, threw a lighted torch under the sacred paneling, the fire took hold so swiftly and so violently that it was impossible to extinguish it. Hadrian, in order to replace the altar of the true God by a sanctuary dedicated to Jupiter Capitolinus, continued the destruction, and it was completed under Julian the Apostate. Anxious to give the lie to Christ's prophecy, Julian gave the Jews permission to rebuild their temple, and himself assumed the expense of the enterprise; but when everything that was left had been demolished, eddies of flame springing up from the foundations made the place untenable for the workmen, many of whom were burned to death. It was necessary to halt the undertaking, and it was never resumed. The fact is recorded not only by Fathers of the Church and Christian historians, but also by an unimpeachable witness who remained faithful to paganism, and who lived at the Emperor's court in Antioch in the very year (363) when the events he reports took place.

2. The Destruction of Jerusalem and the Parousia

Upon reaching the summit of the Mount of Olives, Jesus seated himself apart from the others, silent and thoughtful. From this observation post his gaze embraced the lofty towers of the city, the palaces of Herod and the Hasmoneans, the long colonnades of

[2] Matt. 24:2; Mark 13:2; Luke 21:6. The literal fulfillment of the prophecy is well known. Josephus asserts that Titus wished to spare the Temple, and did all in his power to extinguish the fire (*Bellum,* VI, iv, 3–6); but after the fire had done its work, the General ordered the destruction of the city and *sanctuary* (*Bellum,* VII, i, 1; *καὶ τὸν νεών*), with the exception of three towers and a section of the wall, which were spared to show future generations the strength of the fortification of Jerusalem.

On the vain efforts of Julian the Apostate to re-erect the Temple, read Ammianus Marcellinus (*Rerum Gestarum,* XXIII, 1). The historians Socrates, Sozomen, and Theodoretus on the date 363, St. Gregory of Nazianzus (*Orat.,* V, 4), and St. John Chrysostom (*Adv. Judaeos,* v, 11) testify to the same fact.

the Temple, and the Sanctuary gilded by the last rays of the setting sun.

The four Apostles who enjoyed his most intimate confidence, Peter, John, Andrew, and James, still under the shock of the terrifying prediction they had just heard, approached him. Quite probably the others, too, soon joined them to ask the Master: "When are these things to happen? What will be the prelude to them, and what the sign preceding the consummation of the world?"[3] They ask three questions instead of one; and this fact, fixing in advance a close connection in their minds between the end of Jerusalem and the end of the world, may well have caused some confusion in their minds about the Saviour's answer.

This page of the Gospel is not only a prophecy but an apocalypse, which creates a twofold difficulty for such as are not familiar with this type of literature.

The style of prophecy is not that of history. If the prophet described the future as it will be, his contemporaries would find it not only mysterious but unintelligible. "Continuing to speak his own language, the prophet imprints upon his visions the character of his race, the coloring of his times and of the literary tradition handed on to him, and the stamp of his own native genius. He is the herald of the Great King, not the automatic transmitter of a lesson he has learned."[4] The inspired Seer contemplates the future, so to speak, *sub specie aeternitatis;* he sees it without relief and without perspective. So, indeed, it is in all visual perception. The eye perceives color, lines, and contour, but not the absolute or relative distance of objects. Projected on the retina, these are mixed together and confused. Only experience and education, aided by comparison with known objects, the greater or less distinctness of detail, and the play of light and shadow,

---

[3] Matt. 24:3; Mark 13:4; Luke 21:7. — (1) All three have the question: "When are these things to happen?" (2) Mark and Luke add: "What will be the sign that these things (all this) will begin to come to pass?" So far, there is question only of the ruin of the Temple, or at most, only of Jerusalem. (3) Matthew adds a third question: "What will be the sign of thy coming (*τῆς σῆς παρουσίας*) and of the end of the world (*καὶ τῆς συντελείας τοῦ αἰῶνος*)?" Matthew and Luke attribute the question to the disciples in general; Mark gives the names of the four questioners.

[4] De Grandmaison, *Jésus Christ,* II, 252 (English transl., III, 39).

allow us to appraise dimensions and distances. To place the various elements of his vision on their separate planes the prophet would need another revelation.

Sometimes the prophet's gaze embraces an immense horizon and fixes itself by turns upon points separated by long intervals but linked to one another by a relationship of similarity or a chain of causality. If he describes them thus, in a straight line and without transition, they present themselves to us in apparent confusion. "Prophecy remains upon those lofty summits which dominate the whole course of time. . . . Often overleaping in a bound all intermediate links, it joins together events which are separated from one another by long series of days, years, and even centuries."[5] It happens also that, behind the object directly perceived by the prophet, another shows through which is prefigured by the first and of which the first is a replica in miniature. An ingenious comparison has been thought out to illustrate this curious phenomenon. "Imagine to yourself two palaces unequal in dimensions but almost the same in plan. The smaller one and the closer to you is so placed that, if it is of a crystal transparency, your eye will take in at a glance the corresponding lines and contours of the vaster and more remote. If, on the contrary, the transparency is veiled, uneven, and intermittent, you will need some calculation to complete in your mind the image of the larger edifice, though you will have no doubt of its existence and its main lines."[6]

Much more is this so when the prophecy is an apocalypse. The apocalyptic style is that of prophecy raised to its highest power. It is made up of allusions to past prophecy and of symbols destined to be realized according to a law of proportion which is unknown to us. Thus the eschatological discourse of Jesus abounds in formulas, the key to which is to be found only in ancient prophecy: the Day of the Lord, the abomination of desolation, the physical commotions and the moral convulsions which are like the birth pangs of nature in travail.

For example, the "Day of the Lord" indicates a striking divine intervention into human affairs; but it designates, now a particular event, now the final cataclysm, oftenest the two together.

---

[5] Card. Billot, *La Parousie,* 1920, p. 22.

[6] Le Hir, *Les prophètes d'Israel, Paris,* 1868, pp. 100–110.

God manifests himself as judge, as savior, and as avenger; his coming is accompanied by hope or by terror: hope for the just, terror for sinners. The divine intervention is described in almost all cases in the same terms, either because the particular judgment of a people is a figure of the judgment of the human race, or because the two events fall under the prophet's gaze at the same time. See how Joel describes an invasion of locusts, the scourge inflicted by God on the faithless Jews to arouse them to repentance: "The Day of the Lord cometh, it is nigh at hand . . . before him the earth trembles, the heavens are moved, the sun and the moon are darkened, the stars have withdrawn their shining." Then all of a sudden, when the expiation is complete, Israel's Judge becomes her Avenger: "In that time, I shall bring back the captivity of Juda and Jerusalem, and I will gather together all nations and will bring them down into the Valley of Josaphat, and I will plead with them there for my people." The Day of the Lord seems to continue its course across the ages, and the prophet uses the same colors to paint the invasion of locusts and the consummation of all things. Similar descriptions of the Day of the Lord are to be found in Ezechiel, Amos, Aggeus, Sophonias, and Malachias. The most remarkable of all is, without doubt, the magnificent poem of Isaias on the fall of Babylon.

The Saviour's eschatological discourse is a sort of triptych. The first picture traces in bold strokes the dangers and trials that await the disciples of Christ in the course of history; the second describes the preliminaries to the ruin of Jerusalem, together with the premonitory signs which will enable the faithful to escape it; the third depicts the lightninglike arrival of the Son of Man coming to judge the living and the dead. Here, first of all, is the comprehensive view of the Church Militant up to the end of time:

"Be on your guard against being led astray. For many shall let themselves be led astray by impostors saying: 'I am the Christ.' When you hear of wars and rumors of wars, be not alarmed; these things must come to pass, but the end is not yet. Nation shall rise against nation, and kingdom against kingdom, and there shall be earthquakes and famines in various places. All these things are only the beginning of sorrows.

"Beforehand, they shall deliver you over to affliction and shall put you to death, and you shall be hated by all nations for my name's sake. Then many shall fall away; they shall betray one another and hate one another. False prophets in great numbers shall deceive many. And because iniquity shall abound, the charity of many shall grow cold. But he that shall persevere to the end, he shall be saved. The Gospel shall be preached throughout the world, and then shall come the end."[7]

---

7 *First Tableau — The Future of the Church*

Matthew 24:4–14	Mark 13:5–13	Luke 21:8–19
4. Look to it that no one lead you astray. 5. For many shall come in my name, saying: "I am the Christ," and they shall lead many astray. 6. You shall hear of wars and rumors of war. Take heed not to be alarmed, for these things must come to pass, but the end is not yet. 7. For nation shall be seen rising against nation, and kingdom against kingdom, and there shall be famines and earthquakes in various places. 8. All these things are the beginning of sorrows.	5. Look to it that no one lead you astray. 6. For many shall come in my name saying, "I am he," and they shall lead many astray. 7. When you hear of wars and rumors of war, be not alarmed; these things must come to pass, but the end is not yet. 8. For nation shall be seen rising against nation, and kingdom against kingdom, and there shall be earthquakes in various places and famines. These things are the beginning of sorrows.	8. Look to it that you be not led astray. For many shall come in my name, saying, "I am he, and the time is at hand"; follow them not. 9. When you hear of wars and rebellions, be not fearful, for these things must first come to pass, but the end is not yet. 10. *Then he said to them:* Nation shall be seen rising against nation, and kingdom against kingdom, and there shall be great earthquakes and famines in various places and plagues and frightful prodigies and great signs from heaven.
Persecutions — Matt. 24:9; cf. 10:17–21	*Persecutions — Mark* 13:9–13	*Persecutions* — Luke 21:12–18
13. But he that perseveres to the end, he shall be saved. 14. And this gospel shall be preached in the whole world for a witness to all the nations, and then shall come the end.	13. But he that perseveres to the end, he shall be saved. 10. The Gospel must first be preached to all the nations.	19. By constancy shall you win (the salvation of) your souls.

NOTE — (*a*) St. Matthew, who places the persecutions elsewhere (10:17–21), merely alludes to them here. (*b*) He conducts the history of the Church up to the end of the world (24:13); but in describing the trials of the Church he is careful to note that "the end is not yet" (24:6), that it is only "the beginning of sorrows" (24:8), and that the Gospel must first be preached throughout the

This preliminary picture sketches in prophetic style the history of the Church throughout the ages, especially in moments of great peril and great trials: on the eve of the destruction of Jerusalem and at the approach of the Parousia. Famines, wars, epidemics, frightening phenomena, and cataclysms belong to all times; still, the years which preceded the ruin of Jerusalem were an extraordinarily calamitous epoch. In the year 62 an earthquake destroyed many flourishing cities of Asia; in 64 a frightful fire devoured half the city of Rome; almost the whole reign of Claudius was made desolate by famine; after the death of Nero, wars drenched the whole Empire with blood. One could have believed that the end of the world was coming, if Jesus had not warned his disciples that this was not yet the end, that it was only the beginning of sorrows.

In fact, persecutions followed, violent and atrocious and almost without interruption for three centuries. Persecution is, so to speak, the normal condition of the Church. St. Matthew, having described these trials elsewhere, mentions them here only in passing, but the other Evangelists pause to indicate to the faithful how they should conduct themselves: "You shall be haled before tribunals and beaten in the synagogues and cited before kings and governors, but be not anxious about what you are to say (in your defense). Say what is given to you (by inspiration); for it is not you who speak, but the Holy Spirit (who will speak through your mouths)."

Nevertheless the recurring persecutions, the domestic treasons, and the universal hatred of the Christian name are not yet an indication that the end is near at hand; they are only the prelude of the great sorrows that will mark the final period. Then there will be mass defections; there will be a general cooling of charity and an overflowing of vice, not to speak of the ravages caused by false prophets and false christs. But all this is envisioned in the remote future. The end will not come until the Gospel is preached in the whole world, and it is not said that it will then

---

world (24:14). (*c*) St. Mark includes the same three remarks (7, 8, and 10), which proves that, despite appearances, his picture also embraces a considerable period. (*d*) On the contrary, St. Luke's description could be confined within the horizon of the Apostolic Age. He makes no allusion either to the end of the world or to the conversion of the Gentiles.

come immediately. The Church can therefore still expect long ages of struggle and trials.

If this comprehensive view is still somewhat vague, the same cannot be said of the predictions relating to the ruin of Jerusalem. Certain Rationalists find it too clear to be a prophecy.

"When you see the abomination of desolation of which Daniel the prophet speaks set up in the holy place — reader, take heed! — then let the inhabitants of Judea flee to the mountains. If anyone is on the roof of his house, let him not go down to take anything away; if he is in the fields, let him not turn back again to get his cloak. Woe in those days to the women who are with child or are nursing their young. Pray God that your flight be not in the winter or on the Sabbath day; for that shall be a time of distress such as has not been seen from the beginning of the world and such as shall not be seen again."[8]

[8] *Second Tableau — The Ruin of Jerusalem*

Matthew 24:15–22	Mark 13:14–20	Luke 21:20–24
15. When you see the abomination of desolation, foretold by Daniel the prophet, set up in the holy place — reader, take heed!	14. When you see the abomination of desolation set up where it ought not to be — reader, take heed! Then let those in Judea flee to the mountains.	20. When you see Jerusalem being encompassed by armies, know that her desolation is near.
16. Then let those in Judea flee to the mountains.		21. Then let those in Judea flee to the mountains, and let those in the city go forth, and those in the country not enter it again.
17. Let not him that is upon the housetop come down to take anything from his house,	15. Let not him that is upon the housetop come down and enter his house to take anything thence,	(17:31. On that day, he that shall be on the housetop, let him not come down to take the goods that he has in his house; likewise he that is in the field let him not turn back.)
18. and let not him that is in the field turn back to take his cloak.	16. and let not him that is in the field turn back to take his cloak.	
19. Woe in those days to the women that are with child or have infants at the breast!	17. Woe in those days to the women that are with child or have infants at the breast!	22. For these are the days of vengeance, to accomplish all the Scriptures.
20. Pray that your flight be not in the winter or on the Sabbath,	18. Pray that your flight be not in the winter,	23. Woe in those days to the women that are with child or have infants at the breast!
21. for there shall then be affliction such as has not been from the beginning of the world until now, and never shall be.	19. for those shall be days of affliction such as has not been since the creation until now, and never shall be.	For great distress shall be over the land and wrath upon this people.

The Evangelist invites the reader to ponder this mysterious saying of Daniel: "The abomination of desolation will be over the Temple and will remain there forever." This saying follows another very clear prophecy: "The army of the leader that shall come shall destroy the city and the sanctuary." The profanation of the Temple already perpetrated by Antiochus Epiphanes, which is to be repeated on the eve of the great catastrophe — this is the abomination of desolation of which the prophet speaks. In the year 68, when John of Gishala took possession of the Sanctuary to make it his fortress, human blood flowed in torrents in the Holy Place. Two chief priests and a large group of noble victims fell beneath the daggers of the Zealots. This profanation was a presage of the coming ruin foretold by Daniel.[9] St. Luke replaces this sign by another that is equivalent and more intelligible to his readers: "When you shall see Jerusalem encompassed by armies in the field, know that her desolation is at hand." In the year 69, the Roman legions occupied Hebron, Emmaus, Bethel, and Jericho; the circle of iron contracted around the capital, and its

---

The versions of St. Matthew and St. Mark are almost identical and present scarcely any difficulty, except the sudden transition from the ruin of Jerusalem to the End of the World; but such abrupt transitions are common in the prophets.

St. Luke omits the prophecy of Daniel, which would have been scarcely intelligible to his readers, and speaks in clearer terms of the siege of Jerusalem. He also adds certain elements which fit the capture of any city by assault. In no way do they prove that this Gospel was written after the year A.D. 70. "They shall fall by the edge of the sword, and shall be led away captive to all the nations, and Jerusalem shall be trampled on by the Gentiles, until the time of the nations be fulfilled" (21:24).

[9] The abomination will be standing "where it ought not" (ὅπου οὐ δεῖ, Mark); more precisely, "in the holy place" (ἐν τόπῳ ἁγίῳ, Matthew), that is to say, in the Temple (ἐπὶ τὸ ἱερόν, Daniel). The reference is to the profanation of the Temple which took place in A.D. 68, two years before the destruction of Jerusalem. Cf. Josephus, *Bellum,* IV, v, 1, and IV, vi, 3.

Daniel mentions the "abomination of desolation" three times (Dan. 9:27; 11:31; 12:11). The Gospel allusion does not fit Dan. 11:31 or 12:11, where obviously the reference is to the profanation of the Temple by Antiochus Epiphanes. Hence the passage here referred to is Dan. 9:27. This last passage is almost unintelligible in the present Masoretic text, but the Septuagint translates, with Theodotion: καὶ ἐπὶ τὸ ἱερὸν βδελυγμὸς τῶν ἐρημώσεων ἔσται ἕως συντελείας (*the abomination of desolation will be upon the Temple and will remain there forever*). Cf. Montgomery, *Daniel,* 1927, 386–390, and Swete, *The Old Testament in Greek,* 1891, III, 360 f. The preceding verse, on the destruction of the city and the Temple by "the leader of a people who is to come," is as clear in the Hebrew as it is in the Versions.

investment would have been more rapid but for the revolutions which, in less than two years, cost four emperors their lives.

The Christians did not wait that long to take flight. Under the leadership of St. Simeon, the cousin and successor of St. James the Brother of the Lord, they fled to a city of the Decapolis named Pella, to the south of the Lake of Tiberias. There they awaited the passing of the storm and did not return to Jerusalem until the tempest was over.[10]

The agony of the Jewish nation is a figure of the last convulsions of a dying world. We pass from one to the other without transition, or rather the natural transition is the immensity of disaster common to both, and, as often happens in prophecy, the Evangelist contemplates both in the same perspective. "That will be," they say, "a time of distress such as has never been seen." The hyperbole would be somewhat strong if there were reference only to Jerusalem, though Josephus is not afraid to use it in depicting the ruin of his unhappy country. But if the two catastrophes fall at the same time under the prophet's view, it is no longer hyperbole.[11]

There is, then, no reason for surprise in seeing the Evangelist pass, without warning the reader, from type to antitype, from the destruction of Jerusalem to the end of the world. Thus we come smoothly to the third and last picture representing the Parousia, with its preliminary signs and mysterious distances.

"Then if anyone say to you: 'The Christ is here,' or, 'He is there,' do not believe him. For there shall arise false christs and false prophets who shall work great miracles and prodigies so as to mislead, if possible, even the elect. I tell you beforehand. If,

---

[10] Eusebius (*Hist. eccl.*, III, v, 3) asserts that this was done because of a revelation given to the heads of the community (κατά τινα χρησμόν . . . δι' ἀποκαλύψεως); but the warning of Christ would have been enough. Perhaps the meaning is that the revelation specified the *place* of retreat. Pella was a Greek city, where they would be safe.

[11] "Never was seen such misfortune" is a hyperbole sanctioned by usage: 1 Mach. 9:27; Dan. 12:1; Josephus, *Bellum,* preface; *Assumptio Mosis,* viii. The Evangelists add (Matt. 24:22; Mark 13:20): "And unless those days had been shortened, no flesh would have been saved. But for the sake of the elect those days will be shortened." It is difficult to understand this of the destruction of Jerusalem, unless that be considered as prefiguring the final catastrophe, the Evangelists being allowed to pass without transition from one to the other.

then, they say to you: 'He is in the wilderness,' do not go forth; or, 'He is in the inner parts of the house,' do not believe it. For as the lightning comes forth from the east and shines even to the west, so shall be the coming of the Son of Man. Wherever the corpse lies, the vultures shall be gathered together.

"Immediately after those days of affliction, the sun shall be darkened, the moon shall lose her brightness, the stars shall fall from heaven, and the powers of the heavens shall be shaken. And then shall appear in heaven the sign of the Son of Man. And all the tribes of the earth shall beat their breasts, seeing the Son of Man coming upon the clouds of heaven clothed with power and glory. And he shall send his angels at the sound of the trumpet to gather his elect from the four points of the horizon, from one end of the heavens to the other.

"Learn from the example of the fig tree. When its branches become tender and its leaves begin to sprout, you know that summer is near. So when you see all these things, know that it is very near, that it is at your door."[12]

---

12 *Third Tableau — The End of the World and the Parousia*

Matthew 24:23–33	Mark 13:21–29	Luke 21:25–31
23. Then if anyone say to you: "The Christ is here," or "there," believe it not.	21. Then if anyone say to you: "The Christ is here," or "there," believe it not.	
24. For there shall arise false prophets, who shall work signs and wonders capable of misleading, if possible, even the elect.	22. For there shall arise false christs and false prophets, who shall work signs and wonders so as to mislead, if possible, the elect.	
25. Behold, I have foretold it to you.	23. Be on your guard, I have foretold it all to you.	(Luke 17:23–24 and 37)
26. If therefore they say to you: "Behold, he is in the wilderness," go not forth; "Behold, he is in the store-room," believe it not.		23. They shall say to you: "He is here," "he is there." Go not forth, follow not.
27. For as the lightning comes forth out of the east and shines even to the west, so shall be the coming of the Son of Man.		24. For as the lightning flashes from one end of the heavens and shines even to the other end, so shall it be in the day of the Son of Man.
28. Wherever the corpse is,		37. Where the body is,

The Apostles had asked Jesus by what signs they would recognize the nearness of his coming and the consummation of the world. He answers them now and gives three signs: the appearance of Antichrist and his agents, extraordinary cosmic upheavals, and an almost universal apostasy.

St. Matthew mentions twice the proclamation of false christs, and it might be thought that he is repeating himself; but this is

Matthew 24:23–33	Mark 13:21–29	Luke 21:25–31
there the vultures shall be gathered together.		there shall the vultures gather together.
29. Immediately after those days of affliction the sun shall be darkened, the moon shall not give her light, and the stars shall fall from heaven, and the powers of the heavens shall be shaken	24. In those days after this affliction the sun shall be darkened, the moon shall not give her light, and the stars shall fall from heaven, and the powers of the heavens shall be shaken.	(Luke 21) 25. And there shall be signs in the sun and the moon and the stars, and on earth anguish of nations bewildered by the roaring of the sea and the agitation of the waves.
30. And then shall appear the sign of the Son of Man in the heaven, and all the tribes of the earth shall see the Son of Man coming upon the clouds of heaven with power and great glory.	26. And then shall they see the Son of Man coming in a cloud with power and great glory.	26. Men shall die away from fright in expectation of what is to come upon the world, for the powers of the heavens shall be shaken.
31. And he shall send forth his angels with a great trumpet, and they shall gather together his elect from the four points of the horizon, from end to end of the heavens.	27. And he shall send forth the angels and gather together the elect from the four points of the horizon, from the ends of the earth to the ends of the heavens.	27. And then they shall see the Son of Man coming in a cloud with power and great glory. 28. When these things begin to come to pass, look up and lift up your heads, for your redemption is near at hand.
32. From the example of the fig tree learn. When its young sprouts appear and it puts forth leaves, you know that summer is near.	28. From the example of the fig tree learn. When its young sprouts appear and it puts forth leaves, you know that summer is near.	29. *And he spoke to them a parable.* See the fig tree and all the trees. 30. When you see them budding, you know by them that now summer is near.
33. So too, when you see all these things know that it is near (to you and) at your doors.	29. So too, when you see all these things coming to pass, know that it is near (to you and) at your doors.	31. So too, when you see all these things coming to pass, know that the kingdom of God is near.

not so. There are two distinct periods in the supreme crisis. False christs and false prophets will multiply their prodigies and illusions to mislead mankind. These impostors must not be followed; they must not be believed; but the warning should be heeded, that the Parousia is not far away. A short time before the Parousia, it will be noised about that the Christ is about to appear. This will be nothing but a false report, for the Son of Man will appear with the swiftness of lightning, and all men will find themselves carried in the twinkling of an eye before his judgment seat without warning of his coming.

The cosmic commotions which will precede or accompany the Parousia — the shaking of the world, the darkening of the sun and moon and the falling of the stars, the sound of the trumpet, the shock of the onlookers — are, in great part, borrowed from the theophanies of the Old Testament. In what measure and in what way will these traditional images be verified on the last day? If we flattered ourselves that we knew, the diversity of opinions expressed on the subject since the time of the Fathers should make us pause to reflect. There is no agreement at all. They do not even agree about the *sign of the Son of Man,* which, however, seems to us to designate unequivocally the Cross of Christ. Is it not to be expected that the Saviour should show forth once more, in the sight of the elect and the reprobate, the instrument of Redemption which is the symbol of salvation and the pledge of victory?[13]

The second coming of the Son of Man will be comparable in suddenness and swiftness to lightning, which in an instant cleaves and sets fire to the heavens from one end of the horizon to the other. As soon as he appears, all the living and all the dead will be conveyed to meet him by a spontaneous and irresistible movement, just as vultures, urged on by a marvelous instinct, swoop

[13] Knabenbauer (*In Matthaeum,* II, 336–342), taking everything literally except the trumpet, gives an exposition of the very divergent views of ancient and modern authors. Many of the commentators (SS. Jerome, John Chrysostom, Thomas, etc.) understand the darkening of the sun and even the fall of the stars as referring to the splendor of Christ, which shall eclipse all the heavenly bodies. There would be unanimous agreement that the "Sign of the Son of Man" is the Cross, if many did not suggest an alternative: "*Either* the Cross *or* the standard of victory," without saying what the standard of victory would be as distinct from the Cross. "Signum *aut* crucis intelligamus . . . aut vexillum victoriae triumphantis" (St. Jerome and St. Thomas).

down from all sides on the corpse which has just fallen in the desert sands.[14] St. Paul tells us, without figurative language: "The survivors at the last hour will not precede those who sleep the sleep of death. At the voice of the archangel the Lord will descend from heaven, and then those who have died in Christ will rise first. Then we, who survive, shall be caught up with them upon the clouds into the air to meet him; and so we will be always with the Lord."[15]

The preliminary signs of the Parousia announce it as clearly as the other signs enumerated above announced the catastrophe of Jerusalem and allowed alert Christians to escape it. The budding of the fig tree and of the other trees no more surely presages the coming of summer. "When you see these things," says the Saviour, "know that the Son of Man is near, that he is at your door." The words "this" and "all this" denote clearly the signs preceding the end of the world, which the Synoptics have just described. To make them refer to the destruction of Jerusalem, which has already been placed in remoter perspective and which is announced by different signs, would be the most arbitrary of interpretations.

But men of the last generation will take no heed of these warnings. Neither the decline of faith and charity, nor the overflowing of vice, nor the almost general apostasy, nor the appearance of Antichrist with his deceptive prodigies, nor the quaking of the universe, will awaken them from their torpor.

"As it was in the days of Noe, so shall it be in the days of the Son of Man. Then men were eating and drinking, they were marrying and giving in marriage, up to the day when Noe went into the Ark; and the flood came and engulfed them all. So shall it be in the days of the Son of Man. Of two persons who happen to be in the same field, one shall be taken and the other shall be left; of two women busy grinding at the same millstone, one shall be taken and the other shall be left. Watch, therefore, for you know not at what hour your Master shall come."[16]

---

[14] Cf. Note 10 of Chap. XI, Book III, on p. 157.

[15] 1 Thess. 4:15–17. Cf. Prat, *Théologie de saint Paul,* I, 82–92 (English transl., I, 71–80).

[16] Matt. 24:37–41; Luke 17:26–27, 34–35.

"As to that day and that hour, no one knows them, neither the angels in heaven, nor the Son, but only the Father."[17]

It is certain that the Son of Man knows these things by his divine knowledge and by the beatific knowledge which he has enjoyed from the first moment of his conception. He must also know them by the infused knowledge which he possesses by reason of his office of redeemer and universal judge. If this is so, how can it be said that he does not know them?

In the first centuries of the Church many of the Fathers said simply that, if Jesus Christ is ignorant of anything as man, he knows it as God. This rhetorical concession was enough to close the mouths of the Arians, who denied the divinity of the Saviour. After the Nestorian heresy, the Fathers were not afraid to employ the same formula, while watching their manner of speech, not allowing it to be understood that there were two persons in Jesus Christ, a divine Person and a human person. It did not seem impossible that the Incarnate Word could have accepted, for a time, such ignorance, since he assumes the infirmities inherent in our nature. But St. Augustine reacts forcefully against this assimilation of the Incarnate Word to us: the progress of dogma no longer allows the matter to rest there. What meaning, then, must be given to this mysterious saying of Christ?

The Son of God has the office of teaching men the truths of salvation; but the precise date of the last day does not enter into the object of this revelation, and the Father has reserved the secret to himself. Jesus Christ, having no mission to reveal it, is considered as not knowing it. He does not know it by a *communicable knowledge*, or, as St. Augustine expresses it, "He does not know it to reveal it to us."[18]

[17] Mark 13:32; cf. Matt. 24:36. The limiting phrase, *neque Filius* (οὐδὲ ὁ υἱός), which is *certain* in St. Mark, is doubtful in St. Matthew, though the majority of the critical editors admit its authenticity, since it is found in both codices B and D. If it should be omitted in Matthew as we think it should, the sense of it is there: *nemo novit . . . nisi solus Pater*. The exegesis of this passage in the Fathers has a long history which may be read with profit in the learned note of Lebreton, *Hist. du dogme de la Trinité,* 5 ed., I, 548–590 (English transl., I, 417–432).

[18] St. Augustine, who often treated the question, says, for example: "Hoc nescit quod nescientes facit, id est quod non ita sciebat ut tunc discipulis indicaret." Or more clearly: "Dixit nescire illum diem quia in magisterio ejus non erat

Such is the ordinary solution, and with it one may well be content, since it satisfies so many excellent minds. Still, it must be admitted that it has the appearance of an evasion. Our text would seem rather to approximate this other: "It is not mine to seat you at my right hand or my left; that belongs to those to whom my Father destines it." Christ does not deny that this right belongs to him also; but we know that he always attributes to the Father the initiative in the work of redemption and the effects of predestination. Now the end as well as the beginning of the work of redemption enters into the order of things in which the heavenly Father has the initiative.[19]

Though the date of the Parousia is and will always remain uncertain, the same cannot be said of the fact: "Amen, I say to you, this generation shall not pass away before all these things come to pass. Heaven and earth shall pass away, but my words shall not pass away." The word of Christ is more durable than heaven and earth; and the Jewish nation, the unbelieving race, is sure to see its entire fulfillment.

Some modern authors here become encumbered with shackles which they have forged for themselves, by supposing that the Saviour's prophecy refers solely to the destruction of Jerusalem,

---

ut per eum sciretur a nobis" (*In Ps.,* 36:1; ML, XXXVI, 355). St. Thomas repeats St. Augustine's explanation, adding to it that of Origen (*Comment. in Matth.,* 24:36): "Quod dicitur quod Christus non scit intelligitur quod Ecclesia non scit."

[19] Matt. 20:23; Mark 10:40. Predestination, it seems, is never attributed to the Son or to the Holy Ghost, but always to the Father. The same can be said of the effects of predestination: the call to faith and the election to glory. In general, when Jesus speaks as the envoy of God he attributes to the Father the initiative of his actions: "My doctrine is not from me but from him who sent me" (John 7:16). There are many similar examples in St. John.

Many of the most illustrious of the Fathers, while accepting the common answers: "If Christ does not know it as man, he knows it as God," and "He does not know it to tell it to us," propose another. Thus St. Basil (*Epist. ad Amphilochium,* MG, XXXII, 880): "No one knows the hour, not even the Son, but only the Father; that is to say, the Father is the source of the knowledge of the Son" (*τουτέστιν ἡ αἰτία τοῦ εἰδέναι τὸν υἱὸν παρὰ τοῦ Πατρός*). Also St. Gregory of Nazianzus (*Orat. Theol.,* IV, 16; MG, XXXVI, 124), Didymus of Alexandria, who expressly refers to St. Basil (*De Trinitate,* II, 22; MG, XXXIX, 9), and naturally Amphilochius (*Frag.,* 6; MG, XLIII, 52). St. Irenaeus (*Adv. Haer.,* ii, 28; MG, VII, 811): "For want of a better explanation, we think that the Lord wishes to teach us to place the Father above all things, as when he says: The Father is greater than I."

and that the generation contemporary with him will see its realization. No Father of the Church ever thought of this explanation, which Origen characterizes as excessive simplification. St. Thomas rejects it without examination, and Maldonatus condemns it with a rigor which is, doubtless, excessive. It is not until the fifteenth century that it finds a Catholic defender.[20] In the New Testament, as in the Old, "this generation," with or without an epithet, always has a depreciatory meaning, and denotes the Jewish nation not so much as contemporary with the writer or speaker as bearing the unfavorable mark implied by the term itself. "What characterizes *this generation,*" St. John Chrysostom remarks very correctly, "is less a determined duration than a common origin, an aggregate of political and religious institutions, or a similarity of habits. As long as these characteristics remain, this generation, that is to say, the race remains the same." When Jesus says: "An account shall be demanded of this generation for all the blood spilled by it, from the blood of Abel to the blood of Zacharias, whom you killed between the Temple and the altar," is it not evident that he is speaking of the Jewish nation, and not of

---

[20] The first, to my knowledge, to defend the modern opinion according to which *this generation* means the contemporaries of Christ is Tostado, commenting on Matt. 24:34 (Cologne edition, 1613, Vol. XI, Second Part, p. 525). He was followed by Lucas of Bruges, who thinks that the Saviour intentionally expressed himself in an ambiguous way (*Comment. in Evang.,* Antwerp, 1712, I, 407), and by Calmet, who is able to cite in favor of his opinion only Lucas of Bruges and some Protestant authors (Augsburg edition, 1716, VII, 232). We know what Origen, the most ancient author to mention the opinion, thought of it: "Some *simple persons* refer these words to the destruction of Jerusalem, and believe that they were said of the generation living at the time of Christ, who were witnesses of the Passion, as if that generation were to survive until the ruin of the Holy City" (*In Matth. series,* No. 54; MG, XIII, 1684). When this oversimplifying opinion was brought out, Maldonatus characterized it thus: "Recentiores haereticorum interpretes et nonnulli etiam catholici qui nimis eos avide sequi solent (generationem) aetatem exponunt, quasi sensus sit: antequam illa aetas hominum, qui tunc vivebant, praeteriret, futuram Jerosolymorum vastationem." The censure is much too severe, because, though the new interpretation is false, it is inoffensive and not contrary to the traditional exegesis; for all the Fathers and Doctors agree in taking *generation* in the sense of *nation* or *race,* but they do not agree on the application. The majority rightly believe that the reference is to the Jewish nation; some, however, think of the *human race* or the *Christian society,* influenced, it may be, by the saying in the Psalm, *generatio rectorum,* forgetting that in the New Testament *this generation* always has a depreciatory sense, and denotes the Jewish people. For more details see *Recherches,* 1927, 316–324.

a group of men confined within the compass of thirty or forty years? He means: "The chastisement merited by you and your fathers is to burst upon you and your descendants, who make up with you one moral person."

The uncertainty of the last hour is an exhortation to vigilance, for there will be for each one of us an hour that will be the last; and the date of that hour is unknown to us, as is the date of the end of the world. "Watch, for you do not know the day of my coming. Like servants who are waiting for their master, not knowing whether he will come in the evening or at midnight, or at cock-crow, or in the morning, be fearful lest the Master returning unexpectedly find you sleeping."

The parable of the Ten Virgins, which is a prelude to the description of the Last Judgment, teaches the same lesson.

3. The Last Judgment

(MATTHEW 25:1–13; 31–46)

The kingdom of heaven may be likened to ten virgins who went forth with lamps to meet the bridegroom. Five of them were foolish and five were prudent. The five wise virgins took oil in their vessels with their lamps, but the foolish virgins took none. When the bridegroom delayed in coming, all of them grew drowsy and fell asleep. At midnight the cry rang out: "Behold, the bridegroom is coming. Go forth to meet him." All the virgins awoke and started to trim their lamps. The foolish ones said to the prudent ones: "Give us of your oil, for our lamps are going out." But the latter answered: "For fear that there may not be enough for you and us, go rather to buy some at the market." While they were going, the bridegroom came and those who were ready entered with him into the banquet hall, and the door was closed. Later the others came, saying: "Lord, Lord, open for us." But he gave this answer: "Amen, I say to you, I know you not."[21]

"Watch therefore, for you know neither the day nor the hour."

[21] Matt. 25:1–13. St. Matthew inserts here (25:14–30) the parable of the Talents; but we have seen that the parable of the Talents or the Minas (Luke 19:11–27) had been pronounced at Jericho several days before.

The parable of the Ten Virgins is one that cannot be told in other words without robbing it of half its charm. There is in it no obscurity. The Christian soul must always be ready to receive the divine Bridegroom at whatever hour he presents himself, for that moment upon which depends our eternal fate is uncertain for all of us. The hour of his coming, a different hour for each one of us, is brought forward to the day of the Parousia. Such is the meaning of the parable. It is perfectly clear, provided it is not transformed into an allegory. No theological conclusion may be drawn from the circumstance that the wise and the foolish virgins are equal in number, nor from their qualification as virgins — for they were all virgins — nor from the lack of sympathy shown by the wise virgins, nor from the return of the foolish virgins after the doors were closed. While the delay of the bridegroom may denote the remoteness of the Parousia which the Apostles took to be very close, the hour of midnight and the sleeping of the virgins have no other purpose than to emphasize the delay. It is generally thought that the oil represents charity or sanctifying grace which alone is able to open heaven to God's elect. But the foolish virgins had oil when they left, and they probably succeeded in procuring some, since they came back to knock at the door. Only, they were too late and it availed them nothing. Hence the oil has no special symbolical meaning, any more than the rest.

The only difficulty — and it is an accidental one — is the reconstruction of the scene, taking into account realism and local color. The little drama may be imagined in this way. The bridegroom, accompanied by a noisy escort, comes to rejoin his betrothed in the glare of torches and with the sound of musical instruments. Ten maidens, friends of the bride, have come to her home or to a neighboring house to go out to meet the bridegroom as soon as the signal of his coming is given. He delays longer than was expected, and they all fall asleep. When they awake, the wise virgins are all ready, but the foolish virgins are caught unprepared and are excluded from the wedding feast. In this supposition the feast would take place in the bride's home, which seems to have been the ancient custom of Israel. If we follow the reading of the Latin and the Syriac versions and of some Greek manuscripts, "to go forth to meet the bridegroom *and the bride,"* it must be inferred that the bridegroom has gone to claim his bethrothed and is conducting her ceremoniously to his own house, where the feast is to take place. These different arrangements do not change by one iota the meaning of the parable, the whole moral being contained in this maxim: "Be prepared, for you know neither the day nor the hour." And this advice, repeated several times, leads up to the description of the Last Judgment.

"When the Son of Man shall come in his glory surrounded by all his angels, he shall seat himself on his throne of glory, and all the nations shall be gathered together before him, and he shall separate men from one another as the shepherd separates the sheep from the goats, and he shall place the sheep at his right, and the goats at his left.

"Then the king shall say to the elect placed at his right: 'Come, blessed of my Father, take possession of the kingdom destined to you from the creation of the world. I was hungry and you gave me to eat; I was thirsty and you gave me to drink; I was a stranger and you welcomed me; I was naked and you clothed me; I was sick and you cared for me; I was a prisoner and you visited me.' The just shall say to him: 'When did we see thee suffering from hunger or thirst and give thee to eat or to drink? When did we see thee a stranger or naked and welcome thee or clothe thee? When did we see thee sick or in prison and come to thee?' The king will answer: 'Amen, I say to you, each time that you did these things to the least of my brethren you did them to me.'

"Then he shall say to those placed at his left: 'Depart from me, accursed, into everlasting fire prepared for Satan and his angels. I was hungry and you did not give me to eat; I was thirsty and you did not give me to drink; I was a stranger and you did not welcome me; I was naked and you did not clothe me; I was sick and in prison and you did not visit me.' To excuse themselves, they shall say: 'Lord, when did we see thee suffering from hunger or thirst or a stranger or naked or sick or in prison and neglect to succor thee?' But he shall answer them: 'Each time that you neglected to do these things for one of these little ones, you neglected to do them for me.'

"And they shall go into eternal torment, but the just shall enter into eternal life."[22]

The separation of the good and the bad, already prefigured in the parables of the Net and the Darnel, as well as in the simile of the Winnower, is here more vividly presented with the aid of a picture very familiar to the Palestinian peasant. On the Galilean hillsides one often sees black goats and white sheep grazing together under the care of the same shepherd. From a distance the scene presents nothing but a variegated and confused mass, but upon closer view the goats are readily distinguished from the sheep, less by their darker color than by their skittish behavior. When evening comes the shepherd separates them, or rather they separate themselves from the sheep because of their incompatible disposition.

Something similar will happen when the sovereign Judge, escorted by his angels, comes to render to everyone according to his works, and solemnly to proclaim the sentence already passed in the inner tribunal of conscience. Day of happiness and triumph for the elect: frightful day, day of despair for the reprobate. "Come, blessed of my Father. . . . Depart from me, accursed!" The Evangelist's purpose is not to strike the imagination of the reader, but to present him with a twofold moral lesson. The faults that we most readily condone in ourselves are sins of omission. Now it is precisely these that the Judge enumerates to justify his sentence of condemnation. On the other hand, by attributing to works of mercy alone the efficacy of opening heaven to the elect, he would give us to understand that there exists a mysterious identity between Christ and the Christian, so that by coming to the aid of a member of Christ we come to the aid of Christ himself. Has the reality of the Mystical Christ ever been more strikingly expressed, even in St. Paul?

---

22 Matt. 25:31–46. No parallel in the other Gospels.

CHAPTER V

Wednesday of Holy Week. The Treason

1. The Blinding of the Jewish People

WEDNESDAY was for Jesus a day of recollection. He seems to have spent the entire day at Bethany in private converse with his Apostles, to whom he wished to devote the last hours of his earthly pilgrimage. When he left the Temple on Tuesday evening, his public ministry was closed. Humanly speaking, it had ended in failure. St. John, admitting this, cannot contain his astonishment and seeks an explanation.

"Now though he had worked so many miracles before them, they did not believe in him; that the word of Isaias the prophet might be fulfilled: 'Lord, who has believed our report? To whom has the arm of God been revealed?' They could not believe, because Isaias says again: 'He has blinded their eyes and hardened their heart; thus their eyes see not and their heart understands not, so that they be converted and I heal them.' Isaias said these things, because he saw his glory and spoke of him.

"And yet, even among the rulers, many believed in him; but for fear of the Pharisees, and that they might not be put out of the synagogue, they did not dare to confess their faith; for they loved the glory of men more than the glory of God."[1]

---

[1] John 12:37–43. St. John places the visit of the Gentiles and the incidents associated with it immediately after the triumphal entry into Jerusalem. He closes the story with these words: "Having said these things, he withdrew from their sight." He then adds a reflection on the incredulity of the Jews, together with a short summary of Christ's message. This arrangement evidently disregards chronological order.

The text of Isaias (6:9–10) is cited with notable variants in Matt. 13:14–15;

This general blindness, it is true, admits of many exceptions, even among the ruling classes which St. John has particularly in view. There are men like Nicodemus and Joseph of Arimathea, who are at present paralyzed by human respect, but will soon be emboldened to confess their faith. Later on, the Pharisees will flock into the newborn Church. Nevertheless the incredulity of the mass of the chosen people is a problem and a scandal, and would be so even more, if it had not been foreseen and foretold. He whom Isaias in contemplation saw seated upon his throne of glory, and who in reality was the Word of God, in some way preluding his mission of redemption, had given the prophet the errand to blind and to harden, by a powerful and supreme effort of mercy, a people already hard and blind. We have said elsewhere, in speaking of the parables, that God blinds and hardens by an excess of light and an excess of condescension, but he blinds and hardens only those who are already hard and blind by their own fault. We shall not repeat that explanation here. Jesus had worked in Palestine, and notably in Jerusalem, a multitude of miracles capable of leading to belief the most unbelieving. Of these miracles St. John relates only seven, which allow him to illustrate a dogmatic point, but he tells us that he is deliberately passing over many others, from which the Synoptics have made a choice. If the Scribes and Pharisees and the princes of the priesthood have not perceived these divine signs, it is because pride, self-interest, envy, and ambition have closed their eyes or veiled the light. The blinding is their own work more than God's. It is true that the prophet has foreseen and foretold their blinding, which thereafter will infallibly happen, but it does not happen because the prophet has foreseen and foretold it. On the contrary,

---

Mark 4:12; Luke 8:10; John 12:40; Acts 28:26–27. St. John attributes directly to God what God commands the prophet to say. Cf. Dittmar, *Vetus Testamentum in Novo,* 1899, pp. 30–31. We read with the best manuscripts: "because he saw his glory" (ὅτι), and not, as in the Vulgate, "when he saw" (ὅτε). The variation in meaning is slight.

To understand the text, three peculiarities of St. John's style should be kept in mind: (1) the difference between *believing someone* (αὐτῷ) and believing in someone (εἰς αὐτόν); (2) the difference between *observing his commandments* (τηρεῖν) or putting them into practice, and *keeping his words* (φυλάσσειν), taking account of them, adhering to them, attaching oneself to them; (3) the words *judge* (κρίνειν) and *judgment* (κρίσις) in St. John often mean a condemnatory judgment.

the prophet has foreseen and foretold it because it will some day come to pass. If it be asked why God lavishes his benefits and graces on those who he knows will abuse them and thereby become more culpable, the question is transferred to the sphere of metaphysics. It is asking why God permits evil which he could prevent, or better still, why he has created beings endowed with freedom.[2]

The striking success of Jesus at the outset of his ministry presaged a better result. At his first miracles the masses, who dreamed of a national hero and a conquering Messias, hailed in him the liberator of Israel. The Day of Parables began their disillusionment, and the proclamation of a spiritual kingdom completely broke the charm. Far from heightening enthusiasm, the Saviour seems to assume the task of lulling it. He hides himself and takes to flight in order to escape the demonstrations of the multitudes; he imposes silence upon the beneficiaries of his miracles; to many of those who wish to follow him he speaks of renunciation, of persecutions to be undergone, of carrying the cross. Instead of the temporal advantages that they crave, he proposes to them mysteries to believe and austere precepts to observe. Is it surprising that the common people, their first excitement gone, have little taste for his lessons? The intellectual elite lag behind for other reasons. We have seen what kept the Pharisees back and what alienated the Sadducees. As to the Essenes, those ascetics among the Jewish people, they were always the most obstinate against accepting Christianity, and it does not seem that Jesus ever came into contact with them.

---

[2] Cf. Charue, *L'Incrédulité des Juifs dans le N.T.*, Gembloux, 1929: historical and theological explanation according to St. John, pp. 225–263. The author concludes: "The merciful activity of Jesus, the scandal of a Messianism free of all the vagaries of nationalism, the treacherous enmity of the leaders of the people, the co-ordination by Satan of all the forces of opposition: these are points on which the four Evangelists are in perfect agreement" (p. 261). According to this author, St. John gives, in addition, "the theological explanation of the incredulity of the Jews," or better, of all incredulity. "Antecedently to Jesus' efforts, internal dispositions had already inclined souls toward truth or error, and the incredulity of many of the Jews was no more than the foreseen consequence of a preexisting antipathy to the light. Upright souls, the pure and sincere among them, come to Jesus, while the others remain in the darkness" (p. 263). Is this a complete or only a partial explanation? It is to be noted that "the Fourth Gospel does not ask the further questions about the reconciliation of God's sovereignty and goodness with man's freedom" (p. 262).

The mystery of unbelief, which astonishes St. John, fills the heart of St. Paul with an immense sadness. He consoles himself with the thought that this exclusion of his compatriots is but partial and temporary. Less than thirty years after the Passion, St. James will show him thousands of Jews making up the Christian community of Jerusalem. True, they are only a minority compared with the faithless mass; but are they not the blessed "remnant" of which the prophets speak, the true Israel, the Israel of God?

The unbelief of the Jewish contemporaries of Christ was providential. It hastened the conversion of the Gentiles by accelerating the dispersion of the twelve Apostles. It favored the unity of the newborn Church and preserved it from a very grave peril. If the Jews had embraced the Gospel *en masse,* such a national Church, despite every effort, would have kept something of the particularistic spirit of the Synagogue. It would have wished to impose circumcision and the observance of the law upon all. Now, the world would never have become Jewish. We know what embarrassment the Judaizers of the first centuries, weak minority as they were, created for the preaching of the faith among the Gentiles. Had they been the majority, they might conceivably have divided the infant Church into two heterogeneous factions. There would have been danger of compromising the fusion of the diverse elements into the unity of the Mystical Body, a fusion which St. Paul regarded as the most marvelous fruit of the Redeeming Death.[3]

What, then; was the message of salvation rejected by the Jews? St. John gives it in an abridged form to conclude the first part of his Gospel:

"He that believes in me believes not (solely) in me but in him who sent me; and he that sees me sees him who sent me. As the Light of the world have I come into the world, that he who believes in me may not walk in darkness.

"If anyone hear my words and keep them not, it is not I who will judge him; for I have not come to judge the world, but to save the world. He that spurns me and rejects my word has one to judge him; it is my word that shall judge him on the last

[3] Eph. 2:14–16. Cf. Prat, *Théologie de S. Paul,* Vol. II, pp. 272–284 (English transl., Vol. II, pp. 225–229).

day: For I have not spoken from myself . . . but accordingly as my Father has commanded me."[4]

Perhaps as he spoke these words, marked by melancholy sadness, Jesus was thinking of the unfortunate man who, not content with rejecting his word and despising his benefits, was preparing to sell him to his enemies for thirty pieces of silver.

2. The Bargain of Judas

Wednesday the leaders of the priests and the elders of the people met once more at the house of Caiphas to discuss the situation and to decide what measures should be taken. It was only a private meeting, held outside the customary place for sessions, and it is very probable that the members of the Sanhedrin who were suspected of being favorable to Jesus were not summoned. All present were of the opinion that it was necessary to bring the matter to an end as soon as possible, and to disembarrass themselves, at all costs, of a troublesome adversary. However they were divided on the means to adopt. The majority proposed that they avoid precipitating matters, and hence that they wait at least for the closing of the festival, for fear of provoking a disturbance which the Roman authorities, who were more watchful at such times, might brutally suppress. Others thought that speedy action was imperative lest the opportunity slip away. All agreed in preferring strategy to force.[5]

---

[4] John 12:44–50. "All the ancient writers regarded (this passage) as a distinct discourse (of Jesus). But some recent Catholic writers agree in seeing in it a sort of digest of the discourses pronounced by Jesus, which St. John here attributes to him as a summary of the most essential points of his teaching" (Lagrange, *Saint Jean,* p. 344). Cf. also Schanz, Knabenbauer, Tillman, Durand, etc.

[5] Matt. 26:1–5; Mark 14:1–2; Luke 22:1–2. It was "two days before the Passover" (Matthew); or "before the Passover and the feast of unleavened bread" (Mark); "the feast of the unleavened bread called the Passover was approaching" (Luke). This can only be Wednesday.

The meeting took place in the house of the High Priest Caiphas (Matthew); it included, besides the leaders of the people who were the instigators of the plot, some Scribes (Mark and Luke) and ancients of the people (Matthew), that is to say, some members of the three classes that made up the Sanhedrin. All preferred stratagem and agreed to do nothing on the day of the solemnity itself for fear of creating a disturbance.

While they were still deliberating, without being able to make up their minds which direction to take, help arrived as welcome as it was unexpected. "Satan," says St. Luke, "had entered into the soul of the Iscariot," or rather, had taken possession of it to reign there as master; for the miserable wretch had long since opened the door of his heart to the enemy. Profiting by the freedom which his duties gave him, he had that day left the company of the other Apostles and was prowling around the palace of the High Priest. Perhaps he had waited for the darkness of night before striking the blow. Being led into the presence of the Council, he offered his help, but not without pay: "What will you give me," he said, "and I will guarantee to deliver him to you?" The overjoyed members of the Sanhedrin dissembled their satisfaction, lest the traitor raise his demands, but they finally promised him thirty pieces of silver, if he should succeed. He accepted the bargain. Thirty shekels were scarcely equivalent to twenty-two dollars and fifty cents: a small price for betraying his Master and his God. But Judas was one of those misers over whom the sight of money exercises a fascination.[6]

Next to the revolt of the angels in heaven and the disobedience of Adam in the terrestrial paradise, there is not, perhaps, a spectacle more frightening than the presence of a traitor in the bosom of the Apostolic group, so close to the source of all grace, in the intimate companionship of Jesus himself. Judas was not of a nature different from ours. To say that he was an incarnate devil, or malice personified, explains nothing. He was, as we are, capable of good and of evil. Jesus had discerned in him the making of an Apostle when he associated him with the college of the Twelve. If he was the hateful creature that we know, it was because he became such by his own fault. The premonitory symptoms of his fall were not of recent date. When, shocked by the promise of the Eucharist, the disciples had gradually dispersed, and when St. Peter, in the name of all his colleagues,

---

[6] Matt. 26:14–16; Mark 14:10–11; Luke 22:3–6. The traitor lays plans in concert with the chief priests. St. Luke adds: "and with the chiefs" (of the Temple police, τοῖς στρατηγοῖς). Not only is the pact concluded; plans for its execution are already being made. On the value of thirty pieces of silver, see Note O: *Jewish Money at the Time of Christ.*

had proclaimed their own inviolable fidelity, our Lord had sadly said to them: "Have I not chosen you, the Twelve? Yet one of you is a devil!" "He was speaking," adds St. John, "of Judas the son of Simon Iscariot. He it was, though one of the Twelve, who was to betray him." It is not necessary to suppose that this incident took place immediately after the discourse on the Eucharist, a year before the Passion. It may have been some time after, when the defection of numerous disciples was a recognized fact. It is likewise very probable that the words of Jesus were prophetic and did not reflect the sentiments entertained by the traitor at the time. But nonetheless, it remains true that long before the Passion the unhappy man was already slipping, perhaps unconsciously, down the fatal decline which was to precipitate him into the abyss.[7]

He now abandoned himself without resistance to his evil instincts; we know one of them with certainty, and may suspect others. "He was a thief," says St. John, "and dishonestly abstracted part of the sums cast into the common purse, of which he had charge." Why was he saving it up? It may be that he was already meditating his future desertion and wished to assure for himself an easy life in the time to come; or, as often happens, avarice caressed over a long period turned in his case into a monomania.

Avarice had for company disappointed ambition. Like many another casual disciple, Judas may have attached himself to the Saviour through motives of self-interest, thinking that in the kingdom of heaven there would be temporal advantages to reap and offices to gain by intrigue. He soon found out that he was mistaken, and that the kingdom of heaven would yield him no such return. Besides, the founder of this kingdom was lacking in boldness. Instead of confronting his enemies he fled from them and seemed to be afraid of them. Judas had nothing to hope for from such a leader, who preached only humility and sacrifice.

To ambition and avarice was joined the vilest and most shameful of sentiments, envy. Judas was the only one of the Apostles who was not a Galilean by birth. The surname Iscariot, which he bore like his father, proves that he had left his native place. The

---

[7] On the traitor's psychology, cf. Tasker, in the *Dictionary of Christ and the Gospels,* I, 907–913.

fact that he was a foreigner was likely to give rise to clashes. Judas seems to have had the advantage of an education somewhat superior to that of the other Apostles, and the office that he filled in the Apostolic group must have inspired in him some pretensions. In the list of the Apostles, in which the Evangelists seem to observe a certain hierarchy, Judas is always placed last. When he saw the primacy of Peter proclaimed at Caesarea Philippi, and the favor manifested toward the sons of Zebedee, he understood that he would never play anything more than a secondary role in the Apostolic group. These marks of preference did not leave the other Apostles unaffected, but they were too much of a shock for the venal and naturally jealous soul of Judas.

CHAPTER VI

The Sacrament of Love

1. Preparation for the Passover

THURSDAY morning the Apostles said to Jesus: "Where dost thou wish that we go to prepare what is needed to eat the Passover?" Although the Paschal feast did not begin until nightfall, it was well to make ready beforehand, since the preparations were quite time-consuming, and it was not easy, because of the concourse of pilgrims, to find available places in the city. The Saviour charged the two inseparables, Peter and John, with this task: "As you go into the city, there shall meet you a man carrying a pitcher of water; follow him, and wherever he enters, say to the master of the house, 'The Master says, "Where is my guest chamber that I may eat the Passover there with my disciples?"' And he will show you a large upper room furnished and ready; there prepare the Passover."

Everything happened in order, just as the Saviour had said. The two Apostles entered the city, perhaps by the gate called in Nehemias the Fountain Gate; and, arriving close to the Pool of Siloe, they saw a man who had just filled a pitcher. The duty of drawing water was generally left to the women, who performed this task at twilight. Hence the sign given them by the Saviour was not ambiguous and could not have occurred by chance. Accordingly, the two messengers followed unhesitatingly in the footsteps of their guide, who stopped in front of a fine looking house. Scarcely had they framed their question, when the owner hastened to place the finest room in his house at their disposal. It was a spacious room located on the upper floor, furnished with mats, cushions, and couches. Such rooms were scarcely ever used except for receptions and special dinners. Instead of the simple guest room that Jesus had asked for, the generous disciple, who seems to have been waiting for the request, has reserved for him his best apartment; and he has the delicacy to understand that, despite the extreme scarcity of places, he must yield it to him exclusively, in order to avoid disturbing the intimacy of the feast.[1]

This disciple was well known to Jesus, and the Saviour could have designated him by name to the two messengers. Why, then, so much mystery? Was it that he wished to give the Apostles another proof of his infallible foreknowledge, and thus to fortify them against the scandal of the Passion by robbing the tragic events that were to come of all element of unforeseenness and surprise? Or, as St. Cyril of Alexandria thinks, was it his intention to prevent Judas from advancing the hour of his treason by keeping him until evening in ignorance of the place where he would celebrate the Passover? What makes the latter supposition more likely is that Jesus chose Peter and John to take care of material preparations which belonged rather to the sphere of Judas' duties. The Gospel does not tell us where Jesus spent the rest of the day; perhaps in the hospitable home at Bethany, or else in one of the two retreats to which he used to retire on the slope of the Mount of Olives facing Jerusalem.

The Jewish Pasch or Passover was the annual commemoration

[1] Matt. 26:17–19; Mark 14:12–16; Luke 22:7–13. It is evident that the Cenacle did not belong to any of the Apostles, and it is no less evident that it belonged to a disciple. This may be gathered even from the very succinct narrative of St. Matthew: "Go into the city to a *certain one* and say to him: The Master *informs* thee that *at thy house* he is keeping the Passover with his disciples"; and more clearly still from the more precise and more circumstantial narrative of St. Mark: "Where is *my guest chamber* . . . and he will show you a large room *all ready*." Jesus therefore goes as if to his own house, and he is expected. St. Luke here closely follows St. Mark, whose work he had before him or in his memory. He transcribes the common word ἀνάγαιον (*upper room*), formed after the analogy of κατάγαιον (cf. Moulton-Milligan, for the papyri, and W. Bauer, s.v.), whereas everywhere else he uses the classic word ὑπερῷον (Acts 1:13; 9:37–39; 20:8); but he omits the words *my* (guest chamber) and *all ready,* which bear witness in St. Mark to a personal knowledge.

On the traditions about the Cenacle and its present condition, see Note R: *The Cenacle.*

of the exodus from Egypt. Before leaving the land of exile, each Israelite family had slain a lamb, and had sprinkled the blood on the doorposts and lintels to ward off the exterminating angel. At nightfall the fugitives had eaten the roasted lamb in haste, staff in hand and with shoes upon the feet, as people about to set out upon a journey.

Moses prescribed that the anniversary of this event should be celebrated in perpetuity by a commemorative feast which should last seven days, the first and last days being days of rest from work, like the Sabbath. Throughout the week beginning with the 15th of Nisan, which commenced at sunset on the 14th, only bread without leaven could be eaten, as on the evening of the coming out from Egypt. But the Passover of later times differed much from the first Passover. Only men in the state of legal purity were permitted to eat it; others had to postpone the celebration to the same day of the following month. When the law of one sanctuary forbade sacrifice outside Jerusalem, the lamb was no longer slain except in the Temple. The passage of time brought other departures from the ancient ritual. In the first century of the Christian era, the Jews ate the Passover reclining on couches as became free men, in imitation of the masters of the world. Two points, however, remained untouched, since they were formally prescribed in the law: the prohibition against breaking any bone of the slain lamb, and the prescription that nothing of it be allowed to remain until the morrow.[2]

The casuistry regarding the search for leavened bread and its destruction shows with what childish minuteness the Scribes had regulated the Paschal feast. The Talmud insistently inculcates the obligation of all to empty at least four cups of wine. One could, however, take more than that; and the not very edifying story is told of two Rabbis who celebrated the Passover too well, one

[2] Passages relating to the Passover and the unleavened bread: first Passover, Exod. 12:1–10; commemorative Passover, Exod. 23:14–17; 34:18–25; Lev. 23:5–14; Num. 9:2–14; 28:16–25; 33:3; Deut. 16:1, 8, 16. Originally, the Paschal feast was a meal for men "from the age of twenty years," according to the *Book of Jubilees,* xlix, 17. Later, women also were admitted, as may be concluded from a passage of Josephus (*Bellum,* VI, ix, 3). Still later, no one was excluded, even very small children; and even the Mishnah (*Pesaḥim, x, 4*) supposes that this custom was already in use.

being indisposed up to Pentecost, the other, up to the Feast of Tabernacles. To tell the truth, the whole Rabbinical description of the Paschal feast revolves around these four cups of wine, and one would be led to think that there was nothing else to it.[3]

We purposely omit the description of the Paschal rites for two valid reasons. First, the Gospel makes no allusion to them excepting the final canticle, which was perhaps the chanting of the *Hallel*. Second, it is unknown to what extent these rites were observed at the time of Christ, even by the strictest Pharisees. If we fail to imitate those writers of Lives of Christ who accord a boundless faith to the elucubrations of the Talmud, the specialists most smitten with Rabbinism are of our opinion. "It is difficult to decide," says one of them, "how much of the rubric for the Paschal Supper, as contained in the oldest Jewish documents, may have been obligatory at the time of Christ."[4]

---

[3] The poorest in Israel must empty four cups on that evening (Mishnah, *Pesaḥim,* x, 1). To establish this obligation the Talmud depends upon the following facts: In Exod. 6:6–7, the deliverance of Israel is expressed by four synonyms; in Gen. 40:11–13, the cup of Pharao is mentioned four times: by combining various texts four cups of divine wrath are found, and four cups of consolation and salvation. If the guests were thirsty, they could interject other cups besides the ones in the ritual, but not between the third and fourth. The Jerusalem *Gemara* gives this reason: "For fear of drunkenness. . . . Wine drunk while eating rarely inebriates, whereas that which is taken afterward inebriates" (trans. Schwab, *Pesaḥim,* x, 6, p. 153). Now, after the third cup nothing was eaten.

[4] Edersheim, *Life and Times,* II, 492. See also the reflections of Beer, *Pesaḥim,* 1912, p. 56. The Mishnah, codified some 130 or 140 years after the destruction of Jerusalem, possibly represents *in general the practice of the Pharisees in the time of Christ*. But it cannot be concluded that that was the practice of the people in general or of the Sadducees, of whom we know so little, since we have at our disposal only Pharisaic sources (Talmud, Josephus, Philo, the Book of Jubilees).

Since the majority of authors writing about the life of Christ dwell at length on the ritual of the Paschal feast, we give here a brief summary according to the least troubled source, the Mishnah (*Pesaḥim,* x, 2–3). The first cup is poured and the feast is blessed and then the wine, according to Shammai; or, according to Hillel, first the wine and then the feast. Then in succession the bitter herbs, the unleavened loaves, and the dipping sauce are brought in. While the Temple was standing the Paschal lamb was also brought in.

Pesaḥim, x, 4–5. The second cup is poured and the father of the family instructs those present, above all the children, on the meaning of the feast. Then the first part of the *Hallel* is recited, Ps. 112 (Vulg., 111), as far as Ps. 113(112):8, according to Shammai; as far as Ps. 114(113):9, according to Hillel.

Pesaḥim, x, 6. The third cup is brought, with which the blessing of the repast is recited. The fourth cup will be drunk after the completion of the *Hallel,* up to the end of Ps. 118(117). "Between the first two cups it is permitted to drink others, if one wishes, but this is forbidden between the third and the fourth.

What we regard as certain is that Jesus really celebrated the Passover. Reading St. John alone, one would assert the contrary. He tells us that on Friday morning the Jews did not enter the Praetorium "that they might eat the Passover," and this word can mean nothing else than the Paschal lamb. Again, at the time when Jesus expired, "it was the preparation of the Passover"; and the day that was about to begin at nightfall according to Jewish computation was "an especially great Sabbath," which phrase would have no other meaning than a Sabbath coinciding with the Paschal solemnity. According to these points of information, Jesus died on the 14th of Nisan, at the time when the Paschal lamb was being slain; and, if so, the meal of the previous evening could not have been a Paschal feast. Even in the Synoptics there are several details which are difficult to reconcile with the solemnity of the 15th of Nisan. Such are the meeting of the Sanhedrin, the arrest of Jesus by men carrying arms, Christ's trial before the Procurator, Simon of Cyrene's return from the fields, the freeing of Barabbas. Still, the language of the Synoptics, taken in its entirety, leaves no room for doubt. The eve of the Passion was *the first day of Azymes, the day when the Passover was slain,* or *when it should be slain.* On that day the disciples ask the Saviour where he wishes to *eat the Passover;* at his command they go to *prepare the Passover;* upon taking his place at table Jesus says to them: "I have ardently desired to *eat this Passover* with you."

Briefly, if we had only St. John, we would not hesitate to say that Jesus died on the 14th of Nisan, the eve of the Paschal solemnity; if we had only the Synoptics, we would say with the same assurance that he died on the 15th, the day of the solemnity itself. There is here a problem the difficulty of which is recognized.

After the Paschal lamb, there follows no *Aphiqoman*" (trans. Schwab, p. 153). The last phrase is translated very differently by other authors. Beer, *Pesaḥim,* p. 199, translates it: "After the Paschal feast follows the *Epikomion.*" The variants are unimportant, because no one knows just what the pronunciation, the etymology, and the meaning of *Aphiqoman* or *Epikomion* may be. Some derive it from Arabic, others from Aramaic, the majority from Greek. It could be a chant of praise (*ἐπικώμιον*), or a dessert (*ἐπιγεύομαι*), or sweetmeats or tidbits or something less innocent if one prefers the derivation from *ἐπίκωμος, ἐπικωμάζω.*

A description of a present-day Paschal feast is given by P. Volz, in *Z.N.T.W.,* VII, 1906, pp. 245–251.

The only way to reconcile the Evangelists without doing violence to the texts is to admit that, in that particular year, the Jews did not all celebrate the Passover on the same day, and that what was for some of them the 14th of Nisan was for others the 15th. The solution is not a new one, but today we have many more resources than formerly to show that it is well grounded. Transferring these discussions of secondary importance to a special Note, let us resume the thread of our narrative.[5]

2. The Washing of Feet

"Before the feast of the Passover, Jesus knowing that his hour was come, to pass out of this world to his Father, having constantly loved his own that were in the world, he loved them exceedingly."[6]

Though the love of Jesus for his own is always the same, the visible proofs of this love become more and more striking as he approaches the end. It is the instinct of the human heart to reserve for the moment of parting the most delicate and the most touching proofs of tenderness. The Saviour submits to this law of human nature, and on the eve of parting from his disciples he will prove to them that he loves them exceedingly, even to the folly of the Cross. The last day of his mortal life will offer many occasions.

When night came, the Apostles were gathered around their Master in the upper chamber of the Cenacle, and Jesus, taking his place at table, said to them: "With great desire have I desired to eat this Passover with you before I suffer; for I say to you that I shall eat of it no more until it is fulfilled in the kingdom

---

[5] See Note Q: *The Last Supper, the Passover, and the Passion.*

[6] John 13:1. He loved them εἰς τέλος. This expression could, of course, mean "until the end," *in finem* (Matt. 10:22; 24:13), but this meaning scarcely fits here and does not answer to the solemnity of the introduction. We must therefore fix upon the meaning often found after Polybius, "completely," "altogether," "exceedingly"; Hermas, *Vis.*, III, x, 5: ἱλαρὰ εἰς τέλος, "exceedingly joyful."

This verse takes its place as an introduction to the second part of the Fourth Gospel, which part contains the history of the Passion. The proof of love is, therefore, not only the washing of the feet but all the rest.

of God."[7] Eternal life presented itself to the mind of the Jews under the image of a feast of which the Passover was a figure. The prophets were fond of this symbol, and the Evangelists have not disdained it. At that spiritual banquet, the true banquet of deliverance, Jesus will be at once the host and the guest, and he will drink of the cup of endless happiness with his elect in the kingdom of his Father.

Every great festal meal, and not only the Paschal meal, began with a twofold blessing: that of the wine, and that of the feast. Jesus, as master of the house, in place of the father of the family, must pronounce it. Taking the cup filled with wine, he recited over it the ordinary formula of blessing and gave it to the Apostles, probably after first sipping it himself, and said to them: "Take this cup and share it among you, for I say to you, henceforth I shall not drink of the fruit of the vine, until the kingdom of God come."[8] The strict parallelism with what precedes invites us still to understand here the reign of God in the celestial kingdom, and consequently the cup referred to is the cup of eternal beatitude. There is as yet no question of the Eucharist.

The unleavened bread, together with the bitter herbs and the mixture of fruits called *haroseth,* had been served, when a painful incident occurred which was in singular contrast with the solemnity of the occasion. There arose a contention among the Apostles to know which among them was, or was to be reputed,

---

[7] Luke 22:15–16. The declaration referring to the fruit of the vine, which Jesus will not again drink until he drinks the new wine in the kingdom of his Father, comes after the institution of the Holy Eucharist in St. Mark and St. Matthew, but the more natural place is at the beginning of the meal, as in St. Luke.

[8] Luke 22:17–18. The formula of the blessing of the wine was: "Blessed be thou, Lord God, who hast created the fruit of the vine." Those present answered: "Amen." The formula of blessing for the feast was longer. Cf. Billerbeck, *Kommentar,* Vol. IV, p. 63. This blessing of the wine — St. Luke is not speaking of the blessing of the feast — is not, as has been claimed, a Paschal rite, for it took place at the beginning of every meal.

The text of St. Luke has been variously manipulated by copyists who saw in Verses 17 and 18 a mention of the Eucharistic cup. Some have omitted Verse 20, believing it to be a repetition (so three codices of the Old Latin, and the bilingual D); others on the contrary, but for the same reason, omit Verses 17 and 18 (e.g., the *Peshito*); others again (*Syr-Syn* and *Syr-Cur*) suppress Verse 20 and transpose Verse 19 (consecration of the bread), placing it before Verse 17, which they mistake for the consecration of the chalice. One is astonished to see critics like Westcott-Hort attach any importance to these manipulations, the reasons for which are so clear.

"superior to the others."[9] Questions of precedence can arise at any time and in any place. History tells us what storms they have stirred up. The Pharisees frantically sought the places of honor, and the Apostles were not altogether exempt from this weakness. Among all peoples, it has always been a very delicate matter to assign to each guest the place he should occupy. To avoid complaints and discontent, the master of the house often preferred to allow the guests to select their places as they pleased, at the risk of provoking disorder and disputes. Such, we believe, was the origin of the painful incident recorded by St. Luke. A word of St. John would lead us to think that the pretensions of Judas were not without some influence upon it.

Jesus looked on with sadness in his eyes. His lessons of humility, so often inculcated, apparently had not been grasped. He must strengthen them by a final and striking example. Of a sudden he rose and put aside his cloak and girded his loins with a strip of linen cloth and filled with water a basin which was there for the customary purifications. The dumfounded Apostles watched what was happening, wondering what could be the meaning of this ceremony in the middle of a meal. But what was their stupefaction when they saw their Master, accoutered as a servant, starting to wash their feet and dry them with the towel! The Prince of the Apostles, with whom, apparently, he started, as was very natural, energetically protested:

"Lord, dost thou wash my feet?"

"What I do thou knowest not now, but thou shalt know hereafter."

"Thou shalt never wash my feet."

"If I wash thee not, thou hast no part with me."

"Lord, not my feet only, but also my hands and my head!"

"He who has bathed has no need to wash (except his feet); he is wholly pure. And you too are pure, but not all."[10]

---

[9] Luke 22:24. There was a dispute or rivalry (*φιλονεικία*) about the question: *τὸ τίς αὐτῶν δοκεῖ εἶναι μείζων*: "which among them should pass for the greatest" (Lagrange) or "who among them ought to be considered the greatest" (Joüon).

[10] John 13:6–10. This short dialogue presents certain difficulties.

a) "If I wash thee not, thou shalt have no part with me." Many observing that it is not: "If I do not wash thy *feet*," explain: If I do not wash thee (with my blood), thou shalt have no part (in the fruits of the redemption). It would be a general maxim, and Peter would be the representative of humanity. But this

Judas Iscariot had not yet left the Cenacle, and during this dialogue he was ruminating the plan of treason that Satan had placed in his heart. This it was that prompted Jesus to say, reading the heart of the traitor: "You are pure, but not all." As we see, he passes from the physical sense of bodily cleanness to the idea of moral purity. Was there in his mind a relationship between bodily washing and interior purification? Some exegetes and some theologians have seen in the washing of feet a symbol of Baptism or of Confirmation or of Penance. Such symbolism is not indicated by St. John. At most one may see in Jesus' action a sort of transitory sacrament to purify the Apostles from those lighter faults from which no one is exempt, the better to prepare them to receive the Sacrament of Love. When they had again taken their places at table, Jesus gave to the Twelve the explanation he had promised Peter:

---

is somewhat subtle and does not fit well with the context, where there is question only of a washing of the feet. Others understand thus: "If thou disobeyest me, thou losest my grace and friendship." This, however, is overprecise; the idea of obedience is, at most, only insinuated.

b) "He who has bathed has no need to wash (except his feet); he is wholly clean." Some authorities omit "except his feet." Cf. Lagrange, *Saint Jean,* pp. 353–355. In that case the meaning is clear: there is an opposition between "bathing," i.e., taking a bath (λούεσθαι), which refers to the whole body, and "washing" (νίπτεσθαι), which refers to a part, the hands, the feet, the face. He who has *bathed* is wholly clean, and has no need of *washing*. But it is precisely the ease of meaning obtained by such a reading that could have caused the omission of the phrase in question. With the common reading, the explanation will be: He who has washed his whole body (by bathing) has no need of washing any part, *except, of course, the feet,* which are quickly soiled by the dust and mud of the road.

c) The play on words resulting from the double meaning of καθαρός should be noted: physically "clean," morally "pure." If the first phrase is to be taken in a moral sense, the bath (λούεσθαι) can be the symbol of Baptism, and the washing (νίπτεσθαι) can symbolize Penance. He who has taken the *bath of Baptism* has no further need except recourse to the *washing of Penance*. On this way of explaining the text, see Maldonatus.

d) The exact meaning of "If I do not wash thee, thou *hast no part with me*" is controverted. Note that in the Greek the verb is in the present, not the future, as in the Vulgate (*habebis*). Corluy explains: "Removebo te a meo consortio." Lagrange: "If Peter does not yield, he excludes himself from his Master's company." Westcott: "Thou hast no share in my kingdom, as a faithful soldier in the conquests of his captain." Knabenbauer: "Si non lavero te non accipies quod hac mea actione et significatur et tribuitur." The threat is vague, and should remain so in the translation: "We have nothing in common; we cannot get along together," without saying why. Similar expressions are to be found in 2 Kings 20:1; 3 Kings 12:16.

"Do you understand what I have done to you? You call me Master and Lord; and you say well, for so I am. If then, I have washed your feet, I your Master and your Lord, you also ought to wash one another's feet. I have given you the example, that you in turn may do as I have done to you. Amen, amen, I say to you, the servant is not greater than his master, nor is the one sent greater than he that sent him. Blessed are you, if you know these things and if you do them!"

Peter must now understand — and later on he will understand better — how out of place his obstinacy has been. His refusal had come from a praiseworthy feeling, respect for his Master and repugnance to undergoing treatment which so strangely reversed their roles. But his resistance, were it pushed too far, would turn into insubordination. The Saviour warns him that, if he persists, he will have no part with him. Does he mean that by his disobedience Peter would fall from sanctifying grace, or simply that by failing to enter into the spirit of him who has proclaimed himself meek and humble of heart he would no longer be worthy to share in his work and to be associated with the glory of his apostolate? At all events, the threat is terrifying, and Peter, not content with yielding, falls into excess by claiming even what has not been offered.

St. Luke, who does not record the washing of feet, still gives its moral lesson, precisely with reference to the incident which seems to us to have called it forth:

"The kings of the nations lord it over them, and they who exercise authority over them assume the name 'Benefactor.' But not so with you. Let him who is greatest among you become as the smallest, and him who is the chief as the servant. For who is greater, he that reclines at table, or he that serves? Is it not he that reclines? But I am in your midst as he that serves."

3. The Traitor Unmasked

A certain uneasiness pervaded the little group. What meant those words: "You are pure, but not all"? Our Lord explains himself a little more clearly by quoting a saying of Scripture: "He that eats bread with me shall lift up his heel against me."

When he said these words "he was troubled in spirit," as he had been troubled a few days before at the prospect of the Passion. And he adds: "Amen, I say to you, one of you will betray me." The Apostles looked at one another in consternation, but no thought of crime could be read in any of their faces. Judas remained unmoved. Jesus continued: "He that dips his hand with me in the dish, he shall betray me. The Son of Man indeed goes his way, as it is written of him, but woe to that man by whom the Son of Man is betrayed! It were better for that man if he had not been born." The Apostles still did not grasp the reference to Judas, for Jesus' word, "He that dips his hand with me in the dish" was an allusion to the psalm already quoted, and could apply to all the guests taking food from a common platter. Their fright was extreme. To dissipate the doubt that pressed upon them, like a nightmare, each of them began to ask: "Lord, is it I?" Judas too, feeling that his silence would be tantamount to an avowal, had the effrontery to ask the same question, and Jesus, by a nod or in a voice so low as to be heard by no one else, answered him: "Thou hast said it"; thou art the one. Anguish still gripped the Apostles, suspended as they were between desire of knowing and fear of hearing the answer. Let us hear the witness who is best informed, since he took an active part in the drama.

"One of the disciples, he whom Jesus loved, was reclining on Jesus' bosom. Simon Peter beckoned to him and said: 'Who is it of whom he speaks?' This disciple, leaning back on Jesus' breast, asked him: 'Lord, who is it?' Jesus answered: 'It is he to whom I shall offer a morsel of bread dipped in the sauce.' And dipping a morsel of bread in the sauce he gave it to Judas, son of Simon the Iscariot. . . . And when he had taken the morsel of bread (Satan having taken possession of him), he straightway went out. It was night."

To understand the shifting scenes of this drama and these mute dialogues, it is indispensable to examine briefly the arrangement of places and to bear in mind the positions occupied by the chief actors.[11]

[11] On the banquet customs of antiquity, the order of places at table, the

At the beginning of the Christian era, at formal banquets, the universal custom was to dine reclining on a couch, the breast resting on the left elbow, leaving the right hand free. Originating in Persia, where it was the usage from time immemorial, this custom had been adopted by the Greeks after the wars with the Medes; it then passed to Rome, where it was at first accepted with some reluctance; thence it extended to the rest of the civilized world. Only the Cretans, faithful to their ancient customs, continued to dine seated.

The couches consisted of a low divan, furnished with mats and cushions, and were arranged around three sides of an oval or rectangular table, the fourth side, the one nearer the entrance, being left free for the service. These couches sloped toward the rear, the place for the feet being somewhat lower, and approach to them was made from the back in a space left vacant to provide for moving about. Among the Romans, and the Jews who imitated them, there were three distinct couches, the whole bearing the name *triclinium*. There were often several triclinia in the same room; but we know that Jesus' host had turned over to him the whole upper chamber.

---

disputes caused by the placing of the guests, and other similar questions we refer to our article, *Les places d'honneur chez les Juifs contemporains du Christ,* in *Recherches,* 1925, pp. 512–522.

At the Last Supper we suppose that the disposition was the one generally in use, that of the Roman *triclinium:* three couches placed on three sides of an oval or squared table.

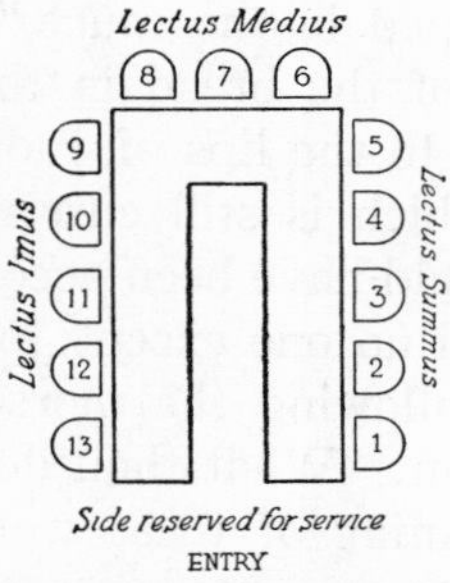

If we number consecutively the places for thirteen guests occupying the three couches of a *triclinium,* the place of honor is in the middle of the *lectus medius* at number 7. This is the place of our Lord, who has at his left St. Peter at number 6, and at his right St. John at number 8. Judas, who is directing the serving, is at the inner end of the *lectus imus* at number 9. If we have this diagram before us, the narrative of the Fourth Gospel presents no difficulty at all.

Two or three guests, sometimes more, took their places on each of the couches. Among the Romans and the Jews, the first place was the one in the middle, and the middle table opposite the entrance was considered the place of honor. Naturally the Saviour occupied this place, having at his right the Beloved Disciple, who could thus, by leaning back, rest his head on Jesus' breast. But we should not conclude from this that John had the place of honor after that of Jesus. According to the ideas of the time, the second place of honor was not at the right, but at the left of the principal guest and near his ear. We would suppose *a priori* that this place fell to St. Peter, and the Gospel narrative shows us that it was so.

Peter was consumed with the desire to know who was the traitor, but he did not dare ask the Saviour himself for fear of another rebuke. Supposing that John already knew, he made a sign to him, whispering with an imperceptible movement of the lips: "Who is it?" To execute this little pantomime without attracting attention and without being seen or heard by anyone, he had to lean over behind the Saviour, whose back was turned to him, and shielding himself behind him, come as close to John's ear as he could. He was therefore placed at Jesus' left, or, as the ancients said, he was *above* him.

The Beloved Disciple leaned his head upon the bosom of his Master — the memory of that privilege was to sweeten his whole life — and asked in a low voice: "Lord, who is it?" He had his answer, also in a very low voice: "It is he to whom I shall offer a morsel of bread dipped in the sauce." And at the same time Jesus dipped a piece of the bread in the sauce, and stretching forth his hand, held it to the lips of Judas. It was a courtesy or mark of preference which is still current in those lands.[12] The other Apostles, who could have been accorded the same attention, were not surprised and no one except John guessed its meaning. Immediately after swallowing the morsel of bread, Judas rose to go. Jesus said to him: "What thou dost, do quickly." No one gathered the true meaning of these words, not even John; for

[12] A description of this courtesy is given by J. Neil, in *Pictured Palestine*, 5 ed., pp. 78–83, or in *Everyday Life in the Holy Land*, 1913, p. 83: "When your host wishes to show you a special kindness or attention, he will take (in his right hand) some dainty piece of meat and put it in your mouth, or else roll up a ball of greasy rice and present it to you in the same way." The author adds that, in general, a European will gladly forego such attentions.

though he now knew the name of the traitor, he did not suspect that the treason was so close. Since Judas filled the office of treasurer in the Apostolic group, the Apostles believed that he was being cautioned to buy as soon as possible what was needed for the next day's feast.

This little piece of information offers us another safe lead. We know that the host of an illustrious personage often took his place to the left of the entrance and at the angle formed by this couch and the one in the middle. This was the most convenient place from which to direct the service and to make sure that nothing should be wanting to the principal guest. This place, one of the less honorable, was the one which his duties assigned to Judas. He was, therefore, separated from Jesus only by the Beloved Disciple, and was almost as close to him as John himself, since the couch on which he was reclining was at right angles to the central couch. This position of his, if one reflects, very naturally explains how the Saviour could speak to him in a low voice and could place in his mouth the morsel of bread dipped in the sauce.

When Judas left the room, it was night: *Nox erat*. These simple words, in the circumstances, have such a doleful sound that we are tempted to see in them a symbolic meaning. It was night; it was the hour of the powers of darkness. Hell was, for the moment, about to triumph, only to be forever vanquished.

The morsel of bread dipped in the sauce, which occasioned the immediate departure of Judas, was not the Eucharist. God forbid! The Holy Eucharist was not instituted until the end of the meal.[13]

---

[13] The only reason for placing the departure of Judas *after* the institution of the Holy Eucharist is that St. Luke adds, *after* the consecration of the wine: "Verumtamen ecce manus tradentis me mecum est in mensa." But the other Evangelists place these words *before* the institution of the Eucharist; and everyone (even Knabenbauer) agrees that in the narrative of the Last Supper, at which St. Luke was not present, this Evangelist does not follow the order of events as they happened.

In St. Augustine's time some negligent readers (quidam negligenter legentes) thought that the morsel of bread dipped in the sauce was the Eucharist. Today such negligent readers are no longer encountered, and the common opinion now is that Judas did not receive Holy Communion. See Salmeron, who develops this opinion at length and answers the objections, which, incidentally, are very weak. Still, many of the ancient Fathers thought differently, but they were not unanimous.

One shudders at the mere thought that, if the traitor had remained to the end, the Saviour would have given to him, as to the others, his body and his blood, since he was not yet a known sinner. If Jesus had ordained him a priest, he would have given him the power to profane at will the Sacrament of Love. Divine Providence would not permit such an abominable sacrilege to profane the banquet of farewell.

Jesus had spared nothing to reclaim this miserable man. He had multiplied his advances, his warnings, his tender reproaches; he had shown himself ready to forgive him at the first sign of repentance. But nothing could move the Son of Perdition. Now, at least, his treason, though it will astound the Apostles, will not be for them a rock of scandal. They will know that their Master had foreseen it and had foretold it; that it was for him neither a mischance nor a surprise; and that, assuredly, he went to death of his own free will.

Judas having gone, the Saviour breathed a sigh of relief. "Now," he said, "the Son of Man is glorified, and God is glorified in him. If God is glorified in him, God will glorify him in turn, and immediately will he glorify him."[14] He will glorify him by his redeeming death, whose corollaries are the Resurrection and the Ascension.

If St. John had wished to relate the institution of the Holy Eucharist, it is here that he would have placed the narrative. But at the time when he wrote, the account of the Synoptics was known to everyone. Even before they wrote — we know it from St. Paul — the celebration of the Eucharist had everywhere entered into the living practice of the Church and was an essential part of divine worship.[15]

4. The Institution of the Holy Eucharist

When the Paschal feast was ended, or about to end, Jesus took into his hand one of the unleavened loaves — there were none

For a good summary of the question see Corluy, *Comment. in Joann.*, 1880, pp. 321–323.

[14] John 13:31–32. Some place the institution of the Eucharist *before* these words. The matter is open to doubt.

[15] See what he writes to the Corinthians in A.D. 56, scarcely twenty-seven years after the Passion (1 Cor. 11:17–34).

other on that particular day — and, lifting his eyes to heaven, he pronounced over it a formula of blessing. This unusual gesture could not but attract the attention of the Apostles and awaken their curiosity, because it was not at the end, but at the beginning of a meal that the food was blessed.

Then Jesus broke the bread into as many morsels as there were guests present, and distributed it saying: "Take ye, eat. This is my body which is given (or delivered up) for you." Then taking a cup filled with wine diluted with water (for it was not customary to drink it pure), he performed the same ritual as for the bread he had consecrated, and presented it to the disciples, saying: "Drink ye all from it, for this is my blood, the blood of the (new) covenant, which is shed for many." The eleven Apostles drank each from the cup, and our Lord added: "Do this in remembrance of me."[16]

In these divinely simple words the Sacrament of Love was instituted. The Apostles, prepared long ago for this great mystery,

---

[16] A comparison of the four narratives of the institution of the Holy Eucharist is interesting. St. Matthew should be compared with St. Mark, and St. Luke with St. Paul, whose version is the most ancient.

Matthew 26:26–28

While they were eating, Jesus taking bread and blessing it, broke it and, giving it to his disciples, said:

TAKE YE, EAT, THIS IS MY BODY.

And taking the chalice and giving thanks, he gave it to them, saying:

DRINK YE ALL FROM IT, FOR THIS IS MY BLOOD (the blood) OF THE COVENANT SHED FOR MANY FOR THE REMISSION OF SINS.

Mark 14:22–24

While they were eating, taking bread, and blessing (it) he broke it, and gave it to them, saying:

TAKE YE, THIS IS MY BODY.

And taking the chalice (and) giving thanks, he gave it to them (and they all drank from it), and he said to them:

THIS IS MY BLOOD (the blood) OF THE ALLIANCE SHED FOR MANY.

Luke 22:19–20

Taking bread (and) giving thanks, he broke it and gave it to them, saying:

THIS IS MY BODY GIVEN FOR YOU. DO THIS IN REMEMBRANCE OF ME.

Likewise (he took) the chalice after the supper, saying:

THIS CHALICE IS THE NEW COVENANT IN MY BLOOD WHICH IS SHED FOR YOU.

1 Corinthians 11:23–25

Jesus took bread and, giving thanks, broke it and said:

THIS IS MY BODY, FOR YOU. DO THIS IN REMEMBRANCE OF ME.

Likewise (he took) the chalice after the supper, saying:

THIS CHALICE IS THE NEW ALLIANCE IN MY BLOOD. DO THIS IN REMEMBRANCE OF ME.

evinced no surprise. Had not Jesus promised them, a year ago in the synagogue of Capharnaum, that he would give them his flesh to eat and his blood to drink? Had he not told them, and repeated in every way, that if they did not eat his flesh and drink his blood they would not have life in them? And when the majority of the disciples, scandalized at this disconcerting manner of speech, had gone away, one after the other, had not Peter in the name of all his colleagues made protestation of their common faith? And now that they see the Saviour's promise fulfilled, they believe more than ever with all their souls in his truthfulness, his power, and his love. *Verba vitae aeternae habes; et nos credidimus.*

These words of Christ have in them nothing ambiguous. To teach that he is truly, really, and substantially present under the Eucharistic species, that he here gives his body for food and his blood for drink, could he have expressed himself with greater clearness? If he had said: "*This bread* is my body, *this wine* is my blood," his assertion would be not only absurd, but unintelligible, as opposed to the principle of contradiction; and the Calvinists, trying to discover a meaning in it, would perhaps be right in resorting to some one of the numerous symbolical systems they have concocted. If he had said: "*Here* is my body, *here* is my blood," the Lutherans would have some authority for holding — strange as it may seem — that nothing is changed in the bread and wine, and that Christ hides himself there as under a veil or a disguise. But he says: "*This* is my body, *this* is my blood," and that can be understood in only one way: "This which I hold in my hands, this which is still bread but will be such no longer as soon as the creative word is pronounced, the word which can neither deceive nor fail in its effect, this is truly and really my body, this body which is about to be delivered up to death for you and for the salvation of the world. In like manner, the content of this chalice is really my blood, the blood which seals the New Covenant, the blood which is about to be shed for you upon the cross." That this be so, it is evident that the bread and wine must cease to be present; to give place to the body and blood of Christ; and it is this change of substance, under the same accidents or sensible species, that the Catholic Church designates by a word, inelegant if you will, but very accurate and very expressive, and filling the need to cut short the quibbling of error — the word Transsubstantiation.

"Do this in remembrance of me; for as often as you eat this bread and drink this chalice, you shall proclaim the death of the Lord until he come."

In virtue of this command and this promise, the Apostles are made associates of the priesthood of Christ and created priests according to the order of Melchisedech, to offer in every place the unblemished victim of which the prophet Malachias speaks. Moreover, they are invested with the power to consecrate in their turn other priests, who will perpetuate the same rites even to the consummation of the world, even to the second coming of the Son of Man: *Donec veniat*.

Christ could have remained content with saying: "This is my body, this is my blood. Do this in remembrance of me," and, in fact, it is in this way that the primitive catechesis summarizes the institution of the Holy Eucharist.[17] If he adds anything, it is to emphasize still more the reality of his true body and his true blood, and to exclude for every unprejudiced mind all idea of symbolism, of figures of speech, of metaphor. It is also to establish a relationship between the Sacrifice of the Cross and the Sacrifice of the Altar.

Faith teaches us that the Sacrifice of the Altar is not only the commemoration and the representation of the Sacrifice of the Cross, but its mystical reproduction. The Church does not rest this dogma on the words of Consecration themselves; but it is a fact well worthy of remark that these words can be applied without strain to both sacrifices. The twofold formula of consecration, like a sword, separates the body and the blood of Christ. This body is delivered for us in the Eucharist as on the Cross, and in both ways it gives life to the world. This blood, mystically shed for us on the altar, as it was shed on Calvary, effects the

---

[17] St. Justin, *Apol.*, I, 66: "This the Apostles have handed down in the Memoirs composed by them which are called Gospels: Jesus, having taken bread and given thanks, gave this command: Do this in memory of me. This is my body. Likewise, having taken the chalice and given thanks, he said: This is my blood."

remission of sins and seals the New Covenant. In both, the Victim is the same, the sacrifice is the same; the only difference is in the manner of offering.[18]

We know beyond all doubt that the consecration of the chalice took place at the end of the meal,[19] and the narrative of the Evangelists leaves no room for supposing any long interval between the two consecrations. On the other hand, the modern hypothesis according to which the wine consecrated was that of the third cup seems to us very precarious. To avoid attributing too much importance to Rabbinical data, we will not emphasize the fact that in the Paschal feast each guest would have his own individual cup, whereas the consecrated chalice passed from hand to hand. We will only observe that this third cup was called the *cup of blessing,* not because it was the object of any special blessing, but because it was at that time that thanks were given to God for the meal, which was concluded before the recitation of the final *Hallel*. Hence it has not the least connection with the chalice of the Lord, which St. Paul calls "the chalice of blessing which we bless."[20]

Did Jesus taste the Eucharistic bread and wine before presenting them to the Apostles? The Gospel does not say that he did and seems to suggest the contrary. Still the Fathers and Doctors almost unanimously think that our Lord himself partook of the Communion.[21] They must be right. Was it not to be expected that Christ, in the celebration of the first Mass, would have wished to serve as an example and model to his new priests, since he was

---

[18] We can indicate these points only in a summary way, for a Life of Christ is not a theological treatise. Consult the magisterial study of P. de la Taille, *Mysterium fidei,* Chap. IX, pp. 101–106: Quaenam sit unitas ex coena et passione (English transl., Bk. I, th. ix, pp. 136–144). The Council of Trent says briefly: "Una eademque est hostia, idem nunc offerens sacerdotum ministerio, qui seipsum tunc in cruce obtulit, sola offerendi ratione diversa" (Denzinger, 15 ed., 940).

[19] 1 Cor. 11:25: *Postquam coenasset,* "after the supper."

[20] 1 Cor. 10:16: *Calix benedictionis cui benedicimus.*

[21] St. Irenaeus and St. John Chrysostom among the Greeks, Tertullian and St. Cyprian among the Latins, St. Ephraem and St. Aphraates among the Syrians are explicit. Vasquez knew no Catholic author of a contrary opinion, aside from certain anonymous writers mentioned by St. Thomas. However, he could have cited Peter of Poitiers. Today other exceptions could be found.

ordaining them to do what they had seen him do himself? The Communion is the complement and the consummation of the sacrifice and is, so to speak, an integral part of it. This is why the priest communicates before leaving the altar, and why the Church wishes those present, united in intention with the sacrificing priest, to unite themselves with him also in the effective partaking of the immolated Victim.

CHAPTER VII

The Discourse After the Last Supper

1. Conversation With the Apostles

(JOHN 13:31–14:31)

THE Paschal feast at no time resembled those pagan orgies which were enlivened by the music of flutists, the whirling of dancing girls, and the histrionics of stage players. The memories which it evoked, and the prayers and hymns which were its framework, always kept its religious character alive. But once the traditional rites were concluded, the conversation could take a freer turn and be prolonged far into the night.

Jesus' farewell discourse to the Apostles takes up five chapters in the Fourth Gospel. It may be asked how St. John could have retrieved so many recollections from the depths of his memory, after the lapse of sixty years. The answer is that, before writing them down, he had recited them hundreds of times in some sort of stereotyped form, even at the risk of hearing it said that he was always repeating the same words. No one maintains that he reproduces these discourses of Jesus in their entirety, word for word, and in the order in which they were originally delivered. He retains only the substance and the essential features, and, as is obvious, he injects into them his own style. But the backward references, the verbal repetitions, the absence of systematic development, and even the occasional lack of connection between the thoughts, are all proof that he did not make the discourses up out of his own mind. They form less one consecutive discourse than a collection of personal memories, the order of which may very well be guided by the natural play of the association of ideas.[1]

First of all there is a familiar exchange with the Apostles. Four speakers — Peter, Thomas, Philip, and Jude — give by turns a new impulse to the conversation, without causing it to deviate from its central theme, which is the imminent departure of Jesus, and his promised return.

"My little children (it is the first and only time that Jesus uses this caressing and tender diminutive), my little children, yet a little while I am with you. You shall seek me, and what I said to the Jews I say again to you: 'Where I go, you cannot come.'

"A new commandment I give to you: that you love one another, as I have loved you. By this sign shall all know that you are my disciples, that you love one another."[2]

It is natural for the new commandment of love to follow so closely the Sacrament of Love. It is called new, not only because, up to the present, it has been ill-understood and badly practiced, but for three reasons that are proper to itself. There now exist between Christians new relationships; a new ideal is proposed to Christ's disciples; and fraternal love is a new characteristic that must distinguish them from all others. Christians do not merely belong to the same human family or to some one religious clan; they are the same Mystical Body of Christ, and as St. Paul says, they are members one of another. Could a more intimate union be conceived? And the ideal of mutual love that is proposed to them is the love of Christ for us, an ideal so sublime that it must always be the goal of our aspiration, and yet we can never hope

[1] This long discourse is divided into three well-marked parts: (1) a conversation with the Apostles (Chaps. 13–14); (2) a monologue of Jesus on various subjects, the allegory of the vine, the sending of the Holy Spirit, future persecutions (Chaps. 15–16); (3) the priestly prayer (Chap. 17). Bossuet in his *Méditations sur l'Evangile* has no less than 172 meditations on the Last Supper and the last discourse of Jesus to the Apostles, for which he draws much of his inspiration from St. Augustine. P. Durand published four articles in *Recherches* (1910–1911) which are reproduced in his *Saint Jean* (*Verbum Salutis,* 1927). A more recent explanation is that of P. Huby, *Le discours de Jésus après la Cène,* Paris, 1932. The monograph of H. B. Swete, *The Last Discourse and Prayer of Our Lord,* London, 1913, deserves mention.

[2] John 13:33–35. The new commandment recurs in John 15:12; 1 John 2:7–10; 3:11; 3:23; 2 John 5. "As I said to the Jews" is an allusion to John 7:33–34 or 8:21.

to reach it. "Love one another!" These words recur again and again under the pen of St. John, just as they came to his lips when, broken down with age and carried in the arms of his disciples to the church in Ephesus, he kept repeating them over and over. To his hearers, weary of hearing them, he thus excused himself: "It is the precept of the Lord, and if it is observed, it is enough." The first Christians never forgot the precept: they were but one heart and one soul. "They loved one another almost before knowing one another," says the apologist, Minucius Felix. This mutual love of the faithful, ready to die for one another, as Tertullian says, was a cause of astonishment to the pagans.[3]

The announcement of an imminent separation has disturbed Peter, and he sees no reason why it should be impossible or forbidden to him to follow his Master:

"Lord, where goest thou?"

"Where I go, thou canst not follow me now; but later thou shalt follow me."

"Why can I not follow thee now? I will lay down my life for thee."

"Thou wilt lay down thy life for me! Amen, amen, I say to thee, the cock shall not crow before thou hast three times denied me."[4]

To all appearances, the prediction of St. Peter's triple denial took place on the way to Gethsemani, but allusion may have been made to it in the Cenacle, and St. John mentions it here to avoid coming back to it. The Apostles in consternation keep silent, not daring to ask more for fear of learning some new misfortune. The Saviour reassures them, gathering together the reasons best calculated to console them:

"Let not your hearts be troubled. You believe in God; believe also in me. In my Father's house there are many mansions — if it were not so, I would have told you — for I go to prepare a place for you. And when I have gone away and have prepared a place for you, I will come again, and I will draw you to myself, that where I am you also may be."[5]

---

[3] Minucius Felix (*Octav.*, 9; ML, III, 261), Tertullian (*Apol.*, 39; ML, I, 471).

[4] John 13:36–38. Peter cannot follow Jesus now, because he has a part to play in the Church; but since Jesus has not explained this, he protests that as far as he is concerned he is ready to follow his Master.

[5] John 14:1–3. There are two difficulties in this passage:

In heaven there are places without number, but to take possession of them, we need a guide to show us the way. Jesus Christ, according to the Epistle to the Hebrews, fills the office of pioneer, and of one who shows the way. His redeeming death gains for us a place in the City of Blessedness; his Ascension opens heaven for us; he alone has the keys, and he must enter in before any other. The places already existed then in divine predestination, but they were not yet ready to receive us. As soon as the Saviour has prepared them, he will come again to conduct his friends to them.

Several returns of Christ are to be distinguished. He returns to meet the Apostles again after his Resurrection; he returns at the death of the just to present them to his Father; he returns at times of religious crisis to succor and to save his Church; he will return at the end of time to judge the living and the dead. Many think that reference is here made to the return at the Parousia; but such a far-off prospect would be little likely to console them; and indeed at the time when St. John was writing his Gospel, all his colleagues had already taken possession of their places in heaven without awaiting that long-delayed date. The context itself shows clearly of what return Jesus wishes to speak. "I will come again, and I will take you to myself, that where I am, you also may be. And where I go, you know the way." But Thomas, distraught, interrupts him: "Lord, we know not even where thou goest. How then can we know the way?" Jesus has just said clearly that he is going to his Father's house to prepare

---

a) In πιστεύετε εἰς τὸν Θεόν, καὶ εἰς ἐμὲ πιστεύετε, the verbs can be either in the indicative or the imperative, which gives a choice of four translations, but that of the Vulgate is certainly the most natural: *Creditis in Deum, et in me credite:* "If you believe in God," or "Since you believe in God, believe also in me." Still, the translation: "Believe in God, believe also in me," is not inadmissible.

b) "Si quo minus dixissem vobis quia vado parare vobis locum." Many take it as a question: "In my Father's house there are many mansions; if it were otherwise, would I have told you that I go to prepare a place for you?" The *quia* and ὅτι can bear this meaning. This sense would be acceptable if Jesus had told them anything of the kind, but he had not. It is better, then, to take "If it were otherwise, I would have told you so" as a parenthesis, and for the sense to combine the two clauses separated by the parenthesis, thus: "In my Father's house there are many places — if it were otherwise, I would have told you so — there are, I say many places, for (or *because*) I go to prepare a place for you." Bernard, *Saint John,* 1928, pp. 523–524, mentions two other explanations which seem less probable.

a place for them; he limits himself, therefore, to this answer:

"I am the Way, the Truth, and the Life. No one comes to my Father except through me. If you knew me, you would also know my Father. And henceforth you know him, and you have seen him."[6]

Almost the whole of St. John's Christology is contained in this definition of the Saviour: "I am the Way, the Truth, and the Life." The paraphrase of it made by the pious author of the Imitation is excellent in its way, but it does not exhaust its riches. "I am the way that you must follow, the truth that you must believe, the life that you must hope for." Jesus Christ is not only a model to imitate; he is also and above all the Mediator through whom we must pass to reach the Father, for there is no salvation save in him. He is not only the road that leads to the Father, or the channel through which life and truth come to us; he is the source of our supernatural life. He is essentially the Way and the Truth, so much so that he is one with the Father, and can say to his disciples: "If you knew me, you would also know my Father, and you already know him and have seen him."

On hearing these words, Philip is thinking of one of those theophanies of the Old Testament when God made visible manifestation of his glory. Philip is conscious that he has never seen anything of this kind. Hence his naïve request: "Lord, show us the Father, and it is enough for us." Jesus, to whom Philip's simplicity is always pleasing, answers him in a tone of gentle reproach: "So long a time have I been with you, and thou dost not yet know me, Philip? He that sees me, sees also my Father. How canst thou say: 'Show us the Father?' Dost thou not believe that I am in my Father, and my Father in me?"

Whether or not he penetrated the mysterious depths of the consubstantiality of the Divine Persons, Philip gave a sign of assent, and Jesus continued:

---

[6] John 14:5–7. We follow the reading of the Vulgate, which is that of all the critical editors except Tischendorf. Another reading, less well attested, allows this translation: "If you know me, you will also know my Father." In this reading, the very ease of which renders it suspect, all hint of reproach or doubt would disappear.

"Believe me, that I am in the Father, and the Father in me. Otherwise, believe because of my works. Amen, amen, I say to you, he that believes in me, the works that I do he also shall do, and greater than these shall he do, because I go to my Father. And whatever you ask my Father in my name, that I will do, in order that the Father may be glorified in the Son.

"I will not leave you orphans: I will come to you. Yet a little while and the world sees me no more; but you see me, because I live and you shall live. In that day you shall know that I am in my Father, and you in me, and I in you. He that loves me and keeps my commandments shall be loved by my Father, and I will love him and manifest myself to him."[7]

Jesus will not leave *orphans* those whom he has just called his *little children*. After a short absence he will come again in glory, and his Apostles will see him with the eyes of the body and with the eyes of the spirit, whereas the world will not see him at all. And this return will be enduring. Beginning on the morning of Easter, it will reach its full splendor on the day of Pentecost, and it will perpetuate itself throughout the ages. Then the disciples will understand — what they are yet incapable of understanding — the intimacy of the union of Christ with his Father and with Christians: "They will know that henceforth Jesus lives a glorious life and they will be conscious of sharing this life. . . . The mutual immanence of the Father and Son, and the reciprocal compenetration of Jesus and his disciples, these are the truths which will be revealed to the faithful. Jesus Christ being in the Father as in the source of divinity, the disciples who are in him will also be in the Father, but through the Son, inasmuch as they are one, they in him and he in them."[8]

At this point Jude — who has nothing in common with the

---

[7] John 14:11–14 and 14:19–21. Between the two fragments there is a promise of the Holy Spirit. There are several points of controversy: (*a*) To which *coming* of Christ is there reference? (*b*) Of what kind of *seeing* is there question here? (*c*) Of what kind of *life* is Jesus speaking? It is impossible for us to enter into this discussion. Let us say only that the present "I come," "you see," "I live" is used by prolepsis for the future, and that in: "You see me, because I live, and shall live," the last two phrases can both depend upon "you see me" (i.e., "you shall see me"), or can be subordinate, one to the other: "because I live, and so you shall live."

[8] Huby, *Le discours après la Cène*, 1932, p. 61.

Iscariot except the name — hazards a question: "Lord, for what reason wilt thou manifest thyself to us and not to the world?" Christ's answer goes farther than the question: "If anyone love me, he will keep my word, and my Father will love him, and we will come to him and make our abode in him. He that does not love me does not keep my words; and the word that you have heard is not mine, but the Father's who sent me."

As may be seen, for these precious teachings we are indebted to four interruptions. Peter's question calls forth the assurance that Jesus will never abandon his own, that he goes to prepare a place for them, and that some day he will come again to take them with him. Thomas' question leads him on to say that he is the Way, the Truth, and the Life, the only Road that can lead to the Father. To Philip's interruption we owe the most precise definition and the most exact formula of the consubstantiality, and what is called the *circuminsession* of the Divine Persons. Finally, though Jude's question is left without a direct answer, the Saviour takes occasion from it to reveal to us the indwelling of the Holy Trinity in our souls by sanctifying grace.

The conversation is over; the Apostles have no more questions to ask. In conclusion, Jesus wishes them peace, and exhorts them to supernatural joyfulness:

"Peace I leave to you; my peace I give to you, but I do not give it as the world gives. Let your heart be untroubled and without fear. You have heard me say: 'I go away and I come to you again.' If you loved me, you would be glad that I go to my Father, for the Father is greater than I. . . . I will no longer speak much with you, for now the prince of this world is coming, and he has no right over me; but the world must know that I love my Father and that I act according to his commands.

"Arise, let us go hence."[9]

---

[9] John 14:28: *My Father is greater than I.*

1. *Exegesis of the Greek Fathers*. There are two explanations. (*a*) The Father is greater *as Father,* because he is the principle (ἀρχή and αἴτιος) of the Son, and in this respect he takes precedence over the Son in order (τάξει), or dignity (ἀξιώματι), without the Son being inferior in essence (οὐσίᾳ) or nature (φύσει), the superiority of the Father coming solely from this, that he is ἄναρχος, ἀναίτιος, ἀγέννητος (St. Basil, *Contra Eunomium,* I, 20 and III, 1). Also Origen, St. Alexander of Alexandria, St. Athanasius, St. Gregory of Nazianzus, St. John

For the Apostles, it is a source of inexhaustible happiness to be assured that their Master is not leaving them forever, that they will see him again, that he destines the Paraclete to take his place, that even after having withdrawn from them his visible presence he will continue to dwell in them, and that he will aid them in his own Person and also through his Spirit. In parting, Jesus does not simply wish them peace, as men do in saying farewell; he gives them peace, for it is his to give. He bequeaths it to them as a heritage. This peace of Christ, says St. Augustine, is "serenity of spirit, tranquility of soul, simplicity of heart, the bond of love, the communion of charity."

The Apostles should be glad to see him go to his Father, for "his Father is greater than he." What connection is there between the greatness of the Father and the joy of the Apostles? And how can the Father be greater than the Son, to whom he communicates his substance? Before the appearance of Arianism, this problem does not seem to have preoccupied the Fathers of the Church. Even after that date, the most illustrious among them understood the words, "the Father is greater than I," of the divine nature of Christ. They recognize in the Father as Father a priority of origin, of order, of dignity, without any pre-eminence

---

Chrysostom, St. Cyril of Alexandria, and St. John Damascene. (*b*) The inferiority of the Son comes from the Incarnation (διὰ τὴν οἰκονομίαν). Many of those who maintained the preceding explanation, such as St. Basil, St. Athanasius, St. John Chrysostom, and St. Cyril of Alexandria, give also this second one.

2. ***Exegesis of the Latin Fathers,*** apart from St. Hilary, who follows the exegesis of the Greeks. The Son is inferior *as man;* but it is doubtful that the human nature is compared with the divine nature. So St. Ambrose (*De fide,* ii, 8: *ex persona hominis*), the so-called Athanasian Creed: *aequalis Patri secundum divinitatem, minor Patre secundum humanitatem.* St. Augustine, who frequently comes back to the text, puts together on one occasion the two explanations of the Greeks: "Sed illa (the texts that affirm the inferiority of the Son) posita sunt propter administrationem (οἰκονομίαν) suscepti hominis qua dicitur: Seipsum exinanivit . . . partim propter hoc quod Filius Patri debet quod est, hoc etiam debens utique Patri quod eidem Patri aequalis aut par est; Pater autem nulli debet quidquid est" (*De fide et symbolo,* ix, no. 18; ML, XL, 191). It is probable that the Latins who express themselves less clearly understand it as Toletus: "Patrem majorem appellat ratione gloriae et majestatis in qua semper erat, non enim se *exinaniverat* Pater." It is not therefore the human nature of Christ that is compared with the nature of the Father, but the Person of the Word Incarnate that is compared with the Word before the Incarnation. So the second explanation of the Greeks would also be that of the Latins. Cf. Westcott, *Saint John,* 14 ed., 1902, pp. 213–216.

of majesty, of power, of nature. The majority of the Latin Fathers found it simpler to say that Jesus speaks here as man; but this involves some difficulty. If a man — were he the greatest that has ever lived on earth — should presume to say: "God is greater than I," would he not fall under suspicion of having lost his reason? In reality, Jesus Christ never speaks as God, or as man; he speaks as the God-Man, as the Incarnate Word. Now, the Word, by becoming man, humbled himself — the word is St. Paul's — he came down from his grandeur; he became inferior to God, by becoming equal to us; he is deprived of the honors which are due him; he must ascend to his Father to regain his glory. At the termination of his redemptive mission, the Father will exalt him, and give to him the name that is above every name. This is what the Apostles would be glad of, if they now fathomed the mystery of the Incarnation as they will after the descent of the Holy Ghost.

2. The Saviour's Monologue

(JOHN 15:1–16:33)

By saying, "Arise, let us go hence," the Saviour was giving the signal to go forth from the Cenacle. This precise order was not a mere advance notice given to no purpose: the Apostles must carry it out at once. Where, then, was the discourse pronounced which St. John summarizes in Chapters 15 and 16 of his Gospel? The narrow, twisting, and precipitous streets of Jerusalem would lend themselves ill to any such coherent address, and the Cenacle was not, in those days, outside the city, as it is now, since the southern wall was at the foot of the hill, running along the ravine of Hinnom.

It has been conjectured that the Evangelist, after composing his book but before making it public, judged proper to add a precious supplement, just as he, perhaps, appended a final chapter to the work, when it was already provided with a conclusion that left nothing to be desired. The words: "Arise, let us go hence," seem to have put an end to the conversation in the Cenacle. What follows is of a different kind. It is not so much a conversation as a monologue which the Apostles do not interrupt except in a body. In the midst of new teachings, there are frequent interruptions, as if to explain points that still remain obscure. The discourse could be described as a collection of memories which the author purposely avoids dating, either because the historical setting is not clearly fixed in his mind, or because he wishes to insert instructions that belong to different periods of time. In itself, this hypothesis contains nothing contrary to the most scrupulous orthodoxy. Composite discourses are frequent in the Gospels, and there are two special reasons for admitting that they are to be found in St. John. The first is that when he introduces a subject he ordinarily treats it fully, to avoid coming back to it; the second, that nowhere else does the book contain a discourse addressed to the Apostles.[10]

Three main ideas are developed: the union of Christ and his followers, illustrated by the allegory of the Vine; the mission and office of the Holy Spirit; the trials which await the faithful in the future.

The True Vine — "I am the true vine, and my Father is the vinedresser. Every branch in me that bears no fruit he cuts off; and every branch that bears fruit, he cleanses, that it may bear more fruit. You are already pure, because of the word which I have spoken to you. Abide in me, and I in you. The branch cannot bear fruit of itself, unless it abide in the vine; so neither can you, unless you abide in me.

---

[10] John 14:31. Many think that the Apostles rose when they heard the words: "Arise, let us go hence"; but did not leave the Cenacle (Maldonatus, Zahn, Knabenbauer, etc.). Others think that they went out, and that all the rest of the discourse was pronounced on the way (Westcott, Godet, Fillion, etc.).

Many Protestants maintain that Chapters 15 and 16 are displaced, and that they should come after 13:20 (Bacon) or after 13:30 (Bernard) or after 13:31a (Wendt). Cf. Moffatt, *Introd. to the N.T.*, 3 ed., 1920, 550–551. This hypothesis, however, is absolutely gratuitous, and the manuscripts and versions give not the slightest indication of any such displacement.

A certain number of Catholic authors are of the opinion that Chapters 15 and 16 form a supplementary collection aimed at strengthening certain previous teachings. The reasons advanced by the sponsors of the opinion may be found in Lepin, *La valeur historique du quatrième Evangile,* 1910, p. 101 ("extra chapters . . . supplement of information . . . by way of an appendix"); Durand, *Evangile selon saint Jean,* 1927, p. 410 ("Far from weakening the historical value of the discourse, this hypothesis strengthens it"); Lagrange, *Evang. selon S. Jean,* 1925, pp. 397–398. The reasons exposed by this last author, while not compelling assent, are not devoid of serious probability. P. Lebreton seems to subscribe to them.

"I am the Vine, you are the branches. He that abides in me, and I in him, he bears much fruit, for without me you can do nothing. If anyone abides not in me, he shall be cast aside as a (sterile) branch and shall wither. He shall be gathered up to be cast into the fire and shall burn."[11]

This lovely picture, which borrows its coloring from country life, is a mixture of allegory and parable. The allegorical elements are the vine, the vinedresser, the branches, and the fruit; representing respectively Jesus Christ, God the Father, the faithful, and meritorious works. All the rest is parabolical, and should be not so much *translated,* by substituting the proper corresponding terms, as *interpreted,* according to the laws of the parable. The general meaning is very clear, and Bossuet sums it up thus: "Our union with Jesus Christ presupposes pre-eminently one same nature in him and us, as the branches from the stalk are of the same nature as the stalk. The words of Jesus presuppose, in the second place, an intimate union between him and us, so far as to make us one body with him, as the shoots and the branches of the vine make one body with the vine. They presuppose, in the third place, an internal influence of Jesus Christ upon us, such as that of the stalk upon the branches, which draw from it all the juices with which they are nourished."[12]

The vine was chosen as the symbol of Israel, in preference to the olive tree, which is the king of Palestinian flora. It was pictured on Jewish coins, and it decorated the pediment of the Temple. There is no tree that requires less care, but none that produces such exquisite fruit, or that propagates more rapidly by layers or by grafting. An ancient author was prompted to say that its growth was limitless. Israel was the vine planted by God on a fertile hillside; its shadow covered the mountains; its

---

[11] John 15:1–6. (*a*) *To be in* Christ as dead or unfruitful wood is quite another matter than *abiding in* Christ. One does not abide in Christ except by charity and sanctifying grace, but Christ abides in all those who abide in him.

b) There is an untranslatable play of words in $\kappa\alpha\theta\alpha\acute{\iota}\rho\epsilon\iota\nu$ and $\kappa\alpha\theta\alpha\rho\acute{o}s$ (v. 2). To *prune* has as its equivalent in Latin *to clean* (*emundare* from *mundus* — "clean," "pure"), particularly with reference to a vine (*putare,* from *putus* — "clean," "neat"); in Greek *to purify* ($\kappa\alpha\theta\alpha\acute{\iota}\rho\epsilon\iota\nu$ from $\kappa\alpha\theta\alpha\rho\acute{o}s$ — "pure"). The vinedresser purifies ($\kappa\alpha\theta\alpha\acute{\iota}\rho\epsilon\iota$, "prunes") the fruitful branch, but you are already pure ($\kappa\alpha\theta\alpha\rho o\acute{\iota}$) and have no need of being further purified.

[12] Bossuet, *Méditations sur l'Evangile,* Second Part, first day.

branches stretched even to the great river; but despite its luxuriant leafage it had frustrated God's designs and had disappointed his expectations. All the prophets represent it as degenerate, decayed, gone wild. Like a wild and meager grapevine, it has borne only bitter fruit and yielded only tart grapes.[13] The True Vine, gifted with inexhaustible fruitfulness and responding to the care of the divine Vinedresser is the Church, the Mystical Body of Christ.

The most necessary and the most delicate task of the vinedresser is the pruning of the vine. He carefully cuts away the branches that are doomed to sterility: greedy boughs, dried-up shoots, and those that are about to wither. He trims the branches that give promise of fruit, so that they may give more. God acts in a similar way with the True Vine. He cuts off the dead branches and superfluous wood; he trims the fertile sprouts to increase their fruitfulness. It would be pushing the allegory too far to seek what corresponds to the various kinds of care given to the vine, and to ask what means the cutting off of the withered branches: namely, Christians who no longer cling to Christ except by a dead faith devoid of charity and good works. The earthly vinedresser is but an imperfect figure of the heavenly Vinedresser; and the persecutions and trials and the deprivation of sensible consolation, which seem to be represented by the operation of pruning, are not the only means that God has at his disposal to increase the fruitfulness of holy souls.

A Christian may *cling* to Christ by a dead and inactive faith, as the withered branch still stays attached to the vine stock. But to bear fruit, that is to say, to do works worthy of a heavenly crown, he must of necessity *abide* in Christ, and Christ must abide in him by charity: "He who abides in me, and I in him, bears much fruit, for without me you can do nothing," nothing that can be called fruit meriting a reward.[14]

---

[13] Ps. 79 (80):8–13; Osee 10:1; Isa. 5.1–5; Jer. 2:21; Ezech. 15:2; 19:10; 2 Esd. 5:3. A difference to be noted is that in the Old Testament the vine is always the *vineyard:* the vine in St. John is always the *stalk of the vine.* Everyone agrees in seeing in the vine of St. John an allusion to the Old Testament. While many think that is called *true* in opposition to that which was only an imperfect figure, others hold that it receives this qualification because it verifies more perfectly what takes place in an ordinary vine. The discussion is unimportant.

[14] The phrase is elliptical, as all the commentators have noted. Toletus completes

A vine is cultivated only for its fruit. A stock that produced only flowers or leaves would be valueless in the eyes of the vinedresser. To speak apart from figurative language, a man who does not abide in Christ by charity, and in whom Christ does not abide through sanctifying grace, can perform naturally good acts, if he obeys the inner voice of conscience; he can, with the aid of actual grace, prepare himself for justification; but he is absolutely incapable of meritorious acts, which can be compared to the fruit.

Friendship is a mutual relationship. If we abide in Christ by charity, he necessarily abides in us through sanctifying grace. His love is assured to us — of this he has given unfailing pledges. It is for us to prove our love for him.

"As my father has loved me, I also have loved you, abide in my love. To that end, keep my commandments, as I keep my Father's commandments to abide in his love.

"My commandment is that you love one another as I have loved you. Greater love than this no one has, than that he lay down his life for his friends. No longer will I call you servants, for the servant knows not what his master is doing. I have called you my friends, because I have made known to you all that I have heard from my Father.

"You have not chosen me: I have chosen you, and have sent you forth to bear fruit, and a fruit that remains, that whatever you ask my Father in my name he may grant you.

---

it thus: "Qui manet in me et ego in eo, hic, *et non alius,* feret fructum multum; quia sine me nihil potestis facere"; and he cites several similar cases of ellipsis, e.g., John 14:21: "Qui habet mandata mea et servat ea, ille est (et ille solus) qui diligit me." What is worth remarking here is that the reason given (*quia* sine me nihil potestis facere) bears upon the phrase that is understood.

All agree that the fruit designates *meritorious* acts, for there is question of those who abide in Christ and in whom Christ abides. Such is the understanding of the Council of Carthage (Denzinger, n. 105, repeated in n. 138): the *gratia justificationis* is necessary to produce *fructus mandatorum*. Also the Council of Trent (Denzinger, nn. 809 and 812): there is question of the *justified,* either as having kept sanctifying grace always, or as having recovered it, and of *the merit of eternal life*. Still, the text could be applied in a *derived sense* to every *supernatural* act done with the aid of *actual* grace before justification, for the reason, *sine me nihil potestis facere,* is the same; but it is not at all applicable to morally good acts which do not rise above the natural sphere.

"This is my commandment: love one another."[15]

The love of God and of neighbor, and the observance of the commandments: these are the fruits which our union with the True Vine assures to us.

Doubtless a difference will be remarked between the Mystical Body in St. Paul and the allegorical Vine in St. John. The latter, borrowing his images from plant life, envisages only the union between Christ and his members, whereas St. Paul, drawing his from the human organism, considers not only the union between the head and the members, but also the connection between the members themselves in that social unit which is the Body of Christ. This may also be the reason why St. Paul always has the Holy Spirit intervening in the constitution of the Mystical Body: because the Holy Spirit is the author of the *charismata* which are, as it were, the joints and ligaments keeping the members of the Christian society united. St. John attributes a different role to the Paraclete.

The Paraclete — Four times during the farewell discourse Jesus promises the Apostles that he will send the Paraclete to take his place and complete his work. The word "Paraclete" means "advocate," "defender," "intercessor," "counselor," and even "witness." As it is natural to expect consolation and comfort from one who is called upon for help, every time that our Lord mentions to his Apostles the coming of the Paraclete, he presents him precisely as a fit compensation to console them for his absence.[16]

---

[15] John 15:9–17. These sentences without apparent links are altogether in the style of St. John. Three connected ideas are mixed and tangled together: (1) Love one another as I have loved you. (2) Prove your love by keeping my word as I keep the word of my Father and am loved by him. (3) This is the way to glorify me and glorify my Father, and it is for this that I have chosen you.

[16] The word "paraclete," used only by St. John, is once applied to Christ (1 John 2:1). Παράκλητος from παρακαλεῖν, "to call to one's aid, one's assistance," corresponds to the Latin *advocatus*. The word παρακαλεῖν also means *to exhort* and, in the Bible, *to console;* but the past participle, *exhorted, consoled,* would not give a meaning applicable to the Holy Spirit. Still, Origen (*De Princip.*, II, vii, 4), Cyril of Jerusalem (*Catech.*, xvi, 20), and St. Gregory of Nyssa (*Contra Eunom.*, ii, 14) relate παράκλητος to παράκλησις, as if it could be taken in the sense of *consoler,* παρακλήτωρ (Job 16:2, Septuagint), which, in fact, Theodotion and Aquila replace by παράκλητος. Cf. Bernard, *St. John,* Edinburgh, 1928, pp. 496–498; and Lagrange, *Saint Jean,* pp. 281–283.

"If you love me, keep my commandments, and I will send you another Paraclete to abide with you forever, the Spirit of truth, whom the world cannot receive because it neither sees him nor knows him. But you know him, because he abides among you, and is in you."[17]

They will receive *another* Paraclete, like to him who intercedes for us with the heavenly Father. This promise is given to the Apostles, but not to them alone, for the presence of the new Paraclete will not be transitory, as was the sojourn on earth of the Incarnate Word. His presence will last to the end of time, and consequently it will outlast the lifetime of all the Apostles. The principal role of the Paraclete will be to complete by his interior light the instruction of the Apostles, now deprived of the visible presence of Jesus:

"These things have I spoken to you while yet abiding with you. But the Paraclete, the Holy Spirit, whom the Father will send in my name, shall teach you all things and bring back to your memory all that I have said to you."[18]

"When the Paraclete comes, whom I will send you from the Father, the Spirit of truth, who proceeds from the Father, he shall bear witness concerning me, and you also shall by my witnesses, because you are with me from the beginning."[19]

The Paraclete is sent by the Father and by the Son; he is sent

---

[17] John 14:15–17. (*a*) The promised Holy Spirit is *another* Paraclete, like to Christ (1 John 2:1), and will assume his office as defender and consoler. (*b*) He will abide *forever* with the disciples; he is therefore promised to the Church, and not to the Apostles only. However, see Corluy, *Comment. in Joan.*, 2 ed., pp. 248–249.

[18] John 14:26. Those who extend the promise to the whole Church explain it thus: "He will teach you nothing new, but he will make you *understand better,* and will recall to you all that I have said to you." That would be to give to the word *teach* (διδάσκειν) an unusual meaning, and it would leave out of consideration the two assertions that enclose the sentence in question: "I say this *to you*" and "what I have said *to you.*" Note that instead of the *suggeret* of the Vulgate, the Greek has ὑπομνήσει, "will recall to *your* memory" all that I have said to you. It is clear that "in my name" should be understood, as in John 5:43; 10:25, not only "in my place" but "as my representative."

[19] John 15:26–27. This is not the place to enter into the controversies aroused by the phrase "who proceeds from the Father." Almost all Catholic commentators understand it of the procession *"ab aeterno."* However, some (Jansenius of Ghent, Schanz), comparing John 16:27–28, think that it should be understood *directly* of the temporal mission, but they recognize that the temporal mission *implies* the procession *ab aeterno.*

by the Father in the name of the Son, and by the Son on the part of the Father. Receiving from the Father and the Son his mission and the object of his mission, he proceeds conjointly from both; for in the intimate life of God, to send and to receive are said only of the eternal processions. It is a very remarkable fact that the sending of the Holy Spirit is never attributed to the Father without mention being made of the Son, nor to the Son without mention being made of the Father. The Father sends the Paraclete "in the name of the Son"; not only at his request, not only to take his place and to fill his office, but to act in his name and, so to speak, at his delegation, as the Son himself acts in the name of the Father and at his delegation.

Some distinguished authors think that here again the promise concerns the entire Church, and that the office of the Spirit will be, not to teach any other truths than Christ has taught, but rather to make those better understood and to recall them at need if they have been forgotten. But it is very clear that in this text our Lord is addressing only the Apostles: "I have spoken these things to you while I was with you . . . but the Paraclete will teach you all things and will recall to you all that I have said to you." Such a promise does not go beyond the Apostolic circle, and there is no reason to restrict "teach" to the less natural sense of "make better understood." There were truths which Jesus had not been able to teach his disciples, because they were not yet able to bear them. It will be the office of the Holy Spirit to reveal these truths to the Apostles, and it will be the exclusive privilege of the Apostles to transmit them to the Church. After the death of the last Apostle, the deposit of revelation will be irrevocably closed, and private revelations, even those that are sanctioned by the authority of the Church, will not enrich the treasury of Christian dogma.

Not content with instructing the Apostles, the Holy Spirit will help them to bear witness to Jesus, and will join his own testimony to theirs.

"I tell you in truth, it is good that I go away. For if I do not go, the Paraclete will not come to you; but if I go, I will send him to you. And when he has come, he shall convince the world of sin, and of justice, and of judgment: of sin, because they have not believed in me; of justice, because I go to my Father and you are to see me no more; of judgment, because the prince of this world is already judged.

"Yet many things I have to say to you, but you cannot bear them now. But when he has come, the Spirit of Truth, he shall guide you to the whole truth; for he shall not speak of himself, but all that he hears he shall speak, and the things that are to come he shall declare to you. He shall glorify me, because he shall receive of what is mine to declare it to you. All that the Father has is mine; for this cause I have said that he shall receive of what is mine to declare it to you."[20]

The Paraclete will convince the world of the sin it has committed in refusing to believe in the Son of God; he will convince it of the justice of Christ, who ascends triumphant to his Father; he will convince it of the judgment of condemnation that is shortly to burst upon it, since Satan, the prince of the world, is already judged and condemned.

But this threefold testimony of the Spirit does not compensate, in the eyes of the Apostles, for the loss of their Master. How can he say to them: "It is expedient for you that I go away"? Could he not fill, in their midst, the office of the Paraclete? He promises to send the Paraclete when he has gone away; but could he not send him without himself departing? What, then, is the meaning of these words: "If I do not go away, the Paraclete will not come"? Obviously there is no question here of absolute impossi-

---

[20] John 16:7–15. On the text, *arguet mundum de peccato et de justitia et de judicio,* Maldonatus writes: "Incidimus in locum, quo vix alius apud ullum evangelistam est, aut majore impeditus difficultate, aut majore interpretationum varietate perplexus, et diligentem interpretem et attentum lectorem postulat." Doubtless; but the great variety of interpretations should cause no disquiet, since the majority of them have no semblance of reason.

The word ἐλέγχειν (*arguere*) means *to convince,* but not *to persuade,* and especially not *to force someone to declare himself convinced;* it could well be translated *to show.* The Holy Spirit will "convince the world of sin": he will so clearly show the sin that the world has committed in refusing to believe in Christ, that all witnesses who are in good faith will be *convinced* of it. In the same way, he will show the *justice* of Jesus, which clearly emerges from the fact of his return to the Father. The only thing that creates difficulty is the phrase "and you shall see me no more"; but this clause, joined generally with the notion of the departure, may have been introduced solely to mark that the departure is definitive. Finally, the world, in seeing its prince Satan condemned to impotency, will be *convinced* of the condemnation that menaces itself. We know that in St. John κρίνειν and κρίσις, like κατακρίνειν, very frequently stand for a judgment of condemnation.

bility, but of an order of Providence such as is known to us through revelation, or such as we deduce from the harmony of the plan of redemption. The Resurrection of the Son of God is the complement of the redemptive death; and the descent of the Holy Ghost is, in some way, the complement of the Resurrection. "Christ's work of mercy has two chief parts: what He did for all men, what He does for each; what He did once for all, what He does for one by one continually; what He did externally to us, what He does within us; what He did on earth, what He does in heaven; what He did in His own Person, what He does by His Spirit."[21]

To perfect his work, he must go away, but he comes again invisibly with the Spirit sent by the Father and by him. "The Spirit will guide them to (the knowledge of) the whole truth." He will cause them to penetrate the depths of truths of which they have seen only the surface, to draw from them other truths which will seem new to them, and may in fact be such. For Jesus Christ has indeed brought to their knowledge all that he was sent to teach; but was it his mission to teach them truth that they could not yet bear? At all events, the teaching of the Holy Spirit will not contradict the teaching of the Son, for he will teach only what the Son conjointly with the Father will give him the mission to teach.

The last benefit of the Spirit will be the aid brought to the faithful in time of trial and persecution, which the Saviour now goes on to sketch for them.

Future Trials — In the Sermon on the Mount, Jesus had proclaimed blessed those who suffer injuries, calumnies, and persecution for his name and for his sake. Later he had revealed a glimpse of a future full of tribulations and struggles for his Church, but it is only on the eve of his death that he explains himself clearly on this subject.

"If the world hates you, know that it has hated me before you. If you were of the world, the world would love its own; but you are not of the world — I have drawn you out of the world by choosing you — for this cause the world hates you. Remember

---

[21] Newman, *Lectures on Justification,* 6 ed., London, 1892, ix, par. 1.

my word: 'The servant is not greater than the master.' If they have persecuted me, they will persecute you also, for my name's sake.

"They shall expel you from their synagogues, and an hour will come when anyone that puts you to death shall believe that he is rendering a service to God. They shall treat you thus because they know neither my Father nor me. And I tell it to you beforehand, that when their hour comes you may remember that I have told you."[22]

If the Evangelist were here speaking in his own name instead of allowing Christ to speak, he would not have failed to emphasize the exceedingly bloody persecutions of Nero and Domitian, of which he had himself been the witness and the victim. But he mentions only the persecutions stirred up by the Jews against the first disciples of the Saviour, and this restraint is another proof of his trustworthiness as a historian.

After this general survey of the fate that awaits the Apostles and their neophytes, our Lord resumes the dominant thought of the whole discourse, his imminent departure and his near return: "A little while and you shall see me no more; and again a little while and you shall see me, because I go to my Father." The Apostles, more perplexed than ever, looked at one another, a question in their eyes: "Soon he shall be seen no more, and soon he shall be seen, because he goes to his Father. What does this mean? We do not understand."

Jesus divined from their attitude and the look on their faces the question they would ask but dared not. He therefore explained to them, by a striking comparison, the meaning of this mysterious "soon":

"Amen, amen, I say to you; you shall weep and lament, while the world shall rejoice; but your sorrow shall be turned into joy. A woman in labor is sorrowful, because her hour has come. But when she has brought forth her child, joy makes her forget her anguish, because a man has come into the world. So, too, you are now in sorrow, but I shall see you again, and you shall feel a joy that no one can snatch from you. And in that day you shall ask questions no longer."[23]

---

[22] John 15:18–20; 16:2–4.

[23] John 16:18–23. We follow the explanation of Toletus, which is that of

This rapid transition from sorrow to joy caused by the Saviour's departure and return, does it not indicate clearly enough his death followed soon by his Resurrection? We are surprised that many interpreters see anything else here. If this were a reference to the return at the Parousia, the comparison of the woman in labor, whose joy follows so swiftly upon her sorrow, would be without meaning. On the other hand, if Jesus wished to speak of Pentecost, and to have it understood that the Apostles would see him again in the Person of the Holy Spirit, and that he himself would see them through the Holy Spirit as an intermediary, the explanation would be more enigmatic than the thing explained. In a few hours he will be in the tomb, and the Apostles will no longer see him; after some hours he will come forth in triumph from the tomb, and the Apostles will see him again with their bodily eyes, as he will see them. Joy will replace their sorrow, and it can be said in all truth that this will be the beginning of a joy without end.

It will also be the beginning of a new relationship between Christ and Christians. "Amen, amen, I say to you, if you ask the Father anything in my name, he will give it to you. Hitherto you have not asked anything in my name. Ask, and you shall receive, that your joy may be perfect." As long as Jesus was on earth, they addressed either him or his Father. They never thought of praying to the Father through the mediation of the Son, or in the name of the Son. Now that he is seated at the right hand of the Father as all-powerful intercessor, the new formula of Christian prayer comes into force: we pray to the Father through the Son, or in the name of the Son. "In that day you shall ask in my name: and I do not say to you that I shall ask the Father for you (there will be no need of that), for the Father himself loves you because you have loved me, and have believed that I came forth from the Father. I came forth from the Father to come into the world. Again I leave the world to go to the Father."[24]

St. Augustine and St. Thomas. But others think (with St. Cyril and St. John Chrysostom) that allusion is made to Pentecost, or that Christ will return invisibly with the Spirit sent by him. Maldonatus believes that there is reference to the return at the Parousia, but that is quite a distance away!

[24] John 16:23–28. In the Vulgate, Verse 23 (in illo die me non *rogabitis* quidquam) seems to contradict Verse 26 (in illo die in nomine meo *petetis*). But *rogare*

Jesus speaks in such clear terms of his birth and his death, of his divine origin and his destiny to glory, that the Apostles finally understand him. It would have been surprising if they had not understood. "Behold," they say, "now thou speakest plainly, in no figurative language. Now we know that thou knowest all things, and dost not need that anyone should question thee." Still, let them be under no illusion. This faith, excellent as it is, is insufficient. It is this that our Lord insinuates in his answer: "Do you now believe? Behold, the hour is coming, and has already come, when each one of you shall go his own way, leaving me alone. And yet, I am not alone, because my Father is with me. These things I have spoken to you that you may enjoy the peace (which I give). In the world you shall have affliction. But have confidence, I have overcome the world."[25] The Cross is the pledge of man's salvation; persecution is for the Church the indication of coming victory. "The disciples," says St. Augustine, "have had confidence in him, and have triumphed through him. He would not have conquered the world, if he had not triumphed through his members."

3. The Priestly Prayer

(JOHN 17:1–26)

The ideal proposed by Jesus to his disciples — that they must pray always and not lose heart — he alone could realize in its fullness. St. Luke thus summarizes the first period of his preaching: "The crowds pressed about him to hear him and to be cured of their infirmities. But he retired to the wilderness and gave himself to prayer." He gave the whole day to men, but he reserved the night for converse with God.

We see him praying at the baptism, in Gethsemani, on Calvary; but it is especially in moments of grave decision that we find him in prayer. He inaugurates his public life by a colloquy with God for forty days; he passes in prayer the whole night preceding

(ἐρωτᾶν) means "to question," "to interrogate," as lower down in Verse 30. In the whole context, *to ask* in the sense of *to pray* is *petere* (αἰτεῖν, four times).

[25] John 16:22–33. Cf. Augustine, *In Joan.*, ciii; ML, XXXV, 1899–1901.

the choice of the Twelve; on the eve of his great discourse on the Eucharist he flees into the mountain to pray. And even in the daytime, when he is about to entrust to Peter the keys of the kingdom of heaven and the dignity of head of the Church, he is discovered at prayer in the outskirts of Caesarea. While his Apostles sleep, he prays upon Thabor, and in the Garden of Olives. But the Evangelists have not preserved for us the formulas of his prayer, except for a few ejaculatory prayers such as: "Father, I praise thee; Father, I thank thee"; "Father, may thy name be sanctified"; "Father, forgive them," and other brief outpourings of soul expressive of gratitude, adoration, and filial submissiveness. St. John recompenses us by reproducing for us the Priestly Prayer, which is, as it were, the testament of the Heart of Jesus and a sublime summary of his teaching.

When he came forth from the city to go to Gethsemani, Jesus raised his eyes to heaven.[26] It was his habitual attitude when he prayed.[27] The long prayer then solemnly pronounced by the High Priest of the New Covenant, as he is about to immolate himself for our salvation, in the presence of the priests whom he has just invested with the priesthood to perpetuate the one Sacrifice of Calvary, can justly be called the *priestly prayer,* though the idea of sacrifice is scarcely more than indicated in passing.[28]

Jesus prays for himself, for the Apostles, and for all the faithful. He prays aloud, not so much to follow the customary usage of his day, as to instruct the Apostles and us with them. In the text handed down by St. John, the conciseness of the language, the loftiness of the thought, and even the sparseness of vocabulary, charging the same words and expressions with different thoughts, make the prayer difficult at times to understand. However, the need to distinguish these various shades of

---

26 Compare John 14:31 ("*let us go from here,* from the Cenacle") and John 18:1 ("*having said this he went out,* from the city").

27 John 11:41; Mark 6:41; and parallels. The gesture is more natural in the open air, but see Acts 7:55.

28 It may have received this name from the Lutheran Cuthraeus, who died in 1600 (Schanz), but it is found *equivalently* in Rupert and in St. Cyril of Alexandria.

meaning, which, for the most part, the context aids us to separate from one another, does not detract from the impression of the whole.

"Father the hour has come: glorify thy Son, in order that he may in turn glorify thee. Thou hast given him power over all flesh, in order that he may give everlasting life to those whom thou hast given him. Now this is everlasting life, to know thee, the only true God, and him whom thou hast sent, Jesus Christ.

"I have glorified thee on earth; I have accomplished the work that thou hast given me to do. And now do thou glorify me, Father, with thyself, with the glory which I had with thee, before the creation of the world."[29]

Jesus has faithfully carried out the mission entrusted to him. By proclaiming himself the Son of God, he has revealed to the world the name of the Father, whom the Jews knew as God but not as Father, since they did not know the Fatherhood of his intimate life. It is thus that Jesus has glorified the Father and given to men the principle of eternal life, which consists in knowing the true God and his envoy. Jesus does not say that the Father alone is the true God to the exclusion of other Divine Persons; but that he is the only God in opposition to the idols, and this can be applied equally to the Son. Eternal life is, in this passage as often elsewhere, the life of grace, of which the life of glory is the later flowering assuredly to come. Faith in God, the Saviour and Rewarder, is, according to the expression of St. Cyril of Alexandria, "the mother and nurse of eternal life"; it brings forth grace which on high is transformed into glory.

The Son having glorified the Father, it is proper that the Father should in turn glorify the Son. The Incarnation has been for the Word an abasement, a descent — St. Paul will say a humiliation. In his form of a slave, men have ignored and contemned and

[29] John 17:1–5. In the whole chapter the Vulgate translates δόξα (*glory*) as *claritas,* and δοξάζειν (to glorify) as *clarificare,* except in Verse 10. It evidently refers to the extrinsic glory either of the Father or of the Son, the intrinsic glory not being susceptible of increase or diminution. It will also be remarked that the word "world" occurs seventeen times with three different acceptations. In the first five verses, *to give* is repeated four times, and *glory* (or *glorify*) five times with different applications.

rejected him. He asks to regain the glory that was his before the creation of the world; he claims for his human nature the honor and adoration which are due to it as to the Word himself, though by a different title. This is not the glory reserved to his human nature by virtue of predestination, for *that* he did not have from all eternity; nor is it the glory intrinsic to his divine nature, for he has never lost that. What he wishes is that the worship to which his divine nature had a right from all eternity be now rendered to all that belongs to his Person, including his humanity. The glorifying of the Son will redound to the Father; or rather, it will pass through the Son to reascend to the Father.

Having prayed for himself, Jesus prays for his Apostles and urges in their favor the four reasons most apt to touch the heart of God. The Apostles are his own; they have glorified him; they will soon find themselves alone; they will be exposed to the hatred of the world.

The Apostles are the common possession of the Father and the Son, and they should be as dear to the one as to the other: "Not for the world do I (now) pray, but for those whom thou hast given me, because they are thine. All things that are mine are thine, and thine are mine." Jesus has already prayed for the world, and he will pray for it again from the height of the Cross; but at this moment he prays only for the friends of God, who are also his friends, and his prayer deserves the more to be granted.

Another claim to the divine favor is that the Apostles have glorified the Father by obeying the Son. "They have kept my word. They have acknowledged that all that thou hast given me comes from thee, for I have handed on to them the things that thou hast confided to me, and they received them, and have acknowledged that I came forth from thee, and they have believed that thou hast sent me."

Still another consideration pleads for them. They will soon find themselves without a guide and without a shepherd, because the earthly career of Jesus is coming to an end. Henceforth the Father must keep them: "And I am no more of this world; but they remain in the world, and I am coming to thee. Holy Father, keep in thy name those whom thou hast given me, that they may be one, even as we are one. While I was with them, I kept them in thy name . . . and not one of them has perished except the son of perdition. But now I am coming to thee; and these things I speak while I am yet in this world, that my joy may be complete in them." In leaving the world he would lack something of his joy, if he were not assured that his Father would watch over his friends.[30]

The last motive — and not the least — for taking compassion on them and for coming to their aid is that they are to be exposed to the hatred of the world for having believed God's word. "I have given them thy word, and the world hates them, because they are not of the world, even as I am not of the world. I do not ask thee to take them out of the world, but to preserve them from evil."

For his Apostles he asks for an unceasing, fatherly, loving protection, like to that which he himself has given them during his mortal life; a protection that does not consist in taking them out of the world, where their presence is needed, but in preserving them from the evil of which the world is full. And then, in conclusion, he makes a more special and more mysterious request:

"Sanctify them in truth. Thy word is truth. Even as thou hast sent me into the world, so I send them into the world. And for them I sanctify myself, that they may be sanctified in truth."[31]

---

30 Note that an exact translation of the text is: "that they may have my joy made full in themselves" (*Translator*).

31 John 17:17–19. *Sanctifica eos in veritate* (ἁγίασον αὐτοὺς ἐν τῇ ἀληθείᾳ). If this were by itself it could be understood: "Sanctify them (increase their sanctity) by the truth," by the Gospel which possesses the power to sanctify. But the context demands another sense. (1) It is impossible to understand *Ego sanctifico meipsum ut sint sanctificati* as referring to sanctifying grace, which in Christ is not susceptible of increase. The word *sanctify* therefore keeps the Biblical sense of *consecrate.* (2) Though the preposition *in* (ἐν) could have the instrumental sense of *by,* it designates in a general way the setting, the sphere of action, in which the Apostles will exercise their ministry. (3) This sphere of action is clearly expressed: "I have sent them into the world as thou hast sent me." St. John Chrysostom explains it admirably: *Sanctifica illos,* "set them apart (ἀφόρισον) for the word and preaching." *Pro eis sanctifico meipsum,* "I offer myself to thee in sacrifice"; *ut sint sanctificati,* "I consecrate them and offer them to thee."

We understand the words *in veritate,* ἐν τῇ ἀληθείᾳ (the σου of the Textus Receptus is lacking in the best manuscripts), of the sphere of the apostolate, of the preaching of the *Truth,* which is the *Word* of the Gospel. The ἐν ἀληθείᾳ can be understood in the same sense in Verse 19, despite the absence of the

The bearing of this astonishing passage cannot be properly grasped except by going back to the Biblical notion of sanctity. In the Bible, *to sanctify* is, properly speaking, to separate a person or thing from profane uses, to consecrate it entirely to God. Moses sanctifies Aaron and his sons in order to devote them to the service of the altar; he sanctifies the sacred vessels and vestments to dedicate them unreservedly to divine worship; he sanctifies the people by a ceremony of expiation in expectation of a theophany. God also sanctifies persons and things that he reserves to his own exclusive service. When he sanctifies the Sabbath, he makes it something holy which cannot be profaned without sacrilege. He had sanctified Jeremias from his mother's womb in order to make him the herald of his vengeance and his mercy. He sanctified his Son by sending him into the world to accomplish in his name the work of the Redemption. In this sense all Christians are sanctified, and St. Paul gives them the title of saints, because by the fact of their Baptism they are dedicated forever and unreservedly to the service of God.

"Sanctify them in truth." Consecrate them to thy service, not simply in a general way, but in the preaching of the Gospel, which is thy word, the word of truth. In the Cenacle, Jesus has consecrated the Apostles priests, by conferring on them the power to offer up the Eucharist; and bishops, by allowing them to hand on the same power to others. He will complete his work after the Resurrection by giving them jurisdiction over his Mystical Body. Now he prays his Father to consecrate them to the apostolate, and this consecration will not be effective without an increase of grace to render them worthy heralds of the Gospel. And he *sanctifies* himself, that is to say, he offers himself, he immolates himself, he consecrates himself to God upon the altar of the Cross where he is at once priest and victim, to make perfect this consecration. Jesus Christ, it is true, immolates himself for all; but at the moment when he is preparing to consummate the sacrifice which solemnizes his High Priesthood of the New Covenant, it is only natural that his thoughts should rest especially upon those whom he has associated with his

definite article; still it could perhaps be an adverbial expression, "that they may be *truly* consecrated."

own priesthood and whom he has chosen to continue his work.

After the Apostles come the simple faithful.

"Yet not for these only do I pray, but for those also who through their preaching are to believe in me, that all may be one. Even as thou, Father, art in me and I in thee, may they also be one in us. . . . And the glory that thou hast given to me, I have communicated to them, that they may be one, even as we are one. I am in them, and thou art in me, that they may be perfected in unity, and that the world may know that thou hast sent me, and that thou hast loved them even as thou hast loved me."

It is impossible to express in more energetic terms the union that Jesus asks for all the faithful. He wills that they be perfected in oneness, that they be one as the Father and the Son are one, that they compenetrate one another, so to speak, as the Father is in the Son, and the Son in the Father. Not only is everything common between the Father and the Son: thought, will, and action; not only are the Three Divine Persons one and the same Substance, but they enjoy this wonderful property: that each is in both the others and contains the perfections of the others. If it be permissible to make use of a crude comparison, it is like a triangle, each angle of which embraces and comprehends the surface of the other two.

"That they may be one as we are one": such is the ideal that Christ offers of the union of Christians. In indicating to them the end he also teaches the means to reach that end: "That they may be one in us." United in faith and charity, they will be but one heart and one soul; God will be not only the model but also the bond of their unity.

"The glory that thou hast given to me, I have communicated to them, that they may be one, as we are one." This glory, which God has given to the Son, and which the Son now communicates to his chosen ones, is not the gift of miracles — not all are favored with that — nor is it the glory of body and soul, which we do not yet possess except in hope, and which could not retroactively produce the union of the faithful with one another. It is the divinity which the humanity of Christ receives at the moment of the Incarnation and which he communicates to us by identifying himself with us, by conferring upon us adoptive sonship, the true foundation of Christian brotherhood.

St. Cyril of Alexandria opens up to us still broader horizons, in some admirable pages too long to transcribe and impossible to abridge. "The Son of God unites himself to us corporally and as man by mingling with us in the divine Eucharist; spiritually and as God through the activity of the Holy Spirit, who creates in us the spirit of regeneration."[32] Hence he communicates his divinity to us in two ways: by the gift of the Holy Spirit, who renders us partakers of the divine nature, and by the Eucharist in which we receive Christ whole and entire, body and soul and divinity. We are not saying that in this passage the Saviour directly envisions the Holy Eucharist, though that would not be impossible after what he had foretold about the effects of the Eucharist, when he promised us the Sacrament of Love. But the ideal of union between Christ and the Christian, and of Christians with one another, which he now proposes to us, would be impossible of realization without the living and life-giving Bread whose partaking makes us all one Mystical Body of Christ, without the sacramental communion which, according to the formula of the Council of Trent, is "the sign of unity, the bond of charity, the symbol of peace and concord." — "Because there is only one (Eucharistic) bread, we (despite our number) are all one body (the Mystical Body of Christ), since we all partake of the same bread."[33]

At its close, the prayer of Christ becomes altogether general; it embraces, with the Apostles, all the faithful, present and future, for all of them have been or will be given to him by his Father:

"Father, those whom thou hast given me, I will that where I am myself they may be with me, in order that they may behold my glory, which thou hast given me, because thou hast loved me before the creation of the world.

"Just Father, the world has not known thee, but I have known

---

[32] St. Cyril, *In Joan.*, lib. XI, cap. 12 (MG, LXXIV, 564). Together with this chapter, the whole preceding chapter on the Eucharist as the principle of union should be cited.

[33] 1 Cor. 10:17. See Prat, *Théologie de saint Paul,* II, 425–426 (English transl., II, 350–351).

thee, and these have known indeed that thou has sent me. I have made known to them thy name, and I will make it known to them (still more), in order that they may have within them the love wherewith thou hast loved me, and that I may be in them."[34]

"I will that wherever I am, they also may be." This is not a simple wish; it is his will, not indeed absolute, but conformed to the will of the Father. Jesus wills to make them witnesses of his glory, the glory which God destined to him from all eternity, and conferred upon him at the moment of the Incarnation. This, then, is not the glory that the Word receives from the Father by virtue of the eternal generation, the moving power of which was not love, but it is the glory of the humanity hypostatically united to the Word. This glory, contemplated in the light of the divinity, will be for the elect the source of ineffable joy. They know it already by faith, but the obscure vision of faith is altogether another matter than the clear view of the beatific vision. This more intimate knowledge of the love of God for his Son will be for them a pledge of God's love for those who are one with the Son. This is the final wish: "That they may have in them the love wherewith thou hast loved me, and that I may be in them."

Such is the Priestly Prayer. Perhaps it would have been better simply to transcribe it, leaving it to the meditation of the reader, rather than to attempt a commentary, since it speaks more to the heart than to the mind. At least, let us not forget the wise counsel of Bossuet: "Read it, then, and reread it. Consider it, ponder it; welcome all the thoughts that will come naturally and

---

[34] John 17:24–26. This passage is the object of very lively controversy.

a) There is no reason to restrict Verse 24 to the Apostles alone. At most it can be said that Jesus is thinking of them in the following verse: "I have made known to them thy name"; but many commentators do not agree.

b) The phrase "before the creation of the world" is to be referred to "because thou hast loved me," and not to "the glory that thou hast given me," which would compel the interpreter to understand it of the glory received by the Son in virtue of the eternal generation. The Father loved the Son from all eternity, but it was not because of this love that he communicated his nature to the Word; on the other hand, it was for love of the humanity of Christ that he united it hypostatically to the Word. And it is this glory of the Incarnate Word that Christ wishes the elect to contemplate as a striking sign of the love of God for the humanity.

simply to your mind. Listen to all, weigh all. Listen principally to what takes possession of the heart and inclines it to God, to Jesus Christ; to what casts it down and humiliates it and lifts it up; to what makes it tremble, and what consoles it. And say within yourself: All this is true; all this is timely. Let us here keep silent, and in silence let us listen to the unfathomable truths of God."

CHAPTER VIII

Gethsemani

1. On the Road to Gethsemani

HERE properly begins the drama of the Passion, to which the struggles of the previous days were but the prologue. The Evangelists narrate this heart-rending drama with an impassivity that is disconcerting. One would say that they had set themselves to achieve that neutrality of attitude which certain modern critics make out to be the capital virtue of the historian. Not a single outbreak of compassionate sorrow in the presence of so much suffering, not a cry of indignation or anger against the executioners, scarcely a word stigmatizing the conduct of the traitor. The explanation is that the Evangelists are not so much biographers as witnesses. They do not describe for the sake of description, and they do not narrate for the sake of narrative. Their purpose is to transmit to future generations what they have seen with their own eyes and have heard from the lips of eyewitnesses. The best guarantee of their testimony is the serene calmness of their attestation. Besides, they are dealing with emotions which cannot be translated into words, which the most vehement rhetoric cannot but weaken. The passionate exclamations of a Tacitus impress the reader less than the apparent coldness of a Thucydides, who allows the facts to speak in all their poignant realism. What in the Greek historian is the supreme effort of consummate art is dictated to the Evangelists by the consciousness of their role, and the instinctive feeling that the language of facts is the most eloquent of languages — and the most pathetic.

It must have been between ten o'clock and midnight when Jesus left the Cenacle with his eleven Apostles. He descended the Tyropoeon ravine, doubtless by the stairway path that recent excavations have brought to light, and left the city by the Fountain Gate. Turning north, and leaving at his right the tombs with which are linked the names of the illustrious dead, he must have crossed the brook, Cedron, at a place near the site of the present bridge. The Cedron is not, properly speaking, either a brook or a torrent. Almost all year long it can be crossed dry-shod, and it does not swell with muddy swirling waves except at the time of the winter rains. Deeply embanked as it is between the Mount of Olives and the Temple hill, the sun does not reach its depths until well after sunrise. *Cedron* in Hebrew means *dark,* and many think that it owes its name to the somber color of its waters or to the semidarkness that reigns there in the early morning and at twilight.

On the way, the Master gave his Apostles his final admonitions: "You shall all be scandalized this night because of me, for it is written: 'I will smite the shepherd, and the sheep of the flock shall be scattered.' But after I have risen, I will go before you into Galilee." Then turning to Peter, he said: "Simon, Simon, behold, Satan has asked to sift (all of) you as wheat (in the sieve). But I have prayed for thee, that thy faith may not fail; and thou, when thou hast returned (from thy wanderings), confirm and strengthen thy brethren." The violent shaking imparted to the grain when it is being sifted often causes the lighter grains to fly up into the air and fall to the ground: an expressive image of the trial which Satan is about to inflict upon the Apostles. Peter will succumb; but, thanks to a grace which he will owe to the Saviour's intercession, his faith will remain intact, and his momentary fall will not deprive him of his office as head of the Church, nor will it take from him his charge of strengthening his brethren in the faith. In fact, his faith did not fail; for though he denied that he knew Jesus of Nazareth, and denied being with him in Gethsemani, he never denied that Jesus was the Messias and the Son of God.

But at this moment Peter is conscious of loving his Master with a sincere and ardent love. He cries out in astonishment: "Lord, with thee I am ready to go both to prison and to death!

Though all the others be scandalized, I will never be scandalized." Presumptuous man! The experience of the inherent frailty of human nature has not yet made him wise. "Amen, amen, I say to thee," Jesus answers, "this very night, before the cock crows twice, thou shalt deny me thrice." And yet, despite this formal assertion, Peter continues to protest, and the others do the same.[1]

There was a moment of silence, and then the conversation took another turn. "When I sent you out before, without purse or wallet or shoes, did you lack anything?" And they answered: "No." "Well then, let him that has a purse or a wallet take it now; and let him that has none sell his cloak to buy a sword. For I say to you, that this word of the Scripture must be fulfilled in me: He was reckoned with the wicked." During their temporary

---

[1] The prediction of Peter's fall is common to all four Gospels (Matt. 26:33–35; Mark 14:26–31; Luke 22:31–34; John 13:37–38) with the variant in Mark: "before the cock crow *twice,* thou shalt deny me thrice." For the time and place, see the Appendix: *Concord of the Gospels.* The promise made to St. Peter is special to St. Luke (21:31–32).

Satan has asked (*and obtained;* the aorist middle ἐξῃτήσατο normally denotes a request that is crowned with success) to pass you through the sieve (σινιάσαι, *to shake you as the grain is shaken in the sieve* or *strainer* commonly called σίνιον). This operation is well described by J. Neil, *Everyday Life in the Holy Land,* 1913, pp. 111–113, or in *Palestine Explored,* by the same author. The sieve, shaped like a shallow basket pierced by holes, is violently shaken. As a result, the earth and the small grains of sand pass through the holes, the chaff flies out, and the other impurities brought to the surface or around the edges are removed by hand. It is clear that the devil's purpose is not to purify the Apostles but to make them fall.

Et tu aliquando conversus confirma fratres tuos (καὶ σύ ποτε ἐπιστρέψας). The verb ἐπιστρέφειν used absolutely means "to return," "to come to oneself," "to re-enter into oneself," "to repent" (Matt. 13:15; Mark 4:12; Acts 28:27, etc.). It is not the equivalent of the Hebrew שׁוּב, as Maldonatus holds: "Sicut ego te confirmo tu *iterum* (ἐπιστρέψας) confirma fratres tuos." This Hebraism has no place except when the same subject performs both actions, and it marks repetition (*iterum*) and not reciprocity (*vicissim*). Still, reciprocity is insinuated by the emphatic opposition of the pronouns (ἐγὼ δέ . . . καὶ σύ): "I have prayed for thee . . . thou on thy part." The transitive sense attributed by Knabenbauer to ἐπιστρέφειν (et tu *converte* et confirma fratres tuos) is generally agreed to be inadmissible. Some Catholics quote with approval the commentary of the Protestant Bengel (*Gnomon N.T.,* Stuttgart, 1892, p. 302): "Totus hic sane sermo Domini praesupponit Petrum esse primum apostolorum quo stante aut cadente ceteri aut magis aut minus periclitantur." Very good, but *in cauda venenum:* "Petri vero successor praetensus, posteaquam a fidei sinceritate descivit, fidei tamen et imperii primatum sibi uni vindicavit, totus misere in cribrum incidit." Before citing a text of a Protestant author apparently favorable to the Church of Rome, it is wise to look around in the vicinity.

mission, the Apostles had been welcomed everywhere, perhaps without enthusiasm, still without hostility. Now, all that is to change. Open warfare is in process of preparation. Each one of them must rely solely upon his own resources to live, and upon his arms to defend himself. The frightened Apostles take this parabolical language literally and imagine that Jesus is inviting them to provide themselves with material arms. This is the meaning of their answer: "There are two swords here." Surprised at their lack of understanding, but judging that remonstrance would be out of season, Jesus adds only this word, emphasized, no doubt, by an indulgent sorrowful gesture: "It is enough."[2]

They came to Gethsemani, a name meaning "oil press." It was a country place planted with a variety of trees, chiefly olives, whose fruit was processed on the spot by means of one of those rock hewn presses that are so often met with in Palestine, especially in Judea. We can picture to ourselves an enclosure encompassed by a wall of loose stones, perhaps reinforced by an impenetrable hedge of cactus. These country establishments on the outskirts of towns were very often large enough to enclose a watchhouse, and sometimes a more or less spacious dwelling where the owner could come on summer days to breathe the fresh air and enjoy the relative coolness in the shade of the big trees. Gethsemani apparently belonged to a friend and disciple of Jesus. At all events, the Saviour had the use of it, and some-

---

[2] Luke 22:35–38. This episode, narrated only by St. Luke, follows the prediction of Peter's denial, which St. Mark and St. Matthew place with more likelihood on the way to Gethsemani.

St. John Chrysostom thinks that the two swords are the two knives used for cutting up the Paschal lamb; but μάχαιρα has not this meaning in the New Testament, and at Gethsemani we find St. Peter using a real sword.

After St. Bernard (*De consider.*, iv, 3) and Boniface VIII (*Unam Sanctam*, Denzinger-Umberg, No. 469), many authors apply this text to the twofold power of the Church, the temporal and the spiritual; but it is evident that this is not the literal sense in St. Luke, and Maldonatus says rightly that, if the Church possesses this twofold power, it is not in virtue of this text.

The answer of Jesus cannot mean: "It is enough to defend us and to plan resistance." The meaning therefore is: "Enough about that; that suffices"; or rather, "That is enough, and more than should be," with a gesture emphasizing the present lack of understanding on the part of the Apostles. "He all but laughed (at them) (μονονουχὶ διαγελᾷ)," says St. Cyril of Alexandria. Later on, they will understand.

times spent the night there when he left Jerusalem too late to go all the way to Bethany.

Leaving eight of his Apostles in the shelter of a cave situated opposite, Jesus went into the garden with the three confidants of his most intimate thoughts, Peter, James, and John.[3] He would not present the spectacle of his soul's distress to any but the three privileged ones who had been permitted to contemplate his glory on the summit of Thabor. To them he said: "My soul is sorrowful unto death. Stay you here and watch with me." And then he withdrew from them the distance of a stone's throw. They saw him fall upon his knees, his face pressed down even to the ground. Close as they were to him, in the brilliant light of the Oriental full moon shining in a cloudless sky, they could distinguish his every move; they could even hear his words, for the Jews, as we know, used to pray aloud, and nothing in the sleeping city nor in the country disturbed the profound silence of midnight.

The appearance of Gethsemani, one of the most venerated spots in the whole world, since its soil was bathed by the tears and blood of God, has changed much, especially during the last century. Many a pilgrim would prefer the austere barrenness of other times to the cultivated flower beds of today, crisscrossed by regularly laid out and carefully raked avenues. Eight giant olive trees are pointed out which are said to date from the time of Christ. It is unlikely, however, that trees so close to the city and so embarrassing to siege operations would have escaped the general clearing of trees which Titus ordered to be effected for a hundred stadia roundabout, in order to permit construction of entrenchments and protected passageways and machines of war.

---

[3] The Cave of the Agony, which should now be called the Cave of the Treason, is separated from the Garden of Gethsemani by the road that goes up to the Mount of Olives. It was always so, because to the east, in the property of the Russians, and on the west, on the land belonging to the Franciscans, one can see the steps carved out of the rock which led from the Golden Gate of the Temple to the summit of the mountain. In the ninth century the stairway path was still intact, and it numbered 537 steps from the level of Cedron to the summit of the Mount of Olives.

The Cave of the Treason forms a very irregular oval about 49 ft. in length by 7 or 8 yds. in width. The rocky vault is sustained by six columns, three of them masonry. The Cave, the garden, and the church belong to the Franciscans,

But these trees may well be descendants of those that witnessed the Saviour's agony, because the olive tree grows again from the roots, and this gives it a reputation of immortality.

In very early times, the faithful came to pray and weep at this place sanctified by the sanguinary prayer of the Saviour. In the reign of Theodosius, about 380, a beautiful basilica was erected here. In the course of centuries it was destroyed and rebuilt and destroyed again several times, and its ruins had so completely disappeared that until recently its site was unknown. Through providential accident, it has been rediscovered at the place where, by a curious transposition, the treason of Judas had been localized. The mistake has been corrected, and henceforth, in conformity with ancient tradition, the arrest of Jesus must be commemorated near the so-called "Cave of the Agony"; and the prayer of Jesus' agonizing Heart, at the church recently erected by the sons of St. Francis, faithful guardians of the Holy Places.[4]

2. The Mystery of the Agony[5]

The agony in the Garden of Olives is, with the temptation on the Mount of Quarantania, perhaps the most frightening mystery of Christ's life. That the Saviour suffered from hunger, thirst, and fatigue, that he experienced heat and cold does not surprise us, because he willed to take a nature like to ours in all things except

---

[4] A description of recent discoveries is given by P. Orfali, O.F.M., *Gethsemani,* Paris, 1924. Historical sketches of the sanctuaries and descriptions of the places are to be found in Vincent and Abel, O.P., *Jérusalem,* II, 301–327, and the *Appendix* (1926), pp. 1006–1013.

The Garden of Gethsemani is a square of about 60 yards. In 1848, it was enclosed by a wall. The ancient Basilica, built on the traditional site of our Saviour's prayer, was contiguous on the south to the present garden. It was rebuilt on a new plan in 1924.

We note that none of the ancient pilgrims mentions the olive trees of Gethsemani. Several of them mention only a palm tree which has now disappeared.

[5] The agony is recounted by the three Synoptics (Matt. 26:36–46; Mark 14:32–42; Luke 22:40–46). St. John, who reports Jesus' agitation at the prospect of his passion (12:27), which is something similar, does not mention the agony. St. Luke, who is the briefest of the three Synoptics, nevertheless has the additional details of the apparition of the angel and the sweat of blood (22:43–44). St. Matthew and St. Mark are very close together, but St. Matthew, contrary to his usual procedure, is a little more detailed in his account.

sin. But how could inner suffering have access to his soul, elevated to the beatific vision from the first instant of his conception? It is true that he voluntarily abandons himself to it, and Pascal's reflection is just: "In the Passion Jesus suffers torments that men inflict upon him, but in the Agony he suffers torments that he inflicts upon himself. It is torture from a hand not human but all-powerful, for he must be all-powerful to sustain it." But that does not solve the mystery.

If pleasure and pain can coexist in us, it is because joy here below is never so intense as to fill the soul so completely that sorrow is excluded. A mother watching by the deathbed of her son, hearing that another child whom she believed to be lost is about to throw himself into her arms, will mingle tears with her smiles. But the happiness of seeing God face to face dries up the source of tears forever. Now, in Jesus it is not only the inferior part of the soul that suffers; his whole soul is overwhelmed with sadness, and his will rigidly withstands his repugnance for the bitter chalice.[6]

Our Saviour's state has been compared to what is sometimes experienced by the mystics inflamed by divine love, to those delicious burnings and inebriating wounds of which St. John of the Cross speaks in the *Living Flame of Love,*[7] and to that "martyrdom of pain and delight" described by St. Theresa in an unforgettable page, when, on the threshold of the Seventh Mansion, she was about to receive the kiss of the Spouse.[8] The vision preluding the mystic marriage, in itself something like a foretaste of the blessed vision, inflames the soul with an ardent desire of the possession and enjoyment of God, and this desire, full of a hope that nothing on earth can gratify, causes in the soul an ineffable happiness mingled with untold suffering.

A comparison closer to minds that have not experienced

---

[6] Pope Innocent XII, in 1699, condemned this proposition: "Inferior Christi pars in cruce non communicavit superiori suas involuntarias perturbationes" (Denziger, 15 ed., 1339).

[7] St. John of the Cross does not say expressly that these "delicious burnings" and "inebriating wounds" were painful, but the words that he uses lead us to suppose it. [Cf. *Complete Works of St. John of the Cross,* trans. by E. Allison Peers, 1946, "The Living Flame of Love," pp. 40–47. *Translator.*]

[8] Life of St. Theresa written by herself, Chap. XX. [Cf. *Complete Works of St. Theresa,* trans. by E. Allison Peers, 1946, Vol. I, pp. 119–130. *Translator.*]

mystical favors is the state of the souls in Purgatory, as depicted by St. Catherine of Genoa. In these souls, now certain of being always loved by God and of loving him always, but kept at a distance from him in the place of expiation, "the love of God causes a happiness beyond what can be told, and still this happiness does not in the least diminish their torment. On the contrary, their great love of God, finding a hindrance to the accomplishment of their desires, is precisely the cause of their pain. Hence there is in them simultaneously an ineffable joy and an untold suffering."[9]

Who can fail to see how imperfect are these comparisons? The martyrdom suffered by the holy soul is the impossibility of possessing fully the object of its love; but when it shall enjoy that object in its fullness, the happiness with which it will be overwhelmed will close the door forever to all pain and sadness. The mystery of the Agony is, therefore, still untouched, and one sees here only a plausible explanation. The twofold natural effect of heavenly glory in him who sees God face to face would be to spiritualize the body and to fill the soul with beatitude. God suspends the first effect during the earthly life of Christ, to permit him to complete the mission of redemption; he suspends momentarily the second effect, to allow his love to suffer in his soul what no one else will ever have to suffer.[10]

There is yet another cause for astonishment: the *way* that Christ suffers. "That the God-Man allows every kind of insult and violence to come upon him from without is something before unheard of; but, after all, it is the logical consequence of the bloody Redemption decreed by his Father and accepted by him. That he lets loose the storm in his own soul, that he abandons his own sensibilities to natural weaknesses such as ours, that he allows himself to fall below the ideal of calm and, as it were, invincible strength after which we love to model our heroes: that

---

[9] St. Catherine of Genoa, *Treatise on Purgatory,* Chap. XIV. [Cf. the work of this name, translated by Balfour and Irvine, 1946, p. 29. *Translator.*] The comparison with Purgatory is also indicated by St. Theresa in the *Interior Castle of the Soul* (*Las Moradas*). [Cf. *Complete Works of St. Theresa,* trans. by E. Allison Peers, 1946, *The Sixth Mansion,* Chap. XI, pp. 323–328. *Translator.*]

[10] We are not saying that the beatific vision itself can be suspended, but only the natural effect of this vision, which would be to confer upon the soul an unalloyed happiness.

is something much more astonishing to our human feelings, something that scandalizes our pride. Nevertheless it is so. Marvel of condescension, priceless lesson and consolation!"[11]

To judge only from externals, certain martyrs have displayed more courage and strength of soul. St. Andrew enthusiastically salutes the cross, and from the height of that improvised pulpit preaches Christ for two whole days. St. Lawrence, half-roasted on the gridiron, offers ironical advice to his executioners. And, to cite an incident whose authenticity cannot be denied, since it is attested by the whole Church of Smyrna in an official document the very year of the martyrdom, St. Polycarp welcomed with charming good humor the myrmidons sent out in pursuit of him; he tranquilly divested himself of his clothes while they were preparing the stake for him; he advised his executioners that it would be superfluous to tie him to the stake, because he for whom he suffered would surely give him the strength to stay in the flames; and finally he breathed forth his soul with a hymn of thanksgiving.[12]

If we should be tempted to attribute to these witnesses to Christ, who were fortified by his example and strengthened by the prospect of the heavenly crown that awaited them, more constancy and strength than that of the King of Martyrs, we should recall that the physical sufferings, cruel as they must have been for so perfect a constitution, were but the smallest part of his agony. It must be remembered that Jesus did not come down from heaven to teach us a stoicism which steels itself against suffering by proclaiming that pain is not an evil. Wishing to show himself true man, and desiring to be a model within our reach, he lowers himself to our level. He is not ashamed to present to us the spectacle of his distress of soul. He seeks out the sympathy of the Apostles; nor does he repel the intervention of the consoling angel. He, the absolute master of the passions and emotions that agitate the human soul, ostensibly abandons himself to them today; he seems to unchain them against himself. But this interior tempest will be calmed in an instant when he

---

[11] Longhaye, *Retraite de huit jours,* p. 435. [The passage may be found in somewhat abridged form in *An Eight Days Retreat . . . adapted from . . . Longhaye,* by B. Wolferstan, 1928, p. 192. *Translator.*]

[12] *Martyrium Polycarpi,* in Funk, *Patres Apostolici,* pp. 320–332.

shall judge it proper; and his attitude in the presence of his judges and his executioners, in the Praetorium and on Calvary, will prove to anyone who can understand, that he has willfully endured the agony, just as he freely embraces death.

In the present order of Providence, it was necessary that Christ should suffer, not indeed the despair of the damned and the torments of hell, as certain blasphemous heretics have dared to maintain, but all the pains that were compatible with his divine Sonship. It was necessary that he suffer them, not only to prove to us the immensity of his love, and the purifying power of suffering, but to make him the ideal High Priest of a regenerated world. Here we may go forward with all assurance by the light of the Epistle to the Hebrews: "It behooved Him who brings many sons into glory, to make perfect through suffering the author of their salvation. . . . It behooved the Christ to be made in all things like unto his brethren, that he might become a merciful High Priest." It was right that, "Son though he was, he should learn obedience in the school of suffering and should thus become for all who obey him the author of eternal salvation."[13] Such are, as far as it is possible for us to grasp them, the providential reasons for the agony of Jesus in the Garden of Olives.

The Greeks gave the name "agony" to those contests in the stadium in which the contestants strained every nerve and energy to gain the palm. We call by the same name that last struggle of man at grips with death, in which death always emerges victorious at the end. The agony of Christ is also a struggle against mortal anguish, but a struggle from which he will come forth the victor. He is assailed at once by fear, by sadness, by weariness, and by disgust.[14]

"Weariness," says Bossuet, "casts the soul into a certain vexation that makes life insupportable and every moment burdensome;

---

[13] Heb. 2:10; 2:17–18; 5:7–10, abridged.

[14] The feelings experienced by Jesus are: (1) *sadness,* excessive sadness, even to death (*περίλυπος ἕως θανάτου*, Matthew and Mark), a sadness which can be called agony (*γενόμενος ἐν ἀγωνίᾳ*, Luke 22:44); (2) *stupor and fright* (*coepit pavere, ἐκθαμβεῖσθαι*, Mark 14:33). The compound verb is stronger than the simple verb *θαμβεῖσθαι*, "to be struck with astonishment or stupor"; (3) *anguish* mingled with weariness and disgust (*coepit taedere, ἀδημονεῖν*, Mark 14:33). This disquiet manifests itself by agitation, by going back and forth from place to place.

fear shakes the soul to its very depths by picturing to it a thousand threatening torments; sadness covers it with a thick veil that makes everything seem a death; and finally languor and exhaustion cause a kind of dejection and prostration of all the forces."[15] There is the picture that the Gospel traces of our Lord's agony.

Fear of death is natural to men. And yet the love of country, or devotion to dear ones, or the defense of a noble cause, or even ostentation and vainglory gives a man the courage to confront it. It is no depreciation of Christ — whatever St. Jerome may say about it,[16] and in this he is contradicted by St. Thomas[17] — to admit in him an instinctive fear. Death is the penalty of sin, and Jesus, all innocent as he was, willed to accept it as such. The circumstances surrounding death are often more terrible than death itself. Many a criminal regards it a favor to escape by a speedy execution the long preparations for a death presented as a public show. Jesus knew in advance, to the smallest detail, all the atrocious vicissitudes of his own death, and he harbored none of the hopes, none of the illusions which the rest of mortals fondle up to the very end. Bound as a malefactor and haled before one tribunal after another, delivered to the brutality of menials and soldiery, scourged and crowned with thorns, he will fall under the weight of the cross, and will languish for long hours nailed to his gibbet, suspended between heaven and earth, the butt of the raillery and insults and blasphemy of a delirious mob, and this under the gaze of his mother who will suffer mortally in seeing him suffer. This somber prospect, presenting itself to him in all its horror, wrests from him the cry: "Father, if it be possible, let this chalice pass from me; but thy will, not mine, be done." If his prayer had been absolute, it would have been granted, but it was conditioned and dependent upon the good pleasure of God.

---

[15] First sermon for Good Friday, first point.

[16] St. Jerome on Matt. 26:1 (ML, XXVI, 190): "Erubescant qui putant Salvatorem timuisse mortem, et passionis pavore dixisse: Pater, si fieri potest transeat a me calix iste." Also on Matt. 26:31 (*ibid.*, 197): "Dominus ut veritatem probaret assumpti hominis, vere quidem contristatus est, sed ne *passio* in animo illius dominaretur, per *propassionem* coepit contristari. Aliud enim est incipere constristari et aliud contristari." What saddens him is not death, but the treason of Judas, the abandonment by the Apostles, the ruin of Jerusalem.

[17] St. Thomas, *Summa,* III, q. xlvi, art. 6, ad 4um.

And God's will was that he should undergo death with all its frightful accompaniment.

During the agony of their Master, the three Apostles were sleeping. Jesus approached them and said to Peter, the responsible head of the group: "Simon, could you not watch one hour with me? Watch and pray, lest you enter into temptation. For the spirit is willing, but the flesh is weak."

Again he withdrew and resumed his communion with God: "My Father, if this chalice cannot pass away unless I drink it, thy will be done." It is substantially the same prayer as before, but with a special accent upon resignation and filial surrender. And now a still more frightful spectacle assails his imagination. He sees heaping up in the course of centuries the iniquities of men, those men for whom he is about to shed all his blood. How many souls, through negligence or malice, in every case through their own fault, will still hold aloof from the fruits of his redeeming death! Even in the Church, how many schisms, how many heresies, what scandals and apostasies and sacrileges! He is prompted to say with the prophet: *Quae utilitas in sanguine meo?* Men are not only ungrateful; they turn his own benefits against him; they outrage him in the Sacrament of his Love. This torrent of iniquity bears down upon him, it overwhelms him, crushes him. An angel must come down from heaven to sustain and comfort him. The consolation, that he needs and has not found in his Apostles, the heavenly messenger brings to him. This intervention of an angel in favor of the God-Man is, with the sweat of blood, a happening so full of mystery that the two episodes are omitted in some ancient manuscripts by scandalized copyists.[18]

The Apostles were still sleeping. It was, says St. Luke, the effect of sadness. Great interior disturbance beats the soul down; it produces a prostration, a sort of drowsiness of all the faculties.

---

[18] Luke 22:43–44. The authenticity of these two verses is admirably defended by Scrivener (*Introduction to the Criticism of the N.T.*, 4 ed., 1894, II, 353–356). The critic carefully examines the testimony of manuscripts, versions, and Fathers. The absence of this passage in the *Vaticanus* has impressed the English critics, Westcott and Hort, who place it in double brackets. But the authorities in favor of a difficult text, which they would be tempted rather to suppress than to add, are so preponderant that even from a critical point of view they leave no room for doubt.

It is not sleep, and yet not waking, but a middle state between consciousness and dream. The Apostles, confused at their collapse, know not how to excuse their sleepiness.

Jesus leaves them once again; again he repeats the same prayer without seeking new formulas. How could he have found a better than the *fiat* of loving resignation? And now he undergoes another trial, the most fearful of all. He feels all the sins of man weighing down upon him; for the Lord, says Isaias, has laid upon him the iniquity of all of us; and, according to the much more forceful words of St. Paul, "God has made him to be *sin* for us, that we may become *justice* in him" and through him. Under the blows of divine malediction which he accepts, he experiences what we ourselves ought to experience when confronted by sin: aversion, shame, horror, disgust, terror of God's judgments. The cup of bitterness is full to overflowing: it surpasses human strength. And then there happens a very rare, though not unexampled phenomenon, explainable partly by the greater delicacy of his organism, partly by his livelier sensibilities, but above all by his keener appreciation of what it is to offend God. A bloody sweat inundates his members and runs down even to the ground in thick drops, like clots of blood.[19]

The storm passes and of a sudden comes the calm. Jesus rises and goes to rejoin the three Apostles. "Sleep on now," he says to them, "and take your rest. Behold, the hour has come when the Son of Man is to be betrayed into the hands of sinners. Arise, let us go."[20] Some authors think that our Lord, with his usual self-possession, is here inviting the Apostles to enjoy a rest during the few minutes of respite left to them before the arrival of Judas. But such delicate attentions, if they may be called such, are little in harmony with the solemnity of the moment and do not fit well into the tenor of the Gospel text. "Sleep on now, and take your rest. It is enough." There is here, rather, a gentle reproach which might be called irony, but an irony devoid of bitterness or raillery.

---

[19] On the phenomenon of the bloody sweat, see the article *Agonie du Christ* in the *Dict. de théol. cath.*, t. I, cols. 621–624. The author distinguishes between a red sweat of microbic origin and the sweat of blood properly so called, for which he cites two well-attested cases. The phenomenon was not unknown to the ancients. Aristotle speaks of a bloody sweat (*Hist. Anim.*, iii, 19 [αἱματώδη ἱδρῶτα]), and Theophrastus, of a sweat which resembles blood.

[20] Matt. 26:45–46; Mark 14:41–42.

"Come, sleep as much as you will; I will not trouble you. But no, arise: the enemy is here."

Saying these words, Jesus went forth with them and directed his steps to the place where he had left the other eight disciples at the entrance to the garden, or rather, as we believe, in the cave mistakenly called the "Cave of the Agony." He had said: "Behold, he who will betray me is at hand." Perhaps the clank of arms could already be heard and the tramp of a troop on the march; and now a sinister gleam of light could be seen shining through the foliage.

3. The Kiss of Judas[21]

Leaving the Cenacle at nightfall, Judas had betaken himself to the house of the High Priest, who was impatiently awaiting him. Though the plot had been woven in its smallest details, there was still the question of carrying it out, and no amount of precaution seemed to be excessive, in order to avoid all mischance. It is true that the High Priest had at his disposal a large staff of servants as well as the guard charged with policing the Temple, which was under his command; but in the event that there should be any disorder or struggle involving bloodshed, he would incur a grave responsibility. The consent and concurrence of the Governor would serve as a shield; hence a detachment of Roman soldiers was requested. St. John's narrative leaves no doubt on this score, for he twice mentions the detachment commanded, not by a mere centurion, but by the tribune himself; and he expressly distinguishes this detachment from the servants of the Sanhedrin.

Judas had assumed the task of acting as guide to the escort. He knew that his Master on leaving the Temple sometimes went to spend the night at Bethany, but he was sure that on this particular night Jesus would not make so long a journey, since, after the eating of the Paschal lamb, it was forbidden to leave

---

[21] Matt. 26:47–56; Mark 14:43–52; Luke 22:47–52; John 18:2–11. The Synoptic versions differ little from one another, except that St. Luke omits the flight of the Apostles, and St. Mark adds the episode of the youth escaping naked from the hands of the guards. St. John completes their narrative without repeating it. He is the only one to mention the falling of the first assailants to the ground; he tells us that Peter was the one who drew his sword to defend Jesus, and that the High Priest's servant, the man wounded by Peter, was named Malchus.

Jerusalem, or the immediate vicinity which lay within the limits of the Sabbath rest. On the Mount of Olives, two caves served as retreats for the Saviour: one near the top (where the Constantinian basilica of Eleona was later erected and still later rebuilt under the title of the Sacred Heart); the other, at the foot of the hill near the Garden of Gethsemani. It may be supposed that the traitor went to prowl in the vicinity, and that, seeing the Saviour stop there, he ran to inform his accomplices.

The Roman soldiers, alerted at their barracks in the Antonia, took with them their usual military equipment and provided themselves besides with lanterns, as they would for any night expedition. They were to be on hand only to lend aid in case of need, the actual arrest of Jesus being left to the Temple police and the servants of the chief priests. This gentry, for the most part, had armed themselves with cudgels; and, since it was necessary to prepare against all contingencies, they had taken care to bring torches, in case any clouds should happen to obscure the full Paschal moon. It is probable, too, that some idlers, curious to see what was going on, joined them. The large procession finally set itself in motion.[22] For a surprise attack, no moment could have been more favorable. Everyone in Jerusalem and its environs was asleep.

Judas had engaged to deliver his Master to the Sanhedrists, and they had promised him thirty pieces of silver; but they had been very careful not to turn the money over to him in advance. The conspirators were too mistrustful of one another to neglect safeguards. The traitor would not get his hands on the money unless

---

[22] The "great multitude" (ὄχλος πολύς, Matthew) was made up as follows: *a*) According to St. Matthew: "those from the chief priests, and elders of the people."

b) According to St. Mark: "those from the chief priests, the Scribes, and the elders."

c) According to St. Luke: "chief priests, and chiefs of the Temple police and elders."

d) According to St. John: "a detachment (σπεῖρα), and the servants of the chief priests and of the Pharisees" (18:3), or: the detachment and the tribune, and the servants of the Jews (18:12: ἡ σπεῖρα καὶ ὁ χιλίαρχος). The σπεῖρα was a maniple, comprising two companies of 100 men each. The term was sometimes used in the sense of "cohort," as the Vulgate has translated it; but it means also, in a more general sense, "detachment, platoon, squad." It is unlikely that a whole cohort (600 men) was sent, despite the presence of the tribune. It is, in fact, doubtful that a whole maniple was sent.

he should succeed. Judas, therefore, was as much interested as anyone else in the success of the venture, perhaps more. The servants of the chief priests had often had occasion to meet Jesus in the Temple, and doubtless they knew him by sight; but at night, in the shadow of leafy trees, it was easy to be mistaken, and it was important to have a sign that would obviate error or hesitancy. Judas said to them: "The man whom I shall kiss, that is he; lay hold of him, and do not let him escape." It may be believed that after this warning the traitor went ahead of them, to avoid the appearance of being part of the band whose scout he was.

To give the signal agreed upon without betraying himself, Judas needed to use guile. We may ask whether disciples were accustomed to kiss the hand of their master whenever they met. It is possible, though the existence of such a custom is not proved by any historical evidence. It was not customary to kiss relatives or friends except at the moment of parting or after a long separation, or in certain exceptional circumstances such as a feast or a family mourning. Now, Judas had left Jesus only a few hours before, and nothing seemed to call for this extraordinary mark of affection. We believe, therefore, that, past master in the art of hypocrisy, and knowing that Jesus was aware of his perfidious intention, the traitor was acting out a comedy of repentance. The Gospels, if attentively read, suggest this conclusion. Judas was not content with kissing Jesus, as he had contracted to do; he effusively embraced him. Catching sight of the Saviour, whom he pretended to be looking for, he threw himself into his arms and pressed him to his breast, pronouncing the customary greeting. "Hail, Rabbi!" as if to say: "Lord, forget the past. I am a changed man."[23] Jesus answered him: "Friend, is it for this that thou hast come?" or — since the meaning of the phrase is uncertain — "Do that for which thou hast come."[24] And then he sadly said: "Judas, dost thou betray the Son of Man with a kiss?"

---

[23] Note the difference between the promise and its execution. "Whomsoever *I kiss,* that is he" (Matthew and Mark: ὃν ἂν φιλήσω); "and immediately going up to him *he embraced him*" (Matthew and Mark: κατεφίλησεν αὐτόν). Καταφιλεῖν is stronger than φιλεῖν. It means *to kiss tenderly,* or *several times, to clasp in one's arms.*

[24] Matt. 26:50: Ἑταῖρε, ἐφ' ὃ (variant, ἐφ' ᾧ) πάρει. *Amice, ad quid venisti?* *a*) The word ἑταῖρος means "companion," "comrade," and not "friend" (φιλός);

Admonished by the countersign, the servants of the Sanhedrin ran forward in disorder. Jesus advanced to meet them and said to them: "Whom do you seek?" — "Jesus of Nazareth." — "I am he." As Jesus said these words, there was something of the superhuman in his look and in his bearing. Those in front, finding themselves thus face to face with him, knowing his miraculous powers, at least by hearsay, and perhaps recalling the terrible vengeance which certain of the prophets had called down upon their persecutors, were seized with a kind of panicky terror and fell back one upon another. By this prodigy, our Lord willed to show that he was not yielding to force, but that he was giving himself up to his enemies of his own free will. When they had picked themselves up from the ground, somewhat recovered from their fright, Jesus said to them: "If it is I that you seek, let these men (these who are with me) go their way." Thus did he keep intact the word that he had spoken in the Priestly Prayer: "Of those whom thou hast given me I have not lost one." The moment he had spoken, the agents of the Sanhedrin threw themselves upon him.

We recall the two swords which had been spoken of on the way to Gethsemani. Some of the Apostles, seeing their Lord brutally bound, asked him if the moment had come to use them; but Peter, in whom patience was not the ruling characteristic, did not wait for the answer. Seizing one of the cutlasses, he cut off the right ear of one of the High Priest's servants named Malchus.

---

but the familiar ἑταῖρε can be rendered by "friend," "my friend."

b) The second person of the present indicative can be that of the verb παριέναι (*thou comest*) or παρεῖναι (*thou art present*). It does not change the meaning.

c) The difficulty is in the expression ἐφ' ὅ, which, in itself, is not interrogative and means, not "why," but "for which." The present Vulgate has *ad quid venisti?* but the Oxford critical edition has *ad quod venisti,* as has the *Brixianus,* the manuscript of the Old Latin Version which is closest to the Vulgate. Something must therefore be understood to complete the sentence. For example: "(Do) that for which thou hast come," or, giving it an interrogative turn by the tone of voice: "(Is that) what thou hast come for?"

Deissmann (*Licht vom Osten,* 4 ed., 1923, pp. 100–105) maintains that in popular language ἐφ' ὅ was interrogative, but the only example he cites is this invitation inscribed on a drinking glass, ΕΥΦΡΑΙΝΟΥΕΦ'ΟΠΑΡΕΙ. He translates: "Why art thou come? Rejoice." But it can also be translated: "Rejoice at having come" or "Rejoice at being here," which is more correct. [Cf. English transl., *Light from the Ancient East,* new ed., 1927, pp. 125–131. *Translator.*]

Jesus healed the ear of the wounded man by a simple touch of his hand, and then said to Peter: "Put back thy sword into its scabbard, for all those who draw the sword shall perish by the sword. Dost thou think that, if I ask it of my Father, he will not forthwith send me more than twelve legions of angels? How then are the Scriptures to be fulfilled, that have predicted all these things?" And then, addressing the mob: "As against a robber you have come out, with swords and clubs to seize me. I was teaching daily in the Temple, where you could have laid hands on me; but it must be that the writings of the prophets have their fulfillment. Now is your hour and (the hour of) the powers of darkness."

"Then all the Apostles, abandoning him, took to flight."

Some very reputable authorities, while not altogether excusing the defection of the Apostles, greatly minimize it.[25] By way of exculpation, they say that excitement and sorrow had robbed them of all power of reflection; that they could not and should not oppose force to force, in order to defend their Master, and therefore they did not believe that they were obliged to expose themselves to death for him; that by asking the Jews to let them go free, Jesus himself had seemed to authorize their flight. For all that, this universal abandonment on the part of those whom he had laden with favors was, perhaps, the blow most deeply felt by the loving Heart of Jesus on that tragic night.

Here is placed a trivial incident which St. Mark, the only one to hand it down to us, has judged worthy of note: "A youth, clad only in a linen cloth (mingling with the crowd), followed Jesus. Someone having seized him, he let go the linen cloth and escaped naked from their hands."[26] Evidently the youth had been sleep-

[25] Suarez, Salmeron, Cornelius a Lapide, etc.

[26] Mark 14:51–52. The hero of this episode was a very young man (νεανίσκος); the only clothing he was wearing was *a linen cloth* wrapped around his body (περιβεβλημένος σινδόνα ἐπὶ γυμνοῦ). This was the night clothing of well-to-do persons (Herodotus, ii, 95; Eusebius, *Hist. Eccl.,* VI, xl, 7).

St. Mark does not say whether the event happened at Gethsemani or in the city. Without specifying the time, he reports it between the flight of the Apostles and the arrival at the house of Caiphas. It could therefore have happened near the Cenacle; but the Cenacle, as we have said elsewhere, probably belonged to the family of Mark. Cf. Note R: *The Cenacle.*

ing, wrapped in one of those fine linen cloths which the well-to-do, instead of going to bed fully clothed like the common people, used to wind around them when they slept. He had been startled out of sleep by the sound of footsteps and the noise of the procession. Boyish curiosity had drawn him out of doors in his scanty attire, leaving him no time to dress more fully. If the Evangelist has seen fit to mention this trivial and pointless incident — pointless as having no connection with the rest of the story — it is doubtless because he is relating a personal recollection of no interest to others, but of capital interest to himself. He had taken no active part in the drama; but he had seen something of it, and he is anxious to tell what he saw. John — this is the name he had in Jerusalem before taking the Latin surname Mark, which has since been his — was at that time a youth, almost a boy, who, perhaps, had not yet reached his sixteenth year; and so his youth explains, or if need be, excuses the incident he reports. Fifteen years later he was still living in the home of his mother Mary, whence he was taken by his cousin Barnabas and the Apostle Paul to serve them in the capacity of helper.

It is he, we believe, that is the hero of this little drama. The hypothesis, to be sure, does not demand assent, but it is based upon solid reasons which have satisfied the most exacting critics.

Some Fathers have thought that the young man was the Apostle John. But St. Mark has just mentioned the flight of *all* the Apostles; and can it be admitted that at Gethsemani St. John was clothed in a tunic? If tradition designated a John, it would be easy to confuse John (Mark) with John (the Apostle). Cf. Wohlenberg, *Evang. des Markus,* Leipzig, 1910, p. 360, and Zahn, *Einleitung,* 3 ed., 1907, II, 216–217 and 248–249.

CHAPTER IX

Jesus Before the Sanhedrin

1. At the House of Annas the High Priest

EVERYTHING had succeeded according to the plans of the Saviour's enemies. It may even be said that their success surpassed their expectations, for even in the most carefully planned projects there is always an element of chance and unexpectedness which baffles all calculation. Here, thanks to the co-operation of the Roman authorities and the favoring night, everything had gone according to their hopes, without any bloodshed or collision, without serious resistance, without even waking up the sleeping city.

Jesus now retraced the journey he had taken two or three hours earlier. The underlings hurried their prisoner along the Valley of Cedron to the gate near the Pool of Siloe; then they climbed the precipitous street that led to the common palace of Annas and Caiphas, on the height that is now called the Hill of Sion. The Roman detachment, its mission over, returned to its quarters, and the Jewish escort conducted the prisoner to the house of Annas, the most active and influential member of the Sanhedrin.

It was commonly said that never had man been more fortunate than he; and if good fortune goes no farther than this earthly horizon, this was true. Annas had held the dignity of High Priest for nine years, and five of his sons, Eleazar, Jonathan, Theophilus, Matthias, and Annas the Younger, and one of his grandsons were raised to that dignity at varying intervals. Caiphas, the High Priest then in office, was his son-in-law. It would seem that the supreme priestly office was a sort of family fief. All that a Jew of his time could ambition: riches, honors, credit, the favor of Rome, Annas possessed. He lacked only the esteem and respect of decent people. The reproaches leveled against the great priestly families of that time were their ostentation, their worldliness, their materialism, and their implacable hardheartedness; but the family of Annas distinguished themselves still more by their malignity and avarice. The hissing of their vipers' tongues was talked about, doubtless because they did not shrink from defamation and calumny to beat down their enemies. Their shops, situated at first on the Mount of Olives and afterward in the vicinity of the Temple, were famous for a long time. On sale there, among other things, were the pigeons and turtledoves which the poor were bound to offer in sacrifice in default of costlier offerings. The Talmud tells us that at one time, no doubt because of a shameless monopoly, the price of these birds reached the exorbitant sum of one gold denarius each. We must always be suspicious of the exaggerations of the Talmud; but the report proves at least what memories the family of Annas bequeathed to posterity.[1]

Why was Jesus brought first before Annas, instead of directly before the High Priest Caiphas? Was it an act of deference on the part of Caiphas, always full of consideration and respect for his powerful father-in-law? Or was it that Annas, accustomed over a long period to speak and act as master, had concocted the whole scheme and set measures afoot and given orders to such an extent that he was now approached as the inspirer and instigator of the plot? The latter hypothesis is the more likely because Annas was still, in the eyes of the common people, the real High Priest, and the title was still linked with his name. Despite his arbitrary dismissal by Valerius Gratus, he could still be regarded as the legitimate successor of Aaron, Caiphas being only a figurehead and a mere agent responsible to the Roman authorities.[2]

---

1 On the bad reputation of the House of Annas according to the Talmud, see Billerbeck, *Kommentar,* Vol. II, pp. 568–571. There were other priestly families that were equally notorious, such as that of Boethus which had six high priests, and that of Cantheras which had two. Cf. Josephus, *Antiq.,* XX, viii, 8; ix, 2.

2 Note the expression of St. Luke: "Under Annas the High Priest and Caiphas" (3:2); "Annas the High Priest and Caiphas" (Acts 4:6). There was only one

The interrogation of Jesus by Annas had nothing judicial about it. There were neither accusers nor witnesses, and the members of the Sanhedrin were not assembled in strength. The only ones present were the fiercest and most fanatical, who had accompanied the night expedition to the Garden of Gethsemani. The others had been hastily summoned, at least those of whom they were sure; but, at that advanced hour of the night, they had to be given time to arrive at Caiphas' house, where the meeting was to be held.

Like a police official profiting by the confusion that seizes a prisoner at the time of his arrest, Annas was hoping to wrest from his captive some compromising admission. He therefore questioned him about his teachings and his disciples; but the answer was not what he was waiting for. "I have spoken openly to the world. I have always taught in the synagogues and in the Temple, where all the Jews are accustomed to gather, and in secret I have said nothing. Why dost thou question me? Question those who have heard what I spoke to them; they know what I have said." It is almost the answer that Plato puts in the mouth of Socrates, accused because of his teaching: "If anyone claims to have learned from me or to have heard me say anything that all the others could not have heard, know you that he has not spoken the truth."[3] Jesus was not like those traffickers in human wisdom who restrict their science to a small group of initiates to make it more sought after and more lucrative. His teaching, accessible to the simplest souls but capable of satisfying the loftiest minds, has nothing secret or esoteric about it. Indeed, his disciples have been commanded to preach it on the housetops.

Jesus had scarcely ceased speaking when a menial of the High Priest struck him in the face, saying: "Is it thus that thou answerest the High Priest?" Since there was nothing official about this questioning, no one in the gathering raised a protest against this shameful treatment inflicted upon a defenseless prisoner still

---

High Priest, but those who had held the office retained the title. Josephus, *Vita,* 38: "He persuaded the High Priests Annas (the younger) and Jesus (son of Gamala)." What is of interest in the language of St. Luke is that he seems to consider the deposed High Priest Annas as the principal person. Forty years later *the tomb of the High Priest Annas* was a landmark of topography (Josephus, *Bellum,* V, xii, 2).

[3] Plato, *Apol. of Socrates,* 33 B.

laden with chains. Without losing his composure, Jesus said to the aggressor: "If I have spoken ill, show what evil I have said; but if I have spoken well, why dost thou strike me?"[4] What wonderful patience and meekness! When St. Paul was struck in the mouth by order of the High Priest Ananias, he addressed him in these terms: "God will strike thee, thou white-washed wall. Thou sittest here to try me by the Law, and in violation of the Law dost order me to be struck!" It may well be that Paul would have spoken differently if he had known that he was addressing the High Priest; still the disciple most anxious to follow in the footsteps of the Master lags far behind him.

2. Jesus Before Caiphas

Annas soon perceived that his questioning would lead to no result, since the prisoner refused to answer. He therefore sent him, still bound, to the house of the High Priest Caiphas.[5] The

[4] John 18:22: *ῥάπισμα* is a blow struck on the face with the fist or a blunt instrument. St. Matthew (26:67) and St. Mark (14:65) distinguish *κολαφίζειν* (*deliver a blow*) from *ῥαπίζειν* (*strike on the head* or *face*).

[5] John 18:24: *Et misit eum Annas ligatum ad Caipham pontificem.* Since the Synoptics do not speak of Annas, many have thought that the whole interrogation took place before Caiphas, and that his father-in-law had sent Jesus to him without having questioned him. They understand *misit* in the pluperfect sense of *miserat,* or they place Verse 24 after Verse 13. Both treatments of the text are equally arbitrary. The aorist has not the sense of the pluperfect except in dependent clauses which are united to the principal proposition by a temporal or a relative particle. In the principal proposition, and with a verb such as *ἀποστέλλειν* whose pluperfect is much used, there would be no reason for such incorrect usage, and it is inadmissible.

As to the verse displacement, which puts Verse 24 after Verse 13, the two witnesses cited (Syr-Sin. and Cyril of Alexandria) are not important enough to authorize it. If this had been the primitive order, no one would have ventured to change it. Hence we follow without hesitation the text of all the Greek manuscripts and all the versions. Zahn supposes that the questioning took place before Annas but that it was conducted by the High Priest (Caiphas). The hypothesis is superfluous: Annas as well as Caiphas bore the title of High Priest.

The house of Annas is now pointed out inside the city 50 or 60 yards from David's Gate, more than 100 yards from the house of Caiphas. "Ancient tradition is entirely ignorant of this artificial distinction between the two residences of the father-in-law and son-in-law" (Vincent, *Jérusalem nouvelle,* 1922, p. 500). A "very plausible conjecture is that they lived in detached lodgings belonging to the same dwelling and looking out upon a common courtyard. We still see something similar in ancient Oriental houses built in the form of a khan where families rising from the same stock have each their own dwelling" (Abel, *ibid.,* p. 483). For description and documentation, *ibid.,* pp. 482–504.

distance was not great. Father-in-law and son-in-law lived in the same palace, which comprised two detached buildings linked by a common courtyard. The reconciliation of the Gospel narratives imposes this hypothesis, which besides is quite natural. As far back as we can go, tradition places the House of Caiphas on the Hill of Sion, in that part of the upper city left outside the enclosure of the Roman encampment, almost coinciding on its southern side with the present wall. According to the data of tradition, it must have been situated not far from the Cenacle, near what is now called David's Gate, between the modern rampart and the recently erected church of the Dormitio. As to the house of Annas, tradition does not concern itself with it at all, and does not distinguish it from the house of Caiphas.[6]

Apart from the role played by him in the Passion of Christ, we know nothing of Joseph Caiphas, except that he was married to Annas' daughter, and that he was named High Priest in A.D. 18 by Valerius Gratus and deposed in the year A.D. 36 by Vitellius, Governor of Syria, at the same time that Pilate was dismissed, and perhaps for the same reasons. He had, therefore, been holding the supreme pontificate for twelve years, and was to keep it for another six or seven. By what prodigies of servility and corruption and base intrigue was he able to keep himself in power for so long a time, when his three predecessors had held office for only one year each, and his five immediate successors were to hold it scarcely longer? How had he been able to keep in the good graces of Pilate, that shifty procurator, authoritarian and covetous, who seemed to make a game of humiliating the priesthood and of suppressing among the Jews the least effort at independence?

---

[6] See Vincent and Abel, *Jérusalem nouvelle,* cc. xviii and xix, pp. 482–515. The Church of Saint Peter was only 197 ft. from the Cenacle. The pilgrim Theodosius says 50 double paces, which is almost the same thing.

P. Marchet in a learned monograph copiously illustrated (*Le véritable emplacement du palais de Caïphe et l'église Saint-Pierre à Jérusalem,* Paris, 1927) and Fr. Power in *Biblica,* 1928, pp. 167–186, have tried to prove that the ancient Church of Saint Peter in Gallicantu was the only church called after St. Peter, and that it occupied the site of the house of Caiphas. Vincent and Lagrange have answered them in the *Revue Biblique* (1929, pp. 135–159).

The Assumptionists have conducted some very interesting excavations in their vast property on the southern slope of Mount Sion. It is there that the stairway street that descended to the lower Pool of Siloe has been discovered. The Church of St. Peter in Gallicantu has just been rebuilt. It is something more than 200 yards to the east of the Cenacle.

This is a problem impossible to solve for lack of documents. And, at any rate, what does it matter? His conduct on this occasion will give us the measure of the man.

The High Priest presided *ex officio* over the Sanhedrin. The history of this celebrated tribunal is somewhat obscure, and the ramblings of the treatise of the Mishnah which deals with it do not contribute much to clarify it.[7] An aristocratic assembly mentioned by Josephus under the name of "Senate" existed among the Jews from the third century B.C., but the name "Sanhedrin" did not appear until the accession of Herod, who put to death all, or almost all, of its members.[8] We do not know how the Sanhedrin was re-established, or how it recruited its membership thereafter, but we know that at the time of Christ it comprised three orders: the chief priests or heads of the principal priestly families, the *elders* or notable laymen of the nation, and finally the Scribes or students of the law. These last were, for the most part, Pharisees, while the majority of the priests belonged to the sect of Sadducees.

The prerogatives of the Sanhedrin differed under different governments. Restricted under Herod to judicial functions, its powers were expanded under the Procurators. The Sanhedrin had its own guard and its own police. It had the right to arrest and to imprison delinquents and to inflict certain penalties such as scourging, not to mention the major and minor excommunications,[9] but its powers went no farther. A Jewish scholar of our time has claimed that this tribunal could pronounce and execute capital sentences without the consent of the procurator.[10] This opinion,

---

[7] On the Sanhedrin, see Schürer, *Geschichte,* 4 ed., II, 237–267. Abundant bibliography.

[8] Josephus makes the first mention of the Sanhedrin under its Greek name (συνέδριον) in *Antiq.,* XIV, ix, 3. Elsewhere he calls it the *senate* (γερουσία, *Antiq.,* XII, iii, 3), *assembly of the ancients* or *notables* (πρεσβυτέριον), *council* (βουλή), *government* (τὸ κοινόν). The Talmud has only two names: *sanhedrin* and *tribunal* (*beth din*). In one text Josephus says that Herod had the members of the Sanhedrin killed (*Antiq.,* XIV, ix, 4) and, in another (*Antiq.,* XV, i, 2), that he had the *forty-five* members who were partisans of his adversary Antigonus killed.

[9] Acts 5:21; 9:1–2; 2 Cor. 11:24 (the five scourgings of St. Paul), etc.

[10] Juster, *Les Juifs dans l'empire romain,* 1914, II, 183: The Sanhedrin could "apply all the penalties prescribed by the Jewish laws, including the different kinds of capital punishment, and could itself execute them." The author gives no proof for his bold assertion. The five-page note that takes the place of a

absolutely devoid of proof and in contradition to the Gospels, is contrary to all likelihood, for Rome, in the provinces annexed to the Empire, always reserved the *jus gladii* to its own representatives, the proconsuls, propraetors, and procurators.

If we are to believe the Talmud, the criminal jurisprudence was regulated by wise laws calculated to ensure every protection to the innocent. A criminal trial could not be conducted at night; everything had to take place in full daylight. The process commenced with the hearing of witnesses for acquittal, and arguments favorable to the accused. The verdict was not pronounced on the same day, but was postponed to the day following. For this reason, a trial which could involve a condemnation to death was never instituted on the eve of a Sabbath or a feast day. The witnesses were duly warned of the seriousness of their act and of the responsibility assumed by them; they were isolated to prevent consultation, and, in a criminal trial, they were asked only what they knew *de visu* and not by hearsay. Finally, the judges gave their opinion in the inverse order of their hierarchical rank for fear that the judgment of those of higher rank, if they should speak first, would influence the others. Side by side with these wise regulations there were many others that were whimsical and inapplicable. While a condemned man was being marched to his punishment, two couriers were stationed in front of the tribunal,

---

proof is nothing but long-winded prattle about the lack of credibility of the Gospels. He finds only one fact to cite, and that fact refutes his thesis. The High Priest Annas, the son of the man spoken of in the Gospels, after the sudden death of Festus and before the arrival of his successor Albinus, profited by the interregnum to have St. James, the cousin of Jesus, condemned and stoned, together with several other Christians. Albinus wrote him a threatening letter in which he reprimanded him for having overstepped his authority. At the same time, King Agrippa II, within whose province it then was to name the High Priests, punished him for the misdemeanor and relieved him of his office which he had occupied for only three months (Josephus, *Antiq.,* XX, ix, 1). There were, perhaps, several riotous executions, like that of St. Stephen, and several clandestine murders, but no legal condemnations pronounced and executed by Jewish authority. About these clandestine murders, which may be compared to those of the *Vehmgericht* and of certain other secret societies, see the curious passage of Origen, *Epist. ad Africanum,* 14 (MG, XI, 81–84). The Jews could execute without trial any stranger who had introduced himself into their Temple, for no one demanded of them an account of what happened in a place into which no pagan had the right to penetrate. Cf. Philo, *Legatio,* 39 (Mangey, II, 591). But to conclude from this that the Sanhedrin could condemn to death and execute a death sentence without the consent of the Procurator is altogether illogical.

one on horseback, the other on foot and holding a flag. If during the course of the journey an argument favorable to the condemned was uncovered, the man with the flag gave a signal and the mounted man rode at full gallop to delay the execution.[11] As has been rightly said, many of these regulations seem to have been contrived to render a condemnation to death impossible, or rather, to create the impression that it was practically impossible.[12] We must remember that the Mishnah was drawn up at an epoch when Judaism had long lost its political autonomy, and when the Pharisees were its sole representatives and could arrange the history of the past to suit their taste. At all events, we know that all the rules of equity and justice were outrageously violated in the trial of Jesus, though perhaps it would be safer to refrain from trying to prove it by the authority of the Talmud.

The place where the Sanhedrin regularly held its sessions was situated on the northern declivity of Mount Sion near the flagstone-paved square called Xystus, and was connected by a bridge with the Temple esplanade not far from the Herodian wall where the Jews assemble to wail every Friday evening. But everything had to be irregular in this singular trial, and the Council met by night in the house of Caiphas. The success of the plot depended upon silence and speed.

As soon as the assembly was complete — or at least as soon as a quorum was present[13] — the presiding officer opened the session, and false witnesses were sought, ready to make a deposition against Jesus that would entail capital punishment. But

---

[11] *Mishnah,* treat. *Sanhedrin,* iv, 1–6; v, 1–2; vi, 1.

[12] Moore, *Judaism,* II, 187. Other critics, even Jews, give a no less severe estimate of this writing. And Edersheim himself, who, as is known, constantly explains the Gospel by the Talmud, admits: "Many of these regulations (as so much in Rabbinic accounts) may represent rather the ideal than the real — what the Rabbis imagined should be, rather than what was, or else what may date from later times" (*Life and Times,* II, pp. 553–554).

[13] St. Mark says (14:53): "*All* the chief priests and the elders and the Scribes gathered together," and later (14:55): "The chief priests and *all* the Sanhedrin sought testimony against Jesus."

The word *all,* which St. Matthew omits in both these texts, should not be taken literally. In the second instance it refers to all the Sanhedrin who are present; it is not necessary to include Nicodemus and Joseph of Arimathea, who were probably not present at the meeting. In the first text, the word *all* refers only to the chief priests, and all of them may be supposed to be included.

everything had been done with such precipitancy and disorder that the witnesses had not had time to come to an agreement, or had learned their lesson badly. Now the Law of Moses was explicit: to condemn a man to death, two or three agreeing witnesses were required. The Rabbis of later times required in this agreement a precision which was almost unattainable. They demanded that the accuser specify exactly the day, the hour, the place, and the smallest circumstances of the crime. At the very least, it was required that the depositions should not be contradictory; and even this they had not managed to obtain against the Saviour, despite the best efforts of the witnesses, the partisanship of the judges, and the number of attempts.

At last two men presented themselves who seemed to have exchanged views and whose testimony instantly gained attention. They affirmed that they had heard Jesus say, according to one of them: "I will destroy the Temple of God, and I will rebuild it in three days"; according to the other: "I will destroy this Temple made by the hand of man, and in three days I will build another not made by the hand of man." The two depositions differed notably from each other; neither of them was in conformity with the letter, and above all, with the spirit, of Jesus' saying: "Destroy this temple" — he was speaking of his body, the sanctuary of divinity — "I will raise it up again at the end of three days." Even if understood in the material sense, of the Temple of Jerusalem, though the proposal might appear extravagant to anyone who did not know Christ's power, it contained nothing blasphemous. To tear down the Temple in order to rebuild it with greater magnificence was no crime. Herod had done it without being accused of impiety, and many thought that the Messias would some day do the same. This was all that could have been stated, if the witnesses were in agreement; but they were not. Besides, even if they were in accord, their testimony would never justify a death sentence. It would merely serve to stir up hatred against Jesus and to alienate from him the sympathy of the people by causing them to believe that he had wished or prophesied the ruin of the Temple. Had not Jeremias been threatened with death for predicting in the name of God that the Temple would be reduced to utter ruin by the enemies of Israel? This was probably Caiphas' intention when he rose from his seat and advanced into the middle of the assembly and thus addressed the prisoner: "Answerest thou nothing to all the accusations directed against thee?" But Jesus was silent. Several members of the Sanhedrin noisily challenged him: "If thou art the Christ, tell us so openly." "If I tell you," answered Jesus, "you will not believe me; if I question you, you will not answer me." This was, in fact, what had happened three days before, when he had asked them whence came the baptism of John, and what was the meaning of the Psalmist's saying: "The Lord said to my Lord."

Caiphas now believed that he had at last found a sure means of overcoming the obstinate silence of the accused and of wresting from him an avowal which would destroy him. He addressed to Jesus these words: "I adjure thee by the living God that thou tell us whether thou art the Christ, the Son of the Blessed One." Such an adjuration was altogether illegal. When the judicial oath was administered to a trustee suspected of infidelity or to a debtor from whom a sum of money was claimed, no titles being produced, the purpose was to provide those who were falsely accused with a simple means of exculpating themselves; but never, in default of witnesses, was anyone adjured to declare himself guilty, and to put an end to the proceedings by pronouncing his own condemnation. Consequently Jesus had no obligation to answer a question which the judge had no right to ask. If he did answer, it was not, as has been maintained, out of deference to the authority of the High Priest. It was because his silence in such circumstances could be taken as a disavowal. He had been asked if he was the Messias and the Son of God; not *a* son in the theocratic sense, as were all the members of the chosen people, but *the* Son *par excellence,* the Son of God properly so called. For us, Messias and Son of God are synonymous terms in the sense that the Messias could be no other than the Son of God; but they were not such for the Jews, and to call oneself Messias did not constitute blasphemy. Why, then, does Caiphas adjure Jesus to tell him if he is the Messias? It is because such a claim, offensive as it is to Rome, will have a capital importance when the case is brought before the tribunal of Pilate.

Though Messianic pretensions were not blasphemous, for one

to arrogate to himself the quality of Son of God, in a sense establishing a transcendent and incommunicable relationship between God and him, was pre-eminently such. Every time that Jesus had given himself this title, the Jews had plotted his death or seized rocks to stone him as a blasphemer. What answer will he give today? Faced with this formal summons of the High Priest, speaking in the name of the Sanhedrin and of the whole Jewish nation, he can no longer be silent. "Thou hast said it. I am. Nevertheless I say to you: Hereafter you shall see the Son of Man seated at the right hand of the (divine) Power and coming upon the clouds of heaven." In these words Jesus brings together two texts — one of them from Daniel, the other from the Psalms — which predict his triumph. From this time forward, beginning with the Resurrection which is so near that it may be said to be now present, the Jews will see the glory of the Son of God. They will see it, not with the eyes of the body, but with the eyes of faith, if they are believers, and with the eyes of the mind, if they have the least sincerity; for the fact of the Resurrection will confirm his right to sit at the right hand of the Father to judge the living and the dead.

Scarcely had the words fallen from Jesus' lips when the High Priest cried out: "You have heard the blasphemy! What further need have we of witnesses? He is worthy of death." And all the members of the Sanhedrin repeated in chorus: "He is worthy of death."[14] As he uttered these words, Caiphas rent a portion of his tunic. It was a gesture of reprobation which every pious Jew was bound to make upon hearing a blasphemy uttered, and the Talmud regulates the ritual of the action in the most minute detail.[15]

---

[14] Matt. 26:57–27:2; Mark 14:53–15:2; Luke 22:54–71.

Comparing the three narratives, it will be remarked that St. Matthew and St. Mark are so close together that the variants are unimportant. St. Luke, on the contrary, deviates notably from the other two, especially as to the order of the events. (1) He passes over the night session in silence and transposes to the morning session the adjuration of the High Priest and the condemnation of Christ. (2) He recounts the three denials of St. Peter immediately after mentioning the arrival of Jesus at the house of Caiphas. (3) He places the scene of derision and insult organized by the guards before any condemnation and even before any questioning of Jesus. On these three points the order followed by the first two Synoptics seems much more natural.

[15] Billerbeck, *Kommentar,* Vol. I, pp. 1007–1019.

However, despite his superficial indignation, the High Priest could scarcely conceal his joy. As has been very well said, "This accusation of blasphemy, which alone could involve condemnation to death, was all that Caiphas had in view in this examination, and we can understand with what eagerness he seized upon it, turning it to his own ends. At last he had his prey within his grasp and on the horns of a fatal dilemma. Either He must deny His mission or condemn Himself to death. He seemed to have triumphed, but the real victor was the Condemned. Jesus was going to His death, and He knew it and willed it too. But He would not undergo this death prepared for Him by His enemies under a pretext that was false. He intended His death to be a martyrdom, which should put upon His teaching the final seal."[16]

It would be impossible to paint more clearly the knavery of Caiphas and the state of Jesus' soul. However, we will not venture to endorse the statement following: "If he is condemned by the Jewish and Roman tribunals, it will be as the Son of God." The question of blasphemy was of no concern to a Roman magistrate. Gallio made this clear when St. Paul was brought before his tribunal on the charge of heresy. Pilate condemns Jesus because he says that he is a king, and because he is accused of aspiring to the throne of Judea. What will put an end to his hesitation and to his wish to save an innocent man will be the cry of the mob: "If thou release this man, thou art no friend of Caesar; for everyone who makes himself king sets himself against Caesar."[17]

The moment the guards saw Jesus condemned by the Sanhedrin as a blasphemer, they furiously threw themselves upon him, overwhelming him with blows and insults. They began by spitting in his face; then, after blindfolding him, they slapped him in the face, saying: "Prophesy who it is that struck thee?"[18] They were

---

16 Lebreton, *La Vie et l'enseignement de Jésus-Christ,* II, 381 (English transl., Vol. II, pp. 351–352).

17 John 19:12–13. Compare the answer of Gallio, Acts 18:14.

18 Matt. 26:67–68; Mark 14:65; Luke 22:63–65. The three texts are complementary. St. Matthew does not say that Jesus' eyes were bandaged, but this is understood, because they ask him to guess who the aggressor is. St. Mark has simply: "Guess" (προφήτευσον), without saying what, but the context indicates sufficiently. St. Luke attributes the ill-treatment to the guards (οἱ συνέχοντες αὐτόν); St. Mark, to the servants (οἱ ὑπηρέται), but he leaves it to be understood that *some* of the Sanhedrists took part.

For the game to which allusion is made, many authors refer to Pollux

at a loss for ways to torture their victim and to satisfy their rage, thinking that no moderation need be observed toward a man who had been convicted of blasphemy. So it will be when Herod's satellites will lavish derisive honors upon Jesus, when they see the Tetrarch treat the Saviour as a fool and a tinsel king; so too the Governor's soldiers will invent the burlesque enthronement, when Pilate condemns the King of the Jews to scourging as a prelude to crucifixion. We know that among the Romans, the populace played the barbarous game of adding to the tortures of men condemned to death, all along the journey from the tribunal to the place of execution. And thus the servants of the High Priest engaged in the cruel pastime of insulting and tormenting their captive to beguile the long hours of night, waiting for the early morning hour when the Sanhedrin must meet again to decide the prisoner's fate.

Another scene, still more painful to the Heart of Jesus, has just taken place a short distance away. We must retrace our steps to recount this lamentable episode.

3. Peter's Triple Denial

Seeing the Saviour brutally seized by the guards and tightly bound, all the Apostles had taken to flight. Peter, after his recent impetuous outbreak, had greater reason than the others to fear reprisals; still, after the first moment of panic, he began little by little to regain control of himself. He followed at some distance the escort which was leading Jesus to the palace of the High Priest. When he arrived there, another disciple, who had come with him or joined him, was able to enter unmolested, because he was an acquaintance of Annas and his household, but Simon Peter had to remain outside, and the door closed in front of him.

(*Onomasticon*, ix, 123, at the word μυῖνδα) but the μυῖνδα was analogous to hide-and-seek or blindman's buff. Rather it is the game described by Pollux (IX, 129) under the word κολλαβίζειν: "One has his eyes closed and someone else slaps him saying: which of my two hands slapped you?" Cf. Van Unnik in *Z.N.T.W.*, 1930, pp. 310–311, and the notes of Dindorf in his edition of Pollux, Vol. V, pp. 1209–1211. Today this children's game is played by several, and the subject must guess which one slapped him, as in the Gospel.

We have no need to ask who this other disciple was. The close bond linking him with the Prince of the Apostles, the discreet and mysterious way in which the Fourth Gospel mentions him, and the precision with which the incident is described, a precision which points to an eyewitness, all lead us to think of the disciple whom Jesus loved. But how could the son of Zebedee have had any connection with the wealthy father-in-law of Caiphas? We must not forget that inequality of rank and fortune did not at that time place between people the distance that differences in social condition nowadays establish among us. Besides, as we have said elsewhere, John's family was relatively well off, and if it had priestly connections, as some think, we may readily suppose that it had trade or business relations with the chief priests. We therefore embrace without hesitation the opinion of St. John Chrysostom, St. Cyril of Alexandria, and St. Jerome, while respecting the candid reserve of St. Augustine, who does not venture to express a firm opinion upon the subject.

John did not take long to notice that his companion had stayed behind. He therefore retraced his steps and, having exchanged a word with the servant girl who was portress, introduced Peter into the palace courtyard.

In order to understand what is to follow, it will be well for us to reconstruct for ourselves the layout of the place, as far as the scanty data of the Evangelists permit. The house of Annas gave upon the street through a main portal, which was closed at nightfall. Below, there was a door guarded by a servant — oftener by a servant maid — which gave entrance to latecomers when the main portal was closed. Passing through this door one found oneself in a sort of corridor or vestibule which led to a central courtyard. The ground floor served as living quarters for the family; the reception rooms were on the upper floor, as is the custom today.[19]

---

[19] We should carefully distinguish the *courtyard,* the *forecourt* (or vestibule), the *portal* (or gateway), and the *door* (or rather, side entrance).

a) The courtyard (αὐλή, the word means "palace" and "courtyard," but here it should be taken in the latter sense). In relation to Jesus, who is inside, on the upper floor, Peter is "below, in the courtyard" (Mark 14:66: κάτω ἐν τῇ αὐλῇ), or "outside, in the courtyard" (Matt. 26:69: ἔξω ἐν τῇ αὐλῇ). The fire is lit *in the middle of the courtyard* and the people are crouched (seated) around the fire. The Vulgate translates αὐλή by *atrium.*

In letting the stranger in, the portress had some suspicions. Distinguishing him imperfectly in the darkness, and impelled by feminine curiosity, she followed him into the courtyard, in the middle of which a fire had been lighted. Toward the end of March and in the beginning of April the nights are chilly in Jerusalem because of the altitude, and the early morning cold is felt the more by contrast with the heat of the day. The servants of the High Priest, and the people who had come in the train of the escort, were warming themselves around a fireplace and talking about the happenings of the night. Peter unconcernedly went and crouched in the midst of them, thinking that this was the best way to pass unobserved. But in the glare of a torch, the suspicious serving maid recognized him as a Galilean, either because of his face and manner or because of some peculiarity of his dress. She abruptly addressed him: "Thou too, thou wast with the Galilean, with Jesus of Nazareth." Peter repelled the imputation as an insult: "I do not know what thou art saying. I do not know this man."

The impetuous nature of the Apostle, his agitation and confusion, had prevented him from reflecting upon the full gravity of his denial. Still, he was not easy in mind. He rose and made his way toward the door, hoping to conceal himself in the shadows of the vestibule from all these peering faces. At that moment, a cock, waking earlier than the rest, made himself heard; but Peter, given over to the turmoil of his own thoughts, did not heed it. Yet the vestibule was for him no safer as a refuge than the fireplace. The portress again confronted him, and she was not alone. She repeated what she had said, and the others

---

b) The *portal* (πυλών, badly translated by *janua*) looked out upon the street. Before the second denial Peter "goes out" (from the courtyard) directing his steps toward the portal in passing through the vestibule (Matt. 26:71: ἐξελθόντα εἰς τὸν πυλῶνα, badly translated by *exeunte illo januam*).

c) The *forecourt* or *vestibule* (προαύλιον, *ante atrium,* which must be read as one word). Peter, making the move described above, "goes out" (from the courtyard) to reach the forecourt or vestibule (Mark 14:68: ἐξῆλθεν ἔξω εἰς τὸ προαύλιον, *exiit foras ante atrium:* i.e., *exiit* [ex atrio] *in anteatrium*). The two texts, badly translated, have misled St. Augustine into thinking that St. Peter went out *into the street,* after the first denial.

d) The *little door* (θύρα, *janua*). Peter waits outside near the *door* (John 18:16: εἱστήκει πρὸς τῇ θύρᾳ ἔξω) guarded by the portress (θυρωρός).

joined in chorus: "Certainly," they said, "he is one of the group." And Peter declared with an oath that he was not.

The die was cast. The unhappy man no longer thought of flight. He was aware that the half-light, far from concealing him, only exposed him the more to suspicion. He returned to the fire and, to keep himself in countenance, joined in the conversation. But this was just what would give him away; for a Galilean was easily recognizable by his accent. In Galilee, the people of the lower classes softened the gutterals which are so characteristic of the Semitic tongues and changed the sound of certain vowels, and this sometimes resulted in very amusing misunderstandings.[20] As soon as Peter opened his mouth, the bystanders said to him: "Surely thou art part of the group, for thou art a Galilean; thy way of speaking betrays thee." He kept protesting until a kinsman of the Malchus, whose ear he had cut off by his impetuous act in the Garden, staring at him said: "Did I not see thee with him in the garden?" Vainly he went on denying it in the face of all evidence, confirming his denials with oaths. They did not believe him.

About an hour had gone by since the first denial. At that very moment the cock crowed for the second time.

By a providential coincidence, our Lord was being led from the tribunal by the servants of the High Priest and was crossing the courtyard. He cast upon Peter a look full of sadness and commiseration.[21] And then it was that Peter remembered the word of the Master: "Before the cock crows twice thou shalt deny me thrice." Aghast, he straightway left the palace, and bursting into tears he fled. Tradition has faithfully preserved the memory of the place where he went to hide his shame and to weep over his fault. A church was built there as far back as the fifth century; in the Middle Ages it bore the name of St. Peter in Gallicantu,

---

20 Examples in Billerbeck, *Kommentar,* Vol. I, pp. 156–159. The best known is the following. A Galilean asked where he could find an *amar* (אמר). A Jew answered him: "Stupid Galilean, what are you looking for: an ass (ḥamôr, חמור), or wine (ḥèmèr, חמר), or wool ('ămar, עמר), or a lamb ('immăr, אמר)?"

21 Luke 22:61: "The Lord turned and looked upon Peter." We are supposing that Jesus is being led from the tribunal to the place where he is to be under guard until morning, and where the scene of derision took place.

in memory of the crowing of the cock. The pilgrims of today are happy to see it rising from its ruins.

St. Peter's triple denial is a cause of the greatest embarrassment to critics too forgetful of the wise principles enunciated by St. Augustine on the freedom which, like others, the sacred writers enjoyed while writing their narratives. Taking into account all the variants, as many as eight or nine distinct denials have been numbered. To solve the discrepancies, the narrative of St. John, the eyewitness, should claim the place of preference; then that of St. Mark, so careful of precise detail with which the other Synoptics are less concerned. St. John places the episode partly before, partly after, the sending of Jesus from Annas to Caiphas. Though St. Matthew and St. Mark recount it before the sentence passed by the High Priest, and St. Luke places it after that event, such inversion, which is frequently met with in the Gospels, should not cause us too much concern. The other divergences are more serious. Meanwhile, it should be noted that the little drama takes place in three acts, with many actors appearing, and this may well have given rise to divergent traditions.[22]

---

[22] Matt. 26:69–75; Mark 14:66–72; Luke 22:56–62; John 18:16–18, 25–27.

ACT I — 1. *The place* — Outside in the courtyard (Matthew), below in the courtyard (Mark), in the middle of the courtyard (Luke).

2. *Peter's position* — He is warming himself (Mark), seated in the light of the fire (Luke).

3. *The person addressing him* — A maidservant (Matthew and Luke), a maidservant of the High Priest (Mark), the maidservant who was guarding the door (John).

4. *The question* — "Thou also wast with Jesus the Galilean" (Matthew); "with Jesus of Nazareth" (Mark); "This man too was with him" (Luke); "Art thou not also one of this man's disciples?" (John.)

5. *The answer* — "I know not what thou sayest" (Matthew); "I neither know nor understand what thou sayest" (Mark); "Woman, I know him not" (Luke); "I am not" (John).

ACT II — 1. *The time* — A little later (Luke); the cock crows (Mark). The other Evangelists do not specify.

2. *Peter's position* — Going out toward the portal (Matthew); going out toward the forecourt (Mark); warming himself (John — this is the case throughout, both before and after).

3. *The person addressing him* — *Another* woman (Matthew); *the* maidservant (Mark); another one, a *man* (Luke); "they" (John).

4. *The question* — "This man also was with Jesus of Nazareth" (Matthew); "This man is one of them" (Mark); "Thou too art one of them" (Luke); "Art thou not also one of his disciples?" (John.)

The first denial took place as soon as Peter entered the courtyard, and in answer to the prying question put to him by the serving maid guarding the door; all the Evangelists agree on this point. They also agree in placing the last denial near the fire, where the people who were warming themselves recognized Peter by his accent and challenged him all together. Only with regard to the second denial does there exist any difficulty. According to St. Matthew, the question was asked by a second serving maid; according to St. Mark, it was asked by the same one; according to St. Luke, the questioner was a man. St. John does not indicate whether it was a man or a woman. The solution, however, is simple, if we reflect that the scene takes place in the forecourt, as the first Evangelist expressly asserts. Is there anything that forbids us to suppose that several persons of both sexes were keeping the portress company and that they joined her in

---

5. *The answer* — Again he denied with an oath (Matthew); again he denied (Mark); "Man, I am not" (Luke); "I am not" (John).

ACT III — 1. *The time* — A little later (Matthew and Mark); at the end of about an hour after the first denial (Luke).

2. *Position* — None of the Evangelists describes it, but Peter is presumed to be near the fire.

3. *The person* — The bystanders (Matthew and Mark); another one (Luke); the kinsman of Malchus (John).

4. *The question* — "Surely thou also art one of them, for even thy speech betrays thee" (Matthew); "Surely thou art one of them, for thou art a Galilean" (Mark); "Surely this man too was with him, for he also is a Galilean" (Luke); "Did I not see thee with him in the garden?" (John.)

5. *The answer* — He curses and swears that he does not know the man (Matthew); "I know not this man of whom you speak" (Mark); "Man, I know not what thou sayest" (Luke); again Peter denied it (John).

CONCLUSION — Immediately the cock crowed (Matthew and John); immediately the cock crowed for the second time (Mark); immediately, while he was still speaking, the cock crowed (John).

The variants, when closely examined, are reduced to very little and can easily be reconciled.

ACT I. Peter on entering goes to the fire, and the portress, who has followed him, denounces him as a disciple of Jesus; he denies it, and the cock crows for the first time.

ACT II. In the forecourt, where he has taken refuge, Peter finds the portress in the company of others. The same denunciation is made by them; the same denial by Peter.

ACT III. Near the fire several bystanders, among them a relative of Malchus, recognize Peter as a Galilean and a companion of Jesus. He denies it more energetically than ever. The cock crows immediately.

[The first part of this note has been edited somewhat. *Translator*.]

challenging the unhappy Apostle? If we were not dealing with captious minds, perhaps it would not be necessary to push the harmonizing process even that far.

Some of the Fathers of the Church, out of regard for the dignity of the Prince of the Apostles, lessen his fault almost to the point of excusing it. St. Jerome puts us on our guard against excessive indulgence; to acquit Peter is to contradict Jesus.[23] True it is that his faith did not fail, but he was lacking in courage; and his fall, while not to be compared to the treason of Judas, is even harder to understand. The traitor had been tending toward his defection for a long time, whereas Peter had been protesting a few hours before that he was ready to die for his Master; and his protestation was sincere. The cause of his undoing was that he counted too much on himself and not enough on divine aid. When Jesus predicted his fall, he refused to believe him. "Jesus insists, Jesus specifies; the prediction of the fall becomes fully explicit; before such and such an hour you will deny me three times. But that makes no difference; once started, Peter does not stop; he takes a stand against our Lord; he contradicts him to his face. He will follow him to prison and to death; he will never deny him. . . . Such noisy presumption is not to be cured by a word; he needs the lesson of facts, a humiliating and dolorous proof. He will have it."[24]

We too had need to learn that in the affair of eternal salvation we can do nothing of ourselves, and that presumption is almost as fatal as despair. To give us this lesson, and to teach us at the same time the power of repentance, God permits this humanly unexplainable fall.

The narrative of the trial of Jesus before the Sanhedrin would doubtless gain in clearness if it were possible for us to fix the order of events with certainty. Unfortunately St. John, who must have followed its various phases, passes it over in silence, either because he supposes it to be well enough known from the text of

---

[23] St. Jerome on Matt. 26:72 (ML, XXVI, 203): "Scio quosdam, pio affectu erga apostolum Petrum, locum hunc ita interpretatos ut dicerent Petrum non Deum negasse sed hominem, et esse sensum: Nescio hominem, quia scio Deum. Hoc quam frivolum sit, prudens lector intelligit." St. Jerome seems to be alluding to St. Ambrose (*In Lucam,* lib. X, 78; edit. Schenkl, p. 485) and to St. Hilary (*In Matthaeum,* Chap. XXXII, No. 4; ML, IX, 1071).

[24] Longhaye, *Retraite annuelle de huit jours,* p. 174.

the Synoptics, or because the verdict of the Sanhedrin had no legal coherence and could not have had any. Still, what he has told us about the triple denial by Peter is a guiding thread which aids us to arrange the rest. We propose the following sequence of events.

The escort which had arrested Jesus led him first of all to the palace of Annas, and it was before the fire lighted in the courtyard of the High Priest that Peter's first denial took place. The questioning before Annas was only a pastime for the curious, or, if you will, an intermission to allow time for the members of the Sanhedrin to arrive at the palace of Caiphas. The Sanhedrin held two sessions: one at night, when the witnesses were summoned; the other at dawn, when it was decided to bring the case before Pilate. St. Luke mentions only the latter, though he supposes the first, for the scene of mockery and violence which he relates before the morning session can be well explained only as happening after a judgment and a condemnation. It was during the night session that the two later denials by St. Peter took place. We have told how Jesus, coming out of the tribunal led by the guards, crossed the courtyard common to the two palaces and cast upon Peter that sad and tender look that pierced his heart. It was also at the night session that the High Priest adjured the Saviour to tell him if he was the Messias and the Son of God. Such a dramatic scene could not have taken place twice. St. Luke places it at the morning session, which he alone reports, but the order observed by the other two Synoptics seems to us to be much more natural.

CHAPTER X

Jesus at the Praetorium

1. Jesus Brought Before Pilate[1]

AT DAYBREAK the members of the Sanhedrin held a second council. Can it be that they wished, because of a tardy scruple, to cover this judicial assassination with a cloak of legality by bringing to an end in the daytime a trial which had begun at night contrary to law? It is scarcely likely. The death sentence had been pronounced; the only point that now gave them any anxiety was to assure its execution. They were well aware that they needed the Procurator's consent, and the question now was how best to secure it. Two courses were open to them: to have their verdict sanctioned by the Roman authority and ask permission to carry it out themselves, or to bring their accusation before Pilate as though they had not yet come to any decision. As to the first plan, the penalty for blasphemy according to the Jewish law was stoning, and it was doubtful whether the Procurator would agree to sanction it. Hence the second course was settled upon as offering two advantages: first, it would place upon the foreigner the odium of passing a sentence of condemnation revolting to the conscience of decent people; secondly, the sentence would be

[1] The older dissertations on the trial of Jesus are now outdated. Among the most recent should be cited two doctoral theses: H. Regnault, *Une province procuratorienne au début de l'empire romain. Le procès de Jésus-Christ,* Paris, 1909; and Kastner, *Jesus vor Pilatus,* Munster-i-W., 1912, completed later in *Jesus vor dem Hohen Rat* (according to St. Mark). Regnault, a Protestant who shows great respect for the sacred text, shows very well that the trial before Pilate is not the continuation nor the confirmation of the trial before the Sanhedrin. The former was political; the latter, religious. The trial before Pilate is a new trial.

carried out without any danger to themselves, thanks to the support of armed force. The deliberations must have taken but a short time, for it was still early when they made their appearance before Pilate.[2]

The people of the ancient world were very early risers. At Rome the patricians used to be up at dawn to give audience to their clients, and the courts opened early, since all serious business came to an end at midday, the remainder of the day being devoted to rest and amusements. So the first rays of the sun were scarcely gilding Mount Sion when Jesus was led to the Praetorium.

Originally the *praetorium* was the tent of the commanding general, a kind of sanctuary where the insignia of the legions were deposited, and where the praetor took the auspices and dealt out justice. Later on, when the Emperor had command of all the armies, the name was given to the imperial abode and to the residences of the Emperor's representatives: proconsuls, propraetors, and procurators, who had the power of life and death. In moving about, the Emperor constantly changed his praetorium.[3] Claudius signed an edict from his praetorium at Baiae. Tiberius barely escaped death at his praetorium in Terracina. When, therefore, we read that Augustus had little taste for vast and sumptuous praetoria, and that, on the contrary, Caligula was fond of the most extravagantly luxurious praetoria, we understand what is meant: the ordinary or temporary dwelling places of the Emperor or his agents armed with the *jus gladii* were their praetoria.[4] It is true that the Roman governors ordinarily installed themselves in the palaces of deposed sovereigns,

---

[2] The morning session took place at a very early hour (πρωΐ, Mark 15:1; Matt. 27:1), more exactly, "as soon as day broke" (Luke 22:66: ὡς ἐγένετο ἡμέρα). This meeting (συνέδριον), which the Sanhedrin seems to have attended in almost full number, decides upon sending the prisoner to Pilate. St. Luke, who does not mention the night session, places here the interrogation of Jesus, and his condemnation by the Sanhedrin. But Maldonatus, with St. Augustine, has very well seen that the condemnation with its tragic circumstances could not have taken place twice, but he is wrong in thinking that the whole trial took place in the morning and that the other Synoptics record it by anticipation. The private morning meeting lasted only a short time, for it was still very early (πρωΐ, John 18:28) when Jesus was led from Caiphas to Pilate.

[3] Daremberg and Saglio, *Dict. des antiquités,* art. *Praetorium.*

[4] *Corpus inscript. lat.,* xiv, 85 (for Claudius); Suetonius, *Tiberius,* 39; *Augustus,* 72; *Caligula,* 37.

but they could have reasons for choosing some other lodging, which accordingly became their praetorium. Hence no argument can be drawn from that fact, to fix upon the palace of Herod as the praetorium of Pilate during his short stay in Jerusalem. We will expose later the reasons for fixing it at the Antonia.

The Procurator of Judea at that time was Pontius Pilate. Named in the year A.D. 26 by the Emperor Tiberius, he occupied the post for ten years and was dismissed only in 36 for having massacred an inoffensive group of Samaritans. On the word of King Agrippa, who, it is true, had no love for him, he was "a man of inflexible character and fierce arrogance."[5] He was charged with venality and rapaciousness, with various acts of violence and all kinds of vexatious measures, with wanton cruelties and butcheries outside any formal trial. This portrait, though emphasizing the shadows, is still recognizable. How was it that Tiberius, generally so zealous for good government in the provinces, left such a man at the helm in Judea? It was because he held the principle that governors, once they grew fat from exactions and rapine, became less voracious, just as flies gorged with blood are less troublesome.[6] Besides, Pilate passed for an active and enterprising administrator, highly capable of maintaining order; and these qualities in the eyes of Tiberius redeemed a multitude of vices.

From the fact that Pilate was brutal and headstrong it should not be concluded that he was endowed with real energy. The most violent characters are sometimes the most timid. They affect brutality to conceal their weakness, and they strive to inspire in others the terror they themselves experience. Two episodes vividly portray this man's character. Upon taking possession of his government, in order from the very start to overawe the Jews, whose obstinacy he knew, he introduced by night into Jerusalem some military insignia adorned with idolatrous images and emblems. The Jews begged him to remove them, and for six whole days they laid bare their breasts before the soldiers who

[5] In Philo, *Legatio ad Caium,* 38 (Mangey, II, 590).

[6] It is also said that he was fond of telling the old fable which has been put into verse by our own fable teller under the title: "The Fox, the Flies, and the Hedgehog." Josephus, *Antiq.,* XVIII, vi, 5. On the long tenure of office by grant of Tiberius, cf. Tacitus, *Annales,* I, 80.

were sent to massacre them. Obliged to yield, Pilate found out what kind of men he was dealing with. On another occasion he had some gilded shields bearing no effigy, but only the name of the reigning Caesar, hung up in the palace of Herod. Tiberius, acting on the complaints of the Jews, censured him severely and ordered him to respect the national customs of the people under his jurisdiction, as his predecessors had always done.[7] The lesson was not wasted. He, before whom everyone trembled, himself trembled before the "solitary of Capri," and it will be fear of denunciation to Tiberius that will wrest from him Christ's condemnation.

The arrival of the Sanhedrists at the Praetorium was no surprise to the Procurator. He must have been well abreast of the whole affair. The tribune in command of the detachment sent to lend a helping hand to the people who were to arrest Jesus must have given him a full account. Deterred by a singular scruple, which however is quite easy to explain in people who would strain out a gnat and swallow a camel, the Saviour's enemies refused to enter the Praetorium. They wished to avoid contracting a legal uncleanness which would prevent them from eating the Passover. To enter the house of a pagan was, at least in Palestine, equivalent to contact with a corpse: it imprinted a stain that lasted seven days. Pilate, therefore, accustomed as were all Roman magistrates to condescend to the religious customs of conquered peoples, went outside to the square adjoining the Praetorium, and asked them what accusation they had to bring against the prisoner. The Jews appeared to be taken aback at this question. Some among them had perhaps deluded themselves into hoping that the Procurator would hand the charge of the whole procedure over to them and would blindly ratify their sentence. They answered: "If this man were not a criminal we would not have handed him over to thee." Pilate thought or pretended to think that there was question of some infraction of the Mosaic Law punishable by excommunication or thirty-nine lashes. In that case, the affair did not concern him, and he answered, as Gallio will later answer St. Paul's accusers: "Take him then, and judge him yourselves according to your law." "But," they objected, "we have not the power to put anyone to death." Many think

[7] Josephus, *Antiq.*, XVIII, iii, 1–2; *Bellum*, II, ix, 2–4.

that the permission granted by Pilate was ironical. The Jews, by saying that they would not have brought Jesus to him unless he were a criminal, appeared to be desirous of dictating the sentence to the judge. Pilate's answer would come to this: "Very well, judge him yourselves, if you can: but you know very well that you cannot." He was thus reminding them of the respect owing to the supreme authority. The explanation is admissible.

In Palestine, as in all the provinces annexed to the Empire, the *jus gladii* belonged solely to the Roman Governor. The Jews were not unaware of this, and the members of the Sanhedrin expressly recognized it. In later years, the murder of St. Stephen will be nothing short of a riotous execution, a sort of lynching during troublous times, and the martyrdom of St. James the Less will gain for the High Priest, who will take advantage of an interregnum to authorize it, a severe censure and deposition.

Pilate, seeing that the matter was serious — they were mentioning capital punishment — became attentive. The members of the Sanhedrin understood that this was the moment to strike a heavy blow. "We have detected this man," they said, "turning our people from obedience, and forbidding them to pay tribute to Caesar, and proclaiming himself the King Messias." The Procurator re-entered the palace and had the accused man brought into his presence, to proceed with the questioning.

Pilate — "Art thou the king of the Jews?"

Jesus — "Sayest thou this of thyself, or have others suggested it to thee?"

Pilate — "Am I a Jew? Thy own nation and the chief priests have arraigned thee before me. What hast thou done?"

Jesus — "My kingdom is not of this world. If my kingdom were of this world my servants would have fought to prevent me from being delivered to the Jews. But my kingdom is not from here below."

Pilate — "Thou art, then, a king?"

Jesus — "Thou hast said it; I am. I was born and have come into the world to bear witness to the truth. Everyone that is (on the side) of the truth hears my voice."

Pilate — "What is truth?"[8]

---

[8] John 18:33–38. According to all the Evangelists, the first question that Pilate asks Jesus is whether he is a king; and the answer is "yes" (Matt. 27:11; Mark 15:2; Luke 23:3); but in St. John, Jesus explains the spiritual nature of his kingship, and this reassures the Procurator.

Without waiting for an answer, Pilate went out. Skeptic and Epicurean that he was, he was little interested in the definition of truth, and he had no craving to learn the obligations associated with it. At all events, he has already made up his mind. The accused is neither a demagogue nor a rabble rouser nor a revolutionary. He is, perhaps, a dreamer, a theorizer, a Utopian; but he is not dangerous to the State. The royalty that he claims is of another sphere; it is no threat to the dominance of the Caesars. He claims to teach the truth; whether it be believed or not, his teaching will harm no one. To dismiss the case and to declare an acquittal, such is the verdict of justice and common sense.

Pilate therefore went out to the square of Lithostrotos, and without doubt, though the Gospel does not say so, ascended the platform where the curule chair was placed, to notify the people of the result of his investigation. He rendered his verdict: "I find no guilt in this man." Immediately violent protests arose from the chief priests. They knew now that, if they did not brazen it out, their game was lost. Furiously they cried out: "This man is arousing and stirring up the people by spreading his teaching throughout all Judea, beginning from Galilee, even to Jerusalem."

2. Jesus Before Herod

(LUKE 23:5–12)

To the Procurator, the name Galilee, pronounced at random, was a gleam of light. He asked if the accused was a Galilean; and learning that he was a subject of Herod Antipas, who was then staying in Jerusalem, he resolved to send the prisoner to the Tetrarch in order to gain time, and, if possible, to rid himself of the whole troublesome affair.[9]

---

[9] "Modern criticism has vigorously attacked this little morsel of the third Gospel, seeing in it a legendary story welcomed by Luke or even invented by him" (Loisy, *Evang. synop.*, II, 636–638). But Loisy had predecessors in Strauss, Renan, and many others of the same stripe. Verrall (*Christ before Herod,* in the *Journal of Th. Studies,* Vol. X, 1909, pp. 321–363) believes that the narrative is simple and natural, if the words "having set him at nought and clothed him with a bright robe" be stricken out, but that if they are kept, it becomes absurd and contradictory. He thinks that the scene had only a dozen or so witnesses, which would explain the silence of the other Evangelists. Those present, according

Antipas had been governing Galilee and Perea for thirty-three years. We have already met the executioner of St. John the Baptist and incestuous husband of Herodias, the sorry character whose distinctive trait was cunning and whom our Lord had stigmatized with the name of fox. Idumeans by race, and brought up for the most part in Rome, the Herods had scarcely anything Jewish about them but the shell. Philip the Tetrarch, living in the midst of a predominantly pagan population, seems to have broken almost entirely with Judaism. He had the image of the ruling Caesar engraved on his coins, and his capital, Caesarea, had a temple of Augustus. The other descendants of Herod did not go as far as that. They built in their towns stadia and amphitheaters, which every true Jew held in abomination, and they adorned their Greek cities with statues and idolatrous temples; but in compensation they erected synagogues and offered sacrifices. Almost all of them affected respect for the Mosaic Law, and at least kept up appearances. They were faithful to the pilgrimages, and no one was surprised to see them engage in certain practices of devotion. It was because of the Passover that Antipas had come to Jerusalem, accompanied by his bodyguards and his small court. He was living in the ancient palace of the Hasmoneans, opposite the Temple, on the other side of the Tyropoeon Valley, close to the bridge linking the square of Xystus to the Court of the Gentiles, and not far from the Antonia.

For more than a year Herod had been anxious to meet Jesus. The thought of the young Galilean teacher, of whom marvelous things were told, haunted his disordered imagination. Some

---

to his view, were Herod and a secretary and a domestic, a messenger and a guard sent by Pilate, and two or three priests who had come to accuse Jesus (p. 334). He maintains that Herod cherished no hostility toward Jesus, and that even the phrase, "Go, tell that fox," had, in the mouth of the Saviour, nothing uncomplimentary to Herod (p. 353). He is as fantastic as Loisy.

St. Luke has more details about Herod than the other Evangelists. Plummer implies that these pieces of information came to him from Joanna the wife of Chusa, Herod's steward, whom he alone mentions (Luke 8:3; 24:10).

The apocryphal *Gospel of Peter* distorts the roles of Herod and of Pilate. The beginning of a fragment recently discovered runs thus: "Among the Jews, no one washed his hands, neither Herod nor any of the judges, and since they refused to wash, Pilate rises. Then Herod ordered Jesus to be seized, saying to them: All that I have ordered you to do to him, do ye" (Vaganay, *L'Evangile de Pierre,* 1930, pp. 203–205). Such a travesty of fact needs no comment.

claimed that the Galilean was John risen from the dead. Antipas did not know what to think. "I had the Baptist beheaded," he said to himself. "Who then is this man?" But Jesus had constantly evaded his curiosity. Great then was the Tetrarch's satisfaction when it was announced to him that the Procurator was sending Jesus to him. It is superfluous to say how much his pride was flattered by such an unexpected courtesy on the part of man who, up to that time, had shown for him nothing but disdain.

Perhaps it will be asked what jurisdiction Herod could have had over Jesus. He had none, either from the religious point of view — that goes without saying — or from the civil, since both he and the accused man were on foreign territory, and it was not in the Procurator's power to delegate authority in criminal cases. Hence it is not for the purpose of obtaining a judicial sentence that Pilate sends Christ to him, but for supplementary information and to fortify himself with the Tetrarch's opinion, if, as he expects, Herod also concludes to the innocence of the accused. Jesus is accused of stirring up trouble and disorder in Galilee and Jerusalem. As to Jerusalem, Pilate knows that there is nothing in the charge; he wants to know if the same is to be said about Galilee, and this the old Tetrarch can tell him better than anyone else. The Acts of the Apostles offer us an altogether similar case. The Procurator Festus, not knowing what report to make to the Emperor about the prisoner Paul, who has made an appeal to Caesar, consults King Agrippa and has him question the captive in his presence.

For the same purpose Pilate sends Jesus to the Tetrarch. Herod is sure that the accused, whose fate he holds in his hands, will not refuse to give a demonstration of his supernatural powers, and this will be a fine spectacle to offer to his little court. Hence he is assiduous and insinuating. He asks a great number of questions, as though eager to be informed. He treats the captive less as an accused man than as a visitor, almost a friend. The excitement and clamorings of the chief priests who have followed the escort and who are striving to force his hand seem to move him not at all. He is waiting for what Jesus will say to defend himself. But Jesus entrenches himself in an absolute and significant silence. The murderer of the Baptist, the scandalous adulterer, the crafty hypocrite deserves no other answer.

In his disappointment, the Tetrarch is incensed at this silence, which he considers an affront. The accusers take heart. More at their ease here than in the presence of Pilate, they can charge the violation of the Sabbath, the remarks passed about the Temple, the pretended blasphemies, and the claims of divine attributes. Still Herod does not listen to them. Exasperated by Jesus' silence, he is thinking of avenging himself in a shabby fashion worthy of him. First he puts on an air of profound contempt for the man whom he has just been treating with so much consideration. Then, bethinking himself of treating Christ as a tinsel king, he has him grotesquely clothed in a bright robe such as Oriental monarchs used to wear on solemn occasions. The Tetrarch's entourage, always ready to ape their master, naturally join in the banter and insults. St. Luke depicts the scene in these energetic words: "Herod with all his retinue scoffed at him and vilified him." The masquerade may be imagined if one recalls that Antipas' bodyguard was made up of Thracian, Gallic, and German mercenaries.

Sworn enemies up to that time, Herod and Pilate became friends, beginning with that day. We do not know the reason for their previous disagreements. They may have had some connection with the massacre of the Galileans who were slain by order of Pilate while they were offering their sacrifices in the Temple. At all events, occasions of friction between the two were not lacking. Today complicity in crime reconciles them; but it will not be for long.

3. The Governor's Perplexities

And so Pilate finds himself again confronting his prisoner. His first attempt to save himself has been checkmated. He will set afoot several others with no better result.

To understand Pilate's role during the Passion, and his attitude toward Jesus, his shufflings and compromises, his wavering between firmness and feebleness, between courage and fear, his character and his situation must be taken into account. He could be cruel by calculation and self-interest without being such by nature. Blood-crazed monsters who kill for the sake of killing are, fortunately, rare. Pitiless in suppressing revolt, Pilate was one of those shortsighted psychologists who flatter themselves that they can always impose obedience by the rigorous use of force, and that they can stifle the murmurs of their subjects by drowning in blood the least spark of insubordination. But he was not the man to commit a cold-blooded judicial murder which would yield him nothing in return. The atmosphere in which he had lived, the offices he had filled, and the habit of seeing justice meted out and of dispensing it himself had in the long run instilled in him some sense of fairness and professional duty. Then too, he had to reckon with his staff of advisers and assistants. Though he was not bound to follow their advice he did not care to defy their opinion. Perfectly convinced of the innocence of the accused and knowing the animosity of the Jews against him, he was not disposed to comply with their demands at the price of a flagrant injustice. Perhaps, too, a little pity was mixed in with these complex feelings, although a human life, especially the life of a member of this contemned and abhorred race, weighed very lightly on the conscience of a Pilate.

However that may be, when he received Jesus whom Herod had sent back to his tribunal with the burlesque honors of which we have just spoken, he addressed the chief priests and notables and people who were waiting in the square: "You have brought this man to me, charging that he was stirring up the people and inciting them to revolt. I have examined him before you, and I find in the accusations brought against him nothing deserving of death. Nor has Herod; for he has sent him back to me without imputing to him any crime deserving capital punishment. Therefore I will set him free after chastising him."[10] What singular justice! Jesus is declared innocent, yet he must be chastised. No doubt Pilate is thinking: "After all, this will be only a salutary warning; for though he is neither a criminal nor a rabble rouser, he is, perhaps, a fanatic or a visionary who needs this lesson.

[10] Luke 23:13–16: "After having *corrected* (παιδεύσας) him, I shall release him." Pilate uses a euphemism: παιδεύειν means properly to raise or instruct (a child), to correct him, to apply the ordinary punishment (the whip). But the *horribile flagellum* (Horace, *Satires,* I, iii, 119) is neither a staff nor rods; it is an instrument comparable to the Russian knout or the English cat-o'-nine-tails of other days. This barbarous punishment aroused the indignation of the pagans themselves (Juvenal, *Satires,* vi, 479–485; Cicero, *In Verrem,* v. 54).

Besides, it will be a satisfaction to the Jews that will calm their fury and rid me of embarrassment."

At this moment, the Procurator's wife intervened. Since she was not allowed to go up to the platform where her husband was seated — Roman custom would not tolerate that — she sent him this message: "Let there be nothing between you and this just man, for today I have been troubled by a dream, because of him." In the time of the Republic, a wife never accompanied her husband to the provinces, but this regulation was relaxed when imperial legations began to be of many years' duration. To take advantage of the relaxation, the example of Augustus and of the son of Tiberius could be urged as a precedent. Hence the presence of Pilate's wife in Jerusalem was nothing unusual. The apocryphal *Gospel of Nicodemus* calls her Procula or Procla and says that she had affiliations with Judaism. A supposed letter of Pilate to Herod tells of her conversion to the Christian religion, and the Greeks have put her name in their Menology. Authentic history gives us no information about her, but her role in the Gospel is all to her honor. If, as the best authorities think, her dream was neither a trick of the imagination nor an illusion of the evil spirit, but an inspiration from on high, we may well believe that her charitable intervention was not wasted in the eyes of God.[11]

The Romans of this period, though skeptics in theory, were in practice the most superstitious of men. They placed a blind faith in dreams and auguries, in sorcery and astrology. Almost all important personages kept in their train a recognized soothsayer to tell their fortunes and to interpret favorable or baneful omens

---

[11] Pilate's wife is mentioned only by St. Matthew (27:19). See the legend of Procla in Fillion, *Vie de J.-C.*, III, 454–455 (English transl., Vol. III, pp. 501–503). The Greeks celebrate her feast on October 27. According to the majority of the Fathers, the dream came from heaven (Origen, Hilary, Ambrose, Augustine, Athanasius, Chrysostom); still Baronius, depending on the Pseudo-Ignatius (*Ad Philipp,* iv), thinks that it came from the devil.

Eight years before, in A.D. 21, the Senate had formally approved the custom which authorized women to accompany their husbands to the provinces (Tacitus, *Annales,* iii, 33–34).

Calpurnia, Caesar's wife, had dreamed during the night of March 14 to 15, 44 B.C., that her husband would fall beneath the thrusts of daggers (Suetonius, *Caesar,* 81). The neglect of this dream cost the dictator his life. Cf. Appian, *Bell. civ.,* ii, 115; Dion Cassius, xliv, 17.

for them. It was said that Julius Caesar fell beneath the dagger of Brutus for having neglected a dream which warned him not to go out on that particular day. Pilate was, therefore, disturbed by his wife's dream, the more so because it was one of those early morning dreams which, they said, were never mistaken.

While Pilate was thinking the matter over, an idea suggested itself to him. It was the eve of the Passover, and it was customary to set free some prisoner on that day to allow him to take part in the feast, which was a commemoration of the deliverance of the Jews from Egyptian captivity. The Romans had respected this usage just as they respected among conquered peoples all national traditions, as far as this tolerance did not involve grave abuses. One may well think that the Jews were tenacious of this annual privilege, and that they would have called it to the Procurator's attention if he had not forestalled them. Accordingly Pilate seated himself on the tribunal and addressed those present: "You have a custom that I should release some prisoner to you on the Passover. Do you wish, therefore, that I release to you the King of the Jews?" Doubtless he was thinking that the title "King of the Jews" would arouse their national self-esteem, and that the mass of the people would never allow their king to be condemned.

But he had left out of his reckoning the cleverness of the heads of the priesthood. They had been busy indoctrinating the fickle multitude, so ready to shift from love to hatred, and soon from all sides was heard the cry raised by a thousand voices: "Barabbas! Barabbas! We choose Barabbas!" The man they were calling for was a notorious criminal, a professional robber whose crimes included a murder committed during a rebellion, perhaps in resisting the armed force sent to arrest him. Provincial governors did not have the power of extending pardon to condemned criminals — that was a right which was reserved to the Emperor alone — but if, as the Gospels seem to imply, Barabbas was merely being detained in custody, his trial having been deferred for some reason or other — for example, in order to discover his accomplices — the Procurator could set him free without seeking special authority from Tiberius. As a fomenter of sedition, Barabbas would enlist the sympathy of the Zealots and of all who secretly detested the Roman yoke; and yet Pilate had not expected that the choice would fall upon him. He weakly demanded: "What then shall I do to Jesus, called the Christ?" With one voice they all cried out: "Crucify him! Crucify him!" Knowing himself to be worsted, the Procurator still hazarded an objection: "Why, what evil has he done?" The multitude, more and more turbulent, answered with a howl: "Away with him! To the cross! Crucify him!"

Pilate finally recognized that, instead of making the crazed populace listen to reason, further argument would only increase the tumult. In circumstances such as these the moderate element is either hesitant or silent, and it is the fanatics who set the tone. The Governor had force at his disposal, and he had shown before that he knew how to use it when his own interest or prestige was at stake, but this time he lacked the courage to use it. In his effort to evade responsibility he put his trust in a theatrical gesture which, as a matter of fact, was to save neither his honor nor his conscience.

He seated himself on the platform in full view of the people and ordered that a ewer of water be brought to him. He then washed his hands before them, saying: "I am innocent of the blood of this just man; see to it yourselves." This symbolic gesture, which would be understood in any country, was even more significant in Palestine, where it had been in use from time immemorial. When the corpse of a murdered man was discovered in a field and the murderer was unknown, all the important people of the nearest town would assemble in the presence of the priests and wash their hands over the corpse of the victim, uttering meanwhile this solemn protestation: "Our hands have not shed this blood, and our eyes have not seen it spilled." By this oath they warded off from themselves all suspicion of homicide or complicity.

Upon hearing Pilate shift upon them the odium and the consequences of the crime, the frenzied people gave voice: "His blood be upon us and upon our children!" Ah, if they had been able with prophetic vision to penetrate the future, they would have seen with what an ocean of blood their unfortunate nation was to be flooded. Within forty years those among them who will survive will assist at the agony of their people and will all be swallowed up together in the immense cataclysm. Foreign war and fratricidal strife, famine and plague and every sort of evil will at once engulf them. Their country devastated, their Sanctuary in flames, their capital in ruins, there will remain to them only a city of the dead. These same Romans whose aid they now implore to assassinate the Just will pitilessly butcher their women and children and old men and every defenseless creature that is devoid of mercenary value; and will not cease crucifying their able-bodied men until the wood for making crosses is exhausted. Only ninety thousand robust young people will be kept for sale at auction; but, for fear that such a multitude of new slaves may glut the market, Titus will distribute them in thousands of towns on days of holiday to feed the bloody games of the amphitheater. The rest will be used to construct the Coliseum or will be entombed in the depths of Phrygian quarries to hew the marbles that will beautify the city of the Caesars. And this will be only the prelude to other visitations of divine vengeance. After another and little longer lapse of time, their children and grandchildren who will have escaped the first extermination will in their turn be struck. The statues of Hadrian and Jupiter will be set up in the place where once stood the altar of the true God. The abomination of desolation will reign forever over the Temple, and the miserable remnants of Israel will be dispersed throughout the whole universe, to carry, to the end of time, the weight of this mysterious malediction.

4. The Scourging and Crowning With Thorns

The narrative of the trial of Jesus is so concise, and leaves so much to be understood, that it would be impossible to fill in the gaps, except that fortunately each of the inspired writers has presented a different phase of it. All agree in showing Pilate persuaded of the innocence of the accused, and seeking a way to set him free; but from a reading of the first two Evangelists, one would gather the impression that, after the incident of Barabbas, he became discouraged and made no further effort. "Then he released to them Barabbas; but Jesus he scourged and delivered him to them to be crucified." In St. Luke, on the contrary, we have seen that the scourging was a cruel expedient to satisfy the Jews without altogether sacrificing an innocent man. That his intention might not be misunderstood, Pilate twice repeated it in the same words: "I find in him no crime deserving of death. I will therefore chastise him and will then acquit him and set him free." Scourging generally preceded crucifixion, but it was also a distinct penalty, and, like the "question," it was often applied without any previous judgment.

Among the Jews, it was customary to limit the strokes of the lash to thirty-nine for fear of infringing, by mistake, upon the letter of the law fixing the maximum at forty. Besides, the condemned man, after examination, had to be adjudged capable of bearing the punishment. But such cautions were unknown to the Romans. Scourging was usually the prelude to crucifixion, and the executioners considered that no moderation was called for in the case of a man who was about to die. The instrument used, the *horribile flagellum,* was made up of thongs of hardened leather studded with small pieces of bone and morsels of lead, and sometimes with sharp points called scorpions. The sufferer, despoiled of his clothes, was bound by the hands to a low column, and was kept from moving out of the bending position, so that all the strokes might reach their mark, and that the executioner might wield them with greater force. At the first blows, the skin became livid and bloody; soon it was torn to shreds, and the flesh came off in strips. There was no limit to the punishment except the fatigue or satiety of the torturers, and often their ferocity was proportioned to the greater patience of the victim. We read in the passions of certain martyrs that veins, muscles, and intestines and the whole anatomy of the body were exposed to the horror-stricken gaze of the onlookers. Not infrequently it happened that the condemned man succumbed during the torture.[12]

[12] The degrading punishment of the lash was inflicted on slaves and inhabitants of the provinces. The words used to describe it mark sufficiently its terrible effects. "To cut (*secare*), tear (*scindere*), break (*rumpere*), pound (*pinsere*), pierce (*forare*), dig (*fodere*), with blows of the scourge, according to the nature of the instrument used. Nothing could be more horrible than the brief description of it given in the letter of the Church of Smyrna on the martyrdom of St. Polycarp (in Eusebius, *Hist. eccl.,* IV, xv, 4). Roman citizens were spared the scourge. It was replaced by the rod, which did not inflict the note of infamy. Even the *Lex Porcia de tergo civium,* passed about 195 B.C., exempted from it Roman citizens

When the executioners were tired of striking Jesus, they gave him back his clothes.[13] And then the thought suggested itself to them, as a pastime, to parody a scene of enthronement, as Herod's guards had done. They substituted for the Saviour's cloak a scarlet rag, draping it over his left shoulder to represent the purple of the Caesars and of Oriental sovereigns. One of them wove a crown of thorns and placed it on his head. Thorny plants are so abundant in Palestine that they are distinguished in the Bible by a score of names. Uprooted by the farmers and dried in the sun, they serve as firewood, and it is doubtless for this purpose that they were on hand in the courtyard of the barracks. What kind of thorn crowned our Saviour's head? Writers have often conjectured that it was a species of jujube, called by naturalists *Sizyphus Spina Christi*. Its sharp-pointed thorns make cruel wounds. But this bush, so common in the environs of Jericho, is scarcely to be found at the altitude of Jerusalem. In Jesus' hands they placed a reed to serve as a scepter, and without doubt, though the Gospel does not say so, they seated him on a stool representing the royal throne. They called the rest of the cohort

---

who *were not condemned to death*. But this law too often remained a dead letter. The exploits of Verres are well known (Cicero, *In Verrem,* v, 54; cf. *Pro Rabir.,* 4). Tiberius had a centurion of a famous cohort scourged; Caligula inflicted the same punishment on his quaestor (Suetonius, *Tiberius,* 60; *Caligula,* 6). Gessius Florus even had Jews who were Roman citizens of equestrian rank scourged (Josephus, *Bellum,* II, xiv, 9). Everything depended on the caprice of powerful people. St. Paul was three times beaten with rods (2 Cor. 11:25). This treatment, which proves that he was a Roman citizen, was still illegal, as he himself declares to the centurion: "Is it legal to scourge anyone who is a Roman citizen, and who has not been condemned?" (Acts 22:25.) There was in this a twofold illegality. It is not permitted in any case to scourge a Roman citizen, and according to the Lex Porcia it is not permitted to strike him with rods unless he has been condemned to death.

[13] Ludolph the Carthusian writes very wisely: "Without a private revelation it is impossible to know exactly the number and severity of the blows which the Saviour received in this atrocious scourging." Still, several people have thought that they knew even more than that. Catherine Emmerich says that the scourging lasted three quarters of an hour. Mary of Agreda says that Jesus received 5115 blows; others say 5375 (Eck) or 5460 (Lansperg); a holy woman, a recluse, according to Ludolph (*Life of Christ,* Part II, Chap. 58), goes as far as 5490. The sober picture given by St. Bridget is more poignant than the long descriptions of other mystics: "Jubente lictore, Jesus seipsum vestibus exuit, columnam sponte amplectens, recte ligatur et flagellis aculeatis, infixis aculeis et retractis, non evellendo sed sulcando totum corpus ejus laceratur" (*Revelationes,* iv, 70).

to share the sport. Then began a scene of derision worthy of these base mercenaries. They came, one after another, to bend the knee before him as though to pay him homage. Again, shifting their role, they took the reed from his hands and, after striking him upon his thorn-crowned head, they slapped him and spat in his face and then retired.

Jesus had predicted that the Son of Man must suffer rebuffs and insults from the ancients, the chief priests, and the students of the law, and that he would be delivered up to the Gentiles to be scoffed at. All was literally fulfilled before Caiphas, before Herod, and before Pilate. Certain authors are surprised that these shameful scenes should have been thrice renewed at such brief intervals, but it would rather have been surprising if they had not happened. In ancient times, in the most barbarous as well as in the most civilized nations, for example at Alexandria and Rome, the populace made sport of adding to the sufferings of those condemned to death. Even today no spectacle draws the people more than does an execution. What scandalous competition for places around the instrument of torture, what debasing puns and pleasantries are bandied about!

The scenes of derision recounted in the Gospel are quite varied and still perfectly accommodated to the situation. Before Caiphas, where Jesus had proclaimed himself the Son of God, he is treated as a blasphemer and false prophet. His eyes are blindfolded to make him guess whose hand had struck him. If he is a prophet, he ought to know. Before Herod and Pilate, there is no longer question of a Son of God, but of the King of the Jews, the pretender to the throne of Judea. Petty and miserable king, weakened by fatigue, abandoned by all his followers, unable to find a word to say in defense of his cause! Evidently he is a fool or one suffering from hallucination. Herod treats him as such. After clothing him in a bright robe, he gives the signal of ironic applause, and Jesus retires under the laughter and insults of the barbarians in the pay of the Jewish Tetrarch. There everything leads to mockery without going as far as blows or bodily brutality.

It is otherwise in the Praetorium. The Saviour has already undergone the scourging which is the forerunner of crucifixion. Everyone knows that he has claimed the title of King and that he will without doubt expiate this alleged crime. The cohort of auxiliaries that formed the garrison of the Antonia was composed entirely of Samaritans and Greeks from Syria, that is to say, of the worst enemies of the Jews. What a fine piece of luck for these mercenaries to have the chance to humiliate and torment a King of the Jews, or anyone who calls himself that! Philo tells of a similar parody organized at Alexandria to ridicule King Agrippa. A buffoon named Carabbas was selected and made to mount a platform so as to be in the full view of all. His head was encircled by a large band of papyrus like a diadem, and an old piece of matting was thrown around his shoulders to represent the royal mantle. A reed was thrust into his hand to serve as a scepter. People armed with truncheons mounted guard before him, while the crowd acclaimed him and saluted him in Syriac with the title of Lord. Such facetious burlesques are found in all countries, and in all periods of time.

5. The Death Sentence

It cannot be that Pilate was ignorant of this masquerade, since the crowning with thorns, like the scourging, took place inside the Praetorium.[14] If he did not order it, at least he did not prevent it, for it served his purpose. He had not given up the attempt to save Jesus, and it seemed to him that if he presented him to the people in the sorry condition in which the soldiers had left him, no hatred could hold out against the spectacle. He therefore bade him come forth from the Praetorium and, exposing him in a place where he could be seen by all, he showed to the multitude the face stained with dirt and streaming with blood and scarcely rec-

---

[14] Mark 15:16: Οἱ δὲ στρατιῶται ἀπήγαγον αὐτὸν ἔσω τῆς αὐλῆς ὅ ἐστιν πραιτώριον. The Vulgate translation (*duxerunt eum in atrium praetorii*) does not correspond to the Greek text, which should be rendered thus: "They led him into the interior of the palace, that is, the Praetorium." Αὐλή means both "court" and "palace." Suidas defines this word: ἡ τοῦ βασιλέως οἰκία, "royal dwelling." Both meanings are found in the New Testament: for example, Matt. 26:3; Luke 11:21, for *palace*. Cf. Thayer, *Lexicon,* 4 ed., 1901, and W. Bauer, *Wörterbuch,* 1928. Since the meaning "courtyard" is a little more frequent, St. Mark, to avoid ambiguity, says: "They led him to the interior of the αὐλή, I mean the Praetorium." From St. John, we know that Jesus was already there; but St. Mark, having failed to mention his entrance at the beginning, mentions it here is retrospect, and it is not necessary to take the aorist ἀπήγαγον as a pluperfect.

ognizable; and he said: *"Behold the man!"* Yes, behold the Man of Sorrows spoken of by the prophet Isaias, the most beautiful of the children of men, who no longer has any beauty to charm the sight or draw the heart. He does not even inspire pity, for the rage of his enemies is not one whit sated. At the sight of him the priests and their fanatical followers cry out the louder: "Crucify him! Crucify him!" "Well then," Pilate says to them, "take him yourselves and crucify him." The Jews well knew that this semblance of permission was nothing but biting irony, and they redoubled their insistence: "We have a law and according to the law he must die, because he pretends to be the Son of God."

"Now when Pilate heard this word," says St. John, "he feared the more." In itself the charge formulated by the Jews left him quite indifferent. He could have answered them as Gallio answered St. Paul's accusers: "If there were question of a misdemeanor or serious crime, I would gladly listen to you; but as soon as questions of your law are brought up, look to it yourselves. I have no wish to decide such matters." In a similar case the Procurator Festus, again with reference to St. Paul, will say: "Having had this man brought to me, his accusers did not charge him with any of the crimes that I had expected. It was only a controversy about their religion and of a certain Jesus who died but who Paul affirmed was alive." It was not Pilate's place to judge heresy, since the Romans did not recognize crimes of opinion, and it was of no importance to him whether the accused had called himself Son of God or not. But a Roman magistrate had to respect and enjoin respect for the national laws of those under his jurisdiction, as long as the laws were not in opposition to the interests of Rome or its principles of government. Thus certain infractions of religious customs of annexed nations were severely punished. A foreigner entering the Temple of Jerusalem or a Jew who brought him in was punishable by death. A soldier who had contemptuously torn the book of the Mosaic Law actually suffered capital punishment, and another who had insulted the Jews by an indecent action would, without doubt, have met the same fate had not the Jews risen in revolt instead of demanding justice. If Pilate refuses to take account of the Jewish law which condemns blasphemers to death, he can be denounced to Tiberius. Hence may arise annoyance, and embarrassment, and other vexations more troublesome still. This is what he fears. He begins to waver; but the decisive blow will not be struck until he hears the threatening cry: "If thou release this man thou art no friend of Caesar."

For the moment he seeks to create a diversion and to gain time. Re-entering the Praetorium with the accused, he asks him: "Whence art thou?" Now, it is not at the conclusion of a questioning but at the beginning of a trial that a culprit is asked about his place of origin. Besides, Pilate already knows that Jesus is a Galilean. If it is about the divine origin of the Son of God that he wishes to be informed, he has neither the right to ask the question nor the ability to understand the answer. And so Jesus is silent. The Procurator is both surprised and irritated.

"Speakest thou not to me? Knowest thou not that I have power to crucify thee, and that I have power to release thee?"

"Thou wouldst have no power over me were it not given thee from above. Therefore he who has delivered me to thee has the greater sin."[15]

The numerous commentaries to which this answer of Jesus has given rise have not shed much light upon it. Without entering into these discussions, which are not to our purpose, we shall only say that there is no question here of the divine origin of power. The power which Pilate has received from above is the power of darkness. It is the permission to make an attempt on the life of the Just One, who had been protected against all the ventures of his enemies so long as his hour had not yet come. Inexcusable as is Pilate's crime, he is less culpable than Judas, who had delivered Jesus to the Sanhedrin to be condemned to death, less culpable

[15] John 19:11. The one who had delivered Jesus to Pilate was Caiphas (or, if you will, the whole Sanhedrin as a body), rather than Judas, who had delivered him to the High Priest and the Sanhedrin.

The phrase "for this reason" (διὰ τοῦτο, "therefore") creates some difficulty. The majority of interpreters understand some such unexpressed reason to explain it, as: "Since you act as an agent in this affair" (Lagrange), you are less culpable. R. Thibaut (*Nouvelle revue théol.*, 1927, pp. 208–211) proposes a solution that would suppress or greatly lessen the difficulty. It is not that Caiphas is more culpable than Pilate; rather, Caiphas would be less culpable, *if Pilate had not received the power to judge,* doubtless because Caiphas would then have committed only a sin of desire. This solution, which is perhaps somewhat oversubtle, had already been proposed by Wetstein, according to Bernard (*Saint John,* 1928, p. 520), who also adopts it.

than Caiphas who has delivered him to Pilate to be crucified. Caiphas and the Sanhedrin have sinned through pure malice. Pilate has yielded to them through weakness and cowardice. He has been their docile tool; but without them he would have done nothing.

Pilate's conscience has been thoroughly enlightened. The language of the accused man is not that of a criminal: Pilate has too much knowledge of men to have escaped conviction on that point. The wonderful calm and patience and wisdom of the prisoner have vividly impressed him. Even after the threatening warning of the Jews: "We have a law that demands his death, for he says he is the Son of God," the Procurator still searches for a way to acquit Jesus and set him free. St. John explicitly affirms it: *"Exinde quaerebat Pilatus dimittere eum."* But he hears the clamor of the crowd, and the cry which freezes him with terror again falls upon his ear: "If thou release this man thou art no longer a friend of Caesar." That threat of being denounced to Tiberius as the accomplice of an agitator and pretender to the throne of the Imperial land of Judea beats down with one blow all his desire of resistance. The fear of displeasing Caesar, and of alienating still more an irascible people, stifles in him every sentiment of justice and compassion. To lose the friendship of Caesar — and of such a Caesar as Tiberius — was to expose himself to the gravest danger.

Accompanied by Jesus, Pilate goes forth from the Praetorium and seats himself upon the judgment seat.

The comings and goings of Pilate during these discussions seem to many authors so complicated that they give up all attempt to unravel them. And yet, there is nothing obscure about them, thanks to the luminous exposition of St. John, provided that we avoid confusing the Praetorium with the tribunal. The Praetorium, as we said above, was the permanent or temporary residence of the Roman Governor; the tribunal was the platform, fixed or mobile, set up generally in front of the Praetorium, always in a place accessible to the public. Pilate goes out of the Praetorium and presents himself before the crowd massed in the square of the tribunal four times: twice alone, twice accompanied by Jesus.

In the morning Jesus is led to the Praetorium by the members of the Sanhedrin and goes in alone, his enemies remaining without to avoid contracting the legal uncleanness that entrance into a pagan dwelling would imprint. The Procurator goes out to the square to demand their complaints against the accused. Then he re-enters the Praetorium to question Jesus and soon comes out again to announce the dismissal of the case. But facing the protests of the aroused people, he hesitates, he discusses, he parleys; incident follows incident; Pilate's wife intervenes; he ostentatiously washes his hands; he proposes to release Jesus because of the festival, and at the people's demand frees Barabbas; finally, for the sake of peace and flattering himself that he may thus appease the hostile multitude, he agrees to have Jesus scourged before releasing him. Going back into the Praetorium, he commands the scourging and, if he does not order the crowning with thorns, tolerates it. He then comes out again to the square to present Jesus to the people in his pitiable condition. But nothing can appease their hatred. Judge and accused man re-enter the Praetorium together, and the Procurator, who has not yet lost all hope, begins a new questioning, soon to be interrupted by the terrifying cry coming from without: "If thou release this man, thou art no friend of Caesar." Hearing these words, Pilate leads Jesus forth from the Praetorium, and this time it is to pronounce in his presence and in the presence of the whole people, from the height of the tribunal, the sentence of condemnation.[16]

In matters of little importance the judge sometimes passed

---

[16] The four times that Pilate comes out from the Praetorium are perfectly clearly distinguished. We translate literally.

1. John 18:28–33. The members of the Sanhedrin "brought Jesus to the Praetorium, but *they did not enter into* the Praetorium. . . . Pilate therefore *went outside* to them. . . . Pilate then *entered again into* the Praetorium and said to Jesus. . . ."

2. John 18:38. "He *went out again* to the Jews" and re-entered to have Jesus scourged.

3. John 19:4–5. "Pilate *went outside again* and said to them: 'Behold, I *lead him outside* to you, that you may know that I find in him no crime.' And Jesus *came outside* wearing the crown of thorns." Since they would not listen to him, "he *entered the Praetorium* and said to Jesus" (19:9) who had re-entered with him.

4. John 19:13. Pilate, hearing these words ("If thou release this man, thou art no friend of Caesar"), *brought Jesus outside* and sat down on the judgment seat, at a place called in Greek Lithostrotos."

sentence *de plano,* but in major cases he took his place upon a high platform surrounded by his assistants and counselors. Provincial governors had their platform set up in any open public place. Pilate on one occasion had his set up in the stadium at Caesarea, perhaps to give more solemnity to the sentence; and the Tetrarch Philip, imitating in this the example of Julius Caesar, had a portable tribunal carried around with him everywhere to be ready for judgment at any time.

On that particular day, Pilate's tribunal was set up in the square adjoining the Antonia, called in Greek *Lithostrotos* and in Aramaic *Gabbatha.* When the Procurator had taken his seat, he said to the Jews, with a gesture toward Jesus standing below at the foot of the platform:

"Behold your king!"

"Away with him! Away with him! Crucify him," cried the enraged people.

"Shall I crucify your king?"

"We have no king but Caesar."

Was this in Pilate's mind a final appeal to their national self-love and a last attempt to save the innocent? Many interpreters have supposed that it was. "He is again trying," says St. Augustine, "to make them ashamed of their own ignominy, because the ignominy of Jesus has failed to touch them." But in reality it would seem that Pilate's mind was made up the moment he heard the howl of the crowd: "If thou release him thou art not Caesar's friend," and came to take his seat on the tribunal. What he now adds has all the air of biting irony: "You ask his death because he called himself your king. Very well. Since you ask it, we shall crucify your king." He then pronounces the death sentence, and it is no longer in his power to recall it, for the right of pardon is the exclusive prerogative of the Emperor.

From concession to concession, Pilate has gone as far as deicide. Not only in the inner court of conscience does he recognize the innocence of Jesus: he has several times proclaimed it aloud. He devises five or six expedients to snatch him from the fury of his enemies: the sending to Herod; the theatrical scene of the washing of hands; the proposal to liberate the prisoner to celebrate the feast of deliverance; the moving spectacle of the Ecce Homo; the horrid scourging, calculated, he thinks, to disarm the fiercest hatred. The Jews, witnessing his vacillation and knowing his weakness, redouble their arrogance; and he ends by yielding all. The incline down which he slips carries him to the abyss almost despite himself.

CHAPTER XI

Jesus on the Cross

1. The Via Dolorosa

IT WOULD be a consolation for Christian piety to be able to follow Jesus step by step along the Via Dolorosa; but, though the terminus of the journey is known with certainty, the same cannot altogether be said of the starting point. Many place it at the palace of Herod, near what is today called the Tower of David and the Jaffa Gate. Others, whose opinion seems to us much more probable, fix it at the Antonia. It is true that the Antonia was a fortress, but it was also a sumptuous palace; and the palace of Herod was equally an entrenched camp flanked by high towers. "The interior of the Antonia," says the historian Josephus, "had the area and the lay-out of a royal dwelling. In fact, it reproduced the plan and the various parts of the abode of a sovereign with its peristyles, and bath chambers, and vast courts for the guards. In the ready provision of everything useful to living it was like a city; in its magnificence, a royal palace. The general impression it presented was that of a fortress. At its four corners were raised as many towers, three of which were fifty cubits in height, and the fourth, at the southeast corner, seventy cubits, so that from the summit the whole Temple lay beneath the view."[1]

No lookout was more suitable for keeping surveillance over the doings of the Jews, and none was more convenient for intervention in case of an alarm. Two stairways led to the roof

[1] Josephus, *Bellum,* V, v, 8. The palace of Herod was also a fortress (*φρούριον*, *Bellum,* II, iii, 2 and 4) and an entrenched camp (*στρατόπεδον*, *Bellum,* II, xv, 6).

of the Temple porticoes and from there into the Court of the Gentiles, which the soldiery could invade at the first signal. It was natural for the Procurator, during the few days that he spent in Jerusalem at the time of feasts, to install himself there rather than in the palace of Herod, which was too far away from the Temple. The skirmish which suddenly flared up when St. Paul was suspected of introducing pagans into the Sanctuary, and which was quieted by the prompt intervention of the tribune Lysias, proves that the presence of the commander could be needed at the most unforeseen moments. His intervention could not have been as rapid or as effective from the Palace of Herod, situated at the other end of the city.

The case of Gessius Florus, which is always cited in favor of the palace of Herod for lack of a better argument, is altogether different. Florus, in the year 66, did not come to Jerusalem to assure the maintenance of order during a festival. He came to punish an insolent city which was almost in a state of revolt. He barracked his numerous effective troops at the entrance of the city at the Palace of Herod, a vast encampment, able to hold all his troops, both infantry and cavalry. He did not push on as far as the Antonia, but for an excellent reason: he was not master of it and two attempts to capture it miserably failed.[2]

But history provides a case altogether similar to that of Pilate. The Procurator Cumanus had come to Jerusalem, like Pilate, to keep order on the occasion of the Passover. The fourth day of the feast, when a Roman soldier insulted the Jews by an indecent action, the crowd became agitated and broke out into shouting and invective against the Procurator, accusing him of having ordered the base gesture of the soldier in order to humiliate the Jews. In vain Cumanus parleyed with them, trying to calm the tumult: it only increased. He was reduced to calling for reinforcements which were held in reserve at the Palace of

[2] Josephus, *Bellum,* II, xiv, 6–9. Gessius Florus tried twice to enter the Antonia, at first by surprise while pursuing fugitives, then with full force, but he was repulsed. Florus had come to Jerusalem with an army of *cavalry and infantry* (μετὰ στρατιᾶς ἱππικῆς καὶ πεζῆς), expecting resistance, which, however, surpassed his expectations.

Herod. At the sight of the troops, the mutineers were overawed and dispersed.[3]

Pilate, as zealous of maintaining order as Cumanus, like him must have been on the watch from the heights of the Antonia. Without doubt, he had been there when he ordered the massacre of the Galileans while they were in the act of offering their sacrifices.[4] Would he then ever have left his comfortable lodgings at Caesarea to come to police Jerusalem, without caring to avail himself of the sure means of avoiding disorder and foreseeing clashes and of repressing instantly the popular uprisings which were always to be feared?

The question of Pilate's Praetorium has recently entered a new phase. St. John tells us that the Governor had his tribunal set up in a place called in Greek "Lithostrotos" and in Hebrew "Gabbatha." Lithostrotos means in Greek "paved with flagstones," and Gabbatha in Aramaic very probably means "height," "elevated place." Now, recent excavations have uncovered to the northwest of the Antonia an ancient square paved with enormous blocks which the centuries have not dislodged. It has every chance of being the ancient Lithostrotos; and the Aramaic name of Gabbatha also fits it, since it occupies the highest point of the eastern hill, at the place where a wide ditch separates it from Bezetha. Henceforth, we may with all confidence place there the trial and condemnation of Jesus and the starting point of the Via Dolorosa.[5]

---

[3] Josephus, *Antiq.*, XX, v, 3. After vainly trying to quiet the multitude, Cumanus ordered all the troops left in reserve at the palace of Herod to arm and *come to the Antonia* where he needed these reinforcements (πάντας πανοπλίαν ἀναλαβόντας ἥκειν εἰς τὴν 'Αντωνίαν).

[4] Luke 13:1. A case of flagrant crime supposing the presence of the Governor. The affair of Paul and Lysias is a typical example of popular effervescence which could not have been foreseen (Acts 21:27–36).

[5] See the article by P. Vincent, O.P., *L'Antonia et Le Prétoire,* in *R.B.,* 1933, pp. 83–113, with ten plates. The Lithostrotos was a square adjoining the Antonia and situated northwest of the fortress. It measured about 55 yards square and was paved with large blocks of hard stone, often a meter square in surface and generally 12 to 14 in. in thickness. Under the square was a cistern cut out of the rock, measuring 55 yds. in length and 16 yds. in width, intended to furnish drinking water for the garrison in case of siege. A specimen of the ancient flagging can be seen under the church of the Dames de Sion.

2. The Ascent of Calvary

The death sentence once passed, the judge could not alter a word or syllable of it.[6] It was the official text which was kept in the provincial archives and which was used as the basis of the official report to the Emperor. From it, too, was transcribed the cause of condemnation, to be presented to the multitude that had not attended the discussions. It was traced on a board coated with white lead or gypsum, in red or black characters, which stood out from the white background and were legible at a distance. This tablet was hung around the neck of the condemned man or carried in front of him by a lackey, to be nailed finally to the tree of torture.

The inscription which was to stand out upon the cross of Jesus was written in three languages: Latin, the language of the masters of the world and the real sovereigns of the country; Greek, the tongue spoken universally in the whole East; and Hebrew, or rather Aramaic, the vernacular of the Jews of Palestine.[7] The wording is not altogether the same in the four Gospels. Either they confined themselves to giving the basically identical meaning, or the three languages employed offered some variants. The text of St. John, with the name and country and alleged

---

[6] Apuleius, *Florida,* ix: "Proconsulis tabella sententia est; quae simul lecta neque augeri littera una neque minui potest; sed, utcumque recitata est, ita provinciae instrumento refertur."

[7] Mark 15:26: The king of the Jews (ὁ βασιλεὺς τῶν Ἰουδαίων). Luke 23:38: This is the king of the Jews (ὁ βασιλεὺς τῶν Ἰουδαίων οὗτος). Matt. 27:37: This is Jesus the king of the Jews (οὗτός ἐστιν Ἰησοῦς ὁ βασιλεὺς τῶν Ἰουδαίων). John 19:19: Jesus of Nazareth, the king of the Jews (Ἰησοῦς ὁ Ναζωραῖος ὁ βασιλεὺς τῶν Ἰουδαίων).

According to the apocryphal *Gospel of Peter* (ed. Harnack, *T.U.,* IX, fasc. 2, p. 9) the inscription was: "This is the king of Israel." This is improbable: Pilate would not speak thus. Some of these inscriptions are known to us. They are always very short. That of the martyr Attallus had in Latin: "This is the *Christian* Attallus" (Eusebius, *Hist. Eccl.,* V, i, 4). The whole crime was in being a Christian. Domitian condemned to the beasts a respectable man who had spoken ill of him, the cause being thus written on the tablet: *Impie locutus parmularius* (Suetonius, *Domit.,* 10). The tablet (τίτλος, πίναξ, αἰτία, ἐπιγραφή, *titulus, inscriptio*) was carried before the condemned man as he walked to his punishment (Eusebius, *loc. cit.,* πίνακος αὐτὸν προάγοντος; Suetonius, *Caligula,* 32, *praecedente titulo*). It was white so that the letters might be seen better (Nicephorus, viii, 29: λευκὴ σανίς; Sozomen, iii, 1: λεύκωμα).

crime of the condemned man, is the most likely: *Jesus of Nazareth, King of the Jews.*

As soon as the Jews noticed the inscription affirming the royalty of Jesus — and without doubt they saw it while is was being transcribed or shortly afterward — they said to Pilate: "Write not, 'The King of the Jews,' but 'He said, I am the King of the Jews.'" But this time the Procurator, tired of their importunity, recaptured his usual arrogance. In a brusque tone, penetrated by scorn and anger, he answered them: "What I have written, I have written." After yielding everything, he is not sorry to get a petty revenge. What a miserable compensation for so much weakness and cowardice!

The execution of condemned men followed immediately after the death sentence. The preparations did not take long. To detail a platoon of soldiers who would fill the office of executioners, to take from their dungeons the two criminals who were to accompany Jesus to Calvary, to construct three roughly squared crosses — unless, as is more probable, provision had been made for unforeseen cases — all this was soon done. The Roman law provided that the condemned man should himself carry the instrument of his punishment. The cross, then, was laid upon the Saviour's shoulders, and at a given signal the dismal procession set itself in motion. At the head rode a mounted centurion, followed by the three condemned men hemmed in by soldiers in field equipment, as for a military expedition. Prisoners were often paraded through the city streets, both to aggravate their sufferings and to inspire in all passers-by a salutary terror. This time, because of the nearness of the feast, the shortest route was taken.

Even if the starting point of the Via Dolorosa were absolutely certain, the route followed by Jesus would not be thereby established, for the direction of the streets may have been changed since, and the ground relief has been profoundly modified, especially in the Tyropoeon Valley. This the Saviour must have crossed, if he came from the Antonia.[8] Whatever it may have been, the journey in a straight line would not require more than

[8] See Note T: *The Way of the Cross.* The distance between the Antonia and Golgotha, as the crow flies, was not more than six or seven hundred yards, but allowance must be made for detours.

a quarter of an hour, but it is likely that progress was retarded on that particular day because of the obstruction of crowds through which it was necessary to open a passage.

Jesus, worn out by a night of sleeplessness, by physical and mental torture, and by the horrible scourging and the crowning with thorns, was at the end of his strength. The Centurion, seeing him stagger and bend under the weight of the cross, realized that it was urgent to give him relief, to avoid delay. At that very moment a peasant was entering the city coming from the fields. He was a man named Simon, a native of Cyrene, where resided a numerous Jewish colony possessing a synagogue in Jerusalem. At all times the military authority has arrogated to itself the right of requisition, and it is preferably upon the common people and peasants that it imposes forced labor. The Centurion therefore impressed the services of Simon of Cyrene to carry the cross of Jesus. Simon submitted: one does not resist armed might. He did not merely help Jesus to carry his cross, as artists imagine; he carried it entirely, walking behind Jesus. The Gospel is explicit on this point. No doubt he inwardly cursed the luckless chance which was to be for him and his family a source of blessings. There is nothing to indicate that he was at that time a disciple of Christ, but we think that he did not wait long to become one. His two sons, Alexander and Rufus, enjoyed a certain prominence in the early Church. The mere fact that St. Mark mentions them by name is a sufficient indication of it.[9]

---

[9] The episode is found in all three Synoptics (Matt. 27:32; Mark 15:21; Luke 23:26). (*a*) Simon was probably returning for the midday meal, for St. Luke says that he was coming *from the fields,* or *from the country* (ἀπ' ἀγροῦ). (*b*) According to St. Matthew, Jesus met him *as he went out of the city* (ἐξερχόμενος); this cannot mean, as he went out of the Praetorium. (*c*) They made him *take up* the cross of Jesus (Matthew and Mark, ἵνα ἄρῃ), or more exactly, *they laid on him the cross to bear it after Jesus* (Luke). Cajetan, whose knowledge of Greek was very limited, translates: "Quam (crucem) non solus portabat, sed post Jesum, ne videretur Simon crucifigendus." This is a misunderstanding of the sense.

St. Mark gives the names of the two sons of Simon: Alexander and Rufus; they are also mentioned in the apocryphal *Gospel of Nicodemus.* It is highly probable that the Rufus of St. Paul (Rom. 16:13) is the same, for Rufus was a very rare name. If he lived in Rome, we can see why St. Mark mentions him. Since Alexander is a very common name, there is no reason to identify the son

Relieved of the burden of the cross and free in his movements, Jesus cast his gaze over the hostile, curious, or indifferent multitude that surrounded him. In the midst of this mob he picked out a group of women who were weeping copiously and beating their breasts, as if assisting at the funeral rites of one of their own dear ones. These are the "daughters of Jerusalem," alien to the hatreds of their fathers and their husbands, touched with pity at the sight of the harsh treatment heaped upon the saintly victim, and desirous of offering him a little compassion. It is worthy of remark that no woman takes an active part in the Passion of Christ. Pilate's wife seeks to ward off from him the death sentence; the daughters of Jerusalem weeping follow him on the road to Calvary; the holy women of Galilee stand at the foot of his cross and care for his burial.

Jesus does not repel the sympathy of the daughters of Jerusalem, but he warns them that their sympathy is mistaken in its object. He is less the object of tears than they; for his death will save the world, and their deaths will be no more than a commonplace incident in the cataclysm that will swallow up their nation. "Daughters of Jerusalem, weep not for me; weep rather for yourselves and for your children. The day shall come when they will say: 'Blessed are the barren! Blessed the womb that has not borne and the breasts that have not suckled!' Then will they say to the mountains: 'Fall upon us,' and to the hills: 'Crush us.' For if they treat thus the green wood, what will they do to the dry?"[10]

This prophecy will be fulfilled to the letter within some forty

---

of Simon with the apostate Alexander of whom St. Paul speaks (1 Tim. 1:20; 2 Tim. 4:14).

About the Jews of Cyrene, established there by Ptolemy, son of Lagus, cf. Josephus, *Antiq.*, XIV, 7, 2 and XVI, vi, 1. In Jerusalem, there was a colony of Jews with a synagogue (Acts 2:10; 6:9).

[10] Luke 23:27–32. It is evident that the *green wood* is a figure of the Saviour, and the *dry wood* represents Israel. These proverbial modes of speech are susceptible of various applications: "If the Romans treat in this manner Jesus, who is innocent, how will they treat the Jews, who are guilty of rebellion?" or, "If God permits that Jesus be treated in this manner, what treatment is he reserving for the deicide nation?"

On the Veronica legend, cf. Hoepfl, *Die Stationen des heiligen Kreuzweges*, Freiburg-i-Br., 1913, pp. 49–55. The documents may be found in the collection of the Bollandists under date of February 4.

years, and many of the women there present will be able to see its accomplishment with their own eyes. Then many mothers will regret their motherhood; others will not escape the horrors of famine except by voluntary death, and some will be so lost to natural instinct as to consume their own infants. Innocent and guilty alike will be enveloped in the common ruin. Like the dry wood, Israel as a people will receive the chastisement of its crimes. As long as it stays green, the tree can recover its fruitfulness; but if it dries up, it is no longer good for anything except to be cut down and cast into the fire. Such is the fate that awaits this unbelieving race.

After passing through the gate, one had only to cross the wide city moat and the foot of Golgotha was reached. This word in Aramaic — like the Latin word corresponding to it, from which comes our Calvary — means "skull." The place was not so called because, as St. Jerome supposed, the skulls of executed criminals left without burial were to be seen there.[11] The Romans never had a fixed place for the execution of those condemned to death, except perhaps of slaves; and the Jews, who regarded the mere contact with human bones as a defilement, would never have left any skulls lying about in the proximity of the city. Another hypothesis mentioned by Origen is no better grounded. "I know a tradition," says he, "according to which the body of Adam was buried at the spot where Christ was crucified. Thus, as on Calvary all died in Adam and all are given life through Christ; the head of the human race received the pledge of resurrection at the place where the Saviour rose from the dead."[12] To bring together the source of death and the source of life is a moving and beautiful thought. Even if it does not correspond to reality, it has a profound symbolism which Christian artists express after their fashion by placing at the foot of the Crucifix a skull sprinkled by the blood of Christ.

But the name "Golgotha" has a less mysterious origin. We ordinarily speak of the foot, the side, the brow of a hill. The

---

[11] St. Jerome, *In Matthaeum,* 27:33; *In Ephesios,* 5:14. Cf. *Epist. ad Marcellam,* xlvi, 3 (ML, XXII, 485), where he refutes the tradition about the skull of Adam, mentioned by Origen.

[12] Origen, *In Matth. series* (MG, XIII, 1717); St. Epiphanius, *Adv. haereses,* xlii, 5 (MG, XLI, 544).

Semites are still freer with such geographical metaphors borrowed from parts of the human body. They speak of the shoulder, the back, the face of a hill. Any promontory which projects toward a plain or a body of water is, in their language, a *head,* just as it is for us a *cape* or headland; and when such a rocky and bald protuberance suggested to them the idea of a skull they would give it that name. The Evangelists never call Calvary a mountain or a hill.[13] It was a bulge of the terrain overhanging the deep moat of the city and was no higher than the ramparts. Two or three similar bulges may yet be seen toward the northeast corner of the present wall.

Among almost all peoples some slight solace is offered *in extremis* to those condemned to death. The Jews gave them a sort of narcotic to drink, basing this custom on the passage in the Book of Proverbs:

> Give strong drink to the man about to die,
> and wine to the man overcome with sadness;
> let him drink it, and he will forget his misery,
> and he will no more think of his ills.

According to the Talmud, the beverage offered to the condemned was pure wine spiced with a grain of incense, the real or assumed property of which was to numb the senses of the sufferer.[14] An ancient Jewish tradition affirms that the most distinguished

---

[13] They say: "*the place* called Golgotha" (Matthew) or "the *place* Golgotha" (Mark) or "the *place* of the skull" (Luke) or "the *place* of the skull which is called in Hebrew Golgotha" (John). The Aramaic *Golgoltha,* in Hebrew *Golgoleth,* is transcribed into Greek *Golgotha* for euphony.

St. Epiphanius, who knew Palestine well — he was born there about 315 — correctly says that Calvary was not on an eminence (ἐν ἄκρᾳ τινί), and that it has less elevation than the surrounding summits, such as Mount Sion and the Mount of Olives (*Haer.,* xli, 5; MG, XLI, 844).

On geographical metaphors and the site of Calvary, read Vincent, *Jérusalem,* II, 92–93.

[14] Billerbeck, *Kommentar,* Vol. I, 1037–1038. The wine offered to Jesus is called *vinum myrrhatum* (ἐσμυρνισμένον) by St. Mark, because myrrh was the substance most commonly used to spice wines (Pliny, *Hist. nat.,* xiv, 15); but the word can mean wine spiced with the juice of any plant. St. Matthew calls it *vinum cum felle mixtum* (οἶνον μετὰ χολῆς μεμιγμένον); but it must be remembered that, in the Bible, gall (*fel,* χολή) translates a Hebrew word meaning *something bitter,* in particular a bitter herb like wormwood (לענה) or another plant called ראש. Hence the variant presents no difficulty.

women of the city took upon themselves the duty of performing this act of mercy at their own expense. If such was the case, have we not good grounds for thinking that the daughters of Jerusalem, met by Jesus on the road to Calvary, had come there for this purpose? To avoid wounding them by declining their charitable offering, Jesus wet his lips with the soporific potion, but when he had tasted it he refused to drink it. Determined to drain the chalice of his Passion to the last drop, he wished no stimulant to blunt the feeling of his sufferings.

Meanwhile the soldiers had set to work to strip the condemned men before nailing them to the cross. Many reputable authorities have asserted that Jesus was crucified in a state of complete nakedness, and some maintain that this was the common opinion of the Fathers of the Church.[15] We do not believe it. The few texts that are offered as proof are almost all ambiguous, for it is well established that the word "naked," in Greek and Latin and Hebrew, is very often applied to partial nudity. The Classical authors describe as *naked* a man wearing no nether garments, and also a soldier not bearing arms. Thus too St. Peter, *naked* as he was, clasped around his body the kind of smock he was wearing, to swim less hampered to the shore where he saw the risen Christ. Thus too Saul prophesied *naked,* one whole day and one whole night, together with other prophets. So, again, Michol reproached David for dancing *naked* before the Ark of the Covenant, because he had put aside his royal vesture.[16]

---

[15] Suarez (*Mysteria Vitae Christi,* Disp. xxxvi, sec. 4) says that this is the *commoner* opinion of the Fathers, but he cites only two: St. Ambrose and St. Athanasius, the latter mistakenly, for the treatise *De passione et cruce Domini* is not his.

[16] See the examples of this word usage in Latin in Freund-Theil, for the Greek in Bailly and Moulton-Milligan (for the papyri). The best known are: Virgil, *Georg.,* I, 299: *Nudus ara, sere nudus;* and Hesiod, *Works and Days,* 389 (or 391): *Γυμνὸν σπείρειν γυμνὸν δὲ βοωτεῖν.* For the Bible, cf. 1 Kings 19:24 (Saul); 2 Kings 6:20 (David); Isa. 58:7: "Si videris nudum operi eum."

Herodotus (i, 10) asserts that all *barbarians* (non-Greeks) considered it shameful to appear naked before anyone. The ancient Greek athletes competed clothed with a loincloth (Homer, *Iliad,* xxiii, 683). The Lacedemonian Acanthus who was the first who dared to compete in the races and in wrestling entirely nude created a scandal. This was in the fifteenth Olympiad. Thucydides remarks in this connection the repugnance of *barbarians,* especially Asiatics, to adopting

Though the soldiers who crucified Jesus would be little disturbed by considerations of decency, they were not the only ones on Calvary. We are not referring to Veronica's veil — the legend is too uncertain — but we decline to believe without proof that no one on Golgotha showed to the divine Crucified One this mark of veneration, or that the Romans, who usually respected the sentiments and even the prejudices of conquered peoples, opposed it.

The sufferer was sometimes bound with ropes to the instrument of torture, there to languish for several days and finally die of hunger and exhaustion, unless birds of prey or wild beasts devoured him alive. Oftener he was fastened to the cross with nails, as the word "crucify" indicates. In the case of our Lord, the matter is beyond all doubt, because after the Resurrection he showed the Apostles his pierced hands and feet, and invited the unbelieving Thomas to place his finger into the wounds. It is the almost unanimous opinion of the ancient authors that four nails were used. Besides, it would be almost impossible to fix both feet of a living man to a cross with one nail without breaking any of his bones, yet we know from St. John that none of the Saviour's bones were broken.

Two malefactors were crucified with Jesus: one on his right, the other on his left. It is not without reason that the Evangelists agree in taking note of this apparently trivial detail. By a supreme irony the place of honor was accorded to the King of

---

this custom. Plato says (*Repub.*, v): "Not so long ago the sight of a naked man in public would have seemed to the Greeks shameful and ridiculous." The Romans did not imitate the Greeks until much later, and reluctantly. Cf. Cicero (*De Officiis*, i, 36) and Dionysius of Halicarnassus (*Antiq. rom.*, vii, 72) who lived in Rome at the beginning of the Christian era.

According to the Mishnah (*Sanhedrin*, vi, 4), persons condemned to stoning were not executed entirely naked. "Four cubits from the place of punishment the condemned is undressed; if a man, he is covered in front; if a woman, both front and back. Such is the opinion of Rabbi Judah. Other teachers say: "A man is stoned naked; but a woman is not stoned naked." Schwab is right in translating thus: "Other teachers say that a woman is not stripped; on the contrary, a man is denuded except for loincloth, of which Rabbi Judah speaks." Thus the opinion of Rabbi Judah does not in any way restrict the opinion of the others. At all events, there is no possible comparison between a condemned man precipitated from a high rock and immediately overwhelmed with stones, and one crucified and exposed for long hours to the gaze of passers-by of both sexes.

the Jews. The soldiery were accustomed to dismal jests of this kind, and the idea may well have come from higher up. He claimed to be a King: they would treat him like a King.

The Saviour's cross did not have the dimensions which artists from the fifteenth century onward have so liberally given it: wood was too scarce in Palestine to be wasted. Besides, the ancient authors tell us that the feet of the crucified almost touched the ground. Still, it is very probable that Jesus' cross rose above the other two, since the soldier who took compassion on him could not reach his lips with the sponge dipped in vinegar even with his arm stretched out. Such derisive distinction was sometimes accorded persons of mark. Galba, having condemned a free man to the torture of the cross, when the man appealed to his standing as a Roman citizen, promised that he should have a cross much higher than usual and all white, so that it could be seen at a great distance. The place of honor between two criminals, and the higher and more prominent cross, which without doubt were not a mere trick of chance but the result of premeditation, would lend more likelihood to the crown of thorns which painters and sculptors have left on the Saviour's head as he hangs on the cross, if that crown were not for them a mere symbol of his royalty.

Their grisly duty done, the four soldiers sat down upon the ground to play at dice. This was the favorite amusement of these rough men to while away the long hours of boredom. On this day, the victim's belongings were the first stake, since by Roman law they became the property of the executioners. First they divided into four parts the clothes which were more or less equal in value. Such were the sandals, the cloak, and the long cloth band wound around the head as a headdress. There remained the linen tunic, hand-woven in one piece, of considerably greater worth than the other articles. To divide it into four parts by tearing it into strips would rob it of all its value. They decided, therefore, to draw lots for it. The winner would be sure to get a high price for it from the relatives or disciples of the condemned man.

The savagery of man, to make still more cruel the frightful torment of the cross, had devised ways of increasing the suffering without hastening death. The piercing of the hands and feet at the most sensitive spots, where bundles of nerves meet, did not cause enough loss of blood to benumb the sufferer and to lessen his pain. The unfortunate man still retained full consciousness, with the prospect of feeling his torture increase hour by hour instead of diminishing. The immobility of the limbs was intolerable, and yet the least movement reopened the wounds. The blood, with its circulation disturbed, rushed to the head, causing a burning fever indescribably agonizing. If, hanging there, the crucified opened his eyes, he saw before him only faces on which were written mockery and insult; if he listened, he heard only words of hatred and contempt.

The Evangelists have drawn a discreet veil over the slow agony of Jesus on the cross. Either they felt themselves powerless to describe it, or they were careful to keep, up to the very end, the impassive attitude of witnesses, which was their role. Or it may be because they were aware that physical suffering carried to such excess inspires rather horror than compassion. We are told that at Rome ecclesiastical authorities forbade the showing of an image in which the Crucifixion was represented in all its frightful realism.

3. The Seven Words of Jesus on the Cross

The last words that fall from the lips of a dying person are piously gathered by friends and dear ones as a sacred heritage and the most precious of memories. Sincere and spontaneous revelation of the last thoughts of the departed, they are something more intimate and more moving that his last will and testament. Jesus on the cross, like the priest at the altar, is performing the august ritual of sacrifice in a low voice, interrupting the sacred silence only at long intervals. Seven only of his words have been preserved for us: three by St. John, three by St. Luke, and one by the first two Evangelists together.

Ordinarily the despair of the crucified was frightful to behold. As long as the preliminary phases lasted — the pronouncement of the sentence, the journey to the place of punishment, the immediate preparations for the execution — they were, to some extent, distracted by the noise and tumult from thinking of the horror of their fate. But when, nailed to the cross and suspended between heaven and earth, delivered defenseless to the insults and raillery of a hostile or curious crowd, they found themselves a prey in all their limbs to unspeakable torture, without any prospect other than an atrocious death at the end of a long agony, their helpless rage vented itself in imprecations, curses, and blasphemies.

1. On this day Calvary presented an altogether different spectacle. Majestic and calm, as he had been before the tribunals of Caiphas, Herod, and Pilate, Jesus is silent. In vain do the chief priests and Scribes, exulting in their triumph, joke with one another as they sneeringly repeat: "He saved others; let him save himself. If he is the Christ, the King of Israel, the Chosen One, the Son of God, let him come down from the cross and we will believe in him." In vain do the passers-by, misled by the priests, nod their heads and repeat: "Thou who destroyest the Temple and in three days buildest it up again, save thyself. If thou art the Son of God, come down from the cross."[17] Jesus is silent. Not a word of reproach, not a sigh, not a single plaint. The first word that he utters aloud is a word of pardon: "Father, forgive them, for they know not what they do."[18] In his capacity as advocate and intercessor he appeals to the mercy of his Father, urging what can, in some measure, lessen the crime of the guilty: "They know not what they do." Pronounced in such circumstances and in favor of such criminals, this word has seemed so strange that many ancient copyists have omitted it from the text of the Gospels; and many com-

[17] The attitude of the spectators is variously described by the Evangelists (Matt. 27:39–43; Mark 15:29–32; Luke 23:35–36). St. Matthew and St. Mark make two categories of insulters: passers-by who wag their heads and curse him, and the chief priests with the Scribes (St. Matthew adds the ancients) who rail at Jesus and joke with one another. In St. Luke, the people look at him, the rulers sneer, the soldiers join in the raillery. Slight differences and easy to reconcile.

[18] This saying is omitted in the Uncials B D W Θ and two cursives, in some manuscripts of the Coptic, in three of the Old Latin. The verse is placed in brackets by Westcott-Hort, without sufficient reason, as Scrivener shows (*Introduction,* 4 ed., II, 356–358). It is admitted without hesitation by other critics, Tischendorf, Von Soden, and Vogels.

mentators, while accepting it, have restricted it, declining to understand it about the Saviour's declared enemies. That the soldiers, blindly executing a sentence whose injustice they were incapable of appreciating, and the common people, led astray by their spiritual guides, may be worthy of pardon and excuse — let that pass; but that the rulers of the priests and of the Pharisees, who have so long been plotting the death of the Just One, who have forced the hand of Pilate to wrest from him a condemnation — that they know not what they do passes belief. And yet it is for them also that he intercedes with his Father. He who had commanded his own to love their enemies and to pray for their persecutors gives them an example in this supreme moment. And it is thus that his true disciples will understand it. The protomartyr, St. Stephen, and St. James the Less, when receiving the death stroke, will repeat the words of Jesus on the cross: "Father, forgive them, for they know not what they do."

There is always in the sin of man a portion of ignorance and blindness that distinguishes it from the sin of the angels. Almost on the morrow of this deicide, St. Peter will not be afraid to say to the Jews: "Brethren, I know that you acted in ignorance, as did also your rulers." Hatred prevented them from measuring the enormity of their crime, nor did they suspect its terrible consequences. "If they had known all these things," says St. Paul, "they never would have crucified the Lord of Glory." Jesus, in pleading their cause before his Father, does not ask for their pardon absolutely and unconditionally. He implores for them the grace to repent and a time of delay for their repentance. And his prayer is not in vain. God will wait forty years before making his hand heavy upon this unbelieving people; and in the interval, the members of the Levitical priesthood and the Pharisees will flock into the Church in such great numbers that they will threaten to falsify its spirit and to disturb its peace.

2. Ordinarily, condemned men who are executed together make common cause. The sympathy of comrades in misfortune appears to every one of them some slight compensation for the hatred and contempt of which they feel themselves the butt. It was not so on Calvary. "One of the two malefactors blasphemed against him, saying: 'Art thou not the Christ? Save thyself, then, and

us with thee.' But the other rebuked him: 'Dost not even thou fear God, thou who art under the stroke of the same condemnation? As for us, our sufferings are the just penalty of our crimes; but this man, what evil has he done?' And then, turning to the Saviour, he said to him: 'O Jesus, remember me when thou shalt be in thy kingdom.'" If, in the beginning, he had associated himself with his comrade's mockeries, as the text of St. Matthew would, at first sight, lead us to think, his reprimand to his companion would be out of place, and he should have begun by asking pardon himself for his insults. But nothing here allows us to read between the lines the sudden conversion of a blasphemer; there is, in the text, no trace of any such rapid change of face.

Without doubt the good thief had heard of Jesus, of his teachings and his miracles; and he had some notion of the kingdom of God. That was the first approach to faith. He must have admired the sweetness, the patience, the calm of the Saviour. He had heard his appeal to divine mercy. Grace, to which he opened his heart, did the rest, and he merited to receive a reply that was capable of alleviating all his ills: "Amen, I say to thee, this day thou shalt be with me in Paradise."[19] He asks only a remembrance, when Jesus shall enter into his kingdom; he receives the assurance that he will reign with the Saviour this very day. Paradise was, for the Jews, the abode of the souls of the just. But of what importance is the precise meaning of

---

[19] Luke 23:39–43. St. Matthew (27:44) and St. Mark (15:32) say: "The robbers crucified with him upbraided him (ὠνείδιζον αὐτόν)." Some reconcile the Evangelists by saying that first both robbers upbraided him (ὠνείδιζον, Matthew and Mark), but that the bad thief alone *cursed and blasphemed* (ἐβλασφήμει, St. Luke's word). The simpler solution, which we have given, is that of St. Augustine (*De cons. evangel.*, III, xvi, 53; ML, XXXIV, 1190–1191). It is admitted by St. Cyril, Maldonatus, Salmeron, Lagrange, Knabenbauer, and many other exegetes. Many (St. Jerome, St. Thomas, etc.) find both explanations admissible and do not commit themselves.

The exact meaning of the phrase Οὐδὲ φοβῇ σὺ τὸν Θεόν, ὅτι ἐν τῷ αὐτῷ κρίματι εἶ presents some difficulty. The Vulgate translation, *Neque tu times Deum quod in eadem damnatione es?* is thoroughly appropriate: "Sharing the same punishment with him and about to die with him, do not even you fear the judgment of God, and do you too, like the others who think they have nothing to fear, insult him?" But many modern commentators (Schanz, Plummer, Lagrange) make the observation that in Greek οὐδέ qualifies φοβῇ and not σύ, and that the translation should be: "Do you not even have the fear of God, you who endure the same punishment?" (Lagrange.) The meaning appears clearer, but the shades of meaning differ little.

the term? To be with the Saviour, to enjoy his company, to share his happiness wherever it be, is not this the true Paradise? Such is the lot promised to the Good Thief, canonized while he was still alive by the voice of God.[20]

3. There were other compassionate souls on Calvary, some kept at a distance by fear of the Jews, others bold enough to come close to the foot of the cross. It is worthy of note that, with the exception of St. John, we find only women there: Mary Magdalene, whom Jesus had freed of seven devils; Mary, the mother of James the Less, called the sister of the Blessed Virgin because she was married to Cleophas, the brother of St. Joseph; Salome, the wife of Zebedee and mother of the two Apostles James and John; Joanna, wife of Chusa, the steward of Herod; and still others who had accompanied the Saviour in his apostolic journeys and had followed him to Jerusalem. The first three Evangelists do not mention the presence of the Blessed Virgin near the cross, doubtless, because they supposed it known to all.

"There were standing by the cross of Jesus his mother, and his mother's sister, Mary of Cleophas, and Mary Magdalene. When Jesus saw his mother and beside her the disciple whom he loved, he said to his mother: 'Behold thy son.' Then he said to the disciple: 'Behold thy mother.' And from that moment, the disciple took her to his own."[21] With his habitual reticence St. John passes over his mother Salome in silence, though she was certainly there,

---

[20] Paradise is evidently not the earthly Paradise, the site of which is unknown, nor the present abode of the elect, to be opened only after the Ascension of the Saviour; it is the abode of just souls, known to the Hebrews under the name *Gan Eden* (Garden of Eden, Paradise). Cf. Billerbeck, *Kommentar,* Vol. II, pp. 264–268. But the reflection made by St. Ambrose is not to be forgotten: "Where Christ is, there is life, there is the Kingdom."

The Apocrypha spread themselves on the history of the two robbers. The *Gospel of Nicodemus* (Chap. X of the Latin version) calls them Dismas and Gestas, names popularly accepted thanks to the "Golden Legend." Elsewhere they were called Titus and Dumachus, Matha and Joca, and even, it would seem, Zustin and Nisimus (Thilo, *Codex apocr. N. T.,* p. 145). According to the Arabic *Gospel of the Infancy* (Chap. XXIII), Titus and Dumachus were brigand chieftains who encountered the Holy Family when they were fleeing into Egypt. Titus defended the travelers whom Dumachus wanted to molest. Jesus predicted that in thirty years they would be crucified with him, Titus at his right and Dumachus at his left: "Titus will go before me (*yasbiquny*) into Paradise."

[21] John 19:25–27. On the question whether St. John enumerates three women or four, see Note I: *The Relatives of Jesus.* The Synoptics do not mention the

and he brings himself upon the stage only to give a meaning to the words of his Master.

The idea that the Beloved Disciple represents all of us at the foot of the cross, an idea now so popular and so sweet to pious souls, seems very natural, since St. John was the only one on Calvary to receive the last testament of Jesus. "All the disciples," says Bossuet, "have abandoned him; only John, his beloved, remains. And so it is that today I am considering him as a man who represents all the faithful. Consequently we should be disposed to apply to ourselves all that refers to him."[22] Still, this simple idea never occurred to any of the Fathers of the Church. The three great commentators of the Fourth Gospel — St. John Chrysostom, St. Cyril of Alexandria, and St. Augustine — see in the touching episode transcribed above only an example of filial piety and a manifestation of the dying Saviour's delicacy toward the disciple of his predilection.[23] The first to make briefly but clearly the application of which Bossuet speaks is, we believe, a fifteenth-century monk, the *ecstatic doctor,* Denis the Carthu-

persons present on Calvary until after the death of Jesus. The first two Synoptics speak only of the holy women, Mary Magdalene, Mary of Cleophas, sister of the Blessed Virgin, and Salome, the wife of Zebedee. St. Luke adds: "all his acquaintances" (πάντες οἱ γνωστοὶ αὐτῷ), friends and disciples. But according to the Synoptics they "looked on from afar" (ἀπὸ μακρόθεν). According to St. John, on the contrary, the Blessed Virgin, her sister Mary of Cleophas, and Mary Magdalene stood beside the cross (παρὰ τῷ σταυρῷ). One should not be disturbed by these slight differences which are susceptible of various solutions. St. Augustine proposes two of them: either they were far off with reference to the guards, but near enough to be seen and heard by Jesus; or they were near at the time when the scene reported by St. John took place, but farther off after the death of Christ, when the Synoptics mention their presence. Other explanations could be found if needed.

22 Bossuet, second sermon for the Friday of Holy Week.

23 St. John Chrysostom, *In Joan.,* hom. lxxxv (lxxxvi), MG, LIX, 462; St. Cyril, *In Joan.,* Lib. XII, MG, LXXIV, 665; St. Augustine, *In Joan.,* tract. cxix, ML, XXXV, 1950.

George of Nicomedia (*Orat.,* VIII; MG, C, 1476) recognizes John's representative role, but he makes him the representative only of the other Apostles: "Be for them what a mother is for her children; and more, what I myself was, when I was with them. In their turn, they will be to you sons and subjects." Mary must be for them a guide and mother, but her role is expressly limited to her mortal life. Nonetheless it is a first step toward John's role of universal representative, and Mary's spiritual motherhood, extending to all the brethren of Jesus without limitation of time or space, such as is envisaged by mystical writers of subsequent ages.

sian: "The Beloved Disciple represents each of the faithful. By saying, 'Behold thy mother,' Jesus has given her as a mother to each and every Christian, so that she is an advocate for everyone of us, and we should love and venerate her above all, after God."[24] Another monk, the Abbot Rupert, of the twelfth century, had shown the way by setting forth the sorrowful maternity of Mary: "The Virgin brought forth without sorrow the author of the salvation of all of us when the Word was made flesh in her womb; now, standing at the foot of the cross, she brings forth again, but with sorrow. . . . Hence she is the mother of all of us, and what Jesus said to the beloved disciple he could appropriately have said to any other disciple, if he had been there."[25]

The role of coredemptrix is the principle of the spiritual maternity of Mary. At the foot of the cross, she offers to the heavenly Father his divine Son, who offers himself on the cross for our salvation. She offers him with the authority of a mother whose consent God asks for. Jesus, in dying for us adopts us as his brothers; and Mary, by sacrificing her Son for us, gives us as brothers to Jesus and adopts us as her own children. The *Fiat* of the Redemption, pronounced from her heart by the Blessed Virgin on Golgotha, answers the *Fiat* of the Incarnation, and, in some way, completes it.

It is clear that the spiritual maternity of Mary has deeper roots than a free and, so to speak, accidental gift of Jesus. It is linked with our status as Christians, which makes of each of us another Christ. It is precisely because of the mystical identity between Christ and the Christian that the words of Christ on the cross addressed to his mother and his disciple are truly applicable to everyone of us. Origen had already remarked this with his perhaps oversubtle penetration: "The perfect Christian lives no longer his own life; it is Christ that lives in him; and it is of him that Christ says to Mary: Behold thy son."[26]

4. Toward the ninth hour, three o'clock in the afternoon, a

---

[24] Denis the Carthusian, ed. of Montreuil-sur-Mer, 1901, XII, 595.

[25] Rupert of Deutz (*Tuitiensis*), in ML, CLXIX, 789–790: "Licet omnium, ut dictum est, mater sit, pulchrius tamen huic, ut virgo virgini, commendari debet."

[26] Origen, Preface of his *Commentary on John* (MG, XIV, 32), reasons thus: Mary has but one son. Now, Jesus in indicating St. John says: "Behold thy son," not: "This is *also* thy son." He therefore identifies himself with St. John. But

comparative silence fell upon Calvary. The curious, sated with the spectacle of death, little by little withdrew; the people with work to do hastened back to their affairs; the Roman soldiers, leaning on their spears or stretched out unconcernedly on the ground, waited for the end. Suddenly, rising above the distant noises of the great city, a cry rent the air: "My God, my God! Why hast thou forsaken me?" *Eli, Eli, lamma sabacthani?* Through an error which the similarity of sounds would explain, or perhaps a willful misunderstanding which furnished them with a new occasion for banter, some of those present thought or pretended to think that Jesus was calling upon the prophet Elias. If he expects Elias to come to his aid, thought they, he will wait a long time, for Elias is not to come until the end of the world or, at soonest, at the dawn of Messianic times. On the lips of Jesus, this cry was neither an appeal nor a plaint nor a cry of desperation: it was a prayer. The Saviour was intoning aloud the first words of the Psalm which contains the prophetic history of the Passion:

> My God, my God! Why hast thou abandoned me? . . .
> I am a worm of the earth and not a man,
> the derision of men and the outcast of the people;
> All that see me laugh me to scorn;
> They whisper and shake their heads:
> He hoped in the Lord; let him deliver him;
> let him save him, since he has complacence in him. . . .
>
> They have dug my hands and my feet.
> I can count all my bones.
> They have divided my garments among them;
> for my tunic they cast lots.[27]

---

what applies to St. John, applies to every perfect Christian. It is clear that this is not the literal sense of the text.

In Terrien, *La Mère des Hommes,* Paris, 1902 (Bk. IV, pp. 247–337), will be found everything that can be said in favor of the modern exegesis, with a long list of authorities (pp. 271–274). The author in concluding wonders: "Is the meaning spiritual and typical? Or is it literal; and, if so, what is the meaning?" He resolutely excludes the *purely accommodated* sense. He holds for the *literal* sense, and not the *derived* but the *immediate,* while admitting that he has not seen it maintained by anyone. "Hence it is not without hesitation," he adds, "that I have embraced it, happy if I may have shown at least its probability" (p. 333). It is a difficult task and his success is open to doubt!

[27] Ps. 21 (22):7–9; 17–19 (after the French translation of Calès).

Jesus is here simply borrowing the language of the Psalmist, just as we recite liturgical prayers, even at times when the sentiments expressed do not correspond to the actual state of our souls. To speak of despair in Jesus because he lovingly repeats the plaint of the Psalmist is to talk pure nonsense.

5. We believe that the fifth word is explained in the same way. The Psalm, of which we have quoted several lines, continues thus:

> My throat is dried up like a potsherd of clay;
> My tongue cleaves to my palate.

The rest of the prophecy has been literally fulfilled; it must be that this last detail have also its accomplishment. For this reason Jesus says: "I thirst." Thirst was, perhaps, the most intolerable torture of the crucified, for the prolonged tension of the nerves and muscles together with the inflammation of the wounds exposed to the air produced a burning fever. Hearing him say: "I thirst," one of the soldiers more compassionate than the others fixed to the end of a stick, or perhaps a javelin, a sponge dipped in a drink called *posca* and brought it to Jesus' lips. This drink was a kind of thin wine or vinegar with which troops in the field or on a military expedition were always supplied. The Saviour took some drops of the liquid with his lips, and having swallowed it, said: "All is consummated."

6. *Consummatum est*. This time all, indeed, is finished. Nothing more in prophecy to be fulfilled; nothing more of type to be made reality; no expiatory act to be added; no new pain to suffer. The work of redemption is completed; the earthly career of Jesus comes to a close. The *consummatum est* finds its commentary in the words of the priestly prayer: "Father, I have accomplished the work that thou hast given me to do"; in the saying of the Epistle to the Hebrews, that he has been *consummated*, that is, he has been raised to the summit of perfection by his sufferings; and much more in the Gospel text that immediately precedes: "Jesus knowing that now all is accomplished, that the Scripture might be fulfilled, said: 'I thirst.'"

7. Then he bowed his head as if to sleep. He did not bow it after death, as other men, but before dying, in order to show that he died voluntarily. And yet, before dying, he gives forth a last cry and breathes out his soul in an act of filial abandonment: "Father, into thy hands I commend my spirit." Again he borrows the formula of the Psalmist, adding only the word, "Father."[28]

Many of the faithful have repeated this prayer of the dying Jesus on their deathbed; but, instead of addressing it to the Father, they address it to Christ himself, as did St. Stephen, to confess the divinity of the Son of God and the efficacy of his redemptive mediation.[29]

4. Jesus' Side Pierced With a Lance

The bodies of executed criminals were scarcely ever refused to relatives and friends who asked for them. Tiberius, toward the end of his reign, aroused more hatred by the unprecedented refusal of such requests than by his numerous other cruelties. There were here and there avaricious magistrates who charged a high price for this concession, which they regarded as a favor, but we find no evidence in the Gospel that Pilate was one of them.[30]

---

[28] Ps. 30 (31):6: "Into thy hands I commend my spirit;
Thou wilt deliver me, God of truth."

[29] Dalman, in *Jesus-Jeshua* (Leipzig, 1922, 176–179; English transl., pp. 195–222), has translated the words of Jesus on the cross into Aramaic. He has rightly left in Hebrew the fourth word, the beginning of Ps. 21 (22):1, which was spoken in Hebrew, as is proved by the mistake made by the bystanders who thought that he was calling upon the prophet Elias. Dalman should have done the same for the seventh word, taken from Ps. 30 (31):6. But here the Aramaic differs very little from the Hebrew. The author translates *consummatum est* by *mushlam,* which corresponds to the Syriac *meshallam* and to the Hebrew *kullá,* and he comments thus: "Jesus does not wish to say only that the word cited by John (19:28) is fulfilled, but that the task which fell to him according to Scripture is accomplished." This is an exact commentary.

He translates "Woman, behold thy son" by *Itta, ha berikh,* and "Behold thy mother" by *Ha immakh.* They could hardly be translated otherwise. The Syriac is identical, with some differences in the pronunciation of the vowels.

[30] *Digest.* xlviii, 24: "Corpora animadversorum quibuslibet petentibus danda sunt." Cf. Quintilian, *Declamat.,* vi, 9: "Cruces succiduntur; percussos sepeliri carnifex non vetat." An exception was made in the case of slaves, who had no civil personality, and of some great criminals. For Tiberius, cf. Suetonius, *Tiberius,* 61; Tacitus, *Annal.,* vi, 19 and 29. Verres demanded payment (Cicero, *In Verrem,* v, 45).

As soon as Jesus had breathed his last, one of his secret disciples boldly presented himself before the Procurator to claim the body. Joseph of Arimathea, a wealthy personage and a member of the Sanhedrin, was a man of straightforward and generous nature; but his timidity and the fear of compromising himself in the eyes of the public and of his colleagues had, up to this time, prevented him from professing his faith openly.[31] Pilate received his request favorably, but he was surprised that Jesus was already dead, because the agony of those who were crucified ordinarily lasted much longer. Before giving a final answer, he wished to make sure of the facts.

Almost at the same time a deputation of Jews presented themselves, coming to formulate another request. They petitioned that the bodies of the executed men be taken down from their crosses and buried as soon as possible. The day was already declining and they were fast approaching the opening of a Sabbath that was doubly solemn, for that year the great feast of the Passover coincided with the Sabbath. Now, according to the Law of Moses, the bodies of those executed must be taken down and buried before nightfall on the same day, and we know from the historian Josephus that this custom was still in force at the beginning of the Christian era.[32] The corpse of a man who had been hanged was cursed by God and was considered a defilement for the whole country. Since the Romans customarily respected the religious scruples of the countries under their administration, Pilate deferred without difficulty to the wishes of the Jews. A new detachment of soldiers provided with the necessary tools was sent to Golgotha to put an end to the condemned men by breaking their legs.

The breaking of bones was sometimes inflicted without any formal trial by potentates impatient to slake their vengeance. Tiberius ordered that two youths whom he had dishonored should have their legs broken; Augustus meted out the same treatment to his secretary because he had allowed himself to be bribed.

---

[31] Matt. 27:57–58; Mark 15:43–44; Luke 23:50–52. Joseph was *rich* (Matthew), distinguished (εὐσχήμων, Mark), a member of the Sanhedrin (βουλευτής, Mark and Luke), good and just (Luke), a disciple of Jesus (Mark and Luke), but in secret and deterred by fear (John).

[32] Deut. 21:23; Josue 8:29, 10:27; Josephus, *Bellum,* IV, v, 2.

Angered masters often threatened their slaves with this punishment. It was also applied to the Christians when it was desired to execute them en masse.[33] But for the *crucified* the breaking of bones was rather an alleviation than an aggravation of their torment: however painful, it shortened their suffering by hastening death. Thus we find no examples of it in profane history, and the case of the Gospel can scarcely be explained except by the request of the Jews demanding respect for their legislation.

The soldiers, armed as usual with lances, and equipped also with hatchets or clubs, broke the legs of the two robbers, who were still breathing. Seeing that Jesus was no longer alive, they judged it superfluous to exert themselves against a corpse, and they were about to retire when one of them, to make sure that Jesus was really dead, struck him with his lance and pierced his side. Immediately blood and water came forth from the wound. The Beloved Disciple affirms this with the greatest emphasis:

"He who saw it bears witness to it, and his witness is true; and he (the Master) knows that he speaks the truth, that you may believe. All these things came to pass that the Scripture might be fulfilled: 'You shall not break any bone of him.' And, as is said in another place: 'They shall look upon him whom they have pierced.' "[34]

John calls Christ to witness that he is not lying, in order to place beyond doubt, by this solemn adjuration, a fact which

---

[33] Suetonius, *Tiberius,* 44; *Octavius,* 67. Examples are not lacking. Also to be cited are Sylla (Seneca, *De Ira,* iii, 18), the Emperor Constantius (Ammianus Marcellinus, xiv, 9), masters threatening their slaves (Plautus, *Asinaria,* II, iv, 68; Seneca, *De Ira,* iii, 22). For the martyrs who had their bones broken see Eusebius, *Hist. eccl.,* viii, 18, and the Martyrology for March 4, May 22, etc. The mercenaries revolting at Carthage broke the arms and legs of seven hundred citizens and threw them pell-mell into a ditch (Polybius, *Hist. rom.,* i, 80).

[34] John 19:34–37. "Unus militum lancea latus ejus aperuit (ἔνυξεν)." The word νύσσειν does not mean merely to "puncture," but "to strike with a lance thrust" or "the stroke of a sword in battle" (*Iliad,* xiii, 147; xv, 278). It is used of a mortal wound (Josephus, *Bellum,* III, vii, 35). The Vulgate translation *aperuit* seems to suppose the reading ἤνοιξεν.

The first text cited by St. John is from the Pentateuch (Exod. 12:46; Num. 9:12); the other is from Zacharias 12:10. The Evangelist does not speak of a miracle; still Origen (*Contra Celsum,* ii, 36) regards the fact as miraculous, because neither blood nor water comes forth from a wound made on a corpse. The majority of authors, even Protestants (for example, Westcott and Godet), think the same.

verifies two prophecies: that of Zacharias in the literal sense, the other in the typical sense; for the Paschal lamb, whose bones it was forbidden to break, was a figure of Jesus Christ.

If, contrary to all likelihood, the Saviour had still been living, the soldier's lance would have killed him, because the stroke delivered with this intention made a wound large enough for St. Thomas to insert his hand. The lance held in the right hand had to strike the left side and reach the heart, whence gushed forth water and blood, the symbols of Baptism and the Eucharist. Grateful tradition has offered a special cultus to the blind agent of this mystery; and, since it did not know his name, it called him Longinus, that is to say, the Lancer.

A doctor of the past century has verified that, in the internal hemorrhage following upon rupture of the heart, the blood decomposes: the red globules fall to the bottom of the pericardium and the lighter serum floats on top in the form of a watery liquid. If the side is pierced shortly after death, before the blood coagulates, the two parts flow out separately. This discovery, which however has been contested, aroused at first very lively controversy.[35] The quick death of Jesus, which had surprised Pilate, would thus find a very natural explanation; and the thought that our Lord's death was hastened by causes of a spiritual kind, and that his heart was literally broken by grief, is of a kind to attract pious souls. There would be nothing unacceptable in believing that spiritual suffering could have hastened the death of the God-Man, who was more sensitive to that kind of suffering than we are. But if, as we are assured is the case, the breaking of the heart always presupposes a morbid organism, the common

[35] Stroud, *The physical cause of the death of Christ,* London, 1847. In an article in the *Expositor* (October, 1911), Simpson enumerates several practitioners who have embraced Stroud's theory. In June, 1916, he adds the authority of the celebrated anatomist, William Turner, who said that he had made several experiments which confirm the theory (*Expositor,* 8 series, Vol. XI, p. 336). Still, Dr. Creighton (*Encyclop. Biblica,* I, 960) disagrees. He believes, with other Rationalist critics who base their opinion on the meaning of νύσσειν (see the previous note), that the wound made by the lance was only a scratch. Cf. Bernard, *Saint John,* Edinburgh, 1928, p. 646.

Innocent III wrote to Hugh of Ferrara on March 5, 1209 (Denzinger, 417): "Quaecumque fuerit illa aqua, sive naturalis, sive miraculosa, sive de novo divina virtute creata, sive ex componentibus ex parte aliqua resoluta, procul dubio vera fuit." The Pontiff argues against those who held that it was a phlegm (*pituita*).

opinion of theologians would not readily admit such a congenital weakness in Christ. Moreover, we know that the Saviour's body remained incorrupt. Now, would not the decomposition of the blood be a kind of corruption?

5. Prodigies Accompanying Jesus' Death

Seven prodigies accompanying the death of Jesus may be enumerated: the darkness at full midday, the rending of the veil of the Temple, the splitting of the rock of Golgotha, the rising of the dead, the cry of Jesus as he died, the mingled blood and water coming forth from his side, and the sudden conversion of some of the spectators.

1. A heavenly light had shone upon the Saviour's cradle to invite the world to rejoice at his birth; thick darkness covers his deathbed, as if to put nature into mourning and to hide from men the horror of the deicide. It prevailed over the whole country from the sixth hour to the ninth, from midday to three in the afternoon. We do not know the cause or extent of this phenomenon. At any rate, it was not the total eclipse of the sun described by Phlegon, the second-century pagan chronicler. This eclipse, which, it was said, changed day into night so that the stars were seen shining in the sky, was not visible at Jerusalem. Besides, no eclipse of the sun can occur at the full moon, the time when the Jews celebrated the Passover. It is true that Pseudo-Dionysius the Areopagite, in his supposed letter to St. Polycarp, affirms that the moon, then in opposition, executed a retrograde movement and came to place itself in front of the sun, and that he had himself been a witness of the occurrence at Heliopolis in Egypt, in company with the pagan philosopher Apollodorus; but we know the value of this late and isolated testimony.[36] By mentioning the precise hour, the Evangelists give

[36] On this eclipse, cf. Eusebius, *Chronicon,* translated by St. Jerome (Helm. ed., 1913, pp. 174–175); Origen, *Contra Celsum,* ii, 33 and 59, and *In Matth. series,* 134 (MG, XIII, 1782). Phlegon, according to Origen, did not say that it took place at the time of the full moon, but Julius Africanus adds this of his own accord (ML, X, 89). Cf. the legend of Pseudo-Dionysius, *Epist. viii ad Polycarpum* (MG, III, 1082).

us to understand that there is question of a local phenomenon, since the hours vary according to the meridian. They do not say that the darkness covered the whole universe, nor even all the inhabited earth, but only the whole country.[37] The sign was of interest to Judea, where it could be understood; elsewhere it would have no significance or object. As to the means God used to bring it about, we will not attempt to say.

2. Toward the ninth hour, "the Veil of the Sanctuary was rent from top to bottom."[38] In the Sanctuary there were two veils, one covering the entrance of the Holy Place, the other the entrance to the Holy of Holies. The first, which was exposed to the view of all the Israelites who could penetrate into the part of the Temple forbidden to the Gentiles, is already known to us. According to Josephus, it was of enormous dimensions: 55 cubits in length by 16 in width, i.e., more than 82 feet by 24. It was a Babylonian carpet woven of multicolored thread — white, purple, blue, and red — symbolizing the four elements of which the world is made up: water, earth, air, and fire.[39] The other veil was seen only by the priests who entered the Holy Place twice a day to burn incense on the Altar of Incense. It was lifted only once a year, by the High Priest, when he penetrated alone into the Holy of Holies on the Day of Atonement. We possess no trustworthy document about the veil which concealed this place "inaccessible, invisible, intangible" from view. The description given of it by the Mishnah is fabulous, except, perhaps, as regards its dimensions: 40 cubits in height by 20 in width, or about 60 by 30 feet.[40]

The eclipse mentioned by Phlegon took place in the fourth year of the 202nd Olympiad (the year A.D. 32), which cannot be the year of Christ's death. The only eclipse of the sun visible at Jerusalem during that period occurred on November 24, A.D. 29, and this is too far from the Jewish Passover.

[37] Matt. 27:45; Mark 15:33; Luke 23:44 agree in writing ἐπὶ πᾶσαν (or ὅλην) τὴν γῆν, and not οἰκουμένην.

[38] Matt. 27:51; Mark 15:38. Identical texts. It is the Sanctuary (ναός), not the outer Temple (ἱερὸν). In the parts of the *Testament of the Prophets* which are interpolated by a Christian hand, the rending of the veil is predicted as a chastisement of the crimes of the Jews (*Levi,* 10; *Benjamin,* 9).

[39] Josephus, *Bellum,* V, v, 5. The same symbolism in Philo, with reference to the tabernacle of Moses (*De Mose,* iii; Mangey, II, 148).

[40] Texts in Billerbeck, *Kommentar,* Vol. I, pp. 1043–1044.

We believe that it was the inner veil that was torn at the time of Christ's death. This prodigy is "the visible sign that the cult of the Old Law has lapsed, that the sacrifices of the Old Covenant are henceforth void of all meaning. Figure and promise yield to reality. For the Jewish cult, attached to one Temple alone, reserved to one people alone, and celebrated by the offering of a victim without intelligence, is substituted a cult as universal as is the kingdom of God, the worship in spirit and in truth, of which Christ is the altar, the victim, and the priest."[41]

3. The theophanies of the Old Testament were almost always preceded by a commotion of nature announcing the arrival of the sovereign Judge. At the death of Christ, the earth quaked and the rocks split, as if to signal the approach of a divine judgment.[42] When Calvary was still visible to the gaze of all, St. Cyril of Jerusalem was accustomed to point out to his hearers the rents in the rock as an irrefutable proof of the veracity of the Gospels. Today, now that the whole surface has been concealed under a covering of marble, this demonstration would be difficult. Still, those who have studied the rent in the rock of Golgotha assert that it was the effect of a seismic disturbance. Indeed, anyone observing it through the opening contrived in the Chapel of the Greeks, or better still below in the Chapel of Adam, can verify that it is vertical, cutting the stratification of the rock at right angles.[43]

---

[41] Huby, *Saint Marc* (*Verbum Salutis*), p. 390. Much the more common opinion is that it was the inner veil that was rent. St. Jerome (*Epist.*, cxx; ML, XXII, 992), followed by St. Thomas, thinks that it was the outer veil, because the miracle ought to be visible. But the principal purpose of the prodigy was not to strike the eye immediately; it was to give a useful lesson for the time to follow.

[42] Matt. 27:51–52. Matthew alone speaks of this earthquake and of the opening of the tombs. One would be tempted to establish a link of causality between the two phenomena; but there is none, since the opening of the tombs occurred after the Resurrection of Jesus. St. Jerome thinks that the tombs were opened at the time of the earthquake, and perhaps as an effect of it, but that the dead did not come forth until after Christ's Resurrection. It is better to say, with Maldonatus, that the opening of the tombs, as well as the coming forth of their occupants, is mentioned here by anticipation.

[43] St. Cyril of Jerusalem, *Catecheses*, i, 1–6; iv, 37. Rufinus (*Hist. eccl.*, ix, 6) puts in the mouth of St. Lucian of Antioch (martyred in 312) a discourse in which he enumerates the prodigies happening at the Saviour's death: "Golgothana

4. The resurrection of the dead, recorded with the other prodigies that accompanied the Saviour's death, was, in reality, subsequent to it. "Coming forth out of the tomb after the resurrection of Jesus, they came into the city and appeared to many." He who is "the first-born from the dead and the first-fruits of the resurrection," after the expression of St. Paul, must be the first to rise; but he wished to associate some of the just with his glorious life, in order to make his own resurrection more credible. If these privileged ones had to die again, or if they had recovered their ordinary life at the risk of falling from the beatitude of which they were certain, their lot would have had in it nothing enviable. There can be no doubt, then, that on the day of the Ascension they formed the escort to the Conqueror of death in his triumphal entry into the abode of glory. Since they were recognized by many, their death cannot have occurred very long before; but to hazard their names — St. Joseph, St. John the Baptist, the Good Thief — would be empty conjecture.

5. A dying person ordinarily gives forth only a rattle, a gasp, a breath. Now, Jesus in dying uttered two great cries: one while intoning the Psalm, "My God, my God, why hast thou forsaken me?" the other in pronouncing his last prayer, "Father, into thy hands I commend my spirit." These death cries, which struck all present with astonishment, had as their purpose to make us all understand that he is Master of life and death; and that, if he dies, he dies of his own free will.

6. Mysterious too — and without doubt miraculous — was the mixture of blood and water that gushed from the pierced side of Jesus. St. John does not speak of miracle, but the emphasis that he places on certifying this phenomenon seems to imply it. Almost

---

rupes sub patibuli onere dirupta." St. Lucian, living before the clearings made by Constantine, had never seen the rent in the rock; but Rufinus, who is putting the words in his mouth, and who lived on the Mount of Olives, had certainly seen it. "It can still be verified that it (Golgotha) is an outcropping of rock, the rents in which, produced at the death of Christ, may be ascertained by everyone" (Vincent-Abel, *Jerusalem,* ii, 186). "One may see, behind an altar dedicated to Melchisedech, the prolongation of the marvelous fissure, stretching two meters below Calvary in an absolutely abnormal way. It presents an opening of fifteen centimeters" (*La Palestine,* 1922, Guide of the Assumptionists, p. 90).

all the Fathers of the Church search here for a symbolical meaning. The majority of them see here the figure of Baptism and of the Eucharist, the two Sacraments that incorporate us into Christ dying for us and living in us; the one infusing into us the life of grace, the other providing us with the nourishment needed to conserve and develop this divine life.[44]

7. The sudden reversal produced in the souls of those present also deserves to be numbered among the signs of Jesus' innocence. All of them, pagans and Jews, were moved by the accumulation of prodigies. The Centurion and the soldiers, accustomed as they were to scenes of blood, and so indifferent that they were unconcernedly playing at dice for the spoils of the victim, now confess that this man was a "son of God." More than that, "all the multitudes that had gathered to this spectacle, on beholding the things that had come to pass, returned beating their breasts."[45] The Gospel is speaking of the common people and the merely curious, not of the Saviour's sworn enemies. These had gone away to attend to their own affairs, or, if they stayed on Golgotha to savor their revenge, no miracle was capable of touching them. They were wantonly committing the sin against the Holy Ghost, which will not be forgiven either in this world or in the world to come, without a special miracle of omnipotent grace.

---

44 The opinions of the Fathers are reduced to these three:

a) The water and blood are figures of the regenerative water of Baptism and the redeeming blood. So St. Ambrose, *In Lucam,* x, 135: "aqua et sanguis exivit: illa quae diluat, iste qui redimat." Since the redeeming blood and the blood of the Eucharist are but one, this opinion is readily reducible to the third.

b) The water and blood are figures of the two baptisms (the Sacrament and martyrdom). Thus Tertullian, *De pudicitia,* 22; *De Baptismo,* 16; *De anima,* 43; St. Cyril of Jerusalem, *Catech.,* iii, 10 (MG, XXXIII, 440); St. Jerome, *Epist. ad Ocean.,* lxix, 6 (ML, XXII, 660); Rufinus, *De symbolo,* 23, etc.

c) The water and the blood are symbols of Baptism and the Eucharist. This is the opinion of the three great commentators on St. John (St. John Chrysostom, St. Augustine, and St. Cyril of Alexandria). Also St. Leo the Great, *Epist. ad Flavianum,* xxviii, 5; St. John Damascene, *De fide,* iv, 9.

45 Luke 23:48. As to the guards, St. Mark (15:39) and St. Luke (23:47) speak only of the Centurion; St. Matthew (27:54) says: "Those who were watching Jesus." St. Luke has the Centurion say: "This man was just"; the other two Evangelists: "This man was Son of God" (υἱὸς Θεοῦ, without the definite article).

CHAPTER XII

Jesus in the Tomb

1. The Burial

IT WAS the eve of the Sabbath and of a Sabbath incomparably greater and holier than ordinary Sabbaths, since it coincided that year with the Paschal solemnity. The feast began on Friday at sunset, or more precisely, when the first three stars appeared. Those among the Jews who had not eaten the Passover on the previous day hastily busied themselves with preparing the Paschal lamb, to take their places, when night should come, around the table laid with the unleavened bread and bitter herbs.[1]

In the words of the Mosaic Law, the lamb should be slain on the 14th day of Nisan "between the two evenings." This expression originally designated the interval between sunset and nightfall, and it is thus that the Samaritans, the Pharisees, and the Karaïtes always understood it. But when the law of one altar came into force, and custom established the slaying of the Paschal lamb in the Temple, the relatively brief Palestinian twilight no longer allowed enough time for the great number of sacrifices. The Pharisees therefore decided that the slaying should commence at three o'clock in the afternoon, or even an hour earlier, on the

[1] John 19:31: "Quoniam Parasceve erat, ut non remanerent in cruce corpora sabbato, erat enim magnus dies ille sabbati." It was the *Preparation* (παρασκευή) of the Sabbath; but it was also, as St. John himself has told us (19:14), the *Preparation* of the Passover. The next day was a *great* day for two reasons: it was a Sabbath and it was the first day of the Unleavened Bread (Exod. 12:16). To say that this Sabbath drew its special solemnity from the offering of the first sheaf — a liturgical ceremony devoid of any special pomp — is altogether arbitrary.

eve of the Sabbath. On this day the fathers of families assumed the role of sacrificers, and the priests intervened only to receive the blood of the victims and to pour it out in front of the altar. According to the Mishnah, this operation was carried out without delays and in the most perfect order. The sacrificers were divided into three groups. As soon as the first had entered the inner Temple, the doors were closed; the same was done for the second group. As far as the third group was concerned, they were so few and acted so expeditiously that they were finished before the Levites had time to complete the chant of the Hallel. Such speed is incredible considering the number of sacrifices. It must be said that in the time of the Mishnah there was no longer any concept of the crowds which used to celebrate the Passover in Jerusalem. Josephus speaks of three million visitors and some two hundred and sixty thousand lambs slain. Even if these figures are considerably reduced, as they should be, one may imagine the tumult and excitement that prevailed around the Temple on the evening of the Parasceve.

There was no less activity on Calvary. The sun was going down, and the bodies of the slain had to be buried before the end of day. The application to Pilate, and the verification of death ordered by him before he would authorize interment, had taken time. It was necessary to make haste. The Apostles, overwhelmed and bewildered by the loss of their Master, were of no assistance. Their presence at this critical time is not even mentioned by the Evangelists. The holy women were there looking on at a distance, but it was not theirs to unfasten the body from the cross, to bathe it and wrap it in linen cloths and bandages. These pious offices were the affair of men.

Fortunately two disciples, Joseph of Arimathea and Nicodemus, assumed the task. It will be remembered that Nicodemus had come by night to meet the Saviour to converse with him at his ease, without compromising himself in the eyes of the Pharisees, to which sect he himself belonged. At the time, the interview had had no decisive results, since Nicodemus, though inwardly convinced, did not dare declare himself openly. Still, on one occasion he had taken the risk of coming to Jesus' defense before the Sanhedrin, and this had caused his colleagues to suspect that he was a secret disciple of Jesus.

Joseph, also a member of the Sanhedrin, was distinguished from the many others who bore the same name by the name of his native city, Ramathaim-Zophim.[2] We do not know what circumstances led him to leave his native place and fix his abode in Jerusalem. He expected to die there; and in a garden which he owned on Golgotha, he had had carved out for himself a tomb which was still unused and probably unfinished, since it contained only one burial chamber. The Gospel renders this testimony to Joseph, that he was "a good and just man," but up to this time he had, like Nicodemus, been paralyzed by fear of his colleagues of the Sanhedrin. The death of Jesus awakened the courage of both these men. Joseph, who was a rich man, purchased a shroud of fine linen and the bandages needed for the burial. The contribution of Nicodemus, who was also rich, was truly regal: one hundred pounds of a mixture of myrrh and aloes.

The mystics are fond of representing Joseph and Nicodemus as taking infinite care to avoid bruising or wounding the body of Jesus, as though he were still alive: "One of them drew the nails from his hands; the other sustained the lifeless body for fear that it might fall to the ground. Then Mary raised her arms, embraced the head of her dear son, and drew it to her, pressing it to her heart and covering it with kisses, clinging to it inseparably. When the holy body had been taken down from the cross, she received it on her lap while Magdalene grasped the feet, before which she had obtained so many graces. The holy women surrounding them shed tears and broke out into lamentations."[3] Can we blame the mystics for trying to make up for the silence of the Evangelists by reconstructing this touching scene from the knowledge we have of the actors and of the sentiments that animated them?

The tomb which Joseph of Arimathea had provided for himself close to Golgotha, or more accurately on Golgotha itself, was no farther than fifty paces from the place where the cross was erected. We know that it was fronted by a vestibule, also cut out

---

[2] Arimathea, in olden times Ramathaim-Zophim, the country of Samuel, is today the village of Rentis, northeast of Lydda (Ludd).

[3] Ludolph the Carthusian, *Life of Christ,* Paris, 1872, VI, 478–479. More detailed descriptions are found in Catherine Emmerich, 3 ed., Paris, 1911, III, 319, and in Mary of Agreda, *The Mystical City,* Bk. VI, Chap. XXIV.

of the rock, accessible to all. The body had to be carried into this vestibule to be washed, as was the custom, and to be wrapped in strips of cloth sprinkled with the pulverized mixture of myrrh and aloes. A napkin covered the head and face. A large piece of linen, the whiteness of which is emphasized by St. Matthew, enveloped the entire body. It was necessary to hurry, since the day was declining. The body was therefore placed in the sepulcher where no one had ever yet been laid, and they rolled in front of the narrow opening the enormous stone, shaped like a millstone, intended to safeguard it.

The holy women examined everything carefully and then retired. Some of them took advantage of the last glimmer of day to buy more perfumes, each of them wishing to contribute according to her means to the burial of their adored Master. That done, they all religiously observed the Sabbath rest.

An impressive calm had of a sudden succeeded to the feverish excitement of the Parasceve. At the close of day the streets were deserted, the houses were closed up, and the city seemed plunged in the sleep of death. Every family was celebrating in privacy the anniversary of the exodus from Egypt. But the true Passover, the feast of Deliverance, was not being celebrated in Jerusalem that year. It was being celebrated in the place where the souls of the just were detained, the just who had died in the grace of God since the beginning of the world.

As soon as Jesus had breathed his last, his soul inseparably united to the divinity, as was also his body, descended into Limbo where, for so many centuries, patriarchs and prophets had been awaiting his coming. Though the primitive Church unanimously accepted the dogma of Christ's descent into hell, there was no agreement about the purpose of this journey. Many, basing their opinion on an obscure text of St. Peter, thought that he went to offer to those who had died before the preaching of the Gospel one last chance of salvation. But it was soon seen that this theory, so acceptable to modern sentimental ways of thinking, was opposed to Catholic teaching. Jesus does not preach the good news to any in hell except those who have merited to hear it. To them he announces that the fullness of time has come; that heaven is about to open so that they may soon enter with him in his glory. All of them will form his escort on the day of the Ascension, and some privileged ones, raised now to life by him, will accompany him both in body and in soul.[4]

The *Gospel of Nicodemus* describes this drama with a realism which calls to mind the mystery plays of the Middle Ages and in a style which at times becomes lyrical.[5] On the evening of Good Friday, a tempestuous wind agitates the subterranean prison of the souls and finally a ray of light penetrates the gloom. Death and Hell personified tremble with fear that they are to have their prey snatched from them. Of a sudden a cry rings out: "Open, ye eternal gates, to give free entrance to the King of Glory!" The saints of the Old Law, beginning with Adam, all file before the Saviour, chanting appropriate canticles. Finally the Good Thief who has just died comes in his turn; he tells his story and the chants of praise and jubilation are redoubled.

2. The Fate of Judas[6]

That same night, Judas the traitor fell to the depths of the abyss where reign disorder and eternal despair. Avarice, which absorbed all his thoughts, at first veiled from him the horror of his crime. In the Cenacle, he had appeared insensible to the advances and warnings of the Saviour. At Gethsemani he had shown neither emotion nor disturbance on hearing the words that could have rent a heart of stone: "My friend, why art thou come here? Judas, dost thou betray the Son of Man with a kiss?" He was thinking only of the promised pay. But when he weighed in his hands those thirty pieces of silver he had so long coveted, the shame of his infamous action rose before his eyes. It was for this that he had sold his benefactor, his Master, and his God!

Up to this time, blinded by passion, he had perhaps calculated that the enemies of Jesus, for fear of the populace, would not dare to make an attempt upon his life, or that Jesus himself, using

---

[4] See the article, *Descente de Jésus aux enfers,* in the *Dict. de théologie,* and the more recent monograph of K. Gschwind, *Die Niederfahrt Christi in die Unterwelt,* Munster-i-W., 1911.

[5] *Gospel of Nicodemus,* Part II, cc. ii–x (Tischendorf, pp. 391–406).

[6] Cf. Note W: *The Fate of Judas.*

his miraculous power, would baffle their plot. But when, on Friday morning, he learned from popular report of the rancor of the priests, when he saw the Saviour condemned by Pilate and loaded with his cross and dragged to Calvary, remorse took hold of him, just as Nero was seized by the consciousness of his matricide as he stood before his mother's corpse.

The money, price of iniquity, now burns his hands; he would rid himself of it at all costs, hoping by such a restitution to obtain a little relief. He directs his steps to the Temple and says to the priests with whom he has made his bargain: "I have sinned by betraying innocent blood." Little does he know them if he is expecting from them a word of comfort. His accomplices, his associates of yesterday evening, have for him now nothing but indifference and contempt. Dryly they answer him: "What is that to us? See thou to it!" We have paid the agreed price; we are quit of you.

Beside himself with anger at this insulting irony, Judas hurled the thirty shekels of silver into the Court of Priests, and they rolled to the entrance of the Sanctuary.[7] Then he fled, rage in his heart and despair in his soul. Alas! his remorse was no true repentance. If he had but gone up to Calvary, if he had implored its grace as did the Good Thief, if he had embraced the feet of the Crucified as had Magdalene, if he had received upon his head one drop of the redemptive blood! There was still time. The heart of Jesus was open to him. But he doubted its love and its mercy. Like Cain, he said: "My sin is too great to be forgiven." Despair was not the greatest of his crimes, but for himself it was the deadliest. It was final impenitence that verified the Saviour's words: "It were better for that man that he had never been born."

We may imagine him in the shadows of evening prowling about

---

[7] Matt. 27:3–5. Judas brings back the money when he sees Jesus condemned to death. Upon the refusal of the priests, he throws the money *into* or *toward the Sanctuary* (εἰς τὸν ναόν). The ναός can designate either the Sanctuary properly so called (the Holy Place and the Holy of Holies) or the entire inner Temple open to the Jews only, in opposition to the exterior Temple (ἱερόν) accessible to Gentiles. Judas, instead of placing the money in one of the boxes provided for the reception of alms, threw it upon the pavement of the Court of Priests which was in front of him — or perhaps, in his rage, he aimed at the entrance of the Holy Place which was not farther from the Court of Israel than some 33 yds.

the city, searching for a suitable place to carry out his fatal design. Finally he finds it in the Valley of Hinnom, that *Gehenna* haunted by specters and peopled by sinister memories, a spot avoided as a place accursed. St. Matthew and the Acts of the Apostles tell of his death in different terms. St. Matthew says briefly: "Judas went away and hanged himself." The Acts are a little less brief: "Falling from a height, he burst in the midst and all his entrails gushed forth."[8] To reconcile the two accounts it suffices to suppose that Judas hanged himself on a tree that overhung one of the precipices bordering the valley. The branch or the rope breaking, he fell on the rocks from a great height and the fall bared his intestines. Legend was not slow to improve the story. A century later it was said that Judas, surviving his attempt at suicide, became so enormously swollen that his eyes disappeared in his puffed-up head and that his deformed abdomen engendered pus and worms. His corpse exhaled such a stench that people passing that way avoided the field in which it was buried. These legendary stories show what horror was inspired in the first Christians by this man who in our day has found admirers and panegyrists.

At first, more indulgence was shown toward Pilate. Had not the Saviour himself said that Pilate was less culpable than Judas or Caiphas? His good intentions made people forget, to some extent, his weakness. The Prince of the Apostles, in his discourse to the people of Jerusalem, makes the greater share of responsibility fall upon the Jews.[9] The aprocryphal *Gospel of Peter* completely exonerates Pilate to heap the blame on Herod. If we were to take the word of this source, it was Herod that judged and condemned Jesus; Pilate takes on the appearance of a supernumerary or a mere spectator.[10] A report to Tiberius was attrib-

[8] Matt. 27:5; Acts 1:18–19. Verses 18 and 19 are a parenthesis inserted by the author into the discourse of St. Peter in the Cenacle. They interrupt the sequence of thought, and if they are taken out, the thoughts are well linked: "It was necessary that the prophecy of David about Judas should be fulfilled . . . for it is written in the Book of Psalms." The Vulgate, *et suspensus crepuit medius,* does not render very exactly the Greek καὶ πρηνὴς γενόμενος ἐλάκησεν μέσος.

[9] Acts 3:13–15: Jesum "negastis ante faciem Pilati, judicante illo dimitti." Tertullian's words about Pilate are famous (Apol. 21): "Jam pro sua conscientia christianus."

[10] *Evangile de Pierre* (edit. Vaganay), 1930, pp. 203–205.

uted to Pilate, in which, after giving a long account of Jesus' miracles, he excuses himself to the Emperor for having condemned him under pressure from the Jews. Decapitated by the order of Tiberius, he was supposed to have implored Christ's pardon before dying and to have obtained the assurance of his salvation.[11] The Coptic Church venerates him as a martyr.[12]

But finally a reaction came. Pilate, it was said, committed suicide, like Judas.[13] His body, cast into the Tiber, was said to have stirred up such storms that it had to be plunged into the Rhone near Vienne; then it was taken to the outskirts of Lausanne, and finally it was thrown into an Alpine lake, whose waters it would sometimes cause to boil, and whence it would rise from time to time, taking the shape of a frightful specter constantly repeating the gesture of washing the hands. These stories would not deserve the honor of being mentioned were it not that they found credence to the extent of being inserted in the *Golden Legend*.[14] In vain did Pilate wash his hands. He remains in the eyes of posterity the responsible author of the death of the God-Man, and to the end of time the Church will associate his name with the crucifixion of Jesus.

Meantime the priests, who had gathered up the thirty pieces thrown by Judas into the Sanctuary, were seized by a delicate scruple. The Law forbade them to apply to divine worship sums that came from an unclean source, and Judas' thirty shekels seemed to them to belong to this category. "Let us not pay them into the Temple treasury," they said, "since they are the price of blood." They decided to devote the money to the purchase of a plot of ground known in the locality as the Potter's Field, to

---

11 *Anaphora Pilati* and *Paradosis Pilati,* in Tischendorf, *Evang. apocr.,* 2 ed., 1876, pp. 443–455. *Mors Pilati, ibid.,* pp. 456–458, and better in James, *Apocrypha of the New Test.,* 1924, pp. 159–161.

12 Feast on June 25. Claudia Procula or Procla, the wife of Pilate, is also venerated by the Copts as a saint. Her feast is celebrated in the Greek Church on October 27.

13 A current opinion was that he committed suicide under Caligula (Eusebius, *Hist. eccl.,* ii, 7). Cf. Müller, *Pontius Pilatus,* Stuttgart, 1888, which has a copious bibliography.

14 This story fills four pages in the *Golden Legend* (Chap. LII). But the author warns that it is apocryphal and that the reader is free to think of it what he wishes.

provide a burial place for strangers dying in Jerusalem during a pilgrimage. At the time when St. Matthew was writing, this ground was still called Haceldama, the Field of Blood.[15]

The sad end of Judas did not prevent the chief priests from savoring their triumph. Still on the following day, upon reflection, a disquiet began to disturb their joy. Jesus had predicted that he would rise again on the third day. The leaders of the priests, for the most part Sadducees, did not believe in the resurrection of the dead, but the people believed in it. What would happen if the Apostles, carrying off the body of the crucified, should spread abroad that he had risen from the dead? The safest thing to do was to cut short the possibility of any such imposture. A private meeting was called despite the Sabbath, and the priests resolved to pay a visit to Pilate and to have him lend them some Roman soldiers to guard the tomb.[16] One can feel in the Procurator's answer the impatience and bad humor of a man at the end of his resources. "You have a guard. Go, secure the tomb as you know how." He places a platoon of soldiers at their disposal to keep watch in the vicinity and to ward off suspected characters, but he will not mix in the affair himself; and he leaves to them the care and the risk. The Jews sealed to the rock wall the stone shaped like a millstone that closed the entrance of the tomb. This last precaution seems to have been taken against the guards. They would be betrayed by the breaking of the seals, if they should let themselves be bribed by the Apostles. The Jews have thought of everything. Now they may sleep secure. The dead body is well guarded.

---

15 Matt. 27:6–8.
16 Matt. 27:62–66.

CHAPTER XIII

Easter Sunday

1. The Resurrection of Jesus

DEATH is not for Jesus, as it is for the rest of men, the term of his earthly career. It is the beginning of a new life, shorter than the first, but as active and, if possible, even more fruitful than the first. He himself tells us in his Gospel that "the Son of Man must rise from the dead," without giving the reason for this necessity. St. Luke gives us a glimpse of that reason and St. Paul reveals it to us. God owed it to his Son to raise him from the dead, and this is why, in more than ten passages of the Scripture, the initiative in the Resurrection is attributed to the Father. "Christ," says St. Paul, "humbled himself, becoming obedient unto death, even to the death of the cross; therefore God has exalted him, and has given him the name which is above every name, that at the name of Jesus every knee should bend in heaven, on earth, and in hell, and every tongue should confess, to the glory of the Father, that Jesus Christ is Lord."[1]

But the Saviour also owed it to himself. When Jesus found his miracles insufficient to authenticate his divine mission, he appealed to his own Resurrection as a decisive and irrefutable sign. "This wicked and adulterous generation seeks for a sign, and a sign shall not be given it except the sign of Jonas the prophet. As Jonas was three days and three nights in the belly of the sea monster, so shall the Son of Man be in the heart of the earth three days and three nights."[2] If this predicted sign were not forthcoming

[1] Phil. 2:7–11.

[2] Matt. 12:39–41; 16:4; Luke 11:29–32.

at the time predicted, the entire work of the Gospel would be destroyed.

Jesus needed to be raised from the dead, not only to confirm his work but to continue it. "The days he spent on earth between the Resurrection and the Ascension," says Pope St. Leo, "were not days lost to the revelation of mysteries. It was then that he breathed upon the Apostles and infused into them the Holy Spirit, and placed St. Peter above the others, confiding to him, with the keys of the kingdom, the care and the guardianship of his flock."[3] Thus he fulfilled the promise he had made to them on the eve of his death: "I will not leave you orphans; I am coming to you." And he will not come with empty hands. He will delegate to them his full powers to remit and retain the sins of men, and he will give them the assurance that he will remain with them, though absent in body, until the consummation of the world.

Without going into an examination of the profound meaning of the words of St. Paul: "Our Lord Jesus Christ was delivered up for our offenses and rose again for our justification," it is easy to show that the Resurrection of Christ contributes to our justification.[4] In the first place, it is the foundation of our faith and the prop of our hope. "If Christ is not risen," says the Apostle, "our preaching is vain; vain also is your faith. . . . You are still in your sins, and the just who died in Christ have utterly perished. If we had no hope in Christ except in this life, we would be the most unfortunate of all men."

What would Christianity be if Christ had not risen from the dead? Without the Resurrection there would be no tabernacle, no altar, no sacrifice, no priests. Baptism itself would lose all its meaning; for by Baptism we mystically die with Christ and with him we mystically rise again. This is why all the Apostles have placed at the foundation of their preaching the Resurrection of Christ as the indispensable complement of the redemptive death. "I have taught you before all else," says St. Paul to the Corinthians, "that Christ died for our sins, according to the Scriptures,

[3] St. Leo, *Sermo de ascensione,* 2 (ML, LIV, 395).

[4] Rom. 4:25. Cf. Prat, *Théologie de S. Paul,* II, 250–252 (English transl., II, 208–211).

that he was buried, and rose again on the third day according to the Scriptures. . . . Whether I or they (the other Apostles), this have we taught and this have you believed."[5] This insistence of the first preachers of the Gospels will, perhaps, help us to understand better the mysterious saying of the Saviour: "My Father loves me because I lay down my life that I may take it up again." Some shortsighted exegetes have been almost scandalized at this saying. Would it not be more worthy of honor, more heroic, to give up life without the design, without the hope of recovering it? St. Augustine, in his brief commentary, has no such scruples: "My Father loves me because I die to rise again." Rightly so. The death of Christ is neither desirable nor conceivable without the Resurrection. In the present order of divine Providence the death of Christ would not be wholly a benefit if the Resurrection had not come to complete the Sacrifice of the Cross.

2. The Empty Tomb

Sunday, at the first glimmer of dawn, a violent earthquake shook the vicinity of the sepulcher, and Jesus came forth glorious, without breaking the seals, as he had once before left the chaste womb of his mother without causing the least injury to her virginal integrity. At the same time, the Angel of the Lord came down from heaven and rolled back in its groove the heavy stone that closed the entrance of the tomb; then he seated himself upon it, as if to forbid access to the sepulcher. His vesture was whiter than snow, and his resplendent face gave forth flashes of lightning.

Such an extraordinary seismic disturbance and the apparition of the angel dazzling with light stupefied the guards, and knowing that there was no longer any reason for them to stay there, they fled to the city, half dead with fear. They did not think at first of the troublesome sequel that this untoward happening might have for them; still, they were not unaware of the consequences to which abandonment of his post exposed a Roman soldier, except when compelled by irresistible force. And so, as dawn gave

---

[5] 1 Cor. 15:3–11. Cf. Prat, *Théologie de S. Paul,* II, 35–36 (English transl., II, 30–31).

place to day, some of them sought out the chief priests, at whose disposal Pilate had placed them, and told in the smallest details what had happened. The priests in a hastily summoned morning session of the Council discussed what measures should be taken to deceive the people and to prevent the truth from becoming known. They gave to each of the guards a large sum of money, with strict instructions to say that Jesus' disciples had carried away the body while they were asleep. What a ridiculous invention! If the guards were asleep, how could they know that the disciples had carried away the body? And if they were not asleep, why had they failed to stop them? Bad as was this explanation, the chief priests could find no better, and they counted on popular credulousness to make it acceptable.[6]

All this, however, did not place the guards beyond pursuit. For a soldier, the abandonment of his post was punishable by death. Accordingly the leaders of the priests reassured the guards, promising that if Pilate should get wind of the affair, they themselves, the chief priests, would stand bail for their safety and would undertake to appease the Procurator. They had too much at stake to fail to keep their promise. Still, even if Pilate should learn what had happened, it was probable that he would not be very much disturbed. It was not he that had thought up the bizarre precaution of setting guard over a dead man. He had loaned the Jews some soldiers at their express request, with the sardonic recommendation that they should guard the tomb carefully. If they had failed, it was their affair; it was no concern of his. Perhaps in his heart he would even be glad at their discomfiture. Besides, if he should put on a show of anger, the Jews knew by experience a sure way to close his mouth by paying the price.[7]

---

[6] St. Matthew is the only one who records the apparition of the angel coming to open the tomb (28:2–4) and the collusion of the guards with the chief priests (28:11–15).

[7] In a confused account full of variants, the *Acta* or *Gesta Pilati,* xiv (Tischendorf, *Evang. apoc.,* 1876, pp. 319 and 374) have Annas and Caiphas saying: "Do not believe the soldiers when they assert that they saw angels; believe rather that the disciples have paid them to carry off the body." According to the worthless Jewish screed called *Toledoth Yeshu,* it was Judas that carried off the body and buried it in a valley, for fear that the disciples would come to take it away to lend credence to the statement that Jesus had risen from the dead.

The absurd tale spread abroad by the soldiers was still current in Palestine at the time when St. Matthew was writing his Gospel. More than a century later, St. Justin reported that emissaries of the Jews had gone forth to spread it everywhere, and that there were not lacking people simple enough to accept it. Such is the credulousness of simple folk that the grossest imposture often finds acceptance among them.[8] Nevertheless, the calumny of the Jews would have exposed the Apostles to grave danger, if Pilate had taken it seriously. An imperial rescript of Augustus or Tiberius, of which we have a Greek translation on a stele said to have come from Nazareth, reads thus: "It is absolutely forbidden for anyone to displace the bodies of the dead. I will that anyone making himself guilty of such an action undergo capital punishment for violation of sepulture."[9] The well-known rigor of Roman law makes still more improbable the bizarre story of the priests.

The risen Saviour was not seen by the guards. He was not to show himself to eyes unworthy of seeing him. St. Peter, in his discourse at Caesarea, gives this reason for it. "God who raised him from the dead on the third day gave him to manifest himself not to all the people, but to witnesses forechosen by God, even ourselves, who ate and drank with him after his resurrection."[10]

No one more than the Blessed Virgin had the right to this favor. Associated with the whole Passion of Jesus, she had drained with him the chalice of bitterness. Was it not just that she before all others should share the joys of his triumph? Can anyone doubt that the first visit of a Son so loving, the perfect model of filial piety, would be to his Mother? Jesus is to show himself to Peter who denied him, to the Apostles who cravenly abandoned him,

---

[8] St. Justin, *Dial. cum Tryph.*, ii, 17 and 108 (MG, VI, 314 and 725).

[9] Phototype and translation of the stele in *R.B.*, 1930, pp. 567–571. F. Cumont, who has a study of it in the *Revue historique* (CLXIII, 1930, pp. 241–266), offers the hypothesis that the rescript could have been addressed by Tiberius to Pilate who had informed the Emperor about the empty tomb. The rescript, translated into Greek and engraved on marble, would then have been exhibited at Nazareth which was believed to be Jesus' birthplace. If such were the case the document would have singular importance, but this is hard to believe.

[10] Acts 10:40–41.

to the disciples of Emmaus who had almost ceased to hope in him. Will he forget or forsake his Mother? Christian feeling refuses to believe it; and this feeling, according to the most esteemed theologians, is conformed to truth.[11] If the Gospel does not mention this first apparition, it is, according to the Abbot Rupert, because the Gospel enumerates only the witnesses to the Resurrection and because a mother's testimony in favor of her son is not acceptable.[12] It is better to say, with St. Ignatius, that the Gospel supposes that we are endowed with intelligence.

But the Gospel, if we know how to read it, is not mute. When it describes the holy women eagerly busying themselves around the Saviour's tomb as soon as the Sabbath rest is over, it makes no reference to Jesus' Mother. Is it not that the Evangelists would have us understand that Mary holds aloof from these loving offices because she knows that they are superfluous?[13] At the time when others went to look for Jesus among the dead, she had already seen him living and glorious. In tears she waited for him during the long night that preceded the Resurrection. Finally a ray of light penetrated into her narrow cell where she was at prayer. Is it the first ray of the newborn day? No, it is he. It is her Jesus. She falls into his arms without any fear of hearing those words that Magdalene will soon hear: "Hold me not, for I have not yet ascended to my Father." Such a prohibition is not for her who is outside all rules. Who can imagine the confidences poured out by such a mother and such a son? Who

---

[11] Suarez (In Part III, q. lv, disp. 49, sect. 1, no. 2) says: "Absque ulla dubitatione credendum." The same is expressed by Benedict XIV, *De festis,* I, viii, 45. Estius objects that Mary, to believe, had no need of an apparition; but that was not the reason why she was favored with one. The first of the ancient authors who speaks of this apparition is Sedulius, a fifth-century poet (*Carmen paschale,* v, 360–366, and the corresponding *Opus paschale* in prose, ML, XIX, 743). St. Ambrose is often, though wrongly, cited (*De virginit.,* 3; ML, XVI, 270); in this passage he is not speaking of the Blessed Virgin, but of that one of the two Mary Magdalenes who, in his theory, was a virgin.

[12] Rupert (*De divinis officiis,* vii, 25; ML, CLXX, 207), with the approval of Salmeron, Maldonatus, and a number of other exegetes, answers the difficulty drawn from Mark (16:9): "apparuit primo Mariae Magdalenae." He thinks that the custom of the Roman Church in placing the *statio* for Easter at St. Mary Major confirms our opinion.

[13] St. Bernard (*Vitis mystica,* ii, no. 4; ML, CLXXXIV, 640) offers this idea with all reserve: "Fortasse propterea . . . non venit cum aliis . . . quia frustra putabat eum ungi quem resurrecturum sciebat."

will dare describe them? Perhaps Mary never made anyone the confidant of those precious exchanges. As in other days at Bethlehem and at Nazareth, she jealously guarded in her heart those secrets of ineffable joy.

3. Magdalene and the Holy Women

The comings and goings of the holy women around the empty tomb are surely one of the thorniest problems of Gospel criticism. The number and identity of the persons, the time of their arrival at the sepulcher, what they saw and what they heard: all are subjects of controversy. One may judge from the following brief summary.

Who were the holy women? — The four Evangelists agree in giving the name of Mary Magdalene, and St. John mentions only her. St. Matthew adds the *other Mary,* who must be the mother of St. James and consequently the sister by marriage of the Blessed Virgin. To these two St. Mark adds Salome, the wife of Zebedee; St. Luke mentions, besides Mary Magdalene and Mary the mother of St. James and Joanna the wife of Chusa, a considerable number of companions whose names he does not give.

At what time did the holy women come to the sepulcher? — It was "very early in the morning" (Luke); or "in the morning while it was yet dark" (John); or "Very early . . . after sunrise" — two indications that seem to be contradictory (Mark); and still more contradictory, it would seem, is the indication given by St. Matthew: "Vespere autem sabbati, quae lucescit in prima sabbati."

What they saw and heard — According to St. Matthew, they saw an angel, who said to them: "Fear not. I know that you seek Jesus the Crucified. He is not here; he is risen, as he said. Come, see the place where he lay. But go quickly and tell his disciples that he is risen from the dead, and that he goes before you into Galilee, where you shall see him." According to St. Mark, the youth whom they saw spoke to them in almost the same words, but he was seated at the right, inside the tomb; whereas the angel of St. Matthew was seated in the vestibule, upon the stone that had been used to close the entrance to the tomb. St. Luke's version is different: "Two men in dazzling raiment stood by them and said to them: 'Why seek you among the dead him who is alive? He is not here, for he is risen. Remember what he said to you when he was still in Galilee: The Son of Man must be delivered into the hands of sinful men and be crucified, but on the third day he will rise again.' " In St. John, the two angels clothed in white, who are seated, one at the head, the other at the foot of the burial slab, did not appear to Magdalene until she came back to the sepulcher, and they said to her only: "Why weepest thou?"

What did they do? — According to St. Matthew, filled with fear mingled with joy, they ran to announce the news to the Apostles. According to St. Mark, they took to flight without saying anything to anyone, because they were afraid. In St. Luke's account, they faithfully reported to the Eleven and all the rest what they had seen and heard. In St. John, Mary Magdalene received no message from the angels, and it was on her own initiative that she hastened to notify the two Apostles.

These word conflicts, difficult as they appear at first reading, are not insoluble. We must admit, however, that the long elucubrations of the commentators do not always shed much light, since most of them are more intent upon refuting the solutions of others than upon solidly establishing their own. Let us recall that the holy women were numerous; that they may have visited the sepulcher in distinct groups and at different hours; and that consequently they may not have seen and heard and reported exactly the same things. We do not, of course, assume, with the author of a discourse wrongly attributed to St. Gregory of Nyssa, that the holy women all together made four journeys to the tomb: one on Saturday evening, another in the course of the night, the third at dawn, and the last after sunrise. Such unlikely hypotheses have all the appearance of an evasion. Nor will we join St. Ambrose in reconciling St. John with the Synoptics by doubling the person of Mary Magdalene, creating two Marys of

Magdala, one of whom was a virgin, the other not a virgin. Neither will we here follow Maldonatus, who (failing his usual inspiration) makes all the holy women stay together at all times, and tortures the text of St. John to accommodate it to the Synoptic narrative, on the supposition that, being three against one, they have the advantage of numbers.[14] We have no need of such subterfuges.

4. Apparition to Mary Magdalene

St. John's narrative, since it is that of an eyewitness, is illuminating; him we shall take as our guide, after some brief topographical indications which will make the understanding of the facts easier.

The Jews of Palestine, when they had the means, used to carve their family tombs out of the soft limestone that forms the rock deposit of their mountains. Sometimes the hollow was dug underground and was reached by steps cut into the rock, the opening of the tomb being closed by a slab placed upon it horizontally. Such was the tomb of Lazarus, as we have already seen. Oftener the tomb rested against the side of a hill and was entered at ground level. The luxurious sepulchers, such as those shown in the environs of Jerusalem under the names of the Tombs

---

[14] The second discourse on the Resurrection attributed to St. Gregory of Nyssa (MG, XLVI, 623–652) is certainly apocryphal. Combefis and Lenain de Tillemont believed it to be the work of Hesychius of Jerusalem; it should rather be ascribed to Severus of Antioch. The author, whoever he is, thinks against all reason, that the *other Mary* in St. Matthew is the Blessed Virgin.— St. Ambrose (*In Lucam,* Bk. X, no. 153; ML, XV, 1242) distinguishes the Mary Magdalene of St. Matthew from the Mary Magdalene of St. John, an opinion which St. Jerome rightly criticizes, without mentioning the name of its author (*Epist. cxx ad Hedibiam,* c. iv; ML, XXII, 988). St. Jerome himself multiplies excessively the visits made by the holy women: "Nobis simplex videtur et aperta responsio sanctas feminas . . . per totam noctem, non semel, nec bis, sed crebro, ad sepulchrum Domini cucurrisse." It is sufficient to distinguish the visit made by Magdalene alone from the visit made by her with others.— Maldonatus admits that here he is going contrary to the general opinion because the language of St. John seems very clear; but "facilius creditu est unum Evangelistam, quam plures, obscure locutum esse"; and he flatters himself that he has proved, though St. John seems to say the opposite, "Magdalenam et reliquas mulieres *semel tantum* ad monumentum venisse." Still, in several places he gives the revealing principle which we have used to explain the Synoptics without doing violence to their text.

of the Kings and Judges and Prophets, were fronted by an open-air courtyard from which there was a passage into a vestibule hollowed out of the rock, and thence into an antechamber, on three sides of which were the carefully sealed burial chambers. The tomb of Joseph of Arimathea, in which Jesus was buried, was much more simple. It consisted of but one burial chamber; but it had a vestibule, as is formally attested by St. Cyril of Jerusalem, who saw it with his own eyes. This vestibule was suppressed by Constantine's architects for reasons of symmetry and perspective. They thought it sufficient to preserve only the tomb itself, and, having cut the surrounding rock away from it, they enclosed it in a richly adorned pavilion surmounted by a cupola.

At the back of the vestibule, a low, narrow entrance, which could be entered only by doubling over and almost crawling, gave access to the tomb itself. This inconvenient doorway was closed by a large stone shaped like a millstone, which could be made to roll in a groove contrived for it along the vertical wall. Since it was very heavy and gave very little purchase, strong arms or the aid of a lever was needed to move it. Beyond the low entrance was a square or oblong room entirely cut into the rock, about as high as a man of medium height and varying in dimensions. On three sides, stone ledges projecting from the rock, or recesses sunk into the side walls were provided to receive the bodies. The place where the head was to rest was somewhat raised and was easily recognizable. The corpse was placed there without any coffin, the head wrapped in a napkin and the rest of the body enveloped in a large piece of linen tightly fastened by bandages, like a child in swaddling clothes.

The tomb of Joseph of Arimathea, comprising only one compartment of narrow dimensions, was entirely new. The Gospel informs us that he had built it only for himself, perhaps putting off the enlargement of it, if that should some day become necessary. As he built it, it could contain only one burial couch located at the right of the entrance, as St. Mark informs us and as we can still verify for ourselves.

This wonderful relic has undergone the ravages of time and the vandalism of man. The fourth-century builders, when they found it necessary to level the soil, hewed the rock containing the Holy Sepulcher into the form of a cube and made it the exact center of the Constantinian cupola. In the tenth century, it was frightfully mutilated by the barbarous Caliph of Egypt. What now remains is concealed beneath costly marbles.[15] So greatly has the appearance of things and places changed that it requires an effort of the imagination to reconstruct in spirit the scenes of the Gospel. These brief indications may help us to understand them better. Let us come back to St. John's narrative.

Very early on Sunday morning, while it was still night, Mary of Magdala came to see the sepulcher. As the sequel will show, she was not alone. During the journey, dawn had dissipated the darkness; and, on arriving, Mary noticed that the tomb was wide open and that the large stone that had closed the opening had been taken away. It did not occur to her that Jesus could have risen from the dead, and she did not take time to enter the vestibule and bend down over the narrow opening of the tomb to assure herself that it was empty.[16] Without doubt, she thought, the violators of the tomb must have carried off the body. Her unnerved state brought on by a day of waiting and two disquieting nights made her a prey to the worst suspicions.

Taken up with this idea, she left her companions there and went straight as an arrow to look for the Apostles. The first she met were the inseparables, Peter and John. Distractedly, she told them: "They have taken the Lord out of the tomb and we know not where they have laid him." She says "we," in the plural, a clear indication that she is speaking for her friends who had stayed near the tomb.

The two Apostles, anxious to verify this surprising news for themselves, made their way across the still almost deserted city. Hope and desire gave them wings. If, as is probable, they were in the vicinity of the Cenacle, a quarter of an hour would be enough to bring them to the sepulcher. John, the younger and more agile of the two, arrived first and, urged by a legitimate curiosity, bent down over the opening to take a furtive look; but

[15] See Note V: *The Holy Sepulcher*.

[16] We may, however, suppose that she cast a furtive glance inside the tomb. The angel who had rolled back the rock was no longer there, or no longer visible; he does not reappear until after her departure.

through deference to his companion, whose dignity he respected even more than his age, he refrained from entering. Hence it was Peter who went in first and attentively examined everything. The cloths and bandages that had been used to enshroud Jesus were lying on the ground. The napkin that had enveloped his head was carefully rolled up and placed aside in a corner. Evidently Magdalene's supposition was contrary to all likelihood. Evildoers working in haste would have carried off the body as it was, without taking the time to undo the bandages and to unwrap the shroud. John entered the empty tomb in his turn and, after making the same investigations, had no doubt that his Master was risen.

Mary Magdalene, perhaps delaying to communicate the news to other disciples, did not return to the sepulcher until after the two Apostles and the holy women had gone away. She remained standing outside the vestibule, her face covered with tears; and then instinctively she leaned down over the low entrance of the tomb and looked inside. What was her surprise and terror when she saw two angels clothed in white — in her distraction she took them for two men — seated one at the head and the other at the foot of the place where the body of Jesus had rested. They said to her: "Woman, why weepest thou?" "Because," she said, "they have taken away the body of my Master and I know not where they have laid it." As she said this, she turned around and saw Jesus standing before her, but, with eyes veiled in tears, she merely glanced at him; and she was so far from believing him alive that she did not recognize him. Thinking that she was addressing the man who was gardener and watchman, she made this naïve request of him: "Sir, if thou hast carried him away, tell me where thou hast laid him, and I will take him away." She believes that everyone must be acquainted with the anxiety that obsesses her; she imagines that she is able, by herself, to replace the body of Jesus. Surely, she no longer knows what she is saying.

And then she hears her name: "Mary!" Her name pronounced by that familiar voice wakes her from her dream. She turns her head and looks. It is he. It is her adored Master. She finds but one word to answer: "Rabboni: My Master!" At once she falls at his feet to embrace them and bathes them with her tears.

But Jesus says to her: "Hold me not, for I have not yet ascended to my Father. But go find my brethren, and say to them: 'I ascend to my Father and your Father, to my God and your God.' "[17]

From St. John's text, it is clear that Mary had already taken hold of Jesus' feet. But why does he now forbid her to make a gesture that he had several times permitted during his mortal life? And what is the meaning of the reason give by Jesus: "I have not yet ascended to my Father"?

None of the explanations proposed by various authors are wholly satisfactory.[18] The best two are these: "Do not touch me now: you will have other occasions, for the time has not yet come for me to ascend to heaven"; or else, "Do not prolong this embrace; there are other more urgent matters; namely, to go carry to my brethren the news of my Resurrection, with the assurance that they will see me soon, for I have not yet ascended to my Father." One is free to choose between the two, or to look for a better. And perhaps the following has a chance of being the closest to the meaning of this mysterious saying. Mary had grasped the Saviour's feet and, in embracing them, had put into the action all her repentance, all her gratitude, all her love. There is nothing blameworthy in her act; Jesus had twice before praised the same action in the highest terms. But it is imperfect in the sense that it is addressed to man more than to God. Now there is something changed in the relationship between Jesus Christ and his disciples. There is no longer place for the effusiveness of former times; that familiar intercourse into which something of the human element entered is no longer fitting. Jesus wishes Magdalene to learn this, and this he charges her to tell the Apostles. He has not yet ascended to his Father, but he will

---

[17] John 20:17: μή μου ἅπτου (in the present) can only mean "Cease holding me." If the aorist were used instead of the present, the meaning would be: "I forbid you to touch me, as you intend to do." The verb ἅπτεσθαι means not simply "to touch" but "to embrace." Thus in Homer the frequent phrase ἅπτεσθαι γούνων designates the gesture of a suppliant embracing the knees of the one whom he is trying to win over. — Mary answers: "Rabboni." It was pronounced either *Rabboni,* as in the Vulgate, or *Rabbouni,* as in the Greek text. Cf. Billerbeck, Vol. II, p. 25. Later, it was *Rabbon.*

[18] A certain number of these explanations may be found in Schanz and Godet; many of them are plainly ridiculous,

soon ascend to him, and from today his relationship with his friends is modified. They will enjoy his bodily presence only at intervals, and these intermittent apparitions will have as their purpose to strengthen their faith and to prepare them for the final separation. When he ascends to his Father, he will establish a still more intimate union between himself and them, but of a different kind. The sentiments that he will inspire will be more purified, more disengaged from all earthly elements, in a word, more supernatural, like those that the elect in heaven have for him.[19]

Mary faithfully carried out her mission to the disciples. She told them: "I have seen the Lord, and this he said to me." But many among them, obstinately skeptical, refused to believe her. This is what we gather from the final words of St. Mark: "Hearing her, they did not believe that Jesus was alive and had appeared to her."[20]

Jesus' Beloved Disciple has left us his personal recollections with a precision and vividness of coloring which only an eyewitness would be able to attain. On the other hand, the Synoptics have transmitted to us a fragment of catechesis of an entirely different kind. Here, first, is St. Matthew's version: "After the Sabbath, toward the dawn of the first day of the week, Mary Magdalene and the other Mary came to see the sepulcher." Then the Evangelist recounts the earthquake, the opening of the sepulcher by an angel who had descended from heaven, and the terror and flight of the guards. He continues thus:

"And the angel said to the women: 'Fear not, for I know that

---

[19] Among the exegetes who come close to our explanation we may cite Schanz and Lagrange and the conservative Protestants, Westcott and Zahn. A word of St. Augustine put them on the right road: "Quod vides, hoc solum me esse putas; noli me tangere." Mary, thinking too much about the man, is in danger of forgetting that he is God. Westcott mistakenly arrests the meaning after "I have not yet ascended to my Father." As Zahn has rightly remarked, the sense is incomplete unless the phrase which follows is added: "I am about to ascend there." Despite the change of construction, which makes the sentence somewhat clumsy, the two phrases give the reason for the γάρ (*for* I have not yet ascended to my Father . . . *but* I am about to ascend there; οὔπω γὰρ ἀναβέβηκα . . . ἀναβαίνω). Lagrange says accurately: "The message given to Magdalene is only a parenthesis and the force of the δὲ should be appended to ἀναβαίνω."

[20] Mark 16:11. St. Mark generalizes, as does St. Luke, 24:11. The incredulity of the disciples is only partial.

you seek Jesus who was crucified. He is not here; he is risen, as he said. Come and see the place where they laid him. And go quickly to tell his disciples that he is risen from the dead, and that he goes before you into Galilee, where you shall see him. Behold, this is what I have to say to you.' They straightway departed from the tomb, filled with fear mingled with joy, and they ran to announce these things to the disciples. And behold, Jesus met them, saying, 'Hail!' And drawing near to him they embraced his feet and adored him. Then Jesus said to them: 'Fear not. Go, tell my brethren to return to Galilee, and there they shall see me.' "[21]

We are already familiar with St. Matthew's literary procedure. We know that he is fond of composite discourses and condensed narrative. He likes to use the categorical plural; that is, as St. Augustine observes, he attributes to a whole group what is done by one member of the group. For example, he says:

---

[21] Matt. 28:1 Ὀψὲ δὲ σαββάτων, τῇ ἐπιφωσκούσῃ εἰς μίαν σαββάτων. *Vespere autem sabbati, quae lucescit in prima sabbati.* The Latin is doubly obscure, because the relative *quae* has no reference to anything, and ὀψέ, instead of being translated by *vespere,* should be rendered *sero,* as St. Ambrose and St. Jerome remark. But the Greek is no clearer. Still the two phrases should be mutually explanatory, and the second can only mean: "at the hour (τῇ, understanding ὥρᾳ) when the first day of the week was beginning to break." It is useless to object that St. Luke (23:54) employs ἐπιφώσκειν to indicate the beginning of the Sabbath. The use of the word there can be justified by the custom of lighting the torches on Friday evening, at the commencement of the Sabbath; but it is inapplicable to any other day of the week. The *Gospel of Peter,* which uses the word capriciously and incorrectly (vv. 8, 33, and 36), cannot be cited as an authority.

Since the second member clearly indicates Sunday morning, ὀψὲ σαββάτων should approximate the same sense. The word ὀψέ means *late, too late,* and, by extension, *after.* It cannot mean "at a late hour on Saturday," as *vespere sabbati* would seem to indicate, for the holy women would not have started out while it was still the Sabbath. Hence it means "after the Sabbath," in whatever way it is understood.

Severus of Antioch, or the author of the discourse mistakenly attributed to St. Gregory of Nyssa (MG, XLVI, 662), cites three examples of ὀψέ meaning *after:* ὀψὲ τοῦ καιροῦ (*when the opportunity had passed*), ὀψὲ τῆς ὥρας (*after the hour*), and ὀψὲ τῆς χρείας. Others could be added: ὀψὲ μυστηρίων, ὀψὲ τούτων (Philostratus, *Vita Apollonii,* iv, 18: vi, 10), ὀψὲ τῆς μάχης (Bauer, *Wörterbuch zum N.T.*). Cf. Tobac, *Revue d'hist. eccl.,* XX, 1924, pp. 229–243.

Billerbeck (*Kommentar,* Vol. I, p. 1052) conjectures that ὀψὲ σαββάτων translates the Hebrew מוצאי שבת, "coming forth from the Sabbath," which means the night after the Sabbath and, by extension, the day following. Dalman proposes the Hebrew אחר לשבת, "after the Sabbath."

"They that sought the life of the child are dead," which refers to Herod alone. He says that the Apostles complained on seeing Martha's sister pour out the costly perfume on Jesus, when only Judas is involved. He frequently uses such generalizations. On Calvary the passers-by blasphemed, the robbers insulted Christ, the chief priests railed at him. St. Matthew does not indicate any exceptions.

The same procedure is followed in the story of the Resurrection. The holy women come to the sepulcher; they find the tomb empty; they see an angel who entrusts to them a message for the disciples; they run full of fear and joy, and announce what they have seen and heard; Jesus appears to them; they embrace his feet and adore him. Thus are facts presented in a catechesis. All, as a matter of fact, is applicable to the *group* and tells in brief form their individual and collective experiences. The hearer or reader who is curious for details must consult the living tradition in order to distinguish times and places and to discover what part belongs to each of the actors.[22] None of the Evangelists have the intention or the time to tell everything.

St. Luke describes another aspect of the same scene:

"After having observed the Sabbath rest, according to the law, the women came to the sepulcher on the first day of the week, very early in the morning, bringing the aromatic spices which they had prepared. They found the stone rolled back close to the tomb, but entering they did not find the Lord Jesus. They knew not what to think of this; whereupon there appeared to them two men clothed in dazzling raiment (of white); in fright they bowed their heads to the ground. They said to them: 'Why seek among the dead him who is living? Remember what he said to you while he was yet in Galilee: The Son of Man must be delivered into the hands of sinners, and be crucified, and rise again on the third day.' They remembered these words and, withdrawing from the tomb, they repeated all these things to the Eleven and to all the rest. They were Mary Magdalene and

[22] About the two robbers, see St. Augustine (*De consensu evangel.*, III, 16, no. 53; ML, XXXIV, 1190–1191). Cf. Levesque, *Nos quatre Évangiles,* 3 ed., Paris, 1923 (*Quelques procédés littéraires de Saint Matthieu,* pp. 273–364). The author proves that the apparition to Magdalene and to the holy women is one and the same incident described in detail by St. John, while St. Matthew traces a simple outline sufficient to the purpose of his Gospel (pp. 320–323).

Joanna and Mary the mother of James and their companions who told these things to the Apostles. And these tales were like nonsense to them and they did not believe them."[23]

This narrative of St. Luke does not mention any apparition of Christ and leaves in the shade the preponderant role of Mary Magdalene, the visit of Peter and John to the tomb, and the message that the holy women were ordered to carry to the Apostles. But in compensation it discloses to us two facts of capital importance for the solution of difficulties: namely, that the women, several of whom had made preparations beforehand, were numerous, and that the Eleven had with them several other disciples. We may consequently conclude that the holy women naturally did not all keep together in one group, that their experiences and impressions were varied, and that many of their listeners ridiculed what they said.

St. Mark's account, again, is different:

"The Sabbath having come to an end, Mary Magdalene, and Mary of James, and Salome brought aromatic spices, that they might anoint (the body of) Jesus. Very early in the morning, the first day of the week, they come to the tomb, after sunrise. And they were saying to one another: 'Who will roll back for us the stone that closes the entrance?' And raising their eyes they see that the stone has been rolled back; now it was very large. And having entered the tomb, they saw a young man seated at the right side, clad in a white robe, and they were frightened. He says to them: 'Fear not. You seek Jesus of Nazareth who was crucified. He is risen, he is not here; behold the place where they laid him. But go, tell his disciples and Peter that he goes before you into Galilee, where you shall see him as he told you.'

---

[23] Luke 24:1–11. In the Vulgate St. Luke adds: "But Peter ran to the sepulcher and, upon stooping down (toward the interior), he saw only the linen cloths; and he went away, marveling at what had come to pass." The authenticity of this verse is disputed by some critics, but it is accepted — rightly, we believe — by Tischendorf, Von Soden, Vogels, and Merk.

According to St. Luke, besides Magdalene, Joanna, and Mary of Cleophas, *other women* who were with them went to see the tomb. They were those who had been present at the drama of Calvary (Luke 23:55–56; cf. 23:49) and who everywhere accompanied Jesus. Now these women were *numerous* (Luke 8:2), which is also gathered from St. Mark (15:41) and St. Matthew (27:55). The large number of holy women is a circumstance worthy of note.

They went forth from the tomb and fled, trembling and beside themselves; and they said nothing to anyone, for they were afraid."[24]

Here St. Mark's narrative abruptly stops; the rest is on another theme and, perhaps, by another hand. This is not the place to study the critical problem here presented, but it is impossible that the author intended that his Gospel should end with the words, "they were afraid." We confine ourselves to noting the apparent conflict between the two indications of time: "very early in the morning," and "after sunrise." It could not have escaped the attention of the Evangelist; a seven-year-old child would notice it. Consequently, either the Evangelist must have combined, in his concise narrative, the departure of two distinct groups of women, or several of them must have delayed on the road to complete their preparations or to wait for latecomers.

It is now possible to unravel this apparently very tangled skein. Early Sunday morning, the holy women make their way to the sepulcher in one or more groups. Mary Magdalene is with them; but on seeing that the heavy stone has been moved back from the tomb, she runs to tell the Apostles. During this time, her companions see the angel and receive his message, and several of them eagerly hurry to deliver it. They have left the tomb when the two Apostles arrive; and these in turn have gone away when Mary Magdalene returns and finds herself alone. The rest is known. She sees two angels at the two extremities of the burial couch. Soon Jesus appears to her; she throws herself at his feet, embracing them. This gesture St. Matthew in his customarily summary and synthetic narrative attributes to the group of holy women. The only difficulty concerns the apparition of the angels in the three Synoptics; but this difficulty is considerably reduced if we reflect that heavenly spirits, unlike men, make themselves visible or invisible as they please. St. Matthew says that the angel rolls the stone back from the tomb and sits upon it; but he does not say that the angel stayed in the same place all the time and kept the same attitude. Hence

[24] Mark 16:1–9.

the holy women, on their arrival, could have failed to see him; he does not appear to them until after the departure of Magdalene.

How much time was consumed in these comings and goings? Two or three hours, perhaps more. When the disciples from Emmaus left Jerusalem, they already knew of the apparition of the angels to the holy women, not the apparition of Christ to Magdalene.

5. The Emmaus Disciples

(LUKE 24:13–32)

It may have been eight or nine o'clock in the morning, or a little later, when two disciples left the Holy City to return to their homes. Pilgrims did not have to spend that whole week in Jerusalem, as was the custom at the Feast of Tabernacles. On the 16th of Nisan, the day following the Paschal solemnity, the first sheaf which had been harvested on the eve of the feast in a sheltered spot in the Valley of Cedron was offered to the Lord; but this ceremony, in which Christians were fond of seeing an image of Christ who finds life in death, as the ear grows from the seed buried in the earth, had no such symbolism for the Jews to attract them or keep them in the city.

One of the travelers was named Cleophas; the name of the other is not given.[25] This has led several authors to think, without the slightest probability, that St. Luke here designates himself under the veil of anonymity. The travelers had learned, before their departure, of the apparition of angels to the holy women and of the visit of the Apostles Peter and John to the empty sepulcher; but they still did not know of the apparition of Christ to Magdalene, much less of the one with which the Prince of the Apostles was favored during the course of the day. While they were walking along, they were conversing about the drama of the past few days, and as they called to mind these events, so disconcerting to their expectations and their hopes, their souls were in complete turmoil.

While they were exchanging these melancholy reflections, a

---

25 St. Cyril of Alexandria thinks that his name was Simon, but he was not one of the Apostles. St. Ambrose, on what grounds we do not know, calls him Ammaus or Ammaon.

traveler, whom they had not noticed before, stopped purposely to wait for them or hastened his steps to join them. It was Jesus; but they did not recognize him. Sadness kept them from looking at him closely, and, by reason of the privilege that glorified bodies have of concealing or manifesting themselves as they please, he did not look the same as usual.

To break the restraint which the unexpected encounter seemed to cause them, Jesus asked in a familiar way: "What was the conversation that you were having together, and what makes you so sad?" Cleophas answered: "Art thou then the only stranger in Jerusalem who knowest not the events that have happened in the last few days?" "What events?" asked the Unknown. "Of Jesus of Nazareth, the prophet mighty in work and word before God and man; and how the chief priests and our rulers caused him to be condemned to death and crucified. We ourselves were hoping that he would be the deliverer of Israel. And it is now three days since all this happened. Some women of our company, it is true, went very early to the tomb, and not finding the body, told us that they had seen angels who declared that he is alive. Then some of our company went to the tomb and found things as the women had said, but him they did not see."

The faith of the disciples was as imperfect as their hope. They regarded in Jesus the prophet, the wonder-worker, the liberator of Israel, rather than the Son of God and the Saviour of the world. Formerly they had hoped in him; now they are very close to despair. The miracle of the empty tomb and the witness of the angels do not satisfy them. Perhaps, like Thomas, they would like to see with their own eyes the risen One, and to touch him with their hands to assure themselves that he is not a phantom. "O undiscerning spirits and hearts slow to believe what the prophets have spoken! Was it not necessary that the Christ should suffer to enter into his glory?" What was paralyzing their faith was the expectation, so common among their fellow countrymen, of a Messias triumphant from the beginning, who would not need to purchase glory at the price of suffering. During the rest of the journey, Jesus set himself to instruct them. He explained to them the meaning of the prophecies concerning him, from Moses down to the last of the seers inspired by God.

The disciples felt themselves stirred and set on fire within as they gave ear to his words, and the hours seemed short. Too soon for them, Emmaus came into sight. It was the end of the journey. The pilgrims started to leave the main road to reach their lodgings, and Jesus made as if to continue on his way. He would indeed have left them, if they had not insisted on detaining him. "Stay with us," they said, "for it grows late and the day is on the decline." At the spring equinox, when the sun sets everywhere at six o'clock, the day may be said to start declining at three o'clock. At least, this was the Semitic manner of speech. And perhaps the disciples, anxious to keep their mysterious companion with them forced the expression a little, insisting on the lateness of the hour.

Jesus was only waiting to yield to their request. He followed them to their lodging, which was probably the house of Cleophas himself, and took his place with them at table. The disciples had already been impressed on the road by his air of authority; but what was their astonishment when they saw him, the guest and the stranger, take bread and bless it and distribute it, as was customary at the beginning of a meal for the master of the household. At that moment their eyes were opened and they recognized him in the breaking of the bread; for they had more than once seen him perform this familiar action. But when they raised their eyes to look at him more closely, he had disappeared.

A certain number of commentators, especially of the sixteenth and seventeenth centuries, thought that the bread distributed was the Lord's body, and from this they drew the authority for defending Communion under one species. This opinion, which is in itself admissible, raises not a few difficulties, and the majority of modern exegetes refuse to subscribe to it. The disciples of Emmaus were not Apostles; they had not been present at the institution of the Eucharist; nothing suggests that they knew anything about it. Is it possible that Jesus would have given them his Body without any previous indication? If, at times, the Eucharistic Bread was distributed to little children who had not reached the age of reason, the universal Church never sanctioned this practice and did not allow it to become general. The Church demands that the communicant be able to distinguish the Eucharist from ordinary bread. It is sometimes said that the *breaking of the bread* naturally designates the Eucharist, but this is not exact. To break bread is a Biblical expression that simply means to take a meal. Except in liturgical ceremonies, it does not take on the sacramental meaning of consecrating the Body of Christ or of partaking of It. As for the texts of the Fathers cited in favor of this opinion, either they do not prove, or they are too few to constitute a tradition.

This episode, "one of the most finished and most suggestive stories to be found in any language," as it is called by an author little open to the suspicion of partiality, has inspired many artists. The place where it unfolded cannot be a matter of indifference to us. Two places vie with each other in claiming to be the Emmaus of the Gospel. Happily, owing to the generosity of the French, both of them are in the hands of Catholics. One of them, entrusted to the sons of St. Francis, has been a much-frequented place of pilgrimage for centuries, and its distance from Jerusalem, eight and a half miles or sixty stadia, corresponds aptly to the data of the Vulgate. The other, favored by a unanimous local tradition up to the Crusades, contains the remains of a magnificent and very ancient church. The Crusaders, in rebuilding it on a more modest plan, took care to respect the triple apse and the remains of the triple nave. This is neither the time nor the place to discuss a question which has divided Catholic authorities and is after all of secondary importance for the understanding of the Gospel.[26]

The disciples, full of joy at seeing the Lord, immediately rose and started back to Jerusalem. They kept saying to each other: "Was not our heart burning in our breast while he was speaking to us on the road and was explaining to us the meaning of the Scriptures?" Had they been attentive, they could have recognized him even before from this sign.

6. Apparitions in the Cenacle[27]

The Emmaus disciples arrived in Jerusalem after nightfall. They immediately sought out the Apostles and found them

[26] See Note Y: *The Question of Emmaus.*

[27] The first apparition in the Cenacle on the evening of Easter is recounted by St. John (20:19–29) and St. Luke (24:36–43). It cannot be doubted that both refer to the same fact, but St. John speaks only of the Apostles and pays

gathered together in a place where all the doors had been carefully closed for fear of the Jews. What was there to be afraid of? Some untoward happening or, perhaps, merely some act of spying. Let us recall that, before the descent of the Holy Ghost, the Apostles did not always give evidence of heroic courage.

As soon as the travelers from Emmaus made themselves known, they were eagerly admitted. They learned that since their departure the Lord had shown himself to Simon Peter, something that does not seem to have caused so much surprise, considering his exceptional position in the Apostolic group. But, when the new arrivals told what had happened to them: how Jesus had accompanied them without their recognizing him, and how their eyes had been opened at the breaking of the bread, doubts arose on all sides, and they were treated as visionaries. This can be inferred from the conclusion of Mark, for he implies at least a partial unbelief.

Such was the state of affairs when Jesus unexpectedly made his appearance through the walls of the closed room without the slightest noise announcing his coming. The laws of gravity and impenetrability, which govern material substances, do not constrain glorified bodies. The first reaction of those present, confronted by a phenomenon so new to them, was a feeling of stupor and fright. Vainly did the Saviour try to reassure them by letting them hear his voice and by wishing them peace; they believed that they were in the presence of a ghost. "What is it that disturbs you," he said to them, "and why do these confused thoughts arise in your hearts? See my hands and my feet; it is I myself. Touch me and bear in mind that a spirit has not flesh and bones, as you see me to have." And speaking thus he showed them not only his hands and his feet, but also his side opened by the soldier's lance.

No reasonable doubt is any longer possible; but, according to the profoundly psychological statement of St. Luke, "excess

---

attention solely to them. St. Luke, who has mentioned the presence of the disciples besides the Eleven, insists chiefly on their incredulity. To convince them, Jesus must show them his wounds and eat some fish in their presence. The Vulgate adds "a honeycomb" (*favum mellis*), but these words are lacking in the majority of Greek manuscripts. The incredulity emphasized by St. Luke (24:37–41) is also attested in Mark's conclusion (16:12–13: "nec illis crediderunt").

of joy and surprise made them incredulous." The reality seemed too wonderful; they could not believe in so much happiness, and they wondered if they were not the plaything of a dream. Jesus said to them: "Have you not something to eat?" They gave him a piece of roasted fish left over from their frugal meal; he took it and ate it in front of them, to complete the effort to convince them that he was not a specter. Then their faith was whole and their joy without alloy.

It was not solely to console the faithful and to strengthen their faith that Jesus showed himself to them on this occasion. He came to bring to the Apostles the complement of the priesthood he had conferred upon them at the Last Supper by ordaining them to perpetuate the Eucharistic sacrifice. He had then given them power over his Sacramental Body; he wishes now to give them power over his Mystical Body. He addresses only the Apostles; St. John, who names only them, leaves no doubt about it. "Peace be to you! As my Father has sent me, I also send you." Then, having breathed upon them, he said: "Receive ye the Holy Ghost; whose sins you shall forgive, they are forgiven them; whose sins you shall retain, they are retained." Today the Saviour is keeping the promise once made to the Apostles, that he would give them the specifically divine power to forgive the sins of those whom they would judge worthy. He confers it upon them by a kind of sacramental rite, breathing upon them to signify the invisible conferring of the Holy Spirit; perhaps also, as some of the Fathers have thought, to teach them that the Holy Ghost proceeds from him. This is not yet the gift of Pentecost, when the Holy Spirit will inaugurate his visible mission to effect the internal transformation of the faithful and to unite them in such a way as to constitute the body of the Church.

One of the eleven Apostles — named Thomas in Hebrew and Didymus in Greek, that is, to say, The Twin — was not present at this reunion. We do not know why he was absent. His obstinate skepticism and his attitude in the whole affair would lead us to suspect that his reasons were not good. But it would be going too far to suppose that he was designedly holding aloof from his colleagues, finding them too credulous and believing himself wiser than they. When they told him of the Saviour's apparition, he refused to believe it: "Unless I see in his hands the imprint of the nails; unless I put my finger into the place of the nails, and put my hand into his side, I will not believe." Impressionable and impulsive, quick to see the dark side of things and to conjure up chimeras, Thomas was one of those men who are disconcerted by disappointment and who cling readily to a fixed idea. He recalled the bruised and bloody corpse as he had seen it the day before yesterday taken down from the cross; and he was not able to persuade himself that that body, having scarcely a human form any longer, should have so quickly recovered life and beauty. Such obstinacy could not have lasted so long in an Apostle without the special permission of God, who wished to teach us a lesson. It is a formidable lesson for anyone who blindly adheres to his own opinion.

The following Sunday the Apostles again happened to be together, and this time Thomas was with them.[28] As on the previous Sunday, Jesus entered through the closed doors and said: "Peace be to you!" Then turning to Thomas, and showing him the scars of his wounds, he said to him: "See my hands and put into them thy finger; and thrust thy hand into my side; and be no longer incredulous but believing." He employs exactly the same words that Thomas had used in phrasing his unreasonable demand, doubtless to shame him and recall him to his senses. Did Thomas persist in his stubbornness? Did he dare make the test that the indulgent goodness of his Master allowed him? Many of the Fathers and commentators think that he did.[29] But need he be brought so low without plausible reasons? We think that he recoiled before such an outrageous act. Jesus' words were a permis-

---

[28] John 20:24–31. "After eight days" (20:26). This brings us to the following Sunday.

[29] Toletus and Maldonatus are of this opinion, but the latter brings forward a proof which everyone will find weak, though it is borrowed from St. Augustine: "Illud *vide* idem est quod *tange;* et hoc *vidisti* idem est quod *tetigisti."* The equivalence of *touch* to *see* is not too obvious. Weaker still is the argument that Belser draws from 1 John 1:1: "Quod vidimus oculis nostris et manus nostrae *contrectaverunt* de Verbo vitae." The reference here is clearly to the whole mortal life of the Incarnate Word and not to the apparition in the Cenacle. Schanz finds the stubbornness of Thomas, who wishes absolutely to touch after having seen, very *psychological.* Westcott, Zahn, Lagrange, etc., think the opposite. Jansenius of Ghent, Knabenbauer, and Corluy give no opinion on this point.

sion, not a command. The mere sight of the pierced hands and the opened side must have been enough to wrest from him that cry of adoration: "My Lord and my God!" What sentiments of faith, of respect, of humble supplication, of ardent prayer, of repentant love were in that weeping exclamation! His eyes revealed to him only a man, but faith led him to adore a God.

St. Thomas' confession goes farther even than that of St. Peter himself. No one up to that time had called Jesus, "My Lord and my God."[30] The simple title of "Lord," which strangers and disciples bestowed upon Jesus, could be no more than a mark of politeness and respect. But after his death when he had solemnly affirmed his royalty before Pilate, and after God had raised him up and had consecrated him "Lord and Christ," the name of Lord was given to him in a wholly different sense. It is well known that in the Septuagint the word "Lord" is the translation of the name of the God of Israel, of the sacred Tetragram which the Jews avoided pronouncing; and that from the time of Augustus the name "Dominus" was attached to the person, or rather the function, of the Roman Emperor. To say to someone "My Lord" was to acknowledge allegiance to him; it was to speak to him as subject to sovereign, as a believer to his God. The prayer *Marana tha* ("Come, Our Lord") contained, for the first Christians, not only an expression of their ardent desire, but also an abridged profession of faith. In pronouncing it they rendered homage to their King and their God.

Jesus said to Thomas: "Because thou hast seen thou hast be-

---

[30] John 20:28: "Thomas answering said to him: 'My Lord and my God'" (*εἶπεν αὐτῷ· ὁ Κύριός μου καὶ ὁ Θεός μου*). Whether these words be taken in the nominative (*You are my Lord and my God*) or, as usage permits, in the vocative (*O my Lord and my God!*), the meaning comes to the same. Note that Thomas speaks to *Jesus* and answers *him*. The exegesis of Theodore of Mopsuestia, who sees here nothing but a cry of surprise or admiration addressed to God, was condemned by the context and by common sense before being condemned by the Church ("Condemnation of the Three Chapters by the Second Council of Constantinople," can. 12; Denzinger-Umberg, 224). On the *strong* meaning of the word "Lord," see L. Cerfaux, *Le titre Kyrios et la dignité royale de Jésus*, in the *Revue des sciences philosophiques et théologiques*, 1922, pp. 40–71, and 1923, pp. 125–153. This study brings into focus the very erudite but tendentious book of Bousset, *Kyrios Christos*, 2 ed., 1922. W. Foerster, *Herr ist Jesus*, Gütersloh, 1924, will be found useful.

lieved. Happy are they who have not seen and have believed." Happier in the sense that the happy witnesses of the Resurrection are those simple souls and docile hearts that respond to testimony, to the affirmation of eyewitnesses, without demanding direct evidence before believing. Do we not read that St. Louis refused to go to see a Eucharistic miracle when everyone was running thither, so as not to lose the merit of his faith in the Real Presence?

Extenuating circumstances may be allowed to have their weight in favor of Thomas, but they cannot altogether excuse him, for Jesus Christ himself blames him for his unbelief. What can be unreservedly admired is his confession of faith, which contains an abbreviated Christology. In St. John's Gospel, Jesus had often proclaimed himself God, but no one before Thomas had given him the title. "By one of those frequent reactions in the moral life, he raises himself by one bound from the lowest degree of faith to the summit, and proclaims the divinity of his Master more explicitly than any of his colleagues."[31]

---

[31] Godet, *Evangile de saint Jean,* 4 ed., III, 500. This sudden transition from the most obstinate unbelief to the most lively faith has impressed all the commentators. P. Lagrange writes (*L'Evangile de J.-C.,* p. 594; English transl., Vol. II, p. 294): "From him, the Unbeliever, came the first explicit act of faith in the divinity of the Risen Christ." And P. Durand (*Saint Jean,* p. 517): "It was reserved to the unbelieving Thomas to be the first to formulate this full profession of faith."

CHAPTER XIV

Apparitions in Galilee

1. On the Shore of the Lake of Tiberias[1]

(JOHN 21)

AFTER the close of the Paschal season, there being nothing to keep the Apostles in Jerusalem, they took the road back to their native country. The Saviour had promised to go there before them and had appointed a meeting, without, however, specifying the time and place. During the period of waiting, time hung heavily on the hands of these men, accustomed as they were from their earliest childhood to the roughest kind of labor. Then too, since they were without resources, they must think of making their living. Thus, when Simon Peter expressed his intention of resuming his former way of life, those of his comrades who were with him at the time instantly answered: "We are going with thee." They were seven in all: Peter, who here as usual takes the initiative; Thomas, called in Greek Didymus or "The Twin"; Nathanael, sometimes called Bartholomew, who was from Cana; the two sons of Zebedee, James and John; and finally, two others whose names the Gospel does not give. There is reason to believe that they were Andrew, the brother of Peter, and Philip who, like them, was from Bethsaida. The Apocryphal *Gospel of Peter* proposes Matthew, the publican from Capharnaum; but nothing picks him out especially for this expedition, and his former profession did not at all prepare him for it.

[1] This chapter is an appendix to the Gospel, the conclusion of which is found in the preceding chapter; but it forms an integral part of it, since it is certainly from the same hand and there is not a Greek manuscript nor a version that does not contain it.

It was easy to find a boat, for the two families of the four great Apostles had each its own. The sequel of the narrative seems to indicate that they used an apparatus very frequently employed in our own time for night fishing. It was a dragnet about a hundred yards or more in length, made up of a triple net attached along its whole length to one cord. Using a boat, the fishermen stretch it out wide in a straight line, and then they row all around the outside to beat into it the fish. These swim very readily through the wide meshes of the two outer nets, but when they reach the net in the middle they get more and more entangled by their very efforts to disengage themselves. The haul is often abundant, but it happens at times that the labor of entire nights results in no catch at all.[2]

On this occasion, the Apostles experienced this at their own expense. And so, seeing that day was beginning to break, they lost courage and were already pulling the net aboard when, in the glimmer of the beginning dawn, they descried a man standing on the beach. They took him for an early morning traveler. "My children," said the Unknown, "have you any provisions?" The familiar address, "My children," did not surprise them, since it was commonly used when speaking to young people or those of lower condition. In the dim early light and at that distance they could not clearly distinguish the one that had spoken to them. Hence they did not suspect that it was Jesus. They thought that the stranger wanted to buy or to ask for some fish. They had nothing either to sell or to give away; so they answered with a dry "No," spoken in the gruff tone that unlucky fishermen or hunters use when asked an indiscreet question. Without allowing himself to be rebuffed by this discourteous reception, the Unknown quietly said: "Cast the net to the right and you will find some." His tone of authority impressed them, and they also knew from experience that a man on the shore is always in a better position

---

[2] On the maneuvering of the dragnet (in Arabic *mebatten*), consult Biever in *Conférences de Saint-Etienne,* 1911, pp. 304–307; or Masterman, *Studies in Galilee,* Chicago, 1909, p. 41. These authors do not agree on details; thus Biever gives the dragnet a length of 328 ft., and Masterman 636; this is the minimum and the maximum. The maneuver of the dragnet requires at least four men; but there are sometimes two boats, the fish being beaten into the nets from both sides. The one boat used by the Apostles seems to have been small (John 21:8: πλοιάριον).

to direct the fishing and to give useful advice. One of them therefore seized a loose net which happened to be in the boat and skillfully gave it a wide, circular sweep.[3] The result was as quick as it was unexpected. The net became so full that the combined efforts of the Apostles were scarcely enough to gather it in, and they were unable to haul it aboard without capsizing the boat.

Such an astounding prodigy could come only from the Master. John, who got the first intimation of it, said confidentially to Peter: "It is the Lord." The same thought had perhaps come confusedly to Peter; but when he heard John say, "It is the Lord," he did not hesitate an instant more. Binding about his loins, for ease in swimming, the kind of smock or sleeveless blouse which was the only clothing he was wearing, he cast himself boldly into the water.[4] They were no farther from land than about two hundred cubits — a hundred yards or so — and Peter easily reached the bank, perhaps without getting beyond his depth, since the beach went down to the lake at a very gentle slope.

Meantime his comrades reached the shore by rowing, dragging behind them the heavily loaded net. On landing they saw a fire lighted, with a fish placed on the embers and beside it some bread.[5] Jesus said to them: "Bring me some of the fish you have

---

[3] There is no longer question of the dragnet, since the setting of it would require too much time, but of the cast net, called in Greek ἀμφίβληστρον. What establishes this are the two verbs employed here: βάλλειν, "to cast," "to throw" (instead of χαλᾶν), and σύρειν, "to draw." These apply to the cast net but not to the dragnet.

[4] John 21:7: τὸν ἐπενδύτην διεζώσατο, *tunica succinxit se.* The word ἐπενδύτης means, according to its etymology, "outer garment." This would be, at that time, the mantle of heavy material which served the peasants as a bed and a covering, but we cannot think that Peter took a garment like that to swim to shore in. Besides the mantle would be *put on* but not *wound around.* Hence we are forced to understand by ἐπενδύτης a kind of blouse or smock which laborers wore at work. Thayer, *Lexicon,* 4 ed., and Billerbeck, *Kommentar,* Vol. II, p. 537, define: "a kind of blouse or frock"; "eine Art Tunika." Note that Peter does not put this garment on; he is already wearing it loosely, and he binds it around his loins (διεζώσατο) to swim more easily. He was *naked* (*erat enim nudus*) only as the laborer in Virgil (*Georg.,* I, 299: Nudus ara, sere nudus) or Hesiod (*Works and Days,* 389: γυμνὸν σπείρειν, γυμνὸν δὲ βοωτεῖν), dressed very lightly.

[5] John 21:9: ἀνθρακιὰν κειμένην καὶ ὀψάριον ἐπικείμενον καὶ ἄρτον. The word ὀψάριον (diminutive of ὄψον, "cooked" or "fried food") means "little foods," especially a small amount of fish, the ordinary meal of the lakeside people and of travelers. The two words ὀψάριον and ἄρτος can be understood in the singular

caught." They had not yet drawn the net up on the shore. Peter therefore leaped into the boat to help. When they had disengaged and spread out on the shore 153 large fish, the Apostles must have cried out, "Miracle!" But what surprised them still more was that the net, overloaded as it was, had not broken. Many of the Fathers of the Church have searched for mysteries in this number of 153, but their conjectures are so divergent that they do not seem to rest on any solid foundation. It is better to see in it nothing more than the exact indication given by an eyewitness, anxious to testify to future generations an extraordinary fact, which he himself guarantees.[6]

And now the Apostles found themselves face to face with Jesus whom they could no longer fail to recognize, though his outward aspect was not altogether the one familiar to them. His features breathed superhuman majesty, his carriage and his manner of acting had something of the ethereal. If, during his mortal life, his mere presence inspired them with respect and reserve, after the Resurrection these two feelings became so lively that they dared not approach too near to him nor address him, and this restraint tempered their joy. Then, too, what would they have said to him? Ask him who he was? But how could they still have any doubt?[7]

It was he who first broke the silence: "Come here, and eat." At the same time, to put them at their ease, he distributed the bread and fish to them with his own hands. Some think that by a new miracle he multiplied, in proportion to their need, the one

---

(a fish, a piece of bread) or in the partitive sense (some fish, some bread). The proof that there were not several fish is that Jesus asks the Apostles for some. If there was only one piece of bread, it must be said that he multiplied it miraculously.

[6] According to some authors, the number 153 symbolizes the totality of the elect, since there are but 153 species of fish (St. Jerome); but Pliny numbers only 144, and modern naturalists find many more. The majority break the number down into three parts (100 — 50 — 3) and in general they see the Trinity in the number 3; 100 can symbolize converts from Gentilism and the 50, those from Judaism (St. Augustine). Abbot Rupert has a lucky discovery, which Maldonatus judges to be very reasonable: 100 would mean married people 50 widows and widowers, 3 virgins. For other *figures* of the kind, see Knabenbauer or Maldonatus.

[7] John 21:12: "None of the disciples dared ask him: 'Who art thou?' knowing that it was the Lord." St. John Chrysostom well describes this embarrassment of the Apostles and explains it (*In Joan. hom.*, lxxxvii; MG, LIX, 496).

fish he had prepared for them before their arrival. This is possible; but why would he have required from them the result of their catch, unless he wished to make use of it? Did he eat with them or not? On this point appropriate reasons are given on both sides, but all rather weak. On the other hand, it is hard to deny all symbolical meaning to the two kinds of food served, for bread is a figure of the Gospel and also of the Eucharist, and it is well known that in the primitive Church the fish became a symbol of Christ.

After the meal, which took but a short time, Jesus addressed Peter, as if he had come only for him. Indeed, it was especially for him that he had come. He is about to keep the promise he had made him seven or eight months before at Caesarea Philippi, when he said to him: "Thou art Peter and upon this Rock I will build my Church, and I will give thee the keys of the kingdom of heaven." Before raising him to the supreme dignity and conferring upon him the guardianship of the flock for which he had shed his blood, he wishes to assure himself that Peter is worthy of it and to make him prove it before the others, and to give Peter himself the occasion to efface his triple denial by a triple protestation of love.

The scene that follows is one of such charming beauty that one would hesitate to analyze it by cold commentary, even if it were possible to translate into our tongue the delicate shadings of the original. The Greeks have two words to express the sentiment which we designate by the general term "love." The first designates purified love, dictated by free choice, proceeding from the will more than the heart, though its intensity at time reacts upon the sense faculties. This is the love of charity which we have for God or for our neighbor for the sake of God. The other love is a spontaneous, I almost said instinctive, feeling which common blood or gratitude or constant and familiar intercourse causes in us. It is the affection we have for our parents, our benefactors, and our intimate friends. The Vulgate attempts to preserve the distinction of the two words by translating the first (ἀγαπᾶν) by *diligere* and the second (φιλεῖν) by *amare*. In the following dialogue these shades of meaning should be kept in mind:

Jesus — "Simon, son of John, lovest thou me (*diligis*) more than do these?"

Peter — "Yea, Lord, thou knowest that I love (*amo*) thee."

Jesus — "Feed my little lambs."

Jesus (*addressing him a second time*) — "Simon, son of John, lovest thou me (*diligis*)?"

Peter — "Yea, Lord, thou knowest that I love (*amo*) thee."

Jesus — "Guide my little sheep."

Jesus (*addressing him a third time*) — "Simon, son of John, lovest thou (*amas*) me?"

Peter — "Lord, thou knowest all things; thou knowest that I love (*amo*) thee."

Jesus — "Feed my sheep."

Hearing himself questioned thus: "Simon, son of John, lovest thou me more than do these?" Peter's confusion reaches the lowest depths. He who a few days before had cravenly denied his Master, could he pretend that he loved Jesus with the love of charity more than all his companions? He answers that he does indeed love him; for he is conscious of loving him more than as a friend, more than as a benefactor, more than as a father. Jesus repeats his question, omitting the comparison that has so much perplexed Peter, and he can do nothing but repeat his protestation. But when Jesus addresses to him the same question for a third time, and in such terms that he seems to doubt even his friendship, Peter in complete distress appeals to the Saviour's divine knowledge. He who knows all things must know, without needing to be told, the tender and generous affection that his disciple has vowed to him.[8]

---

[8] St. Ambrose, with his refined literary taste, has accurately grasped these shades of meaning. He thus presents the dialogue (*In Lucam*, x, 179, ed. Schenkl, 1902, p. 526):

I. *J*. Simon, Johannis, *diligis* (ἀγαπᾷς) me plus his?
P. Utique, tu scis, Domine, quia *amo* (φιλῶ) te.
J. Pasce *agnos* (ἀρνία) meos.
II. *J*. Simon, Johannis, *diligis* (ἀγαπᾷς) me?
P. Utique, tu scis, Domine, quia *amo* (φιλῶ) te.
J. Pasce *oviculas* (προβάτια) meas.
III. *J*. Simon, Johannis, *amas* (φιλεῖς) me?
P. . . . Tu scis quia *amo* (φιλῶ) te.
J. Pasce *oves* (πρόβατα) meas.

He then gives the distinction between *diligere* and *amare* (a distinction which is even truer in the case of ἀγαπᾶν and φιλεῖν): "Videtur mihi dilectio habere

Jesus is not ignorant of Peter's love, but he wishes to hear it from his own lips, and to have the other Apostles know, in order to justify in their eyes the eminent dignity with which he is about to invest him. To him he is confiding, as to his representative on earth, the guardianship and care of his whole flock: lambs, little sheep, and sheep. In our view, these last expressions are only three terms of endearment, serving only to lend variety to the discourse; they designate indiscriminately all the faithful. In one way or another, the whole flock of the Good Shepherd, without distinction, is placed under the shepherd's crook of Peter. He receives the charge, not only to provide it with nourishment, but to lead it. He will discharge the office of pastor in all its fullness. He will guide it to healthy grazing lands and will turn it aside from poisonous pasturage. The ideal picture which the Good Shepherd has traced of himself must henceforth be applied to Peter and his successors; for the privilege conferred upon the chief of the Apostles is not a personal favor; it is granted for the Church, because the sheepfold of Christ can never dispense with its shepherd.

While delegating his sovereign authority to Peter, Jesus is reserving another favor for him, the favor of sharing his cross. After he had said to him, "Feed my sheep," immediately and

---

animi caritatem, amor quemdam aestum conceptum corporis ac mentis ardore." Thus *dilectio* (*caritas*) is in the will, *amor* is in the heart. St. Ambrose rightly supposes that Peter has both, only — and this St. Ambrose does not say — Peter wishes to answer only for his *friendship,* the feeling of which he is conscious, whereas no one can be certain of having the love of charity.

The Saint remarks that the third time Peter "jam non agnos ut primo, nec oviculas ut secundo, sed oves pascere jubetur, perfectiores ut perfectior gubernaret." It seems certain that St. John wished to vary the terms and to establish an ascending gradation: lambs, little sheep, sheep; agnos, oviculas, oves; ἀρνία, προβάτια, πρόβατα. But the difference between προβάτια and πρόβατα is slight and copyists have accidently put one for the other. Editors have failed to notice this: Tischendorf and Hort have πρόβατα, Soden and Vogels have προβάτια in both places.

In the three answers of Jesus, the Vulgate has *pasce,* but in the second, the Greek substitutes ποίμαινε for βόσκε. The two verbs are almost synonymous and can both be used to express the whole charge of a shepherd. Still βόσκειν properly means "to nourish" domestic animals, "to give them pasture"; ποιμαίνειν means "to lead to pasture," "to govern," "to direct." Hence the expression, *pastors of the people* (ποιμένες λαῶν), to designate kings. Philo (*Deter. pot. insid.,* 25, Kohn edit., p. 263) clearly establishes the distinction between βόσκειν and ποιμαίνειν.

without transition he adds: "Amen, amen, I say to thee, when thou wast young thou didst gird thyself and didst go where it seemed good to thee; but when thou shalt be old, thou shalt stretch forth thy hands, and another shall gird thee and lead thee where thou wouldst not go." Peter in his old age will be led in chains to the prisons of Rome and thence to the Hill of the Vatican, to undergo an infamous punishment abhorred by nature, despite the aspirations of grace. Fixed to a gibbet, he will stretch forth his hands to be nailed to the wood of the cross, as his Master had been. The allusion to the kind of death that awaited the Apostle is manifest; the event itself will clarify what prophecy may have left obscure.

Before disappearing, Jesus addressed this word to him: "Follow me!" On the eve of the Passion, Jesus had said to Peter, when he professed to be able to follow him wherever he should go: "Where I go, thou canst not follow me now, but thou shalt follow me later." Then he was going to immolation, to Calvary. He now points out to Peter the same road of sacrifice, opening up to him the more or less distant prospect of martyrdom, as if he were saying to him: "Didst thou wish to follow me to death? Well, this is the time to begin. Follow me!"[9]

But Peter, too much moved to grasp the Saviour's allusion, took his command literally and began to follow Jesus who was departing. When John, by an instinctive movement, began to follow his example, he abruptly turned about and seeing that John was accompanying him, he said to Jesus: "And he, Lord, what of him?" The phrase is elliptical but nowise ambiguous. He wishes to know what fate awaits his companion. His curiosity is, without doubt, legitimate; but it is ill-timed. It draws an answer which has the sound of a rebuke. "If I wish him to remain until I come, what is it to thee? As to thee, follow me." The answer is purposely obscure, since nothing indicates whether the condition is to be fulfilled or not. But among John's disciples there

---

[9] Many think that Jesus commanded Peter to follow him in order to entrust to him a secret. But why such an *aside* when he had nothing more to say to him, and actually says no more? What meaning would such an order have at the moment when Jesus is withdrawing from the sight of all of them while repeating the mysterious "Follow me"?

was no hesitancy in giving it an affirmative meaning. When they saw the Beloved Disciple reach — or perhaps live beyond — the end of the first century, the rumor was spread abroad everywhere that he would not die, and that he would be present in body and soul at the second coming of Christ. In vain did he reopen his Gospel and add a chapter to it to stamp out this error, and clearly specify that Jesus had not said: "I wish him to remain so until I come," but "if I wish him to remain," which is something entirely different.

It made no difference. Even after he breathed his last sigh at Ephesus, his disciples were persuaded that he was not really dead. Some said that he was, indeed, laid to rest in the tomb prepared at his command, but, while the faithful were absent, his body had disappeared; others claimed that he was sleeping a peaceful sleep there, and that the breath of his respiration fluttered the dust on top of his tomb. The legend persisted up to the fifth century. St. Augustine, who reports it, does not conceal his skepticism; but he does not dare to deny the truth of a fact attested, says he, by witnesses deserving of respect. He adds that it belongs to those who are on the spot to verify it.

This was the third apparition of Jesus to all the Apostles or to a group of them. It was not to be the last.

2. On a Mountain in Galilee

On the eve of the Passion, Jesus had promised the Apostles that he would go before them into Galilee when he should come forth from the tomb. After the Resurrection, he notified them of the command that they should go there and await him.[10] He would appear to them on a mountain which he indicated to them, either before their departure from Jerusalem or, more probably, after their return to Galilee. Was it Thabor or the Mount of the Beatitudes? At least it was in the familiar surroundings where they had seen the first flowering of his miracles and teaching.

The Eleven faithfully kept the appointment, and they probably did not come unaccompanied. "When they saw the Lord, they

[10] Before the Passion, Matt. 26:32; Mark 14:28; after it, Matt. 28:7–10; Mark 16:7.

prostrated themselves before him, but some doubted."[11] After the apparitions in Jerusalem, the Apostles could no longer doubt the fact of the Resurrection, but perhaps, seeing the Master so different from what he was formerly, they feared an illusion of the senses. If there is question of real doubt, it must be said, either that other disciples were mingled with the Eleven, or that St. Matthew, in his habitual manner, combines the apparitions of Christ to the Apostles into a single narrative and alludes retrospectively to their past doubts. At all events, it is to the Eleven alone that Christ addresses these last recommendations:

"All power has been given to me in heaven and on earth. Go therefore, teach all nations and baptize them in the name of the Father and of the Son and of the Holy Ghost, instructing them to observe all that I have commanded you. And behold, I am with you unto the consummation of the world."

Not in virtue of the eternal generation, but by the fact of the Incarnation, the Father has given the Son power over every creature. He has established him as the mediator of grace, as supreme legislator, and universal judge, in the world which he came to ransom. In founding the Church, Jesus delegates this power to his Apostles; to them he entrusts the threefold mission of teaching, baptizing, and enforcing the observance of his law. "Teach all the nations," to lead them to the faith that is the principle of salvation; "confer Baptism," which is the seal of faith and the gate of entry into my kingdom; "instruct them to observe my law" in its entirety, without which Baptism and faith would be of no avail to them.

Baptism is the consecration of man to God, and the three divine Persons are named, on a basis of perfect equality, as the term of this consecration. It is true that the Christian could be consecrated to the Trinity without the explicit naming of the Three Persons, but Catholic tradition has from the beginning seen in the words of St. Matthew the obligatory formula of Baptism. If Jesus' hearers did not from the beginning penetrate the full meaning of the formula, "it is directed toward the future, and will shortly be

[11] Matt. 28:18. Levesque (*Nos quatre Évangiles,* 4 ed., 1923, pp. 328 and 336–347) proposes another translation which would eliminate the difficulty, a translation which P. Lagrange accepts (*Saint Matthieu,* p. 543: "Seeing him they prostrated themselves, those who had doubted").

interpreted to the Apostles by the Holy Spirit, together with so many other sayings of Jesus that they have imperfectly understood."[12]

The powers with which the Apostles are invested become the endowment of the Church in the persons of their successors. In order that the deathless Church may be able to carry out her mission, that she may be infallible and indefectible, she has need of the divine assistance that will never be lacking to her. Her Founder has promised to abide with her until the consummation of the ages. He will abide in her through his Spirit, the vivifying soul of the Church; he will abide through his mystical presence in that organism of which the faithful are the living members; he will abide with her through his sacramental presence and by the communion which binds together and perfects the union of Christians with one another and with Christ.

There were several other apparitions of which the Gospel does not speak. St. Paul mentions some of them, when he writes to the Corinthian skeptics: "The risen Christ appeared to Kephas, then to the Twelve, then to more than five hundred brethren together, many of whom are dead, but the greater part are still alive; then he appeared to James, then to all the Apostles."[13] The apparition to Kephas — this is the Aramaic name by which St. Paul ordinarily designates the Prince of the Apostles — was already known to us through an allusion in St. Luke. St. Jerome has preserved for us a curious fragment of the *Gospel according to the Hebrews* on the apparition with which James, the Brother of the Lord, was favored. James had sworn not to taste bread from the hour when he partook of the chalice of the Lord until the day when he should see him risen from the dead. "After the Resurrection the Lord took bread and blessed and broke and gave it to James, saying: 'My brother, eat thy bread, for the Son of Man is risen from the dead.' "[14] As to the apparition to the five hundred brethren together, many of whom were still living twenty-seven

[12] Lebreton, *Dogme de la Trinité,* 6 ed., 1927, p. 340 (English transl., *History of the Dogma of the Trinity,* Lebreton, trans. Thorold, I, p. 258). On the formula of Baptism, see Note Z: *Baptism in the Name Of.*

[13] 1 Cor. 15:5–7. See Note X: *Apparitions of the Risen Christ.*

[14] St. Jerome, *De viris illustr.,* 2.

years later when St. Paul was writing his First Letter to the Corinthians, we would know nothing of it at all were it not for this brief and incidental mention by the Apostle of the Gentiles. Was it such a well-known fact that the Evangelists judged it superfluous to mention it? At all events, their silence should not surprise us. St. John warns us that the whole world could not contain the books if all the deeds and words of Jesus should be written down. And this is particularly true of the period with which we are at present concerned. We know scarcely anything about it, and we are sure that there is much that we do not know. Witness this simple summary by St. Luke, at the beginning of the Acts: "After his passion, Jesus showed his Apostles by many proofs that he was alive, appearing to them during forty days and speaking to them concerning the kingdom of God."[15] The intermittent and rapid apparitions and the short conversations recounted by the Evangelists, even with the supplementary data supplied by St. Paul, present very inadequately the constant meetings of forty days of which St. Luke speaks. In his discourse at Caesarea, St. Peter asserts that the Apostles "ate and drank with the Saviour after his resurrection." He ate in their presence on the evening of Easter, and they ate in his presence on the shore of the Lake of Tiberias. But nowhere is it written that they ate and drank with him, except perhaps on the day of the Ascension; and one isolated incident, it would seem, would be insufficient to justify such a general assertion.

The Evangelists by no means intended to narrate everything. They could not omit the apparition of Christ to the Apostles, who are by reason of their office and their calling the qualified witnesses of the Resurrection of their Master. The other manifestations were of secondary importance; it was enough to mention them all together and to give some examples according to the purpose and convenience of each. The ending of St. Mark furnishes us with a specimen of this primitive catechesis and of the schematic form in which it was clothed:

"Having risen from the dead early in the morning on the first day of the week, he first appeared to Mary Magdalene, out of whom he had cast seven devils. She went and announced it

[15] Acts 1:3.

to the disciples, who were mourning and weeping. And they, when they heard that he was alive and had appeared to her, did not believe it.

"After that he manifested himself in another form to two of them who were traveling to the country. And when they came to tell the rest, even they were not believed.

"Finally he manifested himself to the Eleven, while they were at table, and he reproved them for their want of faith and hardness of heart, because they had not believed those who had seen him risen from the dead."[16]

The difficulty which the disciples had in convincing themselves of the Resurrection, for which they were to be witnesses, is set in high relief by the Evangelist. Mary Magdalene is treated as a fanatic; the pilgrims of Emmaus are considered visionaries; to disarm the unbelief of the Apostles, Jesus must present himself in person, and eat in their presence and severely upbraid them. The picture is complete; the details that might be added would only tax the memory of the readers and hearers to no purpose. Catechetical instruction requires brevity. This one closes with a brief summary that abstracts from time and space:

" 'Go into the whole world to preach the Gospel to every creature. He that believes and is baptized shall be saved, but he that does not believe shall be condemned. And these signs shall attend those that believe: in my name they shall cast out devils, they shall speak new tongues, they shall take up serpents, and if they drink any deadly poison it shall do them no harm; they shall lay hands on the sick and they shall be cured.'

"And the Lord, after speaking to them thus, was taken up into heaven and sits at the right hand of God. But they went forth to preach everywhere, while the Lord gave them aid and confirmed their word by the miracles that accompanied them."[17]

The catechetical style suppresses intervals and distances. If we did not possess the narrative relegated by St. Luke to the Book of Acts, we would believe that all the facts mentioned in St. Mark's ending — the Resurrection, the apparitions, the Ascension,

---

[16] Ending of Mark (16:9–14), first part.

[17] Ending of Mark (16:15–20), second part. On the authority of this ending, see the decree of the Biblical Commission (Denzinger, 2156).

the departure of the Apostles for distant lands — all happened on the same day. To put them in the place that belongs to them, we must have recourse to other sources.

3. The Ascension[18]

The stay of the Apostles in Galilee was at most two or three weeks, for they were on their way back to Jerusalem more than ten days before Pentecost. They were brought back to the places that had witnessed our Redemption either by the need of their hearts or, more probably, by a call from on high. During the forty days that ran their course between the Resurrection and the Ascension, Jesus did not cease to give them numerous and irrefragable proofs of his new life. He allowed them to see him and touch him, he answered their questions, and sometimes he sat down to table with them. Still it was not the constant and easy companionship of other days. He appeared and disappeared unexpectedly, without their being able to call for him or to prolong his visits. The ordinary theme of these conversations was the kingdom of God under its various aspects. He recalled to them the promise he had made them, to send the divine Paraclete to them, and the mission he had given them to preach the Gospel to all peoples by inviting them to repentance. But he kept coming back insistently to a point that had always found them refractory. He kept saying to them, alluding to the events that had happened before their eyes: "These are the words which I spoke to you while I was yet with you: it must be that all that is written of me in the Law of Moses, in the Prophets, and in the Psalms have its fulfillment." We know well how difficult it was for the Jews

[18] Mark's ending (16:19) mentions the Ascension briefly: "The Lord Jesus having said these things was taken up into heaven and sits at the right hand of God." St. Luke, reserving the story of the Ascension for the Acts, narrates in a few words what happened before the Ascension, and he places this summary immediately after the apparition in the Cenacle on the evening of Easter Sunday. It would be unreasonable to conclude, with certain of the critics, that in the author's mind the Ascension took place the night of Easter. The formulas used by St. Luke ("Now he said to them," 24:44; "now he led them forth," 24:50) allow of intervals more or less long between what precedes and what follows. We know from Acts 1:3 that the interval between the Resurrection and the Ascension was forty days.

to accept the idea of a suffering Messias; and the Saviour, despite repeated assertions, had not succeeded in familiarizing the Apostles with the thought of his ignominious death, even if it were to be followed by his triumphant Resurrection. He must even now "open their minds" to inculcate in them the necessity of his death and his Resurrection. This time the Apostles learned the lesson so well that thenceforth they always placed at the foundation of their preaching the twofold dogma of the redemptive death and the glorious Resurrection.

And now, the hour of final separation was about to strike. Jesus visited his own once more, probably in the upper room where he had instituted the Eucharist. Sitting down to table with them,[19] he enjoined upon them not to leave Jerusalem, but to wait for the Paraclete whom he had promised them in the name of the Father. "John," he said, "baptized with water, but you shall be baptized with the Holy Spirit not many days hence." The Apostles listened avidly to his words, for they had the presentiment that they were the last that would fall from his lips. But some of them, their imaginations fired by national dreams, interrupted him with this question: "Lord, wilt thou at this time restore the kingdom of

---

[19] Acts 1:4: *καὶ συναλιζόμενος*. We translate "and eating with them," as do all the ancient versions (Latin, Syriac, Coptic, Ethiopian, Armenian), and all the ancient commentators and a good number of the modern. A very incomplete list may be found in W. Bauer, *Wörterbuch,* 1828, p. 1257. The Greek word in this sense is rare, but less rare than has been thought. Cf. R. Bowen, *The Meaning of συναλιζόμενος in Act. i, 4,* in *Z.N.T.W.*, XIII, 1912, pp. 247–259. It comes from σύναλος, *consalineus* or *consalaneus* (*Thesaurus* of H. Estienne, Paris, Didot). Ducange (*Glossarium,* Niort, 1883) thus explains the *consalaneus,* σύναλος: "contubernalis qui eodem sale utitur, conviva." Literally, therefore, it should be translated "sharing salt with them" (ἅλς, ἁλός). In fact, that is how the Philoxenian Syriac Version translates it. Cf. Zorell, *Lexicon,* 2 ed., 1931.

Others think of the very common word συναλίζω (from ἁλής, *assembled*), which means "to reunite"; but what meaning would the participle συναλιζόμενος have in the context? If taken in the middle voice, it would be "and reuniting, he commanded them." Reuniting whom? A complement is indispensable. If taken in the passive, it is "and being reunited." But an individual cannot be said to be "reunited," at least unless it is said with whom the reunion takes place. Besides, the aorist participle would be used and not the present.

Some adopt the reading of a small number of cursive manuscripts συναυλιζόμενος, "and spending the night with them," "staying with them." But this late reading is negligible. If it were the original reading, no one would have conceived the idea of changing it, easy reading as it is. It is surprising that Milligan (*Vocabulary,* 1928), depending upon Cadbury, is inclined to adopt it. But Cadbury only proves that the change of αυ to α is possible and frequent.

Israel?" It was not the place to explain anew the meaning of the prophecies referring to the restoration of the throne of David, and Jesus confined himself to replying: "It is not for you to know the times or seasons which the Father has fixed by his own authority; but you shall receive the power of the Holy Spirit who shall come down upon you, and you shall be my witnesses in Jerusalem and in all Judea and Samaria, and even to the ends of the earth."

Saying these words, he rose from table and went forth with them from the city. He led them in the direction of Bethany, as far as the summit of the Mount of Olives, where he had been accustomed to instruct them, and where he had pronounced the discourse on the destruction of Jerusalem and the end of the world.[20] Then he raised his hands to heaven to bless them yet once more, and they saw him rise into the air. There, they knew not how, a cloud suddenly hid him from their sight. As they continued to keep their gaze fixed on high, two angels clothed in white approached them and said to them: "Men of Galilee, why stand you here looking up on high? This Jesus, who has been taken up to heaven far from you, will come again some day in the same way as you have seen him ascend into heaven."

Recovered from their shock, the disciples took the road back to Jerusalem, which was distant from them only the distance that it was allowed to journey on a Sabbath day. They ascended to the upper room of the Cenacle, where they stayed assembled

---

20 On the summit of the Mount of Olives, near the place where the road leading to Bethany crosses the saddle of the hill to go down the eastern slope, there used to be two famous sanctuaries: the Eleona or Constantinian basilica of the *Teaching of Christ,* and the *Imbomon* or the Church of the Ascension. These two monuments were not more than 60 or 70 yds. apart. From there, the Temple and the whole City of Jerusalem were spread under the eyes of the spectator as if on a relief map. The Eleona covered the grotto where, according to tradition, Jesus was accustomed to instruct his Apostles and where he sometimes spent the night when the lateness of the hour prevented him from pushing on to Bethany. There he was said to have pronounced the long discourse on the end of the world and the destruction of Jerusalem. The traditional place of the Ascension was to the left, that is to say, to the north of the Bethany road, on a small elevated hillock, which before the end of the fourth century was enclosed in an octagonal church, often reconstructed and now turned into a mosque. On the history and present state of the Church of the Ascension, see Vincent-Abel, *Jérusalem,* II, 36-373.

together under Mary's maternal eye. Thus it is that the Evangelists describe the scene of the Ascension, with a simplicity and calmness of detail which is in happy contrast to the verbose descriptions of the Apocrypha and the mystics.[21]

The Apostles came back from the Mount of Olives filled with a holy cheerfulness. Forty days earlier, when Jesus had announced his coming departure to them, they had been inconsolable. In vain had he told them again and again that he was ascending to his Father to prepare a place for them, that he would not leave them orphans, that he would send the Paraclete, that they would soon see him again; nothing had been able to assuage their grief. And now that they have only the remote prospect of his return at the end of time, they are exultant and overflowing with joy. The explanation is that they are somehow changed. Their love for Jesus, ardent as ever, has become purified, more spiritual, more detached from all that is of the senses. If they have known Christ according to the flesh, they know him so no longer. They are no longer desirous, as was Mary Magdalene, to grasp his adorable feet and bathe them with their tears. The past is no more; it cannot live again; all their thoughts turn to the future. The Ascension fills them with the sentiment that it should inspire in us also: "Being risen with Christ, seek the things that are above, where Christ is seated at the right hand of God. Love the things that are above, and not the things here below."[22] This sentiment the Church suggests to all the faithful by making the Ascension the feast of supernatural joy, of holy desires, and of hope. Everything in the Catholic liturgy bears this mark. The Mass of the day at the Introit, at the Offertory, at the Communion, is a hymn of jubilation and of triumph.

The motive of this joy is easy to grasp. Christ's victory is our

---

[21] *Ascension of Isaias* (Edit. Tisserant), Paris, 1909, xi, 23–32. Isaias sees the Son of God mount to the *seventh* heaven, and traverse in an opposite direction the road which he had descended for the Incarnation. Passing through the various heavens, he is acclaimed and adored by the angels and by Satan himself, who is confined to the lowest heaven in the firmament.

Brentano, *Vie de N.-S. J.-C.*, according to the visions of Anna Catherine Emmerich, Paris, 1861, VI, 199: "When the Lord arrived at the summit of the mountain, he appeared resplendent with whiteness as the light of the sun, and from heaven there descended a luminous sphere from which shone forth all the colors of the rainbow." A long description in this style.

[22] Col. 3:1–2.

victory, the victory of all of us. In his Ascension, he opens up to us heaven, which was closed until now. We know that he ascends there to overwhelm us with blessings.[23] We are sure to have in him a High Priest "always living to make intercession in our behalf."[24] With such an Advocate, who died and is risen for us, seated at the right hand of the Father, "who shall be able to separate us from the love of Christ?"[25] Such is the sustenance of our hope: "Our country is in heaven, whence we await as Saviour our Lord Jesus Christ, who will refashion our perishable body and render it like to his glorious body, in virtue of that sovereign power which subjects all things to him."[26]

---

[23] Eph. 4:8.
[24] Heb. 7:25.
[25] Rom. 8:35.
[26] Phil. 3:21.

CHAPTER XV

Christ Living in the Church

1. The Work Accomplished

OF THE two essential parts of Christ's work — the raising up of fallen humanity, and the foundation of the Church — the first escapes the observation of the senses and is known to us only by faith. On coming into the world, the Son of God said to his Father: "Sacrifice and offering thou hast not desired; in holocausts and sin-offerings thou hast taken no pleasure, but a body thou hast prepared for me. Then I said: 'Behold, I am come, O God, to do thy will.' " The will of the Father is that he die for our salvation, and "we are sanctified with the offering of his body, which he has made once for all." We need not here detail how the Incarnate Word, having clothed himself with our nature in order to embrace our cause, takes upon himself the curse that weighed down upon us, pays our ransom at the price of his own blood, delivers us from the slavery to which sin had reduced us, restores to us the friendship of God, and reopens to us the gates of heaven. We will consider only that part of Christ's work which falls beneath our observation and the historical development of which can be followed.

Jesus Christ survives in his work. As has been excellently said: "It is not enough to be acquainted with a man's perfections and to know how he has lived; it is important to know what he has left after him, and that in which he survives. For, glorious as he may have been in his rapid passage across human generations, all his glory is a small thing, if it does not perpetuate itself in some grand work."[1]

At first glance this work of Jesus is very modest in appearance. He evangelized fewer countries than St. Paul, and personally brought about fewer conversions than St. Francis Xavier. He traversed Samaria, Phoenicia, and the Decapolis only transiently; the theater of his apostolate was a small district of Galilee, a very restricted portion of Perea, and the city of Jerusalem. Within these narrow limits, what was the fruit garnered? The heart-rending farewell addressed to the three Galilean cities and the tears shed over the Holy City, almost on the eve of his death, are a sufficient answer. Humanly speaking, this great effort ended in failure.

But it would be a serious misunderstanding of the economy of salvation to imagine that the Son of God descended from heaven to traverse the continents and islands one by one and to preach the word of salvation to every individual. His work is to announce the good news to a chosen group of witnesses, who will spread it throughout the universe, and to found the Church as the depository of his teachings, his authority, his Sacraments, and his graces. He is the Sower who leaves to others the work of reaping the harvest.

His Person is an integral part of his Gospel. "Among all the religions that claim to be revealed, Christianity is the only one whose revelation, while transcending history by the wealth of its content, is incarnate in a Person, who not only transmits a teaching, but presents himself as the living truth and justice. . . . The founders of other religions preach a doctrine somehow external to their persons; Jesus is the Teacher who presents himself as the object of our faith. He is its author, and he is its finisher; he is at the foundation as the corner stone, and he is at the summit

[1] Monsabré, O.P., *Conférences de Notre-Dame.*, 49th Conf., *Lent,* 1881, consecrated to the work of Christ, treats of the Redemption and the Church. The greater part is devoted to the Church. On the contrary, in a long study entitled *L'Oeuvre de Jésus-Christ* (*Études Bibliques,* second series, pp. 143–194), the Protestant exegete, F. Godet, says not a word of the Church. He considers only the work of Christ *for us,* the reconciliation between God and man, and the work of Christ *in us,* sanctification. The contrast is significant.

as the God who is adored."[2] To preach his doctrine effectively, he must therefore first of all reveal himself and answer by facts the question which will not fail to be presented to him, as it was presented to the Baptist: "What sayest thou of thyself?" He answers it by the miracles which he scatters in profusion during the first part of his ministry, restoring health to lepers, movement to paralytics, sight to the blind, life to the dead.[3] The witnesses of these marvels, dumfounded by what they see, cannot help saying: "This man would not be able to work such signs, if God were not with him."[4] He is no less powerful in word than in work. The four Evangelists agree in noting the admiration of the multitudes that came to hear him: "Never has man spoken as this man."[5] Their minds were thus inclined to believe him when he declared himself to be greater than Moses, and when he claimed for himself the power to forgive sin or to act with freedom on the Sabbath day as God himself acts.[6]

The ascendancy which this man of the people, this apparently uneducated village carpenter, exercised on those about him was still another mystery. The Scribes, so full of pride in their own knowledge, called him "Teacher"; strangers who had never before seen him bowed down before him; the Centurion of Capharnaum declares himself unworthy to receive him under his roof; the Apostles live on terms of familiarity with him and yet lose nothing of their respect and veneration. When he challenges his enemies to convict him of sin, there is no one to take up his challenge. On several occasions, in Jerusalem as at Nazareth, his gaze unnerves the arms of the enemies, who wish to kill him. The minions of the Sanhedrin sent to arrest him dare not lay hands upon him; the servants of the chief priests who come to apprehend him fall back upon the ground. Manifestly, in this man there is something superhuman; in the words of St. Jerome, it is the divinity shining forth.

With the passage of centuries, the figure of Christ only increases in stature. Even those who have broken with Christianity

---

[2] P. Rousselot and J. Huby, *Christus,* 1916, p. 955.
[3] Luke 7:22.
[4] John 9:33.
[5] John 7:46.
[6] Mark 2:10 and parallels; John 5:17.

see no difficulty in admitting that Jesus is the glory of the human race, and that he towers infinitely above the rest of men. Of these, one of the most celebrated, because of his talent as a writer and because of the scandal of his apostasy, thus concludes his too famous book: "All the centuries proclaim that among the children of men there is none greater than Jesus."[7] Another, less gifted but likewise altogether detached from Christian dogma, sees in Jesus the ideal of moral perfection: "By the heroism of his attitude, by his absolute devotedness, and by his tendency exclusively toward the most sublime heights, Jesus places himself at an insuperable distance, on an eminence so steep and so abrupt that it inspires a kind of terror."[8]

The principal task of Jesus during his earthly pilgrimage was the intellectual and spiritual formation of the Apostles, in view of the foundation of the Church, whose columns they were to be. He calls them at the beginning of his ministry and keeps them closely grouped around himself. Then, after some months of trial, he chooses them and sets them apart, to watch over them with the greatest solicitude. The Day of Parables brings about the first selection among his disciples: the curious or indifferent, drawn by the sight of his miracles or the charm of his words rather than by the desire of instruction or of self-reform, neglect to have explained to them what they do not understand, and they remain strangers to the mysteries of the kingdom of God. The promise of the Eucharist in the synagogue of Capharnaum scatters in turn the disciples of wavering faith, so that Jesus remains alone with the little flock of faithful believers. Then we see a kind of hierarchy established among them: at the bottom of the ladder the chance listeners, at the top the Twelve; and in the middle those who have left all things to follow in Jesus' footsteps, ready for all sacrifices in order to share his labors. It is from this elite group that he will choose the Seventy-Two to prepare the way for him during the last half year of his preaching. But it is to the Apostles themselves that he reserves the better part of his time. Sometimes he leads them beyond the frontiers of Palestine — into Phoenicia and the Decapolis — to commune alone with

[7] Renan, *Vie de Jésus,* last sentence.
[8] Bousset, *Jesus,* 3 ed., Tübingen, 1907, p. 72.

them. What authority, what patience, what attentive care, what sweetness mingled with firmness did he have to display to soften their rough Galilean natures, to uproot the prejudices of their unpolished minds, to correct their false notions, and to initiate them little by little into the mysteries of our Faith. The method employed was that of a progressive and wisely graded education.[9]

In the early days, there was no question either of the Son of God or of the Messias. Jesus seemed deliberately to put aside these titles, whose premature use was not without danger. One of the titles collided with nationalistic prejudices hard to exterminate; the other was in apparent conflict with the sovereignty of God as the Jews then understood it. Toward the end of the Galilean period, seven or eight months before the Passion, the people took him, either for the Baptist risen from the dead, or for Elias or Jeremias or one of the prophets of ancient times. None of them yet thought of the Messias. Peter was the first to answer in the name of all the disciples who had been questioned together: "Thou art the Christ, the Son of the living God." He is not repeating a lesson learned; he is expressing a conviction which the person, the acts, and the words of the Saviour — in default of formal assertion — have imposed upon his mind. But what he had seen and heard, all the others had seen and heard, the same as he. To draw the conclusion he needed the inner light of faith, the inspiration of the Father.

At this date, Peter is designated beforehand to be the foundation of the Church; and the Apostles are designated, with him and under him, to receive the absolute power of binding and loosing. Yet these are still promises to be fulfilled after the death and Resurrection, which become more and more frequently and more and more clearly predicted in proportion as the end draws near. The revelation of the greatest mysteries is held in reserve until the final days. These are the subject of the eschatological discourse, of the conversation after the Last Supper, and the brief

[9] P. Delbrel says very rightly: "To expose what Jesus did for the formation of the Apostles is to recount a great part of his history, because Jesus devoted to this ministry a large part of his life. To this he even subordinated to a great extent what today we would call the organization of his life. To enable himself to spend much time on his Apostles, and also to place and keep them constantly under his influence, he constrained himself to live with them, and made them live with him" (*Jésus éducateur des Apôtres,* 1916, pp. 75–76).

instructions of the Risen Christ. Then it is that he confirms the dignity of Peter as the head of the Church, and entrusts to him the guardianship of his whole flock; then too he delegates to the Apostles the full powers which he himself has from the Father. He teaches them that he and his Father are but one, and that he conjointly with the Father sends the Holy Spirit. He inculcates on them the grand precept of fraternal charity founded on the unity of the faithful with him and with one another, a union so close that it is the image of the union of the Divine Persons. Finally he promises that he will not leave them orphans, but will remain with them until the end of time, and will send to them the Paraclete to enlighten them and to take his place.

2. The Descent of the Holy Ghost[10]

(ACTS 2:1–47)

The Ascension does not put an end to Christ's mission. Before dying, he had promised the Apostles that he would send them the Spirit to complete his work. The Paraclete will guide them in the way of all truth; he will teach them what they were hitherto unprepared to understand; he will aid them in building up the Church of which Christ had simply sketched the plan and laid the foundation. The action of the Spirit will therefore be the continuation and the completion of the work of Christ.

The days that followed the Ascension were for the disciples a time of delightful expectation. Met together in the Cenacle, which recalled to their minds so many sweet memories, grouped around Mary who perpetuated in their midst the living image of her Son, in the company of the henceforth loyal Brethren of the Lord, they truly formed but one heart and one soul. From time to time, someone who had disappeared from their midst, a derelict, victim of the recent squalls, came to rejoin them. They

10 For details, see Boudou, *Actes des Apôtres* (*Verbum Salutis,* VII), 1933, pp. 25–60. The author thus concludes his exposition of the miracle of Pentecost: "This admirable mode of life (of the first converts) gained the favor of all the people for Jesus' disciples. . . . The faithful were judged by their fruits, their lives of piety and charity, which placed them in the first rank of those who were zealous for the Law. Thus all of them were, in their own way, and that not the least effective way, the witnesses of Christ."

spent the greater part of the day in the Temple, joining in the public prayers and improvising their own hymns of praise and thanksgiving. These spontaneous outbursts of fervor, contrasted with the cold and rigid formalism of the Pharisees, vividly impressed the multitudes that had been drawn to Jerusalem by the approach of the feast.

St. Peter did not wait any longer to place himself at the head of the little flock entrusted to his care by the divine Shepherd; and no one disputed his prerogative as leader. The question arose of filling the place left vacant in the Apostolic college by the defection of Judas. Assembling all the faithful to the number of about 120, Peter spoke to them in some such words as these: "Brethren, the prophecy of David concerning Judas must be fulfilled. . . . We must therefore choose, as a witness with us of the resurrection of the Lord Jesus, a man who was in his company from his baptism by John up to the day of his ascension." Two of the disciples filled these requirements: Joseph, called Barsabas and surnamed Justus, and Matthias. In order to leave the definitive choice to Heaven, their names were drawn by lot after a prayer to the Lord to make known which of the two was more pleasing to him. The lot fell upon Matthias, and he was thereafter added to the number of the Twelve.

On the morning of Pentecost, the disciples were met together in the Cenacle at an hour when their attendance in the Temple would have been more natural. They may have had a secret presentiment that a great event was impending. This feast, one of the three principal solemnities of the liturgical cycle, was celebrated fifty days or seven weeks after the Passover, which accounts for the Greek name of Pentecost and the common name of Feast of the Weeks. The name which better expressed its nature and purpose was the Feast of Harvest or Feast of First-Fruits. The harvesting of the barley and wheat being completed, or nearly so, thanks were given to God for the fruitfulness of the soil, and the first two loaves of the new harvest were offered to him.

While the crowd of visitors could not be compared to the multitudes attracted by the Passover and the Feast of Tabernacles, it was more diversified and cosmopolitan. Pilgrims in great number came from distant countries, since the season was favorable for travel by land and sea. They came from all parts of the Empire and even from beyond its frontiers. "Parthians, Medes, and Elamites, inhabitants of Mesopotamia and Cappadocia, of Pontus and the Province of Asia, of Phrygia and Pamphilia, of Libya and Cyrene, Romans and Jews, Cretans and Arabians" mingled together in the narrow streets of Jerusalem and crowded into the environs of the Temple.

It was about nine o'clock in the morning when a noise, like the din of a violent tempest, filled the whole house where the disciples were gathered, but without shaking it, as would an earthquake. At the same time, trails of light, like tongues of fire, came down and rested on each of those present. Thus the Spirit of grace and holiness inaugurated his visible mission under the Scriptural symbols of wind and fire, which characterize his activity.

When this tempestuous noise resounded throughout the city, people flocked from all sides to investigate the cause of a phenomenon so extraordinary at a time of year when the sky is always clear. The disciples themselves, filled with a holy enthusiasm, came down from their retreat and mingled with the crowd, celebrating the praises of God in the various tongues of the pilgrims. This prodigy, presaging the universality of the Church which was destined to speak all languages, struck the new arrivals with amazement. There, as everywhere, were skeptics who had made up their minds beforehand; they said mockingly: "These people are drunk; the new wine has gone to their heads" — a ridiculous accusation at such an early hour of the morning. On the other hand, there were honest and sincere spectators who, seeing in this a sign from heaven, could not refrain from saying: "These people, are they not all Galileans? How is it then that each of us hears them speak our own language?" And this reflection set their feet upon the road to the kingdom of God.

And then Peter began to speak. Being able to speak but one language at a time, he naturally made use of his own, pronounced after the fashion of the Galileans. After explaining the meaning of the miracle they had just witnessed, he demonstrated the Resurrection of Jesus with such power that three thousand of his hearers asked for Baptism. A few days later the number of believers reached five thousand, and, far from slowing down, the movement only accelerated. And thus the Church, founded on Peter, mystically united to Christ and animated by his Spirit, began to live its new life.

After hearing the Saviour say to them: "Go, preach the Gospel to all nations," and after seeing the miracle of tongues which presaged and symbolized the Catholicity of the Church, it would seem that the Apostles had nothing else to do but put on their sandals, take in hand the pilgrim's staff, and spread throughout the vast universe, to sow to the four winds of heaven the seed of the word of life. Still, according to a very ancient tradition which has every chance of being the truth, they did not leave the soil of Palestine until the end of a dozen years. They must follow the order prescribed by their Master: first of all Jerusalem, then all of Judea, then schismatical Samaria, and finally the idolatrous nations; for the Jews, who were the holders and depositories of the divine promises, have a right of priority over all others.

Besides, before establishing churches, it was necessary to establish the Church. Now the Church is not a mere aggregate of believers, nor a federation of Christian communities, nor the sum of national churches; but the house of God, the family of Christ, professing one faith, living one and the same life, under the rule of one head. This is why the Twelve remain in Jerusalem, grouped around Peter, who is their guide, their interpreter, and their inspirer. Together they preach beneath the Temple colonnades, together they ordain deacons and confer the Spirit by the imposition of hands, together they govern the newborn Church; but their individuality is somehow effaced behind the person of Peter. If there is need of speaking, acting, deciding, making laws, Peter always takes the initiative. He is the cornerstone and the keystone of this building whose essential characteristic is unity.

When the time came to disperse, James the son of Zebedee had already fallen, or was about to fall, under the stroke of Agrippa; James, the cousin of Jesus, remained until his death at the head of the Mother Church; Peter, after a roundabout journey, made his way to Rome, the capital of the civilized world; John and

Philip established the field of their apostolate in Asia Minor; Andrew went to the Parthians, and Thomas to the Scythians. It is said that Ethiopia fell to Matthew's lot, and India to Bartholomew's. The traditions about the journeys and labors of the Twelve are more or less uncertain. St. John Chrysostom observed, at the end of the fourth century, that the tombs of most of them were unknown. What would we know of St. Paul if St. Luke had not written about him? According to the plan of divine Providence, the Apostles accomplished a collective and, so to speak, anonymous work. They do not preach themselves; they are not the founders of schools; they are the witnesses, the messengers, the heralds of Christ; and they wish to be nothing else than that. It is proper that their individuality be effaced to allow the work of the Saviour to shine forth in all its splendor.

3. The Mystical Christ

The collective entity which is called the Mystical Christ is compared by St. Paul to a living organism, of which the Church is the body, Jesus Christ the head, and the Holy Spirit the soul.

St. Augustine, the one among the Fathers who has studied this marvelous composite with the greatest love and penetration, points out that Jesus Christ is presented in Holy Scripture under three names and three distinct aspects. There is, first of all, the only Son of God, coeternal and consubstantial with the Father, sharing with him, without division or diminution, his power, his glory, and his divinity. There is also the Incarnate Word who humiliated himself by becoming man, and thus becomes our Brother, our Mediator, and our Saviour. Finally there is what St. Augustine calls the *whole* Christ (*totus Christus*), who somehow completes himself by joining the Church to himself in such a way as to form, according to the expression of St. Paul, a perfect man, of whom he personally is the Head and all the faithful are the members.[11]

[11] St. Augustine (*Sermo cccxli,* ML, XXXIX, 1493–1501): "Tertius modus est quodam modo totus Christus in plenitudine ecclesiae, id est, caput et corpus, secundum plenitudinem perfecti cujusdam viri, in quo viro singuli membra sumus" (1493). "Caput et corpus unus est Christus, non quia sine corpore non est integer, sed quia et nobiscum integer esse dignatus est qui et sine nobis semper est integer, non solum in eo quod Verbum est unigenitus Filius aequalis Patri, sed in ipso homine quem suscepit et cum quo simul Deus et homo est" (1499).

The revelation of this mystery was made to the Apostle when he heard himself thus addressed on the road to Damascus: "I am Jesus whom thou art persecuting." Paul had not persecuted Jesus of Nazareth, but he had persecuted his disciples. There was, therefore, between him and them an identity, mystical but real, allowing what concerns them to be attributed to him. We already knew this from the Gospel, in the sentence passed at the Last Judgment: "I was hungry and you gave me to eat; I was thirsty and you gave me to drink. . . . Whenever you did these things to one of my brethren, it was to me that you did them." Thence comes that *communicatio idiomatum* which would appear so strange to us, if we did not know the mystical identity of Christ and Christians. "As the body is one and has many members, and these members, many as they are, do not prevent the body from being one, so also it is with Christ."

The Church is therefore the *pleroma,* the complement of him "who wholly completes himself in all" his members.[12] Not that there is anything lacking to the fullness of Christ. But as the Word, infinite as he is, completes himself in his role as redeemer by uniting himself to human nature, without which, in the present order of providence, he could not be our savior, so too the Incarnate Word completes himself by uniting himself to the Church by a bond of which Christian marriage is the symbol. "Do you understand this, my brethren?" cries St. Augustine. "Admire, exult! We have become Christ. For if he is the head and we the members, the whole man is he and we. Hence the fullness of Christ is the head and the body, Christ and the Church," the Bridegroom and the Bride.[13]

At Nazareth the Incarnate Word "grew in stature, in wisdom, and in grace," not as God, but as man; now he continues to grow, not in the Person of the Incarnate Word, but in the body that forms with him one principle of fruitfulness. He lives in the Church, and the Church lives by him. He infuses the divine life

---

[12] Eph. 1:23. Cf. Prat, *Théologie de Saint Paul,* I, 357–358 (English transl., *Theology of Saint Paul,* trans. Stoddard, Vol. I, pp. 296–299).

[13] St. Augustine (*In Joannem,* tract. xxi, no. 8; ML, XXXV, 1569). There are many similar texts in St. Augustine's works. They will be found quoted, or at least indicated, in Mersch, *Le Corps Mystique du Christ,* Louvain, 1933, II, pp. 34–131 (English transl., pp. 384–440).

throughout this grand organism by faith and charity, which link the members individually to the head; by the Sacraments, which are the ordinary channels of grace; by the *charismata,* conferred with the purpose of perfecting the saints, for the work of the ministry, unto the building up of the Body of Christ. "Through him the whole body, well organized and solidly knit together, thanks to the mutual aid of the members, which operate each according to its measure, increases and builds itself up in charity."[14] And so it will be up to the consummation of the ages, up to the limit fixed by God for the expansion of his Church.

4. Christ the King of Souls

Humanly speaking, the preaching of the Gospel was doomed to certain failure. The dogmatic and moral teaching of the new religion, and still more, if possible, its intransigent exclusiveness, should have fatally arrested its progress. Christian morality runs into conflict with all the passions that rule the world: ambition, pride, covetousness, cupidity, egoism; it preaches virtues most contrary to the instincts of fallen man: chastity, humility, self-forgetfulness, renunciation. Christian dogma is founded on the redemptive death and the Resurrection of Christ. Now if the Saviour's Cross was a scandal to the Jews and folly to the Gentiles, the resurrection of the dead was for the latter an extravagant idea unworthy of examination. When Paul enraptured the Areopagus with his lofty considerations about the Unknown God from whom we derive life, movement, and being, the word "resurrection," by itself, suddenly broke the charm. The greater part of his hearers sneered. The more genteel, wishing to hide their irritation and mockery under a polite formula, said to him: "On these matters we will hear thee some other time." They were referring the Apostle to the Greek Kalends. The Roman Procurator Porcius Festus did not show Paul the same consideration. Hearing the Apostle mention the Resurrection, he gruffly interrupted him: "Paul, thou art talking nonsense! Too much reading has robbed thee of thy senses." Still, despite

[14] Eph. 4:12–16. For the meaning see Prat, *Théologie de Saint Paul,* I, 360–362 (English transl., I, 305–307).

sarcasm and insult, the death of Christ and his Resurrection were always, as was proper, the invariable theme of the first preachers of the Gospel.

Again, the greatest obstacle to the spread of Christianity was its aspiration to be the universal religion which would supplant all others. Such a fantasy appeared to the Romans to be very dangerous to the State. Every citizen was bound to worship the national divinities, adding, if he cared to, the gods of his own choice. What difference would one god, more or less, make in a pantheon peopled by so many idols? The conquerors annexed the divinities of conquered peoples. The Jews alone were exempted from conforming to the State religion, but this was a racial privilege which the Christians could not benefit by except by being confused with the Jews. Once the distinction was made, they were bound, as were all other subjects of the Empire, to the worship of the Caesars, which was an integral part of the religion of Rome. To refuse was the crime of *laesa majestas,* which would place them outside the law. The emperors and proconsuls could never understand their scruples. They would say to them: "Sacrifice to the Genius or the Fortune of Caesar; offer incense to Jupiter, and you will save your life. Otherwise the beasts or the stake awaits you." What was asked of them? Merely to pronounce a word and to make a gesture. What foolishness to persist in refusing! The whole history of the persecutions is there. For three centuries the struggle between the persecutors and victims continued with equal obstinacy on both sides; but the victims finally triumphed over the persecutors.

The definitive triumph of Christianity is ordinarily dated from the Edict of Milan of 313; a manifest error, belied by the facts. Before the battle of the Milvian Bridge and the defeat of Maxentius, an edict signed by the Emperor Galerius and by Licinius and Constantine, still a pagan, was published at Nicomedia on April 30, 311. It stated that the Emperors, for the purpose of reform and public order, had desired to bring the Christians back to the religious institutions of their ancestors, but that the Christians always remained obstinate despite the rigorous measures employed against them; hence it was expedient to authorize them to live as they pleased. In return for this toleration they should pray to their god for the prosperity and security of the Empire.[15] Was not this an official admission that the Church had conquered and that the pagan offensive had wholly failed?

When the Church emerged from the catacombs, its ascendancy over souls was even more astonishing than its prodigious expansion.[16] Has history ever seen a gathering of genius comparable to the defenders of the Church in the second half of the fourth century — men like Basil, the Gregories, and Chrysostom in the East; Ambrose, Jerome, and Augustine in the West, to mention only a few names? Expiring paganism could oppose to them only some grammarians like Symmachus, or prolific writers like Macrobius, or a cloud of rhetoricians, the most celebrated of them being Libanius. The Church preserves across the ages her role of educator of the human race. She saved learning and civilization from barbarism; and if the principles of morality and public law have made any progress in the modern world, it is to the Church that the world owes it without being conscious of the debt.

But it is not enough that Christ should rule over the minds of men; he wishes also to rule over their hearts. A short time before his death he said: "When I am lifted up I shall draw all things to me." Strange paradox, unheard-of marvel, that a crucified man should inspire not pity but love! And this prodigy has been realized. "One man alone has rendered all the ages tributary to him by a love that is never extinguished. King of minds, as he is,

---

[15] The Latin text of the edict is reproduced by Lactantius, *De morte persecutorum,* 34 (ML, VII, 249–250). Galerius was dying at the time — he died the fifth of the following May — and it is possible that the edict was due to the initiative of Licinius and Constantine. The ferocious Maximinus Daia did not subscribe to it; but in the following year, even he ordered his Praetorian prefect to bring an end to the persecution; and the reason he gives is that neither by fear nor by persuasion could anything put an end to the obstinacy of the Christians. Some manuscripts of Eusebius (*Hist. eccl.,* ix, 1, Schwartz ed., 1908, pp. 802–804) have the Greek translation of this document.

The persecutors had come to recognize that it was impossible to exterminate Christianity without ruining the Empire. An end was put to mass executions, and the death penalty was replaced by enforced labor in the mines, the horrible precaution being taken of mutilating those condemned, to prevent them from taking flight.

[16] Harnack (*Die Mission und Ausbreitung des Christentums,* 4 ed., 1924, p. 947, note 1) estimates that in the year 312, before the Edict of Milan, there were 900 episcopal sees in the East and 800 or 900 in the West. Richter (*Das weströmische Reich,* 1865) had arrived at almost the same results.

Jesus Christ is also King of hearts; and by a favor that certifies the perfection belonging to him alone, he has conferred upon his saints the privilege of arousing also in the memory of man a devoted and steadfast remembrance" (Lacordaire).

Who among men was ever more loved than he? Incalculable is the number of those who have rendered to him the testimony of their blood, for the age of martyrs did not close with Constantine. In every period of her history, the Church has passed through persecutions as treacherous as that of Decius, as bloody as that of Diocletian. Without going back any farther than the last century, Christ has found in China, in Tonkin, in the Indies, in Africa, witnesses as heroic as in the time of Nero and Domitian. But there is a proof of love even superior to the sacrifice of life. It is the total gift of self. And this proof Jesus Christ alone has ever demanded; and he alone obtains it from millions of human beings who aspire to impress upon themselves the image of the Crucified. "Anathema," cries St. Paul, "be he that loves not our Lord Jesus Christ."

If his love is not loved by a greater number of men, without doubt it is that it is too little known. May this book, so imperfect and so unworthy of such a subject, so little like the ideal it dreams of, contribute a humble part in making him better known, in his Person that saves us, in his Gospel that enlightens us, and in his Church that makes us live his life.

SUPPLEMENTARY NOTES

NOTE M

The Jewish Calendar at the Time of Christ

1. The Yearly Cycle of Feasts

Jewish Month	*Corresponding to*	*Date*	*Feast or Solemnity*
1. Nisan	March-April	1	New Moon; Liturgical and Religious New Year
		14	Pasch or Passover; Slaying of Paschal Lamb
		15	First Day of Azymes, Unleavened Bread; Solemn Rest
		16	Offering of First Sheaf
		21	Last Day of Unleavened Bread; Close of Paschal Feast
2. Iyyar	April-May	1	New Moon
		14	Second Passover (for those unable to celebrate the first)
3. Siwan	May-June	1	New Moon
		6	Pentecost; Offering of First Fruits
4. Tammuz	June-July	1	New Moon
5. Ab	July-August	1	New Moon
6. Elul	August-September	1	New Moon
7. Tishri	September-October	1	New Moon; *Rosh ha-shanah;* Civil New Year
		10	Feast of Atonement (*Kippur*)
		15–21	Feast of Booths or Tabernacles
		22	Close of Feast; Day of Rest
8. Marḥeshwan	October-November	1	New Moon
9. Kislew	November-December	1	New Moon
		25	Dedication (Ḥanukkah); Eight Days
10. Tebeth	December-January	1	New Moon
11. Shebat	January-February	1	New Moon
12. Adar	February-March	1	New Moon
		14–15	Feast of Lots (*Purim*)

NOTES:

1. The names of the months, which were of Assyro-Babylonian origin, were not introduced into Palestine until after the return from the Captivity. Previously other names were used, only four of which are known to us: Abib (Nisan), Ziw (Iyyar), Ethanim (Tishri), Bul (Marheshwan).

2. The Jews generally indicated the months by their ordinal numbers, beginning with Nisan, the first month of the Liturgical Year.

3. When an intercalary month was added, it was placed at the end of the series and was called *Weadar* or *Adar sheni* (second Adar).

4. Besides the fast of *Kippur* or Atonement (the 10th of Tishri) other fasts were introduced in the course of the centuries and were sanctioned by religious authority or by custom which had the force of law. These were: (*a*) the 17th of Tammuz, commemorating the cessation of the daily sacrifice during the siege of Jerusalem in the year A.D. 70; (*b*) the 9th of Ab, commemorating the two destructions of the Temple by Nebuchodonosor and by Titus, and the capture of Bether (Bettir) in A.D. 135; (*c*) the 10th of Tebeth, calling to mind the beginning of the siege of Jerusalem by Titus; (*d*) the 13th of Adar, commemorating the fast of Esther. A public fast was occasionally prescribed when a great calamity, such as a pest or famine, threatened the nation.

2. The Months and Years

The Hebrew months were lunar months containing 29 or 30 days. Since the moon completes its revolution in 29 days, 12 hours, 44′3″, the year of twelve lunations has a duration of 354 days, 8 hours, 48′3″. It is, therefore, shorter by about 10 days and 21 hours than the solar year, which contains 365 days, 5 hours, 44′48″. Since the cycle of liturgical feasts corresponded to the seasons, it was necessary to effect a harmony between the lunar and the solar year, and an approximate concurrence was obtained by adding at one time or another a thirteenth month to the twelve months of the lunar year. It is a disputed question whether the Jews at the time of Christ made this intercalation by purely empirical methods or by means of calculation.

It is certain that a cycle of eight years, including three intercalary months, was known from most ancient times. In the fifth century B.C., Meton calculated the cycle of nineteen years with seven intercalary months, at the end of which cycle there was a difference of only two hours between the courses of the sun and moon. About 150 B.C., Hipparchus achieved still greater exactness by discovering the precession of the equinoxes. Consequently, the Jews as well as many other peoples of the time could well have employed calculation to regulate their calendar. Good authorities hold that they did; for, they ask, how could the Jews of the Diaspora have attended the annual pilgrimages unless they knew the dates on which they were to fall? How could they have observed the New Moons, the time of Unleavened Bread, and the Fast of the Atonement, if the fixing of the calendar depended on an unpredictable decision of the Sanhedrin?

But, on the other hand, neither Philo nor Josephus makes the slightest allusion to the existence of any cycle established in advance; and, in fact, the legislation of the Mishnah excludes such a hypothesis. A curious passage in the *Preaching of Peter,* cited by Clement of Alexandria, says of the Jews: "If the new moon did not appear, they celebrated neither the Sabbath called the first, nor Neomenia, nor the Azymes, nor any feast, nor any great day." The fixing of the months and years depended, therefore, on observation; and it was not known in advance whether a month would have 29 or 30 days, nor whether a year should have 12 or 13 months. For greater security, in places too remote to receive notice from the Sanhedrin in time, the celebration of New Moons and feasts was doubled.

Still, some elementary rules were necessarily observed. For example, it was well known that, since the lunar month was about equal to 29½ days, a month could not have more than 30 days. Hence, if a cloudy sky on the thirtieth day prevented the sighting of the new moon, the feast of the New Moon was nonetheless fixed for the following day.

Calculation also entered to some degree into the fixing of the intercalary month. The commission of the Sanhedrin took three circumstances into consideration in deciding whether a year would have thirteen months: the condition of the harvests, the state of the fruit-bearing trees, and the course of the sun. At the liturgical New Year, it was necessary that the barley harvest be close enough at hand to provide for the offering of the first sheaf to God on the 16th of Nisan, i.e., the day following the Passover. It was also necessary that the sun should then have reached a point called *Tequphah.* The *Tequphah* was not precisely the spring equinox, but the entry of the sun into the sign of Aries, a phenomenon occurring before the equinox. Josephus, without making any mention of the equinox, says that the Passover was slain on the 14th day of the moon, *when the sun was in the sign of Aries.* Philo mentions the equinox, but does not say that it must precede the Passover. Originally both Jews and Christians made a distinction between the equinox and the Paschal term. At the time of the introduction of the Julian calendar, the equinox had been fixed on the 25th of March, and this date lagged notably behind the true equinox. But neither the official nor the astronomical equinox served for Christians or Jews in fixing the Passover.

3. Sacred Seasons and Feasts

A distinction may be made between major feasts, which included a pilgrimage to the Temple, except when legitimate dispensation intervened (the Passover, Pentecost, and Tabernacles), and minor feasts (the civil New Year or Feast of Trumpets on the 1st of Tishri; Atonement, *Kippur,* on the 10th of Tishri; the Feast of Lots, *Purim,* on the 14th and 15th of Adar; the Feast of Dedication on the 25th of Kislew), and finally sacred days or seasons (Sabbath, New Moon, the Sabbatical Year, and the Year of Jubilee). The feasts named in the New Testament are the Pasch or Passover, Pentecost, Tabernacles, and Dedication, which were celebrated at the time with great solemnity. We have mentioned in the proper place all that is important to know about them and we shall here add but a few notes.

1. *Sabbath* — The institution of the Sabbath is linked with the story of the Creation (Gen 2:3). On this day consecrated to the service of God, Israel imitated the divine repose. The rules of the Sabbath rest had in the course of time gathered extraordinary rigor. Not only was it not permitted to light or extinguish a fire, to tie or untie a knot; it was forbidden, for example, to write *two* characters, even one with the right hand and the other with the left. Two really troublesome prohibitions were the one against going more than 2000 cubits (less than one mile) beyond the walls or beyond the last house of a locality, and the one against transporting from place to place any object whatever which did not serve as clothing or attire. A treatise of the Mishnah entitled *Erubin* had for its purpose to moderate somewhat the rigors of these prohibitions.

2. *The New Moon* — Among nomad and pastoral peoples, the appearance of the new moon is almost everywhere the signal for rejoicing. It was probably celebrated among the Hebrews before the time of Moses. It is generally mentioned with the Sabbath, and it seems, too, that before the Babylonian captivity the custom was to cease work. After that time, it lost its importance and only the women observed the New Moon repose. It is said that even today traces of this custom remain.

3. *The Sabbatical Year* — As the Sabbath was the repose of man, so the Sabbatical Year was the repose of the earth. However, in contrast to the liturgical year which commenced in the spring month of Nisan,

the Sabbatical Year began in autumn in the month of Tishri. From that time, the land lay fallow, debts were canceled, and slaves were set free. The observance of the Sabbatical Year is proved by numerous testimonies. We know, too, that the year *26–27*, the first year of our Lord's preaching, was a Sabbatical Year.

NOTE N

Days and Hours Among the Jews

1. The Day and Its Divisions

The astronomical day of the Babylonians, the civil day of the Romans, and the liturgical day of the Hebrews were all measured by the rotation of the earth on its axis or the apparent revolution of the sun around the earth. The day began for the Romans, as for us, at midnight; for the Babylonians and for some Greek cities (e.g., Pergamus) it began at sunrise, for the Umbrians at midday, and for the majority of the Greeks at sunset.[1] For the Hebrews also the day began at sunset; or perhaps it would be more accurate to say that the liturgical day began at the moment when three stars were distinguishable in the sky. Twilight, which however is very brief in Palestine, was neither day nor night. This Jewish manner of speaking must be borne well in mind. Thus the Paschal lamb was slain on the evening of the 14th of Nisan and was eaten at nightfall, which belonged to the 15th of Nisan.

In principle, the astronomical day was divided into twenty-four hours, but this division of the learned did not enter into current usage, and we need not concern ourselves with it. When we speak of the day, we mean the day popularly so called, the natural daytime as opposed to night.

Daytime as opposed to night is the lapse of time between sunrise and sunset. For the Greeks and Romans and Hebrews daytime was divided into twelve equal hours, which, however, greatly varied in

[1] Pliny, *Hist. Nat.* II, lxxix, 1: "Ipsum diem alii aliter observavere: Babylonii inter duos solis exortus, Athenienses inter duos occasus, Umbri a meridie in meridiem, vulgus omne a luce ad tenebras, sacerdotes Romani et qui diem diffiniere civilem, item Aegyptii et Hipparchus a media nocte ad mediam." This information, according to Aulus Gellius (*Noctes Atticae,* III, 2), comes from Varro: "libro *Rerum Romanarum* quem *De Diebus* inscripsit." *Macrobius* (*Saturnal.*, I, 3) copies Aulus Gellius.

length from season to season.[2] These hours did not correspond to ours, except at the periods of the equinoxes. At Jerusalem, 31°46′30″ north latitude, the longest day, at the summer solstice, lasted 14 hours and 12 minutes; the shortest, at the winter solstice, 9 hours and 48 minutes. The length of daytime hours varied, therefore, between 71 and 49 minutes.

The ancients did not have the means which we have at our disposal for estimating the hours exactly. The first nearly exact sundial did not appear in Rome until 164 B.C., because the one which had been set up 91 years earlier had been calculated for the latitude of Catina. The clepsydra or water clock followed shortly afterward in 159 B.C. From then on, the time of day could be found out at the Forum,[3] but the common people always held to the old division of the day into four parts: morning (*mane*), forenoon (*antemeridiem*), afternoon (*postmeridiem*), and evening (*vespera*). The ancient Greeks had a still simpler division of the day: morning, midday, and evening. This division into three parts seems also to have been in use among the Hebrews, and we find it in the Book of Jubilees.[4]

The night was also divided by the Romans into four watches of three hours each;[5] but it seems that in ancient times among the Hebrews the night, like the day, had but three subdivisions.

2. The Hours of Day and Night

The meaning of the word ὥρα (*hora*) was originally very vague: period, season (of the year), a long or short lapse of time. When the day and night were divided into twelve equal periods, variable in length according to the season, these divisions were called *hours;* but Hebrew has no equivalent term.

---

[2] Censorinus, *Dies Natalis,* xxiii, 6: "In horas duodecim divisum esse diem, noctemque in totidem, vulgo notum est; sed hoc credo Romae post reperta solaria observatum. . . ." The author is right. The division of the day into twelve hours was not altogether practical without the sundial, nor that of the night, without water clocks or sand clocks.

[3] Pliny, *Hist. Nat.,* VII, lx, 1–4. Cf. Dezobry, *Rome au Siècle d'Auguste,* Vol. II, p. 39: "Two sundials were placed in the square near the Rostra, and, to supplement them when the weather was cloudy, a water-clock." But this luxury was not shared by the cities of the provinces.

[4] Theophrastus (*De Sign. Temp., 9*) distinguishes morning (πρωΐ), midday (μεσημβρία), evening (δείλη). Cf. Libanius, *Epist.,* 1084. Homer, in order to express that the hour of death is uncertain, says that it will come in the morning or evening or at midday: Ἔσσεται ἢ ἠὼς ἢ δείλη ἢ μέσον ἦμαρ (*Iliad,* xxi, III).

[5] St. Jerome, *Epist. ad Cyprian,* CLX, 8 (ML, XXII, 1172): "Nox in quatuor vigilias dividitur, quae singulae trium horarum spatio supputantur." The Roman usage was received in Palestine at the time of Christ (Matt. 14:25; Mark 6:48).

The hours were indicated, not as with us, by cardinal numbers, but by ordinals: a usage which lent itself to ambiguity. Thus the *first hour* could mean, either the precise moment when the point of the sundial fell upon the first division of the day (seven o'clock in the morning), or the space of time between sunrise and that precise moment. Sometimes the meaning will be open to doubt, as in the epigram of Martial describing the various occupations of the day. The first two hours (from six to eight) are devoted to visits of clients to their patrons; at nine (or between eight and nine) the courts open and lawsuits begin; then there are various kinds of work, ending at midday for the less active and at one o'clock for the more energetic; the two hours following are given over to rest or the baths or sports; the ninth hour (three o'clock in the afternoon) is the time for banquets and wedding festivities, as we learn also from the Egyptian papyri:

> *Prima* salutantes atque *altera* conterit hora;
> Exercet raucos *tertia* causidicos;
> In *quintam* varios extendit Roma labores;
> *Sexta* quies lassis, *septima* finis erit;
> Sufficit in *nonam* nitidis *octava* palaestris;
> Imperat excelsos frangere *nona* toros, etc.[6]

This division of the day into twelve hours was known in Palestine as in the rest of the Graeco-Roman world: "Are there not twelve hours in the day?" (John 11:9), but it was scarcely ever used. In fact there was no available means of distinguishing with accuracy any two consecutive hours. Jewish legislation is a proof of this. According to the Mishnah, if two witnesses testified that they had seen something or other happen, one of them saying at the second hour, the other at the third, both testimonies were held to be valid, because of the difficulty which the common people had in distinguishing the third hour from the second. Rabbi Judah held that both of two testimonies were acceptable, if one of them designated the third hour and the other the fifth, despite the discrepancy of two hours; not, however, if the first witness designated the fifth hour and the other the seventh, because in this case, the two hours being astride midday, it was easier to tell them apart.[7]

The ancients had only nature's clock of the sun and stars to measure the hours. Thus Socrates could say to Euthydemus: "The gods have given us the sun to mark the hours of day, and the stars to indicate

[6] Martial, *Epigram.*, iv, 8.
[7] *Mishnah,* treatise *Sanhedrin,* v, 3.

the night hours."[8] But this clock is very difficult and sometimes even impossible to read. The Romans had at hand a rich vocabulary to designate the phases of the civil day which began at midnight. There was first of all the decline of night (*mediae noctis inclinatio*); then in succession, cockcrow (*gallicinium*), time of silence (*conticinium*), dawn (*diluculum*), morning (*mane*), forenoon (*a mane ad meridiem*), midday, afternoon (*occiduum*), day's end (*suprema tempestas*), evening (*vespera*), first torch (*prima fax*), bedtime (*concubia*), the dead of night (*intempesta*).[9] But these inexact terms were often interchanged, so difficult was it to distinguish their purport.

Like many ancient peoples and several of their own contemporaries, the Hebrews generally adhered to the division of the day into four parts, and for practical purposes recognized between morning and evening only the third, the sixth, and the ninth hours (nine in the morning, midday, and three in the afternoon), the intervals being joined at a guess to one or another of these divisions.[10]

For the hour of the Crucifixion and the reconciliation of Mark 15:25 and John 19:14, see Note R: *The Cross and the Crucifixion.*

On the subject of this note and the preceding one, Mémain (*La Connaissance des temps Evangéliques,* Sens, 1886) gives much useful information; but the precision which he affects is sometimes deceptive, since precision is often impossible in such matters. The article of Ramsay (*Numbers, Hours, Years and Dates,* in Hastings, *Dict. of the Bible,* Vol. V., pp. 473–484) is instructive. In Schürer (*Geschichte,* 4 ed., Vol. I, pp. 745–760) will be found an abundant bibliography and a comparative table of the Greek, Syrian, Roman, and Christian eras, from 168 B.C. to A.D. 136 (pp. 773–777).

---

[8] Xenophon, *Memorabil.,* IV, iii, 4. It is clear that the word *hour* is not used here in the strict sense.

[9] Macrobius, *Saturnal.,* i, 3: "Haec est diei civilis a Romanis observata divisio."

[10] Censorinus, *Dies Natalis,* xxiii, 9: "Alii diem quadripartito, sed et noctem similiter, dividebant."

NOTE O

Money and Banking in Palestine at the Time of Christ

1. Jewish, Greek, and Roman Money

At no period of their history did the Jews mint gold coinage, and it is very doubtful that they minted silver before the great insurrection which led to the catastrophe of A.D. 70. For gold and silver money they were always dependent upon the foreigner, and, at the time which now concerns us, above all upon the Romans.

The basis of the Jewish system was the shekel; but the shekel was a weight, not a coin. From very ancient times, silver served as a medium of exchange, but it circulated as a commodity valued by weight, a shekel being about 14.20 grams. This was the mean weight of the coins called shekels which were minted, according to some, under Simon Machabeus, according to others, at the time of the insurrection of A.D. 66–67. The latter opinion seems to us to be the more probable.[1]

To estimate the value of ancient moneys in comparison with modern, six elements must be taken into account: the date, the country of origin, the fineness, the standard in vogue, the relationship of gold to silver, and finally the purchasing power. These elements are essentially variable, and neglect of any one of them will lead to very divergent results. Some coins, without changing their name, changed frequently in weight as time went on; and in different countries coins bearing the same name did not have the same value.

Ancient coins differed from ours above all in *fineness:* they were of pure metal, whereas ours are alloyed. In Rome and Greece the alloy was practically nil in gold coins, and almost negligible (scarcely 2 per cent) in silver coins. In order to preserve a sound currency, Augustus expressly reserved to himself the minting of precious metals.

---

[1] On these very complex questions see our article, *Le cours des monnaies en Palestine au temps de Jésus-Christ,* in *Recherches,* Oct., 1925, pp. 441–448.

The *standard* prevailing in the Empire was the gold standard. The value of all coins was linked to that of the *aureus,* a pure gold piece weighing, under Augustus, one forty-second of a Roman pound of 327½ grams, i.e., 7.80 grams. The Roman denarius was equal in weight to one half an aureus (3.90 grams), and was one twenty-fifth of its value. The ratio of silver to gold was therefore 1 to 12½ for equal weight, and not as today, 1 to 15½.

The *drachma* was the monetary unit of Greek countries. Its weight varied from time to time and from place to place. The ancient Attic drachma weighed about 4.30 grams, but this weight was later diminished, and at the epoch in which we are interested the drachma was about equal to the Roman denarius (3.90 grams). Much more widely circulated in Palestine was the Phoenician or Tyrian drachma, the mean weight of which was 3.55 grams. The advantage offered by it was twofold: it corresponded in weight to the Egyptian monetary unit of the Ptolemies; and its multiple, the Tyrian tetradrachma, was exactly equal to the Jewish shekel. There were also Asiatic drachmas weighing 3.25 grams, which continued to be minted at Antioch with the permission and under the control of the Emperor. Though these various drachmas were accepted as currency side by side with the denarius in ordinary dealings, the Roman Treasury insisted on payment in actual denarii and would not accept less than four Antioch drachmas for three denarii. The Tyrian drachma necessarily suffered a similar depression in value.

The Gospel mentions the *mina* (*μνᾶ,* Luke 19:13, 25) and the *talent* (Matt. 18:24–25; 25:16–28), which were only moneys of account, the mina being worth 100 drachmas, and the talent worth 60 minas or 6000 drachmas. Also mentioned are the following coins: the *denarius* (*δηνάριον, passim*), the *drachma* (Luke 15:8–9), the *didrachma* (Matt. 17:24), the *stater* (Matt. 17:27), the *argenteus* (*ἀργύριον,* Matt. 26:16), the *as* (*ἀσσάριον,* Matt. 10:29), the *double as* (*dipondius, ἀσσάρια δύο,* Luke 12:6), the *quarter as* (*quadrans, κοδράντης,* Mark 12:42; Matt. 5:26), the *eighth of an as* (*minutum, λεπτόν,* Mark 12:42; Luke 21:2; 12:59). Shekel, stater, argenteus, and tetradrachma are synonymous terms (four drachmas or four denarii); the same is to be said of the didrachma, and half shekel.

It will now be easy to determine the value of the various coins, linking them to the Roman system, the aureus being worth 25 denarii, and the denarius worth 16 as. The aureus, as we have said, contained 7.80 grams of pure gold. If a gram of pure gold is estimated at 3.444 fr. in our prewar money (before 1914), the aureus will be worth approximately 26.75 fr.

Silver Coins

	Weight in grams	*Value in gold francs*	[*Value in U. S. cents*]
Roman denarius, later Attic drachma.......	3.90	1.07	20.65
Phoenician or Tyrian drachma.............	3.55	0.97	18.72
Asiatic drachma..........................	3.25	0.89	17.18
Tyrian didrachma, half shekel	7.10	1.94	37.44
Tyrian tetradrachma, shekel, stater........	14.20	3.88	74.88

Bronze Coins

	Centimes	[*U. S. cents*]
As, sixteenth of a denarius..........................	6.70	1.29
Quadrans, quarter as (κοδράντης)......................	1.67	0.32
Minutum, eighth of an as (λεπτόν).....................	0.84	0.16

[*Translator's note* — If the value of the "old" *franc d'or* be taken as 19.3 cents in U. S. currency, the values in our money (before 1918) would be approximately those shown in the third column. The *talent* would, on the same scale, be worth $1,239; and the *mina,* $20.65. Note, too, that the purchasing power of money was several times greater in ancient times.]

2. Money-Changers and Bankers

Pilgrims flocking to Jerusalem at the time of feasts brought with them coins of all values: gold darics and staters, Roman aurei and denarii, drachmas, didrachmas, and tetradrachmas of Phoenicia, Antioch, Alexandria, and Rhodes, not to mention ancient coins which were no longer being minted. Since many of these coins were not circulated in Palestine, and because the Temple tax had to be paid in Tyrian silver, it was necessary to have recourse to money-changers. These personages, who enjoyed a considerable role at the time, bear three names in the Gospel: (*a*) κερματιστής (John 2:14), from κέρμα (John 2:15), small change, odd coins with which the money-changer must always be abundantly supplied; (*b*) κολλυβιστής (Matt. 21:12; Mark 11:15), derived from κολλυβός, a small bronze piece; (*c*) τραπεζίτης (Matt. 25:27), from τράπεζα, the small table which served as a desk or counter for the money-changer (Matt. 21:12; Mark 11:15; Luke 19:23; John 2:15). It is seen that τραπεζίτης corresponds etymologically to the word "banker," from "bench." These three words employed in the Gospel as synonymous are translated in the Vulgate by *nummularius* or *numularius,* and the little table (τράπεζα) is translated by *mensa.* They correspond to the Rabbinical Hebrew שׁלחני, from שׁלחן, *table.*

The *nummularii* did not confine themselves to changing money; they also carried on certain banking operations: they issued and paid letters of credit, made loans on security, and received interest-bearing money on deposit (Matt. 25:27; Luke 19:23). According to the Talmud, the fee demanded by the money-changers was generally 4 per cent, but sometimes only 2 per cent. This fee was called, in Rabbinical Hebrew, קלבון, from κολλυβός, *a small coin*. Thus, for an aureus, only 24 denarii were received back instead of 25. If this rate seems high, it must be remembered that the money-changer ran the risk of taking in coins of poor alloy. Hence the saying which an old tradition ascribed to the Saviour: Γίνεσθε δόκιμοι τραπεζῖται (Clement of Alexandria, *Stromata,* I, xxviii, 177): "Be good money-changers, rejecting the bad, keeping the good."

Interest on money (τόκος) was also very high. Except at Rome, where capital was plentiful, the lender usually demanded from 12 per cent to 20 per cent annual interest.

NOTE P

Mary Magdalene, Mary of Bethany, and the Sinner Who Anointed the Saviour's Feet

1. Statement of the Question

St. Luke mentions an unnamed sinful woman who anointed the Saviour's feet (Luke 7:36–50); St. John and St. Luke speak of Mary the sister of Martha, who was the hostess of Jesus at Bethany (John 11:1–44; 12:1–8; Luke 10:39–42); finally, the four Evangelists name a certain Mary Magdalene from whom Jesus had expelled seven devils (Luke 8:2), who played an important part in the Passion (Matt. 27:56–61; Mark 15:40–47; John 19:25), and was favored with an apparition of the risen Christ (Matt. 28:1; Mark 16:1–9; Luke 24:10; John 20:1–18). Are these three distinct persons, or two, or only one? The Gospel knows only one unnamed sinner, one Mary Magdalene, one Mary of Bethany; but under different names and characters they may represent one and the same person. Bossuet correctly observes: "It is not a question of proving that it is impossible for the three to be the same; what must be proved is that the Gospel forces us to believe them to be one, or at least that this is the most natural meaning."[1]

For the Evangelists, these three persons are always distinct, though they have one trait in common, their love of Jesus. But this very love, examined more closely, has not the same characteristics in all three. It is penitent love in the sinful woman of St. Luke, love of gratitude in Mary Magdalene, love of ecstatic contemplation in Mary of Bethany. We shall study the Gospel texts without preconceptions. It will then be necessary to see whether the verdict of exegesis is weakened by tradition or the liturgy.

---

[1] The opusculum, *Sur les Trois Magdalénes,* is in the Lachat edition, Vol. XXVI, pp. 114–116. Bossuet sustains the distinction of the three Marys; Fr. Corluy, who regards their identity as more probable, exposes with clarity the arguments pro and contra (*Comment. in Joan.*, 2 ed., Ghent, 1880, pp. 262–279).

2. Examination of the Gospel Texts

1. *The Unnamed Sinner of St. Luke and Mary of Bethany* — These two women have this in common, that they both anointed the feet of the Saviour, but all the circumstances differ: (*a*) The anointing by the sinful woman, recorded by St. Luke (7:36–50), took place in Galilee toward the middle of the apostolic ministry of Jesus; the anointing by Mary, recounted by St. John (12:1–8), and also by the first two Synoptics without the mention of any name (Matt. 26:6–13; Mark 14:3–9), took place near Jerusalem during the week of the Passion. (*b*) The heroine of St. Luke's story is a sinner known as such throughout the town; the other three Evangelists insinuate nothing of the kind about Mary, the sister of Martha and Lazarus. (*c*) The anointings in the two cases are different and the reflections of the bystanders are different.

But could not the two anointings have been performed by the same person who had, in the interval, changed her way of life, her abode, and her surroundings? The Evangelists do not allow us to affirm it. St. Luke, after having told at length about the anointing by the unnamed sinful woman, introduces the family at Bethany in these words (10:38): "Jesus entered a certain village where a woman called Martha welcomed him into her house: she had a sister named Mary who seated herself at the Lord's feet." Not only does St. Luke fail to establish any link between Mary and the sinful woman, he does not even seem to suspect that any exists. It may be said that he was simply unaware of it, but an escape of that sort should not be resorted to without a serious reason. An any rate, the identity of the two persons is not apparent in his account.

The first time that St. John names Mary of Bethany, he adds this remark: "Mary, whose brother Lazarus was sick, was she who anointed the Saviour with perfume and wiped his feet with her hair" (*ἦν ἡ ἀλείψασα τὸν Κύριον καὶ ἐκμάξασα τοὺς πόδας ταῖς θριξίν*, John 11:2). The aorist participles *ἀλείψασα, ἐκμάξασα* could refer to a fact already mentioned by the author (as in John 18:14 and 19:39); but they could also very well refer to a fact not yet mentioned but known to all (as in Matt. 10:4: Judas who betrayed him, *ὁ καὶ παραδοὺς αὐτόν*, and Mark 3:19; Luke 6:16).

St. John is not alluding to the anointing by the sinful woman of St. Luke, but to the anointing by Mary of Bethany; the difference of the circumstances brings this out: (*a*) The sinful woman of St. Luke's story wipes with her hair the tears shed on the feet of the Saviour (Luke 7:38); the woman of whom St. John speaks here (11:2) wipes with her hair the perfume spread upon his feet, as does Mary of

Bethany (John 12:3). (*b*) The penitent of St. Luke sheds torrents of tears; Mary of Bethany does not weep. (*c*) The sinner of St. Luke wipes only the feet of the Saviour; the woman of whom St. John is speaking anoints the Lord himself (John 11:2), beginning with his head (Matt. 26:7; Mark 14:3).[2]

2. *The Sinful Woman of St. Luke and Mary Magdalene* — Immediately after having told of the anointing by the unnamed sinner, St. Luke mentions Mary Magdalene without seeming to suspect the least link between the two women: "Then Jesus went through the towns and villages having with him the Twelve and some women: Mary named Magdalene, from whom he had expelled seven devils, Joanna the wife of Chusa, Susanna, etc." (Luke 8:1–3.) One could, of course, say that St. Luke, drawing now from a different source, does not think of identifying the unnamed sinner with Magdalene; but, instead of assuming such ignorance, a reason for it should be given. And none is given.

3. *Mary Magdalene and Mary of Bethany* — The first two Evangelists throw no light upon the subject for us, for they name only Mary Magdalene; but St. Luke and St. John distinguish these two clearly enough.

a) Mary Magdalene is *always* so designated; Mary of Bethany is simply called Mary, or Mary the sister of Martha and Lazarus.

b) Mary Magdalene was from Magdala in Galilee; Mary the sister of Martha was from Bethany near Jerusalem, and nowhere is there any indication that she had ever lived elsewhere. She was at Bethany when Jesus came to preach in Judea six months before the Passion (Luke 10:39); and the tone of familiarity which exists between the two

[2] Depending solely on the text of St. John, Fr. Lemonyer makes an able plea for the identity of the Marys (*L'Onction de Bethanie,* in *Recherches,* 1928, pp. 105–117). This is his moderate conclusion: "What shall we finally maintain? That the identity of Mary the sister of Martha and Lazarus with the sinner of St. Luke on the one hand, and with Mary Magdalene on the other, is an established fact? We are not so ingenuous. It suffices that we have pointed out several elements and factual data in the Johannine narrative and, relying on them, have advanced various suggestions which we believe to be plausible, and which, we believe, forbid the theory of the distinction between the Marys to be considered as established." Indeed, if the text of St. John (12:1–8) were the only one, it could be thought that he is here alluding to the anointing by the sinner spoken of by St. Luke (7:37–38); but this is only one of many elements of the question, and as Bossuet says, "the natural meaning" of the accumulated texts is to be sought. As to the identity of Mary of Bethany with Mary Magdalene, we do not see how it can be drawn from the text of St. John, even by reading between the lines.

sisters and the Master shows that this was not the first visit. The same may be inferred from John 11:1–21.

c) Jesus had expelled seven devils from Mary Magdalene (Luke 8:2; Mark 15:9); nothing of the kind is insinuated about Mary of Bethany.

d) Mary of Bethany is always named beside her sister Martha; Mary Magdalene, never.

e) Mary of Magdala was one of the group of holy women who accompanied the Saviour on his apostolic journeys (Luke 8:1). These women had come with him from Galilee (Luke 23:49), and they were in Jerusalem on the day of the Passion and the day of the Resurrection (the four Evangelists). But there is absolutely no indication that either Martha or her sister Mary at any time quitted Bethany.

3. Tradition and Liturgy

Lefèvre d'Etaples was condemned by the Sorbonne in 1521 for denying the identity of the Marys.[3] Later on, even in France, Bossuet, Tillemont, Calmet, and others sustained the same opinion without being disturbed.[4] Still, the Bollandists and the majority of Catholic authorities consider the thesis of the identity of the Marys to be more in accord with the sense of the Church. A Sulpician has vigorously defended it in the name of tradition.[5] Fr. Lagrange has submitted the question to a fresh examination. His conclusion is this: "There does not exist what can be called an exegetical tradition of the Fathers on the unity or plurality (of the Marys). They do not agree and scarcely any of them speak very positively. What is stranger still is that none of them, not one, appeals to the memory of tradition. Since the question came under discussion very early, the reason why this decisive argument was not appealed to was that no one knew anything about it. Hence no historical tradition existed, any more than an exegetical tradition."[6] Fr. Holzmeister also concludes that the Fathers

---

[3] Lefèvre d'Etaples (*Faber Stapulensis*), *De Maria Magdalena,* Paris 1516; *De Tribus et Unica Maria Magdalena,* Paris, 1519. The sentence of the Sorbonne is found in the collection of the Bollandists, under July 22.

[4] Calmet, *Dissertations sur les trois Maries* (*Comment. on Mark and Luke,* Paris ed., 1730, pp. 242–264). After recalling the Sorbonne censure of 1521, he concludes thus: "After that time many learned doctors of the Sorbonne wrote to sustain the distinction of the three Marys, and it is assuredly at present the prevailing opinion among scholars." Perhaps among scholars, but not outside their ranks.

[5] Anonymous priest of Saint-Sulpice (Faillon), *Monuments inédites sur l'apostolat de sainte Marie Madeleine en Province,* Paris, 1848.

[6] Lagrange, *Jésus a-t-il été oint plusieurs fois et par plusieurs femmes?* in *R.B.,* 1912, pp. 504–532. Quotation from p. 529 f.

disagree, but he does not discuss the exegetical question.[7] More recently another Catholic scholar has studied the problem. He concludes flatly to a plurality: "Mary Magdalene, Mary of Bethany, and the sinful woman who anointed the Saviour's feet are three different women. In the interest of historical truth it is desirable that the texts of the Latin liturgy for the feast of St. Mary Magdalene should be changed in consequence, and that preachers together with authors of works of piety should conform."[8] This is going a little too fast! The confusion, if confusion there is, is inoffensive and the liturgy does not always employ Scripture texts literally.

The Greek Church celebrates the feast of the sinful woman of St. Luke on March 31, that of Mary of Bethany on March 18, and that of Mary Magdalene on July 22. The Latin Church, at least at present, celebrates only one feast on July 22 and borrows for the office and the Mass texts and features of all three; but Salmeron proves very thoroughly that this usage of the Church cannot be taken as an argument.[9] True, the Gospel of the sinful woman is read in the Mass of Mary Magdalene; but the Gospel of Mary of Bethany is read in the Mass of the Feast of the Assumption. Would anyone say that the Church confuses Mary the Mother of Jesus with Mary the sister of Lazarus? The feature of resemblance which justifies the accommodated sense is that both, in very different ways, have "chosen the better part."

Despite the objections of exegetes, the theory of identification of the Marys is now and will long remain the more popular one in the West. And basically we see in it no great incongruity, at least for mystics and preachers who are not at all restricted to the literal meaning.

---

[7] Holzmeister, *Die Magdalenenfrage in der kirchl. Überlieferung,* in *Z. f. K.T.,* 1922.

[8] Sickenberger, *Ist die Magdalenen-Frage wirklich unlösbar?* in *Bibl. Zeit.,* Vol. XVI, 1925, pp. 63–74. Citation from p. 74.

[9] Salmeron, Cologne ed., 1604, Vol. IV, Part II, Tr. 6, pp. 289–297.

NOTE Q

The Last Supper, the Passover, and the Passion

1. The Gospel Data

The Evangelists all agree on three points: the Last Supper took place on Thursday, the Passion on Friday, and the Resurrection on Sunday. This needs no proof; the isolated opinion of Westcott, who places the Passion on Thursday, has found no echo.

But, reading the Synoptics without preconceptions, one gets the irresistible impression that Jesus ate the Paschal lamb on the evening of the 14th of Nisan, and that consequently he died on the following day, the 15th of Nisan, the day of the great solemnity. St. John, on the contrary, seems to say no less clearly that Jesus was crucified at the very time when the Jews were slaying the Paschal lamb, that is to say, on the afternoon of the 14th of Nisan. Some of the Rationalist interpreters pronounce in favor of St. John, others in favor of the Synoptics, but they do not take the trouble to reconcile them, and, in fact, declare them to be irreconcilable.

1. *The Data of the Synoptics* — (*a*) On the first day of Azymes (Unleavened Bread), the disciples said to Jesus: "Where wilt thou that we prepare the Passover?" Properly speaking, the *first day of Azymes* was the 15th of Nisan, which began at sunset of the previous evening; but since all unleavened bread had to be destroyed between ten and eleven o'clock on the 14th of Nisan, this day was commonly called the first day of Azymes. Josephus once or twice so designates it (*Bellum,* V, iii, 1; cf. *Antiq.,* II, xv, 1). It must evidently be so understood in St. Matthew (26:17), and in St. Mark, who speaks more precisely (14:12): "When they were accustomed to immolate the Passover" (ὅτε τὸ πάσχα ἔθυον), and in St. Luke, who is still more precise (22:7): "the day on which it was necessary to immolate the Passover" (ἐν ᾧ ἔδει θύεσθαι τὸ πάσχα).

b) Jesus tells the disciples to say to his host: "At thy house I keep the *Passover* with my disciples" (Matt. 26:18), or what comes to the same: "Where is the room where I may *eat the Passover* with my disciples?" (Mark 14:14; Luke 22:11.)

c) The Apostles, carrying out the order they have received, "prepared the *Passover*" (Matt. 26:19; Mark 14:16; Luke 22:11).

d) While they are at table, Jesus says to them: "Greatly have I desired to *eat this Passover* with you before I die" (Luke 22:15).

And yet, the Synoptics give a certain number of details that would seem to exclude the great solemnity of the 15th of Nisan as the day of the Passion. (1) Joseph of Arimathea buys a shroud (Mark 15:46), and the holy women go to buy spices (Luke 23:56). (2) The Jews proceeding to the arrest of Jesus, and also one of the disciples, are bearing arms (Mark 14:47). (3) Simon of Cyrene is returning from the country, more probably from work in the fields, which work customarily ceased around midday of the 14th of Nisan (Mark 15:21; Matt. 27:32; Luke 23:26). (4) The Jews had decided not to lay hold of Jesus to put him to death on the day of the feast (Mark 14:2; Matt. 26:5), and there is no indication that they changed their minds. For the same reason Herod Agrippa waited for the expiration of the feast days to put St. Peter to death (Acts 12:3–4). Father Lagrange writes: "It is absolutely impossible to conceive that the Jews would have engaged in all the undertakings necessary for the condemnation and death of Jesus on the first day of Azymes, a very holy day of rest" (*Saint Marc,* 4 ed., 1929, p. 355).

2. *The Data of St. John* — (*a*) On the day of the Passion, the accusers refrain from entering the Praetorium, in order to avoid contracting a legal uncleanness which would prevent them *from eating the Passover* (John 18:28, ἵνα μὴ μιανθῶσιν ἀλλὰ φάγωσιν τὸ πάσχα). By entering a pagan house they would have contracted a *major* impurity lasting all week, and consequently they would not have been permitted to *eat the Paschal lamb,* even though it were to be eaten at an hour of the night belonging to the following day. The attempts that have been made to prove that the eating of the Passover could here mean the eating of the victims sacrificed during the course of the festival have proved of no avail. To eat the Passover never meant anything else than to eat the Paschal lamb, and to the unprejudiced mind it never will mean anything else (cf. Billerbeck, *Kommentar,* Vol. II, pp. 837–840).

b) At the time when Jesus was crucified, "it was the preparation of the Passover": ἦν δὲ παρασκευὴ τοῦ πάσχα (John 19:14). The word *preparation* (παρασκευή), as an abridgment of "preparation of the Sabbath," is used by itself for Friday, but the *preparation of the*

Passover, corresponding to the Hebrew ערב הפסח, is a consecrated phrase meaning the *eve of the Passover*, that is to say, of the Paschal solemnity, whatever be the day of the week. St. John informs us elsewhere (19:31) that the eve of the Passover in that particular year was a Friday. Cf. Billerbeck, *loc. cit.*, pp. 834–837.

c) The day following the crucifixion was a Sabbath of exceptional greatness (*ἦν γὰρ μεγάλη ἡ ἡμέρα ἐκείνου τοῦ σαββάτου*, John 19:31). If the Paschal solemnity should fall on a Friday, the Saturday following it would have nothing particularly remarkable about it; in comparison with the Passover, it would be a minor feast, as were the other intermediate days between the first and last days. The offering of the first sheaf in the Temple would not confer upon it any special solemnity.

These perfectly clear texts are enough, and we refrain from bringing up other passages that could be discussed: for example, the date of the Last Supper *ante diem festum* (John 13:1) and the allusion to the slaying of the Paschal lamb at the time of Jesus' death (19:36).

2. Solutions Proposed

The proposed solutions are very numerous, and it is difficult to classify the sponsors of various opinions, either because they do not explain themselves clearly enough, or because they are not always self-consistent, or because they do not take into consideration the various shades of meaning which change the basis of the question. Still, all the systems may be reduced to the three following types:

I. Jesus ate the Passover on the same day as the rest of the Jews.

II. Jesus did not eat the Passover on the same day as the rest of the Jews.

III. Not all the Jews ate the Passover on the same day that year; and Jesus ate it on the same day as did one party among them, whereas the others, for some reason or other, ate it on the following day.

FIRST SOLUTION — *Jesus and the Jews ate the Passover on the legal day, the evening of the 14th of Nisan; and Jesus was crucified on the 15th of Nisan, the day of the Paschal solemnity.*

The best-known champions of this system are, on the Catholic side, Patrizi and Corluy; on the Protestant side, Zahn and Edersheim.[1]

---

[1] Patrizi (*De Evangeliis,* Vol. II, pp. 498–515) applies himself chiefly to a refutation of Paul of Burgos and Petau. Corluy (*Comment. in Joan.,* 2 ed., 1880, pp. 311–318) cites in favor of his views Toletus, Lucas of Bruges, Cornelius a Lapide, V. de Buck, Jovino, Hengstenberg, Olshausen, Tholück, Langen. Fillion can now be added. Zahn (*Einleitung in das N.T.,* 3 ed., 1907, Vol. II, pp. 519–536) dwells on points foreign to the question and passes lightly over the difficulties.

They concern themselves less with proving their theory than with exposing the disadvantages of other systems. They rely upon the Synoptics, which, in fact, favor this view, and they seek to answer the texts in which the Synoptics seem to exclude the Paschal solemnity as the day of Christ's death. They say, for example, that Simon of Cyrene was returning from the country, but not from labor in the fields; that the Sanhedrin could, in certain exceptional and urgent circumstances, meet on a feast day and pronounce condemnations to death; that it was not forbidden to buy and sell on that particular day provided that the price agreed upon was not paid then and there, and so on. They are less happy in explaining St. John; and no specialist in Rabbinical studies will ever admit that to "eat the Passover" could mean anything else than to "eat the Paschal lamb," or that the "parasceve of the Passover" could be anything else than the eve of the Paschal solemnity.[2]

Claimed for this opinion are St. Augustine, St. Jerome, Venerable Bede, and Innocent III; but these authors only say that Jesus ate the Passover on the evening of the 14th of Nisan, without concerning themselves with what the other Jews did or did not do.

SECOND SOLUTION — *Jesus did not eat the Passover on the same day as the other Jews, but a day before them.*

This opinion lends itself to numerous variants.

First System — *The Last Supper, celebrated by the Saviour on the evening of the 13th of Nisan, was not a Passover, but a farewell meal.*

Up to the end of the third century, all the authors whose opinions we are acquainted with are in agreement on this point; at least none of them affirm the contrary, but they cannot be quoted as a group. St. Justin and St. Irenaeus say only that the Paschal lamb is the type of Christ, a type fulfilled in the death of the Saviour:[3] "Pascha nostrum immolatus est Christus" (1 Cor. 5:7), which is true whatever opinion be adopted as to the day of his death, but much more strikingly so if Jesus was crucified at the time when the Jews were slaying the Paschal lamb.

Edersheim (*The Life and Times of Jesus,* 1901, Vol. II, pp. 497–512) describes minutely the ritual of the Jewish Passover as it is found in the Talmud and scarcely touches the question of the apparent discord among the Evangelists.

[2] See what we have said about the data of St. John, and for more details, Billerbeck, *Kommentar,* Vol. II, pp. 834–843, or Knabenbauer, ***In Matth.,*** Vol. II, pp. 406–411.

[3] St. Justin, *Dial. cum Trypho,* 40 and 111; St. Irenaeus, *Adv. Haer.,* IV, 10.

On the contrary, Apollinaris of Hierapolis, St. Hippolytus, Clement of Alexandria, whose texts are preserved in the *Chronicon Paschale,* the author of the *Chronicon* himself, Tertullian, Julius Africanus, Lactantius, St. Peter of Alexandria, Ambrosiaster, and the author of a discourse falsely attributed to St. John Chrysostom: all these say expressly that Jesus was crucified on the 14th of Nisan at the time when the Jews were slaying the lamb, and that in that year he did not celebrate the Passover because he was himself the true Passover.[4] Those among the Quartodecimans who differed from other Catholics only about the day on which Easter was to be celebrated were of the same opinion. Relying on St. John, they affirmed that Jesus died on the evening of the 14th of Nisan, and at that time they were accustomed to break their fast and to inaugurate the Easter festival.[5] They are not to be confused with the Judaizing Quartodecimans who, relying on St. Matthew, celebrated on the evening of the 14th of Nisan a supper after the Jewish manner to commemorate the Last Supper.[6] They believed therefore, like the proponents of the preceding solution, that Jesus was crucified on the following day, viz., the 15th of Nisan. It was to refute them that Apollinaris of Hierapolis, Clement of Alexandria, and St. Hippolytus wrote; this was also the purpose of the *Chronicon Paschale.*

The Greek Church, which uses leavened bread in the Eucharist, evidently follows this opinion, which cannot be denied to have real extrinsic probability; but it is not clear how it can be reconciled with the Synoptics.

The opinion which made of the Last Supper an ordinary meal, celebrated on the 13th of Nisan, had almost died out in the West when Calmet, in the eighteenth century, gave it a new lease of life. Let us hear his own words: "Vecchietus was thrown into the prisons of the Inquisition for daring to depart from the common opinion (that Jesus ate the legal Passover). Fr. Lamy, who was the first to make public his system about the Passover, hesitated for many years before de-

[4] Tertullian, *Adv. Judaeos,* 8; Julius Africanus (MG, X, 89); Lactantius, *Epit. Div. Inst.* 45 (or 40); St. Peter of Alexandria (MG, XVIII, 517); Ambrosiaster, *Quaest. Vet. et Nov. Test.,* 55 (MG, XXXV, 2252); Pseudo-Chrysost. (MG, LIX, 547); the texts of Apollinaris, Clement of Alexandria, and St. Hippolytus are reproduced in the *Chronicon Paschale* (MG, LIX, 547).

[5] On the 14th of Nisan, they celebrated the commemoration of the Passion (τὴν μνήμην τοῦ πάθους): Theodoretus, *Haeret. fab.,* III, 11. Cf. Eusebius, *Hist. eccl.,* V, 23.

[6] Their position emerges clearly from the refutations by their Catholic opponents, in the *Chronicon Paschale.* See also Hilgenfeld, *Die Ketzergeschichte des Urchristentums,* Leipzig, 1884, pp. 601–609.

claring himself, and did not do so until he had learned that M. Toynard was formulating the same opinion in his *Harmony,* which he was so long in preparing, and which we did not see until after his death. Hitherto the subject had not been radically examined."[7]

All that can be advanced in favor of the opinion sponsored by Calmet is well exposed by Farrar, to whom we refer the reader who wishes more on the subject.[8]

Second System — *The Last Supper celebrated by Jesus on the 13th of Nisan was an anticipated Passover, or, if you will, a Passover of "intention" or "imitation."*

This is how LeCamus expounds the theory: "There remains but one solution of the difficulty. It is to recognize that Jesus did not eat the real, the legal, Passover, which could not have taken place until the morrow, but a Passover of 'intention' or 'imitation.' Wishing to be immolated at the same time as the Paschal lamb, he had resolved to anticipate the commemorative feast of the past and to inaugurate the banquet of the future." Fouard is of the opinion that Jesus retained all that he could of the Mosaic ritual: the Azymes, the bitter herbs, the *haroseth* sauce, but without the Paschal lamb, which could not be slain on the 13th. But he agrees that one may fall back on the following explanation: "If this supposition (of a Passover without a Paschal lamb) seems too bold, we have then no recourse, except to presume that Jesus caused the Paschal lamb to be immolated by His disciples without first presenting it in the Temple. Lord and Master of the Passover, even as of the Sabbath, He could alter this particular point in a system which He was now about to abrogate, when instituting the sacrifice of the New Covenant."[9]

Third System — *The supper was neither a Paschal feast nor an ordinary meal, but a Qiddush* (a more solemn meal taken on the day before the Sabbath or a great feast, in the evening).

---

[7] Calmet, *Dissertation sur la dernière Pâque de N.-S. J.-C.,* at the beginning of his *Commentaire sur S. Matthieu.* Calmet alludes to Lamy, *Lettre sur la Pâque.*

[8] Farrar, *The Life of Christ,* Excursus X: *Was the Last Supper an Actual Passover?*

[9] LeCamus, *Vie de N.-S. J.-C.,* 8 ed., 1921, Vol. III, p. 183; Fouard, *Vie de N.-S. J.-C.,* 21 ed., 1911, Vol. II, Appendix X, pp. 459–460 (English transl., Vol. II, pp. 394–395). See also Sydney Smith in *The Month,* March, 1891, and Schanz, *Matthäus,* 1879, pp. 509–510: "If he anticipated the Passover, he could also anticipate the entire ritual." And the Paschal lamb? "Because of the great multitude the slaughter probably took place at home."

We say nothing of this system, which is apparently stillborn. In a footnote, we refer to the authorities pro and con.[10]

The texts of the Synoptics, unless violence is done to them, are fatal to the three preceding systems. The Synoptics repeat time and again that Jesus ate the *Passover;* they expressly affirm that he ate it on the day when "it was immolated" or "it was necessary to immolate it," i.e., on the evening of the 14th of Nisan, which was the "first day of Azymes."

Fourth System — *Jesus ate the Passover on the legal day, the evening of the 14th of Nisan; but the Jews, anxious to put him to death, put off the Passover until the following day.*

The Jews willfully violated this law, as they had violated so many other laws, to rid themselves of Jesus as soon as possible, now that he had fallen into their hands. This is the view of Eusebius and of St. John Chrysostom, a view which is altogether unlikely, and which is shared only by Fr. Knabenbauer, who, surprisingly, confuses it with the following system.[11]

Fifth System — *In that year, the Jews, by virtue of the arbitrary law of* badu, *had fixed the slaying of the Paschal lamb on the 15th of Nisan, while Jesus kept the Passover on the legal day, the evening of the 14th.*

Abbot Rupert in the twelfth century, depending on *Jewish traditions,* was the first to propose this system, which was sustained in the fifteenth century by a converted Jew, Paul of Burgos, and embraced by a great number of commentators and exegetes: Salmeron, Jansenius of Ghent, Maldonatus, Estius, Cornely, etc. Unfortunately the rule in question is not earlier than the fourth century.[12] There is not a trace of it in the time of Christ. The Mishnah has not a suspicion of it, since in

---

[10] For the *Qiddush,* see Box, in *Journ. of Th. Stud.,* III, 1902, pp. 357–369; Oesterley and Box, *The Religion and Worship of the Synagogue.* Against the *Qiddush,* see Lambert, in *Journ. Th. Stud.,* IV, 1903, pp. 184–194; Mangenot, in the *Rev. du Clergé,* Feb. 19, 1909; Lagrange, *S. Marc.,* 4 ed., 1929, pp. 357–359.

[11] Eusebius, *De solemnitate paschali,* 12 (MG, XXIV, 706); St. John Chrysostom, *In Matth. hom., 84* (MG, LVIII, 754). Knabenbauer, *In Matth.,* apud 26:17, takes his place beside the partisans of the law of *badu,* which he finds unconvincing; and at the same time he follows Eusebius and Chrysostom.

[12] According to this rule, the Paschal solemnity of the 15th of Nisan could not fall on Monday, Wednesday, or Friday. This is summarized in the word *badu* (בדו): the letters of the word, according to their numerical values, indicate that the 15th of Nisan can be neither the second day of the week (ב = 2) nor the fourth day (ד = 4) nor the sixth day (ו = 6), the week closing with Saturday. But this rule, as also the rule of *adu* (אדו), which forbade the first month of the civil year, Tishri, to fall on a Sunday (א = 1) or a

several passages it mentions cases in which the Paschal solemnity falls on Friday and is not transferred to Saturday, as the rule of *badu* would require. The hypothesis is therefore untenable.

THIRD SOLUTION — *In the year of Christ's death, there was a disagreement between the Pharisees and Sadducees about the fixing of the date of the Passover, and they celebrated it on two consecutive days.*

This solution, which alone satisfactorily harmonizes St. John and the Synoptics, had been glimpsed and even clearly presented some time ago by Petau. The learned Jesuit established these three points: (1) Jesus ate the Passover on the 14th of Nisan *with a minority of the Jews.* (2) This was the legal day, but *because of a disorder introduced into the calendar,* the majority of the Jews did not eat the Passover until the following day. (3) It makes little difference what the cause of the confusion was, provided that its existence be established. Here Petau depends upon an obscure text of Epiphanius, from which not much can be drawn, but his three assertions are to be retained, since this is the direction taken by contemporary Jewish scholars and experts in Rabbinical lore.[13]

Chwolson opened up the way without reaching the end of the road.[14] In conformity with the letter of the law and with ancient usage, the slaying of the Paschal lamb should take place "between the two evenings" (Exod. 12:6; cf. Deut. 16:6), i.e., between sunset and the moment when the first three stars were perceptible in the sky. This was always the understanding of the Sadducees, the Karaites, and the Samaritans. But when the 14th of Nisan fell on a Friday, it was absolutely impossible to slay the lamb in the Temple and to cook it at home without violating the Sabbath, the twilight being relatively short in Palestine. In this case, the lamb was slain on the 13th of Nisan, and some, e.g., the Pharisees, ate it *the same day* to obey the law of Exodus 12:8, while others postponed the eating of it to the following day, the 14th of Nisan, to conform to another law of Exodus 12:6. This hypothesis is very much open to dispute. Even from the time of

---

Wednesday (ד = 4) or a Friday (ו = 6), was formulated only in A.D. 344, when Hillel II replaced the empirical system of the calendar in use before that time by a calendar with a scientific basis.

[13] Petau, *Doctrina Temporum,* and also *Rationarium Temporum,* Second Part, Bk. II, Chap. 4, and especially *De Anno et Die Dominicae Passionis* in his edition of St. Epiphanius (MG, XLII, 839–1016). Hardouin, *De Supremo Christi Paschate,* Paris, 1693, follows Petau, but introduces the rule of *badu,* and holds that Jesus ate the Pasch *with the Galileans* on the evening of the 14th of Nisan, a day earlier than the rest of the Jews.

[14] *Das Letzte Passamahl Christi und der Tag seines Todes,* Leipzig, 1908.

Christ, the Pharisees had adopted the custom of beginning the slaying of the lamb at three o'clock in the afternoon and, according to the Mishnah, even at half past two when the following day was a Sabbath. Again, it cannot be admitted that the Jews would have slain and eaten the Paschal lamb on a day which they knew to be the 13th of Nisan, when the Law of Moses was so formal on this point. However, the Pharisees and the Sadducees may well have differed, as Chwolson thinks, about the date of the eating of the lamb.

A learned Jew, Dr. Klausner, in a work published first in Hebrew and later translated into German, thus modifies Chwolson's theory.[15] A tradition (*halakah*), raised to a principle by the Pharisees in the time of Hillel, taught that the Passover, since it was a *public sacrifice,* took precedence over the Sabbath; the Sadducees, on the contrary, faithful to ancient custom, considered it to be a *private sacrifice* which would yield to the Sabbath. Furthermore, they understood the regulation about the time of immolation, "between the two evenings," in the strict sense as the very brief interval of Jerusalem twilight. Therefore, when the 15th of Nisan fell on a Saturday, they slew the Paschal lamb, not on the 14th of Nisan, which would involve a violation of a Sabbath already begun, but on the 13th of Nisan. They ate the lamb the same evening, together with the obligatory accompaniments of unleavened bread and bitter herbs. According to this theory, Jesus followed the practice of the priestly caste (the Sadducees), who were in possession of authority.

It is readily seen that this hypothesis, which is grafted upon that of Chwolson as an improvement, reconciles St. John and the Synoptics. Klausner adds a reflection which emphatically recommends itself to the attention of Biblical scholars and critics. "We do not know precisely how the Jews at the time of Jesus fixed the date of the new moon, for the Sadducee priests of the faction of Boethus were at that time in control of the Temple." There is the crux of the matter.

Billerbeck, who does not seem to have been acquainted with Klausner's work, explains the disagreement between the Sadducees and Pharisees by having recourse to a hypothesis advanced by Jechiel Lichtenstein in his commentary on St. Matthew (in Hebrew).[16] Strack had already embraced Lichtenstein's opinion, which he knew by hearsay before the publication of the commentary: "The most probable thing," he writes, "is that there existed no unanimous agreement (*Einstimmigheit*) about the beginning of the month of Nisan. Many of the

---

15 J. Klausner, *Jesus von Nazareth,* Berlin, 1930, p. 449 (English transl. by Herbert Danby, p. 326).

16 Lichtenstein, *Kommentar zur Matthäus-Evangelium* (in Hebrew), Leipzig, 1913.

Jews, and among them Jesus, perhaps on the strength of an observation of the new moon, had fixed the beginning of the month, and consequently the 14th of Nisan, a day earlier than the Sadducees and the priests."[17]

A controversy existed between the Pharisees and Sadducees about the date of Pentecost. The Pharisees maintained that the offering of the first sheaf, the commencement of the seven weeks of Pentecost, ought always to be made on the day after the Paschal solemnity, i.e., on the 16th of Nisan; the disciples of Boethus (an influential party among the Sadducees) claimed that it ought to be made on the day after the Saturday following the Passover. When the Sadducees caused their view to prevail, whereas the Pharisees adhered to their own opinion, two Pentecosts were observed: that of the Sadducees which always fell on a Sunday, and that of the Pharisees which fell on a weekday corresponding to the 16th of Nisan. Something similar may have been involved as to the date of the Passover in the year of Christ's death.

Billerbeck places the divergence with regard to the Passover in relationship with the Pentecost controversy.[18] He conjectures that, when the 15th of Nisan was due to fall on Friday or Sunday, the Sadducees contrived to make the month of Nisan begin a day later or a day earlier, so that Pentecost should fall on a Sunday, the same day as for the Pharisees. The task of regulating the calendar was primarily incumbent upon the priests, and their opinion on this point prevailed in the Sanhedrin. At this period the influence of the followers of Boethus was great. During the years preceding and following the Saviour's death, they had no fewer than six of their members elevated to the High Priesthood; they had a reputation for boldness and violence: "Woe to the sons of Boethus because of their grip!" It is likely that, in the year in which Christ died, they had decreed that the first day of Azymes should fall upon a Saturday instead of Friday, as would have been required by the course of the moon.[19]

Hence a rift between Sadducees and Pharisees. The Synoptics would be reflecting the opinion of the Pharisees and the mass of the people, who ate the Passover on Thursday evening; and St. John would be holding to the official date decreed by the priesthood, which fixed the eating of the Paschal lamb on Friday evening.

---

[17] Strack, Edition of the treatise *Pesaḥim,* Leipzig, 1911, p. 10*; cf. p. 7.

[18] Billerbeck, *Kommentar,* Vol. II, pp. 847–853, 1924.

[19] The treatise of the Mishnah entitled *Rosch Ha-Shanah,* ii, 1b (edit. Fiebig, 1914, p. 83 and note) formally accuses the heretics (*Minim*) of having at a certain period caused disorder in the calendar. The *Gemara* of Babylon, as well as a *Tosephta,* I, 15, informs us that these *Minim* were the followers of Boethus.

3. Conclusion

In the year of the Passion, there was a disagreement about the date of the Passover between the Pharisees, who set the tone in religious matters, and the Sadducean chief priests, whose task it was to regulate the calendar. Both dates could be regarded as legitimate: one having in its favor the letter of the Law, the other the interpretation of competent authority. Jesus, knowing that he was about to die, chose the earlier date and ate the Passover Thursday evening with a certain number of his fellow countrymen — it matters little whether Pharisees or Sadducees — and the rest of the people ate it the following evening.

The question is not to be distorted. From the Gospel narrative we conclude that things *must have happened thus,* but we do not attempt to prove it directly. Resting upon the authority of contemporary scholars, Rabbis, or students of Rabbinical lore, we say only that things *could have happened thus,* and that is enough for us to solve the discrepancy.

We are too prone to believe that the religious practices of the Jews were perfectly uniform at that time, or that discrepancies were negligible. The reason for this belief is that we possess only writings that emanate from Pharisaic circles (the Mishnah, Gemara, Philo, Josephus), all others having been systematically suppressed at a time when all Judaism was imbued with the purely Pharisaical spirit. But this conception does not correspond to reality. And the discrepancies bore chiefly upon questions of the calendar.[20]

Let us not forget that many violations of the letter of the Law came about in the course of centuries. The decision of King Ezechias to retard the Passover by a month in order to increase its solemnity and to allow even the unclean to partake, which to us seems a doubly illegal decision, passed without any protest.[21] And when, in the fourth century, Hillel II abolished the empirical regulation of the calendar to replace it by a calendar with a more scientific basis, and when he established the arbitrary rules of *adu* and *badu,* disregarding the ancient system of the New Moons, his system being more convenient was promptly adopted.

It is surprising that the Pharisees and Sadducees should have disagreed on a question of date; but do we not still see Moslems of two neighboring localities celebrating Bairam (the closing of the fast of Ramadan) on two different days because one group has seen, or be-

---

20 Schumacher, *Der 14 Nisan als Kreutzigungstag und die Synoptiker,* in *Biblica,* Vol. IX, 1928, pp. 57–77.

21 Read the whole episode in 2 Para. 30:1–23.

lieves it has seen, the new moon a day before the other group?[22] Again, the famous disagreement of the Churches of Asia over the fixing of the date of Easter is still remembered; the decree of Nicaea on the controversy failed to bring about perfect harmony, because the Churches of Alexandria, Antioch, and Rome used different methods of computation for their calendars.[23] The Gregorian reform, so useful in itself, caused new disagreements, because it was only gradually accepted by the various countries. The Orientals in communion with Rome, with the exception of the Maronites, were late in adopting it, the Melchites or Uniate Greeks in 1857, the Syrians at almost the same time, the Armenians in 1912, the Rumanians in 1924. Do we not, even today, see this or that Catholic rite celebrating the Easter Mass on the evening of Holy Saturday? If such differences have existed and still exist in the Catholic Church, is it surprising that similar ones should have come about in the Synagogue?

Who were the Jews that ate the Paschal lamb a day later than Jesus? The question is of secondary and almost negligible importance. We are inclined to think that they were the chief priests and their adherents among the Sadducees. During the whole drama of the Passion, the chief priests give the cue and direct the movement — the others merely follow. It is to them that Judas sells his Master, to them he restores the price of iniquity. It is also they who decree in advance the death of Jesus (John 11:53), they who deliver him to Pilate and accuse him in the presence of the Governor (Mark 15:3,10; Luke 23:4; 24:20; John 18:35), they who persuade the people to demand Barabbas (Mark 15:11), they who are the first to cry out at the moment of the *Ecce Homo:* "Crucify him!" and who put an end to Pilate's indecision with the cry: "We have no king but Caesar" (John 19:6, 15), etc.

In the fixing of the calendar, the Sadducee priests enjoyed a preponderant authority. We know from the Mishnah that at one period they had succeeded in throwing it into confusion, and we have said that in this particular year they could have had a special reason for retarding the Passover by one day to solemnize it on Saturday.

---

[22] Lagrange, *Saint Marc,* 4 ed., 1929, pp. 262–263.

[23] Duchesne, *Revue des Questions Histor.,* Vol. XXVIII, 1880, pp. 40–42.

NOTE R

The Cenacle

1. Traditions Relating to the Cenacle

Four or five mysteries — the descent of the Holy Ghost on the day of Pentecost, the institution of the Holy Eucharist on the evening of Holy Thursday, the appearances of Christ to his Apostles on the evening of the Resurrection and again eight days later, and finally the falling asleep of the Blessed Virgin Mary — are commemorated in the Cenacle.

After the destruction of Jerusalem in A.D. 70, Mount Sion, where the Cenacle is situated, was left outside the city and given over to farming; the materials of the buildings which it contained were used in rebuilding the rest of Jerusalem. In this state of desolation Eusebius describes it; it was such when the Pilgrim of Bordeaux (in 333) passed through it without stopping. Still, as far back as the second century Christians had erected there a little church of which St. Epiphanius speaks, which, however, must have entirely disappeared by the time of Constantine. Shortly after the visit of the Pilgrim of Bordeaux, St. Cyril of Jerusalem (about 348) mentions there the "upper church of the Apostles," consecrated by the memory of the descent of the Holy Ghost. Before the end of the fourth century, the pilgrim Etheria tells how the Bishop with an escort of the faithful repaired there on the evening of Easter Sunday and the evening of the octave at nightfall, to commemorate the two appearances of the risen Christ, and especially on the day of Pentecost at the third hour (nine o'clock in the morning), to celebrate the descent of the Holy Ghost. In the following century Hezychius of Jerusalem (about 438) localizes very clearly, in the same place, the institution of the Holy Eucharist, the appearances of the risen Christ, and the descent of the Holy Ghost. From that time on the church on Sion was commonly called "the mother of all the churches."

Holy Sion, as it was also called, was rebuilt or restored by Modestus after the fire set by the Persians in 614, and was re-erected by the Crusaders after the capture of Jerusalem in 1099, probably on the same foundations. The pilgrims agree in saying that the church was very large, larger even than the Basilica of Constantine at Bethlehem. Fr. Vincent, after the excavations made by the Germans in order to erect the Church of the Falling Asleep of the Blessed Virgin, estimates it at about 200 feet in length by 110 in width. From the time of the Crusades it was called St. Mary of Mount Sion, because a tradition going back at least as far as the seventh century locates there the dwelling of the Blessed Virgin after the Resurrection. The site of Mary's house was pointed out to the left of the entrance at the northwest, and the Cenacle at the opposite or southwest extremity of the Basilica.

2. The Owner of the Cenacle

The mysteries accomplished in the Cenacle — the institution of the Holy Eucharist, the two appearances of the risen Christ to the Apostles, the election of St. Matthias, and the descent of the Holy Ghost — though differently attested by tradition, are always localized in the same place, on Mount Sion, where from the year 117 a little church existed, and where the upper Basilica of the Apostles, mother of all the churches, was built in the fourth century. If some authors of the sixth century, misled by a false exegesis, placed the washing of the feet in the grotto of Gethsemani, it was because they made a distinction between the supper during which Jesus, according to St. John, washed the feet of his disciples, and the supper during which he instituted the Holy Eucharist, according to the Synoptics. These authors were evidently mistaken, but no one advances the absurd opinion that the Eucharist was instituted outside Jerusalem in the Valley of Cedron.

The *spacious upper hall* where Jesus celebrated the Passover certainly belonged to a disciple, who loaned it to him in its entirety despite the scarcity of quarters during the great influx of people. Now, it is very unlikely that the Apostles would have had at their disposal several halls able to hold the large numbers of disciples who hurried together on the evening of the Resurrection, the hundred and twenty who met for the election of St. Matthias, and the considerable crowd which was gathered together on the day of Pentecost. Very naturally, therefore, the faithful, after the Passion of Christ, would have taken refuge in the large hall belonging to this generous disciple, and they would have continued to assemble there during the period of waiting for the promised coming of the Holy Ghost. So ancient tradition affirms, and no rival tradition counterbalances it.

The objection is sometimes raised that St. Luke, in designating by two different words the upper chamber where the Holy Eucharist was instituted (ἀνάγαιον) and the upper chamber where the Holy Ghost descended (ὑπερῷον), seems to indicate that he is making a distinction between them. The objection would have some force if it were not established that, in his account of the preparation for the Passover (22:7–11), St. Luke is adhering to St. Mark (14:12–16) whom he reproduces almost word for word. From him he borrows the popular word ἀνάγαιον; but on his own account he always uses the word ὑπερῷον, which is classical from the time of Homer (Acts 1:13; 9:37–39; 20:8). The Vulgate, with good reason, translates both words by *coenaculum,* and the Syriac Versions by *alîta.*

To whom did the Cenacle belong? The pilgrim Theodosius (about 530) answers without hesitation: "Ipsa fuit domus sancti Marci evangelistae." The Monk Alexander invokes ancient tradition in support of the same view: "We have from the ancients this tradition, that the man carrying the pitcher of water whom the Apostles followed according to the instructions given them by the Lord was Mark, the son of Mary." Three Biblical texts, if attentively read, confirm this opinion.

1. When the account of the preparation of the Passover in St. Matthew is compared with that of St. Mark, a precision of details is noticeable in the latter which seems to point to a personal knowledge of the situation. St. Luke, following St. Mark, keeps the picturesque detail of the man carrying the pitcher of water, but he tones down several other details, such as: "You shall say to the master of the house: 'The Master says to thee: where is *my* guest-chamber?' And he will show you a large upper room furnished and *all ready.*" St. Luke omits the italicized words, which are significant inasmuch as they show that Jesus is addressing a disciple or friend, and that this disciple is expecting his visit (Mark 14:12–16; Luke 22:7–12; Matt. 26:17–19).

2. The episode of the young man escaping from the hands of the armed horde, an episode peculiar to Mark, seems to have no other reason for insertion than as a personal recollection (Mark 14:51–52).[1]

---

[1] Many authors, Catholics as well as Protestants, take St. Mark to be the hero of this little episode. Knabenbauer (*In Marcum,* 1894, p. 383) names a good number. Several commentators on St. Mark may now be added: Gould (1901); Wohlenberg (1910); Klostermann (1926), with reserve; J. Weiss, *Das älteste Evang.,* p. 303; Burkitt, in *J.T.S.,* xvii, 1917, p. 296; and especially Th. Zahn, *Die Dormitio sanctae Virginis und das Haus des Joannes Marcus* (in *Neue*

Quite insignificant in itself, it has no connection either with what precedes or what follows. The young man is certainly not one of the Apostles; they have all taken to flight (Mark 14:50). If he is not the writer of the narrative why is he brought in at this point?

St. Mark could have been between fifteen and eighteen years old at that time, and the act that he is recording is that of a very young man, bold and curious. At what moment did he awake with a start and sally forth in his scanty attire? Was it when the guard was going down to Gethsemani to arrest Jesus, or when they were coming back to lead him before the High Priest? The text, having no chronological link with the general story, provides no answer, but it was very probably on the return.

3. St. Peter, imprisoned by King Agrippa, was miraculously delivered by an angel, the very night before his decreed execution. "After he had reflected, he betook himself to the house of Mary, the mother of John surnamed Mark, where a great number of the faithful were gathered together to pray" (Acts 12:12). The objection is raised: if the house of Mary was the Cenacle, the official place of prayer, and if it was the eve of the Passover, St. James would have been there, and St. Peter would not have had to send notice to him of his deliverance (Acts 12:17). The ill-founded objection rather strengthens our position. First of all, it was not the eve of the Passover, because St. Peter was arrested during the time of the Unleavened Bread (Acts 12:3) and was not to be put to death until *after the close* of the feast days, the 22nd of Nisan. During the interval, the faithful were taking turns at the house of Mark, praying night and day for the deliverance of St. Peter. At the time when he arrived there he did not find St. James, because the latter could not stay there permanently, and being more in danger than anyone else, as ruler of the Church of Jerusalem, he had probably taken cover. Peter, hurrying to quit the city before daybreak to make for Caesarea, did not have time to seek him out and therefore sent him notice through others who should be acquainted with his place of retreat.

3. Present Condition of the Cenacle

The Cenacle, transformed into a mosque since the sixteenth century, is now surrounded by filthy hovels and access to it is jealously guarded by fanatical Moslems. Entrance to the ground floor, where a supposed tomb of David is venerated by them, is absolutely forbidden to Christians and Jews; the upper floor can be visited for a price,

kirchl. Zeitschrift, 1899, pp. 377–429) and *Einleitung in das N.T.,* 3 ed., 1907, Vol. II, pp. 216–218.

but under the express prohibition against praying there or performing any act of devotion. It is reached from the outside by a lateral staircase containing twenty-four steps in all. "A postern, manifestly contrived at second hand into the massive southern wall, leads into a rectangular room of 15.30 by 9.40 meters on an average, oriented east and west on its main axis. A central row of three columns, to which correspond on both sides pilasters or columns embedded in the wall, divides the hall into two symmetrical naves and three bays of diminishing depth. Thick joists support the slender vaults, which are abundantly lighted by large ogival windows piercing the north wall on the axis of each of the bays. . . . Even the beholder least versed in the technical knowledge of architecture experiences the impression of a splendid Gothic hall soberly and harmoniously ornamented" (Vincent). At the eastern extremity of the Cenacle properly so called, a staircase of eight steps leads to a second hall equal in width to the Cenacle and about sixteen feet in depth. The general make-up indicates a work of the fourteenth century.

Its history is well known. In the thirteenth century the Basilica of the Apostles on Mount Sion, rebuilt by the Crusaders and then belonging to the Treasury of Jerusalem, fell into ruins. Beginning with 1335, thanks to powerful patronage, the Franciscans succeeded in acquiring some parcels of the surrounding ground and even the site of the Cenacle itself, the possession of which was assured to them by the Bull of Clement VI given at Avignon, November 21, 1342. From this period dates the reconstruction of the Cenacle in its present state. Since the absurd rumor that the ground floor enclosed the tomb of David gained circulation from the tenth century and was given more and more credence, the Moslems expelled the Franciscans from the Cenacle on June 2, 1551, and the venerable place was changed into a mosque.

When we say that the Cenacle in its present state dates from the fourteenth century, we are speaking of the upper floor. The exterior walls of the ground floor belong partially to the primitive Basilica whose southeast corner they occupy. For the description of the localities and the history of the successive buildings, no better reference can be had than the monumental work of Frs. Vincent and Abel, *Jérusalem,* Vol. II, pp. 421–481 (la *Sainte Sion*). A good résumé will be found in the *Supplément* to the *Dict. de la Bible,* Vol. I, cols. 1064–1084.

NOTE S

The Cross and Crucifixion

1. The Name and Shape of the Cross

1. *The Name* — The Latin word *crux* meant "torture" (hence *cruciare*); it was applied later to the cross only because that was the most painful form of punishment. The Greek word σταυρός means a "pale" or "post," and σκόλοψ means a "pointed piece of wood" or, as an instrument of punishment, a "stake." These words designate first of all the *simple cross,* i.e., the post to which a culprit was bound, there to die of exhaustion or to be devoured by wild beasts, as also a stake on which the body was impaled. This was the form of cross used from most ancient times, and the authors often allude to it. Speaking of the cross today, we always think of the *complex cross,* of which there are various kinds. Seneca's text is well known: "Video istic, non unius generis, sed aliter ab aliis fabricatas (cruces). Capite quidam conversos in terram suspendere; alii per obscoena stipitem egerunt; alii brachia patibulo explicuerunt."[1]

2. *The Shape* — There were three distinct kinds of complex crosses: (*a*) The *crux decussata,* or St. Andrew's cross, in the shape of a capital X. St. Jerome thus describes it: "Decussare est per medium secare, veluti si duae regulae concurrunt ad speciem litterae X, quae figura est crucis." (*b*) The *crux commissa,* or St. Anthony's cross, formed by a crossbeam placed on top of a post like a capital T. (*c*) The *crux immissa,* formed by two crossbeams cutting each other at right angles. If the four arms are of equal length from the center it is a *Greek cross,* if the upper portion of the vertical upright is shorter than the lower it is the *Latin cross.*

The cross of Jesus certainly had the shape of a Latin cross. The fact alone that the writing (*titulus, inscriptio*) was placed above his

[1] Seneca, *Consol. ad Marciam,* 20; cf. *Epistolae ad Lucil.,* 14.

head and hence at the top of the vertical upright suffices to prove it. St. Justin, St. Irenaeus, Minutius Felix, and many other later Fathers clearly testify in favor of the Latin cross, when they compare it to a plowbeam or to the yard of a ship, and when they say that the crucified nailed to the cross resembles a bird in flight or a man swimming. The satirical cross of the Palatine has also the form of a Latin cross. If some of the Fathers who use these comparisons sometimes ignore the upper extremity, which is less prominent, it is because they wish to give the cross the shape of a capital T (in Latin, Greek, and ancient Hebrew script), and to draw from this fact considerations of symbolism and mystery.[2]

3. *The Support* — Some authors think that the feet of Jesus rested on a support (*suppedaneum*), which artists frequently depict, but which is attested by no ancient document. The first to speak of it is St. Gregory of Tours in the sixth century, and about the eleventh or twelfth century the author of a poem on the Passion, mistakenly attributed to St. Gregory of Nazianzus.[3] On the contrary, it seems certain that the sufferer was seated on a peg or piece of wood fixed in the middle of the upright. This support was necessary to prevent the body from falling, the hands being unable to sustain the weight for long, without being in danger of tearing. The presence of this support is attested by witnesses who wrote at a time when the punishment of crucifixion was still very common: St. Justin, St. Irenaeus, and Tertullian.[4]

St. Justin, describing the cross, finds there five extremities or *horns,* namely, the four ends of the two crossbeams, plus the wood fixed to the center, precisely like a horn, on which the sufferer rests. St. Irenaeus is no less clear: "The cross has five points or extremities, two on its length, two on the width, and one in the middle on which the crucified rests." Tertullian calls the support, now a "projecting

---

[2] References in Justus Lipsius, *De cruce,* Bk. I, Chaps. 9 and 10.

[3] Gregory of Tours, *De gloria martyrum,* vi (MG, LXXI, 711): "Super hanc tabulam, tanquam stantis hominis, suffixae sunt plantae." — *De Christo patiente,* 655 (MG, XXXVIII, 189): *πόδας δὲ καθήλωσαν ἐν πηκτὸν ξύλον.* This last text is not clear: the *πηκτὸν ξύλον* could well be the upright.

[4] St. Justin, *Dial. cum Tryph.,* 91 (MG, VI, 693): *καὶ τὸ ἐν τῷ μέσῳ πηγνύμενον, ὡς κέρας καὶ αὐτὸ ἐξέχον ἐστίν, ἐφ' ᾧ ἐποχοῦνται οἱ σταυρούμενοι.* St. Irenaeus, *Adv. Haer.,* II, xxiv, 4 (MG, VII, 791–792): "Ipse habitus crucis fines et summitates habet quinque, duas in longitudine et duas in latitudine, et unam in medio, in qua requiescit qui clavis affigitur." Tertullian, *Adv. Nationes,* I, 12 (ML, I, 578): "crux cum illo sedilis excessu"; *Adv. Judaeos,* 10 (ML, II, 346): "unicornis autem media stipitis palus." Such a support was in use in Japan, where the punishment of crucifixion was inflicted up to recent times.

seat," or again "a peg fixed to the upright resembling the horn of a rhinoceros." In the Classics also are found such phrases as "seated on the cross," "riding on the cross." It is easily understood why, for aesthetic reasons, this support was suppressed by artists.

2. The Fixing to the Cross

1. *The Nails* — Jesus was not bound to the cross but nailed to it. Not three but four nails were used: such was the Roman custom[5] which almost all the ancient writers imply, v.g., St. Cyprian, Rufinus, St. Augustine, Theodoretus, etc., if we except Nonnus whose text is not clear, and a sixth-century versifier whose *Christus Patiens* is included among the works of St. Gregory of Nazianzus.

The authors who tell of the finding of the holy nails by St. Helena do not inform us how they were identified. The use which was made of them, attested by good authorities, seems to us almost a profanation. According to the story, a bit for Constantine's charger was made from one of them, another was inserted into his crown or helmet, a third was cast into the sea to quell a tempest.[6] The idea of shaping one of the nails into a bit was perhaps suggested by the text of Zacharias (14:20) which the Vulgate translates thus: "In die illa erit *quod supra frenum equi est,* sanctum Domino." But this exegesis does not please St. Jerome: "Audivi a quodam rem, sensu quidem pie dictam, sed ridiculam; clavos dominicae crucis e quibus Constantinus Augustus frenos equo suo fecerat, *sanctum Domini* appellari. Hoc utrum ita accipiendum sit lectoris prudentiae relinquo."[7]

The Greeks have always represented our Lord as fixed to the cross

[5] Plautus, *Mostell.,* II, i, 19: "Affiguntur bis pedes, bis brachia." In Egypt, on the contrary, according to Xenophon of Ephesus, the hands and feet of the condemned were bound to the stake (*Ephesiaca,* iv, 2); cf. Livy, I, 26: "Reste suspendito."

[6] St. Ambrose, *De obitu Theodosii,* 47 (ML, XVI, 1401): "Quaesivit (Helena) clavos quibus crucifixus est Dominus et invenit. De uno clavo frenos fieri praecepit; de altero diadema intexuit; unum ad decorem, alterum ad devotionem avertit." Rufinus, in the continuation of the Ecclesiastical History of Eusebius, expresses himself a little differently: "Clavos quoque quibus corpus dominicum fuerat adfixum, portat ad filium, ex quibus ille frenos composuit quibus uteretur ad bellum, et ex aliis galeam nihilominus belli usibus aptam fertur armasse" (*Hist. eccl.,* x, 8, Mommsen edition in Schwartz, *Eusebius, Kirchengeschichte,* p. 970). Also with variants, Socrates, Sozomen, Theodoretus, St. Cyril of Alexandria, St. Gregory of Tours. The last named writes in his *De gloria martyrum,* i, 6 (ML, LXXI, 711): "Quaeritur quid de his clavis fuerit factum. Duo sunt quos supra diximus aptati in freno; tertius projectus in fretum; quartum asserunt defixum in capite statuae Constantini."

[7] St. Jerome, *Comment. in Zachar.,* 14, 20 (ML, XXV, 1540); St. Gregory of Tours refers expressly to this prophecy.

by four nails. The Latins too, from the satirical crucifix of the Palatine up to the thirteenth century, remained faithful to the tradition thus formulated by Gregory of Tours: "Clavorum ergo dominicorum gratia quod quatuor fuerint haec est ratio: duo sunt affixi in palmis et duo in plantis." Martigny, in his *Dictionnaire des Antiquités Chrétiennes,* asserts that Cimabue and Margaritone were the first to depart from tradition. The departure is justified neither by likelihood nor by aesthetics. Doctors consulted by Rohault de Fleury assured him that it was impossible to fix both feet of a living man with one nail without breaking some bone. "A painter wishing to paint the Crucifixion after the modern Italian manner had tried to have a model pose placing one foot upon the other; he told me that he had never been able to fix them in a satisfactory position."[8]

2. *Erection of the Cross* — Crosses were generally driven down solidly into the ground. Examples are cited of condemned men who were nailed to a cross which was first laid on the ground and then lifted into an excavation which had been prepared in advance, but this was rare, as is plain from the expressions "to climb the cross," "to suspend upon a cross."

3. The Time of the Crucifixion

St. Mark writes (15:23–25): "They gave him wine to drink mixed with aromatics, and he refused it. And they crucify him and divide his garments, casting lots for them. It was the third hour and they crucified him." St. John writes (19:14): "It was the eve of the Passover, toward the sixth hour, and Pilate said to the Jews: 'Behold your king.'" The conflict seems evident. In the latter text, Jesus is not yet condemned at the sixth hour; in the former, Jesus is being crucified and it is the third hour. To solve the difficulty it has been conjectured that in one of the passages an original confusion had occurred between a *gamma* and a *digamma,* the numerical value of the former being three, and that of the latter, six. The confusion could have happened in the first centuries when the uncial script was the only one used. This was St. Jerome's opinion: "Error scriptorum fuit et in Marco hora sexta scriptum fuit; sed multi episemum (the *digamma*) graecum putaverunt esse gamma."[9] This solution would be acceptable if it were better supported, but it is without foundation.

---

[8] Rohault de Fleury, *Mémoire sur les Instruments de la Passion,* Paris, 1871, p. 167.

[9] *Breviarium in Ps. 77* (ML, XXVI, 1046). St. Jerome follows Eusebius; cf. Mai, *Nova Patrum Bibliotheca,* Vol. IV, p. 299. Others, on the contrary, think

The manuscripts which have the sixth hour in St. Mark or the third hour in St. John are an absolutely negligible quantity. Such a striking discrepancy could never have been introduced into almost all the manuscripts if it had not been in the original text. This solution, therefore, has all the appearance of a desperate evasion.[10]

If a choice between St. Mark and St. John were necessary, the latter should be preferred; first because he was an eyewitness, secondly because he is in general much more precise in taking note of the time; and finally because the sixth hour fits in better than the third for several reasons: the darkness prevailing over the earth from the sixth to the ninth hour, Pilate's astonishment upon learning that Jesus had died so soon, and the greater length of time needed for disposing conveniently all the circumstances of the trial.

It is known that theoretically the day was divided into twelve hours (John 11:9), but St. John is the only one of the Evangelists who makes use of this method of computation. He remembers that his first meeting with Jesus took place about the tenth hour (1:40), that Jesus arrived at Jacob's Well about the sixth hour (4:6), and that the son of the royal official was cured at the seventh hour (4:52). When, after recounting the scene of the *Ecce Homo,* he says that it was almost the sixth hour, he is indicating the middle of the day, though the sixth hour can be understood in two ways: for the precise moment when the sundial marks midday, or for the time elapsing between the fifth hour (11 o'clock a.m.) and the sixth (midday).

The Synoptics do not view things with the same exactitude. At a time when there were neither watches nor clocks, and when sand clocks and water clocks served only for certain special uses such as to set limits to an orator's eloquence, and when the few sundials were not consulted by the ordinary people, life was regulated, as even today with the majority of the Orientals, solely by the course of the sun and the stars; and the day was divided into four parts whose limits were sunrise and sunset, with three points of intersection, the third, the sixth, and the ninth hours.

The Synoptics do not appear to know any other computation; for the eleventh hour in St. Matthew (20:5:9) is simply a proverbial

---

that the original text of St. John had the *third hour.* So Corluy (*Comment. in Joan.,* p. 420), who enumerates the sponsors of this opinion.

[10] The same must be said of the hypothesis of Westcott (*St. John,* p. 282) that St. John was counting the hours according to the Roman civil day, which began, as with us, at midnight. The sixth hour would in that case be 6 a.m. But it is impossible that the whole trial of Jesus before Herod and Pilate should have been completed by sunrise. Besides, the hypothesis does not help at all in establishing harmony between John and Mark.

expression to indicate the approach of the close of day. It would have meant the same if he had said the twelfth hour. In this method of computing time, morning lasted up to the third hour (from 6 to 9 a.m.), the third hour lasted up to the sixth, i.e., up to midday, and so on. The four night watches were estimated thus: the first lasted from 6 to 9 p.m., the second from 9 to midnight, etc., without any attempt at greater precision.[11]

Let us return to the text of St. Mark. It is somewhat surprising. The soldiers crucify Jesus (in the present tense), they divide his garments (still in the present). Then of a sudden: "Now it was the third hour and they crucified him." Either the text is misplaced, or rather it is a retreat backwards to repair an oversight, or, if you will, a marginal note which has passed into the text. St. Mark gives this detail in the popular and unprecise form which tradition had preserved. He does not say that the crucifixion followed immediately upon the third hour, if we understand by this the precise time when the sundial marked 9 o'clock, but he says *during* the third hour, i.e., during the time elapsing between 9 o'clock and midday. St. John, when he says "about the sixth hour," does not contradict this.

On the method of computing the time of day and night see Note N: *Days and Hours Among the Jews.*

On the archaeology of the Passion, the two classical works are Justus Lipsius, *De Cruce Libri Tres,* 1592 (a second edition at Antwerp with notes and drawings, 1595; Brunswick ed. with an appendix, 1611), and Gretser, S.J., *De Cruce Christi,* 1598–1605 (three volumes of which the first treats the subject).

Among more recent authors may be cited: Zöckler, *Das Kruez Christi,* Gütersloh, 1875; Fulda, *Das Kreuz und die Kreuzigung,* 1878; G. Martin, *La Passion de J.-C.,* 3 ed. (from an historical and archaeological viewpoint), Paris, 1890; Olivier, O.P., *La Passion, Essai Historique,* Paris, 1892; Rohault de Fleury, *Mémoire sur les Instruments de la Passion de N.-S. J.-C.,* Paris, 1870; J. Hoppenot, S.J., *Le Crucifixe dans l'histoire et dans l'art, dans l'âme des saints et dans notre vie,* 1901.

[11] The division of the day into four parts is well marked in St. Matthew: morning (πρωΐ, 20:1), the third hour (20:3), the sixth and ninth hours (20:5), evening (ὀψία, 20:8). The division of the night into four watches of three hours each is found in St. Luke (12:38). The eleventh hour in St. Matthew is equivalent to the twelfth in Plutarch (*Crassus,* 17). Crassus, mocking the aged King Dejotarus, who was thinking of founding a new city, compares him to a man who begins to build a house at the *twelfth hour.* Here the twelfth hour indicates the interval between the eleventh and twelfth, i.e., between 5 and 6 p.m., just as the sixth hour in St. John designates the interval between the fifth and sixth hours (between 11 o'clock and midday).

NOTE T

The Way of the Cross

1. The Way of the Cross and the Via Dolorosa

In a learned and pious author I find the following reflection: "While the Church enriches the Way of the Cross with indulgences, she has no intention of certifying the historical genuineness of each Station: she wishes rather to instill in the hearts of the faithful a devotion to the sufferings and death of Christ, a devotion which consists above all in the meditation upon the mysteries of the Passion. The various Stations have as their purpose to furnish a sensible support to our imagination."[1] For this purpose it was necessary to place the Stations at fixed points even when no light was shed either by the Gospel or by tradition. For twelve centuries or more, tradition gave no guidance which allowed us to localize certain secondary facts of the Passion, such as the meeting with the women of Jerusalem and with Simon of Cyrene; more obviously there was none about the places associated with certain verified or supposed facts of which the Gospel has nothing to say, such as the three falls of Jesus and the Veronica episode.

Beyond the fact that we have no absolute certainty about the starting point of the Via Dolorosa and that we do not know where the gate was through which Jesus passed in leaving the city, the upheavals undergone by Jerusalem through the course of centuries create another source of uncertainty. And yet the level of the ground in this part of the city has changed less than is generally supposed. LeCamus writes: "Only a simple piety can retrace the footprints of the divine Victim on the Via Dolorosa, following it along modern streets which are more than thirty and often as much as sixty feet above the

[1] Hoepfl, O.S.B., *Die Stationen des Heiligen Kreuzweges in Jerusalem,* Freiburg i. Br., 1914, p. 53.

ruins of ancient Jerusalem."[2] This is an exaggeration. In the Convent of the *Dames de Sion,* near the Arch of the Ecce Homo, the ancient pavement is not more than five feet below the level of the present street. However, it matters little. Nowhere, except on Calvary or at the Holy Sepulcher, can we actually touch the soil trodden by the feet of the Saviour. The direction of the streets may also have changed. Fr. Zanecchia thinks he has proved that "the locations of the first eight stations are completely false." But very probably it is Fr. Zanecchia's theory that is false, since he places the Praetorium, not at the Antonia nor at the Palace of Herod, but at the Turkish tribunal (*Mehkemeh*). He is right however in adding: "It is a pious and praiseworthy practice to visit these Stations, and it is very proper to recall to the mind the facts which are associated with the Passion of our Divine Redeemer."[3]

2. The Origin and Progress of the Devotion

The practice of the Way of the Cross originated outside Palestine, when pilgrimages to the Holy Places sanctified by the Passion of Christ became difficult or impossible. The number of the stations and their order were not everywhere the same. Blessed Alvarez de Cordova, O.P., who died in 1420, had visited Palestine in 1405, and on his return home he had eight oratories built in which the same number of mysteries of the Passion were represented. Toward the end of the fifteenth century, another pilgrim named Ketzel had a Way of the Cross constructed at Nuremberg, beginning at one of the city gates, where the Praetorium was depicted, and finishing at the Monastery of St. John, with seven stations in between. The Louvain Way of the Cross, initiated by Peter Sterckx, dates from 1505; it includes eight stations, different from those at Nuremberg. The one at Romans, dating from 1515, still exists. The number of its stations, which varied from time to time, is thirty-four.

The true initiator of the Way of the Cross in the form we have at present seems to have been John Pascha, who died in 1532 without ever having seen Jerusalem. But his stations numbered only twelve. To reach the fourteen stations which we have at present, two more stations were inserted. This was done by Adrichomius, who knew and quoted John Pascha. His *Jerusalem,* published in 1584, was immensely successful.

Father Thurston has taken pains to go through what may be called

[2] LeCamus, *Vie de Jésus-Christ,* 8 ed., 1921, Vol. III, p. 364.
[3] Zanecchia, O.P., *La Palestine d'aujourd 'hui* (trans. Dorangeon), Vol. I, p. 359.

the attempts at the Way of the Cross between 1320 and 1636. From this study we learn: (*a*) that the Veronica episode does not appear until 1435 and is always placed very close to Calvary; (*b*) that the episodes of Simon of Cyrene and the women of Jerusalem are always placed one after the other and are not separated as now by two other stations. The first to employ the name "Stations" for the Way of the Cross seems to have been the Englishman, Wey, who visited Jerusalem in 1458 and 1462.

All the details which could be desired about the origin and progress of the devotion may be found in a collection of articles published in the *Month* by Fr. Thurston, translated into French by the Abbé Boudinhon under the title, *Ètude Historique sur le Chemin de la Croix,* Paris, 1907. Of interest too are Keppler's *Die XIV Stationen des heiligen Kreuzweges,* Freiburg i. Br., and Hoepfl, O.S.B., *Die Stationen des heiligen Kreuzweges in Jerusalem,* Freiburg i. Br., 1914 (with 16 photographs). About the Way of the Cross at Romans, where the indulgences may be gained despite the very unusual form, cf. *Acta Sanctae Sedis,* XIII, 1880, 319–323.

NOTE U

Calvary

1. The Place Called Golgotha

Nothing is more disconcerting, to the pilgrim who has not been forewarned, than to find the site of the Basilica which encloses both Calvary and the Holy Sepulcher in a depression of ground almost in the center of the city. The ground has been so greatly disturbed that it is now very difficult to reconstruct for oneself the original condition of the place. Dr. Schick tells frankly that, having arrived in Jerusalem, filled with Protestant prejudices against the authenticity of the Holy Sepulcher, he needed forty years of study and research to become convinced.[1] When Schick arrived in Palestine in 1846, the work of Robinson, the first edition of which had appeared in 1841, had acquired great celebrity in England and Germany in Protestant circles.[2] Robinson held that the site of Calvary and the Holy Sepulcher could not be authentic, because the wall of Jerusalem at the time of Christ would have enclosed them; that the tradition in favor of these sanctuaries has no more value than that which is invoked in favor of the sites of the Ascension and the Grotto of Bethlehem. However, he prudently refrains from indicating any other locality. His successors were more courageous. Ferguson, in 1847, was convinced that the Mosque of Omar was the edifice built by Constantine over the tomb of Christ.

---

[1] Schick, *Reflections on the Site of Calvary,* in *Palest. Explor. Fund, Quarterly Statement,* 1893, pp. 119–128.

[2] Robinson, *Biblical Researches in Palestine,* 2 ed., 1856, Vol. I, pp. 407–418 and Vol. III, pp. 254–263. Robinson's book gives evidence of a gift for observation which makes it still useful reading, but the author had a veritable phobia against *the tradition of the monks.* He concludes his dissertation against the authenticity of the Holy Sepulcher with this declaration of principle: "All ecclesiastical tradition respecting the ancient places in and around Jerusalem and throughout Palestine is of NO VALUE," Vol. III, p. 263. We are warned in advance.

Munk, in 1856, placed Calvary someplace on Mount Bezetha; Barclay, in 1857, put it in the Valley of Cedron in front of the present Church of St. Anne; Keim, in 1883, placed it near the Jaffa Gate. But the cleverest discovery of all was that of Thenius, who, in 1842, designated as the location the rock known as the Grotto of Jeremias to the northeast of the Damascus Gate. This opinion was adopted by Conder, Murray (author of a Guide to Palestine), and General Gordon, who gave his name to the new Calvary long visited by English and American tourists. They fancied that this rock, which was pierced by two cavities, resembled a skull.

Such fatuous guessing has passed out of vogue, but the skepticism of the second half of the last century has not been entirely dissipated. C. W. Wilson, who weighed the arguments, pro and con, with a true attempt at impartiality, arrives only at this conclusion: "No reasons of history, tradition, or topography are decisive in proving that Golgotha and the Sepulcher of Christ are in the place pointed out. On the other hand, there is no direct proof against it."[3] Perhaps he would go farther today. The argument from tradition has undergone no change; it had already been evaluated by Chateaubriand and the Marquis de Vogüé.[4] According to the very just estimate of Dalman: "The proof that the tradition indicating the site of Calvary at the place then occupied by the Temple of Venus is well grounded is the very unlikeliness of the location, which was then situated in the middle of the city. Everyone living in Jerusalem must have known that the Crucifixion took place on Golgotha, an Aramaic word meaning 'skull,' and the mention of this by all four of the Evangelists must have impelled all Christian visitors to Jerusalem to ask where the place was."[5]

The principal difficulty, in fact the only one, is a question of topography. It would appear at first sight that the second wall of Jerusalem, which started at the Gennath Gate or Gate of Gardens near the present Jaffa Gate and extended to the Antonia, would have enclosed the present sites of Calvary and the Holy Sepulcher. Recent researches have done much to clear up this point. It now appears to be well established that the second wall did not enclose Golgotha and the tomb of Christ; it was however very close to them. It may be asked why this projection

---

[3] Wilson, *Golgotha and the Holy Sepulcher,* a series of articles published in the *Palest. Explor. Fund, Quarterly Statement,* 1902–1904, gathered into a book after the author's death. An exposition and discussion of the various systems can be found there with accurate references.

[4] Chateaubriand, *Mémoire sur l'authenticité des Traditions Chrétiennes à Jérusalem,* in the Introduction to *Itinéraire de Paris à Jérusalem;* M. de Vogüé, *Les Eglises de Terre Sainte,* 1860, pp. 118–232.

[5] Dalman, *Jerusalem und sein Gelände,* Gütersloh, 1930, p. 72.

of ground was not enclosed within the ramparts. It was because Golgotha is the last spur of a hill which dips down toward Jerusalem from the watershed. If it were desired to have, on this side of the city and in front of the ramparts, ground which did not rise, it would have been necessary to carry the wall a mile and a half farther out from the city.

2. The Present Condition of Calvary[6]

When, in 326, Constantine wished to extend to the Church of Jerusalem the liberality from which Rome and Constantinople had already benefited, he began with the tomb of Christ. The Temple of Venus, built by order of Hadrian on an artificially constructed esplanade, was demolished, and the ground was cleared down to the original soil. Then appeared Calvary and the Holy Sepulcher, providentially authenticated by the very profanation which had been aimed at obliterating their memory. The buildings designed by Constantine's architects measured altogether nearly 492 feet in length, and succeeded one another in the following order beginning from the east: a Propylaeum facing upon the main artery of the city, an atrium encompassed by colonnades, a large basilica with five naves called the *Martyrium,* an open-air court surrounded on three sides by porticoes enclosing Golgotha, and finally the rotunda of the Anastasis covering the tomb of Christ. Since the available ground was uneven, it was necessary to level it in order to have a uniform surface; only Calvary and the Holy Sepulcher were spared, the rock being cut away from this section and leaving it in the form of a cube. These labors are described by Eusebius, with more rhetoric than accuracy, in his Life of Constantine; the description which he had written in simpler style was unfortunately lost.

It is important to note that in the Gospels Calvary is never called either a mountain or a hill. It is "Golgotha, that is the place of the Skull, in Latin Calvariae locus" (Matt. 27:33; Mark 15:22), or "the place called the Skull" (Luke 23:33), "the place called the Skull, in Hebrew Golgotha" (John 19:17). Golgotha was not a point of ground but an extended space: "There was in the place where Jesus was crucified a garden" (John 19:41). It was not called a mountain or hill or prominence until it was cut away and isolated from the rest by Constantine's architects; but then, seen from below, it did look like

[6] On the present position of research, and also the ground relief of this region. no better source can be sought than Fr. Vincent, O.P., *Jerusalem,* Vol. II, pp. 89–104.

a slight eminence.[7] For a long time Calvary remained in the open, in the atrium situated between the rotunda covering the Holy Sepulcher and the Basilica of the Martyrium. It was surrounded by a protective railing and surmounted by a cross of silver adorned with precious stones. The Crusaders enclosed it in the monument, which, despite numerous modifications, corresponded on the whole to the present edifice. Today all lies hidden under a covering of marble and heavy masonry. Fr. Vincent, O.P., has explored with minute care and has described with his usual accuracy the parts of the holy rock which are still visible.[8] The plateau of Calvary, inside the walls surrounding it on three sides, measures 37.56 by 30.35 feet. Fr. Meistermann asserts, I do not know on what grounds, that only a quarter of the pavement which covers the surface rests upon the rock, and that the portion cut away in the form of a die is only 19.68 feet long by 16.40 feet wide.[9] This refers to the part situated in the northeast corner of the present Calvary.

The Gospels inform us that Calvary was outside the city and was near the tomb belonging to Joseph of Arimathea. And, in fact, the Holy Sepulcher is scarcely forty yards in a straight line from the place where the cross was planted, and the difference in elevation between the summit of Golgotha and the Sepulcher level is only sixteen feet. On the other hand, Calvary, though outside the city, was as near to it as possible. It was separated from it only by a wide moat and a much-used thoroughfare.

For more details on the site and history of Calvary and the Holy Sepulcher, we refer the reader to the enlightening and accurate exposition by Fr. Dressaire, in *Jérusalem à travers les siècles,* 1931, pp. 279–323.

---

[7] The Pilgrim of Bordeaux calls it *monticulus Golgotha;* St. Cyril of Jersualem, who pronounced his *Catecheses* at the foot of Calvary, always calls it "this holy Calvary which looks down upon us." Later it was called *mons Calvariae* (*Breviarius de Hierosolyma, etc.*).

[8] Vincent-Abel, *Jérusalem,* Vol. II, pp. 97–104.

[9] *Guide de Terre Sainte,* 1923, p. 135.

NOTE V

The Holy Sepulcher and the Tomb of Lazarus

1. Jewish Burial

Throughout their history the Jews, like the Egyptians and the Chanaanites, disposed of their dead by burial; cremation, which was practiced at Babylon and later at Rome, was altogether unknown among them. At first the numerous caves and grottoes piercing the soil of Palestine served as resting places for their dead, and sometimes also as domiciles for the living. Later on, tombs were carved out of the rock. The soft limestone, which forms the skeletal structure of Western Palestine, lent itself marvelously to this purpose, being soft but hardening upon exposure to the air. What distinguishes the ancient Jewish sepulchers is their great simplicity. There were no inscriptions, little or no ornamentation, nothing above ground level. Desertion of this simplicity betrays Greek influence and is the mark of a later period. This latter is the case with the monuments which are so admired in the valley of Cedron, mistakenly called the tombs of Absalom, of Zacharias, of St. James, and of Josaphat.

The tombs of the time of Christ and of a period before the Christian era show a great deal of variety. A walk in the Valley of Cedron and in the environs of Jerusalem is more instructive with regard to this subject than any number of dissertations. There to be seen are large collective burial places, such as the Tombs of the Kings (the family vault of Queen Helena of Adiabene), the mistakenly named Tomb of the Judges, and the supposed Tomb of the Prophets. Detailed descriptions of these may be found in any "guide" to Palestine.

A less well-known but still interesting and characteristic specimen is the sepulcher discovered in 1899, which is situated some 400 or 500 yards northeast of the Tomb of the Judges. It was fronted by a courtyard, either in the open air, like that of the Tomb of the Kings, or perhaps vaulted over, as was certainly that of the Tomb of the Judges in former times. A large carved door of some ten feet in height and eight in width led into a vestibule cut out of the rock. At the back of this very spacious vestibule and opposite the entrance, an opening scarcely twenty-four inches high gave access (by crawling) to an antechamber about thirteen feet deep. From this antechamber access is had to three burial chambers intended to receive nine bodies each. One of the chambers leads to another built on a different level, doubtless carved out after the first three were filled. This remarkable tomb dates from the Hasmonean period and therefore belongs to a time before the Christian era.[1]

To close the low, narrow opening between the vestibule and the tomb itself, or between the antechamber and the burial chambers, three methods were in use. A vertical slab was placed against the dividing wall; or a rock fitted to the shape of the opening was thrust into it like a stopper; or a rock shaped like a millstone, a little larger in diameter than the height of the opening, was rolled in a track or groove prepared beforehand along the front of the wall.

The places in the burial chamber destined to receive the bodies were also of three kinds. First, there were the *loculi,* which we would call coffin vaults, though the Jews never made use of coffins. These were recesses hewn perpendicularly into the walls of the chamber, except on the side of the entrance. They had more or less the following dimensions: six feet in length and eighteen inches in width, and less than that in height. These *loculi,* numbering three on each side, were situated either at ground level or somewhat higher; sometimes there was a second row placed above the first, thus giving eighteen places instead of nine to the burial chamber. Other tombs had *arcosolia* or depressions cut laterally into each of the sides, presenting below a plane surface the length of a man and assuming above the shape of the arc of a circle. But the commonest arrangement was a stone ledge fixed to the rock, running along the wall on three sides of the chamber. The place intended to receive the head of the corpse was often slightly raised, and sometimes the surface of the ledge, instead of being a plane, was cut into the shape of a trough.

The configuration of the terrain also made necessary other variations. When a vertical wall could be had, as is often the case in the land to the south and east of Jerusalem, either the vestibule of the tomb, or the tomb itself without any vestibule, was cut into this surface after it had been smoothed off. In a flat terrain a simple trench was cut out of the rocky ground for individual tombs, and the tomb was

---

[1] For details, see Macalister, *Quarterly Statement, Palestine Explor. Fund,* 1900, pp. 54–61 (four plates), or Vincent, in *R.B.,* 1899, pp. 287–297.

closed horizontally. For collective tombs, requiring more ample dimensions, a descent of several steps was made, and the horizontal slab was placed over the top of the stairway.

2. The Tomb of Christ

Present Condition — The Holy Sepulcher measures on the inside 6 ft. 8 in. in length and 6 ft. 3 in. in width. The burial couch to the right of the entrance is 25 inches above the ground level and has a width of 3 feet. The Chapel of the Angel, which has replaced the ancient vestibule, is 11 ft. 2 in. by 12 ft. 9 in. But what is now visible, the marble facing that covers everything, does not correspond to reality, for the tomb of Christ is not intact. In 1009 the Egyptian Fatimite Caliph Hakim-bi-amr-Allah, having made himself master of Jerusalem, ordered all Christian buildings to be utterly destroyed. At the Holy Sepulcher the work of demolition was carried on for five days; nothing was spared except what was too hard to demolish or what would take too much time to destroy. In 1809, at the time of the rebuilding of the Basilica which had been burned down the preceding year, Maximus, the monk who supervised the work, had the happy thought of committing to his diary a description of what was left of Christ's tomb. There remained only the north and south lateral walls. Unfortunately Maximus does not say what their height was.[2]

Primitive Condition — The present condition of the sepulcher allows us to estimate the original dimensions of the tomb properly so called. It was unusually small and was made to hold only one body. The burial couch attached to the rock must have been surmounted by a vault in the shape of an arc (*arcosolium*) also cut out of the rock. This has disappeared, together with the upper part of the northern wall. We have said elsewhere that Constantine's architects, for reasons of symmetry or perspective, had suppressed the vestibule. This vestibule must have been on the same level as the surrounding soil, for nowhere is it said that there was a descent.[3] As to the rock shaped like a millstone which sealed the narrow opening of the tomb proper, St. Cyril of Jerusalem mentions it several times beside the tomb. The anonymous Pilgrim of Piacenza saw it in the same place in the

---

[2] See Vincent and Abel, *Jérusalem,* 1914, Vol. II, pp. 248–249 and 299–300; Fr. Meistermann (*Guide de la Terre Sainte,* 1923, p. 126) states that the rock rises to the height of about 3.28 feet.

[3] Cf. Dalman, *Les Itinéraires de Jésus* (enlarged French edition), Paris, 1930, pp. 475–478.

sixth century. In the following century, according to Arculf, it was cut in two and served as an altar.[4] After that it disappeared.

Two tombs, almost contemporary to the tomb of Christ and perfectly intact, were discovered in the spring of 1923 on the property of the Benedictines of Abu Ghosh, nine miles from Jerusalem along the Jaffa road. We paid a visit to them in 1928. They are very interesting as a term of comparison for the Holy Sepulcher. They are 9 ft. 10 inches in length and width and are respectively 5 ft. 3 in. and 4 ft. 3 in. high. Along their sides, except the side of entry, runs a stone bench joined to the rock. In one of the tombs this slab is flat, and in the other it is carved out after the fashion of an uncovered sarcophagus. The opening of the tomb is very low, as is generally the case, and a descent of some steps is hewn into the rock. The particular feature most worthy of remark is the closure in the form of a millstone, which is still to be seen in its groove. One of these rounded stones (in Hebrew *golel*) is 2 ft. 8 in. in diameter and 8½ in. in thickness. The diameter of the other is 2 feet, and its thickness 10 inches.[5]

The differences between these two tombs and that of Christ are as follows:

1. They were notably larger, since they were built to contain three bodies, whereas that of Christ could hold only one.

2. They had no vestibule and there was a descent of several steps, whereas the vestibule before Christ's tomb was entered, it would seem, at ground level.

3. They were lower than is usual, because of the smaller outcropping of rock in this region. The tomb of Christ must have been, as is usually the case, as high as the height of a tall man.[6]

4. The burial couch, where the body of Jesus lay, was surmounted by an *arcosolium* carved out of the rock of the northern wall. The slab itself was neither carved in the shape of a sarcophagus, nor was it entirely flat. At the place for the head it had a sort of cushion, and at the place for the feet an elevation which made it possible to see what the position of the body had been (John 20:12).

5. Finally, the rounded rock which sealed the tomb of Jesus was very large (Mark 16:4), one may say at least 2 ft. 10 in. in diameter and 13 inches in thickness. If so, it would weigh 1102 pounds or more. Since the groove generally had a slight slope, it was easy to

[4] St. Cyril, *Catech.*, XIII, 39 (MG, XXXIII, 820). The anonymous Pilgrim of Piacenza, in Geyer, *Itinera Hierosol.*, p. 171; Arculf, *ibid.*, p. 225.

[5] *R.B.*, 1925, pp. 275–279, with drawings and photographs.

[6] The usual height is at least six and a half feet.

roll this millstone against the entrance of the tomb, but it would require strong arms and suitable appliances to roll it back again, the more so since it offered so little purchase.[7]

3. The Tomb of Lazarus

On flat or only slightly sloping ground the tombs were simple trenches cut out of the rock and sealed by means of a slab placed horizontally. Care was taken to whitewash these slabs from time to time in order to attract the attention of passers-by, because they would contract a legal uncleanness if they should inadvertently tread upon them.

For family vaults, such as the tomb of Lazarus, the task was more complicated. A grave recently discovered between Bethany and Jerusalem gives an accurate idea of them. It is the more interesting in that it has — as is rarely the case — remained unviolated. The entrance has the shape of a rectangle (5 ft. 11 in. by 2 ft. 2 in.) on the surface of the ground, but the slabs which seal it cover a small burial chamber which slants to the right and the left in order to make room for two *loculi* with *acrosolia*. At the further end of the little chamber, a slab placed flat forms a descent of two steps to a lower chamber containing four lateral trough-shaped depressions, two on either side, and a *loculus* in front.[8]

The tomb of Lazarus apparently corresponded to this type; but the entrance of the vestibule was unobstructed, and a descent was made to the single burial room upon lifting a slab which was placed flat in the vestibule. Today it is difficult to reconstruct exactly the original condition of the place, since the ground has been so much disturbed by successive constructions. At one time the entrance was toward the west, i.e., lower down, and it is probable that the vestibule was entered directly. This entrance was walled up by the Moslems in the sixteenth century, when a small mosque was built upon the ruins of the ancient Christian Basilica. It was then that the Franciscans built

---

[7] The diameter of these rounded stones varies greatly. We have given that of the stones at Abu Ghosh. The millstone rock sealing the Tomb of the Kings (of Queen Helena of Adiabene and her family) is 2.62 ft. in diameter; that of the Tomb of the Herods, 5.25 ft. in diameter and 1.15 ft. in thickness. These exceptional dimensions are explained by the circumstance that mobile sarcophagi were introduced into the tomb. Cf. *R.B.*, 1892, pp. 267–270. In contrast, a rounded stone mentioned by Dalman (*Itinéraires de Jésus*, p. 422) is much smaller than the average, and has a diameter of only 1.94 by 0.62 ft. thickness.

[8] Description and engravings in *R.B.*, 1923, pp. 108–111. The grave was found on the property of the Benedictines at *Batn el-Hawa,* popularly called the Mount of Offense.

a stairway of 26 steps leading to the vestibule in a southerly and then westerly direction.

In its present state, the vestibule measures almost ten feet across. A small stairway of three steps, formerly sealed by a horizontal slab, permits descent by a narrow opening into the tomb itself, which is located at a lower level. The tomb is scarcely 6 ft. 6 in. across. It contains three arched loculi carved out of the walls in front and on both sides of the entrance. Since the limestone was very brittle, the walls were coated with cement which at one time was covered with marble plaques; these, however, have now disappeared. It is impossible to say to what extent the original form of the tomb has been altered.

NOTE W

The Fate of Judas

The fate of Judas is recorded by St. Matthew (27:3–10) and St. Luke (Acts 1:18–19). Each of the versions presents difficulties, as does also their reconciliation.

1. The Version of St. Matthew

(MATT. 27:3–10)

"Judas flung the pieces of silver into the sanctuary, and going out hanged himself. The chief priests, who had gathered up the silver, said: 'It is not permitted to put it into the treasury, since it is the price of blood.' After taking counsel together they bought with it the potter's field, for the burial of strangers. For this reason that field is called up to the present day Haceldama, that is, the Field of Blood."

a) "He flung the shekels into the sanctuary" (*εἰς τὸν ναόν*). The sanctuary is either the Sanctuary properly so called, the Holy Place and the Holy of Holies, or the collection of inner Temple buildings where the Jews alone entered, in opposition to the outer Temple (*ἱερόν*), which was accessible to all. Judas rolled the pieces of silver on the pavement of the sacred court, or in his anger aimed at the Holy Place, since it was not much more than some 130 feet from the Court of Israel.

b) "Going out he hanged himself" (*ἀπελθὼν ἀπήγξατο*). The natural sense is that he died by strangulation; but this is not expressly stated, and he could have survived the hanging either by being cut down in time, or by reason of the breaking of the rope.

c) "They bought with it the potter's field." This was a piece of ground known by that name, probably because the clay needed for the making of vessels was extracted from it. Since it was uncultivated ground, the 30 shekels (about 100 francs in former French money) would be enough to buy it.

d) "Since it is the price of blood." The chief priests' scruple comes from Deut. 23:18: "Thou shalt not offer the hire of a strumpet nor the price of a dog in the house of the Lord thy God to fulfill a vow, for both are an abomination before the face of the Lord." The dishonorable bargain of Judas who had trafficked in human life is likened by the chief priests to the shameful gain from prostitution, or to "the price of a dog," whatever be the meaning of that phrase.

2. The Version of St. Luke
(ACTS 1:18–19)

"This man (Judas) obtained a field with the price of iniquity, and falling forward burst asunder in the midst, and all his entrails gushed forth (Οὗτος ἐκτήσατο χωρίον ἐκ μισθοῦ τῆς ἀδικίας καὶ πρηνὴς γενόμενος ἐλάκησεν μέσος καὶ ἐξεχύθη πάντα τὰ σπλάγχνα αὐτοῦ). And the fact was known to all the inhabitants of Jerusalem, so that the field was called in their language Haceldama, that is, the Field of Blood."

We believe that these two verses are a parenthesis inserted by St. Luke into St. Peter's discourse. (1) They break the thread of the discourse, which runs along very consecutively if they are omitted: "It was necessary that the prophecy of David concerning Judas should be fulfilled . . . *for* it is written, etc." (2) St. Luke has a habit of inserting such explanatory parentheses into the speeches which he reports (Acts 1:15; 9:12; 10:29–31). (3) It is improbable that the name "Field of Blood" had already come into general use within forty days after the Passion. (4) St. Peter would not have said that the Jews called it Haceldama *in their language*. However, whether the text be St. Peter's or St. Luke's, the exegesis remains the same.

a) "He obtained a field with the price of iniquity" or the price of his crime. This creates no real difficulty. The 30 shekels rejected by the chief priests would still remain the property of Judas. It is with his money and, so to speak, in his name that the potter's field is bought. It is as though he had obtained it himself.

b) "And falling forward." The word πρηνής is akin to the Latin *pronus* in etymology, and to *praeceps* in meaning. In speaking of objects, it means "sloping," "inclined"; in speaking of persons, it means "leaning forward," "falling head first." The two Anglican versions correctly translate πρηνὴς γενόμενος, "falling headlong." The translation of Crampon in French *"s'étant precipité en avant"* (being precipitated forward) is doubtless somewhat overprecise.

c) The real difficulty is in understanding how, even by falling from a great height, the body of Judas could rend open in the midst so as to allow the intestines to come forth. In a very learned note, Chase has attempted to prove that πρηνής is a medical term equivalent to πρησθείς or πεπρησμένος (*bloated*); but W. Bauer does not accept this meaning of πρηνής. Others have thought that instead of πρηνής St. Luke wrote πρησθείς; but one can see no reason why any copyist would have replaced such a clear word by such an obscure one.

All agree that the translation of the Vulgate, *et suspensus crepuit medius,* is inexact: πρηνής cannot mean *suspensus*. The variant found by St. Augustine in a manuscript of the Old Latin Version, "*et collum sibi alligavit et dejectus in faciem disruptus est medius,*" is an attempt, probably a happy one, to reconcile Matthew and Luke.

3. The Judas Legend

Apollinaris of Laodicea (350–380) states that Judas being cut down in time survived the hanging, as the Acts of the Apostles imply and as Papias of Hierapolis expressly states in the Fourth Book. Papias (about 125–130), after describing the enormously bloated condition of Judas' body as it decomposed, relates that he died in his own field (ἐν ἰδίῳ χωρίῳ), and that thereafter such was the stench from the place that no one could approach it without holding his nose.[1] It is to be noted that Papias does not cite any authority, but reports the thing from hearsay (φασί, twice repeated); in a hundred years legend had time to form and grow.

A *catena* of the Acts in Armenian cites this passage, without naming any author, immediately after an extract from St. John Chrysostom: "Before hanging himself Judas closed the doors behind him and remained hanging Friday and Saturday. But the stench drew the people of Jerusalem, who came to contemplate this hideous spectacle and depressing end, a prelude to the fire of hell."[2]

Euthymius, in the twelfth century, writes: "Judas did not die immediately, as he had wished. Being recognized by certain people and taken down from the halter, he lived for some time in his own dwelling. Enormously swollen he burst in the midst and his entrails gushed out."[3] The point of peculiar interest in Euthymius is that he explains πρηνὴς γενόμενος by πεπρησμένος and ἐξωγκωμένος (*bloated, swollen*). Zonaras does the same in his Lexicon. Oecumenius, in the tenth century, cites Papias by name; Theophylactus also cites him, in the eleventh century, without naming him.

---

[1] Text of Papias in Funk, *Patres Apostolici,* 2 ed., 1901, pp. 360–363.
[2] Cf. Zahn, *Forschungen,* Vol. VI, pp. 153–157 and Vol. IX, 1900, pp. 351–353.
[3] Euthymius, MG, CXXIX, 706.

The monk, George Cedrenus, in the twelfth century, has this new detail: "After his hanging, Judas was daily exhorted by the Apostles to do penance, but in vain. Immediately after the Ascension of Christ, he swelled up and burst in the midst and died." Michael Lycas wrote a refutation of Cedrenus.[4]

Has this legend of Judas any foundation? It can be admitted that Judas may have survived his attempt at suicide by some hours or days. St. Matthew says that he hanged himself, but this does not necessarily mean that he died by strangulation, and the text of St. Luke seems to imply the contrary. St. Luke, for his part, says that Judas "falling from a height burst in the midst and all his entrails gushed forth," but he does not say that he died on the spot.

---

[4] Cedrenus, MG, CXXI, 384; Lycas, MG, CLVIII, 904.

NOTE X

The Apparitions of the Risen Christ

1. The Number and Order of the Apparitions

The apparitions of the risen Christ, during the forty days preceding the Ascension, were frequent (Acts 1:3); but only a few of them are mentioned in the Gospels and in St. Paul:

Two in St. Matthew (28:1–20): (A) to the holy women; (B) to the Eleven in Galilee;

Three in St. Mark (16:9–20): (C) to Mary Magdalene; (D) to two disciples during their journey; (E) to the Apostles in Galilee;

Three in St. Luke (24:13–53): (F) to the two disciples of Emmaus; (G) to Simon Peter; (H) to the disciples and the Apostles;

One in Acts (1:4): (I) to the disciples on the day of the Ascension;

Four in St. John (20:14–21:23): (J) to Mary Magdalene; (K) to the Apostles on the evening of Easter Sunday; (L) to the Apostles eight days later; (M) to the seven on the shore of the lake;

Five in St. Paul (1 Cor. 15:5–7): (N) to Peter (Kephas); (O) to the Twelve; (P) to more than five hundred brethren; (Q) to James the Brother of the Lord; (R) to all the Apostles.

That would be eighteen apparitions in all; but (*a*) the apparition to Magdalene is mentioned twice (C and J) and probably coincides with A (to the holy women); (*b*) the apparition to Peter is mentioned twice (G and N); (*c*) the apparition to the disciples of Emmaus also twice (D and F); (*d*) the apparition to the Apostles on the evening of Easter Sunday, twice (H and K); (*e*) the apparition to the Apostles in Galilee, twice (B and E); (*f*) either the apparition in O should coincide with that of E, or I should coincide with K and R (see below: the apparitions according to St. Paul).

There remain, therefore, ten distinct apparitions, which we may arrange in the following order:

1. To Magdalene (John 20:11–18; Mark 16:9–11) and the holy women (Matt. 28:1–10);
2. To Simon Peter (Luke 24:34) or Kephas (1 Cor. 15:5);
3. To the disciples of Emmaus (Luke 24:13–35; Mark 16:12–13);
4. To the Apostles and disciples in the Cenacle (John 20:19–23; Luke 24:36–43);
5. To the Apostles on the eighth day after Easter (John 20:24–29);
6. To the seven disciples on the shore of the lake (John 21:1–23);
7. To the Apostles in Galilee (Matt. 28:16–17; Mark 16:14–15);
8. To more than five hundred brethren together (1 Cor. 15:6);
9. To James the Brother of the Lord (1 Cor. 15:7);
10. To the Apostles and the faithful on the day of the Ascension (Acts 1:4; Luke 24:50–51).

2. The Apparitions of Christ According to St. Paul

The Apostle writes to the Corinthians (1 Cor. 15:3–8): "I have delivered to you what I received through tradition; namely, that Christ . . . rose again on the third day conformably to the Scriptures and that he appeared to Kephas, *then* to the Twelve; *afterward* he appeared to more than five hundred brethren at one time, of whom some are dead but the greater number are still living; *afterward* he appeared to James, *then* to all the Apostles, and *finally* he appeared to me," etc.

St. Paul does not intend to enumerate all the apparitions of the risen Christ; he omits, perhaps purposely, all mention of the holy women, and he retains only witnesses who were known to the Corinthians; but the words, *then, afterward, finally,* seem to indicate that he is intent upon keeping to the chronological order. There are five apparitions without counting the one with which he himself was favored.

1. The apparition to Kephas (this is the name by which he usually calls Peter) took place the same day as the Resurrection, as St. Luke testifies (24:34).

2. The apparition to the Twelve is that which was accorded to the Apostles on the evening of Easter Sunday (John 20:19–23; Luke 24:33–44). The Apostles numbered only ten, since St. Thomas was absent; but St. Paul can here use the expression, the Twelve (τοῖς δώδεκα is the correct reading, and not *undecim* as the Vulgate has), and St. Luke can call them the Eleven, because the Twelve, or the Eleven if we take into consideration the defection of Judas, was the official name of the Apostolic college whether complete or not.

3. Many authors think that the apparition to the more than five hundred brethren took place at the time of the Ascension of Christ, or that it should be identified with the one which was accorded the Apostles on a mountain in Galilee; but according to St. Luke (24:50–

53) the witnesses of the Ascension would not appear to be as numerous as that, and according to St. Matthew (28:16–20, *οἱ ἕνδεκα*) it seems that only the Eleven were present. It is better, therefore, to count it as a distinct apparition which took place in Galilee at an uncertain date.

4. We know neither the place nor the date of the apparition to James the Less, surnamed the Brother of the Lord. But if St. Paul, as we have said, is following the chronological order, it is probable that it took place in Galilee before the return of the disciples to Jerusalem.

5. When St. Paul says that Jesus appeared to *all* the Apostles, does he wish to indicate that at the time of the apparition mentioned above the Apostolic group was not complete, as Cornely thinks; or does he wish to speak of *apostles in a wider sense,* according to the opinion of Chrysostom, followed by other commentators? In any case, this apparition ought to coincide, either with the one on the mountain in Galilee, or with that of the Ascension; and there is no reason to make of it a distinct apparition.

3. The Farewell Discourse in the Three Synoptics

The three Synoptics, as is known, mention but one apparition to the Apostles. They link it with a definite circumstance and make it follow upon a discourse, which, according to the best Catholic exegetes, does not correspond, at least entirely, to this circumstance. Let us take a closer look.

1. In St. Matthew, the Eleven come to a mountain in Galilee, where Jesus has made an appointment with them. The Lord appears to them and they adore him (Matt. 28:16–17). Without transition, the Evangelist adds: "and drawing near he said to them: All power is given to me. . . . Go therefore, teach all nations, etc." (Matt. 28:18–20.) Who will doubt that the discourse follows the encounter? And still Maldonatus writes: "Sunt qui putant haec non tunc sed postea in ultima demonstratione, qua se Christus discipulis ostendit, cum vellet in caelum ascendere, accidisse; quod valde mihi probabile videtur." Maldonatus is right: this is a discourse of farewell; after having delegated to them all his authority and having given his commands in view of their future apostolate, the Lord has no more to say to his Apostles.

2. The ending of St. Mark's Gospel gives occasion to the same remarks. Jesus appears to the Eleven and reproaches them for their incredulity in having refused to believe those who had seen him (Mark 16:14). The Evangelist continues: "And he said to them: Go into the whole world and preach the Gospel to every creature, etc." Then,

the discourse over, he adds without any transition: "And the Lord Jesus, after he had spoken to them, was taken up into heaven." Reading this account, in which nothing implies any interruption, one could believe, unless warned otherwise, that the three apparitions of Jesus (to Magdalene, to Peter, and to the Eleven), his discourse to the Apostles, and his Ascension all took place on the same day, that is to say, on Easter Sunday. We know, however, from St. Luke that such was not the case. The question then arises, whether the discourse belongs to the first apparition to the Apostles, when Jesus reproaches them for their incredulity, or to the last, when he was about to ascend to heaven. Even Fr. Knabenbauer, who generally adheres to the strictest interpretation, is here forced to remark: "Cum hoc loco narratio sit valde succincta, nullo modo necesse est assumere ea quae v. 15 dicuntur ad eamdem pertinere apparitionem. Uti inter v. 19 et v. 20 longius spatium intercedit, ita quoque inter v. 14 et v. 15, id quod etiam inserto *et dixit illis* haud obscure innuitur." It is, therefore, necessary to establish longer or shorter intervals in this uninterrupted discourse; the evidence demands it. But it is doubtful whether the words *et dixit illis* could inject a suspicion of this if we did not have extrinsic reasons for admitting it.

3. We find something analogous to this in the last chapter of St. Luke. The disciples of Emmaus, having recognized Christ, return to Jerusalem, and while they are telling the Apostles of their adventure, Jesus appears and eats before their eyes to convince them that he is not a phantom. Without any transition, the Evangelist continues (Luke 24:45): *Et dixit ad eos*. And after a discourse, which sounds very much like a discourse of farewell, St. Luke resumes (24:50): *Eduxit autem eos foras in Bethaniam*. Now, in the Acts, St. Luke informs us that this event did not take place until forty days later (Acts 1:3; cf. 1:12). Here again, Catholic exegetes (Schanz, Knabenbauer, Lagrange, etc.) state that an interval must be placed between v. 43 and v. 44. In fact *εἶπεν δὲ αὐτοῖς* is a looser link than *et dixit eis*. Numerous examples show that St. Luke uses this phrase to join together events which are quite distant one from another, but even if he had said *καὶ εἶπεν αὐτοῖς*, as we have seen in the ending of Mark 16:15, it would create no difficulty.

Consequently it is very probable, to say no more than that, that the following passages, Matt. 28:16–20; Mark 16:15–18; Luke 24:44–49; Acts 1:4–8, all belong to a farewell discourse which was pronounced on the Day of the Ascension.

NOTE Y

The Question of Emmaus

Should the Gospel Emmaus be placed at Amwas (the ancient Emmaus-Nicopolis) on the road from Jerusalem to Jaffa, or at Qubeibeh in the same direction but much nearer to the Holy City? Josephus (*Bellum,* VII, vi, 6) was well acquainted with another Emmaus, a little village (χωρίον) 30 stadia from Jerusalem, where Vespasian established a colony of eight hundred veterans, and which is perhaps Qoloniyeh, four miles (35 stadia) from the city. But neither Qoloniyeh nor any of the neighboring places where some have wished to locate the Gospel Emmaus will fit requirements. The distance is too short, and tradition is absolutely lacking.

Textual criticism favors Qubeibeh, but tradition is in favor of Emmaus-Nicopolis. Hence arises a controversy, the elements and history of which may be found in the *Dict. de la Bible* of Vigouroux, Vol. II, cols. 1735–1747 (Heidet), and the *Supplément,* Vol. II, cols. 1049–1063 (Pirot), with maps and charts.

1. Textual Criticism and Tradition

The official Vulgate has (Luke 24:13): *Castellum quod erat in spatio stadiorum sexaginta ab Jerusalem nomine Emmaus.* Still, five important manuscripts have *centum sexaginta:* viz., Fuldensis (sixth century), Oxoniensis (seventh century), Lindisfarnensis (seventh or eighth century), Epternacensis (eighth or ninth century), and Sangermanensis (eighth or ninth century). In support of this latter reading are cited some Syriac and Armenian manuscripts, but none, it would seem, of the Coptic or Old Latin Versions.

The reading *sixty* is also much the commoner reading in Greek. Six Uncials (א I K N Π O) and some cursives read *one hundred and sixty.* The Cursive 194 has this notation: "160 should be read: it is the reading of the exact manuscripts and is confirmed by the authority of Origen." The Cursive 34 has the same note without mentioning Origen; also the manuscripts of the *Catena,* though Cremer's edition suppresses ἑκατόν. The numbers ἑξήκοντα and ἑκατὸν ἑξήκοντα, written in letters representing numerals (ξ', ρξ'), differ very little. Still the divergence in the manuscripts is not due to accident: "A choice must be made: either *one hundred* has been added because it was known that Emmaus was about 160 stadia distant, or this distance being judged too great, *one hundred* was suppressed" (Lagrange, *Saint Luc.*, p. 618). The critics generally adopt the first alternative. According to Hort, the reading *one hundred and sixty* is "an Alexandrine correction" to which Origen cannot have been a stranger. According to Von Soden, all the witnesses to the reading *one hundred and sixty* are linked with the "Palestinian recension," which was influenced by Origen. Tischendorf, despite his weakness for the Sinaiticus, prefers the reading *sixty*, because the number one hundred and sixty seems to him too large. Vogels is also for the shorter reading. Hence textual criticism favors *sixty stadia.*

But local tradition is unanimously in favor of the opposite. "In the fourth and fifth centuries the great tradition of the Holy Land represented by the Palestinians, Eusebius of Caesarea, Jerome of Bethlehem, Hezychius of Jerusalem, and Sozomen of Gaza, with one voice proclaim that the Emmaus of the Gospel is no other than Emmaus-Nicopolis."[1] The pilgrim Theodosius around 530, St. Bede the Venerable in the seventh century, and others echo the ancient traditions, as well as William of Tyre in the twelfth century.

It should be observed: (*a*) that these authors present this identification as a tradition having its roots in the past; (*b*) that they do not seem to suspect that there is any rival tradition; (*c*) that they accept it despite the difficulty in reconciling it with the preponderant reading of St. Luke's text. In fact, no different tradition exists. The one which was thought to be found in the Metropolitan John in the eleventh century rests upon a misunderstanding.[2] And yet Schiffers exaggerates[3] when he affirms that Reland, who published his *Palestina Illustrata* in 1714, is the first to contest the identification of the Gospel Emmaus with Emmaus-Nicopolis. Fabri (about 1480) and Suriano (1541) both preceded him.

In very early times a basilica of three naves was erected at Emmaus-Nicopolis, which must have been held in great veneration, because the Crusaders when they rebuilt it on a much reduced scale respected its ruins which are still admired. Fr. Vincent believes that the ancient

[1] Buzy, *Emmaüs et l'ancienne tradition locale*, in *Recherches*, 1914, pp. 396–397. For the texts, see Eusebius, *Onomasticon;* St. Jerome, *Epist.*, 108 (ML, XXII, 883); Sozomen, *Hist. eccl.*, v. 21; Hezychius (ML, XCIII, 1443); Theodosius, in Geyer, *Itinera Hierosol.*, Vienna, 1898, p. 139; Bede, *In Lucam* (ML, XCII, 625); William of Tyre, *Hist. Rerum Transmarin.*, vii, 24 (ML, CCI, 403).

[2] Van Kasteren, *Emmaüs Nicopolis,* etc., in *R.B.*, 1892, pp. 97–98.

[3] Schiffers, *Amoâs,* Freiburg i. Br., 1890; *R.B.*, 1893, p. 27.

basilica "dates from a Roman period anterior to any Byzantine influence, let us say from the beginning of the fourth century at the latest, and it could easily belong to the beginning of the third."[4]

2. Pros and Cons

1. Qubeibeh has been in possession for many centuries, and it is to this sanctuary that the indulgences for the Holy Places are attached.

2. The distance fits in very well, if *sixty stadia* be read in St. Luke. The length of a stadium varied somewhat in different cities. The Olympic stadium was almost 192 meters, the Delphic was 177 meters, and the Athenian stadium was 600 Greek feet or 185 meters. But in the Gospel the Italic stadium very probably is meant, which was equal to an eighth of a mile, or about 185 meters like the Athenian stadium. Qubeibeh, whose site is now agreed upon, is about 13 kilometers (eight miles) from Jerusalem.[5] That would be 70 stadia; but the difference between 60 and 70 is not very considerable.

3. Fr. Prosper Viaud, O.F.M., who has made a vigorous plea in favor of Qubeibeh, affirms: "There can be no doubt about it: at Qubeibeh we are at the Emmaus of the Gospel, and the house enclosed by the church is the house of Cleophas."[6] Fr. Vincent, O.P., is not of the same opinion. "The church of Qubeibeh, constructed in the twelfth century by the Crusaders on the type of a perfectly normal Roman basilica, is not the successor of any edifice whether religious or profane. Nor does it present to us a single feature whose antiquity can be proved."[7]

4. Emmaus-Nicopolis is 160 stadia from Jerusalem. The Pilgrim of Bordeaux says 22 Roman miles (176 stadia); Peutinger's map, 19 miles (152 stadia); Ptolemy, 20 miles (160 stadia). All depends upon the road one travels. There were three roads: one to the north, passing by the two towns of Beth-horon; one to the south, corresponding to the present route; and a third between these two which was only, it would seem, 18 miles (144 stadia). The 160 stadia of St. Luke would be the average.[8]

5. The other objections against Emmaus-Nicopolis have little force. It is urged that it is a town, whereas the Emmaus of St. Luke was a

[4] Vincent, O.P., in *R.B.*, 1926, *Fouilles d'Amwas,* p. 118. The dimensions of the ancient basilica are 148 by 82 feet.

[5] Cf. *R.B.*, 1931, p. 65.

[6] Prosper Viaud, O.F.M., *Qoubeibeh. Emmaüs évangelique,* Jerusalem, 1930, p. 23.

[7] Vincent, O.P., *Les Monuments de Qoubeibeh,* in *R.B.*, 1931, p. 91, with five cuts.

[8] Cf. Heidet, in *D.B.*, Vol. II, cols. 1739–1741; Abel, *La Distance de Jérusalem à Emmaüs,* in *R.B.*, 1925, pp. 347–367; Dalman, *Les Itinéraires de Jésus,* Paris, 1930, pp. 279–304.

village (κώμη). Emmaus-Nicopolis was always an important strategic point at the entry to the Judean mountains, but the town, whose inhabitants had been sold into slavery by Cassius (43 B.C.), was reduced to ashes by Varus in A.D. 6. We do not know to what degree it was rebuilt from its ruins. At any rate, the distinction between a town and a village is not very sharply defined. Josephus calls Lydda a village (κώμη), though it had been the principal town of a toparchy (*Antiq.*, XX, vi, 2).

Again, it is said that since Emmaus-Nicopolis was 160 stadia from Jerusalem the disciples could not have returned from there on the same day. This objection, which is taken to be decisive, is in reality very weak. Hezychius of Jerusalem has answered it in advance: "It is not strange that they should have made the double journey to Jerusalem and back again in the same day. They arrived at Emmaus when it was getting late and when the day was in decline (toward two or three in the afternoon). . . . The joy of having good news to tell would hasten their pace." The meaning of *advesperascit et inclinata est dies* is just that. To be convinced one need but read the episode narrated in the Book of Judges (19:1–14). If they started from Jerusalem at eight or nine in the morning the travelers would arrive at Nicopolis toward two in the afternoon, and they could have returned to Jerusalem before nine in the evening. At its shortest the double distance from Jerusalem to Emmaus and back is scarcely more than 36 miles, or ten or eleven hours of walking. Not so long ago, when people were still used to walking, any strong man was able to do that much in a day's march. Many have done so without thinking it anything extraordinary.

On the other hand, it is the nearness of Qubeibeh, two hours or two hours and a half from Jerusalem, which creates difficulty. If the disciples did not start until the afternoon, how could they have been unaware of the apparition to Magdalene? And if they started before midday, how could they say upon their arrival: "It is getting late"? And why, upon returning to Jerusalem, would they find the doors of the Cenacle locked for fear of the Jews?

What will always keep the controversy alive is the question whether St. Luke wrote *sixty*, or *one hundred and sixty;* in other words, whether *one hundred* has been suppressed from the manuscripts because the distance was considered too great, or was added to make the text harmonize with a very strong local tradition. Fortunately the sites of both Amwas and Qubeibeh are in Catholic hands: Qubeibeh has long been the property of the Franciscans, and the site of Amwas, acquired in 1880 by a pious French lady, is now a dependency of the Carmel of Bethlehem.

NOTE Z

Baptism in the Name Of

1. The Meaning of the Formula

The authenticity of the verse of St. Matthew (28:16), in which Jesus gives to the Apostles the command to "baptize in the name of the Father, and of the Son, and of the Holy Ghost," is unquestionable. The objections of Conybeare have been so well refuted by Chase (*J. T. S.,* 1905, Vol. VI, pp. 481–499) and by Lebreton (*Dogme de la Trinité,* 6 ed., 1927, Note E, pp. 599–610 [English transl., pp. 436–439]), that it is superfluous to return to the subject.

The meaning of the phrase *εἰς τὸ ὄνομα* is disputed. To confine the question to the Vulgate, *in nomine* could mean merely "by the authority of" or "by order of," but it must be kept in mind that in the language of the Vulgate the difference between *in* with the ablative and *in* with the accusative often disappears; so that, to explain the Latin *in nomine* in the text of St. Matthew, we must go back to the Greek *εἰς τὸ ὄνομα.* The preposition *εἰς* indicates finality or purpose, movement toward something, and with the name of a person, relationship, or connection.

1. The commonest meaning of *εἰς τὸ ὄνομά τινος* is "out of respect for," "in consideration of." Cf. Bauer, *Wörterbuch,* 1928, p. 908. Thus Matt. 10:41–42: "He who receives the prophet *as a prophet* (*εἰς τὸ ὄνομα προφήτου*) in consideration of his mission." Also Heb. 6:10: "God does not forget the charity which you have shown to others *for his name* (*εἰς τὸ ὄνομα αὐτοῦ*), because of him."

2. Often in the papyri *εἰς τὸ ὄνομά τινος* marks a relationship of belonging, and can be translated "to the account of," "to the credit of someone." See the examples in Deissmann, *Biblische Studien,* pp. 144–145, and *Neue bibl. Stud.,* p. 25, or Moulton-Milligan, *Vocabulary,* p. 451.

3. The formula of an oath ὀμνύναι εἰς τὸ ὄνομά τινος indicates a relationship of subjection and obedience (Herodian, *Histor.*, II, ii, 10; II, xiii, 2). The Latins used the same phrase *jurare in nomen alicujus*, "to take the oath of fidelity and obedience" (Suetonius, *Claudius*, 10). *Jurare in verba alicujus* had the same meaning but it was applied to a prescribed form or oath imposed by the one to whom the promise or obedience is made (Livy, xxviii, 29).

4. Finally, then, there is question of God or Christ; the relationship of belonging, expressed by the formula εἰς τὸ ὄνομα Θεοῦ, Χριστοῦ, becomes a relationship of consecration.

As we know, in the Bible, especially when there is question of God, "name" means the *person*. Tertullian thus cites the text: "Ite, docete nationes, tingentes eos *in nomen* Patris et Filii et Spiritus Sancti" (*De Baptismo,* 13), and explains it thus: "Novissime mandans ut tingerent *in* Patrem et Filium et Spiritum Sanctum" (*Adv. Praxeam,* 26; cf. *De Praescrip.* 20). St. Jerome finds the same meaning of consecration in the Latin formula which expresses it less clearly: "Cum *in* Patre et Filio et Spiritu Sancto baptizatus homo templum Domini fiat" (*Dial. cum Lucif.*, 6; ML, XXIII, 161).

2. Inexact and Exaggerated Conceptions

The Anglican Bishop Chase, in an article excellent from other points of view, maintains that the Greek word βαπτίζειν should not be simply transcribed, but should be translated by "plunge," "immerse," because Baptism necessarily implies an *incorporation* (*The Lord's Command to Baptize,* in *J. T. S.,* Vol. VI, 1905, pp. 481–512). J. A. Robinson replies in the same review (*In the Name,* in *J. T. S.,* Vol. VII, 1906, pp. 186–202) that the expressions εἰς τὸ ὄνομα and ἐν τῷ ὀνόματι are equivalent and interchangeable, and that, since "in the name" means "by authority of," the mention of the name is an essential part of the rite of Baptism. Heitmüller had previously sustained that the two expressions are equivalent, and that they both correspond to the Hebrew בשם (*In Namen Jesu,* 1903). These two views sin either by excess or defect.

1. The word βαπτίζειν does not mean merely to "plunge," "immerse," as does βάπτειν, but also to "wash," "purify" (Luke 11:38, "to wash the hands"; Mark 7:4, "to wash vessels"). Besides, this word had already assumed the technical sense of "confer Baptism," without suggesting in any way the idea of immersion (Matt. 3:11, "baptize in the Holy Spirit and fire"; Mark 1:8; Luke 3:16; John 1:33). The concept of incorporation is, of course, found in St. Paul (Gal. 3:27: "You have been baptized in Christ, εἰς τὸν Χριστὸν, you have put on

Christ"; cf. Rom. 6:8), in virtue of the doctrine of the Mystical Christ; but the same does not follow when there is question of the Trinity, and what incorporation into the Divine Persons would mean is very difficult to understand. The ordinary sense of belonging, of subjection, of consecration can therefore be left to the phrase *εἰς τὸ ὄνομα,* without linking it with *βαπτίζειν* in the special sense of immersion.

2. It is not true that the expression *εἰς τὸ ὄνομα* and *ἐν τῷ ὀνόματι* are equivalent and interchangeable in Greek, though this may be so in Latin. One would never say "cast out demons," "work miracles" *εἰς τὸ ὄνομα,* but always *ἐν τῷ ὀνόματι* "by the authority," or "in the name of" (*ἐν τῷ ὀνόματι,* instrumental), "by virtue of the name," "invoking the name." The preposition *εἰς* always differs from *ἐν* when it expresses finality or relationship; the tendency to blend the two is not present except with verbs of motion or rest, because the idea can then bear upon the rest which succeeds the movement, or upon the movement which precedes the rest.

In favor of asserting their equivalence, St. Luke is cited twice using the phrase "to baptize *ἐν τῷ ὀνόματι* I.X." (2:38; 10:48) and twice "to baptize *εἰς τὸ ὄνομα* I.X." (Acts 8:16; 19:5); but it cannot be proved that the meaning is altogether the same: to baptize *εἰς τὸ ὄνομα* can be taken in the Pauline sense of incorporation into the Mystical Christ, and to baptize *ἐν τῷ ὀνόματι* will still keep the normal and usual sense of baptizing "by the authority of" and "at the command of Christ."

Finally, it is inexact to say that both expressions correspond to the Hebrew בשׁם. *Εἰς τὸ ὄνομα* corresponds to the Hebrew לשׁם. Cf. Billerbeck (*Kommentar,* Vol. I, pp. 1054–1055), who well renders the sense of the Baptismal formula in virtue of which the neophyte is "placed in a special relationship to God, the Father, Son, and Holy Ghost," and becomes the common property of the Trinity. Bauer (*Wörterbuch,* p. 908) says the same: "By the baptism *εἰς τὸ ὄνομά τινος* the neophyte becomes the property and thereby the protégé (Besitz und damit Schützling) of the Person named."

If Baptism *εἰς τὸ ὄνομα* consecrates us to the three Divine Persons, to be effective it must demand the mention of these three Persons. This, at least, is what the Church has understood from the beginning. We have heard the words of Tertullian. A century earlier the *Doctrine of the Twelve Apostles* (vii, 1, in Funk, *Patres Apost.,* Vol. I, p. 58) decreed: "Baptize in the name of the Father, and of the Son, and of the Holy Ghost." St. Justin is no less explicit (*Apol.,* i, 61; MG, VI, 421): "Upon those who are to be regenerated *the name* of God the Father *is pronounced,"* etc. And St. Irenaeus (*Demonst. Praed. Apost.*, 3 and 7; trans. Barthoulot in *Recherches,* 1916, pp. 371 and 373): "We are regenerated by Baptism which is given to us in the name of these three Persons."

The Latin *In nomine Patris,* etc., expresses this relationship of consecration and dependence less clearly, because it can mean "by the authority of" or "by order of." Thus Maldonatus can say with many others that this text, *by itself and isolated from the traditional exegesis,* would not, perhaps, convince a *subtle and obstinate reasoner* of the need of mentioning the three Persons in the conferring of Baptism.

Philological Index

This list contains rare words, words which have more than one meaning, and words which are employed in an unusual way. It has been thought advisable to include also certain expressions and turns of speech which are the subject of controversy. The Latin translation given here is always that of the Vulgate, though in some instances another translation was regarded as preferable and was adopted in the course of the book.

'Αγαπᾶν, *diligere* (John 21:15–18), and φιλεῖν, *amare*, II, 442
'Αγιάζειν, *sanctificare* (John 17:17–19), II, 302
Ἄγναφος, *rudis* (Mark 2:21; Matt. 9:16), I, 287
'Αγωνίζεσθαι, *contendere* (Luke 13:24), II, 110
'Αδημονεῖν, *taedere* (Mark 14:33), II, 317
'Αετός, *aquila* (Luke 17:37; Matt. 24:28), II, 157
'Αληθείᾳ (ἐν τῇ), *in veritate* (John 17:17–19), II, 302 f
'Αμφίβληστρον, *rete* (cf. Luke 5:4–6; John 21:6), I, 223; II, 439
'Ανάγαιον, *coenaculum* (Mark 14:15), II, 259
'Ανατάσσεσθαι, *ordinare* (Luke 1:1), I, 19
'Ανατολῇ (ἐν), *in Oriente* (Matt. 2:2), I, 94, 101
Ἄνωθεν, *denuo* (John 3:3–7) and *desursum* (John 3:31), I, 186
'Απολύειν, *dimittere* (Matt. 1:20; 19:9), I, 70; II, 81
'Αποτάσσεσθαι, *dimittere* (Mark 6:46) and *renuntiare* (Luke 9:61; 14:33), II, 10
'Αρχὴν (τὴν) ὅ τι καὶ λαλῶ ὑμῖν, *Principium qui et loquor vobis* (John 8:25), II, 55 f
'Αρχιτρίκλινος, *architriclinus* (John 2:9), I, 179
'Αστήρ, *stella* (Matt. 2:2), I, 98
Αὐλή, *atrium* (Mark 14:66, etc.), II, 340
Ἄχρι καιροῦ, *usque ad tempus* (Luke 4:13), I, 162

Βαριωνᾶς, *Bar Jona* (Matt. 16:17), I, 170, 410
Βασιλεία, *regnum* (passim), I, 217
Βασιλικός or Βασιλίσκος, *regulus* (John 4:46–49), I, 204
Βαστάζειν, *portare* (John 12:7), II, 190
Βάτος, *cadus*, Heb. *bath* (Luke 16:6), II, 128
Βδέλυγμα τῆς ἐρημώσεως, *abominatio desolationis* (Matt. 24:15; Mark 13:14), II, 237
Βεεζεβούλ or Βεελζεβούλ, *Beelzebub* (Matt. 12:24), I, 299
Βιάζεσθαι, *vim facere* (Luke 16:16) and *vim pati* (Matt. 11:12), I, 253
Βούλεσθαι and θέλειν, *velle* (Matt. 1:19), I, 70

Γένεσις, *generatio* (Matt. 24:34), II, 245
Γερασηνῶν, Γαδαρηνῶν, Γεργεσηνῶν, variant readings, I, 334
Γιγνώσκειν, *cognoscere* (Matt. 1:25), I, 70
Γλωσσόκομον, *loculi* (John 12:6), II, 190
Γυμνός, *nudus* (John 21:7), II, 380, 439

Δακρύειν, *lachrymari* (John 11:35), and κλαίειν, *plorare*, II, 195
Δειγματίζειν, *traducere* (Matt. 1:19), I, 70

Διασκορπίζειν, *spargere* (Matt. 25:24–26), II, 180
Δικαιοῦσθαι, *justificari* (Luke 7:35; Matt. 11:19), I, 254
Δίκτυα, *retia* or *rete* (Luke 5:4–6), I, 223
Διχοτομεῖν, *dividere* (Matt. 24:51; Luke 12:46), II, 107
Δόξα and δοξάζειν, *claritas* and *clarificare* John 17:1–5), II, 300
Δυνάμεις, *virtutes* (Luke 19:37), I, 518

Ἐγγίζειν, *appropinquare* (Luke 18:35), II, 175
Ἐγείρειν, *excitare* (John 2:19), I, 182
Ἐγώ εἰμι, *ego sum* (John 8:24), II, 54 f
Εἰρηνοποιός, *pacificus* (Matt. 5:9), I, 262
Εἷς ἐστιν ὁ ἀγαθός, *unus est bonus, Deus* (Matt. 19:17; cf. Mark 10:18; Luke 18:19), II, 160
Ἐκβάλλειν, *expellere* (Mark 1:12), I, 156
Ἐκκλησία, *ecclesia,* Heb. *qahal* (Matt. 16:18; 18:17), I, 413 f
Ἐκμυκτερίζειν, *deridere* (Luke 16:14), II, 131
Ἐκλείπειν, *deficere* (Luke 16:9), II, 130
Ἐλέγχειν, *arguere* (John 16:8), II, 294
Ἐλεήμων, *misericors* (Matt. 5:7), I, 261
Ἐν αὐτῷ ζωὴ ἦν, *in ipso vita erat* (John 1:4), I, 467–470
Ἑνὸς ἐστι χρεία, *unum est necessarium* (Luke 10:42), II, 24 f
Ἐντὸς ὑμῶν ἐστιν, *intra vos est* (Luke 17:21), II, 154
Ἐν τῇ ἑξῆς, *in sequenti die* (Luke 9:37), I, 247
Ἐν τῷ ἑξῆς, *deinceps* (Luke 7:11), I, 247
Ἐξέστη, *in furorem versus est* (Mark 3:21), I, 297
Ἐπιούσιος, *supersubstantialis* (Matt. 6:11) and *quotidianus* (Luke 11:3), II, 32 f
Ἐπιχειρεῖν, *conari* (Luke 1:1), I, 19
Ἐραυνᾶτε, *scrutamini* (John 5:39), I, 392
Ἐργάζεσθαι τὴν βρῶσιν, *operamini cibum* (John 6:27), I, 369
Ἔτι ἐκ κοιλίας, *adhuc ex utero* (Luke 1:15), I, 64
Εὐδοκία, *bona voluntas* (Luke 2:14), I, 86 f
Εὔθετος, *aptus* (Luke 9:62) and *utilis* (Luke 14:35), II, 11
Εὐκαιρεῖν, *spatium habere* (Mark 6:31), I, 359
Ἕως ἄρτι ἐργάζεται, *usque modo operatur* (John 5:17), I, 385

Ζηλωτής, *Zelotes* (Luke 6:15), I, 235
Ζιζάνιον, *zizania,* Arab. *zawan* (Matt. 13:27–40), I, 312
Ζῶν ἀσώτως, *vivendo luxuriose* (Luke 15:13), II, 118

Θεᾶσθαι, *videre* (John 1:32), I, 167
Θέλειν and βούλεσθαι, *velle* (Matt. 1:19), I, 70

Ἰδού, *ecce* (Matt. 2:19), I, 113
Ἰχθύς, *piscis,* symbolism of, I, 226

Καθεξῆς, *ex ordine* (Luke 1:3), I, 20
Καλόν ἐστιν ἡμᾶς ὧδε εἶναι, *bonum est nos hic esse* (Mark 9:5 and parall.), I, 424
Καναναῖος (Matt. 10:4; Mark 3:18) and ζηλωτής (Luke 6:15), I, 235
Καθαρός, *mundus* (John 13:10), II, 266
Καθαίρειν, *purgare* (John 15:2), II, 288
Καθαρισμός, *purgatio* (Luke 2:22), I, 91
Καταλύειν, *solvere* (Matt. 5:17), I, 265
Καταφιλεῖν, *osculari* (Mark 14:45), II, 323
Κατισχύειν, *praevalere* (Matt. 16:18), I, 415 f
Κατ' ὄναρ, *in somnis* (Matt. 1:20), I, 71, 103
Κεράμων (διὰ τῶν), *per tegulas* (Luke 5:19), I, 243
Κλαίειν, *plorare* (Luke 19:41), and δακρύειν, *lachrymari* (John 11:33–35), II, 195
Κόρος, *corus,* Heb. *kor* (Luke 16:7), II, 128
Κράσπεδα, *fimbriae,* Heb. *tsitsioth,* II, 221

Λαῖλαψ, *procella* (Mark 4:37; Luke 8:23), I, 331

Λεπτόν, *minutum,* Heb. *perutah* (Mark 12:42), II, 229
Λόγος, *Verbum* (John 1:1–14), I, 470–475
Λούεσθαι, *lotus esse* (John 13:10), and νίπτεσθαι, *lavari,* II, 266

Μακροθυμεῖ ἐπ' αὐτοῖς, *patientiam habebit in illis* (Luke 18:7), II, 158
Μαμωνᾶς, *mammona,* Aram. *mamona* (Luke 16:9), II, 129 f
Μαρία or Μαριάμ, *Maria* (Luke 1:27), I, 42 f
Μέσον (διὰ) or μέσου, *per medium* (Luke 17:11), II, 151
Μετρητής, *metreta* (John 2:6), I, 178
Μή μου ἅπτου, *noli me tangere* (John 20:17), II, 422

Ναζαρηνός or Ναζωραῖος, *Nazarenus* (Matt. 2:23), I, 115
Ναὶ ναί, οὒ οὔ, *est, est; non, non* (Matt. 5:37), I, 271
Ναός, *templum,* and ἱερόν (Matt. 27:5), II, 406
Νύσσειν, *aperire* (John 19:34), II, 394 f

Οἰκονόμος, *villicus* (Luke 16:1–8), II, 127
Ὄνομα (εἰς τὸ), *in nomine* (Matt. 28:18), II, 536 ff
Ὀρεινή or ὀρινή, *montana* (Luke 1:39, 65), I, 62 f
Ὅρια, *fines* (Matt. 19:1), II, 6
Ὄρος (τὸ), *mons* (Matt. 5:1; 8:1), I, 256
Οὐκ ἀναβαίνω, *non ascendo* (John 7:8), II, 41
Ὀφρύς, *supercilium* (Luke 4:29), I, 357
Ὀψὲ σαββάτων, *vespere sabbati* (Matt. 28:1), II, 424
Ὀψάριον, *piscis* (John 21:9), II, 439 f

Παιδεύειν, *emendare* and *corripere* (Luke 23:16–22), II, 356
Παντελές (εἰς τὸ), *omnino* (Luke 13:11), II, 90
Παράκλητος, *Paraclitus* (John 14:15–17), II, 291
Παραλαβεῖν, *accipere* (Matt. 1:20), I, 70
Παρατήρησις, *observatio* (Luke 17:20), II, 154
Παροιμία, *proverbium* (John 10:6), II, 69
Πειράζειν and ἐκπειράζειν, *tentare* (Matt. 22:35; Luke 10:25), II, 213
Περιβλέπεσθαι, *circumspicere* (Mark 10:23), II, 161
Περίχωρος, *regio* or *regio circa* (Matt. 3:6; Luke 3:3), I, 152
Πέτρα and πέτρος, Aram. *Kepha* (Matt. 16:18), I, 413
Πεφίμωσο, *obmutesce* (Mark 4:39), I, 332
Πιστεύειν, *credere* (John 2:23–24), I, 184
Πιστικός, *spicatus* (Mark 14:3) and *pisticus* (John 12:3), II, 189
Πλὴν τὰ ἔνοντα δότε, *verumtamen quod superest date* (Luke 11:41), II, 84
Πληροῦν, *adimplere* (Matt. 5:17), I, 265
Πληροφορεῖν, *complere* (Luke 1:1), I, 19
Πνεῦμα, *spiritus* (John 3:8), I, 186
Ποίμνη (μία), *unum ovile* (John 10:16), II, 71
Ποιῶν (ὁ) τὴν ἁμαρτίαν, *qui facit peccatum* (John 8:34), II, 57
Πορνεία, *fornicatio* (Matt. 5:32; 19:9), II, 81
Πραιτώριον, *praetorium* (Mark 15:16), II, 364
Πρασιαὶ, πρασιαί, *in partes* (Mark 6:39), I, 362
Πραΰς, *mitis,* Heb. *'anaw* (Matt. 5:6), I, 260
Πρηνὴς γενόμενος, *suspensus* (Acts 1:18), II, 525 f
Πρόβατα and προβάτια, *agnos, oves* (John 21:16–17), II, 442 f
Προβατική, *Probatica* (John 5:2), I, 382
Προσκυνεῖν, *adorare* (passim), I, 101
Πρῶτός μου, *prior me* (John 1:30), I, 166
Πτωχός, *pauper,* Heb. *'ani* (Matt. 5:3), I, 259 f
Πύλαι ᾅδου, *portae inferi* (Matt. 16:18), I, 415 f

Ῥαπίζειν, *palmas in faciem dare* (Matt. 26:67), and κολαφίζειν, *alapis caedere,* II, 330

Sunday Gospel Reference Index

Index

This index embraces both volumes of the work. Reference to the respective volumes is indicated by the Roman numerals I and II.